# THE
# OXFORD-DUDEN
# PICTORIAL
# ITALIAN AND ENGLISH
# DICTIONARY

# THE
# OXFORD-DUDEN
# PICTORIAL
# ITALIAN AND
# ENGLISH
# DICTIONARY

CLARENDON PRESS · OXFORD
1995

Oxford University Press, Walton Street, Oxford OX2 6DP
Oxford New York
Athens Auckland Bangkok Bombay
Calcutta Cape Town Dar es Salaam Delhi
Florence Hong Kong Istanbul Karachi
Kuala Lumpur Madras Madrid Melbourne
Mexico City Nairobi Paris Singapore
Taipei Tokyo Toronto
and associated companies in
Berlin Ibadan

Oxford is a trade mark of Oxford University Press

Published in the United States by
Oxford University Press Inc., New York

British Library Cataloguing in Publication Data
Data available

Library of Congress Cataloging in Publication Data
Data available
ISBN 0–19–864516 3
ISBN 0–19–864517 1 (paperback)

Italian text edited by M. Luisa Heinz-Mazzoni and Paola Scaltriti;
English text edited by Michael Clark and Bernadette Mohan.
Illustrations by Jochen Schmidt, Mannheim.

Printed in Hong Kong

# PREFACE

The *Oxford-Duden Pictorial Italian and English Dictionary* is a new addition to the *Oxford-Duden Pictorial* range. Produced with the assistance of numerous Italian and British companies, institutions, and technical experts, it is part of a family of dictionaries that have a firmly established reputation as uniquely useful learning aids and reference tools.

A picture is worth a thousand words, and this is never more true than when learning a foreign language. A visual clue can guide the user quickly to the appropriate translation and remove the uncertainty of deciding between alternatives offered by traditional bilingual dictionaries. In particular, information about objects and their names can be conveyed more readily and clearly by pictures than by explanations or definitions, however precise and unambiguous, and an illustration will support a bare translation by helping the user to visualize the object referred to by a given word.

The *Oxford-Duden Pictorial Italian and English Dictionary* identifies over 28,000 numbered objects, ranging from the familiar to the highly specialized, and offers at a glance their names in both languages. Each double page contains a plate illustrating the vocabulary of a whole subject, together with the exact Italian names and their correct English translations. Detailed and comprehensive alphabetical indexes in Italian and in English allow the dictionary to be used either way—as an Italian–English or an English–Italian dictionary.

In a convenient, portable format the *Oxford-Duden Pictorial* deals with a vast variety of topics, ranging from domestic situations through to recreation and sport, flora and fauna, industry, science, human biology, the arts, and technology, and reflects recent developments in such fast-changing fields as computing, audio and video, photography, typesetting, communications, and transport. Its wide range of vocabulary, accuracy of translation, and ease of use make it an indispensable supplement to any Italian–English or English–Italian dictionary.

# PREFAZIONE

Il «Dizionario illustrato italiano–inglese» corrisponde per l'accuratezza della presentazione al «Bildwörterbuch», terzo dei dodici volumi Duden della lingua tedesca.

La nuova edizione bilingue presenta la fedele versione dell'originale: un'impresa spesso al limite del possibile nella ricerca di equivalenti, là dove ambiente e consuetudini, e di conseguenza l'uso della lingua, divergono. Nel nostro lavoro ci siamo trovati a volte di fronte ad illustrazioni il cui mondo non appartiene a quello italiano, ad oggetti diversi da quelli a noi propri. In questi casi abbiamo preferito non aggirare l'ostacolo, ma accettarlo nella sua umana inevitabilità.

Le 384 tavole, per un totale di circa 28 000 voci, riportano la terminologia tecnica e specifica dei vari campi dello scibile in forma plastica, secondo il principio: per ogni termine il disegno corrispondente. Qui l'immagine permette di identificare con esattezza l'oggetto indicato senza dover ricorrere a descrizioni astratte.

I singoli temi sono articolati in modo da rendere la consultazione semplice e rapida su due pagine a fronte che riportano, su un unico piano visivo, illustrazione e relativo vocabolario completo in italiano e in inglese.

Grazie alla tecnica di presentazione del vasto materiale e alla presenza di un indice per materie, come pure di un indice alfabetico nelle due lingue, quest'opera offre autorevole supporto alle complesse esigenze del mondo odierno: è dizionario italiano–inglese/inglese–italiano a doppia entrata, è complemento a tutti i vocabolari, compresi quelli tecnici e scientifici, è testo di consultazione per chi desideri arricchire le proprie conoscenze linguistiche o il proprio idioma, è vademecum sicuro nel turismo, nel commercio, nello sport, insomma in ogni attività umana.

Per determinati settori ci siamo rivolti a esperti, tecnici, artigiani, interlocutori occasionali che con generosa disponibilità ci hanno offerto il loro aiuto competente.

# Abbreviazioni

| | |
|---|---|
| *ant.* | antico |
| *f* | femminile |
| *fam.* | familiare |
| *m* | maschile |
| *pl* | plurale |
| *pop.* | popolare |
| *reg.* | regionale |
| *sel.* | selvatico |
| *sim.* | simile |
| *sin.* | sinonimo |
| *sing* | singolare |
| *tec.* | tecnico |

# Abbreviations used in the English text

| | |
|---|---|
| Am. | *American usage* |
| c. | *castrated (animal)* |
| coll. | *colloquial* |
| f. | *female (animal)* |
| form. | *formerly* |
| joc. | *jocular* |
| m. | *male (animal)* |
| poet. | *poetic* |
| sg. | *singular* |
| sim. | *similar* |
| y. | *young (animal)* |

# Indice

*I numeri arabi si riferiscono alle tavole*

# Contents

*The arabic numerals are the numbers of the pictures*

# Indice                                                    Contents

# Indice

# Contents

# Indice

# Contents

# Indice

# Contents

# Indice                                                                 Contents

# Indice

# Contents

**1-8 modelli** *m pl* **atomici (schemi** *m pl* **di strutture** *f pl* **dell'atomo)**
- *atom models*
1 il modello dell'atomo di idrogeno (H)
- *model of the hydrogen (H) atom*
2 il nucleo atomico, un protone
- *atomic nucleus, a proton*
3 l'elettrone *m*
- *electron*
4 lo spin (il moto rotatorio spontaneo dell'elettrone *m*)
- *electron spin*
5 il modello dell'atomo di elio (He)
- *model of the helium (He) atom*
6 lo strato elettronico
- *electron shell*
7 il principio di esclusione *f* di Pauli
- *Pauli exclusion principle (exclusion principle, Pauli principle)*
8 lo strato elettronico chiuso dell'atomo di sodio (Na)
- *complete electron shell of the Na atom (sodium atom)*
**9-14 strutture** *f pl* **molecolari (strutture** *f pl* **reticolari)**
- *molecular structures (lattice structures)*
9 il cristallo del cloruro di sodio
- *crystal of sodium chloride (of common salt)*
10 lo ione cloruro
- *chlorine ion*
11 lo ione sodio
- *sodium ion*
12 il cristallo di cristobalite *f*
- *crystal of cristobalite*
13 l'atomo di ossigeno
- *oxygen atom*
14 l'atomo di silicio
- *silicon atom*
**15 lo schema dei livelli di energia (le transizioni quantistiche permesse) dell'atomo di idrogeno**
- *energy level diagram (term diagram, possible quantum jumps) of the hydrogen atom*
16 il nucleo atomico (il protone)
- *atomic nucleus (proton)*
17 l'elettrone *m*
- *electron*
18 il livello di energia dello stato fondamentale
- *ground state level*
19 lo stato eccitato
- *excited state*
**20-25 le transizioni quantistiche**
- *quantum jumps (quantum transitions)*
20 la serie di Lyman
- *Lyman series*
21 la serie di Balmer
- *Balmer series*
22 la serie di Paschen
- *Paschen series*

23 la serie di Brackett
- *Brackett series*
24 la serie di Pfund
- *Pfund series*
25 l'elettrone libero
- *free electron*
26 il modello di Bohr-Sommerfeld dell'atomo di idrogeno (H)
- *Bohr-Sommerfeld model of the H atom*
27 le orbite dell'elettrone *m*
- *electron orbits of the electron*
**28 il decadimento spontaneo (la disintegrazione spontanea)** di una materia radioattiva
- *spontaneous decay of radioactive material*
29 il nucleo atomico
- *atomic nucleus*
**30 u. 31** la particella alfa ($\alpha$, la radiazione alfa, il nucleo dell'elio)
- *alpha ($\alpha$) particle (alpha ray, helium nucleus)*
30 il neutrone
- *neutron*
31 il protone
- *proton*
32 la particella beta ($\beta$, la radiazione beta, l'elettrone *m*)
- *beta ($\beta$) particle (beta ray, electron)*
33 la radiazione gamma, ($\gamma$, una radiazione X dura)
- *gamma($\gamma$) ray, a hard X-ray*
**34 la fissione nucleare**
- *nuclear fission*
35 il nucleo atomico pesante
- *heavy atomic nucleus*
36 il bombardamento neutronico
- *neutron bombardment*
**37 u. 38** i frammenti della fissione
- *fission fragments*
39 il neutrone libero
- *released neutron*
40 la radiazione gamma ($\gamma$)
- *gamma ($\gamma$) ray*
**41 la reazione a catena**
- *chain reaction*
42 il neutrone incidente
- *incident neutron*
43 il nucleo prima della fissione
- *nucleus prior to fission*
44 il frammento della fissione
- *fission fragment*
45 il neutrone libero
- *released neutron*
46 la fissione ripetuta
- *repeated fission*
47 il frammento della fissione
- *fission fragment*
**48 la reazione a catena controllata in un reattore nucleare**
- *controlled chain reaction in a nuclear reactor*

49 il nucleo atomico di un elemento fissile
- *atomic nucleus of a fissionable element*
50 il bombardamento neutronico
- *neutron bombardment*
51 il frammento della fissione (il nuovo nucleo atomico)
- *fission fragment (new atomic nucleus)*
52 il neutrone rilasciato
- *released neutron*
53 i neutroni assorbiti
- *absorbed neutrons*
54 il moderatore, uno strato ritardante di grafite *f*
- *moderator, a retarding layer of graphite*
55 l'estrazione *f* di calore *m* (la produzione di energia)
- *extraction of heat (production of energy)*
56 la radiazione Röntgen (i raggi X)
- *X-ray*
57 lo schema protettivo di cemento e piombo
- *concrete and lead shield*
**58 la camera a bolle** *f pl* per evidenziare le traiettorie delle particelle ionizzanti a alta energia
- *bubble chamber for showing the tracks of high-energy ionizing particles*
59 la sorgente luminosa
- *light source*
60 l'apparecchio fotografico
- *camera*
61 la linea di espansione *f*
- *expansion line*
62 il percorso dei raggi luminosi
- *path of light rays*
63 il magnete
- *magnet*
64 il punto di ingresso della radiazione
- *beam entry point*
65 lo schema riflettente
- *reflector*
66 la camera
- *chamber*

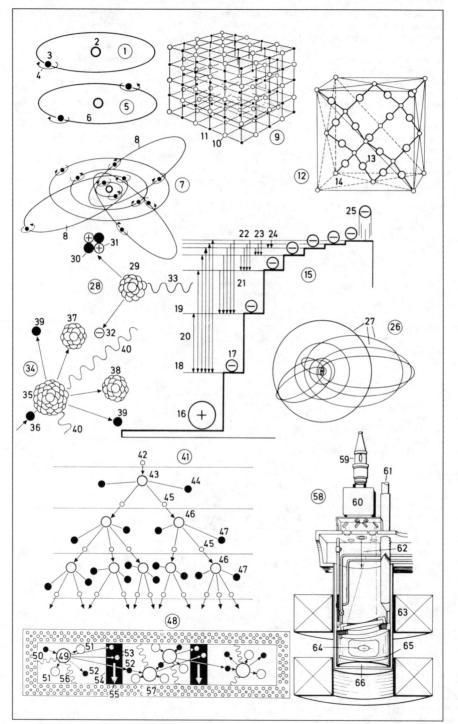

**1-23 strumenti** *m pl* **misuratori (rile-vatori) della radiazione**
– *radiation detectors (radiation meters)*
**1** il misuratore della radiazione, uno strumento protettivo
– *radiation monitor*
**2** la camera di ionizzazione *f*
– *ionization chamber (ion chamber)*
**3** l'elettrodo centrale
– *central electrode*
**4** il selettore dell'intervallo di misura
– *measurement range selector*
**5** la cassa dello strumento
– *instrument housing*
**6** il quadrante di lettura
– *meter*
**7** la manopola per l'azzeramento
– *zero adjustment*
**8-23** dosimetri *m pl*
– *dosimeter (dosemeter)*
**8** il dosimetro a pellicola
– *film dosimeter*
**9** il filtro
– *filter*
**10** la pellicola
– *film*
**11** il dosimetro a pellicola a forma di anello
– *film-ring dosimeter*
**12** il filtro
– *filter*
**13** la pellicola
– *film*
**14** la calotta con filtro
– *cover with filter*
**15** il dosimetro tascabile (camera portatile)
– *pocket meter (pen meter, pocket chamber)*
**16** la finestra d'ispezione *f*
– *window*
**17** la camera di ionizzazione *f*
– *ionization chamber (ion chamber)*
**18** il clip, il fermaglio per fissare il dosimetro al taschino
– *clip (pen clip)*
**19** il contatore Geiger (tubo conta-tore)
– *Geiger counter (Geiger-Müller counter)*
**20** l'involucro del contatore cilindrico
– *counter tube casing*
**21** il contatore cilindrico
– *counter tube*
**22** la cassa dell'apparecchio
– *instrument housing*
**23** il selettore dell'intervallo di misura
– *measurement range selector*
**24** la camera a nebbia di Wilson
– *Wilson cloud chamber (Wilson chamber)*

**25** il piatto di compressione *f*
– *compression plate*
**26** la ripresa fotografica della camera a nebbia
– *cloud chamber photograph*
**27** le tracce di una particella alfa in una camera a nebbia
– *cloud chamber track of an alpha particle*
**28** **il generatore di radiazione** *f* **al cobalto**
– *telecobalt unit* (coll. *cobalt bomb*)
**29** la colonna portante
– *pillar stand*
**30** i cavi di sollevamento
– *support cables*
**31** lo schermo di protezione *f* dalle radiazioni
– *radiation shield (radiation shielding)*
**32** il cursore (schermo semovente)
– *sliding shield*
**33** il diaframma lamellare
– *bladed diaphragm*
**34** il dispositivo ottico di mira
– *light-beam positioning device*
**35** il dispositivo a pendolo
– *pendulum device (pendulum)*
**36** il tavolo d'irradiazione *f* (tavola radioterapica)
– *irradiation table*
**37** la rotaia di scorrimento (la guida)
– *rail (track)*
**38** **il manipolatore a snodo sferico (manipolatore** *m***)**
– *manipulator with sphere unit*
**39** l'impugnatura
– *handle*
**40** la sicura a aletta (leva d'arresto)
– *safety catch (locking lever)*
**41** il giunto (snodo) di raccordo
– *wrist joint*
**42** l'asta (albero) di guida
– *master arm*
**43** il dispositivo di bloccaggio
– *clamping device (clamp)*
**44** la pinza prensile (pinza)
– *tongs*
**45** il pannello (quadro) a fenditure *f pl*
– *slotted board*
**46** lo schermo antiradiazioni, una parete a strato di piombo [sezione]
– *radiation shield (protective shield, protective shielding), a lead shielding wall [section]*
**47** il braccio prensile di due manipo-latori *m pl* paralleli (di un manipolatore Master-Slave)
– *grasping arm of a pair of manipu-lators (of a master/slave manipula-tor)*

**48** la protezione antipolvere
– *dust shield*
**49** **il sincrotrone**
– *synchrotron*
**50** la zona di pericolo
– *danger zone*
**51** il magnete
– *magnet*
**52** le pompe per la disaerazione della camera sotto vuoto (pompe *f pl* aspiranti)
– *pumps for emptying the vacuum chamber*

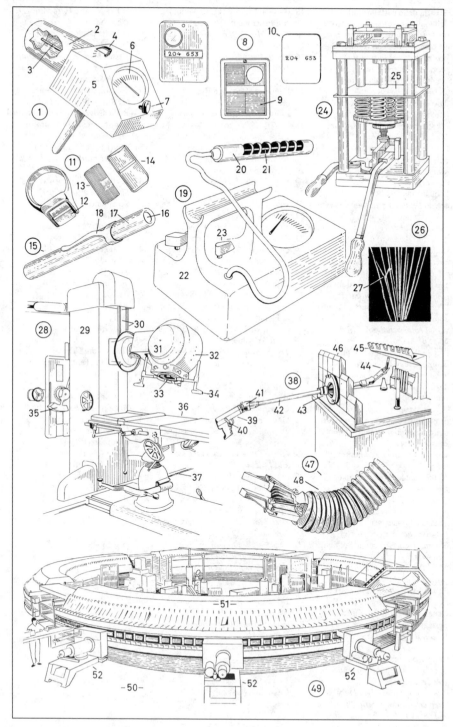

**1-35 carta delle costellazioni**
dell'emisfero celeste settentrionale (dell'emisfero celeste boreale), una carta della volta celeste
– *star map of the northern sky*
*(northern hemisphere)*
**1-8** suddivisione *f* della volta celeste
– *divisions of the sky*
**1** il polo celeste con la Stella polare
(stella del Nord)
– *celestial pole with the Pole Star*
*(Polaris, the North Star)*
**2** l'eclittica (orbita annuale apparente del sole)
– *ecliptic (apparent annual path of*
*the sun)*
**3** l'equatore *m* celeste
– *celestial equator (equinoctial line)*
**4** il tropico del Cancro
– *tropic of Cancer*
**5** il cerchio (la zona) delimitante le
stelle circumpolari
– *circle enclosing circumpolar stars*
**6** *u.* **7** equinozi (i punti in cui i giorni
e le notti hanno la stessa durata)
– *equinoctial points (equinoxes)*
**6** l'equinozio di primavera (il punto
equinoziale in Ariete *m*)
– *vernal equinoctial point (first*
*point of Aries)*
**7** l'equinozio d'autunno (il punto
equinoziale in Bilancia)
– *autumnal equinoctial point*
**8** il solstizio d'estate *f*
– *summer solstice*
**9-48 costellazioni** *f pl* (raggruppa-
mento di **stelle fisse, astri** *m pl* in
figure) e **nomi** *m pl* **delle stelle**
– *constellations (grouping of fixed*
*stars into figures) and names of*
*stars*
**9** Aquila con la stella principale
Altair *m*
– *Aquila (the Eagle) with Altair the*
*principal star (the brightest star)*
**10** Pegaso (Pegasus *m*)
– *Pegasus (the Winged Horse)*
**11** Balena (Cetus *m*) con Mira, una
stella variabile
– *Cetus (the Whale) with Mira, a*
*variable star*
**12** Fiume Eridano (Eridanus *m*)
– *Eridanus (the Celestial River)*
**13** Orione *m* (Orion *m*) con Rigel *f*,
Bételgeuse *f* e Bellatrix *f*
– *Orion (the Hunter) with Rigel,*
*Betelgeuse and Bellatrix*
**14** Cane *m* Maggiore (Canis Major)
con Sirio, *una stella di prima*
*grandezza*
– *Canis Major (the Great Dog, the*
*Greater Dog) with Sirius (the Dog*
*Star), a star of the first magnitude*

**15** Cane *m* Minore (Canis Minor)
con Procione *m* (Procyon)
– *Canis Minor (the Little Dog, the*
*Lesser Dog) with Procyon*
**16** Idra (Hydra)
– *Hydra (the Water Snake, the Sea*
*Serpent)*
**17** Leone *m* (Leo) con Regolo
(Regolus)
– *Leo (the Lion) with Regulus*
**18** Vergine *f* (Virgo) con Spica
– *Virgo (the Virgin) with Spica*
**19** Bilancia (Libra)
– *Libra (the Balance, the Scales)*
**20** Serpente *m* (Serpens)
– *Serpens (the Serpent)*
**21** Ercole *m* (Hercules)
– *Hercules*
**22** Lira (Lyra) con Vega
– *Lyra (the Lyre) with Vega*
**23** Cigno (Cygnus) con Deneb *m*
– *Cygnus (the Swan, the Northern*
*Cross) with Deneb*
**24** Andromeda
– *Andromeda*
**25** Toro (Taurus) con Aldebaran *m*
– *Taurus (the Bull) with Aldebaran*
**26** le Pleiadi (Pleiades, la costel-
lazione di 7 stelle *f pl*), un ammas-
so stellare aperto
– *The Pleiades (Pleiads, the Seven*
*Sisters), an open cluster of stars*
**27** Cocchiere *m* (Auriga) con
Capella (Capra)
– *Auriga (the Wagoner, the*
*Charioteer) with Capella*
**28** Gemelli *m pl* (Gemini) con
Castore *m* e Polluce *m* (Castor et
Pollux)
– *Gemini (the Twins) with Castor*
*and Pollux*
**29** l'Orsa Maggiore (Ursa Major,
Grande Carro, Gran Carro, Carro
Maggiore) con la stella doppia
Mizar *f* ed Alcor *m*
– *Ursa Major (the Great Bear, the*
*Greater Bear, the Plough,*
*Charles's Wain, Am. the Big*
*Dipper) with the double star*
*(binary star) Mizar and Alcor*
**30** Boote *m* (Bootes, Boaro) con
Arturo (Arcturus *m*)
– *Boötes (the Herdsman) with*
*Arcturus*
**31** Corona Boreale (Corona
Borealis)
– *Corona Borealis (the Northern*
*Crown)*
**32** Dragone *m* (Draco)
– *Draco (the Dragon)*
**33** Cassiopea (Cassiopeia)
– *Cassiopeia*

**34** l'Orsa Minore (Urs Minor,
Piccolo Carro, Carro Minore) con
la Stella polare
– *Ursa Minor (the Little Bear,*
*Lesser Bear, Am. Little Dipper)*
*with the Pole Star (Polaris, the*
*North Star)*
**35** la Via Lattea (Galassia)
– *the Milky Way (the Galaxy)*
**36-48 l'emisfero celeste meridionale**
(emisfero celeste australe)
– *the southern sky*
**36** Capricorno (Capricornus)
– *Capricorn (the Goat, the Sea*
*Goat)*
**37** Sagittario (Sagittarius)
– *Sagittarius (the Archer)*
**38** Scorpione *m* (Scorpio)
– *Scorpio (the Scorpion)*
**39** Centauro (Centaurus)
– *Centaurus (the Centaur)*
**40** Triangolo Australe (Triangulum
Australe)
– *Triangulum Australe (the*
*Southern Triangle)*
**41** Pavone *m* (Pavo)
– *Pavo (the Peacock)*
**42** Gru *f* (Grus)
– *Grus (the Crane)*
**43** Ottante *m* (Octans)
– *Octans (the Octant)*
**44** Croce *f* del sud (Crux)
– *Crux (the Southern Cross, the*
*Cross)*
**45** Argo *f*
– *Argo (the Celestial Ship)*
**46** Carena (Carina)
– *Carina (the Keel)*
**47** Pittore *m* (Pictor)
– *Pictor (the Painter)*
**48** Reticolo (Reticulum)
– *Reticulum (the Net)*

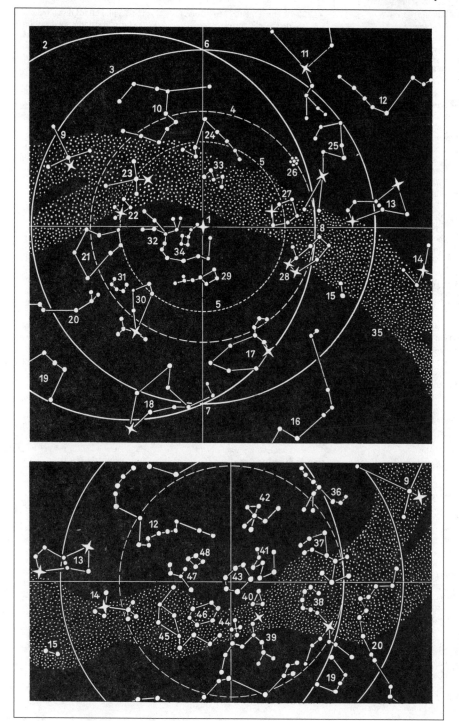

**1-9** la Luna
– *the moon*
**1** l'orbita lunare (la rotazione della luna intorno alla terra)
– *moon's path (moon's orbit round the earth)*
**2-7** le fasi lunari
– *lunar phases (moon's phases) (lunation)*
**2** la luna nuova
– *new moon*
**3** la luna crescente
– *crescent (crescent moon, waxing moon)*
**4** il primo quarto
– *half-moon (first quarter)*
**5** la luna piena
– *full moon*
**6** l'ultimo quarto
– *half-moon (last quarter, third quarter)*
**7** la luna calante
– *crescent (crescent moon, waning moon)*
**8** la Terra (il globo terrestre)
– *the earth (terrestrial globe)*
**9** la direzione della luce solare (dei raggi solari)
– *direction of the sun's rays*
**10-21** il movimento apparente del sole all'inizio delle stagioni
– *apparent path of the sun at the beginning of the seasons*
**10** l'asse *m* celeste
– *celestial axis*
**11** lo Zenit
– *zenith*
**12** il piano orizzontale
– *horizontal plane*
**13** il Nadir
– *nadir*
**14** il punto Est *m*
– *east point*
**15** il punto Ovest *m*
– *west point*
**16** il punto Nord *m*
– *north point*
**17** il punto Sud *m*
– *south point*
**18** il moto apparente del sole il 21 dicembre *m*
– *apparent path of the sun on 21 December*
**19** il moto apparente del sole il 21 marzo e il 23 settembre *m*
– *apparent path of the sun on 21 March and 23 September*
**20** il moto apparente del sole il 21 giugno
– *apparent path of the sun on 21 June*
**21** la zona limite del crepuscolo
– *border of the twilight area*

**22-28** i movimenti di rotazione *f* dell'asse *m* terrestre
– *rotary motions of the earth's axis*
**22** l'asse *m* dell'eclittica
– *axis of the ecliptic*
**23** la sfera celeste
– *celestial sphere*
**24** l'orbita del polo celeste (precessione *f* e nutazione *f* )
– *path of the celestial pole [precession and nutation]*
**25** l'asse *m* istantaneo di rotazione *f*
– *instantaneous axis of rotation*
**26** il polo celeste
– *celestial pole*
**27** l'asse *m* mediano di rotazione *f*
– *mean axis of rotation*
**28** l'altezza del polo
– *polhode*
**29-35** l'eclisse *f* (l'eclissi *f* ) di sole *m* e di luna [*scala non rispettata*]
– *solar and lunar eclipse [not to scale]*
**29** il Sole
– *the sun*
**30** la Terra
– *the earth*
**31** la Luna
– *the moon*
**32** l'eclisse *f* (l'eclissi *f* ) di sole *m*
– *solar eclipse*
**33** l'eclisse (l'eclissi *f* ) totale
– *area of the earth in which the eclipse appears total*
**34** u. **35** l'eclisse *f* (l'eclissi *f* ) di luna
– *lunar eclipse*
**34** la penombra
– *penumbra (partial shadow)*
**35** l'ombra
– *umbra (total shadow)*
**36-41** il Sole
– *the sun*
**36** il disco solare
– *solar disc (disk) (solar globe, solar sphere)*
**37** macchie *f pl* solari
– *sunspots*
**38** turbini *m pl* in prossimità delle macchie solari
– *cyclones in the area of sunspots*
**39** la corona (corona solare), l'alone *m* solare visibile durante l'eclissi *f* totale di sole *m* oppure con strumenti *m pl* speciali
– *corona (solar corona), observable during total solar eclipse or by means of special instruments*
**40** protuberanze *f pl* solari
– *prominences (solar prominences)*
**41** il margine del disco lunare nell'eclissi *f* totale di sole *m*
– *moon's limb during a total solar eclipse*

**42-52** i pianeti *m* (il sistema planetario, il sistema solare) [non in scala] e i simboli dei pianeti
– *planets (planetary system, solar system) [not to scale] and planet symbols*
**42** il Sole
– *the sun*
**43** Mercurio
– *Mercury*
**44** Venere *f*
– *Venus*
**45** la Terra con la Luna, un satellite
– *Earth, with the moon, a satellite*
**46** Marte *m* con due satelliti *m pl*
– *Mars, with two moons*
**47** gli asteroidi (i pianetini)
– *asteroids (minor planets)*
**48** Giove *m*
– *Jupiter*
**49** Saturno
– *Saturn*
**50** Urano
– *Uranus*
**51** Nettuno
– *Neptune*
**52** Plutone *m* con il satellite *m* Caronte *m*
– *Pluto, with the moon Charon*
**53-64** i segni dello Zodiaco (segni *m pl* zodiacali)
– *signs of the zodiac (zodiacal signs)*
**53** Ariete *m* (Aries *m*)
– *Aries (the Ram)*
**54** Toro (Taurus *m*)
– *Taurus (the Bull)*
**55** Gemelli *m pl* (Gemini *m pl*)
– *Gemini (the Twins)*
**56** Cancro (Cancer *m*)
– *Cancer (the Crab)*
**57** Leone *m* (Leo)
– *Leo (the Lion)*
**58** Vergine *f* (Virgo *f*)
– *Virgo (the Virgin)*
**59** Bilancia (Libra)
– *Libra (the Balance, the Scales)*
**60** Scorpione *m* (Scorpio)
– *Scorpio (the Scorpion)*
**61** Sagittario (Sagittarius *m*)
– *Sagittarius (the Archer)*
**62** Capricorno (Capricornus *m*)
– *Capricorn (the Goat, the Sea Goat)*
**63** Acquario (Aquarius *m*)
– *Aquarius (the Water Carrier, the Water Bearer)*
**64** Pesci *m pl* (Pisces *m pl*)
– *Pisces (the Fish)*

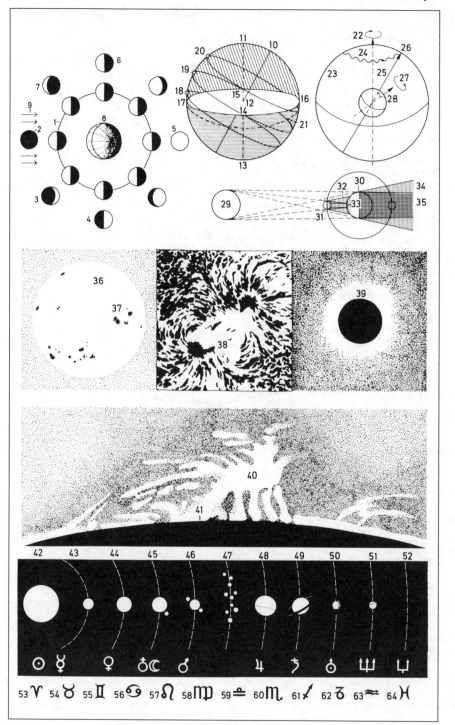

**1-16** l'Osservatorio Meridionale Europeo (ESO) sul Cerro la Silla in Cile, un osservatorio [*sezione*]
– *the European Southern Observatory (ESO) on* Cerro la Silla, Chile, *an observatory [section]*
**1** lo specchio primario (specchio principale) del diametro di 3, 6 metri *m pl*
– *primary mirror (main mirror) with a diameter of 3.6 m (144 inches)*
**2** la cabina dell'obiettivo primario (dello specchio primario) con il supporto degli specchi secondari
– *prime focus cage with mounting for secondary mirrors*
**3** lo specchio piano per la riflessione dei raggi
– *flat mirror for the coudé ray path*
**4** il telescopio di Cassegrain
– *Cassegrain cage*
**5** lo spettografo a grata
– *grating spectrograph*
**6** l'apparecchio fotografico spettografico
– *spectrographic camera*
**7** la guida assiale oraria
– *hour axis drive*
**8** l'asse *m* orario
– *hour axis*
**9** il supporto a ferro di cavallo
– *horseshoe mounting*
**10** il supporto idraulico
– *hydrostatic bearing*
**11** gli obiettivi primario e secondario
– *primary and secondary focusing devices*
**12** la cupola dell'osservatorio (il tetto a cupola, la cupola girevole)
– *observatory dome, a revolving dome*
**13** la fenditura di osservazione *f*
– *observation opening*
**14** la tendina a segmenti *m pl* libera di muoversi verticalmente
– *vertically movable dome shutter*
**15** il paravento
– *wind screen*
**16** il siderostato
– *siderostat*
**17-28** il planetario *di Stoccarda [sezione]*
– *the* Stuttgart *Planetarium [section]*
**17** il settore per amministrazione *f*, officine *f pl*, magazzini *m pl*
– *administration, workshop, and store area*
**18** l'impalcatura in acciaio
– *steel scaffold*
**19** la piramide rivestita in vetro
– *glass pyramid*

**20** la scala graduata circolare girevole
– *revolving arched ladder*
**21** la cupola di proiezione *f*
– *projection dome*
**22** il diaframma
– *light stop*
**23** il proiettore
– *planetarium projector*
**24** il pozzo
– *well*
**25** il foyer (l'atrio)
– *foyer*
**26** la sala delle proiezioni cinematografiche
– *theatre* (Am. *theater*)
**27** la cabina di proiezione *f*
– *projection booth*
**28** i pilastri delle fondamenta
– *foundation pile*
**29-33** l'osservatorio solare «*Kitt Peak*» presso *Tucson*, Arizona *[sezione]*
– *the Kitt Peak solar observatory near* Tucson, Ariz. *[section]*
**29** lo specchio solare (eliostato)
– *heliostat*
**30** il pozzo di osservazione *f* seminterrato
– *sunken observation shaft*
**31** lo schermo paravento raffreddato ad acqua
– *water-cooled windshield*
**32** lo specchio concavo
– *concave mirror*
**33** la sala di osservazione *f* con lo spettografo
– *observation room housing the spectrograph*

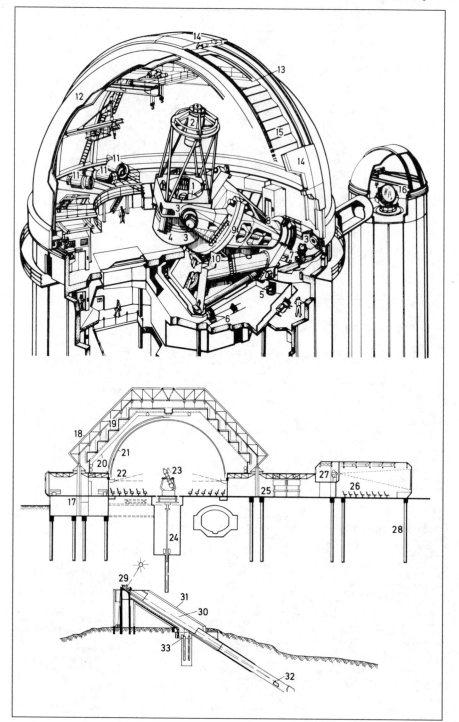

1  l'unità spaziale Apollo (l'astronave f Apollo, il veicolo spaziale Apollo)
–  *Apollo spacecraft*
2  il modulo di servizio (il Service Module, SM)
–  *service module (SM)*
3  l'ugello di scarico del propulsore principale (o del propulsore pilota)
–  *nozzle of the main rocket engine*
4  l'antenna direzionale
–  *directional antenna*
5  il propulsore di assetto
–  *manoeuvring (Am. maneuvering) rockets*
6  i serbatoi dell'ossigeno e dell'idrogeno per l'impianto d'energia a bordo
–  *oxygen and hydrogen tanks for the spacecraft's energy system*
7  il serbatoio del propellente
–  *fuel tank*
8  i radiatori dell'impianto d'energia di bordo
–  *radiators of the spacecraft's energy system*
9  il modulo di comando (capsula spaziale Apollo)
–  *command module (Apollo space capsule)*
10 l'accesso alla capsula spaziale
–  *entry hatch of the space capsule*
11 l'astronauta m
–  *astronaut*
12 il modulo per l'escursione f lunare (il Lunar Module, LEM)
–  *lunar module (LM)*
13 la superficie lunare, una superficie di polvere f
–  *moon's surface (lunar surface), a dust-covered surface*
14 la polvere lunare
–  *lunar dust*
15 il pezzo di roccia
–  *piece of rock*
16 il cratere meteorico
–  *meteorite crater*

17 la terra
–  *the earth*
18-27 la tuta spaziale
–  *space suit (extra-vehicular suit)*
18 il serbatoio di emergenza dell'ossigeno
–  *emergency oxygen apparatus*
19 la tasca per gli occhiali da sole (con occhiali da sole per l'uso a bordo)
–  *sunglass pocket [with sunglasses for use on board]*
20 gli strumenti per la sopravvivenza nello spazio, un'apparecchiatura a zaino
–  *life support system (life support pack), a backpack unit*
21 la linguetta di accesso alla valvola per il condizionamento della tuta
–  *access flap*
22 il casco della tuta spaziale con visiera paraluce (o con visore, con visiera-filtro)
–  *space suit helmet with sun filters*
23 la cassetta di controllo degli strumenti nello zaino (i controlli a distanza dello zaino)
–  *control box of the life support pack*
24 la tasca per la lampada a torcia
–  *penlight pocket*
25 la linguetta di accesso alla valvola di scarico
–  *access flap for the purge valve*
26 attacchi del tubo e dei fili per radio f, pressurizzazione f, e raffreddamento ad acqua
–  *tube and cable connections for the radio, ventilation, and water-cooling systems*
27 la tasca di servizio (con l'occorrente m per scrivere, utensili m pl e altro)
–  *pocket for pens, tools, etc.*
28-36 lo stadio di discesa
–  *descent stage*
28 la guarnizione di collegamento
–  *connector*
29 il serbatoio del propellente
–  *fuel tank*

30 il propulsore
–  *engine*
31 il meccanismo a espansione f del telaio di atterraggio
–  *mechanism for unfolding the legs*
32 la gamba ammortizzatrice
–  *main shock absorber*
33 il disco di atterraggio
–  *landing pad*
34 la piattaforma di salita e discesa
–  *ingress/egress platform (hatch platform)*
35 la scala di accesso
–  *ladder to platform and hatch*
36 il cardamo del propulsore
–  *cardan mount for engine*
37-47 lo stadio di salita
–  *ascent stage*
37 il serbatoio del propellente
–  *fuel tank*
38 il boccaporto di salita e discesa
–  *ingress/egress hatch (entry/exit hatch)*
39 i razzi stabilizzatori
–  *LM manoeuvring (Am. maneuvering) rockets*
40 la finestra
–  *window*
41 l'abitacolo per l'equipaggio
–  *crew compartment*
42 l'antenna radar per il «rendez-vous»
–  *rendezvous radar antenna*
43 il misuratore del coefficiente d'inerzia
–  *inertial measurement unit*
44 l'antenna direzionale per la base sulla terra
–  *directional antenna for ground control*
45 il boccaporto superiore
–  *upper hatch (docking hatch)*
46 l'antenna radioguida di avvicinamento/di arrivo
–  *inflight antenna*
47 l'incavo per il «docking» (o per l'aggancio in orbita)
–  *docking target recess*

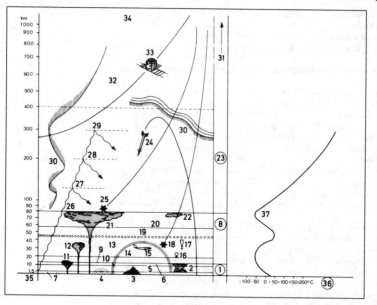

**1 la troposfera**
- *the troposphere*
**2** le nuvole (le nubi) temporalesche
- *thunderclouds*
**3** l'*Everest m*, il monte più alto del mondo (m. 8882)
- *the highest mountain*, Mount Everest *[8,882 m]*
**4** l'arcobaleno
- *rainbow*
**5** lo strato delle correnti a getto
- *jet stream level*
**6** lo strato zero (inversione *f* delle correnti verticali)
- *zero level [inversion of vertical air movement]*
**7** lo strato base (limite *m* inferiore della troposfera)
- *ground layer (surface boundary layer)*
**8 la stratosfera**
- *the stratosphere*
**9** la tropopausa
- *tropopause*
**10** lo strato divisorio (strato di correnti più deboli)
- *separating layer (layer of weaker air movement)*
**11** l'esplosione *f* della bomba atomica
- *atomic explosion*
**12** l'esplosione *f* della bomba a idrogeno
- *hydrogen bomb explosion*
**13** lo strato d'azoto
- *ozone layer*
**14** la propagazione delle onde acustiche
- *range of sound wave propagation*

**15** l'aereo stratosferico (l'aviogetto)
- *stratosphere aircraft*
**16** il pallone con equipaggio
- *manned balloon*
**17** il pallone sonda
- *sounding balloon*
**18** la meteora
- *meteor*
**19** il limite superiore dello strato d'azoto
- *upper limit of ozone layer*
**20** lo strato zero (la stratopausa)
- *zero level*
**21** l'eruzione *f* di Krakatoa
- *eruption of Krakatoa*
**22** nubi *f pl* nottilucenti
- *luminous clouds (noctilucent clouds)*
**23 la ionosfera**
- *the ionosphere*
**24** il campo d'indagine *f* dei missili
- *range of research rockets*
**25** la stella cadente
- *shooting star*
**26** l'onda corta (alta frequenza)
- *short wave (high frequency)*
**27** lo strato E (strato delle onde corte e cortissime)
- *E-layer (Heaviside-Kennelly Layer)*
**28** lo strato F1 (strato delle onde televisive)
- *F₁-layer*
**29** lo strato F2 (strato delle onde televisive)
- *F₂-layer*
**30** l'aurora polare
- *aurora (polar light)*

**31 l'esosfera**
- *the exosphere*
**32** lo strato atomico
- *atom layer*
**33** il campo di rilevazione dei satelliti
- *range of satellite sounding*
**34** il passaggio nello spazio cosmico (o siderale)
- *fringe region*
**35** l'altitudine *f* (la graduazione altimetrica)
- *altitude scale*
**36** la temperatura (la graduazione termometrica)
- *temperature scale (thermometric scale)*
**37** la curva (la linea) delle temperature
- *temperature graph*

**1-19 nubi** *f pl* **(nuvole** *f pl***) e tempo meteorologico**
– *clouds and weather*
**1-4 le nuvole di masse** *f pl* **d'aria omogenee**
– *clouds found in homogeneous air masses*
**1** il cumulo, una nube cumuliforme (nube *f* cumuliforme a base *f* piatta, nube *f* di bel tempo)
– *cumulus (woolpack cloud), a heap cloud; here: cumulus humilis (fair-weather cumulus), a flat-based heap cloud*
**2** il cumulo congesto, una nube cumuliforme gonfia
– *cumulus congestus, a heap cloud with more marked vertical development*
**3** lo stratocumulo, una nube bassa a strati *m pl* articolati cumuliformi
– *stratocumulus, a layer cloud (sheet cloud) arranged in heavy masses*
**4** lo strato (la nebbia alta), una nube bassa a strati *m pl* uniformi
– *stratus (high fog), a thick, uniform layer cloud (sheet cloud)*
**5-12 le nuvole in fronti** *m pl* **caldi**
– *clouds found at warm fronts*
**5** il fronte caldo
– *warm front*
**6** il cirro, una nuvola alta o molto alta formata da cristalli *m pl* di ghiaccio, sottile e di forme *f pl* svariate
– *cirrus, a high to very high ice-crystal cloud, thin and assuming a wide variety of forms*
**7** il cirrostrato, una nuvola a cirri *m pl* formata da cristalli *m pl* di ghiaccio
– *cirrostratus, an ice-crystal cloud veil*
**8** l'altostrato, una nuvola a strati *m pl* di media altezza
– *altostratus, a layer cloud (sheet cloud) of medium height*
**9** l'altostrato precipitans, una nuvola a strati *m pl* con precipitazioni *f pl* in alto
– *altostratus praecipitans, a layer cloud (sheet cloud) with precipitation in its upper parts*
**10** il nembostrato, (il nembo), una nuvola spessa a strati *m pl* apportatrice di precipitazioni *f pl* (pioggia o neve *f*)
– *nimbostratus, a rain cloud, a layer cloud (sheet cloud) of very large vertical extent which produces precipitation (rain or snow)*
**11** il fractostrato, brandelli *m pl* di nuvole *f pl* sottostanti il nembo
– *fractostratus, a ragged cloud occurring beneath nimbostratus*

**12** il fractocumulo, brandelli *m pl* di nuvole *f pl* come il n. 11, ma cumuliformi
– *fractocumulus, a ragged cloud like 11 but with billowing shapes*
**13-17 le nuvole in fronti** *m pl* **freddi**
– *clouds at cold fronts*
**13** il fronte freddo
– *cold front*
**14** il cirrocumulo, una nuvola a fiocchi *m pl* leggeri (*pop.*: il cielo a pecorelle *f pl*)
– *cirrocumulus, thin fleecy cloud in the form of globular masses; covering the sky: mackerel sky*
**15** l'altocumulo, una nuvola ampia e lanuginosa
– *altocumulus, a cloud in the form of large globular masses*
**16** l'altocumulo castellano e l'altocumulo a fiocchi *m pl*, varietà *f pl* del n. 15
– *altocumulus castellanus and altocumulus floccus, species of 15*
**17** il cumulonembo, una nuvola cumuliforme molto spessa, nei temporali di calore da associarsi ai n. 1-4
– *cumulonimbus, a heap cloud of very large vertical extent, to be classified under 1-4 in the case of tropical storms*
**18-19 tipi** *m pl* **di precipitazione** *f*
– *types of precipitation*
**18** la pioggia continua o la caduta estesa di neve *f*, una precipitazione uniforme
– *steady rain or snow covering a large area, precipitation of uniform intensity*
**19** l'acquazzone *m* (il rovescio di pioggia), una precipitazione disuguale (precipitazione *f* a tratti *m pl*)
– *shower, scattered precipitation*

*black arrow = cold air*
*white arrow = warm air*

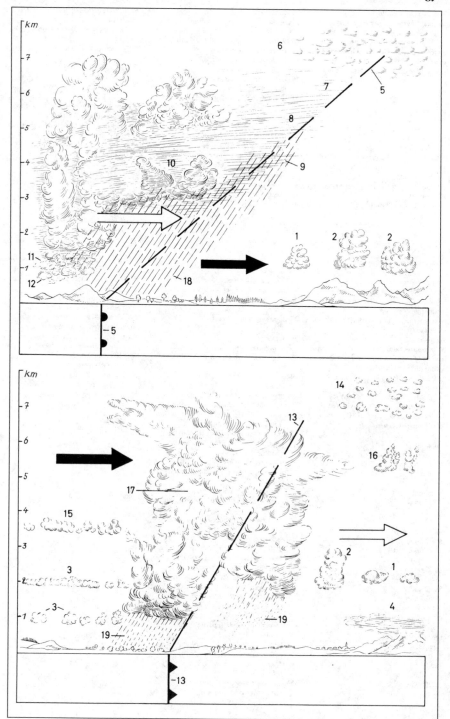

# 9 Meteorologia II e Climatologia

**1-39 la carta meteorologica**
- *weather chart (weather map, surface chart, surface synoptic chart)*
1 la isobara (linea di uguale pressione atmosferica/barometrica al livello del mare)
- *isobar (line of equal or constant atmospheric or barometric pressure at sea level)*
2 la linea pliobara (isobara di pressione f superiore a mb. 1000)
- *pleiobar (isobar of over 1,000 mb)*
3 la linea miobara (isobara di pressione f inferiore a mb. 1000)
- *meiobar (isobar of under 1,000 mb)*
4 l'indicazione f della pressione barometrica (pressione f atmosferica) in millibar m pl (mb.)
- *atmospheric (barometric) pressure given in millibars*
5 l'area di bassa pressione f (il ciclone, la depressione)
- *low-pressure area (low, cyclone, depression)*
6 l'area di alta pressione f (l'anticiclone m)
- *high-pressure area (high, anticyclone)*
7 una stazione meteorologica o una nave di osservazione f meteorologica
- *observatory (meteorological watch office, weather station) or ocean station vessel (weather ship)*
8 la temperatura (indicazione f della temperatura)
- *temperature*

**9-19 la rappresentazione grafica del vento**
- *means of representing wind direction (wind-direction symbols)*
9 la freccia indicante la direzione del vento
- *wind-direction shaft (wind arrow)*
10 la freccia indicante la forza del vento
- *wind-speed barb (wind-speed feather) indicating wind speed*
11 la calma (bonaccia)
- *calm*
12 1-2 nodi m pl (1 nodo = 1,852 km/h)
- *1-2 knots (1 knot = 1,852 kph)*
13 3-7 nodi m pl
- *3-7 knots*
14 8-12 nodi m pl
- *8-12 knots*
15 13-17 nodi m pl
- *13-17 knots*
16 18-22 nodi m pl
- *18-22 knots*
17 23-27 nodi m pl
- *23-27 knots*
18 28-32 nodi m pl
- *28-32 knots*
19 58-62 nodi m pl
- *58-62 knots*

**20-24 nuvolosità f**
- *state of the sky (distribution of the cloud cover)*
20 senza nuvole f pl
- *clear (cloudless)*
21 sereno
- *fair*
22 poco nuvoloso (semicoperto)
- *partly cloudy*
23 nuvoloso
- *cloudy*

24 coperto
- *overcast (sky mostly or completely covered)*

**25-29 fronti m pl e correnti f pl d'aria**
- *fronts and air currents*
25 l'occlusione f
- *occlusion (occluded front)*
26 il fronte di aria calda (fronte m caldo)
- *warm front*
27 il fronte di aria fredda (fronte m freddo)
- *cold front*
28 la corrente di aria calda
- *warm airstream (warm current)*
29 la corrente di aria fredda
- *cold airstream (cold current)*

**30-39 fenomeni m pl atmosferici**
- *meteorological phenomena*
30 l'area di precipitazioni f pl
- *precipitation area*
31 nebbia
- *fog*
32 pioggia
- *rain*
33 pioggia fine
- *drizzle*
34 neve f (caduta di neve f)
- *snow*
35 pioggia mista a neve f (gragnola)
- *ice pellets (graupel, soft hail)*
36 grandine f
- *hail*
37 rovescio di pioggia
- *shower*
38 temporale m
- *thunderstorm*
39 bagliori m pl (lampi m pl di calore m)
- *lightning*

**40-58 la carta climatica**
- *climatic map*
40 la isoterma (linea che congiunge punti m pl di uguale temperatura media)
- *isotherm (line connecting points having equal mean temperature)*
41 la isoterma zero (linea che congiunge punti m pl con temperatura media annuale di 0° C)
- *0° C (zero) isotherm (line connecting points having a mean annual temperature of 0° C)*
42 la isochimena (linea che congiunge punti m pl di uguale temperatura media invernale)
- *isocheim (line connecting points having equal mean winter temperature)*
43 la isotera (linea che congiunge punti m pl di uguale temperatura media estiva)
- *isothere (line connecting points having equal mean summer temperature)*
44 la isoelia (linea che congiunge punti m pl di uguale durata di luce f solare)
- *isohel (line connecting points having equal duration of sunshine)*
45 l'isoieta (linea che congiunge punti m pl con uguali valori m pl di precipitazioni f pl annuali)
- *isohyet (line connecting points having equal amounts of precipitation)*
**46-47 la zona delle calme**
- *calm belts*
**46-52 le coordinate dei venti**
- *atmospheric circulation (wind systems)*

46 la zona delle calme equatoriali (i doldrums)
- *equatorial trough (equatorial calms, doldrums)*
47 le zone delle calme sub-tropicali (le horse latitudes)
- *subtropical high-pressure belts (horse latitudes)*
48 i venti alisei nord-orientali (gli Alisei di Nord-Est)
- *north-east trade winds (north-east trades, tropical easterlies)*
49 i venti alisei sud-orientali (gli Alisei di Sud-Est)
- *south-east trade winds (south-east trades, tropical easterlies)*
50 le zone dei venti variabili occidentali
- *zones of the variable westerlies*
51 le zone dei venti polari
- *polar wind zones*
52 il monsone d'estate f
- *summer monsoon*

**53-58 i climi della terra**
- *earth's climates*
53 il clima equatoriale: la fascia piovosa tropicale
- *equatorial climate: tropical zone (tropical rain zone)*
54 le due fasce secche: le zone dei deserti e delle steppe
- *the two arid zones (equatorial dry zones): desert and steppe zones*
55 le due fasce temperate piovose
- *the two temperate rain zones*
56 il clima boreale (clima m montano)
- *boreal climate (snow forest climate)*
**57 u. 58 i climi polari**
- *polar climates*
57 il clima della tundra
- *tundra climate*
58 il clima dei ghiacci perenni
- *perpetual frost climate*

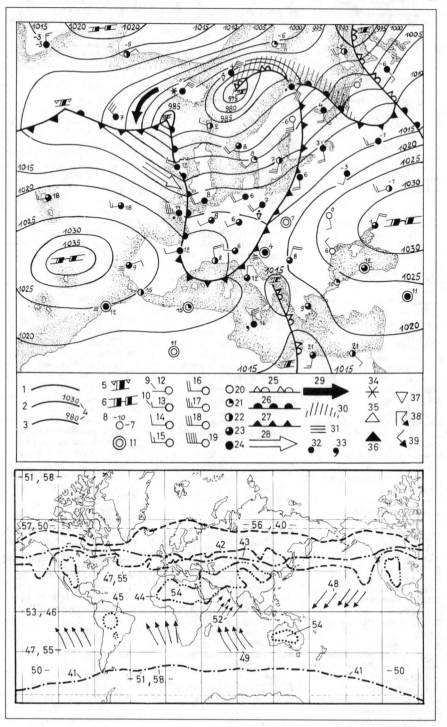

# 10 Strumenti meteorologici

**1**  il barometro a mercurio, un barometro a sifone *m*, un barometro a liquido
– *mercury barometer, a siphon barometer, a liquid-column barometer*
**2**  la colonna di mercurio
– *mercury column*
**3**  la graduazione in millibar *m pl* (scala millimetrica)
– *millibar scale, a millimetre (Am. millimeter) scale*
**4**  il barografo, un barometro aneroide autoregistratore (a registrazione *f* automatica)
– *barograph, a self-registering aneroid barometer*
**5**  il cilindro
– *drum (recording drum)*
**6**  la serie delle scatole aneroidi
– *bank of aneroid capsules (aneroid boxes)*
**7**  la leva scrivente
– *recording arm*
**8**  l'igrografo
– *hygrograph*
**9**  l'elemento misuratore dell'umidità (l'igrometro a capello)
– *hygrometer element (hair element)*
**10**  il regolatore di posizione *f*
– *reading adjustment*
**11**  la leva di amplificazione *f*
– *amplitude adjustment*
**12**  il braccio scrivente
– *recording arm*
**13**  il pennino scrivente
– *recording pen*
**14**  le ruote alternate per l'orologeria
– *change gears for the clockwork drive*
**15**  il dispositivo d'arresto del braccio scrivente
– *off switch for the recording arm*
**16**  il cilindro
– *drum (recording drum)*
**17**  la spartizione del tempo
– *time scale*
**18**  l'involucro
– *case (housing)*
**19**  il termografo
– *thermograph*
**20**  il cilindro
– *drum (recording drum)*
**21**  la leva scrivente
– *recording arm*
**22**  l'elemento misuratore (la lamina sensibile)
– *sensing element*
**23**  il pirœliometro (pireliometro) a disco d'argento (l'attinometro), uno strumento per la misurazione dell'energia solare
– *silver-disc (silver-disk) pyrheliometer, an instrument for measuring the sun's radiant energy*

**24**  il disco d'argento
– *silver disc (disk)*
**25**  il termometro
– *thermometer*
**26**  il rivestimento coibente di legno
– *wooden insulating casing*
**27**  il tubo con diaframma *m*
– *tube with diaphragm (diaphragmed tube)*
**28**  l'anemometro
– *wind gauge (Am. gage) (anemometer)*
**29**  l'indicatore *m* della velocità del vento
– *wind-speed indicator (wind-speed meter)*
**30**  la croce a tazze *f pl* (croce *f* a mulinello)
– *cross arms with hemispherical cups*
**31**  l'indicatore *m* della direzione del vento (l'anemoscopio)
– *wind-direction indicator*
**32**  la banderuola
– *wind vane*
**33**  lo psicometro a aspirazione *f* (psicometro Assmann)
– *aspiration psychrometer*
**34**  il termometro asciutto
– *dry bulb thermometer*
**35**  il termometro umido
– *wet bulb thermometer*
**36**  il tubo protettivo contro le radiazioni solari
– *solar radiation shielding*
**37**  il tubo aspirante
– *suction tube*
**38**  il pluviometro registratore (il pluviografo, pluviografo a sifone *m* Hellmann)
– *recording rain gauge (Am. gage)*
**39**  l'involucro di protezione *f*
– *protective housing (protective casing)*
**40**  il recipiente di captazione *f* (l'imbuto)
– *collecting vessel*
**41**  il tetto parapioggia
– *rain cover*
**42**  il congegno registratore
– *recording mechanism*
**43**  il sifone
– *siphon tube*
**44**  il pluviometro
– *precipitation gauge (Am. gage) (rain gauge)*
**45**  l'imbuto di captazione *f*
– *collecting vessel*
**46**  il recipiente di raccolta (il collettore di pioggia)
– *storage vessel*
**47**  il vaso misuratore (vaso graduato)
– *measuring glass*

**48**  il dispositivo a croce *f* per misurare la precipitazione *f* nevosa
– *insert for measuring snowfall*
**49**  la capanna di termometria
– *thermometer screen (thermometer shelter)*
**50**  l'igrografo
– *hygrograph*
**51**  il termografo
– *thermograph*
**52**  lo psicrometro
– *psychrometer (wet and dry bulb thermometer)*
**53** *u.* **54**  termometri *m pl* per misurare gli estremi di temperatura
– *thermometers for measuring extremes of temperature*
**53**  il termometro di massima
– *maximum thermometer*
**54**  il termometro di minima
– *minimum thermometer*
**55**  la radio-sonda (la radiometeorografa, il pallone radio)
– *radiosonde assembly*
**56**  il pallone a idrogeno
– *hydrogen balloon*
**57**  il paracadute
– *parachute*
**58**  il riflettore radar *m* con cordella distanziatrice
– *radar reflector with spacing lines*
**59**  la cassetta strumenti con sonda radio (un trasmettitore a onde *f pl* corte) e antenna
– *instrument housing with radiosonde [a short-wave transmitter] and antenna*
**60**  il trasmissometro (l'apparecchio per la misurazione delle trasmissioni), un misuratore a vista
– *transmissometer, an instrument for measuring visibility*
**61**  il dispositivo per la registrazione
– *recording instrument (recorder)*
**62**  il trasmettitore
– *transmitter*
**63**  il ricevitore
– *receiver*
**64**  il satellite meteorologico (satellite ITOS)
– *weather satellite (ITOS satellite)*
**65**  valvole *f pl* per la termoregolazione
– *temperature regulation flaps*
**66**  il braccio con le cellule solari
– *solar panel*
**67**  la telecamera
– *television camera*
**68**  l'antenna
– *antenna*
**69**  il sensore solare
– *solar sensor (sun sensor)*
**70**  l'antenna telemetrica
– *telemetry antenna*
**71**  il radiometro
– *radiometer*

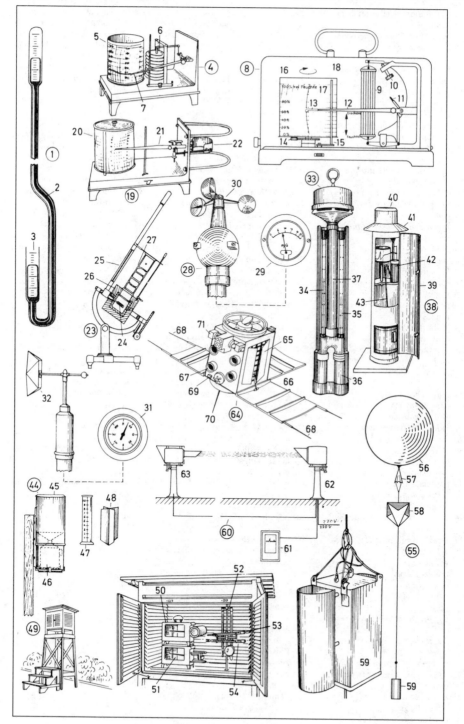

**1-5 la struttura degli strati della terra**
– *layered structure of the earth*
1  la crosta terrestre
– *earth's crust (outer crust of the earth, lithosphere, oxysphere)*
2  l'idrosfera
– *hydrosphere*
3  la litosfera
– *mantle*
4  la geosfera intermedia (il Sima)
– *sima (intermediate layer)*
5  il nucleo centrale della terra (il Nife)
– *core (earth core, centrosphere, barysphere)*
**6-12 la curva ipsometrica (curva ipsografica) della superficie terrestre**
– *hypsographic curve of the earth's surface*
6  il rilievo
– *peak*
7  la piattaforma continentale
– *continental mass*
8  lo zoccolo continentale
– *continental shelf (continental platform, shelf )*
9  la scarpata continentale
– *continental slope*
10  il pavimento abissale
– *deep-sea floor (abyssal plane)*
11  il livello marino
– *sea level*
12  il fosso oceanico
– *deep-sea trench*
**13-28 il vulcanismo**
– *volcanism (vulcanicity)*
13  il vulcano a scudo
– *shield volcano*
14  la crosta lavica (crosta effusiva)
– *lava plateau*
15  il vulcano attivo, un vulcano-strato
– *active volcano, a stratovolcano (composite volcano)*
16  il cratere vulcanico (cratere *m*)
– *volcanic crater (crater)*
17  il camino vulcanico (la gola del vulcano)
– *volcanic vent*
18  la colata lavica
– *lava stream*
19  il tufo (le materie vulcaniche porose)
– *tuff (fragmented volcanic material)*
20  il subvulcano (vulcano senza cono)
– *subterranean volcano*
21  il geyser (la sorgente termale)
– *geyser*
22  il getto di acqua e di vapore *m* (getto del geyser)
– *jet of hot water and steam*

23  le terrazze di geyserite *f*
– *sinter terraces (siliceous sinter terraces, fiorite terraces, pearl sinter terraces)*
24  il cono
– *cone*
25  il Maar (*anche:* lago di cratere *m*)
– *maar (extinct volcano)*
26  il deposito di tufo
– *tuff deposit*
27  la breccia nel camino
– *breccia*
28  il camino del vulcano spento
– *vent of extinct volcano*
**29-31 il magmatismo plutonico (le intrusioni magmatiche)**
– *plutonic magmatism*
29  il batolite (la roccia di origine *f* profonda, roccia plutonica)
– *batholite (massive protrusion)*
30  il laccolite, un'intrusione *f*
– *lacolith, an intrusion*
31  il filone, un giacimento minerario
– *sill, an ore deposit*
**32-38 il terremoto (***tipi:* terremoto tettonico, terremoto vulcanico, terremoto di crollo) **e la sismologia**
– *earthquake* (kinds: *tectonic quake, volcanic quake*) *and seismology*
32  l'ipocentro (la zona di origine del terremoto, il focus)
– *earthquake focus (seismic focus, hypocentre, Am. hypocenter)*
33  l'epicentro (il punto sulla superficie posto sulla verticale dell'ipocentro)
– *epicentre (Am. epicenter), point on the earth's surface directly above the focus*
34  la profondità dell'ipocentro
– *depth of focus*
35  la propagazione delle onde sismiche
– *shock wave*
36  le onde superficiali
– *surface waves (seismic waves)*
37  le isosiste (le isosisme, linee *f pl* che congiungono i punti di uguale intensità sismica)
– *isoseismal (line connecting points of equal intensity of earthquake shock)*
38  la regione dell'epicentro (la zona tellurica macrosismica)
– *epicentral area, an area of macroseismic vibration*
**39 il sismografo** (sismometro) **orizzontale**
– *horizontal seismograph (seismometer)*
40  l'ammortizzatore magnetico
– *electromagnetic damper*

41  la manopola per la regolazione dell'ondulazione *f* del pendolo
– *adjustment knob for the period of free oscillation of the pendulum*
42  l'articolazione *f* a molla di sospensione *f* del pendolo
– *spring attachment for the suspension of the pendulum*
43  la massa pendolare (massa stazionaria)
– *mass*
44  le bobine a induzione *f* per la corrente indicatrice del galvanometro registratore
– *induction coils for recording the voltage of the galvanometer*
**45-54 effetti** *m pl* **dei terremoti (i macrosismi)**
– *effects of earthquakes*
45  la cascata
– *waterfall (cataract, falls)*
46  la frana (smottamento del terreno, caduta di rocce *f pl*)
– *landslide (rockslide, landslip, Am. rock slip)*
47  i detriti (la zona di deposito)
– *talus (rubble, scree)*
48  la nicchia di distacco
– *scar (scaur, scaw)*
49  la dolina
– *sink (sinkhole, swallowhole)*
50  la soliflussione
– *dislocation (displacement)*
51  il cono di fango
– *solifluction lobe (solifluction tongue)*
52  la spaccatura (crepa) del terreno (la litoclasi)
– *fissure*
53  il maremoto causato da un terremoto sottomarino (lo tsumani)
– *tsunami (seismic sea wave) produced by seaquake (submarine earthquake)*
54  la spiaggia sollevata
– *raised beach*

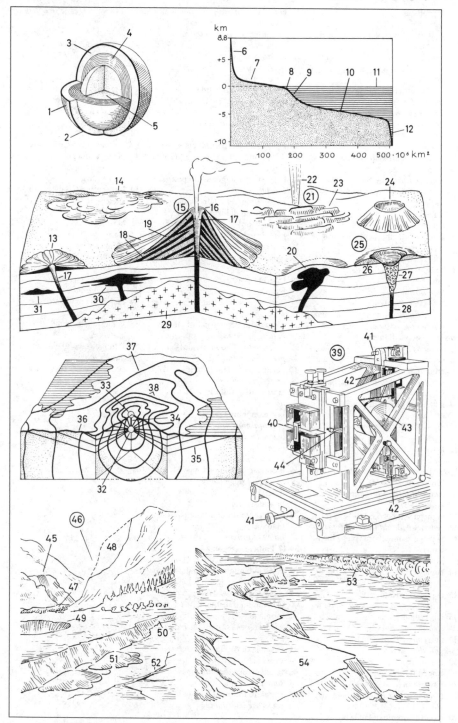

**1-33  geologia**
- *geology*
1  la stratificazione delle rocce sedi-
mentarie
- *stratification of sedimentary rock*
2  la direzione
- *strike*
3  la pendenza (l'immersione *f* )
- *dip (angle of dip, true dip)*
**4-11  la montagna a faglia** (la frattura
delle masse rocciose)
- *fault-block mountain (block
mountain)*
**4-20  i movimenti delle montagne**
(l'orogenesi *f* )
- *orogeny (orogenis, tectogenis,
deformation of rocks by folding
and faulting)*
4  la faglia
- *fault*
5  il piano di faglia (la linea di frattura)
- *fault line (fault trace)*
6  il rigetto della faglia (l'altezza del
salto)
- *fault throw*
7  la faglia normale
- *normal fault (gravity fault, normal
slip fault, slump fault)*
**8-11  il sistema di faglie** *f pl*
- *complex faults*
8  la faglia a gradinata (la frattura a
gradini *m pl*)
- *step fault (distributive fault, multiple fault)*
9  il banco roccioso inclinato
- *tilt block*
10  il pilastro di resistenza
- *horst*
11  la fossa tettonica
- *graben*
**12-20  il corrugamento** (il rilievo montuoso a pieghe *f pl*)
- *range of fold mountains (folded
mountains)*
12  la piega simmetrica
- *symmetrical fold (normal fold)*
13  la piega asimmetrica (piega inclinata)
- *asymmetrical fold*
14  la piega rovesciata
- *overfold*
15  la piega coricata
- *recumbent fold (reclined fold)*
16  l'anticlinale *f*
- *saddle (anticline)*
17  l'asse *m* dell'anticlinale *f*
- *anticlinal axis*
18  la sinclinale
- *trough (syncline)*
19  l'asse *m* della sinclinale
- *trough surface (trough plane, synclinal axis)*
20  il corrugamento a faglia
- *anticlinorium*

21  la falda acquifera sotterranea in
pressione *f*
- *groundwater under pressure (artesian water)*
22  lo strato acquifero
- *water-bearing stratum (aquifer,
aquafer)*
23  la roccia impermeabile
- *impervious rock (impermeable
rock)*
24  l'area d'impluvio (il bacino
imbrifero)
- *drainage basin (catchment area)*
25  il condotto del pozzo artesiano
- *artesian well*
26  l'acqua prorompente, un pozzo
artesiano
- *rising water, an artesian spring*
27  i giacimenti di idrocarburi *m pl*
(di petrolio) in un'anticlinale *f*
- *petroleum reservoir in an anticline*
28  lo strato impermeabile
- *impervious stratum (impermeable
stratum)*
29  lo strato poroso come roccia-ser-
batoio
- *porous stratum acting as reservoir
rock*
30  il gas naturale, una calotta di gas
- *natural gas, a gas cap*
31  il petrolio (l'olio minerale)
- *petroleum (crude oil)*
32  l'acqua (acqua marginale)
- *underlying water*
33  la torre di trivellazione *f*
- *derrick*
34  la mezza montagna
- *mountainous area*
35  la cima arrotondata della montagna
- *rounded mountain top*
36  il dorsale della montagna
- *mountain ridge (ridge)*
37  il pendio
- *mountain slope*
38  la sorgente sul fianco della montagna
- *hillside spring*
**39-47  l'alta montagna**
- *high-mountain region*
39  la catena montuosa, un massiccio
montuoso
- *mountain range, a massif*
40  la sommità (la cima, il picco) della
montagna
- *summit (peak, top of the mountain)*
41  la spalla di roccia
- *shoulder*
42  la sella (sella di montagna)
- *saddle*
43  la parete (parete *f* rocciosa)
- *rock face (steep face)*

44  il canalone (canalone *m* di pendio)
- *gully*
45  la fascia detritica
- *talus (scree, detritus)*
46  la mulattiera
- *bridle path*
47  il passo (passo di montagna)
- *pass (col)*
**48-56  il ghiacciaio**
- *glacial ice*
48  il nevaio
- *firn field (firn basin, nevé)*
49  la lingua del ghiacciaio (il ghiacciaio sceso a valle *f* )
- *valley glacier*
50  il crepaccio (crepaccio di ghiacciaio)
- *crevasse*
51  la fronte (bocca, porta) del ghiacciaio
- *glacier snout*
52  il torrente glaciale
- *subglacial stream*
53  la morena laterale
- *lateral moraine*
54  la morena mediana
- *medial moraine*
55  la morena terminale
- *end moraine*
56  il fungo (tavola) glaciale
- *glacier table*

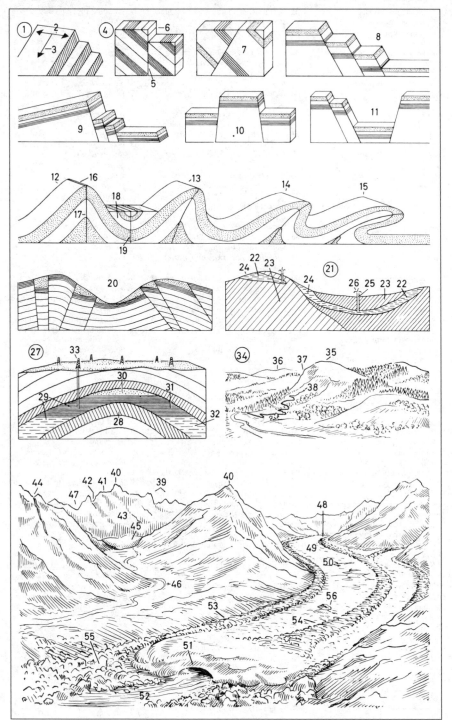

**1-13 il paesaggio fluviale**
– *fluvial topography*
1 la foce del fiume, un delta
– *river mouth, a delta*
2 il braccio del delta, un braccio di un fiume
– *distributary (distributary channel), a river branch (river arm)*
3 il lago
– *lake*
4 la riva
– *bank*
5 la penisola
– *peninsula (spit)*
6 l'isola
– *island*
7 l'insenatura (la baia, il golfo)
– *bay (cove)*
8 il ruscello
– *stream (brook, rivulet, creek)*
9 il cono alluvionale
– *levee*
10 l'area di interramento
– *alluvial plain*
11 il meandro
– *meander (river bend)*
12 il monte raggirato dal meandro
– *meander core (rock island)*
13 la piana alluvionale (la marcita)
– *meadow*
**14-24 la palude** (il terreno paludoso)
– *bog (marsh)*
14 il pantano (la palude bassa)
– *low-moor bog*
15 gli strati di fango (di pantano)
– *layers of decayed vegetable matter*
16 la falda acquifera
– *entrapped water*
17 la torba di canne *f pl* e carici *f pl*
– *fen peat [consisting of rush and sedge]*
18 la torba di ontano (torba di alno)
– *alder-swamp peat*
19 l'alta torbiera (la palude alta)
– *high-moor bog*
20 lo strato recente di torba muscosa
– *layer of recent sphagnum mosses*
21 l'orizzonte limite
– *boundary between layers (horizons)*
22 lo strato antico di torba muscosa
– *layer of older sphagnum mosses*
23 lo stagno (stagno di palude *f* )
– *bog pool*
24 la zona saturata
– *swamp*
**25-31 la costa rocciosa**
– *cliffline (cliffs)*
25 lo scoglio
– *rock*
26 il mare
– *sea (ocean)*
27 il frangente
– *surf*
28 la falesia
– *cliff (cliff face, steep rock face)*
29 i detriti costieri
– *scree*
30 l'erosione *f* del frangente, un'incavatura (una gola)
– *[wave-cut] notch*

31 la superficie di abrasione *f* (spiaggia formata dal frangente)
– *abrasion platform (wave-cut platform)*
32 l'atollo, una scogliera corallina
– *atoll, a ring-shaped coral reef*
33 la laguna
– *lagoon*
34 il canale della laguna
– *breach (hole)*
**35-44 la costa bassa** (la spiaggia)
– *beach*
35 il cordone litoraneo (il limite dell'alta marea)
– *high-water line (high-water mark, tidemark)*
36 le onde di riva
– *waves breaking on the shore*
37 la barriera
– *groyne (Am. groin)*
38 il termine della barriera
– *groyne (Am. groin) head*
39 la duna mobile, una duna
– *wandering dune (migratory dune, travelling, Am. traveling, dune), a dune*
40 la duna falcata (duna a barcone *m*)
– *barchan (barchane, barkhan, crescentic dune)*
41 le ondulazioni (i solchi sulla sabbia, l'increspatura sulla sabbia, i ripplemarks)
– *ripple marks*
42 la cresta di banchisa
– *hummock*
43 l'albero piegato dal vento
– *wind cripple*
44 la laguna litoranea
– *coastal lake*
45 **il canyon** (canon *m*)
– **canyon** *(cañon, coulee)*
46 il tavolato
– *plateau (tableland)*
47 la terrazza rocciosa
– *rock terrace*
48 la stratificazione della roccia (la roccia stratificata)
– *sedimentary rock (stratified rock)*
49 la cengia (il gradino di strato)
– *river terrace (bed)*
50 la frattura
– *joint*
51 il fiume incassato nel canyon
– *canyon river*
**52-56 forme** *f pl* **delle valli** *[sezione trasversale]*
– *types of valley [cross section]*
52 la gola
– *gorge (ravine)*
53 la valle a V stretta
– *V-shaped valley (V-valley)*
54 la valle a V larga
– *widened V-shaped valley*
55 la valle matura
– *U-shaped valley (U-valley, trough valley)*
56 la conca (valle *f* vecchia)
– *synclinal valley*
**57-70 la valle fluviale**
– *river valley*
57 il pendio ripido (la scarpata)
– *scarp (escarpment)*

58 il pendio pianeggiante
– *slip-off slope*
59 il monte tabulare
– *mesa*
60 la catena di colline *f pl*
– *ridge*
61 il fiume
– *river*
62 la marcita (la pianura alluvionale, il prato rivierasco)
– *flood plain*
63 la terrazza rocciosa
– *river terrace*
64 la terrazza fluviale, una terrazza di detriti *m pl*
– *terracette*
65 il pendio
– *pediment*
66 l'altura (la collina)
– *hill*
67 il fondovalle
– *valley floor (valley bottom)*
68 il letto del fiume
– *riverbed*
69 i depositi fluviali
– *sediment*
70 la soletta della roccia
– *bedrock*
**71-83 le formazioni carsiche** in roccia calcarea
– *karst formation in limestone*
71 la dolina, una cavità carsica a forma d'imbuto
– *dolina, a sink (sinkhole, swallowhole)*
72 la valle carsica a forma di bacino
– *polje*
73 il fiume sotterraneo
– *percolation of a river*
74 la sorgente carsica
– *karst spring*
75 la valle secca
– *dry valley*
76 il sistema di grotte ipogee
– *system of caverns (system of caves)*
77 la superficie freatica in una formazione carsica
– *water level (water table) in a karst formation*
78 lo strato roccioso impermeabile
– *impervious rock (impermeable rock)*
79 la grotta carsica
– *limestone cave (dripstone cave)*
80 *u.* 81 le concrezioni calcaree
– *speleothems (cave formations)*
80 la stalattite
– *stalactite (dripstone)*
81 la stalagmite
– *stalagmite*
82 la colonna (il pilastro) di concrezione calcarea
– *linked-up stalagmite and stalactite*
83 il fiume ipogeo (fiume *m* sotterraneo)
– *subterranean river*

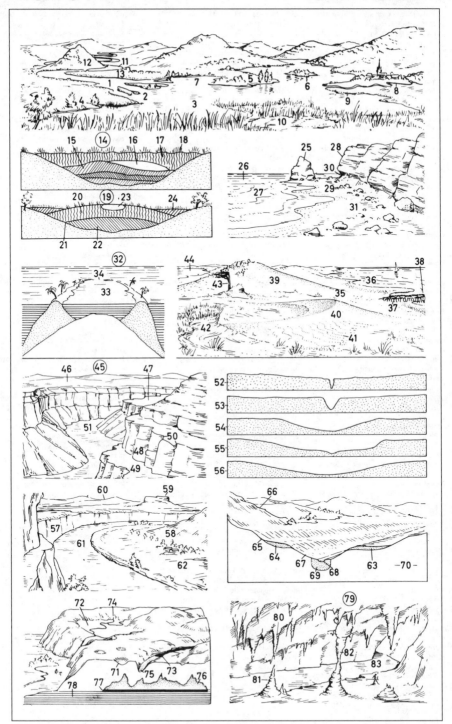

**1-7  il reticolo dei meridiani e dei paralleli sulla superficie terrestre**
- *graticule of the earth (network of meridians and parallels on the earth's surface)*
**1**  l'equatore *m*
- *equator*
**2**  un parallelo
- *line of latitude (parallel of latitude, parallel)*
**3**  il polo (polo nord *o* polo artico; polo sud *o* polo antartico), un polo terrestre
- *pole (North Pole or South Pole), a terrestrial pole (geographical pole)*
**4**  il meridiano (la semicirconferenza del globo terrestre)
- *line of longitude (meridian of longitude, meridian, terrestrial meridian)*
**5**  il meridiano zero (meridiano «O», meridiano di riferimento, meridiano di Greenwich)
- *Standard meridian (Prime meridian, Greenwich meridian, meridian of Greenwich)*
**6**  l'angolo di latitudine *f* geografica (la latitudine geografica)
- *latitude*
**7**  l'angolo di longitudine *f* geografica (la longitudine geografica)
- *longitude*
**8** *u.* **9  proiezioni** *f pl* **cartografiche**
- *map projections*
**8**  la proiezione conica
- *conical (conic) projection*
**9**  la proiezione cilindrica
- *cylindrical projection (Mercator projection, Mercator's projection)*
**10-45  il planisfero (il mappamondo)**
- *map of the world*
**10**  i tropici (le linee dei tropici)
- *tropics*
**11**  i circoli polari
- *polar circles*
**12** *u.* **13**  l'America
- *America*
**12-18  i continenti**
- *continents*
**12**  il Nordamerica, l'America Settentrionale
- *North America*
**13**  il Sudamerica, l'America Meridionale
- *South America*
**14**  l'Africa
- *Africa*
**15** *u.* **16**  l'Eurasia
- *Europe and Asia*
**15**  l'Europa
- *Europe*
**16**  l'Asia
- *Asia*
**17**  l'Australia
- *Australia*
**18**  l'Antartide *f*
- *Antarctica (Antarctic Continent)*
**19-26  i mari del mondo**
- *ocean (sea)*
**19**  l'Oceano Pacifico (il Pacifico)
- *Pacific Ocean*
**20**  l'Oceano Atlantico (l'Atlantico)
- *Atlantic Ocean*
**21**  il Mar (Mare) Glaciale Artico
- *Arctic Ocean*

**22**  il Mar (Mare) Glaciale Antartico
- *Antarctic Ocean (Southern Ocean)*
**23**  l'Oceano Indiano
- *Indian Ocean*
**24**  lo Stretto di Gibilterra, uno stretto
- *Strait of Gibraltar, a sea strait*
**25**  il Mar (Mare) Mediterraneo (il Mediterraneo)
- *Mediterranean (Mediterranean Sea, European Mediterranean)*
**26**  il Mar (Mare) del Nord, un mare epicontinentale
- *North Sea, a marginal sea (epeiric sea, epicontinental sea)*
**27-29  la leggenda (spiegazione** *f* **dei simboli)**
- *key (explanation of map symbols)*
**27**  la corrente marina fredda
- *cold ocean current*
**28**  la corrente marina calda
- *warm ocean current*
**29**  la scala
- *scale*
**30-45  le correnti marine**
- *ocean (oceanic) currents (ocean drifts)*
**30**  la Corrente del Golfo
- *Gulf Stream (North Atlantic Drift)*
**31**  la Corrente Nera (Kuro Shio)
- *Kuroshio (Kuro Siwo, Japan Current)*
**32**  la Corrente Nord-Equatoriale
- *North Equatorial Current*
**33**  la Controcorrente Equatoriale
- *Equatorial Countercurrent*
**34**  la Corrente Sud-Equatoriale
- *South Equatorial Current*
**35**  la Corrente del Brasile
- *Brazil Current*
**36**  la Corrente dei monsoni di Nord-Est
- *Somali Current*
**37**  la Corrente di Las Agulhas, delle Agulhas
- *Agulhas Current*
**38**  la Corrente dell'Australia orientale
- *East Australian Current*
**39**  la Corrente della California
- *California Current*
**40**  la Corrente del Labrador
- *Labrador Current*
**41**  la Corrente delle Canarie
- *Canary Current*
**42**  la Corrente del Perú (la Corrente di Humboldt)
- *Peru Current*
**43**  la Corrente di Benguela
- *Benguela (Benguella) Current*
**44**  la Corrente Antartica
- *West Wind Drift (Antarctic Circumpolar Drift)*
**45**  la Corrente dell'Australia occidentale
- *West Australian Current*
**46-62  la geodesia (le dimensioni di un paese, la misurazione terrestre)**
- *surveying (land surveying, geodetic surveying, geodesy)*
**46**  la livellazione (la misurazione geometrica dell'altezza)
- *levelling (Am. leveling) (geometrical measurement of height)*
**47**  la stadia
- *graduated measuring rod (levelling, Am. leveling, staff )*

**48**  il livello (a cannocchiale), un cannocchiale di puntamento
- *level (surveying level, surveyor's level), a surveyor's telescope*
**49**  il punto trigonometrico
- *triangulation station (triangulation point)*
**50**  il supporto
- *supporting scaffold*
**51**  la torre di segnale *m*
- *signal tower (signal mast)*
**52-62  il teodolite,** uno strumento per la misurazione degli angoli
- *theodolite, an instrument for measuring angles*
**52**  la manopola micrometrica
- *micrometer head*
**53**  l'oculare *m* del microscopio
- *micrometer eyepiece*
**54**  la vite di comando per l'elevazione *f*
- *vertical tangent screw*
**55**  il controdado di elevazione *f*
- *vertical clamp*
**56**  la vite di comando per i movimenti laterali
- *tangent screw*
**57**  il controdado laterale
- *horizontal clamp*
**58**  la manopola per lo specchio riflettore
- *adjustment for the illuminating mirror*
**59**  lo specchio riflettore
- *illuminating mirror*
**60**  il telescopio
- *telescope*
**61**  la livella trasversale
- *spirit level*
**62**  la regolazione (il regolatore) circolare
- *circular adjustment*
**63-66  l'aerofotogrammetria (la fototopografia, la fotografia aerea)**
- *photogrammetry (phototopography)*
**63**  la camera aerofotogrammetrica automatica
- *air survey camera for producing overlapping series of pictures*
**64**  lo stereotopo
- *stereoscope*
**65**  il pantografo
- *pantograph*
**66**  lo stereoplanigrafo
- *stereoplanigraph*

# 15 Carta geografica II

*Map II* 15

**1-114 i simboli cartografici** di una carta
geografica a scala 1 : 25 000, **la leggenda**
- *map signs (map symbols, conventional
signs) on a 1 : 25 000 map*
1 il bosco (la foresta) di conifere *f pl*
- *coniferous wood (coniferous trees)*
2 la radura
- *clearing*
3 l'ente *m* forestale
- *forestry office*
4 il bosco di latifoglie *f pl,* il bosco ceduo
- *deciduous wood (non-coniferous trees)*
5 la brughiera
- *heath (rough grassland, rough pasture,
heath and moor, bracken)*
6 la sabbia
- *sand or sand hills*
7 l'ammofila
- *beach grass*
8 il faro
- *lighthouse*
9 il limite di secca
- *mean low water*
10 la biffa
- *beacon*
11 le isobate (i limiti sottomarini)
- *submarine contours*
12 il traghetto ferroviario
- *train ferry*
13 la nave-faro
- *lightship*
14 il bosco misto
- *mixed wood (mixed trees)*
15 la macchia
- *brushwood*
16 l'autostrada con lo svincolo
- *motorway with slip road (Am. freeway
with on-ramp, freeway with acceleration lane)*
17 la strada nazionale
- *trunk road*
18 il prato
- *grassland*
19 il prato acquitrinoso
- *marshy grassland*
20 l'acquitrino
- *marsh*
21 la linea ferroviaria principale
- *main line railway (Am. trunk line)*
22 il sottopassaggio
- *road over railway*
23 la linea ferroviaria secondaria
- *branch line*
24 il posto di blocco
- *signal box (Am. switch tower)*
25 il trenino locale
- *local line*
26 il passaggio a livello
- *level crossing*
27 la fermata, la stazione
- *halt*
28 la zona residenziale
- *residential area*
29 l'idrometro (l'indicatore *m* del livello
dei fiumi)
- *water gauge (Am. gage)*
30 la strada di terzo ordine; la strada
comunale
- *good, metalled road*
31 il mulino a vento
- *windmill*
32 la salina
- *thorn house (graduation house, salina,
salt-works)*
33 la torre radio, il ripetitore
- *broadcasting station (wireless or television mast)*

34 la miniera
- *mine*
35 la miniera abbandonata
- *disused mine*
36 la strada di secondo ordine, la strada
provinciale
- *secondary road (B road)*
37 la fabbrica, lo stabilimento
- *works*
38 la ciminiera
- *chimney*
39 la recinzione, la rete metallica
- *wire fence*
40 la sovrappassaggio stradale, il cavalcavia
- *bridge over railway*
41 la stazione ferroviaria
- *railway station (Am. railroad station)*
42 il soprappassaggio ferroviario
- *bridge under railway*
43 il sentiero
- *footpath*
44 il passaggio consentito
- *bridge for footpath under railway*
45 il fiume navigabile
- *navigable river*
46 il ponte di barche *f pl*
- *pontoon bridge*
47 la nave-traghetto per auto(mobili) *f pl*
- *vehicle ferry*
48 il molo di massi *m pl*
- *mole*
49 il faro
- *beacon*
50 il ponte di pietra
- *stone bridge*
51 la città
- *town or city*
52 la piazza, la piazza principale
- *market place (market square)*
53 la grande chiesa con due campanili *m pl*
- *large church with two towers*
54 l'edificio pubblico
- *public building*
55 il ponte stradale
- *road bridge*
56 il ponte in ferro
- *iron bridge*
57 il canale
- *canal*
58 la chiusa a conche *f pl*
- *lock*
59 il pontile
- *jetty*
60 il traghetto
- *foot ferry (foot passenger ferry)*
61 la cappella
- *chapel (church) without tower or spire*
62 le isoipse (le curve di livello)
- *contours*
63 il convento (il monastero, il chiostro)
- *monastery or convent [named]*
64 la chiesa visibile da lontano
- *church landmark*
65 il vigneto, la vigna
- *vineyard*
66 lo sbarramento, la cateratta
- *weir*
67 la funivia, la teleferica
- *aerial ropeway*
68 il belvedere
- *view point [tower]*
69 la chiesa di tenuta
- *dam*
70 la galleria, il tunnel
- *tunnel*
71 il punto trigonometrico

- *triangulation station (triangulation
point)*
72 il rudere, le rovine
- *remains of a building*
73 la ruota a vento
- *wind pump*
74 la fortezza
- *fortress [castle]*
75 il meandro morto
- *ox-bow lake*
76 il fiume
- *river*
77 il mulino ad acqua
- *watermill*
78 il ponticello
- *footbridge*
79 lo stagno
- *pond*
80 il ruscello
- *stream (brook, rivulet, creek)*
81 il serbatoio dell'acqua
- *water tower*
82 la sorgente
- *spring*
83 la strada di primo ordine, la strada
statale
- *main road (A road)*
84 la strada incassata
- *cutting*
85 la caverna, la grotta
- *cave*
86 la calcara, la fornace da calce *f*
- *lime kiln*
87 la cava di pietra
- *quarry*
88 la cava d'argilla
- *clay pit*
89 la fornace (la fabbrica) di laterizi *m pl*
- *brickworks*
90 la strada ferrata per trasporto merci *m pl*
- *narrow-gauge (Am. narrow gage) railway*
91 lo scalo merci *m pl*
- *goods depot (freight depot)*
92 il monumento
- *monument*
93 il campo di battaglia
- *site of battle*
94 il podere, la tenuta
- *country estate, a demesne*
95 le mura *f pl*
- *wall*
96 il castello
- *stately home*
97 il parco
- *park*
98 la siepe
- *hedge*
99 la carrareccia
- *poor or unmetalled road*
100 il pozzo a carrucola
- *well*
101 la cascina
- *farm*
102 il sentiero, il viottolo
- *unfenced path (unfenced track)*
103 il confine distrettuale
- *district boundary*
104 il terrapieno
- *embankment*
105 il villaggio, il paese
- *village*
106 il cimitero
- *cemetery [labelled: Cemy]*
107 la chiesa del paese
- *church or chapel with spire*

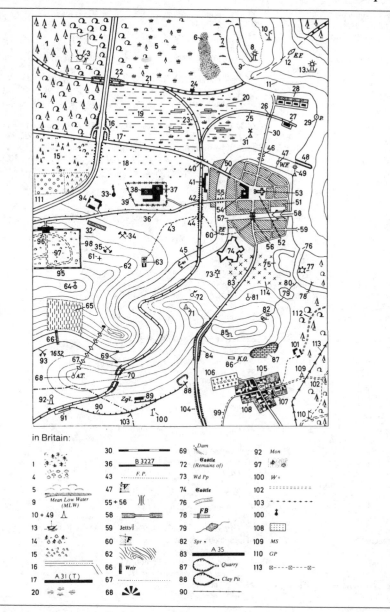

in Britain:

| | | | | | | |
|---|---|---|---|---|---|---|
| 1 | 30 | | 69 | *Dam* | 92 | *Mon* |
| 4 | 36 | B 3227 | 72 | *(Remains of)* | 97 | |
| 5 | 43 | *F. P.* | 73 | *Wd Pp* | 100 | *W* |
| 9 | 47 | *V* | 74 | **Castle** | 102 | |
| 10 + 49 | 55 + 56 | | 76 | | 103 | |
| 13 | 58 | | 78 | *FB* | 100 | |
| 14 | 59 | *Jetty* | 79 | | 108 | |
| 15 | 60 | *F* | 82 | *Spr* | 109 | *MS* |
| 16 | 62 | | 83 | A 35 | 110 | *GP* |
| 17 | A 31 (T) | 66 | *Weir* | 87 | *Quarry* | 113 |
| 20 | 68 | | 88 | *Clay Pit* | 90 | |

- Mean Low Water (MLW)
- Castle (Remains of)

108 il frutteto
– *orchard*
109 la pietra miliare
– *milestone*
110 l'indicatore *m* di direzione *f*
– *guide post*
111 il vivaio
– *tree nursery*
112 il tracciato aperto nel bosco
– *ride (aisle, lane, section line)*
113 la linea ad alta tensione
– *electricity transmission line*

114 la piantagione di luppolo
– *hop garden*

**1-54 il corpo umano**
– *the human body*
**1-18 la testa (il capo)**
– *head*
**1** la testa (il cocuzzolo)
– *vertex (crown of the head, top of the head)*
**2** l'occipite *m*
– *occiput (back of the head)*
**3** i capelli
– *hair*
**4-5** la fronte
– *forehead*
**4-17 la faccia** (il viso, il volto)
– *face*
**4** la bozza frontale
– *frontal eminence (frontal protuberance)*
**5** la circonvoluzione frontale
– *superciliary arch*
**6** la tempia
– *temple*
**7** l'occhio
– *eye*
**8** lo zigomo (l'osso zigomatico)
– *zygomatic bone (malar bone, jugal bone, cheekbone)*
**9** la guancia (la gota)
– *cheek*
**10** il naso
– *nose*
**11** la linea naso-commessura labiale
– *nasolabial fold*
**12** il solco sottonasale
– *philtrum*
**13** la bocca
– *mouth*
**14** la commessura labiale
– *angle of the mouth (labial commissure)*
**15** il mento
– *chin*
**16** la fossetta del mento
– *dimple (fossette) in the chin*
**17** la mascella inferiore (la mandibola)
– *jaw*
**18** l'orecchio
– *ear*
**19-21 il collo**
– *neck*
**19** la gola (*nell'uomo:* il pomo d'Adamo)
– *throat*
**20** l'incavo della gola
– *hollow of the throat*
**21** la nuca (la cervice, la collottola)
– *nape of the neck*
**22-41 il tronco**
– *trunk*
**22-25 la schiena** (il dorso)
– *back*
**22** la spalla
– *shoulder*

**23** la scapola (l'omoplata *m*)
– *shoulderblade (scapula)*
**24** la regione lombare (i lombi)
– *loins*
**25** la regione sacrale
– *small of the back*
**26** l'ascella (la cavitá ascellare)
– *armpit*
**27** i peli ascellari
– *armpit hair*
**28-30 il petto** (la gabbia toracica)
– *thorax (chest)*
**28-29** il petto (*nella donna:* il seno, la mammella)
– *breasts (breast, mamma)*
**28** il capezzolo
– *nipple*
**29** l'areola mammaria
– *areola*
**30** il seno
– *bosom*
**31** la vita
– *waist*
**32** il fianco e la fossa iliaca
– *flank (side)*
**33** l'anca
– *hip*
**34** l'ombelico
– *navel*
**35-37 il ventre** (l'addome *m*, *fam.* la pancia)
– *abdomen (stomach)*
**35** l'epigastrio
– *upper abdomen*
**36** il mesogastrio (la zona periombelicale)
– *abdomen*
**37** l'ipogastrio (la regione soprapubica)
– *lower abdomen*
**38** la regione inguinale (l'inguine *m*)
– *groin*
**39** il pube
– *pudenda (vulva)*
**40** la natica (la regione glutea, *fam.* il sedere)
– *buttock (backside,* coll. *bottom)*
**41** il solco intergluteo
– *anal groove (anal cleft)*
**42** il solco (la piega) della natica
– *gluteal fold (gluteal furrow)*
**43-54 gli arti** (le membra, le estremità)
– *limbs*
**43-48** l'arto superiore (il braccio)
– *arm*
**43** il braccio (la parte superiore del braccio)
– *upper arm*
**44** la piega del braccio
– *crook of the arm*
**45** il gomito
– *elbow*
**46** l'avambraccio
– *forearm*

**47** la mano
– *hand*
**48** il pugno
– *fist (clenched fist, clenched hand)*
**49-54** l'arto inferiore (la gamba)
– *leg*
**49** la coscia
– *thigh*
**50** il ginocchio
– *knee*
**51** il poplite (la regione del poplite, il cavo del poplite, *fam.* la piega del ginocchio)
– *popliteal space*
**52** la gamba (tra ginocchio e piede)
– *shank*
**53** il polpaccio
– *calf*
**54** il piede
– *foot*

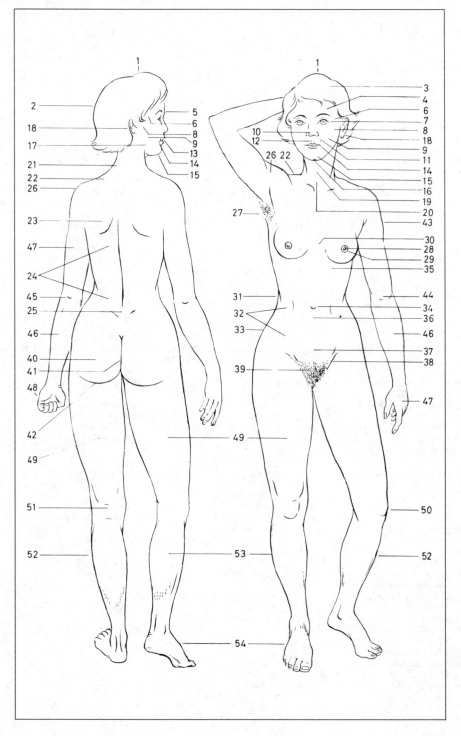

**1-29 lo scheletro** (l'ossatura, le ossa
  *f pl*, la struttura ossea)
– *skeleton (bones)*
**1** il cranio
– *skull*
**2-5 la colonna vertebrale** (*pop.:* la
  spina dorsale)
– *vertebral column (spinal column,
  spine, backbone)*
**2** la vertebra cervicale
– *cervical vertebra*
**3** la vertebra toracica
– *dorsal vertebra (thoracic vertebra)*
**4** la vertebra lombare
– *lumbar vertebra*
**5** il coccige
– *coccyx (coccygeal vertebra)*
**6** *u.* **7** la cintura scapolare
– *shoulder girdle*
**6** la clavicola
– *collarbone (clavicle)*
**7** la scapola (l'omoplata)
– *shoulderblade (scapula)*
**8-11 il torace**
– *thorax (chest)*
**8** lo sterno
– *breastbone (sternum)*
**9** le costole (costole *f pl* sternali)
– *true ribs*
**10** le costole false (costole *f pl*
  spurie) e le costole fluttuanti (costole *f pl* mobili)
– *false ribs*
**11** la cartilagine costale
– *costal cartilage*
**12-14 l'arto superiore** (*pop.:* il braccio)
– *arm*
**12** l'omero
– *humerus*
**13** il radio
– *radius*
**14** l'ulna (cubito)
– *ulna*
**15-17 la mano**
– *hand*
**15** l'osso del carpo
– *carpus*
**16** l'osso metacarpo
– *metacarpal bone (metacarpal)*
**17** la falange del dito della mano
– *phalanx (phalange)*
**18-21 il bacino** (la pelvi, il bacino
  pelvico)
– *pelvis*
**18** l'osso iliaco (l'ileo, la spina iliaca,
  l'anca)
– *ilium (hip bone)*
**19** l'osso ischiatico (l'ischio)
– *ischium*
**20** l'osso del pube
– *pubis*
**21** l'osso sacro
– *sacrum*

**22-25 l'arto inferiore** (*pop.:* la gamba)
– *leg*
**22** il femore
– *femur (thigh bone, thigh)*
**23** la rotula (la patella)
– *patella (kneecap)*
**24** la fibula (il perone)
– *fibula (splint bone)*
**25** la tibia
– *tibia (shinbone)*
**26-29 il piede**
– *foot*
**26** le ossa *f pl* del tarso (il tarso, le
  ossa della caviglia)
– *tarsal bones (tarsus)*
**27** il calcagno
– *calcaneum (heelbone)*
**28** le ossa *f pl* del metatarso
– *metatarsus*
**29** le falangi delle dita *f pl* del piede
– *phalanges*
**30-41 il cranio**
– *skull*
**30** l'osso frontale
– *frontal bone*
**31** l'osso parietale sinistro
– *left parietal bone*
**32** l'osso occipitale
– *occipital bone*
**33** l'osso temporale
– *temporal bone*
**34** il condotto uditivo, il meato uditivo
– *external auditory canal*
**35** l'osso mascellare inferiore (la
  mandibola)
– *lower jawbone (lower jaw,
  mandible)*
**36** l'osso mascellare superiore
– *upper jawbone (upper jaw, maxilla)*
**37** l'osso zigomatico (lo zigomo)
– *zygomatic bone (cheekbone)*
**38** lo sfenoide
– *sphenoid bone (sphenoid)*
**39** l'etmoide *m*
– *ethmoid bone (ethmoid)*
**40** l'osso lacrimale
– *lachrimal (lacrimal) bone*
**41** l'osso nasale
– *nasal bone*
**42-55 il capo** [sezione]
– *head [section]*
**42** l'encefalo (il cervello)
– *cerebrum (great brain)*
**43** l'ipofisi *f* (*ant.:* la ghiandola pitu-
  itaria)
– *pituitary gland (pituitary body,
  hypophysis cerebri)*
**44** il corpo calloso
– *corpus callosum*
**45** il cervelletto
– *cerebellum (little brain)*
**46** il ponte di Varolio
– *pons (pons cerebri, pons cerebelli)*
**47** il midollo allungato (il bulbo)

– *medulla oblongata (brain stem)*
**48** il midollo spinale
– *spinal cord*
**49** l'esofago
– *oesophagus (esophagus, gullet)*
**50** la trachea
– *trachea (windpipe)*
**51** l'epiglottide *f*
– *epiglottis*
**52** la lingua
– *tongue*
**53** la cavità nasale
– *nasal cavity*
**54** il seno sfenoidale
– *sphenoidal sinus*
**55** il seno frontale
– *frontal sinus*
**56-65 l'organo dell'udito e dell'equi-
  librio** (l'orecchio)
– *organ of equilibrium and hearing*
**56-58 l'orecchio esterno**
– *external ear*
**56** il padiglione auricolare
– *auricle*
**57** il lobo dell'orecchio
– *ear lobe*
**58** il meato uditivo
– *external auditory canal*
**59-61 l'orecchio medio**
– *middle ear*
**59** il timpano (la membrana timpanica)
– *tympanic membrane*
**60** la cassa timpanica (cassa del timpano)
– *tympanic cavity*
**61** gli ossicini dell'orecchio: il martello, l'incudine *f*, la staffa
– *auditory ossicles: hammer; anvil,
  and stirrup (malleus, incus, and
  stapes)*
**62-64 l'orecchio interno**
– *inner ear (internal ear)*
**62** il labirinto
– *labyrinth*
**63** la coclea (la chiocciola)
– *cochlea*
**64** il nervo uditivo
– *auditory nerve*
**65** la tromba di Eustachio
– *eustachian tube*

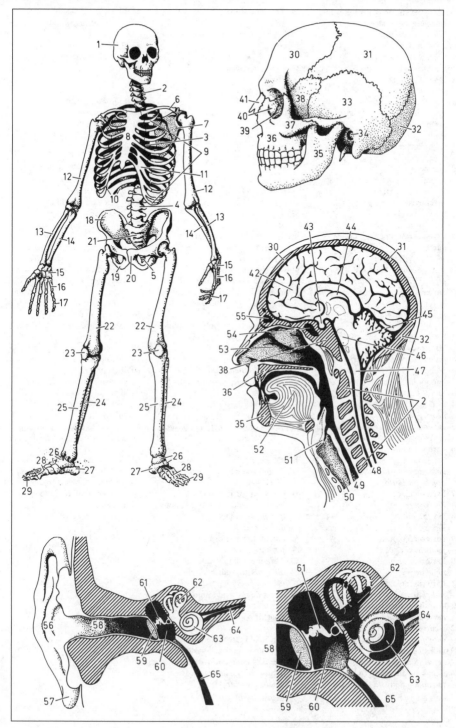

**1-21 l'apparato circolatorio (la cir-
colazione del sangue)**
- *blood circulation (circulatory system)*
1  la carotide, un'arteria
- *common carotid artery, an artery*
2  la vena giugulare
- *jugular vein, a vein*
3  l'arteria temporale
- *temporal artery*
4  la vena temporale
- *temporal vein*
5  l'arteria frontale
- *frontal artery*
6  la vena frontale
- *frontal vein*
7  l'arteria succlavia
- *subclavian artery*
8  la vena succlavia
- *subclavian vein*
9  la vena cava superiore discendente
- *superior vena cava*
10  il grande arco dell'aorta (l'aorta)
- *arch of the aorta (aorta)*
11  l'arteria polmonare (con sangue
*m* venoso)
- *pulmonary artery [with venous
blood]*
12  la vena polmonare (con sangue *m*
arterioso)
- *pulmonary vein [with arterial
blood]*
13  i polmoni
- *lungs*
14  il cuore
- *heart*
15  la vena cava inferiore ascendente
- *inferior vena cava*
16  l'arteria addominale (il ramo discendente dell'aorta)
- *abdominal aorta (descending portion of the aorta)*
17  l'arteria iliaca
- *iliac artery*
18  la vena iliaca
- *iliac vein*
19  l'arteria femorale
- *femoral artery*
20  l'arteria tibiale
- *tibial artery*
21  l'arteria radiale (il polso)
- *radial artery*
**22-33 il sistema nervoso**
- *nervous system*
22  il cervello
- *cerebrum (great brain)*
23  il diencefalo
- *cerebellum (little brain)*
24  il midollo allungato (il bulbo)
- *medulla oblongata (brain stem)*

25  il midollo spinale
- *spinal cord*
26  i nervi toracici (nervi *m pl* inter-
costali)
- *thoracic nerves*
27  il plesso brachiale
- *brachial plexus*
28  il nervo radiale
- *radial nerve*
29  il nervo ulnare (nervo cubitale)
- *ulnar nerve*
30  il grande nervo sciatico [situato
posteriormente]
- *great sciatic nerve [lying posterior-
ly]*
31  il nervo femorale
- *femoral nerve (anterior crural
nerve)*
32  il nervo tibiale
- *tibial nerve*
33  il nervo fibulare (nervo peroneale)
- *peroneal nerve*
**34-64  il sistema muscolare**
- *musculature (muscular system)*
34  il muscolo sternocleidomastoideo
- *sternocleidomastoid muscle (ster-
nomastoid muscle)*
35  il deltoide (il muscolo scapolare,
muscolo deltoide)
- *deltoid muscle*
36  il grande pettorale
- *pectoralis major (greater pectoralis muscle, greater pectoralis)*
37  il bicipite
- *biceps brachii (biceps  of the arm)*
38  il tricipite
- *triceps brachii (triceps of the arm)*
39  il supinatore
- *brachioradialis*
40  il grande palmare
- *flexor carpi radialis (radial flexor
of the wrist)*
41  i muscoli corti del pollice: il
flessore, l'adduttore *m* e l'abduttore *m* del pollice
- *thenar muscle*
42  il dentato anteriore
- *serratus anterior*
43  il grande obliquo addominale
- *obliquus externus abdominis
(external oblique)*
44  il grande retto addominale
- *rectus abdominis*
45  il sartorio
- *sartorius*
46  il muscolo estensore della gamba
(il vasto esterno e il vasto interno)
- *vastus lateralis and vastus medialis*
47  il muscolo tibiale anteriore
- *tibialis anterior*

48  il tendine di Achille
- *tendo calcaneus (Achilles' tendon)*
49  il muscolo pedidio (l'abduttore *m*
dell'alluce *m*), un muscolo del
piede
- *abductor hallucis (abductor of the
hallux), a foot muscle*
50  i muscoli occipitali
- *occipitalis*
51  i muscoli nucali
- *splenius of the neck*
52  il trapezio
- *trapezius*
53  il sottospinoso (il muscolo infra-
spinato)
- *infraspinatus*
54  il piccolo rotondo
- *teres minor (lesser teres)*
55  il grande rotondo
- *teres major (greater teres)*
56  il lungo estensore del radio
- *extensor carpi radialis longus
(long radial extensor of the wrist)*
57  l'estensore *m* comune delle dita *f pl*
- *extensor communis digitorum
(common extensor of the digits)*
58  l'ulnare *m* estensore del carpo
- *flexor carpi ulnaris (ulnar flexor
of the wrist)*
59  il grande dorsale
- *latissimus dorsi*
60  il grande gluteo
- *gluteus maximus*
61  il bicipite femorale
- *biceps femoris (biceps of the
thigh)*
62  il gemello esterno e interno
- *gastrocnemius, medial and lateral
heads*
63  l'estensore *m* delle dita del piede
- *extensor communis digitorum
(common extensor of the digits)*
64  il lungo fibulare (lungo peroneale)
- *peroneus longus (long peroneus)*

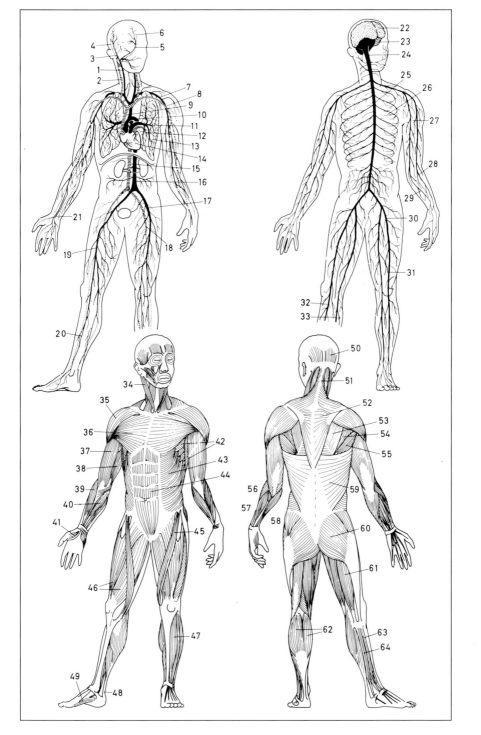

**1-13 la testa e il collo**
– *head and neck*
1 il muscolo sternocleidomastoideo
– *sternocleidomastoid muscle (sternomas-toid muscle)*
2 il muscolo occipitale
– *occipitalis*
3 il muscolo temporale
– *temporalis (temporal, temporal muscle)*
4 il muscolo frontale
– *occipito frontalis (frontalis)*
5 il muscolo orbicolare
– *orbicularis oculi*
6 muscoli *m pl* facciali mimici
– *muscles of facial expression*
7 il massetere (l'elevatore *m* della mandi-bola)
– *masseter*
8 il muscolo orbicolare della bocca
– *orbicularis oris*
9 la ghiandola parotide
– *parotid gland*
10 il nodo linfatico (il linfonodo), *scorret-to:* la ghiandola linfatica
– *lymph node (submandibular lymph gland)*
11 la ghiandola submascellare (ghiandola salivare, ghiandola sottomandibolare)
– *submandibular gland (submaxillary gland)*
12 i muscoli del collo
– *muscles of the neck*
13 il pomo d'Adamo [solo nell'uomo]
– *Adam's apple (laryngeal prominence) [in men only]*
**14-37 la cavità orale e la faringe**
– *mouth and pharynx*
14 il labbro superiore
– *upper lip*
15 la gengiva
– *gum*
**16-18 la dentatura**
– *teeth (set of teeth)*
16 i denti incisivi (gli incisivi)
– *incisors*
17 il dente canino (il canino)
– *canine tooth (canine)*
18 i denti molari (i molari)
– *premolar (bicuspid) and molar teeth (premolars and molars)*
19 la commessura labiale
– *angle of the mouth (labial commissure)*
20 il palato duro (palato osseo, la volta palatina)
– *hard palate*
21 il palato molle (il velo pendulo)
– *soft palate (velum palati, velum)*
22 l'ugola
– *uvula*
23 la tonsilla
– *palatine tonsil (tonsil)*
24 la cavità faringea (la faringe)
– *pharyngeal opening (pharynx)*
25 la lingua
– *tongue*
26 il labbro inferiore
– *lower lip*
27 la mascella superiore
– *upper jaw (maxilla)*
**28-37 il dente**
– *tooth*
28 il periodonto
– *periodontal membrane (periodontium, pericementum)*

29 il cemento
– *cement (dental cementum, crusta pet-rosa)*
30 lo smalto dei denti (la sostanza adamantina)
– *enamel*
31 la dentina (l'avorio dei denti)
– *dentine (dentin)*
32 la polpa dentaria
– *dental pulp (tooth pulp, pulp)*
33 le terminazioni nervose (i nervi) e i vasi sanguigni
– *nerves and blood vessels*
34 il dente incisivo (l'incisivo)
– *incisor*
35 il dente molare (il molare)
– *molar tooth (molar)*
36 la radice
– *root (fang)*
37 la corona
– *crown*
**38-51 l'occhio**
– *eye*
38 il sopracciglio
– *eyebrow (supercilium)*
39 la palpebra superiore
– *upper eyelid (upper palpebra)*
40 la palpebra inferiore
– *lower eyelid (lower palpebra)*
41 la ciglia
– *eyelash (cilium)*
42 l'iride *f*
– *iris*
43 la pupilla
– *pupil*
44 i muscoli oculomotori (muscoli *m pl* ottici)
– *eye muscles (ocular muscles)*
45 il globo oculare
– *eyeball*
46 l'umor *m* vitreo
– *vitreous body*
47 la cornea
– *cornea*
48 il cristallino
– *lens*
49 la retina
– *retina*
50 la macula lutea (il punto cieco)
– *blind spot*
51 il nervo ottico
– *optic nerve*
**52-63 il piede**
– *foot*
52 l'alluce *m*
– *big toe (great toe, first toe, hallux, digi-tus I)*
53 il secondo dito del piede
– *second toe (digitus II)*
54 il terzo dito del piede (il medio)
– *third toe (digitus III)*
55 il quarto dito del piede
– *fourth toe (digitus IV)*
56 il quinto dito del piede (il mignolo)
– *little toe (digitus minimus, digitus V)*
57 l'unghia del dito del piede
– *toenail*
58 la prominenza dell'articolazione *f* metatarso-falangea
– *ball of the foot*
59 il malleolo esterno
– *lateral malleolus (external malleolus, outer malleolus, malleolus fibulae)*

60 il malleolo interno
– *medial malleolus (internal malleolus, inner malleolus, malleolus tibulae, malleolus medialis)*
61 il dorso del piede
– *instep (medial longitudinal arch, dor-sum of the foot, dorsum pedis)*
62 la pianta del piede
– *sole of the foot*
63 il calcagno
– *heel*
**64-83 la mano**
– *hand*
64 il pollice
– *thumb (pollex, digitus I)*
65 il dito indice (l'indice *m*)
– *index finger (forefinger, second finger, digitus II)*
66 il dito medio (il medio)
– *middle finger (third finger, digitus medius, digitus III)*
67 il dito anulare (l'anulare *m*)
– *ring finger (fourth finger, digitus anu-laris, digitus IV)*
68 il dito mignolo (il mignolo)
– *little finger (fifth finger, digitus minimus, digitus V)*
69 il lato radiale della mano
– *radial side of the hand*
70 il lato ulnare della mano
– *ulnar side of the hand*
71 la palma (il palmo) della mano
– *palm of the hand (palma manus)*
**72-74 le linee della mano**
– *lines of the hand*
72 la linea della vita
– *life line (line of life)*
73 la linea della testa (linea dell'intelligen-za)
– *head line (line of the head)*
74 la linea del cuore
– *heart line (line of the heart)*
75 il monte di Venere (l'eminenza tenare)
– *ball of the thumb (thenar eminence)*
76 l'articolazione *f* del polso (articolazione *f* metacarpica)
– *wrist (carpus)*
77 la falange del dito
– *phalanx (phalange)*
78 il polpastrello
– *finger pad*
79 la punta del dito
– *fingertip*
80 l'unghia del dito (l'unghia)
– *fingernail (nail)*
81 la lunula
– *lunule (lunula) of the nail*
82 la nocca
– *knuckle*
83 il dorso della mano
– *back of the hand (dorsum of the hand, dorsum manus)*

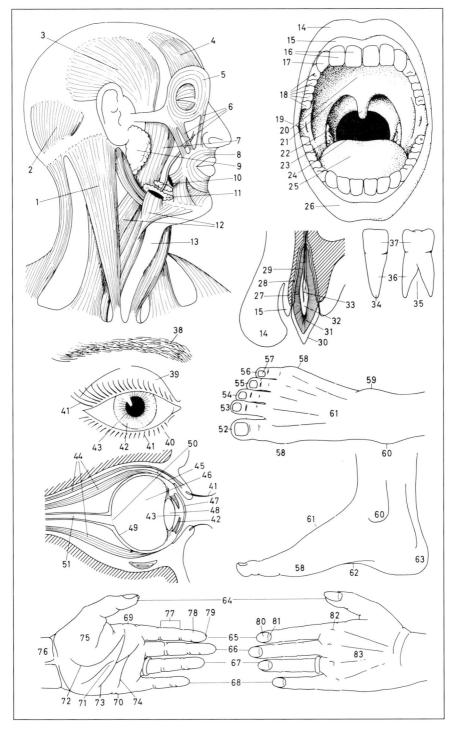

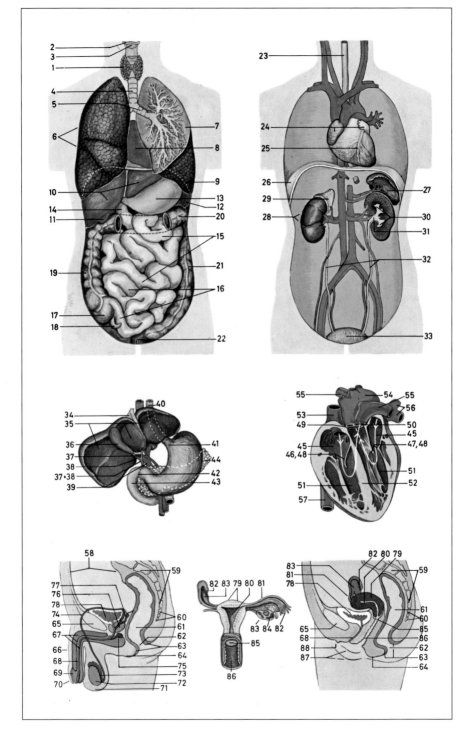

**1-57 gli organi interni** [visti di fronte]
– *internal organs [front view]*
1 la ghiandola tiroide
– *thyroid gland*
2 *u.* **3** la laringe
– *larynx*
2 l'osso ioide (l'ioide *m*)
– *hyoid bone (hyoid)*
3 la cartilagine tiroidea
– *thyroid cartilage*
4 la trachea
– *trachea (windpipe)*
5 i bronchi
– *bronchus*
6 *u.* **7** il polmone
– *lung*
6 il polmone destro
– *right lung*
7 il lobo superiore [sezione]
– *upper pulmonary lobe (upper lobe of the lung) [section]*
8 il cuore
– *heart*
9 il diaframma
– *diaphragm*
10 il fegato
– *liver*
11 la cistifellea
– *gall bladder*
12 la milza
– *spleen*
13 lo stomaco
– *stomach*
**14-22 l'intestino**
– *intestines (bowel)*
**14-16 l'intestino tenue**
– *small intestine (intestinum tenue)*
14 il duodeno
– *duodenum*
15 il digiuno
– *jejunum*
16 l'ileo
– *ileum*
**17-22 l'intestino crasso**
– *large intestine (intestinum crassum)*
17 il cieco
– *caecum (cecum)*
18 l'appendice *f* vermiforme (appendice *f* ciecale)
– *appendix (vermiform appendix)*
19 il colon ascendente
– *ascending colon*
20 il colon traverso
– *transverse colon*
21 il colon discendente
– *descending colon*
22 il retto
– *rectum*
23 l'esofago
– *oesophagus (esophagus, gullet)*
24 *u.* **25** il cuore
– *heart*
24 l'atrio cardiaco (l'orecchietta cardiaca)
– *auricle*
25 il solco longitudinale anteriore
– *anterior longitudinal cardiac sulcus*
26 il diaframma
– *diaphragm*
27 la milza
– *spleen*
28 il rene destro
– *right kidney*
29 la ghiandola surrenale
– *suprarenal gland*

30 *u.* **31** il rene sinistro [sezione longitudinale]
– *left kidney [longitudinal section]*
30 il calice renale
– *calyx (renal calyx)*
31 la pelvi renale (il becinetto renale)
– *renal pelvis*
32 l'uretere *m*
– *ureter*
33 la vescica
– *bladder*
34 *u.* **35** il fegato [superficie inferiore]
– *liver [from behind]*
34 il legamento collaterale del fegato
– *falciform ligament of the liver*
35 il lobo del fegato
– *lobe of the liver*
36 la cistifellea
– *gall bladder*
37 *u.* **38** il canale coledoco
– *common bile duct*
37 il dotto epatico
– *hepatic duct (common hepatic duct)*
38 il dotto cistico
– *cystic duct*
39 la vena porta
– *portal vein (hepatic portal vein)*
40 l'esofago
– *oesophagus (esophagus, gullet)*
41 *u.* **42** lo stomaco
– *stomach*
41 il cardias [*pop.*: la bocca dello stomaco)
– *cardiac orifice*
42 il piloro
– *pylorus*
43 il duodeno
– *duodenum*
44 il pancreas
– *pancreas*
**45-57 il cuore** [sezione longitudinale]
– *heart [longitudinal section]*
45 l'atrio del cuore
– *atrium*
46 *u.* **47** le valvole cardiache
– *valves of the heart*
46 la valvola tricuspidale
– *tricuspid valve (right atrioventricular valve)*
47 la valvola mitrale (valvola bicuspidale)
– *bicuspid valve (mitral valve, left atrioventricular valve)*
48 la cuspide
– *cusp*
49 la valvola semilunare aortica
– *aortic valve*
50 la valvola polmonare
– *pulmonary valve*
51 il ventricolo del cuore
– *ventricle*
52 il setto muscolare del ventricolo cardiaco
– *ventricular septum (interventricular septum)*
53 la vena cava superiore
– *superior vena cava*
54 l'aorta
– *aorta*
55 l'arteria polmonare
– *pulmonary artery*
56 la vena polmonare
– *pulmonary vein*
57 la vena cava inferiore
– *inferior vena cava*
58 il peritoneo
– *peritoneum*

59 l'osso sacro
– *sacrum*
60 il coccige
– *coccyx (coccygeal vertebra)*
61 il retto
– *rectum*
62 l'ano
– *anus*
63 lo sfintere dell'ano
– *anal sphincter*
64 il perineo
– *perineum*
65 la sinfisi pubica
– *pubic symphisis (symphisis pubis)*
**66-77 gli organi sessuali maschili** [sezione longitudinale]
– *male sex organs [longitudinal section]*
66 il pene
– *penis*
67 il corpo cavernoso e spugnoso
– *corpus cavernosum and spongiosum of the penis (erectile tissue of the penis)*
68 l'uretra
– *urethra*
69 il glande
– *glans penis*
70 il prepuzio
– *prepuce (foreskin)*
71 lo scroto
– *scrotum*
72 il testicolo destro
– *right testicle (testis)*
73 l'epididimo
– *epididymis*
74 il dotto (il canale, il vaso) deferente
– *spermatic duct (vas deferens)*
75 la ghiandola periuretrale (ghiandola di Cowper)
– *Cowper's gland (bulbourethral gland)*
76 la prostata
– *prostate (prostate gland)*
77 la vescicola seminale
– *seminal vesicle*
78 la vescica
– *bladder*
**79-88 gli organi sessuali femminili** [sezione longitudinale]
– *female sex organs [longitudinal section]*
79 l'utero
– *uterus (matrix, womb)*
80 la cavità uterina
– *cavity of the uterus*
81 la salpinge uterina
– *fallopian tube (uterine tube, oviduct)*
82 le fimbrie
– *fimbria (fimbriated extremity)*
83 l'ovaio
– *ovary*
84 il follicolo con l'uovo
– *follicle with ovum (egg)*
85 l'orifizio dell'utero
– *os uteri externum*
86 la vagina
– *vagina*
87 i labbri della vulva
– *lip of the pudendum (lip of the vulva)*
88 la/il clitoride
– *clitoris*

**1-13  fasciature** *f pl* **di emergenza**
- *emergency bandages*
**1**  la fasciatura del braccio
- *arm bandage*
**2**  il telo triangolare per sostenere il braccio (la fasciatura triangolare per il braccio)
- *triangular cloth used as a sling (an arm sling)*
**3**  la fasciatura del capo
- *head bandage (capeline)*
**4**  il pacchetto pronto soccorso
- *first aid kit*
**5**  l'occorrente *m* per la fasciatura d'emergenza
- *first aid dressing*
**6**  la garza sterile
- *sterile gauze dressing*
**7**  il cerotto
- *adhesive plaster (sticking plaster)*
**8**  la ferita
- *wound*
**9**  la fascia di garza
- *bandage*
**10**  la fasciatura di emergenza per fratture *f pl*
- *emergency splint for a broken limb (fractured limb)*
**11**  la gamba fratturata
- *fractured leg (broken leg)*
**12**  la stecca
- *splint*
**13**  l'appoggio per la testa (il poggiatesta)
- *headrest*
**14-17  misure** *f pl* **per l'arresto di emorragie** *f pl* (misure per l'emostasi *f*, la legatura di un vaso sanguigno)
- *measures for stanching the blood flow (tying up (ligature) of a blood vessel)*
**14**  i punti di compressione *f* delle arterie
- *pressure points of the arteries*
**15**  la legatura (la compressione) provvisoria dell'arteria femorale
- *emergency tourniquet on the thigh*
**16**  il bastone da passeggio usato come stecca (manico girevole)
- *walking stick used as a screw*
**17**  la fasciatura di compressione *f*
- *compression bandage*
**18-23  il soccorso e il trasporto di un ferito** (di una persona infortunata, della vittima di un incidente)
- *rescue and transport of an injured person*
**18**  la presa Rautek (per estrarre dalla vettura una persona ferita in un incidente stradale)
- *Rautek grip (for rescue of a car accident victim)*

**19**  il soccorritore, l'infermiere *m* del pronto soccorso
- *helper*
**20**  il ferito (l'infortunato, la vittima di un incidente)
- *injured person (casualty)*
**21**  la presa a seggiolino
- *chair grip*
**22**  la presa a barella
- *carrying grip*
**23**  la barella di emergenza formata da bastoni *m pl* e una giacca
- *emergency stretcher of sticks and a jacket*
**24-27  la posizione di persone svenute** (prive di sensi *m pl*) **e la respirazione artificiale** (la rianimazione)
- *positioning of an unconscious person and artificial respiration (resuscitation)*
**24**  la posizione su un fianco
- *coma position*
**25**  la persona priva di sensi *m pl* (la persona svenuta)
- *unconscious person*
**26**  la respirazione bocca a bocca
- *mouth-to-mouth resuscitation (variation: mouth-to-nose resuscitation)*
**27**  il polmone elettrico, un rianimatore (un apparecchio di respirazione *f*, un respiratore)
- *resuscitator (respiratory apparatus, resuscitation apparatus), a respirator (artificial breathing device)*
**28-33  salvataggio in incidenti** *m pl* **su ghiaccio**
- *methods of rescue in ice accidents*
**28**  la persona caduta nella crepa (nel crepaccio)
- *person who has fallen through the ice*
**29**  il soccorritore, la persona che effettua il salvataggio
- *rescuer*
**30**  la fune
- *rope*
**31**  il tavolo (o altro mezzo di emergenza)
- *table (or similar device)*
**32**  la scala a pioli *m pl*
- *ladder*
**33**  l'autosalvataggio
- *self-rescue*
**34-38  il soccorso a chi sta per annegare**
- *rescue of a drowning person*
**34**  la mossa per liberarsi dalla stretta
- *method of release (release grip, release) to free rescuer from the clutch of a drowning person*

**35**  la persona che sta per annegare
- *drowning person*
**36**  il nuotatore che opera il salvataggio
- *lifesaver*
**37** *u.* **38**  il trasporto in acqua (prese *f pl* per il trasporto a nuoto)
- *towing (tows)*
**37**  la presa sotto le ascelle
- *double shoulder tow*
**38**  la presa di (per la) testa
- *head tow*

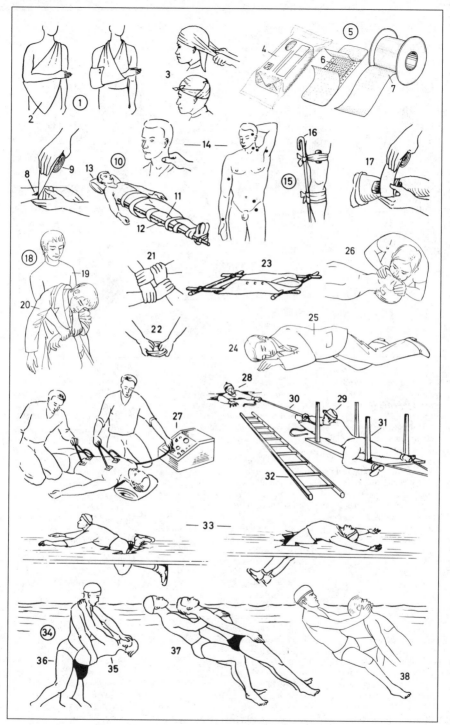

**1-74 l'ambulatorio del medico generico**
- *general practice (*Am. *physician's office)*
**1 la sala d'aspetto**
- *waiting room*
**2** il paziente
- *patient*
**3** i pazienti con appuntamento (per la visita di controllo o per il rinnovo di ricetta)
- *patients with appointments (for a routine check-up or renewal of prescription)*
**4** le riviste a disposizione *f* del pubblico
- *magazines [for waiting patients]*
**5** l'accettazione *f* (la ricezione, la segreteria)
- *reception*
**6** lo schedario dei pazienti
- *patients file*
**7** le cartelle decadute
- *eliminated index cards*
**8** la cartella (la scheda) del paziente
- *medical record (medical card)*
**9** il tagliando della cassa malattia (*Italia:* il libretto della cassa malattia, libretto della mutua)
- *health insurance certificate*
**10** il calendario pubblicitario
- *advertising calendar (publicity calendar)*

**11** l'agenda degli appuntamenti
- *appointments book*
**12** il raccoglitore della corrispondenza
- *correspondence file*
**13** la segreteria telefonica
- *automatic telephone answering and recording set (telephone answering device)*
**14** l'apparecchio per comunicazioni *f pl* radiotelefoniche
- *radiophone*
**15** il microfono
- *microphone*
**16** il cartellone (la tabella, il tabellone)
- *illustrated chart*
**17** il calendario da parete *f*
- *wall calendar*
**18** il telefono
- *telephone*
**19** l'assistente *f* di ambulatorio medico
- *[doctor's] assistant*
**20** la ricetta
- *prescription*
**21** la rubrica telefonica
- *telephone index*
**22** il dizionario medico
- *medical dictionary*
**23** l'elenco dei medicinali ammessi
- *pharmacopoeia (list of registered medicines)*

**24** la macchina affrancatrice
- *franking machine (*Am. *postage meter)*
**25** l'apparecchio appuntagraffette
- *stapler*
**26** lo schedario dei (pazienti) diabetici
- *diabetics file*
**27** il dittafono
- *dictating machine*
**28** la perforatrice
- *paper punch*
**29** il timbro del medico
- *doctor's stamp*
**30** il tampone per timbri *m pl*
- *ink pad*
**31** il portamatite
- *pencil holder*
**32-74 l'ambulatorio**
- *surgery*
**32** il tabellone illustrato della cavità oculare
- *chart of eyegrounds*
**33** la borsa del medico
- *doctor's bag (doctor's case)*
**34** il citofono
- *intercom*
**35** l'armadio dei medicamenti
- *medicine cupboard*
**36** il portatamponi
- *swab dispenser*
**37** la peretta di Politzer
- *inflator (Politzer bag)*

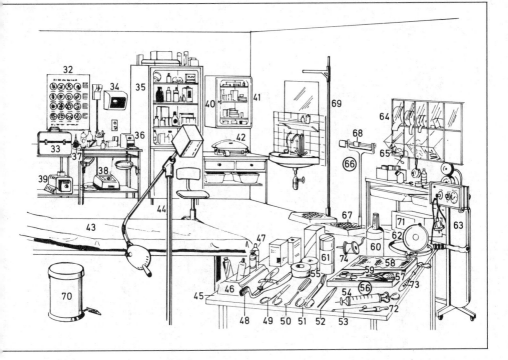

38 l'elettrotomo
– *electrotome*
39 lo sterilizzatore a vapore *m*
– *steam sterilizer*
40 l'armadietto pensile (armadietto da parete *f* )
– *cabinet*
41 i campioni (i medicinali campioni ad uso ambulatoriale)
– *medicine samples (from the pharmaceutical industry)*
42 la bilancia da neonato
– *baby scales*
43 il lettino da ambulatorio (lettino per visita medica)
– *examination couch*
44 il riflettore
– *directional lamp*
45 il carrello (il tavolo) con gli strumenti per medicazioni *f pl*
– *instrument table*
46 il portatubetti
– *tube holder*
47 il tubetto della pomata (la pomata in tubetto)
– *tube of ointment*
48-50 **gli strumenti del medico generico**
– *instruments for minor surgery*
48 l'apribocca
– *mouth gag*
49 la pinza di Kocher
– *Kocher's forceps*

50 il cucchiaio
– *scoop (curette)*
51 le forbici ricurve
– *angled scissors*
52 la pinzetta anatomica
– *forceps*
53 la sonda con punta ad oliva
– *olive-pointed (bulb-headed) probe*
54 la siringa auricolare o per vescica
– *syringe for irrigations of the ear or bladder*
55 il cerotto adesivo
– *adhesive plaster (sticking plaster)*
56 il materiale chirurgico di sutura
– *surgical suture material*
57 l'ago ricurvo
– *curved surgical needle*
58 la garza sterilizzata
– *sterile gauze*
59 il portaghi (porta-aghi *m*)
– *needle holder*
60 il nebulizzatore disinfettante
– *spray for disinfecting the skin*
61 il contenitore del filo (per suturare)
– *thread container*
62 l'oftalmoscopio
– *ophthalmoscope*
63 il dispositivo anestetizzante mediante congelamento per interventi *m pl* di criochirurgia
– *freezer for cryosurgery*

64 il distributore di cerotti *m pl* di grande e piccolo formato
– *dispenser for plasters and small pieces of equipment*
65 gli aghi e le siringhe «usa e getta»
– *disposable hypodermic needles and syringes*
66 la bilancia, una stadera
– *scales, sliding-weight scales*
67 la piattaforma della bilancia
– *weighing platform*
68 il cursore della bilancia
– *sliding weight (jockey)*
69 lo statimetro (il misuratore dell'altezza del corpo)
– *height gauge* (Am. *gage*)
70 la pattumiera
– *waste bin* (Am. *trash bin*)
71 lo sterilizzatore a aria calda
– *hot-air sterilizer*
72 il contagocce (la pipetta contagocce)
– *pipette*
73 il plessimetro (il martello da percussione *f* )
– *percussor*
74 l'otoscopio
– *aural speculum (auriscope, aural syringe)*

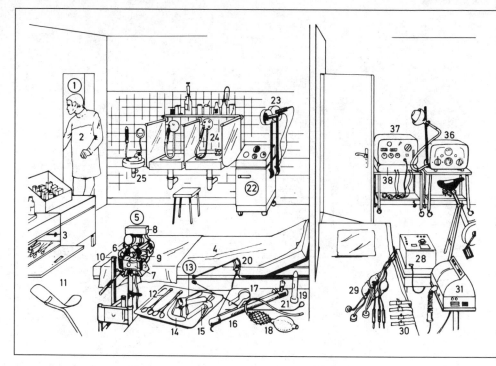

1 l'ambulatorio (lo studio medico)
- *consulting room*
2 il medico generico (medico di base *f*)
- *general practitioner*
**3-21 strumenti** *m pl* **per la visita ginecologica e proctologica**
- *instruments for gynaecological and proctological examinations*
3 il preriscaldamento degli strumenti alla temperatura del corpo
- *warming the instruments up to body temperature*
4 il lettino da ambulatorio (lettino per la visita medica)
- *examination couch*
5 il colposcopio
- *colposcope*
6 l'ispezione *f* binoculare
- *binocular eyepiece*
7 la microcamera (l'apparecchio fotografico per formato piccolo)
- *miniature camera*
8 l'illuminazione *f* a luce *f* fredda
- *cold light source*
9 lo scatto a filo flessibile
- *cable release*
10 l'occhiello per il poggiagamba
- *bracket for the leg support*
11 il poggiagamba
- *leg support (leg holder)*

12 la pinzetta emostatica
- *holding forceps (sponge holder)*
13 lo specchio vaginale
- *vaginal speculum*
14 la linguetta inferiore dello specchio vaginale
- *lower blade of the vaginal speculum*
15 l'ansa di platino (per lo striscio)
- *platinum loop (for smears)*
16 il rettoscopio
- *rectoscope*
17 la pinza bioptica per il rettoscopio
- *biopsy forceps used with the rectoscope (proctoscope)*
18 l'insufflatore *m* d'aria per la rettoscopia
- *insufflator for proctoscopy (rectoscopy)*
19 il protoscopio
- *proctoscope (rectal speculum)*
20 il catetere uretrale (uretroscopio)
- *urethroscope*
21 lo strumento guida per il protoscopio
- *guide for inserting the proctoscope*
22 l'apparecchio per la diatermia (apparecchio ad onde *f pl* corte, apparecchio per l'irradiazione *f* di onde *f pl* corte)
- *diathermy unit (short-wave therapy apparatus)*

23 il radiatore
- *radiator*
24 il dispositivo (l'impianto) per inalazioni *f pl*
- *inhaling apparatus (inhalator)*
25 il lavandino (per l'espettorazione *f*)
- *basin [for sputum]*
**26-31 l'ergometria**
- *ergometry*
26 l'ergometro a bicicletta
- *bicycle ergometer*
27 il monitor (l'indicazione *f* grafica luminosa dell'elettrocardiogramma *m* e della frequenza del polso e del respiro sotto sforzo)
- *monitor (for visual display of the ECG and of pulse and respiratory rates when performing work)*
28 l'apparecchio per elettrocardiogramma *m* (l'elettrocardiografo)
- *ECG (electrocardiograph)*
29 gli elettrodi a ventosa
- *suction electrodes*
30 gli elettrodi di allacciamento agli arti
- *strap-on electrodes for the limbs*
31 lo spirometro (per la misurazione delle funzioni respiratorie)
- *spirometer (for measuring respiratory functions)*

32 la misurazione della pressione
   sanguigna
– *measuring blood pressure*
33 il misuratore di pressione *f* sanguigna
– *sphygmomanometer*
34 il manicotto pneumatico
– *inflatable cuff*
35 lo stetoscopio
– *stethoscope*
36 l'apparecchio a microonde *f pl*
   per irradiazioni *f pl*
– *microwave treatment unit*
37 l'apparecchio di faradizzazione *f*
   (impiego di correnti *f pl* a bassa
   frequenza con diverse forme *f pl*
   di impulso)
– *faradization unit (for applying
   low-frequency currents with different pulse shapes)*
38 l'apparecchio automatico di sintonizzazione *f*
– *automatic tuner*
39 l'apparecchio a onde *f pl* corte
   monodico
– *short-wave therapy apparatus*
40 il timer (il contaminuti)
– *timer*
**41-59 il laboratorio di analisi *f pl***
– ***laboratory***
41 l'assistente *f* tecnico-medica
– *medical laboratory technician*

42 il supporto capillare per la sedi-
   mentazione del sangue
– *capillary tube stand for blood sed-
   imentation*
43 il cilindro graduato
– *measuring cylinder*
44 la pipetta automatica
– *automatic pipette*
45 la vaschetta reniforme
– *kidney dish*
46 l'elettrocardiografo portatile per
   l'impiego nei casi urgenti
– *portable ECG machine for emergency use*
47 il distillatore automatico per
   pipette *f pl*
– *automatic pipetting device*
48 l'acqua termocostante (bagno
   d'acqua termocostante)
– *constant temperature water bath*
49 l'allacciamento dell'acqua con
   pompa a getto
– *tap with water jet pump*
50 la vaschetta di colorazione *f* (per
   la colorazione degli strisci di
   sangue *m* sul vetrino, dei sedimenti e dei prelievi liquidi organi-
   ci)
– *staining dish (for staining blood
   smears, sediments, and other
   smears)*

51 il microscopio sperimentale
   binoculare
– *binocular research microscope*
52 il supporto delle pipette per la
   fotometria
– *pipette stand for photometry*
53 la macchina di misurazione *f* e
   valutazione *f* per la fotometria
– *computer and analyser for photometry*
54 il fotometro
– *photometer*
55 la scrivente di compensazione *f*
– *potentiometric recorder*
56 il livello di trasformazione *f*
– *transforming section*
57 gli strumenti di laboratorio
– *laboratory apparatus (laboratory
   equipment)*
58 la tabella del sedimento urinario
– *urine sediment chart*
59 la centrifuga
– *centrifuge*

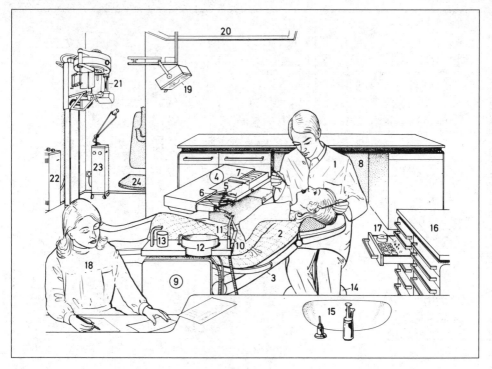

1 il dentista (l'odontoiatra *m*)
– *dentist (dental surgeon)*
2 il paziente
– *patient*
3 la poltrona del dentista
– *dentist's chair*
4 la mensola ondontoiatrica
– *dental instruments*
5 il tray (il tavolino) del dentista
– *instrument tray*
6 i trapani odontoiatrici con diverse
manopole *f pl*
– *drills with different handpieces*
7 la cassetta dei medicamenti
– *medicine case*
8 il vano della mensola
– *storage unit (for dental instruments)*
9 il riunito
– *assistant's unit*
10 l'eiettore *m* a più funzioni *f pl*
(per acqua fredda e calda, spray
*m* o aria)
– *multi-purpose syringe (for cold
and warm water, spray, or air)*
11 l'aspiratore *m* (aspirasaliva *m*)
– *suction apparatus*
12 la sputacchiera
– *basin*
13 il bicchiere dell'acqua a riempimento automatico
– *water glass, filled automatically*

14 lo sgabello del dentista
– *stool*
15 il lavabo (lavandino)
– *washbasin*
16 l'armadietto degli strumenti
– *instrument cabinet*
17 lo scomparto dei trapani
– *drawer for drills*
18 l'assistente *f* del dentista
– *dentist's assistant*
19 la lampada da dentista *m* (su
braccio mobile)
– *dentist's lamp*
20 la plafoniera (a tubo)
– *ceiling light*
21 l'apparecchio radiologico per
raggi X
– *X-ray apparatus for panoramic
pictures*
22 il generatore radiologico
– *X-ray generator*
23 l'apparecchio a microonde *f pl*, un
apparecchio radioterapico
– *microwave treatment unit, a radiation unit*
24 il seggiolino
– *seat*
25 la protesi dentaria (*pop.*: la den-
tiera)
– *denture (set of false teeth)*
26 il ponte (ponte *m* dentario)
– *bridge (dental bridge)*

27 il moncone di dente *m* limato
– *prepared stump of the tooth*
28 la corona dentaria (*tipi*: corona
d'oro, capsula)
– *crown (*kinds: *gold crown, jacket
crown)*
29 il dente di porcellana
– *porcelain tooth (porcelain pontic)*
30 l'otturazione *f* (otturazione *f* dentaria, *ant.*: impiombatura)
– *filling*

**31** il dente a perno (dente *m* a perno
sferico)
– *post crown*
**32** la faccetta (lo smusso)
– *facing*
**33** il diaframma
– *diaphragm*
**34** il perno sferico
– *post*
**35** il disco di carborundum (carburo
di silicio)
– *carborundum disc (disk)*
**36** la rotella smerigliata (il disco
smerigliato)
– *grinding wheel*
**37** trapani *m pl* per cavità
– *burs*
**38** il trapano a fiamma
– *flame-shaped finishing bur*
**39** trapani *m pl* a fessura
– *fissure burs*
**40** il trapano a punta di diamante *m*
– *diamond point*
**41** lo specchietto orale
– *mouth mirror*
**42** la lampada orale
– *mouth lamp*
**43** il cauterio
– *cautery*
**44** l'elettrodo al platino-iridio
– *platinum-iridium electrode*
**45** strumenti *m pl* per la pulizia dei
denti
– *tooth scalers*
**46** la sonda
– *probe*
**47** la pinza per estrazione *f* (pinza da
dentista *m*)
– *extraction forceps*
**48** l'elevatore *m* per estrazioni *f pl* di
radici *f pl*
– *tooth-root elevator*
**49** lo scalpello
– *bone chisel*
**50** la spatola
– *spatula*
**51** il miscelatore dell'amalgama *m*
per otturazioni *f pl*
– *mixer for filling material*
**52** l'interruttore *m* sincrono
– *synchronous timer*
**53** la siringa per l'anestesia (per
l'anestesia locale dei nervi)
– *hypodermic syringe for injection
of local anaesthetic*
**54** l'ago da iniezione *f*
– *hypodermic needle*
**55** il tendicalco (tenditore *m* della
matrice)
– *matrix holder*
**56** il cucchiaio da impronta (cucchiaio da calco)
– *impression tray*
**57** la fiamma a spirito
– *spirit lamp*

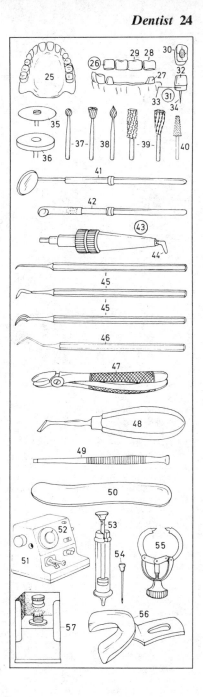

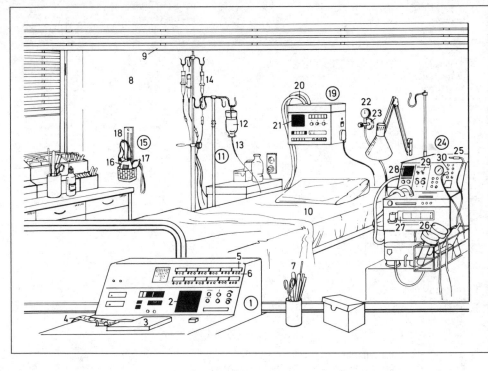

1-30  **il reparto intensivo** (reparto di
    terapia intensiva)
–  *intensive care unit*
1-9  **la sala (di) controllo**
–  *control room*
1  l'impianto centrale di controllo
    del cuore (dell'attività cardiaca,
    del ritmo cardiaco) e della pres-
    sione sanguigna
–  *central control unit for monitoring
    heart rhythm (cardiac rhythm)
    and blood pressure*
2  il monitor per la curva del ritmo
    cardiaco
–  *electrocardiogram monitor (ECG
    monitor)*
3  la scrivente
–  *recorder*
4  la carta per il tracciato
–  *recording paper*
5  la cartella clinica del paziente
–  *patient's card*
6  i segnali luminosi (con pulsanti *m
    pl* di collegamento con ogni
    paziente *m*)
–  *indicator lights (with call buttons
    for each patient)*
7  la spatola
–  *spatula*
8  la vetrata (lo schermo divisorio)
–  *window (observation window,
    glass partition)*

9  la veneziana (la tapparella diviso-
    ria)
–  *blind*
10  il letto del paziente
–  *bed (hospital bed)*
11  il braccio di sostegno per flebo-
    clisi *f* o ipodermoclisi *f*
–  *stand for infusion apparatus*
12  la bottiglia della fleboclisi
–  *infusion bottle*
13  il tubo per fleboclisi *f* a gocce *f pl*
–  *tube for intravenous drips*
14  l'apparecchio per l'infusione *f* di
    medicinali *m pl* idrosolubili
–  *infusion device for water-soluble
    medicaments*
15  lo sfigmomanometro
–  *sphygmomanometer*
16  il manicotto
–  *cuff*
17  la pompetta
–  *inflating bulb*
18  il manometro a mercurio
–  *mercury manometer*
19  il monitor installato sopra il letto
–  *bed monitor*
20  il cavo elettrico di collegamento
    con l'apparecchio centrale di con-
    trollo
–  *connecting lead to the central con-
    trol unit*

21  il monitor per la curva del ritmo
    cardiaco
–  *electrocardiogram monitor (ECG
    monitor)*
22  il manometro per l'alimentazione
    *f* di ossigeno
–  *manometer for the oxygen supply*
23  l'allacciamento a muro per la res-
    pirazione a ossigeno
–  *wall connection for oxygen treat-
    ment*
24  l'apparecchiatura mobile per il
    controllo del paziente
–  *mobile monitoring unit*
25  il cavo dell'elettrodo per il pace-
    maker
–  *electrode lead to the short-term
    pacemaker*
26  gli elettrodi per l'elettrochoc *m*
–  *electrodes for shock treatment*
27  l'apparecchio per la registrazione
    dell'elettrocardiogramma *m*
–  *ECG recording unit*
28  il monitor per il controllo della
    curva del ritmo cardiaco
–  *electrocardiogram monitor (ECG
    monitor)*
29  i tasti per la regolazione del moni-
    tor
–  *control switches and knobs (con-
    trols) for adjusting the monitor*

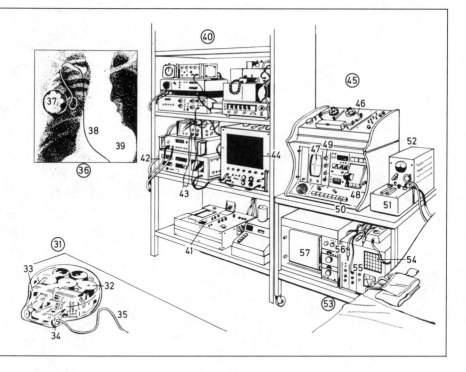

30 i tasti di comando per l'apparecchiatura del pacemaker
– *control buttons for the pacemaker*
*unit*
31 **il pacemaker**
– ***pacemaker (cardiac pacemaker)***
32 la batteria a mercurio
– *mercury battery*
33 il trasmettitore programmabile
del ritmo
– *programmed impulse generator*
34 l'uscita degli elettrodi
– *electrode exit point*
35 l'elettrodo
– *electrode*
36 l'inserimento del pacemaker
– *implantation of the pacemaker*
37 il pacemaker intracorporale
(pacemaker *m*)
– *internal cardiac pacemaker (inter-*
*nal pacemaker, pacemaker)*
38 l'elettrodo introdotto per via
transvenosa
– *electrode inserted through the vein*
39 il profilo del cuore nella radiografia
– *cardiac silhouette on the X-ray*
40 **l'apparecchiatura per il controllo**
**del pacemaker**
– ***pacemaker control unit***
41 la scrivente dell'elettrocardiogramma *m*
– *electrocardiograph (ECG*
*recorder)*

42 il misuratore automatico degli
impulsi
– *automatic impulse meter*
43 il cavo (cavo dell'elettrocardiogramma *m*) di collegamento al
paziente
– *ECG lead to the patient*
44 il monitor per il controllo degli
impulsi del pacemaker
– *monitor unit for visual monitoring*
*of the pacemaker impulses*
45 l'apparecchio di analisi *f* elettrocardiografica a lungo tempo; *tipo:*
holter *m*
– *long-term ECG analyser*
46 il nastro magnetico di registrazione *f* degli impulsi elettrocar-
diografici durante l'esame *m*
– *magnetic tape for recording the*
*ECG impulses during analysis*
47 il monitor di controllo dell'elettrocardiogramma *m*
– *ECG monitor*
48 l'elettrocardiogramma *m* automatico su carta (analisi *f* elettrocardiografica del ritmo cardiaco)
– *automatic analysis on paper of the*
*ECG rhythm*
49 la regolazione del livello di
ampiezza dell'elettrocardiogramma *m*
– *control knob for the ECG ampli-*
*tude*

50 la tastiera di programmazione *f*
per l'analisi *f* elettrocardiografica
– *program selector switches for the*
*ECG analysis*
51 il caricatore delle batterie di
azionamento dell'apparecchio nel
paziente
– *charger for the pacemaker batter-*
*ies*
52 l'apparecchio di verifica delle batterie
– *battery tester*
53 il misuratore di pressione *f* del
catetere cardiaco destro
– *pressure gauge (Am. gage) for the*
*right cardiac catheter*
54 il monitor di controllo del tracciato
– *trace monitor*
55 l'indicatore della pressione
– *pressure indicator*
56 il cavo di collegamento con la
scrivente
– *connecting lead to the paper*
*recorder*
57 la scrivente del tracciato della
pressione
– *paper recorder for pressure traces*

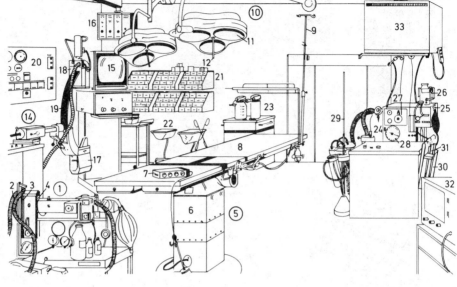

**1-54 il reparto di chirurgia (clinica chirurgica)**
- *surgical unit*
**1-33 la sala operatoria**
- *operating theatre* (Am. *theater*)
1 l'apparecchiatura per narcosi *f* e respirazione *f* artificiale
- *anaesthesia and breathing apparatus (respiratory machine)*
2 i tubi di inalazione *f*
- *inhalers (inhaling tubes)*
3 l'anestetimetro, il dosatore del gas esilarante (protossido di azoto)
- *flowmeter for nitrous oxide*
4 il dosatore di ossigeno
- *oxygen flow meter*
5 il tavolo operatorio
- *pedestal operating table*
6 la colonna
- *table pedestal*
7 l'apparecchio di comando
- *control device (control unit)*
8 il piano regolabile del tavolo operatorio
- *adjustable top of the operating table*
9 il braccio di sostegno per proctoclisi *f* a gocce *f pl*
- *stand for intravenous drips*

10 la lampada parabolica (lampada da sala operatoria) orientabile
- *swivel-mounted shadow-free operating lamp*
11 l'elemento luminoso
- *individual lamp*
12 l'impugnatura (la maniglia)
- *handle*
13 il braccio orientabile
- *swivel arm*
14 l'apparecchio mobile per la radioscopia
- *mobile fluoroscope*
15 il monitor convertitore di immagine *f*
- *monitor of the image converter*
16 il monitor [parte *f* posteriore]
- *monitor [back]*
17 il complesso dei tubi
- *tube*
18 l'unità *f* convertitrice di immagine *f*
- *image converter*
19 l'arco a C
- *C-shaped frame*
20 il quadro degli interruttori (quadro di distribuzione *f* ) dell'impianto di climatizzazione *f*
- *control panel for the air-conditioning*

21 il materiale di sutura
- *surgical suture material*
22 il contenitore (il cestello) a rotelle *f pl* dei rifiuti
- *mobile waste tray*
23 il contenitore di compresse *f pl* non sterilizzate
- *containers for unsterile (unsterilized) pads*
24 l'apparecchiatura per narcosi *f*, anestesia generale e respirazione *f* artificiale
- *anaesthesia and respiratory apparatus*
25 il respiratore
- *respirator*
26 la bombola del fluotano (alotano)
- *fluothane container (halothane container)*
27 la manopola di comando di ventilazione *f*
- *ventilation control knob*
28 il quadro di registrazione *f* con l'indice *m* del volume respiratorio
- *indicator with pointer for respiratory volume*

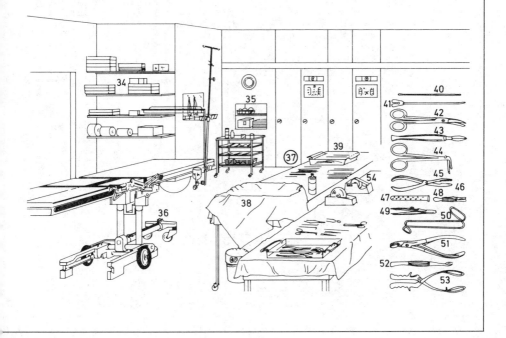

**29** lo stativo con i tubi di inalazione *f*
e i misuratori (riduttori) di pressione *f*
– *stand with inhalers (inhaling
tubes) and pressure gauges (Am.
gages)*
**30** il portacatetere (il contenitore dei
cateteri)
– *catheter holder*
**31** il catetere sterile
– *catheter in sterile packing*
**32** lo sfigmografo
– *sphygmograph*
**33** il monitor
– *monitor*
**34-54 la sala di sterilizzazione *f***
– ***preparation and sterilization
room***
**34** il materiale di medicazione *f*
– *dressing material*
**35** lo sterilizzatore per ferri *m pl*
chirurgici (bollitore *m*)
– *small sterilizer*
**36** il carrello per tavolo operatorio
– *carriage of the operating table*
**37** il tavolo a rotelle *m pl* (tavolo
mobile) degli strumenti
– *mobile instrument table*
**38** il telo (lenzuolo) sterilizzato
– *sterile cloth*
**39** la vaschetta degli strumenti
– *instrument tray*

**40-53 gli strumenti chirurgici**
– *surgical instruments*
**40** lo specillo (sonda con punta ad
oliva)
– *olive-pointed (bulb-headed) probe*
**41** la sonda con foro
– *hollow probe*
**42** le forbici ricurve
– *curved scissors*
**43** il bisturi
– *scalpel (surgical knife)*
**44** la pinza per legatura
– *ligature-holding forceps*
**45** la pinza da sequestro
– *sequestrum forceps*
**46** la branca (le branche)
– *jaw*
**47** il tubo di drenaggio
– *drainage tube*
**48** il compressore emostatico (klem-
mer *m*) per vene *f pl*
– *surgeon's tourniquet*
**49** la pinza emostatica (le pinze emo-
statiche) per arterie *f pl*
– *artery forceps*
**50** il tenacolo
– *blunt hook*
**51** la pinza ortopedica (pinze per le
ossa)
– *bone nippers (bone-cutting forceps)*

**52** la «curette» per il «curettage» (il
cucchiaio per il raschiamento)
– *scoop (curette) for erasion (curettage)*
**53** il forcipe ostetrico
– *obstetrical forceps*
**54** il rotolo di cerotto adesivo (il
cerotto adesivo)
– *roll of plaster*

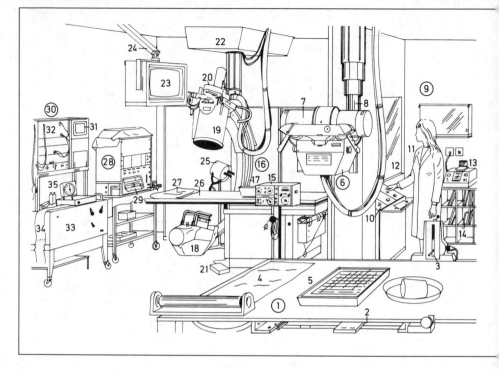

**1-35  la sala di radiografia**
- *X-ray unit*
1  il tavolo per esame *m* radiologico
- *X-ray examination table*
2  il contenitore della cassetta (lastra) radiografica
- *support for X-ray cassettes*
3  il regolatore dell'altezza del raggio principale in radiografie *f pl* sul fianco
- *height adjustment of the central beam for lateral views*
4  la compressa (pezzuola) per radiografia dei reni e della bile
- *compress for pyelography and cholecystography*
5  la vaschetta degli strumenti
- *instrument basin*
6  l'apparecchiatura per radiografia dei reni con mezzo di contrasto
- *X-ray apparatus for pyelograms*
7  il tubo a raggi *m pl* X (tubo per raggi *m pl* Röntgen)
- *X-ray tube*
8  lo stativo allungabile
- *telescopic X-ray support*
9  la centrale di comando
- *central X-ray control unit*
10  il banco di comando
- *control panel (control desk)*
11  l'assistente *f* radiologa
- *radiographer (X-ray technician)*

12  lo schermo visivo sulla sala di angiografia
- *window to the angiography room*
13  l'ossimetro
- *oxymeter*
14  le cassette (lastre *f pl*) per radiografie *f pl* dei reni
- *pyelogram cassettes*
15  l'apparecchio per iniezioni *f pl* a pressione *f* di mezzi *m pl* di contrasto (iniezioni di pasto opaco)
- *contrast medium injector*
16  l'amplificatore *m* della radiografia
- *X-ray image intensifier*
17  la curvatura a C
- *C-shaped frame*
18  la testa con il tubo a raggi *m pl* X
- *X-ray head with X-ray tube*
19  il convertitore d'immagine *f* con il tubo convertitore d'immagine *f*
- *image converter with converter tube*
20  la macchina da presa
- *film camera*
21  l'interruttore *m* a pedale *f*
- *foot switch*
22  il sostegno mobile
- *mobile mounting*
23  il monitor
- *monitor*
24  il braccio girevole del monitor
- *swivel-mounted monitor support*

25  la lampada parabolica (lampada da sala operatoria)
- *operating lamp*
26  il tavolo per l'angiografia (per esame *m* angiografico)
- *angiographic examination table*
27  il cuscino
- *pillow*
28  la scrivente a otto canali *m pl*
- *eight-channel recorder*
29  la carta per il tracciato
- *recording paper*
30  l'ambito di misurazione *f* del catetere per il cateterismo cardiaco
- *catheter gauge (Am. gage) unit for catheterization of the heart*
31  il monitor a sei canali *m pl* per i diagrammi della pressione sanguigna e dell'elettrocardiogramma *m*
- *six-channel monitor for pressure graphs and ECG*
32  gli innesti dei convertitori di pressione *f*
- *slide-in units of the pressure transducer*
33  il dispositivo di registrazione *f* su carta con sviluppo *m* della registrazione fotografica
- *paper recorder unit with developer for photographic recording*

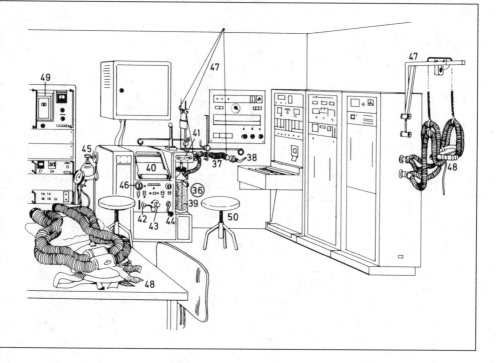

34 la carta per il tracciato
– recording paper
35 il timer
– timer
36-50 spirometria
– spirometry
36 lo spirografo (spirometro, pneu-
madinamometro, pneu-
matometro) per esame della funzione polmonare (per la misurazione del volume respiratorio)
– spirograph for pulmonary function tests
37 il tubo respiratorio
– breathing tube
38 la bocchetta (l'imboccatura)
– mouthpiece
39 l'assorbitore m di calce sodata
– soda-lime absorber
40 la carta per il tracciato
– recording paper
41 il regolatore di erogazione f del
gas
– control knobs for gas supply
42 lo stabilizzatore (stabilizzante m)
di ossigeno (O₂)
– O₂ stabilizer
43 la valvola a farfalla
– throttle valve
44 l'interruttore m dell'assorbitore m
– absorber attachment

45 la bombola di ossigeno
– oxygen cylinder
46 l'erogazione f dell'acqua
– water supply
47 il supporto dei tubi
– tube support
48 la maschera
– mask
49 l'ambito di misurazione f del con-
sumo di anidride f carbonica
(CO₂)
– CO₂ consumption meter
50 lo sgabello per il paziente
– stool for the patient

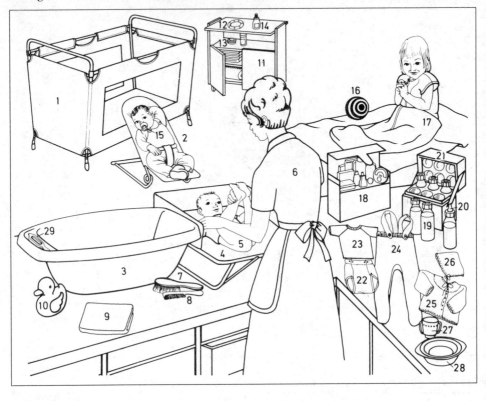

**1** il lettino pieghevole a rotelle *f pl*
– *collapsible cot*
**2** il seggiolino del neonato
– *bouncing cradle*
**3** la vaschetta per il bagno
– *baby bath*
**4** il fasciatoio
– *changing top*
**5** il neonato
– *baby (new-born baby)*
**6** la madre
– *mother*
**7** la spazzola per capelli *m pl*
– *hairbrush*
**8** il pettine
– *comb*
**9** l'asciugamano (la salvietta)
– *hand towel*
**10** il giocattolo galleggiante (*qui:* l'anatroccolo)
– *toy duck*
**11** il fasciatoio
– *changing unit*
**12** l'anello da dentizione *m*
– *teething ring*
**13** la scatola di crema
– *cream jar*
**14** il barattolo del talco
– *box of baby powder*

**15** il succhietto (il succhiotto); *pop.:* il ciuccio
– *dummy*
**16** la palla
– *ball*
**17** il pigiama a sacco
– *sleeping bag*
**18** il cofanetto dei prodotti igienici
– *layette box*
**19** il biberon, il poppatoio
– *feeding bottle*
**20** la tettarella
– *teat*
**21** il termostato per il biberon
– *bottle warmer*
**22** la mutandina di gomma
– *rubber baby pants for disposable nappies* (Am. *diapers*)
**23** la camiciola (allacciata sul dietro)
– *vest*
**24** la mezza tutina con piede *m*
– *leggings*
**25** il golfino
– *baby's jacket*
**26** la cuffietta
– *hood*
**27** la tazza per bebè (con base *f* concava)
– *baby's cup*

**28** il piatto per bebè, un piatto scaldavivande
– *baby's plate, a stay-warm plate*
**29** il termometro
– *thermometer*

**30** la culla a rotelle *f pl*, una culla in giunco
– *bassinet, a wicker pram*
**31** il completo per la culla
– *set of bassinet covers*
**32** la tendina della culla
– *canopy*
**33** il seggiolone, un seggiolone pieghevole
– *baby's high chair, a folding chair*
**34** la carrozzina panoramica
– *pram (baby-carriage) [with windows]*
**35** il tettuccio ribaltabile
– *folding hood*
**36** la finestra
– *window*
**37** il passeggino
– *pushchair (Am. stroller)*
**38** il sacco da passeggino
– *foot-muff (Am. foot-bag)*
**39** il box (*qui:* a rotelle *f pl*)
– *play pen*
**40** il piano del box
– *floor of the play pen*
**41** i cubi per le costruzioni
– *building blocks (building bricks)*
**42** il bambino
– *small child*
**43** il bavaglino
– *bib*

**44** il giocattolo a sonagli *m pl*
– *rattle (baby's rattle)*
**45** le scarpine
– *bootees*
**46** l'orsacchiotto
– *teddy bear*
**47** il vasino (il vaso)
– *potty (baby's pot)*
**48** il baby-pullman
– *carrycot*
**49** la finestra
– *window*
**50** i manici a cinghia
– *handles*

**1-12  gli indumenti da neonato** (il
  corredino per neonato)
– *baby clothes*
1  il completo da passeggio
– *pram suit*
2  la cuffia (la cuffietta)
– *hood*
3  la giacchina (il giacchettino)
– *pram jacket (matinée coat)*
4  il pompon
– *pompon (bobble)*
5  le scarpine (di lana) da neonato
– *bootees*
6  la canottiera (canottierina)
– *sleeveless vest*
7  la maglietta paricollo (maglietta
  all'americana)
– *envelope-neck vest*
8  la maglietta incrociata con allacciatura sul collo
– *wrapover vest*
9  il golfino
– *baby's jacket*
10  la mutandina portapannolini
– *rubber baby pants*
11  la tutina
– *playsuit*
12  il completino
– *two-piece suit*
**13-30  gli indumenti** *m pl* **per bambini**
  *m pl*
– *infants' wear*
13  il vestito estivo, un vestitino
  prendisole
– *child's sundress, a pinafore dress*
14  la manica (*qui:* la spallina) a
  volant
– *frilled shoulder strap*
15  il bustino a nido d'ape *f*
– *shirred top*
16  il cappello estivo (cappello da
  sole *m*)
– *sun hat*
17  la tuta in jersey *m*
– *one-piece jersey suit*
18  la zip (la cerniera lampo, la
  lampo) sul davanti
– *front zip* (Am. *zipper)*
19  la salopette (la tutina)
– *catsuit (playsuit)*
20  l'applicazione
– *motif (appliqué)*
21  il pagliaccetto
– *romper*
22  la tutina a mutandina
– *playsuit (romper suit)*
23  il pigiama (pigiama *m* intero,
  pigiama a tuta)
– *coverall (sleeper and strampler)*
24  l'accappatoio
– *dressing gown (bath robe)*
25  i calzoncini (gli shorts)
– *children's shorts*
26  le bretelle
– *braces* (Am. *suspenders)*

27  il T-shirt (la maglietta)
– *children's T-shirt*
28  il vestitino in tessuto di maglia
  (vestitino di jersey *m*)
– *jersey dress (knitted dress)*
29  il ricamo
– *embroidery*
30  i calzini
– *children's ankle socks*
**31-47  gli indumenti per bambini** *m pl*
  **in età** *f* **scolare**
– *school children's wear*
31  l'impermeabile *m*
– *raincoat*
32  i calzoncini di pelle *f*
– *leather shorts (lederhosen)*
33  i bottoni di osso
– *staghorn button*
34  le bretelle di cuoio
– *braces* (Am. *suspenders)*
35  la brachetta
– *flap*
36  il vestito tirolese
– *girl's dirndl*
37  i lacci incrociati
– *cross lacing*
38  la tuta da sci *m pl* (da neve *f* ),
  una tuta imbottita
– *snow suit (quilted suit)*
39  l'impuntura
– *quilt stitching (quilting)*
40  la salopette (pantaloni *m pl* con
  pettorina)
– *dungarees (bib and brace)*
41  la gonna con pettorina e bretelle *f pl*
– *bib skirt (bib top pinafore)*
42  la calzamaglia
– *tights*
43  il pullover in velluto di cotone
  (pullover *m* in maglia di spugna)
– *sweater (jumper)*
44  la giacca di pelliccia sintetica (di
  pelliccia finta)
– *pile jacket*
45  i pantaloni con le ghette
– *leggings*
46  la gonna
– *girl's skirt*
47  la maglietta
– *child's jumper*
**48-68  l'abbigliamento per ragazzi** *m*
  *pl* **e per ragazze** *f pl*
– *teenagers' clothes*
48  la casacca
– *girl's overblouse (overtop)*
49  i pantaloni da donna
– *slacks*
50  il completo (gonna e giacca) per
  ragazza
– *girl's skirt suit*
51  la giacca
– *jacket*
52  la gonna
– *skirt*

53  i gambaletti (i calzettoni)
– *knee-length socks*
54  il cappotto
– *girl's coat*
55  la cintura
– *tie belt*
56  la borsa (*qui:* borsa a tracolla, la
  tracolla)
– *girl's bag*
57  il berretto di lana
– *woollen* (Am. *woolen) hat*
58  la camicetta, una blusa
– *girl's blouse*
59  la pantagonna (gonna a pantaloni
  *m pl*)
– *culottes*
60  i pantaloni (da ragazzo)
– *boy's trousers*
61  la camicia
– *boy's shirt*
62  il giubbotto impermeabile
– *anorak*
63  le tasche tagliate
– *inset pockets*
64  il cordoncino del cappuccio
– *hood drawstring (drawstring)*
65  il polsino lavorato a maglia
– *knitted welt*
66  il giaccone impermeabile
– *parka coat (parka)*
67  la coulisse in vita
– *drawstring (draw cord)*
68  le tasche applicate
– *patch pockets*

# 30 Abbigliamento per signora I (Abiti invernali)

1 il giacchino di visone *m*
  - *mink jacket*
2 il pull con il collo a anello
  - *cowl neck jumper*
3 il collo rovesciato a anello (ampio collo ad anello)
  - *cowl collar*
4 il pull a casacca (la blusa)
  - *knitted overtop*
5 il colletto rovesciato
  - *turndown collar*
6 la manica con il risvolto
  - *turn-up (turnover) sleeve*
7 la maglietta girocollo
  - *polo neck jumper*
8 lo scamiciato
  - *pinafore dress*
9 la camicetta con il collo a uomo (con il collo a revers *m*)
  - *blouse (with revers collar)*
10 lo chemisier, un abito con abbottonatura intera sul davanti
  - *shirt-waister dress, a button-through dress*
11 la cintura
  - *belt*
12 l'abito invernale
  - *winter dress*
13 la pistagna
  - *piping*
14 il polsino
  - *cuff*
15 la manica lunga
  - *long sleeve*
16 il gilé (gilet *m*) trapuntato (gilé imbottito in ovatta)
  - *quilted waistcoat*
17 l'impuntura
  - *quilt stitching (quilting)*
18 le rifiniture in pelle *f*
  - *leather trimming*
19 i pantaloni invernali
  - *winter slacks*
20 la maglietta a righe
  - *striped polo jumper*
21 la salopette
  - *boiler suit (dungarees, bib and brace)*
22 la tasca applicata
  - *patch pocket*
23 la tasca della pettorina
  - *front pocket*
24 la pettorina
  - *bib*
25 il vestito con gonna a portafoglio
  - *wrapover dress (wrap-around dress)*
26 la camicetta (con il collo) a polo
  - *shirt*
27 il vestito folk
  - *peasant-style dress*
28 la passamaneria a fiori *m pl*
  - *floral braid*
29 la tunica
  - *tunic (tunic top)*

30 il polsino
  - *ribbed cuff*
31 il disegno (il motivo) ricamato (trapuntato)
  - *quilted design*
32 la gonna plissettata (pieghettata)
  - *pleated skirt*
33 il completo di maglia (completo due pezzi *m pl* di maglia)
  - *two-piece knitted dress*
34 la scollatura a barchetta
  - *boat neck, a neckline*
35 il risvolto della manica
  - *turn-up*
36 la manica a chimono (a kimono *m*)
  - *kimono sleeve*
37 il disegno jacquard
  - *knitted design*
38 il blusotto (il giubbotto)
  - *lumber-jacket*
39 il motivo a treccia
  - *cable pattern*
40 la camicia (la blusa)
  - *shirt-blouse*
41 l'abbottonatura a occhiello
  - *loop fastening*
42 il ricamo
  - *embroidery*
43 il colletto alto (colletto alla coreana)
  - *stand-up collar*
44 i pantaloni alla cosacca (alla zuava)
  - *cossack trousers*
45 i due pezzi pantaloni *m pl* e casacca
  - *two-piece combination (shirt top and long skirt)*
46 il fiocco (il nastro)
  - *tie (bow)*
47 la finta
  - *decorative facing*
48 lo spacco della manica
  - *cuff slit*
49 lo spacco laterale
  - *side slit*
50 la casacca senza maniche *f pl*
  - *tabard*
51 la gonna con spacco laterale
  - *inverted pleat skirt*
52 la vista
  - *godet*
53 il vestito (l'abito) da sera
  - *evening gown*
54 la manica a pagoda plissettata
  - *pleated bell sleeve*
55 la camicetta da sera
  - *party blouse*
56 la gonna da sera (gonna lunga)
  - *party skirt*
57 il completo pantalone
  - *trouser suit (slack suit)*
58 la giacca in pelle *f* scamosciata
  - *suede jacket*
59 le rifiniture di pelliccia
  - *fur trimming*

60 la pelliccia (*tipi:* persiano, breitschwanz *m*, visone *m*, zibellino)
  - *fur coat (kinds: Persian lamb, broadtail, mink, sable)*
61 il cappotto invernale (cappotto di panno, cappotto di lana)
  - *winter coat (cloth coat)*
62 il risvolto della manica in pelliccia
  - *fur cuff (fur-trimmed cuff)*
63 il collo di pelliccia
  - *fur collar (fur-trimmed collar)*
64 il loden
  - *loden coat*
65 la mantellina
  - *cape*
66 i bottoni a barretta (di legno o di osso)
  - *toggle fastenings*
67 la gonna di loden *m*
  - *loden skirt*
68 la mantella
  - *poncho-style coat*
69 il cappuccio
  - *hood*

# 31 Abbigliamento per signora II (Abiti estivi)

1 il tailleur (il completo giacca e gonna)
 – skirt suit
2 la giacca del tailleur
 – jacket
3 la gonna del tailleur
 – skirt
4 la tasca tagliata
 – inset pocket
5 la cucitura riportata
 – decorative stitching
6 il completo abito e giacca
 – dress and jacket combination
7 l'orlatura
 – piping
8 il prendisole
 – pinafore dress
9 il vestito estivo (vestito senza maniche f pl, vestito sbracciato)
 – summer dress
10 la cintura
 – belt
11 il completo due pezzi m pl
 – two-piece dress
12 la fibbia della cintura
 – belt buckle
13 la gonna a portafoglio
 – wrapover (wrap-around) skirt
14 il tubino a linea diritta
 – pencil silhouette
15 l'abbottonatura sulla spalla
 – shoulder buttons
16 la manica a pipistrello
 – batwing sleeve
17 il vestito ricercato
 – overdress
18 lo sprone a chimono (la spallina a kimono)
 – kimono yoke
19 la cintura annodata
 – tie belt
20 il soprabito estivo
 – summer coat
21 il cappuccio staccabile (sbottonabile)
 – detachable hood
22 la camicetta estiva (camicetta a maniche f pl corte)
 – summer blouse
23 il collo a uomo
 – lapel
24 la gonna
 – skirt
25 la piega sul davanti
 – front pleat
26 il vestito alla tirolese
 – dirndl (dirndl dress)
27 la manica a sbuffo (a palloncino)
 – puffed sleeve
28 la collana (il collier)
 – dirndl necklace
29 la camicetta alla tirolese
 – dirndl blouse
30 il corsetto (il busto, il bustino)
 – bodice

31 il grembiule alla tirolese
 – dirndl apron
32 la guarnizione di pizzo (il pizzo, il merletto), un pizzo di cotone m: il sangallo
 – lace trimming (lace), cotton lace
33 il grembiule a volant m
 – frilled apron
34 il volant
 – frill
35 la casacca
 – smock overall
36 il vestito da casa
 – house frock (house dress)
37 la giacca di popeline f
 – poplin jacket
38 il T-shirt (qui: la canotta a spalla larga, il top)
 – T-shirt
39 gli shorts (i calzoncini corti)
 – ladies' shorts
40 il risvolto
 – trouser turn-up
41 la cintura
 – waistband
42 il blusotto
 – bomber jacket
43 la cintura elastica (cintura stretch)
 – stretch welt
44 i bermuda
 – Bermuda shorts
45 l'impuntura
 – saddle stitching
46 il colletto con ruche f
 – frill collar
47 il nodo
 – knot
48 la pantagonna (la gonna pantaloni)
 – culotte
49 il completo (i gemelli) di lana
 – twin set
50 il cardigan (il golf )
 – cardigan
51 il pull (il maglioncino)
 – sweater
52 i pantaloni estivi
 – summer (lightweight) slacks
53 la tuta
 – jumpsuit
54 il risvolto della manica
 – turn-up
55 la zip (la cerniera lampo)
 – zip (Am. zipper)
56 la tasca applicata
 – patch pocket
57 il fazzoletto (il foulard) da collo
 – scarf (neckerchief )
58 il completo jeans m (pantaloni m pl e gilé m)
 – denim suit
59 il gilé di jeans m
 – denim waistcoat
60 i jeans (blue jeans m pl)
 – jeans (denims)

61 la tunica (qui: con il colletto aperto)
 – overblouse
62 la manica rimboccata
 – turned-up sleeve
63 la cintura elastica (cintura stretch)
 – stretch belt
64 la maglietta a dorso nudo (maglietta con spallina girocollo)
 – halter top
65 la casacca
 – knitted overtop
66 la cintura a tunnel m
 – drawstring waist
67 la maglia estiva (il pull estivo)
 – short-sleeved jumper
68 la scollatura a V
 – V-neck (vee-neck)
69 il colletto rovesciabile
 – turndown collar
70 il fondomaniche di maglia cannettata (di maglia lavorata a coste f pl)
 – knitted welt
71 lo scialle
 – shawl

**1-15  la biancheria per signora**
(biancheria intima da donna)
- *ladies' underwear (ladies' under-clothes, lingerie)*
1  il reggiseno
- *brassière (bra)*
2  la pancera, la mutanda elastica
- *pantie-girdle*
3  il body, la guaina, il busto; *ant.* la guépière
- *pantie-corselette*
4  il bustino, il reggiseno a bustino
- *longline brassière (longline bra)*
5  il reggicalze elastico
- *stretch girdle*
6  la giarrettiera
- *suspender*
7  la canottiera
- *vest*
8  la mutandina, la mutanda
- *pantie briefs*
9  il gambaletto
- *ladies' knee-high stocking*
10  la mutanda elastica snellente
- *long-legged (long leg) panties*
11  la calzamaglia
- *long pants*
12  il collant
- *tights (pantie-hose)*
13  la sottoveste
- *slip*
14  la sottogonna
- *waist slip*
15  lo slip
- *bikini briefs*
**16-21  l'abbigliamento da notte *f* per signora**
- *ladies' nightwear*
16  la camicia da notte *f*
- *nightdress (nightgown, nightie)*
17  il pigiama (il pigiama da casa)
- *pyjamas* (Am. *pajamas)*
18  la giacca (la maglietta, il T-shirt) del pigiama
- *pyjama top*
19  i pantaloni del pigiama
- *pyjama trousers*
20  la vestaglia; *da bagno:* l'accappa-toio
- *housecoat*
21  il baby-doll
- *vest and shorts set [for leisure wear and as nightwear]*
**22-29  la biancheria da uomo**
- *men's underwear (men's under-clothes)*
22  la canottiera (a rete *f* )
- *string vest*
23  lo slip (a rete *f* )
- *string briefs*
24  la patta
- *front panel*
25  la canottiera
- *sleeveless vest*

26  lo slip
- *briefs*
27  la mutanda da uomo
- *trunks*
28  la canottiera a mezze maniche *f pl*
- *short-sleeved vest*
29  la mutanda lunga (*o* le mutande lunghe)
- *long johns*
30  le bretelle
- *braces* (Am. *suspenders)*
31  il gancio delle bretelle
- *braces clip*
**32-34  calzini *m pl* da uomo**
- *men's socks*
32  i calzettoni, i calzini lunghi
- *knee-length sock*
33  il bordo elastico dei calzini
- *elasticated top*
34  i calzini
- *long sock*
**35-37  l'abbigliamento da notte *f* per uomo**
- *men's nightwear*
35  la vestaglia da uomo
- *dressing gown*
36  il pigiama
- *pyjamas* (Am. *pajamas)*
37  la camicia da notte *f* per uomo
- *nightshirt*
**38-47  camicie *f pl* da uomo**
- *men's shirts*
38  la camicia sportiva
- *casual shirt*
39  la cintura
- *belt*
40  il fazzoletto da collo, il foulard
- *cravat*
41  la cravatta
- *tie*
42  il nodo della cravatta
- *knot*
43  la camicia da smoking *m*
- *dress shirt*
44  le ruches *f pl*
- *frill (frill front)*
45  il polsino
- *cuff*
46  i gemelli
- *cuff link*
47  il papillon, la cravatta a farfalla; *fam.:* il farfallino
- *bow-tie*

**1-67 la moda maschile**
- *men's fashion*
1 l'abito monopetto da uomo
- *single-breasted suit, a men's suit*
2 la giacca
- *jacket*
3 i pantaloni
- *suit trousers*
4 il gilé (gilet *m*)
- *waistcoat (vest)*
5 il revers (il risvolto della giacca)
- *lapel*
6 la gamba dei pantaloni con la piega
- *trouser leg with crease*
7 lo smoking, un abito da sera
- *dinner dress, an evening suit*
8 il revers (il risvolto della giacca) di seta
- *silk lapel*
9 il taschino
- *breast pocket*
10 il fazzoletto da taschino
- *dress handkerchief*
11 il cravattino nero
- *bow-tie*
12 la tasca laterale (tasca esterna)
- *side pocket*
13 il frac (la marsina), un abito da cerimonia
- *tailcoat (tails), evening dress*
14 la falda del frac *m*
- *coat-tail*
15 il gilé bianco
- *white waistcoat (vest)*
16 il cravattino bianco
- *white bow-tie*
17 il completo sportivo
- *casual suit*
18 la patta della tasca
- *pocket flap*
19 il carré (lo sprone)
- *front yoke*
20 il completo jeans
- *denim suit*
21 la giacca jeans
- *denim jacket*
22 i jeans (blue jeans *m pl*)
- *jeans (denims)*
23 la cintura
- *waistband*
24 il completo da spiaggia
- *beach suit*
25 i calzoncini (gli shorts)
- *shorts*
26 la camicia a maniche *f pl* corte alla sahariana
- *short-sleeved jacket*
27 la tuta sportiva
- *tracksuit*
28 la giacca della tuta con la zip
- *tracksuit top with zip*
29 i pantaloni della tuta
- *tracksuit bottoms*
30 la giacca di maglia
- *cardigan*

31 il colletto di maglia a coste *f pl*
- *knitted collar*
32 il pull estivo a maniche *f pl* corte (la maglietta estiva)
- *men's short-sleeved pullover (men's short-sleeved sweater)*
33 la camicia estiva a maniche *f pl* corte (la camiciola)
- *short-sleeved shirt*
34 il bottone della camicia
- *shirt button*
35 il risvolto della manica
- *turn-up*
36 la maglietta polo
- *knitted shirt*
37 la camicia sportiva
- *casual shirt*
38 il taschino applicato
- *patch pocket*
39 la giacca sportiva (giacca da montagna, giacca a vento)
- *casual jacket*
40 i calzoni alla zuava (i knickerbocker)
- *knee-breeches*
41 la fermatura al ginocchio
- *knee strap*
42 il calzettone
- *knee-length sock*
43 la giacca di pelle *f*
- *leather jacket*
44 la tuta da lavoro
- *bib and brace overalls*
45 le bretelle regolabili
- *adjustable braces (Am. suspenders)*
46 la tasca sulla pettorina
- *front pocket*
47 la tasca dei pantaloni
- *trouser pocket*
48 la patta dei pantaloni
- *fly*
49 la tasca per il metro pieghevole
- *rule pocket*
50 la camicia a quadri *m pl* (a quadretti *m pl*)
- *check shirt*
51 il pullover per uomo
- *men's pullover*
52 il maglione da sci *m pl*
- *heavy pullover*
53 il gilé di maglia
- *knitted waistcoat (vest)*
54 il blazer
- *blazer*
55 il bottone della giacca
- *jacket button*
56 il grembiule bianco da lavoro (*tipo*: il camice)
- *overall*
57 il trench, un impermeabile con cintura
- *trenchcoat*
58 il collo
- *coat collar*

59 la cintura
- *coat belt*
60 il soprabito da mezza stagione *f*
- *poplin coat*
61 la tasca del soprabito
- *coat pocket*
62 l'abbottonatura nascosta
- *fly front*
63 il giaccone da marinaio, un giaccone di panno
- *car coat*
64 il bottone del giaccone
- *coat button*
65 la sciarpa
- *scarf*
66 il cappotto di panno (cappotto di lana)
- *cloth coat*
67 i guanti (*qui*: il guanto)
- *glove*

**1-25 fogge** *f pl* **maschili di barba e capelli** (acconciature *f pl* maschili)
– **men's beards and hairstyles** *(haircuts)*
**1** capelli *m pl* lunghi e sciolti
– *long hair worn loose*
**2** la parrucca a riccioli *m pl* (il parruccone), una parrucca; *più corta e liscia:* la mezza parrucca, il parrucchino (il toupet)
– *allonge periwig (full-bottomed wig), a wig;* shorter and smoother: *bob wig, toupet*
**3** i riccioli
– *curls*
**4** la parrucca a borsa (i capelli alla Mozart)
– *bag wig (purse wig)*
**5** la parrucca a codino (parrucca a coda)
– *pigtail wig*
**6** il codino
– *queue (pigtail)*
**7** il nastro del codino
– *bow (ribbon)*
**8** i baffi
– *handlebars (handlebar moustache,* Am. *mustache)*
**9** la scriminatura (la riga) in mezzo
– *centre (*Am. *center) parting*
**10** la barba a punta (il pizzetto, la barba alla francese)
– *goatee (goatee beard), chintuft*
**11** i capelli a spazzola
– *closely-cropped head of hair (crew cut)*
**12** i favoriti (le fedine, la barba alla Cavour, la barba alla Francesco Giuseppe)
– *whiskers*
**13** la barba alla moschettiera (il pizzo a punta, la barba imperiale)
– *Vandyke beard (stiletto beard, bodkin beard), with waxed moustache (*Am. *mustache)*
**14** la scriminatura (la riga) laterale
– *side parting*
**15** la barba intera (barba piena)
– *full beard (circular beard, round beard)*
**16** la barba quadrata
– *tile beard*
**17** la mosca
– *shadow*
**18** i capelli ricci (la testa ricciuta)
– *head of curly hair*
**19** i baffi (baffi *m pl* a spazzola)
– *military moustache (*Am. *mustache) (English-style moustache)*
**20** la testa calva
– *partly bald head*
**21** la calvizie
– *bald patch*
**22** la testa calva (testa pelata)
– *bald head*

**23** la barba lunga (barba non rasata)
– *stubble beard (stubble, short beard bristles)*
**24** le basette
– *side-whiskers (sideboards, sideburns)*
**25** il volto sbarbato
– *clean shave*
**26** l'Afro-Look *m* (per uomini *m pl* e donne *f pl*)
– *Afro look (for men and women)*
**27-38 acconciature** *f pl* **femminili** (pettinature *f pl* da signora e da ragazza)
– **ladies' hairstyles** *(coiffures, women's and girls' hairstyles)*
**27** la coda di cavallo
– *ponytail*
**28** i capelli raccolti
– *swept-back hair (swept-up hair, pinned-up hair)*
**29** lo chignon
– *bun (chignon)*
**30** le trecce
– *plaits (bunches)*
**31** la pettinatura alla vergine (pettinatura a corona, le trecce a corona intorno al capo)
– *chaplet hairstyle (Gretchen style)*
**32** la corona di trecce *f pl*
– *chaplet (coiled plaits)*
**33** i capelli ondulati
– *curled hair*
**34** la pettinatura alla garçonne
– *shingle (shingled hair, bobbed hair)*
**35** la pettinatura alla paggio
– *pageboy style*
**36** la frangia
– *fringe (*Am. *bangs)*
**37** la pettinatura a crocchie
– *earphones*
**38** la crocchia
– *earphone (coiled plait)*

**1-21 cappelli** *m pl* **e berretti** *m pl* **per signora**
- *ladies' hats and caps*
1 la modista mentre confeziona un cappello
- *milliner making a hat*
2 il cono (il fusto di feltro)
- *hood*
3 la forma
- *block*
4 le guarnizioni
- *decorative pieces*
5 il sombrero
- *sombrero*
6 il cappello di lana mohair con piume *f pl*
- *mohair hat with feathers*
7 il cappello con guarnizione *f*
- *model hat with fancy appliqué*
8 il berretto di tela con visiera
- *linen cap (jockey cap)*
9 il berretto di lana grossa a cordoncino
- *hat made of thick candlewick yarn*
10 il berretto lavorato a maglia
- *woollen (Am. woolen) hat (knitted hat)*
11 la calotta in tessuto mohair
- *mohair hat*
12 la cloche con piume *f pl*
- *cloche with feathers*

13 il cappello di foggia maschile in sisal *m* con nastro canneté
- *large men's hat made of sisal with corded ribbon*
14 il cappello di foggia maschile con nastro lavorato
- *trilby-style hat with fancy ribbon*
15 il cappello di feltro morbido
- *soft felt hat*
16 il panama, un cappello di paglia
- *Panama hat with scarf*
17 il berretto di visone *m* con visiera
- *peaked mink cap*
18 il cappello di visone *m*
- *mink hat*
19 il berretto di volpe *f* con calotta in pelle *f*
- *fox hat with leather top*
20 il berretto di visone *m*
- *mink cap*
21 il cappello di paglia di Firenze
- *slouch hat trimmed with flowers*

**22-40 cappelli** *m pl* **e berretti** *m pl* **da uomo**
- *men's hats and caps*
22 il cappello di feltro, la lobbia
- *trilby hat (trilby)*
23 il cappello di loden
- *loden hat (Alpine hat)*
24 il cappello di feltro ruvido di crine *m* con nappa
- *felt hat with tassels (Tyrolean hat, Tyrolese hat)*
25 il berretto di velluto a coste *f pl* (di cord *m*)
- *corduroy cap*
26 il berretto di lana
- *woollen (Am. woolen) hat*
27 il basco
- *beret*
28 il berretto alla marinara (foggia tedesca)
- *German sailor's cap (Prinz Heinrich' cap)*
29 il berretto alla marinara con visiera
- *peaked cap (yachting cap)*
30 il cappello di tela cerata, il sud-ovest
- *sou'wester (southwester)*
31 il berretto di pelliccia di volpe *f* con paraorecchie *m pl*
- *fox cap with earflaps*
32 il berretto di pelle *f* con paraorecchie *m pl* in pelliccia
- *leather cap with fur flaps*

33 il berretto di pelliccia di rat-musqué
- *musquash cap*
34 il colbacco, un berretto di astrakan *m* o di tessuto imitazione astrakan *m*
- *astrakhan cap, a real or imitation astrakhan cap*
35 la paglietta (il cappello di paglia)
- *boater*
36 il cilindro grigio o nero (la tuba) in taffetà di seta; *pieghevole:* il cappello a soffietto (chapeau *m* claque)
- *(grey, Am. gray, or black) top hat made of silk taffeta; collapsible: crush hat (opera hat, claque)*
37 il cappello estivo in tessuto con taschina
- *sun hat (lightweight hat) made of cloth with small patch pocket*
38 il cappello floscio a larghe falde *f pl*
- *wide-brimmed hat*
39 il berretto a punta (berretto da sci *m pl*)
- *toboggan cap (skiing cap, ski cap)*
40 il berretto da lavoro (per agri-coltori *m pl*, guardie *f pl* forestali, manovali *m pl*)
- *workman's cap (for farmers, foresters, craftsmen)*

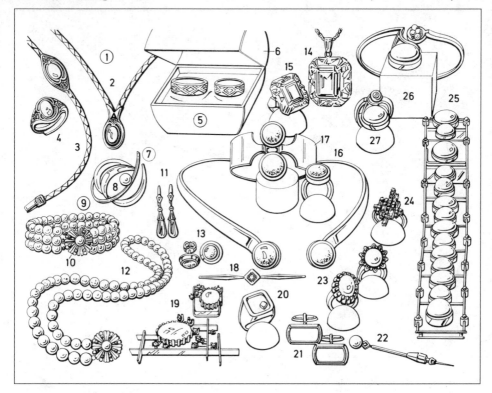

1  la parure di gioielli *m pl*
–  *set of jewellery (Am. jewelry)*
2  il collier
–  *necklace*
3  il braccialetto, il bracciale
–  *bracelet*
4  l'anello
–  *ring*
5  le fedi
–  *wedding rings*
6  il cofanetto delle fedi
–  *wedding ring box*
7  la spilla, una spilla con perla (*oppure:* di perle *f pl*)
–  *brooch, a pearl brooch*
8  la perla
–  *pearl*
9  il braccialetto di perle *f pl* coltivate
–  *cultured pearl bracelet*
10  il fermaglio, un fermaglio in oro bianco
–  *clasp, a white gold clasp*
11  il pendente, l'orecchino a ciondolo
–  *pendant earrings (drop earrings)*
12  la collana di perle *f pl* coltivate
–  *cultured pearl necklace*
13  gli orecchini
–  *earrings*
14  il ciondolo con pietra preziosa
–  *gemstone pendant*
15  l'anello con pietra preziosa
–  *gemstone ring*
16  il collier
–  *choker (collar, neckband)*

17  il braccialetto
–  *bangle*
18  la spilla con brillante *m*
–  *diamond pin*
19  la spilla (la broche) moderna
–  *modern-style brooches*
20  l'anello da uomo
–  *man's ring*
21  i gemelli
–  *cuff links*
22  lo spillo (la spilla) da cravatta
–  *tiepin*
23  l'anello di brillanti *m pl* con perla
–  *diamond ring with pearl*
24  l'anello di brillanti *m pl* moderno
–  *modern-style diamond ring*
25  l'anello con pietre *f pl* preziose
–  *gemstone bracelet*
26  il braccialetto asimmetrico
–  *asymmetrical bangle*
27  l'anello asimmetrico
–  *asymmetrical ring*
28  la collana d'avorio
–  *ivory necklace*
29  la rosetta (la rosa) d'avorio
–  *ivory rose*
30  la spilla (la broche) d'avorio
–  *ivory brooch*
31  il portagioie (il cofanetto per le gioie, per i gioielli)
–  *jewel box (jewel case)*
32  la collana di perle *f pl*
–  *pearl necklace*

33  l'orologio (prezioso, d'oro, di brillanti *m pl*, ecc)
–  *bracelet watch*
34  la collana di corallo
–  *coral necklace*
35  i ciondoli, *fam.* i pendagli
–  *charms*
36  la catena con moneta
–  *coin bracelet*
37  la moneta d'oro
–  *gold coin*
38  la montatura della moneta
–  *coin setting*
39  la maglia della catena
–  *link*
40  l'anello con sigillo
–  *signet ring*
41  l'incisione *f* (il monogramma, le iniziali)
–  *engraving (monogram)*
42-86  i modi e le forme di lavorazione *f* (delle pietre preziose)
–  *cuts and forms*
42-71  pietre *f pl* sfaccettate
–  *faceted stones*
42 *u.* 43  la sfaccettatura standard a taglio rotondo
–  *standard round cut*
44  il taglio a brillante *m*
–  *brilliant cut*
45  il taglio a rosetta
–  *rose cut*
46  il taglio a tavola
–  *flat table*

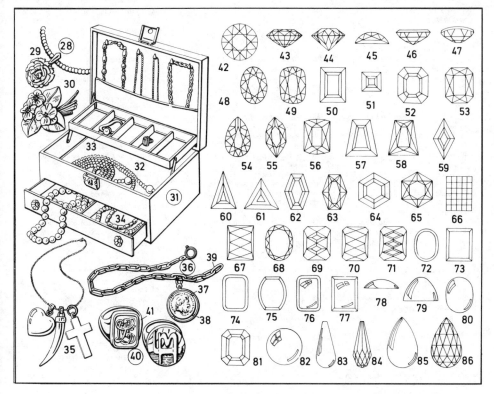

**47** il taglio a cabochon *m*
– *table en cabochon*
**48** il taglio normale a sfaccettatura standard
– *standard cut*
**49** la tradizionale sfaccettatura antica
– *standard antique cut*
**50** il taglio scalare rettangolare
– *rectangular step-cut*
**51** il taglio scalare quadrato
– *square step-cut*
**52** il taglio scalare ottagonale
– *octagonal step-cut*
**53** il taglio ottagonale incrociato
– *octagonal cross-cut*
**54** il taglio a pera a sfaccettatura standard
– *standard pear-shape (pendeloque)*
**55** il taglio a navetta, la navette
– *marquise (navette)*
**56** il taglio a botte *f* a sfaccettatura standard
– *standard barrel-shape*
**57** il taglio scalare a trapezio
– *trapezium step-cut*
**58** il taglio a trapezio incrociato
– *trapezium cross-cut*
**59** il taglio scalare a rombo
– *rhombus step-cut*
**60** *u.* **61** il taglio scalare a triangolo
– *triangular step-cut*
**62** il taglio scalare a esagono
– *hexagonal step-cut*

**63** il taglio incrociato a esagono ovoidale
– *oval hexagonal cross-cut*
**64** il taglio scalare a esagono con lati *m*
*pl* uguali
– *round hexagonal step-cut*
**65** il taglio incrociato a esagono con lati
*m pl* uguali
– *round hexagonal cross-cut*
**66** il taglio a scacchiera
– *chequer-board cut*
**67** il taglio a triangolo
– *triangle cut*
**68-71** tagli *m pl* fantasia
– *fancy cuts*
**72-77** pietre *f pl* per anello
– *ring gemstones*
**72** il taglio a tavola ovale
– *oval flat table*
**73** il taglio a tavola rettangolare
– *rectangular flat table*
**74** il taglio a tavola ottagonale
– *octagonal flat table*
**75** il taglio a botte *f*
– *barrel-shape*
**76** il taglio antico a cabochon *m*
– *antique table en cabochon*
**77** il taglio rettangolare a cabochon *m*
– *rectangular table en cabochon*
**78-81** cabochons *m pl*
– *cabochons*
**78** il cabochon rotondo
– *round cabochon (simple cabochon)*

**79** il cono a punta arrotondata
– *high dome (high cabochon)*
**80** il cabochon ovale
– *oval cabochon*
**81** il cabochon ottagonale
– *octagonal cabochon*
**82-86** sfere *f pl* e forme allungate (pampel)
– *spheres and pear-shapes*
**82** la sfera liscia
– *plain sphere*
**83** il pampel liscio, la forma allungata liscia
– *plain pear-shape*
**84** il pampel sfaccettato, la forma allungata sfaccettata
– *faceted pear-shape*
**85** la goccia liscia
– *plain drop*
**86** la goccia sfaccettata, il briolet
– *faceted briolette*

**1-53 la villetta, la villa**
- *detached house*
1 lo scantinato, il seminterrato
- *basement*
2 il piano terra (il pianterreno)
- *ground floor* (Am. *first floor*)
3 il primo piano
- *upper floor (first floor,* Am. *second floor)*
4 la soffitta
- *loft*
5 il tetto, un tetto a falde *f pl* asimmetriche
- *roof, a gable roof (saddle roof, saddleback roof )*
6 la grondaia
- *gutter*
7 il colmo
- *ridge*
8 la gronda
- *verge with bargeboards*
9 lo sporto del tetto (il cornicione di gronda, la cimasa del tetto), una sporgenza a travi *f pl* inclinate
- *eaves, rafter-supported eaves*
10 il camino (il camignolo)
- *chimney*
11 il canale di gronda
- *gutter*
12 il pluviale
- *swan's neck (swan-neck)*
13 il tubo dell'acqua piovana (la doccia)
- *rainwater pipe (downpipe,* Am. *downspout, leader)*
14 lo stivale, un tubo in ghisa
- *vertical pipe, a cast-iron pipe*
15 il prospetto laterale
- *gable (gable end)*
16 la parete di vetro, una lastra di vetro
- *glass wall*
17 lo zoccolo
- *base course (plinth)*
18 il balcone coperto, *reg.*: la loggia
- *balcony*
19 la ringhiera (il parapetto)
- *parapet*
20 la cassetta portafiori
- *flower box*
21 la porta del balcone a due battenti *m pl* (la portafinestra)
- *French window (French windows) opening on to the balcony*
22 la finestra a due battenti *m pl*
- *double casement window*
23 la finestra a un battente
- *single casement window*
24 il davanzale della finestra con parapetto
- *window breast with window sill*
25 l'architrave *f*
- *lintel (window head)*
26 lo stipite
- *reveal*
27 la finestrella del seminterrato (dello scantinato)
- *cellar window*
28 la persiana avvolgibile (la tapparella)
- *rolling shutter*
29 il dispositivo per spingere in fuori la tapparella
- *rolling shutter frame*
30 l'imposta, il battente
- *window shutter (folding shutter)*
31 il fermaimposta (il nottolino)
- *shutter catch*
32 il garage con ripostiglio per gli attrezzi
- *garage with tool shed*

33 la spalliera
- *espalier*
34 la porta di legno
- *batten door (ledged door)*
35 la finestrella con traversa a crociera
- *fanlight with mullion and transom*
36 il terrazzo
- *terrace*
37 il muro del giardino con lastre *f pl* di rivestimento
- *garden wall with coping stones*
38 la lampada del giardino
- *garden light*
39 la scala di accesso al giardino
- *steps*
40 i massi, una parte del giardino con massi *m pl*
- *rockery (rock garden)*
41 il rubinetto per il tubo d'irrigazione *f*
- *outside tap* (Am. *faucet) for the hose*
42 il tubo d'irrigazione *f*
- *garden hose*
43 l'irrigatore *m* da giardino
- *lawn sprinkler*
44 la vasca
- *paddling pool*
45 il sentiero di beole *f pl*
- *stepping stones*
46 il prato a tappeto (prato)
- *sunbathing area (lawn)*
47 la sedia a sdraio
- *deck-chair*
48 l'ombrellone *m*
- *sunshade (garden parasol)*
49 la sedia da giardino
- *garden chair*
50 il tavolo da giardino
- *garden table*
51 la barra per battere i tappeti (barra stenditappeti)
- *frame for beating carpets*
52 l'accesso al garage
- *garage driveway*
53 la recinzione, una palizzata
- *fence, a wooden fence*
**54-57 il villaggio (il centro) residenziale** (l'agglomerato)
- *housing estate (housing development)*
54 la villetta nel villaggio residenziale (la casa dell'agglomerato)
- *house on a housing estate (on a housing development)*
55 il tetto a una falda
- *pent roof (penthouse roof )*
56 l'abbaino
- *dormer (dormer window)*
57 il giardino della casa
- *garden*
**58-63 la casa (la villetta) a schiera**
- *terraced house [one of a row of terraced houses], stepped*
58 il giardino antistante la casa
- *front garden*
59 la siepe
- *hedge*
60 il marciapiede
- *pavement* (Am. *sidewalk, walkway)*
61 la strada
- *street (road)*
62 il lampione
- *street lamp (street light)*
63 il recipiente dei rifiuti
- *litter bin* (Am. *litter basket)*
**64-68 la casa bifamiliare**
- *house divided into two flats* (Am. *house divided into two apartments, duplex house)*

64 il tetto a padiglione *m* (tetto spiovente, a triangolo)
- *hip (hipped) roof*
65 la porta d'ingresso
- *front door*
66 i gradini
- *front steps*
67 la tettoia (la pensilina)
- *canopy*
68 la vetrata per fiori *m pl* o piante *f pl*
- *flower window (window for house plants)*
**69-71 due case *f pl* gemelle adiacenti con quattro appartamenti** *m pl*
- *pair of semi-detached houses divided into four flats* (Am. *apartments)*
69 il balcone
- *balcony*
70 la veranda
- *sun lounge* (Am. *sun parlor)*
71 la tenda
- *awning (sun blind, sunshade)*
**72-76 il caseggiato a balconate** *f pl*
- *block of flats* (Am. *apartment building, apartment house) with access balconies*
72 la tromba delle scale (le scale)
- *staircase*
73 la balconata di passaggio
- *balcony*
74 l'attico
- *studio flat* (Am. *studio apartment)*
75 la terrazza
- *sun roof, a sun terrace*
76 la zona verde
- *open space*
**77-81 il caseggiato a più piani** *m pl*
- *multi-storey block of flats* (Am. *multistory apartment building, multistory apartment house)*
77 il tetto piano
- *flat roof*
78 il tetto a una falda (tetto a uno spiovente)
- *pent roof (shed roof, lean-to roof )*
79 il garage
- *garage*
80 il pergolato
- *pergola*
81 il finestrone della scala
- *staircase window*
82 il grattacielo
- *high-rise block of flats* (Am. *high-rise apartment building, high-rise apartment house)*
83 l'attico
- *penthouse*
**84-86 la casa di campagna (la seconda casa)** una casa di legno
- *weekend house, a timber house*
84 il rivestimento di tavole *f pl* orizzontali
- *horizontal boarding*
85 lo zoccolo (il basamento) in pietra grezza
- *natural stone base course (natural stone plinth)*
86 la finestra a bande *f* (*qui*: la banda della finestra)
- *strip windows (ribbon windows)*

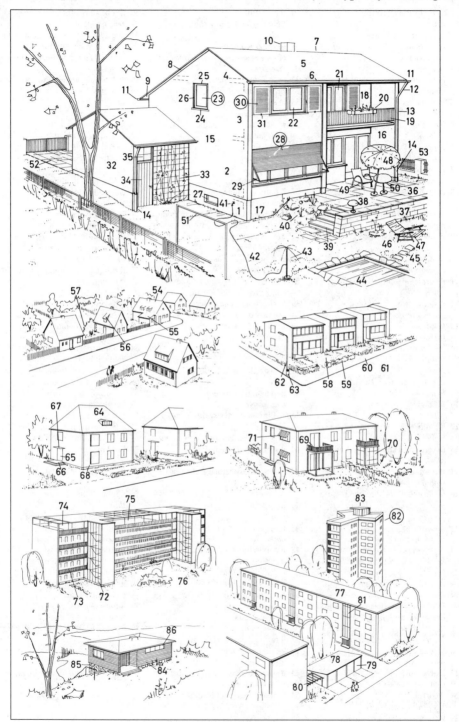

**1-29 la soffitta** (il sottotetto)
– *attic*
1 la copertura del tetto
– *roof cladding (roof covering)*
2 il lucernaio
– *skylight*
3 la passerella
– *gangway*
4 la scala fissa (scala sul tetto)
– *cat ladder (roof ladder)*
5 il camino (il comignolo)
– *chimney*
6 il gancio (l'uncino) per tetto
– *roof hook*
7 l'abbaino
– *dormer window (dormer)*
8 la griglia paraneve (il paraneve)
– *snow guard (roof guard)*
9 la grondaia (il canale di gronda)
– *gutter*
10 il tubo di scarico discendente (il pluviale)
– *rainwater pipe (downpipe,* Am. *downspout, leader)*
11 il cornicione del tetto
– *eaves*
12 il sottotetto
– *pitched roof*
13 la botola
– *trapdoor*
14 l'apertura della botola (del sottotetto)
– *hatch*
15 la scala a pioli *m pl*
– *ladder*
16 lo staggio
– *stile*
17 il piolo
– *rung*
18 la soffitta (il solaio, il granaio)
– *loft (attic)*
19 il tramezzo in legno
– *wooden partition*
20 la porta del ripostiglio in soffitta
– *lumber room door (boxroom door)*
21 il lucchetto
– *padlock*
22 il gancio per la corda del bucato
– *hook [for washing line]*
23 la corda per stendere il bucato
– *clothes line (washing line)*
24 il serbatoio (il vaso) d'espansione *f* dell'impianto di riscaldamento
– *expansion tank for boiler*
25 la scala di legno e la ringhiera
– *wooden steps and balustrade*
26 la longarina
– *string* (Am. *stringer)*
27 il gradino
– *step*
28 il corrimano
– *handrail (guard rail)*
29 il colonnino della ringhiera
– *baluster*

30 il parafulmine
– *lightning conductor (lightning rod)*
31 lo spazzacamino
– **chimney sweep** (Am. *chimney sweeper)*
32 la spazzola col peso
– *brush with weight*
33 la spalla di ferro
– *shoulder iron*
34 il sacco per la fuliggine
– *sack for soot*
35 lo scopino per canna fumaria
– *flue brush*
36 la scopa
– *broom (besom)*
37 il manico della scopa
– *broomstick (broom handle)*
**38-81 il riscaldamento a acqua calda,** un riscaldamento centrale
– *hot-water heating system, full central heating*
**38-43 il locale caldaia**
– *boiler room*
38 l'impianto a carbone *m* coke *m*
– *coke-fired central heating system*
39 lo sportello della cenere
– *ash box door* (Am. *cleanout door)*
40 la canna fumaria
– *flueblock*
41 l'attizzatoio
– *poker*
42 il rastrello da stufa (attizzatoio)
– *rake*
43 la pala da carbone *m*
– *coal shovel*
**44-60 l'impianto di riscaldamento a nafta**
– *oil-fired central heating system*
44 il serbatoio della nafta
– *oil tank*
45 il pozzo d'ispezione *f* (il passo d'uomo)
– *manhole*
46 il portello del pozzo
– *manhole cover*
47 il bocchettone d'immissione *f*
– *tank inlet*
48 il coperchio del duomo
– *dome cover*
49 la valvola di fondo
– *tank bottom valve*
50 la nafta (olio combustibile)
– *fuel oil (heating oil)*
51 il tubo di sfiato
– *air-bleed duct*
52 il tappo di sfiato (la camicia di ventilazione *f,* lo sfiatatoio)
– *air vent cap*
53 il tubo del livello del combustibile
– *oil level pipe*
54 l'indicatore *m* del combustibile
– *oil gauge* (Am. *gage)*
55 il tubo aspirante
– *suction pipe*

56 il tubo di ritorno
– *return pipe*
57 la caldaia del riscaldamento centrale (caldaia a nafta)
– *central heating furnace (oil heating furnace)*
**58-60 il bruciatore a nafta** (bruciatore *m* a olio)
– *oil burner*
58 l'aeratore *m*
– *fan*
59 il motore elettrico
– *electric motor*
60 il getto bruciatore coibentato
– *covered pilot light*
61 lo sportello di alimentazione *f*
– *charging door*
62 la spia
– *inspection window*
63 il misuratore dell'acqua
– *water gauge* (Am. *gage)*
64 il termometro della caldaia
– *furnace thermometer*
65 il rubinetto di alimentazione *f* e di svuotamento
– *bleeder*
66 il basamento della caldaia
– *furnace bed*
67 il quadro di comando
– *control panel*
68 il bollitore (il serbatoio dell'acqua calda, il boiler)
– *hot water tank (boiler)*
69 il tubo di troppopieno
– *overflow pipe (overflow)*
70 la valvola di sicurezza
– *safety valve*
71 il tubo principale di distribuzione *f*
– *main distribution pipe*
72 l'isolante *m*
– *lagging*
73 la valvola
– *valve*
74 il tubo di flusso
– *flow pipe*
75 la valvola di regolazione *f*
– *regulating valve*
76 il radiatore (il calorifero)
– *radiator*
77 l'elemento del radiatore
– *radiator rib*
78 il termostato ambiente *m*
– *room thermostat*
79 il tubo di ritorno
– *return pipe (return)*
80 la conduttura collettrice di ritorno (il ritorno primario)
– *return pipe [in two-pipe system]*
81 la canna fumaria
– *smoke outlet (smoke extract)*

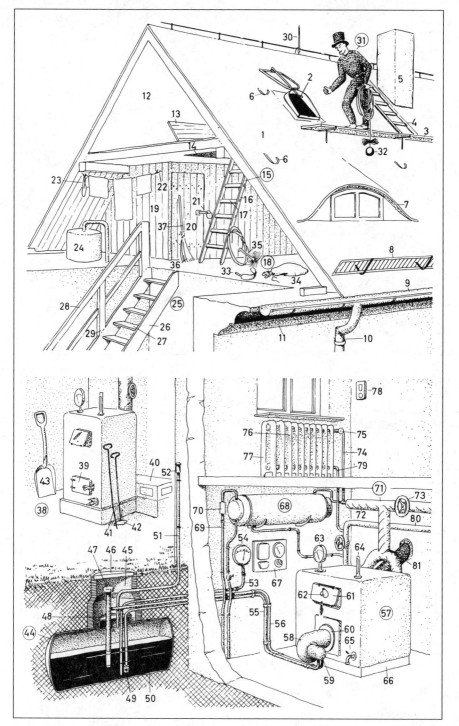

1  il forno a microonde *f pl*
– *microwave oven (microwave)*
2  il frigorifero
– *refrigerator (fridge,* Am. *icebox)*
3  il piano di appoggio (il ripiano) del frigorifero
– *refrigerator shelf*
4  il contenitore della verdura
– *salad drawer*
5  il freezer
– *freezing compartment*
6  la mensola portabottiglie (all'interno dello sportello)
– *bottle rack (in storage door)*
7  il congelatore
– *upright freezer*
8  l'elemento pensile (pensile *m*, armadietto pensile), un armadietto per stoviglie *f pl*
– *wall cupboard, a kitchen cupboard*
9  l'elemento base *f* (armadietto base *f* )
– *base unit*
10  il cassetto delle posate
– *cutlery drawer*
11  il piano di lavoro
– *work surface (worktop)*
**12-17 lo spazio cottura**
– *cooker unit*
12  la cucina elettrica (*anche:* cucina a gas)
– *electric cooker (also: gas cooker)*
13  il forno
– *oven*
14  lo sportello telescopico del forno
– *oven window*
15  la piastra di cottura

– *hotplate, an automatic high-speed plate*
16  il bollitore dell'acqua
– *kettle (whistling kettle)*
17  la cappa aspirante
– *cooker hood*
18  la presina da cucina
– *pot holder*
19  il portapresine (l'appendipresine *m*)
– *pot holder rack*
20  l'orologio da cucina
– *kitchen clock*
21  il timer (il contaminuti)
– *timer*
22  lo sbattitore elettrico
– *hand mixer*
23  la frusta
– *whisk*
24  il macinacaffé elettrico
– *electric coffee grinder (with rotating blades)*
25  il cavo (*pop:* il filo elettrico)
– *lead*
26  la presa di corrente *f* (*qui:* nella parete)
– *wall socket*
27  l'angolare
– *corner unit*
28  il ripiano girevole
– *revolving shelf*
29  la pentola
– *pot (cooking pot)*
30  il bricco
– *jug*
31  il portaspezie
– *spice rack*

32  il vasetto delle spezie
– *spice jar*
**33-36 lo spazio lavello**
– *sink unit*
33  lo scolapiatti
– *dish drainer*
34  il piatto da frutta (piatto da dessert, piattino)
– *tea plate*
35  il lavello (l'acquaio)
– *sink*
36  il rubinetto dell'acqua (il miscelatore)
– *water tap* (Am. *faucet);* here: *mixer tap* (Am. *mixing faucet)*
37  la pianta, una pianta verde
– *pot plant, a foliage plant*
38  la macchina per caffè elettrica
– *coffee maker*
39  il lampadario da cucina
– *kitchen lamp*
40  la lavastoviglie
– *dishwasher (dishwashing machine)*
41  il cestello
– *dish rack*
42  il piatto
– *dinner plate*
43  la sedia da cucina
– *kitchen chair*
44  il tavolo da cucina
– *kitchen table*
45  il tostapane
– *toaster*

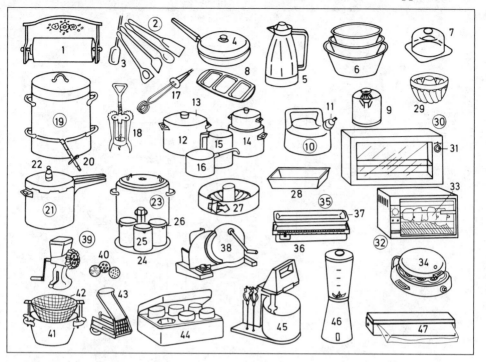

1  il portarotolo con rotolo di carta
–  *general-purpose roll holder with kitchen roll (paper towels)*
2  la serie dei cucchiai o mestoli *m pl* da cucina
–  *set of wooden spoons*
3  il cucchiaione
–  *mixing spoon*
4  la padella
–  *frying pan*
5  la caraffa termoisolante, la caraffa thermos *m*
–  *Thermos jug*
6  i ciotoloni
–  *set of bowls*
7  il portaformaggio con campana trasparente
–  *cheese dish with glass cover*
8  il vassoio (*qui:* vassoio a tre scomparti *m pl*)
–  *three-compartment dish*
9  lo spremiagrumi
–  *lemon squeezer*
10  il bollitore
–  *whistling kettle*
11  il fischietto
–  *whistle*
**12-16  la batteria di tegami *m pl***
–  *pan set*
12  la pentola
–  *pot (cooking pot)*
13  il coperchio
–  *lid*
14  il tegame per arrosti *m pl*
–  *casserole dish*

15  il bollilatte
–  *milk pot*
16  la casseruola
–  *saucepan*
17  il bollitore ad immersione *f*
–  *immersion heater*
18  il cavatappi, il cavaturaccioli
–  *corkscrew [with levers]*
19  l'estrattore *m* di succhi *m pl*
–  *juice extractor*
20  il morsetto
–  *tube clamp (tube clip)*
21  la pentola a pressione *f*
–  *pressure cooker*
22  la valvola di sicurezza
–  *pressure valve*
23  lo sterilizzatore per conserve *f pl*
–  *fruit preserver*
24  il doppio fondo
–  *removable rack*
25  il vasetto di vetro (per conserve *f pl*)
–  *preserving jar*
26  la guarnizione per la chiusura ermetica
–  *rubber ring*
27  la teglia con gancio a molla
–  *spring form*
28  la teglia rettangolare
–  *cake tin*
29  lo stampo per dolci *m pl* e budini *m pl*
–  *cake tin*
30  il forno a microonde *f pl*
–  *microwave oven (microwave)*
31  il timer programmatore di cottura (il programmatore *m* di cottura)
–  *timer*

32  il forno a grill *m*
–  *rotisserie*
33  lo spiedo
–  *spit*
34  l'apparecchio elettrico per le cialde, per i waffel (*in Italia, sim.:* la tostiera)
–  *electric waffle iron*
35  la bilancia da cucina
–  *sliding-weight scales*
36  il peso scorrevole
–  *sliding weight*
37  il piatto della bilancia
–  *scale pan*
38  l'affettatrice *f*
–  *food slicer*
39  il tritacarne
–  *mincer (Am. meat chopper)*
40  i dischetti del tritacarne
–  *blades*
41  la friggitrice
–  *chip pan*
42  il cestello
–  *basket*
43  il tagliapatate
–  *potato chipper*
44  la yogurtiera
–  *yoghurt maker*
45  la macchina elettrica multiusi
–  *mixer*
46  il frullatore
–  *blender*
47  il sigillasacchetti
–  *bag sealer*

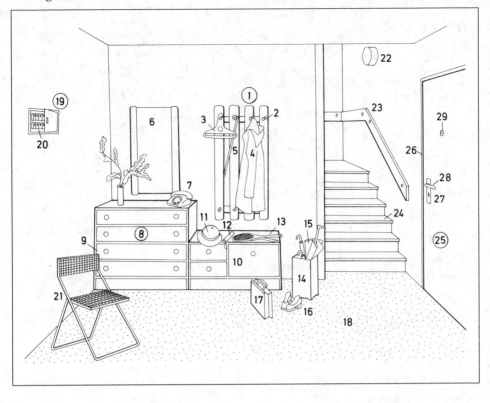

**1-29 l'ingresso,** il vestibolo, il corridoio, l'atrio
– *hall (entrance hall)*
**1** l'attaccapanni *m*
– *coat rack*
**2** il piolo (il gancio) dell'attaccapanni *m, tec.:* il beccatello
– *coat hook*
**3** la gruccia
– *coat hanger*
**4** la mantella impermeabile
– *rain cape*
**5** il bastone da passeggio
– *walking stick*
**6** lo specchio
– *hall mirror*
**7** il telefono
– *telephone*
**8** il mobile portascarpe, il mobile a più usi *m pl*
– *chest of drawers for shoes, etc.*
**9** il cassetto
– *drawer*
**10** la panca
– *seat*
**11** il cappello da donna
– *ladies' hat*
**12** l'ombrello pieghevole
– *telescopic umbrella*

**13** le racchette da tennis *m*
– *tennis rackets (tennis racquets)*
**14** il portaombrelli
– *umbrella stand*
**15** l'ombrello
– *umbrella*
**16** le scarpe
– *shoes*
**17** la borsa portadocumenti, la ventiquattr'ore
– *briefcase*
**18** la moquette
– *fitted carpet*
**19** l'armadietto delle valvole di sicurezza
– *fuse box*
**20** l'interruttore *m* automatico
– *miniature circuit breaker*
**21** la sedia in tubo metallico (in tubo d'acciaio)
– *tubular steel chair*
**22** la lampada a muro (l'applique *f* ) della scala
– *stair light*
**23** il corrimano
– *handrail*
**24** il gradino
– *step*
**25** la porta d'ingresso
– *front door*

**26** lo stipite
– *door frame*
**27** la serratura
– *door lock*
**28** la maniglia
– *door handle*
**29** lo spioncino
– *spyhole*

**1-20 la parete con elementi** *m pl*
**componibili**
- *wall units (shelf units)*
**2** la fiancata
- *side wall*
**3** lo scaffale per i libri
- *bookshelf*
**4** la fila di libri *m pl*
- *row of books*
**5** l'elemento vetrina
- *display cabinet unit*
**6** l'elemento base *f*
- *cupboard base unit*
**7** l'elemento armadio
- *cupboard unit*
**8** il televisore
- *television set (TV set)*
**9** l'impianto stereo
- *stereo system (stereo equipment)*
**10** le casse (gli altoparlanti)
- *speaker (loudspeaker)*
**11** la rastrelliera per le pipe
- *pipe rack*
**12** la pipa
- *pipe*
**13** il mappamondo
- *globe*
**14** il bollitore in ottone *m*
- *brass kettle*

**15** il telescopio
- *telescope*
**16** l'orologio soprammobile *m*
- *mantle clock*
**17** il busto
- *bust*
**18** l'enciclopedia in volumi *m pl*
- *encyclopaedia [in several volumes]*
**19** l'elemento divisore
- *room divider*
**20** l'elemento bar *m* (il mobile bar *m*)
- *drinks cupboard*
**21-26 il salotto (mobili** *m pl* **imbottiti**
**da salotto)**
- *upholstered suite (seating group)*
**21** la poltrona
- *armchair*
**22** il bracciolo
- *arm*
**23** il cuscino del sedile
- *seat cushion (cushion)*
**24** il divano
- *settee*
**25** lo schienale imbottito
- *back cushion*
**26** l'elemento d'angolo del divano
- *[round] corner section*
**27** il cuscino da divano
- *scatter cushion*

**28** il tavolo da salotto (tavolino)
- *coffee table*
**29** il posacenere (il portacenere)
- *ashtray*
**30** il vassoio
- *tray*
**31** la bottiglia di whisky *m*
- *whisky (whiskey) bottle*
**32** la bottiglia di seltz *m*
- *soda water bottle (soda bottle)*
**33-34 l'angolo pranzo**
- *dining set*
**33** il tavolo da pranzo (la tavola)
- *dining table*
**34** la sedia (la seggiola)
- *chair*
**35** la tenda
- *net curtain*
**36** le piante da appartamento
- *indoor plants (houseplants)*

1 l'armadio della camera da letto,
  un armadio guardaroba
– *wardrobe* (Am. *clothes closet*)
2 il ripiano della biancheria
– *linen shelf*
3 la poltrona di vimini *m*
– *cane chair*
**4-13  il letto a due piazze** *f pl* **(il letto
  matrimoniale)**
– *double bed* (sim.: *double divan*)
**4-6  il letto (il fusto del letto)**
– *bedstead*
4 il fondo del letto
– *foot of the bed*
5 la sponda del letto
– *bed frame*
6 la testata (la spalliera del letto)
– *headboard*
7 il copriletto
– *bedspread*
8 la coperta imbottita
– *duvet, a quilted duvet*
9 il lenzuolo
– *sheet, a linen sheet*
10 il materasso, uno strato in
   gommapiuma con fodera di traliccio
   cio
– *mattress, a foam mattress with drill
   tick*

11 il capezzale (il traversino)
– *[wedge-shaped] bolster*
**12 u. 13**  il cuscino (il guanciale)
– *pillow*
12 la federa
– *pillowcase (pillowslip)*
13 la fodera di traliccio
– *tick*
14 il ripiano per i libri (l'alzata a
   scaffale *m*)
– *bookshelf [attached to the head-
   board]*
15 la lampada per leggere
– *reading lamp*
16 la sveglia elettrica
– *electric alarm clock*
17 il comodino (il tavolino da notte *f* )
– *bedside cabinet*
18 il cassetto
– *drawer*
19 la lampada da parete *f* (l'applique *f*)
– *bedroom lamp*
20 il quadro
– *picture*
21 la cornice
– *picture frame*
22 lo scendiletto
– *bedside rug*
23 la moquette
– *fitted carpet*

24 lo sgabello (il pouf)
– *dressing stool*
25 il tavolino da toilette (la specchiera)
– *dressing table*
26 lo spruzzatore del profumo
– *perfume spray*
27 il flacone di profumo
– *perfume bottle*
28 il portacipria
– *powder box*
29 lo specchio
– *dressing-table mirror (mirror)*

**1-11  la tavola da pranzo con sedie** *f pl*
 – *dining set*
**1**  la tavola
 – *dining table*
**2**  il piede della tavola (del tavolo)
 – *table leg*
**3**  il piano della tavola (del tavolo)
 – *table top*
**4**  il servizio all'americana
 – *place mat*
**5**  il servizio da tavola, (*al ristorante:*
   il coperto)
 – *place (place setting, cover)*
**6**  il piatto fondo, *fam.:* la scodella
 – *soup plate (deep plate)*
**7**  il piatto piano, il piatto
 – *dinner plate*
**8**  la zuppiera
 – *soup tureen*
**9**  il bicchiere da vino
 – *wineglass*
**10**  la sedia
 – *dining chair*
**11**  il sedile
 – *seat*
**12**  la lampada (pendente dal soffitto)
 – *lamp (pendant lamp)*
**13**  la soprattenda
 – *curtains*

**14**  le tende
 – *net curtain*
**15**  la guida, *tec.:* **la riloga**
 – *curtain rail*
**16**  il tappeto
 – *rug*
**17**  il mobile pensile
 – *wall unit*
**18**  lo sportello a vetri *m pl*
 – *glass door*
**19**  il ripiano
 – *shelf*
**20**  la credenza (a parallelepipedo), il
   buffet
 – *sideboard*
**21**  il cassetto delle posate
 – *cutlery drawer*
**22**  il cassetto della biancheria da
   tavola
 – *linen drawer*
**23**  lo zoccolo
 – *base*
**24**  il vassoio rotondo
 – *round tray*
**25**  la pianta nel vaso
 – *pot plant*
**26**  la credenza (la vetrina)
 – *china cabinet (display cabinet)*
**27**  il servizio da caffé *m*
 – *coffee set (coffee service)*

**28**  la caffettiera
 – *coffee pot*
**29**  la tazza da caffé *m*
 – *coffee cup*
**30**  il piattino
 – *saucer*
**31**  il bricco del latte
 – *milk jug*
**32**  la zuccheriera
 – *sugar bowl*
**33**  il servizio di piatti *m pl* da tavola
 – *dinner set (dinner service)*

**1** la tavola
- *dining table*
**2** la tovaglia, una tovaglia damascata
- *tablecloth, a damask cloth*
**3-12 il servizio da tavola (per un commensale);** *al ristorante:* **il coperto**
- *place (place setting, cover)*
**3** il sottopiatto
- *bottom plate*
**4** il piatto piano
- *dinner plate*
**5** il piatto fondo; *fam.:* la scodella
- *deep plate (soup plate)*
**6** il piattino (da dolce *m*, da dessert *m*)
- *dessert plate (dessert bowl)*
**7** le posate (coltello e forchetta)
- *knife and fork*
**8** le posate (coltello e forchetta) da pesce *m*
- *fish knife and fork*
**9** il tovagliolo
- *serviette (napkin, table napkin)*
**10** il portatovagliolo
- *serviette ring (napkin ring)*
**11** il reggiposata
- *knife rest*
**12** i bicchieri da vino
- *wineglasses*
**13** il segnaposto
- *place card*
**14** il mestolo
- *soup ladle*
**15** la zuppiera
- *soup tureen (tureen)*
**16** il candelabro da tavola
- *candelabra*

**17** la salsiera
- *sauceboat (gravy boat)*
**18** il cucchiaio della salsiera
- *sauce ladle (gravy ladle)*
**19** la decorazione della tavola
- *table decoration*
**20** il portapane (il cestino del pane)
- *bread basket*
**21** il panino
- *roll*
**22** la fetta di pane *m*
- *slice of bread*
**23** l'insalatiera
- *salad bowl*
**24** le posate da insalata
- *salad servers*
**25** la legumiera
- *vegetable dish*
**26** il piatto di portata (*qui:* per l'arrosto)
- *meat plate (Am. meat platter)*
**27** l'arrosto
- *roast meat (roast)*
**28** il piatto per la frutta cotta (per la composta di frutta), la compostiera
- *fruit dish*
**29** la coppetta per la frutta cotta (per la composta di frutta)
- *fruit bowl*
**30** la frutta cotta (la composta di frutta)
- *fruit (stewed fruit)*
**31** la legumiera coperta per patate *f pl*
- *potato dish*
**32** il carrello delle vivande
- *serving trolley*
**33** il vassoio per le verdure
- *vegetable plate (Am. vegetable platter)*

**34** il pane tostato
- *toast*
**35** il piatto (il vassoio) dei formaggi
- *cheeseboard*
**36** la burriera
- *butter dish*
**37** la tartina
- *open sandwich*
**38** il ripieno della tartina
- *filling*
**39** il panino imbottito (il tramezzino)
- *sandwich*
**40** la fruttiera (il portafrutta)
- *fruit bowl*
**41** le mandorle (*sim.:* le patatine, le noccioline)
- *almonds (also: potato crisps, peanuts)*
**42** l'oliera, (le ampolle per l'olio e l'aceto)
- *oil and vinegar bottle*
**43** il ketchup (una salsa piccante)
- *ketchup (catchup, catsup)*
**44** la credenza
- *sideboard*
**45** lo scaldavivande elettrico
- *electric hotplate*
**46** il cavatappi, il cavaturaccioli
- *corkscrew*

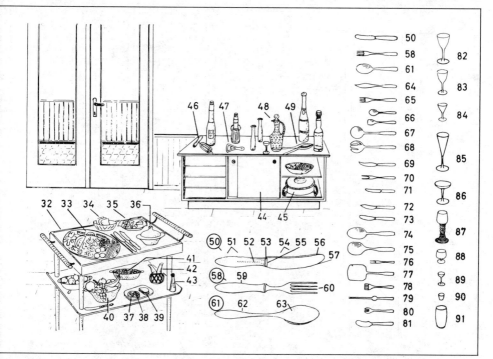

47 l'apribottiglie *m*
– *crown cork bottle opener (crown cork opener), a bottle opener*
48 l'ampolla per liquore *m*
– *liqueur decanter*
49 lo schiaccianoci
– *nutcrackers (nutcracker)*
50 il coltello
– *knife*
51 il manico
– *handle*
52 il codolo
– *tang (tongue)*
53 la ghiera
– *ferrule*
54 la lama
– *blade*
55 la corona
– *bolster*
56 la costa
– *back*
57 il filo della lama
– *edge (cutting edge)*
58 la forchetta
– *fork*
59 il manico
– *handle*
60 la punta della forchetta
– *prong (tang, tine)*
61 il cucchiaio
– *spoon (dessert spoon, soup spoon)*
62 il manico del cucchiaio
– *handle*
63 la parte concava del cucchiaio
– *bowl*

64 il coltello da pesce *m*
– *fish knife*
65 la forchetta da pesce *m*
– *fish fork*
66 il cucchiaio da dolce *m*
– *dessert spoon (fruit spoon)*
67 il cucchiaio (la posata) da insalata
– *salad spoon*
68 la forchetta (la posata) da insalata
– *salad fork*
69 *u.* 70 le posate da portata
– *carving set (serving cutlery)*
69 il coltello da portata
– *carving knife*
70 la forchetta da portata
– *serving fork*
71 il coltello da frutta
– *fruit knife*
72 il coltello da formaggio
– *cheese knife*
73 il coltellino da burro
– *butter knife*
74 il cucchiaio da portata
– *vegetable spoon, a serving spoon*
75 il cucciaio da portata per patate *f pl*
– *potato server (serving spoon for potatoes)*
76 la forchettina per sandwich *m*
– *cocktail fork*
77 la paletta per asparagi *m pl*
– *asparagus server (asparagus slice)*
78 la posata per sardine *f pl*
– *sardine server*
79 la posata per crostacei *m pl*
– *lobster fork*

80 la posata per ostriche *f pl*
– *oyster fork*
81 il coltello per caviale *m*
– *caviare knife*
82 il bicchiere da vino bianco
– *white wine glass*
83 il bicchiere da vino rosso
– *red wine glass*
84 il bicchiere da aperitivo (da porto, da vermuth *m*)
– *sherry glass (madeira glass)*
85 *u.* 86 i bicchieri da spumante *m*
– *champagne glasses*
85 il calice
– *tapered glass*
86 la coppa, un bicchiere di cristallo
– *champagne glass, a crystal glass*
87 il «Römer» (il calice per i vini del Reno; *non in uso in Italia*)
– *rummer*
88 il bicchiere da cognac *m*
– *brandy glass*
89 il bicchierino da liquore *m*
– *liqueur glass*
90 il bicchierino da grappa, da acquavite *f*
– *spirit glass*
91 il bicchiere da birra
– *beer glass*

1 la parete-plurielementi dell'angolo soggiorno (elemento armadio, elemento libreria, elemento scrivania)
– *wall units (shelf units)*
2 l'elemento frontale dell'armadio
– *wardrobe door* (Am. *clothes closet door)*
3 l'elemento armadio (l'armadio)
– *body*
4 la fiancata
– *side wall*
5 la cornice (*anche:* cornice *f* per luce *f* indiretta, cornice *f* paraluce)
– *trim*
6 l'armadietto a due ante *f pl*
– *two-door cupboard unit*
7 lo scaffale per i libri (*qui:* l'elemento libreria a scaffali *m pl* aperti e a vetrina)
– *bookshelf unit (bookcase unit) [with glass door]*
8 i libri
– *books*
9 la vetrina
– *display cabinet*
10 il giradischi
– *record player*
11 il cassetto
– *drawer*

12 la bomboniera
– *decorative biscuit tin*
13 l'animaletto di stoffa (di peluche *f* )
– *soft toy animal*
14 il televisore
– *television set (TV set)*
15 i dischi
– *records (discs)*
16 il letto a cassone *m* (letto con telaio a cassone *m*)
– *bed unit*
17 il cuscino
– *scatter cushion*
18 il cassetto incorporato
– *bed unit drawer*
19 lo scaffale incorporato
– *bed unit shelf*
20 le riviste (i giornali)
– *magazines*
21 lo spazio scrittoio (la nicchia dello scrittoio)
– *desk unit (writing unit)*
22 lo scrittoio
– *desk*
23 la cartella da scrittoio (il sottomano)
– *desk mat (blotter)*
24 la lampada da tavolo
– *table lamp*
25 il cestino per la carta
– *wastepaper basket*

26 il cassetto dello scrittoio
– *desk drawer*
27 la sedia (la poltroncina) da scrittoio
– *desk chair*
28 il bracciolo
– *arm*
29 gli elementi componibili dell'angolo cottura
– *kitchen unit*
30 l'armadietto pensile (il pensile)
– *wall cupboard*
31 la cappa aspirante
– *cooker hood*
32 la cucina elettrica
– *electric cooker*
33 il frigorifero
– *refrigerator (fridge,* Am. *icebox)*
34 il tavolo
– *dining table*
35 il tappeto (tappetino) da tavola (*anche:* il centro da tavola)
– *table runner*
36 il tappeto orientale
– *oriental carpet*
37 la lampada a stelo
– *standard lamp*

1  il lettino, un letto a castello
–  *children's bed, a bunk bed*
2  il cassettone del letto
–  *storage box*
3  il materasso
–  *mattress*
4  il cuscino (il guanciale)
–  *pillow*
5  la scaletta
–  *ladder*
6  l'elefante di stoffa (l'animaletto di stoffa da portare a letto)
–  *soft toy elephant, a cuddly toy animal*
7  il cane di stoffa
–  *soft toy dog*
8  il pouf, uno sgabello imbottito
–  *cushion*
9  la bambola da vestire
–  *fashion doll*
10  la carrozzina della bambola
–  *doll's pram*
11  la bambola (che chiude gli occhi)
–  *sleeping doll*
12  la tendina della carrozzella
–  *canopy*
13  la lavagna
–  *blackboard*
14  il pallottoliere
–  *counting beads*
15  il cavallo a dondolo (ricoperto in peluche *f*) a rotelle *f*
–  *toy horse for rocking and pulling*

16  il telaio a dondolo
–  *rockers*
17  il libro per bambini *m pl*
–  *children's book*
18  il set di giochi *m pl* (scatola di giochi *m pl*)
–  *compendium of games*
19  il gioco «non t'arrabbiare»
–  *ludo*
20  la scacchiera
–  *chessboard*
21  l'armadio della camera dei bambini
–  *children's cupboard*
22  il cassetto della biancheria
–  *linen drawer*
23  il piano per scrivere (lo scrittoio)
–  *drop-flap writing surface*
24  il quaderno
–  *notebook (exercise book)*
25  i libri di scuola (libri *m pl* scolastici)
–  *school books*
26  la matita (*anche*: la matita colorata, il pastello, il pennarello, la biro o penna a sfera)
–  *pencil (also: crayon, felt tip pen, ballpoint pen)*
27  il negozio in miniatura
–  *toy shop*
28  il banco
–  *counter*
29  il portaspezie
–  *spice rack*

30  la merce esposta
–  *display*
31  le caramelle (l'assortimento di caramelle *f pl*)
–  *assortment of sweets* (Am. *candies*)
32  il sacchetto per le caramelle
–  *bag of sweets* (Am. *candies*)
33  la bilancia
–  *scales*
34  la cassa
–  *cash register*
35  il telefono in miniatura
–  *toy telephone*
36  la scansia della merce
–  *shop shelves (goods shelves)*
37  il trenino di legno
–  *wooden train set*
38  l'autocarro a cassone *m* ribaltabile
–  *dump truck, a toy lorry (toy truck)*
39  la gru
–  *tower crane*
40  la betoniera
–  *concrete mixer*
41  il grande cane di peluche *f*
–  *large soft toy dog*
42  il bussolotto dei dadi
–  *dice cup*

**1-20 la scuola materna, l'asilo infantile, l'educazione prescolastica**
- *pre-school education (nursery education)*
**1** l'insegnante *f* di scuola materna (la maestra d'asilo)
- *nursery teacher*
**2** il bambino in età prescolare
- *nursery child*
**3** il lavoro manuale
- *handicraft*
**4** la colla
- *glue*
**5** l'acquerello (acquarello)
- *watercolour (Am. watercolor) painting*
**6** la scatola di colori all'acquerello
- *paintbox*
**7** il pennello
- *paintbrush*
**8** il bicchiere di acqua
- *glass of water*
**9** il puzzle
- *jigsaw puzzle (puzzle)*
**10** il pezzo (l'elemento) del puzzle
- *jigsaw puzzle piece*
**11** le matite colorate (i pastelli, i pastelli di cera)
- *coloured (Am. colored) pencils (wax crayons)*
**12** la plastilina, una sostanza per modellare (*pop.*: il pongo)
- *modelling (Am. modeling) clay (Plasticine)*
**13** le figure modellate con la plastilina
- *clay figures (Plasticine figures)*
**14** la tavoletta per modellare
- *modelling (Am. modeling) board*

**15** il gesso
- *chalk (blackboard chalk)*
**16** la lavagna
- *blackboard*
**17** il pallottoliere, l'abaco
- *counting blocks*
**18** il pennarello da lavagna
- *felt pen (felt tip pen)*
**19** il gioco delle forme (*sim.*: il domino)
- *shapes game*
**20** il gruppo dei giocatori
- *group of players*
**21-32 i giochi (i giocattoli)**
- *toys*
**21** il gioco dei cubi
- *building and filling cubes*
**22** il meccano
- *construction set*
**23** i libri per bambini (i libri illustrati)
- *children's books*
**24** la culla della bambola, una culla di vimini *m*
- *doll's cot, a wicker cot*
**25** il bambolotto
- *baby doll*
**26** la tendina della culla
- *canopy*
**27** le costruzioni di legno
- *building bricks (building blocks)*
**28** l'edificio (la costruzione) di legno
- *wooden model building*
**29** il trenino di legno
- *wooden train set*
**30** l'orsacchiotto a dondolo
- *rocking teddy bear*
**31** il passeggino della bambola
- *doll's pushchair*

**32** la bambola da vestire
- *fashion doll*
**33** il bambino in età prescolare
- *child of nursery school age*
**34** l'attaccapanni *m*
- *cloakroom*

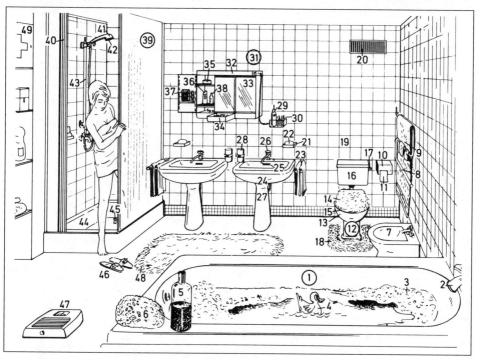

1 la vasca da bagno
– *bath*
2 il rubinetto miscelatore di acqua calda e fredda
– *mixer tap (Am. mixing faucet) for hot and cold water*
3 il bagno-schiuma (la schiuma)
– *foam bath (bubble bath)*
4 il giocattolo galleggiante (*qui:* l'anatroccolo)
– *toy duck*
5 i sali da bagno
– *bath salts*
6 la spugna da bagno
– *bath sponge (sponge)*
7 il bidet
– *bidet*
8 il portasciugamano (l'asta per l'asciugamano)
– *towel rail*
9 l'asciugamano (la salvietta) di spugna
– *terry towel*
10 il portarotolo (per la carta igienica)
– *toilet roll holder (Am. bathroom tissue holder)*
11 la carta igienica
– *toilet paper (coll. loo paper, Am. bathroom tissue)*
12 il water
– *toilet (lavatory, W.C., coll. loo)*
13 la vaschetta del water
– *toilet pan (toilet bowl)*
14 il coperchio del water con ricopertura di spugna
– *toilet lid with terry cover*
15 il sedile del water
– *toilet seat*
16 il sifone del water
– *cistern*

17 lo sciacquone
– *flushing lever*
18 il tappeto girowater
– *pedestal mat*
19 la piastrella da parete *f*
– *tile*
20 l'areatore *m*
– *ventilator (extraction vent)*
21 il portasapone
– *soap dish*
22 il sapone
– *soap*
23 l'asciugamano (la salvietta)
– *hand towel*
24 il lavandino (il lavabo)
– *washbasin*
25 lo sfioratore
– *overflow*
26 il rubinetto dell'acqua calda e fredda
– *hot and cold water tap*
27 la colonna del lavandino (del lavabo) con il sifone
– *washbasin pedestal with trap (antisyphon trap)*
28 il bicchiere per lo spazzolino da denti *m pl* (il bicchiere portaspazzolino da denti *m pl*)
– *tooth glass (tooth mug)*
29 lo spazzolino da denti *m pl* elettrico
– *electric toothbrush*
30 gli apparecchi intercambiabili (dello spazzolino)
– *detachable brush heads*
31 l'armadietto a specchio
– *mirrored bathroom cabinet*
32 la lampada tubolare al neon (il tubo al neon)
– *fluorescent lamp*

33 lo specchio
– *mirror*
34 il cassetto
– *drawer*
35 il portacipria
– *powder box*
36 il collutorio
– *mouthwash*
37 il rasoio elettrico
– *electric shaver*
38 la lozione dopobarba (il dopobarba)
– *aftershave lotion*
39 la cabina della doccia (la doccia)
– *shower cubicle*
40 la tenda della doccia
– *shower curtain*
41 la doccia regolabile
– *adjustable shower head*
42 il bulbo forato della doccia
– *shower nozzle*
43 il braccio di regolazione *f*
– *shower adjustment rail*
44 la vaschetta della doccia (il fondo doccia)
– *shower base*
45 lo scarico
– *waste pipe*
46 le pianelle (le pantofole) da bagno
– *bathroom mule*
47 la bilancia
– *bathroom scales*
48 il tappeto da bagno (il tappeto fuorivasca *m*)
– *bath mat*
49 l'armadietto dei medicinali
– *medicine cabinet*

# 50 Utensili per la casa ed elettrodomestici

**1-20 apparecchi** *m pl* **per stirare**
– *irons*
1 la stiratrice elettrica
– *electric ironing machine*
2 il pedale elettrico
– *electric foot switch*
3 il rullo avvolgente
– *roller covering*
4 la conca ribaltabile
– *ironing head*
5 il lenzuolo
– *sheet*
6 il ferro da stiro elettrico
– *electric iron (lightweight iron)*
7 la piastra del ferro da stiro
– *sole-plate*
8 il termostato (il regolatore della temperatura)
– *temperature selector*
9 l'impugnatura (il manico) del ferro da stiro
– *handle (iron handle)*
10 la lampada spia (spia di controllo, spia)
– *pilot light*
11 il ferro da stiro a vapore *m* con spray (con spruzzatore *m*)
– *steam, spray, and dry iron*
12 il bocchettone di riempimento dell'acqua
– *filling inlet*
13 lo spruzzatore (lo spray nebulizzatore *m*)
– *spray nozzle for damping the washing*
14 i fori di uscita del vapore (fori *m* diffusori del vapore)
– *steam hole (steam slit)*
15 l'asse *f* (il tavolo) da stiro
– *ironing table*
16 l'asse *f* da stiro
– *ironing board (ironing surface)*
17 la copertura dell'asse *f* da stiro
– *ironing-board cover*
18 il poggiaferro
– *iron well*
19 il telaio (la struttura) in alluminio
– *aluminium (Am. aluminum) frame*
20 le stiramaniche
– *sleeve board*
21 il portabiancheria
– *linen bin*
22 la biancheria sporca
– *dirty linen*
**23-34 apparecchi** *m pl* **per lavare e asciugare**
– *washing machines and driers*
23 la lavatrice
– *automatic washing machine*
24 il tamburo della lavatrice
– *washing drum*
25 la chiusura di sicurezza
– *safety latch (safety catch)*
26 la manopola dei programmi (manopola girevole per la scelta dei programmi)
– *program selector control*
27 le vaschette (le camere) per i detersivi in posizione *f* frontale
– *front soap dispenser [with several compartments]*
28 l'asciugatrice *f* elettrica (la macchina elettrica per asciugare)
– *tumble drier*
29 il tamburo dell'asciugatrice *f*
– *drum*
30 la chiusura frontale con gli sfiatatoi
– *front door with ventilation slits*

31 il piano di lavoro
– *worktop*
32 lo stendibiancheria
– *airer*
33 la corda
– *clothes line (washing line)*
34 lo stendibiancheria a cavalletto pieghevole
– *extending airer*
35 la scaletta, una scaletta in metallo leggero
– *stepladder (steps), an aluminium (Am. aluminum) ladder*
36 il fianco (la longarina)
– *stile*
37 il braccio d'appoggio (di sostegno)
– *prop*
38 il gradino
– *tread (rung)*
**39-43 prodotti** *m pl* **e utensili** *m pl* **per le scarpe**
– *shoe care utensils*
39 la scatola di crema da scarpe *f pl* (il lucido da scarpe *f pl*)
– *tin of shoe polish*
40 lo spray da scarpe *f pl*, uno spray impregnante
– *shoe spray, an impregnating spray*
41 la spazzola per le scarpe
– *shoe brush*
42 lo spazzolino per la crema da scarpe *f pl*
– *brush for applying polish*
43 il tubetto di crema da scarpe *f pl*
– *tube of shoe polish*
44 la spazzola da vestiti *m pl*
– *clothes brush*
45 la spazzola da tappeti *m pl*
– *carpet brush*
46 la scopa
– *broom*
47 le setole della scopa
– *bristles*
48 la scopa (senza manico)
– *broom head*
49 il manico della scopa
– *broomstick (broom handle)*
50 la filettatura a vite *f*
– *screw thread*
51 la spazzola per stoviglie *f pl*
– *washing-up brush*
52 la paletta
– *pan (dustpan)*
**53-86 prodotti** *m pl* **e utensili** *m pl* **per pavimenti** *m pl*
– *floor and carpet cleaning*
53 la scopetta
– *brush*
54 il secchio
– *bucket (pail)*
55 lo straccio da pavimenti *m pl*
– *floor cloth (cleaning rag)*
56 il bruschino
– *scrubbing brush*
57 lo scopatappeti
– *carpet sweeper*
58 l'aspirapolvere *m*
– *upright vacuum cleaner*
59 il tasto commutatore della bocchetta
– *changeover switch*
60 il raccordo snodabile
– *swivel head*
61 la spia del sacchetto (spia del livello di riempimento del sacchetto)
– *bag-full indicator*

62 il vano del sacchetto raccoglipolvere
– *dust bag container*
63 la maniglia dell'aspirapolvere *m*
– *handle*
64 il tubo
– *tubular handle*
65 il gancio avvolgicavo (il supporto raccoglicavo)
– *flex hook*
66 il cavo avvolto
– *wound-up flex*
67 la bocchetta multiuso
– *all-purpose nozzle*
68 l'aspirapolvere *m* a carrello
– *cylinder vacuum cleaner*
69 il raccordo snodabile
– *swivel coupling*
70 la prolunga
– *extension tube*
71 la bocchetta scopa (sim.: bocchetta a spazzola)
– *floor nozzle (sim.: carpet beater nozzle)*
72 il regolatore della forza aspirante
– *suction control*
73 la spia del sacchetto (spia del livello di riempimento del sacchetto)
– *bag-full indicator*
74 il soffiatore (il dispositivo regolatore dell'aria)
– *sliding fingertip suction control*
75 il tubo flessibile
– *hose (suction hose)*
76 l'aspirapolvere *m* con battitappeto aggregato
– *combined carpet sweeper and shampooer*
77 il cavo di adduzione *f* elettrica
– *electric lead (flex)*
78 la presa elettrica per il battitappeto
– *plug socket*
79 l'aggregato battitappeto (sim.: l'aggregato lavatappeto con detergente *m* a schiuma, la spazzola per tappeti *m pl*)
– *carpet beater head (sim.: shampooing head, brush head)*
80 il bidone lava e aspira
– *all-purpose vacuum cleaner (wet and dry vacuum cleaner)*
81 la ruota piroettante
– *castor*
82 l'aggregato con il motore (il motore)
– *motor unit*
83 la chiusura del coperchio
– *lid clip*
84 il tubo flessibile per la sporcizia grossa
– *coarse dirt hose*
85 l'accessorio speciale per la sporcizia grossa
– *special accessory (special attachment) for coarse dirt*
86 il bidone della polvere
– *dust container*
87 la borsa carrello
– *shopper (shopping trolley)*

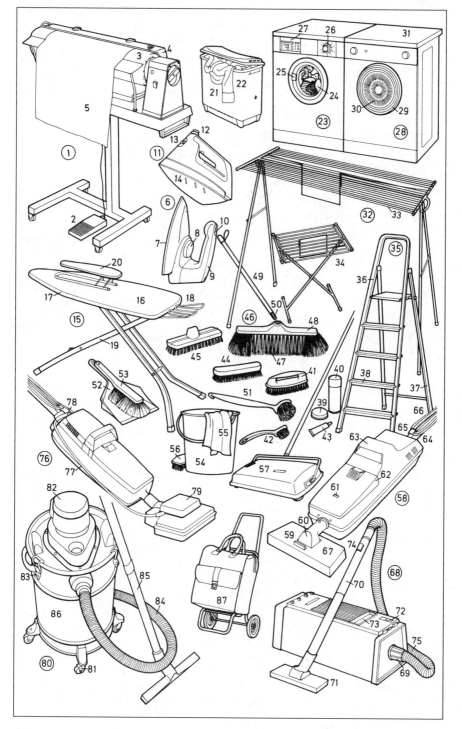

**1-35 il giardino (giardino fiorito)**
- *flower garden*
1 la pergola (il pergolato)
- *pergola*
2 la sedia a sdraio (la sdraia)
- *deck-chair*
3 il rastrello da fogliame *m* (rastrel-lo scopa)
- *lawn rake (wire-tooth rake)*
4 il rastrello
- *garden rake*
5 la vite americana (canadese), una pianta rampicante
- *Virginia creeper (American ivy, woodbine), a climbing plant (climber, creeper)*
6 i massi, una parte del giardino con massi *m pl*
- *rockery (rock garden)*
7 le piante che crescono fra i massi; *tipi:* il riso dei muri, l'erba pigno-la, la sempreviva, il camedrio alpino
- *rock plants;* varieties: *stonecrop (wall pepper), houseleek, dryas, aubretia*
8 l'erba della pampa
- *pampas grass*
9 la siepe del giardino
- *garden hedge*
10 l'abete *m* azzurro di Douglas
- *blue spruce*

11 le ortensie
- *hydrangeas*
12 la quercia
- *oak (oak tree)*
13 la betulla
- *birch (birch tree)*
14 il vialetto (il viale del giardino)
- *garden path*
15 il bordo (la bordura) del vialetto
- *edging*
16 la vasca del giardino
- *garden pond*
17 la lastra di pietra
- *flagstone (stone slab)*
18 la ninfea
- *water lily*
19 le begonie
- *tuberous begonias*
20 le dalie
- *dahlias*
21 l'innaffiatoio
- *watering can* (Am. *sprinkling can)*
22 la zappetta a doppio uso
- *weeding hoe*
23 il lupino
- *lupin*
24 le margherite
- *marguerites (oxeye daisies, white oxeye daisies)*
25 la rosa a alberello
- *standard rose*

26 la gerbera
- *gerbera*
27 l'iris *m* (il giaggiolo)
- *iris*
28 i gladioli
- *gladioli*
29 i crisantemi
- *chrysanthemums*
30 i papaveri
- *poppy*
31 la serretta (la serratola)
- *blazing star*
32 la bocca di leone *m*
- *snapdragon (antirrhinum)*
33 il prato
- *lawn*
34 il tarassaco (il dente di leone *m,* il soffione)
- *dandelion*
35 il girasole
- *sunflower*

**1-32** l'orto (l'orto casalingo, ortaggi *m pl* e frutta)
– **allotment** *(fruit and vegetable garden)*
**1, 2, 16, 17, 29** alberi *m pl* fruttiferi potati a basso fusto (alberi *m pl* fruttiferi a spalliera)
– *dwarf fruit trees (espaliers, espalier fruit trees)*
**1** il cordone quadruplo (la palmetta)
– *quadruple cordon, a wall espalier*
**2** il cordone verticale
– *vertical cordon*
**3** la capanna degli attrezzi
– *tool shed (garden shed)*
**4** la botte per l'acqua piovana
– *water butt (water barrel)*
**5** la pianta rampicante
– *climbing plant (climber, creeper, rambler)*
**6** il mucchio di terriccio
– *compost heap*
**7** il girasole
– *sunflower*
**8** la scala a pioli *m pl* da giardino
– *garden ladder (ladder)*
**9** la pianta perenne (l'arbusto)
– *perennial (flowering perennial)*
**10** lo steccato (la staccionata, la palizzata)
– *garden fence (paling fence, paling)*

**11** l'alberello di bacche *f pl* di alto fusto
– *standard berry tree*
**12** la rosa rampicante (rosa sarmentosa) su pergolato ad arco
– *climbing rose (rambling rose) on the trellis arch*
**13** la rosa a cespuglio
– *bush rose*
**14** il pergolato (il padiglione da giardino)
– *summerhouse (garden house)*
**15** il lampioncino veneziano
– *Chinese lantern (paper lantern)*
**16** l'albero da frutto a piramide *f*, un albero a piramide *f* libera
– *pyramid tree (pyramidal tree, pyramid), a free-standing espalier*
**17** il cordone orizzontale doppio (cordone *m* bilaterale), una spalliera a muro
– *double horizontal cordon*
**18** la bordura di fiori *m pl*, un'aiuola di bordura
– *flower bed, a border*
**19** l'arbusto (l'arbusto di uva spina, il ribes)
– *berry bush (gooseberry bush, currant bush)*
**20** la bordura a lista di cemento
– *concrete edging*

**21** la rosa a alberello
– *standard rose (standard rose tree)*
**22** l'aiuola di piante *f pl* perenni
– *border with perennials*
**23** il vialetto dell'orto
– *garden path*
**24** l'ortolano (l'orticultore *m*, l'ortofrutticultore *m*)
– *allotment holder*
**25** l'aiuola di asparagi *m pl*
– *asparagus patch (asparagus bed)*
**26** l'aiuola di ortaggi *m pl*
– *vegetable patch (vegetable plot)*
**27** lo spaventapasseri
– *scarecrow*
**28** il fagiolo rampicante, una pianta di fagiolo sostenuta da pali (il broncone)
– *runner bean (Am. scarlet runner), a bean plant on poles (bean poles)*
**29** il cordone orizzontale (cordone unilaterale, cordone a un braccio)
– *horizontal cordon*
**30** l'albero da frutta
– *standard fruit tree*
**31** il palo tutore (il tutore)
– *tree stake*
**32** la siepe
– *hedge*

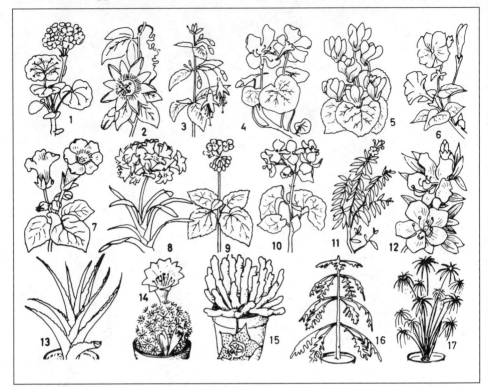

1  il pelargonio (il geranio), una gerani-
acea
–  *pelargonium (crane's bill), a geranium*
2  il fior di passione *f* (la passiflora), una
pianta rampicante
–  *passion flower (Passiflora), a climbing
plant (climber, creeper)*
3  la fucsia, un'enoteracea
–  *fuchsia, an anagraceous plant*
4  la cappuccina (il tropeolo, il nasturzio
indiano)
–  *nasturtium (Indian cress, tropaeolum)*
5  il ciclamino, una primulacea
–  *cyclamen, a primulaceous herb*
6  la petunia, una solanacea
–  *petunia, a solanaceous herb*
7  la gloxinia (sinningia speciosa), una
gesneriacea
–  *gloxinia (Sinningia), a gesneriaceous
plant*
8  la clivia, un'amarillidacea
–  *Clivia minata, an amaryllis (narcissus)*
9  la sparmannia, una tigliacea
–  *African hemp (Sparmannia), a tilia-
ceous plant, a linden plant*
10  la begonia
–  *begonia*
11  il mirto (la mortella)
–  *myrtle (common myrtle, Myrtus)*
12  l'azalea, un'ericacea
–  *azalea, an ericaceous plant*
13  l'aloe *m*, una liliacea (gigliacea)
–  *aloe, a liliaceous plant*
14  l'echinocactus *m*
–  *globe thistle (Echinops)*

15  la stampelia (una pianta che emana
fetore *m*), un'asclepiadacea
–  *stapelia (carrion flower), an asclepiada-
ceous plant*
16  l'araucaria
–  *Norfolk Island Pine (an araucaria
grown as an ornamental)*
17  il cipero (cyperus alternifolius), una
ciperacea
–  *galingale, a cyperacious plant of the
sedge family*

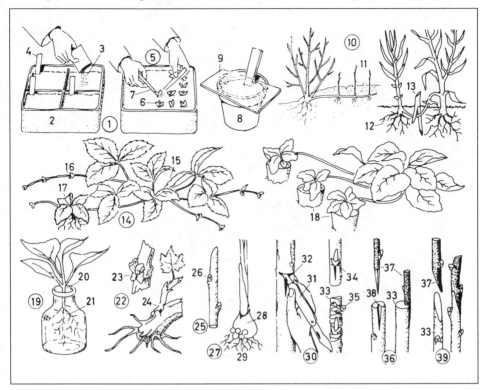

| | | |
|---|---|---|
| **1** la semina | **14** la propaggine per stolone *m* | **30-39 innesto** |
| – *seed sowing (sowing)* | – *propagation by runners* | – *grafting (graftage)* |
| **2** la cassetta di semina | **15** la pianta madre | **30** l'innesto a occhio (innesto a gemma, |
| – *seed pan* | – *parent (parent plant)* | l'inoculazione *f* ) |
| **3** il seme (la semente) | **16** lo stolone | – *budding; here: shield budding* |
| – *seed* | – *runner* | **31** il coltello da innesto |
| **4** il marcapianta (l'etichetta, la targhetta | **17** la pianta figlia radicata | – *budding knife* |
| col nome della pianta) | – *small rooted leaf cluster* | **32** il taglio a T *f* (l'incisione *f* a T) |
| – *label* | **18** la propagazione mediante margotta | – *T-cut* |
| **5** il trapianto (picchettare, diradare, | – *setting in pots* | **33** il portainnesto (il selvatico, il franco, il |
| spostare, rimuovere) | **19** la talea in acqua | soggetto) |
| – *pricking out (pricking off, transplanting)* | – *cutting in water* | – *support (stock, rootstock)* |
| **6** la piantina (la pianta giovane) | **20** la talea | **34** l'occhio innestato (la gemma innestata) |
| – *seedling (seedling plant)* | – *cutting (slip, set)* | – *inserted scion bud* |
| **7** il foraterra (il piantatoio; *in legno:* cav- | **21** la radice | **35** il legaccio di rafia |
| icchio) | – *root* | – *raffia layer (bast layer)* |
| – *dibber (dibble)* | **22** la talea a gemma nella vite *f* | **36** l'innesto a marza (innesto a spacco) |
| **8** il vaso da fiori *m pl* (per piante *f pl* vive, | – *bud cutting on vine tendril* | – *side grafting* |
| un vaso per piante *f pl*) | **23** l'occhio, una gemma | **37** la marza |
| – *flower pot (pot)* | – *scion bud, a bud* | – *scion (shoot)* |
| **9** la lastra di vetro | **24** la talea verde (il germoglio) | **38** l'incisione *f* a cuneo (il taglio) |
| – *sheet of glass* | – *sprouting (shooting) cutting* | – *wedge-shaped notch* |
| **10** la riproduzione per propaggine *f* (per | **25** la talea legnosa | **39** l'innesto per copulazione *f* (innesto a |
| propaggine *f* semplice, per propaggine | – *stem cutting (hardwood cutting)* | becco di clarino, innesto a doppio spac- |
| a archetto), la propagazione | **26** la gemma | co inglese) |
| – *propagation by layering* | – *bud* | – *splice grafting* |
| **11** la propaggine | **27** la propaggine par bulbilli *m pl* | |
| – *layer* | – *propagation by bulbils (brood bud bul-* | |
| **12** la propaggine radicata | *blets)* | |
| – *layer with roots* | **28** il vecchio bulbo | |
| **13** la forcella (ramo biforcuto) per fissare | – *old bulb* | |
| la propaggine | **29** il bulbillo | |
| – *forked stick used for fastening* | – *bulbil (brood bud bulblet)* | |

**1-51 l'azienda di orto-floricoltura**
- *market garden (Am. truck garden, truck farm)*
1 il capanno degli attrezzi
- *tool shed*
2 il serbatoio sopraelevato (la cisterna sopraelevata dell'acqua (la riserva di acqua))
- *water tower (water tank)*
3 il vivaio
- *market garden (Am. truck garden, truck farm), a tree nursery*
4 la serra (serra calda, serra di coltura)
- *hothouse (forcing house, warm house)*
5 il tetto di vetro
- *glass roof*
6 la stuoia avvolgibile (stuoia di paglia, stuoia parasole)
- *[roll of] matting (straw matting, reed matting, shading)*
7 l'ambiente *m* caldaia
- *boiler room (boiler house)*
8 il tubo di riscaldamento (tubo di condotta forzata)
- *heating pipe (pressure pipe)*
9 la tavola di copertura
- *shading panel (shutter)*
10 *u.* 11 l'areazione *f*
- *ventilators (vents)*

10 la finestra di areazione *f* (finestra a vasistas *m*, finestra a cerniera)
- *ventilation window (window vent, hinged ventilator)*
11 l'areazione *f* di colmo
- *ridge vent*
12 il tavolo per invasare
- *potting table (potting bench)*
13 la griglia (settaccio, crivello)
- *riddle (sieve, garden sieve, upright sieve)*
14 la pala da giardino
- *garden shovel (shovel)*
15 il mucchio di terra (composta, terriccio)
- *heap of earth (composted earth, prepared earth, garden mould, Am. mold)*
16 il letto caldo (il lettorino)
- *hotbed (forcing bed, heated frame)*
17 la finestra del lettorino (che attira il calore solare)
- *hotbed vent (frame vent)*
18 il puntello di areazione *f*
- *vent prop*
19 l'irroratore *m* (irrigatore *m* a pioggia)
- *sprinkler (sprinkling device)*
20 il giardiniere (orticoltore *m*)
- *gardener (nursery gardener, grower, commercial grower)*

21 il sarchiatore a mano *f*
- *cultivator (hand cultivator, grubber)*
22 la passerella
- *plank*
23 piantine *f pl* ripicchettate
- *pricked-out seedlings (pricked-off seedlings)*
24 fiori *m pl* forzati (fiori *m pl* primaticci) [forzatura]
- *forced flowers [forcing]*
25 piante *f pl* in vaso
- *potted plants (plants in pots, pot plants)*
26 l'annaffiatoio
- *watering can (Am. sprinkling can)*
27 il manico dell'annaffiatoio
- *handle*
28 il beccuccio traforato dell'annaffiatoio
- *rose*
29 la vasca dell'acqua
- *water tank*
30 il tubo (la conduttura) dell'acqua
- *water pipe*

31 la balla di torba
– *bale of peat*
32 la serra calda
– *warm house (heated greenhouse)*
33 la serra fredda
– *cold house (unheated greenhouse)*
34 l'aeromotore *m*
– *wind generator*
35 la ruota a vento
– *wind wheel*
36 la banderuola
– *wind vane*
37 la striscia di terreno con piante *f pl* perenni (una striscia di terreno coltivato a fiori *m pl*)
– *shrub bed, a flower bed*
38 gli archi di bordura
– *hoop edging*
39 la striscia di terreno coltivato a ortaggi *m pl*
– *vegetable plot*
40 la serra a padiglione *m* in lamina
– *plastic tunnel (polythene greenhouse)*
41 la finestra di aerazione *f* a visistas *m* (a cerniera)
– *ventilation flap*
42 il corridoio centrale (la corsia centrale)
– *central path*
43 la cassetta da spedizione *f* della verdura (cassetta della verdura)
– *vegetable crate*

44 la pianta di pomodoro
– *tomato plant*
45 l'aiutante *m* orticoltore
– *nursery hand*
46 l'aiutante *f* orticoltrice
– *nursery hand*
47 la pianta in vaso da giardino
– *tub plant*
48 il vaso
– *tub*
49 l'alberello di aranci *m pl*
– *orange tree*
50 il cesto (canestro) in fil *m* di ferro
– *wire basket*
51 la cassetta da semina (cassetta di piante *f pl* da semina)
– *seedling box*

1 il piantatoio (il foraterra; *in legno:* il cavicchio)
– *dibber (dibble)*
2 la vanga
– *spade*
3 il rastrello metallico a ventaglio
– *lawn rake (wire-tooth rake)*
4 il rastrello
– *rake*
5 la zappa rincalzatrice (il rincalzatore)
– *ridging hoe*
6 la paletta (il trapiantatoio)
– *trowel*
7 la zappetta a doppio uso
– *combined hoe and fork*
8 la falce
– *sickle*
9 il roncolo (la roncola)
– *gardener's knife (pruning knife, billhook)*
10 il coltello tagliasparagi
– *asparagus cutter (asparagus knife)*
11 lo svettatoio
– *tree pruner (long-handled pruner)*
12 la zappa semiautomatica
– *semi-automatic spade*
13 il sarchiatore a tre denti *m pl* (la zappa tridente)
– *three-pronged cultivator*
14 il raschiatoio (il raschietto)
– *tree scraper (bark scraper)*
15 l'areatore *m* (l'attrezzo per il ricambio dell'aria)
– *lawn aerator (aerator)*
16 la sega da giardiniere *m*
– *pruning saw (saw for cutting branches)*
17 le cesoie a batteria per siepi *f pl*
– *battery-operated hedge trimmer*
18 la sarchiatrice (la zappatrice) a motore *m*
– *motor cultivator*
19 il trapano a mano *f* elettrico
– *electric drill*
20 la trasmissione
– *gear*
21 il tracciasolchi a mano *f* per la semina
– *cultivator attachment*
22 il coglifrutta (il raccoglifrutta)
– *fruit picker*
23 la spazzola per alberi *m pl* (spazzola per scortecciare)
– *tree brush (bark brush)*
24 la pompa per il trattamento antiparassitario
– *sprayer for pest control*
25 il tubo che emette il liquido a spruzzo
– *lance*
26 il carrello avvolgibile
– *hose reel (reel and carrying cart)*
27 il tubo irroratore (tubo d'irrogazione *f*)
– *garden hose*

28 la macchina tosaerba a motore *m* (la tosatrice, la macchina tagliaerba a motore *m*)
– *motor lawn mower (motor mower)*
29 il canestro raccoglierba
– *grassbox*
30 il motore a due tempi *m pl*
– *two-stroke motor*
31 la macchina tosaerba elettrica (la tosatrice, la macchina tagliaerba elettrica)
– *electric lawn mower (electric mower)*
32 il cavo elettrico
– *electric lead (electric cable)*
33 l'elemento falciante
– *cutting unit*
34 la macchina tosaerba a mano *f* (la tosatrice, la macchina tagliaerba a mano *f* )
– *hand mower*
35 il rullo falciante
– *cutting cylinder*
36 la lama
– *blade*
37 il trattore tosaerba (trattore *m* tagliaerba)
– *riding mower*
38 la leva del freno a mano *f*
– *brake lock*
39 l'avviamento elettrico
– *electric starter*
40 la leva del freno a pedale *m* (il pedale del freno)
– *brake pedal*
41 l'elemento falciante
– *cutting unit*
42 il rimorchio ribaltabile
– *tip-up trailer*
43 l'irrigatore *m* (l'irroratore *m*) da giardino
– *revolving sprinkler, a lawn sprinkler*
44 il getto girevole (getto ruotante)
– *revolving nozzle*
45 il nipplo (il raccordo filettato per il tubo)
– *hose connector*
46 l'irrigatore *m* (l'irroratore *m*) tetragonale
– *oscillating sprinkler*
47 la carriola da giardiniere *m*
– *wheelbarrow*
48 le forbici da prato
– *grass shears*
49 le cesoie per siepi *f pl*
– *hedge shears*
50 le forbici per potare
– *secateurs (pruning shears)*

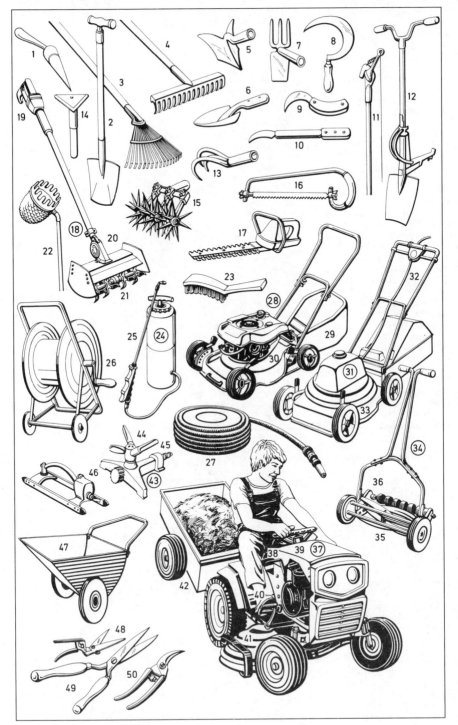

**1-11 legumi** *m pl* (piante *f pl* legumi-
nose)
– *leguminous plants
(Leguminosae)*
**1** la pianta di pisello, una papil-
ionacea
– *pea, a plant with a papilionaceous
corola*
**2** il fiore di pisello
– *pea flower*
**3** la foglia pennata
– *pinnate leaf*
**4** il viticcio di pisello
– *pea tendril, a leaf tendril*
**5** la stipola fogliare
– *stipule*
**6** il guscio, un pericarpo (o pericarpio)
– *legume (pod), a seed vessel (peri-
carp, legume)*
**7** il pisello (il seme)
– *pea [seed]*
**8** il fagiolo, una pianta rampicante;
*tipi:* borlotto, fagiolo rosso, fagiolo bianco; *più piccolo:* fagiolo
nano
– *bean plant (bean), a climbing
plant (climber, creeper);* varieties:
*broad bean (runner bean,* Am.
*scarlet runner), climbing bean
(climber, pole bean), scarlet runner bean;* smaller: *dwarf French
bean (bush bean)*
**9** il fiore del fagiolo
– *bean flower*
**10** il fusto rampicante del fagiolo
– *twining beanstalk*
**11** il fagiolo (guscio e seme *m*)
– *bean [pod with seeds]*
**12** il pomodoro
– *tomato*
**13** il cetriolo
– *cucumber*
**14** l'asparago
– *asparagus*
**15** il ravanello
– *radish*
**16** il ramolaccio
– *white radish*
**17** la carota
– *carrot*
**18** la carota di Liegi (carota rossa
corta)
– *stump-rooted carrot*
**19** il prezzemolo
– *parsley*
**20** il rafano
– *horse-radish*
**21** i porri
– *leeks*
**22** l'erba cipollina
– *chives*
**23** la zucca
– *pumpkin (*Am. *squash);* sim.:
*melon*

**24** la cipolla (cipolla da orto)
– *onion*
**25** la buccia (i catafilli) della cipolla
– *onion skin*
**26** la rapa
– *kohlrabi*
**27** il sedano rapa (sedano di Verona)
– *celeriac*
**28-34 cavoli** *m pl,* piante *f pl* a foglie *f
pl*
– *brassicas (leaf vegetables)*
**28** la bietola da coste *f pl* (le coste)
– *chard (Swiss chard, seakale beet)*
**29** lo spinacio (gli spinaci)
– *spinach*
**30** i broccoletti di Bruxelles
– *Brussels sprouts (sprouts)*
**31** il cavolfiore
– *cauliflower*
**32** il cavolo cappuccio, un cavolo;
*tipi:* cavolo bianco, cavolo rosso
– *cabbage (round cabbage, head of
cabbage), a brassica;* cultivated
races (cultivars): *green cabbage,
red cabbage*
**33** il cavolo verzotto (la verza)
– *savoy (savoy cabbage)*
**34** il cavolo riccio
– *kale (curly kale, kail), a winter
green*
**35** la scorzonera (la radice amara)
– *scorzonera (black salsify)*
**36-40 piante** *f pl* **da insalata**
– *salad plants*
**36** la lattuga (il cespo di lattuga)
– *lettuce (cabbage lettuce, head of
lettuce)*
**37** la foglia di lattuga
– *lettuce leaf*
**38** la valerianella (l'erba pasqualina,
la lattughina)
– *corn salad (lamb's lettuce)*
**39** l'indivia
– *endive (endive leaves)*
**40** la cicoria, la scarola
– *chicory (succory, salad chicory)*
**41** il carciofo
– *globe artichoke*
**42** il peperone (*sim.:* la paprica, il
peperoncino rosso lungo, il peperone messicano)
– *sweet pepper (Spanish paprika)*

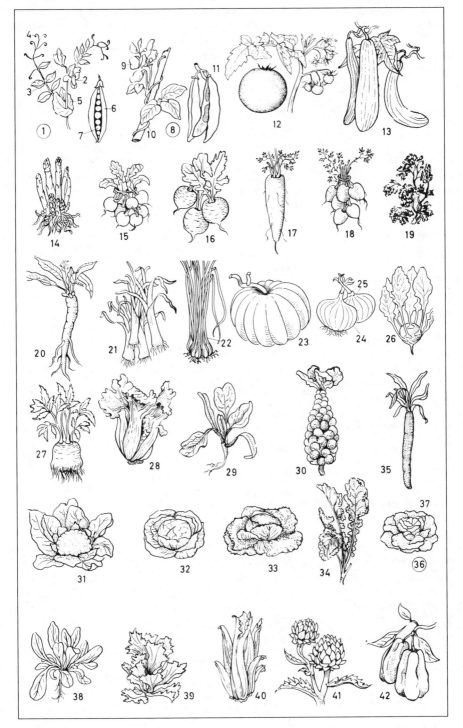

**1-30 frutti** *m pl* **a bacca** (arbusti *m pl* di bacche *f pl*)
– *soft fruit (berry bushes)*
**1-15 sassifragacee** *f pl*
– *Ribes*
**1** l'arbusto di uva spina
– *gooseberry bush*
**2** il rametto di uva spina in fiore *m*
– *flowering gooseberry cane*
**3** la foglia
– *leaf*
**4** il fiore
– *flower*
**5** la falena dell'uva spina (il bruco geometra *m*)
– *magpie moth larva*
**6** il fiore di uva spina
– *gooseberry flower*
**7** l'ovario inferiore
– *epigynous ovary*
**8** il calice (i sepali)
– *calyx (sepals)*
**9** l'uva spina, una bacca
– *gooseberry, a berry*
**10** l'arbusto di ribes *m*
– *currant bush*
**11** il grappolo di ribes *m*
– *cluster of berries*
**12** il ribes
– *currant*
**13** la rachide (il raspo, il graspo)
– *stalk*
**14** il rametto di ribes *m* in fiore *m*
– *flowering cane of the currant*
**15** il grappolo di fiori *m pl*
– *raceme*
**16** la pianta di fragole *f pl; tipi:* fragola di bosco, fragola ananassa, fragola di tutti i mesi (fragola delle quattro stagioni)
– *strawberry plant;* varieties: *wild strawberry (woodland strawberry), garden strawberry, alpine strawberry*
**17** la pianta fruttifera in fiore *m*
– *flowering and fruit-bearing plant*
**18** il rizoma
– *rhizome*
**19** la foglia trifida
– *ternate leaf (trifoliate leaf )*
**20** lo stolone (germoglio laterale, pollone *m*)
– *runner (prostrate stem)*
**21** la fragola, uno pseudocarpo
– *strawberry, a pseudocarp*
**22** il calice
– *epicalyx*
**23** l'achenio (seme *m*, nocciolo)
– *achene (seed)*
**24** la polpa
– *flesh (pulp)*
**25** l'arbusto di lampone *m*
– *raspberry bush*
**26** il fiore di lampone *m*
– *raspberry flower*

**27** il bocciolo fiorale (gemma)
– *flower bud (bud)*
**28** il frutto (lampone *m*), un frutto composto (frutto multiplo)
– *fruit (raspberry), an aggregate fruit (compound fruit)*
**29** la mora
– *blackberry*
**30** il rametto spinoso
– *thorny tendril*
**31-61 piante** *f pl* **da frutto con semi** *m pl* (pomidee *f pl*)
– *pomiferous plants*
**31** il pero; *selv.:* il pero selvatico (peruggine *m*)
– *pear tree;* wild: *wild pear tree*
**32** il ramo di pero in fiore *m*
– *flowering branch of the pear tree*
**33** la pera [sezione longitudinale]
– *pear [longitudinal section]*
**34** il picciolo della pera
– *pear stalk (stalk)*
**35** la polpa
– *flesh (pulp)*
**36** il torsolo (il torso)
– *core (carpels)*
**37** il seme di pera, un nocciolo
– *pear pip (seed), a fruit pip*
**38** il fiore di pero
– *pear blossom*
**39** l'ovulo
– *ovules*
**40** l'ovario
– *ovary*
**41** lo stigma
– *stigma*
**42** lo stilo
– *style*
**43** il petalo
– *petal*
**44** il sepalo
– *sepal*
**45** l'antera (lo stame)
– *stamen*
**46** il cotogno
– *quince tree*
**47** la foglia di cotogno
– *quince leaf*
**48** la stipola
– *stipule*
**49** il cotogno maschio (mela cotogna) [sezione longitudinale]
– *apple-shaped quince [longitudinal section]*
**50** il cotogno femmina (mela cotogna) [sezione longitudinale]
– *pear-shaped quince [longitudinal section]*
**51** il melo; *selv.:* melo selvatico (meluggine *m*)
– *apple tree;* wild: *crab apple tree*
**52** il ramo di melo in fiore *m*
– *flowering branch of the apple tree*
**53** la foglia
– *leaf*

**54** il fiore di melo
– *apple blossom*
**55** il fiore alla caduta dei petali
– *withered flower*
**56** la mela [sezione longitudinale]
– *apple [longitudinal section]*
**57** la buccia della mela (l'esocarpo)
– *apple skin*
**58** la polpa (il mesocarpo)
– *flesh (pulp)*
**59** il torsolo
– *core (apple core, carpels)*
**60** il seme della mela, un seme (un nocciolino) di frutta
– *apple pip, a fruit pip*
**61** il picciolo della mela
– *apple stalk (stalk)*
**62** la carpocapsa (farfalla della mela), una farfalletta
– *codling moth (codlin moth), a small moth*
**63** la galleria del bruco
– *burrow (tunnel)*
**64** la larva (il bruco; *fam.:* il verme) di una farfalletta
– *larva (grub, caterpillar) of a small moth*
**65** il foro di uscita del bruco
– *wormhole*

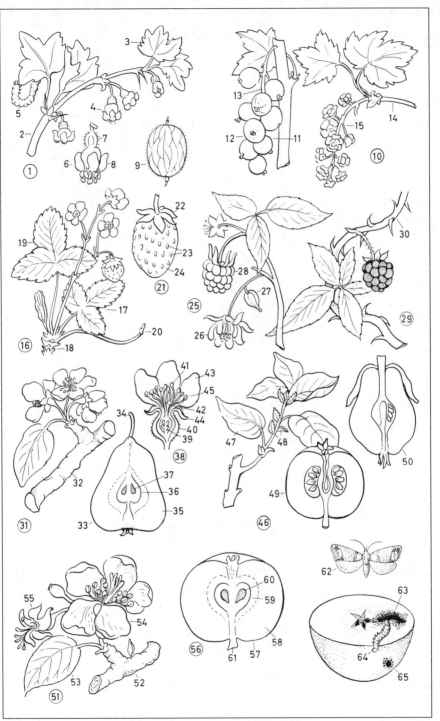

**1-36 drupacee** *f pl*
- *drupes (drupaceous plants)*
**1-18 il ciliegio**
- *cherry tree*
1 il ramo fiorifero di ciliegio
- *flowering branch of the cherry tree (branch of the cherry tree in blossom)*
2 la foglia di ciliegio
- *cherry leaf*
3 il fiore di ciliegio
- *cherry flower (cherry blossom)*
4 il peduncolo fiorale
- *peduncle (pedicel, flower stalk)*
5 la ciliegia; *tipi:* ciliege (ciliegie) *f pl* tenerine e dolci, ciliegie *f pl* duracine, visciole *f pl*, amarene *f pl*
- *cherry;* varieties: *sweet cherry (heart cherry), wild cherry (bird cherry), sour cherry, morello cherry (morello)*
**6-8 la ciliegia** (il frutto del ciliegio) [sezione longitudinale]
- *cherry (cherry fruit) [cross section]*
6 la polpa (il mesocarpo)
- *flesh (pulp)*
7 il nocciolo di ciliegia (l'endocarpo)
- *cherry stone*
8 il seme
- *seed*
9 il fiore [sezione longitudinale]
- *flower (blossom) [cross section]*
10 l'antera
- *stamen*
11 il petalo
- *petal*
12 il sepalo
- *sepal*
13 il pistillo
- *pistil*
14 l'ovulo nell'ovario medio
- *ovule enclosed in perigynous ovary*
15 lo stilo
- *style*
16 lo stigma
- *stigma*
17 la foglia
- *leaf*
18 il nettario figliare
- *nectary (honey gland)*
**19-23 il prugno (il pruno);** *sim:* il susino
- *plum tree*
19 il ramo fruttifero
- *fruit-bearing branch*
20 la prugna; *sim.:* la susina
- *oval, black-skinned plum*
21 la foglia di pruno
- *plum leaf*
22 la gemma
- *bud*

23 il nocciolo di prugna
- *plum stone*
24 la prugna Regina Claudia
- *greengage*
25 la mirabella
- *mirabelle (transparent gage), a plum*
**26-32 il pesco**
- *peach tree*
26 il ramo fiorifero
- *flowering branch (branch in blossom)*
27 il fiore di pesco
- *peach flower (peach blossom)*
28 il germoglio del fiore *m*
- *flower shoot*
29 la foglia in crescenza
- *young leaf (sprouting leaf )*
30 il ramo fruttifero
- *fruiting branch*
31 la pesca
- *peach*
32 la foglia di pesco
- *peach leaf*
**33-36 l'albicocco**
- *apricot tree*
33 il ramo fiorifero di albicocco
- *flowering apricot branch (apricot branch in blossom)*
34 il fiore di albicocco
- *apricot flower (apricot blossom)*
35 l'albicocca
- *apricot*
36 la foglia di albicocco
- *apricot leaf*
**37-51 noci** *f pl*
- *nuts*
**37-43 il noce**
- *walnut tree*
37 il ramo fiorifero di noce *m*
- *flowering branch of the walnut tree*
38 il fiore femminile
- *female flower*
39 l'infiorescenza maschile (il gattino, l'amento)
- *male inflorescence (male flowers, catkins with stamens)*
40 la foglia imparipennata
- *alternate pinnate leaf*
41 la noce, una drupa
- *walnut, a drupe (stone fruit)*
42 il pericarpo (il mallo, lo strato esterno tenero)
- *soft shell (cupule)*
43 la noce, una drupa
- *walnut, a drupe (stone fruit)*
**44-51 il nocciolo** (l'avellano), una pianta anemofila
- *hazel tree (hazel bush), an anemophilous shrub (a wind-pollinating shrub)*

44 il ramo di nocciolo in fiore *m*
- *flowering hazel branch*
45 l'infiorescenza maschile (il gattino, l'amento)
- *male catkin*
46 l'infiorescenza femminile
- *female inflorescence*
47 la gemma fogliare
- *leaf bud*
48 il ramo fruttifero
- *fruit-bearing branch*
49 la nocciola (l'avellana), una drupa
- *hazelnut (hazel, cobnut, cob), a drupe (stone fruit)*
50 la cupola (il pericarpio)
- *involucre (husk)*
51 la foglia di nocciolo (foglia di avellano)
- *hazel leaf*

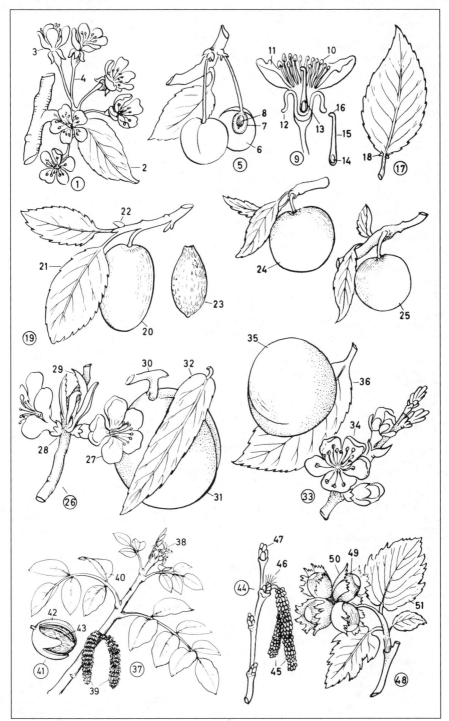

1 il bucaneve
- *snowdrop (spring snowflake)*
2 la viola del pensiero (pensée *f* ),
una viola
- *garden pansy (heartsease pansy), a*
*pansy*
3 il narciso selvatico (la
giunchiglia), un narciso
- *trumpet narcissus (trumpet daf-*
*fodil, Lent lily), a narcissus*
4 il narciso poetico; *sim.*: la tazzetta
selvatica
- *poet's narcissus (pheasant's eye,*
*poet's daffodil); sim.: polyanthus*
*narcissus*
5 il fior di Maria (dicentra
spectabilis), una fumariacea
- *bleeding heart (lyre flower), a*
*fumariaceous flower*
6 il garofanino (il garofano a
mazzetto; *pop.*: speranze *f pl*), un
garofano
- *sweet william (bunch pink), a car-*
*nation*
7 il garofano di giardino
- *gillyflower (gilliflower, clove pink,*
*clove carnation)*
8 il giaggiolo, (acaso falso, ninfea
bianca, dragontea), un'iris
- *yellow flag (yellow water flag, yel-*
*low iris), an iris*
9 la tuberosa
- *tuberose*
10 l'aquilegia
- *columbine (aquilegia)*
11 il gladiolo
- *gladiolus (sword lily)*
12 il giglio
- *Madonna lily (Annunciation lily,*
*Lent lily), a lily*
13 la speronella; *pop.*: il fior cappuccio (delphinium), una ranuncolacea
- *larkspur (delphinium), a ranuncu-*
*laceous plant*
14 la flosside carnicina (il phlox), un
phlox
- *moss pink (moss phlox), a phlox*
15 la rosa (rosa indica, rosa tea)
- *garden rose (China rose)*
16 il boccio di rosa, un bocciolo
- *rosebud, a bud*
17 la rosa doppia
- *double rose*
18 la spina di rosa, una spina
- *rose thorn, a thorn*
19 la gaillardia
- *gaillardia*
20 il tagete (garofano indiano)
- *African marigold (tagetes)*
21 la coda di volpe *f* (amaranthus *m*
caudatus), un amaranto
- *love-lies-bleeding, an amaranthine*
*flower*

22 la zinnia
- *zinnia*
23 la dalia (dahlia), una dalia
(giorgina)
- *pompon dahlia, a dahlia*

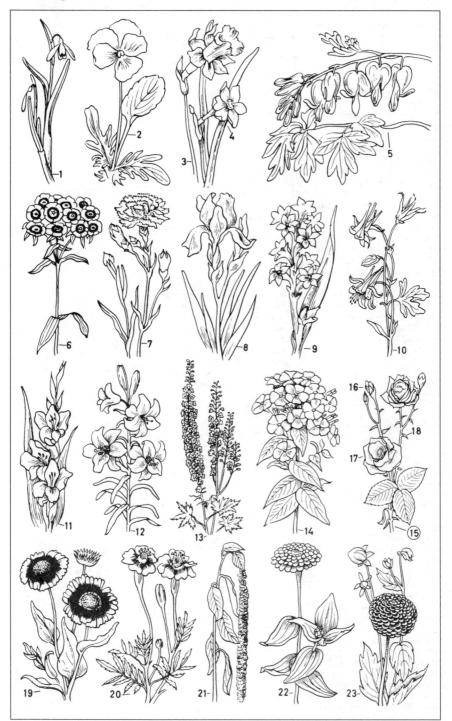

1 il fiordaliso (ciano), una centaurea
– *corn flower (bluebottle), a centaury*
2 il rosolaccio (papavero selvatico;
Austria: papavero dei campi), una
papaveracea
– *corn poppy (field poppy), a poppy*
3 il boccio (bocciolo, bottone *m* floreale)
– *bud*
4 il fiore del rosolaccio (fiore *m* del
papavero)
– *poppy flower*
5 il treto (capsula) con semi *m pl* di
rosolaccio (semi *m pl* di
papavero)
– *seed capsule containing poppy
seeds*
6 il gettaione (gittaione *m*, mazzettone *m*, agrostemma *m*)
– *corn cockle (corn campion,
crown-of-the-field)*
7 il crisantemo delle messi (bambag-
ella, fior *m* d'oro), un crisantemo
– *corn marigold (field marigold), a
chrysanthemum*
8 la camomilla comune (camomilla
selvatica, camomilla bastarda)
– *corn camomile (field camomile,
camomile, chamomile)*
9 la borsa del pastore (borsacchina)
– *shepherd's purse*
10 il fiore
– *flower*
11 il frutto (la siliquetta) a forma di
borsetta
– *fruit (pouch-shaped pod)*
12 la calderugia (senecione *m*, erba
calderina, verzellina)
– *common groundsel*
13 il dente di leone (soffione *m*,
tarassaco, *pop:* bugia, piscialetto)
– *dandelion*
14 il capolino
– *flower head (capitulum)*
15 l'infruttescenza
– *infructescence*
16 l'erisimo, una ruca (ruchetta,
rucola)
– *hedge mustard, a mustard*
17 l'alisso (*pop.:* filograna)
– *stonecrop*
18 la senape (senape *f* selvatica,
senape *f* nera)
– *wild mustard (charlock, runch)*
19 il fiore
– *flower*
20 il frutto, una siliqua
– *fruit, a siliqua (pod)*
21 il ravastrello selvatico (landra,
ramolaccio)
– *wild radish (jointed charlock)*
22 il fiore
– *flower*

23 il frutto (la siliqua)
– *fruit (siliqua, pod)*
24 l'atreplice *f* comune (bietolone *m*)
– *common orache (common orach)*
25 il chenopodio (il piede anserino, il
piè d'oca)
– *goosefoot*
26 il vilucchio (vilucchione *m*), un
convolvolo
– *field bindweed (wild morning
glory), a bindweed*
27 l'anagallide *f* (bellinchina, eufra-
sia, mordigallina, alsina)
– *scarlet pimpernel (shepherd's
weatherglass, poor man's weatherglass, eye-bright)*
28 l'orzo selvatico (forasacco, orzo
murino)
– *wild barley (wall barley)*
29 il loglio (avena selvatica, zizzania)
– *wild oat*
30 la gramigna (caprinella, erba
capriola, malerba); *sim.:* la lattuga
di cane *m*
– *common couch grass (couch,
quack grass, quick grass, quitch
grass, scutch grass, twitch grass,
witchgrass)*; sim.: *bearded couch
grass, sea couch grass*
31 la galinsoga (erba magica, biondella, guada, guaderella)
– *gallant soldier*
32 il cardo selvatico (cardone *m*,
cardo asinino, scardaccione *m*,
eringio), un cardo
– *field eryngo (Watling Street thistle), a thistle*
33 l'ortica maggiore, un'ortica
– *stinging nettle, a nettle*

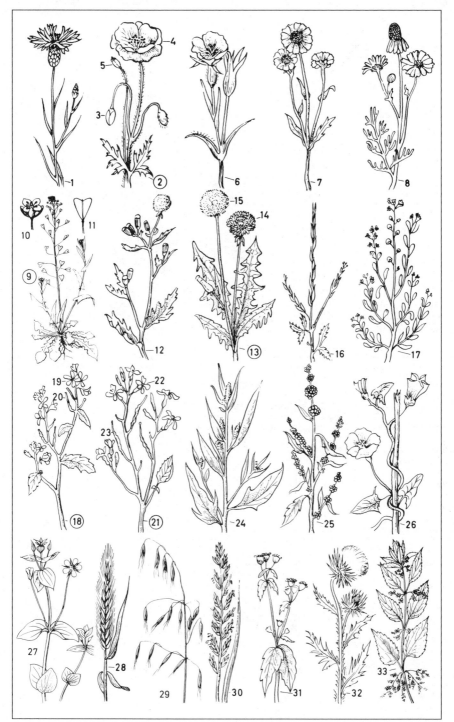

**1** l'abitazione *f*
– *house*
**2** la stalla (la scuderia)
– *stable*
**3** il gatto di casa
– *house cat (cat)*
**4** la contadina
– *farmer's wife*
**5** la scopa
– *broom*
**6** il contadino
– *farmer*
**7** la stalla
– *cowshed*
**8** il porcile
– *pigsty (sty, Am. pigpen, hogpen)*
**9** la mangiatoia all'aperto
– *outdoor trough*
**10** il maiale (il porco, il suino)
– *pig*
**11** il silo da foraggio
– *above-ground silo (fodder silo)*
**12** il tubo di caricamento del silo
– *silo pipe (standpipe for filling the silo)*
**13** la cisterna per il liquame *m*
– *liquid manure silo*
**14** l'edificio annesso
– *outhouse*
**15** la rimessa per le macchine
– *machinery shed*

**16** la porta scorrevole
– *sliding door*
**17** l'ingresso dell'officina
– *door to the workshop*
**18** l'autocarro a cassone *m* ribaltabile su tre lati *m pl*, un veicolo da trasporto
– *three-way tip-cart, a transport vehicle*
**19** il cilindro di ribaltamento
– *tipping cylinder*
**20** il timone
– *shafts*
**21** lo spandiletame
– *manure spreader (fertilizer spreader, manure distributor)*
**22** il gruppo di spandimento
– *spreader unit (distributor unit)*
**23** il rullo di spandimento
– *spreader cylinder (distributor cylinder)*
**24** il piano metallico mobile
– *movable scraper floor*

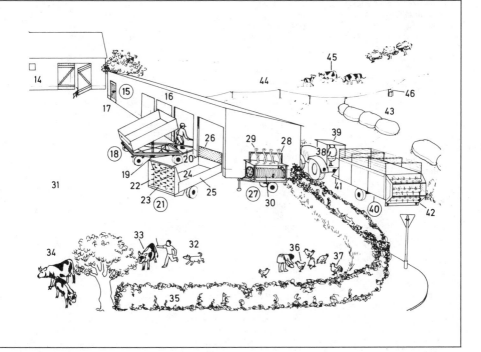

25 la sponda
 – *side planking (side board)*
26 la sponda posteriore a griglia
 – *wire mesh front*
27 il veicolo per l'irrigazione *f* a
 pioggia
 – *sprinkler cart*
28 il supporto degli irrigatori a pioggia
 – *sprinkler stand*
29 l'irrigatore *m* a pioggia, un irrigatore a pioggia rotante
 – *sprinkler, a revolving sprinkler*
30 i tubi dell'irrigatore *m* a pioggia
 – *sprinkler hoses*
31 la corte
 – *farmyard*
32 il cane
 – *watchdog*
33 il vitello
 – *calf*
34 la mucca (la vacca) da latte *m*
 – *dairy cow (milch-cow, milker)*
35 la siepe
 – *farmyard hedge*
36 il pollo (la gallina)
 – *chicken*
37 il gallo
 – *cock* (Am. *rooster*)
38 il trattore
 – *tractor*
39 il trattorista
 – *tractor driver*

40 il carro raccoglitore universale
 – *all-purpose trailer*
41 il dispositivo di raccolta (sollevato)
 – *[folded] pick-up attachment*
42 il dispositivo di scarico
 – *unloading unit*
43 il silo tubolare per foraggio
 – *polythene silo, a fodder silo*
44 il prato a pascolo
 – *meadow*
45 il bestiame al pascolo
 – *grazing cattle*
46 la recinzione elettrica del prato
 – *electrified fence*

**1-41 lavori** *m pl* **dei campi**
- *work in the fields*
**1** il maggese
- *fallow (fallow field, fallow ground)*
**2** la pietra di confine *m*
- *boundary stone*
**3** il confine, il bordo di un campo (il ciglio)
- *boundary ridge, a balk (baulk)*
**4** il campo
- *field*
**5** il bilancino
- *swingletree (Am. whiffletree, whippletree)*
**6** l'aratro
- *plough (Am. plow)*
**7** la zolla
- *clod*
**8** il solco
- *furrow*
**9** la pietra del campo
- *stone*
**10-12** la semina (la seminagione)
- *sowing*
**10** il seminatore
- *sower*
**11** la bisaccia dei semi
- *seedlip*
**12** le sementi
- *seed corn (seed)*
**13** la guardia campestre (il sorvegliante)
- *field guard*
**14** il concime chimico (il fertilizzante; tipi: concime *m* potassico, concime *m* calcareo, concime *m* azotato)
- *chemical fertilizer (artificial fertilizer); kinds: potash fertilizer, phosphoric acid fertilizer, lime fertilizer, nitrogen fertilizer*
**15** il letame (lo stallatico)
- *cartload of manure (farmyard manure, dung)*
**16** la coppia dei buoi
- *oxteam (team of oxen, Am. span of oxen)*
**17** i campi, la campagna, il terreno agricolo
- *fields (farmland)*
**18** la strada di campagna (il sentiero)
- *farm track (farm road)*
**19-30 la raccolta del fieno**
- *hay harvest (haymaking)*
**19** la falciatrice rotante con andana
- *rotary mower with swather (swath reaper)*
**20** la barra di accoppiamento
- *connecting shaft (connecting rod)*
**21** la presa di moto
- *power take-off (power take-off shaft)*
**22** il prato
- *meadow*
**23** l'andana
- *swath (swathe)*
**24** lo spandifieno
- *tedder (rotary tedder)*
**25** il fieno allargato
- *tedded hay*
**26** il ranghinatore rotante
- *rotary swather*
**27** il carro con impianto di raccolta fieno
- *trailer with pick-up attachment*
**28** il pagliaio svedese, un pagliaio
- *fence rack (rickstand), a drying rack for hay*
**29** la struttura cruciforme per il pagliaio
- *rickstand, a drying rack for hay*
**30** la struttura a piramide *f* per il pagliaio
- *hay tripod*
**31-41** la raccolta dei cereali e la preparazione per la semina
- *grain harvest and seedbed preparation*
**31** la mietitrebbia
- *combine harvester*
**32** il campo coltivato a cereali *m pl*
- *cornfield*
**33** il campo di stoppie *f pl*
- *stubble field*
**34** la balla di paglia
- *bale of straw*
**35** la pressa per le balle di paglia, una pressa ad alta pressione *f*
- *straw baler (straw press), a high-pressure baler*
**36** l'andana di paglia
- *swath (swathe) of straw (windrow of straw)*
**37** il caricaballe idraulico
- *hydraulic bale loader*
**38** il carro
- *trailer*
**39** lo spandiletame
- *manure spreader*
**40** l'aratro
- *four-furrow plough (Am. plow)*
**41** la macchina combinata per la preparazione alla semina
- *combination seed-harrow*

**1-33 la mietitrebbia** (la mietitrebbiatrice)
– *combine harvester (combine)*
1 l'andana
– *divider*
2 gli alzaspighe
– *grain lifter*
3 la barra falciante
– *cutter bar*
4 l'aspo sollevatore, un aspo con pettini *m pl* a molle *f pl*
– *pick-up reel, a spring-tine reel*
5 l'azionamento dell'aspo
– *reel gearing*
6 il cilindro alimentatore
– *auger*
7 il nastro trasportatore inclinato a catena
– *chain and slat elevator*
8 il cilindro idraulico per la regolazione del gruppo falciante
– *hydraulic cylinder for adjusting the cutting unit*
9 il dispositivo di raccolta pietre *f pl*
– *stone catcher (stone trap)*
10 il dispositivo di sgranatura
– *awner*
11 la benna trebbiante
– *concave*
12 il rullo trebbiante
– *threshing drum (drum)*
13 il rullo movimentazione paglia
– *revolving beater [for freeing straw from the drum and preparing it for the shakers]*
14 il battitore-griglia
– *straw shaker (strawwalker)*
15 il ventilatore per la pulizia a getto d'aria
– *fan for compressed-air winnowing*
16 la piattaforma di preparazione *f*
– *preparation level*
17 il crivello a lamelle *f pl*
– *louvred-type sieve*
18 il prolungamento del crivello
– *sieve extension*
19 il crivello sussidiario
– *shoe sieve (reciprocating sieve)*
20 la coclea grano
– *grain auger*
21 la chiocciola di mescolamento
– *tailings auger*
22 l'uscita
– *tailings outlet*
23 il serbatoio del grano
– *grain tank*
24 la coclea di riempimento serbatoio
– *grain tank auger*
25 la chiocciola di alimentazione *f* uscita grano
– *augers feeding to the grain tank unloader*
26 il tubo di uscita del serbatoio del grano
– *grain unloader spout*
27 l'apertura per osservazione *f* riempimento serbatoio
– *observation ports for checking tank contents*
28 il motore Diesel a 6 cilindri *m pl*
– *six-cylinder diesel engine*
29 la pompa idraulica con serbatoio olio
– *hydraulic pump with oil reservoir*
30 il rinvio asse *f* di trazione *f*
– *driving axle gearing*
31 il pneumatico dell'asse *f* di trazione *f*
– *driving wheel tyre* (Am. *tire*)
32 il pneumatico dell'asse *f* di sterzo
– *rubber-tyred* (Am. *rubber-tired*) *wheel on the steering axle*
33 il posto guida
– *driver's position*

**34-39 il trinciaforaggi**
– *self-propelled forage harvester (self-propelled field chopper)*
34 il rullo trinciante
– *cutting drum (chopper drum)*
35 il trancia-mais *m*
– *corn head*
36 la cabina di guida
– *cab (driver's cab)*
37 il camino di scarico orientabile
– *swivel-mounted spout (discharge pipe)*
38 la marmitta
– *exhaust*
39 lo sterzo posteriore
– *rear-wheel steering system*

**40-45 il voltafieno**
– *rotary swather*
40 l'albero cardanico
– *cardan shaft*
41 la ruota
– *running wheel*
42 il pettine a doppia molla
– *double spring tine*
43 la manovella
– *crank*
44 il rastrello
– *swath rake*
45 la flangia per collegamento al tre punti
– *three-point linkage*

**46-58 lo spandifieno**
– *rotary tedder*
46 il trattore
– *tractor*
47 il timone del rimorchio
– *draw bar*
48 l'albero cardanico
– *cardan shaft*
49 la presa di forza
– *power take-off (power take-off shaft)*
50 il cambio
– *gearing (gears)*
51 il mozzo
– *frame bar*
52 la trottola
– *rotating head*
53 il portapettini
– *tine bar*
54 il pettine a doppia molla
– *double spring tine*
55 il tubo di protezione *f*
– *guard rail*
56 la ruota
– *running wheel*
57 la manovella per la regolazione dell'altezza
– *height adjustment crank*
58 la regolazione della ruota
– *wheel adjustment*

**59-84 lo scavapatate**
– *potato harvester*
59 le leve di comando per gli organi macchina
– *control levers for the lifters of the digger and the hopper and for adjusting the shaft*
60 il gancio di traino regolabile
– *adjustable hitch*
61 il timone di traino
– *drawbar*
62 il sostegno timone *m*
– *drawbar support*
63 l'attacco albero cardanico
– *cardan shaft connection*
64 il rullo compressore
– *press roller*
65 il cambio per l'idraulica
– *gearing (gears) for the hydraulic system*

66 il coltro a dischi *m pl*
– *disc (disk) coulter* (Am. *colter*) *(rolling coulter)*
67 il vomere a tre corpi *m pl*
– *three-bladed share*
68 la trasmissione del coltro a dischi *m pl*
– *disc (disk) coulter* (Am. *colter*) *drive*
69 la griglia di sterro
– *open-web elevator*
70 il dispositivo di sbattimento della griglia
– *agitator*
71 il cambio a più marce *f pl*
– *multi-step reduction gearing*
72 il nastro di deposito
– *feeder*
73 il defogliatore (il cilindro rotante)
– *haulm stripper (flail rotor)*
74 la ruota di sollevamento
– *rotary elevating drum*
75 il rullo a celle *f pl*
– *mechanical tumbling separator*
76 la griglia di pulitura con elementi *m pl* elastici
– *haulm conveyor with flexible haulm strippers*
77 il dispositivo di sbattimento della griglia
– *haulm conveyor agitator*
78 la trasmissione griglia di pulitura con cinghia
– *haulm conveyor drive with V-belt*
79 il nastro con elementi *m pl* ricoperti in gomma per pulitura fine
– *studded rubber belt for sorting vines, clods and stones*
80 il nastro supplettivo
– *trash conveyor*
81 il nastro di selezione *f*
– *sorting table*
82 i rulli a dischi *m pl* di gomma per la preselezione
– *rubber-disc (rubber-disk) rollers for presorting*
83 il rullo terminale
– *discharge conveyor*
84 la tramoggia
– *endless-floor hopper*

**85-96 la macchina per la raccolta delle rape**
– *beet harvester*
85 lo scollettatore
– *topper*
86 la ruota tastatore
– *feeler*
87 il coltello scollettatore
– *topping knife*
88 la ruota di sostegno del tastatore con regolatore *m* della profondità
– *feeler support wheel with depth adjustment*
89 il dispositivo pulitura rape *f pl*
– *beet cleaner*
90 il sollevatore a pale *f pl*
– *haulm elevator*
91 la pompa idraulica
– *hydraulic pump*
92 il serbatoio aria compressa
– *compressed-air reservoir*
93 il serbatoio dell'olio
– *oil tank (oil reservoir)*
94 il dispositivo tenditore per l'elevatore *m* delle rape
– *tensioning device for the beet elevator*
95 il nastro sollevatore delle rape
– *beet elevator belt*
96 la tramoggia
– *beet hopper*

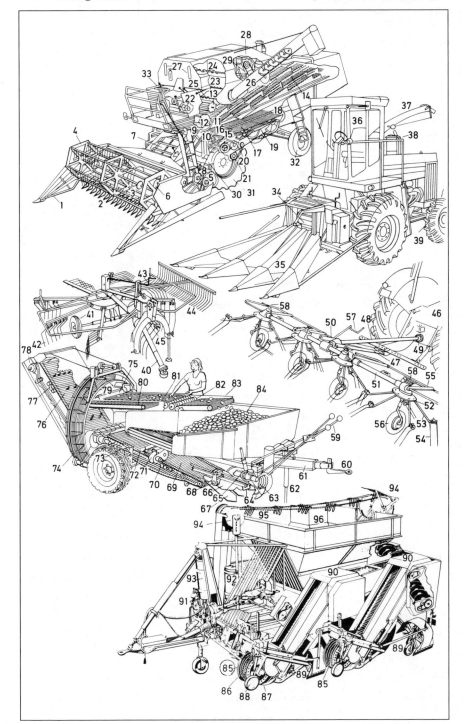

1 **il carro aratro,** un aratro monovomere (ant.)
– *wheel plough* (Am. *plow*), *a single-bottom plough* [form.]
2 le manopole
– *handle*
3 lo sterzo
– *plough* (Am. *plow*) *stilt (plough handle)*
**4-8 il corpo dell'aratro**
– *plough* (Am. *plow*) *bottom*
4 il versoio (l'orecchio)
– *mouldboard* (Am. *moldboard*)
5 la tavola di sostegno
– *landside*
6 la suola
– *sole (slade)*
7 il vomere
– *ploughshare (share,* Am. *plowshare)*
8 la trave
– *frog (frame)*
9 la bure
– *beam (plough beam,* Am. *plowbeam)*
10 il coltro dell'aratro, un coltro
– *knife coulter* (Am. *colter*), *a coulter*
11 il coltro
– *skim coulter* (Am. *colter*)
12 il traversino di guida per collegamento con le catene
– *guide-chain crossbar*
13 la catena di guida
– *guide chain*
**14-19 il carro**
– *forecarriage*
14 il giogo
– *adjustable yoke*
15 la ruota
– *land wheel*
16 la ruota del solco
– *furrow wheel*
17 la catena
– *hake chain*
18 il timone
– *draught beam (drawbar)*
19 il gancio del timone
– *hake*
**20 il trattore**
– *tractor (general-purpose tractor)*
21 il telaio di protezione *f*
– *cab frame (roll bar)*
22 il sedile
– *seat*
23 l'azionamento presa di forza
– *power take-off gear-change (gearshift)*
**24-29 l'idraulica** (il sollevatore)
– *power lift*
24 il pistone idraulico
– *ram piston*
25 il tirante registrabile
– *lifting rod adjustment*
26 la flangia di collegamento
– *drawbar frame*
27 il terzo punto
– *top link*
28 il braccio inferiore
– *lower link*
29 il tirante
– *lifting rod*
30 il gancio di traino
– *drawbar coupling*
31 la presa di forza
– *live power take-off (live power take-off shaft, take-off shaft)*

32 il differenziale
– *differential gear (differential)*
33 l'asse *f* non portante
– *floating axle*
34 la leva del convertitore di coppia
– *torque converter lever*
35 la leva del cambio
– *gear-change (gearshift)*
36 il riduttore
– *multi-speed transmission*
37 la frizione idraulica
– *fluid clutch (fluid drive)*
38 il cambio presa di forza
– *power take-off gear*
39 la frizione di marcia
– *main clutch*
40 la leva presa di forza con frizione *f*
– *power take-off gear-change (gearshift) with power take-off clutch*
41 lo sterzo idraulico con invertitore *m*
– *hydraulic power steering and reversing gears*
42 il serbatoio del carburante
– *fuel tank*
43 la leva del galleggiante
– *float lever*
44 il motore Diesel a quattro cilindri *m pl*
– *four-cylinder diesel engine*
45 la coppa dell'olio con pompa per lubrificazione *f* a circolazione *f* forzata
– *oil sump and pump for the pressure-feed lubrication system*
46 il serbatoio olio fresco
– *fresh oil tank*
47 l'asta regolazione *f* carreggiata
– *track rod* (Am. *tie rod*)
48 il perno collegamento asse *f* anteriore
– *front axle pivot pin*
49 la sospensione anteriore
– *front axle suspension*
50 il gancio di traino anteriore
– *front coupling (front hitch)*
51 il radiatore
– *radiator*
52 il ventilatore
– *fan*
53 la batteria
– *battery*
54 il filtro a bagno d'olio
– *oil bath air cleaner (oil bath air filter)*
**55 il coltivatore**
– *cultivator (grubber)*
56 il telaio
– *sectional frame*
57 i denti a molla
– *spring tine*
58 il vomere
– *share, a diamond-shaped share* (sim.: *chisel-shaped share*)
59 la ruota di sostegno
– *depth wheel*
60 la regolazione della profondità
– *depth adjustment*
61 il gancio di traino
– *coupling (hitch)*
**62 l'aratro voltorecchio a 180°,** un aratro
– *reversible plough* (Am. *plow*), *a mounted plough*
63 la ruota di sostegno
– *depth wheel*
**64-67 il corpo dell'aratro, il corpo di un aratro universale**
– *plough* (Am. *plow*) *bottom, a general-purpose plough bottom*

64 il versoio (l'orecchio)
– *mouldboard* (Am. *moldboard*)
65 il vomere dell'aratro, un vomere a punta
– *ploughshare (share,* Am. *plowshare), a pointed share*
66 la suola
– *sole (slade)*
67 la tavola di sostegno
– *landside*
68 il coltro
– *skim coulter* (Am. *colter*)
69 il coltro a disco
– *disc (disk) coulter* (Am. *colter*) *(rolling coulter)*
70 il telaio
– *plough* (Am. *plow*) *frame*
71 la bure
– *beam (plough beam,* Am. *plowbeam)*
72 l'attacco a tre punti *m pl*
– *three-point linkage*
73 il dispositivo per l'oscillazione *f* laterale
– *swivel mechanism*
**74 la seminatrice a righe *f pl***
– *drill*
75 il portasementi
– *seed hopper*
76 il corpo solcatore
– *drill coulter* (Am. *colter*)
77 il corpo adduttore, un tubo telescopico
– *delivery tube, a telescopic tube*
78 l'uscita sementi *f pl*
– *feed mechanism*
79 la trasmissione
– *gearbox*
80 la ruota di trazione *f*
– *drive wheel*
81 la tracciatura
– *track indicator*
**82 l'erpice *m* a dischi *m pl***
– *disc (disk) harrow, a semimounted implement*
83 la disposizione dei dischi *m pl* in croce *f*
– *discs (disks) in X-configuration*
84 il disco liscio
– *plain disc (disk)*
85 il disco segmentato
– *serrated-edge disc (disk)*
86 l'attacco rapido
– *quick hitch*
**87 l'erpice *m* combinato**
– *combination seed-harrow*
88 l'erpice m. a denti *m pl* a tre piani *m pl*
– *three-section spike-tooth harrow*
89 lo sgretolatore a due file *f pl* a tre piani *m pl*
– *three-section rotary harrow*
90 il telaio
– *frame*

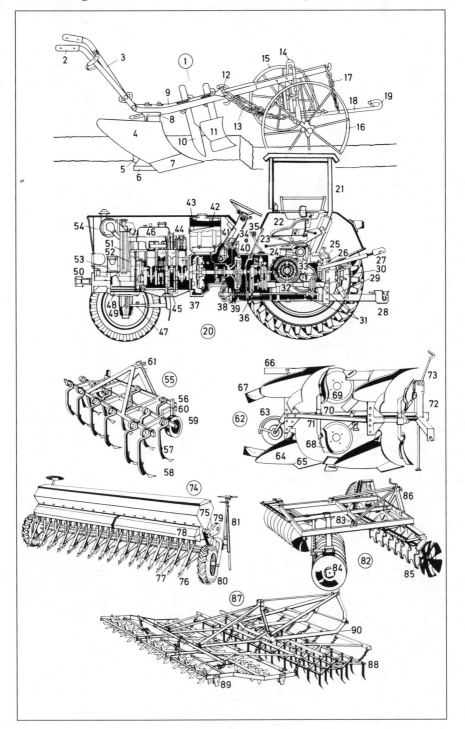

1 la zappa da scavo (zappa scavatrice)
 – *draw hoe (garden hoe)*
2 il manico della zappa
 – *hoe handle*
3 il forcone a tre denti *m pl* per for-
   aggi *m pl* (forcone *m*, forca)
 – *three-pronged (three-tined) hay*
   *fork (fork)*
4 il dente
 – *prong (tine)*
5 il forcone per patate *f pl* (forca
   per patate *f pl*)
 – *potato fork*
6 la zappa scavapatate
 – *potato hook*
7 il forcone a quattro denti *m pl* per
   letame *m* (forca per letame *m*,
   forca)
 – *four-pronged (four-tined) manure*
   *fork (fork)*
8 la zappa per letame *m*
 – *manure hoe*
9 il martello per affilare la falce
 – *whetting hammer [for scythes]*
10 la penna (del martello)
 – *peen (pane)*
11 l'incudine *f* per affilare la falce
 – *whetting anvil [for scythes]*
12 la falce
 – *scythe*
13 la lama della falce
 – *scythe blade*
14 il filo della falce
 – *cutting edge*
15 lo sperone della falce
 – *heel*
16 il manico della falce
 – *snath (snathe, snead, sneath)*
17 l'impugnatura della falce
 – *handle*
18 la guaina della falce (fodero della
   falce)
 – *scythe sheath*
19 la pietra per affilare (cote *f* )
 – *whetstone (scythestone)*
20 la rastrellina per patate *f pl*
 – *potato rake*
21 il recipiente delle patate da
   piantare
 – *potato planter*
22 la forca per scavare
 – *digging fork (fork)*
23 il rastrello di legno (rastrello, rastrello per il fieno)
 – *wooden rake (rake, hayrake)*
24 la zappa (zappa per patate *f pl*)
 – *hoe (potato hoe)*
25 la cesta delle patate, un canestro
   in filo *m* di ferro
 – *potato basket, a wire basket*
26 la carriola per trifoglio, una
   macchina per la semina del trifoglio
 – *clover broadcaster*

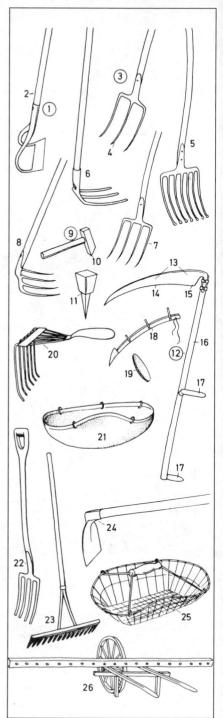

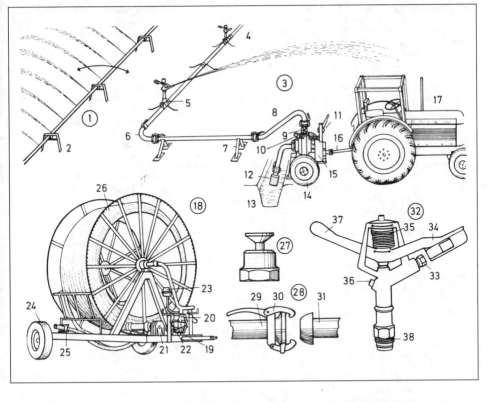

**1**  il tubo irrigatore oscillante
–  *oscillating spray line*
**2**  il cavalletto di sostegno
–  *stand (steel chair)*
**3**  l'impianto di irrigazione *f* a piog-
     gia rotante
–  *portable irrigation system*
**4**  l'irrigatore *m* a pioggia rotante
–  *revolving sprinkler*
**5**  l'attacco del tubo fisso
–  *standpipe coupler*
**6**  il gomito con giunti *m pl* cardanici
–  *elbow with cardan joint (cardan
     coupling)*
**7**  il cavalletto di sostegno
–  *pipe support (trestle)*
**8**  l'arco di collegamento alla pompa
–  *pump connection*
**9**  il raccordo di mandata
–  *delivery valve*
**10**  il manometro
–  *pressure gauge* (Am. *gage)
     (manometer)*
**11**  la pompa di svuotamento
–  *centrifugal evacuating pump*
**12**  la succhieruola (la pesca)
–  *basket strainer*
**13**  il fosso
–  *channel*

**14**  il carrello per la pompa a traino
–  *chassis of the p.t.o.-driven pump
     (power take-off-driven pump)*
**15**  la pompa a traino
–  *p.t.o.-driven (power take-off-dri-
     ven) pump*
**16**  la trasmissione cardanica
–  *cardan shaft*
**17**  il trattore
–  *tractor*
**18**  l'impianto automatico di
     irrigazione *f* a pioggia per superfi-
     ci *f pl* ampie
–  *long-range irrigation unit*
**19**  l'albero per la presa di moto
–  *drive connection*
**20**  la turbina
–  *turbine*
**21**  il cambio
–  *gearing (gears)*
**22**  il supporto regolabile
–  *adjustable support*
**23**  la pompa di svuotamento
–  *centrifugal evacuating pump*
**24**  la ruota portante
–  *wheel*
**25**  il guidatubo
–  *pipe support*
**26**  il tubo in poliestere *m*
–  *polyester pipe*

**27**  la spruzzata (il getto)
–  *sprinkler nozzle*
**28**  il tubo di innesto rapido con giun-
     to cardanico
–  *quick-fitting pipe connection with
     cardan joint*
**29**  la femmina del giunto cardanico
–  *M-cardan*
**30**  l'aggancio
–  *clamp*
**31**  il maschio del giunto cardanico
–  *V-cardan*
**32**  l'irrigatore *m* a pioggia rotante,
     un irrigatore per campi *m pl*
–  *revolving sprinkler, a field sprin-
     kler*
**33**  il giunto
–  *nozzle*
**34**  la leva oscillante
–  *breaker*
**35**  la molla della leva oscillante
–  *breaker spring*
**36**  il tappo
–  *stopper*
**37**  il contrappeso
–  *counterweight*
**38**  il filetto (la filettatura)
–  *thread*

**1-47 prodotti** *m pl* **dei campi**
(prodotti *m pl* agricoli, prodotti *m pl* agrari)
– **arable crops** *(agricultural produce, farm produce)*
**1-37 cereali** *m pl* (granaglie *f pl*, cariossidi *f pl*, grani *m pl*, biade *f pl*)
– **varieties of grain** *(grain, cereals, farinaceous plants, bread-corn)*
**1** la segale (*anche:* il grano; «grano» significa spesso frutto usato di preferenza per ottenere il pane; nella Germania settentrionale: segale *f;* nella Germania meridionale e in Italia: frumento; in Svezia e in Norvegia: orzo; in Scozia: avena; nell'America del Nord: granoturco; in Cina: riso)
– *rye (also: corn, 'corn' often meaning the main cereal of a country or region; in Northern Germany: rye; in Southern Germany and Italy: wheat; in Sweden: barley; in Scotland: oats; in North America: maize; in China: rice)*
**2** la spiga della segale, una spiga
– *ear of rye, a spike (head)*
**3** la spighetta
– *spikelet*
**4** la segale cornuta, una cariosside di segale degenerata da un fungo (parassita *m*) con permanenti filamenti intrecciati
– *ergot, a grain deformed by fungus [shown with mycelium]*
**5** il culmo (il gambo) del cereale dopo accestimento
– *corn stem after tillering*
**6** il culmo
– *culm (stalk)*
**7** il nodo del culmo
– *node of the culm*
**8** la foglia
– *leaf (grain leaf )*
**9** la guaina fogliare (la guaina)
– *leaf sheath (sheath)*
**10** la spighetta (la spicola)
– *spikelet*
**11** la gluma (la pula)
– *glume*
**12** la resta (l'arista, la barba)
– *awn (beard, arista)*
**13** il frutto (la cariosside, il chicco di grano, il seme farinoso)
– *seed (grain, kernel, farinaceous grain)*
**14** la plantula embrionale
– *embryo plant*
**15** la cariosside (il seme)
– *seed*
**16** il germoglio (l'ipocotile *m*)
– *embryo*
**17** la radichetta
– *root*

**18** i peli radicali
– *root hair*
**19** la foglia della pianta cereale
– *grain leaf*
**20** la lamina fogliare
– *leaf blade (blade, lamina)*
**21** la guaina fogliare
– *leaf sheath*
**22** la ligula fogliare
– *ligule (ligula)*
**23** il frumento
– *wheat*
**24** il farro (la spelta)
– *spelt*
**25** la cariosside; *nei paesi nordici un tempo usata immatura* (spelta verde) *come zuppa*
– *seed; unripe: green spelt, a soup vegetable*
**26** l'orzo
– *barley*
**27** l'avena, un pennacchio
– *oat panicle, a panicle*
**28** il miglio
– *millet*
**29** il riso
– *rice*
**30** il grano di riso
– *rice grain*
**31** il granoturco; *anche:* granturco (il mais, il granone, il frumentone, il grano siciliano), *tipi:* pop-corn, granturco dentato (dente di cavallo), granoturco duro, granoturco tenero, granoturco zuccherino
– *maize (Indian corn, Am. corn); varieties: popcorn, dent corn, flint corn (flint maize, Am. Yankee corn), pod corn (Am. cow corn, husk corn), soft corn (Am. flour corn, squaw corn), sweet corn*
**32** l'infiorescenza femminile
– *female inflorescence*
**33** le brattee
– *husk (shuck)*
**34** i pistilli (la barba)
– *style*
**35** l'infiorescenza maschile (il pennacchio)
– *male inflorescence (tassel)*
**36** la pannocchia del granoturco
– *maize cob (Am. corn cob)*
**37** il grano (il chicco, il seme) di mais *m*
– *maize kernel (grain of maize)*
**38-45 tuberi** *m pl* (piante *f pl* tuberose, piante *f pl* da radice *f* )
– **root crops**

**38** la patata, una pianta tuberosa; *tipi:* patata rotonda o tonda, patata ovale appiattita, patata lunga o allungata, patata reniforme; *secondo il colore:* patata bianca, gialla, rossa, blu
– *potato plant (potato), a tuberous plant;* varieties: *round, round-oval (pear-shaped), flat-oval, long, kidney-shaped potato; according to colour: white* (Am. *Irish), yellow, red, purple potato*
**39** il seme (il tubero usato per la semina)
– *seed potato (seed tuber)*
**40** il tubero di patata (patata, tubero)
– *potato tuber (potato, tuber)*
**41** la foglia di patata
– *potato top (potato haulm)*
**42** il fiore
– *flower*
**43** la bacca della patata, il frutto della patata non commestibile
– *poisonous potato berry (potato apple)*
**44** la barbabietola da zucchero, una barbabietola
– *sugar beet, a beet*
**45** la radice (la bietola)
– *root (beet)*
**46** il colletto della barbabietola
– *beet top*
**47** la foglia della barbabietola
– *beet leaf*

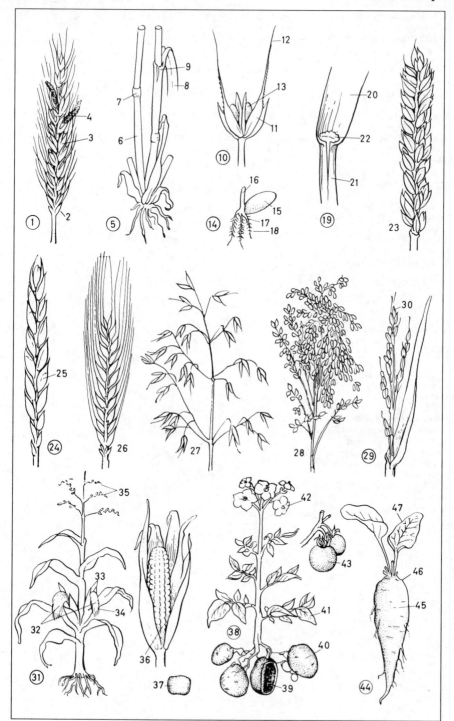

**1-28  piante** *f pl* **da foraggio** (piante coltivate per il foraggio)
– *fodder plants (forage plants) for tillage*
1  il trifoglio rosso (trifoglio comune)
– *red clover (purple clover)*
2  il trifoglio bianco (trifoglio ladino)
– *white clover (Dutch clover)*
3  il trifoglio ibrido
– *alsike clover (alsike)*
4  il trifoglio incarnato
– *crimson clover*
5  il quadrifoglio (*pop.:* il quadrifoglio portafortuna)
– *four-leaf (four-leaved) clover*
6  la vulneraria
– *kidney vetch (lady's finger, ladyfinger)*
7  il fiore della vulneraria
– *flower*
8  il follicolo della vulneraria
– *pod*
9  la medica (l'erba medica)
– *lucerne (lucern, purple medick)*
10  la lupinella
– *sainfoin (cock's head, cockshead)*
11  la serradella (il piede d'uccello)
– *bird's foot (bird-foot, bird's foot trefoil)*
12  la renaiola (la spergula), una cariofillacea
– *corn spurrey (spurrey, spurry), a spurrey (spurry)*
13  la consolida maggiore, una consolida, una borraginacea
– *common comfrey, one of the borage family (Boraginaceae)*
14  il fiore
– *flower (blossom)*
15  la fava da foraggio
– *field bean (broad bean, tick bean, horse bean)*
16  il baccello (il legume)
– *pod*
17  il lupino giallo
– *yellow lupin*
18  la veccia (veccia comune o nera)
– *common vetch*
19  il cece
– *chick-pea*
20  il girasole
– *sunflower*
21  la barbabietola da foraggio
– *mangold (mangelwurzel, mangoldwurzel, field mangel)*
22  l'avena maggiore (avena altissima)
– *false oat (oat-grass)*
23  la spighetta
– *spikelet*

24  la festuca dei prati, una festuca
– *meadow fescue grass, a fescue*
25  l'erba mazzolina (la pannocchina)
– *cock's foot (cocksfoot)*
26  il loglio (il loglio o loieto italico), *sim.:* il loglio perenne (loglio inglese)
– *Italian ryegrass;* sim.: *perennial ryegrass (English ryegrass)*
27  la coda di volpe *f*
– *meadow foxtail, a paniculate grass*
28  la selvastrella maggiore (sanguisorba, pimpinella)
– *greater burnet saxifrage*

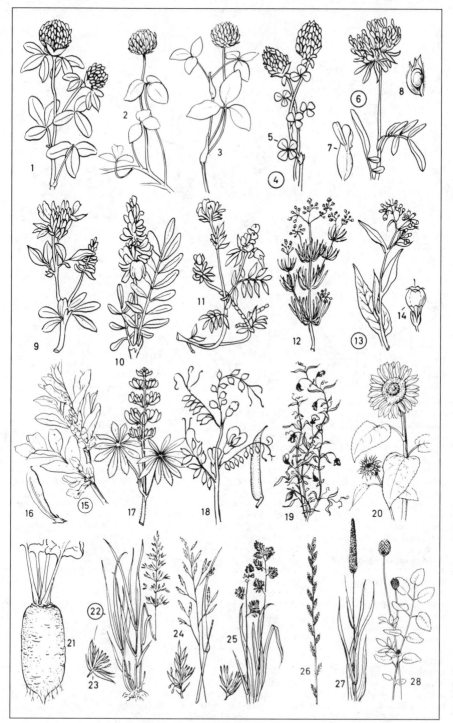

**1-14 bulldogs** *m pl* **(mastini** *m pl* **e alani** *m pl*)
– *mastiffs*
**1** il bulldog inglese (il mastino)
– *bulldog*
**2** l'orecchio, un orecchio rosato
– *ear, a rose-ear*
**3** il muso
– *muzzle*
**4** il naso
– *nose*
**5** la zampa (l'arto) anteriore
– *foreleg*
**6** la zampa (piede *m*) anteriore
– *forepaw*
**7** la zampa (l'arto) posteriore
– *hind leg*
**8** la zampa (piede) posteriore
– *hind paw*
**9** il bulldog francese (molosso)
– *pug (pug dog)*
**10** il boxer
– *boxer*
**11** il garrese
– *withers*
**12** la coda, una coda troncata
– *tail, a docked tail*
**13** il collare del cane
– *collar*

**14** l'alano tedesco (danese *m*)
– *Great Dane*
**15-18 terrier** *m pl*
– *terriers*
**15** il fox-terrier
– *wire-haired fox terrier*
**16** il bullterrier
– *bull terrier*
**17** il terrier scozzese
– *Scotch terrier (Scottish terrier)*
**18** il Bedlington terrier
– *Bedlington terrier*
**19** il pechinese
– *Pekinese (Pekingese, Pekinese dog, Pekingese dog)*
**20-22 volpini** *m pl*
– *spitzes*
**20** il volpino di Pomerania (spitz *m*)
– *spitz (Pomeranian)*
**21** il chow-chow
– *chow (chow-chow)*
**22** il cane esquimese (cane *m* da slitta, husky *m*)
– *husky*
**23 u. 24 levrieri** *m pl*
– *greyhounds* (Am. *grayhounds*)
**23** il levriero (levriere) afgano
– *Afghan (Afghan hound)*

**24** il greyhound (levriero inglese), un cane da inseguimento
– *greyhound* (Am. *grayhound*), *a courser*
**25** il pastore tedesco (cane *m* lupo alsaziano), un cane poliziotto, cane *m* da guardia, cane *m* di scorta
– *Alsatian (German sheepdog, Am. German shepherd), a police dog, watch dog, and guide dog*
**26** le labbra
– *flews (chaps)*
**27** il dobermann
– *Dobermann terrier*

**28-31 il corredo del cane**
- **dog's outfit**
**28** la spazzola per cane *m*
- *dog brush*
**29** il pettine per cane *m*
- *dog comb*
**30** il guinzaglio
- *lead (dog lead, leash);* for hunting: *leash*
**31** la museruola
- *muzzle*
**32** la ciotola (scodella)
- *feeding bowl (dog bowl)*
**33** l'osso
- *bone*
**34** il cane di Terranova
- *Newfoundland dog*
**35** lo schnauzer
- *schnauzer*
**36** il barboncino; *sim. e più piccolo:* il barboncino nano
- *poodle;* sim. and smaller: *pygmy (pigmy) poodle*
**37** il cane di San Bernardo
- *St. Bernard (St. Bernard dog)*
**38-43 cani *m pl* da caccia**
- **hunting dogs**
**38** lo spaniel cocker
- *cocker spaniel*

**39** il bassotto, un cane addestrato alla ricerca di animali *m pl* in tane *f pl* e di tartufi *m pl*
- *dachshund, a terrier*
**40** il bracco tedesco, un cane da ferma
- *German pointer*
**41** il setter inglese, un cane da ferma
- *English setter*
**42** il bracco (segugio)
- *trackhound*
**43** il pointer, un cane segugio
- *pointer, a trackhound*

**1-6 equitazione** *f* (equitazione *f* di alta scuola)
– *equitation (high school riding, haute école)*
**1** la «piaffe» (ciambella, cavallo che raspa)
– *piaffe*
**2** il passo corto (passo di maneggio)
– *walk*
**3** la passata (il passo spagnolo)
– *passage*
**4** la ballottata (la levata, la piroetta)
– *levade (pesade)*
**5** la capriola (il salto del montone)
– *capriole*
**6** la corvetta (la mezza impennata)
– *courbette (curvet)*
**7-25 i finimenti** (la bardatura) del cavallo
– *harness*
**7-13** *u.* **25 l'imbrigliatura** (la briglia)
– *bridle*
**7-11 la testiera**
– *headstall (headpiece, halter)*
**7** la museruola
– *noseband*
**8** la briglia guanciale
– *cheek piece (cheek strap)*
**9** il frontale
– *browband (front band)*
**10** la testiera
– *crownpiece*
**11** il sottogola
– *throatlatch (throatlash)*
**12** il barbazzale
– *curb chain*
**13** il morso
– *curb bit*
**14** il gancio di traino (il portatirelle)
– *hasp (hook) of the hame* (Am. *drag hook)*
**15** il collare per cavallo da tiro, un collare
– *pointed collar, a collar*
**16** la guarnizione del collare
– *trappings (side trappings)*
**17** la selletta (il sellino)
– *saddle-pad*
**18** il sottopancia
– *girth*
**19** la dossiera (la cinghia dorsale)
– *backband*
**20** la catena del rinculo (catena del timone)
– *shaft chain (pole chain)*
**21** il timone (la stanga)
– *pole*
**22** la tirella (il tiro)
– *trace*
**23** il secondo sottopancia (sottopancia *m* di emergenza)
– *second girth (emergency girth)*
**24** il tirante (la tirella, il tiro)
– *trace*

**25** la redine (le redini, la briglia)
– *reins* (Am. *lines)*
**26-36 i finimenti per il tiro pettorale**
– *breast harness*
**26** il paraocchi
– *blinker* (Am. *blinder, winker)*
**27** la catena (anello) di rinculo
– *breast collar ring*
**28** il pettorale
– *breast collar (Dutch collar)*
**29** la forcella (la forchetta)
– *fork*
**30** il sopracollare (la correggia, correggia del collo, cinghia del collo)
– *neck strap*
**31** la selletta (il sellino)
– *saddle-pad*
**32** la groppiera
– *loin strap*
**33** la redine (le redini, la briglia)
– *reins (rein,* Am. *line)*
**34** il sottocoda
– *crupper (crupper-strap)*
**35** la tirella (il tiro)
– *trace*
**36** il sottopancia
– *girth (belly-band)*
**37-49 selle** *f pl* **(selle per cavalcare)**
– *saddles*
**37-44 sella militare**
– *stock saddle* (Am. *western saddle)*
**37** il seggio della sella
– *saddle seat*
**38** l'arcione *m* anteriore (con cintura d'affardellamento)
– *pommel horn (horn)*
**39** l'arcione *m* posteriore
– *cantle*
**40** la falda
– *flap (*Am. *fender)*
**41** la barra, una parte dell'arcione *m*
– *bar*
**42** la cinghia della staffa
– *stirrup leather*
**43** la staffa
– *stirrup (stirrup iron)*
**44** la gualdrappa (coperta da sella, coperta da cavallo)
– *blanket*
**45-49 la sella inglese**
– *English saddle (cavalry saddle)*
**45** il seggio
– *seat*
**46** il pomo della sella
– *cantle*
**47** il quartiere
– *flap*
**48** l'appoggio (il falso quartiere)
– *roll (knee roll)*
**49** il cuscino
– *pad*
**50** *u.* **51 speroni** *m pl* **(sproni** *m pl)*
– *spurs*

**50** lo sperone (sprone *m*) da tacco (sperone *m* con rotella e rampone *m*)
– *box spur (screwed jack spur)*
**51** lo sperone (sprone *m*) da stivale *m* (sperone *m* a cinghia)
– *strapped jack spur*
**52** il morso semplice
– *curb bit*
**53** il morso a paletta (morso a cavaturacciolo)
– *gag bit (gag)*
**54** la striglia
– *currycomb*
**55** la brusca
– *horse brush (body brush, dandy brush)*

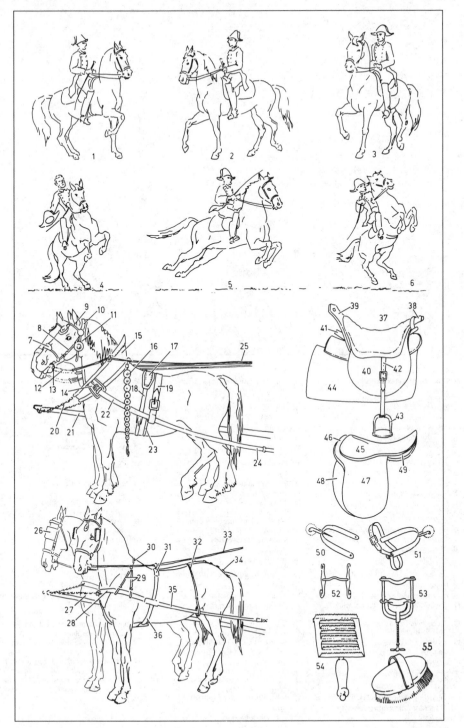

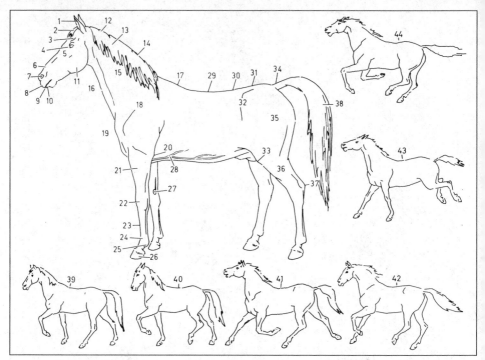

**1-38 la morfologia del cavallo**
– *points of the horse*
**1-11 la testa** (testa del cavallo)
– *head (horse's head)*
**1** l'orecchio
– *ear*
**2** il ciuffo (ciuffo anteriore)
– *forelock*
**3** la fronte
– *forehead*
**4** l'occhio
– *eye*
**5** il muso (faccia)
– *face*
**6** il naso
– *nose*
**7** la frogia (*pl.:* le narici; *pop.:* la narice)
– *nostril*
**8** il labbro superiore
– *upper lip*
**9** la bocca
– *mouth*
**10** il labbro inferiore
– *underlip (lower lip)*
**11** la mascella inferiore (la ganascia)
– *lower jaw*
**12** l'occipite *m* (nuca, cervice *f* )
– *crest (neck)*
**13** la criniera (criniera del cavallo)
– *mane (horse's mane)*
**14** la nuca
– *crest (horse's crest)*
**15** il collo
– *neck*
**16** il margine tracheale (gola)
– *throat (Am. throatlatch, throatlash)*
**17** il garrese
– *withers*

**18-27 il treno anteriore** (la parte anteriore del corpo)
– *forehand*
**18** la spalla
– *shoulder*
**19** il petto
– *breast*
**20** il gomito
– *elbow*
**21** l'avambraccio
– *forearm*
**22-26 il piede anteriore** (piede *m*)
– *forefoot*
**22** il ginocchio (il carpo)
– *knee (carpus, wrist)*
**23** lo stinco (il metacarpo, il cannone)
– *cannon*
**24** il nodello (la nocca)
– *fetlock*
**25** la pastoia
– *pastern*
**26** l'unghia (lo zoccolo)
– *hoof*
**27** la castagna (l'unghiella), una callosità
– *chestnut (castor), a callosity*
**28** la vena pettorale (vena toracica esterna)
– *spur vein*
**29** il dorso (dorso del cavallo)
– *back*
**30** il lombo
– *loins (lumbar region)*
**31** la groppa (groppa del cavallo)
– *croup (rump, crupper)*
**32** l'anca
– *hip*
**33-37 il treno posteriore** (la parte posteriore del corpo)
– *hind leg*

**33** la grassella (grascella; *anche:* la rotula, la patella)
– *stifle (stifle joint)*
**34** l'attacco della coda
– *root (dock) of the tail*
**35** la natica
– *haunch*
**36** la gamba (la sottocoscia)
– *gaskin*
**37** il garretto
– *hock*
**38** la coda (coda del cavallo)
– *tail*
**39-44 le andature del cavallo**
– *gaits of the horse*
**39** il passo
– *walk*
**40** l'ambio
– *pace*
**41** il trotto
– *trot*
**42** il piccolo galoppo
– *canter (hand gallop)*
**43 u. 44** il galoppo a briglia sciolta (galoppo allungato)
– *full gallop*
**43** il galoppo al momento dell'appoggio sul treno anteriore
– *full gallop at the moment of descent on to the two forefeet*
**44** il galoppo nel tempo di sospensione *f* (con i quattro piedi sollevati da terra)
– *full gallop at the moment when all four feet are off the ground*

Abbreviazioni:
*m* = maschio; *c* = castrato;
*f* = femmina; *g* = giovane animale
Abbreviations:
m. = *male;* c. = *castrated;*
f. = *female;* y. = *young*

**1** *u.* **2** bestiame *m* da fattoria (bestiame *m* grosso)
– *cattle and horses*
**1** la mucca, un bovino, un ruminante; *m* il toro; *c* il bue; *f* la vacca, *g* il vitello (*m* il torello, il manzo; *f* la giovenca, la manza)
– *cow, a bovine animal, a horned animal, a ruminant;* m. *bull;* c. *ox;* f. *cow;* y. *calf*
**2** il cavallo; *m* lo stallone; *c* il castrato; *f* la giumenta, *g* il puledro (*m* il puledro, *f* la puledra)
– *horse;* m. *stallion;* c. *gelding;* f. *mare;* y. *foal*
**3** il somaro (l'asino)
– *donkey*
**4** il basto
– *pack saddle (carrying saddle)*
**5** il carico (la soma)
– *pack (load)*
**6** la coda a nappa (coda a ciuffo)
– *tufted tail*
**7** la nappa
– *tuft*
**8** il mulo, un ibrido tra un somaro e una cavalla
– *mule, a cross between a male donkey and a mare*
**9** il maiale (il porco, il suino), un artiodattilo; *m* il verro; *f* la scrofa (la troia); *g* il porcellino, il lattonzolo (*più vecchio:* il magrone)
– *pig, a cloven-hoofed animal;* m. *boar;* f. *sow;* y. *piglet*

**10** il grugno
– *pig's snout (snout)*
**11** l'orecchio del maiale
– *pig's ear*
**12** la coda a cavataraccioli *m*
– *curly tail*
**13** la pecora; *m* l'ariete, *c* il castrato; *g* l'agnello
– *sheep;* m. *ram;* c. *wether;* f. *ewe;* y. *lamb*
**14** la capra
– *goat*
**15** la barba della capra
– *goat's beard*
**16** il cane, un cane di Leonberg; *m* il bracco, il cane; *f* la cagna; *g* il cucciolo
– *dog, a Leonberger;* m. *dog;* f. *bitch;* y. *pup (puppy, whelp)*
**17** il gatto (il micio), un gatto d'Angora; *f* la gatta
– *cat, an Angora cat (Persian cat);* m. *tom (tom cat)*
**18-36 animali** *m pl* **da cortile** *m*
– **small domestic animals**
**18** il coniglio domestico; *m* coniglio; *f* la coniglia
– *rabbit;* m. *buck;* f. *doe*
**19-36 pollame** *m*
– *poultry (domestic fowl)*
**19-26 il pollo**
– *chicken*
**19** la gallina
– *hen*
**20** il gozzo (l'ingluvie *f*)
– *crop (craw)*
**21** il gallo; *c* il cappone
– *cock* (Am. *rooster);* c. *capon*
**22** la cresta del gallo
– *cockscomb (comb, crest)*
**23** il lobo (il cercine, l'orecchio)
– *lap*

**24** i bargigli
– *wattle (gill, dewlap)*
**25** la coda del gallo (coda con piume *f pl* falciformi)
– *falcate (falcated) tail*
**26** lo sperone (lo sprone)
– *spur*
**27** la faraona (la gallina faraona)
– *guinea fowl*
**28** il tacchino; *f* la tacchina
– *turkey;* m. *turkey cock (gobbler);* f. *turkey hen*
**29** la ruota (la coda a ventaglio)
– *fan tail*
**30** il pavone
– *peacock*
**31** la penna di pavone *m*
– *peacock's feather*
**32** l'occhio di pavone *m* (la macchia ocellata della penna)
– *eye (ocellus)*
**33** il colombo domestico (il piccione); *f* la colomba
– *pigeon;* m. *cock pigeon*
**34** l'oca domestica; *m* l'oca maschio; *g* il papero
– *goose;* m. *gander;* y. *gosling*
**35** l'anitra (l'anatra) domestica; *m* anitra (anatra) maschio; *g* l'anatroccolo
– *duck;* m. *drake;* y. *duckling*
**36** la natatoia
– *web (palmations) of webbed foot (palmate foot)*

# 74 Pollicoltura, produzione delle uova

**1-27 la pollicoltura (allevamento intensivo)**
- *poultry farming (intensive poultry management)*

**1-17 l'allevamento al suolo**
- *straw yard (strawed yard) system*

**1** il locale per l'allevamento (il pollaio)
- *fold unit for growing stock (chick unit)*

**2** il pulcino
- *chick*

**3** la cappa calda
- *brooder (hover)*

**4** la mangiatoia lineare regolabile
- *adjustable feeding trough*

**5** il pollaio delle pollastre
- *pullet fold unit*

**6** l'abbeveratoio lineare
- *drinking trough*

**7** l'afflusso dell'acqua
- *water pipe*

**8** la lettiera
- *litter*

**9** la pollastra
- *pullet*

**10** l'impianto di ventilazione *f*
- *ventilator*

**11-17 l'allevamento di polli *m pl* da ingrasso**
- *broiler rearing (rearing of broiler chickens)*

**11** il capannone
- *chicken run (Am. fowl run)*

**12** il pollo da ingrasso
- *broiler chicken (broiler)*

**13** la mangiatoia automatica a tramoggia
- *mechanical feeder (self-feeder, feed dispenser)*

**14** la catena di sostegno
- *chain*

**15** il condotto per il mangime
- *feed supply pipe*

**16** l'abbeveratoio automatico a sifone *m*
- *mechanical drinking bowl (mechanical drinker)*

**17** l'impianto di ventilazione *f*
- *ventilator*

**18** l'allevamento a batteria
- *battery system (cage system)*

**19** la batteria
- *battery (laying battery)*

**20** la gabbia a batteria (la gabbia a scalino)
- *tiered cage (battery cage, stepped cage)*

**21** la mangiatoia lineare
- *feeding trough*

**22** la raccolta delle uova
- *egg collection by conveyor*

**23-27 l'impianto automatico per l'adduzione *f* del mangime e l'evacuazione *f* delle deiezioni**
- *mechanical feeding and dunging (manure removal, droppings removal)*

**23** il sistema di alimentazione *f* rapido per l'alimentazione *f* a batteria
- *rapid feeding system for battery feeding (mechanical feeder)*

**24** la tramoggia di riempimento
- *feed hopper*

**25** il nastro trasportatore per il mangime
- *endless-chain feed conveyor (chain feeder)*

**26** la conduttura dell'acqua
- *water pipe (liquid feed pipe)*

**27** il nastro trasportatore delle deiezioni
- *dunging chain (dunging conveyor)*

**28** l'incubatrice *f* di schiusa
- *setting and hatching machine*

**29** il tamburo di schiusa
- *ventilation drum [for the setting compartment]*

**30** il reparto di schiusa
- *hatching compartment (hatcher)*

**31** il carrello metallico di schiusa
- *metal trolley for hatching trays*

**32** la cassetta metallica di schiusa
- *hatching tray*

**33** la leva d'azionamento dell'impianto di schiusa
- *ventilation drum motor*

**34-53 la produzione di uova *f pl***
- *egg productions*

**34** il dispositivo di raccolta delle uova
- *egg collection system (egg collection)*

**35** il trasporto a livello
- *multi-tier transport*

**36** la raccolta trasversale delle uova
- *collection by pivoted fingers*

**37** il motore di azionamento
- *drive motor*

**38** il calibratore
- *sorting machine*

**39** l'alimentatore *m*
- *conveyor trolley*

**40** l'ovoscopio
- *fluorescent screen*

**41** il dispositivo aspirante per il trasporto uova *f pl*
- *suction apparatus (suction box) for transporting eggs*

**42** il ripiano per contenitori *m pl* pieni o vuoti
- *shelf for empty and full egg boxes*

**43** il carrello portauova
- *egg weighers*

**44** la cernita a seconda delle categorie
- *grading*

**45** il contenitore
- *egg box*

**46** la macchina automatica per l'imballaggio delle uova
- *fully automatic egg-packing machine*

**47** la cabina radioscopica
- *radioscope box*

**48** il tavolo radioscopico
- *radioscope table*

**49-51** l'impianto d'imballaggio delle uova
- *feeder*

**49** il dispositivo di aspirazione *f* a vuoto
- *suction transporter*

**50** il tubo di gomma per il vuoto
- *vacuum line*

**51** il tavolo di trasporto
- *supply table*

**52** il conteggio e la selezione automatica a seconda del peso
- *automatic counting and grading*

**53** il deimpilatore
- *packing box dispenser*

**54** l'anello
- *leg ring*

**55** la piastrina (il contrassegno)
- *wing tally (identification tally)*

**56** il pollo nano
- *bantam*

**57** la gallina ovaiola
- *laying hen*

**58** l'uovo (l'uovo di gallina)
- *hen's egg (egg)*

**59** il guscio (il guscio calcareo)
- *eggshell, an egg integument*

**60** la membrana testacea
- *shell membrane*

**61** la camera d'aria
- *air space*

**62** l'albume *m*
- *white [of the egg] (albumen)*

**63** la calaza
- *chalaza (Am. treadle)*

**64** la membrana vitellina
- *vitelline membrane (yolk sac)*

**65** il disco germinativo
- *blastodisc (germinal disc, cock's tread, cock's treadle)*

**66** la cicatricula (la cellula germinativa)
- *germinal vesicle*

**67** la latebra (il tuorlo bianco)
- *white*

**68** il tuorlo giallo
- *yolk*

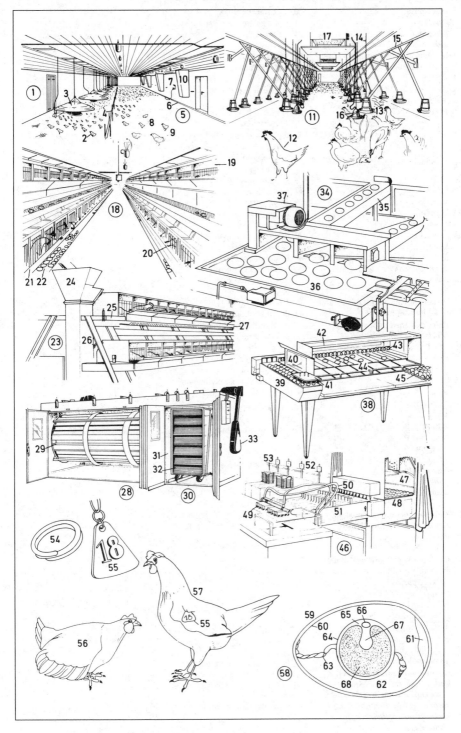

1  **la scuderia**
–  *stable*
2  il box del cavallo
–  *horse stall (stall, horse box, box)*
3  la corsia di alimentazione *f*
–  *feeding passage*
4  il pony
–  *pony*
5  la parete a griglia
–  *bars*
6  lo strame
–  *litter*
7  la balla di paglia
–  *bale of straw*
8  il lucernario
–  *ceiling light*
9  **l'ovile** *m*
–  ***sheep pen***
10  la pecora
–  *mother sheep (ewe)*
11  l'agnello
–  *lamb*
12  la rastrelliera doppia (la greppia)
–  *double hay rack*
13  il fieno
–  *hay*
14  **la stalla bovina,** una stalla a stabu-
   lazione *f* confinata
–  ***dairy cow shed*** *(cow shed) in
   which cows require tying*
15 *u.* **16** l'apparechiatura per tenere
   gli animali legati
–  *tether*
15  la catena
–  *chain*
16  il sostegno
–  *rail*
17  la mucca (la vacca) da latte *m*
–  *dairy cow (milch-cow, milker)*
18  la mammella
–  *udder*
19  il capezzolo
–  *teat*
20  il canale di scolo del colaticcio
–  *manure gutter*
21  l'impianto evacuatore a palette *f pl*
–  *manure removal by sliding bars*
22  il box
–  *short standing*
23  **il box per la mungitura (il mungi-
   toio),** un box a spina di pesce *m*
–  ***milking parlour*** *(Am. parlor), a
   herringbone parlour*
24  la fossa di lavoro
–  *working passage*
25  il mungitore
–  *milker (Am. milkman)*
26  la mungitrice
–  *teat cup cluster*
27  la conduttura del latte
–  *milk pipe*
28  la conduttura dell'aria
–  *air line*
29  la conduttura a vuoto
–  *vacuum line*

30  il portacapezzolo
–  *teat cup*
31  il tubo di livello
–  *window*
32  il raccoglitore del latte e il collettore dell'aria
–  *pulsator*
33  la fase di depressione *f*
–  *release phase*
34  la fase di fuoriuscita del latte
–  *squeeze phase*
35  **il porcile (la porcilaia)**
–  ***pigsty*** *(Am. pigpen, hogpen)*
36  lo stabbiolo dei maialini (dei por-
   cellini)
–  *pen for young pigs*
37  il trogolo
–  *feeding trough*
38  la parete divisoria
–  *partition*
39  il maiale, un maialino
–  *pig, a young pig*
40  lo stabbiolo da parto e da allevamento dei lattonzoli
–  *farrowing and store pen*
41  la scrofa
–  *sow*
42  il lattonzolo (fino a 8 settimane *f
   pl*) (il porcellino, il maialino)
–  *piglets (Am. shoats, shotes) (sucking pigs [for first 8 weeks])*
43  la griglia di protezione *f*
–  *farrowing rails*
44  il canale di scolo del liquame
–  *liquid manure channel*

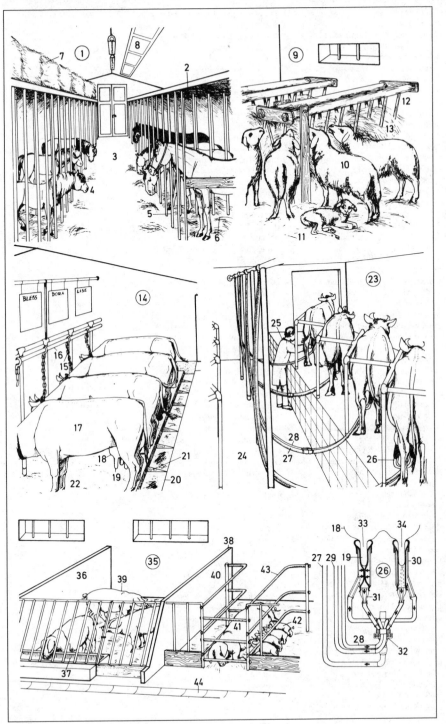

**1-48 la latteria**
- *dairy (dairy plant)*
1 **l'arrivo del latte** (il capannone di scarico dell'autobotte *f* )
- *milk reception*
2 l'autobotte *f* per il trasporto latte *m*
- *milk tanker*
3 la pompa per il latte non lavorato
- *raw milk pump*
4 il misuratore, un contatore ovale
- *flowmeter, an oval (elliptical) gear meter*
5 il serbatoio del latte non lavorato
- *raw milk storage tank*
6 il misuratore di livello
- *gauge* (Am. *gage*)
7 **la sala centrale di comando**
- *central control room*
8 l'organigramma dell'azienda
- *chart of the dairy*
9 lo schema funzionale dell'azienda
- *flow chart (flow diagram)*
10 l'indicatore *m* del livello del serbatoio
- *storage tank gauges* (Am. *gages*)
11 la consolle di comando
- *control panel*
**12-48 il laboratorio**
- *milk processing area*
12 il filtro (l'omogeneizzatore *m*)
- *sterilizer (homogenizer)*
13 il pastorizzatore
- *milk heater;* sim.: *cream heater*
14 il separatore del latte magro
- *cream separator*
15 i serbatoi del latte fresco
- *fresh milk tanks*
16 il serbatoio del latte lavorato
- *tank for sterilized milk*
17 il serbatoio del latte magro
- *skim milk (skimmed milk) tank*
18 il serbatoio del latticello
- *buttermilk tank*
19 il serbatoio della panna
- *cream tank*
20 l'impianto di riempimento e d'imballaggio del latte
- *fresh milk filling and packing plant*
21 la macchina di riempimento dei cartoni del latte
- *filling machine for milk cartons;* sim.: *milk tub filler*
22 il cartone del latte
- *milk carton*
23 il nastro trasportatore
- *conveyor belt (conveyor)*
24 il tunnel per la ritrazione dei fogli di plastica termoretraente
- *shrink-sealing machine*
25 l'imballaggio a dozzine *f pl* in fogli *m pl* di plastica
- *pack of twelve in shrink foil*
26 l'impianto di riempimento da dieci litri *m pl*
- *ten-litre filling machine*

27 l'impianto per la saldatura dei fogli di plastica
- *heat-sealing machine*
28 i fogli di plastica
- *plastic sheets*
29 il sacchetto tubolare
- *heat-sealed bag*
30 la pila delle cassette
- *crate*
31 il serbatoio per la maturazione della panna
- *cream maturing vat*
32 la macchina per la produzione e l'imballaggio del burro
- *butter shaping and packing machine*
33 la macchina per la fabbricazione del burro, un impianto per la fabbricazione del burro con panna dolce, per la produzione continua del burro
- *butter churn, a creamery butter machine for continuous butter making*
34 la linea di trasporto del burro
- *butter supply pipe*
35 l'impianto di formatura
- *shaping machine*
36 l'imballatrice *f*
- *packing machine*
37 il burro di qualità, nella confezione da 250 gr
- *branded butter in 250 g packets*
38 l'impianto di produzione *f* del formaggio fresco
- *plant for producing curd cheese (curd cheese machine)*
39 la pompa del formaggio
- *curd cheese pump*
40 la dosatrice della panna
- *cream supply pump*
41 il separatore del formaggio
- *curds separator*
42 il serbatoio del latte acido
- *sour milk vat*
43 il miscelatore
- *stirrer*
44 l'imballatrice del formaggio
- *curd cheese packing machine*
45 il formaggio imballato
- *curd cheese packet (curd cheese;* sim.: *cottage cheese)*
46 la fase di posa coperchi *m pl*
- *bottle-capping machine (capper)*
47 l'impianto per il formaggio da taglio
- *cheese machine*
48 il serbatoio refrigerante
- *rennet vat*

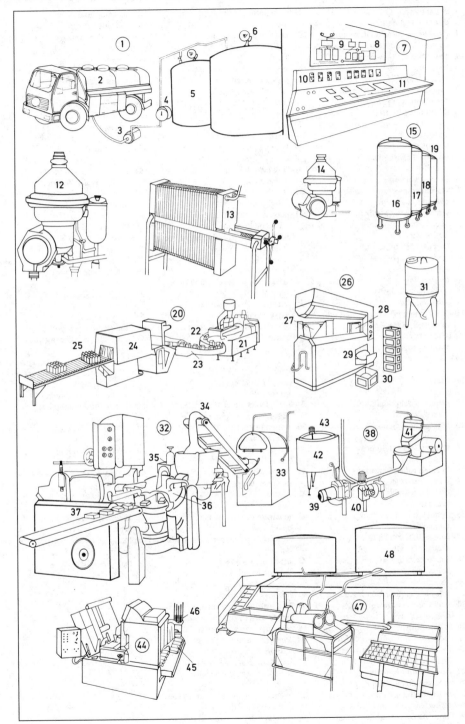

**1-25 l'ape** *f* (ape *f* da miele *m*)
– *bee (honey-bee, hive-bee)*
**1** *u.* **4-5 le classi sociali delle api**
– *castes (social classes) of bees*
**1** l'ape operaia (la pecchia, ape *f* neutra)
– *worker (worker bee)*
**2** i tre occhi composti laterali
– *three simple eyes (ocelli)*
**3** il polline raccolto
– *load of pollen on the hind leg*
**4** l'ape *f* regina
– *queen (queen bee)*
**5** il fuco (il picchione, l'ape *f* maschio)
– *drone (male bee)*
**6-9 la zampa posteriore sinistra dell'ape *f* operaia**
– *left hind leg of a worker*
**6** la cestella del polline
– *pollen basket*
**7** la spazzola
– *pollen comb (brush)*
**8** la pinza
– *double claw*
**9** il cuscinetto adesivo
– *suctorial pad*
**10-19 l'addome** *m* **dell'ape** *f* **operaia**
– *abdomen of the worker*
**10-14 il pungiglione**
– *stinging organs*
**10** l'uncino
– *barb*
**11** l'aculeo
– *sting*
**12** la guaina del pungiglione
– *sting sheath*
**13** la sacca del veleno
– *poison sac*
**14** la ghiandola velenifera
– *poison gland*
**15-19 l'apparato digerente**
– *stomachic-intestinal canal*
**15** l'intestino
– *intestine*
**16** lo stomaco
– *stomach*
**17** il muscolo contrattile
– *contractile muscle*
**18** l'ingluvie *f* (la borsa melaria)
– *honey bag (honey sac)*
**19** l'esofago
– *oesophagus (esophagus, gullet)*
**20-24 l'occhio composto**
– *compound eye*
**20** la faccetta
– *facet*
**21** il cono cristallino (il cristallino)
– *crystal cone*
**22** il segmento sensibile
– *light-sensitive section*
**23** la membrana (la fibra) del nervo ottico
– *fibre (Am. fiber) of the optic nerve*
**24** il nervo ottico
– *optic nerve*

**25** la lamella di cera
– *wax scale*
**26-30 la celletta dell'ape** *f*
– *cell*
**26** l'uovo
– *egg*
**27** la cella contenente l'uovo
– *cell with the egg in it*
**28** il baco
– *young larva*
**29** la larva
– *larva (grub)*
**30** la pupa (la ninfa)
– *chrysalis (pupa)*
**31-43 il favo del miele**
– *honeycomb*
**31** la celletta di covata
– *brood cell*
**32** la celletta chiusa (celletta opercolata) con la pupa
– *sealed (capped) cell with chrysalis (pupa)*
**33** il favo sigillato (la celletta opercolata) con miele *m*
– *sealed (capped) cell with honey (honey cell)*
**34** le cellette delle operaie
– *worker cells*
**35** le cellette d'immagazzinamento con polline *m*
– *storage cells, with pollen*
**36** le celle dei fuchi
– *drone cells*
**37** la cella della regina
– *queen cell*
**38** la regina che esce dalla cella
– *queen emerging from her cell*
**39** l'opercolo
– *cap (capping)*
**40** il telaino
– *frame*
**41** il salvadistanza
– *distance piece*
**42** il favo
– *[artificial] honeycomb*
**43** la parete interna (la base artificiale del favo)
– *septum (foundation, comb foundation)*
**44** la scatola (la gabbietta) per il trasporto delle regine
– *queen's travelling (Am. traveling) box*
**45-50 l'arnia;** *tipo:* arnia Blatt
– *frame hive (movable-frame hive, movable-comb hive [into which frames are inserted from the rear], a beehive (hive))*
**45** il melario con i favi per il miele
– *super (honey super) with honeycombs*
**46** la camera di covata (il nido) con i favi di covata
– *brood chamber with breeding combs*

**47** lo schermo divisorio
– *queen-excluder*
**48** il foro di entrata e di uscita delle api
– *entrance*
**49** il banco d'involo
– *flight board (alighting board)*
**50** la finestra
– *window*
**51** spiario di vecchio tipo
– *old-fashioned bee shed*
**52** l'arnia di paglia (arnia intrecciata)
– *straw hive (skep), a hive*
**53** lo sciame di api *f pl*
– *swarm (swarm cluster) of bees*
**54** la rete per la sciamatura
– *swarming net (bag net)*
**55** il palo uncinato (palo a gancio, a uncino)
– *hooked pole*
**56** l'apiario
– *apiary (bee house)*
**57** l'apicoltore *m*
– *beekeeper (apiarist, Am. beeman)*
**58** la rete di protezione *f*
– *bee veil*
**59** la pipa da apicoltore *m*
– *bee smoker*
**60** il favo naturale
– *natural honeycomb*
**61** lo smielatore (la centrifuga da miele)
– *honey extractor (honey separator)*
**62** *u.* **63** il miele estratto dalla centrifuga (miele *m*)
– *strained honey (honey)*
**62** il recipiente per il miele
– *honey pail*
**63** il barattolo del miele
– *honey jar*
**64** il miele in favi *m pl*
– *honey in the comb*
**65** lo stoppino
– *wax taper*
**66** la candela di cera
– *wax candle*
**67** la cera di api *f pl*
– *beeswax*
**68** l'unguento contro le punture delle api, un antidoto
– *bee sting ointment*

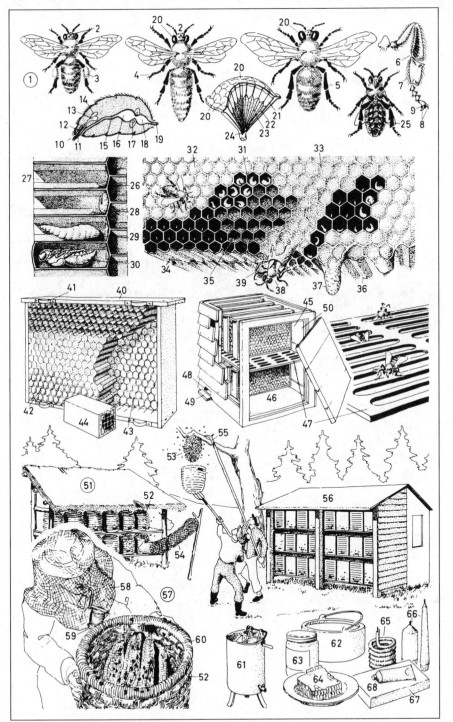

**1-21 il vigneto** (il terreno coltivato a vite *f*)
– *vineyard area*
**1** il vigneto (la vigna) coltivato a spalliera con intelaiatura metallica
– *vineyard using wire trellises for training vines*
**2-9 la vite**
– *vine (*Am. *grapevine)*
**2** il viticcio (il sarmento)
– *vine shoot*
**3** il tralcio (il getto)
– *long shoot*
**4** la foglia della vite
– *vine leaf*
**5** il grappolo con gli acini d'uva (l'uva)
– *bunch of grapes (cluster of grapes)*
**6** il tronco della vite
– *vine stem*
**7** il broncone (il palo di sostegno delle viti)
– *post (stake)*
**8** il fissaggio dell'intelaiatura metallica
– *guy (guy wire)*
**9** l'intelaiatura metallica
– *wire trellis*

**10** il recipiente (il secchio) per la vendemmia
– *tub for grape gathering*
**11** la vendemmiatrice
– *grape gatherer*
**12** la roncola (il potatoio)
– *secateurs for pruning vines*
**13** il viticoltore (il viticultore, il vignaiolo)
– *wine grower (viniculturist, viticulturist)*
**14** il ragazzo con il bigoncio
– *dosser carrier*
**15** il bigoncio (*reg:* la gerla)
– *dosser (pannier)*
**16** la trattrice (il trattore) con la botte di ammostatura
– *crushed grape transporter*
**17** la pigiadiraspatrice
– *grape crusher*
**18** l'imbuto (la tramoggia)
– *hopper*
**19** la parete inseribile su tre lati *m pl*
– *three-sided flap extension*
**20** il ripiano rialzato
– *platform*
**21** la trattrice da vigneto, un trattore a scartamento ridotto
– *vineyard tractor, a narrow-track tractor*

**1-22 la cantina dei vini** (cantina
d'invecchiamento dei vini)
– **wine cellar** *(wine vault)*
**1** la volta
– *vault*
**2** la botte
– *wine cask*
**3** la cisterna del vino (cisterna in
calcestruzzo)
– *wine vat, a concrete vat*
**4** la cisterna in acciaio inossidabile
(*anche:* cisterna in materiale sintetico)
– *stainless steel vat (also: vat made
of synthetic material)*
**5** il miscelatore a elica
– *propeller-type high-speed mixer*
**6** l'elica
– *propeller mixer*
**7** la pompa centrifuga
– *centrifugal pump*
**8** il filtro per sedimenti *m pl* in
acciaio inossidabile
– *stainless steel sediment filter*
**9** la macchina semiautomatica per
imbottigliare
– *semi-automatic circular bottling
machine*

**10** la macchina tappabottiglie *f pl*
semi-automatica con turaccioli *m
pl* di sughero
– *semi-automatic corking machine*
**11** la scansia per le bottiglie
– *bottle rack*
**12** l'aiutante *m* del cantiniere
– *cellarer's assistant*
**13** il canestro delle bottiglie
– *bottle basket*
**14** la bottiglia di vino
– *wine bottle*
**15** la caraffa
– *wine jug*
**16** la degustazione del vino
– *wine tasting*
**17** il capocantiniere (il degustatore
del vino)
– *head cellarman*
**18** il cantiniere
– *cellarman*
**19** il bicchiere da vino
– *wineglass*
**20** l'apparecchiatura per le analisi
all'istante *m*
– *inspection apparatus [for spot-
checking samples]*
**21** il torchio orizzontale
– *horizontal wine press*

**22** il motonebulizzatore
– *humidifier*

# 80 Insetti nocivi alle piante da giardino e da campo

**1-19 insetti nocivi alle piante da frutto**
- *fruit pests*

1 il bombice dispari
- *gipsy (gypsy) moth*

2 il cuscinetto feltroso (il deposito delle uova)
- *batch (cluster) of eggs*

3 il bruco
- *caterpillar*

4 la pupa (la crisalide)
- *chrysalis (pupa)*

5 l'iponomeuta, una tarma
- *small ermine moth, an ermine moth*

6 la larva
- *larva (grub)*

7 la tenda (il nido delle larve)
- *tent*

8 la larva mentre divora la nervatura della foglia
- *caterpillar skeletonizing a leaf*

9 la tortrice del melo (la tignola del melo)
- *fruit surface eating tortrix moth (summer fruit tortrix moth)*

10 l'antonomo, un coleottero parassita di alberi *m pl* da frutto, specialmente del melo
- *appleblossom weevil, a weevil*

11 il bocciolo secco dopo la foratura
- *punctured, withered flower (blossom)*

12 il foro di posa dell'uovo
- *hole for laying eggs*

13 il bombice gallonato (la neutria)
- *lackey moth*

14 il bruco
- *caterpillar*

15 le uova
- *eggs*

16 la falena invernale, una cheimatobia
- *winter moth, a geometrid*

17 il bruco
- *caterpillar*

18 la mosca delle ciliege, un tripetide
- *cherry fruit fly, a borer*

19 la larva
- *larva (grub, maggot)*

**20-27 insetti *m pl* nocivi alla vite**
- *vine pests*

20 il falso oidio, un oidio, una malattia che fa cadere le foglie
- *downy mildew, a mildew, a disease causing leaf drop*

21 l'acino colpito dalla malattia
- *grape affected with downy mildew*

22 la tortrice della vite (la tignola della vite)
- *grape-berry moth*

23 il bruco della tignola della vite, un bruco della prima generazione
- *first-generation larva of the grapeberry moth (Am. grape worm)*

24 il bruco della seconda generazione
- *second-generation larva of the grape-berry moth (Am. grape worm)*

25 la pupa (la crisalide)
- *chrysalis (pupa)*

26 la filossera radicicola, una filossera della vite
- *root louse, a grape phylloxera*

27 la galla della radice (una nodosità, una tuberosità)
- *root gall (knotty swelling of the root, nodosity, tuberosity)*

28 il culo d'oro (un bombice dal ventre bruno)
- *brown-tail moth*

29 il bruco
- *caterpillar*

30 le uova della covata
- *batch (cluster) of eggs*

31 il nido per lo svernamento
- *hibernation cocoon*

32 l'afide *m* sanguigno del melo, un afide *m* (un gorgoglione)
- *woolly apple aphid (American blight), an aphid*

33 il cancro dell'afide *m*, un'escrescenza
- *gall caused by the woolly apple aphid*

34 la colonia degli afidi
- *woolly apple aphid colony*

35 la cocciniglia di san José, (la cocciniglia perniciosa) un pidocchio
- *San-José scale, a scale insect (scale louse)*

36 le larve (*masch.*: lunghe; *femm.*: rotonde)
- *larvae (grubs) [male elongated, female round]*

**37-55 insetti *m pl* nocivi alle piante da campo**
- *field pests*

37 l'elaterio, un elateride
- *click beetle, a snapping beetle (Am. snapping bug)*

38 lo spaghetto, la larva di un elaterio
- *wireworm, larva of the click beetle*

39 la pulce di terra
- *flea beetle*

40 la cecidomia distruttrice, una cecidomia
- *Hessian fly, a gall midge (gall gnat)*

41 la larva
- *larva (grub)*

42 la nottua dei seminati (la nottua delle messi), una nottua
- *turnip moth, an earth moth*

43 la pupa (la crisalide)
- *chrysalis (pupa)*

44 l'agrotide *f*, un bruco
- *cutworm, a caterpillar*

45 la silfa (la blitofaga) della barbabietola
- *beet carrion beetle*

46 la larva
- *larva (grub)*

47 la cavolaia maggiore
- *large cabbage white butterfly*

48 il bruco della cavolaia minore
- *caterpillar of the small cabbage white butterfly*

49 il cleono della barbabietola, un curculione
- *brown leaf-eating weevil, a weevil*

50 il punto cibario
- *feeding site*

51 l'anguillola delle barbabietole, un nematode (una filaria)
- *sugar beet eelworm, a nematode (a threadworm, hairworm)*

52 la dorifora della patata
- *Colorado beetle (potato beetle)*

53 la larva matura
- *mature larva (grub)*

54 la larva giovane
- *young larva (grub)*

55 le uova
- *eggs*

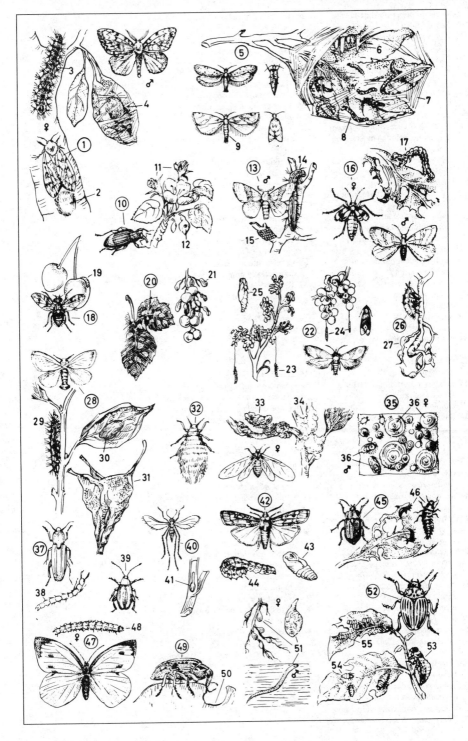

# 81 Insetti nocivi, parassiti

**1-14 insetti** *m pl* **nocivi della casa**
- *house insects*
1 la piccola mosca (mosca canicolare)
- *lesser housefly*
2 la mosca comune (mosca domestica, mosca)
- *common housefly*
3 la pupa (crisalide *f*, crisalide nel pupario)
- *chrysalis (pupa, coarctate pupa)*
4 la mosca cavallina (mosca ippobosca)
- *stable fly (biting housefly)*
5 l'antenna tri-articolata
- *trichotomous antenna*
6 il porcellino di terra (armandillio, iposode *m*)
- *wood louse (slater,* Am. *sow bug)*
7 il grillo del focolare (grillo casalingo, grillo domestico)
- *house cricket*
8 l'elitra con l'apparato sonoro
- *wing with stridulating apparatus (stridulating mechanism)*
9 il ragno domestico
- *house spider*
10 la ragnatela
- *spider's web*
11 la forbicina (forficula, forfecchia)
- *earwig*
12 le cerci (pinze *f pl*) dell'addome *m*
- *caudal pincers*
13 la tignola dei panni (il tarlo, la tarla), una tarma
- *clothes moth, a moth*
14 il lepisma (*pop.*: il pesciolino d'argento) un insetto dei Tisanuri
- *silverfish* (Am. *slicker*), *a bristletail*

**15-30 insetti** *m pl* **nocivi dei commestibili**
- *food pests (pests to stores)*
15 la mosca del formaggio
- *cheesefly*
16 la calandra granaria (calandra del grano)
- *grain weevil (granary weevil)*
17 lo scarafaggio delle cucine (blatta germanica, scarafaggio, blatta)
- *cockroach (black beetle)*
18 il tenebrione mugnaio (*larva:* verme della farina)
- *meal beetle (meal worm beetle, flour beetle)*
19 il tonchio macchiato dei fagioli (a quattro macchie *f pl*)
- *spotted bruchus*
20 la larva
- *larva (grub)*
21 la pupa (crisalide *f*)
- *chrysalis (pupa)*
22 il demeste (lardarius, vulpinus)
- *leather beetle (hide beetle)*

23 il coleottero del pane (sitodrepa panicea)
- *yellow meal beetle*
24 la pupa (crisalide *f* )
- *chrysalis (pupa)*
25 il coleottero del tabacco (lasioderma serricorne)
- *cigarette beetle (tobacco beetle)*
26 la calandra del granoturco
- *maize billbug (corn weevil)*
27 la calandra dei cereali
- *one of the Cryptolestes, a grain pest*
28 la tignola fasciata della frutta
- *Indian meal moth*
29 la tignola del grano
- *Angoumois grain moth (Angoumois moth)*
30 il bruco della tignola del grano nel chicco
- *Angoumois grain moth caterpillar inside a grain kernel*

**31-42 parassiti** *m pl* **dell'uomo**
- *parasites of man*
31 l'ascaride *m*
- *round worm (maw worm)*
32 la femmina
- *female*
33 la testa
- *head*
34 il maschio
- *male*
35 la tenia (*pop.*: verme *m* solitario)
- *tapeworm, a flatworm*
36 la testa (scolice *m*), un organo che si attacca alla parete dell'intestino
- *head, a suctorial organ*
37 la ventosa
- *sucker*
38 la corona di uncini *m pl*
- *crown of hooks*
39 la cimice (cimice *f* dei letti)
- *bug (bed bug,* Am. *chinch)*
40 il pidocchio del pube (piattola, piattone *m*)
- *crab louse (a human louse)*
41 il pidocchio dei vestiti, un parassita del corpo umano
- *clothes louse (body louse, a human louse)*
42 la pulce, un parassita del corpo umano
- *flea (human flea, common flea)*
43 la glossina (la mosca tsè-tsè)
- *tsetse fly*
44 l'anofele *m* della malaria
- *malaria mosquito*

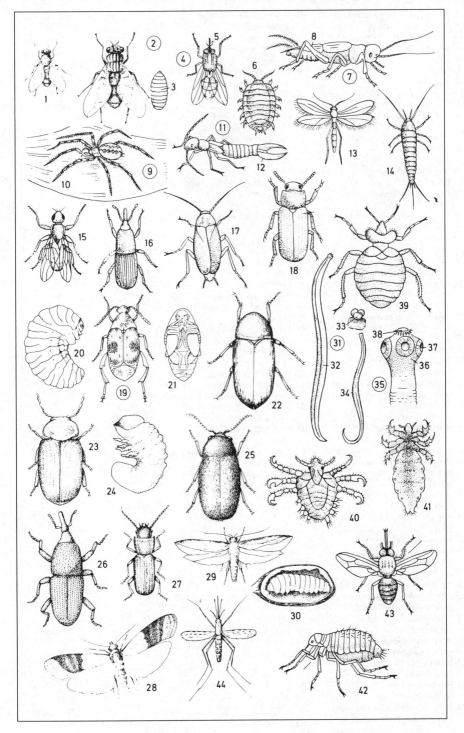

**1** il maggiolino (la melatonta, il ron-
zone), un coleottero
 – *cockchafer (May bug), a lamellicorn*
**2** il capo
 – *head*
**3** l'antenna
 – *antenna (feeler)*
**4** il protorace
 – *thoracic shield (prothorax)*
**5** lo scudetto
 – *scutellum*
**6-8** le zampe
 – *legs*
**6** la zampa anteriore
 – *front leg*
**7** la zampa mediana
 – *middle leg*
**8** la zampa posteriore
 – *back leg*
**9** l'addome *m*
 – *abdomen*
**10** l'elitra
 – *elytron (wing case)*
**11** l'ala membranosa (l'ala
chetinosa)
 – *membranous wing*
**12** la larva di maggiolino; una larva
 – *cockchafer grub, a larva*
**13** la pupa (la crisalide)
 – *chrysalis (pupa)*
**14** la processionaria, una farfalla not-
turna
 – *processionary moth, a nocturnal
moth (night-flying moth)*
**15** la farfalla
 – *moth*
**16** il bruco processionale
 – *caterpillars in procession*
**17** la monaca (la bombice monaca)
 – *nun moth (black arches moth)*
**18** la farfalla
 – *moth*
**19** le uova
 – *eggs*
**20** il bruco
 – *caterpillar*
**21** la pupa (la crisalide)
 – *chrysalis (pupa) in its cocoon*
**22** il bostrico tipografico, uno scoli-
tide (un coleottero)
 – *typographer beetle, a bark beetle*
**23** *u.* **24** le gallerie sotto la corteccia
 – *galleries under the bark*
**23** la galleria del coleottero
 – *egg gallery*
**24** la galleria delle larve
 – *gallery made by larva*
**25** la larva
 – *larva (grub)*
**26** il coleottero
 – *beetle*
**27** la sfinge del pino, una sfingide
 – *pine hawkmoth, a hawkmoth*

**28** il geometra dei pini, un
geometride
 – *pine moth, a geometrid*
**29** la farfalla maschio
 – *male moth*
**30** la farfalla femmina
 – *female moth*
**31** il bruco
 – *caterpillar*
**32** la pupa (la crisalide)
 – *chrysalis (pupa)*
**33** il cinipe della quercia, un cinipide
(un imenottero)
 – *oak-gall wasp, a gall wasp*
**34** la galla
 – *oak gall (oak apple), a gall*
**35** il cinipide
 – *wasp*
**36** la larva nella camera larvale
 – *larva (grub) in its chamber*
**37** la galla del faggio
 – *beech gall*
**38** il chermes dell'abete *m* rosso
 – *spruce-gall aphid*
**39** l'insetto alato
 – *winged aphid*
**40** la galla ad ananasso
 – *pineapple gall*
**41** l'ilobio degli abeti
 – *pine weevil*
**42** il coleottero
 – *beetle (weevil)*
**43** la tortrice della quercia
 – *green oak roller moth (green oak
tortrix), a leaf roller*
**44** il bruco
 – *caterpillar*
**45** la farfalla
 – *moth*
**46** la nottua del pino, una nottuide
 – *pine beauty*
**47** il bruco
 – *caterpillar*
**48** la farfalla
 – *moth*

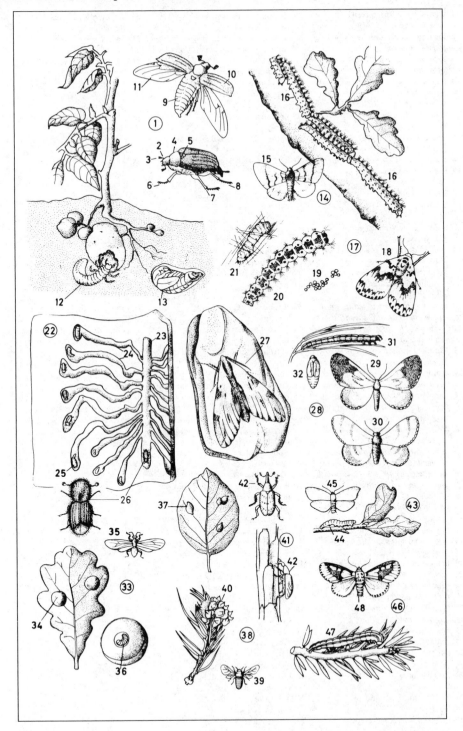

1 l'irrorazione *f* del terreno
– *area spraying*
2 l'irroratore *m* multiplo
– *tractor-mounted sprayer*
3 le barre irroranti
– *spray boom*
4 l'ugello piatto
– *fan nozzle*
5 il serbatoio per il liquido da spargere
– *spray fluid tank*
6 il serbatoio in resina espansa per la schiuma
– *foam canister for blob marking*
7 la sospensione a molle *f pl*
– *spring suspension*
8 il liquido utilizzato (la spruzzaglia)
– *spray*
9 il tracciatore schiumogeno
– *blob marker*
10 la conduttura per la schiuma
– *foam feed pipe*
11 l'impianto di fumigazione *f* sotto vuoto di una manifattura di tabacchi *m pl*
– *vacuum fumigator (vacuum fumigation plant) of a tobacco factory*
12 l'autoclave *f*
– *vacuum chamber*
13 le balle di tabacco greggio
– *bales of raw tobacco*
14 il tubo del gas
– *gas pipe*
15 l'impianto mobile di fumigazione *f* per la fumigazione a acido prussico di piantoni *m pl* da erbaio, barbatelle *f pl*, semi *m pl* e sacchi *m pl* vuoti
– *mobile fumigation chamber for fumigating nursery saplings, vine layers, seeds, and empty sacks with hydrocyanic (prussic) acid*
16 il circuito
– *gas circulation unit*
17 il graticcio
– *tray*
18 la pistola a spruzzo
– *spray gun*
19 la manopola girevole per regolare i getti
– *twist grip (control grip, handle) for regulating the jet*
20 la staffa di protezione *f*
– *finger guard*
21 la leva di azionamento
– *control lever (operating lever)*
22 il tubo
– *spray tube*
23 l'ugello rotondo
– *cone nozzle*
24 lo spruzzatore a mano
– *hand spray*
25 il contenitore di plastica
– *plastic container*

26 la pompa a mano
– *hand pump*
27 la barra oscillante per irrorare il luppolo coltivato in posizione *f* inclinata
– *pendulum spray for hop growing on slopes*
28 l'ugello a pistola
– *pistol-type nozzle*
29 il tubo irrorante
– *spraying tube*
30 il tubo di gomma di allacciamento
– *hose connection*
31 i tubi spargiveleno, per spargere frumento avvelenato
– *tube for laying poisoned bait*
32 lo scacciamosche (l'acchiappamosche *m*)
– *fly swat*
33 la lancia irrorante (l'iniettore *m* di solfuro di carbonio)
– *soil injector (carbon disulphide, Am. carbon disulfide, injector) for killing the vine root louse*
34 il pedale
– *foot lever (foot pedal, foot treadle)*
35 il tubo del gas
– *gas tube*
36 la trappola per topi *m pl*
– *mousetrap*
37 la trappola per microti *m pl* e talpe *f pl*
– *vole and mole trap*
38 l'irroratrice *f* trainata per alberi *m pl* da frutto, un'irroratrice a carriola
– *mobile orchard sprayer, a wheelbarrow sprayer (carriage sprayer)*
39 il serbatoio del liquido
– *spray tank*
40 il coperchio a vite *f*
– *screw-on cover*
41 il gruppo motopompa con motore *m* a benzina
– *direct-connected motor-driven pump with petrol motor*
42 il manometro
– *pressure gauge (Am. gage) (manometer)*
43 l'irroratrice *f* a zaino
– *plunger-type knapsack sprayer*
44 il contenitore con polmone *m* compensatore (a aria compressa)
– *spray canister with pressure chamber*
45 la leva dell'irroratrice *f*
– *piston pump lever*
46 il tubo dell'irroratrice *f* con ugello
– *hand lance with nozzle*
47 l'irroratrice *f* a rimorchio
– *semi-mounted sprayer*
48 il trattore per vigneti *m pl*
– *vineyard tractor*
49 il ventilatore
– *fan*

50 il contenitore del liquido
– *spray fluid tank*
51 il filare
– *row of vines*
52 l'apparecchio per la disinfestazione a secco delle sementi
– *dressing machine (seed-dressing machine) for dry-seed dressing (seed dusting)*
53 il depolverizzatore con motore *m* elettrico
– *dedusting fan (dust removal fan) with electric motor*
54 il filtro pneumatico
– *bag filter*
55 il manicotto per l'insaccatura
– *bagging nozzle*
56 lo schermo antipolvere
– *dedusting screen (dust removal screen)*
57 il contenitore dell'acqua nebulizzata
– *water canister [containing water for spraying]*
58 lo spruzzatore
– *spray unit*
59 l'impianto trasportatore con miscelatore *m*
– *conveyor unit with mixing screw*
60 il serbatoio del disinfestante *m* con dosatore *m*
– *container for disinfectant powder with dosing mechanism*
61 la ruotina
– *castor*
62 l'agitatore *m* meccanico
– *mixing chamber*

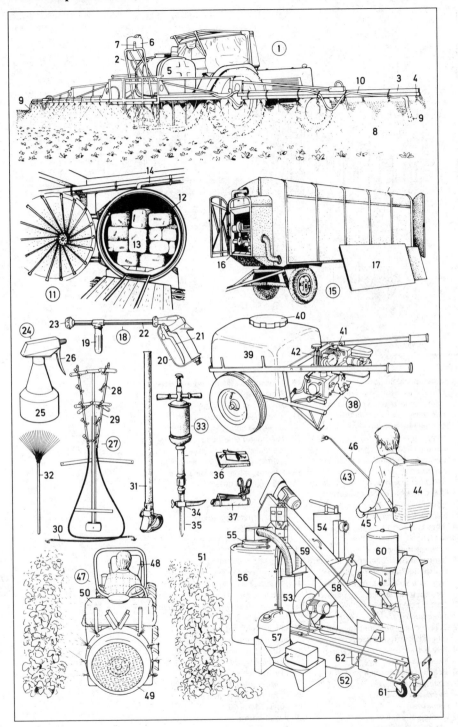

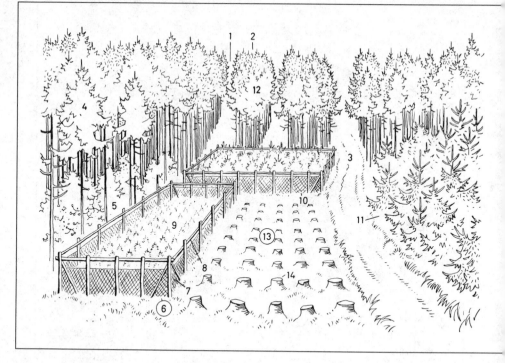

**1-34 la foresta,** un bosco
– *forest, a wood*
**1** la striscia disboscata
– *ride (aisle, lane, section line)*
**2** la zona boschiva
– *compartment (section)*
**3** il sentiero forestale per il
trasporto dei tronchi, un sentiero
nel bosco
– *wood haulage way, a forest track*
**4-14 il sistema di disboscamento
totale**
– *clear-felling system*
**4** il bosco maturo (il legno in piedi
*m pl*)
– *standing timber*
**5** il sottobosco
– *underwood (underbrush, under-
growth, brushwood,* Am. *brush)*
**6** il vivaio forestale, un vivaio; altro
tipo: il semenzaio
– *a tree nursery, seedling nursery*
**7** il recinto, una rete metallica (una
rete di protezione *f* della coltura)
– *deer fence (fence), a wire netting
fence (protective fence for
seedlings);* sim.: *rabbit fence*
**8** la stanga di protezione *f*
– *guard rail*
**9** la coltura
– *seedlings*
**10** *u.* **11** le piante giovani
– *young trees*

**10** il vivaio forestale (la coltura dopo
il trapianto)
– *tree nursery after transplanting*
**11** la boscaglia (la macchia)
– *young plantation*
**12** il bosco giovane (la macchia dopo
la potatura)
– *young plantation after brashing*
**13** il disboscamento (la superficie
disboscata, la radura)
– *clearing*
**14** il ceppo
– *tree stump (stump, stub)*

**15-37 il taglio del bosco**
– *wood cutting (timber cutting, tree felling,* Am. *lumbering)*
**15** i tronchi abbattuti
– *timber skidded to the stack (stacked timber,* Am. *yarded timber)*
**16** la catasta di legname *m,* uno stero, un mucchio di legno
– *stack of logs, one cubic metre (Am. meter) of wood*
**17** il paletto
– *post (stake)*
**18** il boscaiolo mentre fa rotolare un tronco
– *forest labourer (woodsman,* Am. *logger, lumberer, lumberjack, lumberman, timberjack) turning (Am. canting) timber*
**19** il fusto (il tronco)
– *bole (tree trunk, trunk, stem)*
**20** il tecnico forestale mentre numera il tronco
– *feller numbering the logs*
**21** il calibro d'acciaio
– *steel tree calliper (caliper)*
**22** la motosega (mentre taglia un tronco)
– *power saw (motor saw) cutting a bole*
**23** il casco di protezione *f* con visiera e cuffia di protezione *f* acustica
– *safety helmet with visor and ear pieces*

**24** gli anelli annuali
– *annual rings*
**25** il martinetto idraulico
– *hydraulic felling wedge*
**26** la tuta (camicia arancione, calzoni *m pl* verdi)
– *protective clothing [orange top, green trousers]*
**27** l'abbattimento con motosega
– *felling with a power saw (motor saw)*
**28** la tacca direzionale
– *undercut (notch, throat, gullet, mouth, sink, kerf, birdsmouth)*
**29** il taglio
– *back cut*
**30** la tasca con il cuneo
– *sheath holding felling wedge*
**31** la sezione di tronco
– *log*
**32** lo spogliatore per tagliare il sottobosco e le erbacce
– *free-cutting saw for removing underwood and weeds*
**33** la testa con sega circolare (o coltelli *m pl* rotanti)
– *circular saw (or activated blade) attachment*
**34** l'unità motore *m*
– *power unit (motor)*
**35** la lattina col lubrificante per la catena della sega
– *canister of viscous oil for the saw chain*

**36** la tanica
– *petrol canister (*Am. *gasoline canister)*
**37** l'abbattimento delle piante spontanee (lo sfoltimento)
– *felling of small timber (of small-sized thinnings) (thinning)*

**1** l'accetta
– *axe* (Am. *ax)*
**2** il taglio
– *edge (cutting edge)*
**3** il manico
– *handle (helve)*
**4** il cuneo con impugnatura in legno
e anello
– *felling wedge (falling wedge) with
wood insert and ring*
**5** il martello fenditore
– *riving hammer (cleaving hammer,
splitting hammer)*
**6** lo zappino
– *lifting hook*
**7** il giratronchi
– *cant hook*
**8** il ferro per scortecciare
– *barking iron (bark spud)*
**9** la leva di abbattimento e giratronchi *m*
– *peavy*
**10** il calibro a corsoio
– *slide calliper (caliper) (calliper
square)*
**11** la roncola, un coltello da macchia
– *billhook, a knife for lopping*
**12** il punzone a revolver *m*
– *revolving die hammer (marking
hammer, marking iron,* Am.
*marker)*
**13** la motosega
– *power saw (motor saw)*
**14** la catena della sega
– *saw chain*
**15** il freno catena con proteggimano
– *safety brake for the saw chain,
with finger guard*
**16** la spranga di guida
– *saw guide*
**17** la leva di arresto dell'acceleratore *m*
– *accelerator lock*
**18** la macchina per la sramatura
– *snedding machine (trimming
machine,* Am. *knotting machine,
limbing machine)*
**19** i cilindri di avanzamento
– *feed rolls*
**20** il coltello snodato
– *flexible blade*
**21** il braccio idraulico
– *hydraulic arm*
**22** l'utensile *m* tranciapunte
– *trimming blade*
**23** la scortecciatura del tronco
– *debarking (barking, bark stripping) of boles*
**24** il cilindro di avanzamento
– *feed roller*
**25** il rotore
– *cylinder trimmer*
**26** il coltello del rotore
– *rotary cutter*

**27** il trattore (per il trasporto di legname accatastato all'interno del
bosco)
– *short-haul skidder*
**28** la gru di carico
– *loading crane*
**29** la benna
– *log grips*
**30** i montanti di carico
– *post*
**31** lo sterzo articolato
– *Ackermann steering system*
**32** la catasta alla rinfusa di tronchi *m pl*
– *log dump*
**33** la numerazione
– *number (identification number)*
**34** il trattore per il traino dei tronchi
– *skidder*
**35** lo scudo frontale
– *front blade (front plate)*
**36** il telaio di protezione *f* (il roll-
bar)
– *crush-proof safety bonnet* (Am.
*safety hood)*
**37** lo sterzo articolato
– *Ackermann steering system*
**38** il verricello
– *cable winch*
**39** il rullo di guida
– *cable drum*
**40** lo scudo posteriore
– *rear blade (rear plate)*
**41** il tronco sospeso
– *boles with butt ends held off the
ground*
**42** il trasporto stradale di legname *m*
d'alto fusto
– *haulage of timber by road*
**43** la motrice
– *tractor (tractor unit)*
**44** la gru di carico
– *loading crane*
**45** il martinetto idraulico
– *hydraulic jack*
**46** il verricello
– *cable winch*
**47** il montante
– *post*
**48** la ralla
– *bolster plate*
**49** il rimorchio
– *rear bed (rear bunk)*

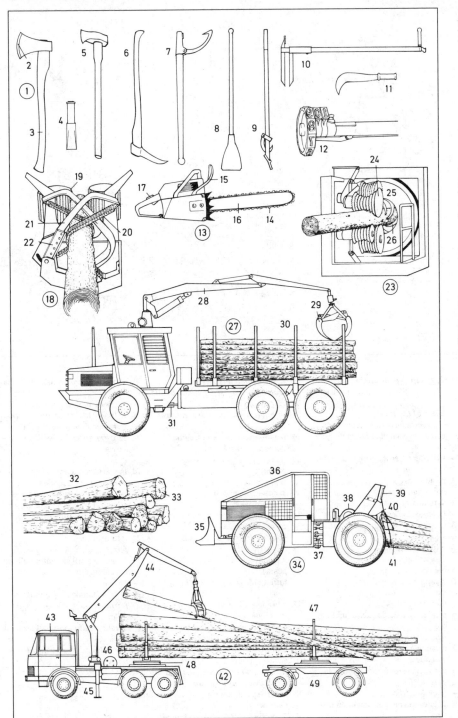

**1-52 generi** *m pl* **di caccia** (tipi *m pl* di caccia, l'arte *f* venatoria, la caccia)
– *kinds of hunting*
**1-8 la caccia da seguito** (caccia alla cerca, caccia nella riserva di caccia)
– *stalking (deer stalking, Am. still-hunting) in the game preserve*
**1** il cacciatore
– *huntsman (hunter)*
**2** la tenuta da caccia
– *hunting clothes*
**3** lo zaino (il sacco da cacciatore *m*)
– *knapsack*
**4** il fucile da caccia
– *sporting gun (sporting rifle, hunting rifle)*
**5** il cappello da cacciatore (da caccia)
– *huntsman's hat*
**6** il cannocchiale da caccia, un binocolo
– *field glasses, binoculars*
**7** il cane da caccia
– *gun dog*
**8** la traccia (l'impronta, l'orma, la pesta)
– *track (trail, hoofprints)*
**9-12 la caccia nel periodo della fregola**
– *hunting in the rutting season and the pairing season*

**9** lo schermo d'appostamento
– *hunting screen (screen, Am. blind)*
**10** lo sgabello da caccia
– *shooting stick (shooting seat, seat stick)*
**11** il gallo di monte *m* in fregola
– *blackcock, displaying*
**12** il cervo in fregola (cervo che branisce)
– *rutting stag*
**13** la cerva alla pastura
– *hind, grazing*
**14-17 la posta** (l'appostamento, la caccia alla posta)
– *hunting from a raised hide (raised stand)*
**14** il palchetto da posta alta (la posta)
– *raised hide (raised stand, high seat)*
**15** il branco (di cervi *m pl*) a tiro
– *herd within range*
**16** il passo della selvaggina
– *game path (Am. runway)*
**17** il capriolo colpito alla spalla ed ucciso con il colpo di grazia
– *roebuck, hit in the shoulder and killed by a finishing shot*
**18** la carrozza da caccia
– *phaeton*
**19-27 caccia a cattura (caccia con le panie)**
– *types of trapping*

**19** la cattura di animali *m pl* predatori
– *trapping of small predators*
**20** la trappola a cateratta (trappola per animali *m pl* predatori)
– *box trap (trap for small predators)*
**21** l'esca
– *bait*
**22** la martora, un animale predatore
– *marten, a small predator*
**23** la caccia col furetto (caccia ai conigli selvatici nella tana)
– *ferreting (hunting rabbits out of their warrens)*
**24** il furetto
– *ferret*
**25** il furettiere (il cacciatore alla caccia col furetto)
– *ferreter*
**26** la tana (tana del coniglio)
– *burrow (rabbit burrow, rabbit hole)*
**27** la rete a cuffia posta all'uscita del cunicolo
– *net (rabbit net) over the burrow opening*

28 la mangiatoia invernale per la
selvaggina
- *feeding place for game (winter
feeding place)*
29 il bracconiere (cacciatore *m* di
frodo)
- *poacher*
30 il fucile a canna corta
- *carbine, a short rifle*
31 la caccia al cinghiale
- *boar hunt*
32 il cinghiale
- *wild sow (sow, wild boar)*
33 il segugio (cane *m* da inseguimento; *più cani:* la muta)
- *boarhound (hound, hunting dog;
collectively: pack, pack of
hounds)*
**34-39 la caccia a battuta** (battuta di
caccia, battuta in cerchio, caccia
alla lepre)
- ***beating (driving, hare hunting)***
34 il fucile spianato
- *aiming position*
35 la lepre, una selvaggina da pelo
- *hare, furred game (ground game)*
36 il riporto
- *retrieving*
37 il battitore
- *beater*
38 la selvaggina abbattuta (la preda)
- *bag (kill)*

39 il carro per il trasporto della selvaggina
- *cart for carrying game*
40 la caccia agli acquatici (caccia
agli anatidi, caccia alle anatre)
- *waterfowling (wildfowling, duck
shooting, Am. duck hunting)*
41 il volo di anatre *f pl* selvatiche, la
selvaggina da penna
- *flight of wild ducks, winged game*
**42-46 la caccia col falcone** (la fal-
coneria)
- ***falconry (hawking)***
42 il falconiere
- *falconer*
43 la ricompensa al falco ritornato,
un pezzo di carne *f*
- *reward, a piece of meat*
44 il cappuccio del falcone
- *falcon's hood*
45 i geti (la pastoia)
- *jess*
46 il falcone, un uccello rapace per
la caccia (un terzuolo) all'attacco
contro un airone
- *falcon, a hawk, a male hawk (tier-
cel) swooping (stooping) on a
heron*
**47-52 la caccia alla posta in capanni**
*m pl*
- ***shooting from a butt***

47 l'albero di calata (degli uccelli)
- *tree to which birds are lured*
48 il gufo (la civetta), un uccello da
richiamo (zimbello)
- *eagle owl, a decoy bird (decoy)*
49 la gruccia
- *perch*
50 l'uccello accivettato, una cornacchia
- *decoyed bird, a crow*
51 il capanno da caccia alle cornac-
chie, un capanno da posta
- *butt for shooting crows or eagle
owls*
52 la guardiola
- *gun slit*

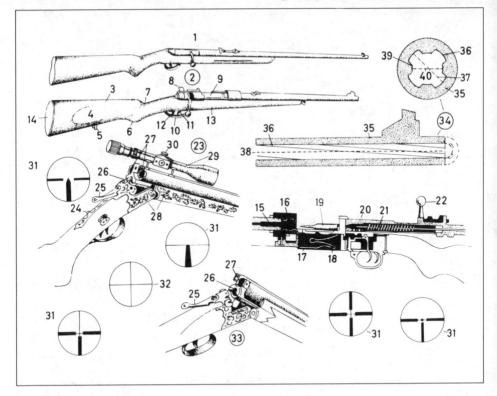

**1-40 fucili** *m pl* **da caccia**
- *sporting guns (sporting rifles, hunting rifles)*
1 il fucile a caricamento semplice
- *single-loader (single-loading rifle)*
2 il fucile a ripetizione *f*, un'arma da fuoco portatile, un ripetitore
- *repeating rifle, a small-arm (fire-arm), a repeater (magazine rifle, magazine repeater)*
3, 4, 6, 13 il fusto di legno
- *stock*
3 il calcio del fucile
- *butt*
4 la guancia del calcio del fucile [lato sinistro]
- *cheek [on the left side]*
5 l'anello per la cinghia (la maglietta)
- *sling ring*
6 l'impugnatura a pistola
- *pistol grip*
7 il collo del calcio del fucile
- *small of the butt*
8 la sicura
- *safety catch*
9 l'otturatore *m*
- *lock*
10 il guardamano
- *trigger guard*
11 il dente di scatto
- *second set trigger (firing trigger)*
12 il grilletto
- *hair trigger (set trigger)*
13 la cassa (la parte anteriore del calcio del fucile)
- *foregrip*

14 il calciolo
- *butt plate*
15 la camera di scoppio
- *cartridge chamber*
16 la testa della culatta mobile
- *receiver*
17 il caricatore
- *magazine*
18 la molla del caricatore
- *magazine spring*
19 la cartuccia
- *ammunition (cartridge)*
20 la camera (il ritegno) dell'otturatore *m*
- *chamber*
21 il percussore
- *firing pin (striker)*
22 il manubrio dell'otturatore *m*
- *bolt handle (bolt lever)*
23 il drilling, un fucile a tre canne *f pl*, un fucile automatico
- *triple-barrelled (triple-barreled) rifle, a self-cocking gun*
24 il bottone di commutazione *f* (*in varie armi:* la sicura)
- *reversing catch; in various guns: safety catch*
25 la chiave di chiusura
- *sliding safety catch*
26 la canna
- *rifle barrel (rifled barrel)*
27 la canna a piombo minuto (canna a pallini *m pl*)
- *smooth-bore barrel*
28 la cesellatura
- *chasing*

29 il cannocchiale di mira
- *telescopic sight (riflescope, telescope sight)*
30 l'aggiustatore *m* di mira
- *graticule adjuster screws*
31 *u.* 32 il mirino
- *graticule (sight graticule)*
31 vari sistemi *m pl* di mira
- *various graticule systems*
32 il reticolo (la croce dei fili di mira, croce di collimazione *f*)
- *cross wires (Am. cross hairs)*
33 la doppietta (il fucile sovrapposto), un fucile a due canne *f pl*
- *over-and-under shotgun*
34 la canna rigata
- *rifled gun barrel*
35 la parete della canna
- *barrel casing*
36 la rigatura
- *rifling*
37 il calibro della rigatura
- *rifling calibre (Am. caliber)*
38 l'asse *m* dell'anima
- *bore axis*
39 la sezione dell'anima (della canna)
- *land*
40 il calibro
- *calibre (bore diameter, Am. caliber)*

**41-48 accessori** *m pl* **per la caccia**
– *hunting equipment*
**41** il coltello da caccia a doppio taglio
– *double-edged hunting knife*
**42** il coltello da caccia a taglio semplice
– *[single-edged] hunting knife*
**43-47 richiami** *m pl* **per la caccia a richiamo**
– *calls for luring game (for calling game)*
**43** il richiamo per il capriolo, un fischietto
– *roe call*
**44** il richiamo per la lepre, un fischietto
– *hare call*
**45** il richiamo per le quaglie
– *quail call*
**46** il richiamo per il cervo
– *stag call*
**47** il richiamo per la pernice
– *partridge call*
**48** la tagliola, una trappola ad archetto
– *bow trap (bow gin), a jaw trap*
**49** la cartuccia a pallini *m pl*
– *small-shot cartridge*
**50** il bossolo di cartone *m*
– *cardboard case*
**51** la carica di pallini *m pl*
– *small-shot charge*
**52** il feltro
– *felt wad*
**53** la polvere da sparo; *tipo:* la polvere nera
– *smokeless powder (different kind: black powder)*
**54** la cartuccia a palla
– *cartridge*
**55** il proiettile (la pallottola) completamente ricoperto di acciaio
– *full-jacketed cartridge*
**56** il nocciolo del proiettile in piombo dolce
– *soft-lead core*
**57** la carica di polvere *f*
– *powder charge*
**58** il fondello
– *detonator cap*
**59** la capsula fulminante (l'innesco)
– *percussion cap*
**60** il corno da caccia
– *hunting horn*
**61-64 accessori** *m pl* per pulire il fucile
– *rifle cleaning kit*
**61** la bacchetta per pulire il fucile
– *cleaning rod*
**62** lo scovolo
– *cleaning brush*
**63** la stoppa
– *cleaning tow*
**64** il doppio tirante
– *pull-through (Am. pull-thru)*
**65** l'alzo di mira, un congegno di puntamento
– *sights*
**66** la tacca di mira
– *notch (sighting notch)*
**67** la foglia dell'alzo
– *back sight leaf*
**68** la graduazione dell'alzo
– *sight scale division*
**69** il cursore dell'alzo
– *back sight slide*
**70** la tacca di ritegno a molla, un dispositivo di arresto
– *notch [to hold the spring]*
**71** il mirino
– *front sight (foresight)*

**72** la punta del mirino (*qui:* punta conica)
– *bead*
**73 balistica**
– *ballistics*
**74** l'orizzonte *m* di tiro
– *azimuth*
**75** l'angolo di tiro
– *angle of departure*
**76** l'angolo di elevazione *f*
– *angle of elevation*
**77** il vertice della traiettoria
– *apex (zenith)*
**78** l'angolo di caduta
– *angle of descent*
**79** la parabola (la traiettoria, la curva) del proiettile
– *ballistic curve*

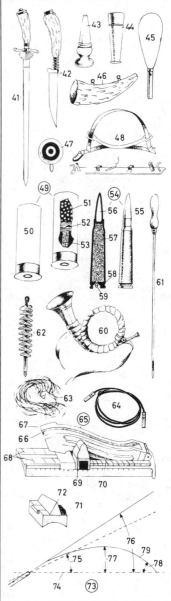

**1-27 i cervi** (cervidi *m pl,* selvaggina nobile)
- *red deer*
**1** il cervo (la cerva), un cervo giovane o una cerva non pregna; *in branco:* femmine *f pl* e piccoli *m pl* senza corna *f pl;* animale giovane: *(femmina)* cerbiatta, *(maschio)* cerbiatto
- *hind (red deer), a young hind or a dam; collectively: antlerless deer,* (y.) *calf*
**2** la lingua
- *tongue*
**3** il collo
- *neck*
**4** il cervo in fregola
- *rutting stag*
**5-11 le corna** (palchi *m pl,* corna *f pl* ramose del cervo)
- *antlers*
**5** la rosa
- *burr (rose)*
**6** il pugnale
- *brow antler (brow tine, brow point, brow snag)*
**7** l'invernino
- *bez antler (bay antler, bay, bez tine)*
**8** il mediano
- *royal antler (royal, tray)*
**9** la corona
- *surroyal antlers (surroyals)*
**10** la punta (l'estremità del ramo)
- *point (tine)*
**11** il fusto
- *beam (main trunk)*
**12** la testa
- *head*
**13** la bocca
- *mouth*
**14** la fossetta lacrimale
- *larmier (tear bag)*
**15** l'occhio
- *eye*
**16** l'orecchio
- *ear*
**17** la spalla (scapola)
- *shoulder*
**18** il lombo
- *loin*
**19** la coda
- *scut (tail)*
**20** lo specchio (macchia bianca sotto la coda)
- *rump*
**21** la coscia
- *leg (haunch)*
**22** l'arto posteriore
- *hind leg*
**23** lo sperone
- *dew claw*
**24** lo zoccolo (unghione *m*)
- *hoof*
**25** l'arto anteriore
- *foreleg*
**26** il fianco
- *flank*
**27** il collare (il velluto)
- *collar (rutting mane)*
**28-39 il capriolo**
- *roe (roe deer)*
**28** il capriolo maschio
- *roebuck (buck)*
**29-31 le corna** (i palchi, la cornatura)
- *antlers (horns)*
**29** la rosa
- *burr (rose)*

**30** il fusto con le gemme
- *beam with pearls*
**31** la punta (estremità del ramo)
- *point (tine)*
**32** l'orecchio
- *ear*
**33** l'occhio
- *eye*
**34** il capriolo femmina (la capriola), una capriola giovane senza corna *f pl* oppure una capriola vecchia non pregna
- *doe (female roe), a female fawn or a barren doe*
**35** il lombo
- *loin*
**36** lo specchio (macchia bianca sotto la coda)
- *rump*
**37** la coscia
- *leg (haunch)*
**38** la spalla
- *shoulder*
**39** il capriolo giovane, *(maschio)* caprioletto, *(femmina)* caprioletta
- *fawn,* (m.) *young buck,* (f.) *young doe*
**40-41 il daino**
- *fallow deer*
**40** il daino (daino maschio), un daino con corna *f pl* a pale *f pl, (femmina)* la daina
- *fallow buck, a buck with palmate (palmated) antlers,* (f.) *doe*
**41** la pala
- *palm*
**42** la volpe rossa, *(maschio)* volpe *f* maschio, *(femmina)* volpe *f* femmina, *il piccolo:* il volpacchiotto (cucciolo)
- *red fox,* (m.) *dog,* (f.) *vixen,* (y.) *cub*
**43** gli occhi
- *eyes*
**44** l'orecchio
- *ear*
**45** le fauci (la bocca)
- *muzzle (mouth)*
**46** le dita unghiate delle zampe
- *pads (paws)*
**47** la coda
- *brush (tail)*
**48** il tasso, *(femmina e maschio)* tasso
- *badger,* (f.) *sow*
**49** la coda
- *tail*
**50** le dita unghiate delle zampe (zampa con unghioni *m pl*)
- *paws*
**51** il cinghiale, *(maschio)* il verro, *(femmina)* la cinghiala (troia selvatica), *(il piccolo)* il cinghialetto
- *wild boar,* (m.) *boar,* (f.) *wild sow (sow),* (y.) *young boar*
**52** le setole
- *bristles*
**53** il grifo (grugno)
- *snout*
**54** il canino inferiore, *i due canini inferiori:* le zanne, *(nella femmina)* i denti, le zanne, *i due canini superiori:* le zanne superiori
- *tusk*
**55** lo scudo (l'ispessimento cutaneo sulla spalla)
- *shield*
**56** il mantello (la pelle)
- *hide*
**57** lo sperone
- *dew claw*

**58** il codino
- *tail*
**59** la lepre, *(maschio)* la lepre maschio, *(femmina)* la lepre femmina
- *hare,* (m.) *buck,* (f.) *doe*
**60** l'occhio
- *eye*
**61** l'orecchio
- *ear*
**62** la coda
- *scut (tail)*
**63** l'arto posteriore (la zampetta)
- *hind leg*
**64** l'arto anteriore
- *foreleg*
**65** il coniglio selvatico
- *rabbit*
**66** il fagiano di monte *m*
- *blackcock*
**67** la coda a lira
- *tail*
**68** le penne falcate
- *falcate (falcated) feathers*
**69** il francolino di monte *m*
- *hazel grouse (hazel hen)*
**70** la pernice (la starna)
- *partridge*
**71** il ferro di cavallo (lo spicchio di luna, la macchia scura sul dorso)
- *horseshoe (horseshoe marking)*
**72** il gallo cedrone (l'urogallo)
- *wood grouse (capercaillie)*
**73** la barba (il pizzo)
- *beard*
**74** lo specchio alare
- *axillary marking*
**75** la coda (coda a ventaglio)
- *tail (fan)*
**76** l'ala
- *wing (pinion)*
**77** il fagiano comune (fagiano da caccia), un fagiano, *(femmina)* fagianella (gallina prataiola)
- *common pheasant, a pheasant,* (m.) *cock pheasant (pheasant cock),* (f.) *hen pheasant (pheasant hen)*
**78** il ciuffo
- *plumicorn (feathered ear, ear tuft, ear, horn)*
**79** l'ala
- *wing*
**80** la coda
- *tail*
**81** la zampa
- *leg*
**82** lo sperone
- *spur*
**83** la beccaccia
- *snipe*
**84** il becco
- *bill (beak)*

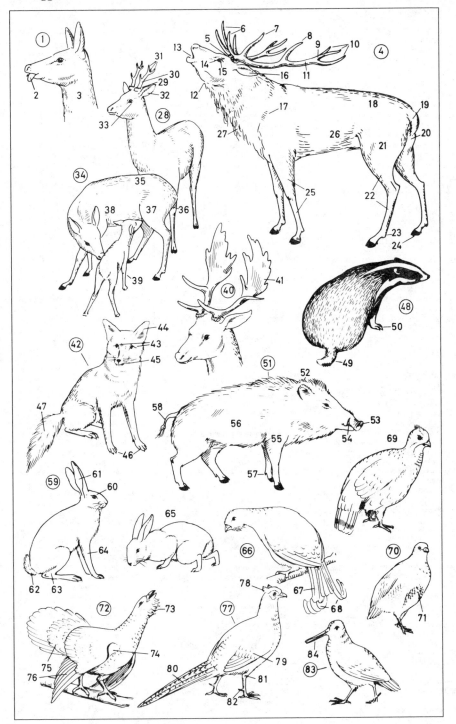

# 89 Piscicoltura e pesca sportiva

**1-19 la piscicoltura**
- *fish farming (fish culture, pisciculture)*
1 la vasca dell'acqua corrente
- *cage in running water*
2 il guadino
- *hand net (landing net)*
3 il barile semiovale per il trasporto dei pesci
- *semi-oval barrel for transporting fish*
4 il tino
- *vat*
5 il contatore del troppo pieno
- *trellis in the overflow*
6 la vasca delle trote; *sim.*: la vasca delle carpe, una vasca per la cova, la preschiusa, la schiusa e la crescita
- *trout pond; sim.: carp pond, a fry pond, fattening pond, or cleansing pond*
7 l'afflusso dell'acqua
- *water inlet (water supply pipe)*
8 il deflusso dell'acqua
- *water outlet (outlet pipe)*
9 lo scarico della vasca
- *monk*
10 la lamiera forata
- *screen*
**11-19 l'avanottiera (l'incubatoio)**
- *hatchery*
11 la spremitura del luccio
- *stripping the spawning pike (seed pike)*
12 l'uova dei pesci (il fregolo)
- *fish spawn (spawn, roe, fish eggs)*
13 il pesce femmina
- *female fish (spawner, seed fish)*
14 l'allevamento delle trote
- *trout breeding (trout rearing)*
15 il truogolo californiano
- *Californian incubator*
16 la cova delle trote
- *trout fry*
17 il recipiente per la cove dei lucci
- *hatching jar for pike*
18 la vasca con acqua corrente
- *long incubation tank*
19 il vassoio contauova
- *Brandstetter egg-counting board*
**20-94 la pesca sportiva**
- *angling*
**20-31 la pesca con la lenza di fondo**
- *bottom fishing (coarse fishing)*
20 il lancio con lenza in mano
- *line shooting*
21 le spirali della lenza
- *coils*
22 lo straccio o il pezzo di carta
- *cloth (rag) or paper*
23 l'appoggiacanne *m*
- *rod rest*
24 la scatola delle esche
- *bait tin*
25 il cestello dei pesci
- *fish basket (creel)*
26 la posta delle carpe dalla barca
- *fishing for carp from a boat*
27 la barca a remi *m pl* (la barca da pesca)
- *rowing boat (fishing boat)*
28 il portapesce
- *keep net*
29 il bilancino (una rete per pesci *m pl* da esca)
- *drop net*
30 la pertica
- *pole (punt pole, quant pole)*
31 la rete da lancio
- *casting net*

32 la canna da lancio a due mani *f pl* con mulinello a tamburo fisso
- *two-handed side cast with fixed-spool reel*
33 la posizione di uscita
- *initial position*
34 il punto di lancio
- *point of release*
35 la traiettoria della punta della canna
- *path of the rod tip*
36 la traiettoria aerea dell'esca
- *trajectory of the baited weight*
**37-94 attrezzi *f pl* per la pesca**
- *fishing tackle*
37 le pinze da pescatore *m*
- *fishing pliers*
38 il coltello da sfilettare i pesci
- *filleting knife*
39 il coltello da pescatore
- *fish knife*
40 lo slamatore
- *disgorger (hook disgorger)*
41 lo spillone per l'esca
- *bait needle*
42 l'apribocca
- *gag*
**43-48 galleggianti *m pl***
- *floats*
43 il galleggiante in sughero
- *sliding cork float*
44 il galleggiante in plastica
- *plastic float*
45 il galleggiante in penna di pavone *m*
- *quill float*
46 il galleggiante in resina espansa
- *polystyrene float*
47 il galleggiante conduttore ovalizzato
- *oval bubble float*
48 il galleggiante piombato
- *lead-weighted sliding float*
**49-58 canne *f pl* da pesca**
- *rods*
49 la canna in fibra di vetro pieno
- *solid glass rod*
50 l'impugnatura in sughero compresso
- *cork handle (cork butt)*
51 l'anello passafilo
- *spring-steel ring*
52 l'anello di punta del cimino
- *top ring (end ring)*
53 la canna telescopica
- *telescopic rod*
54 il pezzo della canna
- *rod section*
55 l'impugnatura fasciata
- *bound handle (bound butt)*
56 l'anello di ancoraggio
- *ring*
57 la canna di vetro tubolare
- *carbon-fibre rod; sim.: hollow glass rod*
58 l'anello per la canna da lancio, un occhiello in acciaio
- *all-round ring (butt ring for long cast), a steel bridge ring*
**59-64 mulinelli *m pl***
- *reels*
59 il mulinello a tamburo rotante
- *multiplying reel (multiplier reel)*
60 il rocchetto
- *line guide*
61 il mulinello a tamburo fisso
- *fixed-spool reel (stationary-drum reel)*
62 l'archetto mulinello
- *bale arm*

63 il filo
- *fishing line*
64 il controllo del lancio coll'indice *m*
- *controlling the cast with the index finger*
**65-76 esche *f pl***
- *baits*
65 la mosca
- *fly*
66 la ninfa
- *artificial nymph*
67 il lombrico
- *artificial earthworm*
68 la cavalletta
- *artificial grasshopper*
69 il pesce galleggiante
- *single-jointed plug (single-jointed wobbler)*
70 il pesce in due pezzi *m pl*
- *double-jointed plug (double-jointed wobbler)*
71 il pesce a palette *f pl*
- *round wobbler*
72 il pesce Devon
- *wiggler*
73 il cucchiaino
- *spoon bait (spoon)*
74 il cucchiaino rotante
- *spinner*
75 il cucchiaino mosca
- *spinner with concealed hook*
76 il cucchiaino ondulante con ancoretta
- *long spinner*
77 la girella
- *swivel*
78 il filo forte
- *cast (leader)*
**79-87 ami *m pl***
- *hooks*
79 l'amo da pesca
- *fish hook*
80 la punta dell'amo con ardiglione *m*
- *point of the hook with barb*
81 il collo dell'amo
- *bend of the hook*
82 la paletta (l'ochiello)
- *spade (eye)*
83 l'amo doppio
- *open double hook*
84 l'amo a forma irlandese (il crystal)
- *limerick*
85 l'amo triplo (l'ancoretta) a forma rotonda
- *closed treble hook (triangle)*
86 l'amo per le carpe
- *carp hook*
87 l'amo per le anguille
- *eel hook*
**88-92 piombi *m pl* da pesca**
- *leads (lead weights)*
88 il piombo a olivetta
- *oval lead (oval sinker)*
89 i pallini di piombo
- *lead shot*
90 il piombo a pera
- *pear-shaped lead*
91 il piombo per la pesca di fondo
- *plummet*
92 il piombo per la pesca in mare *m*
- *sea lead*
93 il passaggio per la risalita dei pesci
- *fish ladder (fish pass, fish way)*
94 la rete a sacco
- *stake net*

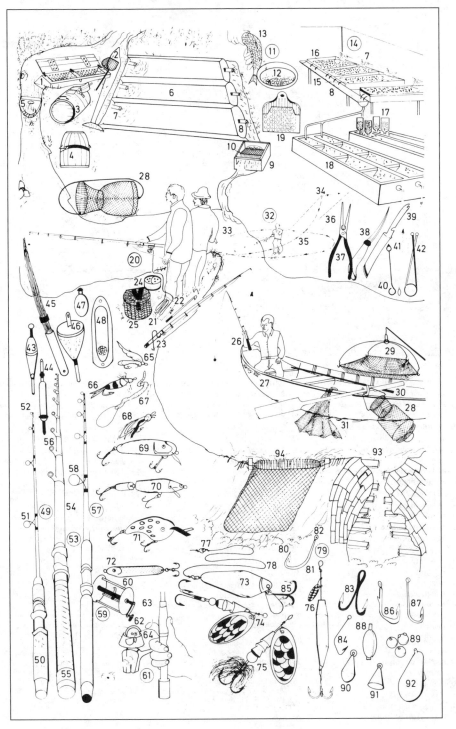

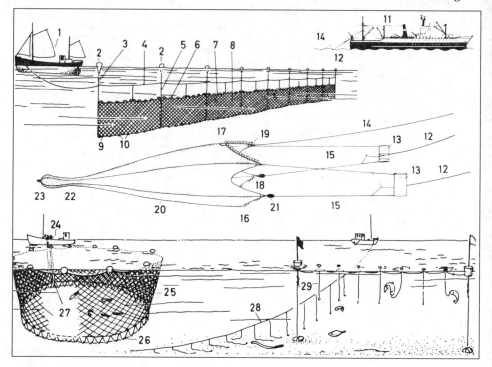

**1-23 la pesca di alto mare** *m*
– *deep-sea fishing*
**1-10 la pesca con rete** *f* **alla deriva**
– *drift net fishing*
**1** il motopeschereccio (il battello
  per la pesca delle aringhe)
– *herring lugger (fishing lugger, lugger)*
**2-10 la rete alla deriva per la pesca
  delle aringhe**
– *herring drift net*
**2** la boa (il gavitello)
– *buoy*
**3** il cavo della boa
– *buoy rope*
**4** la gomena galleggiante
– *float line*
**5** il matafione
– *seizing*
**6** il galleggiante
– *wooden float*
**7** la barriera
– *headline*
**8** la rete
– *net*
**9** il cavo inferiore
– *footrope*
**10** i piombi
– *sinkers (weights)*
**11-23 la pesca a strascico**
– *trawl fishing (trawling)*

**11** il trawler (la nave fattoria), una
  nave con rete *f* a strascico
– *factory ship, a trawler*
**12** il cavo della rete a strascico
– *warp (trawl warp)*
**13** i divergenti
– *otter boards*
**14** il cavo sonda della rete
– *net sonar cable*
**15** il penzolo
– *wire warp*
**16** l'ala
– *wing*
**17** la sonda della rete
– *net sonar device*
**18** il cavo inferiore
– *footrope*
**19** le sferette
– *spherical floats*
**20** il sacco della rete
– *belly*
**21** il peso in ferro da 1800 kg
– *1,800 kg iron weight*
**22** il fondo del sacco
– *cod end (cod)*
**23** la cima Cod per chiudere il fondo
– *cod line for closing the cod end*
**24-29 la pesca costiera**
– *inshore fishing*
**24** il peschereccio
– *fishing boat*

**25** la rete a anello, una rete alla deriva trainata
– *ring net cast in a circle*
**26** la fune metallica per chiudere la
  rete a anello
– *cable for closing the ring net*
**27** il congegno di chiusura
– *closing gear*
**28** *u.* **29** la pesca con palamite *m*
– *long-line fishing (long-lining)*
**28** il palamite
– *long line*
**29** la lenza fissa
– *suspended fishing tackle*

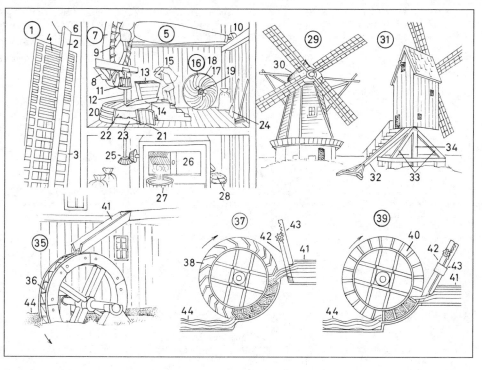

**1-34 il mulino a vento**
- *windmill*
**1** la pala del mulino a vento
- *windmill vane (windmill sail, windmill arm)*
**2** il longherone
- *stock (middling, back, radius)*
**3** il bordo
- *frame*
**4** la feritoia
- *shutter*
**5** l'albero della ruota
- *wind shaft (sail axle)*
**6** la testa della pala
- *sail top*
**7** la ruota dentata
- *brake wheel*
**8** il freno della ruota
- *brake*
**9** il dente di legno
- *wooden cog*
**10** il supporto albero
- *pivot bearing (step bearing)*
**11** il pignone dentato del mulino a vento
- *wallower*
**12** il perno del pignone
- *mill spindle*
**13** la tramoggia
- *hopper*
**14** la cassetta oscillante
- *shoe (trough, spout)*
**15** il mugnaio
- *miller*

**16** la macina (la mola, la molazza)
- *millstone*
**17** la scanalatura per l'aria
- *furrow (flute)*
**18** la scanalatura per macinare
- *master furrow*
**19** l'occhio della macina
- *eye*
**20** la cassa della macina
- *hurst (millstone casing)*
**21** il palmento
- *set of stones (millstones)*
**22** la macina corrente
- *runner (upper millstone)*
**23** la macina fissa
- *bed stone (lower stone, bedder)*
**24** la pala di legno
- *wooden shovel*
**25** la coppia conica
- *bevel gear (bevel gearing)*
**26** il buratto
- *bolter (sifter)*
**27** il tino di legno
- *wooden tub (wooden tun)*
**28** la farina
- *flour*
**29** il mulino a vento olandese
- *smock windmill (Dutch windmill)*
**30** la cupola girevole del mulino a vento
- *rotating (revolving) windmill cap*
**31** il mulino a cavalletto
- *post windmill (German windmill)*
**32** la forcella di sostegno
- *tailpole (pole)*

**33** il cavalletto
- *base*
**34** la colonna portante
- *post*
**35-44 il mulino ad acqua**
- *watermill*
**35** la ruota a cassette *f pl* con alimentazione *f* dall'alto, una ruota da mulino
- *overshot mill wheel (high-breast mill wheel), a mill wheel (water-wheel)*
**36** la cassetta
- *bucket (cavity)*
**37** la ruota alimentata dal centro
- *middleshot mill wheel (breast mill wheel)*
**38** la pala ricurva
- *curved vane*
**39** la ruota alimentata dal basso
- *undershot mill wheel*
**40** la pala dritta
- *flat vane*
**41** il canaletto d'alimentazione *f*
- *headrace (discharge flume)*
**42** la saracinesca
- *mill weir*
**43** la cascata
- *overfall (water overfall)*
**44** il canale derivatore
- *millstream (millrace, Am. raceway)*

**1-41  la maltazione** (il maltaggio)
– *preparation of malt (malting)*
**1** l'impianto di produzione *f* del malto (la torre di maltaggio)
– *malting tower (maltings)*
**2** l'immissione *f* dell'orzo
– *barley hopper*
**3** il piano di lavaggio con lavaggio ad aria
– *washing floor with compressed-air washing unit*
**4** il condensatore di scarico
– *outflow condenser*
**5** il contenitore di raccolta dell'acqua
– *water-collecting tank*
**6** il condensatore dell'acqua dolce
– *condenser for the steep liquor*
**7** il raccoglitore del refrigerante
– *coolant collecting plant*
**8** il piano di germinazione *f*
– *steeping floor (steeping tank, dressing floor)*
**9** il contenitore di acqua fredda
– *cold water tank*
**10** il contenitore di acqua calda
– *hot water tank*
**11** la camera della pompa per l'acqua
– *pump room*
**12** l'impianto pneumatico
– *pneumatic plant*
**13** l'impianto idraulico
– *hydraulic plant*
**14** il pozzo di uscita dell'aria viziata e fresca
– *ventilation shaft (air inlet and outlet)*
**15** l'esaustore *m*
– *exhaust fan*
**16-18  i piani di essicazione *f***
– *kilning floors*
**16** il preessicatoio
– *drying floor*
**17** il ventilatore del bruciatore
– *burner ventilator*
**18** l'essicatoio terminale
– *curing floor*
**19** il pozzetto di scarico dell'essicatoio
– *outlet duct from the kiln*
**20** la tramoggia del malto pronto
– *finished malt collecting hopper*
**21** la stazione di trasformazione *f*
– *transformer station*
**22** i compressori degli impianti frigoriferi
– *cooling compressors*
**23** il malto verde (l'orzo in germinazione *f* )
– *green malt (germinated barley)*
**24** il graticcio rotante
– *turner (plough)*

**25** la consolle di comando centrale con lo schema funzionale
– *central control room with flow diagram*
**26** la coclea di alimentazione *f*
– *screw conveyor*
**27** il piano di lavaggio
– *washing floor*
**28** il piano di germinazione *f*
– *steeping floor*
**29** il preessicatoio
– *drying kiln*
**30** l'essicatoio terminale
– *curing kiln*
**31** il silo dell'orzo
– *barley silo*
**32** la bilancia
– *weighing apparatus*
**33** l'elevatore *m* dell'orzo
– *barley elevator*
**34** la diramazione a tre vie *f pl*
– *three-way chute (three-way tippler)*
**35** l'elevatore *m* del malto
– *malt elevator*
**36** il depuratore
– *cleaning machine*
**37** il silo del malto
– *malt silo*
**38** l'aspirazione *f* del seme germinato
– *corn removal by suction*
**39** l'insaccatrice *f*
– *sacker*
**40** il separatore della polvere
– *dust extractor*
**41** l'entrata dell'orzo
– *barley reception*
**42-53  il processo di fermentazione *f* nella fabbrica della birra**
– *mashing process in the mashhouse*
**42** il preammostatore, per mescolare il tritello con l'acqua
– *premasher (converter) for mixing grist and water*
**43** il tino di ammostatura, per ammostare il malto
– *mash tub (mash tun) for mashing the malt*
**44** la caldaia di ammostatura, per bollire il mosto di birra
– *mash copper (mash tun, Am. mash kettle) for boiling the mash*
**45** il coperchio della caldaia
– *dome of the tun*
**46** l'agitatore *m*
– *propeller (paddle)*
**47** il portello scorrevole
– *sliding door*
**48** la conduttura dell'acqua
– *water (liquor) supply pipe*
**49** il birraio
– *brewer (master brewer, masher)*

**50** il tino di ammostatura per il deposito dei residui e il filtraggio del mosto
– *lauter tun for settling the draff (grains) and filtering off the wort*
**51** la batteria di ammostatura per controllare la limpidezza del mosto
– *lauter battery for testing the wort for quality*
**52** la caldaia del luppolo (la caldaia del mosto) per la cottura del mosto
– *hop boiler (wort boiler) for boiling the wort*
**53** il termometro con recipiente *m*, per prelevare campioni *m pl*
– *ladle-type thermometer (scoop thermometer)*

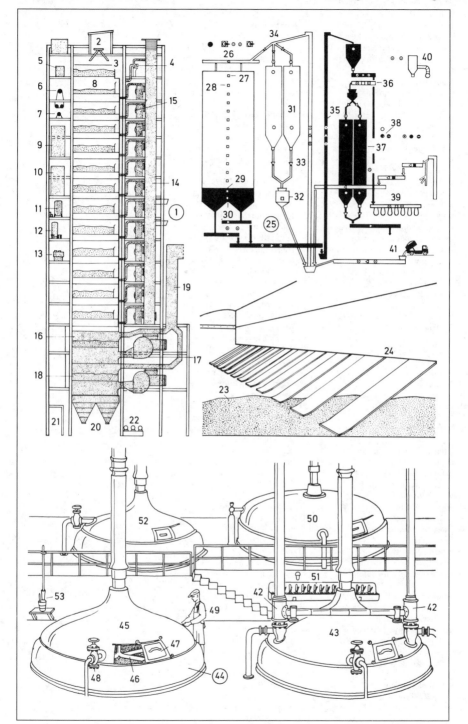

**1-31** la birreria
- *brewery (brewhouse)*
**1-5** il preraffreddamento del mosto
e il deposito del precipitato
- *wort cooling and break removal
(trub removal)*
**1** il banco di comando
- *control desk (control panel)*
**2** la caldaia a mulinello per il deposito del precipitato
- *whirlpool separator for removing
the hot break (hot trub)*
**3** il dosatore dei tripoli (dosatore
della farina fossile)
- *measuring vessel for the kieselguhr*
**4** il filtro dei tripoli
- *kieselguhr filter*
**5** il rinfrescatoio
- *wort cooler*
**6** l'impianto per la cultura del lievito puro (apparecchio per
l'estrazione *f* del lievito biologicamento puro)
- *pure culture plant for yeast (yeast
propagation plant)*
**7** il vano di fermentazione *f*
- *fermenting cellar*
**8** la vasca (il tino) di fermentazione *f*
- *fermentation vessel (fermenter)*
**9** il termometro (termometro di
ammostatura)
- *fermentation thermometer (mash
thermometer)*
**10** il mosto
- *mash*
**11** le serpentine di raffreddamento
- *refrigeration system*
**12** la cantina deposito
- *lager cellar*
**13** il passo d'uomo della cisternadeposito
- *manhole to the storage tank*
**14** il rubinetto di spillatura
- *broaching tap*
**15** il filtro della birra
- *beer filter*
**16** il deposito dei barili (delle botti)
- *barrel store*
**17** il barile (la botte) di birra, un barile (una botte) di alluminio
- *beer barrel, an aluminium (Am.
aluminum) barrel*
**18** l'impianto (di) lavaggio (delle)
bottiglie
- *bottle-washing plant*
**19** la macchina lavabottiglie
- *bottle-washing machine (bottle
washer)*
**20** l'impianto di distribuzione *f*
- *control panel*
**21** le bottiglie lavate
- *cleaned bottles*

**22** l'imbottigliamento (imbottigliatura)
- *bottling*
**23** l'elevatore *m* a forca
- *forklift truck (fork truck, forklift)*
**24** la catasta delle cassette di birra
(cassette *f pl* di birra accatastate)
- *stack of beer crates*
**25** la lattina di birra (la birra in lattina)
- *beer can*
**26** la bottiglia di birra, una bottiglia
formato europeo contenente birra
da bottiglia; *tipi di birra:* birra
chiara (bionda), birra scura
(bruna), birra di Pilsen, birra
bavarese, birra di malto, birra
forte, birra forte marzolina,
Porter, birra chiara forte (Ale),
birra scura forte (Stout), birra
forte bavarese (Salvator), birra
chiara di malto d'orzo e di frumento (birra di Goslar), birra di
frumento, birra leggera
- *beer bottle, a Eurobottle with bottled beer; kinds of beer: light beer
(lager, light ale, pale ale or bitter),
dark beer (brown ale, mild),
Pilsener beer, Munich beer, malt
beer, strong beer (bock beer),
porter, ale, stout, Salvator beer,
wheat beer, small beer*
**27** il tappo a corona
- *crown cork (crown cork closure)*
**28** la confezione non a rendere
- *disposable pack (carry-home
pack)*
**29** la bottiglia non a rendere
- *non-returnable bottle (single-trip
bottle)*
**30** il bicchiere da birra
- *beer glass*
**31** la cresta di schiuma (la schiuma)
- *head*

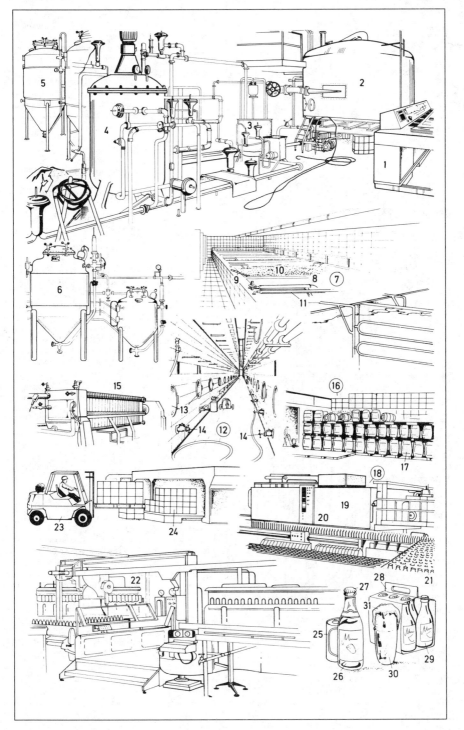

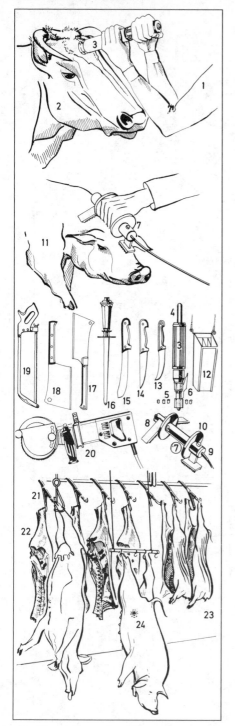

1  il macellaio
–  *slaughterman (Am. slaughterer, killer)*
2  l'animale *m* da macello, un manzo
–  *animal for slaughter, an ox*
3  la pistola sparachiodi, un apparecchio per abbattimento bovini *m pl*
–  *captive-bolt pistol (pneumatic gun), a stunning device*
4  la pistola sparachiodi
–  *bolt*
5  le capsule
–  *cartridges*
6  il ferro per finire l'animale *m*
–  *release lever (trigger)*
7  l'apparecchio elettrico per stordire l'animale *m*
–  *electric stunner*
8  l'elettrodo
–  *electrode*
9  il cavo elettrico di alimentazione *f*
–  *lead*
10  l'isolante *m* di protezione *f*
–  *hand guard (insulation)*
11  il maiale da macello
–  *pig (Am. hog) for slaughter*
12  la vaschetta portacoltelli
–  *knife case*
13  il coltello per scuoiare
–  *flaying knife*
14  il coltello per disossare (per scannare)
–  *sticking knife (sticker)*
15  il coltello per rifilare
–  *butcher's knife (butcher knife)*
16  l'affilacoltelli *m* (acciaiolo)
–  *steel*
17  il marazzo
–  *splitter*
18  la spartitrice
–  *cleaver (butcher's cleaver, meat axe (Am. meat ax))*
19  la sega da ossa *f pl*
–  *bone saw (butcher's saw)*
20  l'elettrosega per sezionare la carne
–  *meat saw for sawing meat into cuts*
**21-24  la cella frigorifera**
–  *cold store (cold room)*
21  il gancio a staffa
–  *gambrel (gambrel stick)*
22  il quarto di manzo
–  *quarter of beef*
23  la mezzena del maiale
–  *side of pork*
24  il marchio di controllo dell'ispettore *m* sanitario
–  *meat inspector's stamp*

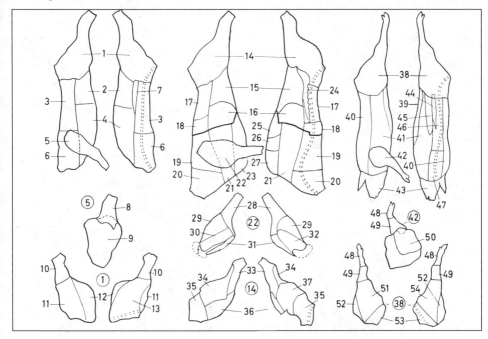

parte *f* sinistra = carne *f*
parte *f* destra = ossa *f pl*
I–IX, a–f: sigla DLG (non in uso in Italia)
*left: meat side;*
*right: bone side*

**1-13 il vitello**
– animal: *calf;* meat: *veal*
**1** la polpa di coscia
– *leg with hind knuckle*
**2** la pancia
– *flank*
**3** la costoletta di vitello
– *loin and rib*
**4** la punta di petto (la punta di petto di vitello)
– *breast (breast of veal)*
**5** la spalla anteriore
– *shoulder with fore knuckle*
**6** il collo
– *neck with scrag (scrag end)*
**7** il filetto (il filetto di vitello)
– *best end of loin (of loin of veal)*
**8** il girello anteriore
– *fore knuckle*
**9** la spalla posteriore
– *shoulder*
**10** il girello posteriore
– *hind knuckle*
**11** la noce
– *roasting round (oyster round)*
**12** il fricandò
– *cutlet for frying or braising*
**13** lo scamone
– *undercut (fillet)*
**14-37 il manzo**
– animal: *ox;* meat: *beef*
**14** la polpa di coscia posteriore
– *round with rump and shank*
**15** *u.* **16** la pancia
– *flank*
**15** il bamborino
– *thick flank*

**16** il bianco costato di pancia
– *thin flank*
**17** il roast-beef
– *sirloin*
**18** la costola della croce
– *prime rib (fore ribs, prime fore rib)*
**19** il reale (la schiena)
– *middle rib and chuck*
**20** il collo (la nuca)
– *neck*
**21** la punta di petto
– *flat rib*
**22** la polpa di spalla
– *leg of mutton piece (bladebone) with shin*
**23** il petto (il petto di manzo)
– *brisket (brisket of beef )*
**24** il filetto (il filetto di manzo)
– *fillet (fillet of beef )*
**25** la punta di petto
– *hind brisket*
**26** lo scalfo
– *middle brisket*
**27** lo sterno
– *breastbone*
**28** il muscolo anteriore
– *shin*
**29** la spalla
– *leg of mutton piece*
**30** la suora (il garetto, la polpa di spalla)
– *part of bladebone*
**31** il fazzoletto
– *part of top rib*
**32** la fesa di spalla
– *part of bladebone*
**33** il ginocchio posteriore
– *shank*
**34** la coda
– *silverside*
**35** il sottofiletto
– *rump*
**36** il condilo
– *thick flank*

**37** lo scamone
– *top side*
**38-54 il suino (il maiale, il porco)**
– animal: *pig;* meat: *pork*
**38** il prosciutto con lo stinco e lo zampetto
– *leg with knuckle and trotter*
**39** la pancia
– *ventral part of the belly*
**40** il carré
– *back fat*
**41** la pancetta
– *belly*
**42** la spalla con stinco e zampetto
– *bladebone with knuckle and trotter*
**43** la testa senza guanciale *m* (la testina del maiale)
– *head (pig's head)*
**44** il filetto (il filetto di maiale *m*)
– *fillet (fillet of pork)*
**45** la sugna
– *leaf fat (pork flare)*
**46** la lombata
– *loin (pork loin)*
**47** il collo (la coppa)
– *spare rib*
**48** lo zampetto
– *trotter*
**49** lo stinco (il gamboncello)
– *knuckle*
**50** il lardo
– *butt*
**51** il prosciutto
– *fore end (ham)*
**52** la noce
– *round end for boiling*
**53** lo speck di prosciutto
– *fat end*
**54** il controgirello
– *gammon steak*

**1-30 la macelleria**
– *butcher's shop*
**1-4 carni** *f pl*
– *meat*
1 il prosciutto
– *ham on the bone*
2 lo speck
– *flitch of bacon*
3 la carne affumicata
– *smoked meat*
4 la lombata
– *piece of loin (piece of sirloin)*
5 lo strutto
– *lard*
**6-11 salumi** *m pl* **(insaccati** *m pl***)**
– *sausages*
6 il cartellino del prezzo
– *price label*
7 la mortadella
– *mortadella*
8 il salsicciotto caldo (il salsicciotto)
– *scalded sausage;* kinds: *Vienna sausage (Wiener), Frankfurter sausage (Frankfurter)*
9 la coppa (il capocollo)
– *collared pork (Am. headcheese)*
10 la salsiccia
– *ring of [Lyoner] sausage*

11 la salsiccia arrostita (la salsiccia da arrostire)
– *bratwurst (sausage for frying or grilling)*
12 il banco frigorifero
– *cold shelves*
13 l'insalata di carne
– *meat salad (diced meat salad)*
14 gli affettati
– *cold meats* (Am. *cold cuts*)
15 il pasticcio di carne *f*
– *pâté*
16 il macinato (la carne macinata)
– *mince (mincemeat, minced meat)*
17 lo stinco di maiale *m*
– *knuckle of pork*
18 il cesto delle offerte speciali
– *basket for special offers*
19 la tabella dei prezzi
– *price list for special offers*
20 l'offerta speciale
– *special offer*
21 il congelatore
– *freezer*
22 l'arrosto confezionato
– *pre-packed joints*
23 il cibo surgelato
– *deep-frozen ready-to-eat meal*

24 il galletto (il galletto amburghese)
– *chicken*
25 cibi *m pl* conservati (a conservazione *f* limitata: conserve *f pl* non completamente sterilizzate)
– *canned food*
26 il barattolo
– *can*
27 la macedonia di verdura (la conserva di verdura)
– *canned vegetables*
28 la conserva di pesce *m*
– *canned fish*
29 la salsa remoulade
– *salad cream*
30 le bibite (le bevande)
– *soft drinks*
**31-59 il locale per la preparazione degli insaccati**
– *kitchen for making sausages*
**31-37 coltelli** *m pl* **da macellaio**
– *butcher's knives*
31 il coltello
– *slicer*
32 la lama (la lama del coltello)
– *knife blade*
33 la lama seghettata (il seghetto)
– *saw teeth*

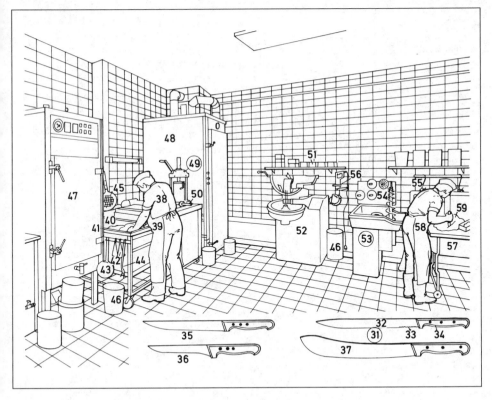

**34** il manico del coltello
– *knife handle*
**35** il coltello da macellaio
– *carver (carving knife)*
**36** il coltello per disossare
– *boning knife*
**37** il falcetto
– *butcher's knife (butcher knife)*
**38** il macellaio
– *butcher (master butcher)*
**39** il grembiule da macellaio
– *butcher's apron*
**40** l'impastatrice *f*
– *meat-mixing trough*
**41** la carne tritata da salsiccia
– *sausage meat*
**42** la campana del macinato (della
carne tritata)
– *scraper*
**43** la schiumarola
– *skimmer*
**44** il forchettone
– *sausage fork*
**45** il colino
– *scalding colander*
**46** la pattumiera
– *waste bin (Am. trash bin)*

**47** il forno con impianto di cottura a
vapore *m* o a aria calda
– *cooker, for cooking with steam or
hot air*
**48** l'affumicatoio
– *smoke house*
**49** l'insaccatrice *f* da tavolo per salumi *m pl* (l'insaccatrice *f* a mano
per salumi *m pl*)
– *sausage filler (sausage stuffer)*
**50** il tubo di riempimento
– *feed pipe (supply pipe)*
**51** i contenitori delle verdure
– *containers for vegetables*
**52** il cutter per la carne macinata (il
coltello da macinato)
– *mincing machine for sausage meat*
**53** il tritacarne
– *mincing machine (meat mincer,
mincer, Am. meat grinder)*
**54** i dischi del tritacarne
– *plates (steel plates)*
**55** il gancio per appendere la carne
– *meathook (butcher's hook)*
**56** la sega per le ossa
– *bone saw*

**57** il banco
– *chopping board*
**58** il macellaio mentre seziona la
carne
– *butcher, cutting meat*
**59** il pezzo di carne *f*
– *piece of meat*

**1-54 la panetteria** (negozio di pane *m* e pasticceria)
– *baker's shop*
1 la commessa (la fornaia)
– *shop assistant* (Am. *salesgirl, saleslady*)
2 il pane (il filone)
– *bread (loaf of bread, loaf )*
3 la mollica
– *crumb*
4 la crosta
– *crust (bread crust)*
5 la parte finale (estremità *f* ) del filone
– *crust* (Am. *heel*)
**6-12 tipi *m pl* di pane *m***
– *kinds of bread (breads)*
6 il pane casareccio (pane *m* a forma rotonda, un pane di cereali *m pl* misti)
– *round loaf, a wheat and rye bread*
7 il pane a forma piccola rotonda
– *small round loaf*
8 il filone, un pane misto di frumento e segale *f*
– *long loaf (bloomer), a wheat and rye bread*
9 il pane bianco
– *white loaf*
10 il pane in cassetta, un pane integrale di cereali *m pl* misti
– *pan loaf, a wholemeal rye bread*
11 lo «stollen» (panettone *m* natalizio, dolce *m* di Natale)
– *yeast bread* (Am. *stollen*)
12 la baguette (il pane francese)
– *French loaf (baguette, French stick)*
**13-16 panini *m pl***
– *rolls*

13 il panino comune
– *roll*
14 il panino di farina di frumento (panino di pasta bianca, *anche:* panino salato, panino con semi *m pl* di papavero, panino al cumino)
– *[white] roll*
15 il panino doppio (pezzatura di due panini *m pl*)
– *double roll*
16 il panino di segale *f*
– *rye-bread roll*
**17-47 pasticceria**
– *cakes (confectionery)*
17 il dolce alla panna (un rotolo farcito di panna)
– *cream roll*
18 il vol-au-vent, una pasta sfoglia
– *ol-au- ent, a puff pastry* (Am. *puff paste*)
19 pan di Spagna spalmato di marmellata un rotolo di pasta biscottata
– *Swiss roll* (Am. *jelly roll*)
20 la tortina (*ital.:* la pasta)
– *tartlet*
21 la bavarese alla crema
– *cream slice*
**22-24 torte *f pl***
– *flans* (Am. *pies*) *and gateaux*
22 la torta di frutta (*tipi:* torta di fragole *f pl*, torta di ciliegie *f pl*, torta di uva spina, torta di pesche *f pl*, torta di rabarbaro)
– *fruit flan (kinds: strawberry flan, cherry flan, gooseberry flan, peach flan, rhubarb flan)*

23 la torta di ricotta
– *cheesecake*
24 la torta alla crema, (*anche:* torta alla panna, *tipi:* torta farcita di crema, torta Schwarzwälder, torta farcita di crema e amarene *f pl*)
– *cream cake* (Am. *cream pie*) *(kinds: butter-cream cake, Black Forest gateau)*
25 il piatto per torte *f pl*
– *cake plate*
26 la meringa
– *meringue*
27 il bignè (*ital.:* bignè *m* alla crema)
– *cream puff*
28 la panna montata
– *whipped cream*
29 il krapfen
– *doughnut* (Am. *bismarck*)
30 la sfogliata
– *Danish pastry*
31 il salatino (*anche:* sfilatino al cumino)
– *saltstick (Salzstange)* (also: *caraway roll, caraway stick*)
32 il cornetto (*tipo:* croissant *m*)
– *croissant (crescent roll,* Am. *crescent)*
33 il dolce focaccia nello stampo col buco (*anche:* pandoro)
– *ring cake*
34 la torta vaniglia in cassetta ricoperta di cioccolato (con «glace» di cioccolato)
– *slab cake with chocolate icing*
35 la focaccina (*anche:* focaccina veneta, con la mousse di farina, zucchero e burro)
– *streusel cakes*

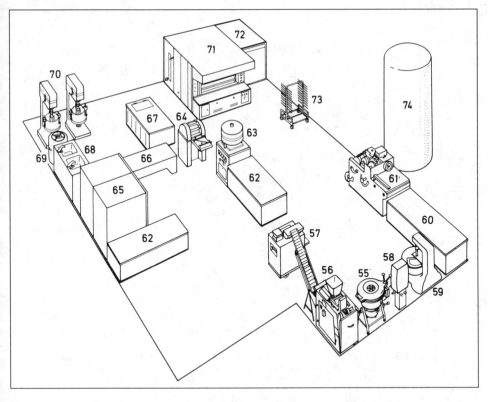

| | | |
|---|---|---|
| **36** l'africano | **49** il pumpernickel, un pane di segale *f* | – *divider and rounder (rounding* |
| – *marshmallow* | – *pumpernickel (wholemeal rye bread)* | *machine)* |
| **37** l'amaretto | **50** il pane croccante di segale *f* | **64** la formatrice dei cornetti (macchina per |
| – *coconut macaroon* | – *crispbread* | formare i cornetti) |
| **38** la pasta (la brioche) a forma di chiocciola (*pop.*: girella, messicano, focaccia con l'uvetta) | **51** il panpepato | – *crescent-forming machine* |
| | – *gingerbread* (Am. *lebkuchen*) | **65** impianti di congelamento |
| | **52** la farina (*tipi:* farina di frumento, farina di segale *f*) | – *freezers* |
| – *schnecke* | | **66** l'apparecchiatura per pane *m* condito (con olio/strutto) |
| **39** l'americano | – *flour (kinds: wheat flour, rye flour)* | |
| – *[kind of] iced bun* | **53** il lievito | – *oven [for baking with fat]* |
| **40** il pane al burro (pane *m* tipo brioche *f*) | – *yeast (baker's yeast)* | **67-70** la pasticceria |
| – *sweet bread* | **54** le fette biscottate | – *confectionery unit* |
| **41** la treccia, una focaccia lievitata | – *rusks (French toast)* | **67** il tavolo di raffreddamento |
| – *plaited bun (plait)* | **55-74** il forno | – *cooling table* |
| **42** la ciambella di pasta lievitata | – *bakery (bakehouse)* | **68** il lavello (l'acquaio) |
| – *Frankfurter garland cake* | **55** l'impastatrice *f* (il robot) | – *sink* |
| **43** la crostata (*tipi:* crostata ricoperta di granelli *m pl* di zucchero, burro e farina, crostata di prugne *f pl*) | – *kneading machine (dough mixer)* | **69** il fornello |
| | **56-57** l'impianto per la produzione del pane | – *boiler* |
| | – *bread unit* | **70** il frullatore (la planetaria) |
| – *slices (kinds: streusel slices, sugared slices, plum slices)* | **56** la spezzettatrice dell'impasto | – *whipping unit [with beater]* |
| | – *divider* | **71** il forno multiplo |
| **44** il (la) brezel, una focaccina salata | **57** l'impianto per le varie forme di pane | – *reel oven (oven)* |
| – *pretzel* | – *moulder* (Am. *molder*) | **72** il vano di lievitazione *f* |
| **45** il wafer (la cialda) | **58** il misuratore e mescolatore *m* dell'acqua | – *fermentation room* |
| – *wafer* (Am. *waffle*) | | **73** il carrello di lievitazione *f* |
| **46** il dolce a piramide | – *premixer* | – *fermentation trolley* |
| – *tree cake* | **59** il miscelatore | **74** il silo (impianto di insilamento della farina) |
| **47** la base di pasta Margherita per torte *f pl* | – *dough mixer* | |
| – *flan case* | **60** il piano (tavolo) di lavoro | – *flour silo* |
| **48-50** tipi *m pl* di pane *m* impacchettato (pane *m* confezionato) | – *workbench* | |
| | **61** l'impianto per la produzione dei panini | |
| – *wrapped bread* | – *roll unit* | |
| **48** il pane integrale di cereali *m pl* misti (*anche:* pane *m* di germi *m pl* di frumento) | **62** il piano (tavolo) di lavoro | |
| | – *workbench* | |
| | | |
| – *wholemeal bread (also: wheatgerm bread)* | **63** la spezzettatrice dell'impasto | |

**1-87 il negozio di generi** *m pl* **alimentari** (negozio di alimentari *m pl;* *ant.:* la drogheria, il negozio di coloniali *m pl*), un negozio di vendita al minuto
– *grocer's shop (grocer's, delicatessen shop, Am. grocery store, delicatessen store), a retail shop (Am. retail store)*
**1** l'esposizione *f* di merce *f* in vetrina
– *window display*
**2** il cartello pubblicitario
– *poster (advertisement)*
**3** la vetrina frigorifero
– *cold shelves*
**4** i salumi
– *sausages*
**5** i formaggi
– *cheese*
**6** il pollo
– *roasting chicken (broiler)*
**7** la gallina, una gallina da ingrasso
– *poulard, a fattened hen*
**8-11 prodotti** *m pl* **per la pasticceria**
– *baking ingredients*
**8** l'uva passa (l'uvetta); *sim.:* l'uva sultanina
– *raisins; sim.: sultanas*
**9** l'uvetta
– *currants*
**10** la scorza (la buccia) di limone *m* candita
– *candied lemon peel*
**11** la scorza (la buccia) di arancia candita
– *candied orange peel*
**12** la bilancia a quadrante *m*
– *computing scale, a rapid scale*

**13** il commesso
– *shop assistant (Am. salesclerk)*
**14** gli scaffali
– *goods shelves (shelves)*
**15-20 prodotti** *m pl* **in scatola** (scatolame *m,* conserve *f pl*)
– *canned food*
**15** il latte in scatola (latte *m* conservato)
– *canned milk*
**16** la frutta in scatola
– *canned fruit (cans of fruit)*
**17** i legumi in scatola
– *canned vegetables*
**18** il succo di frutta
– *fruit juice*
**19** le sardine sott'olio, un pesce in scatola
– *sardines in oil, a can of fish*
**20** la carne in scatola
– *canned meat (cans of meat)*
**21** la margarina
– *margarine*
**22** il burro
– *butter*
**23** il grasso di cocco, un grasso vegetale
– *coconut oil, a vegetable oil*
**24** l'olio; *varietà:* olio da tavola, olio di oliva, di girasole *m,* di semi *m pl,* di arachidi *f pl*
– *oil; kinds: salad oil, olive oil, sunflower oil, wheatgerm oil, groundnut oil*
**25** l'aceto
– *vinegar*
**26** il dado per brodo
– *stock cube*

**27** il dado per consommé
– *bouillon cube*
**28** la senape
– *mustard*
**29** il cetriolo sotto aceto
– *pickled gherkin*
**30** gli aromi per il brodo
– *soup seasoning*
**31** la commessa
– *shop assistant (Am. salesgirl, saleslady)*
**32-34 pasta**
– *pastas*
**32** gli spaghetti
– *spaghetti*
**33** i maccheroni
– *macaroni*
**34** le fettuccine (le tagliatelle)
– *noodles*
**35-39 alimenti** *m pl* **vari**
– *cereal products*
**35** l'orzo perlato (orzo mondato)
– *pearl barley*
**36** il semolino
– *semolina*
**37** i fiocchi d'avena
– *rolled oats (porridge oats, oats)*
**38** il riso
– *rice*
**39** il sagù (il sago)
– *sago*
**40** il sale
– *salt*
**41** il negoziante (il commerciante, il venditore)
– *grocer (Am. groceryman), a shopkeeper (tradesman, retailer, Am. storekeeper)*

42  i capperi
– *capers*
43  la cliente
– *customer*
44  lo scontrino di cassa
– *receipt (sales check)*
45  la borsa della spesa
– *shopping bag*
**46-49  materiale *m pl* d'imballaggio**
(materiale *m* per incartare)
– ***wrapping material***
46  la carta per incartare
– *wrapping paper*
47  lo scotch, il nastro adesivo
– *adhesive tape*
48  il sacchetto di carta
– *paper bag*
49  il sacchetto di carta a cono
– *cone-shaped paper bag*
50  il budino in polvere *f*
– *blancmange powder*
51  la confettura di frutta
– *whole-fruit jam (preserve)*
52  la marmellata
– *jam*
**53-55  zucchero**
– *sugar*
53  lo zuccero in zollette *f pl* (zucchero
in quadretti *m pl*)
– *cube sugar*
54  lo zucchero a velo
– *icing sugar*(Am. *confectioner's*
*sugar)*
55  lo zucchero cristallino, uno zucchero raffinato
– *refined sugar in crystals*
**56-59  alcoolici *m pl***
– ***spirits***

56  l'acquavite *f* (la grappa)
– *schnapps distilled from grain [usu-*
*ally wheat]*
57  il rum
– *rum*
58  il liquore
– *liqueur*
59  il brandy (il cognac)
– *brandy (cognac)*
**60-64  vino in bottiglia** (*qui:* in bottiglie
*f pl*)
– ***wine** in bottles (bottled wine)*
60  il vino bianco
– *white wine*
61  il Chianti
– *Chianti*
62  il vermouth
– *vermouth*
63  lo spumante (il vino frizzante)
– *sparkling wine*
64  il vino rosso
– *red wine*
**65-68  generi *m pl* voluttuari**
– ***tea, coffee, etc.***
65  il caffé (caffé *m* in grani *m pl*)
– *coffee (pure coffee)*
66  il cacao
– *cocoa*
67  la qualità di caffé *m*
– *coffee*
68  il thé (té) in bustine *f pl*
– *tea bag*
69  il macinacaffé
– *electric coffee grinder*
70  la macchina per tostare il caffé
– *coffee roaster*
71  il tamburo di tostatura
– *roasting drum*

72  il provino
– *sample scoop*
73  il listino dei prezzi (listino prezzi *m*
*pl*)
– *price list*
74  il congelatore, il freezer
– *freezer*
**75-86  prodotti *m pl* dolciari (dolciumi**
*m pl*)
– ***confectionery** (Am. candies)*
75  la caramella
– *sweet (Am. candy)*
76  i drops
– *drops*
77  la caramella al latte *m*
– *toffees*
78  la tavoletta di cioccolata
– *bar of chocolate*
79  la scatola (la confezione) di dolciumi *m pl*
– *chocolate box*
80  il cioccolatino ripieno
– *chocolate, a sweet*
81  il nougat
– *nougat*
82  il marzapane
– *marzipan*
83  il cioccolatino al liquore
– *chocolate liqueur*
84  la lingua di gatto
– *cat's tongue*
85  il croccante
– *croquant*
86  il tartufo al cioccolato
– *truffle*
87  l'acqua gassata (acqua minerale)
– *soda water*

**1-95 il supermercato, il supermarket,**
un negozio di generi *m pl* alimentari
self-service
- *supermarket, a self-service food
store*
**1** il carrello
- *shopping trolley*
**2** il cliente (l'acquirente *m*)
- *customer*
**3** la borsa della (per la) spesa
- *shopping bag*
**4** l'ingresso alla vendita
- *entrance to the sales area*
**5** la barriera
- *barrier*
**6** il cartello di divieto d'accesso ai
cani
- *sign (notice) banning dogs*
**7** i cani legati alla barriera
- *dogs tied by their leads*
**8** il cesto
- *basket*
**9 il reparto panetteria e pasticceria**
- *bread and cake counter (bread
counter, cake counter)*
**10** la vetrina
- *display counter for bread and cakes*
**11** le varietà (i tipi) di pane *m*
- *kinds of bread (breads)*
**12** i panini
- *rolls*
**13** i cornetti (i croissant)
- *croissants (crescent rolls, Am. cres-
cents)*
**14** il pane casareccio
- *round loaf (strong rye bread)*
**15** la torta
- *gateau*
**16** il «brezel» (Germania meridionale;
*sim.*: la focaccia)
- *pretzel [made with yeast dough]*

**17** la commessa
- *shop assistant (Am. salesgirl, saleslady)*
**18** la cliente (l'acquirente *f* )
- *customer*
**19** il pannello (il cartello) con le offerte
speciali
- *sign listing goods*
**20** la torta di frutta
- *fruit flan*
**21** il plumcake
- *slab cake*
**22** il dolce lievitato a cupola nello
stampo col buco, (*sim.*: il pan di
Spagna)
- *ring cake*
**23 la scansia dei cosmetici**
- *cosmetics gondola, a gondola (sales
shelves)*
**24** la tenda a baldacchino
- *canopy*
**25** il ripiano delle calze
- *hosiery shelf*
**26** la confezione delle calze
- *pack of stockings (nylons)*
**27-35 prodotti *m pl* igienici**
- *toiletries (cosmetics)*
**27** il vasetto di crema (*tipi*: crema
idratante, crema da giorno, crema
da notte, crema per le mani)
- *jar of cream (cream; kinds: moistur-
ising cream, day cream, night-care
cream, hand cream)*
**28** il pacchetto di cotone *m* idrofilo
- *packet of cotton wool*
**29** la scatola di cipria
- *powder tin*
**30** i batuffoli (i dischi) di cotone per
togliere il trucco
- *packet of cotton wool balls*

**31** il tubetto di dentifricio (il dentifricio)
- *tube of toothpaste*
**32** lo smalto per unghie *f pl*
- *nail varnish (nail polish)*
**33** il tubetto di crema
- *tube of cream*
**34** i sali da bagno
- *bath salts*
**35** gli assorbenti igienici
- *sanitary articles*
**36 *u.* 37 gli alimenti per animali *m pl***
- *pet foods*
**36** il pasto completo per cani *m pl*
- *complete dog food*
**37** il pacchetto di biscotti *m pl* per cani
*m pl*
- *packet of dog biscuits*
**38** il pacco di lettiera (di strame *m*) per
gatti *m pl*
- *bag of cat litter*
**39 il reparto formaggi**
- *cheese counter*
**40** la forma di cacio
- *whole cheese*
**41** l'Emmental *m* (formaggio svizzero
a buchi *m pl*)
- *Swiss cheese (Emmental cheese)
with holes*
**42** il formaggio olandese (formaggio
Edam), un formaggio rotondo
- *Edam cheese, a round cheese*
**43** la scansia dei latticini
- *gondola for dairy products*
**44** il latte a lunga conservazione
- *long-life milk (milk with good keep-
ing properties, pasteurized and
homogenized milk)*
**45** il pacchetto di latte *m*, il latte in
pacchetto
- *carton of milk*

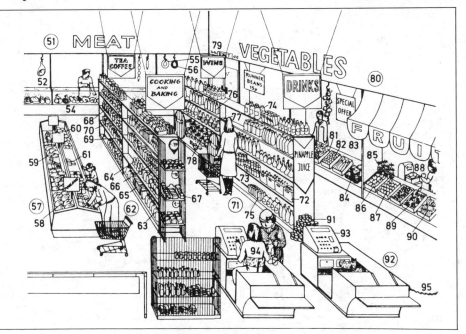

46 la panna
– *cream*
47 il burro
– *butter*
48 la margarina
– *margarine*
49 la scatola di formaggio (il formaggio in scatola)
– *box of cheeses*
50 la scatola delle uova
– *box of eggs*
51 **il reparto carni** *f pl* **e salumi** *m pl*
– **fresh meat counter** *(meat counter)*
52 il prosciutto
– *ham on the bone*
53 la carne
– *meat (meat products)*
54 i salumi
– *sausages*
55 la salsiccia *(diversa in Italia)*
– *ring of [pork] sausage*
56 il sanguinaccio *(diverso in Italia)*
– *ring of blood sausage, black pudding*
57 il congelatore (il freezer)
– *freezer*
**58-61 i prodotti surgelati**
– *frozen food*
58 la pollastra
– *poulard*
59 la coscia di tacchino
– *turkey leg (drumstick)*
60 la gallina da brodo
– *boiling fowl*
61 la verdura surgelata
– *frozen vegetables*
62 **la scansia di prodotti** *m pl* **dolciari e alimentari**
– *gondola for baking ingredients and cereal products*

63 la farina di frumento
– *wheat flour*
64 lo zucchero *(nella confezione a cono)*
– *sugar loaf*
65 il pacchetto di pastina da brodo
– *packet of noodles [for soup]*
66 l'olio
– *salad oil*
67 la bustina di spezie *f pl*
– *packet of spices*
**68-70 thé (té)** *m,* **caffè** *m* **(i generi voluttuari)**
– *tea, coffee, etc.*
68 il caffè
– *coffee*
69 la scatola (il pacchetto) di té (thé)
– *packet of tea*
70 il caffè solubile (caffè *m pl* istantaneo)
– *instant coffee*
71 **la scansia delle bevande**
– **drinks gondola**
72 la confezione (la cassetta) di birra
– *crate of beer*
73 la lattina di birra
– *can of beer*
74 la bottiglia di succo di frutta (il succo di frutta in bottiglia)
– *bottle of fruit juice*
75 la lattina di succo di frutta (il succo di frutta in lattina)
– *can of fruit juice*
76 la bottiglia di vino
– *bottle of wine*
77 il fiasco di Chianti *m*
– *bottle of Chianti*
78 la bottiglia di spumante *m*
– *bottle of sparkling wine*

79 l'uscita di sicurezza
– *emergency exit*
80 **il reparto frutta e verdura**
– **fruit and vegetable counter**
81 il cesto di verdura
– *vegetable basket*
82 i pomodori
– *tomatoes*
83 i cetrioli
– *cucumbers*
84 il cavolfiore
– *cauliflower*
85 l'ananas (l'ananasso)
– *pineapple*
86 le mele
– *apples*
87 le pere
– *pears*
88 la bilancia
– *scales for weighing fruit*
89 l'uva
– *grapes (bunches of grapes)*
90 le banane
– *bananas*
91 la scatola di conserva (di pomodoro, di pelati di frutta, ecc.)
– *can*
92 **la cassa**
– **checkout**
93 il registratore di cassa
– *cash register*
94 la cassiera
– *cashier*
95 la catena divisoria
– *chain*
96 il vice-caporeparto
– *assistant departmental manager*

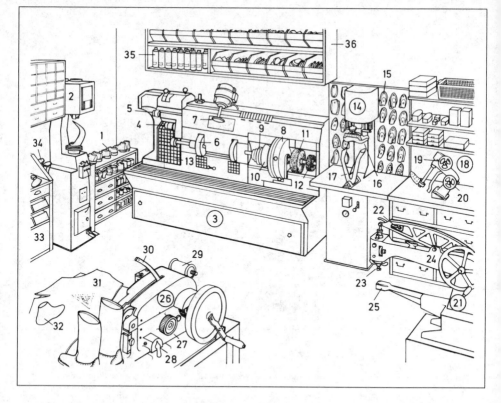

1-68 la bottega del calzolaio (*ant.*:
bottega del ciabattino)
– *shoemaker's workshop (bootmaker's workshop)*
1 le scarpe pronte (riparate)
– *finished (repaired) shoes*
2 la macchina orlatrice (l'orlatrice *f* )
– *auto-soling machine*
3 il banco (il macchinario) di finissaggio
– *finishing machine*
4 la fresa per i tacchi
– *heel trimmer*
5 la fresa a moto alternato (a moto continuo e intermittente)
– *sole trimmer*
6 la mola (il disco) a smeriglio
– *scouring wheel*
7 la piastra rotante di pietra pomice *f*
– *naum keag*
8 l'azionamento
– *drive unit (drive wheel)*
9 l'impianto a pressa per rifinire le suole
– *iron*
10 il disco polimentare (per levigare le suole)
– *buffing wheel*
11 la spazzola polimentare (per lucidare le suole)
– *polishing brush*
12 la spazzola di crine *m*
– *horsehair brush*
13 l'aspirazione *f* (l'impianto di aspirazione *f* )
– *extractor grid*
14 la pressa automatica per suole *f pl*
– *automatic sole press*
15 il piatto premente (piatto della pressa)
– *press attachment*
16 il cuscinetto premente (cuscinetto della pressa)
– *pad*
17 l'archetto di pressione *f*
– *press bar*
18 l'allargatrice *f* (l'apparecchio per allargare le scarpe)
– *stretching machine*
19 il regolatore della larghezza
– *width adjustment*
20 il regolatore della lunghezza
– *length adjustment*
21 la macchina da cucire (la cucitrice)
– *stitching machine*
22 il regolatore dello spessore
– *power regulator (power control)*
23 il piede
– *foot*
24 il volano
– *handwheel*
25 il braccio
– *arm*
26 la macchina per punto doppio (macchina a due aghi *m pl*)
– *sole stitcher (sole-stitching machine)*
27 l'alzapiede *m*
– *foot bar lever*
28 il dispositivo di avanzamento
– *feed adjustment (feed setting)*
29 la bobina portafilo
– *bobbin (cotton bobbin)*
30 il guidafilo
– *thread guide (yarn guide)*
31 il cuoio per suole *f pl*
– *sole leather*
32 la forma
– *[wooden] last*
33 il tavolo da lavoro
– *workbench*
34 la forma di ferro
– *last*

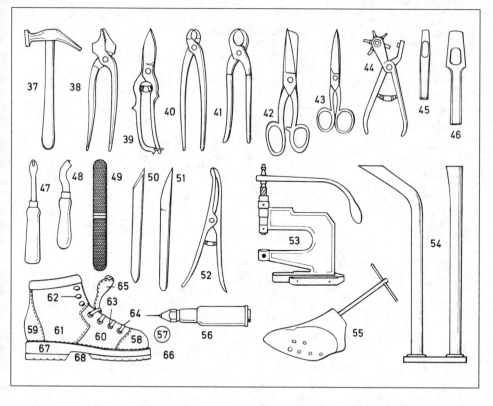

35 la bombola a spray (a spruzzo) del colore
– *dye spray*
36 lo scaffale del materiale di lavoro
– *shelves for materials*
37 il martello del calzolaio
– *shoemaker's hammer*
38 la tenaglia piegatrice (la pinza da cuoio)
– *shoemaker's pliers (welt pincers)*
39 le cesoie per cuoio
– *sole-leather shears*
40 la piccola tenaglia
– *small pincers (nippers)*
41 la tenaglia (il tronchese semplice a taglio orizzontale)
– *large pincers (nippers)*
42 le forbici per tomaia
– *upper-leather shears*
43 le forbici per spago (per refe *m*)
– *scissors*
44 la pinza foratrice a revolver *m*
– *revolving punch (rotary punch)*
45 il foratoio
– *punch*
46 il foratoio con impugnatura
– *punch [with a handle]*
47 il cavachiodi
– *nail puller*

48 il tagliaorli (il coltello tagliaorli)
– *welt cutter*
49 la raspa (la lima) da calzolaio
– *shoemaker's rasp*
50 il trincetto da calzolaio
– *cobbler's knife (shoemaker's knife)*
51 il trincetto per affilare
– *skiving knife (skife knife, paring knife)*
52 la pinza sollevamascherina (pinza sollevapunta)
– *toecap remover*
53 la macchina occhiellatrice, attaccaganci e attaccabottoni automatici
– *eyelet, hook, and press-stud setter*
54 il piede di ferro, un utensile di appoggio
– *stand (with iron lasts)*
55 il tendiscarpe fisso
– *width-setting tree*
56 il fissachiodi
– *nail grip*
57 lo scarpone
– *boot*
58 lo spunterbo (la mascherina, la punta dello scarpone)
– *toecap*

59 il contrafforte
– *counter*
60 la tomaia
– *vamp*
61 il quartiere (la parte laterale della tomaia)
– *quarter*
62 il gancio dello scarpone
– *hook*
63 l'occhiello (foro, asola)
– *eyelet*
64 il laccio (la stringa)
– *lace (shoelace, bootlace)*
65 la linguetta
– *tongue*
66 la suola
– *sole*
67 il tacco
– *heel*
68 il fiosso
– *shank (waist)*

**1** lo stivale invernale (stivale *m* da neve *f,*
moon-boot)
– *winter boot*
**2** la suola in PVC (suola in materiale *m*
sintetico, suola di materia plastica,
suola di plastica)
– *PVC sole (plastic sole)*
**3** l'interno in peluche *m* (interno imbottito,
imbottitura in peluche *m*)
– *high-pile lining*
**4** il tessuto nylon impermeabile
– *nylon*
**5** lo stivaletto da uomo
– *men's boot*
**6** la cerniera lampo interna
– *inside zip (Am. zipper)*
**7** *ant.* lo stivaletto da uomo
– *men's high leg boot*
**8** la suola alta
– *platform sole (platform)*
**9** lo stivaletto alla sceriffo
– *Western boot (cowboy boot)*
**10** lo stivale di pelle *f* di puledro
– *pony-skin boot*
**11** la suola di para (suola di gomma vul-
canizzata)
– *cemented sole*
**12** lo stivale da donna
– *ladies' boot*
**13** lo stivale da uomo
– *men's high leg boot*
**14** lo stivale da pioggia (stivale *m* impermeabile) trattato con PVC, senza cuciture *f pl*
– *seamless PVC waterproof wellington
boot*
**15** la suola a scatola
– *natural-colour (Am. natural-color) sole*
**16** la mascherina
– *toecap*
**17** l'interno in tessuto di maglia
– *tricot lining (knitwear lining)*
**18** la scarpa da montagna, *anche:* le pedule
– *hiking boot*
**19** la suola con profilo (suola tipo carrar-
mato)
– *grip sole*
**20** l'orlo imbottito della tomaia
– *padded collar*
**21** l'allacciatura con cinturini *m pl* (con
legacci *m pl*)
– *tie fastening (lace fastening)*
**22** la pianella da bagno
– *open-toe mule*
**23** la parte superiore in tessuto di spugna
– *terry upper*
**24** la suola sagomata a zeppa
– *polo outsole*
**25** la pantofola
– *mule*
**26** la parte superiore (la tomaia) in cord *m*
(in velluto a coste *f pl* larghe)
– *corduroy upper*
**27** il sandalo con cinturino a collo
– *evening sandal (sandal court shoe)*
**28** il tacco alto
– *high heel (stiletto heel)*
**29** la scarpa décolleté
– *court shoe (Am. pump)*
**30** il mocassino
– *moccasin*
**31** la scarpa chiusa bassa (scarpa stringata,
scarpa con laccetti *m pl*)
– *shoe, a tie shoe (laced shoe, Oxford
shoe, Am. Oxford)*

**32** la linguetta
– *tongue*
**33** la scarpa chiusa a tacco alto
– *high-heeled shoe (shoe with raised
heel)*
**34** il mocassino sfoderato
– *casual*
**35** la scarpa da ginnastica
– *trainer (training shoe)*
**36** la scarpa da tennis *m*
– *tennis shoe*
**37** la tomaia con spunterbo
– *counter (stiffening)*
**38** la suola di gomma a scatola
– *natural-colour (Am. natural-
color) rubber sole*
**39** la scarpa a tomaia alta da lavoro
– *heavy-duty boot (Am. stogy, sto-
gie)*
**40** la punta di rinforzo (punta
antiabrasione)
– *toecap*
**41** la pantofola da casa, *anche:*
pantofola di feltro
– *slipper*
**42** la scarpa après-ski
– *woollen (Am. woolen) slip sock*
**43** il disegno a maglia (la lavorazione) della tomaia
– *knit stitch (knit)*
**44** il clog, uno zoccolo
– *clog*
**45** la suola di legno
– *wooden sole*
**46** la parte superiore (la tomaia) in
pelle *f* di vitello
– *soft-leather upper*
**47** il Töffel, uno zoccolo
– *sabot*
**48** il sandalo alla greca (il sandalo
con cinturino fermadita)
– *toe post sandal*
**49** la pianella ortopedica
– *ladies' sandal*
**50** il sottopiede ortopedico
– *surgical footbed (sock)*
**51** il sandalo; *qui:* la scarpa a sandalo
– *sandal*
**52** la fibbia
– *shoe buckle (buckle)*
**53** il sandalo; *qui:* sandalo a tomaia
chiusa davanti
– *sling-back court shoe (Am. sling
pump)*
**54** la scarpa décolleté di stoffa
– *fabric court shoe*
**55** la zeppa
– *wedge heel*
**56** la scarpina «primi passi» *m pl*
(scarpina da neonato)
– *baby's first walking boot*

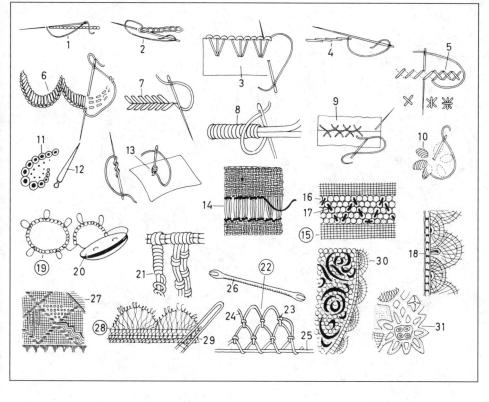

**1** il punto indietro (l'impuntura)
– *backstitch seam*
**2** il punto catenella
– *chain stitch*
**3** il punto ornamentale
– *ornamental stitch*
**4** il punto erba
– *stem stitch*
**5** il punto croce *f*
– *cross stitch*
**6** il punto festone *m*
– *buttonhole stitch (button stitch)*
**7** il punto treccia
– *fishbone stitch*
**8** il punto cordoncino
– *overcast stitch*
**9** il punto strega
– *herringbone stitch (Russian stitch, Russian cross stitch)*
**10** il ricamo a punto passato
– *satin stitch (flat stitch)*
**11** il ricamo a punto inglese
– *eyelet embroidery (broderie anglaise)*
**12** il punteruolo
– *stiletto*
**13** il punto a nodi *m pl* (semplice e doppio)
– *French knot (French dot, knotted stitch, twisted knot stitch)*

**14** il punto a giorno (l'orlo a giorno)
– *hem stitch work*
**15** il ricamo su tulle *m*
– *tulle work (tulle lace)*
**16** il fondo di tulle *m*
– *tulle background (net background)*
**17** la diagonale a punto filza
– *darning stitch*
**18** il pizzo a tombolo; *tipi:* pizzi *m pl* di Valenciennes, pizzi *m pl* di Bruxelles
– *pillow lace (bobbin lace, bone lace); kinds: Valenciennes, Brussels lace*
**19** il chiacchierino (il frivolité)
– *tatting*
**20** la navetta
– *tatting shuttle (shuttle)*
**21** il lavoro a macramé *m*
– *knotted work (macramé)*
**22** il ricamo a rete *f* (il filet)
– *filet (netting)*
**23** il nodo del filet
– *netting loop*
**24** la maglia del filet
– *netting thread*
**25** la stecca del filet
– *mesh pin (mesh gauge)*

**26** l'ago per la lavorazione a filet *m*
– *netting needle*
**27** il ricamo a giorno
– *open work*
**28** il merletto a forcella
– *gimping (hairpin work)*
**29** la forcella da merletto
– *gimping needle (hairpin)*
**30** il pizzo ad ago (il pizzo ricamato); *tipi:* pizzo reticella, pizzo Venezia, pizzo di Alençon; *sim.* con fili *m pl* di metallo: il ricamo a filigrana
– *needlepoint lace (point lace, needlepoint); kinds: reticella lace, Venetian lace, Alençon lace; sim. with metal thread: filigree work*
**31** il ricamo Rinascimento
– *braid embroidery (braid work)*

**1-27 la sartoria da donna (l'atelier *m*)**
- *dressmaker's workroom*
**1** il sarto da donna
- *dressmaker*
**2** il metro (a nastro), un metro
- *tape measure (measuring tape), a metre* (Am. *meter*) *tape measure*
**3** le forbici da sarto
- *cutting shears*
**4** il tavolo (il banco) per tagliare
- *cutting table*
**5** il modello (abito campione)
- *model dress*
**6** il manichino
- *dressmaker's model (dressmaker's dummy, dress form)*
**7** il modello (cappotto campione)
- *model coat*
**8** la macchina da cucire
- *sewing machine*
**9** il motore di avviamento
- *drive motor*
**10** la cinghia di trasmissione *f*
- *drive belt*
**11** il pedale
- *treadle*

**12** il filo per macchina da cucire (il rocchetto di filo)
- *sewing machine cotton (sewing machine thread) (bobbin)*
**13** la squadra
- *cutting template*
**14** la fettuccia
- *seam binding*
**15** la scatola dei bottoni
- *button box*
**16** il ritaglio di stoffa (l'avanzo)
- *remnant*
**17** l'appendiabiti *m* a rotelle *f pl*
- *movable clothes rack*
**18** il piano (il tavolo) da stiro
- *hand-iron press*
**19** la stiratrice
- *presser (ironer)*
**20** il ferro da stiro a vapore *m*
- *steam iron*
**21** il tubo conduttore dell'acqua
- *water feed pipe*
**22** il serbatoio (il contenitore) dell'acqua
- *water container*
**23** il piano inclinabile
- *adjustable-tilt ironing surface*

**24** il dispositivo di sospensione *f* del ferro da stiro
- *lift device for the iron*
**25** la camera per l'aspirazione *f* del vapore
- *steam extractor*
**26** l'interruttore *m* a pedale *m* per l'aspirazione *f* del vapore
- *foot switch controlling steam extraction*
**27** la garza da imbottitura (*fam.* la flisellina)
- *pressed non-woven woollen* (Am. *woolen*) *fabric*

**1-32  la sartoria da uomo (l'atelier *m*)**
– *tailor's workroom*
**1** lo specchio a tre ante *f pl* (a tre pannelli *m pl*)
– *triple mirror*
**2** le pezze (dei tessuti)
– *lengths of material*
**3** la stoffa (il tessuto) per abiti *m pl*
– *suiting*
**4** la rivista di moda
– *fashion journal (fashion magazine)*
**5** il portacenere (posacenere *m*)
– *ashtray*
**6** il catalogo delle ultime novità
– *fashion catalogue*
**7** il tavolo da lavoro
– *workbench*
**8** lo scaffale pensile
– *wall shelves (wall shelf unit)*
**9** il rocchetto di filo
– *cotton reel*
**10** le spagnolette di filo di seta
– *small reels of sewing silk*
**11** le forbici da sarto
– *hand shears*
**12** la macchina da cucire combinata a pedale *m* e elettrica
– *combined electric and treadle sewing machine*

**13** il pedale
– *treadle*
**14** il pararuota
– *dress guard*
**15** il volano
– *band wheel*
**16** lo spolatore
– *bobbin thread*
**17** il piano (il tavolo) della macchina da cucire
– *sewing machine table*
**18** il cassetto (lo scomparto) per gli accessori
– *sewing machine drawer*
**19** la fettuccia
– *seam binding*
**20** il puntaspilli (il cuscinetto puntaspilli)
– *pincushion*
**21** la segnatura della stoffa
– *marking out*
**22** il sarto da uomo
– *tailor*
**23** il braccio imbottito (per dare la forma)
– *shaping pad*
**24** il gesso da sarto (il gessetto)
– *tailor's chalk (French chalk)*
**25** il pezzo in lavorazione *f*
– *workpiece*

**26** l'asse *f* da stiro a vapore *m*
– *steam press (steam pressing unit)*
**27** il braccio girevole
– *swivel arm*
**28** il braccio da stiro
– *pressing cushion (pressing pad)*
**29** il ferro da stiro
– *iron*
**30** il cuscinetto per stirare
– *hand-ironing pad*
**31** la spazzola per abiti *m pl*
– *clothes brush*
**32** la pezza da stiro
– *pressing cloth*

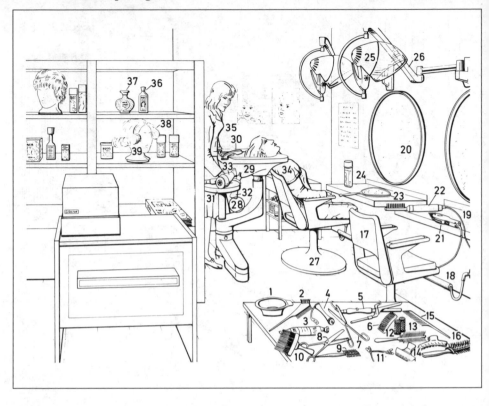

**1-39  il salone per signora** e l'istituto di bellezza
– *ladies' hairdressing salon and beauty salon* (Am. *beauty parlor, beauty shop*)

**1-16  strumenti** *m pl* **da lavoro del parrucchiere**
– *hairdresser's tools*
1  la vaschetta per il decolorante
– *bowl containing bleach*
2  la spazzolina per le mèches
– *highlighting brush*
3  il tubetto di sostanza decolorante
– *bleach tube*
4  il bigodino per la tintura
– *curler [used in dyeing]*
5  il ferro da ricci *m pl* (il ferro per le ondulazioni)
– *curling tongs (curling iron)*
6  il pettine fermacapelli
– *comb (back comb, side comb)*
7  le forbici da parrucchiere *m*
– *haircutting scissors*
8  la sfoltitrice (le forbici per sfoltire)
– *thinning scissors* (Am. *thinning shears*)
9  il rasoio
– *thinning razor*
10  la spazzola per capelli *m pl*
– *hairbrush*
11  la molletta a clip *m* (il beccuccio)
– *hair clip*

12  il bigodino
– *roller*
13  la spazzola Fuller (*fam.* spazzola rotonda)
– *curl brush*
14  il fermaglio per/da capelli *m pl*
– *curl clip*
15  il pettine a coda
– *dressing comb*
16  la spazzola di ferro
– *stiff-bristle brush*
17  la poltrona regolabile da parrucchiere
– *adjustable hairdresser's chair*
18  l'appoggiapiedi *m*
– *footrest*
19  il piano di lavoro (piano di appoggio)
– *dressing table*
20  lo specchio a parete *f*
– *salon mirror (mirror)*
21  la macchinetta elettrica per tagliare i capelli
– *electric clippers*
22  il pettine a fon *m*
– *warm-air comb*
23  lo specchio (a mano)
– *hand mirror (hand glass)*
24  la lacca per capelli *m pl* (il fissatore)
– *hairspray (hair-fixing spray)*
25  il casco asciugacapelli, un casco a braccio mobile
– *drier, a swivel-mounted drier*

26  il braccio mobile del casco
– *swivel arm of the drier*
27  il piede «a piatto»
– *round base*
28  l'impianto per il lavaggio
– *shampoo unit*
29  il lavatesta
– *shampoo basin*
30  la doccia a mano *f*
– *hand spray (shampoo spray)*
31  il tavolo di appoggio
– *service tray*
32  il flacone (la bottiglia) dello shampoo
– *shampoo bottle*
33  l'asciugacapelli *m* elettrico (il fon)
– *hair drier (hand hair drier, hand-held hair drier)*
34  la mantellina
– *cape (gown)*
35  la parrucchiera
– *hairdresser*
36  la bottiglia di profumo
– *perfume bottle*
37  la bottiglia di eau de toilette
– *bottle of toilet water*
38  la parrucca
– *wig*
39  la testiera della parrucca
– *wig block*

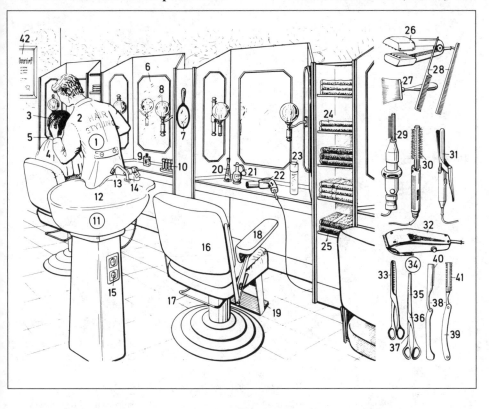

**1-42 il negozio del barbiere (il salone)**
– **men's salon** *(men's hairdressing salon, barber's shop,* Am. *barbershop)*
1 il barbiere (il parrucchiere per uomo, il coiffeur)
– *hairdresser (barber)*
2 il camice del barbiere
– *overalls (hairdresser's overalls)*
3 il taglio
– *hairstyle (haircut)*
4 il telo da barbiere *m*
– *cape (gown)*
5 il colletto di carta
– *paper towel*
6 lo specchio a parete *f*
– *salon mirror (mirror)*
7 lo specchio (a mano *f* )
– *hand mirror (hand glass)*
8 la lampada a parete *f* (l'applique)
– *light*
9 la lozione dopobarba
– *toilet water*
10 la lozione per capelli *m pl* (la frizione)
– *hair tonic*
11 l'impianto per il lavaggio dei capelli
– *shampoo unit*
12 il lavatesta
– *shampoo basin*
13 la doccia a mano *f*
– *hand spray (shampoo spray)*
14 il rubinetto miscelatore
– *mixer tap* (Am. *mixing faucet)*
15 la presa di corrente *f, per es.* per l'attacco dell'asciugacapelli, del fon
– *sockets, e.g. for hair drier*

16 la poltrona regolabile da barbiere
– *adjustable hairdresser's chair (barber's chair)*
17 il pedale regolatore
– *height-adjuster bar (height adjuster)*
18 il braccio della poltrona
– *armrest*
19 l'appoggiapiedi *m*
– *footrest*
20 lo shampoo
– *shampoo*
21 lo spruzzatore (di profumo)
– *perfume spray*
22 l'asciugacapelli *m* (il fon)
– *hair drier (hand hair drier, hand-held hair drier)*
23 la lacca in confezione spray (lacca in bombola spray)
– *setting lotion in a spray can*
24 gli asciugamani per frizionare i capelli
– *hand towels for drying hair*
25 le salviette per compresse *f pl* sul viso
– *towels for face compresses*
26 la piastra
– *crimping iron*
27 lo spazzolino per nuca e collo
– *neck brush*
28 il pettine
– *dressing comb*
29 il pettine a fon *m*
– *warm-air comb*
30 la spazzola termoelettrica
– *warm-air brush*
31 il ferro per ondulazione *f*
– *curling tongs (hair curler, curling iron)*

32 la macchinetta per tagliare i capelli
– *electric clippers*
33 la sfoltitrice (le forbici per sfoltire)
– *thinning scissors* (Am. *thinning shears)*
34 le forbici da barbiere *m*
– *haircutting scissors;* sim.: *styling scissors*
35 la lama delle forbici
– *scissor-blade*
36 il perno
– *pivot*
37 la branca
– *handle*
38 il rasoio
– *open razor (straight razor)*
39 l'impugnatura (il manico) del rasoio
– *razor handle*
40 il filo del rasoio
– *edge (cutting edge, razor's edge, razor's cutting edge)*
41 il rasoio per il taglio sfilato
– *thinning razor*
42 il diploma
– *diploma*

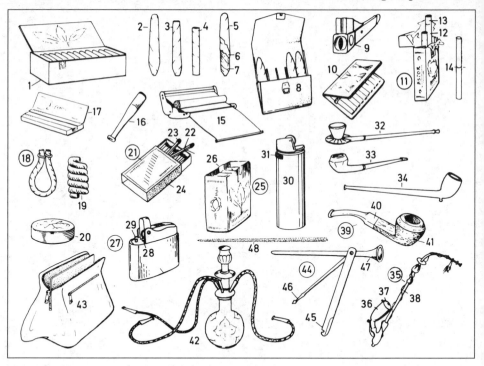

1 la scatola di sigari *m pl*
– *cigar box*
2 il sigaro; *tipi:* Avana, Brasile (sigaro brasiliano), Sumatra
– *cigar; kinds: Havana cigar (Havana), Brazilian cigar, Sumatra cigar*
3 il sigaretto (zigarillo)
– *cigarillo*
4 il mezzo sigaro (*tipo:* sigaro toscano)
– *cheroot*
5 la fascia (foglia che fascia il sigaro)
– *wrapper*
6 la sottofascia
– *binder*
7 il ripieno
– *filler*
8 il portasigari
– *cigar case*
9 lo spuntasigari (il tagliasigari)
– *cigar cutter*
10 il portasigarette
– *cigarette case*
11 il pacchetto di sigarette *f pl*
– *cigarette packet* (Am. *pack*)
12 la sigaretta, una sigaretta con filtro
– *cigarette, a filter-tipped cigarette*
13 la punta (il filtro); *tipi:* la punta (il filtro) in carta sugherata, la punta (il filtro) in carta dorata
– *cigarette tip; kinds: cork tip, gold tip*
14 la sigaretta di tipo russo
– *Russian cigarette*
15 la macchinetta per avvolgere le sigarette
– *cigarette roller*
16 il bocchino
– *cigarette holder*

17 il pacchetto di cartine *f pl* per sigarette *f pl*
– *packet of cigarette papers*
18 il tabacco ritorto
– *pigtail (twist of tobacco)*
19 il tabacco da masticare (tabacco in forma di corda); *un pezzo:* la cicca
– *chewing tobacco; a piece: plug (quid, chew)*
20 la tabacchiera con tabacco da naso
– *snuff box, containing snuff*
21 la scatola di fiammiferi *m pl*
– *matchbox*
22 il fiammifero
– *match*
23 la capocchia di zolfo
– *head (match head)*
24 la superficie di attrito
– *striking surface*
25 il pacchetto di tabacco; *tipi:* trinciato sottile, trinciato medio, Navy Cut
– *packet of tobacco; kinds: fine cut, shag, navy plug*
26 la fascetta fiscale
– *revenue stamp*
27 l'accendino a benzina
– *petrol cigarette lighter (petrol lighter)*
28 la pietrina dell'accendino
– *flint*
29 lo stoppino
– *wick*
30 l'accendino a gas *m* (accendino usa-e-getta)
– *gas cigarette lighter (gas lighter), a disposable lighter*
31 il regolatore della fiamma
– *flame regulator*
32 la pipa turca (pipa araba)
– *chibonk (chibonque)*

33 la pipa corta
– *short pipe*
34 la pipa di terracotta (pipa olandese, pipa abruzzese)
– *clay pipe (Dutch pipe)*
35 la pipa lunga
– *long pipe*
36 il fornello della pipa
– *pipe bowl (bowl)*
37 il coperchio della pipa
– *bowl lid*
38 il cannello (la cannuccia) della pipa
– *pipe stem (stem)*
39 la pipa di rádica
– *briar pipe*
40 il bocchino della pipa
– *mouthpiece*
41 la venatura (la marezzatura: granulosa o levigata) della rádica
– *sand-blast finished or polished briar grain*
42 il narghilé, una pipa ad acqua
– *hookah (narghile, narghileh), a water pipe*
43 la borsa (il sacchetto) del tabacco
– *tobacco pouch*
44 l'accessorio per fumatori *m pl* di pipa (il puliscipipa)
– *smoker's companion*
45 il raschietto
– *pipe scraper*
46 lo scovolino
– *pipe cleaner*
47 il premitabacco
– *tobacco presser*
48 il filo metallico nettapipa
– *pipe cleaner*

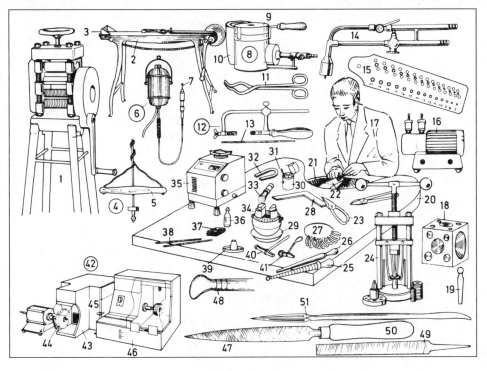

1 il laminatoio
– *wire and sheet roller*
2 la trafilatrice
– *drawbench (drawing bench)*
3 il filo (il filo d'oro o d'argento)
– *wire (gold or silver wire)*
4 il trapano a palla (il trapano a mano, il trapano di Archimede)
– *archimedes drill (drill)*
5 l'impugnatura orizzontale di legno
– *crossbar*
6 il trapano elettrico sospeso
– *suspended (pendant) electric drilling machine*
7 la fresetta sferica con impugnatura (la fresa tonda, la fresa a palla)
– *spherical cutter (cherry)*
8 il forno fusorio
– *melting pot*
9 il coperchio in argilla refrattaria (il coperchio Chamotte)
– *fireclay top*
10 il crogiolo di grafite *f*
– *graphite crucible*
11 la pinza per crogiolo
– *crucible tongs*
12 il seghetto (l'archetto portaseghe)
– *piercing saw (jig saw)*
13 la lama del seghetto da traforo
– *piercing saw blade*
14 il saldatore
– *soldering gun*
15 la filiera (la filiera a cazzuola)
– *thread tapper*
16 il compressore idraulico
– *blast burner (blast lamp) for soldering*
17 l'orafo
– *goldsmith*

18 il punzone per bugnare (l'utensile *m* per bugnare)
– *swage block*
19 il bulino
– *punch*
20 il banco da lavoro
– *workbench (bench)*
21 la pelle di rivestimento del banco da lavoro
– *bench apron*
22 lo stocco
– *needle file*
23 le forbici per lamiera (le cesoie)
– *metal shears*
24 il bilanciere
– *wedding ring sizing machine*
25 la spina graduata per anelli *m pl*
– *ring gauge (Am. gage)*
26 il fuso graduato per anelli
– *ring-rounding tool*
27 l'anelliera
– *ring gauge (Am. gage)*
28 la squadra in acciaio
– *steel set-square*
29 il cuscino delle lenti, un cuscino di pelle *f*
– *(circular) leather pad*
30 la custodia dei punzoni
– *box of punches*
31 il punzone
– *punch*
32 la calamita (il magnete)
– *magnet*
33 la spazzola a pennello
– *bench brush*
34 la boccia universale per incisione *f*
– *engraving ball (joint vice, clamp)*

35 la bilancia per l'oro e l'argento, una bilancia di precisione *f*
– *gold and silver balance (assay balance), a precision balance*
36 il fondente
– *soldering flux (flux)*
37 la lastra di saldatura in carbone *m* di legna
– *charcoal block*
38 il pennello per la saldatura
– *stick of solder*
39 il borace
– *soldering borax*
40 il martello sagomato
– *shaping hammer*
41 il martello da cesello
– *chasing (enchasing) hammer*
42 la pulitrice
– *polishing and burnishing machine*
43 l'aspiratore *m* da tavolo
– *dust exhauster (vacuum cleaner)*
44 la spazzola circolare
– *polishing wheel*
45 l'aspiratore *m*
– *dust collector (dust catcher)*
46 la mola a acqua
– *buffing machine*
47 la lima rotonda
– *round file*
48 il bornitore
– *bloodstone (haematite, hematite)*
49 la lima piatta
– *flat file*
50 il manico della lima
– *file handle*
51 il raschino d'acciaio
– *polishing iron (burnisher)*

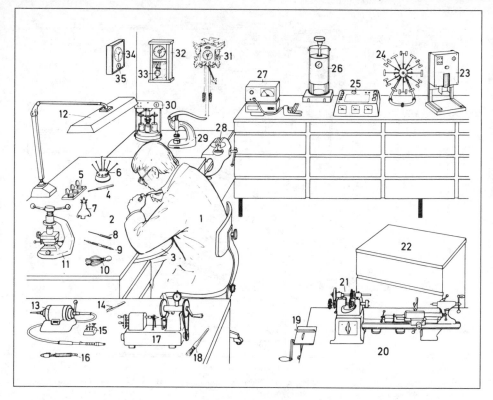

1 l'orologiaio
 – *watchmaker;* also: *clockmaker*
2 il tavolo da lavoro
 – *workbench*
3 l'appoggiabraccio *m*
 – *armrest*
4 l'oliatore *m*
 – *oiler*
5 il recipiente per olio denso
 – *oil stand*
6 la serie dei cacciavite
 – *set of screwdrivers*
7 l'incudine per le lancette
 – *clockmaker's anvil*
8 l'alesatore *m*
 – *broach, a reamer*
9 il punzone
 – *spring pin tool*
10 l'utensile *m* per togliere le
 lancette dagli orologi da polso
 – *hand-removing tool*
11 l'apparecchio per aprire e chiudere le casse
 – *watchglass-fitting tool [for armoured, Am. armored, glass]*
12 la lampada da lavoro, una lampada a più usi *m pl*
 – *workbench lamp, a multi-purpose lamp*
13 il motore universale
 – *multi-purpose motor*

14 la pinzetta
 – *tweezers*
15 gli accessori per la lucidatura
 – *polishing machine attachments*
16 il morsetto autocentrante
 – *pin vice (pin holder)*
17 il brunitore, per brunire, lucidare, arrotondare e accorciare gli alberi
 – *burnisher, for burnishing, polishing, and shortening of spindles*
18 il pennello per la polvere
 – *dust brush*
19 la taglierina per bracciali *m pl* in metallo
 – *cutter for metal watch straps*
20 il tornio di precisione *f* (il tornio da orologiaio)
 – *precision bench lathe (watchmaker's lathe)*
21 il rinvio della cinghia trapezoidale del tornio
 – *drive-belt gear*
22 l'armadietto dei pezzi di ricambio
 – *workshop trolley for spare parts*
23 la pulitrice a vibrazione *f*
 – *ultrasonic cleaner*
24 il simulatore di carica
 – *rotating watch-testing machine for automatic watches*

25 il misuratore per il controllo automatico degli orologi elettronici
 – *watch-timing machine for electronic components*
26 l'apparecchio di controllo per orologi *m pl* subacquei
 – *testing device for waterproof watches*
27 il misuratore
 – *electronic timing machine*
28 la morsa parallela
 – *vice* (Am. *vise*)
29 il dispositivo per il montaggio sulla lunetta dei vetri infrangibili
 – *watchglass-fitting tool for armoured* (Am. *armored*) *glasses*
30 la pulitrice per orologi *m pl* meccanici
 – *[automatic] cleaning machine for conventional cleaning*
31 l'orologio a cucù *m*
 – *cuckoo clock (Black Forest clock)*
32 l'orologio a pendolo (la pendola)
 – *wall clock (regulator)*
33 il pendolo
 – *compensation pendulum*
34 l'orologio da cucina
 – *kitchen clock*
35 il contaminuti
 – *timer*

**1** l'orologio da polso elettrico
– *electronic wristwatch*
**2** l'indicazione *f* digitale (un'indicazione diodica luminosa *anche:* un'indicazione cristallina liquida, un'indicazione LCD)
– *digital display (a light-emitting diode (LED) display; also: a liquid crystal display, LCD)*
**3** il pulsante delle ore e dei minuti (al 6 anche per la messa a punto dell'indicazione *f* analogica)
– *hour and minute button (on 6, also for setting the analogue (Am. analog) display*
**4** il pulsante della data e dei secondi
– *date and second button*
**5** il cinturino
– *strap (watch strap)*
**6** l'orologio elettronico mult'funzionale da polso
– *multifunction electronic watch*
**7** l'indicazione *f* analogica
– *analogue (Am. analog) display*
**8** il pulsante della suoneria (pulsante *m* della sveglia)
– *alarm button*
**9** il pulsante di arresto del programma
– *stopwatch button*
**10** l'anello girevole di regolazione *f* dell'ora
– *rotating bezel (time-lapse indicator ring)*
**11** l'orologio a segnale *m* orario programmato (la sveglia)
– *calendar clock (alarm clock)*
**12** l'indicazione *f* oraria digitale con cifre *f pl* scorrevoli
– *digital display with flip-over numerals*
**13** l'indicazione *f* dell'orario di sveglia
– *alarm indicator*
**14** il tasto d'arresto
– *stop button*
**15** la rotella di regolazione *f* (il bottone regolatore)
– *forward and backward wind knob*
**16** l'orologio a pendolo
– *grandfather clock*
**17** il quadrante
– *face*
**18** la cassa dell'orologio
– *clock case*
**19** il pendolo (il perpendicolo)
– *pendulum*
**20** il peso di rintocco
– *striking weight*
**21** il peso di carica e movimento
– *time weight*
**22** l'orologio solare (la meridiana)
– *sundial*
**23** la clessidra
– *hourglass (egg timer)*

**24-35 gli elementi dell'orologio automatico da polso** (orologio a caricamento automatico)
– **components of an automatic watch** *(automatic wristwatch, self-winding watch)*
**24** la massa oscillante (il rotore)
– *weight (rotor)*
**25** il rubino (la pietra cuscinetto), un rubino sintetico
– *stone (jewel, jewelled bearing) a synthetic ruby*
**26** il nottolino di tensione *f*
– *click*
**27** la ruota di tensione *f*
– *click wheel*
**28** il meccanismo (i congegni) dell'orologio
– *clockwork (clockwork mechanism)*
**29** la placca dell'orologio
– *bottom train plate*
**30** il bariletto
– *spring barrel*
**31** il bilanciere
– *balance wheel*
**32** la ruota dell'ancora
– *escape wheel*
**33** la rotella di caricamento
– *crown wheel*
**34** la corona
– *winding crown*
**35** il meccanismo motore
– *drive mechanism*
**36** il principio dell'orologio elettronico a quarzo
– *principle of the electronic quartz watch*
**37** il quarzo (quarzo oscillatore, quarzo piezoelettrico)
– *quartz*
**38** la fonte motrice (il motore primo), una cellula pulsante
– *power source (a button cell)*
**39** la lancetta delle ore
– *hour hand*
**40** la lancetta dei minuti
– *minute hand*
**41** il movimento (l'ingranaggio delle ruote)
– *wheels*
**42** il motore di comando del movimento
– *stepping motor (stepper motor)*
**43** la ripartizione della frequenza (contatti integrati)
– *frequency divider (integrated circuit)*
**44** il decodificatore
– *decoder*

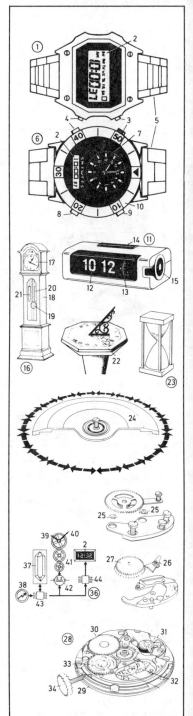

**1-19 il negozio di ottica**
– *sales premises*
**1-4 la prova degli occhiali**
– *spectacle fitting*
**1** l'ottico
– *optician*
**2** il cliente
– *customer*
**3** la montatura degli occhiali (*qui:* montatura di prova)
– *trial frame*
**4** lo specchio
– *mirror*
**5** la colonna-vetrinetta delle montature (la scelta delle montature, la scelta degli occhiali)
– *stand with spectacle frames (display of frames, range of spectacles)*
**6** gli occhiali da sole *m*
– *sunglasses (sun spectacles)*
**7** la montatura di (in) metallo
– *metal frame*
**8** la montatura di (in) corno
– *tortoiseshell frame (shell frame)*
**9** gli occhiali
– *spectacles (glasses)*
**10-14 la montatura degli occhiali**
– *spectacle frame*

**10** il contorno delle lenti (*raro:* la cerchiatura delle lenti)
– *fitting (mount) of the frame*
**11** il ponticello (l'archetto)
– *bridge*
**12** l'aletta (la pinna, il nasello)
– *pad bridge*
**13** la susta (la stanghetta)
– *side*
**14** la cerniera della susta
– *side joint*
**15** la lente degli occhiali, una lente bifocale (lente *f* a due curvature *f pl,* lente a due distanze *f pl* focali)
– *spectacle lens, a bifocal lens*
**16** lo specchietto
– *hand mirror (hand glass)*
**17** il binocolo
– *binoculars*
**18** il cannocchiale (il tubo), un cannocchiale monoculare
– *monocular telescope (tube)*
**19** il microscopio
– *microscope*
**20-47 il laboratorio dell'ottico**
– *optician's workshop*
**20** il tavolo da lavoro
– *workbench*

**21** il frontifocometro (l'apparecchio universale di misura della focale delle lenti)
– *universal centring (centering) apparatus*
**22** il portaventosa
– *centring (centering) suction holder*
**23** la ventosa centratrice
– *sucker*
**24** la mola automatica per sgrossare le lenti e rifinire il contorno
– *edging machine*
**25** le dime (sagome *f pl*) per mola automatica
– *formers for the lens edging machine*
**26** la dima posizionata (la dima nel suo alloggio)
– *inserted former*
**27** il disco copiadima rotante contemporaneamente
– *rotating printer*
**28** il gruppo dei dischi diamantati (dischi *m pl* a sgrezzare)
– *abrasive wheel combination*
**29** l'apparecchio di comando
– *control unit*

**30** l'elemento (il pezzo) della macchina
– *machine part*
**31** l'allacciamento dell'acqua fredda
– *cooling water pipe*
**32** la sostanza liquida detergente (liquido detergente)
– *cleaning fluid*
**33** il tensiometro (misuratore del punto massimo di rottura)
– *focimeter (vertex refractionometer)*
**34** il centratore (apparecchio di centraggio, di pressione *f* della ventosa e di bloccaggio dei due metalli)
– *metal-blocking device*
**35** gruppo di mole *f pl* diamantate e dischi *m pl* di rettifica
– *abrasive wheel combination and forms of edging*
**36** la prima mola (il disco sgrossatore, la mola sgrossatrice)
– *roughing wheel for preliminary surfacing*
**37** la mola a finire per bisello interno o esterno
– *fining lap for positive and negative lens surfaces*

**38** la mola a finire per faccia a nervature *f pl* e faccia piana
– *fining lap for special and flat lenses*
**39** la lente pianoconcava a faccia piana
– *plano-concave lens with a flat surface*
**40** la lente pianoconcava con faccia a nervature *f pl*
– *plano-concave lens with a special surface*
**41** la lente convessoconcava con faccia a nervature *f pl*
– *concave and convex lens with a special surface*
**42** la lente convessoconcava con faccia a bisello interno
– *convex and concave lens with a special surface*
**43** il riunito per l'esame *m* oftalmologico
– *ophthalmic test stand*
**44** il forottero con oftalmometro e rifrattometro dell'occhio
– *phoropter with ophthalmometer and optometer (refractometer)*
**45** la cassetta con le lenti di prova
– *trial lens case*

**46** lo schermo (di collimazione *f* ) dei test visivi
– *collimator*
**47** l'ottotipo a proiezione *f* (proiettore *m* dei test visivi)
– *acuity projector*

1 il microscopio da laboratorio e da ricerca: sistema *m* LEITZ (talvolta in sezione *f* )
– *laboratory and research microscope*, Leitz system
2 lo stativo
– *stand*
3 il piede dello stativo
– *base*
4 lo spostamento grossolano
– *coarse adjustment*
5 lo spostamento di precisione *f*
– *fine adjustment*
6 il percorso del raggio d'illuminazione *f*
– *illumination beam path (illumination path)*
7 l'ottica d'illuminazione *f*
– *illumination optics*
8 il condensatore
– *condenser*
9 il piatto
– *microscope (microscopic, object) stage*
10 il tavolino a croce *f*
– *mechanical stage*
11 il portaobiettivo a revolver *m*
– *objective turret (revolving nosepiece)*
12 il tubo binoculare
– *binocular head*
13 i prismi di deflessione *f*
– *beam-splitting prisms*
14 il microscopio per radioscopia, con macchina fotografica e impianto di polarizzazione *f* sistema *m* Zeiss
– *transmitted-light microscope with camera and polarizer*, Zeiss system
15 la base
– *stage base*
16 l'otturatore *m* del diaframma
– *aperture-stop slide*
17 la tavola rotante universale
– *universal stage*
18 il supporto dell'obiettivo
– *lens panel*
19 gli oculari
– *polarizing filter*
20 il supporto per la macchina fotografica
– *camera*
21 il quadrante
– *focusing screen*
22 la sistemazione dei tubi
– *discussion tube arrangement*
23 il microscopio metallico a grande campo, un microscopio a illuminazione *f* dall'alto
– *wide-field metallurgical microscope, a reflected-light microscope (microscope for reflected light)*
24 lo schermo di proiezione *f* smerigliato
– *matt screen (ground glass screen, projection screen)*
25 la cinepresa a grande campo
– *large-format camera*
26 la cinepresa a piccolo campo
– *miniature camera*

27 la piastra di base *f*
– *base plate*
28 la sede lampada
– *lamphouse*
29 il tavolo girevole
– *mechanical stage*
30 il portaobiettivi a revolver *m*
– *objective turret (revolving nosepiece)*
31 il microscopio chirurgico
– *surgical microscope*
32 lo stativo a colonna
– *pillar stand*
33 l'illuminazione *f* del campo dell'obiettivo
– *field illumination*
34 il microscopio fotografico
– *photomicroscope*
35 il caricatore a piccolo campo
– *miniature film cassette*
36 l'uscita aggiuntiva per macchina da ripresa televisiva o a grande formato
– *photomicrographic camera attachment for large-format or television camera*
37 l'apparecchio di controllo per superfici *f pl*
– *surface-finish microscope*
38 il tubo taglia luce *f*
– *light section tube*
39 la cremagliera
– *rack and pinion*
40 il microscopio stereo a grande campo, con zoom *m*
– *zoom stereomicroscope*
41 l'obiettivo zoom *m*
– *zoom lens*
42 il misuratore del pulviscolo
– *dust counter*
43 la camera di misurazione *f*
– *measurement chamber*
44 l'uscita dati *m pl*
– *data output*
45 l'uscita analogica
– *analogue (Am. analog) output*
46 il selettore del campo di misurazione *f*
– *measurement range selector*
47 l'indicatore *m* digitale dei dati
– *digital display (digital readout)*
48 il rifrattometro ad immersione *f* per l'esame *m* di prodotti *m pl* alimentari
– *dipping refractometer for examining food*
49 il microscopio-fotometro
– *microscopic photometer*
50 la sorgente luminosa del fotometro
– *photometric light source*
51 il fotomoltiplicatore (il moltiplicatore fotoelettronico)
– *measuring device (photomultiplier, multiplier phototube)*
52 la sorgente luminosa per illuminazione *f* panoramica
– *light source for survey illumination*
53 l'armadietto elettronico
– *remote electronics*

54 il microscopio universale a grande campo
– *universal wide-field microscope*
55 il supporto per macchina fotografica o da proiezione *f*
– *adapter for camera or projector attachment*
56 il pulsante regolazione *f* distanza dell'oculare *m*
– *eyepiece focusing knob*
57 il supporto filtri
– *filter pick-up*
58 la base
– *handrest*
59 la sede lampada per l'illuminazione *f* dall'alto
– *lamphouse for incident (vertical) illumination*
60 il collegamento della sede lampada per la radioscopia
– *lamphouse connector for transillumination*
61 il microscopio stereo a grande campo
– *wide-field stereomicroscope*
62 gli obiettivi intercambiabili
– *interchangeable lenses (objectives)*
63 l'illuminazione *f* dall'alto
– *incident (vertical) illumination (incident top lighting)*
64 il microscopio macchina da presa a ripresa automatica, una macchina da presa a mirino
– *fully automatic microscope camera, a camera with photomicro mount adapter*
65 la cassetta
– *film cassette*
66 il condensatore universale per microscopio di ricerca
– *universal condenser for research microscope 1*
67 la macchina da presa universale per fotogrammetria (il fototeodolite)
– *universal-type measuring machine for photogrammetry (phototheodolite)*
68 la macchina fotografica per fotogrammetria
– *photogrammetric camera*
69 il motolivellatore, un livellatore a compensatore *m*
– *motor-driven level, a compensator level*
70 il misuratore di percorso elettrottico
– *electro-optical distance-measuring instrument*
71 la camera da presa stereo
– *stereometric camera*
72 la base orizzontale
– *horizontal base*
73 il teodolite angolare
– *one-second theodolite*

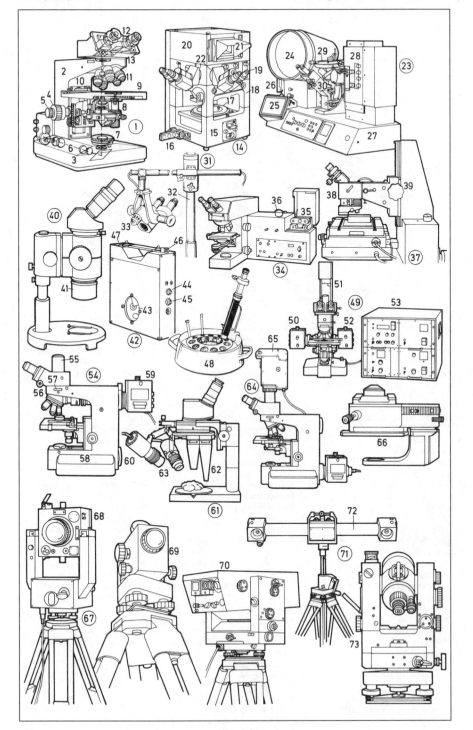

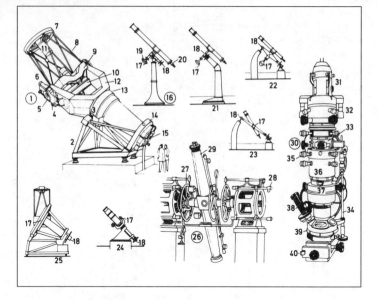

1  **il telescopio riflettore (il telescopio catodico) 2,2 m**
– *2.2 m reflecting telescope (reflector)*
2  la base (il basamento)
– *pedestal (base)*
3  il sistema di supporto assiale-radiale
– *axial-radial bearing*
4  il meccanismo di declinazione *f*
– *declination gear*
5  l'asse *m* di declinazione *f*
– *declination axis*
6  il cuscinetto di declinazione *f*
– *declination bearing*
7  l'anello anteriore
– *front ring*
8  il tubo
– *tube (body tube)*
9  la parte centrale del tubo
– *tube centre (Am. center) section*
10  lo specchio principale
– *primary mirror (main mirror)*
11  lo specchio deflettore
– *secondary mirror (deviation mirror, corrector plate)*
12  la forcella (il traliccio)
– *fork mounting (fork)*
13  la copertura
– *cover*
14  il supporto di guida
– *guide bearing*
15  il comando principale dell'asse *m* orario
– *main drive unit of the polar axis*
16-25  **montature** *f pl* **(montaggi** *f pl*) **di telescopi** *m pl*
– *telescope mountings (telescope mounts)*

16  il telescopio rifrattore (il telescopio diottrico): nella montatura (nel montaggio) tedesca
– *refractor (refracting telescope) on a German-type mounting*
17  l'asse di declinazione *f*
– *declination axis*
18  l'asse polare
– *polar axis*
19  il contrappeso
– *counterweight (counterpoise)*
20  l'oculare *m*
– *eyepiece*
21  la montatura (il montaggio) a colonna articolata
– *knee mounting with a bent column*
22  la montatura (il montaggio) ad asse *m* inglese
– *English-type axis mounting (axis mount)*
23  la montatura (il montaggio) inglese
– *English-type yoke mounting (yoke mount)*
24  la montatura (il montaggio) a forcella
– *fork mounting (fork mount)*
25  la montatura (il montaggio) a ferro di cavallo
– *horseshoe mounting (horseshoe mount)*
26  il cerchio meridiano
– *meridian circle*
27  il cerchio graduato
– *divided circle (graduated circle)*
28  il microscopio di lettura
– *reading microscope*
29  il telescopio meridiano
– *meridian telescope*

30  il microscopio elettronico
– *electron microscope*
31-39  il tubo *m pl* del microscopio
– *microscope tube (microscope body, body tube)*
31  la sorgente di radiazioni *f pl*
– *electron gun*
32  le lenti condensatore *m*
– *condensers*
33  la tavola portaoggetto
– *specimen insertion air lock*
34  il regolatore della tavola portaoggetto
– *control for the specimen stage adjustment*
35  l'azionamento del diaframma
– *control for the objective apertures*
36  la lente obiettivo
– *objective lens*
37  la finestra per osservazione *f* immagine *f* intermedia
– *intermediate image screen*
38  la lente a cannocchiale *m*
– *telescope magnifier*
39  la finestra per osservazione *f* immagine *f* finale
– *final image tube*
40  la cinepresa per pellicole *f pl* o lastre *f pl* a cassetta
– *photographic chamber for film and plate magazines*

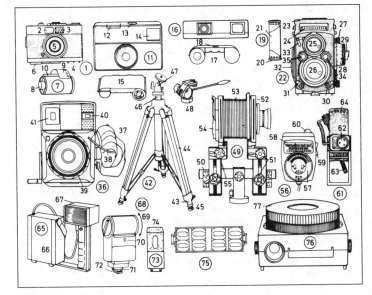

1 la macchina fotografica compatta di piccolo formato
– *miniature camera (35 mm camera)*
2 il mirino
– *viewfinder eyepiece*
3 l'esposimetro
– *meter cell*
4 l'innesto flash
– *accessory shoe*
5 l'obiettivo estraibile
– *flush lens*
6 il bottone riavvolgimento pellicola
– *rewind handle (rewind, rewind crank)*
7 il caricatore di piccolo formato (135)
– *miniature film cassette (135 film cassette, 35 mm cassette)*
8 la bobina
– *film spool*
9 la pellicola con la linguetta d'aggancio e la perforazione
– *film with leader and perforations*
10 l'apertura del caricatore
– *cassette slit (cassette exit slot)*
11 la macchina fotografica con caricatore *m*
– *cartridge-loading camera*
12 il bottone di scatto
– *shutter release (shutter release button)*
13 l'innesto del flash a cubo
– *flash cube contact*
14 il mirino quadrato
– *rectangular viewfinder*
15 il caricatore Instamatic
– *126 cartridge (instamatic cartridge)*
16 la macchina fotografica tascabile
– *pocket camera (subminiature camera)*
17 il caricatore piccolo formato
– *110 cartridge (subminiature cartridge)*
18 la finestrella controllo numero pose *f pl*
– *film window*
19 il rullino
– *120 rollfilm*
20 la bobina
– *rollfilm spool*
21 la carta di protezione *f*
– *backing paper*
22 la macchina a due obiettivi *m pl*
– *twin-lens reflex camera*
23 il mirino a pozzetto a cerniera
– *folding viewfinder hood (focusing hood)*
24 l'esposimetro
– *meter cell*
25 l'obiettivo del mirino
– *viewing lens*
26 l'obiettivo
– *object lens*

27 il bottone della bobina
– *spool knob*
28 la scala delle distanze
– *distance setting (focus setting)*
29 la scala dei diaframmi
– *exposure meter using needle-matching system*
30 l'attacco flash
– *flash contact*
31 la leva dell'autoscatto
– *shutter release*
32 la leva di caricamento
– *film transport (film advance, film wind)*
33 il contatto del flash
– *flash switch*
34 il bottone regolazione *f* diaframma *m*
– *aperture-setting control*
35 il bottone regolazione *f* tempi *m pl*
– *shutter speed control*
36 la macchina fotografica portatile grande formato
– *large-format hand camera (press camera)*
37 l'impugnatura
– *grip (handgrip)*
38 lo scatto a filo
– *cable release*
39 l'anello zigrinato scala distanze *f pl*
– *distance-setting ring (focusing ring)*
40 il telemetro
– *rangefinder window*
41 il mirino a più formati *m pl*
– *multiple-frame viewfinder (universal viewfinder)*
42 il treppiede (lo stativo a telescopio)
– *tripod*
43 la gamba
– *tripod leg*
44 l'asta allungabile
– *tubular leg*
45 il piede di gomma
– *rubber foot*
46 la colonna mediana
– *central column*
47 la testa con giunto sferico
– *ball and socket head*
48 la testa per riprese *f pl* cinematografiche
– *cine camera pan and tilt head*
49 la macchina fotografica a grande formato a soffietto
– *large-format folding camera*
50 il banco ottico
– *optical bench*
51 il basculaggio
– *standard adjustment*
52 gli obiettivi per i vari formati
– *lens standard*

53 il soffietto
– *bellows*
54 la parte posteriore della macchina
– *camera back*
55 il basculaggio posteriore
– *back standard adjustment*
56 l'esposimetro manuale
– *hand-held exposure meter (exposure meter)*
57 il disco calcolatore
– *calculator dial*
58 le scale indicatrici con indice *m* mobile
– *scales (indicator scales) with indicator needle (pointer)*
59 l'interruttore *m* a bilico della misura
– *range switch (high/low range selector)*
60 la calotta diffusore *m* per misurazione *f* luce *f*
– *diffuser for incident light measurement*
61 un esposimetro a cassetta per macchine *f pl* fotografiche a grande formato
– *probe exposure meter for large-format cameras*
62 lo strumento di misura
– *meter*
63 la sonda di misurazione *f*
– *probe*
64 la slitta
– *dark slide*
65 il flash elettronico in due parti *f pl*
– *battery-portable electronic flash (battery-portable electronic flash unit)*
66 il generatore (la batteria)
– *power pack unit (battery)*
67 la torcia flash
– *flash head*
68 il flash elettronico compatto
– *single-unit electronic flash (flashgun)*
69 il riflettore orientabile
– *swivel-mounted reflector*
70 il fotodiodo
– *photodiode*
71 lo zoccolo flash
– *foot*
72 il contatto mediano
– *hot-shoe contact*
73 il flash a cubo
– *flash cube unit*
74 il cubo
– *flash cube*
75 il flash bar (AGFA)
– *flash bar (AGFA)*
76 il proiettore per diapositive *f pl*
– *slide projector*
77 il caricatore circolare
– *rotary magazine*

**1-24 la macchina fotografica reflex** (la macchina fotografica reflex di piccolo formato a specchio ribaltabile monoculare)
- *system camera (fully automatic miniature single-lens reflex camera)*
**1** l'interruttore *m*
- *main switch*
**2** il pulsante di funzione *f* (per impostazione *f* del diaframma e motore *m* autofocus *m*)
- *function adjustment button (to set exposure adjustment value, drive mode, and focus area)*
**3** il pulsante funzioni *f pl* esposizione *f*
- *exposure mode button*
**4** l'innesto per accessori *m pl*
- *accessory shoe*
**5** il tasto riavvolgimento pellicola
- *program reset button*
**6** il display dati *m pl*
- *data panel (data monitor, data display)*
**7** il tasto inserimento scheda
- *card on/off key*
**8** il selettore di funzione *f*
- *function selector key*
**9** la scheda con programmi *m pl* fotografici speciali
- *chip program card*
**10** la chiusura vano inserimento scheda
- *card door*
**11** il visualizzatore scheda
- *card window*
**12** il vano pile *f pl*
- *battery chamber*
**13** il collegamento comando a distanza
- *remote control terminal*
**14** il pulsante di scatto
- *shutter release (shutter release button)*
**15** la finestra per funzione *f* autofocus *m* e segnale luminoso autoscatto
- *autofocus (AF) illuminator and self-timer light*
**16** il pulsante per la regolazione valori *m pl* sensibilità inseriti manualmente
- *manual shutter control [up/down control]*
**17** lo specchio ribaltabile
- *reflex mirror*
**18** il sensore autofocus *m*, un convertitore di immagine *f* CCD
- *autofocus sensor, a CCD image converter (image sensor)*
**19** l'anello di inserimento a baionetta
- *bayonet mounting ring*
**20** il pulsante regolazione *f* diaframma
- *aperture setting button*
**21** il blocco della baionetta
- *lens release*
**22** il commutatore dell'autofocus *m* (per passare a una messa a fuoco manuale)
- *focus-mode switch (to switch to manual focusing)*
**23** l'obiettivo Zoom autofocus *m*, un obiettivo Zoom (35–105)
- *autofocus zoom lens, a x3 zoom lens (35–105 mm)*
**24** la serie contatti *m pl* per diaframma *m* e autofocus *m*
- *aperture and autofocus contacts*

**25-35 i vetri del mirino** (quadrante *m*, volg.: vetro smerigliato, vetro a microprismi *m pl*)
- *viewfinder screen (focusing screen, matt screen), a micro-honeycombed focusing screen*
**25** il segnale inserimento flash
- *flash-on signal*
**26** l'indicatore *m* flash pronto
- *flash-ready signal*
**27** gli indicatori *m* di nitidezza
- *focus signals*
**28** il grande campo autofocus *m*
- *wide focus area*
**29** l'indicatore *m* tempo otturatore *m*
- *shutter speed display*
**30** l'indicatore *m* di sincronizzazione *f* per l'inserimento manuale dell'esposizione *f*
- *manual-exposure compensation-value indicator*
**31** l'indicatore *m* correzione *f* diaframma *m* o esposizione *f*
- *aperture or exposure adjustment indicator*
**32** l'indicatore *m* misurazione *f* spot
- *spot metering indicator*
**33** il cerchio indicatore misurazione *f* spot
- *spot metering area*
**34** il campo centrale autofocus *m*
- *centre focus area*
**35** il selettore del campo di misurazione *f*
- *focus area indicator*
**36-42 il display dati** *m pl* LCD
- *LCD data panel (data monitor)*
**36** l'indicatore *m* di programma *m*
- *program exposure-mode indicator*
**37** l'indicatore *m* numero foto *f pl*
- *frame counter*
**38** gli indicatori di funzione *f*
- *function indicators*
**39** l'indicatore *m* correzione *f* diaframma *m* o esposizione *f*
- *aperture or exposure adjustment indicator*
**40** l'indicatore *m* tempo otturazione *f* o sensibilità pellicola
- *shutter speed or film speed (film sensitivity) indicator*
**41** l'indicatore *m* trasporto pellicola
- *film transport indicator*
**42** la freccia di funzione *f*
- *function pointer*
**43** gli obiettivi intercambiabili (obiettivi autofocus, obiettivi AF )
- *interchangeable lenses (autofocus lenses, AF lenses)*
**44** l'obiettivo occhio di pesce *m*
- *fisheye lens (fisheye)*
**45** l'obiettivo grandangolo (il grandangolo) (distanza focale ridotta)
- *wide-angle lens (short focal-length lens)*
**46** l'obiettivo normale
- *standard lens*
**47** la distanza focale media
- *medium focal-length lens*

**48** il teleobiettivo (la distanza focale lunga), un obiettivo Zoom
- *telephoto lens (long focal-length lens), a zoom lens (variable focus lens, varifocal lens)*
**49** il teleobiettivo fisso
- *long-focus lens*
**50** l'obiettivo a specchio
- *mirror lens*
**51** il teleconvertitore
- *tele converter*
**52** il dorso datario (il data back)
- *data back*
**53** il caricatore pellicola da 10 m
- *ten-metre (Am. ten-meter) film back (magazine back)*
**54-74 l'accessorio per riprese** *f pl* in primo piano e macro
- *accessories for close-up and macro shots*
**54** un tubo intermedio
- *extension tube*
**55** l'anello adattatore
- *adapter ring*
**56** l'anello di inversione *f*
- *reversing ring*
**57** l'obiettivo in posizione *f* retro
- *lens in retrofocus position*
**58** il soffietto (il soffietto per la posizione avvicinata)
- *bellows unit (extension bellows, close-up bellows attachment)*
**59** le slitte di regolazione *f*
- *focusing stage*
**60** il set per duplicare diapositive *f pl*
- *slide-copying attachment*
**61** l'adattatore *m* per il duplicatore
- *slide-copying adapter*
**62** il pulsante a distanza
- *cable release*
**63** lo stativo per riproduzioni *f pl*
- *copying stand (copy stand)*
**64** il braccio per riproduzioni *f pl*
- *arm of the copying stand (copy stand)*
**65** l'impugnatura a spalla
- *rifle grip*
**66** il cavalletto da tavolo (il treppiede, il ministativo)
- *table(-top) tripod (mini tripod)*
**67** la custodia per l'apparecchio fotografico
- *ever-ready case*
**68** la custodia per l'obiettivo
- *lens case*
**69** la custodia in nappa per l'obiettivo
- *soft-leather lens pouch*
**70** la borsa in metallo per l'attrezzatura fotografica
- *camera bag, of metallic construction: aluminium (Am. aluminum) case*
**71** il caricatore pellicola
- *film container*
**72** il portafiltri
- *filter case*
**73** la borsa a più scomparti *m pl*
- *second body*
**74** il flash anulare per riprese *f pl* macro
- *ring flash for macro shots*

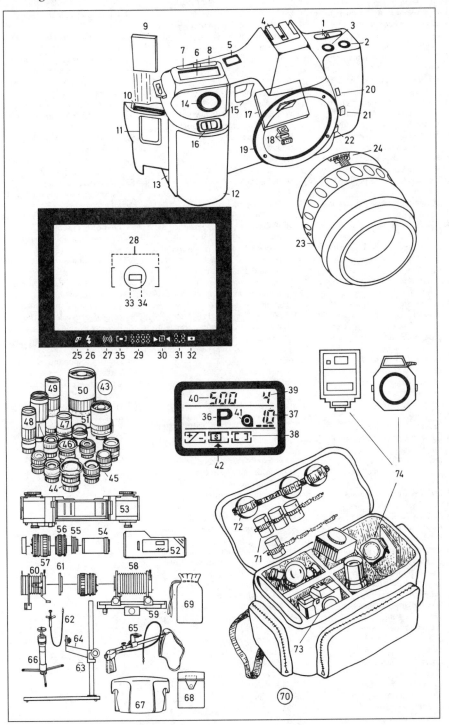

**1-60 attrezzatura della camera oscura**
- *darkroom equipment*
**1** la sviluppatrice (il tank)
- *developing tank*
**2** il rocchetto con scanalature *f pl* a spirale *f*
- *spiral (developing spiral, tank reel)*
**3** la sviluppatrice a più piani *m pl*
- *multi-unit developing tank*
**4** il rocchetto con scanalature *f pl* a spirale *f* a più piani *m pl*
- *multi-unit tank spiral*
**5** la sviluppatrice a luce *f* solare
- *daylight-loading tank*
**6** il caricatore per la pellicola
- *loading chamber*
**7** la manopola per avvolgere la pellicola
- *film transport handle*
**8** il termometro
- *developing tank thermometer*
**9** la bottiglia opaca per la soluzione di sviluppo
- *collapsible bottle for developing solution*
**10** le bottiglie per prodotti *m pl* chimici per il primo sviluppo, il bagno di stop, lo sviluppo cromogeno, il bagno di sbianca-induritore, il fissaggio
- *chemical bottles for first developer, stop bath, colour developer, bleach-hardener, stabilizer*
**11** i cilindri graduati
- *measuring cylinders*
**12** l'imbuto
- *funnel*
**13** il termometro per le bacinelle
- *tray thermometer (dish thermometer)*
**14** le pinzette stendipellicola
- *film clip*
**15** la vaschetta di lavaggio
- *wash tank (washer)*
**16** l'afflusso dell'acqua
- *water supply pipe*
**17** il deflusso dell'acqua
- *water outlet pipe*
**18** il contaminuti (con suoneria)
- *laboratory timer (timer)*
**19** l'agitatore *m* della pellicola
- *automatic film agitator*
**20** la sviluppatrice a tamburo
- *developing tank*
**21** la lampada per l'illuminazione *f* della camera oscura
- *darkroom lamp (safelight)*
**22** la lastra col filtro ottico
- *filter screen*
**23** l'armadio essicatore
- *film drier (drying cabinet)*
**24** il temporizzatore
- *exposure timer*

**25** la bacinella di sviluppo
- *developing dish (developing tray)*
**26** l'ingranditore *m* (l'apparecchio per ingrandimenti *m pl*)
- *enlarger*
**27** la base
- *baseboard*
**28** la colonna portante
- *angled column*
**29** la calotta (la testa portalampada)
- *lamphouse (lamp housing)*
**30** il portanegativi
- *negative carrier*
**31** il soffietto
- *bellows*
**32** l'obiettivo
- *lens*
**33** la manopola
- *friction drive for fine adjustment*
**34** il dispositivo di regolazione *f* di altezza
- *height adjustment (scale adjustment)*
**35** il telaio d'ingrandimento
- *masking frame (easel)*
**36** il fotometro (il densimetro) analizzatore dei colori
- *colour (Am. color) analyser*
**37** la lampada controllo trattamento colori
- *colour (Am. color) analyser lamp*
**38** il cavo
- *probe lead*
**39** il pulsante del tempo di esposizione *f*
- *exposure time balancing knob*
**40** l'ingranditore *m* con testa per le pellicole a colori *m pl* (l'apparecchio per ingrandimento pellicole *f pl* a colori *m pl*)
- *colour (Am. color) enlarger*
**41** la testa dell'apparecchio
- *enlarger head*
**42** la torretta portafiltri
- *column*
**43-45** il pulsante del miscelatore
- *colour-mixing (Am. color-mixing) knob*
**43** il regolatore del filtro Magenta
- *magenta filter adjustment (minus green filter adjustment)*
**44** il regolatore del filtro giallo
- *yellow filter adjustment (minus blue filter adjustment)*
**45** il regolatore del filtro ciano
- *cyan filter adjustment (minus red filter adjustment)*
**46** il regolatore dei filtri
- *red swing filter*
**47** la pinza stendifilm
- *print tongs*
**48** la sviluppatrice
- *processing drum*

**49** il rullo essicatore
- *squeegee*
**50** l'assortimento della carta sensibile
- *range (assortment) of papers*
**51** la carta per ingrandimenti *m pl* a colori *m pl*, una confezione di carta per fotografie *f pl*
- *colour (Am. color) printing paper, a packet of photographic printing paper*
**52** i prodotti chimici per lo sviluppo a colori *m pl*
- *colour (Am. color) chemicals (colour processing chemicals)*
**53** il fotometro
- *enlarging meter (enlarging photometer)*
**54** il pulsante di regolazione *f* con l'indice *m* di sensibilità della carta
- *adjusting knob with paper speed scale*
**55** la sonda di misurazione *f*
- *probe*
**56** la camera di sviluppo termostatico semiautomatica
- *semi-automatic thermostatically controlled developing dish*
**57** il blocco riscaldante
- *rapid print drier (heated print drier)*
**58** la lastra a specchio
- *glazing sheet*
**59** il telo teso (per smaltatrice *f* )
- *pressure cloth*
**60** la sviluppatrice automatica a rulli *m pl*
- *automatic processor (machine processor)*

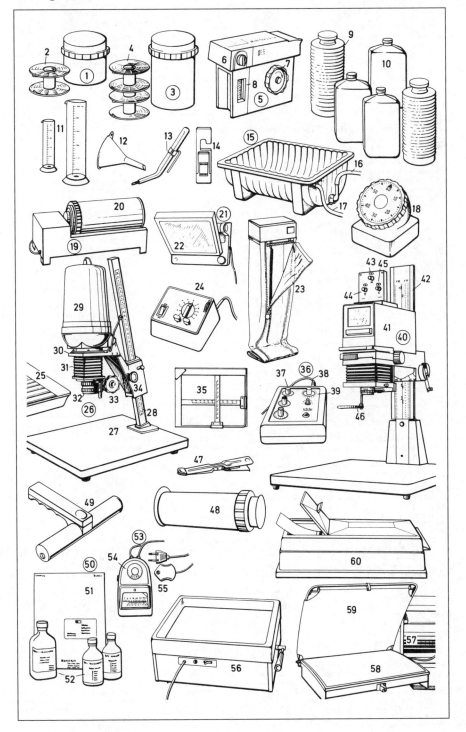

1 la cinepresa per pellicola a passo ridotto, una cinepresa per film *m* sonoro super 8
– *cine camera, a Super-8 sound camera*
2 l'obiettivo zoom variabile (l'obiettivo a focale *m* variabile)
– *interchangeable zoom lens (variable focus lens, varifocal lens)*
3 la regolazione della distanza e la regolazione manuale della distanza focale
– *distance setting (focus setting) and manual focal length setting*
4 l'anello per la regolazione manuale del diaframma
– *aperture ring (aperture-setting ring, aperture control ring) for manual aperture setting*
5 l'impugnatura
– *handgrip with battery chamber*
6 il dispositivo di scatto con allacciamento
– *shutter release with cable release socket*
7 il generatore di impulsi *m pl* per l'impianto di registrazione *f* del suono (nel caso di un funzionamento a due piste *f pl*)
– *pilot tone or pulse generator socket for the sound recording equipment (with the dual film-tape system)*
8 il cavo di collegamento per il microfono o altra fonte *f* sonora (in caso di funzionamento a una pista)
– *sound connecting cord for microphone or external sound source (in single-system recording)*
9 l'allacciamento per comando a distanza
– *remote control socket (remote control jack)*
10 l'allacciamento cuffie *f pl*
– *headphone socket (sim.: earphone socket)*
11 l'interruttore *m* del sistema di regolazione *f*
– *autofocus override switch*
12 l'interruttore *m* velocità pellicola
– *filming speed selector*
13 il selettore registrazione *f* suono per funzionamento automatico o manuale
– *sound recording selector switch for automatic or manual operation*
14 l'oculare *m* con mascherina
– *eyepiece with eyecup*
15 la vite di regolazione *f* diottrie *f pl*
– *diopter control ring (dioptric adjustment ring)*
16 il regolatore modulazione *f* sonora
– *recording level control (audio level control, recording sensitivity selector)*
17 il selettore esposimetro
– *manual/automatic exposure control switch*
18 il regolatore sensibilità pellicola
– *film speed setting*
19 l'impianto power-zoom
– *power zooming arrangement*
20 il diaframma automatico
– *automatic aperture control*
21 il sistema registrazione *f* suono pista
– *sound track system*
22 la cinepresa per film *m* sonoro
– *sound camera*
23 il braccio estraibile del microfono
– *telescopic microphone boom*
24 il microfono
– *microphone*
25 il cavo allacciamento microfono
– *microphone connecting lead (microphone connecting cord)*
26 il tavolo di missaggio
– *mixing console (mixing desk, mixer)*
27 le entrate per diverse fonti *f pl* sonore
– *inputs from various sound sources*
28 il cavo di uscita cinepresa
– *output to camera*
29 la cassetta Super 8 per pellicola sonora
– *Super-8 sound film cartridge*
30 il finestrino (il quadro, il quadruccio)
– *film gate of the cartridge*

31 la bobina di scorta
– *feed spool*
32 la bobina di riavvolgimento
– *take-up spool*
33 la testina di registrazione *f*
– *recording head (sound head)*
34 il rullo di trasporto (il capstan)
– *transport roller (capstan)*
35 il rullo pressore in gomma
– *rubber pinch roller (capstan idler)*
36 la scanalatura di guida
– *guide step (guide notch)*
37 la scanalatura di comando esposizione *f*
– *exposure meter control step*
38 la scanalatura di entrata filtro conversione *f*
– *conversion filter step (colour, Am. color, conversion filter step)*
39 la cassetta Single 8
– *single-8 cassette*
40 l'incavo del finestrino
– *film gate opening*
41 la pellicola non esposta
– *unexposed film*
42 la pellicola esposta
– *exposed film*
43 la cinepresa (la macchina da presa) sedici millimetri *m pl*
– *16 mm camera*
44 il mirino reflex
– *reflex finder (through-the-lens reflex finder)*
45 il caricatore
– *magazine*
46-49 la testa degli obiettivi
– *lens head*
46 la torretta portaobiettivi
– *lens turret (turret head)*
47 il teleobiettivo
– *telephoto lens*
48 l'obiettivo grandangolare (il grandangolo)
– *wide-angle lens*
49 l'obiettivo normale
– *normal lens (standard lens)*
50 la manovella
– *winding handle*
51 la Compact Camera Super 8
– *compact Super-8 camera*
52 il contametri (l'indicatore *m* del passaggio pellicola)
– *footage counter*
53 l'obiettivo macro-zoom
– *macro zoom lens*
54 la leva dello zoom
– *zooming lever*
55 la macro lente per riprese *f pl* ravvicinate
– *macro lens attachment (close-up lens)*
56 la rotaia per riprese *f pl* macro (supporto per piccoli oggetti *m pl*)
– *macro frame (mount for small originals)*
57 la cinepresa per riprese *f pl* subacquee
– *underwater housing (underwater case)*
58 il mirino
– *direct-vision frame finder*
59 il distanziatore
– *measuring rod*
60 il piano di stabilizzazione *f*
– *stabilizing wing*
61 l'impugnatura
– *grip (handgrip)*
62 la leva di chiusura
– *locking bolt*
63 la levetta di comando
– *control lever (operating lever)*
64 il vetro frontale
– *porthole*
65 l'inizio sincronizzato di ripresa
– *synchronization start (sync start)*
66 la cinepresa (la macchina da presa) portatile
– *professional press-type camera*
67 il cameraman
– *cameraman*

68 l'assistente *m* al suono
– *camera assistant (sound assistant)*
69 la battuta di mani *f pl* per indicare il tipo di sincronizzazione *f*
– *handclap marking sync start*
70 la registrazione del suono e delle pellicole a due piste *f pl*
– *dual film-tape recording using a tape recorder*
71 la macchina da riprese che dà gli impulsi *m pl*
– *pulse-generating camera*
72 il cavo
– *pulse cable*
73 il registratore a cassetta
– *cassette recorder*
74 il microfono
– *microphone*
75 la riproduzione del suono e della pellicola a due piste *f pl*
– *dual film-tape reproduction*
76 il registratore a cassette *f pl*
– *tape cassette*
77 il sincronizzatore
– *synchronization unit*
78 il proiettore a passo ridotto
– *cine projector*
79 la bobina di recupero
– *film feed spool*
80 la bobina, una bobina a agganciamento automatico
– *take-up reel (take-up spool), an automatic take-up reel (take-up spool)*
81 il proiettore del film sonoro
– *sound projector*
82 la pellicola sonora con pista magnetica
– *sound film with magnetic stripe (sound track, track)*
83 il tasto di registrazione *f*
– *automatic-threading button*
84 il pulsante per gli effetti speciali
– *trick button*
85 il regolatore del volume
– *volume control*
86 l'interruttore *m*
– *reset button*
87 l'interruttore *m* per gli effetti speciali
– *fast and slow motion switch*
88 l'interruttore *m* per la scelta della cadenza dei fotogrammi
– *forward, reverse, and still projection switch*
89 la giuntatrice per incollature *f pl* a umido
– *splicer for wet splices*
90 il reggipellicola mobile
– *hinged clamping plate*
91 la moviola
– *film viewer (animated viewer editor)*
92 il braccio reggibobina mobile
– *foldaway reel arm*
93 la leva di riavvolgimento
– *rewind handle (rewinder)*
94 lo schermo smerigliato
– *viewing screen*
95 la taglierina
– *film perforator (film marker)*
96 l'apparecchiatura di montaggio a sei piatti *m pl*
– *six-turntable film and sound cutting table (editing table, cutting bench, animated sound editor)*
97 il monitor
– *monitor*
98 il quadro di comando
– *control buttons (control well)*
99 la bobina (la pizza)
– *film turntable*
100 la prima bobina per il suono, per es.: per il suono live (per il suono originale)
– *first sound turntable, e.g. for live sound*
101 la seconda bobina per gli effetti sonori
– *second sound turntable for post-sync sound*
102 l'unità video-audio
– *film and tape synchronizing head*

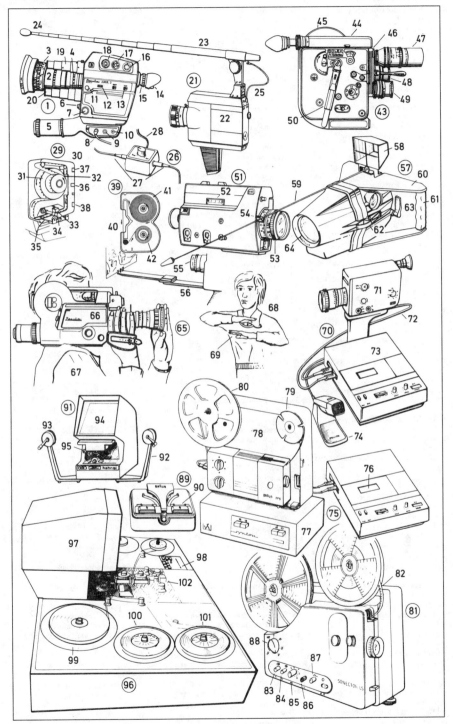

**1-49  il fabbricato in costruzione** *f pl*
(costruzione *f pl* di una casa)
- *carcase (carcass, fabric) [house con-*
*struction, carcassing]*
**1**  lo scantinato in calcestruzzo costipato
(battuto)
- *basement of tamped (rammed) concrete*
**2**  lo zoccolo in calcestruzzo
- *concrete base course*
**3**  la finestra dello scantinato
- *cellar window (basement window)*
**4**  la scala esterna dello scantinato
- *outside cellar steps*
**5**  la finestra del vano-lavanderia
- *utility room window*
**6**  la porta del vano-lavanderia
- *utility room door*
**7**  il pianterreno (piano terra)
- *ground floor (Am. first floor)*
**8**  il muro (la muratura) in mattoni *m pl*
- *brick wall*
**9**  la piattabanda
- *lintel (window head)*
**10**  l'intradosso (l'imbotte *f* ) esterno della
finestra
- *reveal*
**11**  l'introdosso (l'imbotte *f* ) interno della
finestra
- *jamb*
**12**  il davanzale
- *window ledge (window sill)*
**13**  l'architrave *f* in cemento armato
- *reinforced concrete lintel*
**14**  il piano superiore
- *upper floor (first floor, Am. second
floor)*
**15**  il muro in blocchi *m pl* cavi di calcestruzzo
- *hollow-block wall*
**16**  la copertura piena (massiccia)
- *concrete floor*
**17**  l'impalcatura
- *work platform (working platform)*
**18**  il muratore
- *bricklayer (Am. brickmason)*
**19**  il manovale
- *bricklayer's labourer (Am. laborer);*
also: *builder's labourer*
**20**  il giornello (la cassetta per la malta)
- *mortar trough*
**21**  il camino (la canna fumaria)
- *chimney*
**22**  il lucernario (la copertura del vano
scala)
- *cover (boards) for the staircase*
**23**  il palo del ponteggio (dell'impalcatura)
- *scaffold pole (scaffold standard)*
**24**  il corrimano (l'appoggio) del parapetto
- *platform railing*
**25**  la traversa del ponteggio (dell'impalcatura)
- *angle brace (angle tie) in the scaffold*
**26**  il corrente (il palo orizzontale)
- *ledger*
**27**  il correntino
- *putlog (putlock)*
**28**  il tavolato (l'assito)
- *plank platform (board platform)*
**29**  l'asse *f* (la sponda) di protezione *f*
- *guard board*
**30**  la legatura del ponteggio con catene *f*
*pl* o corde *f pl*
- *scaffolding joint with chain or lashing
or whip or bond*

**31**  il montacarichi
- *builder's hoist*
**32**  il manovratore
- *mixer operator*
**33**  la betoniera, un miscelatore a gravità
- *concrete mixer, a gravity mixer*
**34**  il tamburo della betoniera
- *mixing drum*
**35**  la tramoggia di caricamento
- *feeder skip*
**36**  i materiali inerti (sabbia e ghiaia)
- *concrete aggregate [sand and gravel]*
**37**  la carriola
- *wheelbarrow*
**38**  il tubo dell'acqua
- *hose (hosepipe)*
**39**  la vasca della malta (della calce)
- *mortar pan (mortar trough, mortar tub)*
**40**  la catasta di mattoni *m pl* (di forati *m
pl)*
- *stack of bricks*
**41**  il legname per armature accatastato
- *stacked shutter boards (lining boards)*
**42**  la scala a pioli *m pl*
- *ladder*
**43**  il sacco di cemento
- *bag of cement*
**44**  la recinzione del cantiere, una staccionata, un assito
- *site fence, a timber fence*
**45**  il quadro per le affissioni pubblicitarie
- *signboard (billboard)*
**46**  il portone scardinabile
- *removable gate*
**47**  le targhe delle ditte costruttrici
- *contractors' name plates*
**48**  la baracca del cantiere
- *site hut (site office)*
**49**  il gabinetto (il WC del cantiere)
- *building site latrine*
**50-57  gli attrezzi da muratore** *m*
- **bricklayer's** (Am. **brickmason's**) **tools**
**50**  il filo a piombo
- *plumb bob (plummet)*
**51**  la matita da muratore *m*
- *thick lead pencil*
**52**  la cazzuola
- *trowel*
**53**  il martello da muratore *m*
- *bricklayer's (Am. brickmason's) hammer (brick hammer)*
**54**  la mazzuola, un martello di legno
- *mallet*
**55**  la livella a acqua
- *spirit level*
**56**  la cazzuola a punta quadra
- *laying-on trowel*
**57**  il frattazzo
- *float*
**58-68  disposizioni** *f pl* **(committiture** *f pl*)
**dei mattoni**
- **masonry bonds**
**58**  il mattone (di) formato normale
- *brick (standard brick)*
**59**  la disposizione a fascia, una disposizione dei mattoni per il lungo
- *stretching bond*
**60**  la disposizione di testa o di punta dei
mattoni
- *heading bond*
**61**  la scala nella disposizione di testa dei
mattoni
- *racking (raking) back*
**62**  la disposizione (l'apparecchio) a blocco
- *English bond*

**63**  il corso dei mattoni a fascia
- *stretching course*
**64**  il corso dei mattoni di punta (di testa)
- *heading course*
**65**  la disposizione *f* a croce *f*
- *English cross bond (Saint Andrew's
cross bond)*
**66**  la disposizione *f* dei mattoni per
camino
- *chimney bond*
**67**  il primo corso
- *first course*
**68**  il secondo corso
- *second course*
**69-82  lo scavo di fondazione** *f*
- **excavation**
**69**  la spalliera di tracciamento
- *profile (Am. batterboard) [fixed on
edge at the corner]*
**70**  l'incrocio delle corde
- *intersection of strings*
**71**  il filo a piombo
- *plumb bob (plummet)*
**72**  la scarpata dello scavo
- *excavation side*
**73**  la tavola (l'asse *f* ) per il margine superiore
- *upper edge board*
**74**  la tavola (l'asse *f* ) per il margine inferiore
- *lower edge board*
**75**  lo scavo in trincea
- *foundation trench*
**76**  lo sterratore
- *navvy (Am. excavator)*
**77**  il nastro trasportatore
- *conveyor belt (conveyor)*
**78**  lo sterro
- *excavated earth*
**79**  l'assito di accesso
- *plank roadway*
**80**  la protezione degli alberi
- *tree guard*
**81**  l'escavatore *m* a cucchiaia
- *mechanical shovel (excavator)*
**82**  la cucchiaia dell'escavatore *m* per scavi
*m pl* in profondità
- *shovel bucket (bucket)*
**83-91  lavori** *m pl* **d'intonaco (intonacatura)**
- **plastering**
**83**  l'intonacatore *m* (muratore *m* addetto
all'intonaco)
- *plasterer*
**84**  il giornello (la cassetta per la malta)
- *mortar trough*
**85**  il vaglio da sabbia
- *screen*
**86-89  il ponteggio (l'impalcatura) a scale** *f pl*
- **ladder scaffold**
**86**  la scala fissa (scala portante)
- *standard ladder*
**87**  il ponte di tavole *f pl* (la passerella)
- *boards (planks, platform)*
**88**  la diagonale di rinforzo
- *diagonal strut (diagonal brace)*
**89**  l'asse *f* intermedia
- *railing*
**90**  la parete di protezione *f*
- *guard netting*
**91**  l'elevatore *m* a carrucola
- *rope-pulley hoist*

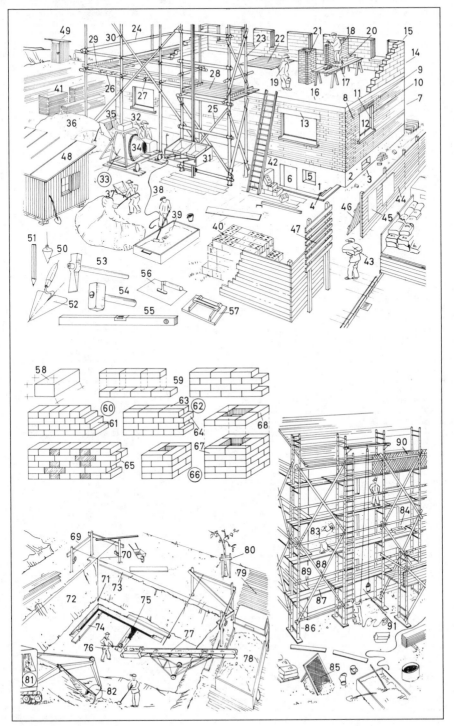

**1-89 la costruzione (l'edificio) in cemento armato**
- *reinforced concrete (ferroconcrete) construction*

**1** la struttura in cemento armato
- *reinforced concrete (ferroconcrete) skeleton construction*

**2** l'intelaiatura in cemento armato
- *reinforced concrete (ferroconcrete) frame*

**3** la trave di banchina (trave *f* portante, trave *f* di sostegno)
- *inferior purlin*

**4** la terzera di cemento armato
- *concrete purlin*

**5** la trave portante (trave *f* di sostegno)
- *ceiling joist*

**6** la modanatura
- *arch (flank)*

**7** il muro in getto di calcestruzzo
- *rubble concrete wall*

**8** la soletta in cemento armato
- *reinforced concrete (ferroconcrete) floor*

**9** il muratore in atto di spianare il calcestruzzo
- *concreter (concretor), flattening out*

**10** i ferri di allacciamento
- *projecting reinforcement (Am. connection rebars)*

**11** la cassaforma di appoggio
- *column box*

**12** la cassaforma della trave portante
- *joist shuttering*

**13** il puntello della cassaforma
- *shuttering strut*

**14** la saetta
- *diagonal bracing*

**15** il cuneo (il concio)
- *wedge*

**16** la tavola
- *board*

**17** la palancolata
- *sheet pile wall (sheet pile, sheet piling)*

**18** il legname (le tavole) per armature *f pl*
- *shutter boards (lining boards)*

**19** la sega a disco (sega circolare)
- *circular saw (buzz saw)*

**20** il tavolo del ferraiolo (tavolo di curvatura)
- *bending table*

**21** il piegaferri
- *bar bender (steel bender)*

**22** la forbice tagliaferro
- *hand steel shears*

**23** il ferro di armatura (tondino per cemento armato)
- *reinforcing steel (reinforcement rods)*

**24** il forato di pomice *f*
- *pumice concrete hollow block*

**25** la parete divisoria, una parete di assi *f pl*
- *partition wall, a timber wall*

**26** gli inerti (ghiaia e sabbia di granulatura diversa)
- *concrete aggregate [gravel and sand of various grades]*

**27** il binario da gru *f*
- *crane track*

**28** il carrello (vagoncino) ribaltabile
- *tipping wagon (tipping truck)*

**29** la betoniera
- *concrete mixer*

**30** il silo del (per) cemento
- *cement silo*

**31** la gru a torre girevole
- *tower crane (tower slewing crane)*

**32** il carrello (della gru)
- *bogie (Am. truck)*

**33** il contrappeso
- *counterweight*

**34** la torre, una torre-traliccio
- *tower*

**35** la cabina del manovratore della gru
- *crane driver's cabin (crane driver's cage)*

**36** il braccio della gru
- *jib (boom)*

**37** il cavo di sollevamento
- *bearer cable*

**38** la benna per il cemento armato
- *concrete bucket*

**39** l'intelaiatura di traversine *f pl*
- *sleepers (Am. ties)*

**40** il ceppo di arresto (ceppo di frenata)
- *chock*

**41** il piano (il tavolaccio) di rampa
- *ramp*

**42** la carriola
- *wheelbarrow*

**43** la sponda di protezione *f* (il parapetto)
- *safety rail*

**44** la baracca del cantiere edile
- *site hut*

**45** la mensa
- *canteen*

**46** il ponteggio tubolare in acciaio (ponteggio in tubi *m pl* d'acciaio)
- *tubular steel scaffold (scaffolding)*

**47** il tubo fisso
- *standard*

**48** la traversa longitudinale del ponteggio
- *ledger tube*

**49** la spranga trasversale
- *tie tube*

**50** la piastra di base *f*
- *shoe*

**51** la contraventatura (diagonali *f pl* di rinforzo)
- *diagonal brace*

**52** il ripiano
- *planking (platform)*

**53** il giunto (l'aggancio, il raccordo)
- *coupling (coupler)*

**54-76 l'armatura (la cassaforma) per la gettata di calcestruzzo**
- *formwork (shuttering) and reinforcement*

**54** la cassaforma per cemento armato
- *bottom shuttering (lining)*

**55** la cassaforma verticale di una trave di banchina
- *side shutter of a purlin*

**56** la sezione del fondo
- *cut-in bottom*

**57** la trave di supporto (la traversa)
- *cross beam*

**58** la grappa per costruzioni *f pl* edili
- *cramp iron (cramp, dog)*

**59** il puntello, un sostegno di testa
- *upright member, a standard*

**60** il coprigiunto di fissaggio
- *strap*

**61** l'incastro, una traversa di legno
- *cross piece*

**62** la tavola di registro (tavola di stretta)
- *stop fillet*

**63** la saetta (la diagonale)
- *strut (brace, angle brace)*

**64** il corrente (in legno) dell'intelaiatura
- *frame timber (yoke)*

**65** la legatura delle tavole
- *strap*

**66** la disposizione dei tenditori in filo di ferro
- *reinforcement binding*

**67** l'assicella di spessore *m* del muro
- *cross strut (strut)*

**68** l'armatura
- *reinforcement*

**69** il distanziatore
- *distribution steel*

**70** la staffa
- *stirrup*

**71** il ferro di presa
- *projecting reinforcement (Am. connection rebars)*

**72** il calcestruzzo (calcestruzzo ordinario)
- *concrete (heavy concrete)*

**73** la cassaforma del pilastro
- *column box*

**74** la cravatta avvitata
- *bolted frame timber (bolted yoke)*

**75** la vite
- *nut (thumb nut)*

**76** la tavola di armamento
- *shutter board (shuttering board)*

**77-89 attrezzatura**
- *tools*

**77** il mordiglione
- *bending iron*

**78** la traversa regolabile per la cassaforma
- *adjustable service girder*

**79** la vite di registro
- *adjusting screw*

**80** il tondo di acciaio
- *round bar reinforcement*

**81** il distanziatore
- *distance piece (separator, spacer)*

**82** l'acciaio di torsione *f*
- *Torsteel*

**83** il costipatore per calcestruzzo
- *concrete tamper*

**84** la forma per i cubi campioni (per i cubi di prova)
- *mould (Am. mold) for concrete test cubes*

**85** le tenaglie da calcestruzzo
- *concreter's tongs*

**86** il puntello della cassaforma
- *sheeting support*

**87** le forbici tagliaferri
- *hand shears*

**88** il vibratore per calcestruzzo
- *immersion vibrator (concrete vibrator)*

**89** la vibro-punta (la punta di vibrazione *f*)
- *vibrating cylinder (vibrating head, vibrating poker)*

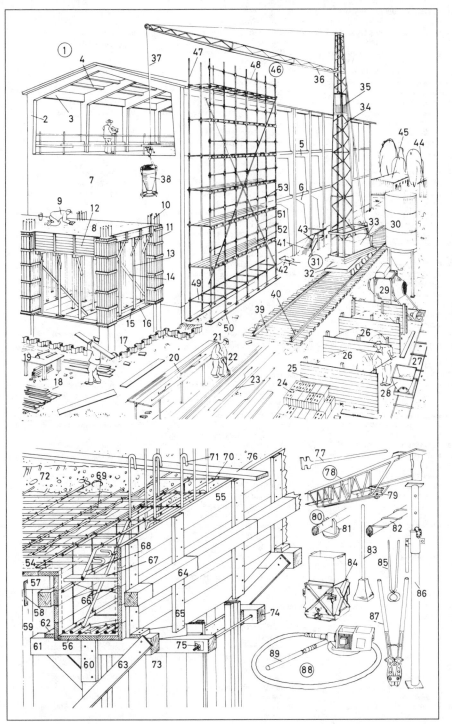

**1-59 il cantiere del carpentiere**
- *carpenter's yard*
1 la catasta di tavole *f pl* da costruzione *f*
- *stack of boards (planks)*
2 le antenne (il legname lungo, legname *m* tagliato in lungo)
- *long timber (Am. lumber)*
3 il capannone (adibito a) segheria
- *sawing shed*
4 l'officina del carpentiere
- *carpenter's workshop*
5 la porta dell'officina
- *workshop door*
6 il carretto a mano *f*
- *handcart*
7 l'armatura (la capriata) del tetto
- *roof truss*
8 l'albero con la corona per festeggiare la copertura del tetto (*Italia:* bandiera, rami *m pl* di alloro o di quercia)
- *tree [used for topping out ceremony], with wreath*
9 l'assito (il rivestimento di tavole *f pl*)
- *timber wall*
10 il legname squadrato (legname *m* da costruzione *f* )
- *squared timber (building timber, scantlings)*
11 il piano di tracciamento
- *drawing floor*
12 il carpentiere
- *carpenter*
13 il berretto (copricapo) da carpentiere *m*
- *carpenter's hat*
14 la sega a catena
- *cross-cut saw, a chain saw*
15 la lama
- *chain guide*
16 la catena della sega
- *saw chain*
17 la mortasatrice (la cavatrice)
- *mortiser (chain cutter)*
18 il cavalletto
- *trestle (horse)*
19 la trave sul cavalletto
- *beam mounted on a trestle*
20 gli utensili da incastro
- *set of carpenter's tools*
21 il trapano elettrico
- *electric drill*
22 il foro per caviglia
- *dowel hole*
23 la marcatura del foro
- *mark for the dowel hole*
24 le travi pronte
- *beams*
25 il montante (il palo)
- *post (stile, stud, quarter)*
26 il saettone
- *corner brace*
27 il puntone (il contraffisso)
- *brace (strut)*
28 lo zoccolo della casa
- *base course (plinth)*
29 il muro (la muratura) della casa
- *house wall (wall)*
30 il vano della finestra
- *window opening*
31 la spalla esterna della finestra
- *reveal*
32 la spalla interna della finestra
- *jamb*

33 il davanzale
- *window ledge (window sill)*
34 l'armatura
- *cornice*
35 l'antenna (il palo rotondo)
- *roundwood (round timber)*
36 la passerella
- *floorboards*
37 la fune montacarichi
- *hoisting rope*
38 la trave del soffitto (trave *f* maestra, trave *f* portante)
- *ceiling joist (ceiling beam, main beam)*
39 la trave della parete
- *wall joist*
40 il dormiente
- *wall plate*
41 il travetto a cravatta
- *trimmer (trimmer joist, Am. header, header joist)*
42 la trave semincastrata (trave *f* a incastro)
- *dragon beam (dragon piece)*
43 il doppiofondo (fondo falso, il controsoffitto)
- *false floor (inserted floor)*
44 la colmata del doppiofondo con cenere *f* di carbone *m* coke, argilla, ecc.)
- *floor filling of breeze, loam, etc.*
45 il listellone di sostegno
- *fillet (cleat)*
46 il vano della scala
- *stair well (well)*
47 la canna fumaria
- *chimney*
48 il muro con intelaiatura a traliccio
- *framed partition (framed wall)*
49 la soglia
- *wall plate*
50 la trave di appoggio
- *girt*
51 la spalletta della finestra, un listello intermedio
- *window jamb, a jamb*
52 il montante di angolo
- *corner stile (corner strut, corner stud)*
53 il listello di legatura
- *principal post*
54 il saettone di contrasto
- *brace (strut) with skew notch*
55 la traversa intermedia
- *nogging piece*
56 la traversa del davanzale
- *sill rail*
57 l'architrave della finestra
- *window lintel (window head)*
58 la traversa superiore (il corrente)
- *head (head rail)*
59 la muratura del traliccio
- *filled-in panel (bay, pan)*

**60-82 attrezzi *m pl* (arnesi *m pl*) del carpentiere**
- *carpenter's tools*
60 il saracco (la sega a lama libera con un'impugnatura)
- *hand saw*
61 la sega intelaiata a lama tesa
- *bucksaw*
62 la lama della sega
- *saw blade*
63 il gattuccio (il foretto)
- *compass saw (keyhole saw)*

64 la pialla
- *plane*
65 la trivella (il succhiello)
- *auger (gimlet)*
66 il sergente
- *screw clamp (cramp, holdfast)*
67 il mazzuolo
- *mallet*
68 la sega a due impugnature *f pl*
- *two-handed saw*
69 la squadra a cappello
- *try square*
70 la scure
- *broad axe (Am. broadax)*
71 lo scalpello
- *chisel*
72 lo scalpello ugnato (scalpello da incastri *m pl*)
- *mortise axe (mortice axe, Am. mortise ax)*
73 l'ascia
- *axe (Am. ax)*
74 il martello da carpentiere *m*
- *carpenter's hammer*
75 il cavachiodi
- *claw head (nail claw)*
76 il metro pieghevole
- *folding rule*
77 la matita da carpentiere *m*
- *carpenter's pencil*
78 la squadra metallica
- *iron square*
79 il coltello a petto
- *drawknife (drawshave, drawing knife)*
80 il truciolo
- *shaving*
81 la falsa squadra (il rapportatore)
- *bevel*
82 la squadra zoppa (squadra a ugnatura)
- *mitre square (Am. miter square, miter angle)*

**83-96 legname *m* da costruzione *f***
- *building timber*
83 il tronco (il tondone)
- *round trunk (undressed timber, Am. rough lumber)*
84 il durame
- *heartwood (duramen)*
85 l'alburno
- *sapwood (sap, alburnum)*
86 la corteccia
- *bark (rind)*
87 il legname a tronco intero
- *baulk (balk)*
88 il legname a mezzo tondo
- *halved timber*
89 la smussatura (lo smusso)
- *wane (waney edge)*
90 il legname a quarto di tronco
- *quarter baulk (balk)*
91 la tavola
- *plank (board)*
92 il legno di testa (legno augnato)
- *end-grained timber*
93 l'anima (la parte interna della tavola)
- *heartwood plank (heart plank)*
94 la tavola non rifilata
- *unsquared (untrimmed) plank (board)*
95 la tavola rifilata
- *squared (trimmed) board*
96 lo sciavero
- *slab (offcut)*

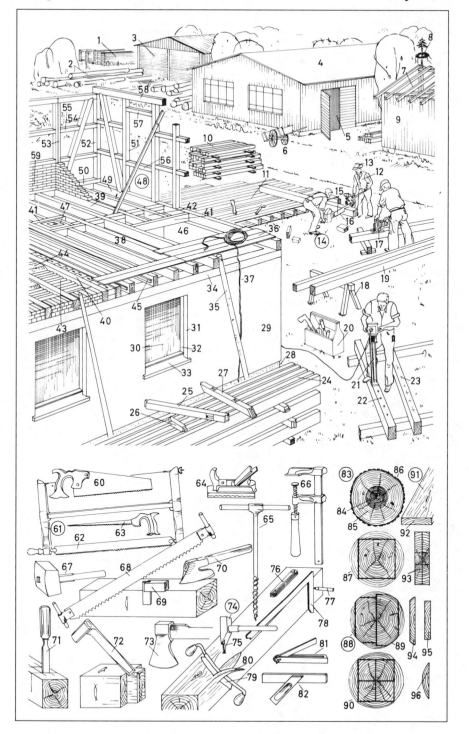

**1-26 forme** *f pl* **e parti** *f pl* **di tetto**
– *styles and parts of roofs*
1 il tetto a capanna (tetto a doppia falda, tetto a due spioventi *m pl*)
– *gable roof (saddle roof, saddleback roof )*
2 la linea di colmo
– *ridge*
3 il bordo del tetto (gronda di frontespizio)
– *verge*
4 la gronda
– *eaves*
5 il timpano
– *gable*
6 l'abbaino rettangolare
– *dormer window (dormer)*
7 il tetto a leggio (tetto a una falda, tetto a uno spiovente)
– *pent roof (shed roof, lean-to roof )*
8 la finestra a lucernaio
– *skylight*
9 il muro tagliafuoco (muro spartifuoco)
– *fire gable*
10 il tetto a padiglione *m*
– *hip (hipped) roof*
11 la falda triangolare (falda di chiusura)
– *hip end*
12 il dipluvio (linea di dipluvio)
– *hip (arris)*
13 l'abbaino triangolare
– *hip (hipped) dormer window*
14 la torretta (*ant.*: torretta campanaria)
– *ridge turret*
15 la conversa (il compluvio del tetto)
– *valley (roof valley)*
16 il tetto a due spioventi *m pl* con falda di chiusura tronca (con falda a timpano)
– *hipped-gable roof (jerkin head roof )*
17 la falda di chiusura tronca (falda a timpano)
– *partial-hip (partial-hipped) end*
18 il tetto a mansarda
– *mansard roof* (Am. *gambrel roof )*
19 la mansarda (finestra a mansarda)
– *mansard dormer window*
20 il tetto a shed *m* (copertura a denti *m pl* di sega)
– *sawtooth roof*
21 la vetrata degli sheds con luce *f* dall'alto
– *north light*
22 il tetto a piramide *f*
– *broach roof*
23 l'abbaino a occhio di bue *m*
– *eyebrow*
24 il tetto conico (tetto a cono)
– *conical broach roof*
25 il tetto a bulbo (la cupola a bulbo)
– *imperial dome (imperial roof )*
26 la banderuola
– *weather vane*
**27-83 capriate** *f pl* **in legno**
– *roof structures of timber*
27 il tetto di puntoni *m pl*, (tetto di travetti *m pl* inclinati)
– *rafter roof*
28 il puntone
– *rafter*
29 la catena (la trave maestra)
– *roof beam*
30 la diagonale di rinforzo
– *diagonal tie (cross tie, sprocket piece, cocking piece)*
31 il correntino
– *arris fillet (tilting fillet)*
32 il muro esterno
– *outer wall*
33 la testa della catena

– *beam head*
34 la capriata con (a) controcatena
– *collar beam roof (trussed rafter roof )*
35 la controcatena
– *collar beam (collar)*
36 il puntone
– *rafter*
37 la duplice capriata con (a) controcatena
– *strutted collar beam roof structure*
38 l'impalcatura a controcatena
– *collar beams*
39 la terzera (l'arcareccio laterale)
– *purlin*
40 il montante
– *post (stile, stud)*
41 la saetta (il saettone)
– *brace*
42 la capriata semplice con arcarecci *m pl*
– *unstrutted (king pin) roof structure*
43 l'arcareccio di colmo
– *ridge purlin*
44 l'arcareccio inferiore (trave *f* di banchina)
– *inferior purlin*
45 la testa del puntone
– *rafter head (rafter end)*
46 la capriata doppia rinforzata con muro d'imposta
– *purlin roof with queen post and pointing sill*
47 il muro d'imposta
– *pointing sill*
48 la traversa di colmo (tavola di colmo)
– *ridge beam (ridge board)*
49 la staffa (la briglia)
– *simple tie*
50 la briglia di collegamento
– *double tie*
51 la terzera (*qui:* posta a metà dei puntoni)
– *purlin*
52 la capriata doppia sostenuta da terzere *f pl*
– *purlin roof structure with queen post*
53 la catena
– *tie beam*
54 la trave del soffitto
– *joist (ceiling joist)*
55 il puntone principale
– *principal rafter*
56 il puntone intermedio
– *common rafter*
57 la seatta
– *angle brace (angle tie)*
58 il contropuntone
– *brace (strut)*
59 le briglie (le controcatene)
– *ties*
60 capriata a padiglione *m* rinforzata con terzere *f pl*
– *hip (hipped) roof with purlin roof structure*
61 il falso puntone
– *jack rafter*
62 il puntone di displuvio
– *hip rafter*
63 il falso puntone della falda triangolare
– *jack rafter*
64 il puntone di compluvio
– *valley rafter*
65 la doppia capriata
– *queen truss*
66 la catena principale
– *main beam*
67 la trave portante (trave *f* di sostegno)
– *summer (summer beam)*
68 il monaco
– *queen post (truss post)*

69 il contropuntone
– *brace (strut)*
70 la catena di rinforzo
– *collar beam (collar)*
71 il travetto a cravatta
– *trimmer* (Am. *header)*
72 la capriata a parete *f* piena
– *solid-web girder*
73 il corrente inferiore
– *lower chord*
74 il corrente superiore
– *upper chord*
75 la nervatura di rinforzo con tavole *f pl*
– *boarding*
76 la terzera
– *purlin*
77 il muro esterno di appoggio
– *supporting outer wall*
78 la capriata a traliccio
– *roof truss*
79 il corrente inferiore
– *lower chord*
80 il corrente superiore
– *upper chord*
81 il montante
– *post*
82 la saetta
– *brace (strut)*
83 l'appogio
– *support*
**84-98 calettature** *f pl* **in legno** (giunture *f pl*, incastri *m pl*)
– *timber joints*
84 il giunto a maschio e femmina
– *mortise (mortice) and tenon joint*
85 l'incastro a tenaglia (la calettatura a canale *m*, calettatura a dente *m*)
– *forked mortise (mortice) and tenon joint*
86 la calettatura a mezzo legno (l'incastro a mezzo e mezzo)
– *halving (halved) joint*
87 il giunto a doppio dente *m* retto (l'incastro a dentatura retta, la calettatura alla greca)
– *simple scarf joint*
88 l'incastro a mezzo legno a dentatura obliqua (la calettatura a dardo di Giove, la parallela a catena)
– *oblique scarf joint*
89 il giunto a coda di rondine *f* (la coda di rondine *f* )
– *dovetail halving*
90 la calettatura a battente *m* semplice
– *single skew notch*
91 la calettatura a doppio battente *m*
– *double skew notch*
92 il chiodo di legno
– *wooden nail*
93 il chiodo grosso senza testa
– *pin*
94 il chiodo (a gambo) quadro
– *clout nail (clout)*
95 la stacchetta (la punta Parigi)
– *wire nail*
96 i cunei (il doppio cuneo) di legno duro
– *hardwood wedges*
97 la grappa
– *cramp iron (timber dog, dog)*
98 il bullone
– *bolt*

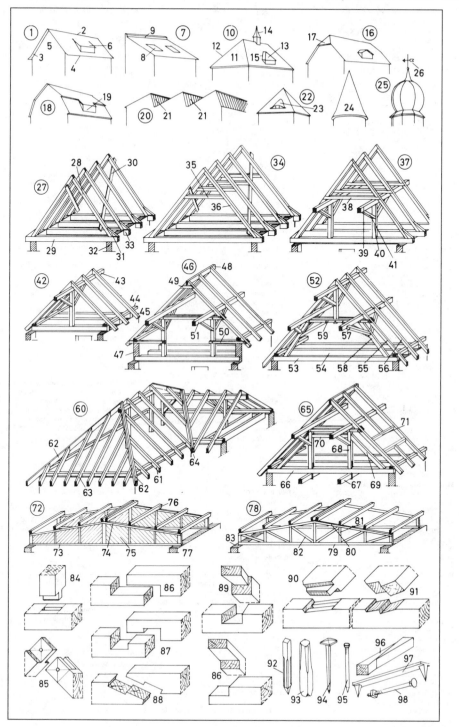

**1** il tetto di tegole *f pl*
– *tiled roof*
**2** la copertura a tegole piane *f pl* sovrapposte (la copertura a due strati *m pl*)
– *plain-tile double-lap roofing*
**3** il tegolone di colmo (coppo di colmo, tegola curva, tegola a canale *m*)
– *ridge tile*
**4** la tegola della fila di colmo
– *ridge course tile*
**5** la tegola di gronda
– *under-ridge tile*
**6** l'embrice *m* (la tegola piana)
– *plain (plane) tile*
**7** la tegola a sfiatatoio
– *ventilating tile*
**8** il tegolone di displuvio (coppo di displuvio)
– *ridge tile*
**9** il tegolone di testa (della linea di displuvio)
– *hip tile*
**10** la falda del tetto
– *hipped end*
**11** la conversa di compluvio
– *valley (roof valley)*
**12** la finestra a lucernaio
– *skylight*
**13** il camino
– *chimney*
**14** lo zoccolo del camino in lamiera di zinco
– *chimney flashing, made of sheet zinc*
**15** il gancio per la scala (gancio fermascala)
– *ladder hook*
**16** il puntello fremaneve
– *snow guard bracket*
**17** i listelli (i correnti)
– *battens (slating and tiling battens)*
**18** il regolo dei listelli (dei correnti)
– *batten gauge (Am. gage)*
**19** il puntone
– *rafter*
**20** il martello da tegola
– *tile hammer*
**21** la scure (l'ascia) del carpentiere
– *lath axe (Am. ax)*
**22** il mastello del copritetto
– *hod*
**23** il gancio del mastello
– *hod hook*
**24** l'apertura per salire e scendere
– *opening (hatch)*
**25** il timpano
– *gable (gable end)*
**26** la cornice dentata
– *toothed lath*
**27** il sottogronda
– *soffit*
**28** la grondaia
– *gutter*
**29** il tubo di discesa (il doccione)
– *rainwater pipe (downpipe)*
**30** il bocchettone
– *swan's neck (swan-neck)*
**31** la staffa (il collarino, il crossante)
– *pipe clip*
**32** la cicogna (il gancio della grondaia)
– *gutter bracket*
**33** il tagliategole
– *tile cutter*
**34** l'impalcatura (il ponteggio di lavoro)
– *scaffold*
**35** la parete (l'assito) di protezione *f*
– *safety wall*
**36** il cornicione del tetto
– *eaves*
**37** il muro esterno
– *outer wall*
**38** l'intonaco
– *exterior rendering*

**39** il muretto di banchina
– *frost-resistant brickwork*
**40** la trave di banchina
– *inferior purlin*
**41** il passafuori
– *rafter head (rafter end)*
**42** la cassaforma del cornicione
– *eaves fascia*
**43** il doppio listello
– *double lath (tilting lath)*
**44** i travelloni isolanti
– *insulating boards*
**45-60 tegole *f pl* e coperture *f pl* di tegole *f pl***
– ***tiles and tile roofings***
**45** il tetto di scandole *f pl* (la copertura a assicelle *f pl*)
– *split-tiled roof*
**46** la tegola piana (tegola semplice, embrice *m*)
– *plain (plane) tile*
**47** la fila di colmo
– *ridge course*
**48** la scandola (l'assicella)
– *slip*
**49** il doppio corso delle tegole in gronda
– *eaves course*
**50** il tetto (la copertura) a cavaliere *m*
– *plain-tiled roof*
**51** il nasello (il risalto)
– *nib*
**52** il tegolone (il coppo) di colmo
– *ridge tile*
**53** il tetto (la copertura) alla fiamminga
– *pantiled roof*
**54** la tegola alla fiamminga (tegola arcuata)
– *pantile*
**55** lo strato di malta
– *pointing*
**56** il tetto (la copertura) in tegole *f pl* curve
– *Spanish-tiled roof* (Am. *mission-tiled roof* )
**57** la tegola rovescia (tegola concava, tegola a canale *m*)
– *under tile*
**58** la tegola dritta (tegola convessa, tegola superiore)
– *over tile*
**59** la tegola a incastro (tegola marsigliese)
– *interlocking tile*
**60** la tegola romana (tegola per tetto piano)
– *flat interlocking tile*
**61-89  il tetto (la copertura) di ardesia**
– *slate roof*
**61** il tavolato (le tavole di rivestimento, la cassaforma)
– *roof boards (roof boarding, roof sheathing)*
**62** il cartone catramato (cartone *m* bitumato)
– *roofing paper (sheathing paper); also: roofing felt* (Am. *rag felt*)
**63** la scala a pioli *m pl* da tetto
– *cat ladder (roof ladder)*
**64** il gancio di prolungamento della scala
– *coupling hook*
**65** il gancio di colmo
– *ridge hook*
**66** il cavalletto del tetto
– *roof trestle*
**67** la corda del cavalletto
– *trestle rope*
**68** il nodo
– *knot*
**69** il gancio per la scala
– *ladder hook*
**70** il tavolone di armatura (la tavola del cavalletto)
– *scaffold board*
**71** il copritetto (l'operaio copritetto)
– *slater*

**72** la borsa (la sacca) dei chiodi
– *nail bag*
**73** il martello per ardesia
– *slate hammer*
**74** il punteruolo del copritetto, una stacchetta zincata
– *slate nail, a galvanized wire nail*
**75** la scarpa del copritetto, una scarpa con suola di rafia o di canapa
– *slater's shoe, a bast or hemp shoe*
**76** la disposizione in gronda delle lastre di ardesia
– *eaves course (eaves joint)*
**77** la lastra di ardesia dell'angolo di gronda
– *corner bottom slate*
**78** la lastra di ardesia di centro
– *roof course*
**79** le lastre di ardesia di colmo
– *ridge course (ridge joint)*
**80** le lastre di angolo dell'abbaino
– *gable slate*
**81** la linea di posa delle lastre di ardesia
– *tail line*
**82** il compluvio
– *valley (roof valley)*
**83** il canale di gronda a cassetta
– *box gutter (trough gutter, parallel gutter)*
**84** la tagliatrice per ardesia (il tagliardesia)
– *slater's iron*
**85** la lastra di ardesia
– *slate*
**86** la parte posteriore (il dorso)
– *back*
**87** la testa
– *head*
**88** la parte anteriore
– *front edge*
**89** la coda
– *tail*
**90-103** copertura in cartone *m* catramato e copertura in eternit *m* ondulato
– *asphalt-impregnated paper roofing and corrugated asbestos cement roofing*
**90** il tetto in cartone *m* catramato (in cartone *m* bitumato)
– *asphalt-impregnated paper roof*
**91** la striscia di cartone catramato (parallela alla gronda)
– *width [parallel to the gutter]*
**92** il canale di gronda
– *gutter*
**93** la striscia di colmo
– *ridge*
**94** il giunto delle strisce
– *join*
**95** la striscia (perpendicolare alla gronda)
– *width [at right angles to the gutter]*
**96** il chiodo per cartone *m* catramato
– *felt nail (clout nail)*
**97** il tetto in eternit *m* ondulato
– *corrugated asbestos cement roof*
**98** la lastra ondulata di eternit *m*
– *corrugated sheet*
**99** la calotta di colmo
– *ridge capping piece*
**100** la sovrapposizione delle lastre
– *lap*
**101** la vite di legno
– *wood screw*
**102** la rondella (la controvite) zincata a ombrello (a forma concava)
– *rust-proof zinc cup*
**103** la rosetta di piombo
– *lead washer*

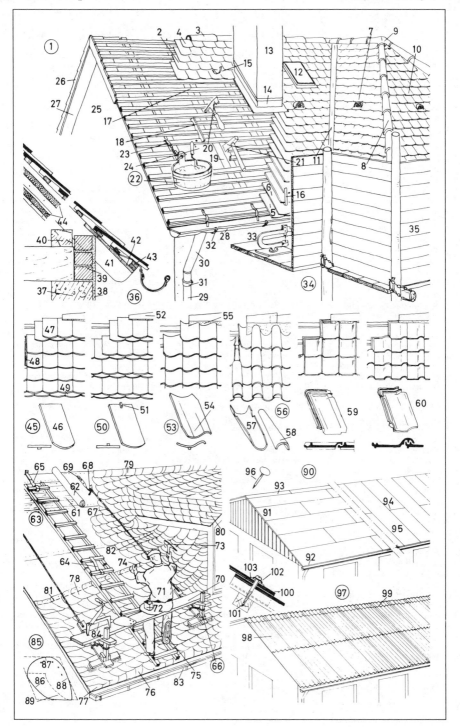

# 123  Pavimento/Soffitto/Costruzione di scale

1 il muro dello scantinato, un muro
  di calcestruzzo
– basement wall, a concrete wall
2 la banchina di fondazione f
– footing (foundation)
3 l'aggetto (lo sporto) di fondazione f
– foundation base
4 lo strato isolante orizzontale
– damp course (damp-proof course)
5 la mano di vernice f protettiva
– waterproofing
6 l'intonaco
– rendering coat
7 l'ammattonato (il pavimento di
  mattoni m pl)
– brick paving
8 il letto di sabbia
– sand bed
9 il suolo (il terreno)
– ground
10 la tavola laterale
– shuttering
11 il picchetto
– peg
12 il vespaio di pietrame m
– hardcore
13 la base in calcestruzzo
– oversite concrete
14 il pavimento di cemento (la passata di cemento)
– cement screed
15 il sottomuro della scala (il muro di
  sostegno della scala)
– brickwork base
16 la scala dello scantinato, una scala
  massiccia
– basement stairs, solid concrete
  stairs
17 il gradino monoblocco
– block step
18 l'invito (il primo gradino)
– curtail step (bottom step)
19 l'ultimo gradino (il gradino del
  pianerottolo)
– top step
20 il paraspigolo
– nosing
21 lo zoccolo (qui: la mattonella dello
  zoccolo)
– skirting (skirting board, Am. mopboard, washboard, scrub board,
  base)
22 la ringhiera di barre f pl metalliche
– balustrade of metal bars
23 il pianerottolo della scala (delle
  scale)
– ground-floor (Am. first-floor)
  landing
24 la porta d'ingresso
– front door
25 lo zerbino
– foot scraper
26 il rivestimento di mattonelle f pl
  (di piastrelle f pl)
– flagstone paving
27 il letto (la gettata) di malta
– mortar bed
28 la soletta piena (qui: soffitto
  pieno), una lastra di cemento
  armato
– concrete ceiling, a reinforced concrete slab

29 il muro del pianterreno (del piano
  terra)
– ground-floor (Am. first-floor)
  brick wall
30 la rampa della scala, una lastra di
  cemento armato
– ramp
31 il gradino cuneiforme
– wedge-shaped step
32 la pedata (del gradino)
– tread
33 l'alzata
– riser
34-41 il pianerottolo
– landing
34 la trave del pianerottolo
– landing beam
35 la soletta nervata in cemento
  armato
– ribbed reinforced concrete floor
36 la nervatura (il travetto)
– rib
37 l'armatura in acciaio (il tondino di
  armatura)
– steel-bar reinforcement
38 la soletta resistente a compressione f
– subfloor (blind floor)
39 lo strato di cemento di copertura
– level layer
40 lo strato di cemento di finitura
– finishing layer
41 il pavimento
– top layer (screed)
42-44 la rampa della scala (delle
  scale)
– dog-legged staircase, a staircase
  without a well
42 l'invito (il primo gradino)
– curtail step (bottom step)
43 il colonnino (il piantone) della
  ringhiera
– newel post (newel)
44 la longarina esterna della scala
– outer string (Am. outer stringer)
45 il fianco interno della scala (lo
  zoccolo della scala)
– wall string (Am. wall stringer)
46 il bullone della scala (in legno)
– staircase bolt
47 la pedata (del gradino)
– tread
48 l'alzata
– riser
49 il gomito
– wreath piece (wreathed string)
50 la ringhiera
– balustrade
51 l'asta della ringhiera
– baluster
52-62 il pianerottolo intermedio
– intermediate landing
52 la curva della ringhiera
– wreath
53 il corrimano
– handrail (guard rail)
54 il colonnino di testa della
  ringhiera
– head post
55 la trave del pianerottolo
– landing beam

56 la tavola di rivestimento
– lining board
57 il coprifilo (il listello di copertura)
– fillet
58 la lastra di materiale m leggero da
  costruzione f
– lightweight building board
59 l'intonaco del soffitto
– ceiling plaster
60 l'intonaco della parete
– wall plaster
61 il soffitto intermedio
– false ceiling
62 la pavimentazione in liste f pl di
  legno
– strip flooring (overlay flooring,
  parquet strip)
63 lo zoccolo
– skirting board (Am. mopboard,
  washboard, scrub board, base)
64 la cornice coprifilo
– beading
65 la finestra della scala
– staircase window
66 la trave portante del pianerottolo
– main landing beam
67 il correntino
– fillet (cleat)
68 u. 69 il soffitto intermedio (il piano
  smorzatore)
– false ceiling
68 il doppiofondo (il controsoffitto)
– false floor (inserted floor)
69 il riempimento (la colmata) del
  doppiofondo
– floor filling (plugging, pug)
70 le traverse di legno
– laths
71 l'incannicciatura (la stuoia di
  canne f pl)
– lathing
72 la superficie intonacata (qui: soffitto intonacato)
– ceiling plaster
73 l'assito (il piano di tavole f pl)
– subfloor (blind floor)
74 il pavimento in parquet m con
  incastro a maschio e femmina
– parquet floor with tongued-and-
  grooved blocks
75 la scala a un quarto di giro
– quarter-newelled (Am. quarter-
  neweled) staircase
76 la scala a chiocciola a anima cava
– winding staircase (spiral staircase)
  with open newels (open-newel
  staircase)
77 la scala a chiocciola a anima piena
– winding staircase (spiral staircase)
  with solid newels (solid-newel
  staircase)
78 l'anima (il piantone, la colonna)
– newel (solid newel)
79 il corrimano
– handrail

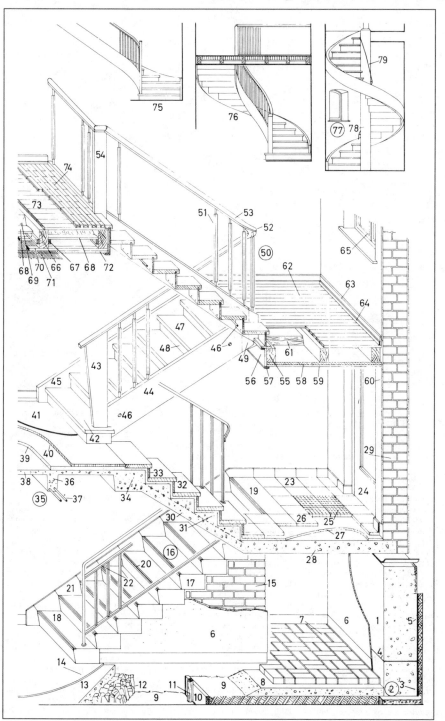

1 il laboratorio del vetraio
– *glazier's workshop*
2 i campioni di telai *m pl* (campioni *m pl* di cornici *f pl*)
– *frame wood samples (frame samples)*
3 il listello
– *frame wood*
4 la giuntura a becco di flauto
– *mitre joint (mitre, Am. miter joint, miter)*
5 il vetro in lastra, *tipi:* vetro per finestre *f pl*, vetro opaco, vetro arabo, cristallo per specchi *m pl*, vetro spesso, vetro opalino, vetro laminato, vetro blindato (vetro di sicurezza o infrangibile)
– *sheet glass; kinds: window glass, frosted glass, patterned glass, crystal plate glass, thick glass, milk glass, laminated glass (safety glass, shatterproof glass)*
6 il vetro lavorato (vetro colato); *tipi:* vetro cattedrale, vetro da ornamento, vetro grezzo, vetro a noduli *m pl*, vetro retinato, vetro striato
– *cast glass; kinds: stained glass, ornamental glass, raw glass, bull's-eye glass, wired glass, line glass (lined glass)*

7 la punzonatrice
– *mitring (Am. mitering) machine*
8 il vetraio (*p. es.:* vetraio per edifici *m pl*, vetraio per cornici *f pl*, vetraio per lavori *m pl* artistici)
– *glassworker (e.g. building glazier, glazier, decorative glass worker)*
9 il portavetro (salvavetro)
– *glass holder*
10 il vetro in frantumi *m pl* (vetro rotto)
– *piece of broken glass*
11 il martello per lavorare il piombo
– *lead hammer*
12 il coltello per lavorare il piombo
– *lead knife*
13 l'asta di piombo
– *came (lead came)*
14 la finestra di vetro al piombo
– *leaded light*
15 il tavolo da lavoro
– *workbench*
16 la lastra di vetro
– *pane of glass*
17 lo stucco (mastice *m*) del vetraio
– *putty*
18 il martello da vetraio
– *glazier's hammer*
19 le tenaglie da vetraio (il topo)
– *glass pliers*
20 la squadra per tagliare il vetro
– *glazier's square*

21 la riga per tagliare il vetro
– *glazier's rule*
22 il compasso per tagliare il vetro
– *glazier's beam compass*
23 l'occhiello
– *eyelet*
24 la punta da vetraio
– *glazing sprig*
25 *u.* 26 tagliavetri *m pl*
– *glass cutters*
25 la punta di diamante *m*, un tagliavetri
– *diamond glass cutter*
26 il tagliavetri di acciaio (tagliavetri a ruota di acciaio)
– *steel-wheel (steel) glass cutter*
27 la spatola per mastice *m*
– *putty knife*
28 il filo di ferro per tracciature
– *pin wire*
29 la punta
– *panel pin*
30 la sega per tagli *m pl* obliqui (sega da [a]ugnatura)
– *mitre (Am. miter) block (mitre box) [with saw]*
31 la cassetta per tagli *m pl* obliqui (cassetta a [a]ugnatura)
– *mitre (Am. miter) shoot (mitre board)*

1 la cesoia per lamiera
- *metal shears (tinner's snips, Am. tinner's shears)*
2 la cesoia sagomata
- *elbow snips (angle shears)*
3 la lastra per spianare
- *gib*
4 la lastra per finitura
- *lapping plate*
5-7 l'apparecchiatura a gas *m* propano per brasatura (saldatura) a stagno
- *propane soldering apparatus*
5 il saldatoio a gas *m* propano, un saldatoio a martello
- *propane soldering iron, a hatchet iron*
6 la pietra per brasare, una pietra di salmiaco
- *soldering stone, a sal-ammoniac block*
7 il fondente per brasature *f pl*
- *soldering fluid (flux)*
8 l'incudine *f* sagomata per rilievi *m pl* (scanalature *f pl*, gole *f pl*)
- *beading iron for forming reinforcement beading*
9 l'alesatore *m* a angolo, un alesatore *m*
- *angled reamer*

10 il banco di lavoro
- *workbench (bench)*
11 il compasso a verga
- *beam compass (trammel, Am. beam trammel)*
12 la filiera regolabile elettrica
- *electric hand die*
13 la fustella
- *hollow punch*
14 il martello per rilievi *m pl*
- *chamfering hammer*
15 il martello per le scorie
- *beading swage (beading hammer)*
16 la smerigliatrice (la macchina per troncare alla mola)
- *abrasive-wheel cutting-off machine*
17 il lattoniere (lo stagnaio)
- *plumber*
18 il mazzuolo di legno
- *mallet*
19 il corno dell'incudine *f*
- *mandrel*
20 l'incudine *f* a pugno
- *socket (tinner's socket)*
21 il ceppo
- *block*
22 l'incudine *f*
- *anvil*

23 il tasso
- *stake*
24 la sega circolare (la troncatrice a disco)
- *circular saw (buzz saw)*
25 la macchina per rilievi *m pl*, bordi *m pl* e introduzione *f* fili *m pl*
- *flanging, swaging, and wiring machine*
26 la cesoia a ghigliottina
- *sheet shears (guillotine)*
27 la filettatrice
- *screw-cutting machine (thread-cutting machine, die stocks)*
28 la piegatubi (la piegatrice per tubi *m pl*)
- *pipe-bending machine (bending machine, pipe bender)*
29 il trasformatore per saldatura
- *welding transformer*
30 la piegatrice conica
- *bending machine (rounding machine) for shaping funnels*

1 l'idraulico
– *gas fitter and plumber*
2 la scala a libretto
– *stepladder*
3 la catena di sicurezza
– *safety chain*
4 la valvola di chiusura (la valvola di arresto)
– *stop valve*
5 il contatore del gas
– *gas meter*
6 la mensola
– *bracket*
7 il tubo montante
– *service riser*
8 la tubazione di derivazione *f*
– *distributing pipe*
9 la tubazione di allacciamento
– *supply pipe*
10 il segatubi
– *pipe-cutting machine*
11 il cavalletto
– *pipe repair stand*
**12-25 impianti** *m pl* **a gas** *m* **e a acqua**
– *gas and water appliances*
**12** *u.* **13** lo scaldacqua fluente, un boiler
– *geyser, an instantaneous water heater*
12 lo scaldacqua istantaneo a gas *m*
– *gas water heater*
13 lo scaldacqua elettrico
– *electric water heater*
14 la cassetta di cacciata del WC
– *toilet cistern*
15 il galleggiante
– *float*
16 la campana
– *bell*
17 il tubo di cacciata
– *flush pipe*
18 il rubinetto d'entrata dell'acqua
– *water inlet*
19 la levetta della cassetta di cacciata
– *flushing lever (lever)*
20 il radiatore (il termosifone)
– *radiator*
21 l'elemento del radiatore
– *radiator rib*
22 il sistema a due tubi *m pl*
– *two-pipe system*
23 il tubo d'entrata (l'entrata)
– *flow pipe*
24 il tubo d'uscita (l'uscita)
– *return pipe*
25 la stufa a gas *m*
– *gas heater*
**26-37 rubinetti** *m pl*
– *plumbing fixtures*
26 il sifone
– *trap (anti-syphon trap)*
27 il miscelatore monoforo da lavabo
– *mixer tap (Am. mixing faucet) for washbasins*
28 il rubinetto dell'acqua calda
– *hot tap*
29 il rubinetto dell'acqua fredda
– *cold tap*
30 la doccetta estraibile a tubo flessibile
– *extendible shower attachment*

31 il rubinetto per lavandino
– *water tap (pillar tap) for washbasins*
32 la rosetta (la maniglia)
– *spindle top*
33 il corpo del rubinetto
– *shield*
34 il rubinetto a maschio
– *draw-off tap (Am. faucet)*
35 il rubinetto a maschio (*fam.* il marziano)
– *supatap*
36 il rubinetto orientabile
– *swivel tap*
37 il rubinetto a pressione *f* (il rubinetto a tempo)
– *flushing valve*
**38-52 raccordi** *m pl*
– *fittings*
38 il nipplo (il raccordo con filettatura esterna maschio e femmina)
– *joint with male thread*
39 la riduzione
– *reducing socket (reducing coupler)*
40 il gomito con bocchettone *m*
– *elbow screw joint (elbow coupling)*
41 la riduzione femmina
– *reducing socket (reducing coupler) with female thread*
42 il bocchettone piano
– *screw joint*
43 il manicotto
– *coupler (socket)*
44 il raccordo a T
– *T-joint (T-junction joint, tee)*
45 il gomito con bocchettone *m* femmina (con filettatura interna)
– *elbow screw joint with female thread*
46 la curva
– *bend*
47 il raccordo a T con filettatura in uscita
– *T-joint (T-junction joint, tee) with female taper thread*
48 l'angolo di copertura
– *ceiling joint*
49 il gomito ridotto
– *reducing elbow*
50 il raccordo a croce *f*
– *cross*
51 il gomito maschio femmina (con filettatura esterna)
– *elbow joint with male thread*
52 il gomito
– *elbow joint*
**53-57 fissaggi** *m pl* **dei tubi**
– *pipe supports*
53 la graffa a sella
– *saddle clip*
54 la staffa a anello
– *spacing bracket*
55 la caviglia (il cavicchio)
– *plug*
56 supporti *m pl* semplici
– *pipe clips*
57 la graffa a spazio doppio
– *two-piece spacing clip*

**58-86 utensili** *m pl* **per idraulico**
– *plumber's tools, gas fitter's tools*
58 la pinza
– *gas pliers*
59 la pinza per tubi *m pl*
– *footprints*
60 la pinza universale
– *combination cutting pliers*
61 la pinza per pompa a acqua (*fam.* la cagna)
– *water pump pliers*
62 la pinza a punte *f pl* piatte
– *flat-nose pliers*
63 il regginipplo
– *nipple key*
64 la pinza a becco tondo
– *round-nose pliers*
65 il tagliatubo di piombo (la tenaglia, la tanaglia)
– *pincers*
66 la chiave prussiana (la chiave registrabile a rullino)
– *adjustable S-wrench*
67 la chiave registrabile a doppio martello
– *screw wrench*
68 la chiave inglese
– *shifting spanner*
69 il cacciavite
– *screwdriver*
70 il foretto o il gattuccio
– *compass saw (keyhole saw)*
71 il seghetto per metalli *m pl*
– *hacksaw frame*
72 il segaccio (il saracco)
– *hand saw*
73 il saldatoio a stagno
– *soldering iron*
74 la lampada per saldare
– *blowlamp (blowtorch) [for soldering]*
75 il nastro isolante
– *sealing tape*
76 lo stagno per brasare
– *tin-lead solder*
77 la mazza
– *club hammer*
78 il martello
– *hammer*
79 la livella a bolla d'aria
– *spirit level*
80 la morsa del meccanico
– *steel-leg vice (Am. vise)*
81 la morsa da tubi *m pl*
– *pipe vice (Am. vise)*
82 la curvatubi (la piegatrice per tubi *m pl*)
– *pipe-bending machine*
83 la forma di curvatura
– *former (template)*
84 il tagliatubi
– *pipe cutter*
85 il portafiliere
– *hand die*
86 la macchina filettatrice
– *screw-cutting machine (thread-cutting machine)*

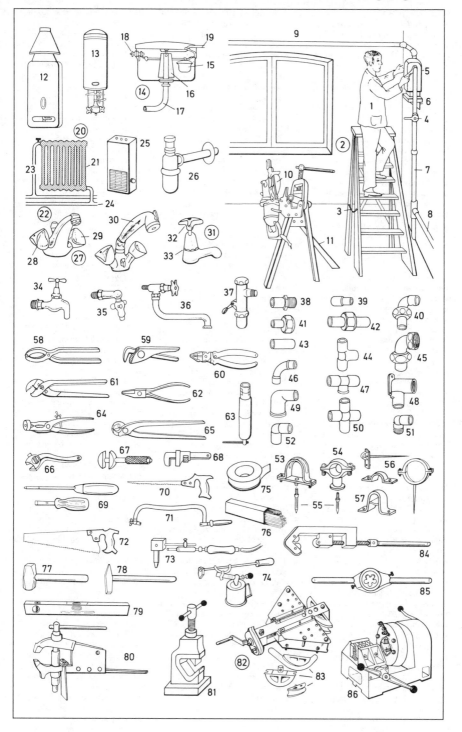

1 l'elettricista *m*
- *electrician (electrical fitter, wireman)*
2 il pulsante del campanello per tensione *f* elettrica inferiore a 42 volt
- *bell push (doorbell) for low-voltage safety current*
3 il citofono con tasto di chiamata
- *house telephone with call button*
4 l'interruttore *m* a bilanciere *m* [incassato, per l'applicazione *f* all'interno della parete]
- *[flush-mounted] rocker switch*
5 la presa di corrente *f* anticontatto [incassata]
- *[flush-mounted] earthed socket (wall socket, plug point, Am. wall outlet, convenience outlet, outlet)*
6 la presa di corrente *f* doppia anticontatto [sporgente, per l'applicazione *f* all'esterno della parete]
- *[surface-mounted] earthed double socket (double wall socket, double plug point, Am. double wall outlet, double convenience outlet, double outlet)*
7 la combinazione (interruttore *m* e presa di corrente *f* anticontatto)
- *switched socket (switch and socket)*
8 la presa di corrente *f* a quattro vie *f pl*
- *four-socket (four-way) adapter (socket)*
9 la spina anticontatto
- *earthed plug*
10 la prolunga
- *extension lead (Am. extension cord)*
11 la spina della prolunga
- *extension plug*
12 la presa della prolunga
- *extension socket*
13 la presa sporgente tripolare (per corrente *f* trifase) anticontatto e con conduttore *m* neutro
- *surface-mounted three-pole earthed socket [for three-phase circuit] with neutral conductor*
14 la spina per corrente *f* trifase
- *three-phase plug*
15 la soneria elettrica (il campanello elettrico)
- *electric bell (electric buzzer)*
16 l'interruttore *m* a strappo con tirante *m*
- *pull-switch (cord-operated wall switch)*
17 il dimmer [per regolare senza scatti *m pl* la luce della lampadina]
- *dimmer switch [for smooth adjustment of lamp brightness]*
18 l'interruttore *m* a pacco in custodia di fusione *f*
- *drill-cast rotary switch*
19 l'interruttore *m* automatico con innesto a vite *f* di sicurezza
- *miniature circuit breaker (screw-in circuit breaker, fuse)*
20 il pulsante di bloccaggio (di sicurezza)
- *resetting button*

21 la vite calibrata, l'inserimento calibrato (per valvole *f pl* fusibili e interruttori *m pl* automatici con innesto a vite *f* di sicurezza)
- *set screw [for fuses and miniature circuit breakers]*
22 l'impianto per (nel) sottosuolo
- *underfloor mounting (underfloor sockets)*
23 l'allacciamento inclinato per la linea di alta tensione *f* e la linea delle telecomunicazioni
- *hinged floor socket for power lines and communication lines*
24 la presa di corrente *f* a muro (a pavimento) con coperchio ribaltabile
- *sunken floor socket with hinged lid (snap lid)*
25 l'alzata della presa di corrente *f*
- *surface-mounted socket outlet (plug point) box*
26 la lampadina tascabile, una lampada a torcia
- *pocket torch, a torch (Am. flash-light)*
27 la batteria a secco (pila per lampadina tascabile)
- *dry cell battery*
28 la molla di contatto
- *contact spring*
29 il morsetto (morsetto per lampadari *m pl*, divisibile, di materiale *m* sintetico termoplastico)
- *strip of thermoplastic connectors*
30 il nastro di acciaio per l'introduzione *f* del cavo con vite *f* sonda e occhiello saldato
- *steel draw-in wire (draw wire) with threading key, and ring attached*
31 l'armadietto del contatore
- *electricity meter cupboard*
32 il contatore della corrente alternata
- *electricity meter*
33 gli interruttori automatici di corrente *f* (le valvole di sicurezza)
- *miniature circuit breakers (miniature circuit breaker consumer unit)*
34 il nastro isolante
- *insulating tape (Am. friction tape)*
35 la cappa filettata
- *fuse holder*
36 il fusibile (la valvola fusibile), una cartuccia con guarnizione *f* fusibile
- *circuit breaker (fuse), a fuse cartridge with fusible element*
37 l'indicatore *m* di fusione *f* (indicata con colori *m pl* diversi a seconda della corrente nominale)
- *colour (Am. color) indicator [showing current rating]*
38 *u.* 39 il punto di contatto (calotta e punta del fusibile)
- *contact maker*
40 il collare per cavo (collare *m* di plastica)
- *cable clip*

41 l'apparecchio di misurazione *f* multipla (tensiometro e amperometro)
- *universal test meter (multiple meter for measuring current and voltage)*
42 il cavo rivestito per ambienti *m pl* umidi, di materiale *m* sintetico termoplastico
- *thermoplastic moisture-proof cable*
43 il conduttore di rame *m*
- *copper conductor*
44 il conduttore a nervatura (a costola)
- *three-core cable*
45 il saldatore elettrico
- *electric soldering iron*
46 il cacciavite
- *screwdriver*
47 la pinza per le pompe dell'acqua
- *water pump pliers*
48 il casco in materiale *m* sintetico antiurto
- *shock-resisting safety helmet*
49 la borsa degli attrezzi (valigetta degli attrezzi)
- *tool case*
50 la pinza a becco rotondo
- *round-nose pliers*
51 la cesoia per profili *m pl*
- *cutting pliers*
52 la seghetta
- *junior hacksaw*
53 la pinza universale
- *combination cutting pliers*
54 l'impugnatura isolante
- *insulated handle*
55 il cercapoli
- *continuity tester*
56 la lampadina elettrica
- *electric light bulb (general service lamp, filament lamp)*
57 il bulbo della lampadina
- *glass bulb (bulb)*
58 il filamento luminoso a doppia spirale *f*
- *coiled-coil filament*
59 l'attacco filettato (la montatura filettata)
- *screw base*
60 la virola
- *lampholder*
61 la lampada a scarica elettrica (lampada con sostanza luminescente)
- *fluorescent tube*
62 il portalampada a scarica elettrica
- *bracket for fluorescent tubes*
63 il coltello a serramanico da elettricista *m*
- *electrician's knife*
64 la pinza dissolante
- *wire strippers*
65 l'attacco a baionetta
- *bayonet fitting*
66 presa tripolare con interruttore
- *three-pin socket with switch*
67 spina tripolare
- *three-pin plug*
68 portafusibile con filo
- *fuse carrier with fuse wire*
69 lampadina a baionetta
- *light bulb with bayonet fitting*

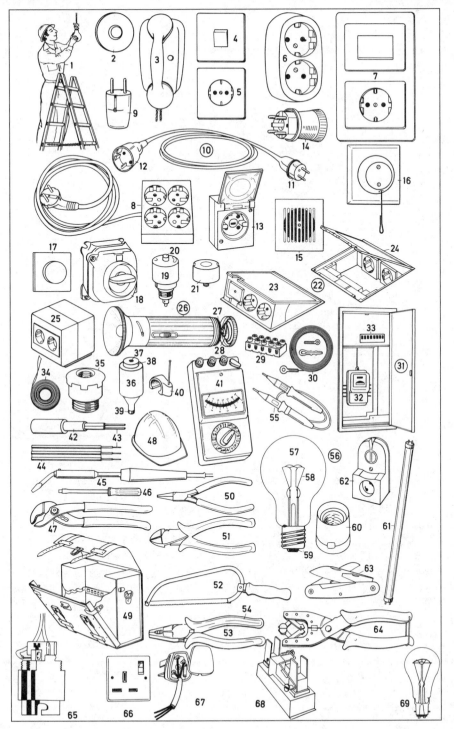

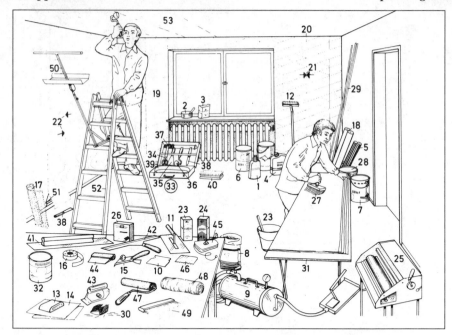

**1-17 la preparazione del fondo** (prima dell'applicazione *f* della tappezzeria)
- *preparation of surfaces*
1 la sostanza per il distacco della tappezzeria (sostanza scrostatrice)
- *wallpaper-stripping liquid (stripper)*
2 il gesso
- *plaster (plaster of Paris)*
3 lo stucco
- *filler*
4 il fondo per la nuova tappezzeria
- *glue size (size)*
5 la carta di fondo (cartaccia)
- *lining paper, a backing paper*
6 il materiale per la prima mano di fondo
- *primer*
7 il silicato di fluoro, una sostanza indurente delle superfici
- *fluate*
8 la seconda mano di fondo
- *shredded lining paper*
9 l'apparecchio per il distacco della tappezzeria
- *wallpaper-stripping machine (stripper)*
10 la spatola giapponese (spatola da stucco)
- *scraper*
11 la liscia (il lisciatoio)
- *smoother*
12 la perforatrice
- *perforator*
13 il blocco di rettifica
- *sandpaper block*
14 la carta smeriglia (carta abrasiva)
- *sandpaper*
15 il raschietto da tappezziere *m*
- *stripping knife*
16 il nastro adesivo di protezione *f* (nastro adesivo coprente)
- *masking tape*
17 il materiale per coprire le crepe (base *f* per crepe *f pl*)
- *strip of sheet metal [on which wallpaper is laid for cutting]*

**18-53 l'applicazione *f* della tappezzeria**
- *wallpapering (paper hanging)*
18 la tappezzeria (*tipi:* tappezzeria di carta da parati *m pl*, di fibra ruvida, di stoffa da parati *m pl*, di materiale *m* sintetico, di metallo, di materiale *m* naturale, a dipinto murale
- *wallpaper (kinds: wood pulp paper, wood chip paper, fabric wallhangings, synthetic wallpaper, metallic paper, natural (e.g. wood or cork) paper, tapestry wallpaper)*
19 la lista (la striscia) di carta da parati *m pl*
- *length of wallpaper*
20 l'attaccatura di cima della tappezzeria (a spigolo)
- *butted paper edges*
21 l'attaccatura rettilinea (rapporto)
- *matching edge*
22 l'attaccatura sfasata
- *non-matching edge*
23 la colla per tappezzieri *m pl* (*anche:* colla di pesce *m*)
- *wallpaper paste*
24 la colla speciale per tappezzieri *m pl*
- *heavy-duty paste*
25 la macchina spalmatrice di colla
- *pasting machine*
26 la colla per spalmatrici *f pl*
- *paste [for the pasting machine]*
27 il pennello da colla
- *paste brush*
28 la colla per grandi superfici *f pl*
- *emulsion paste*
29 il battiscopa (il listello) per tappezzeria
- *picture rail*
30 le punte per battiscopa (punta da listello)
- *beading pins*
31 il tavolo da lavoro del tappezziere
- *pasteboard (paperhanger's bench)*
32 la vernice protettiva per tappezzeria
- *gloss finish*
33 la cassetta degli attrezzi per tappezzieri *m*
- *paperhanging kit*

34 le forbici per tappezziere *m*
- *shears (bull-nosed scissors)*
35 la spatola da stucco
- *filling knife*
36 il rocchetto per cuciture *f pl*
- *seam roller*
37 il coltello per tappezziere *m*
- *hacking knife*
38 il coltello per rifilature *f pl*
- *knife (trimming knife)*
39 la riga del tappezziere
- *straightedge*
40 la spazzola del tappezziere
- *paperhanging brush*
41 la cazzuola del tappezziere
- *wallpaper-cutting board*
42 la riga da strappo
- *cutter*
43 l'apricuciture *m*
- *trimmer*
44 la spatola per materiale *m* sintetico
- *plastic spatula*
45 il cavo retrattile
- *chalked string*
46 la spatola a denti *m pl*
- *spreader*
47 il rullo pressore per tappezzieri *m pl*
- *paper roller*
48 il panno di flanella
- *flannel cloth*
49 il bruschino per tappezzeria
- *dry brush*
50 l'arnese *m* per tappezzare il soffitto
- *ceiling paperhanger*
51 l'angolare per tagli *m pl* di spigolo
- *overlap angle*
52 la scala a cavalletto per tappezzieri *m* (scala doppia, scala a libro)
- *paperhanger's trestles*
53 la tappezzeria del soffitto
- *ceiling paper*

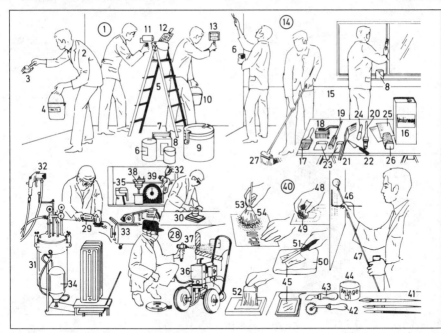

1 **l'imbiancatura (la verniciatura)**
– *painting*
2 l'imbianchino
– *painter*
3 il pennello
– *paintbrush*
4 il colore
– *emulsion paint (emulsion)*
5 la scala doppia
– *stepladder*
6 il barattolo di colore *m*
– *can (tin) of paint*
7 *u.* 8 le taniche del colore
– *cans (tins) of paint*
7 la tanica col manico
– *can (tin) with fixed handle*
8 la tanica con maniglie *f pl*
– *paint kettle*
9 il bidone del colore
– *drum of paint*
10 il secchio
– *paint bucket*
11 il rullo
– *paint roller*
12 il raschiatoio
– *grill [for removing excess paint from the roller]*
13 il rullo finta tappezzeria
– *stippling roller*
14 **la verniciatura**
– *varnishing*
15 lo zoccolo a olio
– *oil-painted dado*
16 la tanica con il solvente
– *canister for thinner*
17 la pennellessa
– *flat brush for larger surfaces (flat wall brush)*
18 la plafoniera
– *stippler*
19 il pennello rotondo
– *fitch*

20 il pennello strozzato
– *cutting-in brush*
21 il pennello per radiatori *m pl* (il pennello per termosifoni *m pl*)
– *radiator brush (flay brush)*
22 la spatola
– *paint scraper*
23 la spatola giapponese
– *scraper*
24 la spatola per mastice *m*
– *putty knife*
25 la carta vetrata (la carta abrasiva)
– *sandpaper*
26 la bietta
– *sandpaper block*
27 il pennello per pavimento
– *floor brush*
28 **la lucidatura e verniciatura a spruzzo**
– *sanding and spraying*
29 la carteggiatrice
– *grinder*
30 la carteggiatrice orbitale
– *sander*
31 la bombola per la verniciatura a spruzzo
– *pressure pot*
32 l'aerografo (la pistola a spruzzo)
– *spray gun*
33 il compressore
– *compressor (air compressor)*
34 l'attrezzo per la verniciatura a spruzzo dei termosifoni
– *flow coating machine for flow coating radiators, etc.*
35 l'aerografo a mano
– *hand spray*
36 l'impianto per la verniciatura a spruzzo senza aria
– *airless spray unit*
37 l'aerografo senza aria
– *airless spray gun*
38 il densimetro DIN per misurare la viscosità
– *efflux viscometer*

39 il contasecondi
– *seconds timer*
40 **scrittura e doratura**
– *lettering and gilding*
41 il pennello per la scrittura
– *lettering brush (signwriting brush, pencil)*
42 la rotella per decorazioni *f pl*
– *tracing wheel*
43 il trincetto
– *stencil knife*
44 l'olio per doratura
– *oil gold size*
45 la foglia d'oro (la lamina d'oro)
– *gold leaf*
46 la profilatura
– *outline drawing*
47 il bastone per dipingere
– *mahlstick*
48 la riproduzione del disegno sulla foglia d'oro
– *pouncing*
49 il sacchetto da spolvero
– *pounce bag*
50 il cuscinetto da doratore *m* (il guancialino)
– *gilder's cushion*
51 il coltello da doratore *m*
– *gilder's knife*
52 l'applicazione *f* della foglia d'oro
– *sizing gold leaf*
53 il riempimento a tampone *m* (a spolvero) delle lettere
– *filling in the letters with stipple paint*
54 il pennello per spolveratura
– *gilder's mop*

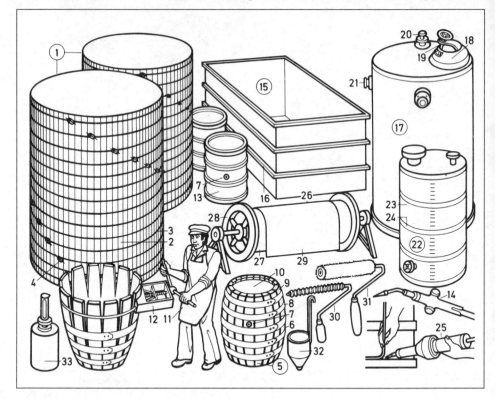

**1-33 il laboratorio del bottaio**
- *cooper's and tank construction engineer's workshops*
1 il tino
- *tank*
2 il rivestimento in legno (le doghe)
- *circumference made of staves (staved circumference)*
3 il cerchio in ferro
- *iron rod*
4 il tenditore a vite *f*
- *turnbuckle*
5 la botte
- *barrel (cask)*
6 il corpo della botte
- *body of barrel (of cask)*
7 lo zaffo (il cocchiume)
- *bunghole*
8 il cerchio della botte
- *band (hoop) of barrel*
9 la doga
- *barrel stave*
10 il fondo della botte
- *barrelhead (heading)*
11 il bottaio
- *cooper*
12 l'arganello (la vite per serrare le doghe)
- *trusser*

13 il barile di ferro
- *drum*
14 il cannello per saldatura autogena
- *gas welding torch*
15 la vasca di decapaggio in termoplasto (in resina termoplastica)
- *staining vat, made of thermoplastics*
16 il cerchio di rinforzo in profilato di ferro
- *iron reinforcing bands*
17 il silo in resina di poliestere *m* con fibra di vetro
- *storage container, made of glass fibre (Am. glass fiber) reinforced polyester resin*
18 il passo d'uomo
- *manhole*
19 il coperchio per il passo d'uomo con vite *f*
- *manhole cover with handwheel*
20 la valvola di sicurezza della flangia
- *flange mount*
21 il volantino di serraggio della flangia
- *flange-type stopcock*
22 il contenitore graduato
- *measuring tank*

23 il rivestimento
- *shell (circumference)*
24 la cerchiatura
- *shrink ring*
25 la pistola a aria calda
- *hot-air gun*
26 il tubo in resina sintetica armata con fibra di vetro
- *roller made of glass fibre (Am. glass fiber) reinforced synthetic resin*
27 il tubo
- *cylinder*
28 la flangia
- *flange*
29 il tessuto di lana di vetro
- *glass cloth*
30 il rullo scanalato
- *grooved roller*
31 il rullo in pelle *f* di pecora
- *lambskin roller*
32 il bicchiere in viscosa
- *ladle for testing viscosity*
33 l'apparecchio per dosare la durezza
- *measuring vessel for hardener*

**1-25 la pellicceria (il laboratorio di pellicceria)**
- *furrier's workroom*
1 il pellicciaio
- *furrier*
2 la pistola a vapore *m,* una pistola a spruzzo
- *steam spray gun*
3 il ferro da stiro a vapore *m*
- *steam iron*
4 il battitoio
- *beating machine*
5 la tagliatrice per pelli *f pl* da pelliccia, una macchina per rifilare le pelli
- *cutting machine for letting out furskins*
6 la pelle intera
- *uncut furskin*
7 le strisce rifilate
- *let-out strips (let-out sections)*
8 la lavorante di pellicceria (la cucitrice)
- *fur worker*
9 la macchina da cucire per pellicceria
- *fur-sewing machine*
10 il soffiatore del sistema di scarico
- *blower for letting out*

**11-21 pelli *f pl* da pelliccia (pelli *f pl*)**
- *furskins*
11 la pelle di visone *m*
- *mink skin*
12 la parte del pelo (parte *f* superiore, pelo)
- *fur side*
13 la parte della pelle (parte *f* inferiore, pelle *f* )
- *leather side*
14 la pelle tagliata (il taglio)
- *cut furskin*
15 la pelle di lince *f* prima della rifilatura
- *lynx skin before letting out*
16 la pelle di lince *f* rifilata
- *let-out lynx skin*
17 la parte del pelo (parte *f* superiore, pelo)
- *fur side*
18 la parte della pelle (parte *f* inferiore, pelle *f* )
- *leather side*
19 la pelle di visone *m* rifilata
- *let-out mink skin*
20 la pelle di lince *f* composta di singoli pezzi *m pl*
- *lynx fur, sewn together (sewn)*

21 la pelle di Breitschwanz *m*
- *broadtail*
22 il chiodo da (per) pelliccia
- *fur marker*
23 la lavorante di pellicceria (la tagliatrice)
- *fur worker*
24 la pelliccia (il mantello) di visone *m*
- *mink coat*
25 la pelliccia (il mantello) di ocelot *m* (di ozelot *m*)
- *ocelot coat*

**1-73 il laboratorio del falegname** (la falegnameria)
– *joiner's workshop*
**1-28 gli utensili del falegname**
– *joiner's tools*
**1** la raspa (da legno)
– *wood rasp*
**2** la lima da legno
– *wood file*
**3** il gattuccio (il foretto)
– *compass saw (keyhole saw)*
**4** l'impugnatura del gattuccio
– *saw handle*
**5** il mazzuolo quadrangolare da legno
– *[square-headed] mallet*
**6** la squadra da falegname *m*
– *try square*
**7-11 scalpelli** *m pl*
– *chisels*
**7** lo scalpello da legno
– *bevelled-edge chisel (chisel)*
**8** il bedano (il pedano)
– *mortise (mortice) chisel*
**9** la sgorbia
– *gouge*
**10** il manico
– *handle*
**11** lo scalpello sbozzatore (lo scalpello a triangolo)
– *framing chisel (cant chisel)*
**12** la pentola da colla con bagno-maria
– *glue pot in water bath*
**13** il pentolino della colla, un recipiente per colla da falegname *m*
– *glue pot (glue well), an insert for joiner's glue*
**14** il morsetto a vite *f* regolabile
– *handscrew*
**15-28 pialle** *f pl*
– *planes*
**15** il pialletto
– *smoothing plane*
**16** la pialla per sgrossare, lo sbozzino
– *jack plane*
**17** il pialletto a denti *m pl*
– *toothing plane*
**18** l'impugnatura
– *handle (toat)*
**19** il cuneo
– *wedge*
**20** il ferro a scalpello
– *plane iron (cutter)*
**21** la cava del cuneo
– *mouth*
**22** la suola
– *sole*
**23** il fianco
– *side*
**24** il ceppo della pialla
– *stock (body)*
**25** la sponderuola
– *rebate (rabbet) plane*

**26** la pialla per scanalature *f pl*
– *router plane (old woman's tooth)*
**27** il raschietto
– *spokeshave*
**28** la pialla per superfici *f pl* curve
– *compass plane*
**29-37 il banco da falegname** *m*
– *woodworker's bench*
**29** il piede
– *foot*
**30** la ganascia anteriore mobile
– *front vice (Am. vise)*
**31** la morsa
– *vice (Am. vise) handle*
**32** la vite della morsa
– *vice (Am. vise) screw*
**33** la ganascia fissa
– *jaw*
**34** il piano del banco
– *bench top*
**35** il bordo (la sponda) del banco
– *well*
**36** il granchio
– *bench stop (bench holdfast)*
**37** la morsa a scorrere (la morsa posteriore)
– *tail vice (Am. vise)*
**38** il falegname
– *cabinet maker (joiner)*
**39** il piallone (la pialla lunga)
– *trying plane*
**40** i trucioli
– *shavings*
**41** la vite da legno
– *wood screw*
**42** la licciaiola a paletta (la licciaiuola, lo stradasega)
– *saw set*
**43** il guida saracco
– *mitre (Am. miter) box*
**44** il saracco
– *tenon saw*
**45** la piallatrice a spessore *m*
– *thicknesser (thicknessing machine)*
**46** la tavola con rulli *m pl* di accompagnamento
– *thicknessing table with rollers*
**47** la protezione per i contraccolpi
– *kick-back guard*
**48** lo scarica trucioli
– *chip-extractor opening*
**49** la mortasatrice a catena
– *chain mortising machine (chain mortiser)*
**50** la catena continua
– *endless mortising chain*
**51** il dispositivo di serraggio legno
– *clamp (work clamp)*
**52** l'alesatrice *f* per nodi *m pl*
– *knot hole moulding (Am. molding) machine*
**53** la fresa
– *knot hole cutter*

**54** la pinza a chiusura rapida
– *quick-action chuck*
**55** la leva a mano
– *hand lever*
**56** la leva di spostamento
– *change-gear handle*
**57** la sega circolare per formatura e rifilatura
– *sizing and edging machine*
**58** l'interruttore *m* principale
– *main switch*
**59** la lama della sega circolare
– *circular-saw (buzz saw) blade*
**60** la manovella d'innalzamento della lama
– *height (rise and fall) adjustment wheel*
**61** la guida prismatica
– *V-way*
**62** il piano con intelaiatura
– *framing table*
**63** il portapezzi
– *extension arm (arm)*
**64** il tavolo per rifilatura
– *trimming table*
**65** la guida diritta
– *fence*
**66** il volantino della guida
– *fence adjustment handle*
**67** la leva di serraggio
– *clamp lever*
**68** la sega circolare a telaio
– *board-sawing machine*
**69** il motore mobile
– *swivel motor*
**70** il supporto del telaio
– *board support*
**71** la slitta della sega
– *saw carriage*
**72** il pedale per sollevare i rulli di trasporto
– *pedal for raising the transport rollers*
**73** la tavola da tagliare
– *blockboard*

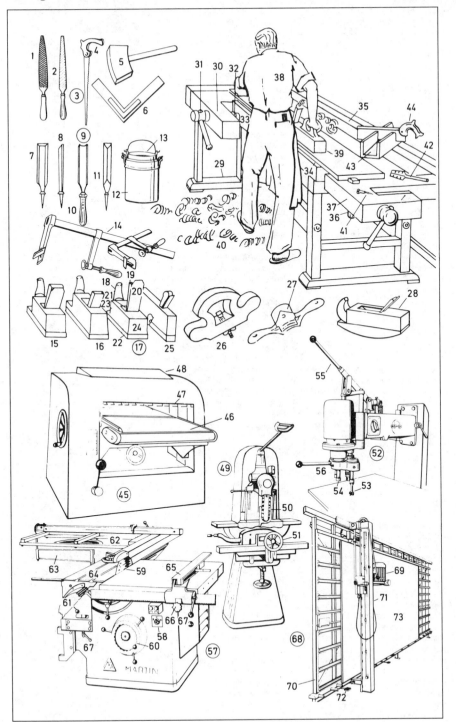

1 la macchina rotativa per tagliare fogli *m pl* per impiallacciature *f pl*
- *veneer-peeling machine (peeling machine, peeler)*
2 il foglio per impiallacciatura
- *veneer*
3 la macchina per incollare i fogli per impiallacciatura
- *veneer-splicing machine*
4 la bobina per il filo di nylon *m*
- *nylon-thread cop*
5 il dispositivo di cucitura
- *sewing mechanism*
6 l'alesatrice *f* per tasselli *m pl*
- *dowel hole boring machine (dowel hole borer)*
7 il motore dell'alesatrice *f* con punta cava
- *boring motor with hollow-shaft boring bit*
8 il volantino per il dispositivo di bloccaggio
- *clamp handle*
9 il dispositivo di bloccaggio
- *clamp*
10 la staffa di montaggio
- *clamping shoe*
11 la guida di arresto
- *stop bar*
12 la levigatrice angolare
- *edge sander (edge-sanding machine)*
13 il tenditore a rullo con regolatore *m*
- *tension roller with extension arm*
14 la vite di regolazione *f* del nastro abrasivo
- *sanding belt regulator (regulating handle)*
15 il nastro abrasivo continuo
- *endless sanding belt (sand belt)*
16 la leva serraggio nastro
- *belt-tensioning lever*
17 il tavolo di appoggio inclinabile
- *canting table (tilting table)*
18 il rullo del nastro
- *belt roller*
19 la riga con angolo per smusso
- *angling fence for mitres* (Am. *miters*)
20 la cuffia sollevabile antipolvere
- *opening dust hood*
21 il dispositivo di abbassamento piano di appoggio
- *rise adjustment of the table*
22 il volantino innalzamento piano
- *rise adjustment wheel for the table*
23 la vite di arresto per la regolazione altezza tavolo
- *clamping screw for the table rise adjustment*
24 la consolle del tavolo
- *console*
25 il basamento della macchina
- *foot of the machine*

26 l'incollatrice *f* a angolo
- *edge-veneering machine*
27 la ruota per carteggiare
- *sanding wheel*
28 l'aspirapolvere *m*
- *sanding dust extractor*
29 l'incollatrice *f*
- *splicing head*
30 la levigatrice a nastro
- *single-belt sanding machine (single-belt sander)*
31 la copertura di protezione *f* del nastro
- *belt guard*
32 la cappottatura del rullo
- *band wheel cover*
33 l'aspiratore *m*
- *extractor fan (exhaust fan)*
34 il pattino di pressione *f*
- *frame-sanding pad*
35 il piano di levigatura
- *sanding table*
36 la regolazione fine
- *fine adjustment*
37 la macchina per assemblaggio e taglio di precisione *f*
- *fine cutter and jointer*
38 la segatrice e piallatrice *f* con trasmissione *f* a catena
- *saw carriage with chain drive*
39 la sospensione ordinata dei cavi
- *trailing cable hanger (trailing cable support)*
40 il supporto dell'aspiratore *m*
- *air extractor pipe*
41 la guida di trasporto
- *rail*
42 la pressa per telai *m pl*
- *frame-cramping (frame-clamping) machine*
43 l'incastellatura per i telai
- *frame stand*
44 il pezzo in lavorazione *f*, un telaio da finestra
- *workpiece, a window frame*
45 la conduttura per l'aria compressa
- *compressed-air line*
46 il cilindro di pressione *f*
- *pressure cylinder*
47 il tampone di pressione *f*
- *pressure foot*
48 il serraggio dei telai
- *frame-mounting device*
49 la pressa per impiallacciatura a azione *f* rapida
- *rapid-veneer press*
50 il piano inferiore della pressa
- *bed*
51 il piano superiore della pressa
- *press*
52 il cilindro di pressione *f*
- *pressure piston*

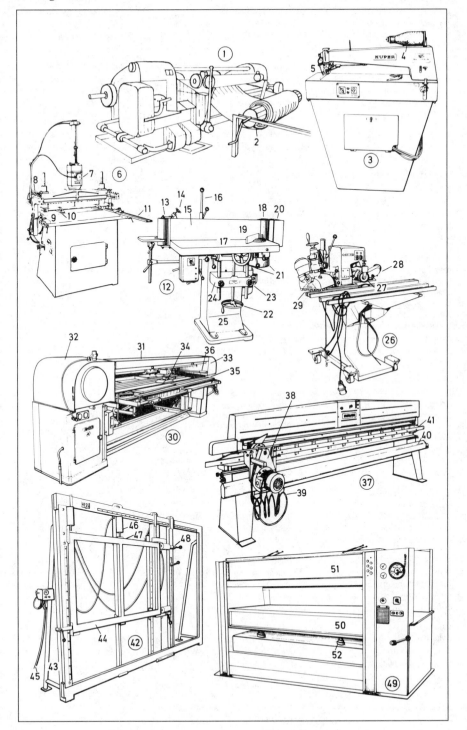

**1-34** l'armadietto degli utensili per il «fai da te»
– *tool cupboard (tool cabinet) for do-it-yourself work*
**1** il pialletto
– *smoothing plane*
**2** la serie delle chiavi fisse
– *set of fork spanners (fork wrenches, open-end wrenches)*
**3** il seghetto a mano
– *hacksaw*
**4** il cacciavite
– *screwdriver*
**5** il cacciavite con punta a croce *f* (con punta a stella)
– *cross-point screwdriver*
**6** la lima da seghe *f pl*
– *saw rasp*
**7** il martello
– *hammer*
**8** la raspa da legno
– *wood rasp*
**9** la lima bastarda
– *roughing file*
**10** la morsa a vite *f* piccola
– *small vice (Am. vise)*
**11** la pinza regolabile
– *corner pipe wrench*
**12** la tenaglia da idraulico (*fam.:* la cagna)
– *water pump pliers*
**13** la tenaglia
– *pincers*
**14** la pinza universale
– *all-purpose wrench*
**15** la pinza isolata
– *wire stripper and cutter*
**16** il trapano elettrico
– *electric drill*
**17** la sega di acciaio
– *hacksaw*
**18** la tazza di gesso
– *plaster cup*
**19** il saldatore (il saldatoio)
– *soldering iron*
**20** il filo di stagno per brasare
– *tin-lead solder wire*
**21** il disco lucidante in pelle *f* di agnello
– *lamb's wool polishing bonnet*
**22** il disco di gomma per il trapano
– *rubber backing disc (disk)*
**23** dischi abrasivi
– *grinding wheel*
**24** la spazzola metallica a disco
– *wire wheel brush*
**25** il disco di carta abrasiva
– *sanding discs (disks)*
**26** la squadra da falegname *m*
– *try square*
**27** il saracco (il segaccio)
– *hand saw*
**28** il coltello universale (il cutter)
– *universal cutter*

**29** la livella a bolla di aria
– *spirit level*
**30** lo scalpello di legno
– *firmer chisel*
**31** il bulino
– *centre (Am. center) punch*
**32** il punteruolo
– *nail punch*
**33** il metro pieghevole
– *folding rule (rule)*
**34** la cassetta minuterie *f pl*
– *storage box for small parts*
**35** la cassetta degli attrezzi
– *tool box*
**36** la colla a freddo
– *woodworking adhesive*
**37** la spatola
– *stripping knife*
**38** il nastro adesivo
– *adhesive tape*
**39** l'assortimento di chiodi *m pl*, viti *f pl*, tasselli *m pl*
– *storage box with compartments for nails, screws, and plugs*
**40** il martello del fabbro
– *machinist's hammer*
**41** il banco da lavoro
– *collapsible workbench (collapsible bench)*
**42** il dispositivo di serraggio
– *jig*
**43** il trapano elettrico
– *electric percussion drill (electric hammer drill)*
**44** l'impugnatura a pistola
– *pistol grip*
**45** l'impugnatura aggiuntiva
– *side grip*
**46** la leva cambio velocità
– *gearshift switch*
**47** l'impugnatura con distanziatore *m*
– *handle with depth gauge (Am. gage)*
**48** il mandrino
– *chuck*
**49** la punta elicoidale (la punta a elica)
– *twist bit (twist drill)*
**50-55** accessori *m pl* per trapano elettrico
– *attachments for an electric drill*
**50** la sega combinata circolare e a nastro
– *combined circular saw (buzz saw) and bandsaw*
**51** il tornio da legno
– *wood-turning lathe*
**52** il rivestimento della sega circolare
– *circular saw attachment*
**53** la levigatrice orbitale
– *orbital sanding attachment (orbital sander)*
**54** la colonna di sostegno del trapano
– *drill stand*

**55** il rivestimento delle cesoie da giardino
– *hedge-trimming attachment (hedge trimmer)*
**56** la pistola per saldature istantanee
– *soldering gun*
**57** il saldatore (il saldatoio)
– *soldering iron*
**58** il saldatore rapido
– *high-speed soldering iron*
**59** l'imbottitura, il rivestimento di una poltrona
– *upholstery, upholstering an armchair*
**60** la stoffa da rivestimento
– *fabric (material) for upholstery*
**61** il bricoleur (l'artigiano dilettante)
– *do-it-yourself enthusiast*

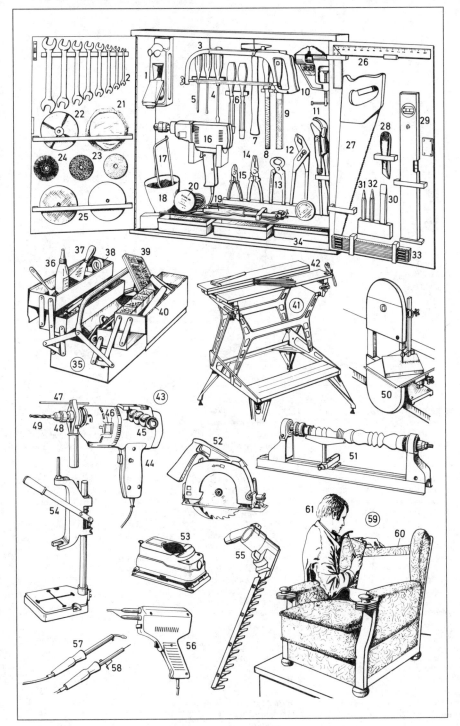

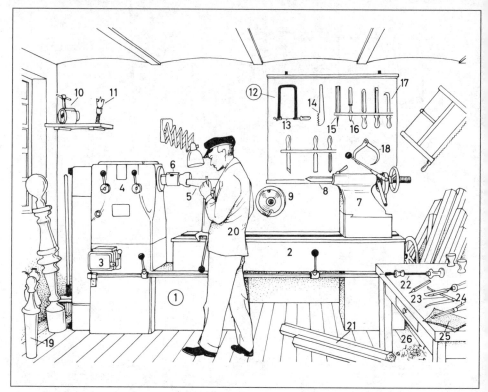

**1-26 l'officina del tornitore**
- *turnery (turner's workshop)*
1 il tornio da (per) legno
- *wood-turning lathe (lathe)*
2 il banco
- *lathe bed*
3 il reostato (la resistenza) di avviamento (la scatola avanzamenti *m
  pl* automatici)
- *starting resistance (starting resistor)*
4 la cassa di protezione *f* degli
  ingranaggi
- *gearbox*
5 la torretta portautensili
- *tool rest*
6 il mandrino
- *chuck*
7 la contropunta (la testa del
  tornio)
- *tailstock*
8 il punto morto
- *centre (Am. center)*
9 la piastra rotante, una puleggia
  con dente *m* di trascinamento
- *driving plate with pin*
10 il mandrino a due ganasce *f pl*
- *two-jaw chuck*

11 la punta a tridente *m*
- *live centre (Am. center)*
12 la sega da trafori *m pl* (l'archetto
  da trafori *m pl*)
- *fretsaw*
13 la lama della sega (lama
  dell'archetto) da traforo
- *fretsaw blade*
14, 15, 24 utensili *m pl* da tornio
  (utensili *m pl* del tornitore)
- *turning tools*
14 il pettine per filettare
- *thread chaser, for cutting threads
  in wood*
15 la sgorbia per sgrossamento
- *gouge, for rough turning*
16 la sgorbia a cucchiaio
- *spoon bit (shell bit)*
17 lo scanalatore
- *hollowing tool*
18 il compasso di spessore *m* (compasso per spessori *m pl*, compasso
  per esterni *m pl*)
- *outside calliper (caliper)*
19 il pezzo tornito (articolo in legno
  tornito)
- *turned work (turned wood)*
20 il tornitore in legno
- *master turner (turner)*

21 il pezzo di legno grezzo (il legno
  da tornire)
- *[piece of] rough wood*
22 il trapano a archetto (trapano a
  spirale *f* )
- *drill*
23 il compasso per fori *m pl*
- *inside calliper (caliper)*
24 lo scalpello del tornitore
- *parting tool*
25 la carta vetrata (carta abrasiva)
- *glass paper (sandpaper, emery
  paper)*
26 i trucioli
- *shavings*

**1-40  il laboratorio (la bottega) del ces-
taio**
– *basket making (basketry, basketwork)*
**1-4  tipi** *m pl* **d'intreccio**
– *weaves (strokes)*
1  l'intreccio a giunchi *m pl* o a vimini *m
pl* accoppiati
– *randing*
2  l'intreccio a trama orizzontale (intreccio a spina)
– *rib randing*
3  l'intreccio a trama obliqua
– *oblique randing*
4  l'intreccio semplice, un intreccio con
giunchi *m pl* o vimini *m pl*
– *randing, a piece of wickerwork (screen
work)*
5  la trama (la verga trasversale)
– *weaver*
6  la bacchetta longitudinale
– *stake*
7  il piano di lavoro
– *workboard; also: lapboard*
8  la lista trasversale
– *screw block*
9  il foro d'inserimento
– *hole for holding the block*
10  il cavalletto mobile del cestaio
– *stand*
11  il cesto fatto con strisce *f pl* di corteccia
– *chip basket (spale basket)*
12  la corteccia lavorata a strisce *f pl*
– *chip (spale)*

13  la tinozza di macerazione *f* (tinozza
d'ammollimento)
– *soaking tub*
14  i rami flessibili di salice *m* (verghe *f pl*)
– *willow stakes (osier stakes)*
15  le canne di salice *m* (canne *f pl*)
– *willow rods (osier rods)*
16  il cesto, un intreccio di vimini *m pl*
– *basket, a piece of wickerwork (basketwork)*
17  la bordura finale (bordo di chiusura
del lavoro)
– *border*
18  l'intreccio laterale
– *woven side*
19  la rosetta di fondo (la base del cesto a
rosetta)
– *round base*
20  l'intreccio della base (del fondo)
– *woven base*
21  la croce di fondo (la base del cesto a
croce *f*)
– *slath*
**22-24  la lavorazione di mobili** *m pl* **di
vimini** *m pl*
– *covering a frame*
22  il telaio
– *frame*
23  l'estremità del giunco
– *end*
24  la stecca
– *rib*
25  l'intelaiatura
– *upsett*

26  le fibre (ricavate da rami *m pl* di
piante *f pl* giunchiformi); *tipi:* fibre *f pl*
di sparto, fibre *f pl* di alfa
– *grass; kinds: esparto grass, alfalfa grass*
27  le canne palustri
– *rush (bulrush, reed mace)*
28  il giunco (matassa di giunco cinese)
– *reed (China reed, string)*
29  la rafia
– *raffia (bast)*
30  la paglia
– *straw*
31  la canna di bambù *m*
– *bamboo cane*
32  la canna d'India
– *rattan (ratan) chair cane*
33  il cestaio
– *basket maker*
34  il ferro flettente (ferro per flessione *f*,
ferro per curvare le canne)
– *bending tool*
35  il trincetto
– *cutting point (bodkin)*
36  il martellone per serraggio (martellone *m* per serrare le verghe trasver-
sali)
– *rapping iron*
37  le tenaglie (la tanaglia, la tenaglia)
– *pincers*
38  il raschietto
– *picking knife*
39  la pialla piatta del cestaio
– *shave*
40  la sega ad archetto
– *hacksaw*

**1-8 l'officina del fabbro con fucina**
- *hearth (forge) with blacksmith's fire*
1 la fucina
- *hearth (forge)*
2 la paletta
- *shovel (slice)*
3 lo spegnitoio
- *swab*
4 l'attizzatoio
- *rake*
5 l'uncino per le scorie
- *poker*
6 il condotto per l'aria
- *blast pipe (tue iron)*
7 la cappa
- *chimney (cowl, hood)*
8 la cassetta per l'acqua
- *water trough (quenching trough, bosh)*
9 il maglio autocompressore
- *power hammer*
10 la mazza battente
- *ram (tup)*
**11-16 l'incudine f**
- *anvil*
11 l'incudine
- *anvil*
12 il corno a sezione f quadrata
- *flat beak (beck, bick)*

13 il corno a sezione f rotonda
- *round beak (beck, bick)*
14 la sporgenza dell'incudine f
- *auxiliary table*
15 la staffa di fissaggio
- *foot*
16 il piede
- *upsetting block*
17 la chiodaia
- *swage block*
18 l'affilatrice f
- *tool-grinding machine (tool grinder)*
19 la mola
- *grinding wheel*
20 il paranco
- *block and tackle*
21 il banco da lavoro
- *workbench (bench)*
**22-39 utensili m pl del fabbro**
- *blacksmith's tools*
22 la mazza
- *sledge hammer*
23 il martello da fucinatore m
- *blacksmith's hand hammer*
24 la tenaglia piatta
- *flat tongs*
25 la tenaglia a punta tonda
- *round tongs*

26 le parti del martello
- *parts of the hammer*
27 la penna
- *peen (pane, pein)*
28 la bocca
- *face*
29 l'occhio
- *eye*
30 il manico
- *haft*
31 il cuneo
- *cotter punch*
32 il tagliolo
- *hardy (hardie)*
33 il martello da spianamento
- *set hammer*
34 il martello per scanalare
- *sett (set, sate)*
35 la presella per spianare
- *flat-face hammer (flatter)*
36 il martello punteruolo
- *round punch*
37 la tenaglia a angolo
- *angle tongs*
38 il tagliolo a freddo
- *blacksmith's chisel (scaling hammer, chipping hammer)*
39 il ferro rotante
- *moving iron (bending iron)*

1  l'impianto dell'aria compressa
–  *compressed-air system*
2  il motore elettrico
–  *electric motor*
3  il compressore
–  *compressor*
4  il serbatoio del compressore
–  *compressed-air tank*
5  la conduttura dell'aria compressa
–  *compressed-air line*
6  l'avvitatrice *f* a aria compressa
–  *percussion screwdriver*
7  la smerigliatrice
–  *pedestal grinding machine (floor grinding machine)*
8  la mola
–  *grinding wheel*
9  il cofano di protezione *f*
–  *guard*
10  il rimorchio
–  *trailer*
11  il tamburo del freno
–  *brake drum*
12  il ceppo del freno
–  *brake shoe*
13  la guarnizione del freno
–  *brake lining*
14  l'apparecchiatura di prova
–  *testing kit*

15  il manometro
–  *pressure gauge (Am. gage)*
16  il banco prova dei freni, un banco a rulli *m pl* per la prova dei freni
–  *brake-testing equipment, a rolling road*
17  la buca per la riparazione dei freni
–  *pit*
18  il rullo per la prova dei freni
–  *braking roller*
19  l'apparecchiatura di registrazione *f*
–  *meter (recording meter)*
20  la rettificatrice per i tamburi dei freni
–  *precision lathe for brake drums*
21  la ruota dell'autocarro
–  *lorry wheel*
22  l'alesatrice *f*
–  *boring mill*
23  la sega meccanica alternativa, una sega a archetto
–  *power saw, a hacksaw (power hacksaw)*
24  la morsa a vite *f*
–  *vice (Am. vise)*
25  l'archetto della sega
–  *saw frame*

26  l'alimentatore *m* del refrigerante
–  *coolant supply pipe*
27  la chiodatrice
–  *riveting machine*
28  il telaio del rimorchio (in costruzione *f*)
–  *trailer frame (chassis) under construction*
29  la saldatrice elettrica a gas *m* inerte
–  *inert-gas welding equipment*
30  il raddrizzatore
–  *rectifier*
31  l'apparecchio di comando
–  *control unit*
32  la bombola di $CO_2$
–  *$CO_2$ cylinder*
33  l'incudine *f*
–  *anvil*
34  la fucina
–  *hearth (forge) with blacksmith's fire*
35  il carrello per saldatura autogena
–  *trolley for gas cylinders*
36  il veicolo in riparazione *f*, un trattore agricolo
–  *vehicle under repair, a tractor*

1  il forno a feritoia e a riverbero
   per riscaldare materiale *m* a
   sezione *f* rotonda
 – *continuous furnace with grid
   hearth for annealing of round
   stock*
2  l'apertura di caduta
 – *discharge opening (discharge
   door)*
3  i bruciatori a gas *m*
 – *gas burners*
4  lo sportello di carico
 – *charging door*
5  il maglio a contraccolpo
 – *counterblow hammer*
6  la mazza battente superiore
 – *upper ram*
7  la mazza battente inferiore
 – *lower ram*
8  la guida della mazza
 – *ram guide*
9  l'azionamento idraulico
 – *hydraulic drive*
10  il montante
 – *column*
11  il maglio di stampaggio a corsa
    corta
 – *short-stroke drop hammer*
12  il maglio
 – *ram (tup)*
13  il maglio superiore
 – *upper die block*
14  il maglio inferiore
 – *lower die block*
15  l'azionamento idraulico
 – *hydraulic drive*
16  l'incastellatura del maglio
 – *frame*
17  l'incudine *f* (il basamento)
 – *anvil*
18  la pressa per calibrare e stampare
 – *forging and sizing press*
19  il montante della macchina
 – *standard*
20  il piano della tavola
 – *table*
21  la frizione a dischi *m pl*
 – *disc (disk) clutch*
22  la conduttura aria compressa
 – *compressed-air pipe*
23  la valvola elettromagnetica
 – *solenoid valve*
24  il maglio pneumatico autocom-
    pressore
 – *air-lift gravity hammer (air-lift
   drop hammer)*
25  il motore di azionamento
 – *drive motor*
26  la mazza battente
 – *hammer (tup)*
27  il comando a pedale *m*
 – *foot control (foot pedal)*
28  il pezzo a fucinatura libera
 – *preshaped (blocked) workpiece*

29  la guida della mazza
 – *hammer guide*
30  il cilindro della mazza
 – *hammer cylinder*
31  l'incudine *f* (il basamento)
 – *anvil*
32  il manipolatore per fucinati *m pl*
    per muovere il pezzo nel corso
    della fucinatura
 – *mechanical manipulator to move
   the workpiece in hammer forging*
33  la pinza
 – *dogs*
34  il contrappeso
 – *counterweight*
35  la pressa idraulica per fucinare
 – *hydraulic forging press*
36  la testa di pressione *f*
 – *crown*
37  la traversa fissa
 – *cross head*
38  lo stampo superiore
 – *upper die block*
39  il controstampo inferiore
 – *lower die block*
40  l'incudine *f* inferiore
 – *anvil*
41  il martinetto idraulico
 – *hydraulic piston*
42  la guida a colonne *f pl*
 – *pillar guide*
43  il voltapezzo
 – *rollover device*
44  la catena della gru
 – *burden chain (chain sling)*
45  il gancio della gru
 – *crane hook*
46  il pezzo
 – *workpiece*
47  il forno a gas *m*
 – *gas furnace (gas-fired furnace)*
48  il bruciatore a gas *m*
 – *gas burner*
49  la bocca per introduzione *f* e
    estrazione *f* pezzi *m pl*
 – *charging opening*
50  la tenda a catena
 – *chain curtain*
51  la porta a saracinesca
 – *vertical-lift door*
52  la condotta aria calda
 – *hot-air duct*
53  il preriscaldatore aria
 – *air preheater*
54  la conduttura del gas
 – *gas pipe*
55  il dispositivo sollevamento porta
 – *electric door-lifting mechanism*
56  il velo di aria
 – *air blast*

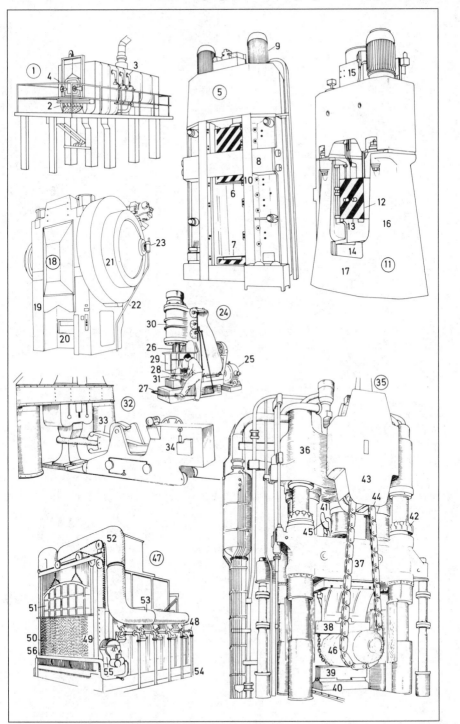

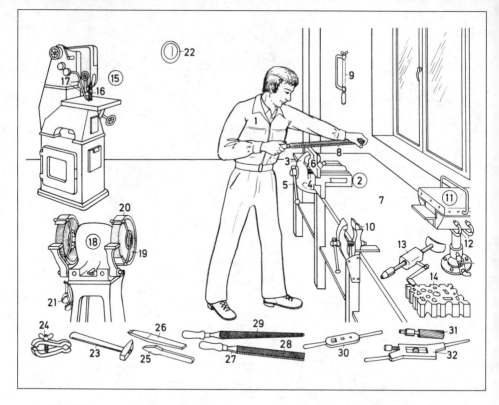

– **metalwork shop** *(mechanic's work-shop, fitter's workshop, locksmith's workshop)*

1 il meccanico (per es. l'operatore *m* alle macchine, il meccanico monta-tore, il carpentiere, il meccanico per chiavi *f pl* e serrature *f pl; ant.:* il fab-bro ferraio), un metalmeccanico

– *metalworker (e.g. mechanic, fitter, locksmith;* form. also: *wrought-iron craftsman)*

2 la morsa parallela
– *parallel-jaw vice (Am. vise)*

3 la ganascia
– *jaw*

4 la vite di serraggio
– *screw*

5 la leva
– *handle*

6 il pezzo
– *workpiece*

7 il banco di lavoro
– *workbench (bench)*

8 la lima (tipi *m pl:* lima a taglio grosso, lima a taglio dolce, lima di precisione *f* )
– *files (kinds: rough file, smooth file, precision file)*

9 il seghetto a mano *f*
– *hacksaw*

10 la morsa articolata a vite *f*, una morsa a tenaglia
– *leg vice (Am. vise), a spring vice*

11 il forno a muffola (il forno per tem-pre), una fucina
– *muffle furnace, a gas-fired furnace*

12 l'alimentazione *f* del gas
– *gas pipe*

13 il trapano a mano
– *hand brace (hand drill)*

14 la chiodaia (la dama chiodiera)
– *swage block*

15 la limatrice
– *filing machine*

16 la lima a nastro
– *file*

17 il soffiatore di trucioli *m pl*
– *compressed-air pipe*

18 la molatrice
– *grinding machine (grinder)*

19 la mola
– *grinding wheel*

20 lo schermo di protezione *f*
– *guard*

21 gli occhiali di protezione *f*
– *goggles (safety glasses)*

22 il casco di protezione *f*
– *safety helmet*

23 il martello
– *machinist's hammer*

24 il morsetto a mano
– *hand vice (Am. vise)*

25 l'ugnetto
– *cape chisel (cross-cut chisel)*

26 lo scalpello piatto
– *flat chisel*

27 la lima piatta
– *flat file*

28 il taglio della lima (il tratto della lima)
– *file cut (cut)*

29 la lima tonda (la lima rotonda; *anche:* la lima mezzatonda)
– *round file (also: half-round file)*

30 il giramaschi
– *tap wrench*

31 l'alesatore *m* (l'alesatoio, l'allisci-atoio)
– *reamer*

32 la filiera regolabile
– *die (die and stock)*

**33-35 la chiave**
– *key*

33 il cannello (il gambo)
– *stem (shank)*

34 l'anello
– *bow*

35 l'ingegno (la mappa)
– *bit*

**36-43 la serratura**
– *door lock, a mortise (mortice) lock*

36 la piastra di base *f*
– *back plate*

37 il saliscendi
– *spring bolt (latch bolt)*

38 il meccanismo di ritenuta (il nottolino)
– *tumbler*

39 il catenaccio (il chiavistello, il paletto)
– *bolt*

**40** il buco della serratura
– *keyhole*
**41** il perno di guida
– *bolt guide pin*
**42** la molla del meccanismo di ritenuta
– *tumbler spring*
**43** la noce con foro quadro
– *follower, with square hole*
**44** la serratura a cilindro (la serratura di sicurezza)
– *cylinder lock (safety lock)*
**45** il cilindro
– *cylinder (plug)*
**46** la molla
– *spring*
**47** la spina di arresto
– *pin*
**48** la chiave di sicurezza, una chiave piatta
– *safety key, a flat key*
**49** la cerniera
– *lift-off hinge*
**50** la piana a angolo
– *hook-and-ride band*
**51** la piana lunga
– *strap hinge*
**52** il calibro a nonio (il calibro a cor-soio)
– *vernier calliper (caliper) gauge (Am. gage)*
**53** il calibro a lame *f pl* (lo spessimetro)
– *feeler gauge (Am. gage)*
**54** il calibro di profondità
– *vernier depth gauge (Am. gage)*
**55** il nonio
– *vernier*
**56** la riga a coltello (la riga a filo)
– *straightedge*
**57** la squadra semplice
– *square*
**58** il trapano a petto
– *breast drill*
**59** la punta elicoidale (la punta a elica)
– *twist bit (twist drill)*
**60** il maschio per filettare
– *screw tap (tap)*
**61** le ganasce per filettare
– *halves of a screw die*
**62** il cacciavite
– *screwdriver*
**63** il raschietto (il raschietto triangolare)
– *scraper* (also: *pointed triangle scraper)*
**64** il bulino (il punzone per centri *m pl*)
– *centre* (Am. *center) punch*
**65** il punzone
– *round punch*
**66** la pinza piatta
– *flat-nose pliers*
**67** il tronchese
– *detachable-jaw cut nippers*
**68** la pinza per tubi *m pl*
– *gas pliers*
**69** la tenaglia (la tanaglia, le tenaglie)
– *pincers*

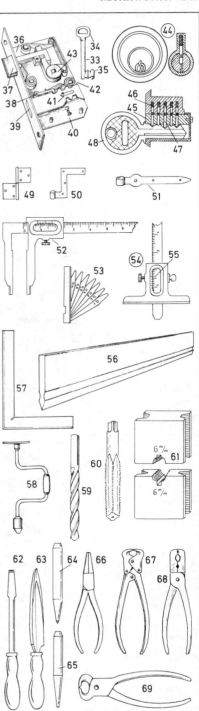

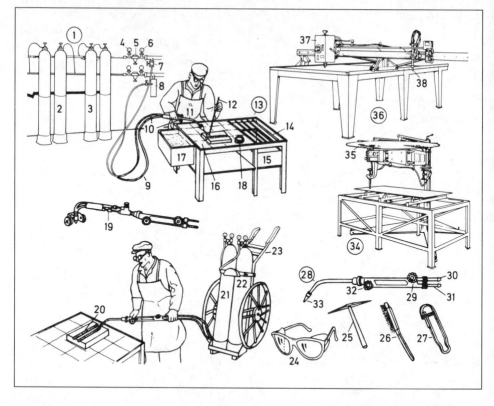

1 la serie delle bombole
– *gas cylinder manifold*
2 il cilindro di acetilene *f* (la bombola d'acetilene *f*)
– *acetylene cylinder*
3 il cilindro d'ossigeno (la bombola d'ossigeno)
– *oxygen cylinder*
4 il manometro alta pressione *f*
– *high-pressure manometer*
5 il riduttore di pressione *f*
– *pressure-reducing valve (reducing valve, pressure regulator)*
6 il manometro bassa pressione *f*
– *low-pressure manometer*
7 il rubinetto di chiusura
– *stop valve*
8 il bariletto d'acqua per bassa pressione *f*
– *hydraulic back-pressure valve for low-pressure installations*
9 il tubo del gas
– *gas hose*
10 il tubo dell'ossigeno
– *oxygen hose*
11 il becco bruciatore (il cannello per la saldatura)
– *welding torch (blowpipe)*
12 la bacchetta di apporto per saldatura
– *welding rod (filler rod)*

13 il banco da lavoro
– *welding bench*
14 la griglia da taglio
– *grating*
15 il cassetto per le scorie
– *scrap box*
16 il piano del banco in argilla refrattaria (chamotte *f*)
– *bench covering of chamotte slabs*
17 la vaschetta per l'acqua
– *water tank*
18 la pasta saldante
– *welding paste (flux)*
19 il cannello da taglio con guida
– *welding torch (blowpipe) with cutting attachment and guide tractor*
20 il pezzo da saldare
– *workpiece*
21 il cilindro d'ossigeno (la bombola d'ossigeno)
– *oxygen cylinder*
22 il cilindro d'acetilene *f* (la bombola d'acetilene *f*)
– *acetylene cylinder*
23 il carrello portabombole
– *cylinder trolley*
24 gli occhiali da saldatore *m* (gli occhiali per saldatura)
– *welding goggles*
25 il martello per le scorie
– *chipping hammer*

26 la spazzola metallica
– *wire brush*
27 l'accenditore *m* per il cannello
– *torch lighter (blowpipe lighter)*
28 il cannello per saldatura
– *welding torch (blowpipe)*
29 la valvola ossigeno
– *oxygen control*
30 il raccordo di entrata del gas comburente (ossigeno)
– *oxygen connection*
31 il raccordo di entrata del gas combustibile (acetilene *f*)
– *gas connection (acetylene connection)*
32 la valvola (il rubinetto) del gas combustibile
– *gas control (acetylene control)*
33 l'ugello
– *welding nozzle*
34 la macchina con cannello da taglio
– *cutting machine*
35 la guida circolare
– *circular template*
36 la macchina universale per taglio al cannello
– *universal cutting machine*
37 la testa di comando
– *tracing head*
38 l'ugello del cannello
– *cutting nozzle*

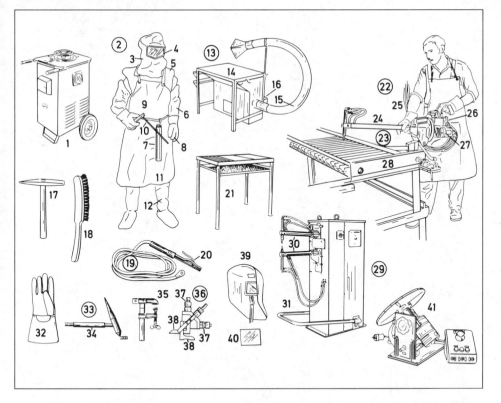

1  il trasformatore per saldatura
– *welding transformer*
**2  il saldatore elettrico**
– *arc welder*
3  la maschera di protezione *f* del
saldatore (elettrico)
– *arc welding helmet*
4  il vetro di protezione *f* sollevabile
– *flip-up window*
5  il proteggispalle
– *shoulder guard*
6  il proteggibraccia
– *protective sleeve*
7  il portaelettrodi
– *electrode case*
8  il guanto a tre dita *f pl* del saldatore
– *three-fingered welding glove*
9  la pinza portaelettrodo
– *electrode holder*
10  l'elettrodo
– *electrode*
11  il grembiule di pelle *f*
– *leather apron*
12  il gambale
– *shin guard*
**13  il tavolo aspirante per saldatura**
– *welding table with fume extraction equipment*
14  la superficie del tavolo aspirante
– *table top*
15  il tubo aspirante orientabile
– *movable extractor duct*

16  il manicotto per l'aria viziata
– *extractor support*
17  la martellina (il martello) per le scorie
– *chipping hammer*
18  la spazzola di filo di acciaio
– *wire brush*
19  il cavo per saldature *f pl*
– *welding lead*
20  la pinza portaelettrodo
– *electrode holder*
21  il banco (il tavolo) per saldatura
– *welding bench*
**22  la saldatura a punti *m pl***
– *spot welding*
23  la pinza per saldatura a punti *m pl*
– *spot welding electrode holder*
24  il braccio degli elettrodi
– *electrode arm*
25  il cavo di alimentazione *f* (il cavo di collegamento)
– *power supply (lead)*
26  il cilindro pneumatico di azionamento elettrodi *m pl*
– *electrode-pressure cylinder*
27  il trasformatore per saldatura
– *welding transformer*
28  il pezzo
– *workpiece*
29  la saldatrice a punti *m pl* azionata a pedale *m*
– *foot-operated spot welder*

30  i bracci oscillanti
– *welder electrode arms*
31  il pedale di azionamento
– *foot pedal for welding pressure adjustment*
32  il guanto a cinque dita *f pl* per saldatore *m*
– *five-fingered welding glove*
33  la torcia per saldatura con gas *m* inerte
– *inert-gas torch for inert-gas welding (gas-shielded arc welding)*
34  la conduttura per gas *m* inerte
– *inert-gas (shielding-gas) supply*
35  il morsetto di terra (il morsetto di massa)
– *work clamp (earthing clamp)*
36  il calibro per saldatura di angolo
– *fillet gauge (Am. gage) (weld gauge) [for measuring throat thickness]*
37  la vite micrometrica
– *micrometer*
38  il braccio graduato
– *measuring arm*
39  lo schermo protettivo (lo schermo protettivo per saldatura)
– *arc welding helmet*
40  il vetro protettivo del casco per saldatura
– *filter lens*
41  il posizionatore a tavola rotante inclinabile
– *small turntable*

# 143 Profilati, viti ed elementi di macchine

*[material: steel, brass, aluminium (Am. aluminum), plastics, etc: in the following, steel was chosen as an example]*

1 il ferro a L *f* (ferro angolare)
– *angle iron (angle)*
2 la flangia
– *leg (flange)*
3-7 **profilati** *m pl* **metallici** (ferro laminato, acciaio laminato)
– *steel girders*
3 il ferro a T *f*
– *T-iron (tee-iron)*
4 l'anima
– *vertical leg*
5 la flangia
– *flange*
6 il ferro a doppia T *f*
– *H-girder (H-beam)*
7 il ferro a E *f*
– *E-channel (channel iron)*
8 la barra rotonda (il tondino, il ferro rotondo)
– *round bar*
9 la barra quadra (il ferro quadro)
– *square iron (Am. square stock)*
10 la barra piatta (il ferro piatto)
– *flat bar*
11 la reggia (reggetta, moietta)
– *strip steel*
12 il filo di ferro
– *iron wire*
13-50 **viti** *f pl*
– *screws and bolts*
13 la vite esagonale (vite *f* a testa esagonale)
– *hexagonal-head bolt*
14 la testa
– *head*
15 il gambo
– *shank*
16 il filetto (il verme)
– *thread*
17 la rondella
– *washer*
18 il dado esagonale (la madrevite esagonale)
– *hexagonal nut*
19 la copiglia
– *split pin*
20 la calotta
– *rounded end*
21 l'apertura della chiave
– *width of head (of flats)*
22 il prigioniero
– *stud*
23 la punta
– *point (end)*
24 il dado a corona (la madrevite a corona)
– *castle nut (castellated nut)*
25 il foro per la copiglia
– *hole for the split pin*
26 la vite con taglio a croce *f*, una vite di latta
– *cross-head screw, a sheet-metal screw (self-tapping screw)*
27 la vite esagonale a sagoma interna
– *hexagonal socket head screw*
28 la vite a testa conica
– *countersunk-head bolt*
29 il naso (nasello)
– *catch*
30 il controdado (dado di bloccaggio)
– *locknut (locking nut)*
31 il maschio
– *bolt (pin)*
32 la vite a colletto
– *collar-head bolt*
33 il colletto della vite
– *set collar (integral collar)*
34 l'anello a molla (maglia a molla, rosetta elastica, rondella elastica)
– *spring washer (washer)*
35 il dado cilindrico a fori *m pl*, un controdado
– *round nut, an adjusting nut*
36 la vite a testa cilindrica, una vite con taglio
– *cheese-head screw, a slotted screw*

37 la spina conica
– *tapered pin*
38 il taglio
– *screw slot (screw slit, screw groove)*
39 la vite a testa quadra
– *square-head bolt*
40 la spina cilindrica
– *grooved pin, a cylindrical pin*
41 la vite a testa di martello
– *T-head bolt*
42 il dado alettato (dado ad alette *f pl*, dado a farfalla, il galletto)
– *wing nut (fly nut, butterfly nut)*
43 il bullone (la chiavarda) da muro (bullone *m* da fondazione *f*)
– *rag bolt*
44 l'uncino (uncinetto)
– *barb*
45 la vite mordente, una vite per legno
– *wood screw*
46 la testa svasata (testa a lenticchia)
– *countersunk head*
47 il filetto mordente da legno
– *wood screw thread*
48 il perno a vite *f* (perno filettato)
– *grub screw*
49 il taglio del perno a vite *f*
– *pin slot (pin slit, pin groove)*
50 la calotta (la punta) sferica
– *round end*
51 il chiodo (la punta Parigi)
– *nail (wire nail)*
52 la testa
– *head*
53 il gambo
– *shank*
54 la punta
– *point*
55 il chiodo per cartone *m* catramato (chiodo per copertura di tetti *m pl*)
– *roofing nail*
56 la chiodatura (la ribaditura, l'unione *f* mediante chiodi *m pl*, l'unione *f* a sovrapposizione *f*)
– *riveting (lap riveting)*
57-60 **il ribattino** (il chiodo da ribaditura); *qui:* il chiodo ribadito
– *rivet*
57 la testa del ribattino; *qui:* testa del chiodo ribadito
– *set head (swage head, die head), a rivet head*
58 il gambo del ribattino
– *rivet shank*
59 la controtesta
– *closing head*
60 il passo dei chiodi
– *pitch of rivets*
61 l'albero
– *shaft*
62 lo smusso
– *chamfer (bevel)*
63 il perno (il maschio)
– *journal*
64 il collare (la gola)
– *neck*
65 la sede
– *seat*
66 l'intaglio (l'alloggiamento) per la chiavetta
– *keyway*
67 la sede conica (il cono)
– *conical seat (cone)*
68 il filetto
– *thread*
69 **il cuscinetto a sfere** *f pl*, un cuscinetto a rotolamento (un supporto a sfere *f pl* o rulli *m pl*)
– *ball bearing, an antifriction bearing*
70 la sfera di acciaio
– *steel ball (ball)*
71 l'anello esterno
– *outer race*
72 l'anello interno
– *inner race*
73 u. 74 **le chiavette incastrate**
– *keys*
73 la chiavetta piatta (chiavetta a molla)
– *sunk key (feather)*

74 la chiavetta a naso
– *gib (gib-headed key)*
75 u. 76 **il cuscinetto a spilli** *m pl* (a aghi *m pl*, a rullini *m pl*)
– *needle roller bearing*
75 la gabbia a spilli *m pl*
– *needle cage*
76 lo spillo
– *needle*
77 il dado a corona
– *castle nut (castellated nut)*
78 la copiglia
– *split pin*
79 l'alloggiamento (la lanterna) dell'albero
– *casing*
80 il coperchio della lanterna (dell'alloggiamento)
– *casing cover*
81 il nipplo ingrassatore
– *grease nipple (lubricating nipple)*
82-96 **gear wheels, cog wheels**
– *gear wheels, cog wheels*
82 l'ingranaggio a gradini *m pl*
– *stepped gear wheel*
83 il dente
– *cog (tooth)*
84 il fondo del dente
– *space between teeth*
85 la scanalatura (scanalatura per chiavetta)
– *keyway (key seat, key slot)*
86 l'alesaggio
– *bore*
87 l'ingranaggio cilindrico a spina di pesce *m* (ruota cilindrica con dentatura a freccia)
– *herringbone gear wheel*
88 i raggi
– *spoke (arm)*
89 l'ingranaggio cilindrico a denti *m pl* inclinati
– *helical gearing (helical spur wheel)*
90 la corona dentata
– *sprocket*
91 l'ingranaggio conico dentato (cono dentato, ruota conica dentata)
– *bevel gear wheel (bevel wheel)*
92 u. 93 **la dentatura a spirale** *f*
– *spiral toothing*
92 il pignone
– *pinion*
93 la corona
– *crown wheel*
94-96 **l'ingranaggio planetario**
– *epicyclic gear (planetary gear)*
94 i satelliti (ruote dentate satelliti)
– *planet wheels*
95 la corona a dentatura interna
– *internal gear*
96 la ruota planetaria
– *sun wheel (sun gear)*
97-107 **freni** *m pl* **dinamometrici**
– *absorption dynamometer*
97 il freno a ceppi *m pl* esterni (freno a ganasce *f pl*)
– *shoe brake (check brake, block brake)*
98 il disco del freno
– *brake pulley*
99 l'albero del freno
– *brake shaft (brake axle)*
100 il ceppo (la ganascia) del freno
– *brake block (brake shoe)*
101 il tirante
– *pull rod*
102 il magnete di apertura del freno
– *brake magnet*
103 il contrappeso del freno
– *brake weight*
104 il freno a nastro
– *band brake*
105 il nastro del freno
– *brake band*
106 la guarnizione
– *brake lining*
107 la vite di registro per un'apertura uniforme
– *adjusting screw, for even application of the brake*

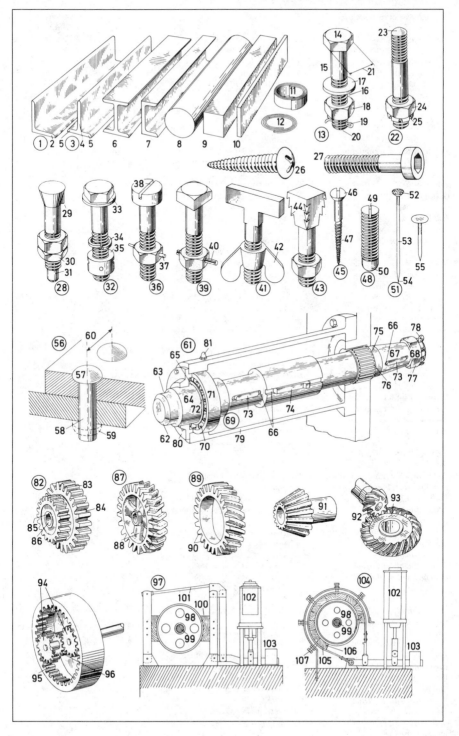

**1-51 la miniera di carbone** *m* (la miniera)
– **coal mine** *(colliery, pit)*
1 il castelletto di estrazione *f*
– *pithead gear (headgear)*
2 la sala macchine *f pl*
– *winding engine house*
3 la torre di estrazione *f*
– *pithead frame (head frame)*
4 gli edifici di collegamento tra i pozzi
– *pithead building*
5 l'impianto di arricchimento
– *processing plant*
6 la segheria
– *sawmill*
**7-11 la cokeria**
– **coking plant**
7 la batteria di storte *f pl* da coke *m*
– *battery of coke ovens*
8 il carrello di riempimento
– *larry car (larry, charging car)*
9 la torre del carbone coke *m*
– *coking coal tower*
10 la torre del polverino
– *coke-quenching tower*
11 il carrello del polverino
– *coke-quenching car*
12 il gasometro
– *gasometer*
13 la centrale elettrica
– *power plant (power station)*
14 il serbatoio d'acqua sopraelevato
– *water tower*
15 la torre di raffreddamento (il refrigeratore a torre *f* )
– *cooling tower*
16 l'areatore *m* della miniera
– *mine fan*
17 il deposito del materiale
– *depot*
18 l'edificio dell'amministrazione *f*
– *administration building (office building, offices)*
19 la discarica
– *tip heap (spoil heap)*
20 il depuratore (l'impianto di depurazione *f* )
– *cleaning plant*
**21-51 gli impianti sotterranei**
– **underground workings** *(underground mining)*
21 il pozzo di ventilazione *f*
– *ventilation shaft*
22 il condotto di ventilazione *f*
– *fan drift*
23 l'estrazione *f* a gabbia con gabbie *f pl*
– *cage-winding system with cages*
24 il pozzo principale
– *main shaft*
25 il trasportatore degli skip
– *skip-winding system*
26 la galleria di riempimento
– *winding inset*

27 il pozzo cieco
– *staple shaft*
28 lo scivolo elicoidale
– *spiral chute*
29 il livello dello strato di minerale *m*
– *gallery along seam*
30 la galleria di livello
– *lateral*
31 la galleria traversobanco
– *cross-cut*
32 la macchina di avanzamento livello
– *tunnelling* (Am. *tunneling*) *machine*
**33-37 fronti** *m pl* **di avanzamento**
– **longwall faces**
33 la piallatura del fronte di avanzamento in posizione orizzontale
– *horizontal ploughed longwall face*
34 il fronte di avanzamento di sottoescavazione *f* in posizione *f* orizzontale
– *horizontal cut longwall face*
35 il fronte di avanzamento con martello pneumatico in posizione *f* inclinata
– *vertical pneumatic pick longwall face*
36 il fronte di avanzamento a battenti *m pl* in posizione *f* inclinata
– *diagonal ram longwall face*
37 la miniera abbandonata
– *goaf (gob, waste)*
38 la chiusa di ventilazione *f*
– *air lock*
39 il trasporto persone *f pl* con vagonetti *m pl*
– *transportation of men by cars*
40 il nastro trasportatore
– *belt conveying, conveyor belt*
41 il deposito del carbone grezzo
– *raw coal bunker*
42 il nastro di caricamento
– *charging conveyor*
43 il trasporto materiale *m* con trasportatore *m* a monorotaia sospesa
– *transportation of supplies by monorail car*
44 il trasporto persone *f pl* con trasportatore *m* a monorotaia sospesa
– *transportation of men by monorail car*
45 il trasporto materiale *m* con carrello
– *transportation of supplies by mine car*
46 l'impianto di prosciugamento (l'impianto di eduzione *f* )
– *drainage*
47 il fondo del pozzo
– *sump (sink)*
48 il terreno di copertura
– *capping*

49 la roccia carbonifera
– *[layer of] coal-bearing rock*
50 lo strato di carbone *m* fossile
– *coal seam*
51 la faglia
– *fault*

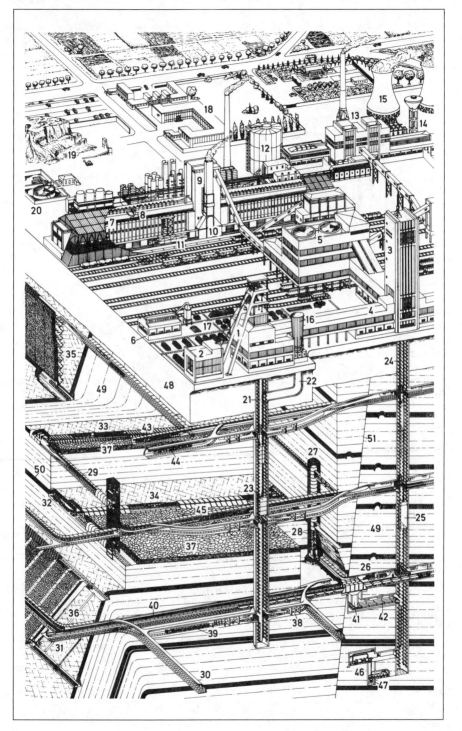

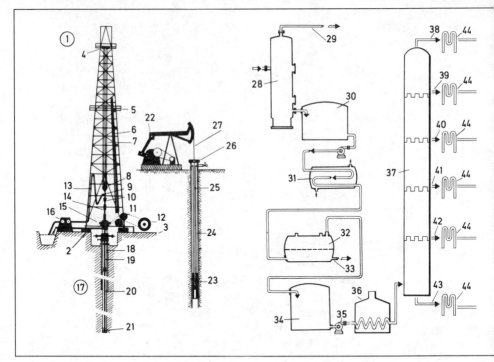

**1-21 la trivellazione del petrolio**
- *oil drilling*
1 la torre di perforazione *f*
- *drilling rig*
2 la fondazione
- *substructure*
3 la piattaforma di servizio (la piattaforma del pontista)
- *crown safety platform*
4 le carrucole della torre
- *crown blocks*
5 la piattaforma per aste *f pl* di perforazione *f*, una piattaforma intermedia
- *working platform, an intermediate platform*
6 i tubi (le aste) di perforazione *f*
- *drill pipes*
7 il cavo di perforazione *f*
- *drilling cable (drilling line)*
8 il paranco
- *travelling* (Am. *traveling*) *block*
9 il gancio di sollevamento
- *hook*
10 la testa di iniezione *f*
- *[rotary] swivel*
11 l'elevatore *m*, un argano
- *draw works, a hoist*
12 il motore di azionamento
- *engine*
13 la sandpipe
- *standpipe and rotary hose*
14 l'asta motrice
- *kelly*

15 la tavola di rotazione *m* (la tavola rotary)
- *rotary table*
16 la pompa
- *slush pump (mud pump)*
17 il foro trivellato
- *well*
18 il tubo fisso
- *casing*
19 l'asta di perforazione *m*
- *drilling pipe*
20 l'intubamento
- *tubing*
21 lo scalpello di perforazione *f;* tipi *m pl:* lo scalpello a coda di pesce *m*, lo scalpello a rulli *m pl*, lo scalpello a nucleo
- *drilling bit; kinds: fishtail (blade) bit, rock* (Am. *roller*) *bit, core bit*

**22-27 l'estrazione *f* del petrolio**
- *oil (crude oil) production*
22 l'articolazione *f* comando pompe *f pl*
- *pumping unit (pump)*
23 la pompa per pozzi *m pl* profondi
- *plunger*
24 i tubi di mandata
- *tubing*
25 l'asta della pompa
- *sucker rods (pumping rods)*
26 il premitreccia
- *stuffing box*
27 l'asta liscia
- *polish (polished) rod*

**28-35 il trattamento del petrolio greggio** (schema *m*)
- *treatment of crude oil [diagram]*
28 il separatore di gas *m*
- *gas separator*
29 la conduttura del gas
- *gas pipe (gas outlet)*
30 il serbatoio del petrolio umido
- *wet oil tank (wash tank)*
31 il preriscaldatore
- *water heater*
32 l'impianto di drenaggio e di desalinizzazione
- *water and brine separator*
33 la conduttura dell'acqua di mare *m*
- *salt water pipe (salt water outlet)*
34 il serbatoio del petrolio purificato
- *oil tank*
35 la conduttura del petrolio purificato (per la raffineria o per la spedizione con autocisterna, navi cisterna o pipeline)
- *trunk pipeline for oil [to the refinery or transport by tanker lorry* (Am. *tank truck), oil tanker or pipeline]*

**36-64 la lavorazione del petrolio** (schema *m*)
- *processing of crude oil [diagram]*
36 il forno tubolare
- *oil furnace (pipe still)*

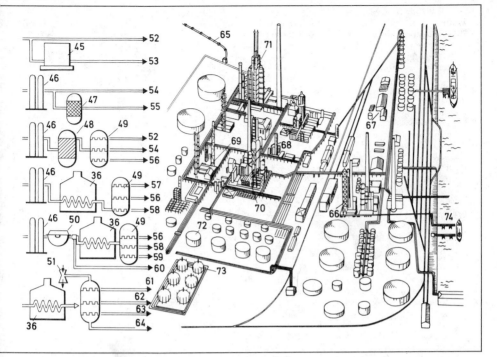

37 la colonna di distillazione *f* (la torre di frazionamento) con i piani della colonna
 – *fractionating column (distillation column) with trays*
38 i gas alti
 – *top gases (tops)*
39 la frazione benzina leggera
 – *light distillation products*
40 la frazione benzina pesante
 – *heavy distillation products*
41 il petrolio
 – *petroleum*
42 la frazione gasolio
 – *gas oil component*
43 il residuo
 – *residue*
44 il refrigeratore
 – *condenser (cooler)*
45 il compressore
 – *compressor*
46 l'impianto di desolforazione *f*
 – *desulphurizing (desulphurization, Am. desulfurizing, desulfurization) plant*
47 l'impianto di reforming
 – *reformer (hydroformer, platformer)*
48 l'impianto di piroscissione *f* catalitico
 – *catalytic cracker (cat cracker)*
49 la colonna di distillazione *f*
 – *distillation column*

50 la deparaffinizzazione
 – *de-waxing (wax separation)*
51 il collegamento al vuoto
 – *vacuum equipment*
52-64 prodotti *m pl* petroliferi
 – *oil products*
52 il gas combustibile
 – *fuel gas*
53 il gas liquido
 – *liquefied petroleum gas (liquid gas)*
54 la benzina normale
 – *regular grade petrol (Am. gasoline)*
55 la benzina super
 – *super grade petrol (Am. gasoline)*
56 il carburante Diesel
 – *diesel oil*
57 la benzina avio (la benzina per aerei *m pl*)
 – *aviation fuel*
58 l'olio combustibile leggero
 – *light fuel oil*
59 l'olio combustibile pesante
 – *heavy fuel oil*
60 la paraffina
 – *paraffin (paraffin oil, kerosene)*
61 l'olio per mandrini *m pl*
 – *spindle oil*
62 l'olio lubrificante
 – *lubricating oil*
63 l'olio per cilindri *m pl*
 – *cylinder oil*

64 il bitume
 – *bitumen*
65-74 la raffineria del petrolio
 – *oil refinery*
65 la pipeline (l'oleodotto)
 – *pipeline (oil pipeline)*
66 gli impianti di distillazione *f*
 – *distillation plants*
67 la raffineria dell'olio lubrificante
 – *lubricating oil refinery*
68 l'impianto di desolforazione *f*
 – *desulphurizing (desulphurization, Am. desulfurizing, desulfurization) plant*
69 l'impianto separazione *f* gas *m*
 – *gas-separating plant*
70 l'impianto di piroscissione *f* catalitico
 – *catalytic cracking plant*
71 l'impianto di reforming catalitico
 – *catalytic reformer*
72 il serbatoio del magazzino
 – *storage tank*
73 l'impianto sferico
 – *spherical tank*
74 il porto petrolifero
 – *tanker terminal*

**1-39  la piattaforma di produzione** *f*
– *drilling rig (oil rig)*
**1-37  la piattaforma della torre di perforazione** *f*
– *drilling platform*
**1**  l'impianto di erogazione *f* energia
– *power station*
**2**  la ciminiera dei gas di scarico del generatore
– *generator exhausts*
**3**  la gru girevole
– *revolving crane (pedestal crane)*
**4**  il deposito dei tubi
– *piperack*
**5**  i tubi di scarico delle turbine
– *turbine exhausts*
**6**  il deposito materiali *m pl*
– *materials store*
**7**  l'elioporto (la piattaforma per gli elicotteri)
– *helicopter deck (heliport deck, heliport)*
**8**  l'ascensore *m*
– *elevator*
**9**  il separatore gas-olio
– *production oil and gas separator*
**10**  il separatore di prova
– *test oil and gas separators (test separators)*
**11**  l'impianto di combustione *f* gas *m pl* superflui
– *emergency flare stack*
**12**  la torre di perforazione
– *derrick*
**13**  il serbatoio Diesel
– *diesel tank*
**14**  il complesso degli uffici
– *office building*
**15**  i serbatoi per la scorta del cemento
– *cement storage tanks*
**16**  il serbatoio acqua potabile
– *drinking water tank*
**17**  il serbatoio di scorta acqua di mare *m*
– *salt water tank*
**18**  i serbatoi per carburante *m* elicotteri *m pl*
– *jet fuel tanks*
**19**  le scialuppe di salvataggio
– *lifeboats*
**20**  il pozzo dell'ascensore *m*
– *elevator shaft*
**21**  il contenitore aria compressa
– *compressed-air reservoir*
**22**  l'impianto di pompaggio (le pompe)
– *pumping station*
**23**  il compressore *m* dell'aria
– *air compressor*
**24**  l'impianto di climatizzazione *f*
– *air lock*
**25**  l'impianto di desalinizzazione *f* acqua di mare *m*
– *seawater desalination plant*
**26**  l'impianto di filtraggio carburante

*m* Diesel
– *inlet filters for diesel fuel*
**27**  l'impianto di raffreddamento gas *m pl*
– *gas cooler*
**28**  il tavolo di comando separatori *m pl*
– *control panel for the separators*
**29**  le toilette (i gabinetti)
– *toilets (lavatories)*
**30**  l'officina
– *workshop*
**31**  la conca del «tritone» *m* (il «tritone» *m* serve per pulire la conduttura principale dell'olio)
– *pig trap [the 'pig' is used to clean the oil pipeline]*
**32**  l'area di controllo
– *control room*
**33**  gli alloggiamenti (gli alloggi)
– *accommodation modules (accommodation)*
**34**  le pompe a alta pressione *m* per cementare
– *high-pressure cementing pumps*
**35**  la coperta inferiore
– *lower deck*
**36**  la coperta mediana
– *middle deck*
**37**  la coperta superiore
– *top deck (main deck)*
**38**  le strutture di sostegno
– *substructure*
**39**  il livello del mare
– *mean sea level*

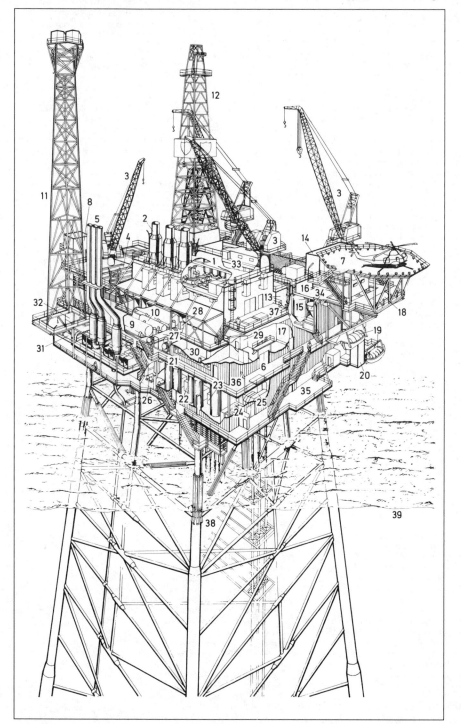

**1-20 l'impianto d'altoforno**
– *blast furnace plant*
1  l'altoforno, un forno a tino
– *blast furnace, a shaft furnace*
2  l'elevatore *m* (il montacarichi)
inclinato per minerale *m*,
fondente *m* o carbone *m* (coke *m*)
– *furnace incline (lift) for ore and*
*flux or coke*
3  il carrello del montacarichi
– *skip hoist*
4  la piattaforma di caricamento
– *charging platform*
5  la benna tramoggia
– *receiving hopper*
6  il cono di chiusura della bocca di
caricamento (la campana)
– *bell*
7  il tino (il pozzo) dell'altoforno
– *blast furnace shaft*
8  la zona di riduzione *f*
– *smelting section*
9  il canale di scarico delle scorie (lo
scarico delle scorie)
– *slag escape*
10  il secchione per le scorie
– *slag ladle*
11  il canale di colata del ferro grezzo
– *pig iron (crude iron, iron) runout*
12  la siviera (il secchio di colata) del
ferro grezzo
– *pig iron (crude iron, iron) ladle*
13  lo scarico dei gas
– *downtake*
14  il sacco per la polvere, un depuratore della polvere
– *dust catcher, a dust-collecting*
*machine*
15  il recuperatore di calore *m* (il
cowper, l'apparecchio Cowper
per il riscaldamento del
vento/dell'aria)
– *hot-blast stove*
16  il pozzo di combustione *f* esterno
– *external combustion chamber*
17  la condotta del vento (dell'aria)
– *blast main*
18  la condotta del gas
– *gas pipe*
19  la condotta del vento riscaldato
(la tubatura del vento caldo,
tubatura dell'aria calda)
– *hot-blast pipe*
20  l'ugello (ugello del vento)
– *tuyère*
**21-69 l'acciaieria**
– *steelworks*
**21-30 il forno Siemens-Martin**
– *Siemens-Martin open-hearth fur-*
*nace*
21  la siviera (il secchio di colata) del
ferro grezzo
– *pig iron (crude iron, iron) ladle*
22  il canale di colata
– *feed runner*
23  il forno fisso
– *stationary furnace*

24  il vano del forno
– *hearth*
25  la macchina di caricamento
– *charging machine*
26  la lingottiera a mitraglia
– *scrap iron charging box*
27  la condotta del gas
– *gas pipe*
28  la camera per il riscaldamento del
gas
– *gas regenerator chamber*
29  la condotta dell'aria
– *air feed pipe*
30  la camera per il riscaldamento
dell'aria
– *air regenerator chamber*
31  la siviera (il secchione di colata)
dell'acciaio con chiusura a turacciolo (a tampone *m*)
– *[bottom-pouring] steel-casting*
*ladle with stopper*
32  la conchiglia (la lingottiera)
– *ingot mould* (Am. *mold*)
33  il lingotto (il blocco) d'acciaio
– *steel ingot*
**34-44 la colatrice di masselli *m pl***
– *pig-casting machine*
34  l'estremità di colata
– *pouring end*
35  il canale di colata
– *metal runner*
36  il nastro trasportatore delle con-
chiglie (delle lingottiere)
– *series (strand) of moulds* (Am.
*molds*)
37  la conchiglia (la lingottiera)
– *mould* (Am. *mold*)
38  la passerella (di manovra)
– *catwalk*
39  il dispositivo di scarico
– *discharging chute*
40  il massello (il ferro grezzo)
– *pig*
41  la gru a ponte *m* scorrevole (gru *f*
mobile)
– *travelling* (Am. *traveling*) *crane*
42  la siviera (il secchione di colata)
con vuotatura dall'alto
– *top-pouring pig iron (crude iron,*
*iron) ladle*
43  il becco della siviera (del secchione di colata)
– *pouring ladle lip*
44  l'incastellatura di ribaltamento
– *tilting device (tipping device,* Am.
*dumping device)*
**45-50 il convertitore per ossidazione**
*f*, (convertitore *m* Linz-Donawitz,
convertitore *m* LD)
– *oxygen-blowing converter (L-D*
*converter, Linz-Donawitz con-*
*verter)*
45  il cappello (la testa) del convertitore
– *conical converter top*
46  l'anello portante
– *mantle*

47  il fondo del convertitore
– *solid converter bottom*
48  il rivestimento in muratura refrat-
tario
– *fireproof lining (refractory lining)*
49  la lancia d'ossigeno
– *oxygen lance*
50  il foro di colata (foro d'uscita)
– *tapping hole (tap hole)*
**51-54 il forno elettrico Siemens a**
**camera (a galleria) bassa**
– *Siemens electric low-shaft fur-*
*nace*
51  il caricamento
– *feed*
52  gli elettrodi [disposti circolar-
mente]
– *electrodes [arranged in a circle]*
53  la condotta a anello per lo scarico
del gas
– *bustle pipe*
54  la colata; *qui:* becco di colata
– *runout*
**55-69 il convertitore Thomas**
– *Thomas converter (basic*
*Bessemer converter)*
55  la posizione di caricamento del
ferro grezzo allo stato fuso
– *charging position for molten pig*
*iron*
56  la posizione di caricamento della
calce
– *charging position for lime*
57  la posizione di soffiatura
– *blow position*
58  la posizione di colata
– *discharging position*
59  il dispositivo di ribaltamento
– *tilting device (tipping device,* Am.
*dumping device)*
60  la siviera da gru *f*
– *crane-operated ladle*
61  la gru ausiliaria
– *auxiliary crane hoist*
62  la tramoggia della calce
– *lime bunker*
63  il tubo di caduta
– *downpipe*
64  il vagoncino (il carrello) a conca
– *tipping car* (Am. *dump truck)*
65  l'apporto del rottame
– *scrap iron feed*
66  la stazione (il banco) di manovra
– *control desk*
67  il camino del convertitore
– *converter chimney*
68  il tubo d'immissione *f* dell'aria di
soffiatura
– *blast main*
69  il fondo ugelli *m pl*
– *wind box*

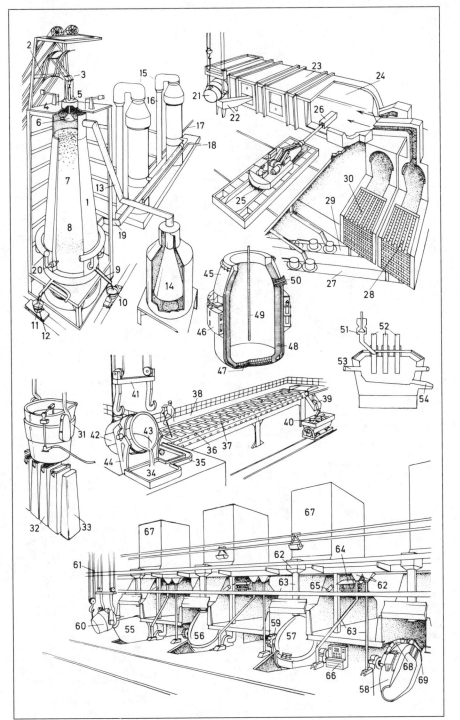

**1-45** la fonderia di ghisa
– *iron foundry*
**1-12 la fusione**
– *melting plant*
**1** il cubilotto, un forno fusorio
– *cupola furnace (cupola), a melting furnace*
**2** la condotta del vento
– *blast main (blast inlet, blast pipe)*
**3** il canale di spillatura (di colata)
– *tapping spout*
**4** il foro d'ispezione *f*
– *spyhole*
**5** l'avancrogiolo ribaltabile
– *tilting-type [hot-metal] receiver*
**6** la siviera a tamburo (la siviera a botte *f*) carrellata
– *mobile drum-type ladle*
**7** il fonditore
– *melter*
**8** il colatore
– *founder (caster)*
**9** l'asta di spillatura
– *tap bar (tapping bar)*
**10** l'asta di tamponatura
– *bott stick (Am. bot stick)*
**11** la ghisa fusa
– *molten iron*
**12** il canale per le scorie
– *slag spout*
**13** la squadra di colata
– *casting team*
**14** la sivierina (la siviera portatile)
– *hand shank*

**15** il forchettone
– *double handle (crutch)*
**16** l'asta del forchettone
– *carrying bar*
**17** la schiumaiola
– *skimmer rod*
**18** la staffa chiusa
– *closed moulding (Am. molding) box*
**19** la staffa superiore
– *upper frame (cope)*
**20** la staffa inferiore (il fondo)
– *lower frame (drag)*
**21** il foro di colata
– *runner (runner gate, down-gate)*
**22** il foro di materozza
– *riser (riser gate)*
**23** la siviera a mano (la tazza di colata)
– *hand ladle*
**24-29 la colata continua**
– *continuous casting*
**24** il tavolo di colata abbassabile
– *sinking pouring floor*
**25** il blocco di metallo da solidificare
– *solidifying pig*
**26** la fase solida
– *solid stage*
**27** la fase liquida
– *liquid stage*
**28** il raffreddamento a acqua
– *water-cooling system*
**29** la parete della conchiglia
– *mould (Am. mold) wall*

**30-37 la formatura**
– *moulding (Am. molding) department (moulding shop)*
**30** il formatore
– *moulder (Am. molder)*
**31** il costipatore pneumatico
– *pneumatic rammer*
**32** il costipatore manuale
– *hand rammer*
**33** la staffa aperta
– *open moulding (Am. molding) box*
**34** la forma (il modello)
– *pattern*
**35** la terra da fonderia
– *moulding (Am. molding) sand*
**36** l'anima
– *core*
**37** la portata di anima
– *core print*
**38-45 il reparto sbavatura**
– *cleaning shop (fettling shop)*
**38** l'alimentazione *f* con graniglia di acciaio o sabbia
– *steel grit or sand delivery pipe*
**39** il soffiatore automatico della piattaforma girevole
– *rotary-table shot-blasting machine*
**40** lo schermo di protezione *f*
– *grit guard*
**41** la piattaforma girevole
– *revolving table*
**42** il getto
– *casting*

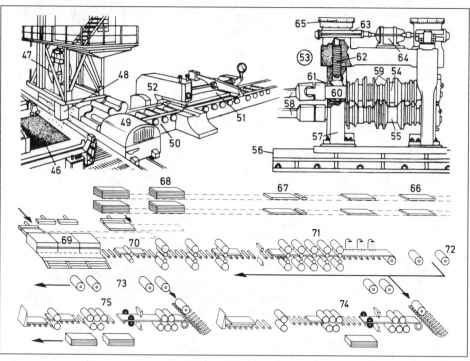

**43** lo sbavatore
– *fettler*
**44** la smerigliatrice a aria compressa
– *pneumatic grinder*
**45** lo scalpello pneumatico
– *pneumatic chisel*
**46-75 il laminatoio**
– *rolling mill*
**46** il forno a pozzo
– *soaking pit*
**47** la gru del forno a pozzo, una gru a tenaglia
– *soaking pit crane*
**48** la bramma grezza (il lingotto di acciaio grezzo fuso)
– *ingot*
**49** il giralingotti
– *ingot tipper*
**50** la linea a rulli *m pl* (il piano a rulli *m pl*)
– *roller table*
**51** il materiale da laminare
– *workpiece*
**52** la cesoia per lingotti *m pl*
– *bloom shears*
**53** la gabbia a due (la gabbia a due cilindri *m pl*, il due)
– *two-high mill*
**54-55 la serie dei cilindri**
– *set of rolls (set of rollers)*
**54** il cilindro superiore
– *upper roll (upper roller)*
**55** il cilindro inferiore
– *lower roll (lower roller)*

**56-60 la gabbia di laminazione** *f*
– *roll stand*
**56** il basamento
– *base plate*
**57** i montanti della gabbia
– *housing (frame)*
**58** l'albero di accoppiamento
– *coupling spindle*
**59** il calibro
– *groove*
**60** il supporto del cilindro
– *roll bearing*
**61-65 il meccanismo di regolazione** *f*
– *adjusting equipment*
**61** il pezzo incorporato
– *chock*
**62** la vite di pressione *f*
– *main screw*
**63** la trasmissione
– *gear*
**64** il motore
– *motor*
**65** l'indicatore *m* di regolazione *f* grossolana e fine
– *indicator for rough and fine adjustment*
**66-75 il treno di laminazione** *f* **per la produzione di nastro di acciaio** (schematico)
– *continuous rolling mill train for the manufacture of strip [diagram]*

**66-68** la preparazione del semilavorato
– *processing of semi-finished product*
**66** il semilavorato
– *semi-finished product*
**67** l'apparecchio per il taglio automatico
– *gas cutting installation*
**68** la pila dei pezzi finiti
– *stack of finished steel sheets*
**69** il meccanismo di spinta
– *continuous reheating furnaces*
**70** il treno sbozzatore
– *blooming train*
**71** il treno finitore
– *finishing train*
**72** il tamburo di avvolgimento (l'aspo)
– *coiler*
**73** il magazzino dei cilindri per la vendita
– *collar bearing for marketing*
**74** il treno di taglio da 5 mm
– *5 mm shearing train*
**75** il treno di taglio da 10 mm
– *10 mm shearing train*

**1** il tornio parallelo e il tornio a barra (tornio)
- *centre* (Am. *center*) *lathe*
**2** la testa motrice con il cambio
- *headstock with gear control (geared headstock)*
**3** la leva di primo innesto
- *reduction drive lever*
**4** la leva per filettature *f pl* normali e rapide
- *lever for normal and coarse threads*
**5** la regolazione della velocità
- *speed change lever*
**6** la leva d'innesto della vite madre *f*
- *leadscrew reverse-gear lever*
**7** la scatola per ingranaggi *m pl* intercambiabili
- *change-gear box*
**8** la scatola di cambio per gli avanzamenti (il cambio Norton, la scatola Norton)
- *feed gearbox (Norton tumbler gear)*
**9** la leva per l'avanzamento e il passo della filettatura
- *levers for changing the feed and thread pitch*
**10** la leva per il cambio di velocità di moto e di avanzamento
- *feed gear lever (tumbler lever)*
**11** la leva di avviamento per rotazione *f* destrorsa o sinistrorsa della vite madre *f*
- *switch lever for right or left hand action of main spindle*
**12** il basamento del tornio
- *lathe foot (footpiece)*
**13** il volantino comando slitta longitudinale
- *leadscrew handwheel for traversing of saddle (longitudinal movement of saddle)*
**14** la leva inversione *f* avanzamento
- *tumbler reverse lever*
**15** la manovella comando slitta trasversale
- *feed screw*
**16** il grembiale
- *apron (saddle apron, carriage apron)*
**17** la leva avanzamento longitudinale e trasversale
- *lever for longitudinal and transverse motion*
**18** il bloccaggio chiocciola su vite madre *f*
- *drop (dropping) worm (feed trip, feed tripping device) for engaging feed mechanisms*
**19** la leva per la chiocciola della vite conduttrice
- *lever for engaging half nut of leadscrew (lever for clasp nut engagement)*
**20** il mandrino
- *lathe spindle*
**21** la torretta quadrata portautensili
- *tool post*
**22** la slitta micrometrica portautensili
- *top slide (tool slide, tool rest)*

**23** la slitta trasversale
- *cross slide*
**24** la slitta longitudinale
- *bed slide*
**25** la conduttura per il liquido di raffreddamento
- *coolant supply pipe*
**26** la contropunta
- *tailstock centre* (Am. *center*)
**27** il cannotto della contropunta
- *barrel (tailstock barrel)*
**28** la leva di serraggio cannotto
- *tailstock barrel clamp lever*
**29** la controtesta
- *tailstock*
**30** il volantino posteriore
- *tailstock barrel adjusting handwheel*
**31** il bancale del tornio
- *lathe bed*
**32** la vite madre
- *leadscrew*
**33** la barra di avanzamento
- *feed shaft*
**34** la barra di inversione *f* per lo spostamento a destra e a sinistra, l'inserimento e il disinserimento
- *reverse shaft for right and left hand motion and engaging and disengaging*
**35** la piattaforma a quattro griffe *f pl*
- *four-jaw chuck (four-jaw independent chuck)*
**36** la griffa
- *gripping jaw*
**37** la piattaforma a tre griffe *f pl*
- *three-jaw chuck (three-jaw self-centring,* Am. *self-centering, chuck)*
**38** il tornio a revolver *m*
- *turret lathe*
**39** la slitta trasversale
- *cross slide*
**40** la torretta esagonale (la testa del revolver)
- *turret*
**41** il portautensile multiplo
- *combination toolholder (multiple turning head)*
**42** la slitta longitudinale
- *top slide*
**43** il volantino comando slitta longitudinale
- *star wheel*
**44** la vasca trucioli *m pl* e liquido refrigerante
- *coolant tray for collecting coolant and swarf*
**45-53 utensili *m pl* da tornio**
- *lathe tools*
**45** l'utensile *m* a inserto per placchette *f pl* a più taglienti *m pl*
- *tool bit holder (clamp tip tool) for adjustable cutting tips*
**46** la placchetta a più taglienti *m pl* in metallo duro o in materiale *m* ceramico
- *adjustable cutting tip (clamp tip) of cemented carbide or oxide ceramic*
**47** forme *f pl* delle placchette in materiale *m* ceramico
- *shapes of adjustable oxide ceramic tips*

**48** l'utensile *m* da tornio con tagliente *m* in metallo duro
- *lathe tool with cemented carbide cutting edge*
**49** il codolo dell'utensile *m*
- *tool shank*
**50** la placchetta di metallo duro brasata
- *brazed cemented carbide cutting tip (cutting edge)*
**51** l'utensile *m* per interni *m pl*
- *internal facing tool (boring tool) for corner work*
**52** l'utensile *m* sgrossatore curvo sinistro
- *general-purpose lathe tool*
**53** l'utensile *m* troncatore
- *parting (parting-off ) tool*
**54** la brida
- *lathe carrier*
**55** il menabride
- *driving (driver) plate*
**56-72 strumenti di misurazione *f***
- *measuring instruments*
**56** il calibro a tampone *m* (il calibro per interni *m pl*)
- *plug gauge* (Am. *gage*)
**57** il lato «passa»
- *'GO' gauging* (Am. *gaging*) *member (end)*
**58** il lato «non passa»
- *'NOT GO' gauging* (Am. *gaging*) *member (end)*
**59** il calibro a forcella per esterni *m pl*
- *calliper (caliper, snap) gauge* (Am. *gage*)
**60** il lato «passa»
- *'GO' side*
**61** il lato «non passa»
- *'NOT GO' side*
**62** il micrometro a vite *f*
- *micrometer calliper (caliper) (micrometer)*
**63** la scala graduata
- *measuring scale*
**64** il tamburo graduato
- *graduated thimble*
**65** il corpo
- *frame*
**66** l'asta di misurazione *f*
- *spindle (screwed spindle)*
**67** il calibro a corsoio (il calibro a cursore *m*)
- *vernier calliper (caliper) gauge* (Am. *gage*)
**68** l'asta per la misurazione delle profondità
- *depth gauge* (Am. *gage*) *attachment rule*
**69** il nonio
- *vernier scale*
**70** i becchi per misurazioni *f pl* esterne
- *outside jaws*
**71** i becchi per misurazioni *f pl* interne
- *inside jaws*
**72** il calibro di profondità
- *vernier depth gauge* (Am. *gage*)

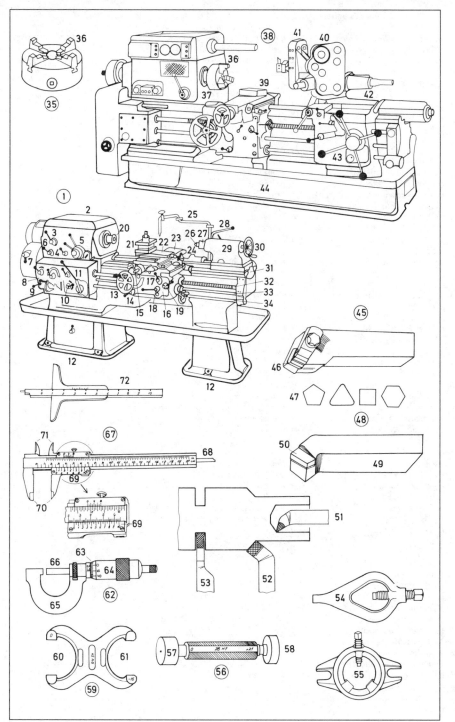

1  **la rettificatrice cilindrica univer-**
   **sale**
–  *universal grinding machine*
2  la testa motrice (la testa porta-
   mandrino)
–  *headstock*
3  il supporto della mola
–  *wheelhead slide*
4  la mola a smeriglio
–  *grinding wheel*
5  la contropunta
–  *tailstock*
6  il basamento della rettificatrice
–  *grinding machine bed*
7  il tavolo della rettificatrice
–  *grinding machine table*
8  **la piallatrice a due montanti** *m pl*
–  *two-column planing machine*
   *(two-column planer)*
9  il motore di comando, un motore
   a corrente *f* continua a velocità
   variabile
–  *drive motor, a direct current motor*
10 il montante
–  *column*
11 il tavolo della piallatrice
–  *planer table*
12 la trave trasversale
–  *cross slide (rail)*
13 il supporto dell'utensile *m*
–  *tool box*
14 **la sega ad archetto**
–  *hacksaw*
15 la morsa di bloccaggio
–  *clamping device*
16 la lama della sega
–  *saw blade*
17 l'archetto della sega
–  *saw frame*
18 **la trapanatrice radiale o il trapano**
   **a bandiera**
–  *radial (radial-arm) drilling*
   *machine*
19 la base (il basamento)
–  *bed (base plate)*
20 il portaoggetto
–  *block for workpiece*
21 il montante
–  *pillar*
22 il motore elevatore
–  *lifting motor*
23 il mandrino
–  *drill spindle*
24 il braccio
–  *arm*
25 **la fresatrice universale**
–  *universal milling machine*
26 il tavolo di fresatura
–  *milling machine table*
27 il tavolo di avanzamento
–  *table feed drive*
28 il commutatore numero giri *m pl*
   mandrino
–  *switch lever for spindle rotation*
   *speed*

29 il quadro di comando
–  *control box (control unit)*
30 il mandrino verticale di fresatura
–  *vertical milling spindle*
31 la testa motrice verticale
–  *vertical drive head*
32 il mandrino orizzontale di fresatura
–  *horizontal milling spindle*
33 il supporto anteriore per stabiliz-
   zare il mandrino orizzontale
–  *end support for steadying horizon-*
   *tal spindle*
34 il maschio per filettare a macchina
–  *machine tap*
35 **il tornio automatico snodato** (un
   robot industriale)
–  *articulated robot, an industrial*
   *robot*
36 la base
–  *base plate*
37 l'unità ruotante (l'asse *m* di
   rotazione *f* )
–  *rotating column (base rotating*
   *axis)*
38 lo snodo della spalla
–  *shoulder joint*
39 la parte superiore del braccio
–  *upper arm*
40 l'articolazione *f* del gomito
–  *elbow joint*
41 l'avambraccio in versione *f* tubolare
–  *tubular forearm*
42 il polso
–  *wrist joint*
43 la flangia di congiunzione *f* pinze *f pl*
–  *gripper mounting flange*
44 la pinza
–  *gripper*
45 le dita
–  *fingers*
46 il robot stativo
–  *upright robot (linear-axis robot,*
   *rectilinear robot)*
47 il robot a portale *m*
–  *portal robot (gantry robot)*

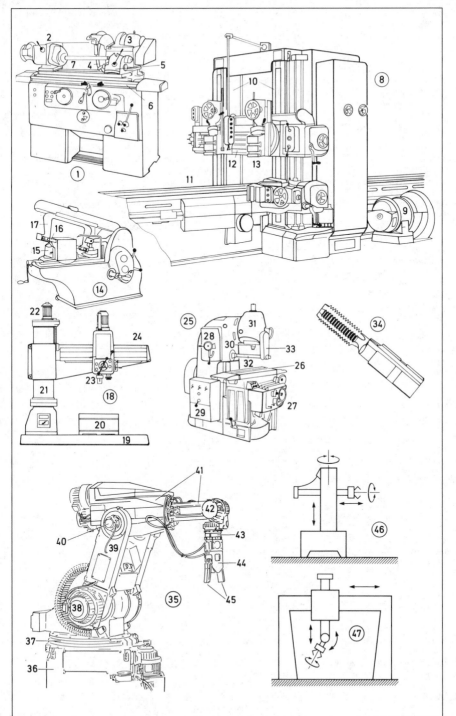

1 il piano del tavolo da disegno
- *drawing board*
2 il tecnigrafo con guida
- *drafting machine with parallel motion*
3 la testa girevole scorrevole
- *adjustable knob*
4 la riga a angolo
- *drawing head (adjustable set square)*
5 il dispositivo di regolazione *f* del tavolo da disegno
- *drawing board adjustment*
6 il tavolo da disegno
- *drawing table*
7 la squadra (la squadra da disegno)
- *set square (triangle)*
8 la squadra a 30°
- *triangle*
9 la riga a T
- *T-square (tee-square)*
10 il rotolo dei disegni
- *rolled drawing*
11 il diagramma (la rappresentazione grafica)
- *diagram*
12 la tavola delle scadenze (lo stereogramma)
- *time schedule*
13 il portacarta
- *paper stand*
14 il rotolo di carta
- *roll of paper*
15 la taglierina
- *cutter*
16 il disegno tecnico
- *technical drawing (drawing, design)*
17 la vista anteriore
- *front view (front elevation)*
18 la vista laterale
- *side view (side elevation)*
19 la vista verticale
- *plan*
20 la superficie non lavorata
- *surface not to be machined*
21 la superficie abbozzata
- *surface to be machined*
22 la superficie rifinita
- *surface to be superfinished*
23 lo spigolo a vista
- *visible edge*
24 lo spigolo non in vista
- *hidden edge*
25 la linea (la linea di quota)
- *dimension line*
26 la freccia (la freccia di quota)
- *arrow head*
27 l'indicazione *f* del tracciato della sezione
- *section line*
28 la sezione A-B
- *section A-B*
29 la superficie tratteggiata
- *hatched surface*

30 l'asse *m* mediano
- *centre (Am. center) line*
31 il riquadro per intestazioni *f pl* e modifiche *f pl*
- *title panel (title block)*
32 i dati tecnici
- *technical data*
33 la riga
- *ruler (rule)*
34 il doppio decimetro
- *triangular scale*
35 la mascherina per cancellare
- *erasing shield*
36 la cartuccia per disegnare a china
- *drawing ink cartridge*
37 il sostegno per riempicartucce
- *holders for tubular drawing pens*
38 il caricatore
- *set of tubular drawing pens*
39 l'igrometro
- *hygrometer*
40 il cappuccio con indicazione *f* gradazioni *f pl*
- *cap with indication of nib size*
41 la matita per cancellare
- *pencil-type eraser*
42 la gomma (la gomma per cancellare, la gomma da cancellare)
- *eraser*
43 il raschietto (il grattino)
- *erasing knife*
44 la lama del raschietto
- *erasing knife blade*
45 il portamine
- *clutch-type pencil*
46 la mina (la mina di grafite *f* )
- *pencil lead (refill lead, refill, spare lead)*
47 la gomma a fibre *f pl* di vetro
- *glass eraser*
48 le fibre di vetro
- *glass fibres (Am. fibers)*
49 il tiralinee
- *ruling pen*
50 la cerniera a croce *f*
- *cross joint*
51 il disco graduato
- *index plate*
52 il compasso (il compasso a punte *f pl* )
- *compass with interchangeable attachments*
53 lo snodo di guida
- *compass head*
54 la punta fissa
- *needle point attachment*
55 la punta articolata
- *pencil point attachment*
56 la punta
- *needle*
57 la prolunga
- *lengthening arm (extension bar)*
58 il tiralinee
- *ruling pen attachment*
59 il balaustrino
- *pump compass (drop compass)*

60 la manopola del balaustrino
- *piston*
61 il tiralinee
- *ruling pen attachment*
62 la punta articolata
- *pencil attachment*
63 il portachina
- *drawing ink container*
64 il compasso regolabile
- *spring bow (rapid adjustment, ratchet-type) compass*
65 la cerniera con molla a anello
- *spring ring hinge*
66 l'avanzamento di precisione *f* a arco
- *spring-loaded fine adjustment for arcs*
67 la punta a gomito
- *right-angle needle*
68 il portachina
- *tubular ink unit*
69 il normografo per lettere *f pl*
- *stencil lettering guide (lettering stencil)*
70 il normografo per cerchi *m pl*
- *circle template*
71 il normografo per ellissi *f pl*
- *ellipse template*

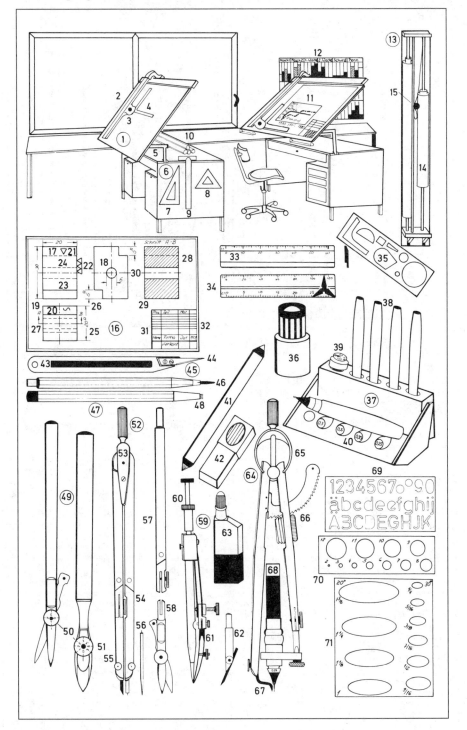

**1-28 la centrale termoelettrica a vapore** *m,* una centrale elettrica
– *steam-generating station, an electric power plant*
**1-21 la sala caldaie** *f pl*
– *boiler house*
**1** il nastro trasportatore del carbone
– *coal conveyor*
**2** il silo (deposito) del carbone
– *coal bunker*
**3** il nastro di deflusso del carbone
– *travelling-grate (Am. traveling-grate) stoker*
**4** il frantoio del carbone
– *coal mill*
**5** la caldaia a vapore *m,* una caldaia tubolare (caldaia a tubi *m pl* bollitori, caldaia a radiazione *f* )
– *steam boiler, a water-tube boiler (radiant-type boiler)*
**6** la camera di combustione *f*
– *burners*
**7** i tubi dell'acqua
– *water pipes*
**8** lo scarico della cenere (scarico delle scorie)
– *ash pit (clinker pit)*
**9** il surriscaldatore
– *superheater*
**10** il preriscaldatore dell'acqua
– *water preheater*

**11** il preriscaldatore dell'aria
– *air preheater*
**12** il condotto del gas combusto
– *gas flue*
**13** il filtro del gas combusto (filtro dei fumi), un elettrofiltro (un filtro elettrostatico)
– *electrostatic precipitator*
**14** il compressore a tiraggio indotto
– *induced-draught (Am. induced-draft) fan*
**15** la ciminiera
– *chimney (smokestack)*
**16** il degassificatore
– *de-aerator*
**17** il serbatoio dell'acqua
– *feedwater tank*
**18** la pompa di alimentazione *f* delle caldaie
– *boiler feed pump*
**19** l'impianto di distribuzione *f*
– *control room*
**20** il piano dei cavi
– *cable tunnel*
**21** il vano sotterraneo dei cavi
– *cable vault*
**22** la sala macchine *f pl* (sala turbine *f pl*)
– *turbine house*
**23** la turbina a vapore *m* con generatore *m* (il turbogeneratore)
– *steam turbine with alternator*

**24** il condensatore in superficie *f* (condensatore in batteria/in quantità)
– *surface condenser*
**25** il preriscaldatore a bassa pressione *f*
– *low-pressure preheater*
**26** il preriscaldatore a alta pressione *f*
– *high-pressure preheater (economizer)*
**27** la conduttura dell'acqua refrigerante
– *cooling water pipe*
**28** la sala controllo (posto di comando)
– *control room*
**29-35 l'impianto esterno di distribuzione** *f,* un impianto di distribuzione *f* a alta tensione *f*
– *outdoor substation, a substation*
**29** la terza rotaia (rotaia conduttrice)
– *busbars*
**30** il trasformatore di tensione *f,* un trasformatore mobile
– *power transformer, a mobile (transportable) transformer*
**31** il ponte degli isolatori
– *stay poles (guy poles)*
**32** il cavo di linea a alta tensione *f*
– *high-voltage transmission line*
**33** il cavo a alta tensione *f*
– *high-voltage conductor*

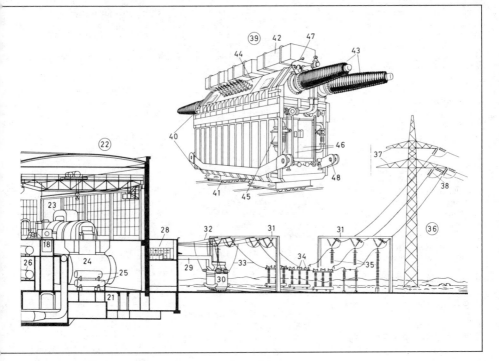

34 l'interruttore *m* rapido a aria
   compressa (interruttore *m* di
   potenza)
 – *air-blast circuit breaker (circuit
   breaker)*
35 lo scaricatore di sovratensione *f*
   (il deviatore di supertensione *f*)
 – *surge diverter (Am. lightning
   arrester, arrester)*
36 il palo della linea aerea, un palo a
   traliccio
 – *overhead line support, a lattice
   steel tower*
37 la traversa (il pezzo a croce *f*)
 – *cross arm (traverse)*
38 l'isolatore *m* di ancoraggio
 – *strain insulator*
39 **il trasformatore mobile** (trasformatore *m* di potenza, trasformatore *m*)
 – ***mobile (transportable) transformer** (power transformer, transformer)*
40 la cassa del trasformatore (dei
   trasformatori)
 – *transformer tank*
41 il carrello
 – *bogie (Am. truck)*
42 il serbatoio di espansione *f*
   dell'olio
 – *oil conservator*

43 i terminali a alta tensione *m*
 – *primary voltage terminal (primary
   voltage bushing)*
44 i terminali a bassa tensione *f*
 – *low-voltage terminals (low-voltage
   bushings)*
45 la pompa di circolazione *f*
   dell'olio
 – *oil-circulating pump*
46 il radiatore dell'olio/dell'acqua
 – *oil cooler*
47 gli elettrodi a corna *f pl* per lo
   scaricamento a arco
 – *arcing horn*
48 l'occhione *m* di traino
 – *transport lug*

**1-8 la sala di comando** (sala di controllo)
– *control room*
**1-6 il leggio di comando** (quadro di distribuzione *f* )
– *control console (control desk)*
**1** il settore dei comandi e controlli per i generatori trifase
– *control board (control panel) for the alternators*
**2** l'interruttore *m* di comando
– *master switch*
**3** il segnale luminoso (la spia)
– *signal light*
**4** il pannello dei comandi selettivi per le derivazioni della rete *f* a alta tensione *f*
– *feeder panel*
**5** gli strumenti di controllo per gli organi di comando
– *monitoring controls for the switching systems*
**6** gli elementi di comando
– *controls*
**7** il quadro di controllo con gli strumenti di misura (con i misuratori) dell'impianto segnalazioni *f pl* di ritorno
– *revertive signal panel*
**8** lo schermo sinottico delle connessioni per la rappresentazione dei potenziali
– *matrix mimic board*
**9-18 il trasformatore**
– *transformer*
**9** il serbatoio di espansione *f* dell'olio
– *oil conservator*
**10** lo sfiatatoio
– *breather*
**11** l'indicatore di livello dell'olio
– *oil gauge (Am. gage)*
**12** l'isolatore passante
– *feed-through terminal (feed-through insulator)*
**13** il commutatore selettivo delle prese di alta tensione *f*
– *on-load tap changer*
**14** il giogo
– *yoke*
**15** l'avvolgimento primario (avvolgimento di alta tensione *f* )
– *primary winding (primary)*
**16** l'avvolgimento secondario (avvolgimento di bassa pressione *f* )
– *secondary winding (secondary, low-voltage winding)*
**17** il nucleo (induttore *m*)
– *core*
**18** i collegamenti di presa
– *tap (tapping)*
**19 il collegamento dei trasformatori**
– *transformer connection*

**20** il collegamento a stella
– *star connection (star network, Y-connection)*
**21** il collegamento a triangolo (chiusa, concatenazione *f* a delta *m*, collegamento poligonale)
– *delta connection (mesh connection)*
**22** il punto morto
– *neutral point*
**23-30 la turbina a vapore *m*,** un gruppo turbogeneratore (un turbosatz)
– *steam turbine, a turbogenerator unit*
**23** il cilindro a alta pressione *f*
– *high-pressure cylinder*
**24** il cilindro a media pressione *f*
– *medium-pressure cylinder*
**25** il cilindro a bassa pressione *f*
– *low-pressure cylinder*
**26** il generatore trifase (generatore *m* a induzione *f* trifase, generatore *m*)
– *three-phase generator (generator)*
**27** il raffreddatore d'idrogeno
– *hydrogen cooler*
**28** la conduttura di «passaggio» (di troppo pieno) del vapore
– *leakage steam path*
**29** la valvola a ugello
– *jet nozzle*
**30** il quadro di controllo della turbina con gli strumenti di misura
– *turbine monitoring panel with measuring instruments*
**31** il regolatore di tensione *f* (graduatore *m*)
– *[automatic] voltage regulator*
**32** l'impianto di sincronizzazione *f* (sincronizzatore *m*)
– *synchro*
**33 il terminale del cavo (il manicotto di estremità del cavo)**
– *cable box*
**34** il conduttore
– *conductor*
**35** l'isolatore passante
– *feed-through terminal (feed-through insulator)*
**36** il cono di avvolgimento
– *core*
**37** il rivestimento
– *casing*
**38** la massa isolante
– *filling compound (filler)*
**39** l'involucro di piombo
– *lead sheath*
**40** la bussola d'ingresso
– *lead-in tube*
**41** il cavo
– *cable*

**42 il cavo a alta tensione** per corrente *f* trifase
– *high voltage cable, for three-phase current*
**43** il conduttore di corrente *f*
– *conductor*
**44** la carta metallizzata
– *metallic paper (metallized paper)*
**45** l'isolamento del conduttore
– *tracer (tracer element)*
**46** la fascia di tela ortica
– *varnished-cambric tape*
**47** l'involucro di piombo
– *lead sheath*
**48** la carta asfaltata
– *asphalted paper*
**49** il rivestimento di juta
– *jute serving*
**50** la corazza di nastro di acciaio o di filo di acciaio
– *steel tape or steel wire armour (Am. armor)*
**51-62 l'interruttore *m* rapido a aria compressa,** un interruttore di potenza
– *air-blast circuit breaker, a circuit breaker*
**51** il serbatoio dell'aria compressa
– *compressed-air tank*
**52** la valvola di comando
– *control valve (main operating valve)*
**53** il collegamento dell'aria compressa
– *compressed-air inlet*
**54** l'isolatore *m* rigido cavo, un isolatore a cappa
– *support insulator, a hollow porcelain supporting insulator*
**55** la camera di disinnesto (camera di spegnimento, camera di annullamento)
– *interrupter*
**56** la resistenza
– *resistor*
**57** i contatti ausiliari
– *auxiliary contacts*
**58** il trasformatore di corrente *f*
– *current transformer*
**59** il trasformatore di tensione *f*
– *voltage transformer (potential transformer)*
**60** la muffola terminale
– *operating mechanism housing*
**61** lo scaricatore a corna *f pl*
– *arcing horn*
**62** la distanza esplosiva
– *spark gap*

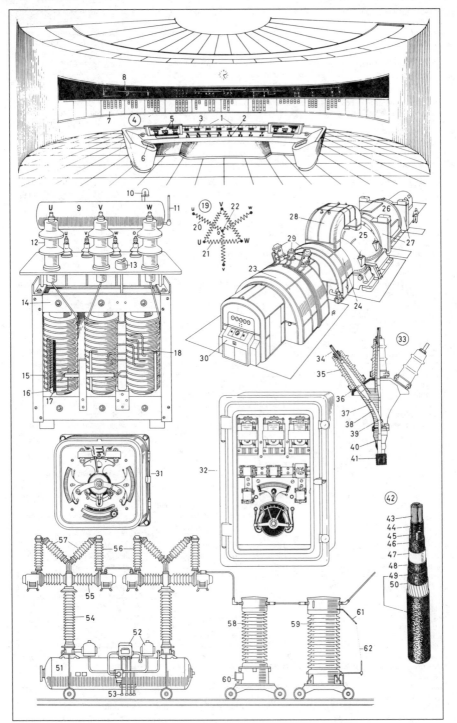

1 **il reattore autofertilizzante** (schema *m*)
 – *fast-breeder reactor (fast breeder) [diagram]*
2 il circuito primario (il circuito al sodio)
 – *primary circuit (primary loop, primary sodium system)*
3 il reattore
 – *reactor*
4 le barre di materiale *m* radioattivo (il combustibile nucleare)
 – *fuel rods (fuel pins)*
5 la pompa di circolazione *f* del circuito primario
 – *primary sodium pump*
6 lo scambiatore di calore *m*
 – *heat exchanger*
7 il circuito secondario (il circuito secondario al sodio)
 – *secondary circuit (secondary loop, secondary sodium system)*
8 la pompa di circolazione *f* del circuito secondario
 – *secondary sodium pump*
9 il generatore di vapore *m*
 – *steam generator*
10 il circuito terziario (il circuito dell'acqua di raffreddamento)
 – *cooling water flow circuit*
11 la conduttura del vapore
 – *steam line*
12 la conduttura dell'acqua di alimentazione *f*
 – *feedwater line*
13 la pompa dell'acqua di alimentazione *f*
 – *feed pump*
14 la turbina a vapore *m*
 – *steam turbine*
15 il generatore
 – *generator*
16 l'alimentazione *f* della rete
 – *transmission line*
17 il condensatore
 – *condenser*
18 l'acqua di raffreddamento
 – *cooling water*
19 **il reattore nucleare,** un reattore a acqua pressurizzata (la centrale elettronucleare; lingua parlata: la centrale atomica)
 – *nuclear reactor, a pressurized-water reactor (nuclear power plant, atomic power plant)*
20 l'incamiciatura in cemento
 – *concrete shield (reactor building)*
21 il contenitore di sicurezza in acciaio con intraferro di aspirazione *f*
 – *steel containment (steel shell) with air extraction vent*
22 il serbatoio a pressione *f* del reattore
 – *reactor pressure vessel*
23 il comando del reattore
 – *control rod drive*
24 le barre di assorbimento
 – *control rods*
25 la pompa principale dell'acqua di raffreddamento
 – *primary coolant pump*
26 il generatore di vapore *m*
 – *steam generator*
27 il montacarichi per il combustibile
 – *fuel-handling hoists*

28 il bacino di deposito del combustibile
 – *fuel storage*
29 la conduttura dell'acqua di raffreddamento del reattore
 – *coolant flow passage*
30 la conduttura dell'acqua di alimentazione *f*
 – *feedwater line*
31 la conduttura del vapore vivo
 – *prime steam line*
32 l'intercapedine *f* per il personale
 – *manway*
33 la serie delle turbine
 – *turbogenerator set*
34 il generatore della corrente trifase
 – *turbogenerator*
35 il condensatore
 – *condenser*
36 l'edificio collaterale
 – *service building*
37 il camino dell'aria viziata
 – *exhaust gas stack*
38 la gru a rotazione *f* concentrica
 – *polar crane*
39 la torre di raffreddamento, una torre di raffreddamento a secco
 – *cooling tower, a dry cooling tower*
40 il sistema a acqua pressurizzata (schema *m*)
 – *pressurized-water system*
41 il reattore
 – *reactor*
42 il circuito primario
 – *primary circuit (primary loop)*
43 la pompa di circolazione *f*
 – *circulation pump (recirculation pump)*
44 lo scambiatore di calore *m* (il generatore di vapore *m*)
 – *heat exchanger (steam generator)*
45 il circuito secondario (il circuito vapore *m* - acqua di alimentazione *f* )
 – *secondary circuit (secondary loop, feedwater steam circuit)*
46 la turbina a vapore *m*
 – *steam turbine*
47 il generatore
 – *generator*
48 il sistema di raffreddamento
 – *cooling system*
49 il sistema a acqua bollente (schema *m*)
 – *boiling water system [diagram]*
50 il reattore
 – *reactor*
51 il circuito condensa-vapore *m*
 – *steam and recirculation water flow paths*
52 la turbina a vapore *m*
 – *steam turbine*
53 il generatore
 – *generator*
54 la pompa di circolazione *f*
 – *circulation pump (recirculation pump)*
55 il sistema a acqua di raffreddamento (il raffreddamento con acqua fluviale)
 – *coolant system (cooling with water from river)*
56 **il deposito delle scorie atomiche** nella miniera di salgemma *m*
 – *radioactive waste storage in salt mine*

57-68 la stratigrafia geologica della miniera di salgemma *m* abbandonata e adattata a deposito per scorie *f pl* radioattive (scorie *f pl* atomiche)
 – *geological structure of abandoned salt mine converted for disposal of radioactive waste (nuclear waste)*
57 la marna iridata inferiore (il triassico superiore)
 – *Lower Keuper*
58 il calcare conchilifero superiore
 – *Upper Muschelkalk*
59 il calcare conchilifero medio
 – *Middle Muschelkalk*
60 il calcare conchilifero inferiore
 – *Lower Muschelkalk*
61 il trias inferiore
 – *Bunter downthrow*
62 i resti di lisciviazione *f* del materiale minerario
 – *residue of leached (lixiviated) Zechstein (Upper Permian)*
63 il salgemma superiore
 – *Aller rock salt*
64 il salgemma inferiore
 – *Leine rock salt*
65 lo strato di sale potassico
 – *Stassfurt seam (potash salt seam, potash salt bed)*
66 lo strato di salgemma *m*
 – *Stassfurt salt*
67 il solfato di calcio anidro limite
 – *grenzanhydrite*
68 l'argilla
 – *Zechstein shale*
69 il pozzo
 – *shaft*
70 gli edifici a cielo aperto
 – *minehead buildings*
71 la camera d'immagazzinamento
 – *storage chamber*
72 l'immagazzinamento di scorie *f pl* medio attive nella miniera di salgemma *m*
 – *storage of medium-active waste in salt mine*
73 la galleria a 511 m
 – *511 m level*
74 il muro di protezione *f* antiradiazioni *f pl*
 – *protective screen (anti-radiation screen)*
75 la finestra di vetro al piombo
 – *lead glass window*
76 la camera di deposito
 – *storage chamber*
77 il barile cerchiato con scorie *f pl* radioattive
 – *drum containing radioactive waste*
78 la telecamera
 – *television camera*
79 la camera di caricamento
 – *charging chamber*
80 il quadro di comando
 – *control desk (control panel)*
81 l'impianto di scarico dell'aria
 – *upward ventilator*
82 lo schermo di protezione *f*
 – *shielded container*
83 la galleria a 490 m
 – *490 m level*

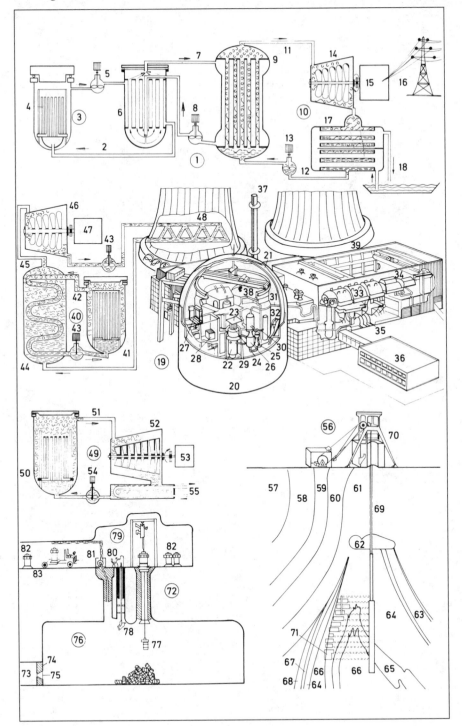

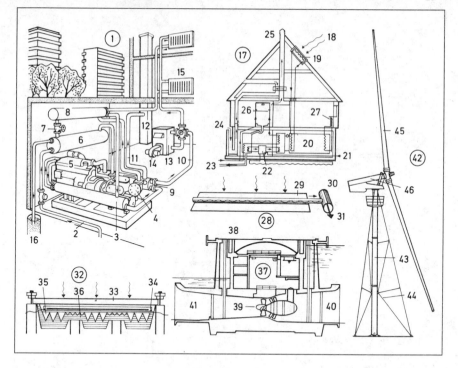

1  il sistema a pompe *f pl* di calore *m*
–  **heat pump system**
2  l'afflusso d'acqua
–  *source water inlet*
3  lo scambiatore acqua fredda acqua calda
–  *cooling water heat exchanger*
4  il compressore
–  *compressor*
5  il motore a metano o Diesel
–  *natural-gas or diesel engine*
6  l'evaporatore *m*
–  *evaporator*
7  il riduttore di pressione *f*
–  *pressure release valve*
8  il condensatore
–  *condenser*
9  lo scambiatore di calore *m* gas di scarico
–  *waste-gas heat exchanger*
10  la mandata
–  *flow pipe*
11  la conduttura di ritorno
–  *vent pipe*
12  il camino
–  *chimney*
13  la caldaia
–  *boiler*
14  il ventilatore
–  *fan*
15  il radiatore
–  *radiator*
16  il pozzetto di sicurezza
–  *sink*
**17-36 lo sfruttamento dell'energia solare**
–  *utilization of solar energy*
17  la casa riscaldata a energia solare
–  *solar (solar-heated) house*

18  le radiazioni solari
–  *solar radiation (sunlight, insolation)*
19  il pannello solare
–  *collector*
20  l'accumulatore *m* termico
–  *hot reservoir (heat reservoir)*
21  l'alimentazione *f* di corrente *f*
–  *power supply*
22  la pompa di calore *m*
–  *heat pump*
23  la conduttura ritorno acqua
–  *water outlet*
24  l'entrata aria
–  *air supply*
25  il camino di deflusso
–  *flue*
26  l'approvvigionamento acqua calda
–  *hot water supply*
27  il radiatore (il termosifone)
–  *radiator heating*
28  il pannello solare
–  *flat plate solar collector*
29  il collettore nero (una lastra di alluminio ricoperta di asfalto)
–  *blackened receiver surface with asphalted aluminium* (Am. *aluminum*) *foil*
30  il tubo d'acciaio
–  *steel tube*
31  il conduttore di calore *m*
–  *heat transfer fluid*
32  il mattone solare
–  *flat plate solar collector, containing solar cell*
33  la copertura in vetro
–  *glass cover*
34  la cellula solare
–  *solar cell*

35  i canali per l'aria
–  *air ducts*
36  l'isolamento
–  *insulation*
37  **la centrale maremotrice** (sezione *f*)
–  *tidal power plant [section]*
38  la diga (la diga di sbarramento)
–  *dam*
39  la turbina a doppia azione *f*
–  *reversible turbine*
40  l'afflusso alla turbina lato mare *m*
–  *turbine inlet for water from the sea*
41  l'afflusso alla turbina lato accumulatore *m*
–  *turbine inlet for water from the basin*
42  **la centrale eolica**
–  **wind power plant** (wind generator, aerogenerator)
43  la torre tubolare
–  *truss tower*
44  l'armatura a cavo metallico
–  *guy wire*
45  il rotore (l'elica)
–  *rotor*
46  il generatore e il motore direzionale
–  *generator with variable pitch for power regulation*

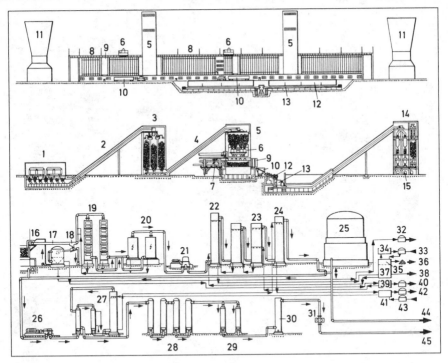

**1-15 la cokeria**
– *coking plant*
**1** lo scarico del coke
– *dumping of coking coal*
**2** il trasportatore a nastro
– *belt conveyor*
**3** il deposito dei componenti del coke
– *blending bunker*
**4** il trasportatore a nastro per la torre del carbone
– *service bunker conveyor*
**5** la torre del carbone
– *service bunker*
**6** il vagonetto di riempimento
– *larry car (larry, charging car)*
**7** la macchina compattatrice del coke
– *pusher ram*
**8** la batteria di storte *f pl* da coke *m*
– *battery of coke ovens*
**9** il vagonetto trasportatore delle formelle del coke
– *coke guide*
**10** il vagonetto del polverino con locomotiva
– *quenching car, with engine*
**11** il serbatoio del polverino
– *quenching tower*
**12** la rampa del coke
– *coke loading bay (coke wharf )*
**13** il nastro trasportatore della rampa del coke
– *coke wharf conveyor*
**14** l'impianto di vagliatura del coke
– *screening of coke and breeze*
**15** il carico del coke
– *coke loading*
**16-45 il trattamento del gas della cokeria**
– *coke-oven gas processing*
**16** l'uscita gas dalla storta da coke *m*
– *discharge (release) of gas from the coke ovens*

**17** la conduttura di raccolta gas (il bariletto)
– *gas-collecting main*
**18** la separazione del catrame denso
– *coal tar extraction*
**19** il refrigeratore del gas
– *gas cooler*
**20** il filtro elettrostatico
– *electrostatic precipitator*
**21** l'aspiratore *m* del gas
– *gas extractor*
**22** lo scrubber (il gorgogliatore di lavaggio) dell'idrogeno solforato
– *hydrogen sulphide (Am. hydrogen sulfide) scrubber (hydrogen sulphide wet collector)*
**23** lo scrubber (il gorgogliatore di lavaggio) dell'ammoniaca
– *ammonia scrubber (ammonia wet collector)*
**24** lo scrubber (il gorgogliatore di lavaggio) del benzolo (del benzene)
– *benzene (benzol) scrubber*
**25** il contenitore dei gas
– *gas holder*
**26** il compressore dei gas
– *gas compressor*
**27** il debenzolaggio con refrigeratore *m* e scambiatore *m* di calore *m*
– *debenzoling by cooler and heat exchanger*
**28** la desolforazione a gas *m* compresso
– *desulphurization (Am. desulfurization) of pressure gas*
**29** il raffreddamento del gas
– *gas cooling*
**30** l'essicazione *m* del gas
– *gas drying*
**31** il contatore del gas
– *gas meter*
**32** il contenitore del catrame grezzo
– *crude tar tank*

**33** l'adduzione *f* di acido solforico
– *sulphuric acid (Am. sulfuric acid) supply*
**34** la produzione di acido solforico
– *production of sulphuric acid (Am. sulfuric acid)*
**35** la produzione di solfato di ammonio
– *production of ammonium sulphate (Am. ammonium sulfate)*
**36** il solfato di ammonio
– *ammonium sulphate (Am. ammonium sulfate)*
**37** l'impianto di rigenerazione *f*, per rigenerare i materiali di lavaggio
– *recovery plant for recovering the scrubbing agents*
**38** l'allontanamento delle acque di rifiuto
– *waste water discharge*
**39** la defenolizzazione dell'acqua di lavaggio del gas
– *phenol extraction from the gas water*
**40** il contenitore di fenolo grezzo
– *crude phenol tank*
**41** la produzione di benzolo (di benzene *m*) grezzo
– *production of crude benzol (crude benzene)*
**42** il serbatoio di benzolo (benzene *m*) grezzo
– *crude benzol (crude benzene) tank*
**43** il serbatoio dell'olio di lavaggio
– *scrubbing oil tank*
**44** la conduttura del gas a bassa pressione *f*
– *low-pressure gas main*
**45** la conduttura del gas a alta pressione *f*
– *high-pressure gas main*

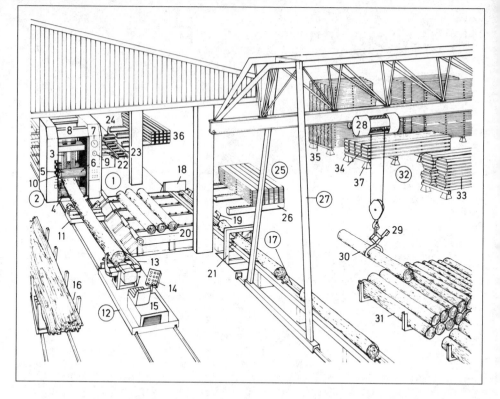

**1 la segheria**
– *sawmill*
**2** la segatrice alternativa multipla
– *vertical frame saw (Am. gang mill)*
**3** le lame della segatrice
– *saw blades*
**4** il cilindro di alimentazione *f*
– *feed roller*
**5** il rullo di guida
– *guide roller*
**6** la scanalatura
– *fluting (grooving, grooves)*
**7** il manometro pressione *f* olio
– *oil pressure gauge* (Am. *gage*)
**8** il telaio della segatrice
– *saw frame*
**9** l'indicatore *m* di avanzamento
– *feed indicator*
**10** la scala per l'altezza di passaggio
– *log capacity scale*
**11** il carrello di sostegno
– *auxiliary carriage*
**12** il carrello di ancoraggio
– *carriage*
**13** la pinza di ancoraggio
– *log grips*
**14** il comando a distanza
– *remote control panel*
**15** il posto di comando del carrello di ancoraggio
– *carriage motor*

**16** il carrello per gli scarti
– *truck for splinters (splints)*
**17** il carrello trasporto tronchi *m pl*
– *endless log chain* (Am. *jack chain*)
**18** la piastra di arresto
– *stop plate*
**19** il dispositivo di espulsione *f*
– *log-kicker arms*
**20** il trasportatore trasversale
– *cross conveyor*
**21** l'impianto di lavaggio
– *washer (washing machine)*
**22** il trasportatore trasversale a catena per le tavole
– *cross chain conveyor for sawn timber*
**23** la tavola a rulli *m pl*
– *roller table*
**24** la sega a disco per la rifilatura
– *undercut swing saw*
**25** la prima impilatura
– *piling*
**26** i supporti a rulli *m pl*
– *roller trestles*
**27** la gru a cavalletto (la gru a portale *m*)
– *gantry crane*
**28** il motore della gru
– *crane motor*
**29** la benna svedese (la benna auto-bloccante)
– *pivoted log grips*

**30** il tronco
– *roundwood (round timber)*
**31** il supporto per i tronchi
– *log dump*
**32** il settore del legno tagliato
– *squared timber store*
**33** i tronchi segati
– *sawn logs*
**34** le tavole
– *planks*
**35** le assi
– *boards (planks)*
**36** il legname squadrato (i travetti)
– *squared timber*
**37** il plinto d'appoggio
– *stack bearer*

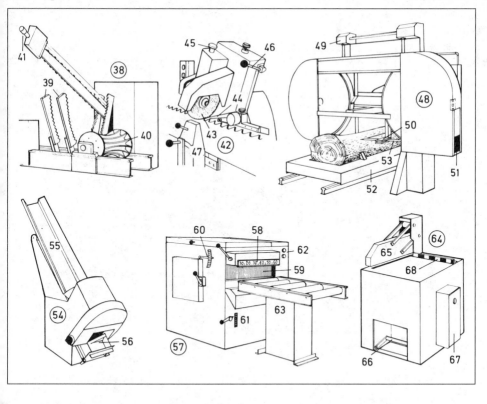

**38** la sega trasversale a catena automatica
 – *automatic cross-cut chain saw*
**39** la pinza di serraggio tronchi *m pl*
 – *log grips*
**40** il cilindro di alimentazione *f*
 – *feed roller*
**41** l'impianto di tensione *f* della catena
 – *chain-tensioning device*
**42** l'affilatrice *f* automatica della sega
 – *saw-sharpening machine*
**43** il disco della mola
 – *grinding wheel (teeth grinder)*
**44** il nottolino di avanzamento
 – *feed pawl*
**45** il regolatore della profondità dell'affilatrice *f*
 – *depth adjustment for the teeth grinder*
**46** la leva d'innalzamento della testa affilante
 – *lifter (lever) for the grinder chuck*
**47** l'arresto della lama della sega
 – *holding device for the saw blade*
**48** la segatrice a nastro orizzontale dei tronchi
 – *horizontal bandsaw for sawing logs*
**49** l'aggiustaggio verticale
 – *height adjustment*

**50** il puliscilama
 – *chip remover*
**51** l'aspiratrucioli *m*
 – *chip extractor*
**52** la slitta di trasporto
 – *carriage*
**53** la lama della sega a nastro
 – *bandsaw blade*
**54** la sega automatica per legna da ardere
 – *automatic blocking saw*
**55** lo scivolo di alimentazione *f*
 – *feed channel*
**56** l'apertura di uscita
 – *discharge opening*
**57** la sega per doppia rifilatura
 – *twin edger (double edger)*
**58** la scala graduata per la distanza dei tagli
 – *breadth scale (width scale)*
**59** le lamelle di sicurezza
 – *kick-back guard (plates)*
**60** la scala graduata per l'altezza
 – *height scale*
**61** la scala graduata per l'alimentazione *f*
 – *in-feed scale*
**62** le spie luminose
 – *indicator lamps*
**63** il tavolo alimentatore
 – *feed table*

**64** la sega a disco di rifilatura
 – *undercut swing saw*
**65** il premilastra automatico (con cappa di protezione *f*)
 – *automatic hold-down with protective hood*
**66** il pedale di comando
 – *foot switch*
**67** la centralina di comando
 – *distribution board (panelboard)*
**68** l'arresto per la lunghezza
 – *length stop*

1 **la cava,** uno sfruttamento a giorno (cava di sgombro)
– *quarry, an open-cast working*
2 lo strato di scoperto (cappellaccio, crosta)
– *overburden*
3 la roccia affiorante
– *working face*
4 la roccia di esplosione *f* (pietrame *m* sciolto/staccato)
– *loose rock pile (blasted rock)*
5 lo spaccapietre, un operaio della cava
– *quarryman (quarrier), a quarry worker*
6 la mazza
– *sledge hammer*
7 il cuneo
– *wedge*
8 il blocco di pietra
– *block of stone*
9 il perforatore (l'addetto alla perforatrice)
– *driller*
10 il casco
– *safety helmet*
11 il martello pneumatico perforatore (perforatrice *f*)
– *hammer drill (hard-rock drill)*
12 il foro (foro di trivellazione *f*)
– *borehole*
13 l'escavatore *m* universale
– *universal excavator*
14 il vagone
– *large-capacity truck*
15 la parete di roccia
– *rock face*

16 l'elevatore *m* inclinato (il montacarichi a salita inclinata)
– *inclined hoist*
17 il frantoio (frantumatrice *f*) preliminare
– *primary crusher*
18 l'impianto di frantumazione *f* (impianto di ricavo del pietrisco)
– *stone-crushing plant*
19 il frantoio rotativo per frantumazione *f* grossa; *sim.*: il frantoio rotativo a frantumazione *f* fine (granulatore *m*, frantumatore *m*)
– *coarse rotary (gyratory) crusher; sim.: fine rotary (gyratory) crusher (rotary or gyratory crusher)*
20 il frantoio a mascelle *f pl*
– *hammer crusher (impact crusher)*
21 il vibrovaglio
– *vibrating screen*
22 la pietra in polvere *f* (polvere *f* di pietra)
– *screenings (fine dust)*
23 il pietrisco (la breccia)
– *stone chippings*
24 la ghiaia
– *crushed stone*
25 il capo artificiere (il brillatore)
– *shot firer*
26 l'asta di misurazione *f* (canna)
– *measuring rod*
27 la cartuccia
– *blasting cartridge*
28 la miccia
– *fuse (blasting fuse)*

29 il secchio di sabbia per otturare
– *plugging sand (stemming sand) bucket*
30 la pietra quadra (pietra squadrata, concio)
– *dressed stone*
31 il piccone
– *pick*
32 il palanchino (piede *m* di capra, barraleva)
– *crowbar (pinch bar)*
33 la forca da pietre *f pl*
– *fork*
34 lo scalpellino (tagliapietre *m*)
– *stonemason*
**35-38 attrezzi** *m pl* **dello scalpellino**
– *stonemason's tools*
35 il maglio
– *stonemason's hammer*
36 il mazzuolo
– *mallet*
37 lo scalpello a punta larga
– *drove chisel (drove, boaster, broad chisel)*
38 l'ascia da tagliapietre *m*
– *dressing axe* (Am. *ax*)

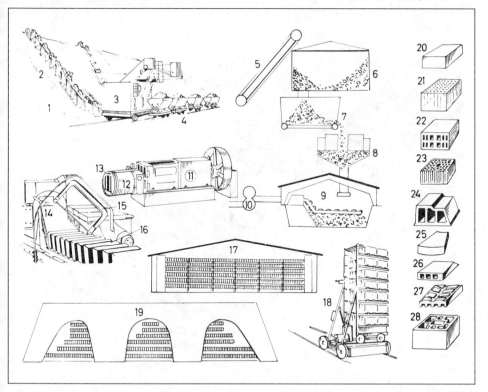

1  la cava di argilla
– *clay pit*
2  l'argilla, un'argilla grezza
– *loam, an impure clay (raw clay)*
3  l'escavatore *m*, un escavatore *m* di grande capacità
– *overburden excavator, a large-scale excavator*
4  la ferrovia decauville, una ferrovia a scartamento ridotto
– *narrow-gauge (Am. narrow-gage) track system*
5  l'elevatore *m* inclinato (montacarichi *m* a salita inclinata)
– *inclined hoist*
6  il deposito
– *souring chambers*
7  la cassa di caricamento (caricatore *m*)
– *box feeder (feeder)*
8  la molazza (macinatoio, macina)
– *edge runner mill (edge mill, pan grinding mill)*
9  l'impianto di rullaggio
– *rolling plant*
10  il miscelatore a due alberi *m pl* (mescolatore *m*)
– *double-shaft trough mixer (mixer)*
11  la pressa per estrusione *f* (pressa per mattoni *m pl*, mattoniera)
– *extrusion press (brick-pressing machine)*
12  la camera sotto vuoto
– *vacuum chamber*
13  la filiera (trafila)
– *die*

14  l'argilla trafilata
– *clay column*
15  la tagliatrice (cesoia per mattoni *m pl*)
– *cutter (brick cutter)*
16  il mattone crudo
– *unfired brick (green brick)*
17  la camera di essicazione *f*
– *drying shed*
18  il carrello elevatore
– *mechanical finger car (stacker truck)*
19  il forno anulare (forno per mattoni *m pl*)
– *circular kiln (brick kiln)*
20  il mattone pieno (mattone *m*, laterizio)
– *solid brick (building brick)*
21 u. 22  i mattoni forati (il forato)
– *perforated bricks and hollow blocks*
21  il forato a foratura verticale
– *perforated brick with vertical perforations*
22  il forato a foratura orizzontale
– *hollow clay block with horizontal perforations*
23  il forato con foratura a griglia
– *hollow clay block with vertical perforations*
24  il laterizio da soletta (mattone *m* da solaio)
– *floor brick*
25  il laterizio da ciminiera (laterizio da pozzo, laterizio radiale)
– *compass brick (radial brick, radiating brick)*
26  il tavellone (laterizio cavo di terracotta)
– *hollow flooring block*

27  il mattone pieno per stalle *f pl*
– *paving brick*
28  il mattone lavorato per camini *m pl*
– *cellular brick [for fireplaces] (chimney brick)*

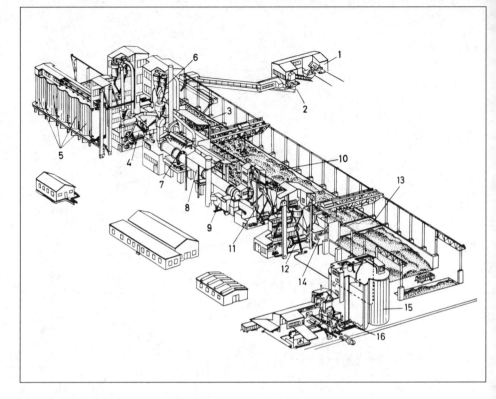

1 le materie prime (calcare *m*, argilla e marna calcarea)
– *raw materials (limestone, clay and marl)*
2 il frantoio a martelli *m pl*
– *hammer crusher (hammer mill)*
3 il deposito delle materie prime
– *raw material store*
4 il mulino di macinazione *f* e simultanea essicazione *f* delle materie prime con impiego dei gas di scarico dello scambiatore di calore *m*
– *raw mill for simultaneously grinding and drying the raw materials with exhaust gas from the heat exchanger*
5 i silos dei materiali grezzi macinati (silos *m pl* omogeneizzatori)
– *raw meal silos*
6 lo scambiatore di calore *m* (impianto a ciclone *m* per lo scambio del calore)
– *heat exchanger (cyclone heat exchanger)*

7 l'impianto di eliminazione *f* della polvere (un filtro elettrico) per i gas di scarico dello scambiatore di calore *m* provenienti dal mulino
– *dust collector (an electrostatic precipitator) for the heat exchanger exhaust from the raw mill*
8 il forno a tubo rotativo
– *rotary kiln*
9 l'impianto di raffreddamento del klinker (delle scorie)
– *clinker cooler*
10 il deposito del klinker
– *clinker store*
11 la soffiatrice di aria primaria
– *primary air blower*
12 l'impianto di macinazione *f* del cemento
– *cement-grinding mill*
13 il deposito del gesso
– *gypsum store*
14 la frantumatrice del gesso
– *gypsum crusher*
15 il silo del cemento
– *cement silo*
16 l'impaccatrice del cemento per sacchi *m pl* di carta a valvola
– *cement-packing plant for paper sacks*

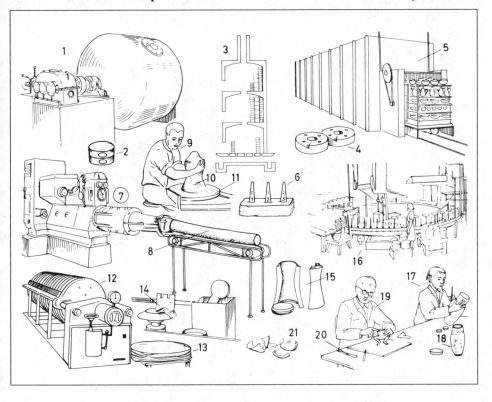

**1** il mulino a tamburo (mulino per impasto, mulino a sfere *f pl*) per la preparazione per via umida della miscela di materie *f pl* prime
– *grinding cylinder (ball mill) for the preparation of the raw material in water*
**2** la capsula dei campioni con apertura per l'osservazione *f* del processo di cottura
– *sample sagger (saggar, seggar), with aperture for observing the firing process*
**3** il forno circolare [schema]
– *bottle kiln (beehive kiln) [diagram]*
**4** la forma di cottura
– *firing mould (Am. mold)*
**5** il forno a tunnel *m*
– *tunnel kiln*
**6** il cono Seger per la misurazione di alti gradi *m pl* di temperatura
– *Seger cone (pyrometric cone, Am. Orton cone) for measuring high temperatures*
**7** l'estrusore *m* a depressione *f*, una pressa per estrudere
– *de-airing pug mill (de-airing pug press), an extrusion press*

**8** il tronco (il tratto) d'impasto
– *clay column*
**9** il ceramista (*anche:* il modellatore, il vasaio) mentre foggia un pezzo sagomato
– *thrower throwing a ball (bat) of clay*
**10** la motta
– *slug of clay*
**11** il tornio del vasaio
– *turntable;* sim.: *potter's wheel*
**12** il filtropressa
– *filter press*
**13** la focaccia d'impasto
– *filter cake*
**14** la tornitura con sagoma (con ronda)
– *jiggering, with a profiling tool;* sim.: *jollying*
**15** la forma da fusione *f* per la colatura dell'impasto umido
– *plaster mould (Am. mold) for slip casting*
**16** la giostra di smaltatura
– *turntable glazing machine*
**17** il decoratore di porcellane *f pl*
– *porcelain painter (china painter)*
**18** il vaso dipinto a mano *f*
– *hand-painted vase*

**19** il ritoccatore
– *repairer*
**20** la stecca di modellatura
– *pallet (modelling,* Am. *modeling, tool)*
**21** i cocci di porcellana (cocci *m pl*)
– *shards (sherds, potsherds)*

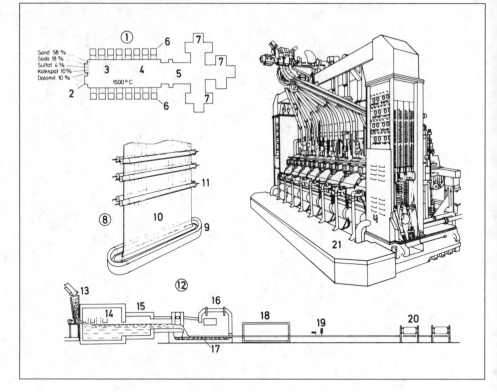

**1-20 la fabbricazione del vetro piano**
- *sheet glass production (flat glass production)*
1 il forno a bacino sistema *m* Fourcault (schema *m*)
- *glass furnace (tank furnace) for the Fourcault process [diagram]*
2 l'infornatrice *f* automatica
- *filling end, for feeding in the batch (frit)*
3 il bacino di fusione *f*
- *melting bath*
4 il bacino di affinaggio
- *refining bath (fining bath)*
5 i bacini di lavorazione *f*
- *working baths (working area)*
6 i bruciatori
- *burners*
7 le macchine di tiraggio
- *drawing machines*
8 la macchina di Fourcault per la produzione di vetro tirato
- *Fourcault glass-drawing machine*
9 la débiteuse
- *slot*
10 il nastro di vetro in ascesa
- *glass ribbon (ribbon of glass, sheet of glass) being drawn upwards*
11 la coppia dei rulli di trasporto (l'apparato di tiraggio)
- *rollers (drawing rolls)*

12 il processo float (schema *m*)
- *float glass process*
13 l'infornatrice *f* a colata
- *batch (frit) feeder (funnel)*
14 il bacino di fusione *f*
- *melting bath*
15 il bacino di raffreddamento
- *cooling tank*
16 il bagno float a gas *m* inerte
- *float bath in a protective inert-gas atmosphere*
17 lo stagno fuso
- *molten tin*
18 il forno di ricottura a rulli *m pl*
- *annealing lehr*
19 l'apparecchiatura di taglio
- *automatic cutter*
20 gli impilatori
- *stacking machines*
21 la macchina IS (individual section), una soffiatrice per bottiglie *f pl*
- *IS (individual-section) machine, a bottle-making machine*
**22-37 gli schemi di soffiatura**
- *blowing processes*
22 il doppio processo di soffiatura
- *blow-and-blow process*
23 l'alimentatore *m* di carica
- *introduction of the gob of molten glass*
24 il presoffiatore
- *first blowing*

25 l'aspiratore *m*
- *suction*
26 il passaggio dallo stampo sbozzatore allo stampo finitore
- *transfer from the parison mould (Am. mold) to the blow mould (Am. mold)*
27 la ricottura
- *reheating*
28 la soffiatura (la formatura sotto vuoto)
- *blowing (suction, final shaping)*
29 la forma finale
- *delivery of the completed vessel*
30 il procedimento di soffiatura e di pressione *f*
- *press-and-blow process*
31 l'alimentatore *m* di carica
- *introduction of the gob of molten glass*
32 il punzone
- *plunger*
33 la pressa
- *pressing*
34 il passaggio dallo stampo a pressione *f* alla soffiatura
- *transfer from the press mould (Am. mold) to the blow mould (Am. mold)*
35 la ricottura
- *reheating*

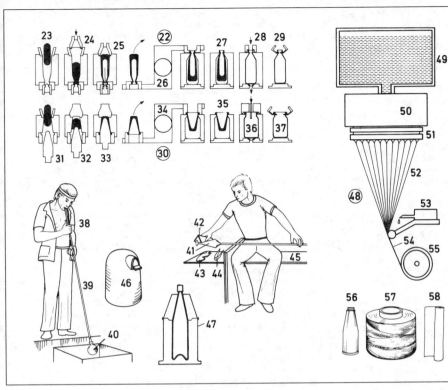

36 la soffiatura (la formatura sotto
    vuoto)
– *blowing (suction, final shaping)*
37 la forma finale
– *delivery of the completed vessel*
38-47 **la soffiatura del vetro** (la sof-
    fiatura a bocca, la formatura)
– ***glassmaking*** *(glassblowing, glass-*
    *blowing by hand, glass forming)*
38 il soffiatore
– *glassmaker (glassblower)*
39 la canna da soffio (la pipa)
– *blowing iron*
40 il bulbo (la goccia)
– *gob*
41 il calice soffiato a bocca
– *hand-blown goblet*
42 la sagoma per la formatura del
    piede del calice
– *clappers for shaping the base*
    *(foot) of the goblet*
43 la sagoma
– *trimming tool*
44 la forbice da vetro
– *tongs*
45 la panca del vetraio
– *glassmaker's chair (gaffer's chair)*
46 il crogiolo da vetraio
– *covered glasshouse pot*
47 lo stampo per la soffiatura della
    goccia preformata
– *mould (Am. mold), into which the*
    *parison is blown*

48-55 **la fabbricazione del vetro per**
    **fibre** *f pl*
– ***production of glass fibre*** *(Am.*
    *glass fiber)*
48 il procedimento di tiraggio del
    vetro
– *continuous filament process*
49 il forno di fusione *f* del vetro
– *glass furnace*
50 il bacino di fusione *f*
– *bushing containing molten glass*
51 la filiera a fori *m pl*
– *bushing tips*
52 i filamenti del vetro per fibre *f pl*
– *glass filaments*
53 l'imbozzimatura
– *sizing*
54 il filamento per fibre *f pl*
– *strand (thread)*
55 il tamburo per fibre *f pl*
– *spool*
56-58 **prodotti** *m pl* **del vetro per**
    **fibre** *f pl*
– ***glass fibre*** *(Am. glass fiber)* **prod-**
    **ucts**
56 il filamento del vetro per fibre *f pl*
– *glass yarn (glass thread)*
57 il filamento del vetro binato
– *sleeved glass yarn (glass thread)*
58 il feltro di vetro tessile
– *glass wool*

**1-13  la consegna del cotone**
- *supply of cotton*
1  la capsula del cotone matura per il raccolto
- *ripe cotton boll*
2  il filato pronto (spola, bobina)
- *full cop (cop wound with weft yarn)*
3  la balla di cotone *m* pressato
- *compressed cotton bale*
4  l'imballo di tela juta
- *jute wrapping*
5  la reggetta (il cerchione) di ferro
- *steel band*
6  il numero del lotto (numero della partita) sulla balla di cotone *m*
- *identification mark of the bale*
7  la macchina per la pulitura del cotone
- *bale opener (bale breaker)*
8  il nastro trasportatore
- *cotton-feeding brattice*
9  il cassone di riempimento (cassa di alimentazione *f* )
- *cotton feed*
10  l'aspirapolvere *m* a imbuto
- *dust extraction fan*
11  il condotto (che arriva) al deposito della polvere
- *duct to the dust-collecting chamber*
12  il motore di propulsione *f*
- *drive motor*
13  il nastro mobile collettatore
- *conveyor brattice*
**14  il battitoio doppio** (battitoio a due volanti *m pl*)
- **double scutcher** (*machine with two scutchers*)
15  la conca di ricezione *f* della falda
- *lap cradle*
16  la testa della crimagliera di compressione *f*
- *rack head*
17  la leva d'innesto della macchina
- *starting handle*
18  il volantino a mano *f* per sollevare e abbassare la testa della crimagliera di pressione *f*
- *handwheel, for raising and lowering the rack head*
19  il dispositivo mobile per voltare la falda
- *movable lap-turner*
20  i cilindri di pressione *f*
- *calender rollers*
21  il coperchio per i due vagli a tamburo
- *cover for the perforated cylinders*
22  il collettore della polvere
- *dust escape flue (dust discharge flue)*
23  i motori di propulsione *f*
- *drive motors (beater drive motors)*
24  l'albero di propulsione *f* delle ali battenti
- *beater driving shaft*

25  il battitore a tre bracci *m pl*
- *three-blade beater (Kirschner beater)*
26  la griglia (il grigliato)
- *grid [for impurities to drop]*
27  il cilindro alimentatore
- *pedal roller (pedal cylinder)*
28  la leva per regolare l'alimentazione *f*, una leva a pedale *m*
- *control lever for the pedal roller, a pedal lever*
29  il cambio continuo di velocità
- *variable change-speed gear*
30  la cassa conica
- *cone drum box*
31  il sistema di leve *f pl* per la regolazione del materiale
- *stop and start levers for the hopper*
32  il cilindro pressore in (di) legno
- *wooden hopper delivery roller*
33  la caricatrice-pesatrice
- *hopper feeder*
**34  la carda a cappelli *m pl*** (carda)
- **carding machine** (*card, carding engine*)
35  il vaso deposito del nastro della carda
- *card can (carding can), for receiving the coiled sliver*
36  il portavaso
- *can holder*
37  i cilindri della calandra
- *calender rollers*
38  il nastro della carda
- *carded sliver (card sliver)*
39  il pettine oscillante
- *vibrating doffer comb*
40  la leva d'arresto
- *start-stop lever*
41  i supporti rettificatori
- *grinding-roller bearing*
42  lo scaricatore (spogliatore *m*, cilindro scaricatore, cilindro spogliatore)
- *doffer*
43  il tamburo
- *cylinder*
44  il pulitore del cappello
- *flat clearer*
45  la catena del cappello
- *flats*
46  i tenditori a rullo per la catena del cappello
- *supporting pulleys for the flats*
47  la falda del battitoio
- *scutcher lap (carded lap)*
48  il portafalda (sostegno della falda)
- *scutcher lap holder*
49  il motore di propulsione *f* con cinghie *f pl* piane
- *drive motor with flat belt*
50  la puleggia motrice principale
- *main drive pulley (fast-and-loose drive pulley)*

51  il principio di funzionamento della carda
- *principle of the card (of the carding engine)*
52  il cilindro alimentatore
- *fluted feed roller*
53  il prerompitore
- *licker-in (taker-in, licker-in roller)*
54  la griglia del prerompitore
- *licker-in undercasing*
55  la griglia del tamburo
- *cylinder undercasing*
**56  la pettinatrice**
- **combing machine** (*comber*)
57  la scatola degli ingranaggi
- *drive gearbox (driving gear)*
58  la falda sulla pettinatrice (falda pronta per la pettinatura)
- *laps ready for combing*
59  la compressione del nastro (dei nastri)
- *calender rollers*
60  lo stiratoio
- *comber draw box*
61  il contatore
- *counter*
62  il deposito del pettinato
- *coiler top*
63  il principio di funzionamento della pettinatrice
- *principle of the comber*
64  il nastro della carda
- *lap*
65  il morsetto inferiore
- *bottom nipper*
66  il morsetto superiore
- *top nipper*
67  il pettine di fissaggio
- *top comb*
68  il pettine circolare
- *combing cylinder*
69  il segmento di cuoio
- *plain part of the cylinder*
70  il segmento a aghi *m pl* (segmento a pettine *m*, segmento dentato)
- *needled part of the cylinder*
71  il cilindro di strappo
- *detaching rollers*
72  il materiale pettinato (il pettinato)
- *carded and combed sliver*

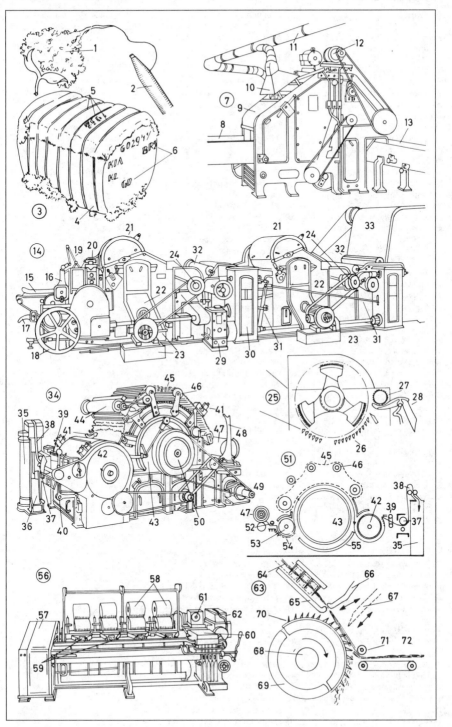

**1** lo stiratoio
– *draw frame*
**2** la scatola degli ingranaggi con motore *m* incorporato
– *gearbox with built-in motor*
**3** i vasi della carda
– *sliver cans*
**4** il cilindro di arresto della macchina per rottura del nastro
– *broken thread detector roller*
**5** la binatura dei nastri
– *doubling of the slivers*
**6** la leva di arresto dello stiratoio
– *stopping handle*
**7** la copertura dello stiratoio
– *draw frame cover*
**8** le lampade spia (lampade *f pl* di segnalazione *f* )
– *indicator lamps (signal lights)*
**9** lo stiratoio semplice a quattro cilindri *m pl* [schema]
– *simple four-roller draw frame [diagram]*
**10** i cilindri inferiori (cilindri *m pl* di acciaio godronati)
– *bottom rollers (lower rollers), fluted steel rollers*
**11** i cilindri superiori ricoperti in materiale *m* sintetico
– *top rollers (upper rollers) covered with synthetic rubber*
**12** il nastro grossolano prima dello stiro
– *doubled slivers before drafting*
**13** il nastro fine dopo lo stiro
– *thin sliver after drafting*
**14** lo stiro [schema]
– *high-draft system (high-draft draw frame) [diagram]*
**15** l'introduzione *f* del lucignolo (introduzione *f* dello stoppino)
– *feeding-in of the sliver*
**16** la cinghia girevole di cuoio
– *leather apron (composition apron)*
**17** la sbarra di guida a inversione *f* di marcia (a passo reversibile)
– *guide bar*
**18** il cilindro superiore leggero (cilindro estrusore)
– *light top roller (guide roller)*
**19** il banco a fusi *m pl* (il filatoio)
– *high-draft speed frame (fly frame, slubbing frame)*
**20** i vasi dei nastri
– *sliver cans*
**21** l'entrata dei nastri nello stiratoio
– *feeding of the slivers to the drafting rollers*
**22** il cilindro stiratore del filatoio con cappello pulitore
– *drafting rollers with top clearers*
**23** le bobine del filatoio (del banco a fusi *m pl*)
– *roving bobbins*

**24** la filatrice
– *fly frame operator (operative)*
**25** l'aletta del filatoio (del banco a fusi *m pl*)
– *flyer*
**26** la spalla del filatoio
– *frame end plate*
**27** il filatoio intermedio
– *intermediate yarn-forming frame*
**28** la rastrelliera portaspole
– *bobbin creel (creel)*
**29** il lucignolo uscente dai cilindri di stiro
– *roving emerging from the drafting rollers*
**30** il carrello di propulsione *f* delle spole
– *lifter rail (separating rail)*
**31** la propulsione dei fusi
– *spindle drive*
**32** la leva di arresto della macchina
– *stopping handle*
**33** la scatola degli ingranaggi con motore incorporato
– *gearbox, with built-on motor*
**34** **il filatoio a anelli** *m pl*
– **ring frame (ring spinning frame)**
**35** il motore a corrente *f* trifase con collettore *m*
– *three-phase motor*
**36** la piastra di base *f* del motore
– *motor base plate (bedplate)*
**37** l'anello di trasporto del motore
– *lifting bolt [for motor removal]*
**38** il regolatore di velocità della filatura (il regolatore di velocità del fuso)
– *control gear for spindle speed*
**39** la scatola degli ingranaggi
– *gearbox*
**40** la ruota del cambio per variare il titolo del filato
– *change wheels for varying the spindle speed [to change the yarn count]*
**41** la rastrelliera piena di spole *f pl*
– *full creel*
**42** gli alberi e i supporti per la propulsione degli anelli di filiera
– *shafts and levers for raising and lowering the ring rail*
**43** i fusi con i separatori dei fili
– *spindles with separators*
**44** la cassa di aspirazione *f* dei fili
– *suction box connected to the front roller underclearers*
**45** **il fuso convenzionale (fuso standard)** del filatoio a anelli *m pl*
– **standard ring spindle**
**46** lo stelo (la cocca) del fuso
– *spindle shaft*
**47** il cuscinetto a rulli *m pl*
– *roller bearing*
**48** la puleggia a gola (la noce)
– *wharve (pulley)*

**49** il gancio del fuso
– *spindle catch*
**50** il banco del fuso
– *spindle rail*
**51** gli organi di filatura
– *ring and traveller* (Am. *traveler*)
**52** il fuso nudo
– *top of the ring tube (of the bobbin)*
**53** il filato (il filo)
– *yarn (thread)*
**54** l'anello di filiera
– *ring fitted into the ring rail*
**55** l'anello cursore
– *traveller* (Am. *traveler*)
**56** il filato avvolto
– *yarn wound onto the bobbin*
**57** **il torcitoio**
– **doubling frame**
**58** la rastrelliera con le spole incrociate
– *creel, with cross-wound cheeses*
**59** il dispositivo d'inoltro del filo
– *delivery rollers*
**60** le spole di torcitura
– *bobbins of doubled yarn*

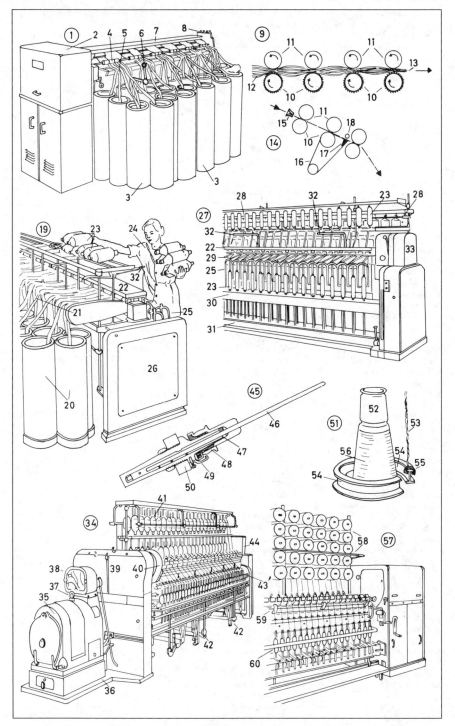

**1-57 la preparazione alla tessitura**
- *processes preparatory to weaving*
1 la roccatrice
- *cone-winding frame*
2 il soffiante mobile
- *travelling (Am. traveling) blower*
3 la guida di scorrimento per il soffiante
- *guide rail, for the travelling (Am. traveling) blower*
4 il ventilatore
- *blowing assembly*
5 l'apertura per l'aria
- *blower aperture*
6 l'arresto di fine corsa per la guida di scorrimento del ventilatore
- *superstructure for the blower rail*
7 l'indicatore del diametro della bobina
- *full-cone indicator*
8 la bobina con avvolgimento a spire *f pl* incrociate
- *cross-wound cone*
9 l'abbinatrice *f*
- *cone creel*
10 il cilindro scanalato guidafili
- *grooved cylinder*
11 la fessura a zig-zag per incrociare i fili
- *guiding slot for cross-winding the threads*
12 il supporto laterale con il motore
- *side frame, housing the motor*
13 la leva di arresto della bobina
- *tension and slub-catching device*
14 la spalla destra con filtro
- *off-end framing with filter*
15 la spola
- *yarn package, a ring tube or mule cop*
16 il contenitore delle spole
- *yarn package container*
17 la leva di avvio e di arresto
- *starting and stopping lever*
18 il dispositivo di infilatura automatica
- *self-threading guide*
19 l'impianto di arresto automatico, in caso di rottura del filo
- *broken thread stop motion*
20 la stribbia
- *thread clearer*
21 il tendifilo
- *weighting disc (disk) for tensioning the thread*
22 l'orditoio
- *warping machine*
23 il ventilatore
- *fan*
24 la bobina
- *cross-wound cone*
25 la cantra
- *creel*
26 il pettine regolabile
- *adjustable comb*

27 il telaio dell'orditoio
- *warping machine frame*
28 il contametri per filo
- *yarn length recorder*
29 il subbio dell'orditoio
- *warp beam*
30 il disco del subbio
- *beam flange*
31 l'asta di protezione *f*
- *guard rail*
32 il cilindro di comando
- *driving drum (driving cylinder)*
33 la trasmissione a cinghia
- *belt drive*
34 il motore
- *motor*
35 il pedale di comando
- *release for starting the driving drum*
36 la vite per la regolazione del pettine
- *screw for adjusting the comb setting*
37 gli aghi per l'arresto automatico in caso di rottura del filo
- *drop pins, for stopping the machine when a thread breaks*
38 l'asta guidafili
- *guide bar*
39 la coppia dei cilindri di serraggio fili *m pl*
- *drop pin rollers*
40 l'imbozzimatrice *f* per tintura indaco
- *indigo dying and sizing machine*
41 il disco di carico
- *take-off stand*
42 il subbio dell'orditoio
- *warp beam*
43 la catena dell'orditoio
- *warp*
44 la vasca di umidificazione *f*
- *wetting trough*
45 il cilindro di immersione *f*
- *immersion roller*
46 il rullo di spremitura
- *squeeze roller (mangle)*
47 la vasca di colorazione *f*
- *dye liquor padding trough*
48 il condotto dell'aria
- *air oxidation passage*
49 la vasca di lavaggio
- *washing trough*
50 il cilindro essicatore per il preessicamento
- *drying cylinders for pre-drying*
51 il compensatore a magazzino
- *tension compensator (tension equalizer)*
52 l'imbozzimatrice *f*
- *sizing machine*
53 il cilindro essicatore
- *drying cylinders*

54 il campo di divisione *f* dei fili asciutti
- for cotton: *stenter;* for wool: *tenter*
55 il subbio di ordito
- *beaming machine*
56 il subbio dell'ordito imbozzimato
- *sized warp beam*
57 i cilindri di compressione *f*
- *rollers*

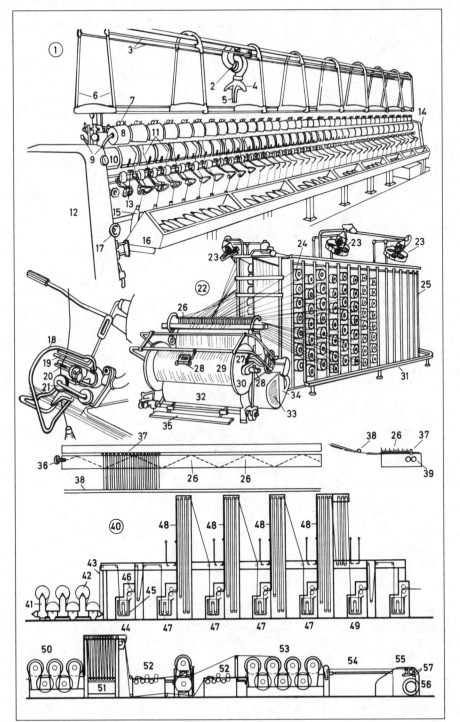

1 **il telaio**
– *weaving machine (automatic loom)*
2 il contagiri
– *pick counter (tachometer)*
3 il guidalicci
– *shaft (heald shaft, heald frame) guide*
4 i licci
– *shafts (heald shafts, heald frames)*
5 il cambiaspole automatico (il cambio a revolver *m* per cambiare le navette)
– *rotary battery for weft replenishment*
6 il coperchio del battente
– *sley (slay) cap*
7 la spola
– *weft pirn*
8 la leva di avviamento e di arresto
– *starting and stopping handle*
9 la cassa delle navette con navette *f pl*
– *shuttle box, with shuttles*
10 il pettine
– *reed*
11 la cimosa (la cimossa)
– *selvedge (selvage)*
12 il tessuto finito
– *cloth (woven fabric)*
13 il tempiale
– *temple (cloth temple)*
14 il guidafili elettrico
– *electric weft feeler*
15 il volano
– *flywheel*
16 la soglia del battente
– *breast beam board*
17 la spada
– *picking stick (pick stick)*
18 il motore elettrico
– *electric motor*
19 gli ingranaggi del cambio
– *cloth take-up motion*
20 il subbio del tessuto
– *cloth roller (fabric roller)*
21 il raccoglitore per i tubetti vuoti (il barilotto)
– *can for empty pirns*
22 la cinghia per il funzionamento della spada
– *lug strap, for moving the picking stick*
23 la valvoliera
– *fuse box*
24 la struttura portante del telaio
– *loom framing*
25 la punta di metallo
– *metal shuttle tip*
26 la navetta
– *shuttle*
27 il liccio
– *heald (heddle, wire heald, wire heddle)*

28 la cruna
– *eye (eyelet, heald eyelet, heddle eyelet)*
29 la cruna della navetta
– *eye (shuttle eye)*
30 la bobina
– *pirn*
31 la capsula di metallo per il contatto col tastatore
– *metal contact sleeve for the weft feeler*
32 la feritoia per il tastatore
– *slot for the feeler*
33 le molle di serraggio delle spole
– *spring-clip pirn holder*
34 il guidafili dell'ordito
– *drop wire*
35 il telaio (vista laterale schematica)
– *weaving machine (automatic loom) [side elevation]*
36 i rulli dei licci
– *heald shaft guiding wheels*
37 il subbiello
– *backrest*
38 la verga
– *lease rods*
39 la catena
– *warp (warp thread)*
40 il passo
– *shed*
41 il battente
– *sley (slay)*
42 il ceppo
– *race board*
43 le trinche per il dispositivo d'arresto
– *stop rod blade for the stop motion*
44 il ceppo di fermo
– *bumper steel*
45 il dispositivo di arresto del telaio
– *bumper steel stop rod*
46 il subbiello
– *breast beam*
47 il cilindro ruvido
– *cloth take-up roller*
48 il subbio dell'ordito
– *warp beam*
49 la flangia
– *beam flange*
50 l'albero principale
– *crankshaft*
51 l'ingranaggio dell'albero a gomiti *m pl*
– *crankshaft wheel*
52 la biella
– *connector*
53 le aste del battente
– *sley (slay)*
54 il tiralicci
– *lam rods*
55 l'ingranaggio dell'albero eccentrico
– *camshaft wheel*
56 l'albero eccentrico
– *camshaft (tappet shaft)*

57 l'eccentrico
– *tappet (shedding tappet)*
58 il braccio dell'eccentrico
– *treadle lever*
59 il freno del subbio
– *let-off motion*
60 il disco del freno
– *beam motion control*
61 la corda del freno
– *rope of the warp let-off motion*
62 la leva del freno
– *let-off weight lever*
63 il peso del freno
– *control weight [for the treadle]*
64 il lancianavetta con rivestimento in pelle *f* o in resina sintetica
– *picker with leather or bakelite pad*
65 il fermatacchetto
– *picking stick buffer*
66 l'eccentrico
– *picking cam*
67 il rullo dell'eccentrico
– *picking bowl*
68 la molla di ritorno della spada
– *picking stick return spring*

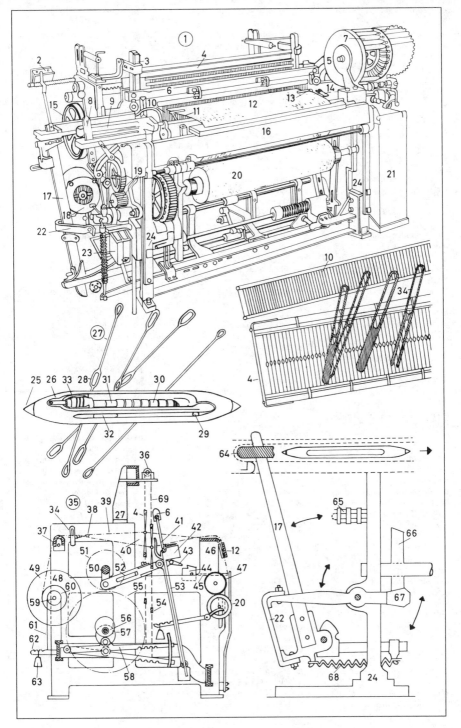

**1-66 la fabbrica di calze** *f pl*
– *hosiery mill*
1 la macchina circolare per
 maglieria, per la produzione di
 tessuto tubolare
– *circular knitting machine for the*
 *manufacture of tubular fabric*
2 l'asta del guidafili
– *yarn guide support post (thread*
 *guide support post)*
3 il guidafili
– *yarn guide (thread guide)*
4 la spola
– *bottle bobbin*
5 il tendifilo
– *yarn-tensioning device*
6 il castello
– *yarn feeder*
7 il volantino per portare il filo
 dietro gli aghi
– *handwheel for rotating the*
 *machine by hand*
8 il cilindro portaaghi *m pl*
– *needle cylinder (cylindrical needle*
 *holder)*
9 il tessuto tubolare (il tessuto di
 maglia)
– *tubular fabric*
10 il contenitore del tessuto
– *fabric drum (fabric box, fabric*
 *container)*
11 il cilindro portaaghi *m pl* (sezione *f* )
– *needle cylinder (cylindrical needle*
 *holder) [section]*
12 gli aghi a linguetta posti radial-
 mente
– *latch needles arranged in a circle*
13 il rivestimento del castello
– *cam housing*
14 le parti del castello
– *needle cams*
15 il canale degli aghi
– *needle trick*
16 il diametro del cilindro; *anche:* la
 larghezza del tessuto tubolare
– *cylinder diameter (also: diameter*
 *of tubular fabric)*
17 il filo
– *thread (yarn)*
18 la macchina Cotton per la fabbricazione di calze *f pl* da donna
– *Cotton's patent flat knitting*
 *machine for ladies' fully-fashioned*
 *hose*
19 la catena comando
– *pattern control chain*
20 la fiancata
– *side frame*
21 la fontura; fonture multiple: la
 produzione contemporanea di
 parecchie calze *f pl*
– *knitting head;* with several knitting heads: *simultaneous produc-*
 *tion of several stockings*

22 l'asta di avvio e di arresto
– *starting rod*
23 il telaio Raschel (il telaio per
 maglieria in catena)
– *Raschel warp-knitting machine*
24 il subbio di ordito
– *warp (warp beam)*
25 il subbiello
– *yarn-distributing (yarn-dividing)*
 *beam*
26 il disco divisore
– *beam flange*
27 la serie degli aghi (la serie degli
 aghi a linguetta)
– *row of needles*
28 la barra di aghi *m pl*
– *needle bar*
29 il tessuto (il tessuto prodotto dal
 telaio Raschel) (tendine *f pl* e reti
 *f pl*) sul subbio
– *fabric (Raschel fabric) [curtain*
 *lace and net fabrics] on the fabric*
 *roll*
30 il volantino per il funzionamento
 a mano
– *handwheel*
31 la puleggia motrice e il motore
– *motor drive gear*
32 il peso della pressa
– *take-down weight*
33 la struttura portante
– *frame*
34 il basamento
– *base plate*
35 la macchina rettilinea per
 maglieria
– *hand flat (flat-bed) knitting*
 *machine*
36 il filo
– *thread (yarn)*
37 la molla di richiamo
– *return spring*
38 la barra di sostegno delle molle
– *support for springs*
39 la slitta mobile
– *carriage*
40 il castello
– *feeder-selecting device*
41 le manopole
– *carriage handles*
42 la scala graduata per la grandezza
 del punto
– *scale for regulating size of stitches*
43 il contagiri
– *course counter (tachometer)*
44 la leva per l'apertura della frontura
– *machine control lever*
45 la guida di scorrimento
– *carriage rail*
46 la serie superiore degli aghi
– *back row of needles*
47 la serie inferiore degli aghi
– *front row of needles*

48 il tessuto
– *knitted fabric*
49 il bordo di tensione *f*
– *tension bar*
50 il peso di tensione *f*
– *tension weight*
51 la frontura degli aghi con lo
 schema di tessitura
– *needle bed showing knitting action*
52 i denti del pettine
– *teeth of knock-over bit*
53 gli aghi paralleli
– *needles in parallel rows*
54 il guidafili (la passetta)
– *yarn guide (thread guide)*
55 la frontura degli aghi
– *needle bed*
56 la lastra di copertura sugli aghi a
 linguetta
– *retaining plate for latch needles*
57 il castello di azionamento degli
 aghi
– *guard cam*
58 l'abbattitura degli aghi
– *sinker*
59 il meccanismo di gettata degli
 aghi
– *needle-raising cam*
60 il piede dell'ago
– *needle butt*
61 l'ago a linguetta
– *latch needle*
62 la maglia
– *loop*
63 il passaggio dell'ago attraverso la
 maglia
– *pushing the needle through the*
 *fabric*
64 l'entrata del filo nell'ago mediante il guidafili
– *yarn guide (thread guide) placing*
 *yarn in the needle hook*
65 la formazione della maglia
– *loop formation*
66 il distacco della maglia
– *casting off of loop*

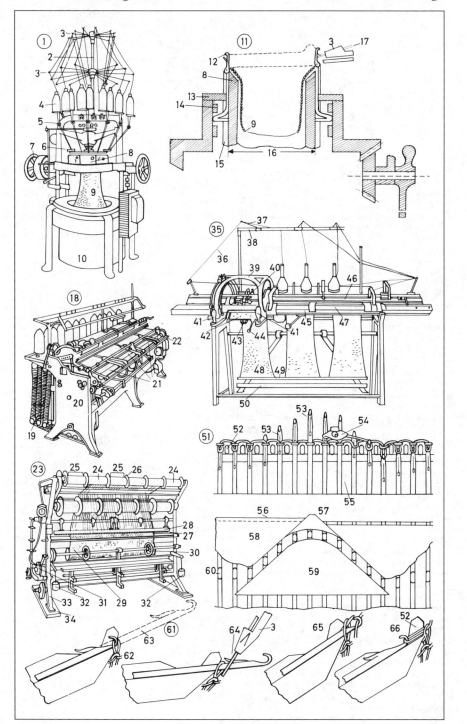

**1-65  il finissaggio dei tessuti**
– *finishing*
1  il follone a cilindri *m pl* per la fol-
   latura dei tessuti di lana
– *rotary milling (fulling) machine*
   *for felting the woollen* (Am.
   *woolen) fabric*
2  il peso
– *pressure weights*
3  il cilindro alimentatore superiore
– *top milling roller (top fulling*
   *roller)*
4  la puleggia motrice del cilindro
   alimentatore inferiore
– *drive wheel of bottom milling*
   *roller (bottom fulling roller)*
5  il cilindro guidapezza
– *fabric guide roller*
6  il cilindro alimentatore inferiore
– *bottom milling roller (bottom*
   *fulling roller)*
7  la tavola di trazione *f*
– *draft board*
8  la macchina per il lavaggio in
   largo dei tessuti delicati
– *open-width scouring machine for*
   *finer fabrics*
9  il rimettaggio del tessuto
– *fabric being drawn off the*
   *machine*
10  la scatola degli ingranaggi
– *drive gearbox*
11  la conduttura dell'acqua
– *water inlet pipe*
12  il cilindro guidapezza
– *drawing-in roller*
13  l'allargapezza (la briglia di tensione *f* )
– *scroll-opening roller*
14  la centrifuga oscillante per la
   disidratazione
– *pendulum-type hydro-extractor*
   *(centrifuge), for extracting liquors*
   *from the fabric*
15  il basamento
– *machine base*
16  la colonna
– *casing over suspension*
17  l'alloggiamento del cilindro interno
   rotante (del cilindro a paniere *m*)
– *outer casing containing rotating*
   *cage (rotating basket)*
18  il coperchio della centrifuga
– *hydro-extractor (centrifuge) lid*
19  il dispositivo di chiusura di
   sicurezza
– *stop-motion device (stopping*
   *device)*
20  il dispositivo di avviamento e di
   arresto automatico
– *automatic starting and braking*
   *device*
21  l'asciugatoio (la rameuse)
– *for cotton: stenter; for wool: tenter*

22  il tessuto umido
– *air-dry fabric*
23  la piattaforma di servizio
– *operator's (operative's) platform*
24  il fissaggio del tessuto con serie *f*
   *pl* di aghi *m pl* o spilli *m pl*
– *feeding of fabric by guides onto*
   *stenter (tenter) pins or clips*
25  il quadro elettrico di comando
– *electric control panel*
26  l'inserimento del tessuto a falde *f*
   *pl* sospese, per evitare l'accorcia-
   mento (il restringimento, la gual-
   citura) all'essicazione *f*
– *initial overfeed to produce shrink-*
   *resistant fabric when dried*
27  il termometro
– *thermometer*
28  la camera di asciugatura
– *drying section*
29  il tubo di uscita dell'aria
– *air outlet*
30  l'uscita dall'asciugatoio (dalla
   rameuse)
– *plaiter (fabric-plaiting device)*
31  la garzatrice cardatrice per
   garzare la superficie del tessuto
   con cardatura, per la formazione
   della garza
– *wire-roller fabric-raising machine*
   *for producing raised or nap sur-*
   *face*
32  la centralina di comando
– *drive gearbox*
33  il tessuto non garzato
– *unraised cloth*
34  i cilindri di garzatura
– *wire-covered rollers*
35  la faldatrice
– *plaiter (cuttling device)*
36  il tessuto garzato
– *raised fabric*
37  il panchetto
– *plaiting-down platform*
38  la calandra per stirare i tessuti
– *rotary press (calendering*
   *machine), for press finishing*
39  il tessuto
– *fabric*
40  i pulsanti e i volantini di comando
– *control buttons and control wheels*
41  il cilindro caldo
– *heated press bowl*
42  l'orditoio meccanico
– *rotary cloth-shearing machine*
43  l'aspirazione *f* del filo di ordito
   tagliato
– *suction slot, for removing loose*
   *fibres* (Am. *fibers*)
44  il cilindro di taglio
– *doctor blade (cutting cylinder)*
45  la griglia di protezione *f*
– *protective guard*
46  la spazzola rotante
– *rotating brush*

47  lo scivolo curvo (il raccoglitessuto)
– *curved scray entry*
48  il pedale di comando
– *treadle control*
49  la macchina di decatissaggio per
   ottenere tessuti *m pl* irrestringibili
– *[non-shrinking] decatizing (decat-*
   *ing) fabric-finishing machine*
50  il cilindro di decatissaggio
– *perforated decatizing (decating)*
   *cylinder*
51  la pezza
– *piece of fabric*
52  la manovella
– *cranked control handle*
53  la macchina da stampa a rullo a
   dieci colori *m pl* (la macchina da
   stampa per tessuti *m pl*)
– *ten-colour* (Am. *ten-color) roller*
   *printing machine*
54  il basamento della macchina
– *base of the machine*
55  il motore
– *drive motor*
56  il tessuto rotante
– *blanket [of rubber or felt]*
57  il tessuto stampato
– *fabric after printing (printed fab-*
   *ric)*
58  il quadro elettrico di comando
– *electric control panel (control*
   *unit)*
59  la stampa a quadro mobile
– *screen printing*
60  il quadro da stampa mobile
– *mobile screen frame*
61  la racla
– *squeegee*
62  la sagoma da stampa
– *pattern stencil*
63  il tavolo di stampa
– *screen table*
64  il tessuto incollato non stampato
– *fabric gummed down on table*
   *ready for printing*
65  lo stampatore
– *screen printing operator (opera-*
   *tive)*

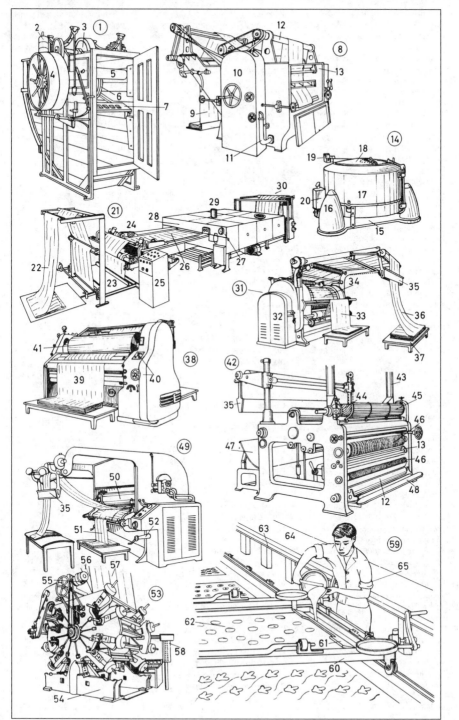

**1-34** la produzione di **fibre** *f pl* **di raion** *m* (filo continuo di raion *m*) e di **fiocco** col procedimento Viscosa

– *manufacture of **continuous filament and staple fibre** (Am. fiber) **viscose rayon yarns** by means of the viscose process*

**1-12** dalla materia prima alla viscosa

– *from raw material to viscose rayon*

**1** la materia prima (cellulosa di faggio e abete *m* rosso in fogli *m pl*, fogli *m pl* di cellulosa)

– *basic material [beech and spruce cellulose in form of sheets]*

**2** il mescolamento dei fogli di cellulosa

– *mixing cellulose sheets*

**3** la soluzione di soda caustica

– *caustic soda*

**4** l'introduzione *f* dei fogli di cellulosa nella soluzione di soda caustica

– *steeping cellulose sheets in caustic soda*

**5** la spremitura per togliere la soluzione di soda caustica in eccedenza

– *pressing out excess caustic soda*

**6** la sfilacciatura dei fogli di cellulosa

– *shredding the cellulose sheets*

**7** la maturazione della cellulosa alcalina

– *maturing (controlled oxidation) of the alkali-cellulose crumbs*

**8** il solfuro di carbonio

– *carbon disulphide (Am. carbon disulfide)*

**9** la solfazione (trasformazione *f* della cellulosa alcalina in xantogenato di cellulosa)

– *conversion of alkali-cellulose into cellulose xanthate*

**10** la dissoluzione dello xantogenato in soluzione *f* di soda caustica per produrre la soluzione di viscosa da inviare alle filiere

– *dissolving the xanthate in caustic soda for the preparation of the viscose spinning solution*

**11** i recipienti per la maturazione

– *vacuum ripening tanks*

**12** il filtropressa

– *filter presses*

**13-27** dalla viscosa al filo continuo di raion *m*

– *from viscose to viscose rayon thread*

**13** la pompa di filatura

– *metering pump*

**14** la filiera

– *multi-holed spinneret (spinning jet)*

**15** il bagno coagulante per la trasformazione della soluzione di viscosa in raion (in filamenti *m pl* di cellulosa plastici)

– *coagulating (spinning) bath for converting (coagulating) viscose (viscous solution) into solid filaments*

**16** il rullo godet, un cilindro di vetro

– *Godet wheel, a glass pulley*

**17** il filatoio centrifugo per avvolgere il filo

– *Topham centrifugal pot (box) for twisting the filaments into yarn*

**18** la focaccia di filatura

– *viscose rayon cake*

**19-27** la lavorazione della focaccia

– *processing of the cake*

**19** la deacidificazione (la neutralizzazione)

– *washing*

**20** la desolforazione

– *desulphurizing (desulphurization, Am. desulfurizing, desulfurization)*

**21** il candeggio

– *bleaching*

**22** l'avvivaggio (il rendere morbido ed elastico il filato)

– *treating of cake to give filaments softness and suppleness*

**23** la centrifugazione per eliminare il liquido in eccedenza

– *hydro-extraction to remove surplus moisture*

**24** l'essicamento nella camera ad aria calda

– *drying in heated room*

**25** l'avvolgimento

– *winding yarn from cake into cone form*

**26** l'aspo

– *cone-winding machine*

**27** il filo di raion *m* su una bobina incrociata conica per l'utilizzo nel settore tessile

– *viscose rayon yarn on cone ready for use*

**28-34** dal filo continuo di raion al fiocco

– *from viscose spinning solution to viscose rayon staple fibre (Am. fiber)*

**28** il cavo (il cordoncino)

– *filament tow*

**29** l'impianto di lavaggio a doccia

– *overhead spray washing plant*

**30** la taglierina per tagliare il cordoncino ad una lunghezza prefissata

– *cutting machine for cutting filament tow to desired length*

**31** l'asciugatoio a piani *m pl* mobili per il fiocco

– *multiple drying machine for cut-up staple fibre (Am. fiber) layer (lap)*

**32** il nastro trasportatore

– *conveyor belt (conveyor)*

**33** la pressa per balle *f pl*

– *baling press*

**34** la balla di fiocco di raion pronta per la spedizione

– *bale of viscose rayon ready for dispatch (despatch)*

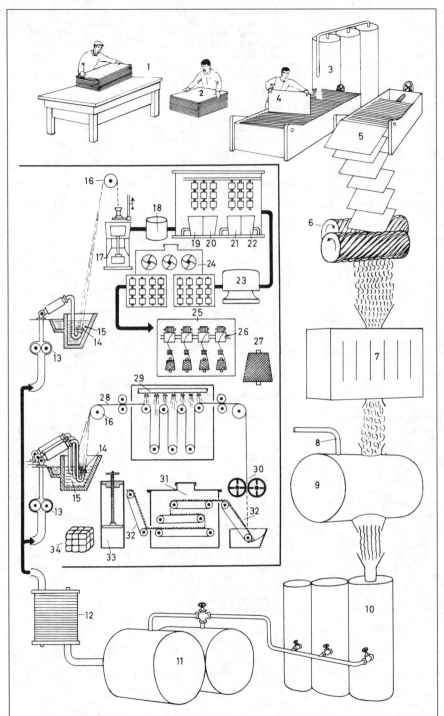

**1-62** la produzione di **fibre** *f pl* **poliammidiche** (nailon)
– *manufacture of* **polyamide** *(nylon 6, perlon)* **fibres** (Am. *fibers)*
**1** il carbone fossile (la materia prima per la produzione di poliammide *m)*
– *coal [raw material for manufacture of polyamide (nylon 6, perlon) fibres* (Am. *fibers)]*
**2** la cockeria (la cocheria) per la distillazione a secco del carbone fossile
– *coking plant for dry coal distillation*
**3** l'estrazione *f* del catrame e del fenolo
– *extraction of coal tar and phenol*
**4** la distillazione progressiva del catrame
– *gradual distillation of tar*
**5** il condensatore
– *condenser*
**6** l'estrazione *f* e il trasporto del benzolo (benzene *m)*
– *benzene extraction and dispatch (despatch)*
**7** il cloro
– *chlorine*
**8** la clorurazione del benzolo (benzene *m)*
– *benzene chlorination*
**9** il clorobenzolo (clorobenzene *m)*
– *monochlorobenzene (chlorobenzene)*
**10** la soluzione di soda caustica
– *caustic soda solution*
**11** l'evaporazione *f* del clorobenzolo (clorobenzene *m)* e della soluzione di soda caustica
– *evaporation of chlorobenzene and caustic soda*
**12** l'autoclave *f*
– *autoclave*
**13** il cloruro di sodio (il sale da cucina), un sottoprodotto
– *sodium chloride (common salt), a by-product*
**14** il fenolo (l'acido fenico)
– *phenol (carbolic acid)*
**15** l'immissione *f* d'idrogeno
– *hydrogen inlet*
**16** l'idrogenazione *f* del fenolo per la produzione di cicloesanolo grezzo
– *hydrogenation of phenol to produce raw cyclohexanol*
**17** la distillazione
– *distillation*
**18** il cicloesanolo puro
– *pure cyclohexanol*
**19** la deidrogenazione
– *oxidation (dehydrogenation)*
**20** la formazione di cicloesanone
– *formation of cyclohexanone (pimehinketone)*
**21** l'introduzione *f* d'idrossilammina
– *hydroxylamine inlet*
**22** formazione di cicloesanonossima
– *formation of cyclohexanoxime*

**23** l'introduzione *f* di acido solforico per lo spostamento molecolare
– *addition of sulphuric acid* (Am. *sulfuric acid) to effect molecular rearrangement*
**24** l'ammoniaca per la neutralizzazione dell'acido solforico
– *ammonia to neutralize sulphuric acid* (Am. *sulfuric acid)*
**25** formazione *f* di lattame *m* oleoso
– *formation of caprolactam oil*
**26** la soluzione di solfato di ammonio
– *ammonium sulphate* (Am. *ammonium sulfate) solution*
**27** il cilindro di raffreddamento
– *cooling cylinder*
**28** il caprolattame
– *caprolactam*
**29** la bilancia
– *weighing apparatus*
**30** la caldaia di fusione *f*
– *melting pot*
**31** la pompa
– *pump*
**32** il filtro
– *filter*
**33** la polimerizzazione in autoclave *f* (serbatoio a pressione *f*, recipiente *m* a pressione *f* )
– *polymerization in the autoclave*
**34** il raffreddamento del poliammide
– *cooling of the polyamide*
**35** lo sminuzzamento del poliammide
– *solidification of the polyamide*
**36** l'ascensore *m* a paternoster (l'elevatore *m* a tazze *f pl)*
– *vertical lift* (Am. *elevator)*
**37** l'estrattore *m* per la separazione del poliammide dal lattame oleoso residuo
– *extractor for separating the polyamide from the remaining lactam oil*
**38** l'essicatoio
– *drier*
**39** le scaglie di poliammide secco
– *dry polyamide chips*
**40** il serbatoio
– *chip container*
**41** la testa di fusione *f*, per la fusione e la filatura a pressione *f* del poliammide
– *top of spinneret for melting the polyamide and forcing it through spinneret holes (spinning jets)*
**42** la filiera
– *spinneret holes (spinning jets)*
**43** la solidificazione dei fili di poliammide *m* nella torre di filatura
– *solidification of polyamide filaments in the cooling tower*
**44** l'avvolgimento del filo
– *collection of extruded filaments into thread form*
**45** la pretorcitura (lo stiro)
– *preliminary stretching (preliminary drawing)*

**46** la torcitura per ottenere maggiore resistenza e flessibilità del filo di poliammide *m*
– *stretching (cold-drawing) of the polyamide thread to achieve high tensile strength*
**47** la torcitura finale (lo stiro finale)
– *final stretching (final drawing)*
**48** il lavaggio delle bobine di filo
– *washing of yarn packages*
**49** la camera di essicazione *f*
– *drying chamber*
**50** la ribobinatura
– *rewinding*
**51** la bobina incrociata
– *polyamide cone*
**52** la bobina incrociata pronta per la spedizione
– *polyamide cone ready for dispatch (despatch)*
**53** il miscelatore
– *mixer*
**54** la polimerizzazione sotto vuoto
– *polymerization under vacua*
**55** lo stiro
– *stretching (drawing)*
**56** il lavaggio
– *washing*
**57** la preparazione per rendere possibile la filatura
– *finishing of tow for spinning*
**58** l'asciugatura del nastro
– *drying of tow*
**59** la crettatura del nastro
– *crimping of tow*
**60** il taglio del nastro alla lunghezza usuale della fibra
– *cutting of tow into normal staple lengths*
**61** il fiocco di poliammide *m*
– *polyamide staple*
**62** la balla del fiocco di poliammide *m*
– *bale of polyamide staple*

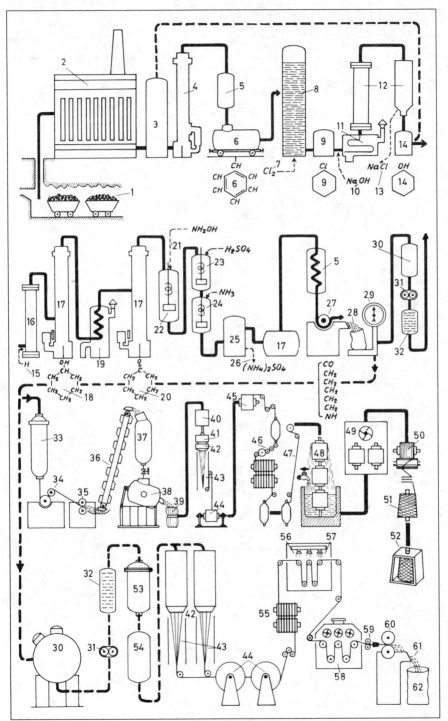

**1-29  intrecci** *m pl (quadrati neri:* filo di ordito alzato, filo di trama abbassato; *quadrati bianchi:* filo di trama alzato, filo di ordito abbassato)
– *weaves [black squares: warp thread raised, weft thread lowered; white squares: weft thread raised, warp thread lowered]*
**1** l'intreccio (l'armatura) del tessuto (visto dall'alto)
– *plain weave (tabby weave) [weave viewed from above]*
**2** il filo di ordito
– *warp thread*
**3** il filo di trama
– *weft thread*
**4** la messa in carta (il cartone) (modello per il tessitore)
– *draft (point paper design) for plain weave*
**5** il rimettaggio nel quadro dei licci
– *threading draft*
**6** la passatura in pettine *m*
– *denting draft (reed-threading draft)*
**7** il filo di ordito alzato
– *raised warp thread*
**8** il filo di ordito abbassato
– *lowered warp thread*
**9** l'annodatura
– *tie-up of shafts in pairs*
**10** l'alzata dei licci sulla trama (i tracciati)
– *treadling diagram*
**11** la messa in carta (il cartone di base *f*) per l'armatura Panama (armatura a scacchi *m pl,* armatura inglese)
– *draft for basket weave (hopsack weave, matt weave)*
**12** il motivo ripetuto
– *pattern repeat*
**13** il cartone per il Reps di trama (Reps longitudinale)
– *draft for warp rib weave*
**14** sezione *f pl* del tessuto del Reps di trama, una sezione di ordito
– *section of warp rib fabric, a section through the warp*
**15** il filo di trama abbassato
– *lowered weft thread*
**16** il filo di trama alzato
– *raised weft thread*
**17** il primo e il secondo filo di ordito (alzati)
– *first and second warp threads [raised]*
**18** il terzo ed il quarto filo di ordito (abbassati)
– *third and fourth warp threads [lowered]*
**19** il cartone per il Reps irregolare trasversale
– *draft for combined rib weave*

**20** il rimettaggio nei licci di cimosa (licci *m pl* aggiuntivi per la cimosa)
– *selvedge (selvage) thread draft (additional shafts for the selvedge)*
**21** il rimettaggio nei licci del tessuto
– *draft for the fabric shafts*
**22** l'annodatura dei licci della cimosa
– *tie-up of selvedge (selvage) shafts*
**23** l'annodatura dei licci del tessuto
– *tie-up of fabric shafts*
**24** la cimosa nell'armatura tela
– *selvedge (selvage) in plain weave*
**25** sezione *f* del tessuto del Reps trasversale irregolare
– *section through combination rib weave*
**26** l'intreccio longitudinale del tessuto a maglia
– *thread interlacing of reversible warp-faced cord*
**27** il cartone per l'intreccio longitudinale del tessuto a maglia
– *draft (point paper design) for reversible warp-faced cord*
**28** i punti di legamento
– *interlacing points*
**29** l'armatura a nido di ape *f*
– *weaving draft for honeycomb weave in the fabric*
**30-48  intrecci** *m pl* **fondamentali dei tessuti a maglia**
– *basic knits*
**30** la maglia, una maglia aperta
– *loop, an open loop*
**31** la testa
– *head*
**32** l'asta (la gamba)
– *side*
**33** il piede
– *neck*
**34** il punto di collegamento delle teste
– *head interlocking point*
**35** il punto di collegamento dei piedi
– *neck interlocking point*
**36** la maglia chiusa
– *closed loop*
**37** lo zig-zag doppio chiuso
– *mesh [with inlaid yarn]*
**38** il filo obliquo
– *diagonal floating yarn (diagonal floating thread)*
**39** il nodo
– *loop interlocking at the head*
**40** il flottante
– *float*
**41** la catenella
– *loose floating yarn (loose floating thread)*
**42** la serie delle maglie
– *course*
**43** la trama (l'intreccio)
– *inlaid yarn*

**44** la maglia dritto-rovescio
– *tuck and miss stitch*
**45** la maglia a zig-zag
– *pulled-up tuck stitch*
**46** la maglia a costa inglese
– *staggered tuck stitch*
**47** il punto perla
– *2×2 tuck and miss stitch*
**48** il punto perla doppio
– *double pulled-up tuck stitch*

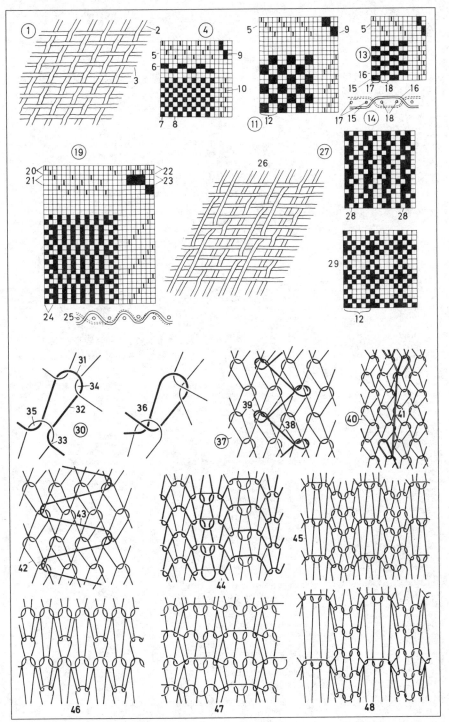

1-52 l'impianto per la produzione della cellulosa al solfato (schema *m*)
– *sulphate* (Am. *sulfate) pulp mill (kraft pulp mill) [in diagram form]*
1 la taglierina con depolverizzatore *m*
– *chippers with dust extractor*
2 il vaglio a cilindri *m pl*
– *rotary screen (riffler)*
3 il dosatore
– *chip packer (chip distributor)*
4 il soffiante
– *blower*
5 il mulino centrifugo
– *disintegrator (crusher, chip crusher)*
6 il soffiante per polvere *f*
– *dust-settling chamber*
7 il bollitore per cellulosa
– *digester*
8 il preriscaldatore per liscivia
– *liquor preheater*
9 la valvola separatrice
– *control tap*
10 il tubo orientabile
– *swing pipe*
11 il diffusore
– *blow tank (diffuser)*
12 la valvola d'iniezione *f*
– *blow valve*
13 la tina per diffusore *m*
– *blow pit (diffuser)*
14 il separatore del terpene
– *turpentine separator*
15 il separatore centrale
– *centralized separator*
16 il condensatore a iniezione *f*
– *jet condenser (injection condenser)*
17 il serbatoio per condensato di alimentazione *f*
– *storage tank for condensate*
18 il cilindro a acqua calda
– *hot water tank*
19 il cambiatore di calore *m*
– *heat exchanger*
20 il filtro
– *filter*
21 il preassortitore
– *presorter*
22 il sabbiere
– *centrifugal screen*
23 l'assortitore *m* rotante
– *rotary sorter (rotary strainer)*
24 il cilindro disidratatore
– *concentrator (thickener, decker)*
25 la tina
– *vat (chest)*
26 il serbatoio per l'acqua di ritorno
– *collecting tank for backwater (low box)*
27 il raffinatore conico
– *conical refiner (cone refiner, Jordan, Jordan refiner)*
28 il filtro per liscivio nero
– *black liquor filter*
29 il serbatoio per liscivio nero
– *black liquor storage tank*
30 il condensatore
– *condenser*
31 i separatori
– *separators*
32 i riscaldatori
– *heaters (heating elements)*
33 la pompa per liscivio
– *liquor pump*
34 la pompa per liscivio condensato
– *heavy liquor pump*
35 il serbatoio di miscelazione *f*
– *mixing tank*

36 il serbatoio per solfato
– *salt cake storage tank (sodium sulphate storage tank)*
37 il serbatoio di diluizione *f*
– *dissolving tank (dissolver)*
38 il generatore di vapore *m*
– *steam heater*
39 il filtro elettrostatico
– *electrostatic precipitator*
40 la pompa a aria
– *air pump*
41 il contenitore per liscivio grigio torbido
– *storage tank for the uncleared green liquor*
42 il concentratore
– *concentrator (thickener, decker)*
43 il preriscaldatore del liscivio grigio
– *green liquor preheater*
44 il concentratore dei liquidi di lavaggio
– *concentrator (thickener, decker) for the weak wash liquor (wash water)*
45 il contenitore del liscivio diluito
– *storage tank for the weak liquor*
46 il contenitore del liscivio di cottura
– *storage tank for the cooking liquor*
47 l'agitatore *m*
– *agitator (stirrer)*
48 il concentratore
– *concentrator (thickener, decker)*
49 l'agitatore *m* di caustificazione *f*
– *causticizing agitators (causticizing stirrers)*
50 il classificatore
– *classifier*
51 il tamburo per lo spegnimento della calce viva
– *lime slaker*
52 la calce ricalcinata
– *reconverted lime*
53-65 la macchina sfibratrice (schema *m*)
– *groundwood mill (mechanical pulp mill) [diagram]*
53 lo sfibratore continuo
– *continuous grinder (continuous chain grinder)*
54 il raccoglischegge
– *strainer (knotter)*
55 la pompa centrifuga
– *pulp water pump*
56 il sabbiere
– *centrifugal screen*
57 l'assortimento grossolano
– *screen (sorter)*
58 l'assortimento fine
– *secondary screen (secondary sorter)*
59 il tamburo per lo scarto
– *rejects chest*
60 il raffinatore conico
– *conical refiner (cone refiner, Jordan, Jordan refiner)*
61 il disidratatore
– *pulp-drying machine (pulp machine)*
62 il tamburo addensatore
– *concentrator (thickener, decker)*
63 la pompa per l'acqua di scarico
– *waste water pump (white water pump, pulp water pump)*
64 la conduttura del vapore
– *steam pipe*
65 la conduttura dell'acqua
– *water pipe*
66 lo sfibratore continuo
– *continuous grinder (continuous chain grinder)*
67 la catena
– *feed chain*

68 i tondelli di legno
– *groundwood*
69 il riduttore per la catena
– *reduction gear for the feed chain drive*
70 il dispositivo per martellinare la pietra
– *stone-dressing device*
71 la pietra (la mola)
– *grinding stone (grindstone, pulpstone)*
72 lo spruzzatore
– *spray pipe*
73 il raffinatore conico verticale (il refiner)
– *conical refiner (cone refiner, Jordan, Jordan refiner)*
74 la ruota per la regolazione della distanza tra le lame
– *handwheel for adjusting the clearance between the knives (blades)*
75 il cono rotante
– *rotating bladed cone (rotating bladed plug)*
76 il cono fisso
– *stationary bladed shell*
77 i fori di entrata per la cellulosa o lo sminuzzato da raffinare
– *inlet for unrefined cellulose (chemical wood pulp, chemical pulp) or groundwood pulp (mechanical pulp)*
78 il foro di uscita per la cellulosa o lo sminuzzato raffinati
– *outlet for refined cellulose (chemical wood pulp, chemical pulp) or groundwood pulp (mechanical pulp)*
79-86 l'impianto di preparazione *f* della cellulosa (schema *f*)
– *stuff (stock) preparation plant [diagram]*
79 il nastro trasportatore per cellulosa o pasta di legno
– *conveyor belt (conveyor) for loading cellulose (chemical wood pulp, chemical pulp) or groundwood pulp (mechanical pulp)*
80 lo spappolatore della cellulosa
– *pulper*
81 la tina di prediluizione *f*
– *dump chest*
82 lo sfibratore conico
– *cone breaker*
83 il raffinatore conico
– *conical refiner (cone refiner, Jordan, Jordan refiner)*
84 il raffinatore a molazza
– *refiner*
85 la tina di stoccaggio
– *stuff chest (stock chest)*
86 la tina di macchina
– *machine chest (stuff chest)*

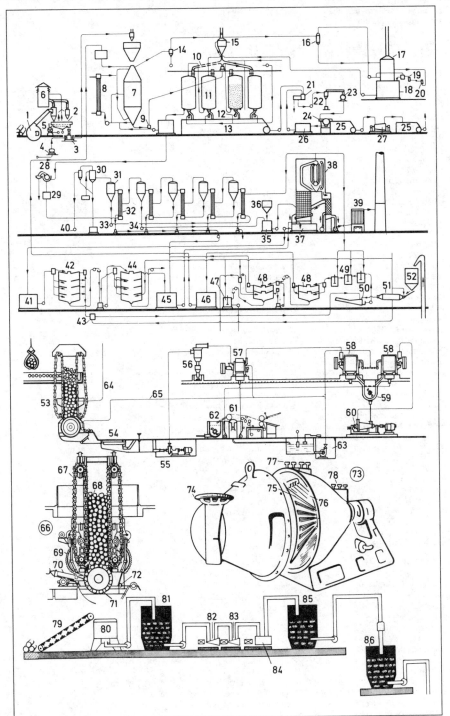

1 la tina di mescolazione *f*, una vasca miscelatrice di pasta per carta
– *stuff chest (stock chest, machine chest), a mixing chest for stuff (stock)*

2-10 apparecchi *m pl* di laboratorio per l'analisi *f* della materia prima e della carta
– *laboratory apparatus (laboratory equipment) for analysing stuff (stock) and paper*

2 il matraccio conico Erlenmeyer
– *Erlenmeyer flask*

3 il cilindro mescolatore
– *volumetric flask*

4 il cilindro misuratore
– *measuring cylinder*

5 il becco Bunsen
– *Bunsen burner*

6 il treppiede
– *tripod*

7 la capsula
– *petri dish*

8 il portaprovette
– *test tube rack*

9 la bilancia per peso lordo
– *balance for measuring basis weight*

10 lo spessimetro
– *micrometer*

11 lo spappolatore cilindrico prima dell'immissione *f* della cellulosa
– *centrifugal cleaners ahead of the breastbox (headbox, stuff box) of a paper machine*

12 il tubo verticale
– *standpipe*

13-28 la macchina continua per la produzione della carta (linea di lavorazione *f* ) (schema *m*)
– *paper machine (production line) [diagram]*

13 la cassa di afflusso con separasabbia e separanodi *m*
– *feed-in from the machine chest (stuff chest) with sand table (sand trap, riffler) and knotter*

14 il vaglio sgocciolatore
– *wire (machine wire)*

15 il cilindro aspirante
– *vacuum box (suction box)*

16 il rullo di ritorno tela
– *suction roll*

17 il primo feltro umido
– *first wet felt*

18 il secondo feltro umido
– *second wet felt*

19 la prima pressa umida
– *first press*

20 la seconda pressa umida
– *second press*

21 la pressa offset
– *offset press*

22 il cilindro essicatore
– *drying cylinder (drier)*

23 il feltro essicatore
– *dry felt (drier felt)*

24 la pressa collante
– *size press*

25 il cilindro raffreddatore
– *cooling roll*

26 i cilindri spianatori
– *calender rolls*

27 la cappa
– *machine hood*

28 l'arrotolatore *m*
– *delivery reel*

29-35 la macchina laminatrice
– *blade coating machine (blade coater)*

29 la carta grezza
– *raw paper (body paper)*

30 il nastro di carta
– *web*

31 l'impianto di patinatura per la parte anteriore
– *coater for the top side*

32 il forno essicatore a infrarossi *m pl*
– *infrared drier*

33 il cilindro essicatore riscaldato
– *heated drying cylinder*

34 l'impianto di patinatura per la parte posteriore
– *coater for the underside (wire side)*

35 il rotolo di carta patinata (il tamburo)
– *reel of coated paper*

36 la calandra
– *calender (super-calender)*

37 la pressa idraulica
– *hydraulic system for the press rolls*

38 il cilindro della calandra
– *calender roll*

39 l'impianto di sbobinatura
– *unwind station*

40 il ponte elevatore per persone *f pl*
– *lift platform*

41 l'impianto di bobinatura
– *rewind station (rewinder, re-reeler, reeling machine, re-reeling machine)*

42 la taglierina a rulli *m pl*
– *roll cutter*

43 il quadro elettrico
– *control panel*

44 il coltello di taglio
– *cutter*

45 il nastro di carta
– *web*

46-51 la produzione della carta a mano
– *papermaking by hand*

46 il cartaio
– *vatman*

47 la tina
– *vat*

48 la forma a mano
– *mould* (Am. *mold*)

49 il pressatore
– *coucher (couchman)*

50 la pila pronta per essere pressata
– *post ready for pressing*

51 il feltro
– *felt*

1 la composizione a mano
- *hand-setting room (hand-composing room)*
2 il bancone del compositore
- *composing frame*
3 la cassa tipografica
- *case (typecase)*
4 la cassa per i corpi grossi
- *case cabinet (case rack)*
5 il compositore a mano (il compositore)
- *hand compositor (compositor, typesetter, maker-up)*
6 il manoscritto
- *manuscript (typescript)*
7 i caratteri
- *sorts (types, type characters, characters)*
8 la cassa per marginature *f pl* e bianco
- *rack (case) for furniture (spacing material)*
9 il bancone per la composizione in piedi *m pl*
- *standing type rack (standing matter rack)*
10 il piano scorrevole
- *storage shelf (shelf for storing formes, Am. forms)*
11 la composizione in piedi
- *standing type (standing matter)*
12 il vantaggio
- *galley*
13 il compositoio
- *composing stick (setting stick)*
14 l'interlinea alta (il cavarighe)
- *composing rule (setting rule)*
15 la composizione
- *type (type matter, matter)*
16 lo spago per le pagine composte
- *page cord*
17 il punteruolo
- *bodkin*
18 la pinzetta
- *tweezers*
19 la macchina compositrice «Linotype», una compositrice monolineare
- *Linotype line-composing (linecasting, slug-composing, slugcasting) machine, a multi-magazine machine*
20 lo scompositore
- *distributing mechanism (distributor)*
21 i magazzini delle matrici
- *type magazines with matrices (matrixes)*
22 la pinza per portare le matrici alla scomposizione
- *elevator carrier for distributing the matrices (matrixes)*
23 il raccoglitore
- *assembler*

24 il serraforme per la spaziatura
- *spacebands*
25 la fonditrice
- *casting mechanism*
26 l'alimentazione *f* del metallo
- *metal feeder*
27 la composizione a macchina
- *machine-set matter (cast lines, slugs)*
28 le matrici a mano
- *matrices (matrixes) for hand-setting (sorts)*
29 la matrice per «Linotype»
- *Linotype matrix*
30 la sbarra dentata di scomposizione *f*
- *teeth for the distributing mechanism (distributor)*
31 la matrice
- *face (type face, matrix)*
32-45 la macchina «Monotype», una macchina tipografica compofonditrice
- *monotype single-unit composing (typesetting) and casting machine (monotype single-unit composition caster)*
32 la «Monotype», tipo normale
- *monotype standard composing (typesetting) machine (keyboard)*
33 la torretta portanastro di carta
- *paper tower*
34 la striscia di nastro perforato
- *paper ribbon*
35 il cilindro
- *justifying scale*
36 l'indice *m* (l'indicatore *m*) delle unità
- *unit indicator*
37 la tastiera
- *keyboard*
38 il tubo flessibile dell'aria compressa
- *compressed-air hose*
39 la «Monotype» fonditrice
- *monotype casting machine (monotype caster)*
40 l'alimentatore *m* automatico del metallo
- *automatic metal feeder*
41 la molla di compressione *f* della pompa
- *pump compression spring (pump pressure spring)*
42 il telaio portamatrici
- *matrix case (die case)*
43 la torretta portacarta
- *paper tower*
44 il vantaggio con caratteri *m pl* (caratteri *m pl* mobili fusi)
- *galley with types (letters, characters, cast single types, cast single letters)*

45 il riscaldamento elettrico
- *electric heater (electric heating unit)*
46 il telaio portamatrici
- *matrix case (die case)*
47 le matrici
- *type matrices (matrixes) (letter matrices)*
48 l'attacco per innestare il telaio nella guida della slitta a croce *f*
- *guide block for engaging with the cross-slide guide*

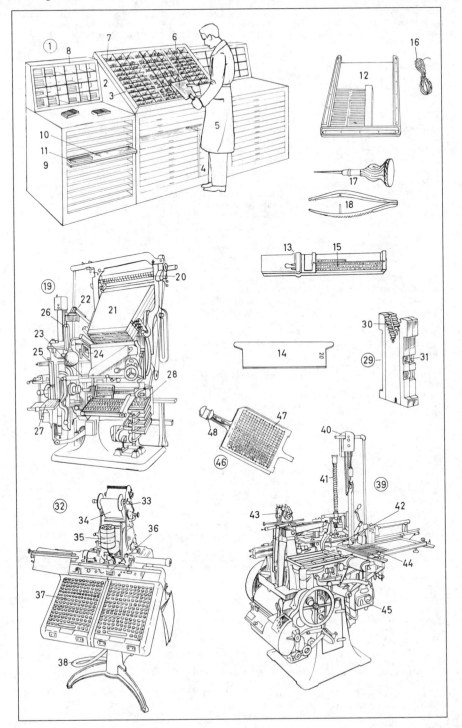

**1-17 la composizione**
- *composition (type matter, type)*
1 l'iniziale *f*
- *initial (initial letter)*
2 il carattere nero
- *bold type (bold, boldfaced type, heavy type, boldface)*
3 il carattere neretto (il grassetto)
- *semibold type (semibold)*
4 la linea
- *line*
5 l'interlinea
- *space*
6 la legatura (il logotipo)
- *ligature (double letter)*
7 il carattere corsivo (il corsivo)
- *italic type (italics)*
8 il carattere magro
- *light face type (light face)*
9 il carattere nerissimo
- *extra bold type (extra bold)*
10 il carattere nero stretto
- *bold condensed type (bold condensed)*
11 la maiuscola (la lettera maiuscola, il carattere maiuscolo)
- *majuscule (capital letter, capital, upper case letter)*
12 la minuscola (la lettera minuscola, il carattere minuscolo)
- *minuscule (small letter, lower case letter)*
13 la spazieggiatura
- *letter spacing (interspacing)*
14 i maiuscoletti
- *small capitals*
15 la nuova riga (il paragrafo)
- *break*
16 il capoverso
- *indention*
17 la spaziatura
- *space*
18 **corpo dei caratteri** (un punto tipografico = 0,376 mm; *ant.*)
- *type sizes [one typographic point = 0.376 mm (Didot system), 0.351 mm (Pica system). The German size-names refer to exact multiples of the Didot (Continental) system. The English names are now obsolete: current English type-sizes are exact multiples of the Pica]*
19 corpo due (due punti *m pl*)
- *six-to-pica (2 points)*
20 corpo tre (tre punti *m pl*)
- *half nonpareil (four-to-pica) (3 points)*
21 corpo quattro (diamante *m*) (quattro punti *m pl*)
- *brilliant (4 points); sim.: diamond (4 ¹/₂ points)*
22 corpo cinque (cinque punti *m pl*)
- *pearl (5 points); sim.: ruby (Am. agate) (5 ¹/₂ points)*
23 corpo sei (sei punti *m pl*)
- *nonpareil (6 points); sim.: minionette (6 ¹/₂ points)*
24 corpo sette (sette punti *m pl*)
- *minion (7 points)*

25 corpo otto (otto punti *m pl*)
- *brevier (8 points)*
26 corpo nove (nove punti *m pl*)
- *bourgeois (9 points)*
27 corpo dieci (dieci punti *m pl*)
- *long primer (10 points)*
28 corpo dodici (dodici punti *m pl*)
- *pica (12 points)*
29 corpo quattordici (quattordici punti *m pl*)
- *English (14 points)*
30 corpo sedici (sedici punti *m pl*)
- *great primer (two-line brevier, Am. Columbian) (16 points)*
31 corpo venti (venti punti *m pl*)
- *paragon (two-line primer) (20 points)*
**32-37 la fabbricazione dei caratteri**
- *typefounding (type casting)*
32 l'incisore *m*
- *punch cutter*
33 il bulino
- *graver (burin, cutter)*
34 la lente d'ingrandimento
- *magnifying glass (magnifier)*
35 il punzone
- *punch blank (die blank)*
36 il punzone finito (il controstampo)
- *finished steel punch (finished steel die)*
37 la matrice incisa
- *punched matrix (stamped matrix, strike, drive)*
38 il carattere
- *type (type character, character)*
39 il terminale
- *head*
40 il rilievo interno
- *shoulder*
41 l'occhio del carattere
- *counter*
42 l'asta
- *face (type face)*
43 la spalla inferiore (l'allineamento del carattere)
- *type line (bodyline)*
44 l'altezza totale
- *height to paper (type height)*
45 l'altezza base *f* spalla
- *height of shank (height of shoulder)*
46 il corpo del carattere
- *body size (type size, point size)*
47 la tacca
- *nick*
48 il piede
- *set (width)*
49 **la fresatrice per l'incisione** *f* **a pantografo,** un trapano speciale
- *matrix-boring machine (matrix-engraving machine), a special-purpose boring machine*
50 lo stativo
- *stand*
51 la fresa
- *cutter (cutting head)*
52 il piano di fresatura
- *cutting table*

53 il supporto del pantografo
- *pantograph carriage*
54 la guida del prisma
- *V-way*
55 la matrice
- *pattern*
56 il piano della matrice
- *pattern table*
57 la punta di copiatura
- *follower*
58 il pantografo
- *pantograph*
59 il dispositivo di fissaggio
- *matrix clamp*
60 il mandrino portafresa
- *cutter spindle*
61 il motore di azionamento
- *drive motor*

Meyer, **Joseph,** Verlagsbuchhändler, Schriftstel- ler und Industrieller, *9. 5. 1796 Gotha, †27. 6. 1856 Hildburghausen, erwies sich nach mißglückten Börsen- (1816-20 in London) und industriellen Unterneh- mungen (1820-23 in Thüringen) als origineller Shake- speare- und Scott-Übersetzer und fand mit seinem „Korrespondenzblatt für Kaufleute" 1825 Anklang. 1826 gründete er den Verlag *„Bibliographisches In- stitut"* in Gotha (1828 nach Hildburghausen verlegt), den er durch die Vielseitigkeit seiner eigenen Werke (**„Universum", „Das Große Konversations- lexikon für die gebildeten Stände", „Meyers Universal-Atlas"** 1830-37) sowie durch die Wohlfeil- heit und die gediegene Ausstattung seiner volkstüm- lichen Verlagswerke („Klassikerausgaben", „Meyers Familien- und Groschenbibliothek", „Volksbibliothek für Naturkunde", „Geschichtsbibliothek", „Meyers Pfennig-Atlas" u. a.) sowie durch die Entwicklung neuer Absatzwege (lieferungsweises Erscheinen auf Subskription und Vertrieb durch Reisebuch- handel) zum Welthaus machte. Besonders durch das **„Universum",** ein historisch-geographisches Bilderwerk, das in 80000 AUFLAGE und in 12 SPRACHEN erschien, wirkte er auf breiteste Kreise. — Seit Ende der 1830er Jahre trat er unter großen Opfern für ein einheitliches deutsches Eisen- bahnnetz ein, doch scheiterten seine Pläne und seine

19

20

21   N n

22   N n

23   N n

24   N n

25   N n

26   N n

27   N n

28   N n

29   N n

30   N n

31   N n

# 176 Composizione III (fotocomposizione)

1-21 **i subsistemi multipli** per la fotocomposizione
– *phototypesetting configurations*
1 il subsistema off-line
– *off-line configuration*
2 u. 3 i terminali di composizione *f*
– *data capture*
2 la tastiera chilometrica
– *terminal for keying unformatted text*
3 la tastiera di composizione *f* e correzione *f*
– *text capture and correction terminal*
4 lo schermo di impostazione *f*
– *layout terminal (page-layout terminal)*
5 il supporto dati *m pl*, un dischetto
– *data carrier, a diskette (floppy disk)*
6 l'unità di esposizione *f*
– *(photo)typesetting unit (phototypesetter)*
7 il subsistema on-line
– *on-line configuration*
8 il terminale d'impaginazione *f*
– *make-up terminal (page make-up terminal)*
9 il calcolatore centrale (il calcolatore di composizione *f*, il computer di composizione *f* )
– *central processing unit (typesetting computer)*
10 l'unità centrale di magnetizzazione *f*
– *magnetic tape unit (magnetic tape drive)*
11 la pila di dischi *m pl* magnetici
– *disk store*
12 la stampante (printer), una stampante laser (laserprinter)
– *printer, a laser printer*
13 l'impianto di esposizione *f*
– *phototypesetting machine (phototypesetter)*
14 la composizione testi *m pl* (il visualizzatore di composizione *f* testi *m pl*)
– *text capture (text-capture terminal)*
15 il compositore (il compositore dei testi o tipografo)
– *typesetter (keyboarder or typographer)*
16 lo schermo (il monitor)
– *screen (monitor)*
17 il caricamento dei dischetti (il caricamento)
– *floppy disk drive*
18 l'unità di calcolo e di memoria con l'unità centrale e disco rigido (memoria a disco rigido)
– *computer and memory unit with central processing unit and hard disk*
19 il mouse, un apparecchio per l'immissione *f* dati *m pl*
– *mouse, an input device*

20 la tavoletta del mouse
– *mouse mat*
21 la tastiera, un apparecchio per l'immissione *f* dati *m pl*
– *keyboard, an input device*
22 **l'impianto di fotocomposizione *f* compatto**
– *direct-entry phototypesetter*
23-33 **il desktop publishing (DTP)**
– *desktop publishing (DTP)*
23 il dischetto con programmi del testo, del layout e di grafica
– *diskette (floppy disk) with text, layout, and graphics programs*
24 lo scanner, un analizzatore
– *scanner (flat-bed scanner)*
25 il personal computer (PC) o la workstation
– *personal computer (PC) or workstation*
26 il terminale (il terminale del computer)
– *printout (computer printout)*
27 il raster image processor (RIP)
– *raster image processor (RIP)*
28 l'esposimetro laser
– *laser phototypesetter*
29 la bozza (la bozza di stampa)
– *proof*
30 lo schermo grafico a alta risoluzione *f*, uno schermo gigante a colori *m pl*
– *high-resolution graphics screen, a large-format colour monitor*
31 l'immagine *f* visualizzata
– *display window*
32 i parametri tipografici
– *typographic parameters*
33 il visualizzatore per correzioni *f pl* e acquisizioni *f pl*
– *(typographic) command window*
34 l'apparecchio automatico duplicazione *f* film
– *film copier*
35-46 **l'esposimetro a raggi *m pl* catodici**
– *cathode ray tube (CRT) typesetter*
35 il sistema di esplorazione *f*
– *scanning system*
36 i tubi a raggi *m pl* catodici o sorgente *f* luminosa
– *scan-generating (scanning) cathode ray tube (CRT)*
37 la lente
– *lens*
38 la matrice a telaio
– *character grid (matrix case)*
39 la lente condensatrice
– *condenser lens*
40 il fotomoltiplicatore
– *photomultiplier*
41 il sistema di riproduzione *f*
– *output system*
42 il videoamplificatore
– *video amplifier*

43 i tubi scriventi
– *character-generating tube (CRT character generator)*
44 il piano di esposizione *f*
– *exposure plane*
45 la matrice a telaio
– *matrix case*
46 l'innesto
– *guide claw*

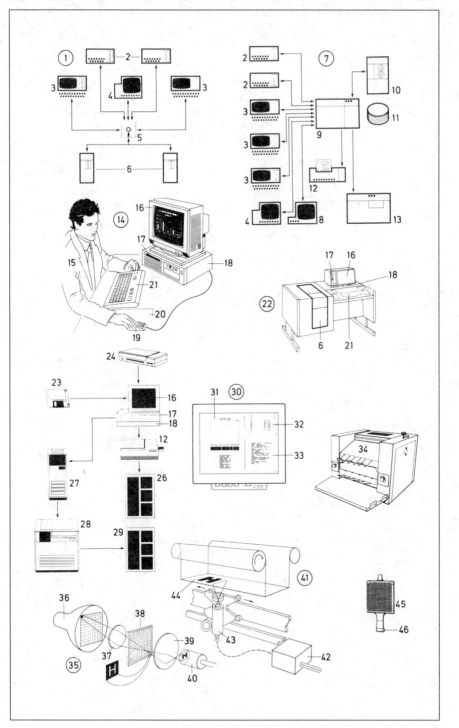

1 la macchina per riproduzioni *f pl* a ponte *m*
– *overhead process camera (overhead copying camera)*
2 la lastra smerigliata (il vetro smerigliato)
– *focusing screen (ground glass screen)*
3 il telaio girevole del vetro smerigliato
– *hinged screen holder*
4 il sistema di coordinate *f pl* (gli assi cartesiani)
– *graticule*
5 la pulsantiera di comando
– *control console*
6 il quadro a leggio pensile
– *hinged bracket-mounted control panel*
7 le scale percentuali
– *percentage focusing charts*
8 il contenitore a vuoto della lastra
– *vacuum film holder*
9 il magazzino dei retini
– *screen magazine*
10 il soffietto
– *bellows*
11 lo stativo
– *standard*
12 il regolatore
– *register device*
13 lo stativo del ponte
– *overhead gantry*
14 il portaoriginali
– *copyboard*
15 il montante portaoriginali
– *copyholder*
16 il braccio mobile delle lampade
– *lamp bracket*
17 la lampada a xeno
– *xenon lamp*
18 l'originale *m*
– *copy (original)*
19 il tavolo di montaggio e ritocco
– *retouching and stripping desk*
20 il piano luminoso
– *illuminated screen*
21 il dispositivo di regolazione *f* dell'inclinazione *f*
– *height and angle adjustment*
22 il portaoriginali
– *copyboard*
23 il contafili pieghevole, una lente (una lente d'ingrandimento)
– *linen tester, a magnifying glass*
24 la macchina universale per riproduzioni *f pl*
– *universal process and reproduction camera*
25 il contenitore dell'apparecchio fotografico
– *camera body*
26 il soffietto
– *bellows*

27 il gruppo ottico
– *lens carrier*
28 lo specchio angolare
– *angled mirror*
29 il sostegno a T
– *stand*
30 il portaoriginali
– *copyboard*
31 la lampada alogena
– *halogen lamp*
32 l'apparecchio verticale, un apparecchio fotografico compatto
– *vertical process camera, a compact camera*
33 il contenitore dell'apparecchio fotografico
– *camera body*
34 il vetro smerigliato
– *focusing screen (ground glass screen)*
35 il coperchio a vuoto
– *vacuum back*
36 il quadro di comando
– *control panel*
37 la lampada di preilluminazione *f*
– *flash lamp*
38 gli specchi per riprese *f pl* laterali
– *mirror for right-reading images*
39 lo scanner (l'apparecchio per la correzione dei colori)
– *scanner (colour,* Am. *color, correction unit)*
40 il telaio inferiore
– *base frame*
41 lo spazio per le lampade
– *lamp compartment*
42 l'alloggiamento della lampada a xeno
– *xenon lamp housing*
43 i motori di avanzamento
– *feed motors*
44 il braccio per diapositive *f pl*
– *transparency arm*
45 il rullo esploratore
– *scanning drum*
46 la testina esploratrice
– *scanning head*
47 la testina esploratrice a maschera
– *mask-scanning head*
48 il rullo a maschera
– *mask drum*
49 lo scrivente
– *recording space*
50 il cassetto
– *daylight cassette*
51 il cassetto per caricare e scaricare la pellicola con filtro correttivo variabile
– *colour (*Am. *color) computer with control unit and selective colour correction*
52 l'impianto per i clichés
– *engraving machine*
53 il mascheramento delle cuciture
– *seamless engraving adjustment*

54 la presa motore *m*
– *drive clutch*
55 la flangia di accoppiamento
– *clutch flange*
56 la colonna di comando
– *drive unit*
57 il bancale della macchina
– *machine bed*
58 il portatrezzi
– *equipment carrier*
59 il carrello
– *bed slide*
60 il quadro di comando
– *control panel*
61 il supporto del cuscinetto
– *bearing block*
62 la contropunta
– *tailstock*
63 il pulsante di esplorazione *f*
– *scanning head*
64 il rullo portaoriginali
– *copy cylinder*
65 il supporto mediano
– *centre (*Am. *center) bearing*
66 il sistema d'incisione *f*
– *engraving system*
67 il cilindro di stampa
– *printing cylinder*
68 il braccio del cilindro
– *cylinder arm*
69 l'armadio di montaggio
– *electronics (electronic) cabinet*
70 i calcolatori
– *computers*
71 l'inserimento dei programmi
– *program input*
72 la macchina automatica per lo sviluppo delle pellicole scanner
– *automatic film processor for scanner films*

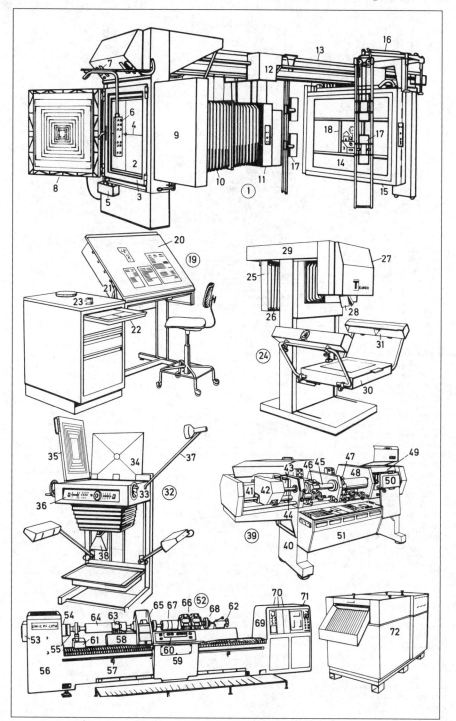

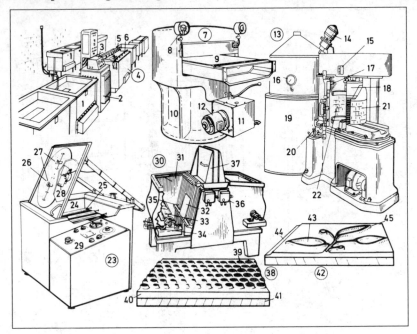

**1-6 il procedimento galvanoplastico**
- *electrotyping plant*
1 la vasca di lavaggio
- *cleaning tank*
2 il raddrizzatore
- *rectifier*
3 l'impianto di misurazione *f* e regolazione *f*
- *measuring and control unit*
4 la vasca per galvanostegia
- *electroplating tank (electroplating bath, electroplating vat)*
5 gli anodi di rame *m*
- *anode rod (with copper anodes)*
6 il catodo (la matrice metallica)
- *plate rod (cathode)*
7 **la pressa idraulica per incidere le matrici**
- *hydraulic moulding* (Am. *molding*) *press*
8 il manometro
- *pressure gauge* (Am. *gage*) *(manometer)*
9 il piano d'incisione *f*
- *apron*
10 il piede del cilindro
- *round base*
11 la pompa idraulica di pressione *f*
- *hydraulic pressure pump*
12 il motore di azionamento
- *drive motor*
13 **la fonditrice (per lastre *f pl* stereotipiche semicilindriche)**
- *curved plate casting machine* (*curved electrotype casting machine*)
14 il motore
- *motor*
15 i pulsanti di comando
- *control knobs*

16 il pirometro
- *pyrometer*
17 la bocca di fusione *f*
- *mouth piece*
18 l'anima di fusione *f*
- *core*
19 il forno fusorio
- *melting furnace*
20 l'interruttore
- *starting lever*
21 la lastra stereotipica fusa per la stampa rotativa
- *cast curved plate (cast curved electrotype) for rotary printing*
22 la conchiglia di colata
- *fixed mould* (Am. *mold*)
23 **la macchina per incidere i clichés**
- *etching machine*
24 la vasca d'incisione *f* con liquido per incisione *f* e la protezione sui fianchi
- *etching tank with etching solution (etchant, mordant) and filming agent (film former)*
25 i cilindri a pale *f pl*
- *paddles*
26 il piatto rotante
- *turntable*
27 il supporto delle lastre
- *plate clamp*
28 il motore di azionamento
- *drive motor*
29 la consolle di comando
- *control unit*
30 **la macchina binata per incidere i clichés**
- *twin etching machine*
31 la vasca d'incisione *f* (in sezione *f*)
- *etching tank (etching bath) [in section]*

32 la lastra d'zinco copiata
- *photoprinted zinc plate*
33 la ruota a pale *f pl*
- *paddle*
34 il rubinetto di scarico
- *outlet cock (drain cock, Am. faucet)*
35 il supporto della lastra
- *plate rack*
36 l'interruttore *m*
- *control switches*
37 il coperchio della vasca
- *lid*
38 **l'autotipia (la fotozincotipia),** un cliché
- *halftone photoengraving (halftone block, halftone plate), a block (plate, printing plate)*
39 il retino a punti *m pl*, un elemento di stampa
- *dot (halftone dot), a printing element*
40 la lastra di zinco incisa
- *etched zinc plate*
41 il piede del cliché (lo zoccolo in legno del cliché)
- *block mount (block mounting, plate mount, plate mounting)*
42 **l'incisione *f* a tratto**
- *line block (line engraving, line etching, line plate, line cut)*
43 le parti da non stampare incise profondamente
- *non-printing, deep-etched areas*
44 il supporto del cliché
- *flange (bevel edge)*
45 il lato inciso (il lato)
- *sidewall*

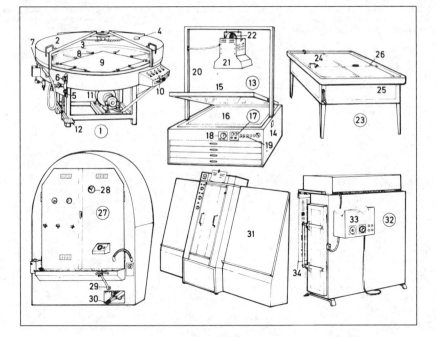

1 la centrifuga per sensibilizzare le lastre offset (la tournette)
– *plate whirler (whirler, plate-coating machine) for coating offset plates*
2 il coperchio scorrevole
– *sliding lid*
3 l'impianto di riscaldamento elettrico
– *electric heater*
4 il termometro rotondo
– *temperature gauge* (Am. *gage)*
5 il bocchettone per l'acqua
– *water connection for the spray unit*
6 l'impianto per il lavaggio del circuito
– *spray unit*
7 la doccia a mano
– *hand spray*
8 le barre portalastre
– *plate clamps*
9 la lastra di zinco (*anche:* lastra di magnesio o di rame *m*)
– *zinc plate (*also: *magnesium plate, copper plate)*
10 la consolle di comando
– *control panel*
11 il motore di azionamento
– *drive motor*
12 la leva del freno a pedale *m*
– *brake pedal*
13 il telaio pneumatico per riproduzione *f*
– *vacuum printing frame (vacuum frame, printing-down frame)*
14 il basamento del telaio pneumatico
– *base of the vacuum printing frame (vacuum frame, printing-down frame)*
15 la parte superiore del telaio con la lastra di vetro a specchio
– *plate glass frame*

16 la lastra offset sensibilizzata
– *coated offset plate*
17 il quadro di comando
– *control panel*
18 il regolatore dell'esposizione *f* (l'apparecchio per la regolazione del tempo di posa)
– *exposure timer*
19 gli interruttori *m* per la produzione del vuoto (la pompa a vuoto)
– *vacuum pump switches*
20 i bracci di sostegno
– *support*
21 la lampada a luce *f* puntiforme per le copie, una lampada alogena
– *point light exposure lamp, a quartz-halogen lamp*
22 il ventilatore della lampada
– *fan blower*
23 il tavolo per il montaggio della pellicola
– *stripping table (make-up table) for stripping films*
24 la lastra di cristallo
– *crystal glass screen*
25 la cassa per l'illuminazione *f*
– *light box*
26 la sagoma
– *straightedge rules*
27 l'idroestrattore *m* verticale
– *vertical plate-drying cabinet*
28 l'igrometro
– *hygrometer*
29 il regolatore della velocità
– *speed control*
30 la leva del freno a pedale *m*
– *brake pedal*

31 la macchina di sviluppo per lastre *f pl* sensibilizzate
– *processing machine for presensitized plates*
32 il forno, un forno per lastre *f pl* di diazonio
– *burning-in oven for glue-enamel plates (diazo plates)*
33 il quadro di comando
– *control box (control unit)*
34 la lastra di diazonio
– *diazo plate*

1 la macchina offset a quattro colori *m pl*
– *four-colour* (Am. *four-color) rotary off-set press (rotary offset machine, web-offset press)*
2 il rotolo di carta non stampata
– *roll of unprinted paper (blank paper)*
3 il supporto stellare dei rotoli (il supporto per il rotolo di carta non stampata)
– *reel stand (carrier for the roll of unprinted paper)*
4 i cilindri trasportatori
– *forwarding rolls*
5 il dispositivo di conversione *f* (il tamburo voltafogli)
– *side margin control (margin control, side control, side lay control)*
6-13 i calamai
– *inking units (inker units)*
6 *u.* 7 il doppio rullo stampante giallo
– *perfecting unit (double unit) for yellow*
6, 8, 10, 12 i calamai nel rullo dosatore (nel rullo stampante superiore)
– *inking units (inker units) in the upper printing unit*
7, 9, 11, 13 i calamai nel rullo pescatore (nel rullo stampante inferiore)
– *inking units (inker units) in the lower printing unit*
8 *u.* 9 il doppio rullo stampante ciano
– *perfecting unit (double unit) for cyan*
10 *u.* 11 il doppio rullo stampante magenta
– *perfecting unit (double unit) for magenta*
12 *u.* 13 il doppio rullo stampante nero
– *perfecting unit (double unit) for black*
14 l'impianto di essicazione *f*
– *drier*
15 l'impianto di piegatura
– *folder (folder unit)*
16 il quadro di comando
– *control desk*
17 il foglio di stampa
– *sheet*
18 la macchina cilindrica offset a quattro colori *m pl* (schema *m*)
– *four-colour* (Am. *four-color) rotary off-set press (rotary offset machine, web-offset press) [diagram]*
19 il supporto stellare dei rotoli
– *reel stand*
20 il dispositivo di conversione *f* (il tamburo voltafogli)
– *side margin control (margin control, side control, side lay control)*
21 i rulli inchiostratori
– *inking rollers (ink rollers, inkers)*
22 il calamaio
– *ink duct (ink fountain)*
23 i rulli bagnatori
– *damping rollers (dampening rollers, dampers, dampeners)*
24 il cilindro caucciù *m*
– *blanket cylinder*
25 il cilindro portalastra
– *plate cylinder*
26 il percorso della carta
– *route of the paper (of the web)*
27 l'impianto di essicazione *f*
– *drier*
28 i cilindri raffreddatori
– *chilling rolls (cooling rollers, chill rollers)*
29 l'impianto di piegatura
– *folder (folder unit)*

30 la macchina offset a quattro colori *m pl* (schema *m*)
– *four-colour* (Am. *four-color) sheet-fed offset machine (offset press) [diagram]*
31 il mettifoglio
– *sheet feeder (feeder)*
32 il piano automatico di puntatura
– *feed table (feed board)*
33 il percorso del foglio verso il tamburo di accumulo attraverso la pinza
– *route of the sheets through swing-grippers to the feed drum*
34 il tamburo di accumulo
– *feed drum*
35 il cilindro di stampa
– *impression cylinder*
36 i tamburi di trasferimento
– *transfer drums (transfer cylinders)*
37 il cilindro caucciù *m*
– *blanket cylinder*
38 il cilindro portalastra
– *plate cylinder*
39 il cilindro bagnatore
– *damping unit (dampening unit)*
40 il calamaio
– *inking unit (inker unit)*
41 il gruppo stampante
– *printing unit*
42 il tamburo di trasferimento
– *delivery cylinder*
43 il sollevatore a catene *f pl* continue
– *chain delivery*
44 la pila di uscita (il levafoglio)
– *delivery pile*
45 la catena di trasferimento
– *delivery unit (delivery mechanism)*
46 la macchina offset monocolore
– *single-colour* (Am. *single-color) offset press (offset machine)*
47 la pila di fogli *m pl* (la carta da stampare)
– *pile of paper (sheets, printing paper)*
48 il mettifoglio automatico
– *sheet feeder (feeder), an automatic pile feeder*
49 il piano automatico di puntatura
– *feed table (feed board)*
50 i rulli inchiostratori
– *inking rollers (ink rollers, inkers)*
51 il calamaio
– *inking unit (inker unit)*
52 i rulli bagnatori
– *damping rollers (dampening rollers, dampers, dampeners)*
53 il cilindro portalastra, una lastra di zinco
– *plate cylinder, a zinc plate*
54 il cilindro caucciù *m*, un cilindro di acciaio rivestito in caucciù *m*
– *blanket cylinder, a steel cylinder with rubber blanket*
55 il tamburo di trasferimento dei fogli stampati
– *pile delivery unit for the printed sheets*
56 le pinze montate su catene *f pl*
– *gripper bar, a chain gripper*
57 la pila di carta stampata
– *pile of printed paper (printed sheets)*
58 la lamiera di protezione *f* per la trasmissione a cinghia trapezoidale
– *guard for the V-belt (vee-belt) drive*
59 la macchina offset monocolore (schema *m*)
– *single-colour* (Am. *single-color) offset press (offset machine) [diagram]*

60 il calamaio con i rulli inchiostratori
– *inking unit (inker unit) with inking rollers (ink rollers, inkers)*
61 il bagnatore con i rulli bagnatori
– *damping unit (dampening unit) with damping rollers (dampening rollers, dampers, dampeners)*
62 il cilindro portalastra
– *plate cylinder*
63 il cilindro caucciù *m*
– *blanket cylinder*
64 il cilindro stampa
– *impression cylinder*
65 il tamburo di trasferimento con sistema di pinze *f pl*
– *delivery cylinders with grippers*
66 la puleggia di trasmissione *f*
– *drive wheel*
67 la tavola di alimentazione *f* (la tavola d'immissione *f*)
– *feed table (feed board)*
68 il mettifoglio
– *sheet feeder (feeder)*
69 la pila di carta non stampata
– *pile of unprinted paper (blank paper, unprinted sheets, blank sheets)*
70 la macchina da stampa offset Rotaprint (macchina offset di piccolo formato)
– *small sheet-fed offset press*
71 il calamaio
– *inking unit (inker unit)*
72 il mettifoglio a aspirazione *f*
– *suction feeder*
73 la pila dei fogli
– *pile feeder*
74 la consolle di comando con contafogli *m*, manometro, regolatore *m* dell'aria e interruttore *m* per l'avanzamento della carta
– *instrument panel (control panel) with counter, pressure gauge* (Am. *gage), air regulator, and control switch for the sheet feeder (feeder)*
75 il torchio offset semiautomatico
– *flat-bed offset press (offset machine) ('Mailänder' proofing press, proof press)*
76 il calamaio
– *inking unit (inker unit)*
77 i rulli inchiostratori
– *inking rollers (ink rollers, inkers)*
78 il piano portalastra
– *bed (press bed, type bed, forme bed, Am. form bed)*
79 il cilindro con rivestimento in tessuto gommato
– *cylinder with rubber blanket*
80 la leva per aumentare e diminuire la pressione di stampa
– *starting and stopping lever for the printing unit*
81 la manovella regolatrice della pressione
– *impression-setting wheel (impression-adjusting wheel)*

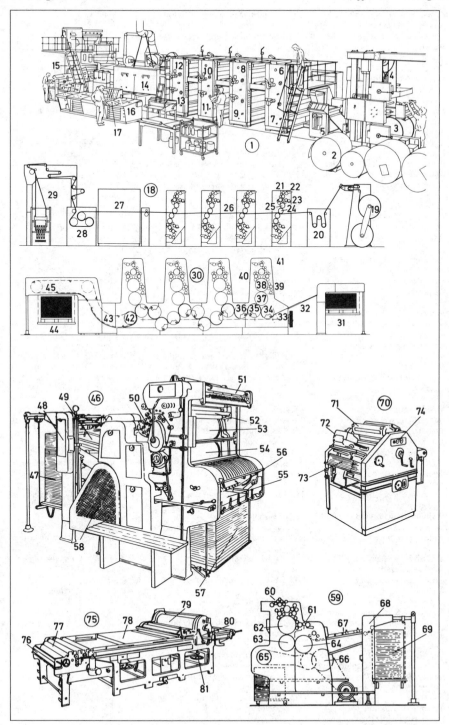

**1-65 macchine** *f pl* **tipografiche**
– *presses (machines) for letterpress printing (letterpress printing machines)*
**1 la macchina da stampa veloce a due giri** *m pl*
– *two-revolution flat-bed cylinder press*
**2** il cilindro di stampa
– *impression cylinder*
**3** la leva sollevamento e abbassamento cilindro
– *lever for raising or lowering the cylinder*
**4** il piano automatico di puntatura
– *feed table (feed board)*
**5** il mettifoglio automatico (azionato con aria aspirante e soffiante)
– *automatic sheet feeder (feeder) [operated by vacuum and air blasts]*
**6** la pompa a aria per mettifoglio e levafoglio
– *air pump for the feeder and delivery*
**7** il gruppo di macinazione *f* e di inchiostrazione *f*
– *inking unit (inker unit) with distributing rollers (distributor rollers, distributors) and forme rollers (Am. form rollers)*
**8** il gruppo inchiostratore
– *ink slab (ink plate) inking unit (inker unit)*
**9** la pila carta uscita foglio, per carta stampata
– *delivery pile for printed paper*
**10** lo spruzzatore a polvere *f*
– *sprayer (anti set-off apparatus, anti set-off spray) for dusting the printed sheets*
**11** l'impianto di trasferimento foglio
– *interleaving device*
**12** il pedale di avvio e di arresto stampa
– *foot pedal for starting and stopping the press*
**13 la platina (una pressa a mano** *f* **)** (sezione *f* )
– *platen press (platen machine, platen) [in section]*
**14** il metti- e levafoglio
– *paper feed and delivery (paper feeding and delivery unit)*
**15** la platina
– *platen*
**16** il comando a leva ginocchiera
– *toggle action (toggle-joint action)*
**17** il piano portaforma
– *bed (type bed, press bed, forme bed, Am. form bed)*
**18** i rulli inchiostratori a colori *m pl*
– *forme rollers (Am. form rollers) (forme-inking, Am. form-inking, rollers)*
**19** il cilindro macinatore (per macinare l'inchiostro da stampa)
– *inking unit (inker unit) for distributing the ink (printing ink)*

**20 la macchina da stampa a arresto del cilindro**
– *stop-cylinder press (stop-cylinder machine)*
**21** la tavola di puntatura
– *feed table (feed board)*
**22** il mettifoglio
– *feeder mechanism (feeding apparatus, feeder)*
**23** la pila di carta non stampata
– *pile of unprinted paper (blank paper, unprinted sheets, blank sheets)*
**24** la griglia di protezione *f*
– *guard for the sheet feeder (feeder)*
**25** la pila di carta stampata
– *pile of printed paper (printed sheets)*
**26** il quadro di comando
– *control mechanism*
**27** il gruppo inchiostratore
– *forme rollers (Am. form rollers) (forme-inking, Am. form-inking, rollers)*
**28** il cilindro di stampa
– *inking unit (inker unit)*
**29 la platina, una pressa a mano** (Heidelberg)
– *[Heidelberg] platen press (platen machine, platen)*
**30** il mettifoglio con la pila di carta non stampata
– *feed table (feed board) with pile of unprinted paper (blank paper, unprinted sheets, blank sheets)*
**31** il piano portaforma
– *delivery table*
**32** la leva di avvio e di arresto
– *starting and stopping lever*
**33** l'aspiratore *m*
– *delivery blower*
**34** la pistola a spruzzo
– *spray gun (sprayer)*
**35** la pompa a aria per aspirare e soffiare
– *air pump for vacuum and air blasts*
**36 la fustellatura**
– *locked-up forme (Am. form)*
**37** la forma (la composizione)
– *type (type matter, matter)*
**38** il telaio serraforma
– *chase*
**39** il dispositivo di chiusura forma
– *quoin*
**40** la marginatura
– *length of furniture*
**41 la macchina rotativa a alta pressione** *f* **per giornali** *m pl* **fino a 16 pagine** *f pl*
– *rotary letterpress press (rotary letterpress machine, web-fed letterpress machine) for newspapers of up to 16 pages*
**42** i coltelli tagliatori per il taglio longitudinale della bobina
– *slitters for dividing the width of the web*

**43** la bobina
– *web*
**44** il cilindro di pressione *f*
– *impression cylinder*
**45** il rullo pivottante
– *jockey roller (compensating roller, compensator, tension roller)*
**46** il rotolo di carta
– *roll of paper*
**47** l'arresto automatico del rotolo di carta
– *automatic brake*
**48** la stampa in bianca
– *first printing unit*
**49** la stampa in volta
– *perfecting unit*
**50** il rullo inchiostratore
– *inking unit (inker unit)*
**51** il cilindro di forma
– *plate cylinder*
**52** la stampa a colori *m pl*
– *second printing unit*
**53** il cono di piega
– *former*
**54** il tachimetro con contafogli *m*
– *tachometer with sheet counter*
**55** la piegatrice
– *folder (folder unit)*
**56** il giornale piegato
– *folded newspaper*
**57 il gruppo inchiostratore** per rotativa (sezione *f* )
– *inking unit (inker unit) for the rotary press (web-fed press) [in section]*
**58** il nastro di carta
– *web*
**59** il cilindro di stampa
– *impression cylinder*
**60** il cilindro di pressione *f*
– *plate cylinder*
**61** i rulli inchiostratori a colori *m pl*
– *forme rollers (Am. form rollers) (forme-inking, Am. form-inking, rollers)*
**62** il cilindro di stampa con racla
– *distributing rollers (distributor rollers, distributors)*
**63** il cilindro di pressione *f*
– *lifter roller (ductor, ductor roller)*
**64** il cilindro iniettore
– *duct roller (fountain roller, ink fountain roller)*
**65** il calamaio
– *ink duct (ink fountain)*

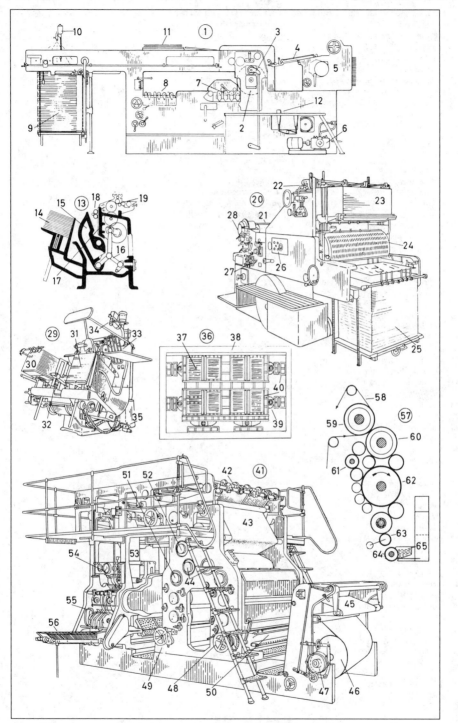

1 l'esposizione *f* alla luce della carta
al pigmento
– *exposure of the carbon tissue (pig-*
*ment paper)*
2 il telaio a vuoto
– *vacuum frame*
3 la lampada per l'esposizione *f*,
una lampada alogena in piano
– *exposing lamp, a bank of quartz-*
*halogen lamps*
4 la lampada a luce *f* puntiforme
– *point source lamp*
5 la cappa termica
– *heat extractor*
6 la macchina di avanzamento della
carta al pigmento
– *carbon tissue transfer machine*
*(laydown machine, laying*
*machine)*
7 il cilindro di rame *m*
– *polished copper cylinder*
8 il cilindro di pressione *f* in caucciù
*m* per forzare la carta al pigmento
negli alveoli
– *rubber roller for pressing on the*
*printed carbon tissue (pigment*
*paper)*
9 la macchina sensibilizzatrice
– *cylinder-processing machine*
10 il cilindro calcografico sensibiliz-
zato con carta al pigmento
– *gravure cylinder coated with car-*
*bon tissue (pigment paper)*
11 la vasca di sviluppo
– *developing tank*
12 la correzione del cilindro
– *staging*
13 il cilindro sviluppato
– *developed cylinder*
14 il ritoccatore
– *retoucher painting out (stopping*
*out)*
15 la macchina per incidere i clichés
– *etching machine*
16 la conca dell'acido
– *etching tank with etching solution*
*(etchant, mordant)*
17 il cilindro per calcografia inciso
– *printed gravure cylinder*
18 il calcografo
– *gravure etcher*
19 il disco calcolatore
– *calculator dial*
20 l'orologio di controllo
– *timer*
21 il correttore dell'incisione *f*
– *revising (correcting) the cylinder*
22 il cilindro calcografico trattato
con acido
– *etched gravure cylinder*
23 il lardone correttore
– *ledge*

24 la macchina calcografica per
stampa policroma
– *multicolour (Am. multicolor)*
*rotogravure press*
25 il tubo di scarico per i vapori del
solvente
– *exhaust pipe for solvent fumes*
26 la pinza raddrizzatrice
– *reversible printing unit*
27 la piegatrice
– *folder (folder unit)*
28 la consolle di comando
– *control desk*
29 l'impianto di composizione *f* del
giornale
– *newspaper delivery unit*
30 il nastro trasportatore
– *conveyor belt (conveyor)*
31 la pila dei giornali imballati
– *bundled stack of newspapers*

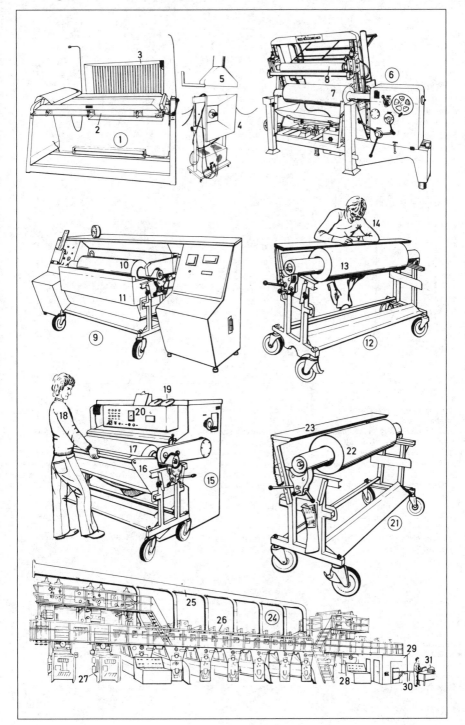

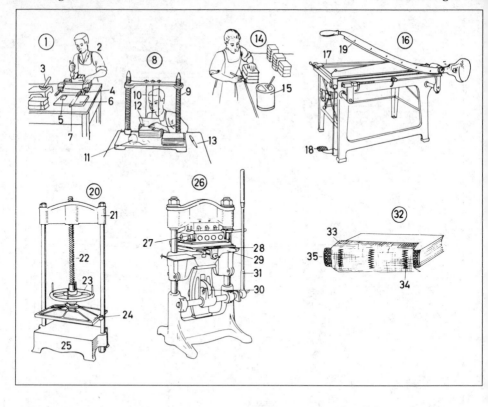

**1-35 la legatura (la rilegatura) a mano di un libro**
– *hand bookbindery (hand bindery)*
1 la doratura del dorso del libro
– *gilding the spine of the book*
2 il doratore, un rilegatore (un legatore)
– *gold finisher (gilder), a bookbinder*
3 il filetto
– *fillet*
4 lo strettoio
– *holding press (finishing press)*
5 l'oro in foglie *f pl*
– *gold leaf*
6 il cuscinetto da doratore *m* (il guancialino)
– *gold cushion*
7 il coltello da doratore *m*
– *gold knife*
8 la cucitura
– *sewing (stitching)*
9 il telaio per la cucitura
– *sewing frame*
10 il filo (per cucire)
– *sewing cord*
11 il gomitolo di filo
– *ball of thread (sewing thread)*
12 la posizione della cucitura
– *section (signature)*

13 il cutter (il coltello del legatore)
– *bookbinder's knife*
14 l'incollatura del dorso
– *gluing the spine*
15 il barattolo della colla
– *glue pot*
16 il tagliacartone (la cesoia per il cartone, la taglierina)
– *board cutter (guillotine)*
17 lo squadro
– *back gauge (Am. gage)*
18 il bloccafoglio a pedale *m*
– *clamp with foot pedal*
19 il coltello superiore
– *cutting blade*
20 il torchio
– *standing press, a nipping press*
21 la parte superiore
– *head piece (head beam)*
22 la vite
– *spindle*
23 il volantino
– *handwheel*
24 il piano di pressione *f*
– *platen*
25 la base
– *bed (base)*

26 la pressa per doratura e stampa in rilievo, una pressa (a leva) manuale – *sim.:* una pressa a ginocchiera
– *gilding (gold blocking) and embossing press, a hand-lever press;* sim.: *toggle-joint press (toggle-lever press)*
27 il riscaldatore
– *heating box*
28 la lastra supplettiva estraibile
– *sliding plate*
29 la platina per rilievi *m pl*
– *embossing platen*
30 il sistema a leva ginocchiera
– *toggle action (toggle-joint action)*
31 la leva a mano
– *hand lever*
32 il libro fissato sulla garza, il libro cucito
– *book sewn on gauze (mull, scrim) (book block)*
33 la garza
– *gauze (mull, scrim)*
34 la cucitura
– *sewing (stitching)*
35 il capitello
– *headband*

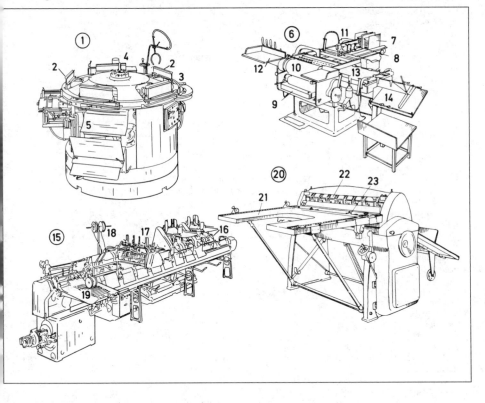

1-23 **macchine** *f pl* **per la legatoria**
– *bookbinding machines*
1 **la macchina incollatrice**
– *adhesive binder (perfect binder)*
  *for short runs*
2 l'alimentatore *m* manuale
– *manual feed station*
3 il settore di fresatura e irruvidi-
  mento
– *cutoff knife and roughing station*
4 il rullo spalmatore
– *gluing mechanism*
5 l'uscita del manufatto
– *delivery (book delivery)*
6 **la copertinatrice (la cartellatrice)**
– *case maker (case-making*
  *machine)*
7 i magazzini per le copertine di
  cartone *m*
– *board feed hoppers*
8 l'estrattore *m* dei cartoni
– *pick-up suckers*
9 l'incollatrice *f*
– *glue tank*
10 il rullo incollatore
– *cover cylinder*
11 la ventosa di aspirazione *f*
– *picker head*
12 il magazzino del materiale da
  rivestimento (lino, carta, pelle *f* )
– *feed table for covering materials*
  *[linen, paper, leather]*

13 la pressa
– *pressing mechanism*
14 l'uscita dei manufatti
– *delivery table*
15 **la macchina accavallatrice-**
  **cucitrice a punto metallico**
– *gang stitcher (gathering and wire-*
  *stitching machine, gatherer and*
  *wire stitcher)*
16 il mettifoglio
– *sheet feeder (sheet-feeding station)*
17 la piegatrice
– *folder-feeding station*
18 la testa della cucitrice a punti *m pl*
  metallici
– *stitching wire feed mechanism*
19 l'uscita del manufatto
– *delivery table*
20 **la cesoia circolare per legatoria**
  **(la taglierina)**
– *rotary board cutter (rotary board-*
  *cutting machine)*
21 il piano di appoggio del materiale
  con rientranza
– *feed table with cut-out section*
22 il coltello circolare
– *rotary cutter*
23 la sella di avanzamento
– *feed guide*

**1-35 le macchine per legatoria**
- *bookbinding machines*
1 la macchina tagliacarta (la taglie-rina)
- *guillotine (guillotine cutter, automatic guillotine cutter)*
2 il pannello di controllo
- *control panel*
3 il meccanismo di chiusura al vano del taglio
- *clamp*
4 il piano di caricamento
- *back gauge* (Am. *gage)*
5 l'indicatore *m* di pressione *f*
- *calibrated pressure adjustment [to clamp]*
6 il misuratore ottico
- *illuminated cutting scale*
7 la manopola di sollevamento della sella
- *single-hand control for the back gauge* (Am. *gage)*
8 la macchina combinata rifilatrice-aggraffatrice
- *combined buckle and knife folding machine (combined buckle and knife folder)*
9 il mettifoglio
- *feed table (feed board)*
10 la piegatrice
- *fold plates*
11 l'arresto dei fogli per la rifilatura dei bordi
- *stop for making the buckle fold*
12 il coltello per pieghe *f pl* incrociate
- *cross fold knives*
13 il nastro per piegature *f pl* parallele
- *belt delivery for parallel-folded signatures*
14 la terza piega
- *third cross fold unit*
15 il cassetto raccoglitore alla terza piega
- *delivery tray for cross-folded signatures*
16 la cucitrice a filo di refe *m*
- *sewing machine (book-sewing machine)*
17 il portabobine
- *spool holder*
18 la bobina
- *thread cop (thread spool)*
19 il supporto della bobina del refe
- *gauze roll holder (mull roll holder, scrim roll holder)*
20 il refe
- *gauze (mull, scrim)*
21 le teste di cucitura con aghi *m pl*
- *needle cylinders with sewing needles*
22 il libro cucito
- *sewn book*
23 la tavola di uscita
- *delivery*

24 la sella mobile
- *reciprocating saddle*
25 il mettifoglio
- *sheet feeder (feeder)*
26 il magazzino d'introduzione *f* fogli *m pl*
- *feed hopper*
27 la brossuratrice
- *casing-in machine*
28 l'incollatrice *f*
- *joint and side pasting attachment*
29 la racla
- *blade*
30 il preriscaldatore
- *preheater unit*
31 l'incollatrice *f* per incollatura completa di dorsi *m pl*, margini *m pl* e risguardi *m pl*
- *gluing machine for whole-surface, stencil, edge, and strip gluing*
32 la vasca della colla
- *glue tank*
33 il rullo incollatore
- *glue roller*
34 il tavolo di alimentazione *f*
- *feed table*
35 l'uscita
- *delivery*
**36 il libro**
- *book*
37 la sovraccoperta
- *dust jacket (dust cover, book jacket, wrapper), a publisher's wrapper*
38 il risvolto
- *jacket flap*
39 la scheda (la nota) bibliografica
- *blurb*
40-42 la copertina (la coperta)
- *binding*
40 la copertina del libro
- *cover (book cover, case)*
41 il dorso
- *spine (backbone, back)*
42 il capitello
- *tailband (footband)*
43-47 i preliminari
- *preliminary matter (prelims, front matter)*
43 il falso frontespizio
- *half-title*
44 l'occhiello
- *half-title (bastard title, fly title)*
45 il frontespizio
- *title page*
46 il titolo
- *full title (main title)*
47 il sottotitolo
- *subtitle*
48 la sigla della casa editrice
- *publisher's imprint (imprint)*
49 il risguardo
- *fly leaf (endpaper, endleaf )*
50 la dedica manoscritta
- *handwritten dedication*

51 l'ex-libris *m*
- *bookplate (ex libris)*
52 il libro aperto
- *open book*
53 la pagina
- *page*
54 la piega
- *fold*
55-58 il margine
- *margin*
55 il margine di cucitura
- *back margin (inside margin, gutter)*
56 il margine di testa
- *head margin (upper margin)*
57 il margine esterno
- *fore edge margin (outside margin, fore edge)*
58 il margine inferiore
- *tail margin (foot margin, tail, foot)*
59 la luce di composizione *f* (la stampa)
- *type area*
60 il titolo del capitolo
- *chapter heading*
61 l'asterisco
- *asterisk*
62 la nota a piè *m* di pagina, una nota
- *footnote, a note*
63 il numero della pagina
- *page number*
64 la composizione a due colonne *f pl*
- *double-column page*
65 la colonna
- *column*
66 il titolo della colonna
- *running title (running head)*
67 il titolo intermedio
- *caption*
68 la nota a margine *m*
- *marginal note (side note)*
69 la norma (la segnatura)
- *signature (signature code)*
70 il segnalibro fisso
- *attached bookmark (attached bookmarker)*
71 il segnalibro
- *loose bookmark (loose bookmarker)*

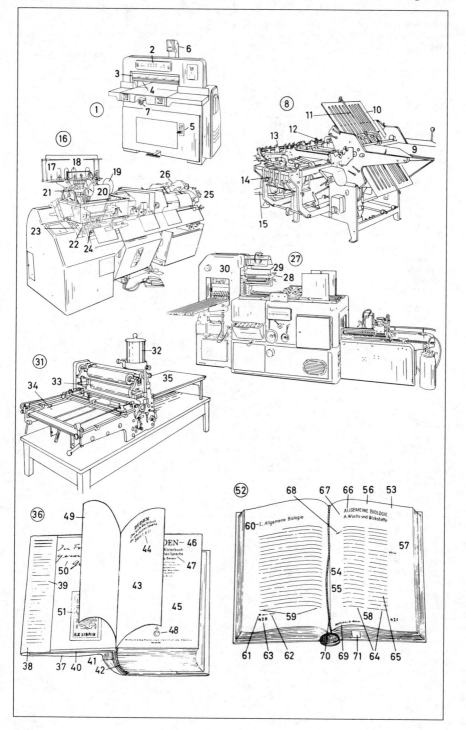

**1-54** carrozze *f pl* (veicoli *m pl*, carri *m pl*, vetture *f pl*)
– *carriages (horse-drawn vehicles)*
**1-3, 26-39, 45, 51-54** carrozze *f pl* a cavalli *m pl*
– *carriages and coaches (coach wagons)*
**1** la berlina
– *berlin*
**2** il break
– *wagonette; larger: brake (break)*
**3** il coupé
– *coupé; sim.: brougham*
**4** la ruota anteriore
– *front wheel*
**5** la cassa della carrozza
– *coach body*
**6** il parafango
– *dashboard (splashboard)*
**7** la pedana
– *footboard*
**8** la cassetta (il sedile del cocchiere)
– *coach box (box, coachman's seat, driver's seat)*
**9** il fanale (la lanterna)
– *lamp (lantern)*
**10** il finestrino
– *window*
**11** lo sportello
– *door (coach door)*
**12** la maniglia
– *door handle (handle)*
**13** il predellino
– *footboard (carriage step, coach step, step, footpiece)*
**14** il tetto fisso
– *fixed top*
**15** la molla
– *spring*
**16** il freno (il ceppo del freno)
– *brake (brake block)*
**17** la ruota posteriore
– *back wheel (rear wheel)*
**18** il dogkart, una carrozza a un cavallo
– *dogcart, a one-horse carriage*
**19** il timone
– *shafts (thills, poles)*
**20** il lacché (il servo, il servitore)
– *lackey (lacquey, footman)*
**21** la livrea (l'uniforme *f*, la divisa del lacché)
– *livery*
**22** il colletto gallonato
– *braided (gallooned) collar*
**23** la giacca gallonata
– *braided (gallooned) coat*
**24** la manica gallonata
– *braided (gallooned) sleeve*
**25** il cappello a cilindro (il cilindro)
– *top hat*
**26** il fiacre (la vettura da piazza a cavalli *m pl*)
– *hackney carriage (hackney coach, cab, growler, Am. hack)*

**27** il groom (lo stalliere)
– *stableman (groom)*
**28** il cavallo
– *coach horse (carriage horse, cab horse, thill horse, thiller)*
**29** l'hansom cab *m*, una carrozza a due ruote *f pl* con mantice *m*, un cabriolet a un cavallo
– *hansom cab (hansom), a cabriolet, a one-horse chaise (one-horse carriage)*
**30** il timone a due stanghe *f pl*
– *shafts (thills, poles)*
**31** le redini
– *reins (rein, Am. line)*
**32** il cocchiere con la mantellina
– *coachman (driver) with inverness*
**33** il char à bancs, una vettura per comitive *f pl*
– *covered char-a-banc (brake, break), a pleasure vehicle*
**34** il cab
– *gig (chaise)*
**35** il calesse
– *barouche*
**36** il landò (il landau), una carrozza a due cavalli *m pl*
– *landau, a two-horse carriage; sim.: landaulet, landaulette*
**37** l'omnibus *m* (l'omnibus *m* a cavalli *m pl*)
– *omnibus (horse-drawn omnibus)*
**38** il phaeton
– *phaeton*
**39** la diligenza (la vettura di posta)
– *Continental stagecoach (mailcoach, diligence); also: road coach*
**40** il postiglione (il cocchiere)
– *mailcoach driver*
**41** il corno del postiglione
– *posthorn*
**42** il mantice
– *hood*
**43** i cavalli di posta (i cavalli di ricambio)
– *post horses (relay horses, relays)*
**44** il tilbury
– *tilbury*
**45** la troika (la troica); in Russia: un tiro a tre cavalli *m pl*
– *troika (Russian three-horse carriage)*
**46** il cavallo posto tra le stanghe
– *leader*
**47** il cavallo laterale
– *wheeler (wheelhorse, pole horse)*
**48** il buggy inglese
– *English buggy*
**49** il buggy americano
– *American buggy*
**50** il tiro a due
– *tandem*
**51** il vis-à-vis
– *vis-à-vis*

**52** il mantice
– *collapsible hood (collapsible top)*
**53** il mailcoach (la vettura di posta inglese)
– *mailcoach (English stagecoach)*
**54** il dorsay
– *covered (closed) chaise*

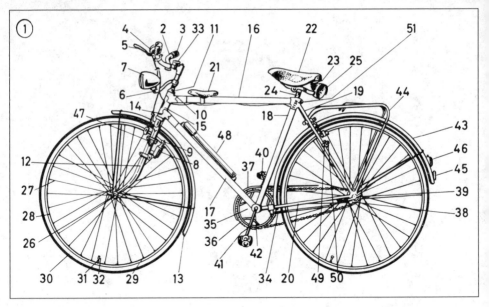

1 la bicicletta (la bici), una bicicletta da uomo, una bicicletta da turismo
– bicycle (cycle, coll. bike, Am. wheel), a gent's bicycle, a touring bicycle (touring cycle, roadster)
2 il manubrio, un manubrio da turismo
– handlebar (handlebars), a touring cycle handlebar
3 la manopola
– handlebar grip (handgrip, grip)
4 il campanello
– bicycle bell
5 il freno a mano f
– hand brake (front brake, a rim brake)
6 il portafanale
– lamp bracket
7 il fanale
– headlamp (bicycle lamp)
8 la dinamo
– dynamo
9 la rotellina della dinamo
– pulley
10-12 la forcella anteriore
– front forks
10 il cannotto della forcella anteriore
– handlebar stem
11 la testa del cannotto
– steering head
12 la forcella
– fork blades (fork ends)
13 il parafango anteriore
– front mudguard (Am. front fender)
14-20 il telaio
– bicycle frame

14 la pipa inferiore dello sterzo
– steering tube (fork column)
15 la marca
– head badge
16 la canna superiore
– crossbar (top tube)
17 la canna inferiore
– down tube
18 la canna verticale
– seat tube
19 la canna superiore della forcella posteriore
– seat stays
20 la canna inferiore della forcella posteriore
– chain stays
21 il sedile del bambino
– child's seat (child carrier seat)
22 il sellino (la sella)
– bicycle saddle
23 le molle del sellino
– saddle springs
24 il tubo reggisella
– seat pillar
25 la borsetta portaccessori
– tool bag
26-32 la ruota (ruota anteriore)
– wheel (front wheel)
26 il mozzo
– hub
27 il raggio
– spoke
28 il cerchio
– rim (wheel rim)
29 il nippel
– spoke nipple (spoke flange, spoke end)

30 il pneumatico (la gomma, il tubolare); all'interno: la camera di aria; all'esterno: il copertone
– tyre (Am. tire) (pneumatic tyre, high-pressure tyre); inside: tube (inner tube); outside: tyre (outer case, cover)
31 la valvola, una valvola della camera di aria, una valvola brevettata
– valve, a tube valve with valve tube or a patent valve with ball
32 la valvola a farfalla
– valve sealing cap
33 il tachimetro della bicicletta con contachilometri m
– bicycle speedometer with milometer
34 il cavalletto
– kick stand (prop stand)
35-42 la trasmissione a catena della bicicletta
– bicycle drive (chain drive)
35-39 la trasmissione a catena
– chain transmission
35 la ruota dentata anteriore
– chain wheel
36 la catena, una catena a rulli m pl
– chain, a roller chain
37 il carter
– chain guard
38 il rocchetto posteriore (la corona dentata)
– sprocket wheel (sprocket)
39 il galletto
– wing nut (fly nut, butterfly nut)

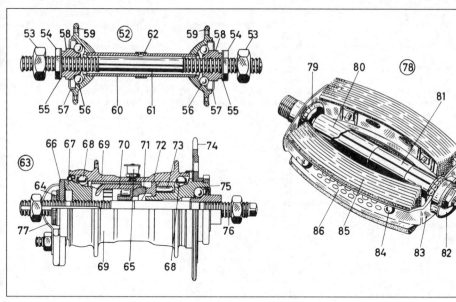

| | | |
|---|---|---|
| **40** il pedale | **56** la sfera | **71** il cono del freno |
| – *pedal* | – *ball bearing* | – *brake cone* |
| **41** la pedivella | **57** il coperchio parapolvere | **72** l'anello guidarulli |
| – *crank* | – *dust cap* | – *driver* |
| **42** il perno centrale | **58** il cono | **73** il rullo |
| – *bottom bracket bearing* | – *cone (adjusting cone)* | – *driving barrel* |
| **43** il parafango posteriore | **59** la bussola (la boccola) portaraggi | **74** la corona dentata |
| – *rear mudguard* (Am. *rear fender*) | – *centre* (Am. *center*) *hub* | – *sprocket* |
| **44** il portapacchi | **60** il tubo | **75** la testa filettata |
| – *luggage carrier (carrier)* | – *spindle* | – *thread head* |
| **45** il catarifrangente (*fam.*: la gemma) | **61** l'asse *m* | **76** l'asse *m* |
| – *reflector* | – *axle* | – *axle* |
| **46** il fanale anteriore elettrico | **62** l'ingrassatore *m* | **77** la fascetta fissaggio leva freno |
| – *rear light (rear lamp)* | – *clip covering lubrication hole (lubricator)* | – *bracket* |
| **47** il poggiapiedi | **63** il mozzo libero con freno contropedale | **78** il pedale della bicicletta (il pedale, il pedale con catarifrangente *m*) |
| – *footrest* | – *free-wheel hub with back-pedal brake (with coaster brake)* | – *bicycle pedal (pedal, reflector pedal)* |
| **48** la pompa | **64** il dado di sicurezza | **79** la bussola (la boccola) |
| – *bicycle pump* | – *safety nut* | – *cup* |
| **49** il catenaccio della bicicletta, un bloccaraggi | **65** l'oliatore *m* | **80** il tubo del pedale |
| – *bicycle lock, a wheel lock* | – *lubricator* | – *spindle* |
| **50** la serratura brevettata | **66** la leva del freno | **81** l'asse *m* del pedale |
| – *patent key* | – *brake arm* | – *axle* |
| **51** il numero del telaio | **67** il cono della leva | **82** il coperchio parapolvere |
| – *cycle serial number (factory number, frame number)* | – *brake arm cone* | – *dust cap* |
| **52** il mozzo anteriore | **68** la gabbia portasfere, con sfere *f pl* nel cuscinetto a sfere *f pl* | **83** la gabbia del pedale |
| – *front hub (front hub assembly)* | – *bearing cup with ball bearings in ball race* | – *pedal frame* |
| **53** il dado | **69** il manicotto del mozzo | **84** la vite fissaggio gomma |
| – *wheel nut* | – *hub shell (hub body, hub barrel)* | – *rubber stud* |
| **54** il controdado con fermo a stella | **70** il mantello del freno | **85** il panetto di gomma |
| – *locknut (locking nut)* | – *brake casing* | – *rubber block (rubber tread)* |
| **55** la rondella col nasello | | **86** il vetro catarifrangente |
| – *washer (slotted cone adjusting washer)* | | – *glass reflector* |

1 la bicicletta pieghevole
– *folding bicycle*
2 la cerniera
– *hinge* (also: *locking lever*)
3 il manubrio regolabile
– *adjustable handlebar (handlebars)*
4 la sella regolabile
– *adjustable saddle*
5 le ruotine di sostegno per principianti *m pl*
– *stabilizers*
6 il ciclomotore (*fam.*: il motorino)
– *motor-assisted bicycle*
7 il motore a due tempi *m pl* con raffreddamento a aria
– *air-cooled two-stroke engine*
8 la forcella telescopica
– *telescopic forks*
9 il telaio tubolare
– *tubular frame*
10 il serbatoio per il carburante
– *fuel tank (petrol tank, Am. gasoline tank)*
11 il manubrio sollevato
– *semi-rise handlebars*
12 il cambio a due marce *f pl*
– *two-speed gear-change (gearshift)*
13 la sella sagomata
– *high-back polo saddle*
14 la sospensione della ruota posteriore
– *swinging-arm rear fork*
15 il tubo di scappamento sollevato
– *upswept exhaust*
16 l'isolamento termico
– *heat shield*
17 la catena
– *drive chain*
18 il paramotore
– *crash bar (roll bar)*
19 il tachimetro
– *speedometer* (coll. *speedo*)
20 la city-bike, un veicolo elettrico
– *battery-powered moped, an electrically-powered vehicle*
21 la sella regolabile
– *swivel saddle*
22 il contenitore dell'accumulatore *m*
– *battery compartment*
23 il cestino in metallo
– *wire basket*
24 il ciclomotore (*fam.*: il motorino)
– *touring moped (moped)*
25 il pedale di avviamento
– *pedal crank (pedal drive, starter pedal)*
26 il motore monocilindrico a due tempi *m pl*
– *single-cylinder two-stroke engine*
27 il filo della candela con innesto
– *spark-plug cap*
28 il serbatoio per il carburante (per la miscela)
– *fuel tank (petrol tank, Am. gasoline tank)*

29 il fanale
– *moped headlamp (front lamp)*
30-35 gli strumenti sul manubrio
– *handlebar fittings*
30 la manopola del gas *m*
– *twist grip throttle control (throttle twist grip)*
31 la manopola di avviamento
– *twist grip (gear-change, gearshift)*
32 la leva del cambio
– *clutch lever*
33 la leva del freno a mano
– *hand brake lever*
34 il tachimetro
– *speedometer* (coll. *speedo*)
35 lo specchietto retrovisore
– *rear-view mirror (mirror)*
36 il freno a tamburo
– *front wheel drum brake (drum brake)*
37 i flessibili Bowde
– *Bowden cables (brake cables)*
38 il fanalino per il freno e lo stop
– *stop and tail light unit*
39 la motocicletta
– *light motorcycle with kickstarter*
40 il cockpit (il cruscotto) con il tachimetro e il contagiri elettronico
– *housing for instruments with speedometer and electronic rev counter (revolution counter)*
41 la forcella telescopica con soffietto
– *telescopic shock absorber*
42 la sella doppia
– *twin seat*
43 la leva di avviamento
– *kickstarter*
44 l'appoggiapiede per il passeggero
. – *pillion footrest, a footrest*
45 il manubrio sportivo
– *handlebar (handlebars)*
46 il carter chiuso della catena
– *chain guard*
47 lo scooter
– *motor scooter (scooter)*
48 la scocca laterale rimovibile
– *removable side panel*
49 il telaio tubolare
– *tubular frame*
50 la scocca di lamiera
– *metal fairings*
51 il cavalletto
– *prop stand (stand)*
52 il freno a pedale *m*
– *foot brake*
53 il clacson
– *horn (hooter)*
54 il gancio per i guanti o la borsa
– *hook for handbag or briefcase*
55 il freno a pedale *m*
– *foot gear-change control (foot gearshift control)*
56 la high-riser
– *high-riser;* sim.: *Chopper*

57 il manubrio in due parti *f pl*
– *high-rise handlebar (handlebars)*
58 l'imitazione *f* della forcella della motocicletta
– *imitation motorcycle fork*
59 la sella a banana
– *banana saddle*
60 il ferro cromato
– *chrome bracket*

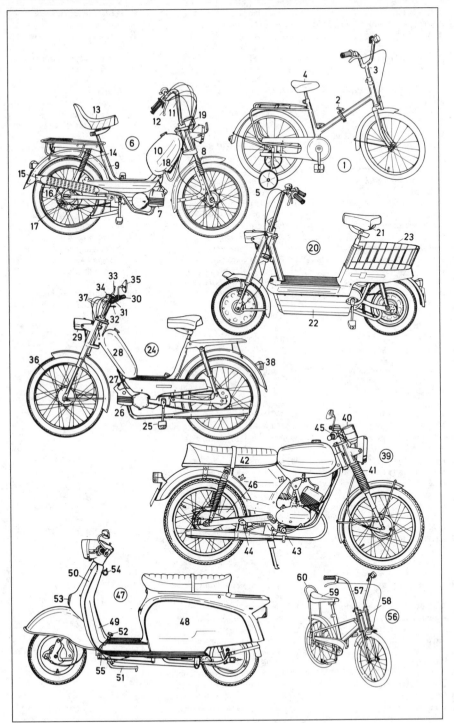

1 il ciclomotore (50 cm³)
– *lightweight motorcycle (light motorcycle) [50 cc]*
2 il serbatoio
– *fuel tank (petrol tank, Am. gasoline tank)*
3 il motore monocilindrico a quattro tempi *m pl*, raffreddato ad aria (con albero a camme *f pl* in testa)
– *air-cooled single-cylinder four-stroke engine (with overhead camshaft)*
4 il carburatore
– *carburettor (Am. carburetor)*
5 il tubo di aspirazione *f*
– *intake pipe*
6 il cambio a cinque marce *f pl*
– *five-speed gearbox*
7 il braccio oscillante della ruota posteriore
– *swinging-arm rear fork*
8 la targa di immatricolazione *f* (la targa)
– *number plate (Am. license plate)*
9 la luce di arresto e posteriore (lo stop)
– *stop and tail light (rear light)*
10 il fanale
– *headlight (headlamp)*
11 il freno a tamburo anteriore
– *front drum brake*
12 il cavo del freno, un cavo Bowde
– *brake cable (brake line), a Bowden cable*
13 il freno a tamburo posteriore
– *rear drum brake*
14 la sella sportiva
– *racing-style twin seat*
15 il tubo di scappamento alto
– *upswept exhaust*
16 la motocicletta (la moto) da cross (125 cm³), la moto sportiva fuori strada, una motoleggera
– *scrambling motorcycle (cross-country motorcycle) [125 cc], a light motorcycle*
17 il telaio a doppia culla
– *lightweight cradle frame*
18 il numero di partenza
– *number disc (disk)*
19 la sella monoposto
– *solo seat*
20 le alette di raffreddamento
– *cooling ribs*
21 il cavalletto centrale
– *motorcycle stand*
22 la catena
– *motorcycle chain*
23 la forcella telescopica
– *telescopic shock absorber*
24 i raggi
– *spokes*

25 il cerchione
– *rim (wheel rim)*
26 il pneumatico
– *motorcycle tyre (Am. tire)*
27 la scolpitura del pneumatico (il profilo del pneumatico)
– *tyre (Am. tire) tread*
28 la leva del cambio di marcia
– *gear-change lever (gearshift lever)*
29 la manopola del gas
– *twist grip throttle control (throttle twist grip)*
30 lo specchietto retrovisore
– *rear-view mirror (mirror)*
31-58 moto *f pl* pesanti
– *heavy (heavyweight, large-capacity) motorcycles*
31 la moto pesante con motore *m* raffreddato a liquido
– *heavyweight motorcycle with water-cooled engine*
32 il freno a disco anteriore
– *front disc (disk) brake*
33 la pinza del freno a disco
– *disc (disk) brake calliper (caliper)*
34 l'asse *m* della ruota
– *floating axle*
35 il radiatore
– *water cooler*
36 il serbatoio
– *fuel tank (petrol tank, Am. gasoline tank)*
37 l'indicatore *m* di direzione *f* (il lampeggiatore)
– *indicator (indicator light, turn indicator light)*
38 il pedale d'avviamento
– *kickstarter*
39 il motore raffreddato a liquido
– *water-cooled engine*
40 il tachimetro
– *speedometer*
41 il contagiri
– *rev counter (revolution counter)*
42 il lampeggiatore posteriore
– *rear indicator (indicator light)*
43 la moto pesante carenata (1000 cm³)
– *heavy (heavyweight, high-performance) machine with fairing [1000 cc]*
44 il cockpit integrale, una carenatura integrale
– *integrated streamlining, an integrated fairing*
45 il lampeggiatore
– *indicator (indicator light, turn indicator light)*
46 il parabrezza antiappannante
– *anti-mist windscreen (Am. windshield)*
47 il motore boxer a due cilindri *m pl* con trasmissione *f* cardanica
– *horizontally-opposed twin engine with cardan transmission*

48 la ruota in lega leggera
– *light alloy wheel*
49 la moto a quattro cilindri *m pl* (400 cm³)
– *four-cylinder machine [400 cc]*
50 il motore a quattro tempi *m pl* a quattro cilindri *m pl* raffreddato ad aria
– *air-cooled four-cylinder four-stroke engine*
51 il tubo di scappamento quattro in uno
– *four-pipe megaphone exhaust pipe*
52 l'avviatore *m* elettrico
– *electric starter button*
53 la motocarrozzetta
– *sidecar machine*
54 il sidecar
– *sidecar body*
55 la barra paraurti
– *sidecar crash bar*
56 le luci d'ingombro
– *sidelight (Am. sidemarker lamp)*
57 la ruota del sidecar
– *sidecar wheel*
58 il parabrezza del sidecar
– *sidecar windscreen (Am. windshield)*

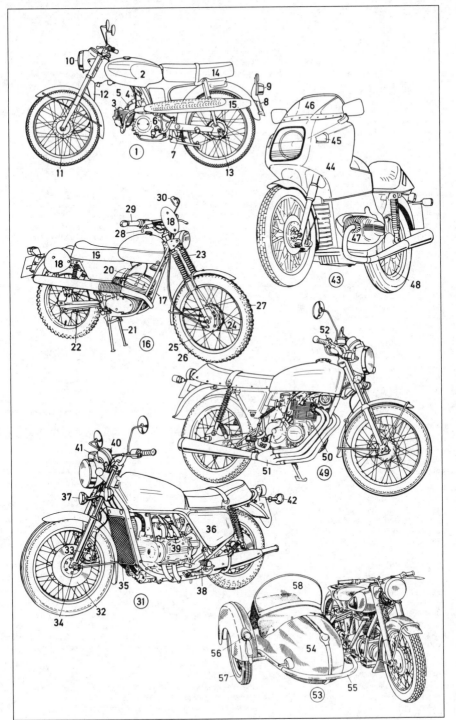

1  il motore a ciclo Otto, a V con otto cilindri *m pl* a iniezione *f* di benzina, in sezione *f* longitudinale
–  *eight-cylinder V (vee) fuel-injection spark-ignition engine (Otto-cycle engine)*
2  il motore a ciclo Otto in sezione *f* trasversale
–  *cross-section of spark-ignition engine (Otto-cycle internal combustion engine)*
3  il motore Diesel a cinque cilindri *m pl* in linea, in sezione *f* longitudinale
–  *sectional view of five-cylinder in-line diesel engine*
4  il motore Diesel in sezione *f* trasversale
–  *cross-section of diesel engine*
5  il motore Wankel (motore *m* a stantuffo rotante)
–  *two-rotor Wankel engine (rotary engine)*
6  il motore a ciclo Otto monocilindrico a due tempi *m pl*
–  *single-cylinder two-stroke internal combustion engine*
7  il ventilatore
–  *fan*
8  il supporto in plastica del ventilatore
–  *fan clutch for viscous drive*
9  il distributore di accensione *f* con camera a depressione *f* per l'anticipo di accensione *f*
–  *ignition distributor (distributor) with vacuum timing control*
10  la catena di distribuzione *f* doppia
–  *double roller chain*
11  il vano dell'albero a camme *f pl*
–  *camshaft bearing*
12  il tubo di sfiato
–  *air-bleed duct*
13  il tubo dell'olio per la lubrificazione dell'albero a camme *f pl*
–  *oil pipe for camshaft lubrication*
14  l'albero a camme *f pl*, un albero a camme *f pl* in testa
–  *camshaft, an overhead camshaft*
15  il collettore della valvola a farfalla
–  *venturi throat*
16  il silenziatore di ammissione *f*
–  *intake silencer (absorption silencer, Am. absorption muffler)*
17  il regolatore di pressione *f* del carburante
–  *fuel pressure regulator*
18  il tubo di aspirazione *f*
–  *inlet manifold*
19  il basamento (incorporato al monoblocco)
–  *cylinder crankcase*
20  il volano
–  *flywheel*
21  il corpo della biella
–  *connecting rod (piston rod)*
22  il cappello di banco
–  *cover of crankshaft bearing*
23  l'albero a gomiti *m pl*
–  *crankshaft*
24  il tappo di scarico dell'olio
–  *oil bleeder screw (oil drain plug)*

25  la catena di azionamento della pompa dell'olio
–  *roller chain of oil pump drive*
26  l'antivibratore *m*
–  *vibration damper*
27  l'albero conduttore per il distributore di accensione *f*
–  *distributor shaft for the ignition distributor (distributor)*
28  il bocchettone di riempimento per l'olio
–  *oil filler neck*
29  la cartuccia del filtro
–  *diaphragm spring*
30  la tiranteria di regolazione *f*
–  *control linkage*
31  la conduttura di alimentazione *f* a anello
–  *fuel supply pipe (Am. fuel line)*
32  la valvola d'iniezione *f*
–  *fuel injector (injection nozzle)*
33  il bilanciere
–  *rocker arm*
34  il vano dei bilancieri
–  *rocker arm mounting*
35  la candela di accensione *f* con cappuccio antiradiodisturbi
–  *spark plug (sparking plug) with suppressor*
36  il collettore di scarico
–  *exhaust manifold*
37  il pistone con segmenti *m pl* e anello raschiaolio
–  *piston with piston rings and oil scraper ring*
38  il supporto del motore
–  *engine mounting*
39  la flangia intermedia
–  *dog flange (dog)*
40  la parte superiore della coppa dell'olio
–  *crankcase*
41  la parte inferiore della coppa dell'olio
–  *oil sump (sump)*
42  la pompa dell'olio
–  *oil pump*
43  il filtro dell'olio
–  *oil filter*
44  il motorino di avviamento
–  *starter motor (starting motor)*
45  la testa del cilindro
–  *cylinder head*
46  la valvola di scarico
–  *exhaust valve*
47  l'astina di livello dell'olio
–  *dipstick*
48  il coperchio testa cilindri *m pl*
–  *cylinder head cover*
49  il fodero della catena doppia di distribuzione *f*
–  *double bushing chain*
50  il rilevatore della temperatura
–  *warm-up regulator*
51  il tirante per la regolazione della corsa a vuoto
–  *tapered needle for idling adjustment*
52  il tubo di mandata del carburante
–  *fuel pressure pipe (fuel pressure line)*
53  la tubazione di recupero del carburante
–  *fuel leak line (drip fuel line)*

54  il polverizzatore
–  *injection nozzle (spray nozzle)*
55  il raccordo per il riscaldamento
–  *heater plug*
56  il disco equilibratore
–  *thrust washer*
57  l'albero dentato intermedio per l'azionamento della pompa dell'olio
–  *intermediate gear shaft for the injection pump drive*
58  il regolatore della fasatura d'immissione *f*
–  *injection timer unit*
59  la pompa di depressione *f*
–  *vacuum pump (low-pressure regulator)*
60  la camma a disco per la pompa di depressione *f*
–  *cam for vacuum pump*
61  la pompa per l'acqua di raffreddamento
–  *water pump (coolant pump)*
62  il termostato per l'acqua di raffreddamento
–  *cooling water thermostat*
63  l'interruttore *m* termico
–  *thermo time switch*
64  la pompa a mano del carburante *m*
–  *fuel hand pump*
65  la pompa d'iniezione *f*
–  *injection pump*
66  la candela di avviamento a incandescenza
–  *glow plug*
67  la valvola regolatrice della pressione dell'olio
–  *oil pressure limiting valve*
68  lo stantuffo rotante
–  *rotor*
69  la guarnizione di tenuta a listello
–  *seal*
70  il variatore di coppia
–  *torque converter*
71  la frizione monodisco
–  *single-plate clutch*
72  il cambio a più marce *f pl*
–  *multi-speed gearing (multi-step gearing)*
73  i condotti del collettore per diminuire la nocività dei gas di scarico
–  *port liners in the exhaust manifold for emission control*
74  il freno a disco
–  *disc (disk) brake*
75  il cambio differenziale assiale
–  *differential gear (differential)*
76  la dinamo
–  *generator*
77  il pedale di avviamento
–  *foot gear-change control (foot gearshift control)*
78  la frizione a secco a più dischi *m pl*
–  *dry multi-plate clutch*
79  il carburatore esterno
–  *cross-draught (Am. cross-draft) carburettor (Am. carburetor)*
80  le alette di raffreddamento
–  *cooling ribs*
81  la cinghia trapezoidale
–  *V-belt (fan belt)*

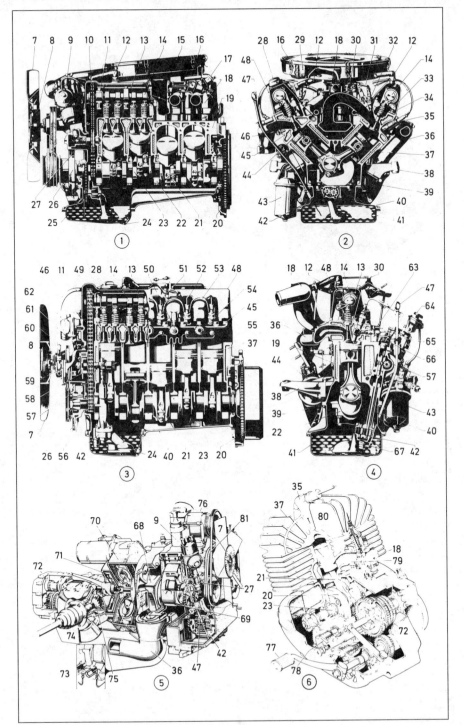

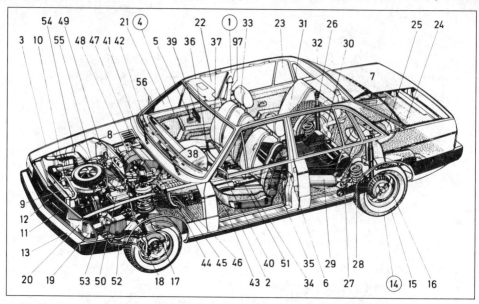

1-56 l'automobile *f* (l' auto *f* )
– *motor car (car, Am. automobile, auto), a passenger vehicle*
1 la carrozzeria portante
– *monocoque body (unitary body)*
2 il telaio (lo chassis), il pianale della carrozzeria
– *chassis, the understructure of the body*
3 il parafango anteriore
– *front wing (Am. front fender)*
4 la portiera
– *car door*
5 la maniglia
– *door handle*
6 la serratura
– *door lock*
7 il coperchio del bagagliaio
– *boot lid (Am. trunk lid)*
8 il cofano anteriore
– *bonnet (Am. hood)*
9 il radiatore
– *radiator*
10 la conduttura del liquido di raffreddamento
– *cooling water pipe*
11 la griglia del radiatore
– *radiator grill*
12 la marca dell'auto
– *badging*
13 il paraurti anteriore con rivestimento in gomma
– *rubber-covered front bumper (Am. front fender)*
14 la ruota dell'auto *f*, una ruota a disco
– *car wheel, a disc (disk) wheel*
15 il pneumatico
– *car tyre (Am. automobile tire)*
16 il cerchione
– *rim (wheel rim)*
17-18 il freno a disco
– *disc (disk) brake*
17 il disco del freno
– *brake disc (disk) (braking disc)*

18 la pinza del freno
– *calliper (caliper)*
19 l'indicatore *m* di direzione *f* anteriore
– *front indicator light (front turn indicator light)*
20 il fanale (il proiettore) con luci *f pl* abbaglianti, antiabbaglianti e di posizione *f* (luci *f pl* d'ingombro)
– *headlight (headlamp) with main beam (high beam), dipped beam (low beam), sidelight (side lamp, Am. sidemarker lamp)*
21 il parabrezza, un parabrezza panoramico
– *windscreen (Am. windshield), a panoramic windscreen*
22 il finestrino abbassabile
– *crank-operated car window*
23 il finestrino posteriore fisso
– *quarter light (quarter vent)*
24 il bagagliaio
– *boot (Am. trunk)*
25 la ruota di scorta
– *spare wheel*
26 l'ammortizzatore *m*
– *damper (shock absorber)*
27 il puntone longitudinale articolato
– *trailing arm*
28 la sospensione
– *coil spring*
29 la marmitta di scarico
– *silencer (Am. muffler)*
30 la ventilazione forzata
– *automatic ventilation system*
31 i sedili posteriori
– *rear seats*
32 il lunotto posteriore
– *rear window*
33 il poggiatesta regolabile
– *adjustable headrest (head restraint)*
34 il sedile dell'autista, un sedile ribaltabile
– *driver's seat, a reclining seat*

35 lo schienale regolabile
– *reclining backrest*
36 il sedile del passeggero
– *passenger seat*
37 il volante
– *steering wheel*
38 il cruscotto con tachimetro, contagiri *m*, orologio, indicatore *m* del livello della benzina, termometro del liquido di raffreddamento, termometro dell'olio
– *centre (Am. center) console containing speedometer (coll. speedo), revolution counter (rev counter, tachometer), clock, fuel gauge (Am. gage), water temperature gauge, oil temperature gauge*
39 lo specchietto retrovisore
– *inside rear-view mirror*
40 lo spechietto esterno sinistro
– *left-hand wing mirror*
41 il tergicristallo
– *windscreen wiper (Am. windshield wiper)*
42 la bocchetta dello sbrinatore
– *defroster vents*
43 la moquette
– *carpeting*
44 il pedale della frizione (la frizione)
– *clutch pedal (coll. clutch)*
45 il pedale del freno (il freno)
– *brake pedal (coll. brake)*
46 il pedale dell'acceleratore *m* (l'acceleratore *m*)
– *accelerator pedal (coll. accelerator)*
47 la griglia ingresso aria
– *inlet vent*
48 il ventilatore per l'areazione *f*
– *defroster vents*
49 il serbatoio liquido freni *m pl*
– *brake fluid reservoir*
50 l'accumulatore *m* (la batteria)
– *battery*

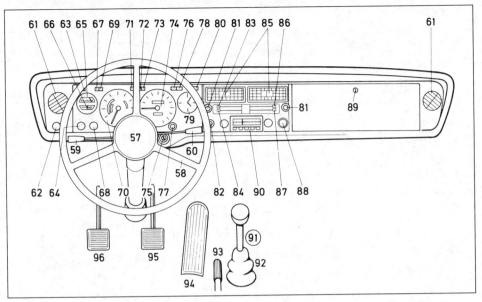

**51** il tubo di scappamento
 – *exhaust pipe*
**52** l'articolazione *f* della ruota anteriore con trazione *f* anteriore
 – *front running gear with front wheel drive*
**53** il supporto motore *m*
 – *engine mounting*
**54** il silenziatore *m* di ammissione *f*
 – *intake silencer (Am. intake muffler)*
**55** il filtro dell'aria
 – *air filter (air cleaner)*
**56** lo specchietto esterno destro
 – *right-hand wing mirror*
**57-90** il cruscotto
 – *dashboard (fascia panel)*
**57** il mozzo del volante *m*, con funzione *f* di protezione *f* anticollisione
 – *controlled-collapse steering column*
**58** la razza del volante
 – *steering wheel spoke*
**59** il cambio luci *f pl*
 – *indicator and dimming switch*
**60** la leva comando tergicristallo, lavaggio, indicatore *m* acustico
 – *wiper/washer switch and horn*
**61** l'ugello di areazione *f* del finestrino laterale
 – *side window blower*
**62** il comando luci *f pl* di posizione *f*, fanali *m pl* e parcheggio
 – *sidelight, headlight, and parking light switch*
**63** la lampada controllo luci *f pl* fendinebbia
 – *fog lamp warning light*
**64** il comando fanali *m pl* fendinebbia e luce *f* posteriore fendinebbia
 – *fog headlamp and rear lamp switch*
**65** l'indicatore *m* livello carburante *m*
 – *fuel gauge (Am. gage)*

**66** il termometro liquido di raffreddamento
 – *water temperature gauge (Am. gage)*
**67** la lampada controllo luce *f* posteriore fendinebbia
 – *warning light for rear fog lamp*
**68** il comando del lampeggiatore *m*
 – *hazard flasher switch*
**69** la lampada controllo abbaglianti *m pl*
 – *main beam warning light*
**70** il contagiri elettrico
 – *electric rev counter (revolution counter)*
**71** la lampada (la spia) controllo carburante *m*
 – *fuel warning light*
**72** la lampada (la spia) controllo freno a mano e impianto sdoppiato di frenatura
 – *warning light for the hand brake and dual-circuit brake system*
**73** la lampada (la spia) controllo pressione *f* olio
 – *oil pressure warning light*
**74** il tachimetro con contachilometri parziale
 – *speedometer (coll. speedo) with trip mileage recorder*
**75** il commutatore di accensione *f*
 – *starter and steering lock*
**76** la lampada (la spia) controllo lampeggiatori *m pl*
 – *warning lights for turn indicators and hazard flashers*
**77** il regolatore illuminazione *f* interna e azzeramento contachilometri *m* parziale
 – *switch for the courtesy light and reset button for the trip mileage recorder*
**78** la lampada (la spia) controllo batteria
 – *ammeter*
**79** l'orologio elettrico
 – *electric clock*

**80** la lampada (la spia) controllo riscaldamento lunotto posteriore
 – *warning light for heated rear window*
**81** il comando areazione inferiore abitacolo
 – *switch for the leg space ventilation*
**82** il comando riscaldamento lunotto posteriore
 – *rear window heating switch*
**83** la leva regolazione *f* areazione *f*
 – *ventilation switch*
**84** la leva regolazione *f* temperatura
 – *temperature regulator*
**85** la bocchetta orientabile aria fredda
 – *fresh-air inlet and control*
**86** la leva regolazione *f* aria fredda
 – *fresh-air regulator*
**87** la leva regolazione *f* aria calda
 – *warm-air regulator*
**88** l'accendisigaro
 – *cigar lighter*
**89** la serratura del cassetto ripostiglio
 – *glove compartment (glove box) lock*
**90** l'autoradio *f*
 – *car radio*
**91** la leva del cambio
 – *gear lever (gearshift lever), a floor-type gear-change*
**92** il manicotto in pelle *f*
 – *leather gaiter*
**93** la leva del freno a mano
 – *hand brake lever*
**94** il pedale dell'accelleratore *m*
 – *accelerator pedal*
**95** il pedale del freno
 – *brake pedal*
**96** il pedale della frizione
 – *clutch pedal*
**97** la cintura di sicurezza
 – *seat belt (safety belt)*
 – *blower fan*

**1-15 il carburatore,** un carburatore invertito
- **carburettor** (Am. *carburetor*), a down-draught (Am. *down-draft*) carburettor
1 il getto del minimo
- *idling jet (slow-running jet)*
2 il calibratore aria del minimo
- *idling air jet (idle air bleed)*
3 il calibratore aria principale
- *air correction jet*
4 l'aria calibrata
- *compensating airstream*
5 l'aria principale
- *main airstream*
6 la farfalla dello starter (la valvola di chiusura dell'aria)
- *choke flap*
7 il braccio di uscita
- *plunger*
8 il diffusore
- *venturi*
9 la valvola a farfalla
- *throttle valve (butterfly valve)*
10 il tubetto emulsionatore
- *emulsion tube*
11 la valvola a spillo di regolazione *f* del minimo
- *idle mixture adjustment screw*
12 il getto principale
- *main jet*
13 l'alimentazione *f* del carburante
- *fuel inlet* (Am. *gasoline inlet*) *(inlet manifold)*
14 la vaschetta del galleggiante
- *float chamber*
15 il galleggiante
- *float*
**16-27 la lubrificazione forzata**
- *pressure-feed lubricating system*
16 la pompa dell'olio
- *oil pump*
17 la coppa dell'olio
- *oil sump*
18 il filtro dell'olio
- *sump filter*
19 il refrigeratore dell'olio
- *oil cooler*
20 il filtro a maglia fine
- *oil filter*
21 il passaggio principale dell'olio
- *main oil gallery (drilled gallery)*
22 il condotto di lubrificazione *f*
- *crankshaft drilling (crankshaft tributary, crankshaft bleed)*
23 il cuscinetto di banco
- *crankshaft bearing (main bearing)*
24 il cuscinetto dell'albero a camme *f pl*
- *camshaft bearing*
25 il cuscinetto di biella (il perno di biella)
- *connecting-rod bearing*
26 il foro di passaggio dell'olio per la lubrificazione del perno di manovella
- *gudgeon pin (piston pin)*
27 la conduttura secondaria
- *bleed*
**28-47 il cambio sincronizzato a quattro marce *f pl***
- *four-speed synchromesh gearbox*
28 il pedale della frizione
- *clutch pedal*
29 l'albero motore *m*
- *crankshaft*

30 l'albero primario
- *drive shaft (propeller shaft)*
31 la corona dentata per l'avviamento
- *starting gear ring*
32 il manicotto scorrevole per la terza e la quarta marcia
- *sliding sleeve for 3rd and 4th gear*
33 la sfera del sincronizzatore
- *synchronizing cone*
34 l'ingranaggio elicoidale per la terza marcia
- *helical gear wheel for 3rd gear*
35 il manicotto scorrevole per la prima e seconda marcia
- *sliding sleeve for 1st and 2nd gear*
36 l'ingranaggio elicoidale per la prima marcia
- *helical gear wheel for 1st gear*
37 il contralbero (l'albero ausiliario)
- *lay shaft*
38 la presa di moto del tachimetro
- *speedometer drive*
39 l'ingranaggio elicoidale per il tachimetro
- *helical gear wheel for speedometer drive*
40 l'albero primario
- *main shaft*
41 l'albero del cambio marcia
- *gearshift rods*
42 la forcella del cambio per la prima e seconda marcia
- *selector fork for 1st and 2nd gear*
43 l'ingranaggio elicoidale per la seconda marcia
- *helical gear wheel for 2nd gear*
44 l'albero d'innesto per la retromarcia
- *selector head with reverse gear*
45 la forcella del cambio per la terza e quarta marcia
- *selector fork for 3rd and 4th gear*
46 la leva del cambio
- *gear lever (gearshift lever)*
47 lo schema delle marce
- *gear-change pattern (gearshift pattern, shift pattern)*
**48-55 il freno a disco**
- *disc (disk) brake [assembly]*
48 il disco del freno
- *brake disc (disk) (braking disc)*
49 la pinza frenante, una pinza fissa con pastiglie *f pl* frenanti
- *calliper (caliper), a fixed calliper with friction pads*
50 il tamburo del freno a mano
- *servo cylinder (servo unit)*
51 il ceppo del freno (la ganascia del freno)
- *brake shoes*
52 il ferodo
- *brake lining*
53 la giunzione per la tubazione del freno
- *outlet to brake line*
54 il cilindretto
- *wheel cylinder*
55 la molla di richiamo
- *return spring*
**56-59 la scatola dello sterzo** (con vite *f* senza fine *f* )
- **steering gear** (*worm-and-nut steering gear*)

56 il piantone dello sterzo
- *steering column*
57 il settore dentato
- *worm gear sector*
58 la leva di comando sterzo
- *steering drop arm*
59 la filettatura della vite
- *worm*
**60-64 l'impianto di riscaldamento a acqua** (il riscaldamento dell'automobile *f* )
- **water-controlled heater**
60 l'ingresso dell'aria fredda
- *air intake*
61 lo scambiatore di calore *m*
- *heat exchanger (heater box)*
62 il ventilatore
- *blower fan*
63 la valvola di regolazione *f*
- *flap valve*
64 il getto sbrinatore
- *defroster vent*
**65-71 l'assale *m* rigido**
- **live axle** (*rigid axle*)
65 il tubo di reazione *f*
- *propeller shaft*
66 il braccio longitudinale (il puntone longitudinale articolato)
- *trailing arm*
67 il cuscinetto di gomma
- *rubber bush*
68 la molla elicoidale
- *coil spring*
69 l'ammortizzatore *m*
- *damper (shock absorber)*
70 l'asta Panhard
- *Panhard rod*
71 lo stabilizzatore
- *stabilizer bar*
**72-84 il braccio ammortizzatore McPherson**
- **MacPherson strut unit**
72 il supporto per la carrozzeria
- *body-fixing plate*
73 il supporto di base *f* per il braccio ammortizzatore
- *upper bearing*
74 la molla elicoidale
- *suspension spring*
75 la biella
- *piston rod*
76 l'ammortizzatore *m* del braccio
- *suspension damper*
77 il cerchione
- *rim (wheel rim)*
78 il perno del fuso a snodo
- *stub axle*
79 la leva del tirante trasversale
- *steering arm*
80 lo snodo di guida
- *track-rod ball-joint*
81 il tirante di guida
- *trailing link arm*
82 il supporto di gomma
- *bump rubber (rubber bonding)*
83 il cuscinetto portante
- *lower bearing*
84 il supporto dell'avantreno
- *lower suspension arm*

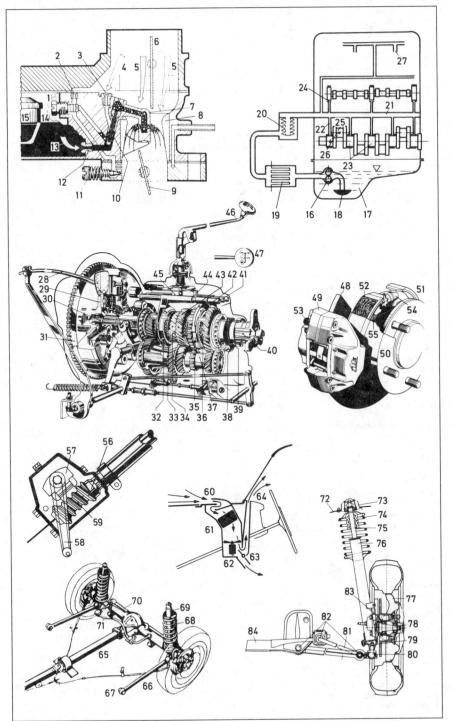

**1-36 tipi** *m pl* **d'automobili** *f pl* (tipi *m pl* di vetture *f pl*)
– *car models (Am. automobile models)*
**1 la berlina a quattro porte** *f pl* (berlina della classe medio-alta)
– *four-door touring saloon (Am. four-door sedan) in the upper-middle range*
**2** la portiera anteriore sinistra
– *driver's door*
**3** la portiera posteriore
– *rear door*
**4-10 le berline a quattro porte** *f pl* della classe media
– *four-door saloon (Am. four-door sedan)* **and four-door hatchback in the middle range**
**4 la berlina classica a tre volumi** *m pl* (con la parte posteriore tronca)
– *saloon (Am. sedan)*
**5** i poggiatesta
– *headrests (head restraints)*
**6** il sedile anteriore
– *front seat*
**7** il sedile posteriore
– *rear seat (back seat)*
**8 la berlina a due volumi** *m pl* **media** (con la parte posteriore a spoiler *m*)
– *fastback saloon (Am. fastback sedan) (stubback saloon, Am. stubback sedan)*
**9** il cofano del bagagliaio
– *tailgate*
**10** il portellone posteriore
– *fastback (stubback)*
**11 la vettura fuoristrada** con quattro ruote *f pl* motrici
– *cross-country vehicle with all-wheel drive (four-wheel drive)*
**12** la ruota di scorta
– *spare wheel*
**13** la barra di protezione *f*, il Roll bar
– *roll bar*
**14 la spider** (il cabrio)
– *cabriolet sports coupé (cabriolet sports car)*
**15** il sedile integrale
– *integral seat*
**16** il tettuccio automatico (la capote richiusa)
– *automatic hood (Am. top) (power-operated hood, Am. top)*
**17 la vettura famigliare** (la giardinetta, la station wagon)
– *estate car (estate, shooting brake, Am. station wagon)*
**18** lo spazio utile di carico (bagagliaio)
– *boot space (luggage compartment)*
**19 l'utilitaria a tre porte** *f pl*
– *small three-door car*
**20** il portellone posteriore
– *back (tailgate)*

**21** il bordo del bagagliaio
– *sill*
**22** il sedile posteriore ribaltabile
– *folding back seat*
**23** il bagagliaio
– *boot (luggage compartment, Am. trunk)*
**24** il tettuccio apribile (il tettuccio apribile di acciaio)
– *(sliding) sunroof (steel sliding sunroof )*
**25 la berlina famigliare a tre porte** *f pl*
– *three-door hatchback*
**26** la vettura sportiva cabrio (la sport cabrio), una due posti *m pl*
– *roadster (sports cabrio, sports cabriolet), a two-seater*
**27** l'hard-top *m* (il tettuccio rigido amovibile)
– *hard top*
**28 la vettura sportiva coupé,** una due più due (due sedili *m pl* con strapuntini *m pl*)
– *sports coupé, a two-plus-two (two-seater with occasional seats)*
**29** il montante posteriore
– *fastback*
**30** lo strapuntino
– *occasional seat*
**31** il pneumatico a sezione *f* ribassata e larga
– *low-profile tyre (Am. tire) (wide wheel)*
**32 la vettura GT** (Gran Turismo), la coupé sportiva
– *gran turismo car (GT car)*
**33** il paraurti integrato
– *integral bumper (Am. integral fender)*
**34** lo spoiler posteriore
– *rear spoiler*
**35** il cofano motore posteriore
– *back*
**36** lo spoiler anteriore
– *front spoiler*

1 il camioncino fuoristrada con quattro ruote *f pl* motrici
– *light cross-country lorry (light truck, pick-up truck) with all-wheel drive (four-wheel drive)*
2 la cabina
– *cab (driver's cab)*
3 il cassone (il pianale di carico)
– *loading platform (body)*
4 il pneumatico di scorta, un pneumatico per fuoristrada
– *spare tyre (Am. spare tire), a cross-country tyre*
5 il piccolo autocarro da trasporto
– *light lorry (light truck, pick-up truck)*
6 l'autocarro a pianale *m*
– *platform truck*
7 l'autocarro a cassone *m* coperto
– *medium van*
8 la portiera laterale scorrevole (la portiera per il carico)
– *sliding side door [for loading and unloading]*
9 il pullmino (un piccolo autobus)
– *minibus*
10 il tettuccio apribile
– *folding top (sliding roof)*
11 la portiera posteriore (lo sportello posteriore)
– *rear door*
12 la portiera laterale incernierata
– *hinged side door*
13 il bagagliaio (il portabagagli)
– *luggage compartment*
14 il sedile per i passeggeri
– *passenger seat*
15 la cabina per l'autista
– *cab (driver's cab)*
16 la presa di aria
– *air inlet*
17 l'autobus (il pullman)
– *motor coach (coach, bus)*
18 il bagagliaio
– *luggage locker*
19 il bagaglio (la valigia)
– *hand luggage (suitcase, case)*
20 l'autocarro pesante
– *heavy lorry (heavy truck, heavy motor truck)*
21 la motrice
– *tractive unit (tractor, towing vehicle)*
22 il rimorchio
– *trailer (drawbar trailer)*
23 il container
– *swop platform (body)*
24 l'autocarro ribaltabile
– *three-way tipper (three-way dump truck)*
25 il cassone ribaltabile
– *tipping body (dump body)*
26 il cilindro idraulico
– *hydraulic cylinder*

27 il container sul pallet
– *supported container platform*
28 l'autobotte *f*
– *articulated vehicle, a vehicle tanker*
29 la motrice
– *tractive unit (tractor, towing vehicle)*
30-33 il rimorchio cisterna
– *semi-trailer (skeletal)*
30 la cisterna
– *tank*
31 il perno rotante di trazione *f*
– *turntable*
32 il carrello di sostegno
– *undercarriage*
33 la ruota di scorta
– *spare wheel*
34 l'autobus *m* di linea di piccolo formato, in versione *f* da città
– *midi bus [for short-route town operations]*
35 la porta esterna oscillante
– *outward-opening doors*
36 l'autobus *m* a due piani *m pl*
– *double-deck bus (double-decker bus)*
37 il piano inferiore
– *lower deck (lower saloon)*
38 il piano superiore
– *upper deck (upper saloon)*
39 la salita
– *boarding platform*
40 il tram (il tram snodato)
– *trolley bus*
41 il braccio per la presa di corrente *f*
– *current collector*
42 il trolley
– *trolley (trolley shoe)*
43 la linea aerea di alimentazione *f*
– *overhead wires*
44 il rimorchio del tram
– *trolley bus trailer*
45 il passaggio a soffietto
– *pneumatically sprung rubber connection*

**1-55 l'officina specializzata**
- *agent's garage (distributor's garage,* Am. *specialty shop)*
**1-23** il settore diagnosi
- *diagnostic test bay*
**1** l'apparecchiatura per effettuare la diagnosi
- *computer*
**2** la presa di corrente centrale
- *main computer socket*
**3** il cavo di diagnosi *f*
- *computer harness (computer cable)*
**4** il commutatore per il misuratore manuale o automatico
- *switch from automatic to manual*
**5** l'inserimento del programma
- *slot for program cards*
**6** la stampante
- *printout machine (printer)*
**7** il modulo con la diagnosi
- *condition report, a data printout*
**8** l'apparecchiatura per il comando manuale
- *master selector (hand control)*
**9** gli indicatori luminosi (*verde:* a posto; *rosso:* non a posto)
- *light read-out [green: OK; red: not OK]*
**10** la cassetta per i programmi
- *rack for program cards*

**11** l'interruttore *m* di avviamento
- *mains button*
**12** il tasto per il programma veloce
- *switch for fast readout*
**13** l'indicatore *m* di divieto d'inserimento programma
- *firing sequence insert*
**14** il piano di appoggio
- *shelf for used cards*
**15** il reggicavo
- *cable boom*
**16** il cavo per la misurazione della temperatura dell'olio
- *oil temperature sensor*
**17** l'apparecchio di controllo per la misurazione della convergenza e della campanatura delle ruote sulla destra
- *test equipment for wheel and steering alignment*
**18** la lastra ottica sulla destra
- *right-hand optic plate*
**19** i transistor di scatto
- *actuating transistors*
**20** l'interruttore *m* del proiettore
- *projector switch*
**21** la fascia luminosa per misurare la campanatura
- *check light for wheel alignment, a row of photocells*

**22** la fascia luminosa per misurare la convergenza
- *check light for steering alignment, a row of photocells*
**23** il cacciavite elettrico
- *power screwdriver*
**24** l'apparecchio per controllare l'inclinazione *f* dei fari
- *beam setter*
**25** il ponte elevatore idraulico
- *hydraulic lift*
**26** il braccio mobile del ponte elevatore
- *adjustable arm of hydraulic lift*
**27** il tampone del ponte elevatore
- *hydraulic lift pad*
**28** il vano per la ruota
- *excavation*
**29** il manometro
- *pressure gauge (Am. gage)*
**30** il lubrificatore a pressione *f*
- *grease gun*
**31** la cassetta delle minuterie
- *storage box for small parts*
**32** l'elenco dei pezzi di ricambio
- *wall chart [of spare parts]*
**33** la diagnosi automatica
- *automatic computer test*

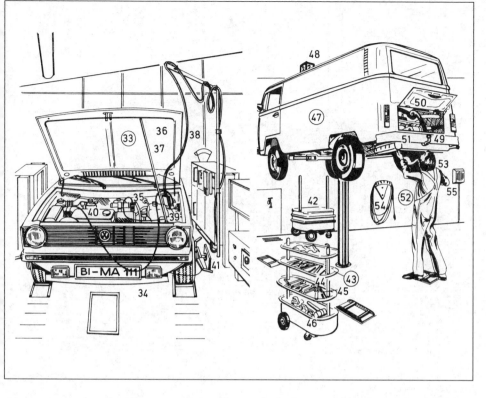

34 il veicolo, un'automobile
(un'auto)
– *motor car (car, Am. automobile,
auto), a passenger vehicle*
35 il vano motore *m*
– *engine compartment*
36 il cofano
– *bonnet (Am. hood)*
37 l'asta di sostegno del cofano
– *bonnet support (Am. hood support)*
38 il cavo per la diagnosi
– *computer harness (computer
cable)*
39 la presa di corrente *f* per la diagnosi (la presa di corrente *f* centrale)
– *main computer socket*
40 il cavo per misurare la temperatura dell'olio
– *oil temperature sensor*
41 lo specchio della ruota per la misurazione ottica della convergenza
e della campanatura
– *wheel mirror for visual wheel and
steering alignment*
42 il carrello portautensili
– *tool trolley*

43 l'utensile *m*
– *tools*
44 la chiave per dadi *m pl*
– *impact wrench*
45 la chiave dinamometrica
– *torque wrench*
46 il martello per spianare
– *body hammer (roughing-out hammer)*
47 il veicolo in riparazione *f*, un
pullmino
– *vehicle under repair, a minibus*
48 il numero della riparazione *f*
– *car location number*
49 il motore posteriore
– *rear engine*
50 il coperchio ribaltabile del motore *m*
– *tailgate*
51 l'impianto di scarico (il sistema di
scarico)
– *exhaust system*
52 la riparazione dello scarico (dello
scappamento)
– *exhaust repair*
53 il meccanico auto (l'automeccani-
co, il riparatore auto)
– *motor car mechanic (motor vehicle mechanic, Am. automotive
mechanic)*

54 il tubo per l'aria compressa
– *air hose*
55 il citofono
– *intercom*

1-29  la stazione di servizio, una
stazione di servizio self-service
– *service station (petrol station, filling station, Am. gasoline station,
gas station), a self-service station*
1  il distributore di carburante *m* (la
colonnina; *ant.*: la pompa della
benzina) per benzina normale e
super senza piombo (*sim.*: per
carburante *m* Diesel)
– *petrol (Am. gasoline) pump
(blending pump) for lead-free pre-
mium grade and regular petrol
(Am. gasoline) (sim.: for derv)*
2  il tubo
– *hose (petrol pump, Am. gasoline
pump, hose)*
3  l'erogatore *m* di benzina
– *nozzle*
4  l'importo indicato
– *cash readout*
5  l'indicatore *m* dei litri
– *volume readout*
6  l'indicatore *m* del prezzo
– *price display*
7  il segnale luminoso
– *indicator light*
8  l'automobilista *m* mentre si serve
– *driver using self-service petrol
pump (Am. gasoline pump)*
9  l'estintore *m*
– *fire extinguisher*

10  il distributore di fazzoletti *m pl* di
carta
– *paper-towel dispenser*
11  il fazzoletto di carta
– *paper towel*
12  il cestino dei rifiuti
– *litter receptacle*
13  il contenitore della miscela
– *two-stroke blending pump*
14  il misuratore
– *meter*
15  l'olio del motore
– *engine oil*
16  l'oliatore *m*
– *oil can*
17  il misuratore della pressione dei
pneumatici
– *tyre pressure gauge (Am. tire pressure gage)*
18  il tubo dell'aria compressa
– *air hose*
19  il serbatoio per l'aria compressa
– *static air tank*
20  il manometro
– *pressure gauge (Am. gage)
(manometer)*
21  il tubo erogatore di aria
– *air filler neck*
22  il box (il box per le riparazioni)
– *repair bay (repair shop)*
23  la pompa di lavaggio, una pompa
per l'acqua
– *car-wash hose, a hose (hosepipe)*

24  il negozio di accessori *m pl* per
l'auto
– *accessory shop*
25  la tanica da benzina
– *petrol can (Am. gasoline can)*
26  la mantellina impermeabile
– *rain cape*
27  i pneumatici per l'automobile *f*
– *car tyres (Am. automobile tires)*
28  l'accessorio per l'automobile *f*
– *car accessories*
29  la cassa
– *cash desk (console)*

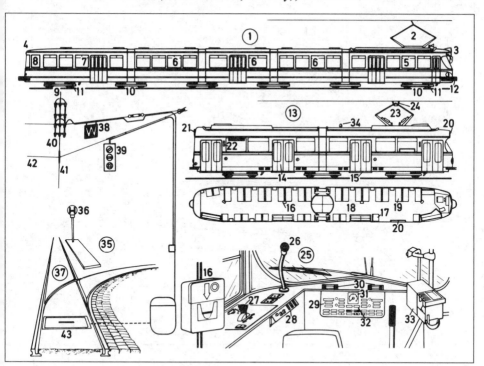

1 la motrice articolata a dodici assi *m pl,* per il funzionamento del tram
– *twelve-axle articulated railcar for interurban rail service*
2 la presa di corrente
– *current collector*
3 il frontale (il muso) della vettura
– *head of the railcar*
4 la parte posteriore della vettura
– *rear of the railcar*
5 la parte «A» della vettura con motore *m* a trazione *f*
– *carriage A containing the motor*
6 la parte «B» della vettura (*anche:* parte *f* «C» e «D» della vettura)
– *carriage B (also: carriages C and D)*
7 la parte «E» della vettura con motore *m* a trazione *f*
– *carriage E containing the motor*
8 il combinatore di marcia posteriore (il controller)
– *rear controller*
9 il carrello motore
– *driving bogie*
10 il carrello portante
– *carrying bogie*
11 il cacciapietre
– *wheel guard*
12 il paraurti
– *bumper (Am. fender)*
13 la motrice articolata a sei assi *m pl,* tipo «Mannheim», per il funzionamento dei tram e delle ferrovie urbane
– *six-axle articulated railcar ('Mannheim' type) for tram (Am. streetcar, trolley) and urban rail services*
14 la porta di salita e di discesa per i passeggeri, una porta doppia a soffietto
– *entrance and exit door, a double folding door*

15 il piano del gradino
– *step*
16 la macchina obliteratrice
– *ticket-cancelling machine*
17 il posto a sedere singolo
– *single seat*
18 il settore per i posti in piedi *m pl*
– *standing room portion*
19 il posto a sedere doppio
– *double seat*
20 la targa con l'indicazione *f* della linea e della destinazione
– *route (number) and destination sign*
21 la targa con l'indicazione *f* della linea
– *route sign (number sign)*
22 l'indicatore *m* di direzione *f* (il segnale luminoso)
– *indicator (indicator light)*
23 il pantografo
– *pantograph (current collector)*
24 il pattino di carbone *m* o di lega di alluminio
– *carbon or aluminium (Am. aluminium) alloy trolley shoes)*
25 la cabina di guida
– *driver's position*
26 il microfono
– *microphone*
27 il combinatore di marcia (il controller)
– *controller*
28 la radio
– *radio equipment (radio communication set)*
29 il cruscotto
– *dashboard*
30 l'illuminazione *f* del cruscotto
– *dashboard lighting*
31 il tachimetro
– *speedometer*

32 i pulsanti per apertura delle porte, tergicristallo, illuminazione *f* esterna e interna
– *buttons controlling doors, windscreen wipers, internal and external lighting*
33 la cassa
– *ticket counter with change machine*
34 l'antenna radiofonica
– *radio antenna*
35 l'area di fermata
– *tram stop (Am. streetcar stop, trolley stop)*
36 il cartello di fermata
– *tram stop sign (Am. streetcar stop sign, trolley stop sign)*
37 il deviatore elettrico (lo scambio elettrico)
– *electric change points*
38 il segnale elettrico di deviazione *f* (di scambio)
– *points signal (switch signal)*
39 l'indicatore *m* di direzione *f*
– *points change indicator*
40 la linea di contatto
– *trolley wire contact point*
41 il filo di contatto
– *trolley wire (overhead contact wire)*
42 il tirante trasversale della linea di contatto
– *overhead cross wire*
43 l'azionamento elettromagnetico (*anche:* elettroidraulico, e elettromotore) dello scambio
– *electric (also: electrohydraulic, electro-mechanical) points mechanism*

**1-5 gli strati del piano stradale**
- *road layers*
1 lo strato di protezione *f* antigelo
- *anti-frost layer*
2 lo strato portante bituminoso
- *bituminous sub-base course*
3 lo strato inferiore a volto
- *base course*
4 lo strato superiore a volto
- *binder course*
5 il manto coprente bituminoso (la copertura del piano stradale)
- *bituminous surface*
6 lo spigolo del marciapiede
- *kerb (curb)*
7 il cordone superiore del marciapiede
- *kerbstone (curbstone)*
8 la pavimentazione del marciapiede
- *paving (pavement)*
9 il marciapiede
- *pavement* (Am. *sidewalk, walkway*)
10 il tombino (il pozzetto)
- *gutter*
11 il passaggio pedonale (le zebre)
- *pedestrian crossing (zebra crossing*, Am. *crosswalk)*
12 l'angolo della strada
- *street corner*

13 la carreggiata
- *road*
14 il cavo per la fornitura dell'energia elettrica
- *electricity cables*
15 il cavo telefonico
- *telephone cables*
16 la linea di passaggio del cavo telefonico
- *telephone cable pipeline*
17 il pozzetto per i cavi con coperchio
- *cable manhole with cover (with manhole cover)*
18 il palo della luce
- *lamp post with lamp*
19 il cavo di corrente *f* per impianti *m pl* tecnici
- *electricity cables for technical installations*
20 la tubazione di allacciamento per la centrale telefonica
- *subscribers' (Am. customers') telephone lines*
21 la conduttura del gas
- *gas main*
22 la conduttura dell'acqua potabile
- *water main*
23 il pozzetto di raccolta
- *drain*
24 la caditoia
- *drain cover*

25 la tubazione di allacciamento del pozzetto di raccolta
- *drain pipe*
26 la tubazione di allacciamento dell'acqua sporca di uso domestico
- *waste pipe*
27 il collettore principale delle acque (la fognatura)
- *combined sewer*
28 la conduttura del teleriscaldamento
- *district heating main*
29 il tunnel della metropolitana
- *underground tunnel*

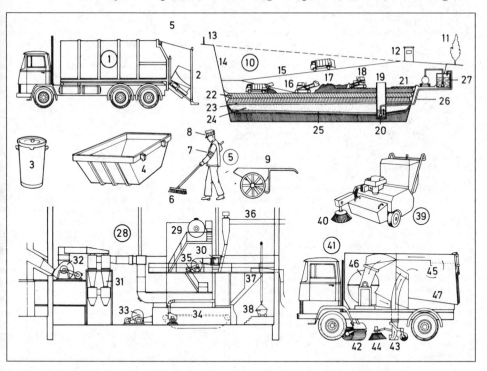

1 l'autocarro per il trasporto dei rifiuti, un compattatore
– refuse collection vehicle (Am. garbage truck)
2 il dispositivo di sollevamento dei contenitori, un sistema di carico con bocca antipolvere f
– dustbin-tipping device (Am. garbage can dumping device), a dust-free emptying system
3 il bidone delle immondizie
– dustbin (Am. garbage can, trash can)
4 il cassonetto dei rifiuti
– refuse container (Am. garbage container)
5 il netturbino (lo spazzino)
– road sweeper (Am. street sweeper)
6 la scopa (la ramazza)
– broom
7 il bracciale catarifrangente
– fluorescent armband
8 il berretto con il contrassegno catarifrangente
– cap with fluorescent band
9 il carretto dello spazzino
– road sweeper's (Am. street sweeper's) barrow
10 la discarica controllata delle immondizie
– controlled tip (Am. sanitary landfill, sanitary fill)
11 il mascheramento
– screen
12 il controllo di entrata
– weigh office
13 la staccionata di recinzione f
– fence
14 la parete della discarica
– embankment

15 la rampa d'ingresso
– access ramp
16 il bulldozer
– bulldozer
17 l'immondizia fresca
– refuse (Am. garbage)
18 il costipatore della discarica
– bulldozer for dumping and compacting
19 il pozzo con pompa
– pump shaft
20 la pompa per l'acqua di scarico
– waste water pump
21 lo strato permeabile di copertura
– porous cover
22 l'immondizia compressa e sminuzzata
– compacted and decomposed refuse
23 lo strato filtrante di ghiaia
– gravel filter layer
24 lo strato filtrante morenico
– morainic filter layer
25 lo strato di drenaggio
– drainage layer
26 la conduttura dell'acqua di scolo
– drain pipe
27 il serbatoio di raccolta dell'acqua di scolo
– water tank
28 l'inceneritore m
– refuse (Am. garbage) incineration unit
29 la caldaia
– furnace
30 l'impianto di combustione f a nafta
– oil-firing system
31 il separatore di polveri f pl (il depolverizzatore)
– separation plant
32 il ventilatore aspirante
– extraction fan

33 il ventilatore con soffiaggio dal di sotto per la griglia
– low-pressure fan for the grate
34 la griglia amovibile
– continuous feed grate
35 il ventilatore per l'impianto di combustione f a nafta
– fan for the oil-firing system
36 l'impianto di trasporto per rifiuti m pl combustibili speciali
– conveyor for separately incinerated material
37 l'impianto di caricamento del carbone
– coal feed conveyor
38 il trasportatore per le ceneri
– truck for carrying fuller's earth
39 la macchina spazzatrice
– mechanical sweeper
40 la spazzola rotante
– circular broom
41 il veicolo per la pulizia delle strade
– road-sweeping lorry (street-cleaning lorry, street cleaner)
42 la spazzola laterale
– cylinder broom
43 la bocca di aspirazione f
– suction port
44 la spazzola convogliatrice
– feeder broom
45 il condotto dell'aria
– air flow
46 il ventilatore
– fan
47 il contenitore delle immondizie
– dust collector

# 200 Costruzione delle strade

**1-54 macchine** *f pl* **per costruzioni** *f pl* **stradali**
– *road-building machinery*
1 l'escavatore *m* a cucchiaio spingente
– *shovel (power shovel, excavator)*
2 la cabina
– *machine housing*
3 i cingoli
– *caterpillar mounting (Am. caterpillar tractor)*
4 il braccio dell'escavatore *m*
– *digging bucket arm (dipper stick)*
5 il cucchiaio dell'escavatore *m*
– *digging bucket (bucket)*
6 le punte di scavo
– *digging bucket (bucket) teeth*
7 l'autocarro ribaltabile posteriormente, un autocarro pesante
– *tipper (dump truck), a heavy lorry (Am. truck)*
8 il cassone ribaltabile
– *tipping body (Am. dump body)*
9 la nervatura di rinforzo
– *reinforcing rib*
10 il riparo per la cabina di guida
– *extended front*
11 la cabina di guida
– *cab (driver's cab)*
12 il materiale scaricato
– *bulk material*
13 l'escavatore *m* a benna trascinata, una betoniera con escavatore *m*
– *concrete scraper, an aggregate scraper*
14 la tramoggia di caricamento
– *skip hoist*
15 la betoniera, un miscelatore
– *mixing drum (mixer drum), a mixing machine*
16 la ruspa a cingoli *m pl*
– *caterpillar hauling scraper*
17 la ruspa
– *scraper blade*
18 la pala livellatrice
– *levelling (Am. leveling) blade (smoothing blade)*
19 il motolivellatore stradale; *anche:* un livellatore di terreno
– *grader (motor grader)*
20 lo scarificatore stradale
– *scarifier (ripper, road ripper, rooter)*
21 la lama livellatrice
– *grader levelling (Am. leveling) blade (grader ploughshare, Am. plowshare)*
22 il dispositivo di regolazione *f* della lama
– *blade-slewing gear (slew turntable)*
23 la ferrovia Decauville
– *light railway (narrow-gauge, Am. narrow-gage, railway)*

24 la locomotiva Diesel per ferrovia Decauville, una locomotiva a scartamento ridotto
– *light railway (narrow-gauge, Am. narrow-gage) diesel locomotive*
25 il vagonetto ribaltabile (il vagonetto Decauville)
– *trailer wagon (wagon truck, skip)*
26 il costipatore a scoppio, una mazzaranga; *più pesante:* la mazzaranga con motore *m* a scoppio
– *tamper (rammer) [with internal combustion engine];* heavier: *frog (frog-type jumping rammer)*
27 le guide della mazzaranga
– *guide rods*
28 il bulldozer
– *bulldozer*
29 la pala livellatrice
– *bulldozer blade*
30 il portapala
– *pushing frame*
31 lo spandipietrisco
– *road-metal spreading machine (macadam spreader, stone spreader)*
32 la piastra costipatrice
– *tamping beam*
33 il pattino
– *sole-plate*
34 la sponda di arresto
– *side stop*
35 la parete laterale del contenitore del pietrisco
– *side of storage bin*
36 il rullo compressore a motore *m* a tre ruote *f pl*, un compressore stradale
– *three-wheeled roller, a road roller*
37 il rullo
– *roller*
38 il tetto di protezione *f* della cabina
– *all-weather roof*
39 il trattore Diesel per compressori *m pl*
– *mobile diesel-powered air compressor*
40 la bombola di ossigeno
– *oxygen cylinder*
41 lo spandipietrisco semovente
– *self-propelled gritter*
42 la fessura di spandimento del pietrisco
– *spreading flap*
43 la pavimentatrice per asfalto
– *surface finisher*
44 la sponda di arresto
– *side stop*
45 il contenitore del materiale
– *bin*
46 la catramatrice a spruzzo con riscaldatore *m* per catrame *m* e bitume *m*
– *tar-spraying machine (bituminous distributor) with tar and bitumen heater*

47 la caldaia del catrame
– *tar storage tank*
48 l'impianto automatico a rulli *m pl* per l'essicamento e il mescolamento dell'asfalto
– *fully automatic asphalt drying and mixing plant*
49 l'elevatore *m* a tazze *f pl*
– *bucket elevator (elevating conveyor)*
50 il tamburo miscelatore dell'asfalto
– *asphalt-mixing drum (asphalt mixer drum)*
51 il sollevatore-riempitore
– *filler hoist*
52 il materiale di alimentazione *f*
– *filler opening*
53 l'iniezione *f* dei leganti bituminosi
– *binder injector*
54 l'uscita dell'asfalto miscelato
– *mixed asphalt outlet*
55 la sezione trasversale di una strada
– *typical cross-section of a bituminous road*
56 la banchina stradale
– *grass verge*
57 la pendenza
– *crossfall*
58 la pavimentazione in asfalto
– *asphalt surface (bituminous layer, bituminous coating)*
59 la fondazione (la massicciata)
– *base (base course)*
60 il vespaio, o massicciata di ghiaia, una protezione antigelo
– *hardcore sub-base course (Telford base) or gravel sub-base course, an anti-frost layer*
61 il pozzetto di drenaggio
– *sub-drainage*
62 il tubo di cemento forato
– *perforated cement pipe*
63 il canaletto di raccolta delle acque
– *drainage ditch*
64 la copertura del terreno
– *soil covering*

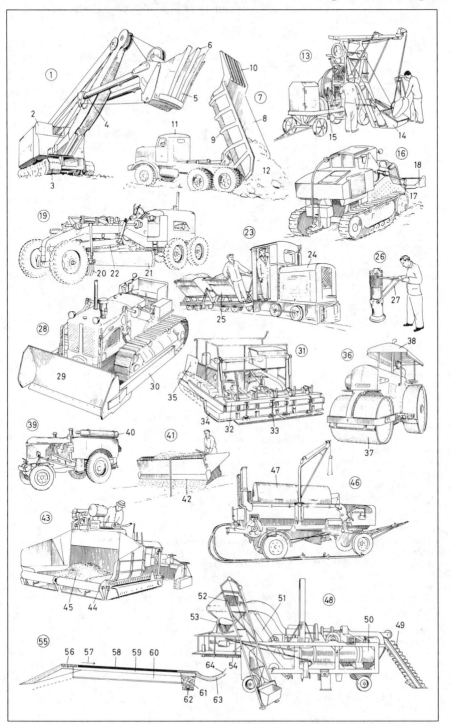

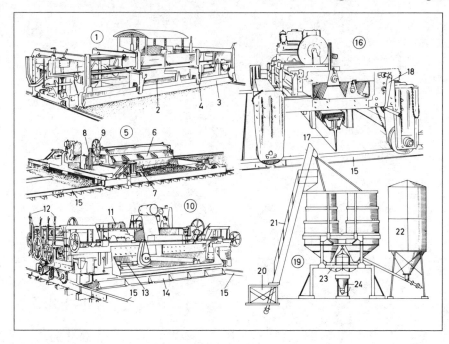

**1-24 costruzione** *f* **di strade** *f pl* **in calcestruzzo** (costruzione *f* di autostrade *f pl*)
– *concrete road construction (highway construction)*
**1** la finitrice della piattaforma stradale, una macchina per costruzioni *f pl* stradali
– *subgrade grader, a road-building machine*
**2** la palancola di asfalto compresso
– *tamping beam (consolidating beam)*
**3** la trave battente (la trave livellatrice)
– *levelling (Am. leveling) beam*
**4** la guida a rulli *m pl* per la trave battente
– *roller guides for the levelling (Am. leveling) beam*
**5** la pavimentatrice stradale per calcestruzzo
– *concrete spreader*
**6** il distributore di calcestruzzo
– *concrete spreader box*
**7** la guida a funi *f pl*
– *cable guides*
**8** la leva di comando
– *control levers*
**9** la manovella per vuotare il distributore di calcestruzzo
– *handwheel for emptying the boxes*

**10** la vibrofinitrice
– *concrete-vibrating compactor*
**11** l'unità motore
– *gearing (gears)*
**12** la leva di comando
– *control levers (operating levers)*
**13** l'albero motore per i vibratori dell'asse *f* di vibrazione *f*
– *axle drive shaft to vibrators (tampers) of vibrating beam*
**14** la livellatrice
– *screeding board (screeding beam)*
**15** il supporto rotaie *f pl* di scorrimento
– *road form*
**16** la macchina per il taglio dei giunti
– *joint cutter*
**17** la lama della macchina per giunti *m pl*
– *joint-cutting blade*
**18** la manovella di azionamento
– *crank for propelling machine*
**19** la betoniera, un impianto automatico di dosatura e di mescolazione *f*
– *concrete-mixing plant, a stationary central mixing plant, an automatic batching and mixing plant*
**20** la vasca di raccolta
– *collecting bin*
**21** l'elevatore *m* a tazze *f pl*
– *bucket elevator*

**22** il silo del cemento
– *cement store*
**23** il miscelatore
– *concrete mixer*
**24** la secchia per calcestruzzo
– *concrete pump hopper*

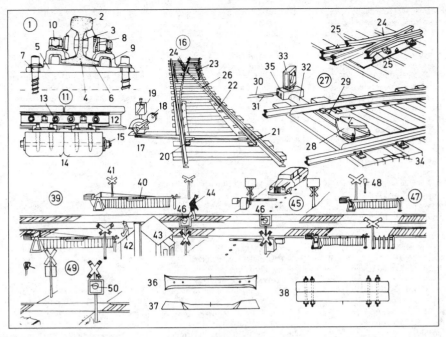

**1-38 il binario**
- *line (track)*
1 la rotaia (la rotaia ferroviaria)
- *rail*
2 il fungo della rotaia
- *rail head*
3 l'anima della rotaia
- *web (rail web)*
4 la base della rotaia (la suola della rotaia)
- *rail foot (rail bottom)*
5 la piastra di appoggio
- *sole-plate (base plate)*
6 il distanziatore (lo spessore)
- *cushion*
7 la caviglia per traversine *f pl*
- *coach screw (coach bolt)*
8 le rondelle elastiche
- *lock washers (spring washers)*
9 la piastra di fissaggio
- *rail clip (clip)*
10 la caviglia a becco
- *T-head bolt*
11 il giunto delle rotaie
- *rail joint (joint)*
12 la stecca (la ganascia) per rotaie *f pl*
- *fishplate*
13 il perno della ganascia
- *fishbolt*
14 la traversina dell'asse *m* accoppiato
- *coupled sleeper (Am. coupled tie, coupled crosstie)*
15 la vite dell'asse *m* accoppiato
- *coupling bolt*
16 il deviatoio a mano (lo scambio a mano)
- *manually-operated points (manually-operated switch)*
17 il cavalletto di manovra a mano
- *switch stand*
18 il contrappeso
- *weight*

19 il segnale di scambio
- *points signal (switch signal, points signal lamp, switch signal lamp)*
20 l'asta di comando
- *pull rod*
21 l'ago dello scambio
- *switch blade (switch tongue)*
22 il cuscinetto di scorrimento
- *slide chair*
23 la controrotaia
- *check rail (guard rail)*
24 il cuore semplice
- *frog*
25 la guancia (la rotaia di ala, la zampa di lepre *f* )
- *wing rail*
26 la rotaia intermedia
- *closure rail*
27 lo scambio comandato a distanza
- *remote-controlled points (remote-controlled switch)*
28 la chiusura della punta dello scambio
- *point lock (switch lock)*
29 il supporto
- *stretcher bar*
30 il tirante a filo
- *point wire*
31 il tenditore a vite *f*
- *turnbuckle*
32 il canale
- *channel*
33 il segnale di scambio illuminato elettricamente
- *electrically illuminated points signal (switch signal)*
34 la piastra dello scambio
- *trough*
35 il comando dello scambio con cassetta di distribuzione *f*
- *points motor with protective casing*
36 la traversina di ferro
- *steel sleeper (Am. steel tie, steel crosstie)*

37 la traversina di cemento armato
- *concrete sleeper (Am. concrete tie, concrete crosstie)*
38 la traversina di accoppiamento
- *coupled sleeper (Am. coupled tie, coupled crosstie)*
**39-50 passaggi *m pl* a livello**
- *level crossings (Am. grade crossings)*
39 il passaggio a livello custodito
- *protected level crossing (Am. protected grade crossing)*
40 la sbarra (la barriera) del passaggio a livello
- *barrier (gate)*
41 la croce di S. Andrea, per indicare pericolo
- *warning cross (Am. crossbuck)*
42 il cantoniere (il casellante)
- *crossing keeper (Am. gateman)*
43 il casello (la casa cantoniera)
- *crossing keeper's box (Am. gateman's box)*
44 il guardalinee (il cantoniere addetto alla vigilanza della linea ferroviaria)
- *linesman (Am. trackwalker)*
45 la mezza sbarra (barriera) del passaggio a livello
- *half-barrier crossing*
46 il segnale intermittente
- *warning light*
47 la sbarra (la barriera) del passaggio a livello apribile a chiamata
- *intercom-controlled crossing; sim.: telephone-controlled crossing*
48 l'impianto a comunicazione *f* alternata nei due sensi
- *intercom system*
49 il passaggio a livello incustodito
- *unprotected level crossing (Am. unprotected grade crossing)*
50 il segnale intermittente
- *warning light*

# 203 Linea ferroviaria II (Segnali)

**1-6 segnali** *m pl* **principali**
– *stop signals (main signals)*
**1** il segnale principale, un segnale sulla posizione «via impedita»
– *stop signal (main signal), a semaphore signal in 'stop' position*
**2** l'aletta *f* del semaforo
– *signal arm (semaphore arm)*
**3** il segnale elettrico principale (segnale *m* luminoso su «via impedita»)
– *electric stop signal (colour light, Am. color light, signal) at 'stop'*
**4** la posizione del segnale su «via libera con avviso di via impedita»
– *signal position: 'proceed at low speed'*
**5** la posizione del segnale *m* su «via libera»
– *signal position: 'proceed'*
**6** il segnale sostitutivo di «chiamata d'emergenza»
– *substitute signal*
**7-24 presegnali** *m pl*
– *distant signals*
**7** il segnale su «via impedita»
– *semaphore signal at 'be prepared to stop at next signal'*
**8** la pala sussidiaria
– *supplementary semaphore arm*
**9** il presegnale luminoso su «via impedita»
– *colour light (Am. color light) distant signal at 'be prepared to stop at next signal'*
**10** il segnale su «via libera con attesa di via impedita»
– *signal position: 'be prepared to proceed at low speed'*
**11** il segnale su «attesa di via libera»
– *signal position: 'proceed main signal ahead'*
**12** il presegnale con tavola ausiliaria, per diminuzione *f* dello spazio di frenata di più del 5%
– *semaphore signal with indicator plate showing a reduction in braking distance of more than 5%*
**13** la tavola triangolare
– *triangle (triangle sign)*
**14** il presegnale luminoso con luce *f* sussidiaria per distanza ridotta sul binario di arrivo
– *colour light (Am. color light) distant signal with indicator light for showing reduced braking distance*
**15** la luce sussidiaria bianca
– *supplementary white light*
**16** l'annuncio di presegnale *m* «attesa di via libera» (segnale *m* giallo di attenzione *f* )
– *distant signal indicating 'be prepared to stop at next signal' (yellow light)*
**17** il ripetitore del presegnale (il presegnale con luce *f* sussidiaria senza tavola)
– *second distant signal (distant signal with supplementary light, without indicator plate)*

**18** il presegnale con indicazione *f* di velocità
– *distant signal with speed indicator*
**19** il preindicatore di velocità
– *distant speed indicator*
**20** il presegnale con indicazione *f* di direzione *f*
– *distant signal with route indicator*
**21** il preindicatore di direzione *f*
– *route indicator*
**22** il presegnale senza tavola sussidiaria in posizione *f* «via impedita»
– *distant signal without supplementary arm in position: 'be prepared to stop at next signal'*
**23** il presegnale senza tavola sussidiaria in posizione *f* «attesa di via libera»
– *distant signal without supplementary arm in 'be prepared to proceed' position*
**24** la tavola di presegnale *m*
– *distant signal identification plate*
**25-44 segnali** *m pl* **sussidiari**
– *supplementary signals*
**25** la tavola trapezoidale per definire i punti di arresto prima di un punto di assistenza
– *stop board for indicating the stopping point at a control point*
**26-29 le tavole di presegnalazione** *f*
– *approach signs*
**26** la tavola di presegnalazione a 100 m di distanza dal presegnale
– *approach sign 100 m from distant signal*
**27** la tavola di presegnalazione *f* a 175 m di distanza dal presegnale
– *approach sign 175 m from distant signal*
**28** la tavola di presegnalazione *f* a 250 m di distanza dal presegnale
– *approach sign 250 m from distant signal*
**29** la tavola di presegnalazione *f* a una distanza inferiore al 5% dallo spazio di fermata della linea
– *approach sign at a distance of 5% less than the braking distance on the section*
**30** la tavola scaccata per segnare i segnali principali distanti
– *chequered sign indicating stop signals (main signals) not positioned immediately to the right of or over the line (track)*
**31** *u.* **32** le tavole di stop, per indicare il punto di arresto della testa del treno
– *stop boards to indicate the stopping point of the front of the train*
**33** la tavola di stop (ci si deve aspettare un arresto)
– *stop board indicating 'be prepared to stop'*
**34** *u.* **35** tavole *f pl* con indicazione *f* di spartineve *m*
– *snow plough (Am. snowplow) signs*

**34** la tavola «sollevare il cuneo»
– *'raise snow plough (Am. snowplow)' sign*
**35** la tavola «abbassare il cuneo»
– *'lower snow plough (Am. snowplow)' sign*
**36-44 segnali** *m pl* **di rallentamento**
– *speed restriction signs*
**36-38 il disco di rallentamento** [velocità massima 3 x 10 = 30 km/h]
– *speed restriction sign [maximum speed 3 x 10 = 30 kph]*
**36** l'indicazione *f* del giorno
– *sign for day running*
**37** l'indicatore della velocità
– *speed code number*
**38** l'indicatore notturno
– *illuminated sign for night running*
**39** l'inizio del tratto a velocità momentaneamente ridotta
– *commencement of temporary speed restriction*
**40** la fine del tratto di velocità momentaneamente ridotta
– *termination of temporary speed restriction*
**41** la tavola che indica un tratto a velocità ridotta costante [velocità massima: 5 x 10 = 50 km/h]
– *speed restriction sign for a section with a permanent speed restriction [maximum speed 5 x 10 = 50 kph]*
**42** l'inizio della velocità ridotta costante
– *commencement of permanent speed restriction*
**43** la tavola che indica la velocità [solo nelle stazioni principali]
– *speed restriction warning sign [only on main lines]*
**44** il segnale di velocità (solo nelle stazioni principali)
– *speed restriction sign [only on main lines]*
**45-52 gli indicatori di direzione** *f* **per deviata**
– *point signals (switch signals)*
**45-48 deviazioni** *f pl* **semplici**
– *single points (single switches)*
**45** l'istradamento dritto
– *route straight ahead (main line)*
**46** l'istradamento con curva [a destra]
– *[right] branch*
**47** l'istradamento con curva [a sinistra]
– *[left] branch*
**48** l'istradamento con curva [vista da cuore *m*]
– *branch [seen from the frog]*
**49-52 doppi scambi** *m pl* **inglesi**
– *double crossover*
**49** l'istradamento dritto da sinistra a destra
– *route straight ahead from left to right*

50 l'istradamento dritto da destra a sinistra
– *route straight ahead from right to left*
51 la curva da sinistra a sinistra
– *turnout to the left from the left*
52 la curva da destra a destra
– *turnout to the right from the right*
53 **la cabina di blocco manuale**
– ***manually-operated signal box***
(Am. *signal tower, switch tower*)
54 la leva di comando
– *lever mechanism*
55 la leva di deviazione *f* (bleu), una leva di blocco
– *points lever (switch lever) [blue], a lock lever*
56 la leva segnaletica (rossa)
– *signal lever [red]*
57 l'impugnatura a paletto
– *catch*
58 la leva di passaggio a livello
– *route lever*
59 il blocco di sezione *f*
– *block instruments*
60 il relais di blocco
– *block section panel*
61 **il banco di blocco elettrico**
– ***electrically-operated signal box***
(Am. *signal tower, switch tower*)
62 il pulsante d'itinerario
– *points (switch) and signal knobs*
63 l'indicazione *f* dell'avvenuta registrazione *f* del comando
– *lock indicator panel*
64 il campo di controllo
– *track and signal indicator*
65 **l'apparato centrale**
– ***track diagram control layout***
66 il tavolo dell'apparato centrale
– *track diagram control panel (domino panel)*
67 i pulsanti
– *push buttons*
68 gli itinerari e gli istradamenti
– *routes*
69 l'impianto di interfono
– *intercom system*

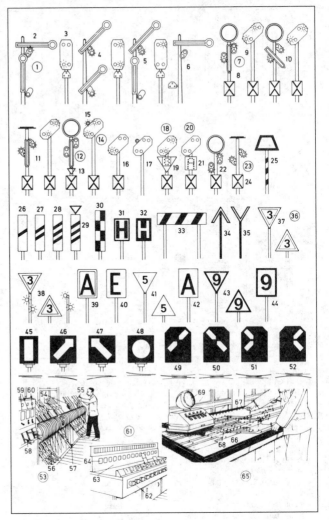

1 l'ufficio spedizione *f* merce *f*
espresso (accettazione *f* e ritiro
merce *f* espresso)
– *parcels office*
2 la merce, spedita per espresso (il
collo)
– *parcels*
3 la cesta da viaggio con chiusura
– *basket [with lock]*
4 l'ufficio spedizione *f* bagagli *m pl*
– *luggage counter*
5 la bilancia automatica
– *platform scale with dial*
6 la valigia
– *suitcase (case)*
7 l'etichetta
– *luggage sticker*
8 lo scontrino
– *luggage receipt*
9 l'addetto ai bagagli
– *luggage clerk*
10 il cartellone pubblicitario
– *poster (advertisement)*
11 la cassetta per le lettere della
stazione
– *station post box (Am. station mail-box)*
12 il pannello segnaletico
– *station guide*
13 il ristorante della stazione
– *station restaurant*

14 la sala di aspetto
– *waiting room*
15 la pianta della città
– *map of the town (street map)*
16 l'orario ferroviario generale
– *timetable (Am. schedule)*
17 il distributore automatico dei
biglietti
– *ticket machine*
18 l'orario ferroviario a parete *f*
(coll'indicazione *f* dei binari)
– *arrivals and departures board (timetable)*
19 il quadro degli arrivi
– *arrival timetable (Am. arrival schedule)*
20 il quadro delle partenze
– *departure timetable (Am. depar-ture schedule)*

21 le cassette per deposito bagagli *m pl*
– *left luggage lockers*
22 il distributore automatico per cambio del denaro
– *change machine*
23 il sottopassaggio di accesso ai binari
– *tunnel to the platforms*
24 i viaggiatori – le viaggiatrici
– *passengers*
25 la scala di accesso ai binari
– *steps to the platforms*
26 la libreria della stazione (*anche:* l'edicola della stazione)
– *station bookstall (Am. station bookstand) (also: magazine kiosk)*
27 il deposito bagagli *m pl*
– *left luggage office (left luggage)*
28 l'agenzia di viaggio, *anche:* l'ufficio informazioni per alberghi *m pl* e camere *f pl*
– *travel centre (Am. center); also: accommodation bureau*
29 l'ufficio informazioni *f pl*
– *information office (Am. information bureau)*
30 l'orologio della stazione
– *station clock*
31 la filiale della banca, con ufficio cambio
– *bank branch with foreign exchange counter*

32 il listino dei cambi (listino delle valute estere)
– *indicator board showing exchange rates*
33 la pianta della rete ferroviaria
– *railway map (Am. railroad map)*
34 la distribuzione dei biglietti
– *ticket office*
35 lo sportello
– *ticket counter*
36 il biglietto
– *ticket*
37 il piatto girevole
– *revolving tray*
38 la membrana attraverso la quale parlare
– *grill*
39 il bigliettario
– *ticket clerk (Am. ticket agent)*
40 la lastra di vetro
– *pane of glass (window)*
41 l'orario ferroviario tascabile
– *pocket timetable (Am. pocket train schedule)*
42 la panca per i bagagli
– *luggage rest*
43 l'infermeria
– *first aid station*
44 la missione della stazione
– *Travellers' (Am. Travelers') Aid*

45 l'addetto alle informazioni (il funzionario ferroviario; *qui:* il conduttore)
– *railway (Am. railroad) information clerk (railway [Am. railroad] employee; here: the guard, conductor)*
46 l'orario ufficiale
– *official timetable (official railway guide, Am. train schedule)*

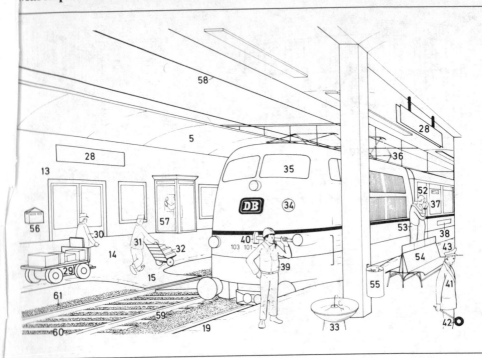

1 il marciapiede della stazione ferroviaria (il marciapiede)
- *platform*
2 la scala di accesso ai binari
- *steps to the platform*
3 il sovrappassaggio
- *bridge*
4 il numero del binario
- *platform number*
5 la pensilina (la tettoia)
- *platform roofing*
6 i viaggiatori, le viaggiatrici
- *passengers*
7-12 i bagagli
- *luggage*
7 la valigia
- *suitcase (case)*
8 il cartellino della valigia
- *luggage label*
9 l'etichetta dell'albergo
- *hotel sticker*
10 la borsa da viaggio
- *travelling (Am. traveling) bag*
11 la cappelliera
- *hat box*
12 l'ombrello
- *umbrella, a walking-stick umbrella*
13 l'ufficio di ricevimento per la clientela
- *main building (offices)*

14 il marciapiede di servizio
- *platform*
15 la passerella
- *crossing*
16 l'edicola mobile
- *news trolley*
17 il venditore di giornali *m pl*
- *news vendor (Am. news dealer)*
18 la lettura da viaggio
- *reading matter for the journey*
19 il cordolo del marciapiede
- *edge of the platform*
20 l'agente *m* della polizia ferroviaria
- *railway policeman (Am. railroad policeman)*
21 il cartello indicatore della direzione
- *destination board*
22 lo spazio riservato all'indicazione *f* della stazione di destinazione *f*
- *destination indicator*
23 lo spazio riservato all'orario di partenza previsto
- *departure time indicator*
24 lo spazio riservato all'annuncio del ritardo dei treni
- *delay indicator*
25 il treno della ferrovia urbana, una motrice
- *suburban train, a railcar*

26 lo scompartimento riservato (il compartimento riservato)
- *special compartment*
27 l'altoparlante della stazione
- *platform loudspeaker*
28 il cartello indicatore di località
- *station sign*
29 il carrello manovrato elettricamente
- *electric trolley (electric truck)*
30 l'assistente *m* addetto al carico
- *loading foreman*
31 il facchino
- *porter (Am. redcap)*
32 il carrello a mano (del facchino)
- *barrow*
33 la fontanella
- *drinking fountain*
34 l'Eurocity *m*, anche: l'Intercity *m*
- *electric Eurocity express; also: IC express (Intercity express)*
35 una locomotiva elettrica per espressi *m pl*
- *electric locomotive, an express locomotive*
36 il pantografo
- *collector bow (sliding bow)*

22 der Geldwechselautomat (Geld-
   wechsler)
– *change machine*
23 der Bahnsteigtunnel
– *tunnel to the platforms*
24 die Reisenden *m u. f*
– *passengers*
25 der Bahnsteigaufgang
– *steps to the platforms*
26 die Bahnhofsbuchhandlung (*auch:*
   das Zeitschriftenkiosk)
– *station bookstall (Am. station*
   *bookstand) (*also: *magazine kiosk)*
27 die Handgepäckaufbewahrung
– *left luggage office (left luggage)*
28 das Reisebüro; *auch:* der Hotel- und
   Zimmernachweis
– *travel centre (Am. center); also:*
   *accommodation bureau*
29 die Auskunft
– *information office (Am. information*
   *bureau)*
30 die Bahnhofsuhr
– *station clock*
31 die Bankfiliale, mit Wechselstelle *f*
– *bank branch with foreign exchange*
   *counter*
32 die Geldkurstabelle (Währungs-
   tabelle)
– *indicator board showing exchange*
   *rates*
33 der Streckennetzplan
– *railway map (Am. railroad map)*

34 die Fahrkartenausgabe
   (Fahrausweisausgabe)
– *ticket office*
35 der Fahrkartenschalter
   (Fahrausweisschalter)
– *ticket counter*
36 die Fahrkarte (der Fahrausweis)
– *ticket*
37 der Drehteller
– *revolving tray*
38 die Sprechmembran
– *grill*
39 der Schalterbeamte (Fahrkarten-
   verkäufer)
– *ticket clerk (Am. ticket agent)*
40 die Glasscheibe
– *pane of glass (window)*
41 der Taschenfahrplan
– *pocket timetable (Am. pocket train*
   *schedule)*
42 die Gepäckbank
– *luggage rest*
43 die Sanitätswache
– *first aid station*
44 die Bahnhofsmission
– *Travellers' (Am. Travelers') Aid*
45 der Auskunftsbeamte (Bahn-
   angestellte, *hier:* der Schaffner,
   Zugführer)
– *railway (Am. railroad) information*
   *clerk (railway [Am. railroad]*
   *employee; here: the guard,*
   *conductor)*

46 das amtliche Kursbuch
– *official timetable (official railway*
   *guide, Am. train schedule)*

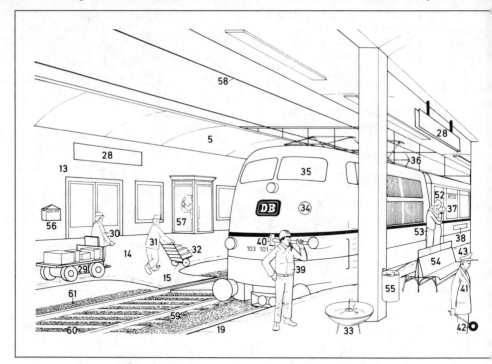

1 il marciapiede della stazione ferroviaria (il marciapiede)
– *platform*
2 la scala di accesso ai binari
– *steps to the platform*
3 il sovrappassaggio
– *bridge*
4 il numero del binario
– *platform number*
5 la pensilina (la tettoia)
– *platform roofing*
6 i viaggiatori, le viaggiatrici
– *passengers*
**7-12  i bagagli**
– *luggage*
7 la valigia
– *suitcase (case)*
8 il cartellino della valigia
– *luggage label*
9 l'etichetta dell'albergo
– *hotel sticker*
10 la borsa da viaggio
– *travelling* (Am. *traveling*) *bag*
11 la cappelliera
– *hat box*
12 l'ombrello
– *umbrella, a walking-stick umbrella*
13 l'ufficio di ricevimento per la
  clientela
– *main building (offices)*

14 il marciapiede di servizio
– *platform*
15 la passerella
– *crossing*
16 l'edicola mobile
– *news trolley*
17 il venditore di giornali *m pl*
– *news vendor* (Am. *news dealer*)
18 la lettura da viaggio
– *reading matter for the journey*
19 il cordolo del marciapiede
– *edge of the platform*
20 l'agente *m* della polizia ferroviaria
– *railway policeman* (Am. *railroad
  policeman*)
21 il cartello indicatore della
  direzione
– *destination board*
22 lo spazio riservato all'indicazione
  *f* della stazione di destinazione *f*
– *destination indicator*
23 lo spazio riservato all'orario di
  partenza previsto
– *departure time indicator*
24 lo spazio riservato all'annuncio
  del ritardo dei treni
– *delay indicator*
25 il treno della ferrovia urbana, una
  motrice
– *suburban train, a railcar*

26 lo scompartimento riservato (il
  compartimento riservato)
– *special compartment*
27 l'altoparlante della stazione
– *platform loudspeaker*
28 il cartello indicatore di località
– *station sign*
29 il carrello manovrato elettricamente
– *electric trolley (electric truck)*
30 l'assistente *m* addetto al carico
– *loading foreman*
31 il facchino
– *porter* (Am. *redcap*)
32 il carrello a mano (del facchino)
– *barrow*
33 la fontanella
– *drinking fountain*
34 l'Eurocity *m*, anche: l'Intercity *m*
– *electric Eurocity express;* also: *IC
  express (Intercity express)*
35 una locomotiva elettrica per
  espressi *m pl*
– *electric locomotive, an express
  locomotive*
36 il pantografo
– *collector bow (sliding bow)*

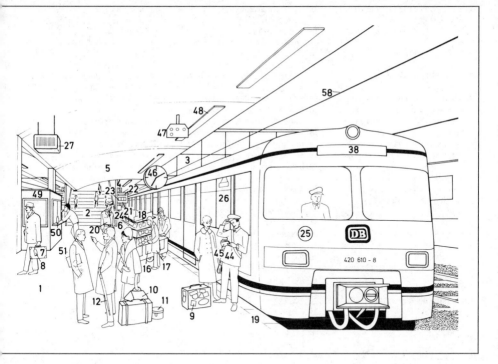

37 il compartimento riservato al personale di scorta al treno
– *secretarial compartment*
38 il cartello di direzione *f*
– *destination board*
39 il verificatore di materiale *m* rota-
bile
– *wheel tapper*
40 il martelletto di verifica ruote *f pl*
– *wheel-tapping hammer*
41 il capostazione
– *station-master*
42 la paletta del capostazione
– *signal*
43 il berretto rosso
– *red cap*
44 lo steward a terra (l'addetto alle
informazioni)
– *inspector*
45 l'orario ferroviario tascabile
– *pocket timetable (Am. pocket
train schedule)*
46 l'orologio
– *platform clock*
47 il segnale di partenza
– *starting signal*
48 l'illuminazione *f* del marciapiede
– *platform lighting*

49 il chiosco per bevande *f pl* e
generi *m pl* alimentari per il viaggio
– *refreshment kiosk*
50 la bottiglia di birra
– *beer bottle*
51 il giornale
– *newspaper*
52 il bacio di addio
– *parting kiss*
53 l'abbraccio
– *embrace*
54 la panchina
– *platform seat*
55 il cestino dei rifiuti
– *litter bin (Am. litter basket)*
56 la cassetta delle lettere
– *platform post box (Am. platform
mailbox)*
57 il telefono
– *platform telephone*
58 il filo di linea (il filo di contatto)
– *trolley wire (overhead contact
wire)*
59-61 il binario
– *track*
59 la rotaia
– *rail*

60 la traversina
– *sleeper (Am. tie, crosstie)*
61 il pietrisco (lo strato di pietrisco,
il ballast)
– *ballast (bed)*

1 la rampa di carico (la rampa per il bestiame)
- *ramp (vehicle ramp);* sim.: *livestock ramp*
2 la motrice elettrica
- *electric truck*
3 il carrello trasportatore
- *trailer*
4 la merce a collettame *m* (i colli); nella spedizione collettiva: collo in spedizione *f* di merce *f* a collettame *m*
- *part loads (Am. package freight, less-than-carload freight); in general traffic: general goods in general consignments (in mixed consignments)*
5 la gabbia d'imballaggio
- *crate*
6 il carro merci *f pl*
- *goods van (Am. freight car)*
7 il magazzino merci *f pl* (il deposito merci *f pl*)
- *goods shed (Am. freight house)*
8 la strada di carico
- *loading strip*
9 la rampa del deposito (il piano caricatore)
- *loading dock*
10 la balla di torba
- *bale of peat*
11 la balla di lino
- *bale of linen (of linen cloth)*
12 la legatura
- *fastening (cord)*
13 la damigiana
- *wicker bottle (wickered bottle, demijohn)*
14 il carrello a due ruote *f pl* per sacchi *m pl*
- *trolley*
15 l'autocarro per trasporto merci *f pl* in collettame *m*
- *goods lorry (Am. freight truck)*
16 il muletto
- *forklift truck (fork truck, forklift)*
17 il binario di caricamento
- *loading siding*
18 la merce ingombrante
- *bulky goods*
19 il piccolo container ferroviario
- *small railway-owned (Am. railroad-owned) container*
20 il vagone del circo
- *showman's caravan (sim. circus caravan)*
21 il pianale in esecuzione *f* normale
- *flat wagon (Am. flat freight car)*
22 la sagoma di carico
- *loading gauge (Am. gage)*
23 la balla di paglia
- *bale of straw*
24 il carro piatto con stanti *m pl*
- *flat wagon (Am. flatcar) with side stakes*

25 il parco macchine *f pl*
- *fleet of lorries (Am. trucks)*
26-39 il deposito merci *f pl*
- *goods shed (Am. freight house)*
26 la spedizione *f* merci *f pl* (l'inoltro)
- *goods office (forwarding office, Am. freight office)*
27 la merce in collettame *m*
- *part-load goods (Am. package freight)*
28 l'addetto alla merce in collettame *m*
- *forwarding agent (Am. freight agent, shipper)*
29 il capo caricatore
- *loading foreman*
30 la lettera di carico (la lettera di vettura)
- *consignment note (waybill)*
31 la bascula
- *weighing machine*
32 il pallet
- *pallet*
33 il lavoratore del magazzino
- *porter*
34 il carrello elettrico
- *electric cart (electric truck)*
35 il carrello trasportatore
- *trailer*
36 lo spedizioniere
- *loading supervisor*
37 il portone
- *goods shed door (Am. freight house door)*
38 la rotaia di scorrimento
- *rail (slide rail)*
39 la carrucola di guida
- *roller*
40 la pesa (l'edificio per la pesa)
- *weighbridge office*
41 la stadera a ponte *m*
- *weighbridge*
42 la stazione di smistamento
- *marshalling yard (Am. classification yard, switch yard)*
43 la locomotiva di smistamento
- *shunting engine (shunting locomotive, shunter, Am. switch engine, switcher)*
44 la cabina di manovra smistamento
- *marshalling yard signal box (Am. classification yard switch tower)*
45 il manovratore capo
- *yardmaster*
46 la schiena di asino
- *hump*
47 il binario di manovra
- *sorting siding (classification siding, classification track)*
48 il freno su rotaia
- *rail brake (retarder)*
49 la scarpa di arresto
- *slipper brake (slipper)*
50 il binario morto
- *storage siding (siding)*

51 il fermacarri
- *buffer (buffers, Am. bumper)*
52 la carrata
- *wagon load (Am. carload)*
53 il magazzino (il deposito)
- *warehouse*
54 la stazione dei container
- *container station*
55 la gru a portale *m*
- *gantry crane*
56 l'elevatore *m*
- *lifting gear (hoisting gear)*
57 il container
- *container*
58 il carrello porta container
- *container wagon (Am. container car)*
59 il semirimorchio
- *semi-trailer*

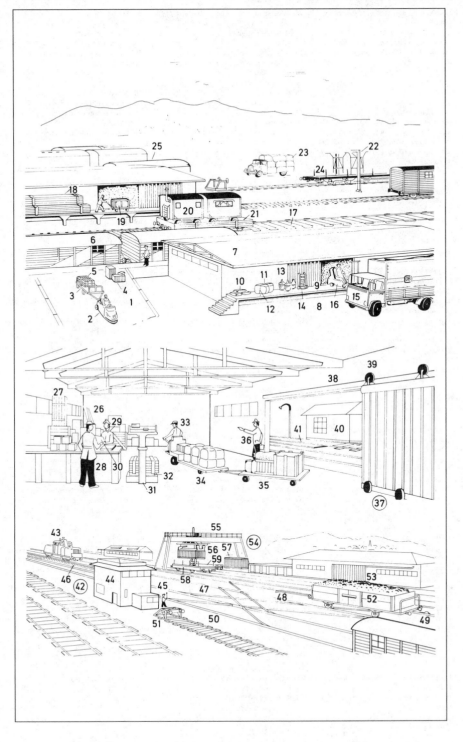

**1-21  la vettura per treni** *m pl* **espressi e rapidi**
– *express train coach (express train carriage, express train car, corridor compartment coach), a passenger coach*
1  la vista laterale
– *side elevation (side view)*
2  la fiancata della vettura
– *coach body*
3  il telaio inferiore
– *underframe (frame)*
4  il carrello girevole con sospensione *f* in acciaio-gomma e ammortizzatori *m pl*
– *bogie (truck) with steel and rubber suspension and shock absorbers*
5  le casse contenimento batterie *f pl*
– *battery containers (battery boxes)*
6  lo scambiatore di calore *m* elettrico e a vapore *m* per il riscaldamento
– *steam and electric heat exchanger for the heating system*
7  il finestrino
– *sliding window*
8  il mantice di gomma di collegamento
– *rubber connecting seal*
9  il ventilatore (la presa di aria) statico
– *ventilator*
**10-21  la vista in pianta**
– *plan*
10  la seconda classe
– *second-class section*
11  il corridoio laterale
– *corridor*
12  il sedile ribaltabile
– *folding seat (tip-up seat)*
13  il compartimento (*fam.:* lo scompartimento)
– *passenger compartment (compartment)*
14  la porta del compartimento (dello scompartimento)
– *compartment door*
15  il vano lavamani (il locale lavamani)
– *washroom*
16  il WC (la toilette)
– *toilet (lavatory, WC)*
17  la prima classe
– *first-class section*
18  la porta a vento (la porta apribile nei due sensi)
– *swing door*
19  la porta scorrevole del passaggio d'intercomunicazione *f*
– *sliding connecting door*
20  la porta di accesso
– *door*
21  il vestibolo
– *vestibule*
**22-32  il vagone ristorante** *m*
– *dining car (restaurant car, diner)*
**22-25  la vista laterale**
– *side elevation (side view)*
22  la porta di accesso
– *door*
23  la porta di carico vivande *f pl*
– *loading door*
24  il pantografo di alimentazione *f* per l'approvvigionamento della corrente nelle soste (la presa di corrente *f* per la produzione di energia elettrica nelle soste)
– *current collector for supplying power during stops*

25  le casse di contenimento batterie *f pl*
– *battery boxes (battery containers)*
**26-32  la vista in pianta**
– *plan*
26  il WC (la toilette) del personale
– *staff washroom*
27  il ripostiglio
– *storage cupboard*
28  il cucinotto
– *washing-up area*
29  la cucina
– *kitchen*
30  la piastra elettrica di cottura a otto fuochi *m pl*
– *electric oven with eight hotplates*
31  il buffet
– *counter*
32  il ristorante
– *dining compartment*
33  la cucina del vagone ristorante
– *dining car kitchen*
34  il cuoco (il cuoco del treno)
– *chef (head cook)*
35  la dispensa
– *kitchen cabinet*
36  il vagone letto
– *sleeping car (sleeper)*
37  la vista laterale
– *side elevation (side view)*
**38-42  la vista in pianta**
– *plan*
38  lo scompartimento T 2 (a due posti *m pl* letto)
– *two-seat twin-berth compartment (two-seat two-berth compartment, Am. bedroom)*
39  la porta a soffietto girevole
– *folding doors*
40  il lavabo
– *washstand*
41  lo spazio riservato al personale di servizio
– *office*
42  il WC (la toilette)
– *toilet (lavatory, WC)*
43  il compartimento dell'espresso (dell'intercity, dell'IC)
– *express train compartment*
44  il sedile imbottito allungabile
– *upholstered reclining seat*
45  il bracciolo
– *armrest*
46  il posacenere (il portacenere) del bracciolo
– *ashtray in the armrest*
47  l'appoggiatesta imbottito spostabile
– *adjustable headrest*
48  la fodera in tessuto
– *antimacassar*
49  lo specchio
– *mirror*
50  l'attaccapanni *m* (il gancio)
– *coat hook*
51  il portapacchi
– *luggage rack*
52  il finestrino
– *compartment window*
53  il tavolinetto ribaltabile
– *fold-away table (pull-down table)*
54  il regolatore del riscaldamento
– *heating regulator*
55  il recipiente per i rifiuti
– *litter receptacle*

56  la tendina
– *curtain*
57  l'appoggiapiedi
– *footrest*
58  il posto vicino al finestrino
– *corner seat*
59  la vettura pullman
– *open car*
60  la vista laterale
– *side elevation (side view)*
**61-72  la vista in pianta**
– *plan*
61  lo scompartimento della vettura pullman
– *open carriage*
62  la corsia ad un sedile
– *row of single seats*
63  la corsia a due sedili *m pl*
– *row of double seats*
64  il sedile girevole
– *reclining seat*
65  il sedile imbottito
– *seat upholstery*
66  lo schienale
– *backrest*
67  l'appoggiatesta
– *headrest*
68  il cuscino di piuma con la fodera in nylon *m*
– *down-filled headrest cushion with nylon cover*
69  il bracciolo con il posacenere (il portacenere)
– *armrest with ashtray*
70  il reparto guardaroba (il reparto appendiabiti)
– *cloakroom*
71  il reparto portabagagli
– *luggage compartment*
72  il WC (la toilette)
– *toilet (lavatory, WC)*
73  il vagone self-service
– *buffet car (quick-service buffet car), a self-service restaurant car*
74  la vista laterale
– *side elevation (side view)*
75  la presa di corrente *f* per la produzione di energia elettrica nelle soste
– *current collector for supplying power during stops*
76  la vista in pianta
– *plan*
77  il ristorante self-service
– *dining compartment*
**78-79  i servizi per il vagone self-service**
– *buffet (buffet compartment)*
78  la parte riservata ai passeggeri
– *customer area*
79  la parte riservata al personale
– *serving area*
80  la cucina
– *kitchen*
81  il settore riservato al personale
– *staff compartment*
82  il WC (la toilette) del personale
– *staff toilet (staff lavatory, staff WC)*
83  i portavivande
– *food compartments*
84  i piatti
– *plates*
85  le posate
– *cutlery*
86  la cassa
– *till (cash register)*

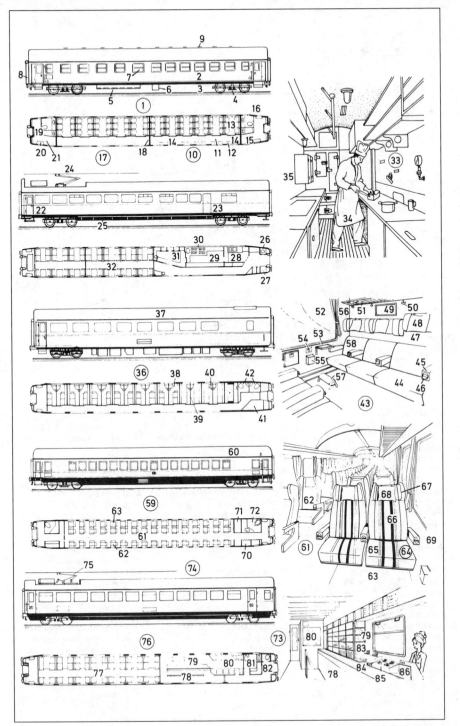

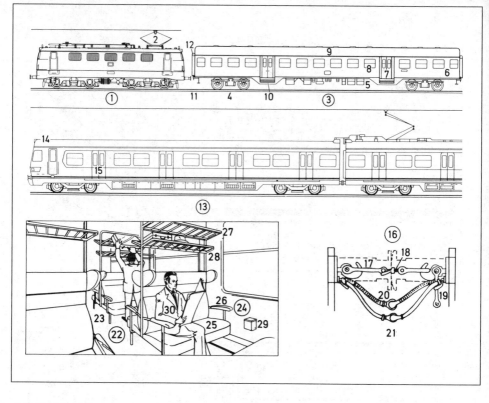

**1-30  il traffico locale**
- *local train service*

**1-12  il treno locale**
- *local train (short-distance train)*

**1**  la locomotiva elettrica
- *electric locomotive*

**2**  il pantografo
- *current collector*

**3**  il treno locale a quattro assi *m pl*, una carrozza viaggiatori *m pl*
- *four-axled coach (four-axled car) for short-distance routes, a passenger coach (passenger car)*

**4**  il carrello girevole (con freni *m pl* a disco)
- *bogie (truck) [with disc (disk) brakes]*

**5**  la cassa contenimento batterie *f pl*
- *underframe (frame)*

**6**  lo scatolato metallico
- *coach body with metal panelling (Am. paneling)*

**7**  la doppia porta a soffietto automatica
- *double folding doors*

**8**  il finestrino del compartimento (dello scompartimento)
- *compartment window*

**9**  la vettura pullman
- *open carriage*

**10**  la porta di accesso
- *entrance*

**11**  il passaggio d'intercomunicazione *f*
- *connecting corridor*

**12**  il mantice di gomma di collegamento
- *rubber connecting seal*

**13**  l'automotrice *f*, un'automotrice per il traffico locale
- *light railcar, a short-distance railcar*

**14**  la cabina dell'automotrice *f*
- *cab (driver's cab, Am. engineer's cab)*

**15**  la porta della carrozza
- *carriage door*

**16**  l'aggancio e il raccordo delle vetture
- *connecting hoses and coupling*

**17**  la maglia del tenditore
- *coupling link*

**18**  il tenditore filettato (il doppio tenditore con il bilanciere)
- *tensioning device (coupling screw with tensioning lever)*

**19**  il giunto non innestato
- *unlinked coupling*

**20**  l'accoppiamento flessibile del condotto di riscaldamento
- *heating coupling hose (steam coupling hose)*

**21**  l'accoppiamento del freno a aria
- *coupling hose (connecting hose) for the compressed-air braking system*

**22**  il compartimento (lo scompartimento) di II classe *f*
- *second-class section*

**23**  il corridoio centrale
- *central gangway*

**24**  il compartimento (lo scompartimento)
- *compartment*

**25**  il sedile imbottito
- *upholstered seat*

**26**  il bracciolo
- *armrest*

**27**  il portapacchi
- *luggage rack*

**28**  la reticella per i cappelli e i bagagli meno ingombranti
- *hat and light luggage rack*

**29**  il posacenere (il portacenere) ribaltabile
- *ashtray*

**30**  il viaggiatore (il passeggero)
- *passenger*

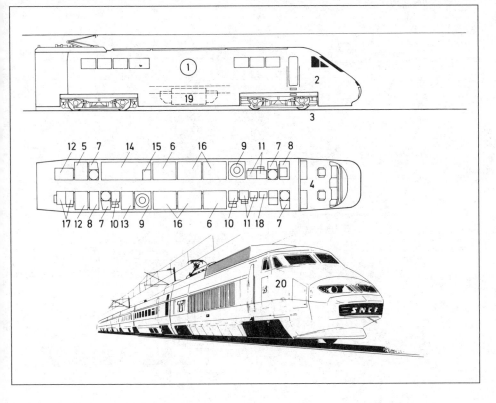

**1-19  il treno ICE** (intercity express, intercity sperimentale)
– *Intercity Express (*formerly: *Intercity Experimental)*
**1**  la motrice delle ferrovie tedesche (DB)
– *German Federal Railway engine*
**2**  l'automotrice *f*
– *driving unit (power car)*
**3**  la serie delle ruote motrici con motori *m pl* di trazione *f*
– *driving bogie with traction motors*
**4**  la cabina del macchinista
– *cab (driver's cab, Am. engineer's cab)*
**5**  l'alimentatore *m*
– *power supply (traction current filter)*
**6**  la bobina di reattanza (la bobina d'impedenza)
– *contactors (converters, inductance)*
**7**  il raffreddamento a aria dei motori di trazione *f*
– *traction motor blower*
**8**  il convertitore
– *inductance protection (converter)*

**9**  l'impianto di raffreddamento a olio
– *oil-cooling plant*
**10**  il convertitore di frequenza degli impianti ausiliari
– *converter for the auxiliaries*
**11**  l'elettronica
– *electronics*
**12**  l'impianto della corrente di comando
– *control current equipment*
**13**  gli impianti ausiliari (i teleruttori di comando)
– *auxiliaries (switchgear)*
**14**  l'impianto per l'aria compressa
– *pneumatic equipment*
**15**  il condizionatore
– *air-conditioning plant*
**16**  il convertitore della corrente di trazione *f*
– *main current converters*
**17**  l'unità tecnica di diagnosi *f*
– *measuring equipment (diagnosis)*
**18**  l'interferenza dei treni di linea
– *continuous automatic train-running control*

**19**  il trasformatore
– *transformer*
**20**  **il TGV** (Train à Grande Vitesse) della Société Nationale des Chemins de Fer Français (SNCF)
– *TGV (Train à Grande Vitesse) of the Société Nationale des Chemins de Fer Français (SNCF)*

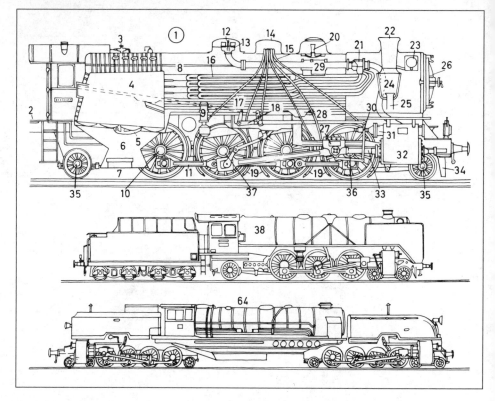

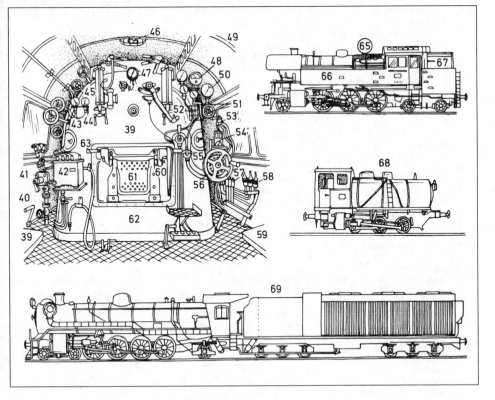

**38** il tender per locomotive *f pl* veloci
– *express locomotive with tender*
**39-63 la cabina del macchinista della locomotiva a vapore** *m*
– **cab** *(driver's cab,* Am. *engineer's cab)*
**39** il sedile del fuochista
– *fireman's seat*
**40** la leva della griglia inclinabile
– *drop grate lever*
**41** l'iniettore *m* idraulico
– *line steam injector*
**42** la pompa automatica di lubrificazione *f*
– *automatic lubricant pump (automatic lubricator)*
**43** il manometro del preriscaldatore
– *preheater pressure gauge* (Am. *gage)*
**44** il manometro del circuito di riscaldamento
– *carriage heating pressure gauge* (Am. *gage)*
**45** l'indicatore *m* del livello dell'acqua
– *water gauge* (Am. *gage)*
**46** l'illuminazione *f* della cabina
– *light*
**47** il manometro della caldaia
– *boiler pressure gauge* (Am. *gage)*

**48** il teletermometro
– *distant-reading temperature gauge* (Am. *gage)*
**49** la cabina del macchinista
– *cab (driver's cab,* Am. *engineer's cab)*
**50** il manometro del freno
– *brake pressure gauge* (Am. *gage)*
**51** la leva del fischio a vapore *m*
– *whistle valve handle*
**52** il regolatore (la leva a mano del regolatore)
– *driver's timetable* (Am. *engineer's schedule)*
**53** il rubinetto freno
– *driver's brake valve* (Am. *engineer's brake valve)*
**54** il tachigrafo
– *speed recorder (tachograph)*
**55** il rubinetto dello spandisabbia
– *sanding valve*
**56** il volantino di comando
– *reversing wheel*
**57** la valvola del freno di emergenza
– *emergency brake valve*
**58** la valvola di scarico
– *release valve*
**59** il sedile del macchinista
– *driver's seat* (Am. *engineer's seat)*
**60** lo schermo di protezione *f*
– *firehole shield*

**61** il portello del focolare
– *firehole door*
**62** la caldaia
– *vertical boiler*
**63** la maniglia del portello del focolare
– *firedoor handle handgrip*
**64** la locomotiva articolata (la locomotiva Garratt)
– *articulated locomotive (Garratt locomotive)*
**65** la locomotiva tender *m*
– *tank locomotive*
**66** il serbatoio dell'acqua
– *water tank*
**67** il tender (il carroscorta)
– *fuel tender*
**68** la locomotiva a accumulatore *m* termico (la locomotiva senza focolaio)
– *steam storage locomotive (fireless locomotive)*
**69** la locomotiva a condensazione *f*
– *condensing locomotive (locomotive with condensing tender)*

1 **la locomotiva elettrica**
- *electric locomotive*
2 la presa di corrente f a pantografo
- *current collector*
3 l'interruttore m principale
- *main switch*
4 il trasformatore di tensione f primaria
- *high-tension transformer*
5 la conduttura del tetto
- *roof cable*
6 il motore di trazione f
- *traction motor*
7 l'arresto di sicurezza induttivo (Indusi)
- *inductive train control system*
8 il serbatoio principale aria compressa
- *main air reservoir*
9 il segnalatore acustico
- *whistle*
10-18 **la vista in pianta della locomotiva**
- *plan of locomotive*
10 il trasformatore con meccanismo di commutazione f
- *transformer with tap changer*
11 il refrigeratore dell'olio con ventilatore m
- *oil cooler with blower*
12 la pompa pneumatica dell'olio
- *oil-circulating pump*
13 il comando del meccanismo di commutazione f
- *tap changer driving mechanism*
14 il compressore di aria
- *air compressor*
15 il ventilatore del motore di trazione f
- *traction motor blower*
16 la muffola terminale
- *terminal box*
17 condensatori m pl per motori m pl ausiliari
- *capacitors for auxiliary motors*
18 il teleruttore del commutatore
- *commutator cover*
19 **la cabina del macchinista della locomotiva**
- *cab (driver's cab, Am. engineer's cab)*
20 il volantino comando marcia
- *controller handwheel*
21 il dispositivo di uomo morto (Sifa)
- *dead man's handle*
22 il rubinetto comando freno
- *driver's brake valve (Am. engineer's brake valve)*
23 il comando freno ausiliario
- *ancillary brake valve (auxiliary brake valve)*
24 il manometro dell'aria
- *pressure gauge (Am. gage)*

25 l'interruttore m shunt del Sifa
- *bypass switch for the dead man's handle*
26 l'indicatore m forza trazione f
- *tractive effort indicator*
27 l'indicatore m tensione f riscaldamento
- *train heating voltage indicator*
28 l'indicatore m tensione f filo di contatto
- *contact wire voltage indicator (overhead wire voltage indicator)*
29 l'indicatore m tensione f primaria
- *high-tension voltage indicator*
30 il comando abbassamento e innalzamento pantografo
- *on/off switch for the current collector*
31 l'interruttore m principale
- *main switch*
32 l'interruttore m sabbia
- *sander switch (sander control)*
33 l'interruttore m freno centrifugo di protezione f
- *anti-skid brake switch*
34 l'indicatore m ottico impianti m pl ausiliari
- *visual display for the ancillary systems*
35 l'indicatore m velocità
- *speedometer*
36 l'indicatore m posizioni f pl di marcia del combinatore
- *running step indicator*
37 l'orologio segnatempo
- *clock*
38 il comando indusi
- *controls for the inductive train control system*
39 l'interruttore m riscaldamento cabina macchinista
- *cab heating switch*
40 la leva indicatore m acustico
- *whistle lever*
41 **l'automotrice f a torre f per la manutenzione,** un'automotrice Diesel
- *contact wire maintenance vehicle (overhead wire maintenance vehicle), a diesel railcar*
42 la piattaforma di servizio
- *work platform (working platform)*
43 la scala
- *ladder*
44-54 **la disposizione macchinari automotrice f a torre f**
- *mechanical equipment of the contact wire maintenance vehicle*
44 il compressore aria
- *air compressor*
45 il ventilatore pompa olio
- *blower oil pump*
46 la dinamo
- *generator*

47 il motore Diesel
- *diesel engine*
48 la pompa d'iniezione f
- *injection pump*
49 la marmitta di scarico
- *silencer (Am. muffler)*
50 il cambio
- *change-speed gear*
51 la trasmissione cardanica
- *cardan shaft*
52 il lubrificatore del bordino
- *wheel flange lubricator*
53 l'invertitore m assiale
- *reversing gear*
54 il montante del momento torcente
- *torque converter bearing*
55 **l'automotrice f a accumulatori m pl**
- *accumulator railcar (battery railcar)*
56 il contenitore delle batterie
- *battery box (battery container)*
57 la cabina del macchinista
- *cab (driver's cab, Am. engineer's cab)*
58 la sistemazione dei posti a sedere in seconda classe f
- *second-class seating arrangement*
59 la toilette (il WC)
- *toilet (lavatory, WC)*
60 **l'automotrice f rapida elettrica**
- *fast electric multiple-unit train*
61 la motrice terminale
- *front railcar*
62 la motrice intermedia
- *driving trailer car*

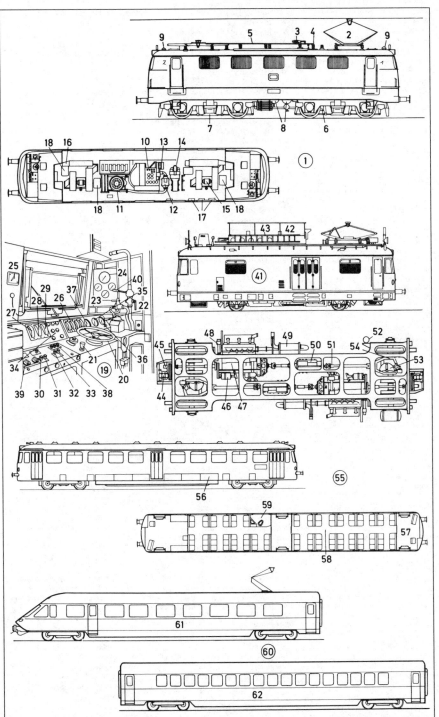

**1-84 locomotive** *f pl* **(con motore** *m***) Diesel**
– *diesel locomotives*
**1** la locomotiva dieselidraulica, una locomotiva Diesel di linea per servizio passeggeri *m pl* e merci *f pl* medio pesanti
– *diesel-hydraulic locomotive, a main-line locomotive (diesel locomotive) for medium passenger and goods service (freight service)*
**2** il carrello
– *bogie (truck)*
**3** la sala montata
– *wheel and axle set*
**4** il serbatoio principale del combustibile
– *main fuel tank*
**5** il banco di manovra della locomotiva Diesel
– *cab (driver's cab, Am. engineer's cab) of a diesel locomotive*
**6** il manometro per la condotta principale dell'aria
– *main air pressure gauge (Am. gage)*
**7** il manometro del cilindro freno
– *brake cylinder pressure gauge (Am. gage)*
**8** il manometro del serbatoio principale dell'aria compressa
– *main air reservoir pressure gauge (Am. gage)*
**9** il tachimetro
– *speedometer*
**10** il freno ausiliario
– *auxiliary brake*
**11** il rubinetto di comando del freno
– *driver's brake valve (Am. engineer's brake valve)*
**12** il volantino del comando di marcia
– *controller handwheel*
**13** il dispositivo di uomo morto (Sifa)
– *dead man's handle*
**14** la sicurezza induttiva del treno (Indusi)
– *inductive train control system*
**15** l'indicatore *m* delle luci
– *signal lights*
**16** l'orologio
– *clock*
**17** il voltmetro del riscaldamento
– *voltage meter for the train heating system*
**18** l'amperometro del riscaldamento
– *current meter for the train heating system*
**19** il termometro dell'olio motore
– *engine oil temperature gauge (Am. gage)*
**20** il termometro dell'olio del cambio
– *transmission oil temperature gauge (Am. gage)*
**21** il termometro dell'acqua di raffreddamento
– *cooling water temperature gauge (Am. gage)*
**22** il contagiri del motore
– *revolution counter (rev counter, tachometer)*
**23** il radiotelefono
– *radio telephone*
**24** la locomotiva dieselidraulica (in pianta e in prospetto)
– *diesel-hydraulic locomotive [plan and elevation]*

**25** il motore Diesel
– *diesel engine*
**26** l'impianto di raffreddamento
– *cooling unit*
**27** il cambio idraulico
– *fluid transmission*
**28** il ponte riduttore
– *wheel and axle drive*
**29** la trasmissione cardanica (l'albero cardanico)
– *cardan shaft*
**30** il generatore di corrente elettrica per l'illuminazione *f*
– *starter motor*
**31** la consolle di comando
– *instrument panel*
**32** la consolle del macchinista
– *driver's control desk (Am. engineer's control desk)*
**33** il freno a mano
– *hand brake*
**34** il compressore con motore *m* elettrico
– *air compressor with electric motor*
**35** l'armadietto degli strumenti
– *equipment locker*
**36** lo scambiatore di calore *m* per l'olio del cambio
– *heat exchanger for transmission oil*
**37** il ventilatore della sala macchine *f pl*
– *engine room ventilator*
**38** il magnete per la sicurezza induttiva del treno
– *magnet for the inductive train control system*
**39** il generatore del riscaldamento
– *train heating generator*
**40** l'armadio del convertitore del riscaldamento
– *casing of the train heating system transformer*
**41** l'apparecchio di preriscaldamento
– *preheater*
**42** il silenziatore gas di scarico
– *exhaust silencer (Am. exhaust muffler)*
**43** lo scambiatore di calore *m* ausiliario per l'olio del cambio
– *auxiliary heat exchanger for the transmission oil*
**44** il freno idraulico
– *hydraulic brake*
**45** la cassetta degli attrezzi
– *tool box*
**46** la batteria di avviamento
– *starter battery*
**47** **la locomotiva dieselidraulica a tre assi** *m pl* per il servizio di manovra leggero e medio
– *diesel-hydraulic locomotive for light and medium shunting service*
**48** il silenziatore gas di scarico
– *exhaust silencer (Am. exhaust muffler)*
**49** la sirena e il fischio
– *bell and whistle*
**50** la radio di manovra
– *yard radio*
**51-67** il prospetto della locomotiva a tre assi *m pl*
– *elevation of locomotive*
**51** il motore Diesel con turbina di sovralimentazione *f*
– *diesel engine with supercharged turbine*
**52** il cambio idraulico
– *fluid transmission*

**53** il riduttore ausiliario
– *output gear box*
**54** il radiatore
– *radiator*
**55** lo scambiatore di calore *m* per l'olio motore *m*
– *heat exchanger for the engine lubricating oil*
**56** il serbatoio del combustibile
– *fuel tank*
**57** il serbatoio principale dell'aria compressa
– *main air reservoir*
**58** il compressore dell'aria
– *air compressor*
**59** le casse sabbia
– *sand boxes*
**60** il serbatoio di riserva del combustibile
– *reserve fuel tank*
**61** il serbatoio ausiliario dell'aria
– *auxiliary air reservoir*
**62** il motore idrostatico del ventilatore
– *hydrostatic fan drive*
**63** il sedile con scomparto per i vestiti
– *seat with clothes compartment*
**64** la ruota del freno a mano
– *hand brake wheel*
**65** il serbatoio di espansione *f* dell'acqua di raffreddamento
– *cooling water*
**66** la zavorra
– *ballast*
**67** il volantino di servizio per la regolazione del motore e del cambio
– *engine and transmission control wheel*
**68** **la piccola locomotiva Diesel** per servizio di manovra
– *small diesel locomotive for shunting service*
**69** la marmitta di scarico
– *exhaust casing*
**70** la tromba di segnalazione *f*
– *horn*
**71** il serbatoio principale dell'aria
– *main air reservoir*
**72** il compressore dell'aria
– *air compressor*
**73** il motore Diesel a otto cilindri *m pl*
– *eight-cylinder diesel engine*
**74** il cambio Voith con invertitore *m*
– *Voith transmission with reversing gear*
**75** il serbatoio dell'olio di riscaldamento
– *heating oil tank (fuel oil tank)*
**76** la cassa sabbia
– *sand box*
**77** l'impianto di raffreddamento
– *cooling unit*
**78** il serbatoio di espansione *f* per l'acqua di raffreddamento
– *header tank for the cooling water*
**79** il filtro dell'aria a bagno di olio
– *oil bath air cleaner (oil bath air filter)*
**80** il volantino del freno a mano
– *hand brake wheel*
**81** il volantino di comando
– *control wheel*
**82** il giunto
– *coupling*
**83** la trasmissione cardanica (l'albero cardanico)
– *cardan shaft*
**84** la griglia a persiana
– *louvred shutter*

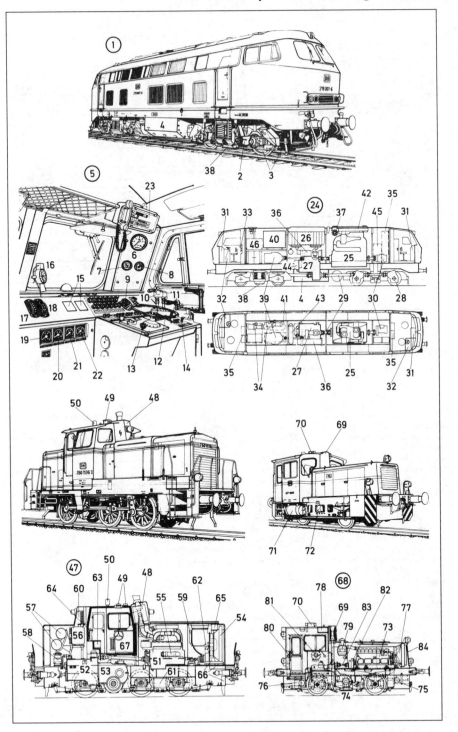

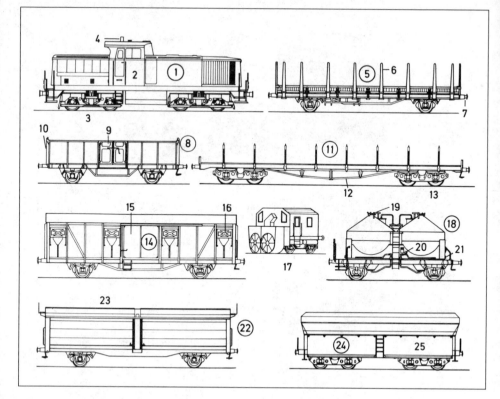

1 la locomotiva dieselidraulica
– *diesel-hydraulic locomotive*
2 la cabina del macchinista
– *cab (driver's cab, Am. engineer's cab)*
3 la sala montata
– *wheel and axle set*
4 l'antenna per l'impianto radiofonico di manovra
– *aerial for the yard radio*
5 il pianale in esecuzione *f* normale
– *standard flat wagon (Am. standard flatcar)*
6 il montante ribaltabile
– *hinged steel stanchion (stanchion)*
7 i respingenti
– *buffers*
8 il carro merci *f pl* aperto in esecuzione *f* normale
– *standard open goods wagon (Am. standard open freight car)*
9 le porte laterali girevoli
– *revolving side doors*
10 la parete frontale ribaltabile
– *hinged front*
11 il pianale su carrello girevole in esecuzione *f* normale
– *standard flat wagon (Am. standard flatcar) with bogies*

12 il longherone di rafforzamento
– *sole bar reinforcement*
13 il carrello girevole
– *bogie (truck)*
14 il carro merci coperto
– *covered goods van (covered goods wagon, Am. boxcar)*
15 la porta scorrevole
– *sliding door*
16 la presa di aria
– *ventilation flap*
17 lo spazzaneve centrifugo
– *snow blower (rotary snow plough, Am. snowplow), a track-clearing vehicle*
18 il serbatoio con scarico a aria compressa
– *wagon (Am. car) with pneumatic discharge*
19 l'apertura di riempimento
– *filler hole*
20 il collegamento per l'aria compressa
– *compressed-air supply*
21 il collegamento per lo svuotamento
– *discharge connection valve*
22 il carro a tetto scorrevole
– *goods van (Am. boxcar) with sliding roof*

23 l'apertura del tetto
– *roof opening*
24 il carro aperto autoscaricante su carrello girevole (la tramoggia)
– *bogie open self-discharge wagon (Am. bogie open self-discharge freight car)*
25 lo sportello ribaltabile per lo scarico
– *discharge flap (discharge door)*

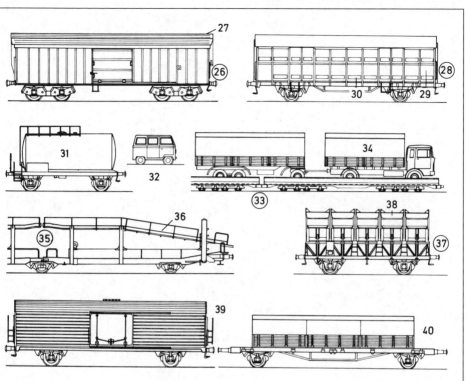

26 il carro a tetto orientabile su carrello girevole
– *bogie wagon with swivelling (Am.*
  *swiveling) roof*
27 il tetto orientabile
– *swivelling (Am. swiveling) roof*
28 il carro gabbia per il trasporto di
  animali *m pl* da cortile *m*
– *large-capacity wagon (Am. large-*
  *capacity car) for small livestock*
29 la parete laterale (la parete in
  lamiera) permeabile all'aria
– *sidewall with ventilation flaps*
  *(slatted wall)*
30 la presa di aria
– *ventilation flap*
31 il carro cisterna
– *tank wagon (Am. tank car)*
32 il carrello a motore *m*
– *track inspection railcar*
33 il carro tipo «canguro» per
  trasporti *m pl* combinati
– *open special wagons (Am. open*
  *special freight cars)*
34 l'autocarro con rimorchio
– *lorry (Am. truck) with trailer*
35 il carro a due piani *m pl* per il
  trasporto auto
– *two-tier car carrier (double-deck*
  *car carrier)*

36 il piano superiore ribaltabile
– *hinged upper deck*
37 il carro tramoggia
– *tipper wagon (Am. dump car)*
  *with skips*
38 la conca ribaltabile
– *skip*
39 il carro frigorifero universale
– *general-purpose refrigerator*
  *wagon (refrigerator van, Am.*
  *refrigerator car)*
40 le sagome di carico tipo per
  pianali *m pl*
– *interchangeable bodies for flat*
  *wagons (Am. flatcars)*

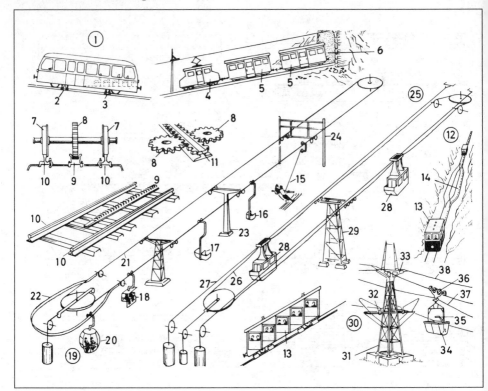

**1-14 ferrovie** *f pl* **di montagna su rotaie** *f*
*pl*
– *mountain railways* (Am. *mountain rail-*
*roads)*
**1** l'automotrice *f* a aderenza forzata
– *adhesion railcar*
**2** la trasmissione di moto
– *drive*
**3** il freno di emergenza
– *emergency brake*
**4** *u.* **5** la ferrovia a cremagliera
– *rack mountain railway (rack-and-pinion*
*railway, cog railway, Am. cog railroad,*
*rack railroad)*
**4** la locomotiva elettrica
– *electric rack railway locomotive (Am.*
*electric rack railroad locomotive)*
**5** i vagoni
– *rack railway coach (rack railway trailer,*
Am. *rack railroad car)*
**6** la galleria (il tunnel)
– *tunnel*
**7-11** ferrovie *f pl* a cremagliera (sistemi *m*
*pl)*
– *rack railways (rack-and-pinion rail-*
*ways,* Am. *rack railroads) [systems]*
**7** la ruota portante
– *running wheel (carrying wheel)*
**8** la ruota dentata di trasmissione *f* di
moto
– *driving pinion*
**9** la cremagliera
– *rack [with teeth machined on top edge]*
**10** la rotaia
– *rail*

**11** la doppia cremagliera
– *rack [with teeth on both outer edges]*
**12** la funicolare
– *funicular railway (funicular, cable rail-*
*way)*
**13** il vagone (trainato da fune *f* )
– *funicular railway car*
**14** la fune traente
– *haulage cable*
**15-38 funivie** *f pl*
– *cableways (ropeways, cable suspension*
*lines)*
**15-24** funivie *f pl* monofune, funivie *f pl*
continue
– *single-cable ropeways (single-cable sus-*
*pension lines), endless cableways, end-*
*less ropeways*
**15** lo ski-lift (la sciovia)
– *drag lift*
**16-18** la seggiovia
– *chair lift*
**16** il seggiolino, un seggiolino singolo
– *lift chair, a single chair*
**17** il seggiolino doppio
– *double lift chair, a two-seater chair*
**18** il seggiolino doppio accoppiabile
– *double chair (two-seater chair) with*
*coupling*
**19** l'ovoia, una funivia continua
– *gondola cableway, an endless cableway*
**20** la cabinetta
– *gondola (cabin)*
**21** la fune, una fune portante e traente
– *endless cable, a suspension (supporting)*
*and haulage cable*

**22** la monorotaia di riserva
– *U-rail*
**23** il pilone di sostegno
– *single-pylon support*
**24** il portante
– *gantry support*
**25** la funivia bifune, una funivia va e vieni
– *double-cable ropeway (double-cable*
*suspension line), a suspension line with*
*balancing cabins*
**26** la fune traente
– *haulage cable*
**27** la fune portante
– *suspension cable (supporting cable)*
**28** la cabina passeggeri *m pl*
– *cabin*
**29** il pilone intermedio (il cavalletto)
– *intermediate support*
**30** la teleferica, una funivia va e vieni
– *cableway (ropeway, suspension line), a*
*double-cable ropeway (double-cable*
*suspension line)*
**31** il traliccio
– *pylon*
**32** la carrucola della fune traente
– *haulage cable roller*
**33** la scarpa della corda portante
– *cable guide rail (suspension cable bear-*
*ing)*
**34** il vagoncino ribaltabile
– *skip, a tipping bucket (Am. dumping*
*bucket)*
**35** il dispositivo di ribaltamento
– *stop*

36 il carrello di vettura
– *pulley cradle*
37 la fune traente
– *haulage cable*
38 la fune portante
– *suspension cable (supporting cable)*
39 **la stazione a valle** *f*
– ***valley station*** *(lower station)*
40 il pozzo di contrappeso
– *tension weight shaft*
41 il contrappeso della fune portante
– *tension weight for the suspension cable (supporting cable)*
42 il contrappeso della fune traente
– *tension weight for the haulage cable*
43 la puleggia tendifune *f*
– *tension cable pulley*
44 la fune portante
– *suspension cable (supporting cable)*
45 la fune traente
– *haulage cable*
46 la fune inferiore (la fune di zavorra)
– *balance cable (lower cable)*
47 la fune di sicurezza
– *auxiliary cable (emergency cable)*
48 l'apparecchio di tensione *f* della fune di sicurezza
– *auxiliary-cable tensioning mechanism (emergency-cable tensioning mechanism)*
49 le carrucole della fune traente
– *haulage cable rollers*
50 il respingente a molla
– *spring buffer (Am. spring bumper)*
51 il marciapiede della stazione a valle *f*
– *valley station platform (lower station platform)*
52 la cabina passeggeri *m pl* (la telecabina, il bidone)
– *cabin (cableway gondola, ropeway gondola, suspension line gondola), a large-capacity cabin*
53 il carrello
– *pulley cradle*
54 il carrello cabina
– *suspension gear*
55 l'ammortizzatore *m*
– *stabilizer*
56 la trave di protezione *f*
– *guide rail*
57 **la stazione a monte** *m*
– ***top station*** *(upper station)*
58 la scarpa per la fune portante
– *suspension cable guide (supporting cable guide)*
59 l'ancoraggio a tamburi *m pl* per fune portante
– *suspension cable anchorage (supporting cable anchorage)*
60 la serie delle carrucole della fune traente
– *haulage cable rollers*
61 la puleggia di rinvio della fune traente
– *haulage cable guide wheel*
62 la puleggia motrice della fune traente
– *haulage cable driving pulley*
63 il motore principale
– *main drive*
64 il motore di riserva
– *standby drive*
65 la cabina di manovra
– *control room*
66 **il carrello di vettura**
– ***cabin pulley cradle***
67 il sostegno principale
– *main pulley cradle*

68 la traversa oscillante doppia
– *double cradle*
69 la traversa a due ruote *f pl*
– *two-wheel cradle*
70 le ruote del carrello
– *running wheels*
71 il freno della ruota portante, un freno di emergenza in caso di rottura della fune traente
– *suspension cable brake (supporting cable brake), an emergency brake in case of haulage cable failure*
72 il perno della sospensione
– *suspension gear bolt*
73 l'attacco a manicotto della fune traente
– *haulage cable sleeve*
74 l'attacco a manicotto della fune inferiore
– *balance cable sleeve (lower cable sleeve)*
75 la protezione antisviamento
– *derailment guard*
76 **tralicci** *m pl* (piloni *m pl*)
– *cable supports (ropeway supports, suspension line supports, intermediate supports)*
77 il pilone a traliccio di acciaio, un sostegno a traliccio
– *pylon, a framework support*
78 il pilone in tubi *m pl* di acciaio, un sostegno in tubi *m pl* di acciaio
– *tubular steel pylon, a tubular steel support*
79 la scarpa della fune portante
– *suspension cable guide rail (supporting cable guide rail, support guide rail)*
80 la struttura di protezione *f*, un'impalcatura di montaggio per lavori *m pl* alla fune
– *support truss, a frame for work on the cable*
81 il basamento
– *base of the support*

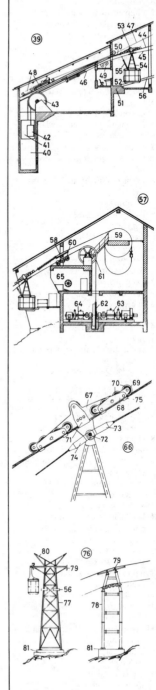

**1** la sezione del ponte
– *cross-section of a bridge*
**2** l'impalcato del piano stradale coperto con lamiera ortotropa
– *orthotropic roadway (orthotropic deck)*
**3** il saettone (la saetta)
– *truss (bracing)*
**4** la controventatura
– *diagonal brace (diagonal strut)*
**5** l'impalco
– *hollow tubular section*
**6** la lamiera del piano stradale
– *deck slab*
**7** il ponte a travata (il ponte a trave *f* )
– *solid-web girder bridge (beam bridge)*
**8** lo spigolo superiore del piano stradale
– *road surface*
**9** il corrente superiore
– *top flange*
**10** il corrente inferiore
– *bottom flange*
**11** l'appoggio fisso
– *fixed bearing*
**12** l'appoggio mobile
– *movable bearing*
**13** la luce
– *clear span*
**14** la distanza tra gli appoggi
– *span*
**15** la passerella sospesa (il ponte sospeso)
– *rope bridge (primitive suspension bridge)*
**16** la fune portante
– *carrying rope*
**17** la fune di sospensione *f*
– *suspension rope*
**18** la passerella intrecciata
– *woven deck (woven decking)*
**19** il ponte a arco in pietra, un ponte in muratura
– *stone arch bridge, a solid bridge*
**20** l'arcata del ponte
– *arch*
**21** la pila del ponte (il pilone del ponte, la pila in corrente)
– *pier*
**22** la statua del ponte
– *statue of saint on bridge*
**23** il ponte a travata (il ponte a trave *f* reticolare)
– *trussed arch bridge*
**24** l'elemento del traliccio
– *truss element*
**25** l'arco reticolato (l'arco a traliccio)
– *trussed arch*
**26** la luce del ponte
– *arch span*
**27** la pila in golena
– *abutment (end pier)*
**28** il ponte a arco su pilastri *m pl*
– *spandrel-braced arch bridge*

**29** l'imposta dell'arco
– *abutment (abutment pier)*
**30** il piedritto (il pilastro del ponte)
– *bridge strut*
**31** la chiave dell'arco
– *crown*
**32** il ponte medievale con abitazioni *m pl* (il Ponte Vecchio a Firenze)
– *covered bridge of the Middle Ages (the* Ponte Vecchio *in Florence)*
**33** le gioiellerie (i negozi dei gioiellieri)
– *goldsmiths' shops*
**34** il ponte a piloni *m pl* a traliccio
– *steel lattice bridge*
**35** l'asta diagonale della travata del ponte
– *counterbrace (crossbrace, diagonal member)*
**36** l'asta verticale della travata del ponte
– *vertical member*
**37** il nodo del traliccio
– *truss joint*
**38** il pilone terminale
– *portal frame*
**39** il ponte sospeso
– *suspension bridge*
**40** il cavo portante
– *suspension cable*
**41** l'asta di sospensione *f*
– *suspender (hanger)*
**42** il pilone terminale
– *tower*
**43** l'ancoraggio del cavo portante
– *suspension cable anchorage*
**44** il tirante (con il piano stradale)
– *tied beam [with roadway]*
**45** la spalla del ponte
– *abutment*
**46** il ponte con funi *f pl* di sospensione *f*
– *cable-stayed bridge*
**47** la fune di sospensione *f*
– *inclined tension cable*
**48** l'ancoraggio della fune di sospensione *f*
– *inclined cable anchorage*
**49** il ponte in cemento armato
– *reinforced concrete bridge*
**50** l'arco in cemento armato
– *reinforced concrete arch*
**51** il sistema a funi *f pl* di sospensione *f*
– *inclined cable system (multiple cable system)*
**52** il ponte piatto, un ponte a trave *f* con parete *f* piena
– *flat bridge, a plate girder bridge*
**53** il rinforzo trasversale
– *stiffener*
**54** la pila in corrente
– *pier*
**55** l'appoggio (l'appoggio del ponte)
– *bridge bearing*

**56** il paraghiaccio
– *cutwater*
**57** il ponte in elementi *m pl* prefabbricati
– *straits bridge, a bridge built of precast elements*
**58** l'elemento prefabbricato
– *precast construction unit*
**59** il viadotto
– *viaduct*
**60** il fondovalle
– *valley bottom*
**61** il pilastro in cemento armato
– *reinforced concrete pier*
**62** l'impalcatura in aggetto
– *scaffolding*
**63** il ponte girevole a traliccio
– *lattice swing bridge*
**64** la corona girevole
– *turntable*
**65** il pilone girevole
– *pivot pier*
**66** la metà del ponte girevole
– *pivoting half (pivoting section, pivoting span, movable half ) of bridge*
**67** il ponte girevole piatto
– *flat swing bridge*
**68** la parte mediana
– *middle section*
**69** il perno girevole
– *pivot*
**70** il parapetto del ponte
– *parapet (handrailing)*

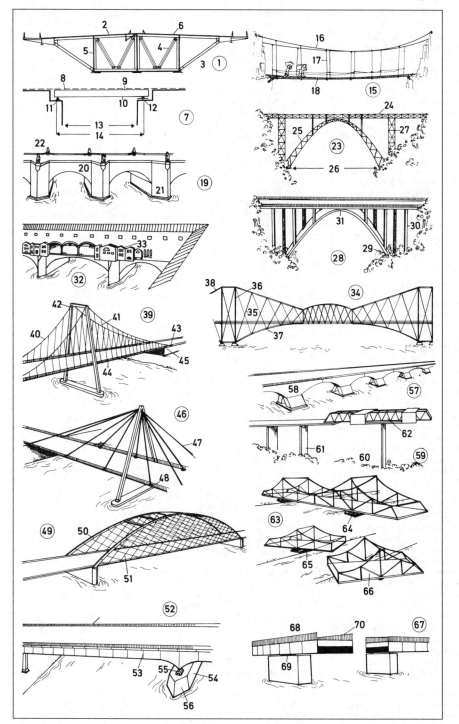

1  **il traghetto a cavo** (*anche:* il
   traghetto a catena), un traghetto
   passeggeri *m pl*
–  ***cable ferry*** (also: *chain ferry*), a
   *passenger ferry*
2  il cavo
–  *ferry rope (ferry cable)*
3  il braccio fluviale
–  *river branch (river arm)*
4  l'isolotto
–  *river island (river islet)*
5  l'erosione *f* sulla riva del fiume,
   un danno provocato dalla piena
–  *collapsed section of riverbank,*
   *flood damage*
6  **il traghetto a motore** *m*
–  ***motor ferry***
7  il pontile di attracco per il
   traghetto (per barche *f pl* a
   motore)
–  *ferry landing stage (motorboat*
   *landing stage)*
8  i pali di sostegno
–  *pile foundations*
9  la corrente
–  *current (flow, course)*
10 **il traghetto a spola** (il  traghetto
   fluviale, il traghetto)
–  ***flying ferry*** (*river ferry*), a car
   ferry
11 il traghetto
–  *ferry boat*
12 il galleggiante
–  *buoy (float)*
13 l'ancoraggio
–  *anchorage*
14 la darsena
–  *harbour* (Am. *harbor*) *for laying*
   *up river craft*
15 la barca sospinta con pertiche *f pl,*
   una chiatta-traghetto
–  ***ferry boat*** (*punt*)
16 la pertica
–  *pole (punt pole, quant pole)*
17 il traghettatore
–  *ferryman*
18 l'alveo abbandonato
–  *blind river branch (blind river*
   *arm)*
19 il pennello (il repellente)
–  *groyne* (Am. *groin*)
20 la punta del repellente
–  *groyne* (Am. *groin*) *head*
21 il canale navigabile
–  *fairway (navigable part of river)*
22 **il convoglio d'imbarcazioni** *f pl*
–  ***train of barges***
23 il rimorchiatore fluviale
–  *river tug*
24 il cavo da traino
–  *tow rope (tow line, towing hawser)*
25 la chiatta rimorchiata
–  *barge (freight barge, cargo barge,*
   *lighter)*

26 il barcaiolo
–  *bargeman (bargee, lighterman)*
27 l'alaggio
–  *towing (hauling, haulage)*
28 l'albero
–  *towing mast*
29 il motore di alaggio
–  *towing engine*
30 la strada alzaia
–  *towing track;* form.: *tow path*
   *(towing path)*
31 il fiume dopo la regolazione
–  *river after river training*
32 **l'argine** *m* **per livello invernale**
–  ***dike*** (*dyke, main dike, flood wall,*
   *winter dike*)
33 i fossi di scolo
–  *drainage ditch*
34 la chiusa di argine *m*
–  *dike (dyke) drainage sluice*
35 il muro di ala
–  *wing wall*
36 il canale di raccolta
–  *outfall*
37 il cunettone per le acque d'infil-
   trazione *f*
–  *drain (infiltration drain)*
38 la berma
–  *berm (berme)*
39 il coronamento (la cresta)
   dell'argine *m*
–  *top of dike (dyke)*
40 la scarpa esterna (la spalla)
   dell'argine *m*
–  *dike (dyke) batter (dike slope)*
41 la golena
–  *flood bed (inundation area)*
42 la zona inondata
–  *flood containment area*
43 l'indicatore *m* della corrente
–  *current meter*
44 il segnale con l'indicazione *f* della
   distanza
–  *kilometre* (Am. *kilometer*) *sign*
45 la casa del sorvegliante
–  *dikereeve's (dykereeve's) house*
   *(dikereeve's cottage);* also: *ferry-*
   *man's house (cottage)*
46 il sorvegliante della diga
–  *dikereeve (dykereeve)*
47 la rampa dell'argine *m*
–  *dike (dyke) ramp*
48 l'argine *m* per livello estivo
–  *summer dike (summer dyke)*
49 la diga fluviale
–  *levee (embankment)*
50 i sacchi di sabbia
–  *sandbags*
51-55 **le opere di difesa delle sponde**
–  ***bank protection*** (*bank stabiliza-*
   *tion, revetment*)
51 la gettata di pietre *f pl*
–  *riprap*
52 il terreno alluvionale
–  *alluvial deposit (sand deposit)*

53 la fascina
–  *fascine (bundle of wooden sticks)*
54 la fascinata
–  *wicker fences*
55 la mantellata in pietrame *m*
–  *stone pitching*
56 **la draga,** una draga a catena di
   tazze *f pl*
–  ***floating dredging machine***
   (*dredger*), *a multi-bucket ladder*
   *dredge*
57 la catena di tazze *f pl* (l'elevatore
   *m* a tazze *f pl*)
–  *bucket elevator chain*
58 la tazza dell'elevatore *m*
–  *dredging bucket*
59 **la draga succhiante** con aspiratore
   *m* a testa da traino o da chiatta
–  ***suction dredger*** (*hydraulic*
   *dredger*) *with trailing suction pipe*
   *or barge sucker*
60 la pompa dell'acqua motrice
–  *centrifugal pump*
61 la valvola di depressione *f*
–  *back scouring valve*
62 la pompa aspirante
–  *suction pump, a jet pump with*
   *scouring nozzles*

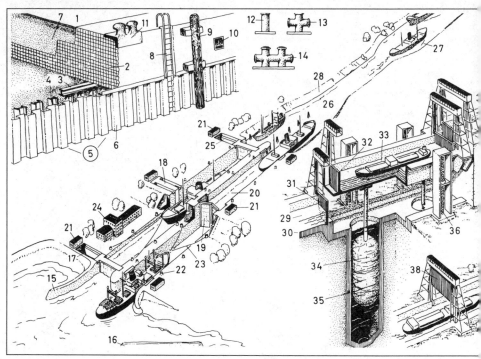

**1-14 il molo**
- *quay wall*
1 il manto stradale
- *road surface*
2 il corpo del muro
- *body of wall*
3 la trave di acciaio
- *steel sleeper*
4 il palo di acciaio
- *steel pile*
5 la palancolata
- *sheet pile wall (sheet pile bulkhead, sheet piling)*
6 la palancola di legno (l'asse-palo, il palo-piano)
- *box pile*
7 il materiale di riempimento
- *backfilling (filling)*
8 la scaletta metallica
- *ladder*
9 il parabordo di accosto
- *fender (fender pile)*
10 la nicchia di ormeggio
- *recessed bollard*
11 la bitta abbinata
- *double bollard*
12 la bitta
- *bollard*
13 la bitta a croce *f*
- *cross-shaped bollard (cross-shaped mooring bitt)*
14 la bitta doppia a doppia croce *f* abbinata
- *double cross-shaped bollard (double cross-shaped mooring bitt)*
15 *u.* 16 l'entrata del canale (l'entrata)
- *canal entrance*
**15-28 il canale**
- *canal*

15 il molo
- *mole*
16 il frangionde (il frangiflutti)
- *breakwater*
**17-25** le conche in serie *f*
- *staircase of locks*
17 la parte inferiore
- *lower level*
18 la porta di chiusa, una porta scorrevole
- *lock gate, a sliding gate*
19 lo sbarramento a portoni *m pl*
- *mitre* (Am. *miter*) *gate*
20 la chiusa (la conca, il bacino)
- *lock (lock chamber)*
21 la sala macchine *f pl*
- *power house*
22 l'argano di traino, un argano
- *warping capstan (hauling capstan), a capstan*
23 il cavo (la gomena) di traino, un cavo
- *warp*
24 gli uffici (*per es.:* l'amministrazione *f* del canale, la polizia fluviale, l'ufficio doganale)
- *offices (e.g. canal administration, river police, customs)*
25 la testa del molo
- *upper level (head)*
26 l'avanporto (l'antiporto) della chiusa
- *lock approach*
27 l'allargamento del canale
- *lay-by*
28 la scarpata
- *bank slope*
**29-38 l'impianto di sollevamento per natanti *m pl***
- *boat lift* (Am. *boat elevator*)

29 la parte inferiore del canale
- *lower pound (lower reach)*
30 il fondo del canale
- *canal bed*
31 la paratoia, una paratoia sollevabile
- *pound lock gate, a vertical gate*
32 la paratoia della conca
- *lock gate*
33 la conca di elevazione *f* della nave
- *boat tank (caisson)*
34 il galleggiante, un corpo di spinta
- *float*
35 il pozzo del galleggiante
- *float shaft*
36 la vite di sollevamento
- *lifting spindle*
37 la parte superiore del canale
- *upper pound (upper reach)*
38 la paratoia a gargani *m pl*
- *vertical gate*
**39-46 il serbatoio raccolta acque**
- *pumping plant and reservoir*
39 il serbatoio di ristagno
- *forebay*
40 la camera di carico
- *surge tank*
41 la condotta forzata
- *pressure pipeline*
42 la sala saracinesche *f pl*
- *valve house (valve control house)*
43 la sala turbine *f pl* (la sala delle pompe)
- *turbine house (pumping station)*

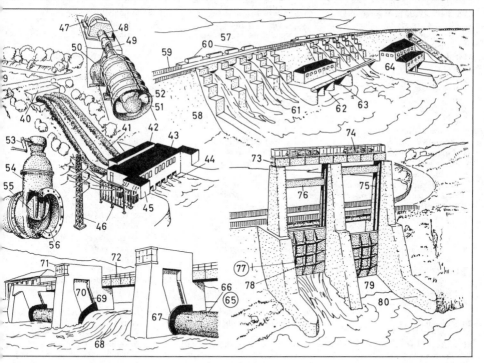

**44** il canale di scarico
– *discharge structure (outlet structure)*
**45** la centrale di distribuzione *f*
– *control station*
**46** l'impianto di trasformazione *f*
– *transformer station*
**47-52 la pompa a elica**
– *axial-flow pump (propeller pump)*
**47** il motore di propulsione *f*
– *drive motor*
**48** la trasmissione di moto
– *gear*
**49** l'albero di trasmissione *f*
– *drive shaft*
**50** la condotta forzata
– *pressure pipe*
**51** il tubo di aspirazione *f*
– *suction head*
**52** l'elica
– *impeller wheel*
**53-56 la valvola a saracinesca** (la saracinesca)
– *sluice valve (sluice gate)*
**53** il volantino
– *crank drive*
**54** il corpo della saracinesca
– *valve housing*
**55** la saracinesca
– *sliding valve (sliding gate)*
**56** la lente (la luce di deflusso)
– *discharge opening*
**57-64 la diga**
– *dam (barrage)*
**57** il lago artificiale
– *reservoir (storage reservoir, impounding reservoir, impounded reservoir)*
**58** la diga di sbarramento
– *masonry dam*

**59** il coronamento del muro
– *crest of dam*
**60** lo stramazzo libero (lo sfioratore)
– *spillway (overflow spillway)*
**61** il bacino di smorzamento, il dissipatore *m*
– *stilling basin (stilling box, stilling pool)*
**62** lo scarico della paratoia
– *scouring tunnel (outlet tunnel, waste water outlet)*
**63** la sala saracinesche *f pl*
– *valve house (valve control house)*
**64** la sala macchine *f pl*
– *power station*
**65-72 la traversa cilindrica** (la diga, un impianto di sbarramento; altro sistema: la diga a battenti *m pl*)
– *rolling dam (weir), a barrage; other system: shutter weir*
**65** il cilindro, una traversa di sbarramento
– *roller, a barrier*
**66** la calotta del cilindro
– *roller top*
**67** la pianta laterale
– *flange*
**68** il cilindro a scomparsa
– *submersible roller*
**69** la cremagliera
– *rack track*
**70** la nicchia
– *recess*
**71** la cabina di manovra verricelli *m pl*
– *hoisting gear cabin*
**72** la passerella di servizio
– *service bridge (walkway)*
**73-80 lo sbarramento con paratoie piane**
– *sluice dam*
**73** il ponte dei verricelli
– *hoisting gear bridge*

**74** il verricello
– *hoisting gear (winding gear)*
**75** la scanalatura di guida
– *guide groove*
**76** il contrappeso
– *counterweight (counterpoise)*
**77** la paratoia (la chiusa)
– *sluice gate (floodgate)*
**78** la nervatura di rinforzo
– *reinforcing rib*
**79** la suola della diga
– *dam sill (weir sill)*
**80** il muro laterale
– *wing wall*

**1-6  barca a remi** *m pl* **germanica** [400 d. C. circa]; la Nydam
– *Germanic rowing boat [ca. AD 400]; the Nydam boat*
**1**  il dritto di poppa (la ruota di poppa)
– *stern post*
**2**  il timoniere
– *steersman*
**3**  i rematori
– *oarsman*
**4**  il dritto di prua (la ruota di prua)
– *stem post (stem)*
**5**  il remo per vogare
– *oar, for rowing*
**6**  il remo-timone, un remo laterale per pilotare (governare) la nave
– *rudder (steering oar), a side rudder, for steering*
**7  la piroga,** un tronco di albero scavato
– *dugout, a hollowed-out tree trunk*
**8**  la pagaia
– *paddle*
**9-12  la trireme,** una nave da guerra romana
– *trireme, a Roman warship*
**9**  il rostro (lo sperone)
– *ram*
**10**  il castello
– *forecastle (fo'c'sle)*
**11**  l'asta per l'arrembaggio (asta per trattenere la nave nemica)
– *grapple (grapnel, grappling iron), for fastening the enemy ship alongside*
**12**  i tre ordini di remi *m pl*
– *three banks (tiers) of oars*
**13-17  la nave vichinga** [antica nave nordica]
– *Viking ship (longship, dragon ship) [Norse]*
**13**  la barra del timone
– *helm (tiller)*
**14**  i sostegni della tenda, con teste *f pl* di cavalli *m pl* incise
– *awning crutch with carved horses' heads*
**15**  la tenda
– *awning*
**16**  la polena a testa di drago
– *dragon figurehead*
**17**  lo scudo di protezione *f* (lo scudo)
– *shield*
**18-26  la cocca** (la cocca anseatica)
– *cog (Hansa cog, Hansa ship)*
**18**  la gomena (il cavo) dell'ancora
– *anchor cable (anchor rope, anchor hawser)*
**19**  il castello di prua (di prora)
– *forecastle (fo'c'sle)*
**20**  l'albero di bompresso (il bompresso)
– *bowsprit*
**21**  la vela quadra imbrogliata
– *furled (brailed-up) square sail*
**22**  il vessillo della città
– *town banner (city banner)*

**23**  il castello di poppa
– *aftercastle (sterncastle)*
**24**  il timone, un timone a ruota
– *rudder, a stem rudder*
**25**  la poppa arrotondata
– *elliptical stern (round stern)*
**26**  il parabordi di legno
– *wooden fender*
**27-43  la caravella** [«Santa Maria» 1492]
– *caravel (carvel) ['Santa Maria' 1492]*
**27**  la cabina dell'ammiraglio
– *admiral's cabin*
**28**  la boma di mezzana
– *spanker boom*
**29**  la vela di mezzana, una vela latina
– *mizzen (mizen, mutton spanker, lateen spanker), a lateen sail*
**30**  il picco di mezzana
– *lateen yard*
**31**  l'albero di mezzana
– *mizzen (mizen) mast*
**32**  la trinca
– *lashing*
**33**  la vela maestra, una vela quadrata
– *mainsail (main course), a square sail*
**34**  la bonnetta, una striscia staccabile
– *bonnet, a removable strip of canvas*
**35**  la bulina (la bolina, la burina)
– *bowline*
**36**  gli imbrogli laterali
– *bunt line (martinet)*
**37**  il pennone di maestra
– *main yard*
**38**  la gabbia (la vela di gabbia)
– *main topsail*
**39**  il pennone di gabbia
– *main topsail yard*
**40**  l'albero di maestra (l'albero maestro)
– *mainmast*
**41**  il trinchetto
– *foresail (fore course)*
**42**  l'albero di trinchetto
– *foremast*
**43**  la vela di civada
– *spritsail*
**44-50  la galea** [15. mo–18. mo sec.], una nave i cui rematori *m pl* erano forzati *m pl*
– *galley [15th to 18th century], a slave galley*
**44**  la lanterna (il fanale)
– *lantern*
**45**  la cabina
– *cabin*
**46**  il passaggio centrale
– *central gangway*
**47**  il capo ciurma (il sorvegliante dei forzati), con la frusta
– *slave driver with whip*
**48**  i forzati della galea (i forzati, i rematori, gli schiavi, i reclusi, la ciurma)
– *galley slaves*

**49**  la rembata, una piattaforma coperta sulla prua
– *covered platform in the forepart of the ship*
**50**  il cannone (il pezzo di artiglieria)
– *gun*
**51-60  la nave di linea,** una nave a tre ponti *m pl* [18. mo–19. mo sec.]
– *ship of the line (line-of-battle ship) [18th to 19th century], a three-decker*
**51**  l'asta di fiocco
– *jib boom*
**52**  il velaccino
– *fore topgallant sail*
**53**  il gran velaccio
– *main topgallant sail*
**54**  il mizzen (mizen) topgallant sail
– *mizzen (mizen) topgallant sail*
**55-57**  la poppa ornata
– *gilded stern*
**55**  lo specchio di coronamento
– *upper stern*
**56**  la balconata di poppa
– *stern gallery*
**57**  la balconata all'anca, un ampliamento con finestre *f pl* laterali ornate
– *quarter gallery, a projecting balcony with ornamental portholes*
**58**  lo specchio inferiore (lo specchio)
– *lower stern*
**59**  le batterie di cannoni *m pl* per il fuoco di bordata
– *gunports for broadside fire*
**60**  il portello della bocca da fuoco
– *gunport shutter*

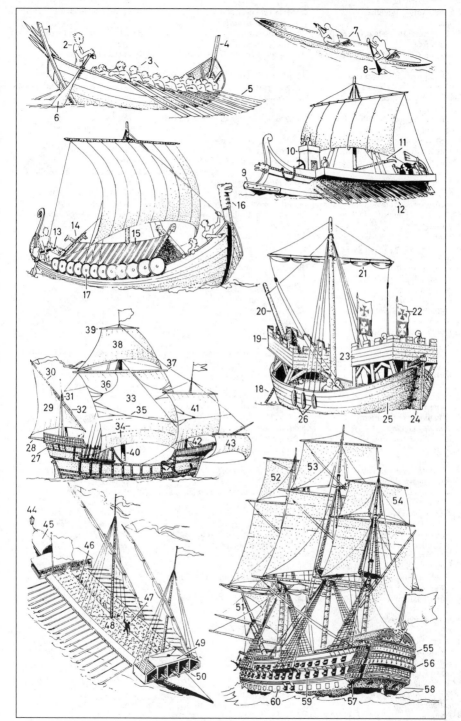

**1-9 l'alberatura (gli alberi)**
– *masts*
**1-72 l'attrezzatura e la velatura di
una barca**
– *rigging (rig, tackle) and sails of a
bark (barque)*
**1** il bompresso col bastone di fiocco
– *bowsprit with jib boom*
**2-4** l'albero di trinchetto
– *foremast*
**2** il fuso maggiore dell'albero di
trinchetto
– *lower foremast*
**3** l'albero di gabbia dell'albero di
trinchetto
– *fore topmast*
**4** l'albero di velaccio dell'albero di
trinchetto
– *fore topgallant mast*
**5-7** l'albero di maestra (l'albero
maestro)
– *mainmast*
**5** il fuso maggiore dell'albero di
maestra
– *lower mainmast*
**6** l'albero di gabbia dell'albero
maestro
– *main topmast*
**7** l'albero di velaccio dell'albero
maestro
– *main topgallant mast*
**8** *u.* **9** l'albero di mezzana
– *mizzen (mizen) mast*
**8** il fuso maggiore dell'albero di
mezzana
– *lower mizzen (lower mizen)*
**9** l'alberetto (l'albero di gabbia)
– *mizzen (mizen) topmast*
**10-19 le manovre dormienti**
– *standing rigging*
**10** lo strallo di trinchetto
– *forestay, mizzen (mizen) stay,
mainstay*
**11** lo strallo di parrocchetto
– *fore topmast stay, main topmast
stay, mizzen (mizen) topmast stay*
**12** lo stralletto di velaccio
– *fore topgallant stay, mizzen
(mizen) topgallant stay, main topgallant stay*
**13** lo stralletto di controvelaccino
– *fore royal stay (main royal stay)*
**14** la draglia di falso fiocco (la
draglia di fiocco di fuori)
– *jib stay*
**15** la briglia di bompresso
– *bobstay*
**16** le sartie maggiori
– *shrouds*
**17** le sartie di parrocchetto
– *fore topmast rigging (main topmast rigging, mizzen (mizen) topmast rigging)*
**18** le sartiole di velaccino
– *fore topgallant rigging (main topgallant rigging)*
**19** i paterazzi
– *backstays*

**20-31 le vele di strallo**
– *fore-and-aft sails*
**20** la trinchettina
– *fore topmast staysail*
**21** il gran fiocco (il fiocco di dentro)
– *inner jib*
**22** il falso fiocco (il fiocco di fuori)
– *outer jib*
**23** il controfiocco
– *flying jib*
**24** la vela di strallo di gabbia (la cavalla, la carbonera)
– *main topmast staysail*
**25** la vela di strallo di gran velaccio
– *main topgallant staysail*
**26** la vela di strallo di controvelaccio
– *main royal staysail*
**27** la vela di strallo di contromezzana
– *mizzen (mizen) staysail*
**28** la vela di strallo di belvedere *m*
– *mizzen (mizen) topmast staysail*
**29** la vela di strallo di contro-
belvedere *m*
– *mizzen (mizen) topgallant staysail*
**30** la randa di poppa
– *mizzen (mizen, spanker, driver)*
**31** la controranda di poppa
– *gaff topsail*
**32-45 i pennoni**
– *spars*
**32** il pennone di trinchetto
– *foreyard*
**33** il pennone di basso parrocchetto
– *lower fore topsail yard*
**34** il pennone di parrocchetto
volante
– *upper fore topsail yard*
**35** il pennone di basso velaccino
– *lower fore topgallant yard*
**36** il pennone di velaccino volante
– *upper fore topgallant yard*
**37** il pennone di controvelaccino
– *fore royal yard*
**38** il pennone di maestra
– *main yard*
**39** il pennone di bassa gabbia
– *lower main topsail yard*
**40** il pennone di gabbia volante
– *upper main topsail yard*
**41** il pennone di basso velaccio
– *lower main topgallant yard*
**42** il pennone di velaccio volante
– *upper main topgallant yard*
**43** il pennone di controvelaccio
– *main royal yard*
**44** la boma (il bome della randa di
poppa)
– *spanker boom*
**45** il picco della randa
– *spanker gaff*
**46** il marciapiede
– *footrope*
**47** il mantiglio
– *lifts*
**48** il mantiglio della boma
– *spanker boom topping lift*
**49** la drizza del picco della randa
– *spanker peak halyard*

**50** la coffa di trinchetto
– *foretop*
**51** la crocetta dell'albero di parrocchetto
– *fore topmast crosstrees*
**52** la coffa di maestra
– *maintop*
**53** la crocetta dell'albero di gabbia
– *main topmast crosstrees*
**54** la coffa
– *mizzen (mizen) top*
**55-66 le vele quadre**
– *square sails*
**55** la vela di trinchetto
– *foresail (fore course)*
**56** la vela di basso parrocchetto
– *lower fore topsail*
**57** la vela di parrocchetto volante
– *upper fore topsail*
**58** la vela di basso velaccino
– *lower fore topgallant sail*
**59** la vela di controvelaccino
– *upper fore topgallant sail*
**60** la vela di velaccino volante
– *fore royal*
**61** la vela di maestra
– *mainsail (main course)*
**62** la vela di bassa gabbia
– *lower main topsail*
**63** la vela di gabbia volante
– *upper main topsail*
**64** la vela di velaccio
– *lower main topgallant sail*
**65** la vela di controvelaccio
– *upper main topgallant sail*
**66** la vela di velaccio volante
– *main royal sail*
**67-71 le manovre correnti**
– *running rigging*
**67** i bracci
– *braces*
**68** le scotte
– *sheets*
**69** il paranco della scotta
– *spanker sheet*
**70** gli ostini della randa
– *spanker vangs*
**71** gli imbrogli
– *bunt line*
**72** il terzarolo
– *reef*

**1-5 velature** *f pl*
- *sail shapes*
1 la randa (la vela di randa)
- *gaffsail* (small: *trysail, spencer*)
2 il fiocco
- *jib*
3 la vela latina
- *lateen sail*
4 la vela aurica
- *lugsail*
5 la vela a tarchia
- *spritsail*
**6-8 imbarcazioni** *f pl* **a un albero**
- *single-masted sailing boats (*Am.
  *sailboats)*
6 il veliero a vela aurica e fiocco
- *tjalk*
7 la deriva (la deriva laterale)
- *leeboard*
8 il cutter
- *cutter*
**9** *u.* **10 imbarcazioni** *f pl* **a due alberi**
  *m pl* **uno più grande e uno più pic-**
  **colo**
- *mizzen (mizen) masted sailing*
  *boats (*Am. *sailboats)*
9 la yawl (la iolla)
- *ketch-rigged sailing barge*
10 il bovo
- *yawl*
**11-13** la goletta a gabbiola
- *topsail schooner*
**11-17 imbarcazioni** *f pl* **a due alberi** *m*
  *pl*
- *two-masted sailing boats (*Am.
  *sailboats)*
11 la randa di maestra
- *mainsail*
12 la randa di trinchetto
- *boom foresail*
13 il grande fiocco
- *square foresail*
14 il brigantino goletta
- *brigantine*
15 l'albero di maestra
- *half-rigged mast with fore-and-aft*
  *sails*
16 l'albero con vela quadra
- *full-rigged mast with square sails*
17 il brigantino
- *brig*
**18-27 imbarcazioni** *f pl* **a tre alberi** *m pl*
- *three-masted sailing vessels*
  *(three-masters)*
18 la goletta a palo
- *three-masted schooner*
19 la nave goletta
- *three-masted topsail schooner*
20 il brigantino a palo
- *bark (barque) schooner*
**21-23** il brigantino [cfr. l'alberatura e
  la velatura tav. 219]
- *bark (barque) [cf. illustration of*
  *rigging and sails in plate 219]*

21 l'albero di trinchetto
- *foremast*
22 l'albero di maestra (l'albero maestro)
- *mainmast*
23 l'albero di mezzana
- *mizzen (mizen) mast*
**24-27** il veliero (la nave)
- *full-rigged ship*
24 l'albero di mezzana
- *mizzen (mizen) mast*
25 la randa
- *crossjack yard (crojack yard)*
26 la vela di mezzana
- *crossjack (crojack)*
27 i portelli
- *ports*
**28-31 imbarcazioni** *f pl* **a quattro**
  **alberi** *m pl*
- *four-masted sailing ships (four-*
  *masters)*
28 la goletta a quattro alberi *m pl*
- *four-masted schooner*
29 la nave a palo
- *four-masted bark (barque)*
30 l'albero di mezzana
- *mizzen (mizen) mast*
31 la nave a quattro alberi *m pl*
- *four-masted full-rigged ship*
**32-34 nave** *f* **a cinque alberi** *m pl* **a**
  **palo**
- *five-masted bark (barque)*
32 il controvelaccio
- *skysail*
33 l'albero di contromaestra
- *middle mast*
34 l'albero di mezzana
- *mizzen (mizen) mast*
**35-37 sviluppo dei velieri** in 400 anni
  *m pl*
- *development of sailing ships over*
  *400 years*
35 la nave a cinque alberi *m pl*
  «Preussen» 1902–1910
- *five-masted full-rigged ship*
  *'Preussen' 1902-10*
36 il veliero inglese «Spindrift» 1867
- *English clipper ship 'Spindrift'*
  *1867*
37 la caravella «Santa Maria» 1492
- *caravel (carvel) 'Santa Maria'*
  *1492*

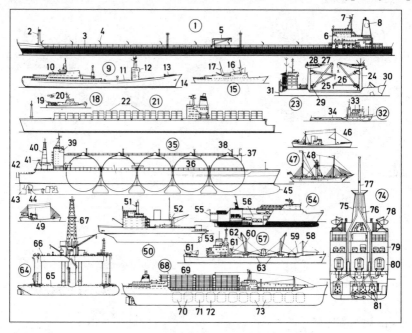

1 **la nave cisterna gigante** (ULCC, ultra large crudeoil carrier) del tipo All-aft
– *ULCC (ultra-large crude carrier) of the 'all-aft' type*
2 l'albero di prua
– *foremast*
3 la passerella con le condutture
– *catwalk with the pipes*
4 le lance antincendio
– *fire gun (fire nozzle)*
5 la gru di coperta
– *deck crane*
6 la tuga (il casotto di coperta) con il ponte
– *deckhouse with the bridge*
7 il pilone poppiero per antenna radar e segnali *m pl*
– *aft signal (signalling) and radar mast*
8 il fumaiolo
– *funnel*
9 **la nave per ricerche** *f pl* **oceanografiche a energia nucleare** «Otto Hahn», una nave trasporto merci *f pl* alla rinfusa
– *nuclear research ship 'Otto Hahn', a bulk carrier*
10 la soprastruttura poppiera (la sala macchine *f pl*)
– *aft superstructure (engine room)*
11 il boccaporto di carico (la stiva), per merci *f pl* alla rinfusa
– *cargo hatchway for bulk goods (bulk cargoes)*
12 il ponte di comando (la plancia)
– *bridge*
13 il castello di prua
– *forecastle (fo'c'sle)*
14 la ruota di prua
– *stem*
15 **la nave di linea per stazioni** *f pl* **balneari** (fam. il vaporetto)
– *seaside pleasure boat*
16 il fumaiolo cieco
– *dummy funnel*
17 l'albero dei gas di scarico
– *exhaust mast*
18 **la nave di salvataggio** in alto mare *m*
– *rescue cruiser*
19 la piattaforma per elicotteri *m pl*
– *helicopter platform (working deck)*
20 l'elicottero di salvataggio
– *rescue helicopter*

21 **la nave portacontainer**
– *all-container ship*
22 il carico container di coperta
– *containers stowed on deck*
23 **il mercantile da carico pesante**
– *cargo ship*
24-29 le apparecchiature di carico
– *cargo gear (cargo-handling gear)*
24 il pilone da carico pesante
– *bipod mast*
25 la boma da carico pesante
– *jumbo derrick boom (heavy-lift derrick boom)*
26 l'apparecchiatura di caricamento
– *derrick boom (cargo boom)*
27 il paranco (la taglia)
– *tackle*
28 il bozzello
– *block*
29 il piedritto
– *thrust bearing*
30 il portello di prua
– *bow doors*
31 il portello di carico poppiero
– *stern loading door*
32 **l'offshore** (il mezzo di approvvigionamento piattaforma di estrazione *f* )
– *offshore drilling rig supply vessel*
33 la soprastruttura compatta
– *compact superstructure*
34 la coperta di carico
– *loading deck (working deck)*
35 **la nave cisterna per gas** *m pl* **liquidi**
– *liquefied-gas tanker*
36 il serbatoio sferico
– *spherical tank*
37 l'albero televisivo per navigazione *f*
– *navigational television receiver mast*
38 lo sfiatatoio
– *vent mast*
39 la tuga (il casotto di coperta)
– *deckhouse*
40 il fumaiolo
– *funnel*
41 il ventilatore
– *ventilator*
42 la poppa quadra
– *transom stern (transom)*
43 la pala del timone
– *rudder blade (rudder)*

44 l'elica
– *ship's propeller (ship's screw)*
45 il bulbo di prua
– *bulbous bow*
46 il peschereccio (il battello da pesca)
– *steam trawler*
47 **la nave faro**
– *lightship (light vessel)*
48 il faro
– *lantern (characteristic light)*
49 la motonave da pesca
– *smack*
50 **il rompighiaccio** (la nave rompighiaccio)
– *ice breaker*
51 l'albero a torre *f*
– *steaming light mast*
52 l'hangar *m* per gli elicotteri
– *helicopter hangar*
53 la scia di poppa per l'inserimento delle navi
– *stern towing point, for gripping the bow of ships in tow*
54 **il Roll-on-roll-off-trailer** (il Roro-trailer)
– *roll-on-roll-off (ro-ro) trailer ferry*
55 il portellone di poppa con rampa di uscita
– *stern port (stern opening) with ramp*
56 l'ascensore *m* per autocarri *m pl*
– *heavy vehicle lifts (Am. heavy vehicle elevators)*
57 **il mercantile universale** (la nave da carico universale)
– *multi-purpose freighter*
58 il pilone di carico e di ventilazione *f*
– *ventilator-type samson (sampson) post (ventilator-type king post)*
59 l'apparecchiatura di caricamento
– *derrick boom (cargo boom, cargo gear, cargo-handling gear)*
60 l'albero di caricamento
– *derrick mast*
61 la gru di coperta
– *deck crane*
62 la boma da carico pesante
– *jumbo derrick boom (heavy-lift derrick boom)*
63 il boccaporto di carico (la stiva) per merci *f pl* alla rinfusa
– *cargo hatchway*
64 **la piattaforma di trivellazione** *f* **galleggiante**
– *semisubmersible drilling vessel*

65 il galleggiante con i macchinari
 – *floating vessel with machinery*
66 la piattaforma di lavoro
 – *drilling platform*
67 la torre di trivellazione *f*
 – *derrick*
68 **la nave trasporto bestiame** *m* (livestock-carrier)
 – **cattleship** *(cattle vessel)*
69 la soprastruttura per trasporto bestiame *m*
 – *superstructure for transporting livestock*
70 i serbatoi di acqua fresca
 – *fresh water tanks*
71 il serbatoio di gasolio
 – *fuel tank*
72 il serbatoio per il letame
 – *dung tank*
73 i serbatoi per il mangime
 – *fodder tanks*
74 **il traghetto ferroviario** (in sezione *f* )
 – **train ferry** *[cross section]*
75 il fumaiolo
 – *funnel*
76 le condutture dei gas di scarico
 – *exhaust pipes*
77 l'albero
 – *mast*
78 la scialuppa di salvataggio appesa ad una gru brevettata per imbarcazioni *f pl*
 – *ship's lifeboat hanging at the davit*
79 la coperta per le automobili
 – *car deck*
80 la coperta per i vagoni
 – *main deck (train deck)*
81 i motori principali
 – *main engines*
82 **il piroscafo passeggeri** *m pl* (il transatlantico)
 – *passenger liner (liner, ocean liner)*
83 la prua atlantica
 – *stem*
84 il fumaiolo con rivestimento a traliccio
 – *funnel with lattice casing*
85 il gran pavese (il pavese di bandiera – *per es.*: per il viaggio inaugurale)
 – *flag dressing (rainbow dressing, string of flags extending over mastheads, e.g., on the maiden voyage)*

86 **il peschereccio a vapore** *m* con rete *f* a strascico a poppa, un peschereccio con prima lavorazione *f* del pesce
 – **trawler,** *a factory ship*
87 il braccio di carico di poppa
 – *gallows*
88 la rete a strascico di poppa
 – *stern ramp*
89 **la nave container**
 – **container ship**
90 la plancia di carico
 – *loading bridge (loading platform)*
91 la scala di corda
 – *sea ladder (jacob's ladder, rope ladder)*
92 **l'abbinamento di rimorchiatori** *m pl* **a spinta,** due imbarcazioni *f pl* per navigazione *f* interna
 – **barge and push tug assembly**
93 lo spintore (il rimorchiatore a spinta)
 – *push tug*
94 il rimorchiatore di alleggio, un alleggio cisterna per trasporto gas *m*
 – *tug-pushed dumb barge (tug-pushed lighter)*
95 il battello pilota *m*
 – *pilot boat*
96 **la nave di linea per trasporto passeggeri** *m pl* **e merci** *f pl*
 – *combined cargo and passenger liner*
97 la lancia trasporto passeggeri *m pl*
 – *the ship's boat, launch*
98 la scaletta
 – *accommodation ladder*
99 la motonave costiera
 – *coaster (coasting vessel)*
100 l'incrociatore *m* leggero della polizia e della polizia doganale
 – *customs or police launch*
101-128 **il vaporetto** (il battello per il trasporto di comitive *f pl* di gitanti *m pl*)
 – *excursion steamer (pleasure steamer)*
101-106 la gru della scialuppa di salvataggio
 – *lifeboat launching gear*
101 la gru per imbarcazioni *f pl*
 – *davit*
102 il supporto
 – *wire rope span*
103 il guardamano (il guardacorpo)
 – *lifeline*
104 **il paranco (la taglia)**
 – *tackle*

105 il bozzello
 – *block*
106 il tirante del paranco
 – *fall*
107 la scialuppa di salvataggio coperta da tela incerata
 – *ship's lifeboat (ship's boat) covered with tarpaulin*
108 il dritto di prua
 – *stem*
109 il passeggero
 – *passenger*
110 lo steward
 – *steward*
111 la sedia a sdraio
 – *deck-chair*
112 il mozzo
 – *deck hand*
113 il secchio
 – *deck bucket*
114 il marinaio
 – *boatswain (bo's'n, bo'sun, bosun)*
115 la litweca
 – *tunic*
116 la tenda (da sole *m*)
 – *awning*
117 i sostegni della tenda
 – *stanchion*
118 la tavola della tenda
 – *ridge rope (jackstay)*
119 la legatura
 – *lashing*
120 il parapetto di murata
 – *bulwark*
121 il parapetto
 – *guard rail*
122 il corrimano
 – *handrail (top rail)*
123 la scaletta di boccaporto
 – *companion ladder (companionway)*
124 il salvagente
 – *lifebelt (lifebuoy)*
125 la spia luminosa (del salvagente)
 – *lifebuoy light (lifebelt light, signal light)*
126 l'ufficiale *m* di guardia
 – *officer of the watch (watchkeeper)*
127 la giacca di bordo
 – *reefer (Am. pea jacket)*
128 il binocolo
 – *binoculars*

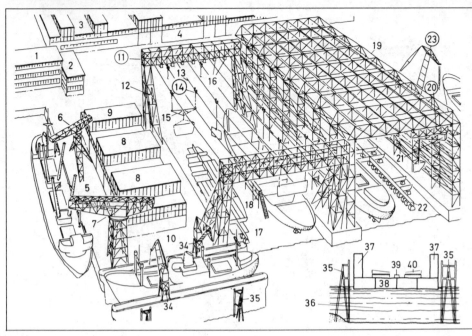

1-43 **il cantiere navale** (l'arsenale *m*)
- *shipyard (shipbuilding yard, dock-*
  *yard, Am. navy yard)*
1 gli uffici dell'amministrazione *f*
- *administrative offices*
2 l'ufficio progetti *m pl*
- *ship-drawing office*
3 *u.* 4 l'officina allestimento
- *shipbuilding sheds*
3 la sala a tracciare (la sala di tracciatura)
- *mould (Am. mold) loft*
4 l'officina
- *erection shop*
5-9 la banchina di allestimento
- *fitting-out quay*
5 la banchina
- *quay*
6 la gru a tre gambe *f pl*
- *tripod crane*
7 la gru a martello
- *hammer-headed crane*
8 l'officina macchine *f pl*
- *engineering workshop*
9 l'officina di costruzione *f* caldaie *f pl*
- *boiler shop*
10 la banchina per le riparazioni
- *repair quay*
11-26 il bacino (lo scalo) di costruzione
  *f* navale
- *slipways (slips, building berths,*
  *building slips, stocks)*
11-18 il blondin portuale
- *cable crane berth, a slipway (building*
  *berth)*
11 la torre
- *slipway portal*

12 il montante della torre
- *bridge support*
13 il cavo della gru
- *crane cable*
14 il carrello
- *crab (jenny)*
15 la traversa
- *cross piece*
16 la cabina di manovra della gru
- *crane driver's cabin (crane driver's*
  *cage)*
17 il piano del bacino di costruzione *f*
- *slipway floor*
18 il ponte, un'impalcatura (un ponteggio)
- *staging, a scaffold*
19-21 l'impalcatura del bacino di
  costruzione *f*
- *frame slipway*
19 l'impalcatura
- *slipway frame*
20 la gru a ponte *m* a vie *f pl* di corsa
  superiori
- *overhead travelling (Am. traveling)*
  *crane (gantry crane)*
21 il paranco girevole
- *slewing crab*
22 la chiglia in posizione *f* di varo
- *keel in position*
23 la gru a piattaforma girevole
- *luffing jib crane, a slipway crane*
24 le rotaie della gru
- *crane rails (crane track)*
25 la gru a cavalletto (a portale *m*)
- *gantry crane*
26 il ponte della gru
- *gantry (bridge)*

27 la trave principale del ponte
- *trestles (supports)*
28 il carroponte (la gru a carroponte)
- *crab (jenny)*
29 la struttura interna dello scafo
- *hull frames in position*
30 la nave pronta per il varo
- *ship under construction*
31-33 il bacino di carenaggio
- *dry dock*
31 la platea del bacino
- *dock floor (dock bottom)*
32 la chiusura del bacino (la porta del
  bacino)
- *dock gates (caisson)*
33 la sala pompe *f pl* (la sala macchine *f pl*)
- *pumping station (power house)*
34-43 il bacino di carenaggio galleggiante
- *floating dock (pontoon dock)*
34 la gru, una gru a portale *m*
- *dock crane (dockside crane), a jib*
  *crane*
35 il parabordo
- *fender pile*
36-43 la disposizione del bacino
- *working of docks*
36 la conca del bacino
- *dock basin*
37 *u.* 38 la struttura del bacino
- *dock structure*
37 il serbatoio laterale
- *side tank (side wall)*
38 il serbatoio inferiore
- *bottom tank (bottom pontoon)*

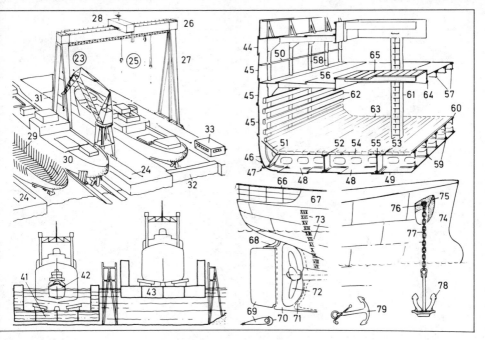

39  la taccata di bacino
 – *keel block*
40  il tacco
 – *bilge block (bilge shore, side support)*
41-43  la messa in bacino di una nave
 – *docking a ship*
41  il bacino galleggiante allagato
 – *flooded floating dock*
42  il rimorchiatore in azione *f*
 – *tug towing the ship*
43  il bacino prosciugato
 – *emptied (pumped-out) dock*
44-61  **gli elementi costruttivi**
 – **structural parts of the ship**
44-56  i corsi longitudinali
 – *longitudinal structure*
44-49  il fasciame esterno
 – *shell (shell plating, skin)*
44  la cinta
 – *sheer strake*
45  la sottocinta
 – *side strake*
46  il ginocchio
 – *bilge strake*
47  la chiglia antirollio
 – *bilge keel*
48  il fondo
 – *bottom plating*
49  la carena piatta
 – *flat plate keel (keel plate)*
50  il trincarino
 – *stringer (side stringer)*
51  il marginale
 – *tank margin plate*
52  il paramezzale laterale
 – *longitudinal side girder*

53  il paramezzale centrale
 – *centre (Am. center) plate girder (centre girder, kelson, keelson, vertical keel)*
54  il cielo del doppio fondo
 – *tank top plating (tank top, inner bottom plating)*
55  il corso centrale del doppio fondo
 – *centre (Am. center) strake*
56  la lamiera del ponte
 – *deck plating*
57  il baglio
 – *deck beam*
58  la costola (l'ossatura)
 – *frame (rib)*
59  il madiere
 – *floor plate*
60  il doppio fondo
 – *cellular double bottom*
61  il puntale di stiva
 – *hold pillar (pillar)*
62 *u.* 63  il fasciame interno
 – *dunnage*
62  il fasciame interno laterale
 – *side battens (side ceiling, spar ceiling)*
63  il pagliuolo
 – *ceiling (floor ceiling)*
64 *u.* 65  il boccaporto
 – *hatchway*
64  la mastra di boccaporto
 – *hatch coaming*
65  il portello di boccaporto
 – *hatch cover (hatchboard)*
66-72  la poppa
 – *stern*

66  il parapetto di murata aperto (la battagliola)
 – *guard rail*
67  il parapetto di murata
 – *bulwark*
68  l'asse *f* del timone (l'anima del timone)
 – *rudder stock*
69 *u.* 70  il timone Oertz
 – *Oertz rudder*
69  la pala del timone
 – *rudder blade (rudder)*
70 *u.* 71  il dritto di poppa
 – *stern frame*
70  il dritto del timone
 – *rudder post*
71  il dritto dell'elica
 – *propeller post (screw post)*
72  l'elica
 – *ship's propeller (ship's screw)*
73  la marca d'immersione *f* (la marca di pescaggio)
 – *draught (draft) marks*
74-79  la prua
 – *bow*
74  la ruota di prua, una prua a bulbo
 – *stem, a bulbous stem (bulbous bow)*
75  la cubia (l'occhio di cubia)
 – *hawse*
76  il foro della cubia
 – *hawse pipe*
77  la catena dell'ancora
 – *anchor cable (chain cable)*
78  l'ancora senza ceppo
 – *stockless anchor (patent anchor)*
79  l'ancora con ceppo
 – *stocked anchor*

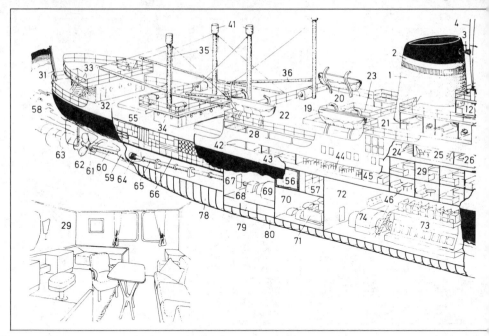

**1-71 la nave combinata per passeg-geri** *m pl* **e merci** *f pl*
– *combined cargo and passenger ship [of the older type]*
**1** il fumaiolo
– *funnel*
**2** il contrassegno (i colori del fumaiolo, il contrassegno della compagnia armatrice)
– *funnel marking*
**3** la sirena
– *siren (fog horn)*
**4-11 le sovrastrutture aeree**
– *compass platform (compass bridge, compass flat, monkey bridge)*
**4** la discesa (la coda) dell'antenna
– *antenna lead-in (antenna down-lead)*
**5** l'antenna radiogoniometrica
– *radio direction finder (RDF) antenna (direction finder antenna, rotatable loop antenna, aural null loop antenna)*
**6** la bussola magnetica
– *magnetic compass (mariner's compass)*
**7** la lampada Morse (il telegrafo ottico)
– *morse lamp (signalling, Am. signaling, lamp)*
**8** l'antenna radar
– *radar antenna (radar scanner)*
**9** la bandiera a segnali *m pl*
– *code flag signal*
**10** la cima di segnalazione *f*
– *code flag halyards*

**11** lo straglio (lo strallo)
– *triatic stay (signal stay)*
**12-18 il ponte di comando** (il ponte di coperta, il ponte)
– *bridge deck (bridge)*
**12** la cabina radio
– *radio room*
**13** la cabina del capitano
– *captain's cabin*
**14** la sala nautica
– *navigating bridge*
**15** il fanale laterale destro (di dritta) verde; il fanale laterale di sinistra: rosso
– *starboard sidelight [green; port sidelight red]*
**16** la varea
– *wing of bridge*
**17** il parapetto di murata
– *shelter (weather cloth, dodger)*
**18** la plancia (il ponte di coperta)
– *wheelhouse*
**19-21 il ponte della lancia**
– *boat deck*
**19** la scialuppa (la lancia) di salvataggio
– *ship's lifeboat*
**20** la gru della lancia di salvataggio
– *davit*
**21** il quadrato degli ufficiali
– *officer's cabin*
**22-27 il ponte di passeggiata**
– *promenade deck*
**22** il ponte di riposo
– *sun deck (lido deck)*
**23** la piscina
– *swimming pool*

**24** la scaletta
– *companion ladder (companion-way)*
**25** la biblioteca
– *library (ship's library)*
**26** il salone
– *lounge*
**27** la passeggiata
– *promenade*
**28-30 il ponte di seconda classe** *f*
– *A-deck*
**28** il ponte semicoperto
– *semi-enclosed deck space*
**29** la cabina doppia, una cabina
– *double-berth cabin, a cabin*
**30** la cabina di lusso
– *de luxe cabin*
**31** l'asta della bandiera di poppa
– *ensign staff*
**32-47 il ponte di prima classe** *f* (il ponte principale)
– *B-deck (main deck)*
**32** il ponte di poppa (il ponte poppiero)
– *after deck*
**33** il cassero di poppa
– *poop*
**34** la tuga
– *deckhouse*
**35** la colonna di carico
– *samson (sampson) post (king post)*
**36** il braccio di carico
– *derrick boom (cargo boom)*
**37** la crocetta (la barra)
– *crosstrees (spreader)*

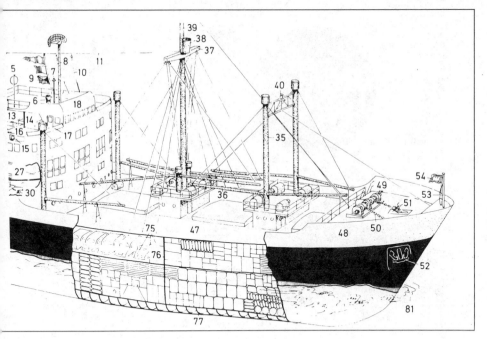

| | |
|---|---|
| **38** la coffa (la gabbia) | **54** la bandiera di bompresso |
| – *crow's nest* | – *jack* |
| **39** l'albero di gabbia | **55** la stiva di poppa |
| – *topmast* | – *after holds* |
| **40** il fanale del piroscafo | **56** la cella frigorifera |
| – *forward steaming light* | – *cold storage room (insulated hold)* |
| **41** gli aeratori | **57** il deposito viveri *m pl* |
| – *ventilator lead* | – *store room* |
| **42** la cucina della nave | **58** la scia |
| – *galley (caboose, cookroom, ship's kitchen)* | – *wake* |
| **43** la cambusa | **59** il supporto dell'albero portaelica |
| – *ship's pantry* | – *shell bossing (shaft bossing)* |
| **44** la sala da pranzo | **60** l'estremità dell'albero portaelica |
| – *dining room* | – *tail shaft (tail end shaft)* |
| **45** l'ufficio del commissario di bordo | **61** il braccio dell'albero portaelica |
| – *purser's office* | – *shaft strut (strut, spectacle frame, propeller strut, propeller bracket)* |
| **46** la cabina singola | **62** l'elica a tre pale *f pl* |
| – *single-berth cabin* | – *three-blade ship's propeller (ship's screw)* |
| **47** la coperta di prua | **63** il timone |
| – *foredeck* | – *rudder blade (rudder)* |
| **48** il castello di prua | **64** il premitreccia |
| – *forecastle (fo'c'sle)* | – *stuffing box* |
| **49-51 il paranco delle ancore** | **65** l'albero portaelica |
| – **ground tackle** | – *propeller shaft* |
| **49** il verricello salpa ancora | **66** il tunnel dell'asse *f* |
| – *windlass* | – *shaft alley (shaft tunnel)* |
| **50** la catena dell'ancora | **67** il cuscinetto reggispina |
| – *anchor cable (chain cable)* | – *thrust block* |
| **51** lo strozzatoio | **68-74 la propulsione dieselelettrica** |
| – *compressor (chain compressor)* | – *diesel-electric drive* |
| **52** l'ancora | **68** la sala macchine elettriche |
| – *anchor* | – *electric engine room* |
| **53** l'asta della bandiera di bompresso | |
| – *jackstaff* | |

| |
|---|
| **69** il motore elettrico |
| – *electric motor* |
| **70** la sala macchine ausiliarie |
| – *auxiliary engine room* |
| **71** le macchine ausiliarie |
| – *auxiliary engines* |
| **72** la sala macchine principale |
| – *main engine room* |
| **73** la macchina principale, un motore Diesel |
| – *main engine, a diesel engine* |
| **74** il generatore |
| – *generator* |
| **75** le stive di prua |
| – *forward holds* |
| **76** l'interponte *m* |
| – *tween deck* |
| **77** il carico |
| – *cargo* |
| **78** la cisterna per la zavorra liquida |
| – *ballast tank (deep tank) for water ballast* |
| **79** il serbatoio per l'acqua potabile |
| – *fresh water tank* |
| **80** il serbatoio per il gasolio |
| – *fuel tank* |
| **81** l'onda di prua |
| – *bow wave* |

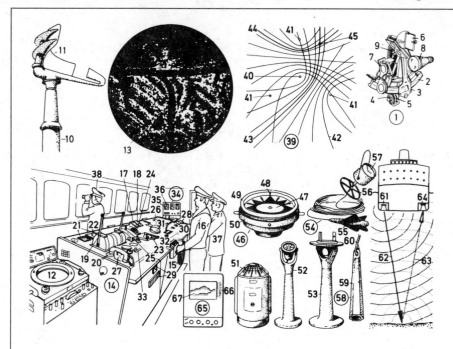

1 **il sestante**
– *sextant*
2 l'arco graduato
– *graduated arc*
3 l'alidada
– *index bar (index arm)*
4 il rullo graduato
– *decimal micrometer*
5 il nonio
– *vernier*
6 lo specchio mobile (lo specchio grande)
– *index mirror*
7 lo specchio fisso (lo specchio piccolo)
– *horizon glass (horizon mirror)*
8 il cannocchiale
– *telescope*
9 l'impugnatura
– *grip (handgrip)*
10-13 **il radar**
– *radar equipment (radar apparatus)*
10 il sostegno del radar
– *radar pedestal*
11 l'antenna di riflessione *f* girevole
– *revolving radar reflector*
12 lo schermo radar
– *radar display unit (radar screen)*
13 l'immagine *f* radar
– *radar image (radar picture)*
14-38 **il ponte di comando** (la timoneria)
– *wheelhouse*
14 il posto di manovra e di comando
– *steering and control position*
15 la ruota del timone
– *ship's wheel for controlling the rudder mechanism*
16 il timoniere
– *helmsman (Am. wheelsman)*
17 l'indicatore *m* dell'angolo di barra del timone
– *rudder angle indicator*
18 l'indicatore *m* della rotta
– *automatic pilot (autopilot)*
19 la leva azionamento elica a passo variabile
– *control lever for the variable-pitch propeller (reversible propeller, feathering propeller, feathering screw)*

20 l'indicatore *m* del passo dell'elica
– *propeller pitch indicator*
21 l'indicatore *m* dei giri dei motori principali
– *main engine revolution indicator*
22 l'indicatore *m* della velocità della nave
– *ship's speedometer (log)*
23 il comando timone *m* di prua
– *control switch for bow thruster (bow-manoeuvring, Am. maneuvering, propeller)*
24 l'ecografo
– *echo recorder (depth recorder, echograph)*
25 il telegrafo di macchina doppia
– *engine telegraph (engine order telegraph)*
26 gli apparecchi di comando e controllo per lo stabilizzatore di rullio
– *controls for the anti-rolling system (for the stabilizers)*
27 il telefono a batteria locale
– *local-battery telephone*
28 il telefono dell'impianto telefonico per il traffico marittimo
– *shipping traffic radio telephone*
29 il quadro delle luci di posizione *f*
– *navigation light indicator panel (running light indicator panel)*
30 il microfono
– *microphone for ship's address system*
31 la girobussola, una bussola ripetitrice
– *gyro compass (gyroscopic compass), a compass repeater*
32 il pulsante per la sirena della nave
– *control button for the ship's siren (ship's fog horn)*
33 l'apparecchio controllo sovraccarico motori *m pl* principali
– *main engine overload indicator*
34 l'apparecchio Decca per il controllo punto nave *f*
– *Decca position-finder (Decca Navigator)*
35 l'indicatore *m* di sintonia piatta
– *rough focusing indicator*
36 l'indicatore *m* di sintonia acuta
– *fine focusing indicator*
37 l'ufficiale *m* di rotta
– *navigating officer*

38 il capitano
– *captain*
39 **il sistema Decca, un sistema di radionavigazione** *f*
– *Decca navigation system*
40 la stazione padrona
– *master station*
41 la stazione schiava
– *slave station*
42 l'iperbole *f* zero
– *null hyperbola*
43 la linea iperbolica di rilevamento 1
– *hyperbolic position line 1*
44 la linea iperbolica di rilevamento 2
– *hyperbolic position line 2*
45 la linea di posizione *f*
– *position (fix, ship fix)*
46-53 **bussole** *f pl*
– *compasses*
46 la bussola a liquido, una bussola magnetica
– *liquid compass (fluid compass, spirit compass, wet compass), a magnetic compass*
47 la rosa della bussola
– *compass card*
48 la linea di fede *f*
– *lubber's line (lubber's mark, lubber's point)*
49 il mortaio della bussola
– *compass bowl*
50 il sostegno cardanico
– *gimbal ring*
51-53 la girobussola (la bigiroscopica)
– *gyro compass (gyroscopic compass, gyro compass unit)*
51 la girobussola madre *f*
– *master compass (master gyro compass)*
52 la bussola ripetitrice
– *compass repeater (gyro repeater)*
53 la bussola ripetitrice con grafometro
– *compass repeater with pelorus*
54 **il solcometro**
– *patent log (screw log, mechanical log, towing log, taffrail log, speedometer), a log*
55 l'elica del solcometro
– *rotator*

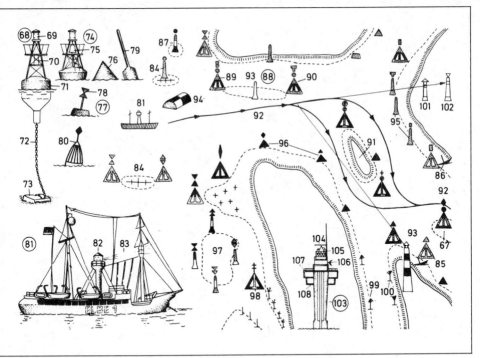

56  il regolatore del volano
– governor
57  il totalizzatore (l'orologio del solcometro)
– log clock
58-67 scandagli m pl
– leads
58  lo scandaglio manuale
– hand lead
59  il corpo dello scandaglio
– lead (lead sinker)
60  la corda dello scandaglio
– leadline
61-67 lo scandaglio acustico
– echo sounder (echo sounding machine)
61  l'emittente f suoni m pl
– sound transmitter
62  l'impulso dell'onda sonora
– sound wave (sound impulse)
63  l'eco f
– echo (sound echo, echo signal)
64  il ricevitore eco f
– echo receiver (hydrophone)
65  l'ecografo
– echograph (echo sounding machine
recorder)
66  la scala di profondità
– depth scale
67  il grafico
– echogram (depth recording, depth reading)
68-108 segnali m pl marini
– sea marks (floating navigational marks)
for buoyage and lighting systems
68-83 segnali m pl per acque navigabili
– fairway marks (channel marks)
68  la boa luminosa con sirena
– light and whistle buoy
69  la lanterna
– light (warning light)
70  la sirena
– whistle
71  il galleggiante
– buoy
72  la catena dell'ancora
– mooring chain

73  l'ancora di boa
– sinker (mooring sinker)
74  la boa luminosa con campana
– light and bell buoy
75  la campana
– bell
76  la boa a punta
– conical buoy
77  la boa a tronco di cono
– can buoy
78  il segnale a clessidra
– topmark
79  la boa a albero
– spar buoy
80  la boa di segnalazione f
– topmark buoy
81  il battello faro
– lightship (light vessel)
82  la torre del faro
– lantern mast (lantern tower)
83  il faro
– beam of light
84-102 i contrassegni per la navigazione
– fairway markings (channel markings)
[German type]
84  relitto (boa verde)
– wreck [green buoys]
85  relitto a dritta dell'acqua navigabile
– wreck to starboard
86  relitto a sinistra dell'acqua navigabile
– wreck to port
87  bassofondo
– shoals (shallows, shallow water, Am.
flats)
88  secca a sinistra dell'acqua principale
– middle ground to port
89  divisione f (l'inizio della secca: boa =
cilindro rosso su palla rossa)
– division (bifurcation) [beginning of the
middle ground; topmark: red cylinder
above red ball]
90  unione f (la fine della secca; boa = croce f
di S. Antonio rossa su palla rossa)
– convergence (confluence) [end of the middle ground; topmark: red St. Antony's
cross above red ball]

91  secca
– middle ground
92  la via d'acqua navigabile principale
– main fairway (main navigable channel)
93  la via d'acqua navigabile secondaria
– secondary fairway (secondary navigable
channel)
94  la boa a botte f
– can buoy
95  boe f pl di sinistra (rosse)
– port hand buoys (port hand marks) [red]
96  boe f pl di dritta (nere)
– starboard hand buoys (starboard hand
marks) [black]
97  bassofondo al di fuori della via d'acqua
navigabile
– shoals (shallows, shallow water, Am.
flats) outside the fairway
98  centro della via d'acqua navigabile (boa =
croce f doppia)
– middle of the fairway (mid-channel)
99  pali m pl di dritta (scopa all'ingiù)
– starboard markers [inverted broom]
100 pali m pl di sinistra (scopa all'insù)
– port markers [upward-pointing broom]
101 u. 102 luci f pl direzionali
– range lights (leading lights)
101 luce f inferiore
– lower range light (lower leading light)
102 luce f superiore
– higher range light (higher leading light)
103 il faro
– lighthouse
104 l'antenna radar
– radar antenna (radar scanner)
105 la lanterna
– lantern (characteristic light)
106 l'antenna di trasmissione f per ponte m
radio
– radio direction finder (RDF) antenna
107 la coperta per le macchine e di sosta
– machinery and observation platform
(machinery and observation deck)
108 i locali di abitazione f
– living quarters

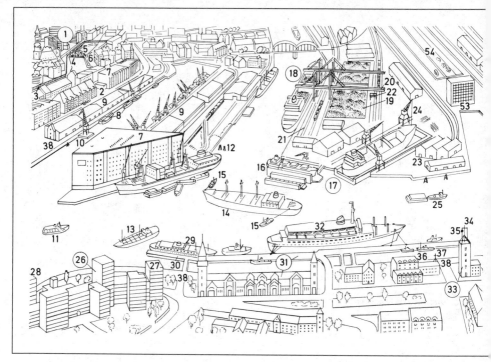

1 il porto (i quartieri del porto, la zona portuale)
– *dock area*
2 il porto franco
– *free port (foreign trade zone)*
3 la dogana del porto
– *free zone frontier (free zone enclosure)*
4 la barriera doganale
– *customs barrier*
5 il passaggio (il transito)
– *customs entrance*
6 l'ufficio doganale (la dogana)
– *port custom house*
7 il magazzino (il deposito) delle merci
– *entrepôt*
8 la chiatta
– *barge (dumb barge, lighter)*
9 il capannone (la rimessa) del collettame
– *break-bulk cargo transit shed (general cargo transit shed, package cargo transit shed)*
10 la gru galleggiante
– *floating crane*
11 il traghetto (il ferry-boat)
– *harbour (Am. harbor) ferry (ferryboat)*
12 il pilone di attracco
– *fender (dolphin)*

13 la bettolina per bunkeraggio (la bettolina per rifornimento combustibile *m*), una grossa chiatta
– *bunkering boat*
14 la nave da carico per collettame *m*
– *break-bulk carrier (general cargo ship)*
15 il rimorchiatore
– *tug*
16 il bacino galleggiante
– *floating dock (pontoon dock)*
17 il bacino di carenaggio
– *dry dock*
18 la calata del carbone
– *coal wharf*
19 il deposito del carbone
– *coal bunker*
20 il ponte di carico
– *transporter loading bridge*
21 lo scalo ferroviario
– *quayside railway*
22 il casello della pesa
– *weighing bunker*
23 il capannone (la rimessa) del cantiere navale
– *warehouse*
24 la gru del cantiere navale
– *quayside crane*
25 la motolancia con chiatta
– *launch and lighter*
26 l'ospedale del porto (la sanità)
– *port hospital*

27 l'ospedale *m* contumaciale
– *quarantine wing*
28 l'istituto di medicina tropicale
– *Institute of Tropical Medicine*
29 il vaporetto
– *excursion steamer (pleasure steamer)*
30 il pontile di sbarco
– *jetty*
31 le strutture a disposizione *f* dei passeggeri
– *passenger terminal*
32 la nave di linea (la nave passeggeri *m pl*, il transatlantico)
– *liner (passenger liner, ocean liner)*
33 l'ufficio meteorologico, una stazione meteorologica
– *meteorological office, a weather station*
34 il semaforo, una stazione costiera per vedetta e comunicazioni *f pl*
– *signal mast (signalling mast)*
35 il segnale di tempesta
– *storm signal*
36 l'ufficio portuale
– *port administration offices*
37 il mareografo (l'indicatore *m* del livello dell'acqua)
– *tide level indicator*
38 la banchina
– *quayside road (quayside roadway)*

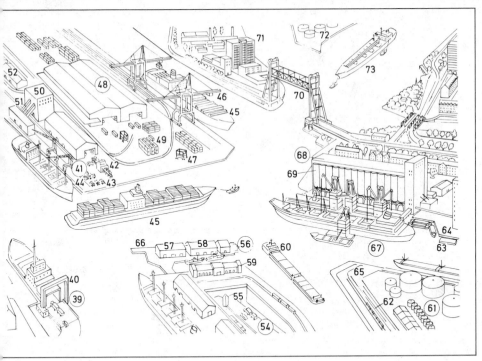

**39** il trasporto con nave *f* Ro-Ro (la
nave Roll-on-roll-off, la nave per
il trasporto di automezzi *m pl*
carichi)
– *roll-on roll-off (ro-ro) system
(roll-on roll-off operation)*
**40** l'ascensore *m* del ponte
– *gantry*
**41** il trasporto con nave *f* per carico
pallettizzato (truck-to-truck)
– *truck-to-truck system (truck-to-
truck operation)*
**42** la catasta di merce *f* imballata
– *foil-wrapped unit loads*
**43** i pallet
– *pallets*
**44** il carrello elevatore
– *forklift truck (fork truck, forklift)*
**45** la nave portacontainer
– *container ship*
**46** il ponte a bilico
– *transporter container-loading
bridge*
**47** il carrello elevatore per container
– *container carrier truck*
**48** il terminal dei container
– *container terminal (container
berth)*
**49** la catasta dei container
– *unit load*
**50** l'impianto frigorifero
– *cold store*

**51** il nastro trasportatore
– *conveyor belt (conveyor)*
**52** il magazzino per la frutta
– *fruit storage shed (fruit warehouse)*
**53** gli uffici
– *office building*
**54** l'autostrada
– *urban motorway (Am. freeway)*
**55** il tunnel sotto il porto
– *harbour (Am. harbor) tunnels*
**56** il porto di pesca
– *fish dock*
**57** il magazzino del pesce
– *fish market*
**58** il magazzino per le vendite
all'asta
– *auction room*
**59** la fabbrica di conserve *f pl* di
pesce *m* (la fabbrica per l'incato-
lamento di prodotti *m pl* ittici)
– *fish-canning factory*
**60** la maona
– *push tow*
**61** il deposito carburante *m*
– *tank farm*
**62** i binari
– *railway siding*
**63** il pontile di approdo (di attracco)
– *landing pontoon (landing stage)*
**64** la banchina
– *quay*

**65** la punta di terra
– *breakwater (mole)*
**66** il molo
– *pier (jetty), a quay extension*
**67** la nave rinfusiera (il bulk carrier,
la nave destinata a merci *f pl*
solide non imballate)
– *bulk carrier*
**68** il silo
– *silo*
**69** lo scomparto del silo
– *silo cylinder*
**70** il ponte sollevabile
– *lift bridge*
**71** la zona industriale del porto
– *industrial plant*
**72** il deposito dei liquidi
– *storage tanks*
**73** la nave cisterna
– *tanker*

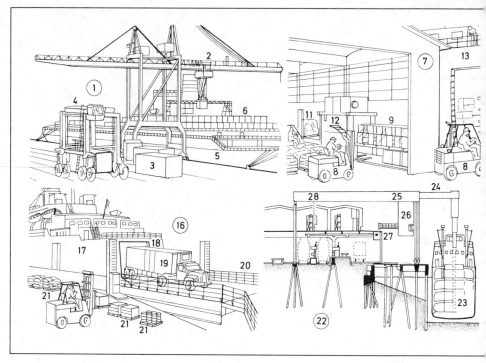

**1** il terminal dei container, un impianto moderno per il trasbordo merci *f pl*
– *container terminal (container berth), a modern cargo-handling berth*
**2** il ponte dei container (il ponte a bilico) *sim.:* la gru per il trasporto container
– *transporter container-loading bridge (loading bridge); sim.: transtainer crane (transtainer)*
**3** il container
– *container*
**4** il carrello elevatore a portale *m*
– *truck (carrier)*
**5** la nave portacontainer
– *all-container ship*
**6** il carico di coperta (container)
– *containers stowed on deck*
**7** il trasbordo truck-to-truck (il trasbordo pallettizzato di merce)
– *truck-to-truck handling (horizontal cargo handling with pallets)*
**8** il carrello elevatore (il truck)
– *forklift truck (fork truck, forklift)*
**9** il carico unificato imballato in fogli *m pl* di plastica termoretraente (unit load)
– *unitized foil-wrapped load (unit load)*
**10** il pallet piatto, un pallet normale
– *flat pallet, a standard pallet*

**11** il collettame unificato
– *unitized break-bulk cargo*
**12** il forno per la ritrazione dei fogli di plastica termoretraente
– *heat sealing machine*
**13** la nave da trasporto per il collettame
– *break-bulk carrier (general cargo ship)*
**14** il boccaporto di carico
– *cargo hatchway*
**15** il muletto
– *receiving truck on board ship*
**16** l'all-round terminal
– *multi-purpose terminal*
**17** la nave Roll-on-roll-off (la nave Ro-Ro)
– *roll-on roll-off ship (ro-ro-ship)*
**18** il portello di poppa
– *stern port (stern opening)*
**19** il carico semovente, un camion
– *driven load, a lorry (Am. truck)*
**20** l'impianto di trasporto Ro-Ro
– *ro-ro depot*
**21** gli imballaggi unificati
– *unitized load (unitized package)*
**22** l'impianto di trasbordo delle banane (sezione *f*)
– *banana-handling terminal [section]*
**23** il Turas, lato acqua
– *seaward tumbler*

**24** il braccio (la trave)
– *jib*
**25** il ponte elevatore
– *elevator bridge*
**26** il supporto della catena
– *chain sling*
**27** il segnale luminoso
– *lighting station*
**28** il Turas, lato terra (per il carico ferroviario e stradale)
– *shore-side tumbler [for loading trains and lorries (Am. trucks)]*
**29** il trasbordo di merce *f* alla rinfusa e risucchiata
– *bulk cargo handling*
**30** la nave rinfusiera (il bulk-carrier)
– *bulk carrier*
**31** il sifone galleggiante
– *floating bulk-cargo elevator*
**32** le condutture del tubo aspirante
– *suction pipes*

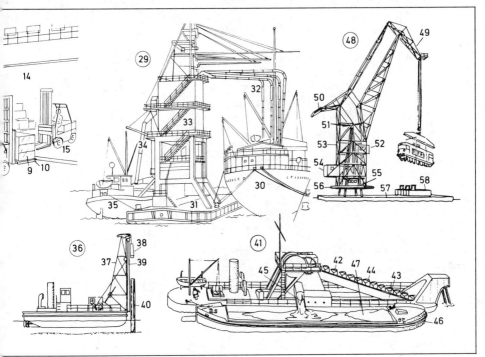

**33** il serbatoio
– *receiver*
**34** il tubo di carico
– *delivery pipe*
**35** la chiatta rinfusiera
– *bulk transporter barge*
**36** il battipalo
– *floating pile driver*
**37** l'intelaiatura del battipalo
– *pile driver frame*
**38** la mazza battente
– *pile hammer*
**39** la guida
– *driving guide rail*
**40** il supporto oscillante
– *pile*
**41** la draga a catena di tazze *f pl*, una
    draga
– *bucket dredger, a dredger*
**42** la catena di tazze *f pl*
– *bucket chain*
**43** il trascinatore delle tazze
– *bucket ladder*
**44** la tazza dello scavatore
– *dredger bucket*
**45** il piano inclinato
– *chute*
**46** la chiatta della draga
– *hopper barge*
**47** il materiale scavato
– *spoil*

**48** la gru galleggiante
– *floating crane*
**49** il braccio della gru
– *jib (boom)*
**50** il contrappeso
– *counterweight (counterpoise)*
**51** la colonna centrale
– *adjusting spindle*
**52** la cabina di manovra
– *crane driver's cabin (crane driver's*
    *cage)*
**53** la struttura della gru
– *crane framework*
**54** la cabina
– *winch house*
**55** il ponte di comando
– *control platform*
**56** la piattaforma girevole
– *turntable*
**57** il pontone (una chiatta)
– *pontoon, a pram*
**58** il gruppo motori *m pl*
– *engine superstructure (engine*
    *mounting)*

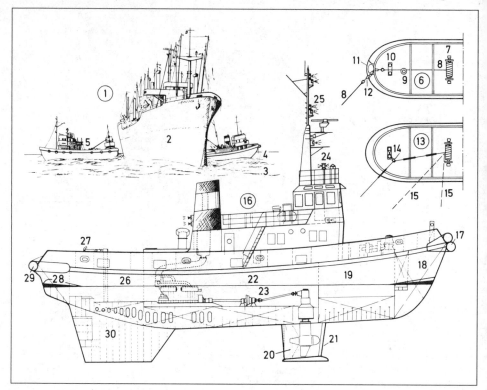

**1** il ricupero di una nave incagliata
– *salvaging (salving) of a ship run aground*
**2** la nave incagliata (la nave in avaria)
– *ship run aground (damaged vessel)*
**3** la secca
– *sandbank; also: quicksand*
**4** l'alto mare *m* (*anche:* il mare aperto)
– *open sea*
**5** il rimorchiatore
– *tug (salvage tug)*
**6-15** il paranco di traino
– *towing gear*
**6** il paranco per il rimorchio marino
– *towing gear for towing at sea*
**7** il verricello di traino
– *towing winch (towing machine, towing engine)*
**8** la gomena da traino (la gomena)
– *tow rope (tow line, towing hawser)*
**9** la guida della gomena
– *tow rope guide*
**10** la bitta
– *cross-shaped bollard*
**11** la cubia (l'occhio di cubia)
– *hawse hole*

**12** la catena dell'ancora
– *anchor cable (chain cable)*
**13** il paranco di traino per il rimorchio nel porto
– *towing gear for work in harbours (Am. harbors)*
**14** lo strozzatoio
– *guest rope*
**15** la direzione della gomena in caso di rottura dello strozzatoio
– *position of the tow rope (tow line, towing hawser)*
**16** il rimorchiatore (vista di prospetto)
– *tug (salvage tug) [vertical elevation]*
**17** il parabordo di accosto di prua
– *bow fender (pudding fender)*
**18** il gavone di prua
– *forepeak*
**19** gli alloggi (le cabine)
– *living quarters*
**20** l'involucro cilindrico intorno all'elica
– *Schottel propeller*
**21** l'ugello Kort
– *Kort vent*
**22** sala macchine *f pl* e trasmissione *f*
– *engine and propeller room*
**23** il giunto cardanico
– *clutch coupling*

**24** le sovrastrutture aeree
– *compass platform (compass bridge, compass flat, monkey bridge)*
**25** l'estintore *m*
– *fire-fighting equipment*
**26** il compartimento stagno
– *stowage*
**27** il gancio per il rimorchio
– *tow hook*
**28** la balumina
– *afterpeak*
**29** il parabordo di poppa (il paglietto di poppa)
– *stern fender*
**30** la chiglia di manovra
– *main manoeuvring (Am. maneuvering) keel*

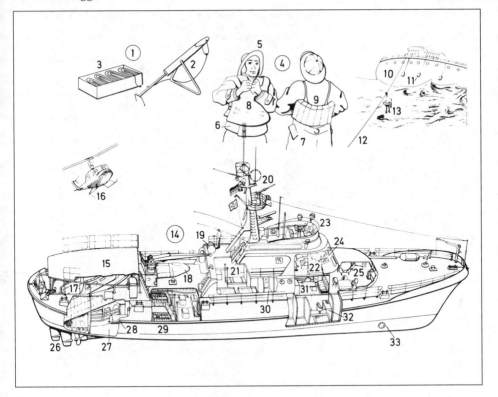

1 il lanciarazzi
– *rocket apparatus (rocket gun, line-throwing gun)*
2 il razzo
– *life rocket (rocket)*
3 la sagola di salvataggio
– *rocket line (whip line)*
4 gli indumenti di tela cerata
– *oilskins*
5 il cappello di tela cerata
– *sou'wester (southwester)*
6 il giubbotto di tela cerata
– *oilskin jacket*
7 l'impermeabile di tela cerata
– *oilskin coat*
8 il giubbotto di salvataggio gonfiabile
– *inflatable life jacket*
9 il giubbotto di salvataggio in sughero
– *cork life jacket (cork life preserver)*
10 la nave in avaria
– *stranded ship (damaged vessel)*
11 il contenitore dell'olio per versare olio sulla superficie del mare
– *oil bag, for trickling oil on the water surface*
12 la gomena di salvataggio
– *lifeline*

13 il salvagente a calzoni *m pl*
– *breeches buoy*
14 la nave di salvataggio «John T. Essberger» della Società tedesca per il salvataggio dei naufraghi
– *rescue cruiser*
15 la piattaforma di decollo per gli elicotteri
– *helicopter landing deck*
16 l'elicottero di salvataggio
– *rescue helicopter*
17 la scialuppa (la lancia) di salvataggio
– *daughter boat*
18 il gommone
– *inflatable boat (inflatable dinghy)*
19 la zattera di salvataggio
– *life raft*
20 l'estintore *m* per combattere gli incendi sulla nave
– *fire-fighting equipment for fires at sea*
21 l'ospedale *m* con reparto operatorio e vasca ipotermica
– *hospital unit with operating cabin and exposure bath*
22 la sala nautica
– *navigating bridge*
23 il ponte di comando superiore
– *upper tier of navigating bridge*

24 il ponte di comando inferiore
– *lower tier of navigating bridge*
25 il quadrato
– *messroom*
26 il gruppo timone-elica
– *rudders and propeller (screw)*
27 il compartimento stagno
– *stowage*
28 l'estintore *m* a schiuma
– *foam can*
29 i motori laterali
– *side engines*
30 la doccia
– *shower*
31 la cabina del comandante
– *coxswain's cabin*
32 la cabina singola per i membri dell'equipaggio
– *crew member's single-berth cabin*
33 il tappo a vite *f* di prua
– *bow propeller*

**1-14 la collocazione delle superfici portanti**
- *wing configurations*
1 l'aeroplano a ala alta
- *high-wing monoplane (high-wing plane)*
2 l'apertura di ala (l'apertura alare)
- *span (wing span)*
3 l'aeroplano a ala alta inserita nella fusoliera
- *shoulder-wing monoplane (shoulder-wing plane)*
4 l'aeroplano a ala media
- *midwing monoplane (midwing plane)*
5 l'aeroplano a ala bassa
- *low-wing monoplane (low-wing plane)*
6 il triplano
- *triplane*
7 l'ala superiore
- *upper wing*
8 l'ala media
- *middle wing (central wing)*
9 l'ala inferiore
- *lower wing*
10 il biplano
- *biplane*
11 il montante
- *strut*
12 il tirante
- *cross bracing wires*
13 il sesquiplani
- *sesquiplane*
14 il diedro A W
- *low-wing monoplane (low-wing plane) with cranked wings (inverted gull wings)*
**15-22 forme delle superfici portanti** (forme *f pl* delle ali)
- *wing shapes*
15 l'ala ellittica
- *elliptical wing*
16 l'ala rettangolare
- *rectangular wing*
17 l'ala trapezoidale
- *tapered wing*
18 l'ala a freccia crescente
- *crescent wing*
19 l'ala a delta *m*
- *delta wing*
20 l'ala a freccia con freccia positiva poco pronunciata
- *swept-back wing with semi-positive sweepback*
21 l'ala a freccia con freccia positiva molto marcata
- *swept-back wing with positive sweepback*
22 l'ala a delta *m* ogivale
- *ogival wing (ogee wing)*
**23-36 le forme degli impennaggi**
- *tail shapes (tail unit shapes, empennage shapes)*

23 l'impennaggio normale
- *normal tail (normal tail unit)*
24 *u.* 25 l'impennaggio verticale
- *vertical tail (vertical stabilizer and rudder)*
24 la deriva (la parte fissa)
- *vertical stabilizer (vertical fin, tail fin)*
25 il timone (la parte mobile)
- *rudder*
26 *u.* 27 l'impennaggio orizzontale
- *horizontal tail*
26 lo stabilizzatore (la parte fissa)
- *tailplane (horizontal stabilizer)*
27 l'equilibratore *m* (la parte mobile)
- *elevator*
28 l'impennaggio cruciforme
- *cruciform tail (cruciform tail unit)*
29 l'impennaggio a T
- *T-tail (T-tail unit)*
30 il cono antivortice *m*
- *lobe*
31 l'impennaggio a V (impennaggio a farfalla)
- *V-tail (vee-tail, butterfly tail)*
32 l'impennaggio bideriva
- *double tail unit (twin tail unit)*
33 la deriva
- *end plate*
34 l'impennaggio bideriva di un aereo con due fusoliere *f pl*
- *double tail unit (twin tail unit) of a twin-boom aircraft*
35 l'impennaggio bideriva con impennaggio orizzontale alto
- *raised horizontal tail with double booms*
36 l'impennaggio trideriva
- *triple tail unit*
**37 il sistema degli ipersostentatori**
- *system of flaps*
38 l'alula anteriore mobile
- *extensible slat*
39 lo spoiler
- *spoiler*
40 l'ipersostentatore *m* fowler a scorrimento
- *double-slotted Fowler flap*
41 l'alettone *m* esterno (il low speed aileron)
- *outer aileron (low-speed aileron)*
42 lo spoiler interno (lift dump)
- *inner spoiler (landing flap, lift dump)*
43 l'alettone *m* interno (all speed aileron)
- *inner aileron (all-speed aileron)*
44 l'ipersostentatore *m* frenante
- *brake flap (air brake)*
45 il profilo base *f*
- *basic profile*
**46-48** gli ipersostentatori posteriori
- *plain flaps (simple flaps)*

46 l'ipersostentatore *m* normale
- *normal flap*
47 l'ipersostentatore *m* a fessura
- *slotted flap*
48 l'ipersostentatore *m* a doppia fessura
- *double-slotted flap*
49 *u.* 50 gli ipersostentatori a spacco
- *split flaps*
49 l'ipersostentatore *m* a spacco semplice
- *plain split flap (simple split flap)*
50 l'ipersostentatore *m* zapp
- *zap flap*
51 l'ipersostentatore *m* Junkers
- *extending flap*
52 l'ipersostentatore *m* Fowler (a scorrimento)
- *Fowler flap*
53 l'alula fissa a fessura
- *slat*
54 l'ipersostentatore *m* a becco profilato
- *profiled leading-edge flap (droop flap)*
55 l'aletta Krüger
- *Krüger flap*

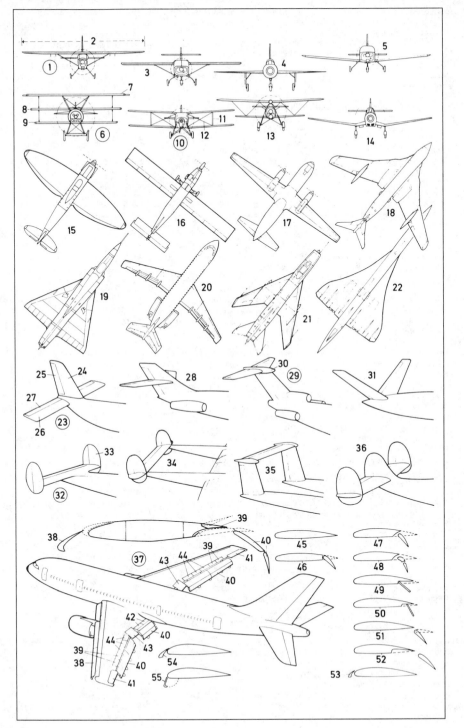

**1-31 il cockpit** di un aeroplano monomotore sportivo e da turismo
– *cockpit of a single-engine (single-engined) racing and passenger aircraft (racing and passenger plane)*
**1** il cruscotto (il cruscotto degli strumenti)
– *instrument panel*
**2** l'anemometro
– *air-speed (Am. airspeed) indicator*
**3** l'orizzone *m* artificiale
– *artificial horizon (gyro horizon)*
**4** l'altimetro
– *altimeter*
**5** la radiobussola
– *radio compass (automatic direction finder)*
**6** la bussola magnetica
– *magnetic compass*
**7** il manometro pressione alimentazione *f*
– *boost gauge (Am. gage)*
**8** il contagiri
– *tachometer (rev counter, revolution counter)*
**9** il misuratore temperatura cilindri *m pl*
– *cylinder temperature gauge (Am. gage)*
**10** l'accelerometro
– *accelerometer*
**11** l'orologio di bordo
– *chronometer*
**12** l'indicatore *m* di virata con livella a pallina
– *turn indicator with ball*
**13** la bussola giroscopica
– *directional gyro*
**14** il variometro
– *vertical speed indicator (rate-of-climb indicator, variometer)*
**15** l'indicatore *m* di rotta (VOR: very high frequency omnidirectional range)
– *VOR radio direction finder* [VOR: very high frequency omnidirectional range]
**16** l'indicatore *m* livello carburante *m* serbatoio di sinistra
– *left tank fuel gauge (Am. gage)*
**17** l'indicatore *m* livello carburante *m* serbatoio di destra
– *right tank fuel gauge (Am. gage)*
**18** l'amperometro
– *ammeter*
**19** il manometro carburante *m*
– *fuel pressure gauge (Am. gage)*
**20** il manometro olio
– *oil pressure gauge (Am. gage)*
**21** il termometro olio
– *oil temperature gauge (Am. gage)*
**22** l'apparecchiatura per radionavigazione *f* e radiotelefonia
– *radio and radio navigation equipment*
**23** l'illuminazione *f* per le carte
– *map light*

**24** la barra di comando (la cloche) azionamento alettone *m pl* equilibratore *m*
– *wheel (control column, control stick) for operating the ailerons and elevators*
**25** la barra di comando per il copilota
– *co-pilot's wheel*
**26** le apparecchiature elettriche di manovra
– *switches*
**27** la pedaliera timone *m* di direzione *f*
– *rudder pedals*
**28** la pedaliera timone *m* di direzione *f* del copilota
– *co-pilot's rudder pedals*
**29** il microfono comunicazioni *f pl* in radiotelefonia
– *microphone for the radio*
**30** la leva del gas
– *throttle lever (throttle control)*
**31** il regolatore della miscela (la leva della miscela)
– *mixture control*
**32-66 l'aeroplano monomotore sportivo e da turismo**
– *single-engine (single-engined) racing and passenger aircraft (racing and passenger plane)*
**32** l'elica
– *propeller (airscrew)*
**33** l'ogiva dell'elica
– *spinner*
**34** il motore boxer a quattro cilindri *m pl*
– *flat four engine*
**35** il cockpit
– *cockpit*
**36** il sedile del pilota
– *pilot's seat*
**37** il sedile del copilota
– *co-pilot's seat*
**38** i sedili dei passeggieri
– *passenger seats*
**39** il tettuccio (della cabina di pilotaggio)
– *hood (canopy, cockpit hood, cockpit canopy)*
**40** la ruota anteriore orientabile
– *steerable nose wheel*
**41** il carrello principale
– *main undercarriage unit (main landing gear unit)*
**42** il gradino d'imbarco
– *step*
**43** la superficie portante (l'ala)
– *wing*
**44** la luce di posizione *f* destra
– *right navigation light (right position light)*
**45** il longherone
– *spar*
**46** la centina
– *rib*

**47** il corrente
– *stringer (longitudinal reinforcing member)*
**48** il serbatoio carburante *m*
– *fuel tank*
**49** il faro di atterraggio
– *landing light*
**50** la luce di posizione *f* di sinistra
– *left navigation light (left position light)*
**51** il dispersore elettrostatico
– *electrostatic conductor*
**52** l'alettone *m*
– *aileron*
**53** l'ipersostentatore *m* di atterraggio (il flap)
– *landing flap*
**54** la fusoliera
– *fuselage (body)*
**55** l'ordinata
– *frame (former)*
**56** il corrente laterale
– *chord*
**57** il corrente
– *stringer (longitudinal reinforcing member)*
**58** l'impennaggio verticale
– *vertical tail (vertical stabilizer and rudder)*
**59** la deriva laterale
– *vertical stabilizer (vertical fin, tail fin)*
**60** il timone di direzione *f*
– *rudder*
**61** l'impennaggio orizzontale
– *horizontal tail*
**62** il piano stabilizzatore
– *tailplane (horizontal stabilizer)*
**63** l'equilibratore *m* (il timone di profondità)
– *elevator*
**64** la luce intermittente
– *warning light (anticollision light)*
**65** l'antenna dipolo
– *dipole antenna*
**66** l'antenna a filo
– *long-wire antenna (long-conductor antenna)*
**67-72 i movimenti principali** dell'aeroplano
– *principal manoeuvres (Am. maneuvers) of the aircraft (aeroplane, plane, Am. airplane)*
**67** il beccheggio
– *pitching*
**68** l'asse *m* trasversale
– *lateral axis*
**69** l'imbardata
– *yawing*
**70** l'asse *m* normale (l'asse *m* verticale)
– *vertical axis (normal axis)*
**71** il rollio
– *rolling*
**72** l'asse *m* longitudinale
– *longitudinal axis*

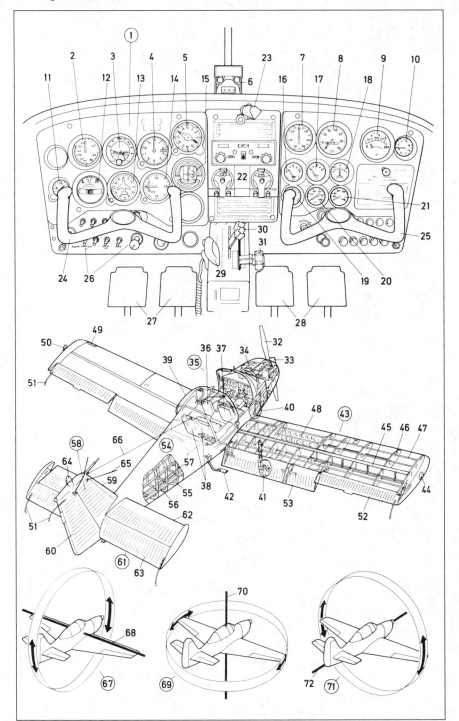

**1-33 tipi** *m pl* **di aeroplani** *m pl*
- *types of aircraft (aeroplanes, planes,* Am. *airplanes)*
**1-6 aeroplani** *m pl* **a elica**
- *propeller-driven aircraft (aeroplanes, planes,* Am. *airplanes)*
**1** l'aeroplano monomotore *m* da turismo a ala bassa
- *single-engine (single-engined) racing and passenger aircraft (racing and passenger plane), a low-wing monoplane (low-wing plane)*
**2** l'aeroplano monomotore *m* da turismo a ala alta
- *single-engine (single-engined) passenger aircraft, a high-wing monoplane (high-wing plane)*
**3** il bimotore da trasporto passeggeri *m pl* e merci *f pl*
- *twin-engine (twin-engined) business and passenger aircraft (business and passenger plane)*
**4** l'aeroplano da trasporto passeggeri *m pl* a medio e breve raggio, un aeroplano turboelica
- *short/medium haul airliner, a turboprop plane (turbopropeller plane, propeller-turbine plane)*
**5** la turbina
- *turboprop engine (turbopropeller engine)*
**6** la pinna
- *vertical stabilizer (vertical fin, tail fin)*
**7-33 aeroplani** *m pl* **a reazione** *f* (jet)
- *jet planes (jet aeroplanes, jets,* Am. *jet airplanes)*
**7** il bireattore da trasporto passeggeri *m pl* e merci *f pl*
- *twin-jet business and passenger aircraft (business and passenger plane)*
**8** l'aletta antiscorrimento
- *fence*
**9** il serbatoio alare
- *wing-tip tank (tip tank)*
**10** la gondola motore *m* di poppa
- *rear engine*
**11** il bireattore da trasporto passeggeri *m pl* a medio e breve raggio
- *twin-jet short/medium haul airliner*
**12** il trimotore a reazione *f* da trasporto passeggeri *m pl* a medio raggio
- *tri-jet medium haul airliner*
**13** il quadrimotore a reazione *f* da trasporto passeggeri *m pl* a lungo raggio
- *four-jet long haul airliner*
**14** il jumbo jet
- *wide-body long haul airliner (jumbo jet)*

**15** l'aereo supersonico (tipo: Concorde *f* )
- *supersonic airliner* [Concorde]
**16** il muso abbassabile
- *droop nose*
**17** **l'airbus** *m*, **un bireattore**, a medio e breve raggio
- *twin-jet wide-body airliner for short/medium haul routes (airbus)*
**18** il radom (il radome) con l'antenna meteorologica radar *m*
- *radar nose (radome, radar dome) with weather radar antenna*
**19** il cockpit (la cabina di pilotaggio)
- *cockpit*
**20** la cucina di bordo
- *galley*
**21** il bagagliaio
- *cargo hold (hold, underfloor hold)*
**22** la cabina per i passeggeri con i sedili
- *passenger cabin with passenger seats*
**23** il carrello retrattile
- *retractable nose undercarriage unit (retractable nose landing gear unit)*
**24** il portello copriruota anteriore
- *nose undercarriage flap (nose gear flap)*
**25** il portello mediano per i passeggeri
- *centre (*Am. *center) passenger door*
**26** la gondola col motore (turboreattore *m*, reattore *m* a turbina)
- *engine pod with engine (turbojet engine, jet turbine engine, jet engine, jet turbine)*
**27** i dispersori di corrente *f* elettrostatica
- *electrostatic conductors*
**28** il carrello principale retrattile
- *retractable main undercarriage unit (retractable main landing gear unit)*
**29** il finestrino laterale
- *side window*
**30** il portello posteriore per i passeggeri
- *rear passenger door*
**31** la toilette
- *toilet (lavatory, WC)*
**32** la paratia stagna
- *pressure bulkhead*
**33** il gruppo elettrogeno ausiliario
- *auxiliary engine (auxiliary gas turbine) for the generator unit*

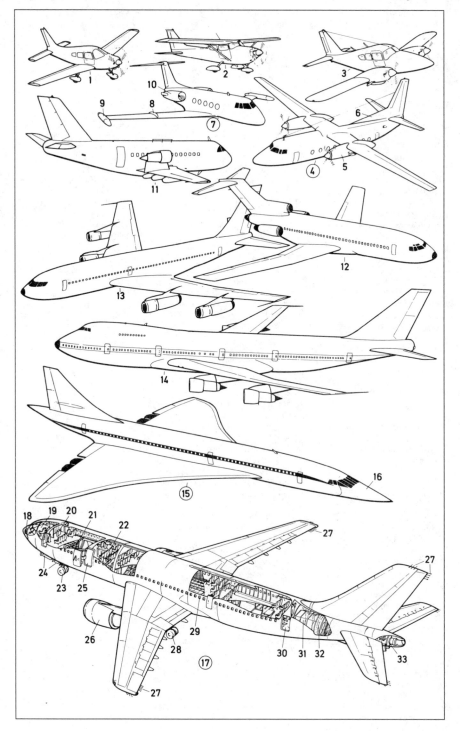

1 l'idrovolante *m* a scafo centrale
– *flying boat, a seaplane*
2 lo scafo
– *hull*
3 l'aletta laterale
– *stub wing (sea wing)*
4 la controventatura degli impennaggi
– *tail bracing wires*
5 l'idrovolante *m* a due galleggianti
*m pl*
– *floatplane (float seaplane), a seaplane*
6 il galleggiante
– *float*
7 il pattino di coda
– *vertical stabilizer (vertical fin, tail
fin)*
8 **l'aeroplano anfibio**
– **amphibian** *(amphibian flying
boat)*
9 lo scafo
– *hull*
10 il carrello retrattile
– *retractable undercarriage
(retractable landing gear)*
11-25 **elicotteri** *m pl*
– *helicopters*
11 l'elicottero leggero a più usi *m pl*
– *light multirole helicopter*
12 *u.* 13 il rotore principale
– *main rotor*
12 la pala rotante
– *rotary wing (rotor blade)*
13 il mozzo del rotore
– *rotor head*
14 il rotore di coda (il rotore stabilizzatore, il rotore di direzione *f* )
– *tail rotor (anti-torque rotor)*
15 il carrello a pattini *m pl*
– *landing skids*
16 l'elicottero gru *f*
– *flying crane*
17 i motori a turbina
– *turbine engines*
18 il carrello trasportatore
– *lifting undercarriage*
19 la piattaforma di carico
– *lifting platform*
20 il serbatoio ausiliario
– *reserve tank*
21 l'elicottero da trasporto
– *transport helicopter*
22 i rotori in tandem *m*
– *rotors in tandem*
23 il supporto del rotore
– *rotor pylon*
24 il motore a turbina
– *turbine engine*
25 il portello posteriore di carico
– *tail loading gate*
26-32 **gli aeroplani VSTOL** (aeroplani *m pl* vertical-short-take-off-
and-landing)
– **V/STOL aircraft** *(vertical/short
take-off and landing aircraft)*

26 l'aeroplano a ala a incidenza variabile, un aeroplano VTOL (verti-
cal-take-off-and-landing, un aeroplano a decollo verticale)
– *tilt-wing aircraft, a VTOL aircraft
(vertical take-off and landing aircraft)*
27 l'ala a incidenza variabile, in
posizione *f* verticale
– *tilt wing in vertical position*
28 i rotori posteriori di controllo
– *contrarotating tail propellers*
29 il convertiplano composito
– *gyrodyne*
30 il motore a turboelica
– *turboprop engine (turbopropeller
engine)*
31 il convertiplano
– *convertiplane*
32 il rotore orientabile in posizione *f*
verticale
– *tilting rotor in vertical position*
33-50 turboreattori *m pl* (motori *m pl*
a turbina)
– *jet engines (turbojet engines, jet
turbine engines, jet turbines)*
33-60 **motori** *m pl* **di aeroplani** *m pl*
– *aircraft engines (aero engines)*
33 il propulsore turboventola
frontale
– *front fan-jet*
34 il fan (la ventola)
– *fan*
35 il compressore a bassa pressione *f*
– *low-pressure compressor*
36 il compressore a alta pressione *f*
– *high-pressure compressor*
37 la camera di combustione *f*
– *combustion chamber*
38 la turbina a alta pressione *f*
– *fan-jet turbine*
39 l'ugello propulsivo
– *nozzle (propelling nozzle, propulsion nozzle)*
40 le turbine
– *turbines*
41 il canale della corrente secondaria
– *bypass duct*
42 il propulsore a turboventola posteriore
– *aft fan-jet*
43 il fan (la ventola)
– *fan*
44 il canale della corrente secondaria
– *bypass duct*
45 l'ugello propulsivo
– *nozzle (propelling nozzle, propulsion nozzle)*
46 il turboreattore assiale
– *bypass engine*
47 le turbine
– *turbines*
48 il miscelatore
– *mixer*

49 l'ugello propulsivo
– *nozzle (propelling nozzle, propulsion nozzle)*
50 la corrente secondaria di raffreddamento
– *secondary air flow (bypass air
flow)*
51 il motore turboelica, un motore
con doppio compressore *m* assiale
– *turboprop engine (turbopropeller
engine), a twin-shaft engine*
52 la presa di aria a anello
– *annular air intake*
53 la turbina a alta pressione *f*
– *high-pressure turbine*
54 la turbina a bassa pressione *f*
– *low-pressure turbine*
55 l'ugello propulsivo
– *nozzle (propelling nozzle, propulsion nozzle)*
56 l'albero motore *m*
– *shaft*
57 l'albero intermedio
– *intermediate shaft*
58 l'albero di potenza
– *gear shaft*
59 il riduttore
– *reduction gear*
60 l'albero dell'elica
– *propeller shaft*

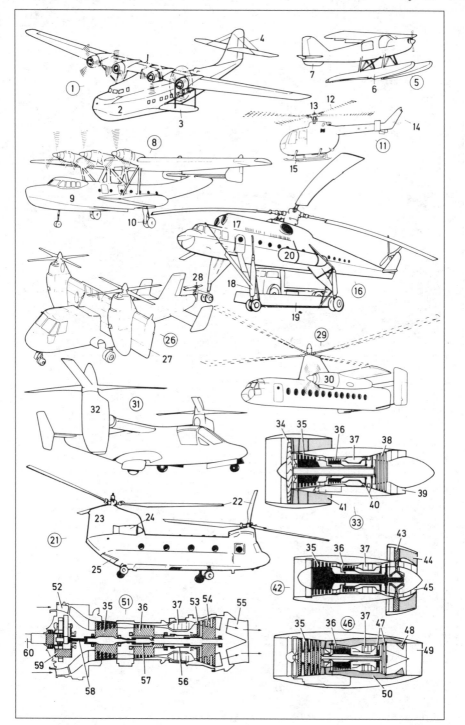

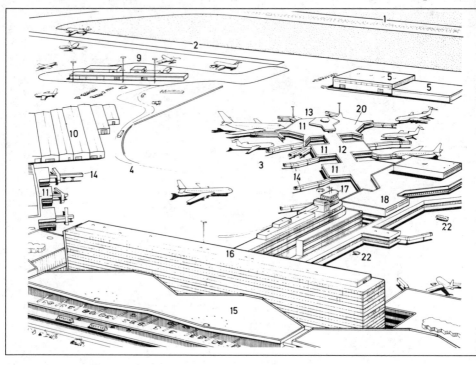

1 la pista (la pista di decollo e di atterraggio, la pista principale)
– *runway*
2 la pista di rullaggio
– *taxiway*
3 il piazzale
– *apron*
4 la strada di accesso al piazzale
– *apron taxiway*
5 il deposito bagagli *m pl*
– *baggage terminal*
6 l'ingresso tunnel *m* bagagli *m pl*
– *tunnel entrance to the baggage terminal*
7 i vigili del fuoco dell'aeroporto
– *airport fire service*
8 il capannone degli attrezzi
– *fire appliance building*
9 il capannone spedizione *f* merci *f pl* e
  posta
– *mail and cargo terminal*
10 il deposito merci *f pl*
– *cargo warehouse*
11 l'aerostazione *f*
– *assembly point*
12 la proboscide (la passerella di collegamento aereo-aerostazione *f*)
– *pier*
13 la testa della passerella
– *pierhead*
14 il ponte passeggeri *m pl*
– *airbridge*
15 il terminal
– *departure building (terminal)*
16 l'edificio amministrativo
– *administration building*
17 la torre di controllo
– *control tower (tower)*
18 la hall di attesa dei passeggeri
– *waiting room (lounge)*
19 il ristorante dell'aeroporto
– *airport restaurant*

20 la terrazza dei visitatori
– *spectators' terrace*
21 l'aereo in posizione *f* di partenza, una
  posizione nose-in
– *aircraft in loading position (nosed in)*
22 veicoli *m pl* di manutenzione *f* e di
  servizio, per es. per trasporto bagagli *m
  pl*, trasporto acqua, cucina, toilette *f*,
  alimentazione *f* elettrica, autocisterna
– *service vehicles, e.g. baggage loaders,
  water tankers, galley loaders, toilet-
  cleaning vehicles, ground power units,
  tankers*
23 il rimorchio aereo
– *aircraft tractor (aircraft tug)*
24-53 i cartelli indicatori
– *airport information symbols (pic-
  tographs)*
24 «aeroporto»
– *'airport'*
25 «decollo»
– *'departures'*
26 «arrivi»
– *'arrivals'*
27 «coincidenza»
– *'transit passengers'*
28 «sala di attesa»
– *'waiting room' ('lounge')*
29 «punto d'incontro»
– *'assembly point' ('meeting point', 'rendezvous point')*
30 «terrazza visitatori *m pl*»
– *'spectators' terrace'*
31 «informazioni *f pl*»
– *'information'*
32 «tassi *m pl*»
– *'taxis'*
33 «macchine *f pl* a noleggio» (rent a car)
– *'car hire'*
34 «ferrovia»
– *'trains'*

35 «bus (autobus) *m*»
– *'buses'*
36 «entrata»
– *'entrance'*
37 «uscita»
– *'exit'*
38 «consegna bagagli *m pl*»
– *'baggage reclaim'*
39 «deposito bagagli *m pl*»
– *'luggage lockers'*
40 «chiamata di emergenza»
– *'telephone–emergency calls only'*
41 «uscita di sicurezza»
– *'emergency exit'*
42 «controllo passaporti *m pl*»
– *'passport check'*
43 «ufficio stampa»
– *'press facilities'*
44 «infermeria»
– *'doctor'*
45 «farmacia»
– *'chemist' (Am. 'druggist')*
46 «docce *f pl*»
– *'showers'*
47 «toilette *f* uomini *m pl*»
– *'gentlemen's toilet' ('gentlemen')*
48 «toilette *f* donne *f pl*»
– *'ladies toilet' ('ladies')*
49 «cappella»
– *'chapel'*
50 «ristorante *m*»
– *'restaurant'*
51 «cambio»
– *'change'*
52 «duty free *m*»
– *'duty free shop'*
53 «parrucchiere *m*»
– *'hairdresser'*

1 il razzo vettore Saturno V con capsula «Apollo» (vista d'insieme *m*)
– *Saturn V 'Apollo' booster (booster rocket) [overall view]*
2 il razzo vettore Saturno V con
capsula «Apollo» (spaccato)
– *Saturn V 'Apollo' booster (booster
rocket) [overall sectional view]*
3 il primo stadio S-IC
– *first rocket stage (S-IC)*
4 motori *m pl* razzo F-1
– *F-1 engines*
5 lo scudo termico (lo schermo di
protezione *f* termica)
– *heat shield (thermal protection
shield)*
6 il rivestimento aerodinamico dei
motori razzo
– *aerodynamic engine fairings*
7 stabilizzatori *m pl* aerodinamici
– *aerodynamic stabilizing fins*
8 retrorazzi *m pl* per il distacco
degli stand, 8 razzi *m pl* a 4 coppie
*f pl*
– *stage separation retro-rockets, 8
rockets arranged in 4 pairs*
9 il serbatoio del cherosene raffinato (RP-1) (811.000 l)
– *kerosene (RP-1) tank [capacity:
811,000 litres]*
10 tubi *m pl* convogliatori ossigeno
liquido, *in totale* 5
– *liquid oxygen (LOX, LO₂) supply
lines, total of 5*
11 il sistema antivortice (impianto
per impedire la formazione di
vortici *m pl* nel carburante)
– *anti-vortex system (device for pre-
venting the formation of vortices
in the fuel)*
12 il serbatoio ossigeno liquido
(1.315.000 l)
– *liquid oxygen (LOX, LO₂) tank
[capacity: 1,315,000 litres]*
13 l'ammortizzatore *m*
– *anti-slosh baffles*
14 bombole *f pl* a pressione *f* per elio
– *compressed-helium bottles (helium pressure bottles)*
15 il diffusore ossigeno gassoso
– *diffuser for gaseous oxygen*
16 il vano di collegamento tra i serbatoi
– *inter-tank connector (inter-tank
section)*
17 unità strumentale
– *instruments and system-monitor-
ing devices*
18 il secondo stadio S-II
– *second rocket stage (S-II)*
19 motori *m pl* razzo J-2
– *J-2 engines*
20 lo scudo termico (lo schermo di
protezione *f* termica)
– *heat shield (thermal protection
shield)*
21 l'incastellatura dei motori e complesso di spinta
– *engine mounts and thrust structure*

22 razzi *m pl* di accelerazione *f*
– *acceleration rockets for fuel acqui-
sition*
23 il tubo aspirante dell'idrogeno liquido
– *liquid hydrogen (LH₂) suction line*
24 il serbatoio ossigeno liquido
(1.315.000 l)
– *liquid oxygen (LOX, LO₂) tank
[capacity: 1,315,000 litres]*
25 il tubo verticale
– *standpipe*
26 il serbatoio idrogeno liquido
(1.020.000 l)
– *liquid hydrogen (LH₂) tank
[capacity: 1,020,000 litres]*
27 il sensore verticale del propellente
– *fuel level sensor*
28 la piattaforma di servizio
– *work platform (working platform)*
29 il pozzetto del cavo
– *cable duct*
30 il passaggio per l'uomo
– *manhole*
31 l'anello intermedio di raccordo
tra S-IC/S-II
– *S-IC/S-II inter-stage connector
(inter-stage section)*
32 il contenitore del gas compresso
– *compressed-gas container (gas
pressure vessel)*
33 il terzo stadio S-IVB
– *third rocket stage (S-IVB)*
34 il motore J-2
– *J-2 engine*
35 il cono di spinta
– *nozzle (thrust nozzle)*
36 il cono di raccordo tra S-II/S-IVB
– *S-II/S-IVB inter-stage connector
(inter-stage section)*
37 retrorazzi *m pl* per il distacco
degli stadi per S-II, 4 razzi *m pl*
– *four second-stage (S-II) separation retro-rockets*
38 razzi *m pl* controllo assetto
– *attitude control rockets*
39 il serbatoio ossigeno liquido
(77.200 l)
– *liquid oxygen (LOX, LO₂) tank
[capacity: 77,200 litres]*
40 il pozzo di conduttura
– *fuel line duct*
41 il serbatoio idrogeno liquido
(253.000 l)
– *liquid hydrogen (LH₂) tank
[capacity: 253,000 litres]*
42 sonde *f pl* di livello
– *measuring probes*
43 serbatoi *m pl* gas *m* compresso
elio
– *compressed-helium tanks (helium
pressure vessels)*
44 lo sfiato del serbatoio
– *tank vent*
45 l'anello anteriore a celle *f pl*
– *forward frame section*
46 la piattaforma di servizio
– *work platform (working platform)*

47 il pozzetto del cavo
– *cable duct*
48 razzi *m pl* di accelerazione *f*
– *acceleration rockets for fuel acqui-
sition*
49 l'anello posteriore a celle *f pl*
– *aft frame section*
50 serbatoi *m pl* gas *m* compresso
elio
– *compressed-helium tanks (helium
pressure vessels)*
51 la conduttura dell'idrogeno liquido
– *liquid hydrogen (LH₂) line*
52 la conduttura dell'ossigeno liquido
– *liquid oxygen (LOX, LO₂) line*
53 il modulo di strumentazione *f* con
24 pannelli *m pl*
– *24-panel instrument unit*
54 l'hangar *m* LEM
– *LM hangar (lunar module
hangar)*
55 il LEM (lunar module, il modulo
lunare)
– *LM (lunar module)*
56 la capsula «Apollo»-SM (service
module), un modulo di servizio
Apollo per l'approvvigionamento
– *Apollo SM (service module), containing supplies and equipment*
57 l'ugello propulsore SM, modulo
di servizio
– *SM (service module) main engine*
58 il serbatoio principale propellente *m*
– *fuel tank*
59 il serbatoio tetrossido di azoto
– *nitrogen tetroxide tank*
60 il sistema di alimentazione *f* del
gas compresso
– *pressurized gas delivery system*
61 serbatoi *m pl* ossigeno
– *oxygen tanks*
62 celle *f pl* propellenti *m*
– *fuel cells*
63 quadranti *m pl* getto di controllo
assetto
– *manoeuvring (Am. maneuvering)
rocket assembly*
64 il gruppo di antenne *f pl* a alto
guadagno
– *directional antenna assembly*
65 il modulo di comando (la capsula,
cabina di discesa)
– *space capsule (command section)*
66 la torre di salvataggio per la fase
di partenza
– *launch phase escape tower*

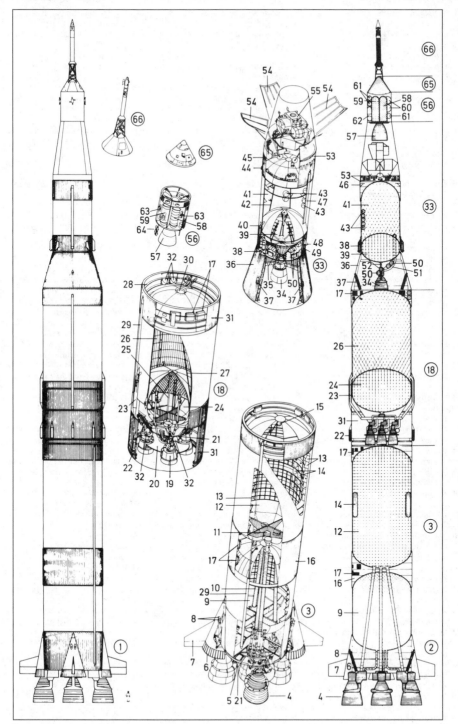

**1-45 lo Space Shuttle-Orbiter** (la navetta spaziale)
– *Space Shuttle-Orbiter*
1 la deriva a due longheroni *m pl*
– *twin-spar (two-spar, double-spar) vertical fin*
2 l'incastellatura del gruppo propulsore
– *engine compartment structure*
3 il longherone laterale
– *fin post*
4 la staffa collegamento fusoliera
– *fuselage attachment [of payload bay doors]*
5 il tirante superiore
– *upper thrust mount*
6 il tirante inferiore
– *lower thrust mount*
7 la struttura di carenatura
– *keel*
8 lo scudo termico
– *heat shield*
9 il longherone della fusoliera mediana
– *waist longeron*
10 l'ordinata maestra integrale fresata
– *integrally machined (integrally milled) main rib*
11 il rivestimento in lega leggera integrale irrigidito
– *integrally stiffened light alloy skin*
12 le travi a traliccio
– *lattice girder*
13 il rivestimento isolante del vano di carico
– *payload bay insulation*
14 il portello dello spazio utile di carico
– *payload bay door*
15 il rivestimento resistente al freddo
– *low-temperature surface insulation*
16 il compartimento equipaggio
– *flight deck (crew compartment)*
17 il sedile del comandante
– *captain's seat (commander's seat)*
18 il sedile del pilota
– *pilot's seat (co-pilot's seat)*
19 l'ordinata anteriore di spinta
– *forward pressure bulkhead*
20 il naso della fusoliera (il muso della navetta), uno scudo in fibre *f pl* di carbonio
– *nose-section fairings, carbon fibre reinforced nose cone*
21 il serbatoio anteriore
– *forward fuel tanks*
22 le consolle dell'avionica
– *avionics consoles*
23 la consolle controllo e comando volo automatico
– *automatic flight control panel*
24 le finestre di osservazione *f* superiori
– *upward observation windows*
25 le finestre di osservazione *f* anteriori
– *forward observation windows*

26 il portello di accesso al vano di carico
– *entry hatch to payload bay*
27 la camera di decompressione *f*
– *air lock*
28 la scaletta accesso ponte *m* di volo
– *ladder to lower deck*
29 il braccio manipolatore esterno
– *payload manipulator arm*
30 il carrello anteriore a comando idraulico
– *hydraulically steerable nose wheel*
31 il carrello principale azionato idraulicamente
– *hydraulically operated main landing gear*
32 il rivestimento amovibile in RCC (reinforced carbon-carbon)
– *removable (reusable) carbon fibre reinforced leading edge [of wing]*
33 le parti mobili dell'alettone *m*
– *movable elevon sections*
34 la struttura termoresistente dell'alettone *m*
– *heat-resistant elevon structure*
35 la conduttura principale dell'idrogeno
– *main liquid hydrogen ($LH_2$) supply*
36 il motore principale a combustibile *m* liquido
– *main liquid-fuelled rocket engine*
37 l'ugello
– *nozzle (thrust nozzle)*
38 la conduttura di raffreddamento
– *coolant feed line*
39 l'apparecchiatura azionamento motori *m pl*
– *engine control system*
40 lo scudo termico
– *heat shield*
41 la pompa alimentazione *f* idrogeno
– *high-pressure liquid hydrogen ($LH_2$) pump*
42 la pompa alimentazione *f* ossigeno
– *high-pressure liquid oxygen ($LOX$, $LO_2$) pump*
43 il sistema di comando a spinta
– *thrust vector control system*
44 il gruppo propulsore principale per manovre *f pl* spaziali a comando elettromeccanico
– *electromechanically controlled orbital manoeuvring (Am. maneuvering) main engine*
45 i serbatoi carburante *m*
– *nozzle fuel tanks (thrust nozzle fuel tanks)*
**46 il serbatoio di ossigeno e idrogeno sganciabile**
– *jettisonable liquid hydrogen and liquid oxygen tank (fuel tank)*
47 l'ordinata a anello integrale irrigidita
– *integrally stiffened annular rib (annular frame)*

48 l'ordinata terminale semisferica
– *hemispherical end rib (end frame)*
49 il ponte di collegamento posteriore all'Orbiter
– *aft attachment to Orbiter*
50 la conduttura idrogeno
– *liquid hydrogen ($LH_2$) line*
51 la conduttura ossigeno
– *liquid oxygen ($LOX$, $LO_2$) line*
52 il portello ingresso equipaggio
– *manhole*
53 il sistema di stabilizzazione *f*
– *surge baffle system (slosh baffle system)*
54 la conduttura di mandata per serbatoio idrogeno
– *pressure line to liquid hydrogen tank*
55 la conduttura collettrice elettrica
– *electrical system bus*
56 il condotto esterno ossigeno
– *liquid oxygen ($LOX$, $LO_2$) line*
57 la conduttura di mandata per il serbatoio ossigeno
– *pressure line to liquid oxygen tank*
**58 il razzo ausiliario a propellente *m* solido riutilizzabile**
– *recoverable solid-fuel rocket (solid rocket booster)*
59 il vano paracaduti *m pl* ausiliari
– *auxiliary parachute bay*
60 il vano paracaduti *m pl* principali e razzi *m pl* ausiliari anteriori
– *compartment housing the recovery parachutes and the forward separation rocket motors*
61 la conduttura cavi *m pl*
– *cable duct*
62 i razzi ausiliari posteriori
– *aft separation rocket motors*
63 il cono aerodinamico posteriore
– *aft skirt*
64 l'ugello propulsore orientabile
– *swivel nozzle (swivelling, Am. swiveling, nozzle)*
**65 lo Space-lab** (il laboratorio spaziale, la stazione spaziale)
– *Spacelab (space laboratory, space station)*
66 il laboratorio
– *multi-purpose laboratory (orbital workshop)*
67 l'astronauta *m*
– *astronaut*
68 il telescopio a supporto cardanico
– *gimbal-mounted telescope*
69 la piattaforma per apparecchiature *f pl* scientifiche
– *measuring instrument platform*
70 il modulo spaziale
– *spaceflight module*
71 il tunnel di accesso
– *crew entry tunnel*

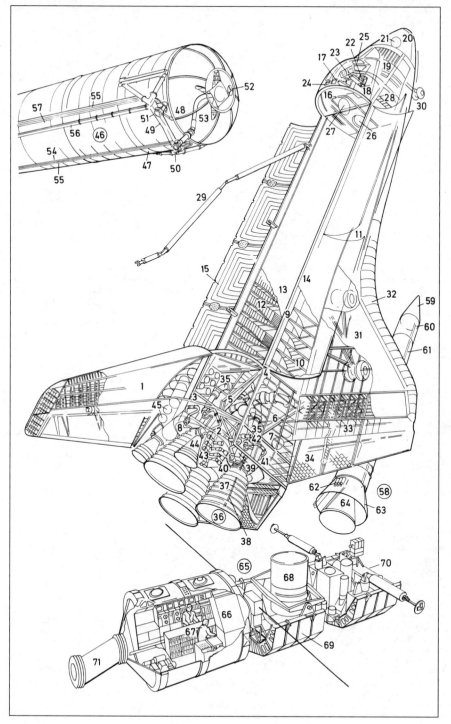

**1-30 il settore di retrosportelleria**
- *main hall*
1 lo sportello accettazione *f* pacchi *m pl*
- *parcels counter*
2 la bilancia (il pesalettere)
- *parcels scales*
3 il pacco
- *parcel*
4 l'indirizzo con l'etichetta e il numero del pacco
- *stick-on address label with parcel registration slip*
5 il vasetto della colla
- *glue pot*
6 il pacchetto
- *small parcel*
7 la macchina per affrancare i bollettini di spedizione *f* dei pacchi postali
- *franking machine (Am. postage meter) for parcel registration cards*
8 la cabina telefonica
- *telephone box (telephone booth, telephone kiosk, call box)*
9 il telefono a gettoni *m pl*
- *coin-box telephone (pay phone, public telephone)*
10 il contenitore degli elenchi del telefono
- *telephone directory rack*
11 il braccio oscillante
- *directory holder*
12 l'elenco del telefono
- *telephone directory (telephone book)*
13 il casellario
- *post office boxes*
14 la casella postale
- *post office box*
15 lo sportello per la vendita dei valori bollati
- *stamp counter*
16 l'impiegato allo sportello
- *counter clerk (counter officer)*
17 l'agente *m* interno
- *company messenger*
18 il bollettario ricevute *f pl* postali
- *record of posting book*
19 lo sportello per distribuzione *f* automatica valori *m pl* bollati
- *counter stamp machine*
20 la cartella raccoglitore valori *m pl* bollati
- *stamp book*
21 il foglio dei valori bollati
- *sheet of stamps*
22 il cassetto
- *security drawer*
23 la cassa
- *change rack*
24 la bilancia per le lettere (il pesalettere)
- *letter scales*

25 lo sportello per i versamenti, il risparmio postale e il pagamento delle pensioni
- *paying-in (Am. deposit), post office savings, and pensions counter*
26 la macchina contabile
- *accounting machine*
27 l'annullatrice *f* postale per vaglia *m pl* e moduli *m pl* di versamento
- *franking machine for money orders and paying-in slips (Am. deposit slips)*
28 il rendiresto (non in uso in Italia)
- *change machine (Am. changemaker)*
29 il timbro obliterazione *f* ricevute *f pl*
- *receipt stamp*
30 il passaoggetti
- *hatch*
31-44 la macchina per lo smistamento della posta
- *letter-sorting installation*
31 l'inserimento degli oggetti
- *letter feed*
32 i contenitori impilati delle lettere
- *stacked letter containers*
33 la linea meccanizzata smistamento oggetti *m pl*
- *feed conveyor*
34 la macchina smistamento
- *intermediate stacker*
35 il posto operatore *m* di codifica
- *coding station*
36 la linea scorrimento oggetti *m pl* per prima suddivisione *f*
- *pre-distributor channel*
37 il calcolatore
- *process control computer*
38 la smistatrice oggetti *m pl* per destinazioni *f pl*
- *distributing machine*
39 il posto operatore *m* codifica video (non in uso in Italia)
- *video coding station*
40 lo schermo
- *screen*
41 l'immagine degli indirizzi
- *address display*
42 l'indirizzo
- *address*
43 il codice di avviamento postale (CAP)
- *post code (postal code, Am. zip code)*
44 la tastiera
- *keyboard*
45 il timbro a mano (il timbro Guller)
- *handstamp*
46 il timbro a rulli *m pl*
- *roller stamp*
47 la timbratrice automatica
- *franking machine*

48 l'impilatore *m* oggetti *m pl* da obliterare
- *feed mechanism*
49 il contenitore per raccolta oggetti *m pl* obliterati
- *delivery mechanism*
50-55 la vuotatura delle cassette della posta in partenza
- *postal collection and delivery*
50 la cassetta postale (la buca delle lettere)
- *postbox (Am. mailbox)*
51 il sacco di raccolta della posta
- *collection bag*
52 l'auto della posta
- *post office van (mail van)*
53 il postino (il portalettere)
- *postman (Am. mail carrier, letter carrier, mailman)*
54 la borsa del portalettere
- *delivery pouch (postman's bag, mailbag)*
55 la consegna della posta
- *letter-rate item*
56-60 le obliterazioni (gli annulli)
- *postmarks*
56 l'annullo pubblicitario
- *postmark advertisement*
57 il bollo Guller a data e ora
- *date stamp postmark*
58 l'annullo con tassa affrancatura
- *charge postmark*
59 l'annullo commemorativo
- *special postmark*
60 l'annullo meccanizzato con data e ora
- *roller postmark*
61 il francobollo
- *stamp (postage stamp)*
62 la dentellatura
- *perforations*

**1-41 il telefono**
– *telephone*
**1** il telefono a disco
– *dial telephone*
**2** la cornetta
– *handset (telephone receiver)*
**3** il cavo della cornetta
– *receiver cord (handset cord)*
**4** il filo del telefono
– *telephone cable (telephone cord)*
**5** la base del telefono
– *telephone casing (telephone cover)*
**6** i numeri per le chiamate di emergenza
– *emergency numbers*
**7** il numero dell'apparecchio
– *line number*
**8** il disco teleselettivo
– *dial*
**9** il microtelefono (il telefono addizionale)
– *compact telephone (slimline telephone), an added-feature telephone*
**10** l'auricolare *m* (il ricevitore)
– *earpiece (receiver)*
**11** la tastiera con numeri *m pl* e tasti *m pl* di funzione *f*
– *keypad with number and function keys (feature keys)*
**12** il tasto di memoria (il memory)
– *last number redial button*
**13** il tasto per numeri *m pl* brevi (redial)
– *abbreviated dialling key*
**14** il tasto di amplificazione *f*
– *speaker key (loudspeaker key)*
**15** il microfono
– *mouthpiece*
**16** il tasto mute
– *line reset button*
**17** l'altoparlante *m*
– *speaker (loudspeaker)*
**18** l'indicatore *m* ottico di chiamata
– *call indicator*
**19** il telefono a tastiera
– *push-button telephone, an added-feature telephone*
**20** il display
– *display*
**21** il lucchetto
– *lock*
**22** il telefono design
– *novelty telephone, an added-feature telephone*
**23** la forcella
– *(telephone) cradle*
**24** la manovella
– *dummy crank*
**25** la console ribaltabile con tastiera
– *detachable keypad*
**26** il telefono portatile (senza fili *m pl*)
– *cordless (tele)phone (radiophone, mobile phone)*
**27** l'antenna
– *aerial*
**28** la spia della batteria
– *battery strength light*
**29** la spia della portata
– *out of signal-range indicator*
**30** l'interruttore *m* principale
– *power switch*
**31** l'apparecchio telefonico a carta telefonica
– *cardphone*
**32** il display per gli scatti
– *split display showing call charges*

**33** il tasto di scelta della lingua del display
– *language select button for the display*
**34** il tasto per telefonate *f pl* in serie *f*
– *follow-on call button*
**35** la fessura per la carta telefonica
– *phonecard slot*
**36** la carta telefonica (*qui:* la telecarta)
– *phonecard (here: telephone credit card)*
**37** il simbolo del telefono a carta telefonica
– *phonecard symbol*
**38** il nome dell'utente *m*
– *cardholder's name*
**39** il numero della carta
– *card number*
**40** il senso d'inserimento
– *arrow indicating direction of insertion*
**41** i chip
– *chips*
**42-62 I.S.D.N.** (la rete di telecomunicazioni *f pl* digitale integrativa del servizio)
– *ISDN (Integrated Services Digital Network)*
**42** il terminale di telecomunicazione *f* multifunzionale
– *multifunction telecommunications terminal (ISDN workstation)*
**43** lo schermo (monitor) per videotelefono e videotel
– *screen (monitor) for viewdata, video telephone, and Teletex*
**44** l'unità di memoria e di calcolo
– *central processing and memory unit*
**45** il telefax (il fax)
– *fax unit (fax)*
**46** la tastiera
– *input device (keyboard)*
**47** la cornetta del telefono (il collegamento colla rete delle telecomunicazioni)
– *telephone receiver (link to the telephone network)*
**48** l'accoppiatore *m* (anche: il modem)
– *acoustic coupler (modem)*
**49** la rete telecomandata (la rete TEMEX)
– *telecontrol network (TEMEX network)*
**50** l'antenna telefonica
– *public telephone network (switched telephone network)*
**51** i punti di comando della rete telecomandata
– *telecontrol centres*
**52** la centrale TEMEX
– *TEMEX main control centre*
**53** l'impianto di trasmissione *f* TEMEX
– *TEMEX transmission equipment*
**54** la conduttura telefonica
– *telecommunications line (telephone line)*
**55** l'inserimento in rete *f*
– *TEMEX network termination*
**56** la sottostazione
– *slave station*
**57** gli apparecchi di telecomando
– *telecontrol terminal equipment*
**58** gli impianti di teletelettura (il rilevatore, il sensore, il regolatore)
– *telecontrol terminal equipment (detector, sensor, or control equipment)*

**59** il segnalatore di guasto
– *glass-break detector*
**60** il regolatore di temperatura
– *temperature controller*
**61** la chiamata urgente
– *emergency call*
**62** il contatore
– *meter (electricity meter)*
**63** il satellite delle telecomunicazioni
– *communications satellite*
**64** il pannello solare (il pannello a cellule *f pl* solari, il generatore solare)
– *solar panel (solar paddle, solar array, solar generator)*
**65** il supporto dell'antenna
– *antenna module*
**66** l'antenna ricevente per comandi *m pl* di manovra
– *receiving antenna for control commands*
**67** le antenne paraboliche
– *parabolic antennas*
**68** il modulo (satellite *m* per telecomunicazioni *f pl*)
– *communications module*
**69** il modulo di comando
– *propulsion module*
**70** il modulo radiofonico (il modulo televisivo)
– *broadcasting satellite (television satellite)*
**71** il modulo di alimentazione *f*
– *service module*
**72** i serbatoi del carburante
– *fuel tanks*
**73** i reattori di comando
– *control jets*
**74** la stazione radio terrestre
– *earth station*
**75** l'antenna parabolica
– *parabolic antenna*
**76** il riflettore principale
– *main reflector*
**77** il riflettore ricevente
– *feed antenna*
**78** le onde elettromagnetiche
– *radio beams*
**79** la trasmissione radiotelevisiva via satellite *m* e la televisione via cavo
– *satellite broadcasting, satellite television, and cable television*
**80** il satellite radiofonico
– *broadcasting satellite*
**81** lo studio televisivo
– *television studio*
**82** l'antenna televisiva
– *television tower*
**83** la stazione via cavo ricevente
– *cablehead station*
**84** la radiodiffusione
– *terrestrial broadcasting*
**85** la trasmissione via satellite *m*
– *satellite broadcasting*
**86** la trasmissione per ponte *m* radio
– *line-of-sight link (microwave link)*
**87** la rete collegamenti *m pl* a cavo
– *cable network*
**88** i collegamenti ai cavi *m pl*
– *cable connections*

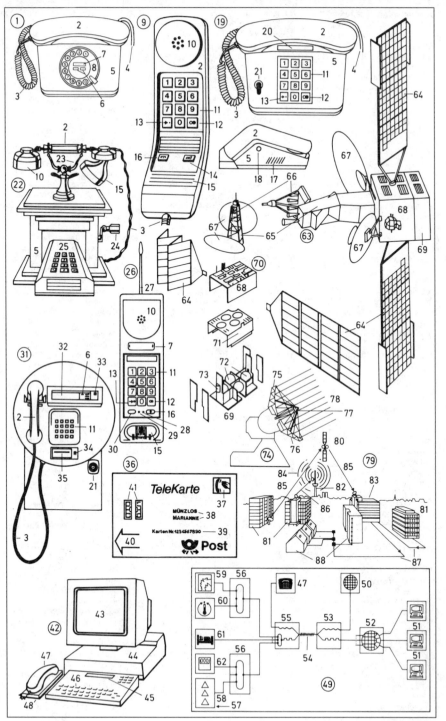

**1-6 lo studio centrale di radiodiffusione** f
- *central recording channel of a radio station*

1 l'apparecchiatura di controllo e monitoraggio
- *monitoring and control panel*

2 il videomonitor per l'indicazione f ottica del programma guidato dal computer
- *data display terminal (video data terminal, video monitor) for visual display of computer-controlled programmes (Am. programs)*

3 il gruppo di altoparlanti m pl e alimentatori m pl
- *amplifier and mains power unit*

4 il gruppo registrazione f e riproduzione f a banda magnetica da un quarto di pollice m
- *magnetic sound recording and playback deck for ¼″ magnetic tape*

5 il nastro magnetico, un nastro da ¼ di pollice m
- *magnetic tape, a ¼″ tape*

6 la bobina del rotolo di pellicola
- *film spool holder*

**7-15 lo studio** del centro radiotrasmissioni
- *radio switching centre (Am. center) control room*

7 l'apparecchiatura di controllo e monitoraggio
- *monitoring and control panel*

8 l'altoparlante m centrale
- *talkback speaker*

9 il telefono a batteria locale (il telefono OB)
- *local-battery telephone*

10 il microfono centrale
- *talkback microphone*

11 il video-monitor
- *data display terminal (video data terminal)*

12 il telex
- *teleprinter*

13 la tastiera d'immissione f dati m pl nel computer
- *input keyboard for computer data*

14 la tastiera della centralina telefonica
- *telephone switchboard panel*

15 l'altoparlante m di ascolto
- *monitoring speaker (control speaker)*

**16-26 lo studio di radiotrasmissione** f
- *broadcasting centre (Am. center)*

16 il settore audio
- *recording room*

17 la cabina di regia
- *production control room (control room)*

18 la cabina dello speaker (dell'annunciatore m)
- *studio*

19 il tecnico del suono
- *sound engineer (sound control engineer)*

20 la consolle di regia
- *sound control desk (sound control console)*

21 lo speaker (l'annunciatore m)
- *newsreader (newscaster)*

22 il direttore di trasmissione f
- *duty presentation officer*

23 il telefono per i reportage
- *telephone for phoned reports*

24 il giradischi
- *record turntable*

25 la consolle di missaggio del settore audio
- *recording room mixing console (mixing desk, mixer)*

26 l'addetta al sonoro
- *sound technician (sound mixer, sound recordist)*

**27-53 lo studio di postsincronizzazione** f **alla televisione**
- *television post-sync studio*

27 lo studio di regia del suono
- *sound production control room (sound control room)*

28 lo studio di sincronizzazione f
- *dubbing studio (dubbing theatre, Am. theater)*

29 il tavolo dello speaker (dell'annunciatore m)
- *studio table*

30 l'indicazione f ottica del segnale
- *visual signal*

31 l'orologio elettronico di stop
- *electronic stopclock*

32 lo schermo di proiezione f
- *projection screen*

33 il monitor
- *monitor*

34 il microfono dello speaker (dell'annunciatore m)
- *studio microphone*

35 l'apparecchiatura per i rumori
- *sound effects box*

36 la tavola di collegamento microfoni m pl
- *microphone socket panel*

37 l'altoparlante m d'incisione f
- *recording speaker (recording loudspeaker)*

38 lo sportello di controllo
- *control room window (studio window)*

39 il microfono centrale del produttore
- *producer's talkback microphone*

40 il telefono a batteria locale
- *local-battery telephone*

41 la consolle di regia
- *sound control desk (sound control console)*

42 il commutatore
- *group selector switch*

43 l'indice m luminoso
- *visual display*

44 il limitatore
- *limiter display (clipper display)*

45 le cassette di regolazione f e di comando
- *control modules*

46 i tasti di preascolto
- *pre-listening buttons*

47 il regolatore della pista piana
- *slide control*

48 il dispositivo antidistorsione f (l'equilibratore m) universale
- *universal equalizer (universal corrector)*

49 il selettore d'ingresso
- *input selector switches*

50 l'altoparlante m di preascolto
- *pre-listening speaker*

51 il misuratore del livello del suono
- *tone generator*

52 l'altoparlante m centrale
- *talkback speaker*

53 il microfono centrale
- *talkback microphone*

**54-59 lo studio di premissaggio** per registrazioni f pl e missaggi m pl di film m pl magnetici perforati a 16 mm, 17.5 mm, 35 mm
- *pre-mixing room for transferring and mixing 16 mm, 17.5 mm, 35 mm perforated magnetic film*

54 la consolle di regia del suono
- *sound control desk (sound control console)*

55 l'impianto compact per registrazione f e riproduzione f
- *compact magnetic tape recording and playback equipment*

56 il dispositivo monopista per la riproduzione
- *single playback deck*

57 l'impianto centrale di comando
- *central drive unit*

58 il dispositivo monopista per registrazione f e riproduzione f
- *single recording and playback deck*

59 il tavolo di riavvolgimento
- *rewind bench*

**60-65 lo studio di controllo finale delle immagini**
- *final picture quality checking room*

60 il monitor di controllo
- *preview monitor*

61 il monitor del programma
- *programme (Am. program) monitor*

62 l'orologio dello stop
- *stopclock*

63 la consolle di missaggio video
- *vision mixer (vision-mixing console, vision-mixing desk)*

64 l'impianto centrale
- *talkback system (talkback equipment)*

65 il monitor della telecamera
- *camera monitor (picture monitor)*

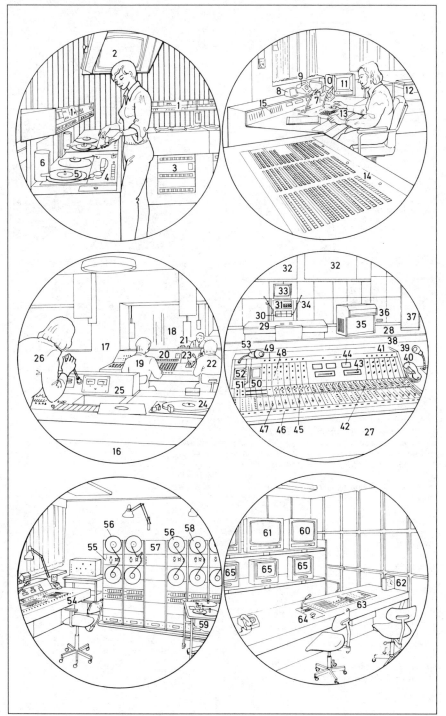

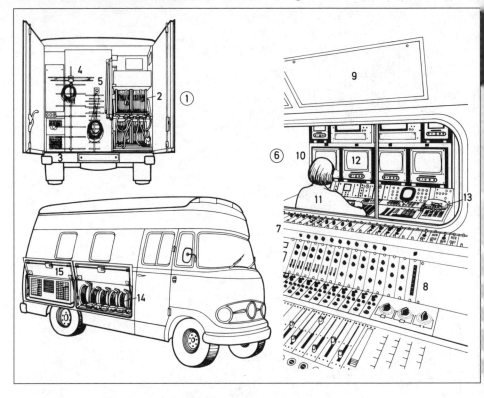

**1-15 la stazione mobile per riprese** *f pl* **televisive e radiofoniche**
– *outside broadcast (OB) vehicle (television OB van; also: sound OB van, radio OB van)*
**1-4 l'attrezzatura posteriore della stazione mobile**
– *rear equipment section of the OB vehicle*
**2** i cavi della telecamera
– *camera cable*
**3** il quadro allacciamento cavi *m pl*
– *cable connection panel*
**4** l'antenna ricevente per il primo programma
– *television (TV) reception aerial (receiving aerial) for Channel I*
**5** l'antenna televisiva per il secondo programma
– *television (TV) reception aerial (receiving aerial) for Channel II*
**6 le apparecchiature interne della stazione mobile**
– *interior equipment (on-board equipment) of the OB vehicle*
**7** il settore regia suoni
– *sound production control room (sound control room)*

**8** la consolle regia suoni
– *sound control desk (sound control console)*
**9** l'altoparlante *m* di controllo
– *monitoring loudspeaker*
**10** il settore regia video
– *vision control room (video control room)*
**11** la tecnica video
– *video controller (vision controller)*
**12** il monitor della telecamera
– *camera monitor (picture monitor)*
**13** il telefono di bordo
– *on-board telephone (intercommunication telephone)*
**14** i cavi del microfono
– *microphone cables*
**15** il condizionatore
– *air-conditioning plant*

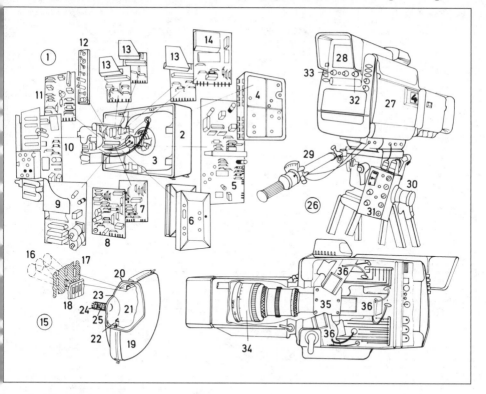

1  **il televisore a colori** *m pl*
(l'apparecchio televisivo a colori)
–  *colour* (Am. *color*) *television
(TV) receiver (colour television
set) of modular design*
2  il mobile esterno
–  *television cabinet*
3  il tubo catodico (il cinescopio)
–  *television tube (picture tube)*
4  il modulo media frequenza
(l'amplificatore *m* ZF)
–  *IF (intermediate frequency) amplifier module*
5  il modulo colore *m*
–  *colour* (Am. *color*) *decoder module*
6  il tuner VHF e UHF (il gruppo
sintonizzatore)
–  *VHF and UHF tuner*
7  il modulo del sincronismo orizzontale
–  *horizontal synchronizing module*
8  il modulo deflessione *f* verticale
–  *vertical deflection module*
9  il modulo Est-Ovest
–  *horizontal linearity control module*
10 il modulo deflessione *f* orizzontale (il modulo sincronismi *m pl*)
–  *horizontal deflection module*
11 il modulo alimentazione *f*
–  *control module*

12 il modulo di convergenza
–  *convergence module*
13 il modulo croma
–  *colour* (Am. *color*) *output stage
module*
14 il modulo audio
–  *sound module*
15 il cinescopio a colori *m pl*
–  *colour* (Am. *color*) *picture tube*
16 i raggi elettronici dei catodi
–  *electron beams*
17 la maschera
–  *shadow mask with elongated holes*
18 i fosfori a strisce *f pl*
–  *strip of fluorescent (luminescent,
phosphorescent) material*
19 lo strato di sostanza fluorescente
–  *coating (film) of fluorescent material*
20 lo schermo magnetico interno
–  *inner magnetic screen (screening)*
21 il vuoto
–  *vacuum*
22 le molle di aggancio della
maschera isolate termicamente
–  *temperature-compensated shadow
mask mount*
23 il giogo di deflessione *f*
–  *centring* (Am. *centering*) *ring for
the deflection system*

24 il sistema di raggi elettronici (il
collo del cinescopio)
–  *electron gun assembly*
25 il catodo a riscaldamento veloce
–  *rapid heat-up cathode*
26 **la telecamera**
–  *television (TV) camera*
27 il corpo
–  *camera head*
28 il monitor
–  *camera monitor*
29 la leva di comando
–  *control arm (control lever)*
30 la messa a fuoco
–  *focusing adjustment*
31 la tastiera di comando
–  *control panel*
32 la regolazione del contrasto
–  *contrast control*
33 la regolazione della luce
–  *brightness control*
34 l'obiettivo zoom (lo zoom)
–  *zoom lens*
35 il prisma deviazione *f* raggi *m pl*
–  *beam-splitting prism (beam splitter)*
36 l'unità di ripresa (i tubi del colore)
–  *pick-up unit (colour,* Am. *color,
pick-up tube)*

**1-17 l'impianto stereo** (l'impianto Hi-Fi), un impianto di medie dimensioni *f pl*
– *stereo system (hi-fi system), a midi system*
**1 la torre Hi-Fi** (Hi-Fi Tower)
– *hi-fi stack*
**2** il coperchio copridisco
– *rack lid (rack dust cover, [housing] lid)*
**3** il rack (lo chassis dell'impianto) con sportello frontale in vetro
– *rack (housing) with glass door*
**4** il giradischi
– *record player (record deck, analogue [Am. analog] record player)*
**5** il tuner (il ricevitore, il radioricevitore, il sintonizzatore)
– *tuner (receiver, radio tuner)*
**6** l'amplificatore *m*
– *amplifier (power amplifier)*
**7** il registratore a doppio nastro
– *double cassette deck (double cassette recorder)*
**8** il lettore compact disc (il lettore compact)
– *CD player (compact disc player)*
**9** il vano cassette audio
– *cassette rack*
**10** il vano dischi *m pl* e CD
– *record and compact disc rack*
**11** la ruotina
– *castor*
**12 il box degli altoparlanti** (il box), un box a tre diffusori *m pl* con registro basso
– *speaker (loudspeaker), a three-way bass reflex speaker*
**13** l'altoparlante *m* toni *m pl* alti (tweeter, il sistema a note *f pl* alte), un altoparlante a calotta o piezo
– *tweeter, a dome tweeter or piezo tweeter*
**14** l'altoparlante *m* toni *m pl* medi (il sistema toni *m pl* medi)
– *mid-range speaker (squawker)*
**15** l'altoparlante *m* toni *m pl* bassi (il woofer, il sistema per i toni bassi)
– *bass speaker (woofer)*
**16** il foro del risuonatore
– *port*
**17** il telecomando a raggi *m pl* infrarossi
– *infrared remote control [unit] (IR remote control [unit])*
**18 il giradischi**
– *record player (record deck, analogue [Am. analog] record player)*
**19** il piatto del giradischi con trascinamento diretto (direct drive) o trascinamento a cinghia (belt drive)
– *turntable with direct drive or belt drive*
**20** lo stroboscopio luminoso
– *strobe light (strobe speed control)*
**21** la regolazione volume *m* suono (il pitch)
– *pitch control*
**22** l'indicatore *m* numero giri *m pl*
– *rpm display*
**23** il tasto di stop
– *stop button*
**24** il tasto avvio automatico
– *auto-return button*
**25** il selettore numero giri *m pl* disco
– *rpm selector (speed selector)*
**26** il tasto discesa pick up
– *cue button (down)*
**27** il tasto sollevamento pick up (il lift)
– *cue button (up)*

**28** la puntina
– *stylus (needle)*
**29** il pick up
– *pick-up*
**30** il selettore diametro dischi *m pl*
– *size selector (record size selector)*
**31** il braccio del pick up
– *tone arm (pick-up arm)*
**32** il sostegno del braccio
– *tone arm support (pick-up arm support)*
**33** il regolatore peso pick up
– *stylus pressure control*
**34** il regolatore ritorno braccio
– *anti-skate control*
**35** il contrappeso braccio
– *tone arm counterweight (pick-up arm counterweight)*
**36** il coperchio
– *lid (dust cover)*
**37 il tuner** (il ricevitore, il radioricevitore, il sintonizzatore)
– *tuner (receiver, radio tuner)*
**38** l'interruttore *m* di accensione *f* (power)
– *power switch*
**39** il sintonizzatore
– *tuning button (tuning control)*
**40** il selettore sintonizzazione *f* stazione *f* e ricerca automatica con regolazione *f* silenziosa (muting)
– *manual and automatic tuning selection button with muting*
**41** il selettore funzionamento stereo o mono
– *stereo/mono selection button*
**42** l'indicatore *m* intensità di campo
– *strength-of-signal display button*
**43** il tasto di memorizzazione *f*
– *memory button*
**44** i tasti delle stazioni
– *station selection buttons*
**45** i selettori bande *f pl* frequenza
– *frequency selection buttons ([wave] band selection buttons)*
**46** l'indicatore *f* luminoso della stazione
– *station select display*
**47** il display per banda di frequenza, frequenza e intensità di campo
– *fluorescent digital display indicating wave band, frequency, and strength of signal*
**48** l'indicatore *m* luminoso a diodi *m pl* (l'indicatore *m* LED), per ricezioni *f pl* stereo, mono e ricerca stazioni *f pl*
– *LED indicator for stereo and mono mode and automatic tuning*
**49 l'amplificatore *m***
– *amplifier (power amplifier)*
**50** i selettori comando giradischi *m*, tuner, registratore *m* a cassette *f pl*, lettore *m* CD e monitor *m*
– *function select buttons for the turntable, tuner, cassette deck (tape deck), CD player, and monitor (tape monitor)*
**51** i tasti dei filtri (il tasto per il filtro alto e basso)
– *filter buttons (high and low filter buttons)*
**52** il regolatore dei bassi
– *bass control*
**53** il regolatore degli alti
– *treble control*

**54** il regolatore di bilanciamento (il balance)
– *balance control*
**55** il tasto loudness
– *loudness button*
**56** il regolatore volume *m*
– *volume control*
**57** la presa jack della cuffia
– *headphone socket*
**58** i selettori degli altoparlanti
– *speaker select buttons*
**59** l'indicatore *m* luminoso a diodi *m pl* (l'indicatore *m* LED) per livello intensità
– *LED display, a multifunction display*
**60** il pittogramma funzioni *f pl* (il pittogramma)
– *function display*
**61 il receiver** (il ricevitore), una combinazione di ricevitore *m* e amplificatore *m*
– *receiver, a combined tuner-amp[lifier]*
**62** il selettore a display
– *display select button*
**63** l'indicatore *m* a cristalli *m pl* liquidi (l'indicatore *m* LCD), un indicatore multifunzione
– *liquid crystal display (LCD), a multifunction display*
**64** l'equalizzatore *m*, un dispositivo antidistorsione $2 \times 7$ bande *f pl* di frequenza
– *[graphic] equalizer, a $2 \times 7$ band [graphic] equalizer*
**65** i regolatori a slitta di banda di frequenza
– *equalizer slide controls*
**66** l'indicatore *m* luminoso a diodi *m pl* (l'indicatore *m* LED) per l'intensità del segnale banda frequenza
– *LED-display spectrum analyser*
**67 la cuffia** (la cuffia stereo)
– *headphones (stereo headphones)*
**68** gli auricolari *m* imbottiti
– *ear pads (ear cushions)*
**69** u. **70 i microfoni**
– *microphones*
**69** il microfono unidirettivo (il microfono unidirettivo stereo)
– *directional microphone (stereo directional microphone)*
**70** il microfono a condensatore *m* elettrete con caratteristica isotropa
– *electret condenser microphone with omnidirectional pick-up characteristic*

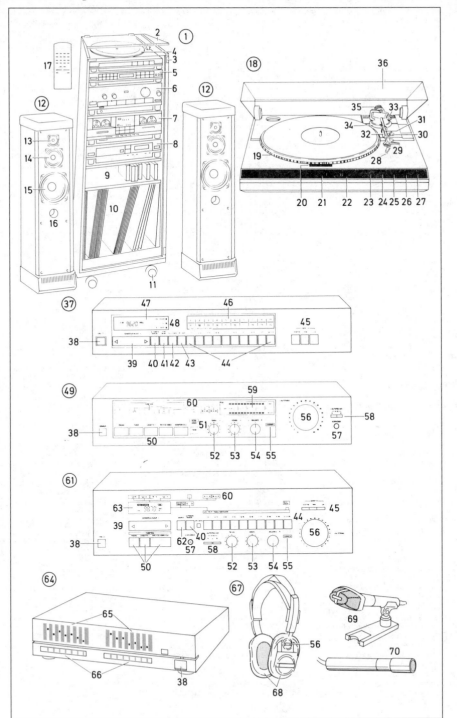

1 **la piastra di registrazione** *f*
- *cassette deck (cassette recorder)*
2 l'interruttore *m* di accensione *f* e di spegnimento (power)
- *power switch*
3 il tasto arresto automatico funzioni *f pl,* al momento dell'estrazione *f* della cassetta
- *[stop and] eject button*
4 l'alloggiamento cassetta
- *cassette holder (cassette drive, cassette transport)*
5 il coperchio di protezione *f*
- *dust cover*
6 il contagiri di funzionamento (counter)
- *counter (tape counter)*
**7-12 i tasti**
- *transport buttons*
7 il tasto di stop (<stop>)
- *stop button*
8 il tasto di riavvolgimento veloce (<review>)
- *rewind button*
9 il tasto di riproduzione *f* (<play>) bidirezionale
- *play buttons for both directions (bidirectional play buttons)*
10 il tasto di avanzamento veloce (<cue>)
- *fast forward button*
11 il tasto di registrazione *f* (<record>)
- *record button*
12 il tasto di pausa (<pause>)
- *pause button*
13 il tasto di azzeramento contagiri (<reset>)
- *counter reset button*
14 i tasti di filtro dolby
- *noise reduction buttons (Dolby select buttons)*
15 i tasti di autoreverse (per LP)
- *auto-reverse buttons*
16 il regolatore di livello di registrazione *f* (record level)
- *recording level control*
17 le prese per il microfono
- *microphone sockets*
18 la presa per la cuffia
- *headphone socket*
19 l'indicatore *m* del livello di registrazione *f,* un indicatore a diodi *m pl* luminosi (l'indicatore *m* LED)
- *level indicator display (VU meter), an LED display*
20 l'indicatore *m* del tipo di nastro, un indicatore a diodi *m pl* luminosi (l'indicatore *m* LED)
- *tape type indicator (tape-bias indicator), an LED display*
21 **la piastra doppia di registrazione** *f* (il registratore a due cassette *f pl*)
- *double cassette deck (double cassette recorder)*
22 il tasto di riproduzione *f* (<play>)
- *play button*
23 il tasto di arresto e espulsione *f* cassette *f pl* (<eject>)
- *[stop and] eject button*
24 il tasto di duplicazione *f* veloce (high speed dubbing)
- *high-speed dubbing button*
25 il tasto scelta funzioni *f pl*
- *function select button*

26 l'indicatore *m* luminoso di registrazione *f*
- *recording indicator light*
27 l'indicatore *m* luminoso di funzionamento
- *on-off light (power indicator light)*
28 **il CD player** (il compact disc player, il lettore compact)
- *CD player (compact disc player, digital compact disc player)*
29 l'alloggiamento CD
- *CD drawer*
30 il tasto apertura e chiusura alloggiamento CD
- *open/close button for the CD drawer*
31 il tasto avanzamento, ritorno e ricerca indice *m*
- *search button and index search button*
32 i tasti ricerca brano
- *skip buttons (skip-track buttons)*
33 il regolatore di volume *m* per la cuffia
- *headphone volume control*
34 i tasti scelta funzioni *f pl*
- *function select buttons*
35 gli indicatori luminosi di funzione *f* per programmazione *f,* ripetizione *f,* riproduzione *f* e pausa
- *programming, track and disc repeat, and pause indicators*
36 l'indicatore *m* luminoso a diodi *m pl* (l'indicatore *m* LED, il display)
- *LED display*
37 gli indicatori luminosi di funzione *f* per il tempo restante e l'indice *m* dei brani
- *remaining time and track-index indicators*
38 **il radioregistratore portatile** con lettore *m* CD incorporato
- *portable radio recorder with integral CD player*
39 il manico per il trasporto
- *handle*
40 il receiver (l'elemento pilota *m,* il ricevitore amplificatore)
- *[radio] receiver (receiver and amplifier)*
41 il lettore CD
- *CD player*
42 l'orologio al quarzo con indicatore *m* digitale e timer *m*
- *quartz clock with digital display and timer*
43 il registratore a due cassette *f pl*
- *double cassette recorder*
44 l'altoparlante *m*
- *loudspeaker*
**45-47 i tipi di nastro**
- *types of tape*
**45-49 la cassetta audio** (cassetta)
- *audio-cassette (cassette)*
45 la cassetta a ossidi *m pl* di ferro (la cassetta normale)
- *ferric cassette (iron oxide cassette, normal cassette)*
46 la cassetta a diossido di cromo
- *chrome dioxide cassette (chrome cassette)*
47 la cassetta a ossido metallico
- *metal cassette (metal oxide cassette)*
48 la linguetta prevenzione *f* cancellazioni *f pl*
- *tape type indication (indicating hole)*
49 le cassette non duplicabili
- *record-protected cassettes*
50 **il radioricevitore universale** (world

receiver) per ricevere le onde ultracorte (UKW), medie (MW), lunghe (LW), e corte (KW)
- *world receiver for receiving ultra-short wave (USW), medium wave (MW), long wave (LW), and short wave (SW)*
51 l'antenna (l'antenna a stilo), un'antenna telescopica
- *aerial (rod aerial), a telescopic aerial*
52 i tasti di funzione *f*
- *function buttons*
53 i tasti di sintonia
- *station select buttons*
54 il regolatore manuale di sintonia
- *manual tuning knob*
55 l'indicatore *m* a cristalli *m pl* liquidi (il display) per settore *m* di frequenza, frequenza e memoria
- *liquid crystal display (LCD) showing waveband, frequency, and memory number*
56 il potenziometro volume *m*
- *(sliding) volume control*
57 **il riproduttore per cassette** *f pl* a cuffia (Walkman®), con radio *f* incorporata
- *cassette player (Walkman® with radio)*
58 la cuffia
- *headphones*
59 l'equalizzatore *m,* l'equalizzatore *m* a tre vie *f pl*
- *equalizer, a 3-band equalizer*
60 **il lettore CD portatile**
- *portable CD player (Discman®)*
61 il compact disc (CD)
- *compact disc (CD)*
62 il coperchio di protezione *f*
- *lid*
63 lo chassis con lettore *m,* altoparlante *m,* display *m* e tasti *m pl* di funzione *f*
- *casing with transport, amplifier, display, and function buttons*
64 **l'impianto compatto Hi-Fi** (l'impianto compatto stereo)
- *compact hi-fi system (compact stereo system)*
65 l'amplificatore *m*
- *amplifier section*
66 **il DAT recorder** (il registratore digitale a cassetta; DAT = digital audio tape)
- *DAT recorder (digital cassette recorder) (DAT = Digital Audio Tape)*
67 il sensore a infrarossi *m pl* (sensore *m* IR) per comando a distanza
- *infrared sensor (IR sensor) for the remote control*
68 i tasti ricerca segnali *m pl* in entrata per funzionamento mono, analogico e digitale
- *input selection buttons for mono, analogue (Am. analog), and digital signals*
69 i tasti ricerca brani *m pl* e programmi *m pl*
- *index and program selection buttons*
70 l'indicatore *m* numero brano
- *index number display*
71 l'accensione *f* automatica col timer *m*
- *auto-scan button*
72 il tasto ricerca parti *f pl* non registrate
- *end-record search button*

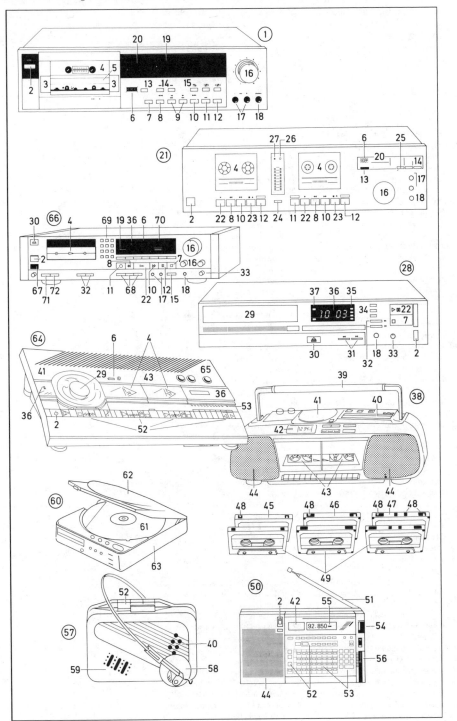

**1** la videocamera, l'impianto a due componenti *m pl* (telecamera e videoregistratore separati)
– *camcorder (camera recorder),* form: *two-component system (separate camera and recorder)*
**2** la videocamera portatile, un Video-8
– *pocket camcorder, a video-8 camcorder*
**3** l'obiettivo, un obiettivo zoom a sei ingrandimenti *m pl* (11–66 mm)
– *lens, a x 6 zoom lens (11–66 mm)*
**4** l'oculare *m*
– *viewfinder (ocular)*
**5** il sensore d'immagine *f* CCD, e High-Speed-Shutter, un Chip mezzo pollice *m*, con funzioni *f pl* di chiusura
– *CCD image converter (image sensor) and high-speed shutter, a half-inch chip with shutter functions*
**6** la videocassetta
– *video cassette*
**7** il videonastro
– *videotape*
**8** il tamburo testina video
– *head drum*
**9** il servocomando autofocus
– *autofocus motor*
**10** il microfono integrato
– *built-in microphone (integral microphone)*
**11** il tamburo testina VHS (VHS: Video Home System)
– *VHS head drum (VHS: Video Home System)*
**12** la testina di cancellazione *f*
– *erase head*
**13** il perno di guida
– *guide pin*
**14** il tendinastro
– *tape guide*
**15** la testina incisione *f* sonoro
– *capstan*
**16** la testina sincro
– *audio sync head*
**17** il rullo pressore
– *pinch roller*
**18** la testina video
– *video head*
**19** le piste nella parete *f* del tamburo della testina, per la formazione di cuscini *m pl* di aria
– *grooves in the wall of the head drum to promote air cushion formation*
**20** lo schema delle piste VHS
– *VHS track format*
**21** il senso di rotazione *f* nastro
– *direction of tape movement*
**22** il senso di rotazione *f* testina video
– *direction of recording*

**23** la pista video, una pista obliqua (sono indicate solamente poche piste *f*)
– *video track, a slant track (only a few tracks shown)*
**24** la colonna sonora
– *sound track (audio track)*
**25** la pista dei sincronismi (la pista di sincronizzazione *f*)
– *sync track*
**26** la testina sincro
– *sync head*
**27** la testina del sonoro
– *sound head (audio head)*
**28** la testina video
– *video head*
**29** il videoregistratore
– *video recorder*
**30** il telecomando a raggi *m pl* infrarossi
– *infrared remote control*
**31** la scala dei programmi *m pl*, un multidisplay
– *program scale (program dial), a multidisplay*
**32** il vano portacassetta
– *cassette compartment*
**33** il Jog Shuttle per il comando movimenti *m pl* avanti-indietro dell'immagine *f* video
– *jog shuttle knob for forward or reverse movement of the [video] picture*
**34** il multi-disc-player
– *multidisc player*
**35** il telecomando a raggi *m pl* infrarossi
– *infrared remote control*
**36** il cassetto dei dischi
– *disc drawer*
**37-41 i formati dei dischi**
– *disc formats*
**37** il compact-disc single (il CD single)
– *single compact disc (single CD)*
**38** il CD audio
– *audio CD*
**39** il CD video
– *video CD*
**40** il disco laser piccolo (il disco laser: 20 cm ø)
– *small laser disc (20 cm)*
**41** il disco laser grande (il disco laser: 30 cm ø)
– *large laser disc (30 cm)*
**42** il sistema di lettura laser
– *laser scanning system*
**43** l'asse *m* del disco
– *[disc] spindle*
**44** l'asse *m* alimentazione *f* testina laser
– *laser-head tracing spindle*
**45** la testina laser (il gruppo laser)
– *laser head (laser unit)*

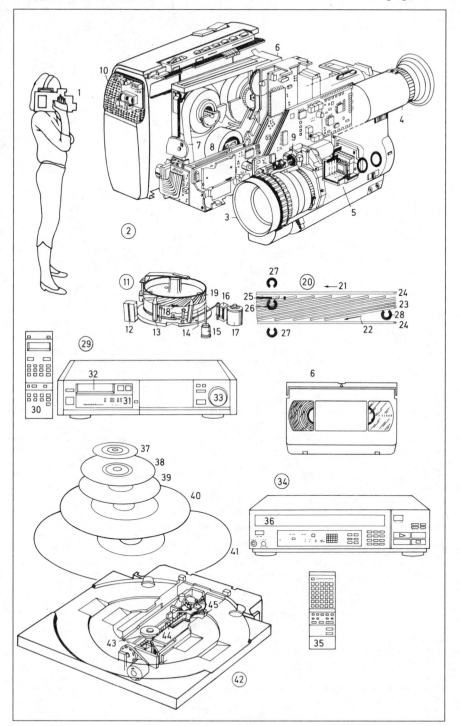

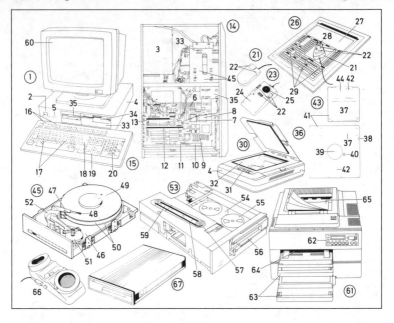

1 **il personal computer** (PC)
– *personal computer* (*PC*; sim.: *laptop*)
2 il pulsante di accensione *f*
– *power switch*
3 l'alimentatore *m*
– *power supply (power pack)*
4 la base
– *housing*
5 la spia dell'hard disc
– *fixed-disk access light*
6 la memoria di lavoro (RAM)
– *main memory*
7 lo zoccolo del coprocessore *m*
– *coprocessor socket*
8 l'unità centrale (CPU, central process-ing unit), un microprocessore
– *central processing unit (CPU), a micro-processor*
9 la memoria cachée (caché-controller)
– *cache memory (cache controller)*
10 la porta d'inserimento (slot) per la scheda di ampliamento memoria
– *expansion memory slot*
11 la porta d'inserimento (slot) per la scheda di grafica
– *graphics card slot*
12 il dispositivo commutabile sul drive e sull'hard disc
– *combined fixed and floppy disk con-troller*
13 la scheda d'inserimento per i punti di sezione *f* seriali e paralleli
– *serial and parallel communication card*
14 **la torre PC (tower) vista dall'interno**
– *PC tower interior view*
15-67 **gli accessori**
– *peripherals*
15-32 **gli apparecchi d'immissione *f* dati** *m pl*
– *built-in devices*
15 la tastiera
– *keyboard*
16 i tasti di funzione *f*
– *function keys*

17 i tasti lettere *f pl* e cifre *f pl*
– *letter keys and number keys (numeric keys)*
18 il tasto return
– *enter key (return key)*
19 i tasti di posizione *f* cursore *m*
– *cursor keys*
20 il blocco numerico
– *number [key]pad (numeric [key]pad)*
21 **il mouse**
– *mouse*
22 i tasti del mouse
– *mouse buttons*
23 **il track ball**
– *trackerball (trackball)*
24 l'impugnatura
– *handrest*
25 la pallina di rotolamento
– *roller ball*
26 **il digitizer**
– *digitizing tablet (digitizer,* also: *graph-ics tablet)*
27 il campo grafico
– *graphics area*
28 il reticolo
– *cross hairs*
29 i campi di funzione *f*
– *receiving grids*
30 **lo scanner**
– *scanner*
31 il settore comandi con tasti *m pl* di fun-zione *f*
– *control panel with function keys*
32 la lastra di appoggio
– *scanning surface*
33-59 **le memorie di massa** (i memorizza-tori magnetici)
– *mass storage devices (magnetic stores, magnetic memories)*
33-44 **i dispositivi di caricamento dischetti** *m pl* (i dispositivi di caricamento dei floppy)
– *disk drives (drives, floppy disk drives)*

33 il dispositivo di caricamento dei mini disc (5 ¹/₄ pollici *m pl*) (il mini drive)
– *minifloppy disk drive (5 ¹/₄ inch [flop-py] disk drive)*
34 la leva di chiusura
– *latch*
35 il dispositivo di caricamento dei micro disc (3 ¹/₂ pollici *m pl*)
– *microfloppy disk drive (3 ¹/₂ inch [flop-py] disk drive)*
36-44 **i dischetti** (floppy disc)
– *diskettes (disks, floppy disks, floppies)*
36 il mini dischetto (il minidisc, il dischetto da 5 ¹/₄ pollici *m pl*)
– *minifloppy (minifloppy disk, 5 ¹/₄ inch disk, flexible disk)*
37 l'etichetta (lo spazio per le scritte)
– *label*
38 la fessura di protezione *f*
– *write-protect notch*
39 il foro di trascinamento
– *hole for engaging the drive hub*
40 il foro dell'indice *m*
– *registration hole*
41 l'involucro del dischetto
– *disk cover (envelope)*
42 l'apertura per la testina di lettura e scrittura
– *access slot for the read-write head*
43 il microdischetto (il microdisc, dischetto da 3 ¹/₂ pollici *m pl*)
– *microfloppy (3 ¹/₂ inch [floppy] disk)*
44 la lastrina di protezione *f* mobile
– *sliding shutter*
45 **il dispositivo di funzionamento dell'hard disc** (hard disc drive)
– *fixed-disk drive (fixed disk, hard disk)*
46 la base (la base dell'hard disc)
– *base plate*

47–67 → S. 431

244:

**47** l'actuator (il braccio)
– *access arm (actuator)*
**48** la testina per scrittura e lettura
– *read-write head*
**49** il motore di trascinamento per i piatti di alluminio, un mandrino a motore *m*
– *drive motor for the aluminium (Am. aluminum) platters, a spindle drive motor*
**50** le lastre di alluminio rivestite di materiale *m* magnetico (hard disc)
– *magnetic-coated aluminium (Am. aluminum) platters*
**51** il motore di spostamento della testina lettura-scrittura, un motore lineare o passo a passo
– *read-write head drive motor, a linear motor or stepping motor (stepper motor)*
**52** la banda di trasferimento dati *m pl* (bus dati *m pl*)
– *data, address, and control bus*
**53** **la memoria a banda magnetica** (lo streamer)
– *magnetic tape unit (magnetic tape drive, streamer)*
**54** la banda magnetica
– *magnetic tape*
**55** la bobina
– *magnetic tape reel*
**56** la cassetta
– *magnetic tape cassette (magnetic tape cartridge)*
**57** la puleggia azionamento banda
– *drive post*
**58** la cinghia di trascinamento
– *drive band*
**59** il motore
– *drive motor*
**60-65** **gli apparecchi di visualizzazione *f* e riproduzione *f* dati *m pl***
– *output devices*
**60** lo schermo (il monitor, il display), uno schermo a colori *m pl* a alta definizione *f*
– *screen (monitor, display) a high-resolution colour (Am. color) monitor*
**61** **la stampante,** una stampante a matrice *f* di punti *m pl* (qui: la stampante laser, anche: la stampante a aghi *m pl*)
– *printer, a dot-matrix printer (here: laser printer; also: inkjet printer, needle printer)*
**62** la consolle di comando con tasti di funzione *f* e display
– *control panel with function keys and display*
**63** il contenitore della carta
– *paper tray (paper cassette)*
**64** il vano inserimento carta
– *paper feed path*
**65** l'uscita carta
– *paper output tray*
**66** *u.* **67 apparecchiature *f pl* per la trasmissione a distanza dati *m pl***
– *devices for long-distance data transmission*
**66** l'accoppiatore acustico
– *acoustic coupler*
**67** il modem
– *modem*

**1-33** **l'ufficio della segretaria** (delle segretarie)
– *receptionists office (secretary's office)*
**1** il sistema della telecopia (sistema *m* di trasmissione *f* di facsimili *m pl*, sistema *m* di comunicazione *f* per telefax *m pl*)
– *fax machine*
**2** il telefax (la telecopia, la teleriproduzione)
– *transmitted or received copy*
**3** il calendario da parete *f*
– *wall calendar*
**4** l'armadio per pratiche *f pl*
– *filing cabinet*
**5** lo sportello avvolgibile
– *tambour door (roll-up door)*
**6** il raccoglitore (qui: raccoglitore *m* di pratiche *f pl*)
– *file (document file)*
**7** la macchina (autografica) per indirizzi *m pl*
– *transfer-type addressing machine*
**8** il contenitore delle piastrine incise (delle sagome)
– *vertical stencil magazine*
**9** il piano di appoggio delle piastrine (delle sagome)
– *stencil ejection*
**10** la custodia delle piastrine (delle sagome)
– *stencil storage drawer*
**11** il piano di alimentazione *f* della carta (il guidacarta)
– *paper feed*
**12** la scorta (le scorte, la riserva) della carta da lettere *f pl*
– *stock of notepaper*
**13** il centralino privato (centralino telefonico)
– *switchboard (internal telephone exchange)*
**14** il quadro dei pulsanti per gli allacciamenti interni
– *push-button keyboard for internal connections*
**15** il ricevitore
– *handset*

**16** il disco combinatore (disco selettore)
– *dial*
**17** l'elenco dei numeri telefonici interni (elenco telefonico degli apparecchi interni, elenco degli allacciamenti interni)
– *internal telephone list*
**18** l'orologio
– *master clock (main clock)*
**19** la cartella delle lettere da firmare (cartella delle lettere alla firma)
– *folder containing documents, correspondence, etc. for signing (to be signed)*
**20** il citofono
– *intercom (office intercom)*
**21** la matita (anche: penna)
– *pen*
**22** il portamatite (qui: portamatite *m* a vaschetta)
– *pen and pencil tray*
**23** lo schedario
– *card index*
**24** la pila (la catasta) dei moduli
– *stack (set) of forms*
**25** il tavolo per la macchina da scrivere
– *typing desk*
**26** la macchina da scrivere elettronica con memorizzatore *m*
– *electronic memory typewriter*
**27** la tastiera
– *keyboard*
**28** i tasti di funzione *f*
– *function keys*
**29** il blocco da stenografia (blocco steno)
– *shorthand pad(Am. steno pad)*
**30** il cestino di appoggio delle pratiche
– *letter tray*
**31** la calcolatrice
– *office calculator*
**32** il meccanismo (il blocco) impressore
– *printer*
**33** la lettera di ufficio (anche: lettera di affari *m pl*, lettera commerciale, ecc.)
– *business letter*

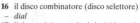

**1-36 l'ufficio del direttore** (del principale, del capo)
- *executive's office*
1 la sedia (la poltrona) da scrivania
- *swivel chair*
2 la scrivania (lo scrittoio)
- *desk*
3 il piano della scrivania
- *desk top*
4 il cassetto della scrivania
- *desk drawer*
5 lo scomparto ribaltabile
- *cupboard (storage area) with door*
6 la cartella da scrittoio (il sottomano)
- *desk mat (blotter)*
7 la lettera di ufficio (*anche:* lettera di
affari *m pl*, lettera commerciale,
ecc.)
- *business letter*
8 l'agenda (taccuino degli appuntamenti)
- *appointments diary*
9 il portapenne (la vaschetta portapenne)
- *desk set*
10 il citofono
- *intercom (office intercom)*
11 la lampada da scrittoio
- *desk lamp*
12 la calcolatrice tascabile (calcolatrice
*m* elettronica)
- *pocket calculator (electronic calculator)*

13 il telefono, un impianto ricevente-
emittente fra segretaria e capo
- *telephone, an executive-secretary system*
14 il disco combinatore (disco selettore); *anche:* la tastiera (quadro
selettore a tasti *m pl*)
- *dial; also: push-button keyboard*
15 i tasti per chiamata rapida diretta
- *call buttons*
16 il ricevitore
- *receiver (telephone receiver)*
17 il dittafono
- *dictating machine*
18 l'indicazione *f* della lunghezza del
dettato
- *position indicator*
19 i tasti di comando
- *control buttons (operating keys)*
20 l'armadio a cassone *m*
- *cabinet*
21 la poltrona per gli ospiti
- *visitor's chair*
22 la cassaforte (cassaforte *f* blindata)
- *safe*
23 la chiavarda della serratura
- *bolts*
24 l'interno dello sportello blindato
- *armour-plated* (Am. *armor-plated)
lock area*
25 i documenti segreti (documenti *m pl*
riservati)
- *confidential documents*

26 l'atto del brevetto
- *patent*
27 il denaro contante (denaro in con-
tanti *m pl*)
- *petty cash*
28 il quadro (*qui:* quadro alla parete *f* )
- *picture*
29 il mobile bar *m*
- *bar (drinks cabinet)*
30 il servizio di bicchieri per il mobile
bar
- *bar set*
**31-36** l'angolo per riunioni *f pl*
- *conference grouping*
31 il tavolo
- *conference table*
32 il dittafono tascabile
- *pocket-sized dictating machine, a
micro-cassette recorder*
33 il posacenere
- *ashtray*
34 il tavolino di angolo
- *corner table*
35 la lampada da tavolo
- *table lamp*
36 la poltrona (*qui:* il divanetto biposto)
- *two-seater sofa [part of the conference grouping]*

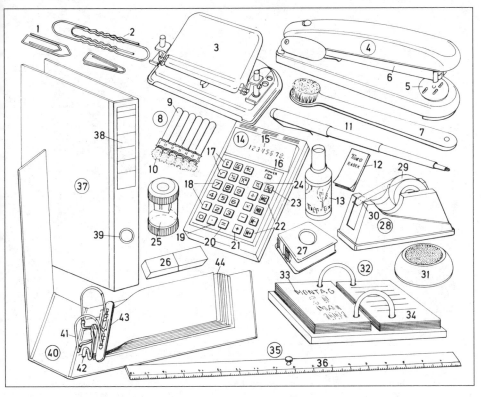

**1-44 materiale *m* da ufficio**
- *office equipment (office supplies, office materials)*
1 il fermaglio (la graffetta)
- *[small] paper clip*
2 il fermaglio (per incartamenti *m pl*)
- *[large] paper clip*
3 il perforatore
- *punch*
4 la cucitrice (*pop.:* la spillatrice)
- *stapler (stapling machine)*
5 la matrice
- *anvil*
6 il cursore di alimentazione *f* (caricatore *m* scorrevole)
- *spring-loaded magazine*
7 lo spazzolino per i caratteri
- *type-cleaning brush*
8 l'utensile *m* per pulire i caratteri (il nettacaratteri)
- *type cleaner (type-cleaning kit)*
9 il contenitore del liquido detergente
- *fluid container (fluid reservoir)*
10 la spazzola
- *cleaning brush*
11 il pennarello
- *felt tip pen*
12 la mascherina per cancellare
- *correcting paper [for typing errors]*
13 la cancellina (il liquido per cancellare)
- *correcting fluid [for typing errors]*
14 la calcolatrice elettronica
- *electronic pocket calculator*
15 il visore luminoso di otto cifre *f pl*
- *eight-digit fluorescent display*

16 l'interruttore *m* (per accendere e spegnere)
- *on/off switch*
17 i tasti delle funzioni *f pl*
- *function keys*
18 i tasti delle cifre (cifre *f pl*)
- *number keys*
19 il tasto della virgola (virgola)
- *decimal key*
20 il tasto di «uguale»
- *'equals' key*
21 i tasti di comando delle singole operazioni
- *instruction keys (command keys)*
22 i memorizzatori (tasti *m pl* di memoria)
- *memory keys*
23 il tasto per il calcolo percentuale
- *percent key (percentage key)*
24 il tasto del π (il π) per la misurazione del cerchio
- *π-key (pi-key) for mensuration of circles*
25 il temperamatite
- *pencil sharpener*
26 la gomma per macchina da scrivere
- *typewriter rubber*
27 il caricatore del nastro adesivo (portanastro adesivo chiuso)
- *adhesive tape dispenser*
28 il portanastro adesivo aperto
- *adhesive tape holder (roller-type adhesive tape dispenser)*
29 il rotolo di nastro adesivo
- *roll of adhesive tape*
30 il bordo dentellato per lo strappo
- *tear-off edge*

31 la spugna
- *moistener*
32 l'agenda da tavolo
- *desk diary*
33 la pagina con la data
- *date sheet (calendar sheet)*
34 la pagina per annotazioni *f pl* (pagina per appunti *m pl*)
- *memo sheet*
35 la riga
- *ruler*
36 la suddivisione (la graduazione) in centimetri *m pl* e millimetri *m pl*
- *centimetre and millimetre (Am. centimeter and millimeter) graduations*
37 il raccoglitore
- *file (document file)*
38 l'etichetta sul dorso del raccoglitore
- *spine label (spine tag)*
39 il buco (il foro) per la presa (la presa a foro)
- *finger hole*
40 il raccoglitore delle pezze giustificative
- *arch board file*
41 il congegno del raccoglitore
- *arch unit*
42 la levetta (levetta a mano *f*)
- *release lever (locking lever, release/lock lever)*
43 la spranghetta di bloccaggio
- *compressor*
44 l'estratto conto
- *bank statement (statement of account)*

**1-48 la sala multiuffici**
- *open plan office*
1 la parete divisoria
- *partition wall (partition screen)*
2 il mobile archivio con schedario
- *filing drawer with suspension file system*
3 il raccoglitore delle schede
- *suspension file*
4 il cavaliere
- *file tab*
5 il raccoglitore delle pratiche
- *file (document file)*
6 l'addetto (l'addetta) all'archivio
- *filing clerk*
7 l'impiegata
- *clerical assistant*
8 l'annotazione *f*
- *note for the files*
9 il telefono
- *telephone*
10 lo scaffale per pratiche *f pl*
- *filing shelves*
11 il tavolo dell'impiegato (dell'impiegata)
- *clerical assistant's desk*
12 l'armadio da ufficio
- *office cupboard*
13 la vaschetta portapiante
- *plant stand (planter)*
14 le piante da interni *m pl* (piante *f pl* da appartamento)
- *indoor plants (houseplants)*

15 la programmatrice
- *programmer*
16 il visualizzatore dei dati
- *data display terminal (visual display unit)*
17 l'impiegato addetto al servizio clienti *m pl*
- *customer service representative*
18 il cliente
- *customer*
19 il disegno grafico eseguito col computer
- *computer-generated design*
20 la parete divisoria fonoassorbente
- *sound-absorbing partition*
21 la stenodattilografa
- *typist*
22 la macchina da scrivere
- *typewriter*
23 il cassetto schedario
- *filing drawer*
24 lo schedario clienti *m pl*
- *customer card index*
25 la sedia da ufficio, una sedia girevole
- *office chair, a swivel chair*
26 il tavolo per macchina da scrivere
- *typing desk*
27 la cassetta delle pratiche
- *card index box*
28 lo scaffale pluriuso
- *multi-purpose shelving*

29 il capo (il direttore)
- *proprietor*
30 la lettera di ufficio
- *business letter*
31 la segretaria del direttore (segretaria di direzione *f*)
- *proprietor's secretary*
32 il blocco steno (blocco per stenografia)
- *shorthand pad (Am. steno pad)*
33 la fonodattilografa
- *audio typist*
34 il dittafono
- *dictating machine*
35 l'auricolare *m*
- *earphone*
36 il grafico (la statistica)
- *statistics chart*
37 la parte inferiore della scrivania (l'armadietto incorporato nella scrivania)
- *pedestal containing a cupboard or drawers*
38 l'armadietto a ante *f pl* scorrevoli
- *sliding-door cupboard*
39 i mobili da ufficio a angolo
- *office furniture arranged in an angular configuration*
40 lo scaffale pensile
- *wall-mounted shelf*
41 il contenitore delle pratiche (*qui:* il cestino delle pratiche)
- *letter tray*

**42** il calendario da parete *f*
– *wall calendar*
**43** la centrale (dei) dati
– *data centre (Am. center)*
**44** il prelievo di informazioni *f pl* dal
visualizzatore dei dati
– *calling up information on the data
display terminal (visual display
unit)*
**45** il cestino per la carta
– *waste paper basket*
**46** il grafico del volume di affari *m pl*
(grafico delle vendite, grafico del
fatturato), una statistica
– *sales statistics*
**47** i dati elaborati, un foglio ripiegato
a fisarmonica
– *EDP print-out, a continuous fan-
fold sheet*
**48** l'elemento di congiunzione *f*
– *connecting element*

1  **la macchina da scrivere elettronica,**
una macchina da scrivere con testina sferica
– *electric typewriter, a golf ball type-*
*writer*
2-6  la tastiera
– *keyboard*
2  la barra spaziatrice (lo spaziatore)
– *space bar*
3  il liberamaiuscole (tasto delle
maiuscole)
– *shift key*
4  il tasto automatico di interlinea
– *line space and carrier return key*
5  il tasto fissamaiuscole
– *shift lock*
6  il liberamargine
– *margin release key*
7  il tasto incolonnatore (tasto del tab-
ulatore)
– *tabulator key*
8  il tasto di annullamento del tabula-
tore
– *tabulator clear key*
9  l'interruttore *m* (interruttore *m*
inseritore e esclusore)
– *on/off switch*
10  il regolatore dell'intensità delle battute
– *striking force control (impression*
*control)*
11  il commutatore del nastro inchiostrato
– *ribbon selector*
12  la graduazione per la messa a punto
del margine
– *margin scale*
13  il marginatore sinistro
– *left margin stop*
14  il marginatore destro
– *right margin stop*
15  la testina sferica con i caratteri
– *golf ball (spherical typing element)*
*bearing the types*
16  la cassetta del nastro inchiostrato
– *ribbon cassette*
17  il reggifoglio con i rulli guida
– *paper bail with rollers*
18  il rullo della macchina da scrivere
– *platen*
19  la finestra guidacaratteri
– *typing opening (typing window)*
20  l'inseritore automatico del foglio (il
mettifoglio)
– *paper release lever*
21  il ritorno del carrello
– *carrier return lever*
22  la manopola del rullo
– *platen knob*
23  il regolatore dell'interlinea
– *line space adjuster*
24  il liberacarrello (liberarullo)
– *variable platen action lever*
25  il bottone della frizione
– *push-in platen variable*
26  l'appoggio per cancellare
– *erasing table*
27  il coperchio trasparente del corpo
scrivente
– *transparent cover*

28  la testina sferica di ricambio
– *exchange golf ball (exchange typing*
*element)*
29  il carattere
– *type*
30  la calotta della testina
– *golf ball cap (cap of typing element)*
31  i segmenti dentati
– *teeth*
32  **la copiatrice** (fotocopiatrice *f,*
macchina fotocopiatrice)
– **photocopier** *(copier, photocopying*
*machine)*
33  il tappetino (tettuccio, coperchio)
coprioriginale, per emissione *f* di
copie *f pl* singole
– *copyboard cover with single-copy*
*(single-sheet) delivery tray*
34  la cassetta portacarta universale
– *universal paper cassette*
35  le cassette portacarta regolabili
– *adjustable paper cassettes*
36  lo sportello ribaltabile della carrozzeria (carter *m*, cover-part ribaltabile)
– *front door*
37  il gruppo di trasporto carta per
copiatura in fronte e retro
– *dual vertical transport unit*
38  il fascicolatore
– *sorter*
39  il vassoio raccoglicopia
– *copy delivery bins*
40-43  il pannello con i tasti di comando
– *control panel displays and control*
*keys*
40  i tasti di comando per copia
ingrandita, rimpicciolita e per programmi *m pl*
– *enlargement, reduction, and pro-*
*gram selection keys*
41  i tasti di comando per copie *f pl* fas-
cicolate e copie *f pl* in fronte e retro
– *sort mode and two-sided copy keys*
42  il visualizzatore (display *m*) con
tasti di comando per colore *m*,
impressione *f*, formato del foglio,
numero delle copie
– *display with colour, exposure, for-*
*mat, and copy number selection keys*
43  il tasto per copiare
– *start key (copy start key)*
44  **la pieghettatrice delle lettere**
– *letter-folding machine*
45  l'immissione *f* (introduzione *f* )
della carta
– *paper feed*
46  il verso della piega
– *folding mechanism*
47  il vassoio di raccolta
– *receiving tray*
48  **la microstampa offset**
– *small offset press*
49  il contenitore della carta
– *paper feed*
50  la leva per inchiostrazione *f* della
lastra litografica
– *lever for inking the plate cylinder*
51 *u.* 52  il meccanismo d'inchiostrazione *f*
– *inking unit (inker unit)*

51  il rullo di attrito
– *distributing roller (distributor)*
52  il rullo inchiostratore
– *ink roller (inking roller, fountain*
*roller)*
53  il regolatore di pressione *f*
– *pressure adjustment*
54  il vassoio portacarta
– *sheet delivery (receiving table)*
55  la regolazione della velocità di
stampa
– *printing speed adjustment*
56  **il vibratore** per tener compatta e
allineata la pila dei fogli di carta
– *jogger for aligning the piles of sheets*
57  la pila dei fogli di carta
– *pile of paper (pile of sheets)*
58  **la macchina piegatrice**
– *folding machine*
59  la macchina raccoglitrice (la raccoglitrice) dei fogli per piccole tira-
ture *f pl*
– *gathering machine (collating*
*machine, assembling machine) for*
*short runs*
60  la stazione di raccolta
– *gathering station (collating station,*
*assembling station)*
61  **l'apparecchio incollatore** nella ter-
molegatura
– *adhesive binder (perfect binder) for*
*hot adhesives*
62  **il dittafono a nastro magnetico** (il
magnetodittafono)
– *magnetic tape dictating machine*
63  l'auricolare *m*
– *headphones (headset, earphones)*
64  l'interruttore *m* (per accendere e
spegnere)
– *on/off switch*
65  la staffa del microfono (staffa
appoggiamicrofono/reggimicro-
fono)
– *microphone cradle*
66  la presa dell'interruttore *m* a pedale *m*
– *foot control socket*
67  la presa del telefono
– *telephone adapter socket*
68  la presa dell'auricolare *m*
– *headphone socket (earphone socket,*
*headset socket)*
69  la presa del microfono
– *microphone socket*
70  l'altoparlante *m* incorporato
– *built-in loudspeaker*
71  la spia luminosa
– *indicator lamp (indicator light)*
72  il vano portacassetta
– *cassette compartment*
73  i tasti di avanzamento, di ritorno e
di stop *m*
– *forward wind, rewind, and stop but-*
*tons*
74  la scala cronometrica graduata
(timer *m*)
– *time scale with indexing marks*
75  lo stop della scala cronometrica
– *time scale stop*

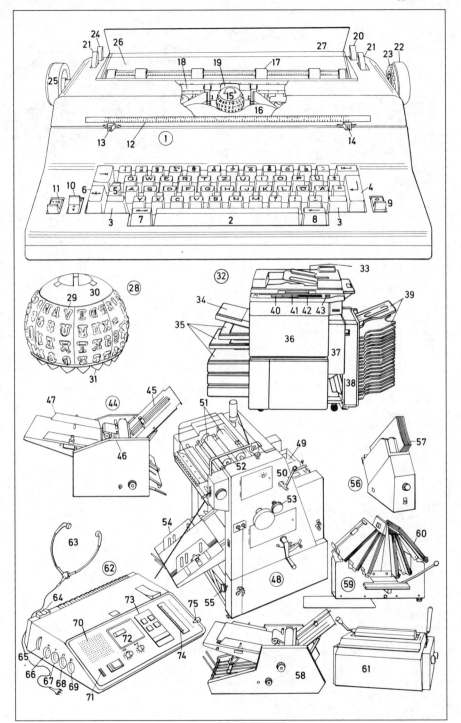

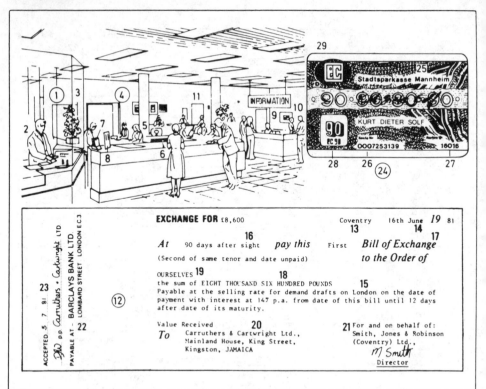

1-11 la sala sportelli *m pl*
- *main hall*
1 la cassa
- *cashier's desk (cashier's counter)*
2 il cassiere
- *teller (cashier)*
3 il vetro blindato antiproiettile
- *bullet-proof glass*
4 il banco (per il) servizio clienti *m pl* (il banco per il pubblico, servizio informazione *f pl* per conti di risparmio, conti privati o di ditte *f pl*, crediti *m pl*)
- *service counters (for service and advice on savings accounts, private and company accounts, personal loans)*
5 l'impiegata di banca
- *bank clerk*
6 la cliente della banca
- *customer*
7 i dépliant (i prospetti)
- *brochures*
8 il listino di borsa (listino delle quotazioni)
- *stock list (price list, list of quotations)*
9 lo stand informazioni *f pl* (l'informazione *f*)
- *information counter*

10 lo sportello del cambio
- *foreign exchange counter*
11 l'entrata alle cassette di sicurezza
- *entrance to strong room*
12 la cambiale; *qui:* la tratta, una cambiale accettata
- *bill of exchange (bill); here: a draft, an acceptance (bank acceptance)*
13 il luogo di emissione *f*
- *place of issue*
14 la data di emissione *f*
- *date of issue*
15 la piazza di pagamento
- *place of payment*
16 la scadenza (data di scadenza)
- *date of maturity (due date)*
17 la clausola cambiaria
- *bill clause (draft clause)*
18 l'importo della cambiale
- *value*
19 il beneficiario (il prenditore) cambiario
- *payee (remittee)*
20 il trattario (trassato)
- *drawee (payer)*
21 il traente
- *drawer*

22 la domiciliazione (il luogo di pagamento)
- *domicilation (paying agent)*
23 l'accettazione *f*
- *acceptance*
24 la carta dell'Eurochèque *m*
- *Eurocheque card*
25 l'istituto bancario emittente
- *issuing bank (drawee bank)*
26 il numero del conto
- *account number*
27 il numero della carta
- *card number*
28 l'ologramma *m*, un ologramma in luce *f* bianca (ologramma *m* di volume *m*)
- *hologram, a white light hologram (rainbow hologram)*
29 (*sul retro:*) la striscia magnetica
- *(on the back:) magnetic strip*

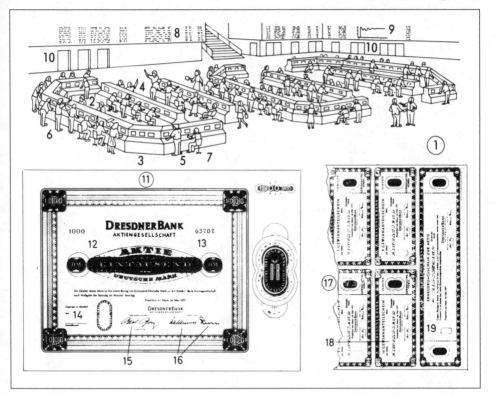

**1-10 la Borsa** (Borsa Valori, Borsa Titoli)
– *stock exchange*
**1** la sala Borsa
– *exchange hall (exchange floor)*
**2** la piazza per la trattazione dei titoli
– *market for securities*
**3** il recinto degli agenti di borsa (il ring)
– *broker's post*
**4** l'agente *m* di cambio, un pubblico ufficiale (un agente giurato)
– *sworn stockbroker (exchange broker, stockbroker, Am. specialist), an inside broker*
**5** l'agente *m* di cambio operante sul mercato libero (agente *m* di contrattazioni *f pl* fuori Borsa)
– *kerbstone broker (kerbstoner, curbstone broker, curbstoner, outside broker), a commercial broker dealing in unlisted securities*
**6** il membro della Borsa, un privato ammesso alle contrattazioni di Borsa
– *member of the stock exchange (stockjobber, Am. floor trader, room trader)*

**7** il commissario di Borsa, un impiegato di banca
– *stock exchange agent (boardman), a bank employee*
**8** il quadro (quadrante *m*) delle quotazioni (il listino di Borsa, listino dei cambi)
– *quotation board*
**9** il diagramma dell'indice *m*
– *index curve*
**10** la cabina telefonica
– *telephone box (telephone booth, telephone kiosk, call box)*
**11-19 titoli** *m pl* (effetti *m pl; tipi:* azioni *f pl*, titoli *m pl* a tasso fisso, buoni *m pl* di Stato, prestiti *m pl*, ipoteche *f pl*, obbligazioni *f pl* comunali, obbligazioni *f pl* industriali, prestiti *m pl* convertibili)
– *securities; kinds: share (Am. stock), fixed-income security, annuity, bond, debenture bond, municipal bond (corporation stock), industrial bond, convertible bond*
**11** il certificato azionario (il titolo); *qui:* l'azione *f* al portatore
– *share certificate (Am. stock certificate); here: bearer share (share warrant)*

**12** il valore nominale dell'azione *f*
– *par (par value, nominal par, face par) of the share*
**13** il numero di serie *f*
– *serial number*
**14** il numero di registrazione *f* sul registro azionario della banca
– *page number of entry in bank's share register (bank's stock ledger)*
**15** la firma del presidente del consiglio di amministrazione *f*
– *signature of the chairman of the board of governors*
**16** la firma del direttore generale
– *signature of the chairman of the board of directors*
**17** il foglio (delle) cedole (cartella dei tagliandi, cartella dei coupons)
– *sheet of coupons (coupon sheet, dividend coupon sheet)*
**18** la cedola del dividendo (il coupon)
– *dividend warrant (dividend coupon)*
**19** il tagliando per il rinnovo del foglio cedole *f pl* (la cedola di riaffogliamento)
– *talon*

# 252 Denaro (monete e banconote)

**1-29 monete** *f pl* (pezzi *m pl*, tipi:
monete *f pl* d'oro, d'argento, di
nichel *m*, di rame *m oppure* di
alluminio)
- *coins (coin, coinage, metal money,
specie,* Am. *hard money);* kinds:
*gold, silver, nickel, copper, or alu-
minium,* Am. *aluminum, coins*
**1** Atene: tetradramma *m* in forma
di pepita
- *Athens: tetradrachm (tetradrach-
mon, tetradrachma)*
**2** la civetta (l'uccello simbolo della
città di Atene)
- *the owl, emblem of the city of
Athens*
**3** aureo di Costantino il Grande
- *aureus of Constantine the Great*
**4** bratteato dell'Imperatore *m*
Federico I Barbarossa
- *bracteate of Emperor Frederick I
Barbarossa*
**5** Francia: luigi *m s* d'oro di Luigi
XIV
- *Louis XIV louis-d'or*
**6** Prussia: tallero imperiale di
Federico il Grande
- *Prussia: I reichstaler (speciestaler)
of Frederick the Great*
**7** Repubblica Federale Tedesca: 5
marchi *m pl* (marchi *m pl*
tedeschi); 1 marco tedesco = 100
pfennig *m*
- *Federal Republic of Germany: 5
Deutschmarks (DM); 1 DM = 100
pfennigs*
**8** il diritto (il recto)
- *obverse*
**9** il rovescio
- *reverse (subordinate side)*
**10** l'indicazione *f* della zecca (lettere
*f pl* e cifre *f pl*)
- *mint mark (mintage, exergue)*
**11** la leggenda (l'iscrizione *f* ) del
bordo
- *legend (inscription on the edge of
a coin)*
**12** l'effige *f*, uno stemma nazionale
- *device (type), a provincial coat of
arms*
**13** Austria: 25 scellini *m pl;* 1 scellino
= 100 groschen *m*
- *Austria: 25 schillings; 1 sch = 100
groschen*
**14** gli stemmi regionali
- *provincial coats of arms*
**15** Svizzera: 5 franchi; 1 franco = 100
centesimi *m pl* (rappen)
- *Switzerland: 5 francs; 1 franc =
100 centimes*
**16** Francia: 1 franco = 100 centesimi
*m pl* (centimes)
- *France: 1 franc = 100 centimes*

**17** Belgio: 100 franchi *m pl*
- *Belgium: 100 francs*
**18** Lussemburgo: 1 franco
- *Luxembourg (Luxemburg): 1
franc*
**19** Olanda: 2 ¹/₂ fiorini *m pl;* 1 fiorino
= 100 cents *pl*
- *Netherlands: 2 ¹/₂ guilders; 1
guilder (florin, gulden) = 100 cents*
**20** Italia: 200 lire *f pl* (*sing.*: lira)
- *Italy: 200 lire (sg. lira)*
**21** Città del Vaticano: 100 lire *f pl*
(*sing.*: lira)
- *Vatican City: 100 lire (sg. lira)*
**22** Spagna: peseta = 100 centesimi *m pl*
- *Spain: 1 peseta = 100 céntimos*
**23** Portogallo: 1 scudo = 100 centesimi *m pl*
- *Portugal: 1 escudo = 100 centavos*
**24** Danimarca: 1 corona = 100 ore *pl*
- *Denmark: 1 krone = 100 øre*
**25** Svezia: 1 corona = 100 ore *pl*
- *Sweden: 1 krona = 100 öre*
**26** Norvegia: 1 corona = 100 ore *pl*
- *Norway: 1 krone = 100 öre*
**27** Repubblica Cecoslovacca: 1 corona = 100 halèru *pl*
- *Czechoslovakia: 1 koruna = 100
heller*
**28** Jugoslavia: 1 dinaro = 100 para *pl*
- *Yugoslavia: 1 dinar = 100 paras*
**29** Regno Unito di Gran Bretagna e
Irlanda del Nord: 1 sterlina = 100
new pence *m pl;* (*sing.*: new
penny)
- *United Kingdom of Great Britain
and Northern Ireland: 1 pound
sterling (£1) = 100 new pence (100
p)* (sg. *new penny, new p*)
**30-39 banconote** *f pl* (cartamoneta,
biglietti *m pl* di banca, tagli *m pl*)
- *banknotes* (Am. *bills) (paper
money, notes, treasury notes)*
**30** Repubblica Federale Tedesca:
100 marchi *m pl*
- *Federal Republic of Germany: 100
DM*
**31** la banca d'emissione *f*
- *bank of issue (bank of circulation)*
**32** l'effige *f* in filigrana
- *watermark [a portrait]*
**33** l'indicazione *f* del valore
- *denomination*
**34** USA (Stati Uniti d'America): 1
dollaro ($) = 100 cents *m pl*
- *USA: 1 dollar ($1) = 100 cents*
**35** le firme in facsimile *m*
- *facsimile signatures*
**36** il contrassegno di Stato
- *impressed stamp*
**37** l'indicazione *f* della serie
- *serial number*

**38** Grecia: 1000 dramme *f pl* (dracme
*f pl*); 1 dracma *m* = 100 lepta *m pl*
(*sing.*: lepton)
- *Greece: 1,000 drachmas (drach-
mae); 1 drachma = 100 lepta* (sg.
*lepton)*
**39** l'effige *f* (il ritratto)
- *portrait*
**40-44 la coniatura delle monete**
- *striking of coins (coinage,
mintage)*
**40** *u.* **41** i controstampi per coniare (i
punzoni per coniare)
- *coining dies (minting dies)*
**40** lo stampo superiore
- *upper die*
**41** lo stampo inferiore
- *lower die*
**42** l'anello del conio (anello di centraggio)
- *collar*
**43** la piastrina del conio
- *coin disc (flan, planchet, blank)*
**44** il tavolo per coniare
- *coining press (minting press)*

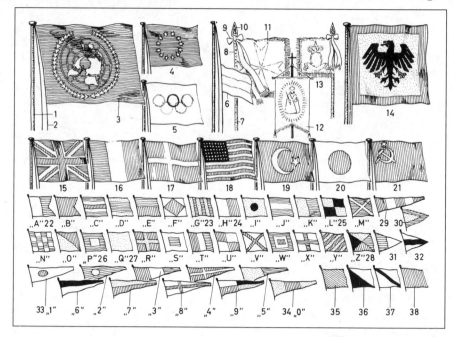

1-3 la bandiera delle Nazioni Unite
– *flag of the United Nations*
1 l'asta della bandiera con il pomo dell'asta
– *flagpole (flagstaff) with truck*
2 la sagola (funicella) della bandiera
– *halyard (halliard, haulyard)*
3 il drappo, la stamigna (la stamina)
– *hunting*
4 la bandiera del Consiglio di Europa (la bandiera europea)
– *flag of the Council of Europe*
5 la bandiera olimpica
– *Olympic flag*
6 la bandiera a mezz'asta (in segno di lutto)
– *flag at half-mast (Am. at half-staff) [as a token of mourning]*
7-11 la bandiera (il gonfalone, lo stendardo, il vessillo)
– *flag*
7 l'asta della bandiera (il pennone)
– *flagpole (flagstaff)*
8 la borchia
– *ornamental stud*
9 il nastro della bandiera
– *streamer*
10 la punta della bandiera
– *pointed tip of the flagpole*
11 il drappo (la stamigna, la stamina)
– *hunting*
12 il gonfalone (lo stendardo, il vessillo, il labaro, la bandiera)
– *banner (gonfalon)*
13 lo stendardo (il vessillo, l'insegna) della cavalleria
– *cavalry standard (flag of the cavalry)*
14 lo stendardo del Presidente della Repubblica Federale Tedesca (l'emblema *m* di un Capo di Stato)
– *standard of the German Federal President [ensign of head of state]*

15-21 bandiere *f pl* nazionali
– *national flags*
15 l'Union Jack *m* (Gran Bretagna)
– *the Union Jack (Great Britain)*
16 il Tricolore (Francia)
– *the Tricolour (Am. Tricolor) (France)*
17 il Danebrog (Danimarca)
– *the Danebrog (Dannebrog) (Denmark)*
18 la bandiera Stelle *f pl* e Strisce *f pl* (Stati Uniti d'America)
– *the Stars and Stripes (Star-Spangled Banner) (USA)*
19 la Mezzaluna (Turchia)
– *the Crescent (Turkey)*
20 il Sol Levante (Giappone)
– *the Rising Sun (Japan)*
21 la bandiera Falce *f* e Martello (URSS)
– *the Hammer and Sickle (USSR)*
22-28 bandierine *f pl* a numerazione *f* alfabetica
– *letter flags*
22-34 bandierine *f pl* di segnalazione *f*, una serie di bandierine *f pl*
– *signal flags, a hoist*
22 lettera A, un gagliardetto
– *letter A, a burgee (swallow-tailed flag)*
23 lettera G, il segnale di chiamata del pilota
– *G, pilot flag*
24 lettera H («pilota *m* a bordo»)
– *H ('pilot on board')*
25 lettera L («stop *m*, comunicazione *f* importante»)
– *L ('you should stop, I have something important to communicate')*
26 lettera P, il segnale di partenza
– *P, the Blue Peter ('about to set sail')*
27 lettera W, il segnale sanitario
– *W ('I require medical assistance')*
28 lettera Z, un gagliardetto rettangolare
– *Z, an oblong pennant (oblong pendant)*

29 il gagliardetto del Codice dei Segnali, un gagliardetto del Codice Internazionale dei Segnali
– *code pennant (code pendant), used in the International Signals Code*
30-32 gagliardetti *m pl* di richiesta di aiuto, gagliardetti *m pl* triangolari
– *substitute flags (repeaters), triangular flags (pennants, pendants)*
33 *u.* 34 segnali *m pl* numerici
– *numeral pennants (numeral pendants)*
33 il numero 1
– *number 1*
34 il numero 0
– *number 0*
35-38 bandierine *f pl* doganali
– *customs flags*
35 la bandierina (il gagliardetto) delle imbarcazioni doganali
– *customs boat pennant (customs boat pendant)*
36 «la nave ha passato la dogana»
– *'ship cleared through customs'*
37 il segnale di chiamata dei doganieri
– *customs signal flag*
38 il segnale di carico esplosivo («carico infiammabile»)
– *powder flag ['inflammable (flammable) cargo']*

**1-36** araldica (scienza degli stemmi gentilizi)
- *heraldry (blazonry)*
**1, 11, 30-36** cimiero *m*
- *crests*
**1-6** lo stemma
- *coat-of-arms (achievement of arms, hatchment, achievement)*
**1** il cimiero
- *crest*
**2** la goletta (il cercine)
- *wreath of the colours (Am. colors)*
**3** il mantello (i lambrecchini)
- *mantle (mantling)*
**4, 7-9** elmi *m pl*
- *helmets (helms)*
**4** l'elmo
- *tilting helmet (jousting helmet)*
**5** lo scudo
- *shield*
**6** la banda diagonale
- *bend sinister wavy*
**7** l'elmo chiuso
- *pot-helmet (pot-helm, heaume)*
**8** l'elmo con sbarre *f pl*
- *barred helmet (grilled helmet)*
**9** l'elmo aperto
- *helmet affronty with visor open*
**10-13** lo stemma coniugale (stemma *m* di alleanza, stemma *m* combinato dei coniugi)
- *marital achievement (marshalled, Am. marshaled, coat-of-arms)*
**10** lo stemma dell'uomo
- *arms of the baron (of the husband)*
**11-13** lo stemma della donna
- *arms of the family of the femme (of the wife)*
**11** il busto
- *demi-man; also: demi-woman*
**12** la corona di fogliame *m* (corona dell'elmo)
- *crest coronet*

**13** il giglio
- *fleur-de-lis*
**14** il padiglione araldico (il manto araldico, il drappo araldico)
- *heraldic tent (mantling)*
**15** *u.* **16** i tenenti (i supporti), animali *m pl* araldici
- *supporters (heraldic beasts)*
**15** il toro
- *bull*
**16** l'unicorno
- *unicorn*
**17-23** la descrizione dello stemma (del blasone, ordine dei campi dello stemma)
- *blazon*
**17** il cuore
- *inescutcheon (heart-shield)*
**18** *u.* **19** testa
- *chief*
**18, 20, 22** destra
- *dexter (right)*
**18-23** campi *m pl* 1–6 (campi *m pl* dello stemma; *qui:* campo dello stemma)
- *quarterings one to six*
**19, 21, 23** sinistra
- *sinister (left)*
**22** *u.* **23** base *f*
- *base*
**24-29** i colori
- *tinctures*
**24** *u.* **25** metalli *m pl*
- *metals*
**24** oro
- *or (gold) [yellow]*
**25** argento
- *argent (silver) [white]*
**26** nero
- *sable*
**27** rosso
- *gules*
**28** azzurro
- *azure*
**29** verde
- *vert*

**30** le piume di struzzo
- *ostrich feathers (treble plume)*
**31** il bastone araldico (per le elezioni)
- *truncheon*
**32** la mezza capra
- *demi-goat*
**33** i pennoncini (le banderuole) da torneo
- *tournament pennons*
**34** le corna di bufalo
- *buffalo horns*
**35** l'arpia
- *harpy*
**36** le piume di pavone *m*
- *plume of peacock's feathers*
**37, 38, 42-46** corone *f pl*
- *crowns and coronets [continental type]*
**37** la tiara
- *tiara (papal tiara)*
**38** la corona imperiale (ted. fino al 1806)
- *Imperial Crown [German, until 1806]*
**39** la corona ducale
- *ducal coronet (duke's coronet)*
**40** la corona principesca
- *prince's coronet*
**41** il copricapo del principe elettore (berretto elettorale)
- *elector's coronet*
**42** la corona reale inglese
- *English Royal Crown*
**43-45** corone *f pl* nobiliari
- *coronets of rank*
**43** la corona nobiliare
- *baronet's coronet*
**44** la corona di barone *m* (corona baronale)
- *baron's coronet (baronial coronet)*
**45** la corona di conte *m* (corona comitale)
- *count's coronet*
**46** la corona murale di uno stemma cittadino (corona di città)
- *mauerkrone (mural crown) of a city crest*

**1-96** l'armamento dell'esercito
– *army armament (army weaponry)*
**1-28** armi *f pl* individuali (armi *f pl* portatili)
– *hand weapons*
**1** la pistola P1
– *P 1 pistol*
**2** la canna
– *barrel*
**3** il mirino
– *front sight (foresight)*
**4** il cane (la leva di percussione *f* )
– *hammer*
**5** il grilletto
– *trigger*
**6** l'impugnatura
– *pistol grip*
**7** il caricatore
– *magazine holder*
**8** il mitra (il fucile mitragliatore MP2)
– *MP 2 submachine gun*
**9** il calcio
– *shoulder rest (butt)*
**10** la scatola di culatta
– *casing (mechanism casing)*
**11** la ghiera fissaggio canna
– *barrel clamp (barrel-clamping nut)*
**12** il nottolino dell'otturatore
– *cocking lever (cocking handle)*
**13** il paramano
– *palm rest*
**14** la sicura d'impugnatura
– *safety catch*
**15** il caricatore
– *magazine*
**16** il fucile G3–A3
– *G3-A3 self-loading rifle*
**17** il rompifiamma
– *flash hider (flash eliminator)*
**18** il dispositivo di scatto
– *trigger mechanism*
**19** la tacca di mira
– *notch (sighting notch, rear sight)*
**20** il mirino protetto
– *front sight block (foresight block) with front sight (foresight)*
**21** il calcio del fucile
– *rifle butt (butt)*
**22** il lanciarazzi leggero (il lanciarazzi anticarro 44 2A1)
– *44 2A1 light anti-tank rocket launcher*
**23** la granata
– *rocket (projectile)*
**24** il cannocchiale di puntamento
– *telescopic sight (telescope sight)*
**25** il proteggiguancia
– *cheek rest*
**26** la mitragliatrice MG 3
– *MG3 machine gun (Spandau)*
**27** il rinforzatore di rinculo
– *recoil booster*
**28** la leva sbloccaggio canna
– *belt-changing flap*
**29-61** armi *f pl* di artiglieria su affusti *m pl* semoventi
– *artillery weapons mounted on self-propelled gun carriages*
**29** l'obice *m* SF M 110 A2
– *SFM 110 A2 self-propelled howitzer*
**30-32** le sospensioni
– *gun carriage*
**30** la ruota motrice
– *drive wheel*
**31** il cingolo
– *track*
**32** la ruota portante
– *road wheel*
**33** lo scafo
– *hull*

**34** lo sperone a vomere *m*
– *spade*
**35** il cilindro del vomere
– *spade piston*
**36** l'impianto idraulico
– *hydraulic system*
**37** il pistone di rilevamento
– *elevating piston*
**38** la parte fissa
– *breech ring*
**39** la canna
– *barrel*
**40** il freno di bocca (il freno di rinculo alla volata)
– *muzzle*
**41** il freno idraulico a tubo
– *buffer (buffer recuperator)*
**42** l'obice *m* corazzato M 109 A3 G
– *M 109 A3 G self-propelled howitzer*
**43** la torretta blindata
– *armoured (Am. armored) turret*
**44** la cabina di combattimento
– *fighting compartment*
**45** il puntello della canna
– *barrel clamp*
**46** l'evacuatore *m* del fumo
– *fume extractor*
**47** il recuperatore di rinculo
– *barrel recuperator*
**48** la mitragliatrice per difesa contraerea (Fla-MG)
– *light anti-aircraft (AA) machine gun*
**49** il semovente di lancio per razzi *m pl* (il lanciarazzi) SF Lance
– *SF Lance missile launch system (missile launcher)*
**50** lo schermo di protezione *f* cingolo
– *skirt*
**51** il veicolo cingolato
– *tracked vehicle*
**52** il razzo mobile
– *missile (guided missile)*
**53** il meccanismo di alzo (di puntamento)
– *elevating gear*
**54** la rampa di lancio
– *launching ramp*
**55** il lanciarazzi 110 SF 2
– *110 SF 2 rocket launcher*
**56** la centrale di puntamento
– *fire control system*
**57** il contenitore razzi *m pl*
– *launching tubes*
**58** la blindatura del contenitore
– *tube bins*
**59** l'affusto orientabile
– *turntable*
**60** il sostegno idraulico del veicolo
– *jack*
**61** la cabina di guida
– *driver's cab*
**62-87** carri *m pl* armati
– *armoured (Am. armored) vehicles*
**62** il carro armato da combattimento Leopard 2
– *Leopard 2 tank*
**63** il cannone a anima liscia
– *smooth-barrelled gun*
**64** la feritoia del carrista
– *driver's hatch*
**65** il periscopio del comandante
– *commander's periscope*
**66** il mortaio lanciafumogeni
– *smoke canister (smoke dispenser)*
**67** il carro armato da ricognizione *f* Luchs, un anfibio
– *Luchs armoured (Am. armored) reconnaissance vehicle, an amphibious vehicle*

**68** il cannone automatico di bordo
– *cannon*
**69** il portello stagno
– *hatch*
**70** l'antenna
– *antenna*
**71** l'elica di propulsione *f* (per spostamenti *m pl* in acqua)
– *propeller (for propulsion in water)*
**72** il carro armato leggero Jaguar 1 (HOT)
– *Jagdpanzer Jaguar 1 ATGW vehicle (HOT)*
**73** la cabina di guida con apparecchiature *f pl* di puntamento (parte *f* superiore)
– *guidance system (upper part) with guidance unit*
**74** il contenitore di lancio per razzi *m pl* guidati (HOT)
– *HOT guided-missile launcher*
**75** l'apparecchiatura di sparo (parte *f* superiore)
– *firing mechanism (upper part)*
**76** la cupola del capopezzo
– *commander's cupola*
**77** il carro armato da tiro Marder
– *Marder armoured (Am. armored) personnel carrier*
**78** il faro
– *searchlight*
**79** il gruppo di missili *m pl* anticarro Milan
– *MILAN anti-tank guided-missile system*
**80** il carro armato da trasporto Fuchs, un anfibio
– *Fuchs armoured (Am. armored) personnel and load carrier, an amphibious vehicle*
**81** la porta posteriore
– *rear door*
**82** il carro armato antiaereo (Flak-Panzer) Gepard
– *Gepard anti-aircraft tank*
**83** il ricercatore radar
– *surveillance radar*
**84** il radar di puntamento
– *tracking radar for fire control*
**85** il cannone a canne *f pl* binate
– *twin 35 mm cannon*
**86** il carro trasporto truppe *f pl* (MTW) M 113 A1 G
– *M113 A1 G armoured (Am. armored) personnel carrier*
**87** la mitragliatrice (MG) su affusto orientabile
– *machine gun on a traversing mount*
**88-96** elicotteri *m pl*
– *helicopters*
**88** l'elicottero da trasporto CH-53 G
– *CH-53 G transport helicopter*
**89** il rotore principale
– *single rotor*
**90** la turbina
– *turbine*
**91** il rotore di coda
– *stabilizing tail rotor*
**92** la fusoliera
– *fuselage*
**93** la cabina di pilotaggio
– *cockpit*
**94** l'elicottero anticarro BO-105P
– *BO-105P anti-tank helicopter*
**95** il pattino di atterraggio
– *skid*
**96** il contenitore razzo guidato anticarro HOT
– *HOT anti-tank guided-missile launcher*

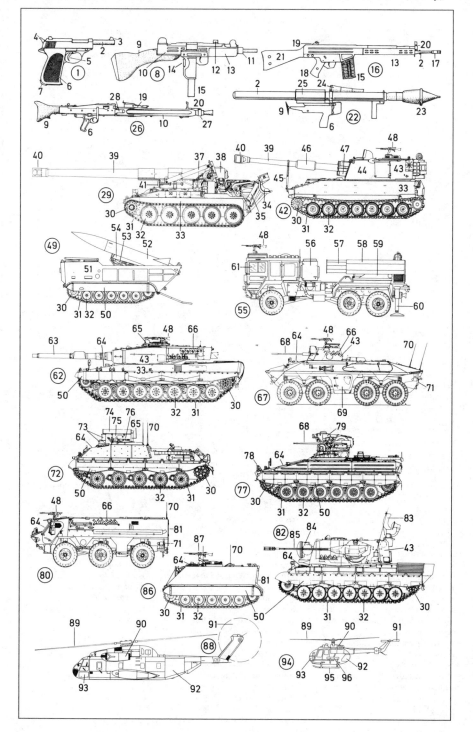

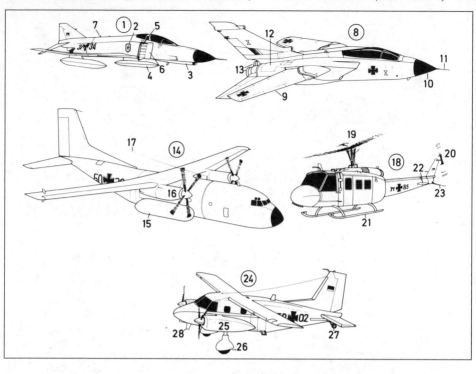

1 **l'aereo da caccia e cacciabom-
bardiere** *m* (McDonnel-Douglas
F-4F Phantom II)
– McDonnell-Douglas F-4F
Phantom II *interceptor and fight-
er-bomber*
2 il simbolo dello stormo
– *squadron marking*
3 il cannone di bordo
– *aircraft cannon*
4 il serbatoio alare (il serbatoio
sotto l'ala)
– *wing tank (underwing tank)*
5 la presa di aria
– *air intake*
6 la linea di confine *m* dello strato
limite
– *boundary layer control flap*
7 il bocchettone di rifornimento in
volo
– *in-flight refuelling* (Am. *refueling*)
*probe (flight refuelling probe, air
refuelling probe)*
8 **l'aereo da combattimento multi-
ruolo** (MRCA, Multirolo Combat
Aircraft) Panavia 200 Tornado
– Panavia 2000 Tornado *multirole
combat aircraft (MRCA)*
9 l'ala a geometria variabile
– *swing wing*
10 il radom (il radome)
– *radar nose (radome, radar dome)*

11 il tubo pressostatico (il tubo di
Pitot)
– *pitot-static tube (pitot tube)*
12 l'aerofreno (il freno aerodinamico)
– *brake flap (air brake)*
13 l'effusore *m* del postbruciatore
– *afterburner exhaust nozzles of the
engines*
14 **l'aereo da trasporto a medio raggio** C 160 Transall
– C160 Transall *medium-range
transport aircraft*
15 la gondola del carrello
– *undercarriage housing (landing
gear housing)*
16 il gruppo propulsore turboelica
– *propeller-turbine engine (turboprop engine)*
17 l'antenna
– *antenna*
18 **l'elicottero leggero da trasporto e
di salvataggio** Bell UH-1D
Iroquois
– Bell UH-1D Iroquois *light transport and rescue helicopter*
19 il rotore principale
– *main rotor*
20 il rotore di coda (l'elica)
– *tail rotor*
21 i pattini di atterragio
– *landing skids*

22 le pinne di stabilizzazione *f*
– *stabilizing fins (stabilizing surfaces, stabilizers)*
23 il pattino di coda
– *tail skid*
24 **l'aereo STOL da trasporto e da
collegamento** Dornier DO 28 D-2
Sky-servant
– Dornier DO 28 D-2 Skyservant
*transport and communications
aircraft*
25 la gondola del motore
– *engine pod*
26 il carrello principale
– *main undercarriage unit (main
landing gear unit)*
27 il ruotino di coda
– *tail wheel*
28 l'antenna a spada
– *sword antenna*

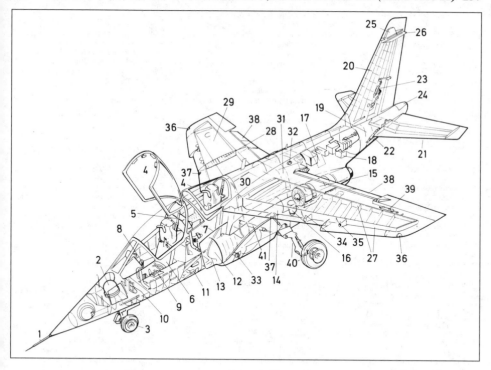

1-41 il turbogetto di addestramento franco tedesco Dornier-Dassault-Breguet
Alpha Jet
– Dornier-Dassault-Breguet Alpha Jet
*Franco-German jet trainer*
1 il tubo pressostatico
– *pitot-static tube (pitot tube)*
2 il serbatoio di ossigeno
– *oxygen tank*
3 la ruota anteriore retrattile
– *forward-retracting nose wheel*
4 la capote
– *cockpit canopy (cockpit hood)*
5 il cilindro azionamento capote *f*
– *canopy jack*
6 il sedile (il sedile dell'allievo pilota *m*)
un sedile eiettabile (un sedile a espulsione *f*)
– *pilot's seat (student pilot's seat), an ejector seat (ejection seat)*
7 il sedile dell'osservatore *m* (il sedile
dell'istruttore *m*), un sedile eiettabile
– *observer's seat (instructor's seat), an
ejector seat (ejection seat)*
8 la cloche (la barra di comando)
– *control column (control stick)*
9 la leva comando motore *m*
– *thrust lever*
10 la pedaliera con freni *m pl*
– *rudder pedals with brakes*
11 il vano avionica frontale
– *front avionics bay*
12 la presa di aria della turbina
– *air intake to the engine*
13 la linea di divisione *f* dello strato limite
– *boundary layer control flap*
14 il condotto ingresso aria
– *air intake duct*

15 il propulsore a turbine *f pl*
– *turbine engine*
16 il serbatoio idraulico
– *reservoir for the hydraulic system*
17 il vano batterie *f pl*
– *battery housing*
18 il vano avionica di coda
– *rear avionics bay*
19 il bagagliaio
– *baggage compartment*
20 l'impennaggio verticale a tre
longheroni *m pl*
– *triple-spar tail construction*
21 l'impennaggio orizzontale
– *horizontal tail*
22 il servocomando impennaggio orizzontale
– *servo-actuating mechanism for the elevator*
23 il servocomando impennaggio verticale (il
servocomando timone *m* di direzione *f*)
– *servo-actuating mechanism for the rudder*
24 il vano freno aerodinamico di atterraggio
– *brake chute housing (drag chute housing)*
25 l'antenna VHF (l'antenna UKW)
(VHF = Very high frequency)
– *VHF (very high frequency) antenna
(UHF antenna)*
26 l'antenna VOR (VOR = Very high frequency omnidirectional range)
– *VOR (very high frequency omnidirectional range) antenna*
27 la semiala a due longheroni *m pl*
– *twin-spar wing construction*
28 il rivestimento integrato
– *former with integral spars*

29 i serbatoi integrali
– *integral wing tanks*
30 il serbatoio centrale della fusoliera
– *centre-section (Am. center-section) fuel
tank*
31 i serbatoi della fusoliera
– *fuselage tanks*
32 il bocchettone di riempimento a gravità
– *gravity fuelling (Am. fueling) point*
33 il raccordo rifornimento a pressione *f*
– *pressure fuelling (Am. fueling) point*
34 la sospensione interna all'ala
– *inner wing suspension*
35 la sospensione esterna all'ala
– *outer wing suspension*
36 le luci di posizione *f*
– *navigation lights (position lights)*
37 i fanali di atterraggio
– *landing lights*
38 l'ipersostentatore *m* di atterraggio
– *landing flap*
39 il servocomando alettoni *m pl·*
– *aileron actuator*
40 il carrello principale retrattile anteriore
– *forward-retracting main undercarriage
unit (main landing gear unit)*
41 il cilindro azionamento carrello
– *undercarriage hydraulic cylinder (landing gear hydraulic cylinder)*

1 **il cacciatorpediniere** classe *f* «Hamburg»
– *Hamburg* class **guided-missile destroyer**
2 lo scafo a coperta rasa
– *hull of flush-deck vessel*
3 la prua (la prora)
– *bow (stem)*
4 l'asta della bandiera
– *flagstaff (jackstaff)*
5 l'ancora, un'ancora brevettata
– *anchor, a stockless anchor (patent anchor)*
6 l'argano dell'ancora
– *anchor capstan (windlass)*
7 il paraonde
– *breakwater (Am. manger board)*
8 il fondo angolare
– *chine strake*
9 il ponte di coperta (la coperta)
– *main deck*
10-28 la sovrastruttura
– *superstructures*
10 la controcoperta
– *superstructure deck*
11 i mezzi di salvataggio
– *life rafts*
12 l'imbarcazione *f* di servizio (il cutter)
– *cutter (ship's boat)*
13 la gru (la gru di ammarraggio)
– *davit (boat-launching crane)*
14 il ponte (il ponte di comando)
– *bridge (bridge superstructure)*
15 il fanale di posizione *f* laterale
– *side navigation light (side running light)*
16 l'antenna
– *antenna*
17 l'antenna radiogoniometro
– *radio direction finder (RDF) frame*
18 l'albero a traliccio
– *lattice mast*
19 il fumaiolo di prua
– *forward funnel*
20 il fumaiolo di poppa
– *aft funnel*
21 la parte superiore del fumaiolo
– *cowl*
22 il cassero (la sovrastruttura di poppa)
– *aft superstructure (poop)*
23 l'argano
– *capstan*
24 la scaletta del boccaporto (il boccaporto)
– *companion ladder (companionway, companion hatch)*
25 l'asta della bandiera di poppa
– *ensign staff*
26 la poppa, una poppa quadra
– *stern, a transom stern*
27 la linea di galleggiamento
– *waterline*
28 il fanale
– *searchlight*
29-37 l'armamento
– *armament*
29 la torre di artiglieria 100 mm
– *100 mm gun turret*
30 il lanciamissili antisommergibili
– *four-barrel anti-submarine rocket launcher (missile launcher)*
31 il cannone contraereo binato da 40 mm
– *40 mm twin anti-aircraft (AA) gun*
32 il lanciatore singolo per missili *m pl* MM 38, nel contenitore *m* di lancio
– *MM 38 anti-aircraft (AA) rocket launcher (missile launcher) in launching container*
33 il lanciasiluri
– *anti-submarine torpedo tube*

34 la rampa di lancio per bombe *f pl* di profondità
– *depth-charge thrower*
35 il radar guidamissili
– *weapon system radar*
36 l'antenna radar
– *radar antenna (radar scanner)*
37 il misuratore ottico di distanza
– *optical rangefinder*
38 **il cacciatorpediniere** della classe *f* «Lutjens»
– *Lütjens* class **guided-missile destroyer**
39 l'ancora di prua
– *bower anchor*
40 il paraelica
– *propeller guard*
41 l'albero prodiero a tripode *m*
– *tripod lattice mast*
42 l'albero principale
– *pole mast*
43 le prese di aria
– *ventilator openings (ventilator grill)*
44 il tubo di scarico gas combusti
– *exhaust pipe*
45 la pinaccia
– *ship's boat*
46 l'antenna
– *antenna*
47 il cannone teleguidato da 127 mm nella torre *f* di artiglieria
– *radar-controlled 127 mm all-purpose gun in turret*
48 il cannone da 127 mm
– *127 mm all-purpose gun*
49 il lanciamissili per missili *m pl* Tartar
– *launcher for Tartar missiles*
50 il lanciamissili antisommergibili Asroc
– *anti-submarine rocket (ASROC) launcher (missile launcher)*
51 le antenne radar controllo tiro
– *fire control radar antennas*
52 il radom (il radome)
– *radome (radar dome)*
53 la fregata classe *f* «Bremen»
– *Bremen* class **frigate**
54 il cannone da 76 mm, a tiro rapido teleguidato
– *radar-controlled 76 mm rapid-fire gun*
55 i lanciatori per missili *m pl* navali superficie *f* – aria «Sea Sparrow»
– *Sea Sparrow surface-to-air missiles*
56 il sistema di controllo radar del tiro
– *radar and fire control system*
57 i missili antinave «Harpoon»
– *Harpoon surface-to-surface missiles*
58 il fumaiolo
– *funnel*
59 la parte superiore del fumaiolo
– *cowl*
60 il locale radar poppiero
– *air/surface search radar*
61 l'imbarcazione *f* di servizio (il cutter)
– *cutter*
62 i missili navali superficie *f* – aria a corto raggio
– *close-range surface-to-air missiles*
63 il ponte di volo elicotteri *m pl*
– *helicopter deck*
64 **il sottomarino** (il sommergibile) della classe 206
– *type 206* **submarine**
65 la struttura di prua rialzata
– *flooded foredeck*
66 lo scafo esterno non resistente alla pressione dell'acqua
– *pressure hull*

67 la torretta
– *turret*
68 le apparecchiature di sollevamento
– *retractable instruments*
69 **la vedetta portamissili** della classe 148
– *type 148* **missile-firing fast attack craft**
70 il cannone da 76 mm con torre *f* di artiglieria
– *76 mm all-purpose gun with turret*
71 il container per i lanciamissili
– *missile-launching housing*
72 la tuga
– *deckhouse*
73 il cannone Fla da 40 mm
– *40 mm anti-aircraft (AA) gun*
74 il paraelica
– *propeller guard moulding (Am. molding)*
75 **la vedetta portamissili** della classe 143
– *type 143* **missile-firing fast attack craft**
76 il paraonde
– *breakwater (Am. manger board)*
77 il radom (il radome)
– *radome (radar dome)*
78 il lanciasiluri
– *torpedo tube*
79 la bocca di scarico per gas *m pl* combusti
– *exhaust escape flue*
80 **il dragamine (il cacciamine)** della classe 331
– *type 331* **mine hunter**
81 il parabordo con rinforzo
– *reinforced rubbing strake*
82 il mezzo di salvataggio
– *inflatable boat (inflatable dinghy)*
83 la gru manovra battellini *m pl* di salvataggio
– *davit*
84 **il dragamine (il cacciamine)** veloce della classe 341
– *type 341* **minesweeper**
85 il verricello del tamburo per cavi *m pl*
– *cable winch*
86 il verricello da traino
– *towing winch (towing machine, towing engine)*
87 il veicolo subacqueo neutralizzazione *f* mine *f pl*
– *mine-sweeping gear (paravanes)*
88 la gru
– *crane (davit)*
89 **il mezzo da sbarco** della classe «Barbe»
– *Barbe* class **landing craft**
90 la rampa di prua
– *bow ramp*
91 la rampa di poppa
– *stern ramp*
92 **il tender** (la nave di appoggio) della classe «Rhein»
– *Rhein* class **tender**
93 **l'unità di sostegno logistico** della classe «Luneburg»
– *Lüneburg* class **support ship**
94 **l'unità navale posamine** della classe «Sachsenwald»
– *Sachsenwald* class **mine transport**
95 **il rimorchiatore di alto mare** *m* della classe «Helgoland»
– *Helgoland* class **salvage tug**
96 **la nave cisterna** «Eifel»
– *replenishment tanker* 'Eifel'

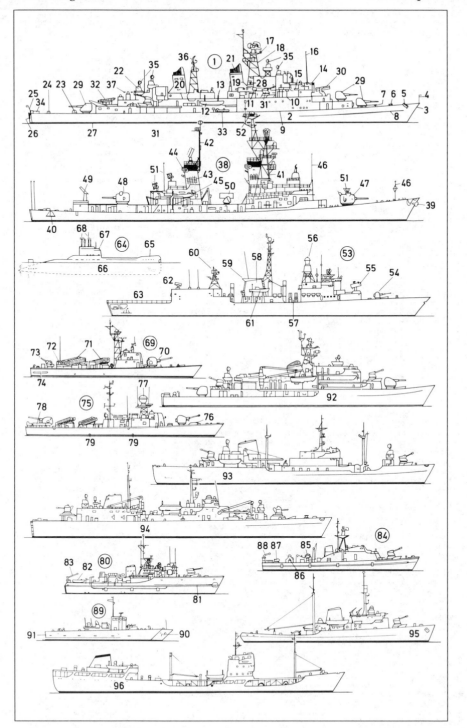

# 259 Navi da guerra II (navi da guerra moderne)

**1** la portaerei a propulsione *f* nucleare «Nimitz ICVN 68» (USA)
- *nuclear-powered aircraft carrier* Nimitz ICVN68 *(USA)*

**2-11** la sezione
- *body plan*

**2** il ponte di volo
- *flight deck*

**3** l'isola (il ponte di comando)
- *island (bridge)*

**4** l'elevatore *m* per i velivoli
- *aircraft lift (Am. aircraft elevator)*

**5** il lanciatore ottuplo per missili *m pl*
- *eight-barrel anti-aircraft (AA) rocket launcher (missile launcher)*

**6** l'albero principale (porta antenna)
- *pole mast (antenna mast)*

**7** l'antenna
- *antenna*

**8** l'antenna radar
- *radar antenna (radar scanner)*

**9** la prua Uragano chiusa
- *fully enclosed bow*

**10** la gru di bordo
- *deck crane*

**11** la poppa quadra
- *transom stern*

**12-20** la planimetria della coperta
- *deck plan*

**12** il ponte angolato (il ponte di volo)
- *angle deck (flight deck)*

**13** l'elevatore *m* per i velivoli
- *aircraft lift (Am. aircraft elevator)*

**14** la catapulta binata
- *twin launching catapult*

**15** la paratia antifiamma ripiegabile
- *hinged (movable) baffle board*

**16** il cavo di arresto
- *arrester wire*

**17** la barriera (la rete di arresto)
- *emergency crash barrier*

**18** il corridoio di lancio
- *safety net*

**19** la piattaforma di armamento
- *caisson (cofferdam)*

**20** il lanciatore ottuplo per missili *m pl*
- *eight-barrel anti-aircraft (AA) rocket launcher (missile launcher)*

**21** l'incrociatore *m* **lanciamissili** della classe «Kara» (URSS)
- *Kara class **rocket cruiser** (missile cruiser) (USSR)*

**22** lo scafo a coperta rasa
- *hull of flush-deck vessel*

**23** l'insellatura
- *sheer*

**24** il lanciarazzi antisommergibili a dodici canne *f pl*
- *twelve-barrel underwater salvo rocket launcher (missile launcher)*

**25** il lanciamissili antiaereo binato
- *twin anti-aircraft (AA) rocket launcher (missile launcher)*

**26** la rampa per quattro missili *m pl* a corto raggio
- *launching housing for 4 short-range rockets (missiles)*

**27** la paratia antifiamma
- *baffle board*

**28** il ponte
- *bridge*

**29** l'antenna radar
- *radar antenna (radar scanner)*

**30** la torre binata Fla da 76 mm
- *twin 76 mm anti-aircraft (AA) gun turret*

**31** il torrione
- *turret*

**32** il fumaiolo
- *funnel*

**33** il lanciamissili binato Fla
- *twin anti-aircraft (AA) rocket launcher (missile launcher)*

**34** la mitragliera Fla
- *automatic anti-aircraft (AA) gun*

**35** l'imbarcazione *f* di servizio
- *ship's boat*

**36** la serie dei lanciasiluri quintupli
- *underwater 5-torpedo housing*

**37** il lanciarazzi antisommergibili a sei canne *f pl*
- *underwater 6-salvo rocket launcher (missile launcher)*

**38** l'hangar *m* per elicotteri *m pl*
- *helicopter hangar*

**39** la piattaforma per elicotteri *m pl*
- *helicopter landing platform*

**40** l'apparecchio Sonar a immersione *f* variabile (VDS)
- *variable depth sonar (VDS)*

**41** l'**incrociatore** *m* **a propulsione** *f* **atomica** della classe «California» (USA)
- *California class **rocket cruiser** (missile cruiser) (USA)*

**42** lo scafo
- *hull*

**43** il torrione prodiero
- *forward turret*

**44** il torrione poppiero
- *aft turret*

**45** la riservetta per missili *m pl*
- *forward superstructure*

**46** le lance di salvataggio
- *landing craft*

**47** l'antenna
- *antenna*

**48** l'antenna radar
- *radar antenna (radar scanner)*

**49** il radom (il radome)
- *radome (radar dome)*

**50** la rampa per missili *m pl* Harpoon
- *surface-to-air rocket launcher (missile launcher)*

**51** il lanciamissili antisommergibili
- *underwater rocket launcher (missile launcher)*

**52** il cannone automatico leggero da 127 mm con torre *f* di artiglieria
- *127 mm gun with turret*

**53** la piattaforma per elicotteri *m pl*
- *helicopter landing platform*

**54** il **sottomarino di attacco a propulsione** *f* **nucleare**
- *nuclear-powered fleet submarine*

**55-74** la sezione mediana
- *middle section [diagram]*

**55** lo scafo esterno non resistente alla pressione dell'acqua
- *pressure hull*

**56** il locale per macchinari *m pl* ausiliari
- *auxiliary engine room*

**57** la pompa centrifuga turbo
- *rotary turbine pump*

**58** il generatore della turbina a vapore *m*
- *steam turbine generator*

**59** l'albero portaelica
- *propeller shaft*

**60** il cuscinetto di spinta
- *thrust block*

**61** il riduttore
- *reduction gear*

**62** la turbina a alta e bassa pressione *f*
- *high and low pressure turbine*

**63** la conduttura del vapore a alta pressione *f* del circuito secondario
- *high-pressure steam pipe for the secondary water circuit (auxiliary water circuit)*

**64** il condensatore
- *condenser*

**65** il circuito primario
- *primary water circuit*

**66** lo scambiatore di calore *m*
- *heat exchanger*

**67** il rivestimento del reattore nucleare
- *nuclear reactor casing (atomic pile casing)*

**68** il nucleo del reattore
- *reactor core*

**69** le barre attive
- *control rods*

**70** lo schermo di piombo
- *lead screen*

**71** la torretta
- *turret*

**72** lo Snorkel
- *snorkel (schnorkel)*

**73** la presa di aria
- *air inlet*

**74** le apparecchiature di sollevamento
- *retractable instruments*

**75** il **sottomarino da pattugliamento** a propulsione *f* Diesel-elettrica
- ***patrol submarine** with conventional (diesel-electric) drive*

**76** lo scafo esterno non resistente alla pressione dell'acqua
- *pressure hull*

**77** la struttura di prua rialzata
- *flooded foredeck*

**78** il cappello dei tubi lanciasiluri
- *outer flap (outer doors) [for torpedoes]*

**79** il lanciasiluri
- *torpedo tube*

**80** il vano di sentina prodiero
- *bow bilge*

**81** l'ancora
- *anchor*

**82** il verricello
- *anchor winch*

**83** la batteria
- *battery*

**84** locali *m pl* con cuccette *f pl* ribaltabili
- *living quarters with folding bunks*

**85** l'alloggio del comandante
- *commanding officer's cabin*

**86** il boccaporto centrale
- *main hatchway*

**87** l'asta per la bandiera
- *flagstaff*

**88-91** le apparecchiature di sollevamento
- *retractable instruments*

**88** il periscopio (il periscopio di attacco)
- *attack periscope*

**89** l'antenna
- *antenna*

**90** lo Snorkel
- *snorkel (schnorkel)*

**91** l'antenna radar
- *radar antenna (radar scanner)*

**92** le feritoie di scarico dei gas
- *exhaust outlet*

**93** la serra
- *heat space (hot-pipe space)*

**94** il gruppo Diesel
- *diesel generators*

**95** il timone poppiero di profondità e direzione *f*
- *aft diving plane and vertical rudder*

**96** il timone prodiero di profondità
- *forward vertical rudder*

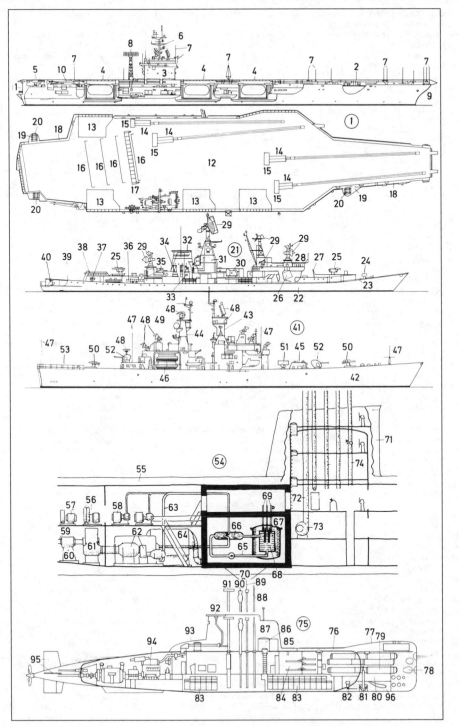

**1-85 la Scuola d'obbligo** (la Scuola Elementare e la Scuola Media)
– *primary and secondary school*
**1-45 l'aula**
– *classroom*
**1** la disposizione dei banchi a «u» (a ferro di cavallo)
– *arrangement of desks in a horse-shoe*
**2** i banchi uniti a due a due (non in uso)
– *double desk*
**3** gli scolari ordinati per gruppi *m pl*
– *pupils (children) in a group (sitting in a group)*
**4** il quaderno degli esercizi
– *exercise book*
**5** la matita (matita da disegno)
– *pencil*
**6** il pastello di cera
– *wax crayon*
**7** la cartella
– *school bag*
**8** il manico
– *handle*
**9** la cartella a zaino
– *school satchel (satchel)*
**10** la tasca della cartella
– *front pocket*
**11** la cinghia dello zaino
– *strap (shoulder strap)*
**12** l'astuccio (il portapenne)
– *pen and pencil case*
**13** la cerniera-lampo
– *zip* (Am. *zipper*)
**14** la penna stilografica
– *fountain pen (pen)*
**15** il quaderno a fogli *m pl* mobili
– *loose-leaf file (ring file)*
**16** il libro di lettura
– *reader*
**17** il dizionario di ortografia
– *spelling book*
**18** il quaderno a righe *f pl*
– *lined exercise book (notebook)*
**19** il pennarello
– *felt tip pen*
**20** l'alzata di mano
– *raising the hand*
**21** l'insegnante *m* (il maestro)
– *teacher*
**22** la cattedra
– *teacher's desk*
**23** il registro
– *register*
**24** la vaschetta portapenne
– *pen and pencil tray*
**25** il sottomano (da scrivania)
– *desk mat (blotter)*
**26** la pittura su vetro con colori da distendere con le dita *(non in uso)*
– *window painting with finger paints (finger painting)*
**27** gli acquerelli degli allievi
– *pupils' (children's) paintings (watercolours,* Am. *watercolors)*
**28** il crocifisso
– *cross*

**29** la lavagna a tre ante *f pl* (lavagna, lavagna a muro)
– *three-part blackboard*
**30** il sostegno per la carta geografica, per i cartelloni didattici
– *bracket for holding charts*
**31** la mensola per il gesso
– *chalk ledge*
**32** il gesso
– *chalk*
**33** il disegno sulla lavagna
– *blackboard drawing*
**34** lo schema (l'illustrazione *f* schematica)
– *diagram*
**35** l'anta laterale apribile della lavagna
– *reversible side blackboard*
**36** lo schermo (la parete) per le proiezioni
– *projection screen*
**37** la squadra
– *triangle*
**38** il gognometro
– *protractor*
**39** la scala dei gradi (i gradi)
– *divisions*
**40** il compasso da lavagna
– *blackboard compass*
**41** il portaspugna
– *sponge tray*
**42** la spugna (lo strofinaccio)
– *blackboard sponge (cloth)*
**43** l'armadio (l'armadietto)
– *classroom cupboard*
**44** la carta geografica
– *map (wall map)*
**45** la parete in pietra a vista
– *brick wall*
**46-85  il laboratorio per i lavori manuali**
– *craft room*
**46** il tavolo da lavoro
– *workbench*
**47** il morsetto
– *vice* (Am. *vise*)
**48** la maniglia del morsetto
– *vice* (Am. *vise*) *bar*
**49** le forbici
– *scissors*
**50-52** l'incollaggio (il lavoro d'incollaggio)
– *working with glue (sticking paper, cardboard, etc.)*
**50** la superficie da incollare
– *surface to be glued*
**51** il tubetto della colla *(fam.:* l'attaccatutto *m)*
– *tube of glue*
**52** il tappo del tubetto
– *tube cap*
**53** la seghetta
– *fretsaw*
**54** la lama della seghetta
– *fretsaw blade (saw blade)*
**55** la raspa
– *wood rasp (rasp)*

**56** il pezzo di legno stretto nella morsa
– *piece of wood held in the vice* (Am. *vise*)
**57** il barattolo della colla (per legno)
– *glue pot*
**58** lo sgabello
– *stool*
**59** la scopetta
– *brush*
**60** la paletta
– *pan (dustpan)*
**61** i trucioli
– *wood shaving*
**62** il lavoro a smalto
– *enamelling* (Am. *enameling)*
**63** il forno elettrico per smaltare
– *electric enamelling* (Am. *enameling) stove*
**64** il pezzo grezzo di rame *m*
– *unworked copper*
**65** lo smalto in polvere *f*
– *enamel powder*
**66** il colino
– *hair sieve*
**67-80  i lavori degli scolari**
– *pupils' (children's) work*
**67** i lavori in creta
– *clay models (models)*
**68** la decorazione in vetro colorato per finestre *f pl*
– *window decoration of coloured* (Am. *colored) glass*
**69** il quadro a mosaico di vetro
– *glass mosaic picture (glass mosaic)*
**70** l'aeternum mobile
– *mobile*
**71** l'aquilone *m*
– *paper kite (kite)*
**72** la costruzione di legno
– *wooden construction*
**73** il poliedro
– *polyhedron*
**74** le marionette
– *hand puppets*
**75** le maschere di creta
– *clay masks*
**76** le candele di cera
– *cast candles (wax candles)*
**77** i lavori d'incisione *f* su legno
– *wood carving*
**78** il vaso di creta
– *clay jug*
**79** le forme geometriche in creta
– *geometrical shapes made of clay*
**80** il giocattolo di legno
– *wooden toys*
**81** il materiale da lavoro
– *materials*
**82** le scorte di legno
– *stock of wood*
**83** i colori a stampo (per legno)
– *inks for wood cuts*
**84** i pennelli
– *paintbrushes*
**85** il sacco di farina di gesso
– *bag of plaster of Paris*

**1-45 il ginnasio (il liceo)** (*Germania:* scuola di 8/9 anni *m pl* di insegnamento; vi si accede dopo la 4. classe elementare e termina con la maturità classica/scientifica), *anche:* il ramo ginnasiale di una scuola collettiva
– **grammar school;** also: *upper band of a comprehensive school* (Am. *alternative school*)

**1-13 la lezione di chimica**
– *chemistry*

**1** l'aula di chimica con le file dei banchi degradanti, *anche:* aula a anfiteatro
– *chemistry lab (chemistry laboratory) with tiered rows of seats*

**2** l'insegnante *m* (il professore, *pop.:* prof) di chimica
– *chemistry teacher*

**3** il tavolo (il banco) degli esperimenti
– *demonstration bench (teacher's bench)*

**4** l'allacciamento dell'acqua
– *water pipe*

**5** il piano di lavoro piastrellato
– *tiled working surface*

**6** l'acquaio (la vasca di scarico)
– *sink*

**7** il monitor, un teleschermo per programmi *m pl* didattici
– *television monitor, a screen for educational programmes* (Am. *programs*)

**8** l'overhead, un proiettore
– *overhead projector*

**9** la superficie di appoggio per i fogli trasparenti (per i trasparenti)
– *projector top for transparencies*

**10** l'ottica di proiezione *f* con specchio angolare
– *projection lens with right-angle mirror*

**11** il banco (il tavolo) degli allievi attrezzato per esperimenti *m pl*
– *pupils' (Am. students') bench with experimental apparatus*

**12** l'allacciamento elettrico (la presa di corrente *f* )
– *electrical point (socket)*

**13** il tavolo di proiezione *f*
– *projection table*

**14-34 l'aula di biologia**
– **biology preparation room** (*biology prep room)*

**14** lo scheletro
– *skeleton*

**15** la serie dei crani, copie *f pl* (imitazioni *f pl*, calchi *m pl*) di crani *m pl*
– *collection of skulls, models (casts) of skulls*

**16** la calotta cranica del pitecantropo eretto
– *calvarium of Pithecanthropus erectus*

**17** il cranio dell'uomo dell'età della pietra
– *skull of Steinheim man*

**18** la calotta cranica del sinantropo
– *calvarium of Peking man (of Sinanthropus)*

**19** il cranio dell'uomo di Neandertal, un cranio dell'uomo primitivo
– *skull of Neanderthal man, a skull of primitive man*

**20** il cranio australopiteco
– *Australopithecine skull (skull of Australopithecus)*

**21** il cranio dell'uomo di oggi
– *skull of present-day man*

**22** il tavolo con gli oggetti di studio
– *dissecting bench*

**23** i flaconi di prodotti *m pl* chimici
– *chemical bottles*

**24** l'allacciamento del gas
– *gas tap*

**25** la vaschetta di Petri, un vaso per le culture batteriologiche
– *petri dish*

**26** il cilindro graduato
– *measuring cylinder*

**27** i fogli (il materiale didattico)
– *work folder containing teaching material*

**28** il libro di testo
– *textbook*

**29** le culture batteriologiche
– *bacteriological cultures*

**30** l'incubatrice *f*
– *incubator*

**31** l'essicatore delle provette
– *test tube rack*

**32** la boccia di lavaggio a gas
– *washing bottle*

**33** la vaschetta per l'acqua
– *water tank*

**34** l'acquaio (lo scarico)
– *sink*

**35 il laboratorio linguistico**
– **language laboratory**

**36** la lavagna da (a) muro
– *blackboard*

**37** il banco di comando
– *console*

**38** la cuffia
– *headphones (headset)*

**39** il microfono
– *microphone*

**40** la conchiglia (l'auricolare *m*)
– *earcup*

**41** il supporto imbottito della cuffia
– *padded headband (padded headpiece)*

**42** il magnetofono per il programma registrato, un registratore per cassette *f pl*
– *programme* (Am. *program*) *recorder, a cassette recorder*

**43** il regolatore del volume di voce *f* dell'allievo
– *pupil's* (Am. *student's*) *volume control*

**44** il regolatore del volume della cassetta
– *master volume control*

**45** i tasti di comando
– *control buttons (operating keys)*

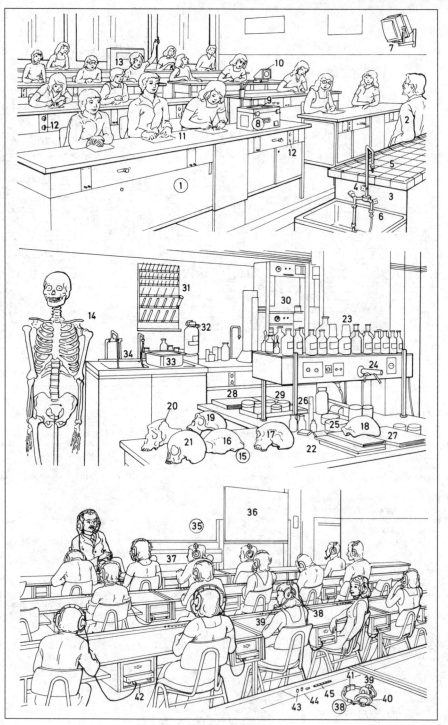

**1-28 l'Università** *f* (Università *f* degli Studi)
– *university (college)*
**1** la lezione universitaria
– *lecture*
**2** l'aula
– *lecture room (lecture theatre,* Am. *theater)*
**3** il docente, un professore universitario (libero docente), professore *m* associato, lettore *m*
– *lecturer (university lecturer, college lecturer,* Am. *assistant professor), a university professor or assistant lecturer*
**4** la cattedra
– *lectern*
**5** il microfono
– *microphone*
**6** la lavagna a comando automatico
– *remote-controlled blackboard*
**7** il proiettore overhead
– *overhead projector*
**8** lo schermo per proiezioni *f pl* con proiettore *m* cinematografico o con diascopio oppure con episcopio
– *projection screen for projecting pictures by means of a film projector, slide projector, or an epidiascope*

**9** lo studente
– *student*
**10** la studentessa
– *student*
**11-28 la biblioteca universitaria;** *sim.:* biblioteca nazionale, biblioteca comunale
– *university library;* sim.: *national library, regional or municipal scientific library*
**11** l'archivio con la raccolta dei libri
– *stack (book stack) with the stock of books*
**12** lo scaffale, uno scaffale di acciaio
– *bookshelf, a steel shelf*
**13** la sala di lettura
– *reading room*
**14** la sorvegliante, una bibliotecaria
– *member of the reading room staff, a librarian*
**15** lo scaffale delle riviste, con riviste *f pl*
– *periodicals rack with periodicals*
**16** lo scaffale dei giornali, dei quotidiani
– *newspaper shelf*
**17** la sala di consultazione *f,* con manuali *m pl*, dizionari *m pl*, enciclopedie *f pl*, vocabolari *m pl*
– *reference library with reference books (handbooks, encyclopedias, dictionaries)*

**18** la sala di prestito dei libri e la sala dei cataloghi
– *lending library and catalogue* (Am. *catalog) room*
**19** il bibliotecario
– *librarian*
**20** il banco di consegna dei libri in prestito
– *issue desk*
**21** il catalogo generale
– *main catalogue* (Am. *catalog)*
**22** lo schedario
– *card catalogue* (Am. *catalog)*
**23** il cassetto con le schede
– *card catalogue* (Am. *catalog) drawer*
**24** l'utente *m* della biblioteca
– *library user*
**25** la scheda (il modulo) di prestito
– *borrower's ticket (library ticket)*
**26** il terminale dei prestiti
– *issue terminal*
**27** le microfiche
– *microfiche (fiche)*
**28** l'apparecchio di lettura delle microfiche
– *microfiche reader*

**1-15** il comizio elettorale (adunanza), un raduno popolare
– *election meeting, a public meeting*
**1** *u.* **2** il comitato
– *committee*
**1** il presidente dell'assemblea
– *chairman*
**2** il membro del comitato
– *committee member*
**3** il tavolo del comitato (della presi-
denza)
– *committee table*
**4** il volantino
– *pamphlet*
**5** l'oratore *m*
– *election speaker (speaker)*
**6** il podio dell'oratore *m*
– *rostrum*
**7** il microfono
– *microphone*
**8** l'adunanza (il raduno; *anche:*
l'auditorio, i partecipanti)
– *meeting (audience)*
**9** l'addetto alla distribuzione dei
volantini
– *man distributing leaflets*
**10** gli addetti al servizio di ordine *m*
– *stewards*

**11** il bracciale (la fascia al braccio)
– *armband (armlet)*
**12** il manifesto (lo striscione)
– *banner*
**13** il cartello elettorale
– *placard*
**14** il manifesto
– *proclamation*
**15** l'interlocutore *m*
– *heckler*
**16-29** l'elezione *f* (le elezioni)
– *election*
**16** il seggio elettorale
– *polling station (polling place)*
**17** i membri della commissione elettorale
– *polling officers*
**18** la lista degli elettori (il registro
elettorale)
– *electoral list*
**19** il certificato elettorale con il
numero di registrazione *f*
– *polling card with registration number (polling number)*
**20** la scheda elettorale con le indicazioni dei partiti e i nomi dei
candidati
– *ballot paper with the names of the
parties and candidates*

**21** la busta della scheda elettorale
*(non in uso)*
– *ballot envelope*
**22** l'elettrice *f*
– *voter*
**23** la cabina elettorale
– *polling booth*
**24** l'elettore *m* (l'avente diritto al
voto)
– *elector (qualified voter)*
**25** il regolamento elettorale
– *election regulations*
**26** lo schedario elettorale (schedario
degli elettori)
– *electoral register*
**27** il presidente del seggio
– *election supervisor*
**28** l'urna
– *ballot box*
**29** la fessura dell'urna
– *slot*

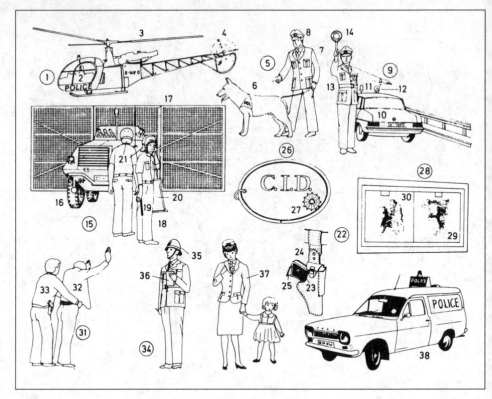

**1-33 l'organo esecutivo della polizia**
(polizia)
– *police duties*
**1** l'elicottero della polizia per il controllo stradale dall'alto
– ***police helicopter** (traffic helicopter) for controlling traffic from the air*
**2** la cabina piloti *m pl*
– *cockpit*
**3** il rotore (elica di quota)
– *rotor (main rotor)*
**4** l'elica di coda
– *tail rotor*
**5 l'impiego dei cani poliziotti**
– *use of police dogs*
**6** il cane poliziotto
– *police dog*
**7** l'uniforme *f* (abito di servizio)
– *uniform*
**8** il berretto di ordinanza, un berretto a visiera con coccarda
– *uniform cap, a peaked cap with cockade*
**9 il controllo stradale** di una pattuglia della polizia stradale
– ***traffic control** by a mobile traffic patrol*
**10** l'automobile *f* (vettura) della polizia
– *patrol car*
**11** la luce azzurra
– *blue light*

**12** l'altoparlante *m*
– *loud hailer (loudspeaker)*
**13** l'agente *m* di polizia (guardia di pubblica sicurezza, poliziotto)
– *patrolman (police patrolman)*
**14** la paletta della polizia
– *police signalling* (Am. *signaling) disc (disk)*
**15 l'impiego durante dimostrazioni** *f pl*
– *riot duty*
**16** la vettura speciale
– *special armoured* (Am. *armored) car*
**17** il reticolo di sgombro
– *barricade*
**18** l'agente *m* in divisa protettiva (divisa antiproiettile)
– *policeman (police officer) in riot gear*
**19** lo sfollagente, un'arma contundente (*pop.:* il manganello)
– *truncheon (baton)*
**20** lo schermo di protezione *f*
– *riot shield*
**21** il casco protettivo (casco)
– *protective helmet (helmet)*
**22 la pistola di ordinanza**
– *service pistol*
**23** l'impugnatura della pistola
– *pistol grip*
**24** la fendina della pistola
– *quick-draw holster*
**25** il caricatore della pistola
– *magazine*

**26 la targa di servizio** della polizia giudiziaria, un distintivo
– *police identification disc (disk)*
**27** la stella (*non in uso in Italia*)
– *police badge*
**28 la dattiloscopia** (il confronto delle impronte digitali)
– ***fingerprint identification** (dactyloscopy)*
**29** l'impronta digitale
– *fingerprint*
**30** il quadrante luminoso
– *illuminated screen*
**31 la perquisizione personale**
– *search*
**32** la persona sospetta (il sospettato)
– *suspect*
**33** il funzionario di polizia giudiziaria in civile *m*
– *detective (plainclothes policeman)*
**34** poliziotto inglese
– *English policeman*
**35** elmetto
– *helmet*
**36** taccuino
– *pocket book*
**37** donna poliziotto
– *policewoman*
**38** furgone della polizia
– *police van*

**1-31 il caffé** con pasticceria; *sim.:* il
bar, la sala da té *m*, la gelateria
– *café, serving cakes and pastries;*
*sim.: espresso bar, tea room, ice-*
*cream parlour* (Am. *parlor)*
**1** il banco
– *counter (cake counter)*
**2** la macchina da caffé *m*, macchina
da caffé elettrica
– *coffee urn, coffee machine*
**3** il vassoio per il denaro
– *tray for the money*
**4** la torta
– *gateau*
**5** la meringa, un composto di chiara
di uovo montata con zucchero a
velo e panna
– *meringue with whipped cream*
**6** l'apprendista *m* pasticciere *m*
– *trainee pastry cook*
**7** la cameriera al banco
– *girl (lady) at the counter*
**8** l'armadietto dei giornali
– *newspaper shelves (newspaper*
*rack)*
**9** l'applique *f*, una lampada da
parete *f*
– *wall lamp*

**10** la panca da angolo, un divanetto
imbottito
– *corner seat, an upholstered seat*
**11** il tavolino
– *café table*
**12** la lastra di marmo
– *marble top*
**13** la cameriera
– *waitress*
**14** il vassoio
– *tray*
**15** la bottiglia di limonata (di gazzosa)
– *bottle of lemonade*
**16** il bicchiere da (per la) gazzosa
– *lemonade glass*
**17** i giocatori di scacchi *m pl* (partita
a scacchi *m pl*)
– *chess players playing a game of*
*chess*
**18** il servizio (per uno) da caffé *m*
– *coffee set*
**19** la tazzina (*Germania:* la tazza) di
caffé *m*
– *cup of coffee*
**20** la zuccheriera
– *small sugar bowl*

**21** il bricco della panna (*Italia:* bricco
del latte)
– *cream jug* (Am. *creamer)*
**22-24** clienti (frequentatori) del caffé
– *café customers*
**22** il signore
– *gentleman*
**23** la signora
– *lady*
**24** il lettore del giornale (un cliente
che legge il giornale)
– *man reading a newspaper*
**25** il giornale (il quotidiano)
– *newspaper*
**26** il listello reggigiornale
– *newspaper holder*
**27** il caffé espresso (l'espresso)
– *espresso*
**28** il gelato misto (il gelato)
– *ice cream in assorted flavours*
(Am. *flavors)*
**29** la coppa di gelato
– *ice-cream dish (sundae dish)*
**30** l'eiskaffee *m* (il caffé freddo con
gelato e panna)
– *iced coffee*
**31** la cannuccia
– *(drinking) straw*

**42** il secchiello per tenere in fresco il vino
– *wine cooler*
**43** la bottiglia di vino
– *bottle of wine*
**44** i cubetti di ghiaccio
– *ice cubes (ice, lumps of ice)*
**45-78 il ristorante con self-service**
– *self-service restaurant (cafeteria)*
**45** la pila dei vassoi
– *stack of trays*
**46** le cannucce
– *drinking straws (straws)*
**47** i tovaglioli (di carta)
– *serviettes (napkins)*
**48** gli scomparti delle posate
– *cutlery holders*
**49** il banco di refrigerazione per piatti *m pl* freddi
– *cool shelf*
**50** la fetta di melone *m*
– *slice of honeydew melon*
**51** il piatto d'insalata
– *plate of salad*
**52** il piatto di formaggio
– *plate of cheeses*
**53** il piatto di pesce
– *fish dish*
**54** il panino imbottito
– *filled roll*
**55** il piatto di carne *m* con contorno
– *meat dish with trimmings*

**56** il mezzo pollo
– *half chicken*
**57** il cestino (la cesta) della frutta
– *basket of fruit*
**58** il succo di frutta
– *fruit juice*
**59** il ripiano delle bevande
– *drinks shelf*
**60** la bottiglia di latte *m*
– *bottle of milk*
**61** la bottiglia di acqua minerale
– *bottle of mineral water*
**62** il piatto (menu *m*) di vegetali *m pl* crudi
– *vegetarian meal (diet meal)*
**63** il vassoio
– *tray*
**64** la guida per i vassoi, una guida su cui scorrono i vassoi
– *tray counter*
**65** il quadro delle vivande
– *food price list*
**66** il passavivande
– *serving hatch*
**67** il menu (piatto) caldo
– *hot meal*
**68** l'apparecchio per spillare la birra alla spina
– *beer pump (beerpull)*
**69** la cassa
– *cash desk*
**70** la cassiera
– *cashier*

**71** il proprietario (il capo)
– *proprietor*
**72** la barriera
– *rail*
**73** la sala ristorante
– *dining area*
**74** il tavolo
– *table*
**75** il panino con formaggio, una porzione di formaggio con pane *m*
– *open sandwich*
**76** la coppa di gelato
– *ice-cream sundae*
**77** la saliera e la pepaiola (il sale e pepe *m*)
– *salt cellar and pepper pot*
**78** la decorazione del tavolo, una decorazione floreale
– *table decoration (flower arrangement)*

**461**

**1-26 la hall** (la recezione, l'ingresso)
- *vestibule (foyer, reception hall)*
**1** il portiere
- *doorman (commissionaire)*
**2** lo scaffale con gli scomparti per la posta
- *letter rack with pigeon holes*
**3** il pannello portachiavi
- *key rack*
**4** il lampadario a globo, una sfera di vetro opaco
- *globe lamp, a frosted glass globe*
**5** il centralino (il quadro con i numeri delle camere)
- *indicator board*
**6** il segnale luminoso di chiamata
- *indicator light*
**7** il caporecezione (receptionist *m*)
- *chief receptionist*
**8** il registro dei clienti (degli ospiti)
- *register (hotel register)*
**9** la chiave della camera
- *room key*
**10** la targhetta col numero della camera
- *number tag (number tab) showing room number*
**11** il conto dell'albergo
- *hotel bill*
**12** il blocco per le registrazioni (i moduli di registrazione *m*)
- *block of registration forms*

**13** il passaporto
- *passport*
**14** l'ospite *m* (il cliente) dell'albergo
- *hotel guest*
**15** la valigia per aereo, una valigia leggera per viaggi *m pl* aerei
- *lightweight suitcase [for air travel]*
**16** la scrivania a leggio (lo scrittoio con piano inclinato)
- *wall desk*
**17** l'inserviente *m* (portabagagli *m*)
- *porter (Am. baggage man)*
**18-26** la hall
- *lobby (hotel lobby)*
**18** il lift
- *page (pageboy, Am. bell boy)*
**19** il direttore dell'albergo
- *hotel manager*
**20** la sala da pranzo (il ristorante)
- *dining room (hotel restaurant)*
**21** il lampadario, un lampadario a bracci *m pl*
- *chandelier*
**22** l'angolo del caminetto
- *fireside*
**23** il caminetto
- *fireplace*
**24** la mensola del caminetto
- *mantelpiece (mantelshelf)*
**25** il fuoco
- *fire*

**26** la poltrona
- *armchair*
**27-38 la camera di albergo,** una (camera) doppia con bagno
- *hotel room, a double room with bath*
**27** la porta doppia
- *double door*
**28** il pannello dei campanelli
- *service bell panel*
**29** l'armadio
- *wardrobe (Am. clothes closet)*
**30** lo scomparto per gli abiti
- *clothes compartment*
**31** lo scomparto per la biancheria
- *linen compartment*
**32** il lavandino doppio
- *double washbasin*
**33** il cameriere
- *room waiter*
**34** il telefono
- *room telephone*
**35** il tappeto di velluto
- *velour (velours) carpet*
**36** lo sgabello per i fiori
- *flower stand*
**37** la disposizione dei fiori
- *flower arrangement*
**38** il letto matrimoniale
- *double bed*
**39 la sala di riunione** *f* (salone *m*)
- *function room (banqueting hall)*

**40-43** il banchetto, una riunione conviviale (tavolata) al pranzo di gala
– *party (private party) at table (at a banquet)*
**40** il brindisi (il commensale che pronuncia il brindisi)
– *speaker proposing a toast*
**41** il vicino di tavola del 42
– *42's neighbour (Am. neighbor)*
**42** il vicino di tavola (il cavaliere) del 43
– *43's partner*
**43** la vicina di tavola del 42
– *42's partner*
**44** l'orchestrina del caffé concerto, un'orchestrina di tre elementi *m pl*
– *bar trio*
**45** il suonatore di violino
– *violinist*
**46** la coppia che balla (coppia danzante)
– *couple dancing (dancing couple)*
**47** il cameriere
– *waiter*
**48** il tovagliolo
– *napkin*
**49** la sigaretta
– *cigarette*
**50** il posacenere
– *ashtray*
**51** il bar dell'albergo
– *hotel bar*

**52** l'appoggiapiedi *m* (la lista poggiapiedi)
– *foot rail*
**53** lo sgabello da bar *m*
– *bar stool*
**54** il banco del bar
– *bar*
**55** il cliente del bar
– *bar customer*
**56** il bicchiere da cocktail *m*
– *cocktail glass (Am. highball glass)*
**57** il bicchiere da whisky *m*
– *whisky (whiskey) glass*
**58** il tappo dello spumante
– *champagne cork*
**59** il secchiello per lo spumante
– *champagne bucket (champagne cooler)*
**60** il recipiente graduato (misurino)
– *measuring beaker (measure)*
**61** lo shaker
– *cocktail shaker*
**62** il barman (barista *m*)
– *bartender (barman, Am. barkeeper, barkeep)*
**63** la barista
– *barmaid*
**64** il ripiano per le bottiglie
– *shelf for bottles*
**65** lo scaffale per i bicchieri
– *shelf for glasses*

**66** la parete a specchi *m pl*, un rivestimento della parete a specchi *m pl*
– *mirrored panel*
**67** il portaghiaccio
– *ice bucket*
**68** il foyer dell'albergo
– *hotel foyer*

1  il parchimetro
– *parking meter*
2  la pianta della città
– *map of the town (street map)*
3  il quadro illustrativo illuminato (quadrante *m* luminoso)
– *illuminated board*
4  la leggenda (la didascalia)
– *key*
5  il cestino dei rifiuti
– *litter bin (Am. litter basket)*
6  il lampione
– *street lamp (street light)*
7  la targa col nome della strada
– *street sign showing the name of the street*
8  il pozzetto; *pop.:* il tombino
– *drain*
9  il negozio di abbigliamento
– *clothes shop (fashion house)*
10  la vetrina
– *shop window*
11  l'esposizione *f* della vetrina (vetrina)
– *window display (shop window display)*
12  la decorazione della vetrina
– *window decoration (shop window decoration)*
13  l'entrata
– *entrance*
14  la finestra
– *window*

15  la cassetta dei fiori
– *window box*
16  l'insegna pubblicitaria luminosa
– *neon sign*
17  l'atelier del sarto (la sartoria)
– *tailor's workroom*
18  il passante
– *pedestrian*
19  la borsa della spesa
– *shopping bag*
20  il netturbino (lo spazzino)
– *road sweeper (Am. street sweeper)*
21  la scopa del netturbino
– *broom*
22  l'immondizia
– *rubbish (litter)*
23  le rotaie del tram
– *tramlines (Am. streetcar tracks)*
24  il passaggio pedonale (le strisce pedonali; *pop.:* zebra)
– *pedestrian crossing (zebra crossing, Am. crosswalk)*
25  la fermata del tram
– *tram stop (Am. streetcar stop, trolley stop)*
26  il cartello della fermata
– *tram stop sign (Am. streetcar stop sign, trolley stop sign)*
27  l'orario delle corse
– *tram timetable (Am. streetcar schedule, trolley schedule)*

28  il distributore automatico dei biglietti
– *ticket machine*
29  il segnale (stradale) di «passaggio pedonale»
– *'pedestrian crossing' sign*
30  il vigile che regola il traffico (vigile *m* addetto al regolamento del traffico)
– *traffic policeman on traffic duty (point duty)*
31  la mezza manica bianca (la manichetta, il manicotto)
– *traffic control cuff*
32  il berretto bianco
– *white cap*
33  la segnalazione del vigile
– *hand signal*
34  il motociclista
– *motorcyclist*
35  la motocicletta, *pop.:* la moto
– *motorcycle*
36  il passeggero
– *pillion passenger (pillion rider)*
37  la libreria
– *bookshop*
38  il negozio di cappelli *m pl* (per cappelli da uomo: cappelleria)
– *hat shop (hatter's shop); for ladies' hats: milliner's shop*
39  l'insegna del negozio
– *shop sign*

**40** l'istituto di assicurazione *f*
– *insurance company office*
**41** i grandi magazzini
– *department store*
**42** il fronte delle vetrine
– *shop front*
**43** l'insegna pubblicitaria (cartellone *m* pubblicitario)
– *advertisement*
**44** le bandiere (*raro:* l'imbandieramento)
– *flags*
**45** la pubblicità (réclame *f*) sul tetto con lettere cubitali luminose
– *illuminated letters*
**46** il tram (il tranvai, la vettura tranviaria)
– *tram (Am. streetcar, trolley)*
**47** il camion (furgone *m*) per trasporto mobili *m pl*, camion per traslochi *m pl*)
– *furniture lorry (Am. furniture truck)*
**48** il cavalcavia tranviario
– *flyover*
**49** l'illuminazione *f* stradale, una lampada al centro della strada
– *suspended street lamp*
**50** la linea di arresto
– *stop line*
**51** la marcatura del passaggio pedonale
– *pedestrian crossing (Am. crosswalk)*

**52** il semaforo
– *traffic lights*
**53** il palo del semaforo
– *traffic light post*
**54** i segnali luminosi
– *set of lights*
**55** i segnali luminosi per pedoni *m pl*
– *pedestrian lights*
**56** la cabina telefonica
– *telephone box (telephone booth, telephone kiosk, call box)*
**57** il cartellone del cinema (il manifesto)
– *cinema (Am. movie) advertisement (film poster, Am. movie poster)*
**58** la zona pedonale
– *pedestrian precinct (paved zone)*
**59** il caffè all'aperto
– *street café*
**60** il tavolino e le sedie
– *group seated (sitting) at a table*
**61** l'ombrellone *m*
– *sunshade*
**62** la discesa alle toilettes
– *steps to the public lavatories (public conveniences)*
**63** il posteggio dei tassi
– *taxi rank (taxi stand)*
**64** il tassi
– *taxi (taxicab, cab)*
**65** l'insegna del tassi
– *taxi sign*

**66** il segnale stradale di «posteggio tassi»
– *'taxi rank' ('taxi stand') sign*
**67** il telefono del posteggio
– *taxi telephone*
**68** l'ufficio postale
– *post office*
**69** il distributore automatico di sigarette *f pl*
– *cigarette machine*
**70** la colonna delle (per le) affissioni
– *advertising pillar*
**71** il cartello pubblicitario
– *poster (advertisement)*
**72** la linea di demarcazione delle carreggiate
– *white line*
**73** la freccia segnaletica di corsia per «svolta a sinistra»
– *lane arrow for turning left*
**74** la freccia segnaletica di corsia per «proseguire diritto»
– *lane arrow for going straight ahead*
**75** lo strillone
– *news vendor (Am. news dealer)*

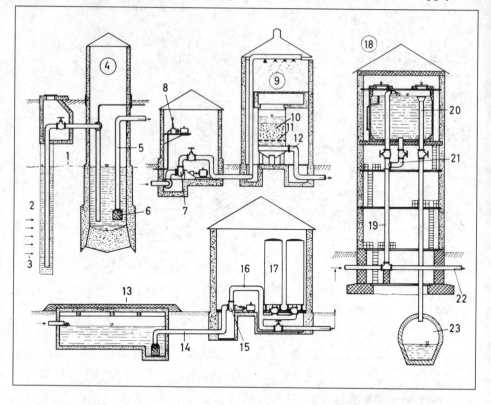

**1-66 l'erogazione *f* dell'acqua pota-
bile**
– *drinking water supply*
**1** il livello dell'acqua
– *water table (groundwater level)*
**2** la falda acquifera (lo strato
acquifero)
– *water-bearing stratum (aquifer,
aquafer)*
**3** la corrente sotterranea
– *groundwater stream (underground
stream)*
**4** il pozzo di raccolta dell'acqua
grezza
– *collector well for raw water*
**5** il tubo aspirante
– *suction pipe*
**6** la succhieruola con valvola di
fondo
– *pump strainer with foot valve*
**7** la pompa aspirante con motore *m*
– *bucket pump with motor*
**8** la pompa per vuoto (il depres-
sore) con motore *m*
– *vacuum pump with motor*
**9** l'impianto di filtrazione *f* primaria
(impianto di filtrazione *f* a alta
velocità)
– *rapid-filter plant*

**10** la ghiaia di filtrazione *f*
– *filter gravel (filter bed)*
**11** il filtro (*qui*: base *f* del filtro), una
griglia (un filtro a rete *f* )
– *filter bottom, a grid*
**12** la conduttura di scarico dell'acqua
filtrata
– *filtered water outlet*
**13** il serbatoio dell'acqua depurata
– *purified water tank*
**14** il tubo aspirante con succhieruola
e valvola di fondo
– *suction pipe with pump strainer
and foot valve*
**15** la pompa principale con motore *m*
– *main pump with motor*
**16** il tubo di mandata
– *delivery pipe*
**17** il polmone compensatore (polmone *m* di aria compressa)
– *compressed-air vessel (air vessel,
air receiver)*
**18** la torre dell'acqua (il serbatoio di
acqua sopraelevato)
– *water tower*
**19** il tubo (la colonna) montante
– *riser pipe (riser)*
**20** il tubo di troppopieno
– *overflow pipe*

**21** il tubo di alimentazione *f* (per
gravità)
– *outlet*
**22** il tubo d'innesto nella rete di distribuzione *f*
– *distribution main*
**23** il canale di scarico
– *excess water conduit*
**24-39** lo sfruttamento di una fonte
– *tapping a spring*
**24** l'incameramento della sorgente
– *chamber*
**25** il dissabbiatore (fermassabbia *m*,
separatore *m* di sabbia)
– *chamber wall*
**26** il pozzo d'ispezione *f*
– *manhole*
**27** il ventilatore
– *ventilator*
**28** i gradini di ferro
– *step irons*
**29** la gettata di pietrame *m*
– *filling (backing)*
**30** la valvola di arresto (valvola di
intercettazione *f* )
– *outlet control valve*
**31** la valvola di scarico a cassetto
– *outlet valve*
**32** il filtro
– *strainer*

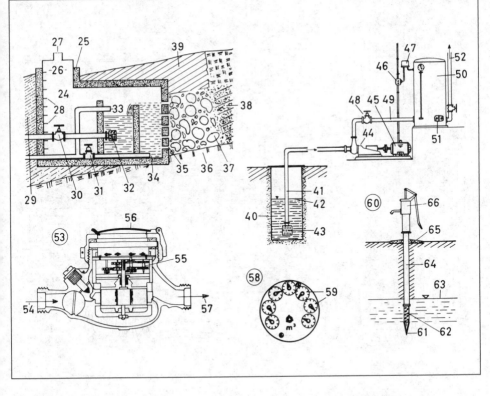

**33** il troppopieno (lo sfiatatore, il tracimatore)
– *overflow pipe (overflow)*
**34** lo scaricatore di fondo
– *bottom outlet*
**35** i tubi di grès *m*
– *earthenware pipes*
**36** lo strato impermeabile
– *impervious stratum (impermeable stratum)*
**37** i sassi depositati intorno alla camera
– *rough rubble*
**38** lo strato acquifero
– *water-bearing stratum (aquifer, aquafer)*
**39** il mantello di argilla compressa (mantello di argilla monolitica)
– *loam seal (clay seal)*
**40-52** l'impianto singolo di erogazione *f* dell'acqua
– *individual water supply*
**40** il pozzo
– *well*
**41** il tubo aspirante
– *suction pipe*
**42** il livello della falda freatica (orizzonte *m* freatico)
– *water table (groundwater level)*

**43** la succhieruola con valvola di fondo
– *pump strainer with foot valve*
**44** la pompa centrifuga
– *centrifugal pump*
**45** il motore
– *motor*
**46** il salvamotore
– *motor safety switch*
**47** il pressostato, un apparecchio di commutazione *f*
– *manostat, a switching device*
**48** la saracinesca (rubinetto a saracinesca)
– *stop valve*
**49** il tubo di mandata
– *delivery pipe*
**50** il polmone compensatore (polmone *m* di aria compressa)
– *compressed-air vessel (air vessel, air receiver)*
**51** il passo d'uomo
– *manhole*
**52** il condotto di allacciamento all'utente *m*
– *delivery pipe*
**53** il contatore di acqua, un contatore di acqua a palette *f pl*
– *water meter, a rotary meter*

**54** l'afflusso dell'acqua
– *water inlet*
**55** il contatore
– *counter gear assembly*
**56** il coperchio a periscopio (coperchio con calotta di vetro)
– *cover with glass lid*
**57** il canale di scarico
– *water outlet*
**58** il quadrante del contatore
– *water-meter dial*
**59** il contatore
– *counters*
**60** il pozzo battuto
– *driven well (tube well, drive well)*
**61** la punta della trivella
– *pile shoe*
**62** il filtro
– *filter*
**63** il livello dell'acqua di sottosuolo (orizzonte *m* freatico)
– *water table (groundwater level)*
**64** il tubo da pozzo
– *well casing*
**65** la bocca del pozzo
– *well head*
**66** la pompa a mano *f*
– *hand pump*

1-46 **l'esercitazione** *f* **dei vigili del fuoco** (esercitazione *f* antincendio, di salita sulla scala, di salvataggio)
– *fire service drill (extinguishing, climbing, ladder, and rescue work)*
1-3 il distaccamento dei vigili del fuoco
– *fire station*
1 l'autorimessa e il magazzino attrezzature *f pl*
– *engine and appliance room*
2 la caserma dei vigili del fuoco
– *firemen's (Am. firefighters') quarters*
3 il castello di manovra
– *drill tower*
4 la sirena di allarme *m*
– *fire alarm (fire alarm siren, fire siren)*
5 l'autopompa serbatoio
– *fire engine*
6 il lampeggiatore, una luce intermittente
– *blue light (warning light), a flashing light* (Am. *flashlight)*
7 il segnalatore acustico (la sirena)
– *horn (hooter)*
8 l'autopompa, una pompa centrifuga
– *motor pump, a centrifugal pump*

9 l'autoscala (una scala girevole montata su automezzo)
– *motor turntable ladder* (Am. *aerial ladder)*
10 la scala autocarrozzata, una scala di acciaio (scala meccanica)
– *ladder, a steel ladder (automatic extending ladder)*
11 il meccanismo della scala
– *ladder mechanism*
12 il braccio meccanico di sostegno
– *jack*
13 l'operatore *m* della scala meccanica
– *ladder operator*
14 la scala estensibile
– *extension ladder*
15 il rampone (per demolire)
– *ceiling hook* (Am. *preventer)*
16 la scala a ganci *m pl*
– *hook ladder* (Am. *pompier ladder)*
17 la squadra di salvataggio
– *holding squad*
18 il telo di salvataggio
– *jumping sheet (sheet)*
19 l'autoambulanza (l'ambulanza)
– *ambulance car (ambulance)*
20 l'apparecchiatura di rianimazione *f* (un rianimatore)
– *resuscitator (resuscitation equipment), oxygen apparatus*

21 l'infermiere *m*
– *ambulance attendant (ambulance man)*
22 il bracciale
– *armband (armlet, brassard)*
23 la barella
– *stretcher*
24 lo svenuto
– *unconscious man*
25 l'idrante *m* interrato
– *pit hydrant*
26 la colonnina idrante
– *standpipe (riser, vertical pipe)*
27 la chiave dell'idrante *m*
– *hydrant key*
28 l'avvolgitubo portatile
– *hose reel* (Am. *hose cart, hose wagon, hose truck, hose carriage)*
29 il raccordo del tubo
– *hose coupling*
30 il tubo di aspirazione *f*
– *soft suction hose*
31 la conduttura a alta pressione
– *delivery hose*
32 il divisore
– *dividing breeching*
33 la lancia
– *branch*
34 la squadra d'intervento
– *branchmen*
35 l'idrante *m* a colonna
– *surface hydrant (fire plug)*

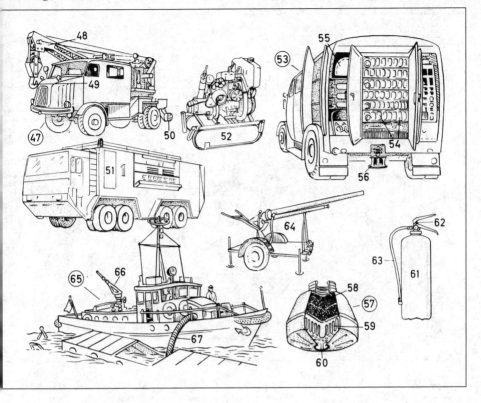

36 il caposquadra *m* dei vigili del
   fuoco
 – *officer in charge*
37 il vigile del fuoco
 – *fireman (Am. firefighter)*
38 il casco protettivo con protegginu-
   ca *m*
 – *helmet (fireman's helmet, Am. fire
   hat) with neck guard (neck flap)*
39 l'autoprotettore *m*
 – *breathing apparatus*
40 la maschera antigas
 – *face mask*
41 il radiotelefono portatile
 – *walkie-talkie set*
42 la lampada portatile a batteria
 – *hand lamp*
43 la piccozza del vigile del fuoco
 – *small axe (Am. ax, pompier hatchet)*
44 il cinturone di salvataggio
 – *hook belt*
45 la corda di salvataggio
 – *beltline*
46 la tuta di protezione *f*
 – *protective clothing of asbestos
   (asbestos suit) or of metallic fabric*
47 l'autogru *f*
 – *breakdown lorry (Am. crane
   truck, wrecking crane)*
48 il braccio di sollevamento
 – *lifting crane*

49 il gancio di sollevamento
 – *load hook (draw hook, Am. drag
   hook)*
50 lo stabilizzatore
 – *support roll*
51 l'autobotte *f*, un veicolo antincendio
 – *water tender, a large fire engine*
52 la motopompa barellata
 – *portable pump*
53 il carro attrezzi a manichette *f pl*
 – *hose layer*
54 i tubi di mandata
 – *flaked lengths of hose*
55 la bobina per cavi elettrici
 – *cable drum*
56 l'argano (il verricello)
 – *winch*
57 il filtro della maschera antigas
 – *face mask filter*
58 il carbone attivo
 – *active carbon (activated carbon,
   activated charcoal)*
59 il filtro per la polvere
 – *dust filter*
60 l'apertura per l'entrata dell'aria
 – *air inlet*
61 l'estintore *m* portatile
 – *portable fire extinguisher*
62 la leva di funzionamento
 – *operating valve*

63 il tubo con spruzzatore
 – *hose with spray nozzle*
64 il cannone-lancia per acqua e
   schiuma
 – *foam-making branch (Am. foam
   gun)*
65 la motobarca con pompa
 – *fireboat*
66 il cannone a acqua
 – *monitor (water cannon)*
67 il tubo di aspirazione *f*
 – *suction hose*

**1** la cassiera
– *cashier*
**2** il registratore di cassa elettronico
– *electronic cash register (till) (scanner till)*
**3** i tasti delle cifre (le cifre)
– *number keys*
**4** lo scanner (il ricercatore di frequenza)
– *scanner (light pen)*
**5** la cassetta del contante, una cassetta a scatto
– *cash drawer (till)*
**6** gli scomparti per monete *f pl* e banconote *f pl*
– *compartments (money compartments) for coins and notes (Am. bills)*
**7** lo scontrino di cassa
– *receipt (sales check)*
**8** l'importo da pagare (la somma registrata)
– *amount [to be paid]*
**9** i tasti di funzione *f*
– *function keys*
**10** la merce
– *goods*
**11** il cortile interno coperto a vetrata (patio coperto a vetrata)
– *glass-roofed well*
**12** il reparto articoli *m pl* per uomo
– *men's wear department*

**13** la vetrinetta
– *showcase (display case, indoor display window)*
**14** la consegna della merce
– *wrapping counter*
**15** il cestello per acquisti *m pl*
– *tray for purchases*
**16** la cliente
– *customer*
**17** il reparto calze *f pl*
– *hosiery department*
**18** la commessa
– *shop assistant (Am. salesgirl, saleslady)*
**19** il cartello del prezzo
– *price card*
**20** il supporto per guanti *m pl*
– *glove stand*
**21** il trequarti, un giaccone trequarti
– *duffle coat, a three-quarter length coat*
**22** la scala mobile
– *escalator*
**23** i tubi fluorescenti
– *fluorescent light (fluorescent lamp)*
**24** l'ufficio (*p. e.*: ufficio crediti *m pl*, ufficio viaggi *m pl*, direzione *f*)
– *office (e.g. customer accounts office, travel agency, manager's office)*
**25** il cartello pubblicitario
– *poster (advertisement)*

**26** il botteghino (la prevendita dei biglietti)
– *theatre (Am. theater) and concert booking office (advance booking office)*
**27** lo scaffale
– *shelves*
**28** il reparto confezioni *f pl* per donna
– *ladies' wear department*
**29** l'abito confezionato
– *ready-made dress (ready-to-wear dress, coll. off-the-peg dress)*
**30** il sacco antipolvere
– *dust cover*
**31** la stanga appendiabiti
– *clothes rack*
**32** la cabina (cabina per la prova)
– *changing booth (fitting booth)*
**33** lo specchio
– *mirror*
**34** il manichino
– *dummy*
**35** la poltrona
– *seat (chair)*
**36** la rivista di moda
– *fashion journal (fashion magazine)*
**37** il sarto mentre appunta le modifiche
– *tailor marking a hemline*
**38** il metro
– *measuring tape (tape measure)*

**39** il gessetto da sarta
– *tailor's chalk (French chalk)*
**40** il segnaorlo (l'apparecchio pareg-
giatore dell'orlo)
– *hemline marker*
**41** il cappotto
– *loose-fitting coat*
**42** lo stand disposto a quadrato
– *sales counter*
**43** l'uscita dell'aria calda (cortina
dell'aria calda)
– *warm-air curtain*
**44** la scala
– *stairs*
**45** l'ascensore *m*
– *lift (Am. elevator)*
**46** la cabina dell'ascensore *m*
– *lift cage (lift car, Am. elevator car)*
**47** le freccie di direzione *f*
– *direction indicators*
**48** la pulsantiera di comando
– *controls (lift controls, Am. eleva-*
*tor controls)*
**49** l'indicatore dei piani
– *floor indicator*
**50** la porta scorrevole
– *sliding door*
**51** la tromba dell'ascensore *m*
– *lift shaft (Am. elevator shaft)*
**52** il cavo portante
– *bearer cable*

**53** il cavo di controllo
– *control cable*
**54** la rotaia di guida
– *guide rail*
**55** il cliente
– *customer*
**56** gli articoli di maglieria
– *hosiery*
**57** la biancheria (biancheria da
tavola e da letto)
– *linen goods (table linen and bed*
*linen)*
**58** il reparto stoffe *f pl*
– *fabric department*
**59** il rotolo di stoffa
– *roll of fabric (roll of material, roll*
*of cloth)*
**60** il caporeparto
– *head of department (department*
*manager)*
**61** il banco di vendita
– *sales counter*
**62** il reparto bigiotteria
– *jewellery (Am. jewelry) depart-*
*ment*
**63** la dimostratrice (*anche:* informa-
trice *f*)
– *customer assistant*
**64** il banco per vendita straordinaria
– *special counter (extra counter)*
**65** il cartello con l'offerta speciale
– *placard advertising special offers*

**66** il reparto tendaggi *m pl*
– *curtain department*
**67** la decorazione (*qui:* decorazione *f*
sugli scaffali)
– *display on top of the shelves*

**1-40 il parco alla francese** (parco
barocco), un parco di un castello
– *formal garden (French Baroque
garden), palace gardens*
1 la grotta
– *grotto (cavern)*
2 la statua, una ninfa delle fonti
– *stone statue, a river nymph*
3 l'orangerie
– *orangery (orangerie)*
4 il boschetto
– *boscage (boskage)*
5 il labirinto con vialetti delimitati
da siepi f
– *maze (labyrinth of paths and
hedges)*
6 il teatro all'aperto
– *open-air theatre (Am. theater)*
7 il castello barocco
– *Baroque palace*
8 le fontane ornamentali (i giochi di
acqua)
– *fountains*
9 la cascata artificiale a gradini
– *cascade (broken artificial waterfall, artificial falls)*
10 la statua, un monumento
– *statue, a monument*
11 il piedistallo del monumento
– *pedestal*

12 l'albero a forma tonda
– *globe-shaped tree*
13 l'albero a forma conica
– *conical tree*
14 il cespuglio ornamentale
– *ornamental shrub*
15 la fontana a muro
– *wall fountain*
16 la panchina del parco
– *park bench*
17 il pergolato (la pergola)
– *pergola (bower, arbour, Am.
arbor)*
18 il sentiero coperto di ghiaia
– *gravel path (gravel walk)*
19 l'albero a forma di piramide f
– *pyramid tree (pyramidal tree)*
20 l'amorino
– *cupid (cherub, amoretto, amorino)*
21 la fontana a zampillo
– *fountain*
22 lo zampillo (il getto di acqua)
– *fountain (jet of water)*
23 la tazza della fontana (la vasca del
troppopieno)
– *overflow basin*
24 il bacino (la vasca esterna)
– *basin*
25 il bordo della fontana
– *kerb (curb)*

26 il passeggiatore
– *man out for a walk*
27 la guida
– *tourist guide*
28 il gruppo dei turisti
– *group of tourists*
29 il regolamento del parco
– *park by-laws (bye-laws)*
30 il guardiano (il custode) del parco
– *park keeper*
31 il cancello del parco (un cancello
di ferro battuto)
– *garden gates made of wrought
iron*
32 l'ingresso del parco
– *park entrance*
33 la cancellata del parco
– *park railings*
34 l'asta della cancellata
– *railing (bar)*
35 il vaso di pietra
– *stone vase*
36 il prato (un manto erboso)
– *lawn*
37 la bordura del sentiero (una siepe
potata)
– *border, a trimmed (clipped) hedge*
38 il sentiero del parco
– *park path*
39 l'aiuola ornamentale
– *parterre*

40 la betulla
– birch (birch tree)

**41-72 il parco all'inglese** (il giardino all'inglese)
– **landscaped park** (jardin anglais)

41 il bordo fiorito
– flower bed

42 la panchina del giardino
– park bench (garden seat)

43 il cestino dei rifiuti
– litter bin (Am. litter basket)

44 il prato per i giochi
– play area

45 il corso di acqua
– stream

46 la passerella
– jetty

47 il ponte
– bridge

48 la sedia spostabile del parco
– park chair

49 il recinto per gli animali
– animal enclosure

50 lo stagno
– pond

**51-54 gli uccelli acquatici**
– waterfowl

51 l'anatra selvatica con i piccoli
– wild duck with young

52 l'oca
– goose

53 il fenicottero
– flamingo

54 il cigno
– swan

55 l'isola
– island

56 la ninfea
– water lily

57 il bar all'aperto
– open-air café

58 l'ombrellone m
– sunshade

59 l'albero del parco
– park tree (tree)

60 la chioma dell'albero
– treetop (crown)

61 il gruppo di alberi
– group of trees

62 lo zampillo
– fountain

63 il salice piangente
– weeping willow

64 la scultura moderna
– modern sculpture

65 la serra
– hothouse

66 il giardiniere
– park gardener

67 il rastello (popolare: rastrello) per le foglie f pl
– rake

68 il minigolf
– minigolf course

69 il giocatore di minigolf
– minigolf player

70 la pista del minigolf
– minigolf hole

71 la mamma con la carrozzina
– mother with pram (baby carriage)

72 la coppia d'innamorati
– courting couple (young couple)

**1** il tennis da tavolo (*fam.* il ping-pong)
– *table tennis game*
**2** il tavolo da ping-pong
– *table*
**3** la reticella del ping-pong
– *table tennis net*
**4** la racchetta da ping-pong
– *table tennis racket (raquet) (table tennis bat)*
**5** la pallina da ping-pong
– *table tennis ball*
**6** il gioco del volano (il badminton)
– *badminton game (shuttlecock game)*
**7** il volano
– *shuttlecock*
**8** la giostra volante (in questa forma non in uso in Italia)
– *maypole swing*
**9** il triciclo
– *child's bicycle*
**10** il gioco del calcio
– *football game (soccer game)*
**11** la porta
– *goal (goalposts)*
**12** il pallone
– *football*

**13** il cannoniere (il marcatore)
– *goal scorer*
**14** il portiere
– *goalkeeper*
**15** il salto alla corda (saltare alla corda)
– *skipping* (Am. *jumping rope*)
**16** la corda
– *skipping rope* (Am. *skip rope, jump rope, jumping rope*)
**17** la torre per arrampicarsi
– *climbing tower*
**18** l'altalena
– *rubber tyre* (Am. *tire*) *swing*
**19** il pneumatico da autocarro
– *lorry tyre* (Am. *truck tire*)
**20** il pon-pon (una palla su cui saltare)
– *bouncing ball*
**21** il parco dei giochi avventurosi
– *adventure playground*
**22** la scala a pioli *m pl*
– *log ladder*
**23** il posto di osservazione *f* (la vedetta)
– *lookout platform*
**24** lo scivolo
– *slide*

**25** il cestino dei rifiuti
– *litter bin* (Am. *litter basket*)
**26** l'orsacchiotto
– *teddy bear*
**27** il trenino di legno
– *wooden train set*
**28** la piscina per bambini
– *paddling pool*
**29** la barca a vela
– *sailing boat (yacht,* Am. *sailboat)*
**30** l'ochetta
– *toy duck*
**31** la carrozzina
– *pram (baby carriage)*
**32** la sbarra fissa
– *high bar (bar)*
**33** il go-kart
– *go-cart (soap box)*
**34** la bandierina di partenza
– *starter's flag*
**35** l'altalena a bilico
– *seesaw*
**36** il robot
– *robot*
**37** il lancio dell'aeromodello
– *flying model aeroplanes* (Am. *airplanes*)
**38** l'aeromodello
– *model aeroplane* (Am. *airplane*)

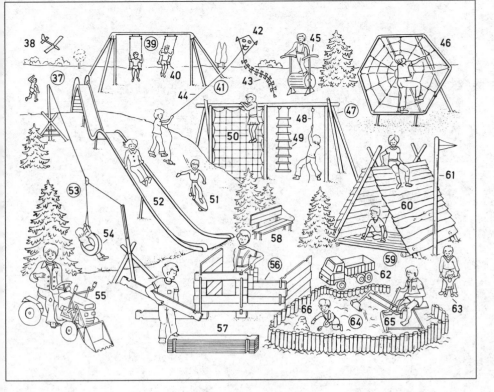

39 l'altalena doppia
– *double swing*
40 il sedile dell'altalena
– *swing seat*
41 l'ascesa dell'aquilone *m*
– *flying a kite*
42 l'aquilone
– *kite*
43 la coda dell'aquilone *m*
– *tail of the kite*
44 il filo dell'aquilone *m*
– *kite string*
45 il tamburo rotolante
– *revolving drum*
46 la ragnatela
– *spider's web*
47 il sostegno per i giochi di arrampicata
– *climbing frame*
48 la corda
– *climbing rope*
49 la scala di corda
– *rope ladder*
50 la rete
– *climbing net*
51 lo skate-board
– *skateboard*

52 lo scivolo
– *up-and-down slide*
53 la funicolare
– *rubber tyre (Am. tire) cable car*
54 il pneumatico usato come sedile *m*
– *rubber tyre (Am. tire)*
55 il trattore
– *tractor, a pedal car*
56 la casetta componibile
– *den*
57 le tavole modulari
– *presawn boards*
58 la panchina
– *seat (bench)*
59 la tenda indiana
– *Indian hut*
60 il tetto per l'arrampicata
– *climbing roof*
61 l'asta della bandiera
– *flagpole (flagstaff)*
62 l'automobilina
– *toy lorry (Am. toy truck)*
63 la bambola che cammina
– *walking doll*
64 il recinto con la sabbia
– *sandpit (Am. sandbox)*

65 la scavatrice giocattolo
– *toy excavator (toy digger)*
66 la montagna di sabbia
– *sandhill*

1-7 le terme salsoiodiche
– *salina, spa*
1-21 il parco delle terme
– *spa gardens*
1 lo stabilimento di gradazione *f*
– *thorn house (graduation house)*
2 le fascine
– *thorns (brushwood)*
3 la grondaia di distribuzione *f*
dell'acqua salmastra
– *brine channels*
4 l'adduzione *f* dell'acqua salmastra
tramite pompa
– *brine pipe from the pumping station*
5 l'addetto all'impianto
– *salt works attendant*
6 *u.* 7 l'inalazione *f* (la terapia inala-
toria)
– *inhalational therapy*
6 l'inalazione *f* all'aria aperta
– *open-air inhalatorium (outdoor
inhalatorium)*
7 il paziente durante l'inalazione *f*
– *patient inhaling (taking an inhala-
tion)*

8 le terme (lo stabilimento termale)
con il Kursaal
– *hydropathic (pump room) with
kursaal (casino)*
9 il portico delle terme
– *colonnade*
10 la passeggiata
– *spa promenade*
11 il viale delle fonti termali
– *avenue leading to the mineral
spring*
12-14 la terapia del riposo (all'aria
aperta)
– *rest cure*
12 il prato per riposare (riservato
alle sedie a sdraio)
– *sunbathing area (lawn)*
13 la sedia a sdraio
– *deck-chair*
14 la tenda da sole *m* (il tendone)
– *sun canopy*
15 il padiglione delle acque termali
– *pump room*
16 il posto dei bicchieri
– *rack for glasses*

17 la mescita
– *tap*
18 l'ospite *m* delle terme alla cura
delle acque
– *patient taking the waters*
19 il padiglione dei concerti
– *bandstand*
20 l'orchestra delle terme mentre
esegue un concerto nel giardino
delle terme
– *spa orchestra giving a concert*
21 il direttore di orchestra
– *conductor*

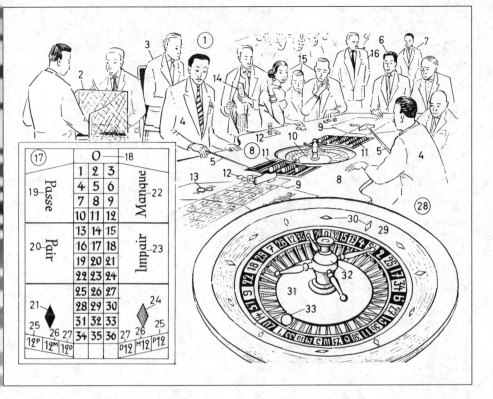

**1-33 la roulette,** un gioco di azzardo
– *roulette, a game of chance (gambling game)*
**1** la sala da gioco, nel casinó
– *gaming room in the casino (in the gambling casino)*
**2** la cassa
– *cash desk*
**3** lo chef de partie *f*
– *tourneur (dealer)*
**4** il croupier
– *croupier*
**5** il rastrello del croupier
– *rake*
**6** il primo croupier
– *head croupier*
**7** il direttore di sala (il caposala)
– *hall manager*
**8** il tavolo della roulette
– *roulette table (gaming table, gambling table)*
**9** il tavolo da gioco (il tavolo delle puntate)
– *roulette layout*
**10** la roulette (la ruota della roulette)
– *roulette wheel*
**11** il pool
– *bank*

**12** la fiche (il gettone)
– *chip (check, plaque)*
**13** la puntata
– *stake*
**14** la scheda di accesso al casinò
– *membership card*
**15** il giocatore di roulette *f*
– *roulette player*
**16** il detective privato
– *private detective (house detective)*
**17** il tavolo delle puntate (detto pure: roulette *f* )
– *roulette layout*
**18** lo zero
– *zero (nought, 0)*
**19** passe (numeri *m pl* dal 19 al 36)
– *passe (high) [numbers 19 to 36]*
**20** pair (numeri *m pl* pari)
– *pair (even numbers)*
**21** noir (nero)
– *noir (black)*
**22** manque (numeri *m pl* dall'1 al 18)
– *manque (low) [numbers 1 to 18]*
**23** impair (numeri *m pl* dispari)
– *impair [odd numbers]*
**24** rouge (rosso)
– *rouge (red)*

**25** douze premiers (prima dozzina; numeri *m pl* dall'1 al 12)
– *douze premier (first dozen) [numbers 1 to 12]*
**26** douze milieu (seconda dozzina; numeri *m pl* dal 13 al 24)
– *douze milieu (second dozen) [numbers 13 to 24]*
**27** douze derniers (terza dozzina; numeri *m pl* dal 25 al 36)
– *douze dernier (third dozen) [numbers 25 to 36]*
**28** la ruota della roulette (la roulette)
– *roulette wheel (roulette)*
**29** il piatto della roulette
– *roulette bowl*
**30** l'arresto
– *fret (separator)*
**31** il disco girevole della roulette (con i numeri dallo 0 al 36)
– *revolving disc (disk) showing numbers 0 to 36*
**32** il perno girevole
– *spin*
**33** la pallina della roulette
– *roulette ball*

**1-16 il gioco degli scacchi** (gli scacchi), un gioco di combinazione *f* o di posizione *f*
– *chess, a game involving combinations of moves, a positional game*
**1** la scacchiera con i pezzi in posizione di apertura
– *chessboard (board) with the men (chessmen) in position*
**2** la casella (la casa) bianca
– *white square (chessboard square)*
**3** la casella (casa) nera
– *black square*
**4** gli scacchi bianchi (i bianchi)
– *white chessmen (white pieces) [white = W]*
**5** gli scacchi neri (i neri)
– *black chessmen (black pieces) [black = B]*
**6** le lettere e i numeri per la designazione *f* delle caselle, per la notazione delle mosse (i tratti), delle partite e dei problemi degli scacchi
– *letters and numbers for designating chess squares in the notation of chess moves and chess problems*
**7** i singoli pezzi (i singoli scacchi)
– *individual chessmen (individual pieces)*
**8** il re
– *king*
**9** la regina
– *queen*
**10** l'alfiere *m*
– *bishop*
**11** il cavallo
– *knight*
**12** la torre
– *rook (castle)*
**13** il pedone
– *pawn*
**14** le mosse dei singoli pezzi
– *moves of the individual pieces*
**15** il matto (lo scacco matto), uno scacco dato da un cavallo (S f3 #)
– *mate (checkmate), a mate by knight [kt f3 ≠]*
**16** l'orologio da torneo, un orologio doppio per tornei di scacchi
– *chess clock, a double clock for chess matches (chess championships)*
**17-19 il gioco della dama**
– *draughts (Am. checkers)*
**17** la scacchiera per la dama (la damiera)
– *draughtboard (Am. checkerboard)*

**18** la pedina bianca; *anche:* pedina per tric trac e per il gioco del mulino (filetto)
– *white draughtsman (Am. checker, checkerman); also: piece for backgammon and nine men's morris*
**19** la pedina nera
– *black draughtsman (Am. checker, checkerman)*
**20 il gioco del «Salta»** (gioco tedesco)
– *salta*
**21** la pedina del salta
– *salta piece*
**22** la scacchiera per il **tric trac** (backgammon)
– *backgammon board*
**23-25 il gioco del filetto** (gioco del mulino)
– *nine men's morris*
**23** la scacchiera per il gioco del filetto
– *nine men's morris board*
**24** il filetto
– *mill*
**25** il filetto doppio
– *double mill*
**26-28 l'Halma**
– *halma*
**26** la scacchiera per l'Halma
– *halma board*
**27** il campo
– *yard (camp, corner)*
**28** le diverse pedine del gioco dell'Halma
– *halma pieces (halma men) of various colours (Am. colors)*
**29 il gioco dei dadi** (i dadi)
– *dice (dicing)*
**30** il bussolotto
– *dice cup*
**31** i dadi
– *dice*
**32** i punti
– *spots (pips)*
**33 il gioco del domino** (il domino)
– *dominoes*
**34** la tessera del domino
– *domino (tile)*
**35** la pariglia (il doppio sei)
– *double*
**36 le carte da gioco**
– *playing cards*
**37** la carta da gioco francese (la carta)
– *French playing card (card)*
**38-45** i colori (i semi)
– *suits*

**38** fiore
– *clubs*
**39** picche *f pl*
– *spades*
**40** cuori
– *hearts*
**41** quadri
– *diamonds*
**42-45** i colori tedeschi
– *German suits*
**42** i bastoni
– *acorns*
**43** le spade
– *leaves*
**44** le coppe
– *hearts*
**45** i denari (gli ori)
– *bells (hawkbells)*

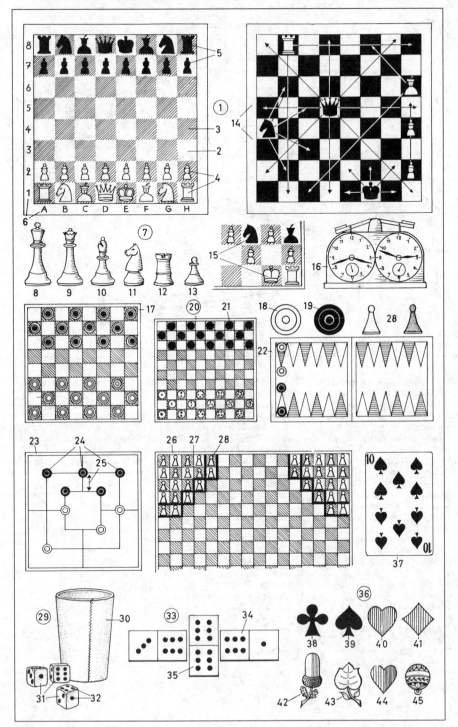

**1-19** il biliardo (gioco del biliardo)
– *billiards*
**1** la bilia (la palla da biliardo), una palla di avorio o di materiale *m* sintetico
– *billiard ball, an ivory or plastic ball*
**2-6** i colpi del biliardo
– *billiard strokes*
**2** il colpo al centro
– *plain stroke (hitting the cue ball dead centre,* Am. *center)*
**3** il colpo di testa (la palla è spinta in avanti)
– *top stroke [promotes extra forward rotation]*
**4** il colpo sotto (la palla è spinta indietro)
– *screw-back [imparts a direct recoil or backward motion]*
**5** il colpo con effetto a sinistra
– *side (running side,* Am. *English)*
**6** il colpo con effetto a destra
– *check side*
**7-19** la sala da biliardo
– *billiard room (*Am. *billiard parlor, billiard saloon, poolroom)*

**7** il biliardo (col colpo) a carambola (la carambola); *sim.:* il biliardo tedesco o inglese (biliardo a buche *f pl*)
– *French billiards (carom billiards, carrom billiards); sim.: German or English billiards (pocket billiards,* Am. *pool billiards)*
**8** il giocatore di biliardo
– *billiard player*
**9** la stecca da biliardo
– *cue (billiard cue, billiard stick)*
**10** la punta della stecca, una punta di cuoio
– *leather cue tip*
**11** la bilia bianca (la prima palla)
– *white cue ball*
**12** la bilia rossa
– *red object ball*
**13** il pallino (bianco), (il boccino, il grillo)
– *white spot ball (white dot ball)*
**14** il tavolo da biliardo (il biliardo)
– *billiard table*
**15** il piano da gioco ricoperto di panno verde
– *table bed with green cloth (billiard cloth, green baize covering)*

**16** la sponda (sponda di gomma, sponda elastica)
– *cushions (rubber cushions, cushioned ledge)*
**17** il segnatempo (il marcatempo), un orologio di controllo
– *billiard clock, a timer*
**18** la lavagna segnapunti (il segnapunti)
– *billiard marker*
**19** la rastrelliera delle stecche
– *cue rack*

**1-59 il campeggio**
– *camp site (camping site, Am. campground)*
**1** la reception (l'ufficio di recezione, l'ufficio)
– *reception (office)*
**2** il guardiano del camping (il guardiano del campeggio)
– *site warden*
**3** la roulotte pieghevole
– *folding trailer (collapsible caravan, collapsible trailer)*
**4** l'amaca
– *hammock*
**5** *u.* **6** le attrezzature igieniche
– *washing and toilet facilities*
**5** le toilette e i lavatoi
– *toilets and washrooms (Am. lavatories)*
**6** i lavandini e i lavelli
– *washbasins and sinks*
**7** il bungalow
– *bungalow (chalet)*
**8-11 la tendopoli**
– *scout camp*
**8** la tenda a campana
– *bell tent*
**9** la banderuola
– *pennon*
**10** il fuoco da campo
– *camp fire*
**11** il giovane esploratore (il boy scout)
– *boy scout (scout)*
**12** la barca a vela
– *sailing boat (yacht, Am. sailboat)*
**13** il pontile (il pontile di attracco)
– *landing stage (jetty)*
**14** il gommone, un battello pneumatico
– *inflatable boat (inflatable dinghy)*
**15** il motore fuoribordo (il fuoribordo)
– *outboard motor (outboard)*
**16** il trimarano
– *trimaran*
**17** l'asse *f* per sedersi (la panchetta per sedersi)
– *thwart (oarsman's bench)*

**18** lo scalmo
– *rowlock (oarlock)*
**19** il remo
– *oar*
**20** il carrello (il trailer)
– *boat trailer (boat carriage)*
**21 la tenda canadese**
– *ridge tent*
**22** il telo esterno
– *flysheet*
**23** il tirante
– *guy line (guy)*
**24** il paletto
– *tent peg (peg)*
**25** il mazzuolo
– *mallet*
**26** l'anello di tensione *f*
– *groundsheet ring*
**27** l'abside *f* della tenda
– *bell end*
**28** la veranda
– *erected awning*
**29** la lampada della tenda, una lampada a petrolio
– *storm lantern, a paraffin lamp*
**30** il sacco a pelo
– *sleeping bag*
**31** il materassino pneumatico (il materassino gonfiabile)
– *air mattress (inflatable air-bed)*
**32** la borraccia
– *water carrier (drinking water carrier)*
**33** il fornello a gas a due fuochi *m pl* per gas butano o propano
– *double-burner gas cooker for propane gas or butane gas*
**34** la bombola del gas propano (butano)
– *propane or butane gas bottle*
**35** la pentola a pressione *f*
– *pressure cooker*
**36 la tenda a casetta**
– *frame tent*
**37** la veranda
– *awning*
**38** il palo della tenda
– *tent pole*

**39** l'ingresso a arco
– *wheelarch doorway*
**40** la finestra per l'areazione *f*
– *mesh ventilator*
**41** la finestra trasparente (la zanzariera)
– *transparent window*
**42** il numero del posto tenda
– *pitch number*
**43** la seggiola da campeggio, una seggiola pieghevole
– *folding camp chair*
**44** il tavolo da campeggio, un tavolo pieghevole
– *folding camp table*
**45** le stoviglie da campeggio
– *camping eating utensils*
**46** il campeggiatore
– *camper*
**47** il barbecue
– *charcoal grill (barbecue)*
**48** il carbone di legna (la carbonella)
– *charcoal*
**49** il soffietto
– *bellows*
**50** il portapacchi
– *roof rack*
**51** la rete di fissaggio
– *roof lashing*
**52 la roulotte**
– *caravan (Am. trailer)*
**53** il contenitore delle bombole di gas liquido
– *box for gas bottle*
**54** la ruota del timone di traino
– *jockey wheel*
**55** il gancio di traino
– *drawbar coupling*
**56** il tetto apribile (il tettuccio)
– *roof ventilator*
**57** la veranda della roulotte
– *caravan awning*
**58** la tenda gonfiabile a igloo
– *inflatable igloo tent*
**59** la sedia a sdraio del campeggio
– *camp bed (Am. camp cot)*

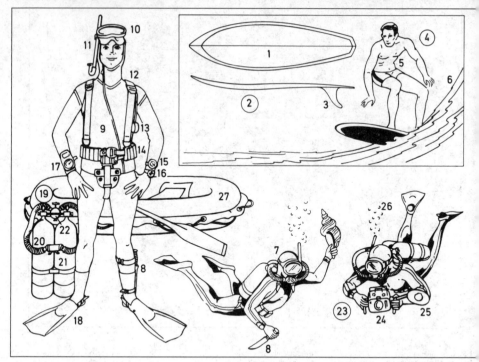

**1-6**  il surfing
– *surf riding (surfing)*
**1**  la tavola del wind-surf vista
  dall'alto
– *plan view of surfboard*
**2**  la tavola del wind-surf vista di
  fianco
– *section of surfboard*
**3**  la deriva
– *skeg (stabilizing fin)*
**4**  il big-wave-riding
– *big wave riding*
**5**  il surfer
– *surfboarder (surfer)*
**6**  il frangente (la grande onda)
– *breaker*
**7-27**  l'immersione *f*
– *skin diving (underwater swimming)*
**7**  il sub (il subacqueo)
– *skin diver (underwater swimmer)*
**8-22**  l'attrezzatura del sub
– *underwater swimming set*
**8**  il coltello del sub
– *knife*
**9**  la muta in neoprene *m*, una tenuta per proteggersi dal freddo
– *neoprene wetsuit*
**10**  la maschera da sub (la maschera),
  una maschera per compensare la
  pressione
– *diving mask (face mask, mask), a
  pressure-equalizing mask*

**11**  lo snorkel (il respiratore)
– *snorkel (schnorkel)*
**12**  i cinghiaggi per le bombole a aria
  compressa
– *harness of diving apparatus*
**13**  il manometro per la pressione
  delle bombole
– *compressed-air pressure gauge
  (Am. gage)*
**14**  la cintura di piombo
– *weight belt*
**15**  il misuratore di profondità
– *depth gauge (Am. gage)*
**16**  l'orologio subacqueo per controllare il tempo d'immersione *f*
– *waterproof watch for checking
  duration of dive*
**17**  il decompressimetro, per indicare
  i livelli di risalita (i dati di decompressione)
– *decometer for measuring stages of
  ascent*
**18**  la pinna
– *fin (flipper)*
**19**  le bombole da immersione *f*
– *diving apparatus (aqualung,
  scuba) with two cylinders (bottles)*
**20**  il boccaglio per la respirazione a
  due tubi *m pl*
– *two-tube demand regulator*
**21**  la bombola di aria compressa
– *compressed-air cylinder (compressed-air bottle)*

**22**  la valvola della bombola
– *on/off valve*
**23**  la fotografia subacquea
– *underwater photography*
**24**  il contenitore stagno per la
  macchina fotografica
– *underwater camera housing
  (underwater camera case); sim.:
  underwater camera*
**25**  il flash subacqueo
– *underwater flashlight*
**26**  l'aria espirata
– *exhaust bubbles*
**27**  il battello pneumatico (il gommone)
– *inflatable boat (inflatable dinghy)*

1 il bagnino
 – *lifesaver (lifeguard)*
2 la corda di salvataggio
 – *lifeline*
3 il salvagente
 – *lifebelt (lifebuoy)*
4 il segnale di tempesta (la bandiera rossa)
 – *storm signal*
5 l'indicatore *m* del tempo (non in uso in Italia)
 – *time ball*
6 il cartello di pericolo
 – *warning sign*
7 l'indicatore *m* delle maree, un cartello che indica la bassa e l'alta marea
 – *tide table, a notice board showing times of low tide and high tide*
8 il cartello con l'indicazione *f* della temperatura dell'acqua e dell'aria
 – *board showing water and air temperature*
9 il pontile
 – *bathing platform*
10 l'asta del pennone
 – *pennon staff*
11 il pennone
 – *pennon*
12 il pedalò (il pattino, il moscone)
 – *paddle boat (pedal boat)*
13 lo sci d'acqua, dietro il motoscafo
 – *surf riding (surfing) behind motorboat*
14 lo sciatore acquatico (nautico)
 – *surfboarder (surfer)*
15 la tavola per lo sci acquatico (nautico)
 – *surfboard*

16 lo sci d'acqua
 – *water ski*
17 il materassino pneumatico
 – *inflatable beach mattress*
18 la palla da acqua
 – *beach ball*
19-23 abbigliamento da spiaggia
 – *beachwear*
19 il prendisole (il vestito da spiaggia)
 – *beach suit*
20 il cappello da spiaggia
 – *beach hat*
21 la giacca da spiaggia
 – *beach jacket*
22 i calzoni da spiaggia
 – *beach trousers*
23 il sandalo da spiaggia (il sandalo da mare *m*)
 – *beach shoe (bathing shoe)*
24 la borsa da spiaggia (la borsa da mare *m*)
 – *beach bag*
25 l'accappatoio
 – *bathing gown (bathing wrap)*
26 il bikini (il due pezzi *m pl*, il costume a due pezzi *m pl*)
 – *bikini (ladies' two-piece bathing suit)*
27 i calzoncini da bagno
 – *bikini bottom*
28 il reggiseno
 – *bikini top*
29 la cuffia da bagno
 – *bathing cap (swimming cap)*
30 il bagnante
 – *bather*
31 il gioco dei cerchietti *m pl*
 – *deck tennis (quoits)*

32 il cerchietto (l'anello) di gomma
 – *rubber ring (quoit)*
33 l'animale *m* di gomma, un oggetto gonfiabile
 – *inflatable rubber animal*
34 il bagnino
 – *beach attendant*
35 il castello di sabbia
 – *sand den [built as a wind-break]*
36 la poltroncina da spiaggia in vimini *m*, una poltrona coperta
 – *roofed wicker beach chair*
37 il pescatore subacqueo (il sub)
 – *underwater swimmer*
38 la maschera subacquea
 – *diving goggles*
39 il respiratore
 – *snorkel (schnorkel)*
40 l'arpione *m* (l'arpone *m*)
 – *hand harpoon (fish spear, fish lance)*
41 le pinne per il nuoto subacqueo
 – *fin (flipper) for diving (for underwater swimming)*
42 il costume da bagno
 – *bathing suit (swimsuit)*
43 i calzoncini da bagno
 – *bathing trunks (swimming trunks)*
44 la cuffia da bagno
 – *bathing cap (swimming cap)*
45 la tenda da spiaggia (una canadese)
 – *beach tent, a ridge tent*
46 la stazione di soccorso
 – *lifeguard station*

**1-9** piscina con onde *f pl* artificiali
– *wave pool, an indoor pool*
**1** l'onda artificiale
– *artificial waves*
**2** la spiaggia
– *beach area*
**3** il bordo della piscina
– *edge of the pool*
**4** il maestro di nuoto
– *swimming pool attendant (pool attendant, swimming bath attendant)*
**5** la sedia a sdraio
– *sun bed*
**6** il salvagente
– *lifebelt*
**7** i bracciali
– *water wings*
**8** la cuffia da bagno
– *bathing cap*
**9** la bocchetta per il movimento ondoso in piscina
– *channel to outdoor mineral bath*
**10** il solarium
– *solarium*
**11** l'area per la cura del sole
– *sunbathing area*
**12** la ragazza che fa la cura del sole
– *sunbather*
**13** il sole artificiale
– *sun ray lamp*
**14** il telo da bagno
– *bathing towel*
**15** la zona riservata ai nudisti
– *nudist sunbathing area*
**16** il nudista
– *nudist (naturist)*
**17** la siepe di protezione *f*
– *screen (fence)*
**18** la sauna (la sauna finlandese), una sauna comune
– *mixed sauna*
**19** il rivestimento di legno
– *wood panelling (Am. paneling)*
**20** i ripiani per sedersi e sdraiarsi
– *tiered benches*
**21** la stufa della sauna
– *sauna stove*
**22** le pietre
– *stones*
**23** l'igrometro (il misuratore di umidità)
– *hygrometer*
**24** il termometro
– *thermometer*
**25** il telo
– *towel*
**26** il secchio per spruzzare le pietre della stufa
– *water tub for moistening the stones in the stove*

**27** le verghe di betulla per flagellare il corpo (la pelle)
– *birch rods (birches) for beating the skin*
**28** la stanza di raffreddamento, per rinfrescarsi dopo la sauna
– *cooling room for cooling off (cooling down) after the sauna*
**29** la doccia tiepida
– *lukewarm shower*
**30** la vasca d'acqua fredda
– *cold bath*
**31** la vasca per l'idromassaggio (lo jaccuzzi)
– *hot whirlpool (underwater massage bath)*
**32** il gradino per scendere
– *step into the bath*
**33** l'idromassaggio
– *massage bath*
**34** la bocchetta
– *jet blower*
**35** la vasca per l'idromassaggio (lo jaccuzzi) (schema *m*)
– *hot whirlpool [diagram]*
**36** la sezione della vasca
– *section of the bath*
**37** la discesa
– *step*
**38** la panca circolare
– *circular seat*
**39** l'aspiratore *m* (lo sfioratore) per l'acqua
– *water extractor*
**40** il canale per l'immissione *f* dell'acqua
– *water jet pipe*
**41** il canale per l'immissione *f* dell'aria
– *air jet pipe*

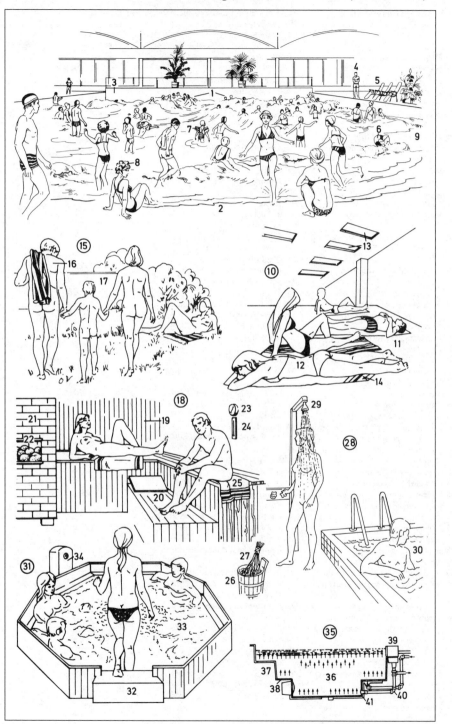

1-32 **la piscina,** una piscina all'aperto
- *swimming pool, an open-air swimming pool*
1 la cabina
- *changing cubicle*
2 la doccia
- *shower (shower bath)*
3 lo spogliatoio
- *changing room*
4 la cura del sole
- *sunbathing area*
5-10 **l'impianto per i tuffi**
- *diving boards (diving apparatus)*
5 il tuffatore
- *diver (highboard diver)*
6 il trampolino
- *diving platform*
7 la piattaforma dei dieci metri
- *ten-metre* (Am. *ten-meter) platform*
8 la piattaforma dei cinque metri
- *five-metre* (Am. *five-meter) platform*
9 il trampolino dei tre metri
- *three-metre* (Am. *three-meter) springboard (diving board)*
10 il trampolino di un metro
- *one-metre* (Am. *one-meter) springboard*
11 la piscina per i tuffi
- *diving pool*
12 il tuffo di testa
- *straight header*
13 il tuffo di piedi *m pl*
- *feet-first jump*
14 il tuffo da seduto
- *tuck jump (haunch jump)*
15 il bagnino
- *swimming pool attendant (pool attendant, swimming bath attendant)*
16-20 **la lezione di nuoto**
- *swimming instruction*
16 il maestro di nuoto (l'istruttore *m*)
- *swimming instructor (swimming teacher)*
17 l'allievo mentre nuota
- *learner-swimmer*
18 la tavoletta gonfiabile
- *float;* sim.: *water wings*
19 il salvagente (la cintura di salvataggio, il giubbotto di salvataggio)
- *swimming belt (cork jacket)*
20 il nuoto a secco (gli esercizi a secco, il condizionamento a terra)
- *land drill*
21 la piscina per i principianti
- *non-swimmers' pool*
22 la vasca bagnapiedi (il bagnapiedi)
- *footbath*
23 la piscina
- *swimmers' pool*

24-32 **la staffetta a stile *m* libero**
- *freestyle relay race*
24 il cronometrista
- *timekeeper (lane timekeeper)*
25 l'arbitro di arrivo
- *placing judge*
26 l'arbitro di virata
- *turning judge*
27 il blocco di partenza
- *starting block (starting place)*
28 la battuta contro la parete di un nuotatore in gara
- *competitor touching the finishing line*
29 il tuffo (il salto) di partenza
- *starting dive (racing dive)*
30 lo starter
- *starter*
31 la corsia
- *swimming lane*
32 il galleggiante di sughero
- *rope with cork floats*
33-39 **gli stili**
- *swimming strokes*
33 la rana (il nuoto a rana)
- *breaststroke*
34 la farfalla (il nuoto a farfalla)
- *butterfly stroke*
35 il delfino (il nuoto a delfino)
- *dolphin butterfly stroke*
36 il dorso (il nuoto a dorso)
- *side stroke*
37 lo stile libero (il crawl): *sim.* il nuoto a braccio
- *crawl stroke (crawl);* sim.: *trudgen stroke (trudgen, double overarm stroke)*
38 il nuoto subacqueo
- *diving (underwater swimming)*
39 il camminare nell'acqua
- *treading water*
40-45 **i tuffi**
- *diving (acrobatic diving, fancy diving, competitive diving, highboard diving)*
40 il tuffo carpiato dalla piattaforma
- *standing take-off pike dive*
41 il tuffo in avanti
- *one-half twist isander (reverse dive)*
42 il doppio salto all'indietro
- *backward somersault (double backward somersault)*
43 il tuffo avvitato con rincorsa
- *running take-off twist dive*
44 il tuffo con doppio avvitamento
- *screw dive*
45 il tuffo verticale (il tuffo a candela)
- *armstand dive (handstand dive)*
46-50 **la pallanuoto**
- *water polo*

46 la porta
- *goal*
47 il portiere
- *goalkeeper*
48 la palla
- *water polo ball*
49 il difensore
- *back*
50 l'attaccante *m*
- *forward*

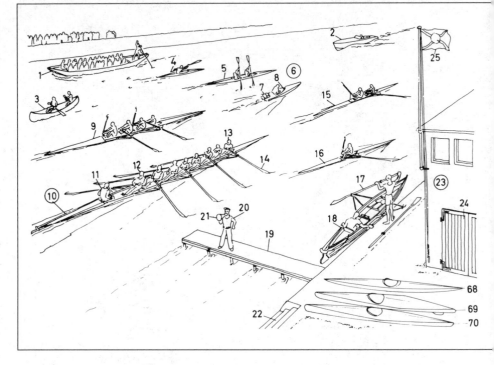

1-18  la partenza per la regata
– *taking up positions for the regatta*
1  il barcone, un barcone da diporto
– *punt, a pleasure boat*
2  la barca a motore *m*
– *motorboat*
3  la canadese, una canoa
– *Canadian canoe*
4  il kayak, una canoa eschimese
– *kayak (Alaskan canoe, slalom
   canoe), a canoe*
5  il kayak biposto
– *tandem kayak*
6  il fuoribordo
– *outboard motorboat (outboard
   speedboat, outboard)*
7  il motore fuoribordo
– *outboard motor (outboard)*
8  il pozzetto (il cockpit, il sedile)
– *cockpit*
9-15  barche *f pl* a remi *m pl*
– *shells (rowing boats, Am. row-
   boats)*
9-16  imbarcazioni *f pl* da corsa
   (imbarcazioni *f pl* sportive)
– *racing boats (sportsboats, outrig-
   gers)*
9  il quattro senza (il quattro senza
   timoniere *m*)
– *coxless four, a carvel-built boat*

10  l'otto con (l'otto con timoniere *m*)
– *eight (eight-oared racing shell)*
11  il timoniere
– *cox*
12  il capovoga, un rematore
– *stroke, an oarsman*
13  l'uomo di prua (il «numero uno»)
– *bow ('number one')*
14  il remo
– *oar*
15  il due senza
– *coxless pair*
16  il singolo, il monoposto
– *single sculler (single skuller, racing sculler, racing skuller, skiff)*
17  la pagaia
– *scull (skull)*
18  il singolo con timoniere *m*
– *coxed single, a clinker-built single*
19  la passerella
– *jetty (landing stage)*
20  l'allenatore *m*
– *rowing coach*
21  il megafono
– *megaphone*
22  la scaletta per le barche
– *quayside steps*
23  il club nautico (la club house)
– *clubhouse (club)*

24  la rimessa per le barche
– *boathouse*
25  il vessillo del club
– *club's flag*
26-33  la iole a quattro vogatori *m pl*
– *four-oared gig, a touring boat*
26  il timone
– *oar*
27  il sedile del timoniere
– *cox's seat*
28  il sedile del rematore
– *thwart (seat)*
29  lo scalmo
– *rowlock (oarlock)*
30  il bordo
– *gunwale (gunnel)*
31  il rivestimento interno
– *rising*
32  la chiglia (la chiglia esterna)
– *keel*
33  il rivestimento esterno a fasciame
   *m* sovrapposto
– *skin (shell, outer skin) [clinker-
   built]*
34  la pagaia semplice
– *single-bladed paddle (paddle)*
35-38  il remo
– *oar (scull, skull)*
35  l'impugnatura
– *grip*

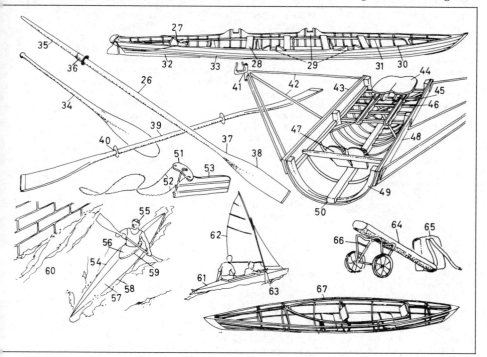

36  la fasciatura in pelle *f*
–  *leather sheath*
37  il collo del remo
–  *shaft (neck)*
38  la pala
–  *blade*
39  la pagaia biposto
–  *double-bladed paddle (double-ended paddle)*
40  l'anello paragocce
–  *drip ring*
41-50  il posto di voga
–  *sliding seat*
41  lo scalmo girevole
–  *rowlock (oarlock)*
42  il tirante
–  *outrigger*
43  il bordo del pozzetto
–  *saxboard*
44  il sedile scorrevole
–  *sliding seat*
45  le corsie
–  *runner*
46  il fine corsa
–  *strut*
47  l'asse *f* di appoggio
–  *stretcher*
48  il rivestimento esterno
–  *skin (shell, outer skin)*
49  l'ordinata
–  *frame (rib)*

50  la chiglia (la chiglia interna)
–  *kelson (keelson)*
51-53  il timone
–  *rudder (steering rudder)*
51  il giogo del timone
–  *yoke*
52  il cavo del timone
–  *lines (steering lines)*
53  la pala del timone
–  *blade (rudder blade, rudder)*
54-66  canoe *f pl* pieghevoli
–  *folding boats (foldboats, canoes)*
54  la canoa monoposto
–  *one-man kayak*
55  il canoista
–  *canoeist*
56  il paraspruzzi
–  *spraydeck*
57  la capote
–  *deck*
58  il rivestimento esterno in gomma
–  *rubber-covered canvas hull*
59  il lembo di chiusura del pozzetto
–  *cockpit coaming (coaming)*
60  la corrente della diga
–  *channel for rafts alongside weir*
61  la canoa biposto
–  *two-seater folding kayak, a touring kayak*
62  la vela della canoa
–  *sail of folding kayak*

63  la deriva laterale
–  *leeboard*
64  il fodero per la canoa
–  *bag for the rods*
65  lo zaino
–  *rucksack*
66  il carrello
–  *boat trailer (boat carriage)*
67  l'ossatura della canoa pieghevole
–  *frame of folding kayak*
68-70  kayak *m pl*
–  *kayaks*
68  il kayak eschimese
–  *Eskimo kayak*
69  il kayak da corsa
–  *wild-water racing kayak*
70  il kayak da turismo
–  *touring kayak*

**1-9 il Windsurf**
- *windsurfing*
**1** il surfista
- *windsurfer*
**2** la vela
- *sail*
**3** il finestrino della vela
- *transparent window (window)*
**4** l'albero
- *mast*
**5** la tavola del surf (lo scafo)
- *surfboard*
**6** il piede dell'albero regolabile, per dirigere lo scafo
- *universal joint (movable bearing) for adjusting the angle of the mast and for steering*
**7** il boma
- *wishbone*
**8** la deriva a scomparsa
- *retractable centreboard (Am. centerboard)*
**9** la pinna
- *rudder*
**10-48 la barca a vela**
- *yacht (sailing boat, Am. sailboat)*
**10** la coperta di prua
- *foredeck*
**11** l'albero
- *mast*
**12** la randa a trapezio
- *trapeze*
**13** il saling
- *crosstrees (spreader)*
**14** l'appendisartie *m*
- *hound*
**15** la trinchettina
- *forestay*
**16** il trinchetto
- *jib (Genoa jib)*
**17** l'ammainatrinchetto
- *jib downhaul*
**18** la sartia
- *side stay (shroud)*
**19** il tendisartie
- *lanyard (also: turnbuckle)*
**20** il piede dell'albero
- *foot of the mast*
**21** l'ammainaboma *m*
- *kicking strap (vang)*
**22** il fermascotta
- *jam cleat*
**23** la scotta di trinchetto
- *foresheet (jib sheet)*
**24** la scatola per la deriva
- *centreboard (Am. centerboard) case*
**25** la bitta a cricco
- *bitt*
**26** la deriva mobile
- *centreboard (Am. centerboard)*
**27** il cursore
- *traveller (Am. traveler)*
**28** la scotta di maestra
- *mainsheet*

**29** il conduttore della scotta di trinchetto
- *foresheet fairlead (jib fairlead)*
**30** la cinghia
- *toestraps (hiking straps)*
**31** il buttafuori della barra del timone
- *tiller extension (hiking stick)*
**32** la barra del timone
- *tiller*
**33** la testa del timone
- *rudderhead (rudder stock)*
**34** la pala del timone
- *rudder blade (rudder)*
**35** la poppa quadra
- *transom*
**36** il foro di sentina
- *drain plug*
**37** la mura della vela maestra
- *gooseneck*
**38** la finestra della vela
- *window*
**39** la boma
- *boom*
**40** il gratile (la ralinga di bordame *m*)
- *foot*
**41** il corno di trinchetto
- *clew*
**42** la ralinga di caduta prodiera
- *luff (leading edge)*
**43** la ripresa della randa
- *leech pocket (batten cleat, batten pocket)*
**44** la randa
- *batten*
**45** la balumina
- *leech (trailing edge)*
**46** la vela maestra
- *mainsail*
**47** la testa della vela maestra
- *headboard*
**48** la banderuola segnavento
- *racing flag (burgee)*
**49-65 le classi delle barche a vela**
- *yacht classes*
**49** il flying-dutchman
- *Flying Dutchman*
**50** la iolla
- *O-Joller*
**51** il finn
- *Finn dinghy (Finn)*
**52** il pirata
- *pirate*
**53** lo sharpie da 12 m²
- *12.00 m² sharpie*
**54** il tempest
- *tempest*
**55** la star
- *star*
**56** il soling
- *soling*
**57** il dragone
- *dragon*
**58** la classe 5,5 m
- *5.5-metre (Am. 5.5-meter) class*

**59** la classe 6 m R
- *6-metre (Am. 6-meter) R-class*
**60** lo sloop da crociera da 30 m²
- *30.00 m² cruising yacht (coastal cruiser)*
**61** lo iolla da crociera da 30 m²
- *30.00 m² dinghy cruiser*
**62** lo yacht monochiglia da 25 m²
- *25.00 m² one-design keelboat*
**63** la classe KR
- *KR-class*
**64** il catamarano
- *catamaran*
**65** il doppio scafo
- *twin hull*

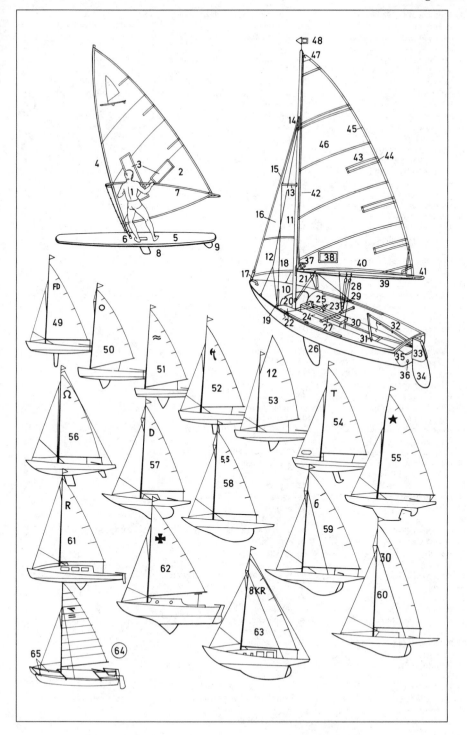

**1-13 posizioni** *f pl* della vela e
   direzioni *f pl* del vento
 – *points of sailing and wind direc-*
   *tions*
1 l'andatura di poppa
 – *sailing downwind (running)*
2 la randa
 – *mainsail*
3 il fiocco
 – *jib*
4 la posizione a farfalla della vela
 – *sails set goose-winged*
5 il timone con la barra al centro
 – *centre* (Am. *center) line*
6 la direzione del vento
 – *wind direction*
7 la barca ferma con vento in prua
 – *yacht stopped head to wind*
8 la vela in sbando
 – *sail, shivering*
9 l'andatura di bolina
 – *luffing*
10 l'andatura di bolina stretta
 – *sailing close-hauled*
11 l'andatura al traverso
 – *sailing with wind abeam*
12 l'andatura di gran lasco
 – *sailing with free wind*
13 la brezza sulla vela di strallo (di
   straglio)
 – *quartering wind (quarter wind)*
**14-24 il percorso di regata**
 – *regatta course*
14 le boe di partenza e di arrivo
 – *starting and finishing buoy*
15 il battello della giuria
 – *committee boat*
16 il percorso a triangolo (il percorso
   di regata)
 – *triangular course (regatta course)*
17 la boa di virata
 – *buoy (mark) to be rounded*
18 la boa di percorso
 – *buoy to be passed*
19 il primo giro
 – *first leg*
20 il secondo giro
 – *second leg*
21 il terzo giro
 – *third leg*
22 il tratto di bolina
 – *windward leg*
23 il tratto col vento in poppa
 – *downwind leg*
24 il tratto a gran lasco
 – *reaching leg*
**25-28 le andature**
 – *tacking*
25 il tratto di bolina
 – *tack*
26 la strambata
 – *gybing (jibing)*
27 la virata
 – *going about*

28 la perdita contro vento nel caso di
   strambata
 – *loss of distance during the gybe*
   *(jibe)*
**29-34** lo yacht con chiglia da crociera
 – *cruiser keelboat*
**29-41 le forme della poppa delle**
   **barche a vela**
 – *types of yacht hull*
29 la poppa
 – *stern*
30 la prua
 – *spoon bow*
31 la linea di galleggiamento
 – *waterline*
32 la chiglia
 – *keel (ballast keel)*
33 il bulbo
 – *ballast*
34 il timone
 – *rudder*
35 lo yacht con chiglia da regata
 – *racing keelboat*
36 la pinna di piombo
 – *lead keel*
**37-41** la iole
 – *keel-centreboard* (Am. *center-*
   *board) yawl*
37 il timone retrattile
 – *retractable rudder*
38 il pozzetto
 – *cockpit*
39 la cabina
 – *cabin superstructure (cabin)*
40 il dritto di prua
 – *straight stem*
41 la chiglia mobile
 – *retractable centreboard* (Am. *cen-*
   *terboard)*
**42-49 le forme della poppa delle**
   **barche a vela**
 – *types of yacht stern*
42 la poppa dello yacht
 – *yacht stern*
43 lo specchio di poppa
 – *square stern*
44 la poppa a canoa
 – *canoe stern*
45 la poppa affusolata
 – *cruiser stern*
46 la targhetta col nome della barca
 – *name plate*
47 la chiglia
 – *deadwood*
48 lo specchio di poppa
 – *transom stern*
49 lo specchio
 – *transom*
**50-52** il rivestimento a fasciame *m*
   sovrapposto
 – *clinker planking (clench planking)*
**50-57 il rivestimento degli scafi di**
   **legno**
 – *timber planking*

50 la centinatura esterna
 – *outside strake*
51 l'ordinata, una ordinata trasversale
 – *frame (rib)*
52 il chiodo ribattuto
 – *clenched nail (riveted nail)*
53 il rivestimento a paro (il rivestimento a comenti *m pl* appaiati)
 – *carvel planking*
54 il rivestimento continuo
 – *ribband-carvel construction*
55 l'ordinata longitudinale
 – *ribband, a stringer*
56 il rivestimento a paro diagonale
 – *diagonal carvel planking*
57 il rivestimento interno
 – *inner planking*

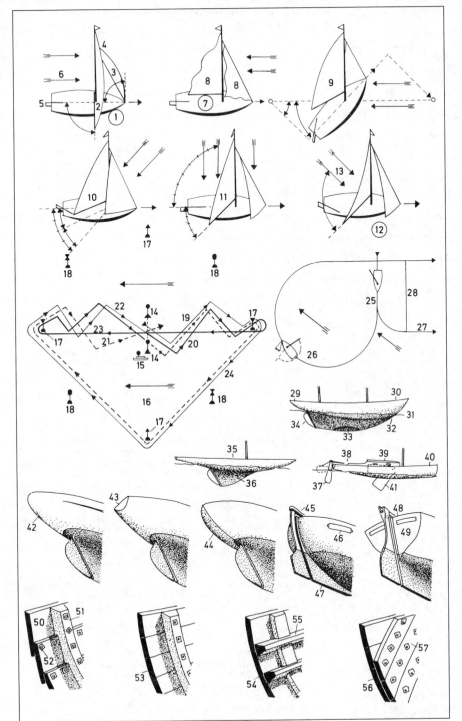

**1-5** motoscafi *m pl*
- *motorboats (powerboats, sports-boats)*
**1** il battello pneumatico (il gommone) con motore *m* fuoribordo
- *inflatable sportsboat with outboard motor (outboard inflatable)*
**2** il motoscafo entrobordo (con propulsione *f* bielica)
- *Z-drive motorboat (outdrive motorboat)*
**3** il cabinato
- *cabin cruiser*
**4** il motoscafo da crociera
- *motor cruiser*
**5** lo yacht d'alto mare *m* da 30 m
- *30-metre (Am. 30-meter) ocean-going cruiser*
**6** il vessillo della federazione
- *association flag*
**7** il nome del battello (o: il numero di matricola)
- *name of craft (or: registration number)*
**8** l'indicazione *f* di appartenenza a un club e porto d'origine *f*
- *club membership and port of registry (Am. home port)*
**9** il vessillo della federazione sulla dritta di prua
- *association flag on the starboard crosstrees*
**10-14** la disposizione delle luci sui motoscafi per le acque costiere e lacustri (i fanali di posizione *f*)
- *navigation lights of sportsboats in coastal and inshore waters*
**10** la luce bianca di testa d'albero
- *white top light*
**11** la luce verde della dritta (il fanale di dritta)
- *green starboard sidelight*
**12** la luce rossa di sinistra (il fanale di sinistra)
- *red port sidelight*
**13** la luce verde-rossa di prua
- *green and red bow light (combined lantern)*
**14** la luce bianca di poppa
- *white stern light*
**15-18** ancore *f pl*
- *anchors*
**15** l'ancora con ceppo, un'ancora pesante
- *stocked anchor (Admiralty anchor), a bower anchor*
**16-18** ancore *f pl* leggere
- *lightweight anchor*
**16** l'ancora a vomere *m*
- *CQR anchor (plough, Am. plow, anchor)*
**17** l'ancora senza ceppi *m pl*
- *stockless anchor (patent anchor)*
**18** l'ancora Danforth
- *Danforth anchor*

**19** l'isola di salvataggio (la zattera di salvataggio)
- *life raft*
**20** il giubbotto salvagente
- *life jacket*
**21-44** corse *f pl* di motoscafi *m pl*
- *powerboat racing*
**21** il catamarano fuoribordo
- *catamaran with outboard motor*
**22** l'imbarcazione *f* da corsa idroplano
- *hydroplane*
**23** il fuoribordo da corsa
- *racing outboard motor*
**24** la barra del timone
- *tiller*
**25** la conduttura della benzina
- *fuel pipe*
**26** lo specchio di poppa
- *transom*
**27** lo scafo portante
- *buoyancy tube*
**28** partenza e arrivo
- *start and finish*
**29** la zona di partenza
- *start*
**30** la linea di partenza e di arrivo
- *starting and finishing line*
**31** la boa di virata
- *buoy to be rounded*
**32-34** la barca a ordinata rotonda
- *round-bilge boat*
**32-37** le barche da diporto
- *displacement boats*
**32** la vista in pianta
- *view of hull bottom*
**33** la sezione trasversale della prua
- *section of fore ship*
**34** la sezione trasversale della poppa
- *section of aft ship*
**35-37** l'imbarcazione *f* col corpo a V
- *V-bottom boat (vee-bottom boat)*
**35** la vista in pianta
- *view of hull bottom*
**36** la sezione trasversale della prua
- *section of fore ship*
**37** la sezione trasversale della poppa
- *section of aft ship*
**38-41** lo scafo con redan
- *stepped hydroplane (stepped skimmer)*
**38-44** idroscivolanti *m pl*
- *planing boats (surface skimmers, skimmers)*
**38** la vista laterale
- *side view*
**39** la vista in pianta
- *view of hull bottom*
**40** la sezione trasversale della prua
- *section of fore ship*
**41** la sezione trasversale della poppa
- *section of aft ship*
**42** l'imbarcazione *f* a tre punti *m pl*
- *three-point hydroplane*

**43** la chiglia a pinna
- *fin*
**44** il galleggiante
- *float*
**45-62** sci *m* nautico (sci *m* d'acqua)
- *water skiing*
**45** la sciatrice
- *water skier*
**46** la partenza sott'acqua
- *deep-water start*
**47** la corda di traino
- *tow line (towing line)*
**48** il bilancino
- *handle*
**49-55** la lingua dello sci nautico (i segnali di comunicazione *f* dello sciatore)
- *water-ski signalling (code of hand signals from skier to boat driver)*
**49** il segnale «più veloce»
- *signal for 'faster'*
**50** il segnale «più adagio»
- *signal for 'slower' ('slow down')*
**51** il segnale «velocità OK»
- *signal for 'speed OK'*
**52** il segnale «girare»
- *signal for 'turn'*
**53** il segnale «alt»
- *signal for 'stop'*
**54** il segnale «ferma il motore»
- *signal for 'cut motor'*
**55** il cenno «torna al pontile»
- *signal for 'return to jetty' ('back to dock')*
**56-62** sci *m* d'acqua (sci *m* nautico)
- *types of water ski*
**56** il monosci
- *trick ski (figure ski), a monoski*
**57** u. **58** l'attacco in gomma
- *rubber binding*
**57** la pantella anteriore in gomma
- *front foot binding*
**58** la pantella posteriore in gomma
- *heel flap*
**59** l'appoggio per il secondo piede
- *strap support for second foot*
**60** lo sci da slalom
- *slalom ski*
**61** la pinna
- *skeg (fixed fin, fin)*
**62** lo sci da salto
- *jump ski*
**63** l'hovercraft *m*
- *hovercraft (air-cushion vehicle)*
**64** l'elica
- *propeller*
**65** il timone aereo
- *rudder*
**66** il cuscino d'aria
- *skirt enclosing air cushion*

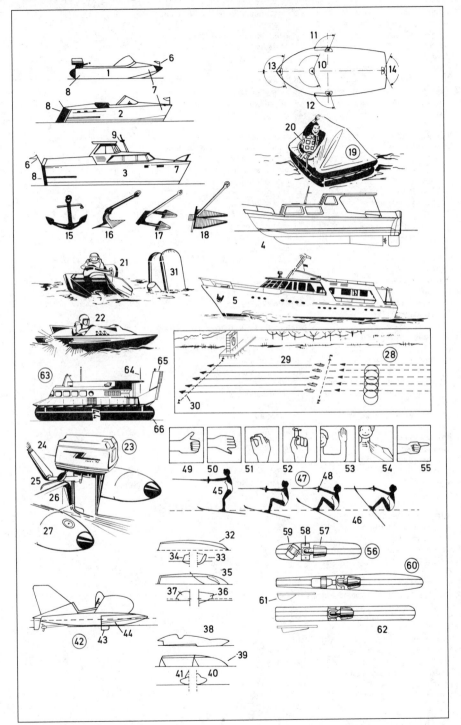

1 il tipo di rimorchio aereo (il traino aereo, il rimorchio aereo, il volo rimorchiato)
– *aeroplane* (Am. *airplane*) *tow launch (aerotowing)*
2 l'aereo a motore *m* trainante
– *tug (towing plane)*
3 l'aliante *m*, il veleggiatore trainato
– *towed glider (towed sailplane)*
4 il cavo di traino
– *tow rope*
5 il lancio con verricello
– *winched launch*
6 il verricello a motore *m*
– *motor winch*
7 il paracadute del cavo di traino
– *cable parachute*
8 il motoaliante (l'aliante *m* a motore *m*)
– *motorized glider (powered glider)*
9 l'aliante *m* da alte prestazioni *f pl*
– *high-performance glider (high-performance sailplane)*
10 l'impennaggio a T
– *T-tail (T-tail unit)*
11 la manica a vento
– *wind sock (wind cone)*
12 la torre di controllo
– *control tower (tower)*
13 la zona di atterraggio degli alianti
– *glider field*
14 l'hangar *m* (l'aviorimessa)
– *hangar*
15 la pista di volo per decolli *m pl* e atterraggi *m pl* per aerei *m pl* a motore *m*
– *runway for aeroplanes* (Am. *airplanes*)
16 il volo a spirale *f*
– *wave soaring*
17 il volo sottovento
– *lee waves (waves, wave system)*
18 il rotore
– *rotor*
19 le nuvole lenticolari
– *lenticular clouds (lenticulars)*
20 il volo a vela in termica
– *thermal soaring*
21 il cono della termica (della corrente d'aria ascendente)
– *thermal*
22 la nuvola a cumulo (il cumulo)
– *cumulus cloud (heap cloud, cumulus, woolpack cloud)*
23 il volo a vela sul fronte temporalesco
– *storm-front soaring*
24 il fronte temporalesco
– *storm front*
25 la corrente d'aria ascendente del fronte temporalesco
– *frontal upcurrent*

26 il cumulonembo (la nuvola cumulonembo)
– *cumulonimbus cloud (cumulonimbus)*
27 il volo in pendio
– *slope soaring*
28 la corrente d'aria ascendente del volo in pendio
– *hill upcurrent (orographic lift)*
29 la semiala, una superficie portante
– *multispar wing, a wing*
30 il longherone principale scatolato
– *main spar, a box spar*
31 un innesto a baionetta
– *connector fitting*
32 la centina di ancoraggio
– *anchor rib*
33 il longherone obliquo
– *diagonal spar*
34 il bordo d'attacco
– *leading edge*
35 la centina principale
– *main rib*
36 la centina ausiliaria
– *nose rib (false rib)*
37 il bordo d'uscita
– *trailing edge*
38 il diruttore (il freno aerodinamico)
– *brake flap (spoiler)*
39 il bordo d'attacco antitorsione
– *torsional clamp*
40 la ricopertura delle ali
– *covering (skin)*
41 l'alettone
– *aileron*
42 l'estremità alare
– *wing tip*
43 il volo col deltaplano
– *hang gliding*
44 il deltaplano
– *hang glider*
45 il deltaplanista
– *hang glider pilot*
46 il triangolo di guida (la barra)
– *control frame*

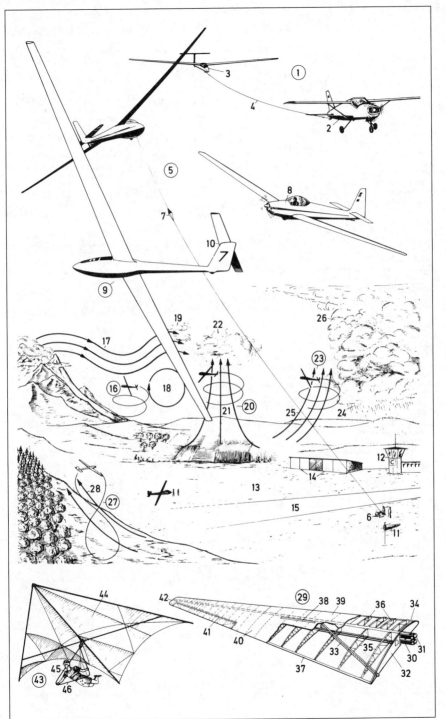

**1-9 il volo acrobatico**
- *aerobatics* (aerobatic manoeuvres, Am. *maneuvers*)
**1** il looping
- *loop*
**2** l'otto orizzontale
- *horizontal eight*
**3** il cerchio
- *rolling circle*
**4** la scampanata
- *stall turn (hammer head)*
**5** la caduta a foglia morta
- *tail slide (whip stall)*
**6** la vite
- *vertical flick spin*
**7** l'avvitamento
- *spin*
**8** il tonneau
- *horizontal slow roll*
**9** il volo rovescio
- *inverted flight (negative flight)*
**10** **il cockpit**
- ***cockpit***
**11** il cruscotto (il quadro degli strumenti)
- *instrument panel*
**12** la bussola
- *compass*
**13** il dispositivo radio e di navigazione *f*
- *radio and navigation equipment*
**14** la cloche (la barra di comando)
- *control column (control stick)*
**15** la leva del gas
- *throttle lever (throttle control)*
**16** la leva dosaggio miscela (il dosatore miscela)
- *mixture control*
**17** il microfono
- *radio equipment*
**18** **il biposto sportivo per volo acrobatico**
- ***two-seater plane for racing and aerobatics***
**19** la cabina di pilotaggio
- *cabin*
**20** l'antenna
- *antenna*
**21** la deriva laterale
- *vertical stabilizer (vertical fin, tail fin)*
**22** il timone laterale
- *rudder*
**23** lo stabilizzatore orizzontale
- *tailplane (horizontal stabilizer)*
**24** il timone orizzontale
- *elevator*
**25** il correttore di assetto
- *trim tab (trimming tab)*
**26** la fusoliera
- *fuselage (body)*
**27** la superficie alare (la superficie portante)
- *wing*
**28** l'alettone *m*
- *aileron*
**29** l'ipersostentatore di atterraggio (il flap)
- *landing flap*
**30** il correttore di assetto
- *trim tab (trimming tab)*
**31** la lampada di posizione *f* (rossa)
- *navigation light (position light) [red]*
**32** il faro di atterraggio
- *landing light*
**33** il carrello principale
- *main undercarriage unit (main landing gear unit)*
**34** la ruota anteriore
- *nose wheel*

**35** il motore propulsore
- *engine*
**36** l'elica
- *propeller (airscrew)*
**37-62** **il paracadutismo** (il paracadutismo sportivo)
- ***parachuting*** *(sport parachuting)*
**37** il paracadute (il paracadute per lanci *m pl* sportivi)
- *parachute*
**38** la velatura (la calotta)
- *canopy*
**39** l'estrattore
- *pilot chute*
**40** i tiranti (le funi, il fascio funicolare)
- *suspension lines*
**41** il comando
- *steering line*
**42** l'imbracatura
- *riser*
**43** la bretella
- *harness*
**44** il sacco
- *pack*
**45** la velatura del paracadute per lanci sportivi
- *system of slots of the sports parachute*
**46** gli ugelli direzionali
- *turn slots*
**47** il foro apicale
- *apex*
**48** il bordo di attacco
- *skirt*
**49** il pannello di stabilizzazione *f*
- *stabilizing panel*
**50** *u.* **51** il lancio di stile *m* (l'acrobazia)
- *style jump*
**50** il rovesciamento
- *back loop*
**51** il looping (la spirale)
- *spiral*
**52-54** i segnali visivi esplicativi
- *ground signals*
**52** il segnale «salto permesso» (il bersaglio a croce *f* )
- *signal for 'permission to jump' ('conditions are safe') (target cross)*
**53** il segnale «divieto di salto – nuovo volo»
- *signal for 'parachuting suspended–repeat flight'*
**54** il segnale «divieto di salto – atterrare subito»
- *signal for 'parachuting suspended–aircraft must land'*
**55** il lancio di precisione *f*
- *accuracy jump*
**56** il bersaglio a croce *f*
- *target cross*
**57** il cerchio piccolo del bersaglio (il cerchio dei 25 m)
- *inner circle [radius 25 m]*
**58** il cerchio medio del bersaglio (il cerchio dei 50 m)
- *middle circle [radius 50 m]*
**59** il cerchio grande del bersaglio (il cerchio dei 100 m)
- *outer circle [radius 100 m]*
**60-62** cadute *f pl* libere
- *free-fall positions*
**60** la posizione a X
- *full spread position*
**61** la posizione «deriva lenta»
- *frog position*

**62** la posizione a T
- *T position*
**63-84** **la navigazione in pallone** *m* (la navigazione aerostatica)
- ***ballooning***
**63** il pallone a gas (il pallone libero)
- *gas balloon*
**64** la navicella (la gondola)
- *gondola (balloon basket)*
**65** la zavorra (i sacchi di sabbia)
- *ballast (sandbags)*
**66** l'ormeggio del pallone
- *mooring line*
**67** l'anello del pallone
- *hoop*
**68** gli strumenti di bordo
- *flight instruments (instruments)*
**69** il cavo di guida
- *trail rope*
**70** l'appendice *f* di gonfiamento
- *mouth (neck)*
**71** gli ormeggi dell'appendice *f* di gonfiamento
- *neck line*
**72** la tela da strappo (il pannello da strappo) di emergenza
- *emergency rip panel*
**73** la cordicella da strappo di emergenza
- *emergency ripping line*
**74** i piedi di oca
- *network (net)*
**75** la tela da strappo (il pannello da strappo)
- *rip panel*
**76** la cordicella da strappo
- *ripping line*
**77** la valvola
- *valve*
**78** la cordicella della valvola
- *valve line*
**79** la mongolfiera (il pallone a aria calda)
- *hot-air balloon*
**80** la piattaforma per il bruciatore
- *burner platform*
**81** l'apertura ingresso aria calda
- *mouth*
**82** la valvola
- *vent*
**83** la tela (il pannello) da strappo
- *rip panel*
**84** l'ascesa dei palloni
- *balloon take-off*
**85-91** **il modellismo**
- ***flying model aeroplanes*** (Am. *airplanes*)
**85** il volo di aeromodelli *m pl* radiocomandati
- *radio-controlled model flight*
**86** l'aeromodello libero comandato a distanza
- *remote-controlled free flight model*
**87** la radio trasmittente
- *remote control radio*
**88** l'antenna (l'antenna trasmittente)
- *antenna (transmitting antenna)*
**89** l'aeromodello controllato (l'aeromodello U-control)
- *control line model*
**90** il comando unifilare per volo controllato
- *mono-line control system*
**91** la cuccia volante, un aeromodello grottesco
- *flying kennel, a K9-class model*

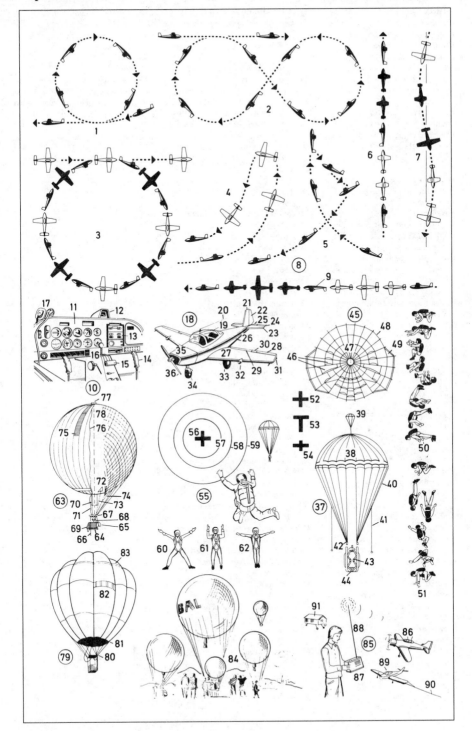

**1-7 il dressage**
- *dressage*
1 il rettangolo da dressage *m*
- *arena (dressage arena)*
2 il margine del recinto
- *rail*
3 il cavallo da dressage *m*
- *school horse*
4 la giacca nera
- *dark coat (black coat)*
5 i pantaloni bianchi da cavallerizzo
- *white breeches*
6 il cilindro (la bombetta)
- *top hat*
7 il passo
- *gait (also: school figure)*
**8-14 il salto a ostacoli *m pl***
- ***show jumping***
8 l'ostacolo (il barrage), un ostacolo
semi-fisso; *simili:* la barriera, le
stanghe accoppiate, la palizzata,
l'oxer *m* la siepe, il terrapieno, il
fossato, il fosso, il muro
- *obstacle (fence), an almost-fixed
obstacle); sim.: gate, gate and rails,
palisade, oxer, mound, wall*
9 il cavallo da salto (il saltatore)
- *jumper*
10 la sella da salto
- *jumping saddle*
11 il sottopancia
- *girth*
12 il filetto del morso
- *snaffle*
13 la giacca rossa (*anche:* la giacca
nera)
- *red coat (hunting pink, pink; also:
dark coat)*
14 il cap nero
- *hunting cap (riding cap)*
15 la fasciatura
- *bandage*
**16-19 il military**
- ***three-day event***
16 la cavalcata in aperta campagna
- *endurance competition*
17 la scarpata
- *cross-country*
18 il casco di sicurezza (il cap con
sottogola)
- *helmet (also: hard hat, hard hunting cap)*
19 le bandierine marca percorso
- *course markings*
**20-22 la corsa a ostacoli *m pl***
- ***steeplechase***
20 la siepe (con fossato), un ostacolo
fisso
- *water jump, a fixed obstacle*
21 il salto
- *jump*
22 il frustino
- *riding switch*

**23-40 il trotto (le corse al trotto)**
- ***harness racing (harness horse racing)***
23 la pista per le corse al trotto (la
pista)
- *harness racing track (track)*
24 il sulky
- *sulky*
25 la ruota a raggi *m pl* con protezione *f* di plastica
- *spoke wheel (spoked wheel) with
plastic wheel disc (disk)*
26 il fantino, con la casacca da trotto
- *driver in trotting silks*
27 le redini
- *rein*
28 il cavallo da trotto, il trottatore
- *trotter*
29 il cavallo pezzato
- *piebald horse*
30 il morso
- *shadow roll*
31 il parastinchi
- *elbow boot*
32 la protezione di gomma
- *rubber boot*
33 il numero di partenza
- *number*
34 la tribuna vetrata con lo sportello
del totalizzatore (la cassa)
- *glass-covered grandstand with
totalizator windows (tote windows) inside*
35 la tabella del totalizzatore
- *totalizator (tote)*
36 il numero di partenza
- *number [of each runner]*
37 la quotazione
- *odds (price, starting price, price
offered)*
38 l'indicazione *f* del vincitore
- *winners' table*
39 la quota vincente
- *winner's price*
40 i tempi (il tabellone dei tempi)
- *time indicator*
**41-49 la caccia a cavallo, una caccia a
strascico**
- ***hunt, a drag hunt;*** *sim.: fox hunt,
paper chase (paper hunt, hare-
and-hounds)*
41 il gruppo
- *field*
42 la giacca rossa da caccia
- *hunting pink*
43 il piqueur
- *whipper-in (whip)*
44 il corno da caccia
- *hunting horn*
45 il capo caccia
- *Master (Master of foxhounds,
MFH)*

46 la muta dei cani
- *pack of hounds (pack)*
47 il cane da cervi *m pl*
- *staghound*
48 la «volpe»
- *drag*
49 lo strascico, la finta pista
- *scented trail (artificial scent)*
**50 la corsa al galoppo (il galoppo)**
- ***horse racing (racing)***
51 la pista
- *field (racehorses)*
52 il favorito
- *favourite (Am. favorite)*
53 l'outsider
- *outsider*

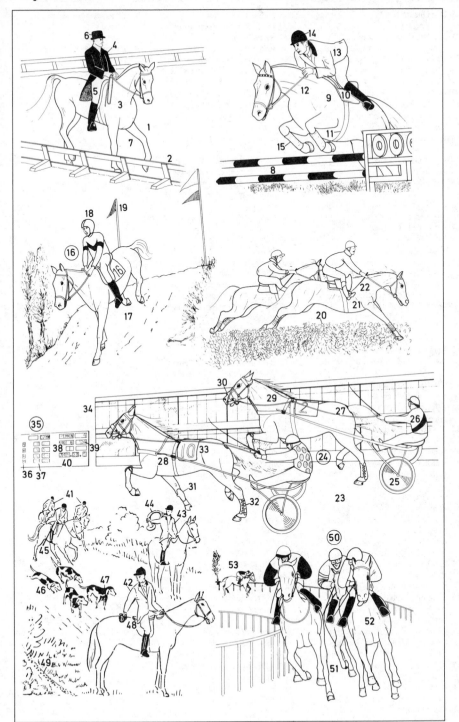

**1-23 ciclismo**
- *cycle racing*
**1** la pista, qui pista indoor
- *cycling track (cycle track); here: indoor track*
**2-7** la seigiorni
- *six-day race*
**2** il corridore della seigiorni, un pistard in azione *f*
- *six-day racer, a track racer (track rider) on the track*
**3** il casco di protezione *f*
- *crash hat*
**4** la giuria (della corsa)
- *stewards*
**5** il giudice di arrivo
- *judge*
**6** il giudice addetto a contare i giri
- *lap scorer*
**7** il box (la cabina) dei ciclisti
- *rider's box (racer's box)*
**8-10** la corsa su strada
- *road race*
**8** il corridore su strada, un corridore ciclista
- *road racer, a racing cyclist*
**9** la maglia da ciclista
- *racing jersey*
**10** la borraccia
- *water bottle*
**11-15** la corsa dietro motori *m pl*
- *motor-paced racing (long-distance racing)*
**11** il battistrada, un motociclista
- *pacer, a motorcyclist*
**12** la motocicletta battistrada
- *pacer's motorcycle*
**13** il rullo poggia-ruote, una protezione
- *roller, a safety device*
**14** il ciclista dietro motori *m pl*
- *stayer (motor-paced track rider)*
**15** la bicicletta da corsa per gare *f pl* dietro motori *m pl*
- *motor-paced cycle, a racing cycle*
**16** la bicicletta da corsa per gare *f pl* su strada
- *racing cycle (racing bicycle) for road racing (road race bicycle)*
**17** la sella da corsa, una sella senza molle *f pl*
- *racing saddle, an unsprung saddle*
**18** il manubrio da corsa
- *racing handlebars (racing handlebar)*
**19** il tubolare (la gomma da corsa)
- *tubular tyre (Am. tire) (racing tyre)*
**20** la catena
- *chain*
**21** il fermapiedi
- *toe clip (racing toe clip)*
**22** il cinghietto
- *strap*

**23** la gomma di scorta
- *spare tubular tyre (Am. tire)*
**24-38 motociclismo**
- *motorsports*
**24-28** le corse in motocicletta: discipline *f pl*: corse *f pl* su erba, corse *f pl* su strada, corse *f pl* su piste *f pl* di sabbia, corse *f pl* su piste *f pl* di cemento, corse *f pl* su piste *f pl* di cenere *f*, corse *f pl* in montagna, corse *f pl* su ghiaccio (speedway), sport *m* campestre, trial, motocross *m*
- *motorcycle racing; disciplines: grasstrack racing, road racing, sand track racing, cement track racing, speedway [on ash or shale tracks], mountain racing, ice racing (ice speedway), scramble racing, trial, moto cross*
**24** la pista di sabbia
- *sand track*
**25** il corridore motociclista
- *racing motorcyclist (rider)*
**26** la tuta di protezione *f* in pelle *f*
- *leather overalls (leathers)*
**27** la motocicletta da corsa (una monoposto)
- *racing motorcycle, a solo machine*
**28** il numero di partenza
- *number (number plate)*
**29** la coppia dei corridori in curva
- *sidecar combination on the bend*
**30** il sidecar
- *sidecar*
**31** la motocicletta da corsa carenata [500 cm³]
- *streamlined racing motorcycle [500 cc.]*
**32** la gimcana (la gimkana, la gincana), una gara di abilità; *qui:* il motociclista durante lo slalom
- *gymkhana, a competition of skill; here: motorcyclist performing a jump*
**33** la gara campestre, una prova di abilità
- *cross-country race, a test in performance*
**34-38** auto *f pl* da corsa
- *racing cars*
**34** l'automobile da corsa di Formula 1 (una monoposto)
- *Formula One racing car (a mono posto)*
**35** lo spoiler posteriore
- *rear spoiler (aerofoil, Am. airfoil)*
**36** l'automobile *f* da corsa di Formula 2 (una macchina da corsa)
- *Formula Two racing car (a racing car)*

**37** l'automobile *f* sportiva da corsa Super V
- *Super-Vee racing car*
**38** il prototipo, una macchina sportiva
- *prototype, a racing car*

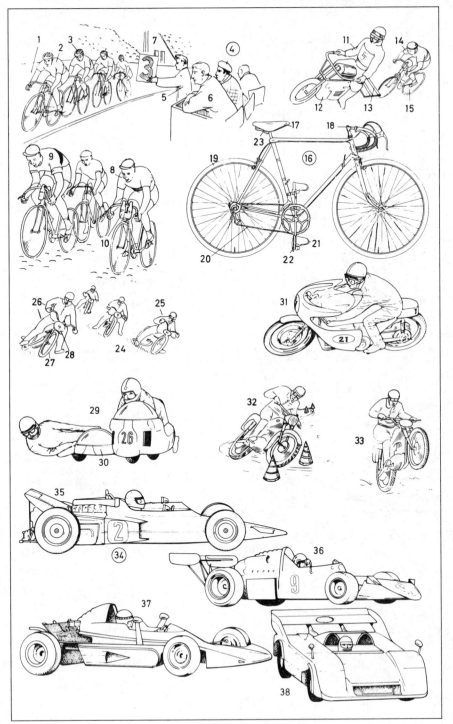

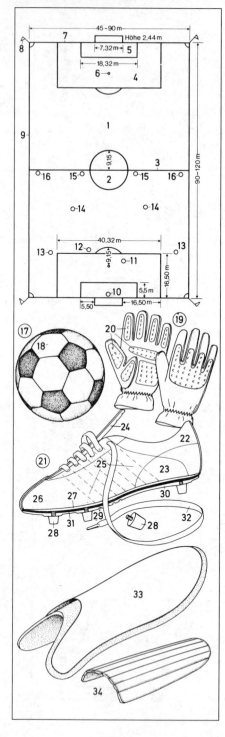

1-16 il terreno di gioco
– *football pitch*
1 il campo di calcio
– *field (park)*
2 il centro campo
– *centre (Am. center) circle*
3 la linea di metà campo
– *half-way line*
4 l'area di rigore *m*
– *penalty area*
5 l'area di porta
– *goal area*
6 il cerchietto del calcio di rigore *m*
– *penalty spot*
7 la linea di fondo
– *goal line (by-line)*
8 la bandierina di calcio d'angolo
– *corner flag*
9 la linea laterale
– *touch line*
10 il portiere
– *goalkeeper*
11 il libero
– *sweeper (libero)*
12 lo stopper
– *inside defender*
13 il difensore esterno
– *outside defender*
14 il centrocampista (il mediano)
– *midfield players*
15 la mezz'ala
– *inside forward (striker)*
16 l'ala
– *outside forward (winger)*
17 il pallone
– *football*
18 la valvola
– *valve*
19 i guanti del portiere
– *goalkeeper's gloves*
20 il rinforzo di gomma piuma
– *foam rubber padding*
21 la scarpa da calcio
– *football boot*
22 il rivestimento di pelle *f*
– *leather lining*
23 il contrafforte
– *counter*
24 la linguetta di gomma piuma
– *foam rubber tongue*
25 le cuciture
– *bands*
26 il rinforzo in pelle *f*
– *shaft*
27 la suola
– *insole*
28 i chiodi
– *screw-in stud*
29 le scanalature per l'articolazione *f*
– *groove*
30 la suola di nylon *m*
– *nylon sole*

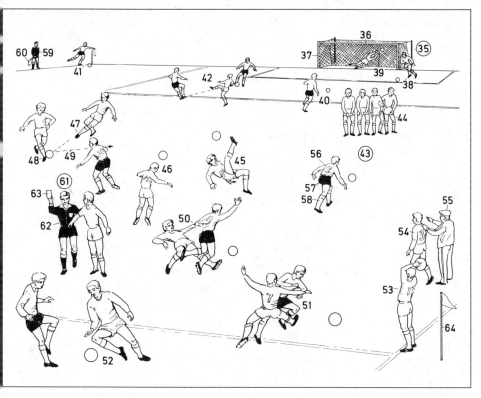

31 la tramezza
– *inner sole*
32 i lacci delle scarpe
– *lace (bootlace)*
33 il parastinchi con ginocchiera
– *football pad with knee guard*
34 il parastinchi
– *shin guard*
35 la porta
– *goal*
36 la traversa
– *crossbar*
37 il palo (il palo della porta)
– *post (goalpost)*
38 il calcio di rinvio
– *goal kick*
39 la respinta di pugno
– *save with the fists*
40 il calcio di rigore *m* (il rigore)
– *penalty (penalty kick)*
41 il calcio d'angolo (il corner)
– *corner (corner kick)*
42 il fuorigioco
– *offside*
43 il calcio di punizione *f*
– *free kick*
44 la barriera
– *wall*

45 la rovesciata
– *bicycle kick (overhead bicycle kick)*
46 il colpo di testa
– *header*
47 il passaggio diretto (della palla)
– *pass (passing the ball)*
48 l'arresto (della palla)
– *receiving the ball (taking a pass)*
49 il passaggio corto
– *short pass (one-two)*
50 il fallo
– *foul (infringement)*
51 l'ostruzione *f*
– *obstruction*
52 il dribbling
– *dribble*
53 la rimessa laterale
– *throw-in*
54 la riserva (il giocatore di riserva)
– *substitute*
55 l'allenatore *m*
– *coach*
56 la maglia
– *shirt (jersey)*
57 i calzoncini
– *shorts*
58 i calzini (le calze da giocatore *m*)
– *sock (football sock)*

59 il guardalinee (il segnalinee, l'arbitro di linea)
– *linesman*
60 la bandierina (del guardalinee)
– *linesman's flag*
61 l'ammonizione *f*
– *sending-off*
62 l'arbitro
– *referee*
63 il cartellino, rosso per l'espulsione *f*, giallo per l'ammonizione *f*
– *red card; as a caution also: yellow card*
64 la bandierina della linea di centro campo
– *centre (Am. center) flag*

505

1 **la pallamano**
– *handball (indoor handball)*
2 il giocatore di pallamano
– *handball player, a field player*
3 il pivot (l'attaccante *m*) in fase *f* di attacco
– *attacker, making a jump throw*
4 il difensore
– *defender*
5 la linea di tiro
– *penalty line*
6 **l'hockey su prato**
– *hockey*
7 la porta
– *goal*
8 il portiere
– *goalkeeper*
9 il parastinchi (la ginocchiera, la bardatura)
– *pad (shin pad, knee pad)*
10 le scarpe da calcio
– *kicker*
11 la maschera
– *face guard*
12 il guanto
– *glove*
13 il bastone da hockey
– *hockey stick*
14 la palla da hockey
– *hockey ball*
15 il giocatore di hockey
– *hockey player*
16 l'area di tiro
– *striking circle*
17 la linea laterale
– *sideline*
18 il corner
– *corner*
19 **il rugby**
– *rugby (rugby football)*
20 la mischia
– *scrum (scrummage)*
21 la palla da rugby
– *rugby ball*
22 il football (il calcio americano)
– *American football (Am. football)*
23 il tide-hand, un giocatore di foot-ball
– *player carrying the ball, a football player*
24 il casco
– *helmet*
25 la maschera di protezione *f* del viso
– *face guard*
26 il paraspalle (il shoulder pads)
– *padded jersey*
27 la palla da football
– *ball (pigskin)*
28 **il basket (la pallacanestro)**
– *basketball*
29 il pallone da basket
– *basketball*
30 il tabellone (lo specchio)
– *backboard*

31 il supporto
– *backboard support*
32 il canestro
– *basket*
33 l'anello
– *basket ring*
34 il quadratino
– *target rectangle*
35 il tiratore, un giocatore di palla-canestro
– *basketball player shooting*
36 la linea di fondo
– *end line*
37 l'area di tiro libero
– *restricted area*
38 la linea di tiro libero
– *free-throw line*
39 il giocatore di riserva (la riserva)
– *substitute*
**40-69 il baseball**
– *baseball*
**40-58** il campo da gioco (il diamante)
– *field (park)*
40 la zona riservata agli spettatori
– *spectator barrier*
41 il giocatore esterno (l'esterno)
– *outfielder*
42 il giocatore interno (l'interno)
– *short stop*
43 la seconda base
– *second base*
44 il giocatore di seconda base *f*
– *baseman*
45 il corridore
– *runner*
46 la prima base
– *first base*
47 la terza base
– *third base*
48 la linea di fallo
– *foul line (base line)*
49 la base di lancio
– *pitcher's mound*
50 il pitcher
– *pitcher*
51 la casa base
– *batter's position*
52 il battitore
– *batter*
53 la base di battuta
– *home base (home plate)*
54 il ricevitore (il catcher)
– *catcher*
55 il primo arbitro
– *umpire*
56 il coach-box
– *coach's box*
57 l'allenatore *m* (il coach)
– *coach*
58 il battitore successivo
– *batting order*
**59** *u.* **60** guanti *m pl* da baseball
– *baseball gloves (baseball mitts)*
59 il guanto del giocatore
– *fielder's glove (fielder's mitt)*

60 il guanto del ricevitore (il guanto del catcher)
– *catcher's glove (catcher's mitt)*
61 la palla
– *baseball*
62 la mazza
– *bat*
63 il battitore al tiro
– *batter at bat*
64 il ricevitore (il catcher)
– *catcher*
65 il giudice arbitro
– *umpire*
66 il corridore
– *runner*
67 il cuscinetto di base *f*
– *base plate*
68 il lanciatore
– *pitcher*
69 la pedana di lancio
– *pitcher's mound*
**70-76 il cricket**
– *cricket*
70 la porta con l'asticella
– *wicket with bails*
71 la linea di porta
– *bowling crease*
72 la linea di corsa
– *popping crease*
73 il ricevitore
– *wicket keeper of the fielding side*
74 il ribattitore
– *batsman*
75 la mazza
– *bat (cricket bat)*
76 il lanciatore
– *fielder (bowler)*
**77-82 il croquet**
– *croquet*
77 il picchetto di arrivo
– *winning peg*
78 l'archetto
– *hoop*
79 il picchetto di girata
– *corner peg*
80 il giocatore di croquet *m*
– *croquet player*
81 il maglio da croquet *m*
– *croquet mallet*
82 la pallina da croquet *m*
– *croquet ball*

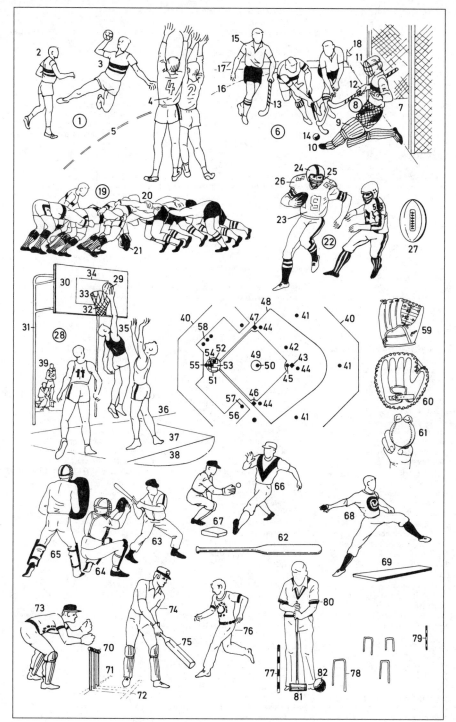

**1-42 il tennis** (il gioco del tennis)
– _tennis_
**1** il campo da tennis _m_
– _tennis court_
**2** _bis_ **3** la linea laterale per il doppio (doppio; doppio maschile, doppio femminile, doppio misto)
– _sideline for doubles match (doubles; men's doubles, women's doubles, mixed doubles) (doubles sideline)_
**3** _bis_ **10** la linea di fondo
– _base line_
**4** _bis_ **5** la linea laterale per il singolare (singolare; signolare maschile, singolare femminile)
– _sideline for singles match (singles; men's singles, women's singles) (singles sideline)_
**6** _bis_ **7** la linea di servizio
– _service line_
**8** _bis_ **9** la linea mediana
– _centre (Am. center) line_
**11** il segno di centrocampo
– _centre (Am. center) mark_
**12** il rettangolo di servizio (il campo di servizio)
– _service court_
**13** la rete
– _net (tennis net)_
**14** il tendirete
– _net strap_
**15** i pali
– _net post_
**16** il giocatore di tennis; qui: il battitore
– _tennis player_
**17** la schiacciata (la battuta)
– _smash_
**18** il partner (_qui:_ il ribattitore)
– _opponent_
**19** l'arbitro
– _umpire_
**20** il seggiolone dell'arbitro
– _umpire's chair_
**21** il microfono dell'arbitro
– _umpire's microphone_
**22** il raccattapalle
– _ball boy_
**23** il giudice di net _m_
– _net-cord judge_
**24** il giudice di linea laterale
– _foot-fault judge_
**25** il giudice di linea mediana
– _centre (Am. center) line judge_
**26** il giudice di linea di fondo
– _base line judge_
**27** il giudice di linea di servizio
– _service line judge_
**28** la palla da tennis _m_
– _tennis ball_
**29** la racchetta da tennis _m_ (la racchetta)
– _tennis racket (tennis racquet, racket, racquet)_
**30** l'impugnatura
– _racket handle (racquet handle)_
**31** l'incordatura (la raccordatura)
– _strings (striking surface)_
**32** la pressa
– _press (racket press, racquet press)_
**33** il tirante a vite _f_
– _tightening screw_
**34** il tabellone dei risultati
– _scoreboard_

**35** i risultati del gioco (delle partite)
– _results of sets_
**36** il nome del giocatore
– _player's name_
**37** il numero dei set (delle partite)
– _number of sets_
**38** il numero dei game (dei giochi)
– _state of play_
**39** il rovescio
– _backhand stroke_
**40** il diritto
– _forehand stroke_
**41** la volée
– _volley (forehand volley at normal height)_
**42** lo smash (la battuta)
– _service_
**43** _u._ **44 il badminton** (il gioco del volano)
– _badminton_
**43** la racchetta da badminton
– _badminton racket (badminton racquet)_
**44** il volano
– _shuttle (shuttlecock)_
**45-55 il tennis da tavolo** (il ping pong)
– _table tennis_
**45** la racchetta da ping pong
– _table tennis racket (racquet) (table tennis bat)_
**46** l'impugnatura
– _racket (racquet) handle (bat handle)_
**47** il rivestimento della racchetta
– _blade covering_
**48** la pallina da ping pong
– _table tennis ball_
**49** i giocatori di ping pong; qui: il doppio misto
– _table tennis players; here: mixed doubles_
**50** il ribattitore (il ricevente)
– _receiver_
**51** il giocatore alla battuta (il giocatore al servizio, il battitore)
– _server_
**52** il tavolo da ping pong
– _table tennis table_
**53** la rete da ping pong
– _table tennis net_
**54** la linea mediana
– _centre (Am. center) line_
**55** la linea laterale
– _sideline_
**56-71 la pallavolo** (il volley ball)
– _volleyball_
**56** _u._ **57** la posizione corretta delle mani
– _correct placing of the hands_
**58** il pallone da pallavolo (il pallone da volley)
– _volleyball_
**59** la battuta (il servizio)
– _serving the volleyball_
**60** il difensore (il centrale)
– _blocker_
**61** la zona di battuta
– _service area_
**62** il battitore
– _server_
**63** il giocatore a rete _f_ (l'attaccante _m_)
– _front-line player_
**64** la zona di attacco
– _attack area_

**65** la linea di attacco
– _attack line_
**66** la zona di difesa (la sconda linea)
– _defence (Am. defense) area_
**67** il primo arbitro
– _referee_
**68** il secondo arbitro
– _umpire_
**69** il giudice di linea
– _linesman_
**70** il tabellone
– _scoreboard_
**71** il segnapunti (il giudice a tavolino)
– _scorer_
**72-78 il gioco della palla a pugno** (non giocato in Italia)
– _faustball_
**72** la linea di battuta
– _base line_
**73** la corda
– _tape_
**74** la palla
– _faustball_
**75** lo schiacciatore
– _forward_
**76** il mediano
– _centre (Am. center)_
**77** il difensore
– _back_
**78** la battuta
– _hammer blow_
**79-82** il percorso (le buche)
– _course (holes)_
**79-93 il gioco del golf** (il golf)
– _golf_
**79** il teeing-ground
– _teeing ground_
**80** il rough
– _rough_
**81** il bunker
– _bunker (Am. sand trap)_
**82** il green
– _green (putting green)_
**83** il giocatore mentre lancia
– _golfer, driving_
**84** l'arco dello swing (lo swing verticale)
– _follow-through_
**85** la sacca
– _golf trolley_
**86** il putten (il mettere in buca)
– _putting (holing out)_
**87** la buca
– _hole_
**88** la bandierina
– _pin (flagstick)_
**89** la palla da golf _m_
– _golf ball_
**90** il marchino (il tee)
– _tee_
**91** il bastone da golf _m_, un driver (_sim.:_ il brassie)
– _wood, a driver; sim.: brassie (brassy, brassey)_
**92** il ferro
– _iron_
**93** il putter
– _putter_

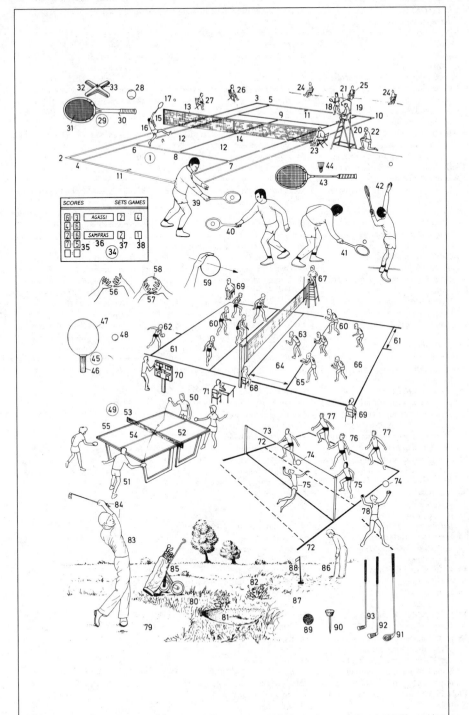

**1-33 la scherma**
- *fencing (modern fencing)*

**1-18** la scherma di fioretto (il fioretto)
- *foil*

**1** il maestro di scherma
- *fencing master (fencing instructor)*

**2** la pedana
- *piste*

**3** la linea di messa in guardia
- *on guard line*

**4** la linea centrale
- *centre (Am. center) line*

**5** *u.* **6** gli schermidori (gli schermidori di fioretto, i fiorettisti) in
combattimento
- *fencers (foil fencers, foilsmen,
foilists) in a bout*

**5** l'attaccante *m* nella posizione *f* di
affondo
- *attacker (attacking fencer) in lunging position (lunging)*

**6** l'attaccato in posizione *f* di
guardia
- *defender (defending fencer), par-
rying*

**7** il colpo dritto (la botta dritta, le
coup droit), un'azione
- *straight thrust, a fencing movement*

**8** la parata di terza
- *parry of the tierce*

**9** la linea di combattimento
- *line of fencing*

**10** le tre misure (le tre distanze di
combattimento): misura di allun-
go o giusta misura, misura cammi-
nando, stretta misura
- *the three fencing measures (short,
medium, and long measure)*

**11** il fioretto, un'arma bianca
(un'arma da combattimento)
- *foil, a thrust weapon*

**12** il guanto
- *fencing glove*

**13** la maschera
- *fencing mask (foil mask)*

**14** la gorgiera della maschera
- *neck flap (neck guard) on the
fencing mask*

**15** il giubbetto metallico
- *metallic jacket*

**16** la divisa
- *fencing jacket*

**17** le scarpe da scherma senza tacco
- *heelless fencing shoes*

**18** la prima posizione per il saluto e
per la discesa in guardia
- *first position for fencer's salute
(initial position, on guard position)*

**19-24** la scherma di sciabola (la sciabola)
- *sabre (Am. saber) fencing*

**19** lo schermidore di sciabola (lo
sciabolatore)
- *sabreurs (sabre fencers Am. saber
fencers)*

**20** la sciabola leggera
- *(light) sabre (Am. saber)*

**21** il guanto
- *sabre (Am. saber) glove (sabre
gauntlet)*

**22** la maschera
- *sabre (Am. saber) mask*

**23** la punta di testa, un'azione
- *cut at head*

**24** la parata di quinta
- *parry of the fifth (quinte)*

**25-33** la scherma con sistema di segnalazione *f* elettrica di stoccata
- *épée, with electrical scoring equipment*

**25** lo schermidore
- *épéeist*

**26** la spada elettrica; *anche:* il fioretto elettrico
- *electric épée; also: electric foil*

**27** la punta della spada
- *épée point*

**28** il segnalatore ottico di stoccata
- *scoring lights*

**29** il rullo avvolgitore
- *spring-loaded wire spool*

**30** la lampada di segnalazione *f*
- *indicator light*

**31** il cavo (il filo di corpo o passante)
- *wire*

**32** l'apparecchio segnalatore
- *electronic scoring equipment*

**33** la posizione di guardia
- *on guard position*

**34-45 le armi bianche**
- *fencing weapons*

**34** la sciabola leggera, un'arma da
taglio e da punta
- *light sabre (Am. saber), a cut and
thrust weapon*

**35** l'elsa
- *guard*

**36** la spada, un'arma da punta e da
taglio
- *épée, a thrust weapon*

**37** il fioretto francese, un'arma da
punta e da taglio
- *French foil, a thrust weapon*

**38** la coccia
- *guard (coquille)*

**39** il fioretto italiano
- *Italian foil*

**40** il pomolo
- *foil pommel*

**41** l'impugnatura
- *handle*

**42** il gavigliano
- *cross piece (quillons)*

**43** la coccia
- *guard (coquille)*

**44** la lama
- *blade*

**45** la punta
- *button*

**46** i legamenti
- *engagements*

**47** il legamento di quarta
- *quarte (carte) engagement*

**48** il legamento di terza
- *tierce engagement (also: sixte
engagement)*

**49** il legamento di mezzo cerchio
- *circling engagement*

**50** il legamento di seconda
- *seconde engagement (also: octave
engagement)*

**51-53** le superfici valide
- *target areas*

**51** tutto il corpo, negli schermidori di
spada (uomini *m pl*)
- *the whole body in épée fencing
(men)*

**52** testa e busto fino all'inguine *m*
negli schermidori di sciabola
(uomini *m pl*)
- *head and upper body down to the
groin in sabre (Am. saber) fencing
(men)*

**53** il busto dal collo all'inguine *m*
negli schermidori di fioretto
(donne *f pl* e uomini *m pl*)
- *trunk from the neck to the groin in
foil fencing (ladies and men)*

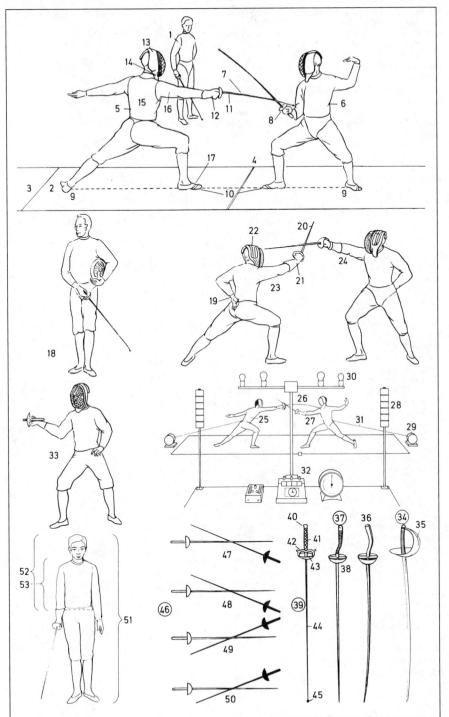

1 la posizione iniziale (di partenza)
 – *basic position (starting position)*
2 la posizione di corsa
 – *running posture*
3 la posizione laterale a gambe *f pl*
 divaricate
 – *side straddle*
4 la posizione trasversale a gambe *f*
 *pl* divaricate
 – *straddle (forward straddle)*
5 la posizione sugli avampiedi
 – *toe stand*
6 la posizione raccolta
 – *crouch*
7 la posizione in ginocchio
 – *upright kneeling position*
8 la posizione seduta sui talloni
 – *kneeling position, seat on heels*
9 la posizione seduta a gambe *f pl*
 piegate
 – *squat*
10 la posizione seduta distesa
 – *L seat (long sitting)*
11 la posizione raccolta a gambe *f pl*
 incrociate
 – *tailor seat (sitting tailor-style)*
12 la posizione seduta con gamba a
 ostacolo
 – *hurdle (hurdle position)*
13 la posizione seduta con gambe *f pl*
 a squadra
 – *V-seat*
14 la staccata sagittale
 – *side split*
15 la staccata frontale
 – *forward split*
16 l'appoggio a angolo
 – *L-support*
17 l'appoggio a angolo acuto
 – *V-support*
18 il sostegno Stalder (il sostegno a
 angolo a gambe *f pl* divaricate)
 – *straddle seat*
19 il ponte
 – *bridge*
20 l'appoggio sulle ginocchia
 – *kneeling front support*
21 l'appoggio in avanti disteso
 – *front support*
22 l'appoggio dorsale disteso
 – *back support*
23 l'appoggio raccolto
 – *crouch with front support*
24 l'appoggio a angolo
 – *arched front support*
25 l'appoggio laterale
 – *side support*
26 la verticale sull'avambraccio
 – *forearm stand (forearm balance)*
27 la verticale ritta
 – *handstand*
28 la verticale sulla fronte
 – *headstand*

29 la candela
 – *shoulder stand (shoulder balance)*
30 la posizione orizzontale prona
 – *forward horizontal stand
 (arabesque)*
31 la posizione laterale
 – *rearward horizontal stand*
32 la flessione laterale del busto
 – *trunk-bending sideways*
33 la flessione del busto in avanti
 – *trunk-bending forwards*
34 la flessione dorsale del busto
 – *arch*
35 il salto a corpo disteso
 – *astride jump (butterfly)*
36 il salto raccolto
 – *tuck jump*
37 il salto a gambe *f pl* divaricate
 – *astride jump*
38 il salto carpiato
 – *pike*
39 il salto a forbice *f*
 – *scissor jump*
40 il salto del cervo
 – *stag jump (stag leap)*
41 il passo di corsa
 – *running step*
42 il passo di affondo
 – *lunge*
43 il passo sorpassato
 – *forward pace*
44 la posizione supina
 – *lying on back*
45 la posizione prona
 – *prone position*
46 la posizione laterale
 – *lying on side*
47 la stazione eretta
 – *holding arms downwards*
48 la stazione a gambe *f pl* divaricate
 – *holding (extending) arms sideways*
49 la posizione distesa sugli avampiedi in fuori
 – *holding arms raised upward*
50 la posizione delle braccia in avanti
 – *holding (extending) arms forward*
51 la posizione delle braccia all'indietro
 – *arms held (extended) backward*
52 la posizione delle braccia sulla
 nuca
 – *hands clasped behind the head*

**1-11  gli attrezzi ginnici** nella ginnastica olimpica maschile
  – *gymnastics apparatus* in men's Olympic gymnastics
**1**  il cavallo senza maniglie *f pl* (il cavallo)
  – *long horse (horse, vaulting horse)*
**2**  le parallele
  – *parallel bars*
**3**  lo staggio
  – *bar*
**4**  gli anelli
  – *rings (stationary rings)*
**5**  il cavallo con maniglie *f pl*
  – *pommel horse (side horse)*
**6**  la maniglia
  – *pommel*
**7**  la sbarra
  – *horizontal bar (high bar)*
**8**  il montante
  – *bar*
**9**  il sostegno della sbarra
  – *upright*
**10**  il tirante (l'estensore *m*)
  – *stay wires*
**11**  la pedana del corpo libero (la pedana 12 x 12 m)
  – *floor (12 m × 12 m floor area)*
**12-21  attrezzi** *m pl* **ausiliari e attrezzi** *m pl* **didattici**
  – *auxiliary apparatus and apparatus for school and club gymnastics*
**12**  la pedana elastica
  – *springboard (Reuther board)*
**13**  il materassino paracadute
  – *landing mat*
**14**  la panca
  – *bench*
**15**  il plinto
  – *box*
**16**  il plinto piccolo
  – *small box*
**17**  la cavallina
  – *buck*
**18**  il materasso paracadute
  – *mattress*
**19**  la fune
  – *climbing rope (rope)*
**20**  la spalliera
  – *wall bars*
**21**  il quadro svedese
  – *window ladder*
**22-39  il comportamento all'attrezzo** (le posizioni)
  – *positions in relation to the apparatus*
**22**  la posizione ritta di fronte all'attrezzo
  – *side, facing*
**23**  la posizione ritta dorso all'attrezzo
  – *side, facing away*

**24**  la posizione longitudinale all'attrezzo
  – *end, facing*
**25**  la posizione trasversale all'attrezzo
  – *end, facing away*
**26**  la posizione di partenza esterna fronte all'attrezzo
  – *outside, facing*
**27**  la posizione di partenza fra gli staggi
  – *inside, facing*
**28**  l'appoggio frontale
  – *front support*
**29**  l'appoggio dorsale
  – *back support*
**30**  l'appoggio a gambe *f pl* divaricate
  – *straddle position*
**31**  la posizione seduta esterna
  – *seated position outside*
**32**  la posizione trasversale esterna (la sedia)
  – *riding seat outside*
**33**  la sospensione frontale
  – *hang*
**34**  la sospensione dorsale
  – *reverse hang*
**35**  la sospensione a braccie flesse
  – *hang with elbows bent*
**36**  la kippe (il voltabraccia dorsale)
  – *piked reverse hang*
**37**  la verticale rovesciata
  – *straight inverted hang*
**38**  l'oscillazione *f* in appoggio ritto
  – *straight hang*
**39**  l'appoggio a braccie *f pl* piegate
  – *bent hang*
**40-46  le impugnature**
  – *grasps (kinds of grasp)*
**40**  l'impugnatura dorsale alla sbarra
  – *overgrasp on the horizontal bar*
**41**  l'impugnatura palmare alla sbarra
  – *undergrasp on the horizontal bar*
**42**  l'impugnatura mista alla sbarra
  – *combined grasp on the horizontal bar*
**43**  l'impugnatura incrociata alla sbarra
  – *cross grasp on the horizontal bar*
**44**  l'impugnatura cubitale alla sbarra
  – *rotated grasp on the horizontal bar*
**45**  l'impugnatura a anello alle parallele
  – *outside grip on the parallel bars*
**46**  l'impugnatura cubitale alle parallele
  – *rotated grasp on the parallel bars*
**47**  il paracallo
  – *leather handstrap*
**48-60  esercizi** *m pl* **agli attrezzi**
  – *(apparatus) exercises*
**48**  la planche al cavallo
  – *long-fly on the horse*

**49**  la squadra alle parallele
  – *rise to straddle on the parallel bar.*
**50**  la croce agli anelli
  – *crucifix on the rings*
**51**  la forbice al cavallo con maniglie *f p*
  – *scissors (scissors movement) on the pommel horse*
**52**  la sospensione verticale di forza
  – *legs raising into a handstand on the floor*
**53**  il salto a gambe *f pl* flesse al cavallo
  – *squat vault on the horse*
**54**  il mulinello al cavallo con maniglie *f pl*
  – *double leg circle on the pommel horse*
**55**  l'oscillazione *f* in avanti agli anelli
  – *hip circle backwards on the rings*
**56**  la posizione distesa agli anelli
  – *lever hang on the rings*
**57**  l'oscillazione *f* in presa ascellare alle parallele
  – *rearward swing on the parallel bars*
**58**  la kippe alle parallele
  – *forward kip into upper arm hang on the parallel bars*
**59**  l'uscita in fioretto alla sbarra
  – *backward underswing on the horizontal bar*
**60**  la gran volta dorsale alla sbarra
  – *backward grand circle on the horizontal bar*
**61-63  l'abbigliamento per la ginnastica**
  – *gymnastics kit*
**61**  la maglietta da ginnastica
  – *singlet (vest, Am. undershirt)*
**62**  i calzoni lunghi da ginnastica artistica
  – *gym trousers*
**63**  le scarpe da ginnastica
  – *gym shoes*
**64**  la fasciatura (il bandage)
  – *wristband*

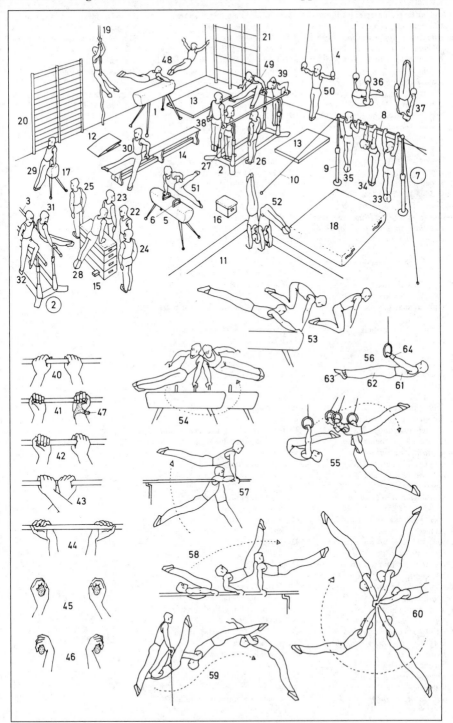

# 297 Ginnastica agli attrezzi II (ginnastica femminile)

**1-6 gli attrezzi ginnici** (nella ginnastica olimpica femminile)
- *gymnastics apparatus in women's Olympic gymnastics*
**1** il cavallo senza maniglie *f pl* (il cavallo)
- *horse (vaulting horse)*
**2** la trave
- *beam*
**3** le parallele asimmetriche
- *asymmetric bars (uneven bars)*
**4** lo staggio
- *bar*
**5** l'estensore *m* (il divaricatore)
- *stay wires*
**6** la pedana del corpo libero (la pedana 12 × 12 m)
- *floor (12 m × 12 m floor area)*
**7-14 attrezzi** *m pl* **ausiliari e didattici**
- *auxiliary apparatus and apparatus for school and club gymnastics*
**7** il materasso paracadute
- *landing mat*
**8** la pedana elastica
- *springboard (Reuther board)*
**9** il plinto piccolo
- *small box*
**10** il trampolino elastico
- *trampoline*
**11** il telo
- *sheet (web)*
**12** il telaio
- *frame*
**13** gli elastici
- *rubber springs*
**14** il mini trampolino elastico
- *springboard trampoline*
**15-32 esercizi** *m pl* **agli attrezzi**
- *apparatus exercises*
**15** il salto all'indietro raccolto
- *backward somersault*
**16** l'assistenza
- *spotting position (standing-in position)*
**17** il salto all'indietro teso al trampolino
- *vertical backward somersault on the trampoline*
**18** il salto in avanti raccolto al mini trampolino
- *forward somersault on the springboard trampoline*
**19** la capovolta al suolo
- *forward roll on the floor*
**20** il tuffo con capovolta al suolo
- *long-fly to forward roll on the floor*
**21** la ruota sulla trave
- *cartwheel on the beam*
**22** il salto capovolto al cavallo
- *handspring on the horse*

**23** la rovesciata indietro a terra
- *backward walkover*
**24** il flick-flack al suolo
- *back flip (flik-flak) on the floor*
**25** la butterfly al suolo (la rovesciata avanti libera)
- *free walkover forward on the floor*
**26** la ribaltata avanti al suolo
- *forward walkover on the floor*
**27** la kippe di fronte al suolo
- *headspring on the floor*
**28** la kippe alle parallele asimmetriche
- *upstart on the asymmetric bars*
**29** il giro addominale libero all'indietro alle parallele asimmetriche
- *free backward circle on the asymmetric bars*
**30** il passaggio al cavallo
- *face vault over the horse*
**31** il volteggio con passaggio laterale al cavallo
- *flank vault over the horse*
**32** il volteggio dorsale al cavallo
- *back vault (rear vault) over the horse*
**33-50 ginnastica con piccoli attrezzi** *m pl*
- *gymnastics with hand apparatus*
**33** il lancio a arco
- *hand-to-hand throw*
**34** la palla da ginnastica ritmica
- *gymnastic ball*
**35** il lancio in alto
- *high toss*
**36** il palleggio
- *bounce*
**37** il mulinello con due clavette *f pl*
- *hand circling with two clubs*
**38** la clavetta
- *gymnastic club*
**39** l'oscillazione *f*
- *swing*
**40** il salto sopra la bacchetta
- *tuck jump*
**41** la bacchetta
- *bar*
**42** il saltello
- *skip*
**43** la funicella
- *rope (skipping rope)*
**44** il saltello incrociato
- *criss-cross skip*
**45** il passaggio dentro al cerchio
- *skip through the hoop*
**46** il cerchio da ginnastica ritmica
- *gymnastic hoop*
**47** i giri intorno alla mano
- *hand circle*
**48** la serpentina
- *serpent*
**49** il nastro da ginnastica ritmica
- *gymnastic ribbon*

**50** la spirale
- *spiral*
**51** u. **52** l'abbigliamento per la ginnastica
- *gymnastics kit*
**51** il costume ginnico
- *leotard*
**52** le scarpette da ginnastica
- *gym shoes*

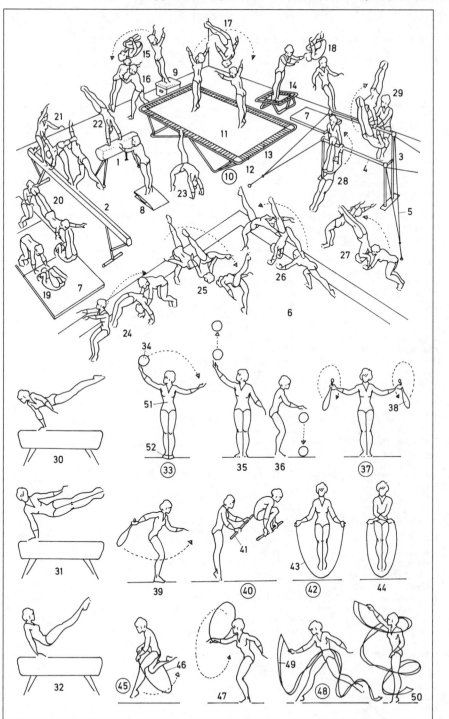

**1-8 la corsa**
- *running*
**1-6** la partenza (lo start)
- *start*
**1** il blocco di partenza
- *starting block*
**2** il piano regolabile
- *adjustable block (pedal)*
**3** la linea di partenza
- *start*
**4** la partenza dai blocchi
- *crouch start*
**5** il corridoio, un velocista (uno sprinter); *anche:* un mezzo-fondista, un fondista
- *runner, a sprinter; also: middle-distance runner, long-distance runner*
**6** la pista, una pista di carbonella o una pista in tartan *m*
- *running track (track), a cinder track or synthetic track*
**7** *u.* **8** la corsa a ostacoli *m pl*
- *hurdles (hurdle racing); sim.: steeplechase*
**7** il superamento dell'ostacolo
- *clearing the hurdle*
**8** l'ostacolo
- *hurdle*
**9-41 il salto**
- *jumping and vaulting*
**9-27** il salto in alto
- *high jump*
**9** il salto alla Fosbury (lo scarica-mento dorsale, il Fosbury flop)
- *Fosbury flop (Fosbury, flop)*
**10** il saltatore in alto
- *high jumper*
**11** la rotazione del corpo lungo l'asse *f* longitudinale e trasversale
- *body rotation (rotation on the body's longitudinal and latitudinal axes)*
**12** l'atterraggio di spalle *f pl*
- *shoulder landing*
**13** il ritto (il saltometro ritto)
- *upright*
**14** l'asticella per il salto in alto (l'asticella)
- *bar (crossbar)*
**15** il salto a forbice *f* (il salto con spalle *f pl* parallele all'asse *f* )
- *Eastern roll*
**16** il salto ventrale
- *Western roll*
**17** lo stacco
- *roll*
**18** la tecnica di superamento
- *rotation*
**19** l'atterraggio
- *landing*
**20** il misuratore dell'altezza del salto
- *height scale*

**21** la tecnica a sforbiciata
- *Eastern cut-off*
**22** la sforbiciata
- *scissors (scissor jump)*
**23** lo scavalcamento ventrale
- *straddle (straddle jump)*
**24** la tecnica dello scavalcamento ventrale
- *turn*
**25** la posizione di stacco-slancio
- *vertical free leg*
**26** lo stacco
- *take-off*
**27** l'arto di stacco
- *free leg*
**28-36** il salto con l'asta
- *pole vault*
**28** l'asta per il salto
- *pole (vaulting pole)*
**29** il saltatore nella fase di slancio
- *pole vaulter (vaulter) in the pull-up phase*
**30** la tecnica di slancio (il flyaway)
- *swing*
**31** il valicamento dell'asticella
- *crossing the bar*
**32** l'impianto di salto con l'asta
- *high jump apparatus (high jump equipment)*
**33** il ritto
- *upright*
**34** l'asticella per il salto
- *bar (crossbar)*
**35** la cassetta di imbucata
- *box*
**36** la zona di caduta
- *landing area (landing pad)*
**37-41** il salto in lungo
- *long jump*
**37** lo stacco
- *take-off*
**38** l'asse *f* di stacco (la tavoletta di stacco)
- *take-off board*
**39** la buca
- *landing area*
**40** la tecnica dei passi in aria (lo step-style)
- *hitch-kick*
**41** la tecnica dell'estensione *f* (lo hang)
- *hang*
**42-47** il lancio del martello
- *hammer throw*
**42** il martello
- *hammer*
**43** la testa del martello
- *hammer head*
**44** il filo di collegamento
- *handle*
**45** la maniglia triangolare
- *grip*

**46** l'impugnatura
- *holding the grip*
**47** il guanto
- *glove*
**48** il lancio del peso
- *shot put*
**49** il peso
- *shot (weight)*
**50** lo stile O'Brien
- *O'Brien technique*
**51-53** il lancio del giavellotto
- *javelin throw*
**51** l'impugnatura con il medio e l'indice *m*
- *grip with thumb and index finger*
**52** l'impugnatura con il medio e il pollice
- *grip with thumb and middle finger*
**53** l'impugnatura a tenaglia
- *horseshoe grip*
**54** la fasciatura
- *binding*

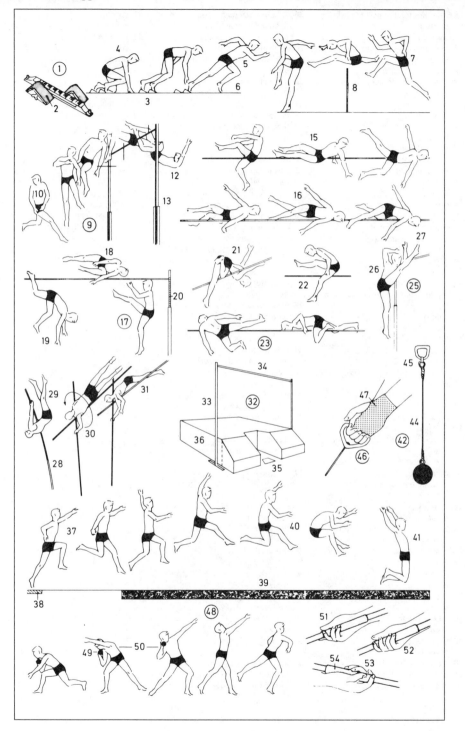

**1-5 il sollevamento pesi** *m pl* (la pesistica)
– *weightlifting*
**1** lo strappo (il sollevamento a strappo)
– *squat-style snatch*
**2** il sollevatore di pesi *m pl* (il pesista)
– *weightlifter*
**3** il bilanciere
– *disc (disk) barbell*
**4** lo slancio
– *jerk with split*
**5** il peso immobile
– *maintained lift*
**6-12 la lotta**
– *wrestling*
**6-9** la lotta greco-romana
– *Greco-Roman wrestling*
**6** la lotta in piedi *m pl*
– *standing wrestling (wrestling in standing position)*
**7** il lottatore
– *wrestler*
**8** la lotta sul tappeto (*qui:* la cintura)
– *on-the-ground wrestling (here: the referee's position)*
**9** il ponte
– *bridge*
**10-12** la lotta libera
– *freestyle wrestling*
**10** la presa di braccia
– *bar arm (arm bar) with grapevine*
**11** la presa di gamba
– *double leg lock*
**12** il tappeto
– *wrestling mat (mat)*
**13-17 il judo** (*sim.:* lo ju-jutsu)
– *judo* (sim.: *ju-jitsu, jiu-jitsu, ju-jutsu)*
**13** lo sbilanciamento verso destra in avanti
– *drawing the opponent off balance to the right and forward*
**14** lo judoka
– *judoka (judoist)*
**15** la cintura colorata come indicazione *f* del grado Dan
– *coloured* (Am. *colored*) *belt, as a symbol of Dan grade*
**16** l'arbitro
– *referee*
**17** la proiezione (il lancio)
– *judo throw*
**18** *u.* **19 il karaté**
– *karate*
**18** il karateka
– *karateka*
**19** il calcio volante laterale, una tecnica di piede *m*
– *side thrust kick, a kicking technique*

**20-50 la boxe** (il pugilato) (l'incontro di boxe *f*, l'incontro di pugilato)
– *boxing (boxing match)*
**20-24** gli attrezzi usati in allenamento
– *training apparatus (training equipment)*
**20** il punching-ball fisso
– *[spring-supported] punch ball*
**21** il sacco
– *punch bag* (Am. *punching bag)*
**22** il punching-ball piccolo
– *speed ball*
**23** la pera
– *[suspended] punch ball*
**24** il punching-ball
– *punch ball*
**25** il pugile, un pugile dilettante (combatte con la maglietta), o un pugile professionista (combatte senza maglietta)
– *boxer, an amateur boxer (boxes in a singlet, vest, Am. undershirt) or a professional boxer (boxes without singlet)*
**26** il guantone (il guantone da boxe *f*)
– *boxing glove*
**27** lo sparring-partner
– *sparring partner*
**28** il diretto
– *straight punch (straight blow)*
**29** la schivata
– *ducking and sidestepping*
**30** il casco di protezione *f*
– *headguard*
**31** il corpo a corpo; *qui:* il clinch
– *infighting; here: clinch*
**32** il montante (l'uppercut *m*)
– *uppercut*
**33** il gancio (il crochet)
– *hook to the head (hook, left hook or right hook)*
**34** il colpo basso, un colpo proibito
– *punch below the belt, a foul punch (illegal punch, foul)*
**35-50** l'incontro di boxe *f*, un incontro per il titolo
– *boxing match (boxing contest), a title fight (title bout)*
**35** il ring (il quadrato)
– *boxing ring (ring)*
**36** le corde
– *ropes*
**37** il tirante delle corde
– *stay wire (stay rope)*
**38** l'angolo
– *neutral corner*
**39** il vincitore
– *winner*
**40** lo sconfitto per fuori combattimento (knock-out, KO)
– *loser by a knockout*

**41** l'arbitro
– *referee*
**42** il conteggio
– *counting out*
**43** il giudice
– *judge*
**44** il secondo
– *second*
**45** il manager (il procuratore)
– *manager*
**46** il gong
– *gong*
**47** il cronometrista
– *timekeeper*
**48** il commissario di gara
– *record keeper*
**49** il fotografo
– *press photographer*
**50** il cronista sportivo (il reporter)
– *sports reporter (reporter)*

**1-57 l'alpinismo** (l'escursione *f*, la gita in montagna, il turismo di alta montagna)
– **mountaineering** *(mountain climbing, Alpinism)*
**1** il rifugio (rifugio del Club Alpino, rifugio alpino)
– *hut (Alpine Club hut, mountain hut, base)*
**2-13 la scalata** (scalata in roccia, l'arrampicata in parete *f* ) la tecnica di scalata su roccia
– **climbing** *(rock climbing) [rock climbing technique]*
**2** la parete (parete *f* rocciosa, grado di pendenza delle pareti)
– *rock face (rock wall)*
**3** il canale (il colatoio, la fenditura) (canale verticale, orizzontale, diagonale)
– *fissure, (vertical, horizontal, or diagonal fissure)*
**4** la cengia (rocciosa, erbosa, di massi *m pl*, di neve *f*, di ghiaccio)
– *ledge, (rock ledge, grass ledge, scree ledge, snow ledge, ice ledge)*
**5** lo scalatore (il rocciatore, l'alpinista *m*)
– *mountaineer (climber, mountain climber, Alpinist)*
**6** la giacca a vento (giacca a vento da alpinista *m*, giacca da neve *f*, il piumino)
– *anorak (high-altitude anorak, snowshirt, padded jacket)*
**7** i pantaloni da roccia
– *breeches (climbing breeches)*
**8** il camino
– *chimney*
**9** l'appiglio
– *belay (spike, rock spike)*
**10** la sicura (la sicurezza)
– *belay*
**11** il cappio di appiglio (l'anello di corda, il nodo di cordino)
– *rope sling (sling)*
**12** la corda
– *rope*
**13** la cornice, una cengia
– *spur*
**14-21 la scalata su neve *f* e su ghiaccio** (tecnica di scalata su ghiaccio)
– **snow and ice climbing** *[snow and ice climbing technique]*
**14** la parete di ghiaccio (il pendio ghiacciato o innevato, il ghiacciaio, il nevaio)
– *ice slope (firn slope)*
**15** lo scalatore di ghiacciai *m pl*
– *snow and ice climber*
**16** la piccozza
– *ice axe* (Am. *ax*)
**17** lo scalino nel ghiaccio
– *step (ice step)*

**18** gli occhiali da ghiacciaio (occhiali *m pl* da neve *f* )
– *snow goggles*
**19** il cappuccio (cappuccio della giacca a vento, il passamontagna)
– *hood (anorak hood)*
**20** il tetto di neve *f* (la cornice di neve *f* )
– *cornice (snow cornice)*
**21** la cresta (cresta di ghiaccio)
– *ridge (ice ridge)*
**22-27 la cordata** (la traversata di un ghiacciaio in cordata)
– **rope** *(roped party) [roped trek]*
**22** il ghiacciaio
– *glacier*
**23** il crepaccio
– *crevasse*
**24** il ponte di neve *f*
– *snow bridge*
**25** il capocordata
– *leader*
**26** il secondo in cordata
– *second man (belayer)*
**27** il terzo in cordata (ultimo della cordata)
– *third man (non-belayer)*
**28-30 la discesa con la corda**
– **roping down** *(abseiling, rapelling)*
**28** il cappio di appiglio per la discesa
– *abseil sling*
**29** la discesa con moschettoni *m pl*
– *sling seat*
**30** la discesa Dülfer
– *Dülfer seat*
**31-57 l'equipaggiamento dello scalatore** (equipaggiamento alpinistico, equipaggiamento per alta montagna, equipaggiamento per l'attraversata dei ghiacciai)
– **mountaineering equipment** *(climbing equipment, snow and ice climbing equipment)*
**31** la piccozza
– *ice axe (Am. ax)*
**32** la cinghia da polso
– *wrist sling*
**33** il becco (la parte aguzza della testa della piccozza)
– *pick*
**34** la paletta (la parte piatta della testa della piccozza)
– *adze (Am. adz)*
**35** il buco (foro) per il moschettone
– *karabiner hole*
**36** la piccozza da ghiaccio
– *short-shafted ice axe* (Am. *ax*)
**37** il martello da ghiaccio (il martello a doppio uso per ghiaccio e roccia, martello)
– *hammer axe* (Am. *ax*)
**38** il chiodo da roccia (tipo universale)
– *general-purpose piton*

**39** il gancio per la discesa (gancio circolare)
– *abseil piton (ringed piton)*
**40** la vite da ghiaccio (gancio da ghiaccio a semivite *f* )
– *ice piton (semi-tubular screw ice piton, corkscrew piton)*
**41** il gancio da ghiaccio a spirale *f*
– *drive-in ice piton*
**42** lo scarpone da montagna
– *mountaineering boot*
**43** la suola con il profilo
– *corrugated sole*
**44** lo scarpone da roccia (scarpone *m* per scalate *f pl*)
– *climbing boot*
**45** la bordatura ruvida in ebanite *f*
– *roughened stiff rubber upper*
**46** il moschettone
– *karabiner*
**47** il morsetto
– *screwgate*
**48** i ramponi (ramponi *m pl* leggeri, ramponi *m pl* a dieci chiodi *m pl*, ramponi *m pl* a dodici chiodi *m pl*)
– *crampons (lightweight crampons, twelve-point crampons, ten-point crampons)*
**49** i chiodi frontali
– *front points*
**50** il parachiodi
– *point guards*
**51** le stringhe fissaramponi
– *crampon strap*
**52** gli attacchi a cavo dei ramponi
– *crampon cable fastener*
**53** il casco da montagna
– *safety helmet (protective helmet)*
**54** la lampada frontale
– *helmet lamp*
**55** i gambali da neve *f*
– *snow gaiters*
**56** l'imbragatura a cintura
– *climbing harness*
**57** l'imbragatura a sedile *m*
– *sit harness*

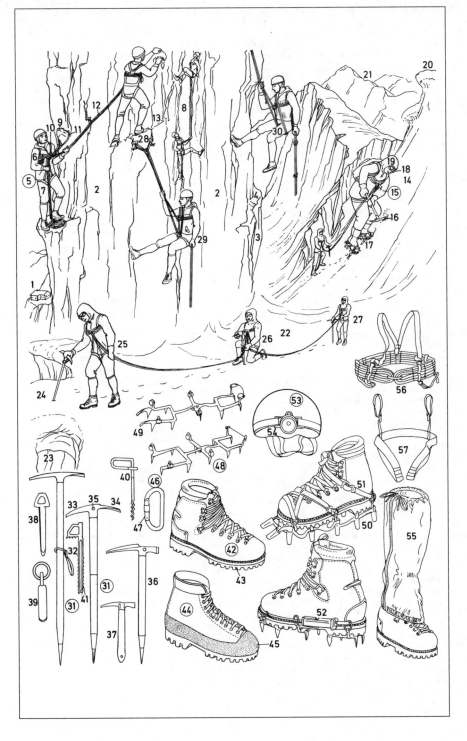

**1-72 lo sport dello sci** (lo sci)
– *skiing*
**1** lo sci (lo sci compatto)
– *compact ski*
**2** l'attacco (gli attacchi) di sicurezza
– *safety binding (release binding)*
**3** la cinghia
– *strap*
**4** la lamina di acciaio
– *steel edge*
**5** il bastone (bastoncino) da sci *m pl*
– *ski stick (ski pole)*
**6** l'impugnatura
– *grip*
**7** il collare (il cappio)
– *loop*
**8** la racchetta
– *basket*
**9** la tuta da sci *m pl* per donna
– *ladies' one-piece ski suit*
**10** il berretto da sci *m pl*
– *skiing cap (ski cap)*
**11** gli occhiali da sci *m pl*
– *skiing goggles*
**12** lo scarpone da sci (con suola a guscio)
– *cemented sole skiing boot*
**13** il casco
– *crash helmet*
**14-20** l'equipaggiamento (l'attrezzatura) per il fondo
– *cross-country equipment*
**14** lo sci da fondo
– *cross-country ski*
**15** l'attacco per sci *m pl* da fondo
– *cross-country rat trap binding*
**16** la scarpa da fondo
– *cross-country boot*
**17** la tuta da fondo
– *cross-country gear*
**18** il berretto con visiera
– *peaked cap*
**19** gli occhiali da sole *m*
– *sunglasses*
**20** i bastoni (bastoncini *m pl* ) da fondo, di bambù
– *cross-country poles made of bamboo*
**21-24** gli accessori per la sciolinatura
– *ski-waxing equipment*
**21** la sciolina
– *ski wax*
**22** la lampada (per la cera)
– *waxing iron (blowlamp, blowtorch)*
**23** il sughero
– *waxing cork*
**24** il raschietto
– *wax scraper*
**25** il bastone per gare *f pl* di velocità
– *downhill racing pole*
**26** il passo a spina di pesce *m* (salita a spina di pesce *m*, salita a lisca)
– *herringbone, for climbing a slope*

**27** il passo a scala (passo a scaletta, salita a gradini *m pl*, salita a scale *f pl*)
– *sidestep, for climbing a slope*
**28** il marsupio
– *ski bag*
**29** lo slalom
– *slalom*
**30** il paletto (*anche:* bandierina) della porta
– *gate pole*
**31** la tuta per gare *f pl* di velocità
– *racing suit*
**32** la discesa (*anche:* discesa libera)
– *downhill racing*
**33** la posizione a «ovo» («uovo»), la posizione ideale per la discesa
– *'egg' position, the ideal downhill racing position*
**34** lo sci da discesa
– *downhill ski*
**35** il salto
– *ski jumping*
**36** la posizione a «pesce» *m*, la posizione per il salto
– *lean forward*
**37** il numero di partenza
– *number*
**38** lo sci per il salto
– *ski jumping ski*
**39** le scanalature di direzione *f* (da 3 a 5 scanalature *f pl*)
– *grooves (3 to 5 grooves)*
**40** l'attacco per sci *m* da salto, un attacco con cavo in tensione *f*
– *cable binding*
**41** lo scarpone da salto
– *ski jumping boots*
**42** il fondo
– *cross-country*
**43** la tuta (overall *m*) per gare *f pl* di fondo
– *cross-country stretch-suit*
**44** la pista di fondo
– *course*
**45** la bandierina di segnalazione *f* (la segnalazione della pista di fondo)
– *course-marking flag*
**46** gli strati (lamine *f pl* ) degli sci moderni
– *layers of a modern ski*
**47** l'anima (nucleo speciale)
– *special core*
**48** i laminati
– *laminates*
**49** lo strato di smorzamento
– *stabilizing layer (stabilizer)*
**50** il bordo di acciaio
– *steel edge*
**51** il bordo superiore in alluminio
– *aluminium (*Am. *aluminum)* upper edge*

**52** la superficie di scorrimento in materiale *m* plastico
– *synthetic bottom (artificial bottom)*
**53** la staffa di sicurezza
– *safety jet*
**54-56** gli elementi degli attacchi
– *parts of the binding*
**54** il blocca-tallone automatico
– *automatic heel unit*
**55** la parte anteriore degli attacchi (la punta)
– *toe unit*
**56** lo stopper
– *ski stop*
**57-63** l'impianto di risalita
– *ski lift*
**57** la seggiovia biposto
– *double chair lift*
**58** l'asta del seggiolino e il poggiapiedi
– *safety bar with footrest*
**59** lo ski-lift (sciovia)
– *ski lift*
**60** la pista
– *track*
**61** l'impugnatura con staffa di appoggio
– *hook*
**62** l'avvolgitore automatico della funicella
– *automatic cable pulley*
**63** il cavo traente (monofune *f* traente)
– *haulage cable*
**64** lo slalom
– *slalom*
**65** la porta aperta
– *open gate*
**66** la porta cieca verticale
– *closed vertical gate*
**67** la porta aperta verticale
– *open vertical gate*
**68** la porta doppia diagonale
– *transversal chicane*
**69** la curva a gomito
– *hairpin*
**70** la porta doppia verticale sfalsata
– *elbow*
**71** il corridoio
– *corridor*
**72** l'Allais-Schikane (Chicane-Allais)
– *Allais chicane*

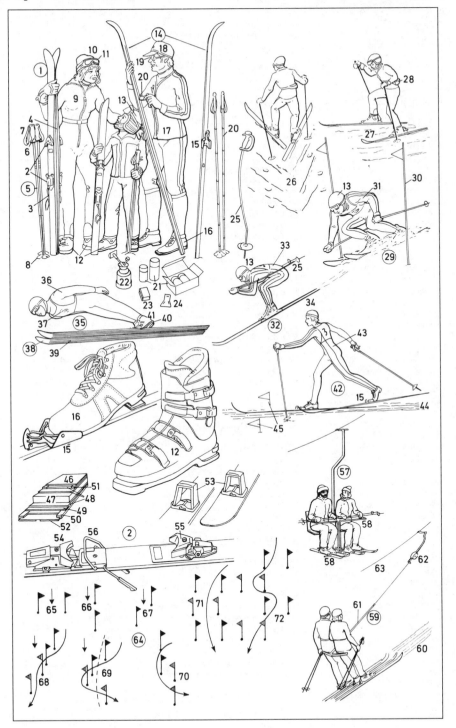

**1-26 il pattinaggio su ghiaccio** (pattinaggio artistico)
– *ice skating*
1 la pattinatrice su ghiaccio (il pattinatore, il pattinaggio individuale, *qui:* il pattinatore di pattinaggio individuale)
– *ice skater, a solo skater*
2 la gamba portante (il piede portante)
– *tracing leg*
3 la gamba libera (il piede libero)
– *free leg*
4 il pattinaggio a coppia (*qui:* i pattinatori di pattinaggio a coppia)
– *pair skaters*
5 il giro della morte (la spirale della morte)
– *death spiral*
6 l'arco
– *pivot*
7 il salto (salto del capriolo)
– *stag jump (stag leap)*
8 la piroetta seduta (piroetta di Jackson Haines)
– *jump-sit-spin*
9 la piroetta (la trottola)
– *upright spin*
10 la presa del piede
– *holding the foot*
**11-19** le figure obbligatorie
– *compulsory figures*
11 l'otto (il doppio cerchio)
– *curve eight*
12 la curva a S (l'S)
– *change*
13 il tre
– *three*
14 il doppio tre
– *double-three*
15 il nodo
– *loop*
16 la curva a S con nodo
– *change loop*
17 il controtrè
– *bracket*
18 il controgiro con il cambio di piede *m*
– *counter*
19 il giro con cambio di piede *m*
– *rocker*
**20-25** pattini *m pl*
– *ice skates*
20 il pattino da corsa
– *speed skating set (speed skate)*
21 lo spigolo
– *edge*
22 la rettifica concava
– *hollow grinding (hollow ridge, concave ridge)*
23 il pattino da hockey su ghiaccio
– *ice hockey set (ice hockey skate)*

24 il pattino a stivaletto
– *ice skating boot*
25 il salvapattino (la protezione, il fodero)
– *skate guard*
26 il pattinatore di velocità (il corridore su ghiaccio)
– *speed skater*
**27 u. 28 il pattinaggio a vela**
– *skate sailing*
27 il pattinatore a vela
– *skate sailor*
28 la vela a mano *f*
– *hand sail*
**29-37 l'hockey su ghiaccio**
– *ice hockey*
29 il giocatore di hockey su ghiaccio
– *ice hockey player*
30 il bastone da hockey su ghiaccio
– *ice hockey stick*
31 l'impugnatura del bastone
– *stick handle*
32 la lama (la spatola, la pala) del bastone
– *stick blade*
33 il parastinchi (con ginocchiera)
– *shin pad*
34 il casco
– *headgear (protective helmet)*
35 il disco da hockey su ghiaccio (un disco in ebanite *f* )
– *puck, a vulcanized rubber disc (disk)*
36 il portiere
– *goalkeeper*
37 la porta
– *goal*
**38-40 l'«eisschießen»** *m* (*sim.:* il curling)
– *ice-stick shooting (Bavarian curling)*
38 il tiratore di «eisstock» (*sim.:* il giocatore di curling *m*)
– *ice-stick shooter (Bavarian curler)*
39 l'eisstock *m* (*sim.:* la pietra da curling *m*)
– *ice stick*
40 la meta (la doga)
– *block*
**41-43 il curling**
– *curling*
41 il giocatore di curling *m*
– *curler*
42 la pietra da curling *m* (il curling *m*)
– *curling stone (granite)*
43 la granata
– *curling brush (curling broom, besom)*
**44-46 la corsa a vela su ghiaccio**
– *ice yachting (iceboating, ice sailing)*

44 lo scooter (la slitta a vela, un'imbarcazione *f* da ghiaccio)
– *ice yacht (iceboat)*
45 il pattino dello scooter
– *steering runner*
46 il buttafuori
– *outrigged runner*

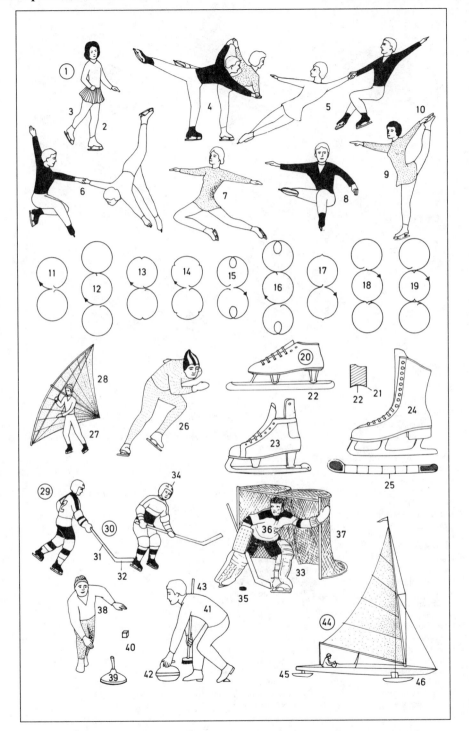

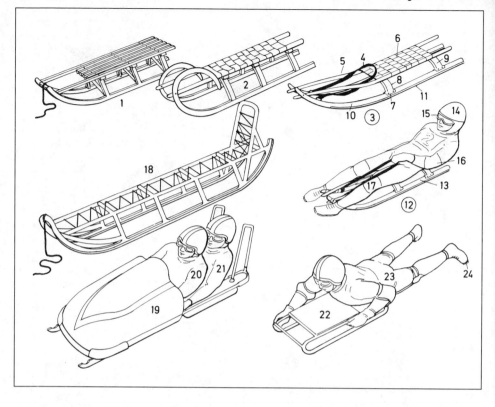

1 la slitta comune
– *toboggan (sledge,* Am. *sled)*
2 la slitta comune con sedile *m* a
   cinghia
– *toboggan (sledge,* Am. *sled) with
   seat of plaid straps*
3 la slitta per ragazzi *m pl*
– *junior luge toboggan (junior luge,
   junior toboggan)*
4 la cinghia per sterzare
– *rein*
5 la barra
– *bar (strut)*
6 il sedile
– *seat*
7 la piastra di fissaggio
– *bracket*
8 il piede anteriore
– *front prop*
9 il piede posteriore
– *rear prop*
10 il pattino mobile
– *movable runner*
11 il treno del pattino
– *metal face*
12 il corridore su slittino
– *luge tobogganer*

13 lo slittino (la slitta per gare *f pl* di
   velocità)
– *luge toboggan (luge, toboggan)*
14 il casco
– *crash helmet*
15 gli occhiali da corsa
– *goggles*
16 la fascia paragomito
– *elbow pad*
17 la ginocchiera
– *knee pad*
18 la slitta Nansen, una slitta polare
   (slitta eschimese)
– *Nansen sledge, a polar sledge*
19-21 lo sport del bob
– *bobsleigh (bobsledding)*
19 il bob, un bob a due
– *bobsleigh (bobsled), a two-man
   bobsleigh (a boblet)*
20 il pilota del bob (bobista pilota)
– *steersman*
21 il frenatore (bobista frenatore)
– *brakeman*
22-24 lo skeleton (lo sport dello
   skeleton)
– *skeleton tobogganing (Cresta
   tobogganing)*

22 lo skeleton
– *skeleton (skeleton toboggan)*
23 il corridore di skeleton (lo skele-
   tonista)
– *skeleton rider*
24 il pattino (raschietto) di ferro per
   sterzare e frenare
– *rake, for braking and steering*

**1** la valanga (lavina, slavina); *tipi:*
valanga polverosa, valanga di
fondo
– *avalanche (snow avalanche, Am.*
*snowslide); kinds: wind avalanche,*
*ground avalanche*
**2** la barriera frangivalanghe, un
muro deviavalanghe; *sim.:* cuneo
di arresto della valanga
– *avalanche wall, a deflecting wall*
*(diverting wall); sim.: avalanche*
*wedge*
**3** la galleria frangivalanghe
– *avalanche gallery*
**4** la nevicata
– *snowfall*
**5** il cumulo di neve *f*
– *snowdrift*
**6** il paraneve (la palizzata paraneve)
– *snow fence*
**7** la riserva forestale
– *avalanche forest [planted as pro-*
*tection against avalanches]*
**8** lo spazzaneve
– *street-cleaning lorry (street cleaner)*
**9** lo spartineve
– *snow plough (Am. snowplow)*
*attachment*

**10** la catena antineve (catena *f pl*
antisdrucciolevole)
– *snow chain (skid chain, tyre chain,*
Am. *tire chain)*
**11** il cofano
– *radiator bonnet (Am. radiator*
*hood)*
**12** la grata del cofano e la gelosia
– *radiator shutter and shutter open-*
*ing (louvre shutter)*
**13** il pupazzo di neve *f*
– *snowman*
**14** la battaglia con palle *f pl* di neve *f*
– *snowball fight*
**15** la palla di neve *f*
– *snowball*
**16** il monopattino da neve *f*
– *ski bob*
**17** la pista ghiacciata per lo scivolo
(scivolo)
– *slide*
**18** il ragazzo che scivola o pattina
– *boy, sliding*
**19** la superficie ghiacciata
– *icy surface (icy ground)*
**20** lo strato di neve *f* sul tetto
– *covering of snow, on the roof*
**21** il ghiacciolo
– *icicle*

**22** lo spalatore di neve *f*
– *man clearing snow*
**23** la pala da neve *f*
– *snow push (snow shovel)*
**24** il mucchio di neve *f*
– *heap of snow*
**25** la slitta a cavalli *m pl*
– *horse-drawn sleigh (horse sleigh)*
**26** i sonagli
– *sleigh bells (bells, set of bells)*
**27** il sacco scaldapiedi
– *foot muff (Am. foot bag)*
**28** il paraorecchi
– *earmuff*
**29** la slitta a seggiola; *sim.:* la slitta
spinta a mano *f*
– *handsledge (tread sledge); sim.:*
*push sledge*
**30** la fanghiglia di neve *f*
– *slush*

**1-13 il gioco dei birilli** (i birilli)
– *skittles*
**1-11** lo schieramento (disposizione *f* ) dei birilli
– *skittle frame*
**1** il primo birillo (birillo dello spigolo anteriore)
– *front pin (front)*
**2** il birillo della fila anteriore sinistra, una dama
– *left front second pin (left front second)*
**3** la fila anteriore sinistra
– *running three [left]*
**4** il birillo della fila anteriore destra, una dama
– *right front second pin (right front second)*
**5** la fila anteriore destra
– *running three [right]*
**6** il birillo dell'angolo sinistro (birillo di angolo)
– *left corner pin (left corner), a corner (copper)*
**7** il re
– *landlord*
**8** il birillo dell'angolo destro (birillo di angolo)
– *right corner pin (right corner), a corner (copper)*
**9** il birillo della fila posteriore sinistra, una dama
– *back left second pin (back left second)*
**10** il birillo della fila posteriore destra, una dama
– *back right second pin (back right second)*
**11** l'ultimo birillo (birillo dello spigolo posteriore)
– *back pin (back)*
**12** il birillo
– *pin*
**13** il re
– *landlord*
**14-20 il bowling**
– *tenpin bowling*
**14** lo schieramento (disposizione *f* ) dei birilli nel bowling
– *frame*
**15** la palla da bowling
– *bowling ball (ball with finger holes)*
**16** il foro per la presa (la presa a foro)
– *finger hole*
**17-20** i tiri (tipi *m pl* di tiro)
– *deliveries*
**17** il tiro dritto (straight *m*)
– *straight ball*
**18** il tiro a angolo (hook *m*)
– *hook ball (hook)*
**19** il tiro a curva (curve *f* )
– *curve*
**20** il tiro a curva di rovescio (back-up *m*)
– *back-up ball (back-up)*
**21 il gioco delle bocce,** *sim.:* il gioco francese delle bocce, il bowl inglese
– *boules;* sim.: *Italian game of boccie, green bowls (bowls)*
**22** il giocatore di bocce *f pl*
– *boules player*
**23** il pallino
– *jack (target jack)*
**24** la boccia a superficie zigrinata (palla di lancio)
– *grooved boule*
**25** la squadra dei giocatori
– *group of players*
**26 il tiro al fucile**
– *rifle shooting*
**27-29** posizioni *f pl* di tiro
– *shooting positions*
**27** la posizione eretta
– *standing position*
**28** la posizione a ginocchio piegato
– *kneeling position*

**29** la posizione supina
– *prone position*
**30-33** bersagli *m pl*
– *targets*
**30** il bersaglio per arma da fuoco con gittata di 50 m
– *target for 50 m events (50 m target)*
**31** il cerchio
– *circle*
**32** il bersaglio per arma da fuoco con gittata di 100 m
– *target for 100 m events (100 m target)*
**33** il bersaglio mobile
– *bobbing target (turning target, running-boar target)*
**34-39** munizioni *f pl* per gare *f pl* sportive
– *ammunition*
**34** il proiettile per fucile a aria compressa (proiettile *m* diabolo)
– *air rifle cartridge*
**35** la cartuccia a spoletta marginale per fucile *m* a canna corta
– *rimfire cartridge for zimmerstutzen (indoor target rifle), a smallbore German single-shot rifle*
**36** il bossolo della cartuccia
– *case head*
**37** la pallottola a testa tonda
– *caseless round*
**38** la cartuccia calibro 22 *long rifle*
– *.22 long rifle cartridge*
**39** la cartuccia calibro 222 *Remington*
– *.222 Remington cartridge*
**40-49** fucili *m pl* per gare *f pl* sportive (per gare *f pl* di tiro)
– *sporting rifles*
**40** il fucile a aria compressa
– *air rifle*
**41** la diottra
– *optical sight*
**42** il mirino
– *front sight (foresight)*
**43** il fucile standard di piccolo calibro
– *smallbore standard rifle*
**44** l'arma franca internazionale di piccolo calibro
– *international smallbore free rifle*
**45** l'appoggio della mano per il tiro in posizione *f* eretta
– *palm rest for standing position*
**46** il cappuccio del calcio con gomito
– *butt plate with hook*
**47** il fusto
– *butt with thumb hole*
**48** il fucile di piccolo calibro per bersaglio mobile
– *smallbore rifle for bobbing target (turning target)*
**49** il cannocchiale di puntamento
– *telescopic sight (riflescope, telescope sight)*
**50** la mira della diottra con mirino circolare
– *optical ring sight*
**51** la mira della diottra con mirino a trave *f*
– *optical ring and bead sight*
**52-66 il tiro con l'arco**
– *archery (target archery)*
**52** il tiro
– *shot*
**53** il tiratore (*ant.:* arciere *m*)
– *archer*
**54** l'arco
– *competition bow*
**55** l'elemento flessibile
– *riser*
**56** l'alzo (la mira)
– *point-of-aim mark*
**57** l'impugnatura
– *grip (handle)*
**58** lo stabilizzatore
– *stabilizer*

**59** la corda dell'arco (corda)
– *bow string (string)*
**60** la freccia (*ant.:* il dardo)
– *arrow*
**61** la punta della freccia
– *pile (point) of the arrow*
**62** le penne timoniere (penne *f pl* di tacchino, l'impennaggio)
– *fletching*
**63** la cocca
– *nock*
**64** l'asta della freccia
– *shaft*
**65** il segno di riconoscimento (contrassegno) del tiratore
– *cresting*
**66** il bersaglio
– *target*
**67 il gioco della pelota** basca (*sim.:* jai alai *m*)
– *Basque game of pelota (jai alai)*
**68** il giocatore di pelota
– *pelota player*
**69** la cesta
– *wicker basket (cesta)*
**70-78 il tiro a volo** (tiro al piattello, tiro al piccione)
– *skeet (skeet shooting), a kind of clay pigeon shooting*
**70** la doppietta
– *skeet over-and-under shotgun*
**71** la volata con il foro per il tiro a volo
– *muzzle with skeet choke*
**72** la posizione di partenza
– *ready position on call*
**73** la posizione di tiro
– *firing position*
**74** l'impianto del tiro a volo (impianto del tiro al piattello, impianto del tiro al piccione)
– *shooting range*
**75** la gabbia alta
– *high house*
**76** la gabbia bassa
– *low house*
**77** la traiettoria
– *target's path*
**78** la posizione del tiratore
– *shooting station (shooting box)*
**79 il cerchio acrobatico**
– *aero wheel*
**80** l'impugnatura
– *handle*
**81** l'asse *f* di appoggio per i piedi
– *footrest*
**82 il kartismo** (lo sport del kart)
– *go-karting (karting)*
**83** il go-kart
– *go-kart (kart)*
**84** il numero di partenza
– *number plate (number)*
**85** i pedali
– *pedals*
**86** il (lo) pneumatico liscio (slick *m*)
– *pneumatic tyre (Am. tire)*
**87** il serbatoio per il carburante
– *petrol tank (Am. gasoline tank)*
**88** il telaio
– *frame*
**89** il volante
– *steering wheel*
**90** il sedile orbicolare (sedile *m* a guscio)
– *bucket seat*
**91** il rivestimento antincendio
– *protective bulkhead*
**92** il motore a due tempi *m pl*
– *two-stroke engine*
**93** il silenziatore
– *silencer (Am. muffler)*

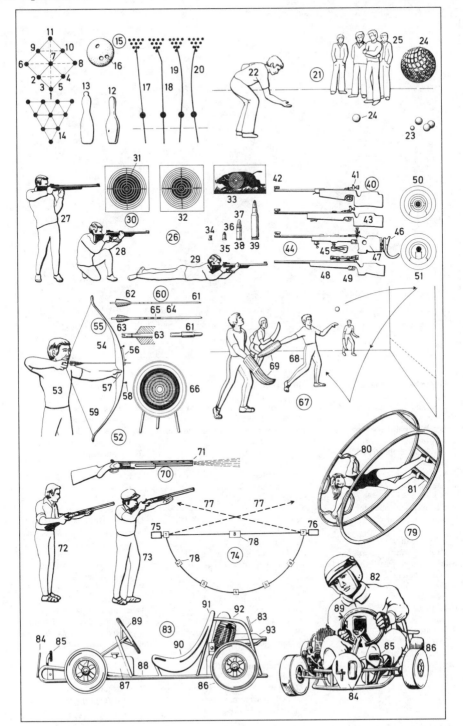

**1-48 il ballo in maschera** (la festa mascherata, la festa in costume *m*)
– **masked ball** *(masquerade, fancy-dress ball)*
**1** la sala da ballo (il salone)
– *ballroom*
**2** l'orchestra pop, un'orchestra da ballo
– *pop group, a dance band*
**3** il musicista pop
– *pop musician*
**4** il lampioncino alla veneziana (il lampione di carta)
– *paper lantern*
**5** il festone di carta
– *festoon (string of decorations)*
**6-48** i costumi (i travestimenti) per la mascherata
– *disguise (fancy dress) at the masquerade*
**6** la strega
– *witch*
**7** la maschera
– *mask*
**8** il cacciatore di animali *m pl* da pelliccia (Davy Crockett)
– *fur trapper (trapper)*
**9** la donna dell'apache *m*
– *Apache girl*

**10** la calza a rete *f*
– *net stocking*
**11** il primo premio della tombola, un cesto di regali *m pl*
– *first prize in the tombola (raffle), a hamper*
**12** la Pierrette
– *pierette*
**13** la bautta
– *half mask (domino)*
**14** il diavolo
– *devil*
**15** il domino
– *domino*
**16** l'hawaiana
– *hula-hula girl (Hawaii girl)*
**17** la collana di fiori *m pl*
– *garland*
**18** il gonnellino hawaiano
– *grass skirt (hula skirt)*
**19** il Pierrot
– *pierrot*
**20** il colletto da Pierrot (un collare increspato)
– *ruff*
**21** la midinette (la sartina)
– *midinette*
**22** l'abito ottocentesco (abito dell'epoca romantica)
– *Biedermeier dress*

**23** la cuffietta
– *poke bonnet*
**24** il decolleté con nei *m pl* di bellezza
– *décolletage with beauty spot*
**25** la bajadera (danzatrice indiana)
– *bayadère (Hindu dancing girl)*
**26** il grande di Spagna
– *grandee*
**27** la Colombina
– *Columbine*
**28** il maragià
– *maharaja (maharajah)*
**29** il mandarino, un dignitario cinese
– *mandarin, a Chinese dignitary*
**30** la donna esotica
– *exotic girl (exotic)*
**31** il cow-boy; *sim.*: il gaucho
– *cowboy;* sim.: *gaucho (vaquero)*
**32** la vamp, in costume fantasia
– *vamp, in fancy dress*
**33** il damerino (il dandy), una maschera da caratterista *m*
– *dandy (fop, beau), a disguise*
**34** la rosetta da ballo
– *rosette*
**35** l'Arlecchino
– *harlequin*
**36** la zingara (la gitana)
– *gipsy (gypsy) girl*

47 la cocotte (la demi-mondaine)
– *cocotte (demi-monde, demi-mondaine, demi-rep)*
48 il buffone, un matto
– *owl-glass, a fool (jester, buffoon)*
49 il berretto del buffone
– *foolscap (jester's cap and bells)*
40 il sonaglio
– *rattle*
41 l'odalisca (donna orientale), una schiava dell'harem *m*
– *odalisque, Eastern female slave in Sultan's seraglio*
42 i pantaloni alla turca (pantaloni a sbuffo)
– *chalwar (pantaloons)*
43 il pirata (il corsaro)
– *pirate (buccaneer)*
44 il tatuaggio
– *tattoo*
45 il cappello di carta
– *paper hat*
46 il naso finto (il naso di cartone *m*)
– *false nose*
47 la raganella
– *clapper (rattle)*
48 il bastone (il bastone d'Arlecchino)
– *slapstick*
49-54 **i fuochi d'artificio**
– *fireworks*

49 la capsula per pistola giocattolo
– *percussion cap*
50 la bombetta di carta
– *cracker*
51 la castagnola
– *banger*
52 il petardo
– *jumping jack*
53 il petardo a cascata di fuoco
– *cannon cracker (maroon, maroon)*
54 il razzo
– *rocket*
55 la pallina di carta
– *paper ball*
56 la scatola a sorpresa (Jack-in-the-box), un articolo da carnevale *m*
– *jack-in-the-box, a joke*
57-70 **la sfilata di carnevale** *m*
– **carnival procession**
57 il carro mascherato
– *carnival float (carnival truck)*
58 il re del carnevale *m*
– *King Carnival*
59 lo scettro del re di carnevale *m*
– *bauble (fool's sceptre,* Am. *scepter)*
60 l'onorificenza carnevalesca
– *fool's badge*
61 la regina di carnevale *m*
– *Queen Carnival*

62 i coriandoli
– *confetti*
63 il gigante, una figura grottesca
– *giant figure, a satirical figure*
64 la reginetta di bellezza
– *beauty queen*
65 un personaggio fiabesco
– *fairy-tale figure*
66 la stella filante
– *paper streamer*
67 la majorette
– *majorette*
68 la guardia del re
– *king's guard*
69 il pagliaccio
– *buffoon, a clown*
70 il tamburo
– *lansquenet's drum*

**1-63** il circo equestre (circo ambulante)
- *travelling (Am. traveling) circus*
**1** il tendone del circo (chapiteau)
- *circus tent (big top), a four-pole
tent*
**2** l'antenna centrale
- *tent pole*
**3** il riflettore
- *spotlight*
**4** il tecnico delle luci
- *lighting technician*
**5** la piattaforma per l'acrobata *m*
(la sbarra fissa)
- *trapeze platform*
**6** il trapezio (trapezio volante)
- *trapeze*
**7** il trapezista (l'acrobata *m*, l'uomo
volante)
- *trapeze artist*
**8** la scala di corda
- *rope ladder*
**9** il podio dell'orchestra
- *bandstand*
**10** l'orchestra del circo
- *circus band*
**11** l'ingresso alla pista
- *ring entrance (arena entrance)*
**12** il retropista (le quinte)
- *wings*

**13** il palo perimetrale del tendone
- *tent prop (prop)*
**14** la rete di protezione *f*
- *safety net*
**15** le gradinate
- *seats for the spectators*
**16** il palco
- *circus box*
**17** il direttore del circo
- *circus manager*
**18** l'agente *m* teatrale
- *artiste agent (agent)*
**19** l'ingresso e l'uscita
- *entrance and exit*
**20** la rampa di accesso
- *steps*
**21** la pista
- *ring (arena)*
**22** il bordo della pista
- *ring fence*
**23** il clown musicista
- *musical clown (clown)*
**24** il clown (il pagliaccio)
- *clown*
**25** il «numero comico», un numero
dello spettacolo
- *comic turn (clown act), a circus
act*
**26** i cavallerizzi acrobati
- *circus riders (bareback riders)*

**27** l'inserviente *m* di pista, un
inserviente del circo
- *ring attendant, a circus attendant*
**28** la piramide umana
- *pyramid*
**29** il porteur (il portatore, la colonna)
- *support*
**30** *u.* **31** il numero del cavallo
ammaestrato
- *performance by liberty horses*
**30** il cavallo del circo (il cavallo
ammaestrato) in impennata (en
debout)
- *circus horse, performing the levade (pesade)*
**31** il domatore
- *ringmaster, a trainer*
**32** il volteggiatore
- *vaulter*
**33** l'uscita di sicurezza
- *emergency exit*
**34** il carrozzone (il carrozzone del
circo)
- *caravan (circus caravan, Am.
trailer)*
**35** l'acrobata *m* saltatore
- *springboard acrobat (springboard
artist)*

**6** la bascula (l'asse *f* del trampolino)
– *springboard*
**7** il lanciatore di coltelli *m pl*
– *knife thrower*
**8** il tiratore
– *circus marksman*
**9** l'assistente *f*
– *assistant*
**0** la ballerina sulla corda
– *tightrope dancer*
**1** la corda metallica
– *tightrope*
**2** la pertica per esercizi *m pl* di equi-
librio (la pertica da funambulo)
– *balancing pole*
**3** il numero di lancio dell'acrobata *m*
– *throwing act*
**4** il numero di equilibrismo
– *balancing act*
**5** il porteur (il portatore, la colonna)
– *support*
**6** la pertica (pertica di bambù *m*)
– *pole (bamboo pole)*
**7** l'acrobata *m*
– *acrobat*
**8** l'equilibrista *m*
– *equilibrist (balancer)*
**9** la gabbia delle bestie feroci (una
gabbia rotonda)
– *wild animal cage, a round cage*

**50** la sbarra della gabbia
– *bars of the cage*
**51** il tunnel (il corridoio) a inferriate
*f pl* per il passaggio delle bestie
feroci
– *passage (barred passage, passage
for the wild animals)*
**52** il domatore (delle bestie feroci)
– *tamer (wild animal tamer)*
**53** la frusta (la frusta del domatore)
– *whip*
**54** il forcone di protezione *f*
– *fork (protective fork)*
**55** il piedistallo
– *pedestal*
**56** la bestia feroce (la tigre, il leone)
– *wild animal (tiger, lion)*
**57** lo sgabello
– *stand*
**58** il cerchio (attraverso il quale
saltano le bestie feroci)
– *hoop (jumping hoop)*
**59** la bascula (un'altalena a bilico)
– *seesaw*
**60** il pallone
– *ball*
**61** la tendopoli
– *camp*
**62** la vettura gabbia
– *cage caravan*

**63** il serraglio
– *menagerie*

**1-69** il parco dei divertimenti (il
luna park)
– *fair (annual fair)*
**1** l'area destinata al luna park
– *fairground*
**2** la giostra
– *children's merry-go-round,
(whirligig), a roundabout (Am.
carousel)*
**3** il banco dei rinfreschi
– *refreshment stall (drinks stall)*
**4** la giostra volante
– *chairoplane*
**5** la giostra del bacio
– *up-and-down roundabout*
**6** il baraccone da fiera
– *show booth (booth)*
**7** la cassa
– *box (box office)*
**8** l'imbonitore *m*
– *barker*
**9** la/il medium
– *medium*
**10** il banditore
– *showman*
**11** il misuratore della forza
– *try-your-strength machine*
**12** il venditore ambulante
– *hawker*

**13** il palloncino
– *balloon*
**14** la lingua di Menelik (la lingua
delle donne)
– *paper serpent*
**15** la girandola
– *windmill*
**16** il borsaiolo (il ladruncolo)
– *pickpocket (thief )*
**17** il venditore
– *vendor*
**18** il miele turco (non in uso in
Italia)
– *nougat*
**19** la casa delle streghe
– *ghost train*
**20** il mostro
– *monster*
**21** il drago
– *dragon*
**22** il mostro
– *monster*
**23** la birreria sotto il tendone (non in
uso in Italia)
– *beer marquee*
**24** il baraccone da fiera
– *sideshow*

**25-28** artisti *m pl* girovaghi (i
girovaghi)
– *travelling (Am. traveling) artistes
(travelling show people)*
**25** il mangiatore di fuoco
– *fire eater*
**26** il mangiatore di spade *f pl*
– *sword swallower*
**27** l'uomo forzuto (il carnera)
– *strong man*
**28** l'uomo che spezza le catene
– *escapologist*
**29** gli spettatori
– *spectators*
**30** il gelataio (il venditore di gelati *m pl*)
– *ice-cream vendor (ice-cream man)*
**31** il cono gelato
– *ice-cream cornet, with ice cream*
**32** la bancarella con le salsicce calde
– *sausage stand*
**33** la griglia (il barbecue)
– *grill (Am. broiler)*
**34** la salsiccia arrostita
– *bratwurst (grilled sausage, Am.
broiled sausage)*
**35** le pinze per la salsiccia
– *sausage tongs*

36 la chiromante (l'indovina), una veggente
– *fortune teller*
37 la ruota gigante
– *big wheel (Ferris wheel)*
38 l'organetto (l'organetto di Barberia), uno strumento musicale mobile
– *orchestrion (automatic organ), an automatic musical instrument*
39 l'ottovolante (le montagne russe)
– *scenic railway (switchback)*
40 il toboga
– *toboggan slide (chute)*
41 l'altalena
– *swing boats*
42 l'altalena con capovolta
– *swing boat, turning full circle*
43 la capovolta
– *full circle*
44 il baraccone della lotteria
– *lottery booth (tombola booth)*
45 la ruota della fortuna
– *wheel of fortune*
46 la ruota del diavolo
– *devil's wheel (typhoon wheel)*
47 il gioco dei cerchietti
– *throwing ring (quoit)*
48 i premi
– *prizes*

49 l'uomo «sandwich» (l'uomo sui trampoli)
– *sandwich man on stilts*
50 il cartellone pubblicitario
– *sandwich board (placard)*
51 il venditore di sigarette *f pl*
– *cigarette seller, an itinerant trader (a hawker)*
52 la cassetta appesa al collo
– *tray*
53 il banco della frutta
– *fruit stall*
54 il pilota del giro della morte
– *wall-of-death rider*
55 il gabinetto degli specchi deformanti
– *hall of mirrors*
56 lo specchio concavo
– *concave mirror*
57 lo specchio convesso
– *convex mirror*
58 il baraccone del tiro a segno (del tiro al bersaglio)
– *shooting gallery*
59 la nave pirata (il vascello pirata *m*)
– *giant swing boat*
60 il mercato delle pulci (il mercatino delle cose vecchie)
– *junk stalls (second-hand stalls)*

61 la tenda del pronto soccorso
– *first aid tent (first aid post)*
62 l'autodromo
– *dodgems (bumper cars)*
63 l'autoscontro
– *dodgem (bumper car)*
64-66 il banco delle terraglie
– *pottery stand*
64 l'imbonitore *m*
– *barker*
65 la venditrice
– *market woman*
66 le terraglie
– *pottery*
67 i visitatori del parco dei divertimenti
– *visitors to the fair*
68 il gabinetto delle cere
– *waxworks*
69 la statua di cera
– *wax figure*

**1** la macchina da cucire a pedale *m*
– *treadle sewing machine*
**2** il vaso da fiori *m pl*
– *flower vase*
**3** la specchiera
– *wall mirror*
**4** la stufa cilindrica
– *cylindrical stove*
**5** il tubo della stufa
– *stovepipe*
**6** il gomito del tubo della stufa
– *stovepipe elbow*
**7** lo sportello della stufa
– *stove door*
**8** il paravento
– *stove screen*
**9** la cassetta per le mattonelle combustibili
– *coal scuttle*
**10** il cesto di vimini
– *firewood basket*
**11** la bambola
– *doll*
**12** l'orsacchiotto
– *teddy bear*
**13** la pianola
– *barrel organ*
**14** l'organetto meccanico
– *orchestrion*
**15** il disco metallico (il foglio musicale traforato)
– *metal disc (disk)*

**16** la radio (l'apparecchio radio, il
radioricevitore) un ricevitore
supereterodina
– *radio (radio set, joc.: 'steam
radio'), a superheterodyne (super-
het)*
**17** la parete di rimando del suono
– *baffle board*
**18** l'occhio magico
– *'magic eye', a tuning indicator
valve*
**19** l'apertura per l'altoparlante *m*
– *loudspeaker aperture*
**20** i tasti selettori
– *station selector buttons (station
preset buttons)*
**21** il bottone di sintonia
– *tuning knob*
**22** la scala di frequenza
– *frequency bands*
**23** il detector
– *crystal detector (crystal set)*
**24** la cuffia
– *headphones (headset)*
**25** la macchina fotografica a soffietto
– *folding camera*
**26** il soffietto
– *bellows*
**27** lo sportello di chiusura
– *hinged cover*
**28** le leve di bloccaggio
– *spring extension*

**29** il venditore
– *salesman*
**30** la macchina fotografica a fuoco
fisso
– *box camera*
**31** il grammofono (il giradischi)
– *gramophone*
**32** il disco
– *record (gramophone record)*
**33** il pick-up (il microfono a membrana con puntina)
– *needle head with gramophone needle*
**34** la tromba (la tromba del grammofono)
– *horn*
**35** la cassa del grammofono
– *gramophone box*
**36** il portadischi
– *record rack*
**37** il registratore a nastro, un registratore a valigetta
– *tape recorder, a portable tape
recorder*
**38** il flash
– *flashgun*
**39** la lampadina del flash
– *flash bulb*
**40** *u.* **41** il flash elettronico
– *electronic flash (electronic flashgun)*
**40** il portalampada
– *flash head*

41 il portapile
 – *accumulator*
42 il proiettore per diapositive *f pl*
 – *slide projector*
43 la slitta portadiapositive *f pl*
 – *slide holder*
44 il vano per la lampada
 – *lamphouse*
45 il candeliere
 – *candlestick*
46 la conchiglia portata sul cappello dai pellegrini (la conchigilia St. Jacques)
 – *scallop shell*
47 le posate
 – *cutlery*
48 il piatto ricordo (il souvenir)
 – *souvenir plate*
49 il sostegno per l'asciugatura delle lastre fotografiche
 – *drying rack for photographic plates*
50 la lastra fotografica
 – *photographic plate*
51 l'autoscatto
 – *delayed-action release*
52 i soldatini di stagno (*simile:* i soldatini di piombo)
 – *tin soldiers* (sim.: *lead soldiers*)
53 il boccale da birra
 – *beer mug (stein)*
54 la trombetta
 – *bugle*
55 i libri antichi
 – *second-hand books*

56 l'orologio a pendolo
 – *grandfather clock*
57 la cassa dell'orologio
 – *clock case*
58 il pendolo dell'orologio
 – *pendulum*
59 il peso
 – *time weight*
60 il contrappeso
 – *striking weight*
61 la sedia a dondolo
 – *rocking chair*
62 la divisa da marinaio
 – *sailor suit*
63 il berretto da marinaio
 – *sailor's hat*
64 il lavabo portatile
 – *washing set*
65 il catino
 – *washing basin*
66 la brocca (la brocca per l'acqua)
 – *water jug*
67 il sostegno
 – *washstand*
68 la ventosa
 – *dolly*
69 la tinozza
 – *washtub*
70 l'asse *f* da bucato
 – *washboard*
71 la trottola
 – *humming top*
72 la lavagna di ardesia
 – *slate*
73 l'astuccio portapenne di legno
 – *pencil box*

74 la macchina calcolatrice
 – *adding and subtracting machine*
75 il rotolo di carta
 – *paper roll*
76 i tasti
 – *number keys*
77 il pallottoliere
 – *abacus*
78 il calamaio, un calamaio apribile
 – *inkwell, with lid*
79 la macchina da scrivere
 – *typewriter*
80 la calcolatrice meccanica
 – *[hand-operated] calculating machine (calculator)*
81 la manovella di azionamento
 – *operating handle*
82 il totalizzatore
 – *result register (product register)*
83 il contatore
 – *rotary counting mechanism (rotary counter)*
84 la bilancia da cucina
 – *kitchen scales*
85 il pettycoat
 – *waist slip (underskirt)*
86 il carro a rastrelliera
 – *wooden handcart*
87 l'orologio a parete *f* (la pendola)
 – *wall clock*
88 la borsa dell'acqua calda
 – *bed warmer*
89 il bidone del latte
 – *milk churn*

1-13 **Cinecittà**
- *film studios (studio complex, Am.*
  *movie studios)*
1 l'area dei teatri di posa (l'area per le
  riprese esterne, l'area degli stabilimenti)
- *lot (studio lot)*
2 gli stabilimenti di sviluppo e stampa
- *processing laboratories (film laborato-*
  *ries, motion picture laboratories)*
3 gli stabilimenti di montaggio
- *cutting rooms*
4 l'edificio dell'amministrazione f
- *administration building (office building,*
  *offices)*
5 l'archivio cinematografico
- *film (motion picture) storage vault (film*
  *library, motion picture library)*
6 i laboratori
- *workshop*
7 le costruzioni (esterne) per riprese f pl
  cinematografiche
- *film set (Am. movie set)*
8 la centrale di alimentazione f elettrica
- *power house*
9 i laboratori di ricerca e tecnici
- *technical and research laboratories*
10 i teatri di posa
- *groups of stages*
11 la piscina per le riprese acquatiche
- *concrete tank for marine sequences*
12 il ciclorama (il falso orizzonte)
- *cyclorama*

13 la collina artificiale di sfondo
- *hill*
14-60 **le riprese cinematografiche**
- *shooting (filming)*
14 lo studio di registrazione f sonora
- *music recording studio (music recording*
  *theatre, Am. theater)*
15 il rivestimento «acustico» delle pareti
- *'acoustic' wall lining*
16 lo schermo
- *screen (projection screen)*
17 l'orchestra (per l'esecuzione f pl della
  musica da film)
- *film orchestra*
18 la ripresa esterna
- *exterior shooting (outdoor shooting,*
  *exterior filming, outdoor filming)*
19 la macchina da presa di sincronizzazione f
- *camera with crystal-controlled drive*
20 il cameraman (l'operatore m della
  fotografia)
- *cameraman*
21 l'assistente m alla regia
- *assistant director*
22 l'assistente m al suono
- *boom operator (boom swinger)*
23 il tecnico del suono
- *recording engineer (sound recordist)*
24 il registratore portatile al quarzo
- *portable sound recorder with crystal-*
  *controlled drive*

25 la giraffa
- *microphone boom*
26-60 la ripresa interna (nel teatro di posa)
  per film sonori (studio per lungome-
  traggi m pl nel teatro di posa)
- *shooting (filming) in the studio (on the*
  *sound stage, on the stage, in the filming*
  *hall)*
26 il direttore di produzione f
- *production manager*
27 l'attrice f protagonista (l'attrice f cinematografica, la star, la stella del cinema)
  *ant.:* la diva (la diva cinematografica)
- *leading lady (film actress, film star, star)*
28 l'attore m principale (l'attore m cinematografico, l'eroe m cinematografico,
  l'eroe m); *ant.:* il divo
- *leading man (film actor, film star, star)*
29 la comparsa cinematografica (la comparsa)
- *film extra (extra)*
30 la serie di microfoni per riprese f pl
  stereo e per effetti m pl sonori speciali
- *arrangement of microphones for stereo*
  *and sound effects*
31 il microfono del teatro di posa
- *studio microphone*
32 il cavo del microfono
- *microphone cable*
33 le scene cinematografiche e il fondale
- *side flats and background*

**4** l'uomo che dà il ciac (il ciacchista)
- *clapper boy*
**5** il ciac (la tavoletta di legno per il titolo del film, il numero dell'inquadratura, il numero della ripresa)
- *clapper board (clapper) with slates (boards) for the film title, shot number (scene number), and take number*
**6** il truccatore (il parrucchiere)
- *make-up artist (hairstylist)*
**7** il tecnico delle luci
- *lighting electrician (studio electrician, lighting man, Am. gaffer)*
**8** lo schermo diffusore
- *diffusing screen*
**9** la segretaria di produzione *f* (la script)
- *continuity girl (script girl)*
**0** il regista cinematografico (il regista)
- *film director (director)*
**1** il cameraman (l'operatore *m* alla fotografia)
- *cameraman (first cameraman)*
**2** l'aiuto operatore *m*, un assistente alla fotografia
- *camera operator, an assistant cameraman (camera assistant)*
**3** lo scenografo
- *set designer (art director)*
**4** l'operatore *m* capo
- *director of photography*
**5** la sceneggiatura cinematografica (la sceneggiatura, il manoscritto del film, il manoscritto, lo script)
- *filmscript (script, shooting script, Am. movie script)*

**46** l'assistente *m* alla regia
- *assistant director*
**47** la cinepresa (la macchina da presa, una cinepresa cinemascope)
- *soundproof film camera (soundproof motion picture camera), a wide screen camera (cinemascope camera)*
**48** lo schermo di protezione *m* acustica (blimp)
- *soundproof housing (soundproof cover, blimp)*
**49** il dolly (una gru per la macchina da presa)
- *camera crane (dolly)*
**50** il supporto idraulico
- *hydraulic stand*
**51** lo schermo per togliere le luci di disturbo (il negro)
- *mask (screen) for protection from spill light (gobo, nigger)*
**52** il riflettore fisso
- *tripod spotlight (fill-in light, filler light, fill light, filler)*
**53** il ponte delle luci
- *spotlight catwalk*
**54** la cabina per la ripresa sonora
- *recording room*
**55** il tecnico del suono
- *recording engineer (sound recordist)*
**56** la consolle di missaggio
- *mixing console (mixing desk)*
**57** l'assistente *m* del tecnico del suono
- *sound assistant (assistant sound engineer)*

**58** il registratore magnetico
- *magnetic sound recording equipment (magnetic sound recorder)*
**59** l'amplificatore *m* e l'impianto per effetti *m pl* sonori speciali (*per es.*: l'eco *f* )
- *amplifier and special effects equipment, e.g. for echo and sound effects*
**60** la cinepresa con ripresa diretta del suono
- *sound recording camera (optical sound recorder)*

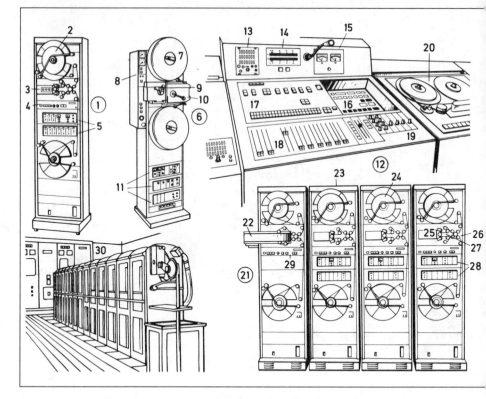

**1-46 sonorizzazione *f* del film e copia**
- *sound recording and re-recording (dubbing)*
**1** il registratore magnetico
- *magnetic sound recording equipment (magnetic sound recorder)*
**2** la bobina per il film magnetico
- *magnetic film spool*
**3** la testina magnetica del registratore
- *magnetic head support assembly*
**4** il pannello di comando
- *control panel*
**5** l'amplificatore *m* magnetico
- *magnetic sound recording and playback amplifier*
**6** il registratore ottico per il suono
- *optical sound recorder (sound recording camera, optical sound recording equipment)*
**7** la cassetta paraluce
- *daylight film magazine*
**8** il pannello di controllo e di comando
- *control and monitoring panel*

**9** l'oculare *m* per il controllo visivo della sonorizzazione ottica
- *eyepiece for visual control of optical sound recording*
**10** il dispositivo di trascinamento
- *deck*
**11** l'amplificatore *m* e alimentatore *m* di rete *f*
- *recording amplifier and mains power unit*
**12** la consolle
- *control desk (control console)*
**13** l'altoparlante *m*
- *monitoring loudspeaker (control loudspeaker)*
**14** gli strumenti per la modulazione
- *recording level indicators*
**15** gli strumenti di controllo
- *monitoring instruments*
**16** la pulsantiera
- *jack panel*
**17** il pannello dei comandi
- *control panel*
**18** il regolatore a cursore *m*
- *sliding control*

**19** il dispositivo antidistorsione *f*
- *equalizer*
**20** il registratore magnetico
- *magnetic sound deck*
**21** l'impianto di missaggio per film magnetici
- *mixer for magnetic film*
**22** il proiettore
- *film projector*
**23** l'impianto di registrazione *f* e di riproduzione *f*
- *recording and playback equipment*
**24** la bobina del film
- *film reel (film spool)*
**25** il supporto per la testina di registrazione *f*, riproduzione *f* e cancellazione *f*
- *head support assembly for the recording head, playback head, and erase head*
**26** il rocchetto di trascinamento del film
- *film transport mechanism*

7 il compensatore di movimento (di moto)
- *synchronizing filter*
8 l'amplificatore *m*
- *magnetic sound amplifier*
9 il pannello di comando
- *control panel*
) le macchine da sviluppo dei film nel laboratorio di sviluppo
- *film-processing machines (film-developing machines) in the processing laboratory (film laboratory, motion picture laboratory)*
1 la camera anecoica (antiriverbero, antieco)
- *echo chamber*
2 l'altoparlante *m* per camera anecoica
- *echo chamber loudspeaker*
3 il microfono per camera anecoica
- *echo chamber microphone*
4-36 il missaggio (il missaggio delle varie colonne sonore)
- *sound mixing (sound dubbing, mixing of several sound tracks)*
4 la sala di doppiaggio
- *mixing room (dubbing room)*

35 la consolle di missaggio per colonne sonore mono o stereofoniche
- *mixing console (mixing desk) for mono or stereo sound*
36 i tecnici del suono (gli addetti al doppiaggio, gli addetti al missaggio)
- *dubbing mixers (recording engineers, sound recordists) dubbing (mixing)*
37-41 la sincronizzazione (il doppiaggio)
- *synchronization (syncing, dubbing, post-synchronization, post-syncing)*
37 la sala di sincronizzazione *f* (la sala di doppiaggio)
- *dubbing studio (dubbing theatre, Am. theater)*
38 il direttore del doppiaggio
- *dubbing director*
39 la doppiatrice
- *dubbing speaker (dubbing actress)*
40 il microfono su giraffa
- *boom microphone*

41 il cavo del microfono
- *microphone cable*
42-46 il montaggio
- *cutting (editing)*
42 la moviola
- *cutting table (editing table, cutting bench)*
43 il montatore (cutter)
- *film editor (cutter)*
44 i piatti di svolgimento o riavvolgimento delle pellicole e delle colonne sonore
- *film turntables for picture and sound tracks*
45 il visore dell'immagine *f*
- *projection of the picture*
46 l'altoparlante *m*
- *loudspeaker*

**1-23 la proiezione cinematografica**
– *film projection (motion picture projection)*
1 il cinematografo (il cinema, la sala cinematografica)
– *cinema (picture house, Am. movie theater, movie house)*
2 la biglietteria (la cassa)
– *cinema box office (Am. movie theater box office)*
3 il biglietto (il biglietto d'ingresso)
– *cinema ticket (Am. movie theater ticket)*
4 la maschera
– *usherette*
5 gli spettatori
– *cinemagoers (filmgoers, cinema audience, Am. moviegoers, movie audience)*
6 l'illuminazione *f* di sicurezza
– *safety lighting (emergency lighting)*
7 l'uscita di sicurezza
– *emergency exit*
8 la ribalta (il palcoscenico)
– *stage*
9 le file
– *rows of seats (rows)*
10 il sipario
– *stage curtain (screen curtain)*

11 lo schermo (lo schermo di proiezione *f*)
– *screen (projection screen)*
12 la cabina di proiezione *f*
– *projection room (projection booth)*
13 la macchina da proiezione *f* di sinistra
– *lefthand projector*
14 la macchina da proiezione *f* di destra
– *righthand projector*
15 lo spioncino della cabina per la proiezione e il controllo
– *projection room window with projection window and observation port*
16 la bobina
– *reel drum (spool box)*
17 il regolatore luci *f pl* sala
– *house light dimmers (auditorium lighting control)*
18 il raddrizzatore, un raddrizzatore al selenio o a vapori *m pl* di mercurio per le lampade di proiezione *f*
– *rectifier, a selenium or mercury vapour rectifier for the projection lamps*

19 l'amplificatore *m*
– *amplifier*
20 l'operatore *m*
– *projectionist*
21 il tavolo di riavvolgimento bobine *f p*
– *rewind bench for rewinding the film*
22 il collante per pellicole *f pl*
– *film cement (splicing cement)*
23 il diascopio per diapositive *f pl* pubblicitarie
– *slide projector for advertisements*
**24-52 proiettori *m pl* per film *m***
– *film projectors*
24 il proiettore per film *m pl* sonori
– *sound projector (film projector, cinema projector, theatre projector, Am. movie projector)*
**25-38 il percorso della pellicola**
– *projector mechanism*
25 le scatole parafuoco
– *fireproof reel drums (spool boxes) with circulating oil cooling system*
26 il rocchetto dentato alimentazione *f* pellicola
– *feed sprocket (supply sprocket)*
27 il rocchetto dentato recupero pellicola
– *take-up sprocket*

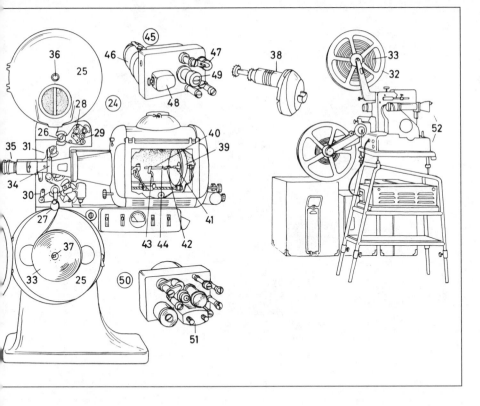

il sistema lettura magnetica
- *magnetic head cluster*
il rullino tendipellicola per lettura magnetica
- *guide roller (guiding roller) with framing control*
il rullino tendipellicola per testina sonora (lettura ottica)
- *loop former for smoothing out the intermittent movement; also: film break detector*
la guida di scorrimento pellicola
- *film path*
2 la bobina
- *film reel (film spool)*
la pellicola
- *reel of film*
la mascherina raffreddata a aria
- *film gate (picture gate, projector gate) with cooling fan*
5 l'obiettivo
- *projection lens (projector lens)*
6 il perno bobina
- *feed spindle*
7 il perno di riavvolgimento, con frizione *f*
- *take-up spindle with friction drive*
il blocco a croce *f* di Malta
- *maltese cross mechanism (Maltese cross movement, Geneva movement)*

39-44 la sede lampada
- *lamphouse*
39 la lampada a arco con specchio concavo asferico e soffiatore *m* magnetico per la stabilizzazione dell'arco voltaico (*anche:* lampada a Xenon)
- *mirror arc lamp, with aspherical (non-spherical) concave mirror and blowout magnet for stabilizing the arc ( also: high-pressure xenon arc lamp)*
40 il carbone positivo
- *positive carbon (positive carbon rod)*
41 il carbone negativo
- *negative carbon (negative carbon rod)*
42 l'arco voltaico
- *arc*
43 la pinza dei carboni
- *carbon rod holder*
44 il cratere (il cratere dei carboni)
- *crater (carbon crater)*
45 la testa sonora per lettura ottica mono e stereo Dolby
- *optical sound unit [also designed for multi-channel optical stereophonic sound and for push-pull sound tracks]*

46 il cannocchiale lettore
- *sound optics*
47 la testa sonora
- *sound head*
48 la lampada per il sonoro nella custodia
- *exciter lamp in housing*
49 la fotocellula nel tamburo
- *photocell in hollow drum*
50 l'accessorio per la lettura magnetica a quattro canali *m pl*
- *attachable four-track magnetic sound unit (penthouse head, magnetic sound head)*
51 la testina magnetica a quattro piste *f pl*
- *four-track magnetic head*
52 una macchina portatile per pellicola a 16 mm
- *narrow-gauge (Am. narrow-gage) cinema projector for mobile cinema*

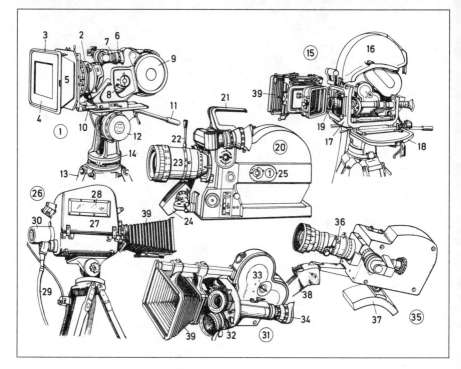

1-39 Cineprese *f pl*
- *motion picture cameras (film cameras)*
1 la cinepresa normale (cinepresa a 35 mm)
- *standard-gauge* (Am. *standard-gage)
motion picture camera (standard-gauge,
Am. standard-gage, 35 mm camera)*
2 l'obiettivo
- *lens (object lens, taking lens)*
3 il compendium (il paraluce con portafil-
tro e portamaschera)
- *lens hood (sunshade) with matte box*
4 la maschera
- *matte (mask)*
5 il paraluce
- *lens hood barrel*
6 l'oculare *m* del mirino
- *viewfinder eyepiece*
7 il regolatore dell'oculare *m*
- *eyepiece control ring*
8 la manopola di serraggio del coperchio
- *opening control for the segment disc
(disk) shutter*
9 il caricatore
- *magazine housing*
10 la slitta di fissaggio
- *slide bar for the lens hood*
11 la leva di direzione
- *control arm (control lever)*
12 la ghiera d'inclinazione *f*
- *pan and tilt head*
13 il treppiede di legno
- *wooden tripod*
14 la scala graduata
- *degree scale*
15 la cinepresa isolata acusticamente
- *soundproof (blimped) motion picture
camera (film camera)*

16-18 la cassa di isolamento acustico (il
blimp)
- *soundproof housing (blimp)*
16 la parte superiore del blimp
- *upper section of the soundproof housing*
17 la parte inferiore del blimp
- *lower section of the soundproof housing*
18 lo sportello laterale apribile del blimp
- *open sidewall of the soundproof housing*
19 l'obiettivo
- *camera lens*
20 la macchina da presa da studio
- *lightweight professional motion picture
camera*
21 l'impugnatura
- *grip (handgrip)*
22 la leva dello zoom
- *zooming lever*
23 l'obiettivo zoom con apertura variabile
continua
- *zoom lens (variable focus lens, varifocal
lens) with infinitely variable focus*
24 l'impugnatura con dispositivo di scatto
- *handgrip with shutter release*
25 lo sportello della cinepresa
- *camera door*
26 la cinepresa sonora, per riprese
d'immagini e di suoni
- *sound camera (newsreel camera) for
recording sound and picture*
27 la cassa di isolamento acustico (il
blimp)
- *soundproof housing (blimp)*
28 il finestrino di controllo per il contametri
- *window for the frame counters and indicator scales*

29 il cavo di sincronizzazione *f*
- *pilot tone cable (sync pulse cable)*
30 il sincronizzatore
- *pilot tone generator (signal generator,
pulse generator)*
31 la cinepresa a 16 mm (a passo ridotto)
- *professional narrow-gauge* (Am. *narrow-gage) motion picture camera, a 16
mm camera*
32 la torretta (il revolver) porta obiettivi
- *lens turret (turret head)*
33 la chiusura del corpo della cinepresa
- *housing lock*
34 l'oculare *m*
- *eyecup*
35 la cinepresa a alta velocità, una cinepresa speciale a 16 mm
- *high-speed camera, a special narrow-
gauge* (Am. *narrow-gage) camera*
36 la leva dello zoom
- *zooming lever*
37 l'appoggiaspalla *m*
- *rifle grip*
38 l'impugnatura con dispositivo di scatto
- *handgrip with shutter release*
39 il paraluce a soffietto del compendium
- *lens hood bellows*

**1–6** le cinque posizioni
*the five positions (ballet positions)*
la prima posizione
*first position*
la seconda posizione
*second position*
la terza posizione
*third position*
la quarta posizione (aperta)
*fourth position [open]*
la quarta posizione [incrociata; quinta posizione aperta]
*fourth position [crossed; extended fifth position]*
la quinta posizione
*fifth position*
**7–10** i ports de bras (atteggiamenti delle braccia)
*ports de bras (arm positions)*
il port de bras à côté
*port de bras à coté*
il port de bras en bas
*port de bras en bas*
il port de bras en avant
*port de bras en avant*
il port de bras en haut
*port de bras en haut*
il dégagé à la quatrième devant
*dégagé à la quatrième devant*
il dégagé à la quatrième derrière
*dégagé à la quatrième derrière*

**13** l'effacé *m*
– *effacé*
**14** il sur le cou-de-pied
– *sur le cou-de-pied*
**15** l'écarté *m*
– *écarté*
**16** il croisé
– *croisé*
**17** l'attitude *f*
– *attitude*
**18** l'arabesque *m*
– *arabesque*
**19** la punta
– *à pointe (on full point)*
**20** la spaccata
– *splits*
**21** l'arabesque *m* en plié
– *cabriole (capriole)*
**22** l'entrechat *m* (entrechat quatre)
– *entrechat (entrechat quatre)*
**23** la preparazione [*per es.* alla pirouette *f*]
– *préparation [e.g. for a pirouette]*
**24** la pirouette
– *pirouette*
**25** il corps de ballet (il corpo di ballo)
– *corps de ballet*
**26** la ballerina (la danzatrice)
– *ballet dancer (ballerina)*
**27** *u.* **28** il pas de trois
– *pas de trois*

**27** la prima ballerina
– *prima ballerina*
**28** il primo ballerino (il solista)
– *principal male dancer (leading soloist)*
**29** il tutù
– *tutu*
**30** la scarpetta a punta, una scarpetta da ballo
– *point shoe, a ballet shoe (ballet slipper)*
**31** il tutù romantico
– *ballet skirt*

**1-4  i sipari**
- *types of curtain operation*
1  il sipario alla greca
- *draw curtain (side parting)*
2  il sipario all'italiana
- *tableau curtain (bunching up sideways)*
3  il sipario alla tedesca
- *fly curtain (vertical ascent)*
4  il sipario combinato (alla greca e alla tedesca)
- *combined fly and draw curtain*
**5-11  il guardaroba**
- *cloakroom hall* (Am. *checkroom hall*)
5  il guardaroba
- *cloakroom* (Am. *checkroom*)
6  la guardarobiera (l'addetta al guardaroba)
- *cloakroom attendant* (Am. *checkroom attendant*)
7  la contromarca (lo scontrino)
- *cloakroom ticket* (Am. *check*)
8  lo spettatore
- *playgoer (theatregoer,* Am. *theatergoer)*
9  il binocolo da teatro
- *opera glass (opera glasses)*
10  la maschera (l'addetto al controllo biglietti *m pl*)
- *commissionaire*
11  il biglietto, un biglietto d'ingresso
- *theatre* (Am. *theater) ticket, an admission ticket*
**12 u. 13  il foyer**
- *foyer (lobby, crush room)*
12  la maschera
- *usher;* form.: *box attendant*
13  il programma
- *programme* (Am. *program)*
**14-27  il teatro**
- *auditorium and stage*
14  il palcoscenico, un palcoscenico circolare
- *stage*
15  il proscenio
- *proscenium*
**16-20  lo spazio riservato agli spettatori**
- *auditorium*
16  la terza fila di palchi *m pl* (il loggione)
- *gallery (balcony)*
17  la seconda fila di palchi *m pl*
- *upper circle*
18  la prima fila di palchi *m pl*
- *dress circle* (Am. *balcony, mezzanine)*
19  la platea
- *front stalls*
20  il posto a sedere (la poltrona, la poltroncina)
- *seat (theatre seat,* Am. *theater seat)*

**21-27  la prova**
- *rehearsal (stage rehearsal)*
21  il coro
- *chorus*
22  il cantante
- *singer*
23  la cantante
- *singer*
24  la fossa dell'orchestra (il golfo mistico)
- *orchestra pit*
25  l'orchestra
- *orchestra*
26  il direttore di orchestra (il maestro)
- *conductor*
27  la bacchetta del direttore di orchestra (la bacchetta)
- *baton (conductor's baton)*
**28-42  la stanza dei pittori** (un atelier teatrale)
- *paint room, a workshop*
28  l'operatore *m* scenico
- *stagehand (scene shifter)*
29  la passerella
- *catwalk (bridge)*
30  l'elemento scenografico
- *set piece*
31  l'intelaiatura
- *reinforcing struts*
32  il rivestimento
- *built piece (built unit)*
33  il fondale
- *backcloth (backdrop)*
34  la scatola portatile dei colori
- *portable box for paint containers*
35  il pittore di scene *f pl*, un decoratore
- *scene painter, a scenic artist*
36  la tavolozza portatile
- *paint trolley*
37  lo scenografo
- *stage designer (set designer)*
38  il costumista (il disegnatore dei costumi di scena)
- *costume designer*
39  lo schizzo
- *design for a costume*
40  il figurino
- *sketch for a costume*
41  il plastico
- *model stage*
42  il modello di una scena
- *model of the set*
**43-52  il camerino** (il camerino degli artisti)
- *dressing room*
43  lo specchio per il trucco
- *dressing room mirror*
44  la salvietta per il trucco
- *make-up gown*
45  il tavolo da trucco
- *make-up table*

46  il rossetto
- *greasepaint stick*
47  il truccatore
- *chief make-up artist (chief make up man)*
48  il parrucchiere (il parrucchiere teatro)
- *make-up artist (hairstylist)*
49  la parrucca
- *wig*
50  gli accessori
- *props (properties)*
51  il costume teatrale
- *theatrical costume*
52  la spia luminosa (la chiamata de direttore di scena)
- *call light*

**1-60 il palcoscenio con la macchineria** (macchineria superiore e inferiore)
– *stagehouse with machinery (machinery in the flies and below stage)*
**1** la cabia di regia
– *control room*
**2** la consolle con comando centralizzato dei riflettori
– *control console (lighting console, lighting control console) with preset control for presetting lighting effects*
**3** il leggio per le indicazioni di regia
– *lighting plot (light plot)*
**4** la graticciata (la soffitta per il macchinista)
– *grid (gridiron)*
**5** la passerella di servizio
– *fly floor (fly gallery)*
**6** l'impianto d'irrigazione *f* antincendio
– *sprinkler system for fire prevention (for fire protection)*
**7** il macchinista (l'addetto ai tiri delle scene)
– *fly man*
**8** i tiri delle scene
– *fly lines (lines)*
**9** il ciclorama
– *cyclorama*
**10** i fondali
– *backcloth (backdrop, background)*
**11** l'arco scenico (l'arcata centrale)
– *arch, a drop cloth*
**12** il celeto (il soffitto)
– *border*
**13** l'assicella di carico
– *compartment (compartment-type, compartmentalized) batten (Am. border light)*
**14** gli impianti d'illuminazione *f* scenica
– *stage lighting units (stage lights)*
**15** l'illuminazione *f* dei fondali (l'illuminazione *f* dell'orizzonte *m*)
– *horizon lights (backdrop lights)*
**16** i riflettori orientabili per il campo di azione *f*
– *adjustable acting area lights (acting area spotlights)*
**17** gli apparecchi di proiezione *f* scenici
– *scenery projectors (projectors)*
**18** l'idrante *m* (un apparecchio di sicurezza)
– *monitor (water cannon) (piece of safety equipment)*
**19** il ponte mobile delle luci
– *travelling (Am. traveling) lighting bridge (travelling lighting gallery)*

**20** il tecnico delle luci
– *lighting operator (lighting man)*
**21** il riflettore del boccascena
– *portal spotlight (tower spotlight)*
**22** il boccascena
– *adjustable proscenium*
**23** il sipario
– *curtain (theatrical curtain)*
**24** il sipario di ferro
– *iron curtain (safety curtain, fire curtain)*
**25** il proscenio (la ribalta)
– *forestage (apron)*
**26** le luci della ribalta
– *footlight (footlights, floats)*
**27** la buca del suggeritore
– *prompt box*
**28** la suggeritrice (*masch.* il suggeritore)
– *prompter*
**29** il box (la consolle) del direttore di scena
– *stage manager's desk*
**30** il direttore di scena
– *stage director (stage manager)*
**31** il palcoscenico girevole
– *revolving stage*
**32** il trabocchetto (la botola)
– *trap opening*
**33** il coperchio della botola
– *lift (Am. elevator)*
**34** il ponte mobile
– *bridge (Am. elevator), a rostrum*
**35** le decorazioni sceniche
– *pieces of scenery*
**36** la scena
– *scene*
**37** l'attore *m*
– *actor*
**38** l'attrice *f*
– *actress*
**39** le comparse *f pl*
– *extras (supers, supernumeraries)*
**40** il regista
– *director (producer)*
**41** la sceneggiatura (il copione)
– *prompt book (prompt script)*
**42** il tavolo di regia
– *director's table (producer's table)*
**43** l'assistente *m* alla regia
– *assistant director (assistant producer)*
**44** il copione (il copione del regista)
– *director's script (producer's script)*
**45** il capomacchina
– *stage carpenter*
**46** il macchinista (l'addetto alle scene)
– *stagehand (scene shifter)*
**47** l'elemento scenico mobile
– *set piece*
**48** il riflettore
– *mirror spot (mirror spotlight)*

**49** l'apparecchio per cambiare il filtro (con filtro colorato)
– *automatic filter change (with colour filters, colour mediums, gelatines)*
**50** la centrale che fornisce pressione *f* idraulica
– *hydraulic plant room*
**51** il contenitore dell'acqua
– *water tank*
**52** la conduttura aspirante
– *suction pipe*
**53** la pompa a pressione *f* idraulica
– *hydraulic pump*
**54** la conduttura a pressione *f*
– *pressure pipe*
**55** l'accumulatore *m*
– *pressure tank (accumulator)*
**56** il manometro
– *pressure gauge (Am. gage)*
**57** l'indicatore *m* del livello dell'acqua
– *level indicator (liquid level indicator)*
**58** la leva di comando
– *control lever*
**59** il tecnico addetto alle macchine
– *operator*
**60** le colonne a stantuffo
– *rams*

| | |
|---|---|
| **1** il bar | **14** l'illuminazione *f* della pista da |
| – *bar* | ballo |
| **2** la barista | – *dance floor lighting* |
| – *barmaid* | **15** la cassa dell'altoparlante *m* |
| **3** lo sgabello del bar | (l'altoparlante *m*) |
| – *bar stool* | – *speaker (loudspeaker)* |
| **4** il ripiano per le bottiglie | **16** la pista da ballo |
| – *shelf for bottles* | – *dance floor* |
| **5** il ripiano per i bicchieri | **17** *u.* **18** la coppia dei ballerini |
| – *shelf for glasses* | – *dancing couple* |
| **6** il bicchiere da birra | **17** la ballerina |
| – *beer glass* | – *dancer* |
| **7** i bicchieri da vino e da liquore *m* | **18** il ballerino |
| – *wine and liqueur glasses* | – *dancer* |
| **8** la spina (per la birra alla spina) | **19** il giradischi |
| – *beer tap (tap)* | – *record player* |
| **9** il banco | **20** il microfono |
| – *bar* | – *microphone* |
| **10** il frigorifero | **21** il registratore a nastro |
| – *refrigerator (fridge,* Am. *icebox)* | – *tape recorder* |
| **11** le lampade | **22** *u.* **23** l'impianto stereo |
| – *bar lamps* | – *stereo system (stereo equipment)* |
| **12** l'illuminazione *f* indiretta | **22** il tuner |
| – *indirect lighting* | – *tuner* |
| **13** le luci psichedeliche | **23** l'amplificatore *m* |
| – *colour* (Am. *color*) *organ (clav-* | – *amplifier* |
| *ilux)* | |

| |
|---|
| **24** i dischi |
| – *records (discs)* |
| **25** il disk-jockey (il DJ) |
| – *disc jockey* |
| **26** la consolle di missaggio |
| – *mixing console (mixing desk,* |
| *mixer)* |
| **27** il tamburello |
| – *tambourine* |
| **28** la parete a specchio |
| – *mirrored wall* |
| **29** il rivestimento del soffitto |
| – *ceiling tiles* |
| **30** gli impianti di areazione *f* |
| – *ventilators* |
| **31** le toilette |
| – *toilets (lavatories, WC)* |
| **32** il long drink |
| – *long drink* |
| **33** il cocktail |
| – *cocktail* (Am. *highball*) |

| | | |
|---|---|---|
| **1-33 il locale notturno** (il night club) | **13** il bar | **25** l'illuminazione *f* del celetto |
| – *nightclub (night spot)* | – *bar* | – *festoon lighting* |
| **1** il guardaroba | **14** la barista | **26** la lampadina a bulbo |
| – *cloakroom (Am. checkroom)* | – *barmaid* | – *festoon lamp (lamp, light bulb)* |
| **2** la guardarobiera | **15** il banco | **27-32** lo spogliarello (lo striptease) |
| – *cloakroom attendant (Am. check-* | – *bar* | – *striptease act (striptease number)* |
| *room attendant)* | **16** lo sgabello del bar | **27** la spogliarellista (la striptiseuse) |
| **3** l'orchestrina | – *bar stool* | – *striptease artist (stripper)* |
| – *band* | **17** il registratore a nastro | **28** la giarrettiera |
| **4** il clarinetto | – *tape recorder* | – *suspender (Am. garter)* |
| – *clarinet* | **18** il receiver (l'amplificatore *m*) | **29** il reggiseno (il reggipetto) |
| **5** il clarinettista | – *receiver* | – *brassière (bra)* |
| – *clarinettist (Am. clarinetist)* | **19** gli alcoolici | **30** la stola di pelliccia (il boa di pel- |
| **6** la tromba | – *spirits* | liccia) |
| – *trumpet* | **20** il proiettore a passo ridotto per | – *fur stole* |
| **7** il trombettista | film *m pl* pornografici (per film *m* | **31** i guanti |
| – *trumpeter* | *pl* porno) | – *gloves* |
| **8** la chitarra | – *cine projector for porno films (sex* | **32** la calza |
| – *guitar* | *films, blue movies)* | – *stocking* |
| **9** il chitarrista | **21** il contenitore dello schermo | **33** l'entraineuse *f* |
| – *guitarist (guitar player)* | – *box containing screen* | – *hostess* |
| **10** la batteria | **22** la scena | |
| – *drums* | – *stage* | |
| **11** il batterista | **23** l'illuminazione *f* per la scena | |
| – *drummer* | – *stage lighting* | |
| **12** la cassa dell'altoparlante *m* | **24** il riflettore per la scena | |
| (l'altoparlante *m*) | – *spotlight* | |
| – *speaker (loudspeaker)* | | |

**1-33 la corrida**
- *bullfight (corrida, corrida de toros)*
1 la simulazione
- *mock bullfight*
2 il novillero (il torero della novillada)
- *novice (aspirant matador, novillero)*
3 il finto toro
- *mock bull (dummy bull)*
4 il banderillero della novillada
- *novice banderillero (apprentice banderillero)*
5 l'arena (la plaza de toros) [schema]
- *bullring (plaza de toros) [diagram]*
6 l'ingresso principale
- *main entrance*
7 le tribune
- *boxes*
8 i posti a sedere (le gradinate)
- *stands*
9 l'arena (il ruedo)
- *arena (ring)*
10 l'entrata dei toreri
- *bullfighters' entrance*
11 l'entrata dei tori
- *torril door*
12 la porta di uscita per i tori uccisi
- *exit gate for killed bulls*
13 il macello
- *slaughterhouse*
14 la stalla dei tori (il toril)
- *bull pens (corrals)*
15 la corte per i cavalli
- *paddock*
16 il picador
- *lancer on horseback (picador)*
17 il pungolo del picador
- *lance (pike pole, javelin)*
18 il cavallo corazzato
- *armoured (Am. armored) horse*
19 la gambiera di acciaio
- *leg armour (Am. armor)*
20 il cappello rotondo del picador
- *picador's round hat*
21 il banderillero, un torero
- *banderillero, a torero*
22 le banderillas
- *banderillas (barbed darts)*
23 la fascia
- *shirtwaist*
24 la corrida
- *bullfight*
25 il matador, un torero
- *matador (swordsman), a torero*
26 il codino, un simbolo del matador
- *queue, a distinguishing mark of the matador*

27 il drappo rosso (la cappa rossa)
- *red cloak (capa)*
28 il toro da combattimento
- *fighting bull*
29 la montera (il cappello del matador)
- *montera [hat made of tiny black silk chenille balls]*
30 la morte del toro (la stoccata)
- *killing the bull (kill, estocada)*
31 il matador durante uno spettacolo di beneficenza [senza costume *m*]
- *matador in charity performances [without professional uniform]*
32 la spada (l'espada)
- *estoque (sword)*
33 la muleta
- *muleta*
**34 il rodeo**
- *rodeo*
35 il torello
- *young bull*
36 il cow-boy
- *cowboy*
37 lo stetson (il cappello da cow-boy)
- *stetson (stetson hat)*
38 la bandana (il fazzoletto da collo; *fam.* il bandana)
- *scarf (necktie)*
39 il cavaliere da rodeo
- *rodeo rider*
40 il laccio
- *lasso*

**1** *u.* **2 note** *f pl* **medievali**
– *medieval (mediaeval) notes*
**1** la notazione dei corali (la notazione quadrata)
– *plainsong notation (neumes, neums, pneumes, square notation)*
**2** la notazione mensurata
– *mensural notation*
**3-7 la nota musicale** (nota)
– *musical note (note)*
**3** la testa della nota
– *note head*
**4** il gambo della nota (il collo della nota)
– *note stem (note tail)*
**5** la coda della nota (la cediglia della nota)
– *hook*
**6** la linea orizzontale che unisce più note *f pl* dello stesso valore
– *stroke*
**7** il punto di valore *m*
– *dot indicating augmentation of note's value*
**8-11 le chiavi**
– *clefs*
**8** la chiave di violino (la chiave di sol)
– *treble clef (G-clef, violin clef )*
**9** la chiave di basso (la chiave di fa)
– *bass clef (F-clef )*
**10** la chiave di contralto (la chiave di do) per viola
– *alto clef (C-clef )*
**11** la chiave di tenore *m* (la chiave di do) per violoncello
– *tenor clef*
**12-19 i valori delle note**
– *note values*
**12** la breve (*ant.*: brevis)
– *breve (brevis, Am. double-whole note)*
**13** la semibreve (*ant.*: semibrevis)
– *semibreve (Am. whole note)*
**14** la minima
– *minim (Am. half note)*
**15** la semiminima
– *crotchet (Am. quarter note)*
**16** la croma (*ant.*: fusa)
– *quaver (Am. eighth note)*
**17** la semicroma (*ant.*: semifusa)
– *semiquaver (Am. sixteenth note)*
**18** la biscroma
– *demisemiquaver (Am. thirty-second note)*
**19** la semibiscroma
– *hemidemisemiquaver (Am. sixty-fourth note)*
**20-27 le pause**
– *rests*
**20** la pausa di una breve
– *breve rest*
**21** la pausa di una semibreve
– *semibreve rest (Am. whole rest)*
**22** la pausa di una minima
– *minim rest (Am. half rest)*
**23** la pausa di una semiminima (il sospiro)
– *crotchet rest (Am. quarter rest)*
**24** la pausa di una croma
– *quaver rest (Am. eighth rest)*

**25** la pausa di una semicroma
– *semiquaver rest (Am. sixteenth rest)*
**26** la pausa di una biscroma
– *demisemiquaver rest (Am. thirty-second rest)*
**27** la pausa di una semibiscroma
– *hemidemisemiquaver rest (Am. sixty-fourth rest)*
**28-42 il tempo** (le misure, le battute, le indicazioni di tempo)
– *time (time signatures, measure, Am. meter)*
**28** il tempo (la misura) di due ottavi *m pl*
– *two-eight time*
**29** il tempo (la misura) di due quarti *m pl*
– *two-four time*
**30** il tempo (la misura) di due mezzi *m pl*
– *two-two time*
**31** il tempo (la misura) di quattro ottavi *m pl*
– *four-eight time*
**32** il tempo (la misura) di quattro quarti *m pl* (tempo ordinario)
– *four-four time (common time)*
**33** il tempo (la misura) di quattro mezzi *m pl*
– *four-two time*
**34** il tempo (la misura) di sei ottavi *m pl*
– *six-eight time*
**35** il tempo (la misura) di sei quarti *m pl*
– *six-four time*
**36** il tempo (la misura) di tre ottavi *m pl*
– *three-eight time*
**37** il tempo (la misura) di tre quarti *m pl*
– *three-four time*
**38** il tempo (la misura) di tre mezzi *m pl*
– *three-two time*
**39** il tempo (la misura) di nove ottavi *m pl*
– *nine-eight time*
**40** il tempo (la misura) di nove quarti *m pl*
– *nine-four time*
**41** il tempo (la misura) di cinque quarti *m pl*
– *five-four time*
**42** la stanghetta (la barra) (la linea di divisione *f* della battuta)
– *bar (bar line, measure line)*
**43** *u.* **44 il pentagramma**
– *staff (stave)*
**43** la linea
– *line of the staff*
**44** lo spazio
– *space*
**45-49 le scale musicali**
– *scales*
**45** la scala in do maggiore, suoni *m pl* naturali: do, re, mi, fa, sol, la, si, do
– *C major scale naturals: c, d, e, f, g, a, b, c*
**46** la scala in la minore [scala naturale], suoni *m pl* naturali. la, si, do, re, mi, fa, sol, la
– *A minor scale [natural] naturals: a, b, c, d, e, f, g, a*
**47** la scala in la minore [armonica]
– *A minor scale [harmonic]*
**48** la scala in la minore [melodica]
– *A minor scale [melodic]*
**49** la scala cromatica
– *chromatic scale*

**50** *u.* **51** i segni di alterazione *f* ascendenti
– *signs indicating the raising of a note*
**50-54 i segni di alterazione** *f* (gli accidenti)
– *accidentals (inflections, key signatures)*
**50** il diesis (l'elevazione *f* della nota di un semitono)
– *sharp (raising the note a semitone or half-step)*
**51** il doppio diesis (l'elevazione *f* della nota di due semitoni *m pl*)
– *double sharp (raising the note a tone or full-step)*
**52** *u.* **53** segni *m pl* di alterazione *f* discendenti
– *signs indicating the lowering of a note*
**52** il bemolle (l'abbassamento della nota di un semitono)
– *flat (lowering the note a semitone or half-step)*
**53** il doppio bemolle (l'abbassamento della nota di due semitoni *m pl*)
– *double flat (lowering the note a tone or full-step)*
**54** il bequadro
– *natural*
**55-68 le tonalità** (le tonalità maggiori e le loro parallele tonalità minori, di volta in volta con le loro indicazioni)
– *keys (major keys and the related minor keys having the same signature)*
**55** do maggiore (la minore)
– *C major (A minor)*
**56** sol maggiore (mi minore)
– *G major (E minor)*
**57** re maggiore (si minore)
– *D major (B minor)*
**58** la maggiore (fa diesis minore)
– *A major (F sharp minor)*
**59** mi maggiore (do diesis minore)
– *E major (C sharp minor)*
**60** si maggiore (sol diesis minore)
– *B major (G sharp minor)*
**61** fa diesis maggiore (re diesis minore)
– *F sharp major (D sharp minor)*
**62** do maggiore (la minore)
– *C major (A minor)*
**63** fa maggiore (re minore)
– *F major (D minor)*
**64** si bemolle maggiore (sol minore)
– *B flat major (G minor)*
**65** mi bemolle maggiore (do minore)
– *E flat major (C minor)*
**66** la bemolle maggiore (fa minore)
– *A flat major (F minor)*
**67** re bemolle maggiore (si minore)
– *D flat major (B flat minor)*
**68** sol bemolle maggiore (mi bemolle minore)
– *G flat major (E flat minor)*

**1-5 l'accordo**
- *chord*

**1-4 gli accordi perfetti (le triadi)**
- *triad*

**1** l'accordo maggiore
- *major triad*

**2** l'accordo minore
- *minor triad*

**3** l'accordo perfetto diminuito
- *diminished triad*

**4** l'accordo perfetto aumentato
- *augmented triad*

**5** l'accordo di settima
- *chord of four notes, a chord of the seventh (seventh chord, dominant seventh chord)*

**6-13 gli intervalli**
- *intervals*

**6** la prima (l'unisono)
- *unison (unison interval)*

**7** la seconda maggiore
- *major second*

**8** la terza maggiore
- *major third*

**9** la quarta
- *perfect fourth*

**10** la quinta
- *perfect fifth*

**11** la sesta maggiore
- *major sixth*

**12** la settima maggiore
- *major seventh*

**13** l'ottava
- *perfect octave*

**14-22 gli abbellimenti**
- *ornaments (graces, grace notes)*

**14** l'appoggiatura lunga
- *long appoggiatura*

**15** l'appoggiatura breve
- *acciaccatura (short appoggiatura)*

**16** l'acciaccatura (la doppia appoggiatura)
- *slide*

**17** il trillo senza nota finale (il trillo senza risoluzione *f* )
- *trill (shake) without turn*

**18** il trillo con nota finale (il trillo con risoluzione *f* )
- *trill (shake) with turn*

**19** il trillo di rimbalzo (il mordente superiore)
- *upper mordent (inverted mordent, pralltriller)*

**20** il mordente inferiore
- *lower mordent (mordent)*

**21** il gruppetto
- *turn*

**22** l'arpeggio
- *arpeggio*

**23-26** altri segni di notazione *f*
- *other signs in musical notation*

**23** la terzina; variazioni analoghe: duina, quartina, quintina, sestina, settina
- *triplet;* corresponding groupings: *duplet (couplet), quadruplet, quintuplet, sextolet (sextuplet), septolet (septuplet, septimole)*

**24** la legatura
- *tie (bind)*

**25** la pausa, un segno di arresto (la corona)
- *pause (pause sign)*

**26** il segno di ripetizione *f* (il segno di ritornello, da capo)
- *repeat mark*

**27-41 i segni di espressione *f***
- *expression marks (signs of relative intensity)*

**27** marcato
- *marcato (marcando, markiert, attack, strong accent)*

**28** presto
- *presto (quick, fast)*

**29** portato
- *portato (lourer, mezzo staccato, carried)*

**30** tenuto
- *tenuto (held)*

**31** crescendo
- *crescendo (increasing gradually in power)*

**32** decrescendo
- *decrescendo (diminuendo, decreasing or diminishing gradually in power)*

**33** legato
- *legato (bound)*

**34** staccato
- *staccato (detached)*

**35** piano
- *piano (soft)*

**36** pianissimo
- *pianissimo (very soft)*

**37** pianissimo piano
- *pianissimo piano (as soft as possible)*

**38** forte
- *forte (loud)*

**39** fortissimo
- *fortissimo (very loud)*

**40** forte fortissimo
- *forte fortissimo (double fortissimo, as loud as possible)*

**41** fortepiano
- *forte piano (loud and immediately soft again)*

**42-50 la divisione dell'ambito tonale**
- *divisions of the compass*

**42** la 1. ottava (la tessitura bassa)
- *subcontra octave (double contra octave)*

**43** la 2. ottava (la tessitura bassa)
- *contra octave*

**44** la 3. ottava (la tessitura bassa)
- *great octave*

**45** la 4. ottava (la tessitura centrale)
- *small octave*

**46** la 5. ottava (la tessitura centrale)
- *one-line octave*

**47** la 6. ottava (la tessitura centrale)
- *two-line octave*

**48** la 7. ottava (la tessitura acuta)
- *three-line octave*

**49** la 8. ottava (la tessitura acuta)
- *four-line octave*

**50** la 9. ottava (la tessitura acuta)
- *five-line octave*

1 la lura, un corno di bronzo
- *lur, a bronze trumpet*
2 il flauto di Pan (la siringa, il flauto pastorale)
- *panpipes (Pandean pipes, syrinx)*
3 il diaulos, un doppio piffero (la cennamella)
- *aulos, a double shawm*
4 l'aulos *m*
- *aulos pipe*
5 la phorbeia (il capestro)
- *phorbeia (peristomion, capistrum, mouth band)*
6 il cromorno
- *crumhorn (crummhorn, cromorne, krumbhorn, krummhorn)*
7 il flauto a becco (il flauto dolce o diritto)
- *recorder (fipple flute)*
8 la cornamusa (la zampogna, la piva); *simile:* la musette
- *bagpipe;* sim.: *musette*
9 l'otre *m*
- *bag*
10 la canna melodica
- *chanter (melody pipe)*
11 il bordone (la canna di bordone)
- *drone (drone pipe)*
12 il cornetto curvo
- *curved cornett (zink)*
13 il serpentone
- *serpent*
14 il piffero; *più grande:* la bombarda
- *shawm (schalmeyes);* larger: *bombard (bombarde, pommer)*
15 la cetra (la citera); *simile e più piccola:* la lira
- *cythara (cithara);* sim. and smaller: *lyre*
16 il braccio verticale
- *arm*
17 il ponticello
- *bridge*
18 la cassa di risonanza
- *sound box (resonating chamber, resonator)*
19 il plettro (la penna), una lamina per pizzicare
- *plectrum, a plucking device*
20 la pochette (violino da tasca)
- *kit (pochette), a miniature violin*
21 la citara, uno strumento cordofono (*corrente:* uno strumento a pizzico); *simile:* la pandora
- *cittern (cithern, cither, cister, citole), a plucked instrument;* sim.: *pandora (bandora, bandore)*
22 il foro di risonanza (la rosa)
- *sound hole*

23 la viola, strumento da gamba; *più grande:* la viola da gamba, il violone
- *viol (descant viol, treble viol, a viola da gamba);* larger: *tenor viol, bass viol (viola da gamba, gamba), violone (double bass viol)*
24 l'arco da viola (l'archetto)
- *viol bow*
25 l'organino (la viola a manovella, l'organino dei mendicanti, la ghironda)
- *hurdy-gurdy (vielle à roue, symphonia, armonie, organistrum)*
26 la ruota impeciata
- *friction wheel*
27 il coperchio di protezione *f*
- *wheel cover (wheel guard)*
28 la tastiera
- *keyboard (keys)*
29 la cassa di risonanza
- *resonating body (resonator, sound box)*
30 le corde melodiche
- *melody strings*
31 le corde di accompagnamento (le corde di bordone *m*)
- *drone strings (drones, bourdons)*
32 il cimbalon (il salterio tedesco)
- *dulcimer*
33 la fascia
- *rib (resonator wall)*
34 il martelletto per il cimbalon vallese
- *beater for the Valasian dulcimer*
35 il martelletto per il cimbalon di Appenzell
- *hammer (stick) for the Appenzell dulcimer*
36 il clavicordo; *tipi:* il clavicordo legato o sciolto
- *clavichord;* kinds: *fretted or unfretted clavichord*
37 la meccanica del clavicordo
- *clavichord mechanism*
38 la leva (la leva del tasto)
- *key (key lever)*
39 il bilanciere
- *balance rail*
40 la piastrina metallica di guida del tasto
- *guiding blade*
41 la sede della guida
- *guiding slot*
42 l'appoggio
- *resting rail*
43 la tangente
- *tangent*

44 la corda
- *string*
45 il clavicembalo (cembalo), uno strumento a corda; *simile:* la spinetta (il virginale)
- *harpsichord (clavicembalo, cembalo), a wing-shaped stringed keyboard instrument;* sim.: *spinet (virginal)*
46 la tastiera superiore (il manuale superiore)
- *upper keyboard (upper manual)*
47 la tastiera inferiore (il manuale inferiore)
- *lower keyboard (lower manual)*
48 la meccanica del clavicembalo
- *harpsichord mechanism*
49 la leva dei tasti
- *key (key lever)*
50 il saltarello
- *jack*
51 i registri (la rastrelliera)
- *slide (register)*
52 il becco (la linguetta)
- *tongue*
53 la penna (il becco)
- *quill plectrum*
54 la sordina
- *damper*
55 la corda
- *string*
56 l'organo portativo, un organo portatile; *più grande:* l'organo fisso (il positivo)
- *portative organ, a portable organ;* larger: *positive organ (positive)*
57 la canna
- *pipe (flue pipe)*
58 il mantice (il soffietto)
- *bellows*

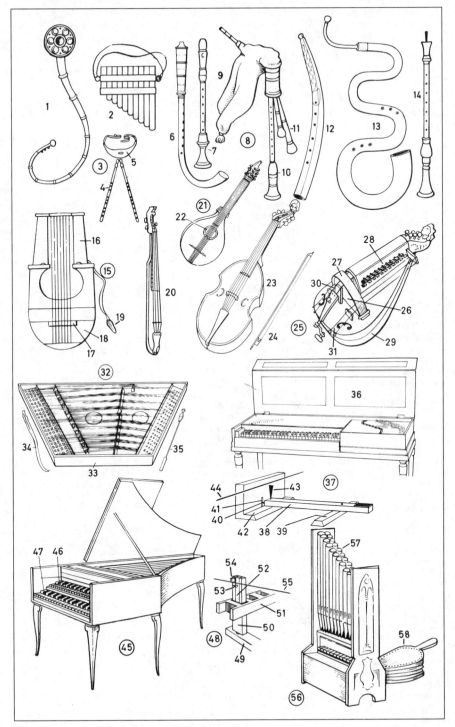

1-62 **gli strumenti dell'orchestra**
– *orchestral instruments*
1-27 **gli strumenti a corda,** strumenti a arco
– *stringed instruments, bowed instruments*
1 il violino
– *violin*
2 il manico del violino
– *neck of the violin*
3 la cassa di risonanza (la cassa del violino)
– *resonating body (violin body, sound box of the violin)*
4 la fascia
– *rib (side wall)*
5 il ponticello, il ponticello del violino
– *violin bridge*
6 la effe (la f), un foro di risonanza
– *F-hole, a sound hole*
7 la cordiera
– *tailpiece*
8 la mentoniera
– *chin rest*
9 le corde (corde del violino), la corda di sol, la corda di re, la corda di la, la corda di mi
– *strings (violin strings, fiddle strings): G-string, D-string, A-string, E-string*
10 la sordina
– *mute (sordino)*
11 la colofonia
– *resin (rosin, colophony)*
12 l'arco da violino (l'archetto)
– *violin bow (bow)*
13 il nasetto
– *nut (frog)*
14 la bacchetta
– *stick (bow stick)*
15 l'incrinatura di crini di cavallo
– *hair of the violin bow (horsehair)*
16 il violoncello
– *violoncello (cello), a member of the da gamba violin family*
17 il riccio
– *scroll*
18 il pirolo (la chiave, il bischero)
– *tuning peg (peg)*
19 il cavigliere
– *pegbox*
20 il capotasto superiore
– *nut*
21 la tastiera
– *fingerboard*
22 il puntale
– *spike (tailpin)*
23 il contrabbasso
– *double bass (contrabass, violone, double bass viol, Am. bass)*
24 la tavola
– *belly (top, soundboard)*

25 la fascia
– *rib (side wall)*
26 i filetti
– *purfling (inlay)*
27 la viola
– *viola*
28-38 **i legni** (strumenti *m pl* a fiato di legno)
– *woodwind instruments (woodwinds)*
28 il fagotto; *più grande:* il controfagotto
– *bassoon; larger: double bassoon (contrabassoon)*
29 il bocchino a doppia ancia
– *tube with double reed*
30 il flauto piccolo
– *piccolo (small flute, piccolo flute, flauto piccolo)*
31 il flauto traverso
– *flute (German flute), a cross flute (transverse flute, side-blown flute)*
32 la chiave
– *key*
33 il foro
– *fingerhole*
34 il clarinetto; *più grande:* il clarinetto basso
– *clarinet; larger: bass clarinet*
35 la chiave doppia (chiave)
– *key (brille)*
36 il bocchino
– *mouthpiece*
37 la campana
– *bell*
38 l'oboe *m; tipi:* oboe d'amore, oboe tenore, oboe da caccia, il corno inglese, l'oboe baritono
– *oboe (hautboy); kinds: oboe d'amore; tenor oboes: oboe da caccia, cor anglais; heckelphone (baritone oboe)*
39-48 **gli ottoni**
– *brass instruments (brass)*
39 il corno tenore
– *tenor horn*
40 il pistone
– *valve*
41 il corno da caccia
– *French horn (horn, waldhorn), a valve horn*
42 il padiglione
– *bell*
43 la tromba; *più grande:* la tromba bassa; *più piccola:* la cornetta
– *trumpet; larger: Bb cornet; smaller: cornet*
44 il basso-tuba (la tuba, il bombardino); *simili:* l'elicona, il contrabbasso tuba
– *bass tuba (tuba, bombardon); sim.: helicon (pellitone), contrabass tuba*

45 l'anello metallico per il pollice
– *thumb hold*
46 il trombone; *tipi:* il trombone alto, il trombone tenore, il trombone basso
– *trombone; kinds: alto trombone, tenor trombone, bass trombone*
47 la coulisse (il tiro)
– *trombone slide (slide)*
48 il padiglione
– *bell*
49-59 **strumenti** *m pl* **a percussione** *f*
– *percussion instruments*
49 il triangolo
– *triangle*
50 il piatto
– *cymbals*
51-59 membranofoni *m pl*
– *membranophones*
51 il tamburo rullante
– *side drum (snare drum)*
52 la membrana (la pelle, la pelle del tamburo)
– *drum head (head, upper head, batter head, vellum)*
53 il tirante a vite *f*
– *tensioning screw*
54 la bacchetta
– *drumstick*
55 il tamburo (il tamburo militare, la grancassa)
– *bass drum (Turkish drum)*
56 la mazza
– *stick (padded stick)*
57 il timpano, uno strumento membranofono a percussione *f* diretta; *simile:* il timpano meccanico
– *kettledrum (timpano), a screw-tensioned drum; sim.: machine drum (mechanically tuned drum)*
58 la membrana del timpano (la pelle del timpano)
– *kettledrum skin (kettledrum vellum)*
59 la chiave di registrazione *f*
– *tuning screw*
60 l'arpa, un'arpa a pedali *m pl*
– *harp, a pedal harp*
61 le corde
– *strings*
62 il pedale (il pedale dell'arpa)
– *pedal*

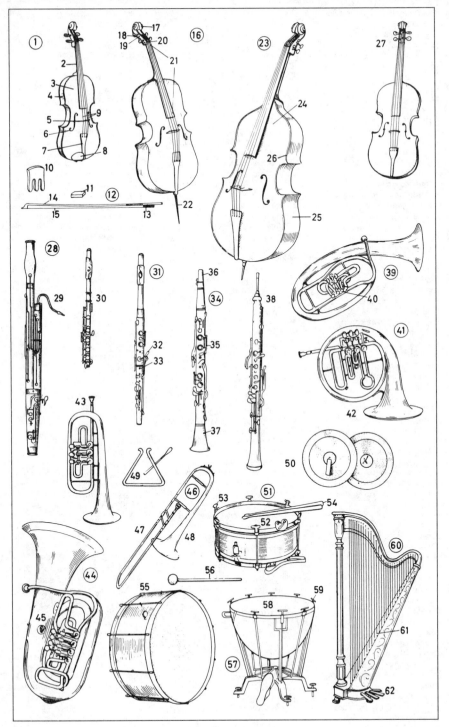

**1-46  Strumenti** *m pl* **per musica popolare**
– *popular musical instruments (folk instruments)*

**1-31**  strumenti *m pl* a corda
– *stringed instruments*

**1**  il liuto; *più grande:* la tierba, il chitarrone
– *lute* larger: *theorbo, chitarrone*

**2**  la cassa di risonanza
– *resonating body (resonator)*

**3**  la tavola armonica
– *soundboard (belly, table)*

**4**  la cordiera
– *string fastener (string holder)*

**5**  il foro di risonanza (la rosa)
– *sound hole (rose)*

**6**  la corda, una corda di budello
– *string, a gut (catgut) string*

**7**  il manico
– *neck*

**8**  la tastiera
– *fingerboard*

**9**  il tasto
– *fret*

**10**  il cavigliere
– *head (bent-back pegbox, swan-head pegbox, pegbox)*

**11**  il pirolo
– *tuning peg (peg, lute pin)*

**12**  la chitarra
– *guitar*

**13**  la cordiera
– *string holder*

**14**  la corda, una corda di budello o di perlon
– *string, a gut (catgut) or nylon string*

**15**  la cassa armonica (cassa di risonanza)
– *resonating body (resonating chamber, resonator, sound box)*

**16**  il mandolino
– *mandolin (mandoline)*

**17**  la cordiera
– *sleeve protector (cuff protector)*

**18**  il manico
– *neck*

**19**  il cavigliere
– *pegdisc*

**20**  il plettro (la penna)
– *plectrum*

**21**  la cetra (cetra da tavolo)
– *zither (plucked zither)*

**22**  il somiere
– *pin block (wrest pin block, wrest plank)*

**23**  la chiave
– *tuning pin (wrest pin)*

**24**  le corde di bordone (corde di accompagnamento)
– *accompaniment strings (bass strings, unfretted strings, open strings)*

**25**  le corde di melodia
– *melody strings (fretted strings, stopped strings)*

**26**  l'allargamento della cassa di risonanza
– *semicircular projection of the resonating sound box (resonating body)*

**27**  il plettro a anello
– *ring plectrum*

**28**  la balalaika
– *balalaika*

**29**  il banjo
– *banjo*

**30**  la cassa armonica (il tamburino)
– *tambourine-like body*

**31**  la membrana
– *parchment membrane*

**32**  l'ocarina
– *ocarina, a globular flute*

**33**  il bocchino
– *mouthpiece*

**34**  il foro
– *fingerhole*

**35**  l'armonica a bocca
– *mouth organ (harmonica)*

**36**  la fisarmonica, *simili:* l'accordeon, il bandoleon
– *accordion; sim.: piano accordion, concertina, bandoneon*

**37**  il mantice (il soffietto)
– *bellows*

**38**  il blocca-mantice
– *bellows strap*

**39**  la tastiera melodica (tastiera di canto)
– *melody side (keyboard side, melody keys)*

**40**  la tastiera
– *keyboard (keys)*

**41**  il registro melodico
– *treble stop (treble coupler, treble register)*

**42**  il tasto del registro (della tastiera)
– *stop lever*

**43**  la tastiera dei bassi
– *bass side (accompaniment side, bass studs, bass press-studs, bass buttons)*

**44**  il registro grave
– *bass stop (bass coupler, bass register)*

**45**  il tamburello (il tamburo basso)
– *tambourine*

**46**  le nacchere
– *castanets*

**47-78**  strumenti *m pl* jazz
– *jazz band instruments (dance band instruments)*

**47-58**  strumenti *m pl* a percussione *f*
– *percussion instruments*

**47-54**  la batteria
– *drum kit (drum set, drums)*

**47**  la grancassa
– *bass drum*

**48**  il tamburo rullante
– *small tom-tom*

**49**  il tom-tom
– *large tom-tom*

**50**  l'hi-hat (charleston), un piatto doppio
– *high-hat cymbals (choke cymbals, Charleston cymbals, cup cymbals)*

**51**  il piatto (cimbalino)
– *cymbal*

**52**  l'asta del piatto
– *cymbal stand (cymbal holder)*

**53**  la spazzola metallica
– *wire brush*

**54**  il pedale
– *pedal mechanism*

**55**  la conga (la tumba)
– *conga drum (conga)*

**56**  l'anello di tensione
– *tension hoop*

**57**  i timbali
– *timbales*

**58**  i bongos
– *bongo drums (bongos)*

**59**  le maracas
– *maracas;* sim.: *shakers*

**60**  il guiro
– *guiro*

**61**  lo xilofono; *simili:* il vibrafono, il metallofono
– *xylophone;* form.: *straw fiddle;* sim.: *marimbaphone (steel marimba), tubaphone*

**62**  la bacchetta di legno
– *wooden slab*

**63**  la cassa di risonanza
– *resonating chamber (sound box)*

**64**  la sbarretta di legno (o lamina di metallo)
– *beater*

**65**  la tromba da jazz
– *jazz trumpet*

**66**  il pistone
– *valve*

**67**  l'appoggio per il dito
– *finger hook*

**68**  la sordina
– *mute (sordino)*

**69**  il sassofono
– *saxophone*

**70**  il padiglione (la campana)
– *bell*

**71**  l'imboccatura
– *crook*

**72**  il bocchino
– *mouthpiece*

**73**  la chitarra folk (chitarra country)
– *struck guitar (jazz guitar)*

**74**  la spalla mancante (cutaway)
– *hollow to facilitate fingering*

**75**  il vibrafono
– *vibraphone (Am. vibraharp)*

**76**  il telaio metallico
– *metal frame*

**77**  la limina metallica
– *metal bar*

**78**  i tubi metallici
– *tubular metal resonator*

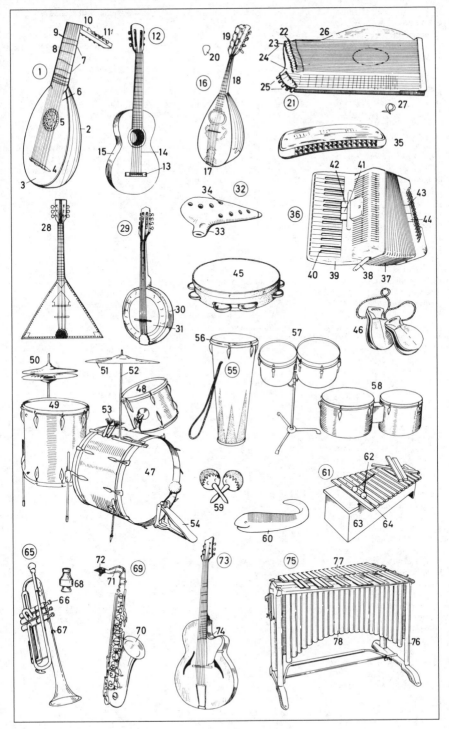

**1** il pianoforte (pianoforte verticale), uno strumento a tastiera;
*forma più piccola:* pianoforte da
appartamento; *forme anteriori:* il
pantaleon, il pianoforte a martelli
*m pl*, la celesta con piastre *f pl* di
acciaio al posto delle corde *f pl*
– *piano (pianoforte, upright piano,
upright, vertical piano, spinet
piano, console piano), a keyboard
instrument (keyed instrument);
smaller form: cottage piano
(pianino); earlier forms: pantaleon; celesta, with steel bars instead
of strings*
**2-18** la meccanica del pianoforte
– *piano action (piano mechanism)*
**2** il telaio (la griglia) di ghisa
– *iron frame*
**3** il martelletto (martelletto del
pianoforte, martelletto con feltro;
*tutti insieme:* la martelliera)
– *hammer; collectively: striking
mechanism*
**4** *u.* **5** la tastiera (i tasti) del
pianoforte
– *keyboard (piano keys)*
**4** il tasto bianco (il tasto di avorio)
– *white key (ivory key)*
**5** il tasto nero (il tasto di ebano)
– *black key (ebony key)*
**6** il mobile esterno
– *piano case*
**7** le corde del pianoforte
– *strings (piano strings)*
**8** *u.* **9** i pedali del pianoforte
– *piano pedals*
**8** il pedale di destra (*impropria-
mente:* pedale *m* del forte *m*) per
sollevare gli smorzatori
– *right pedal (sustaining pedal,
damper pedal; loosely: forte pedal,
loud pedal) for raising the
dampers*
**9** il pedale di sinistra (*impropria-
mente:* pedale del piano) per
diminuire la sonorità
– *left pedal (soft pedal; loosely:
piano pedal) for reducing the
striking distance of the hammers
on the strings*
**10** le corde centro-acute
– *treble strings*
**11** il ponticello delle corde centro-
acute
– *treble bridge (treble belly bridge)*
**12** le corde basse
– *bass strings*
**13** il ponticello delle corde basse
– *bass bridge (bass belly bridge)*
**14** la punta di aggancio della corda
sul telaio
– *hitch pin*

**15** il supporto della meccanica
– *hammer rail*
**16** il compressore (la barra di compressione *f* delle corde)
– *brace*
**17** la caviglia
– *tuning pin (wrest pin, tuning peg)*
**18** il somiere
– *pin block (wrest pin block, wrest
plank)*
**19** il metronomo
– *metronome*
**20** la chiave per l'accordatura del
pianoforte
– *tuning hammer (tuning key, wrest)*
**21** il cuneo per l'accordatura
– *tuning wedge*
**22-39** la meccanica del tasto del
pianoforte
– *key action (key mechanism)*
**22** la barra centrale
– *beam*
**23** la leva degli smorzatori (levatutti)
– *damper-lifting lever*
**24** la testa del martelletto, ricoperta
di feltro
– *felt-covered hammer head*
**25** la gamba del martelletto (stiletto)
– *hammer shank*
**26** la barra appoggia martelletti
– *hammer rail*
**27** il paramartelletto
– *check (back check)*
**28** il feltro del paramartelletto
– *check felt (back check felt)*
**29** l'astina del paramartelletto
– *wire stem of the check (wire stem
of the back check)*
**30** il montante o spingitore *m*
– *sticker (hopper, hammer jack,
hammer lever)*
**31** la nocetta
– *button*
**32** il bilanciere
– *action lever*
**33** il pilota
– *pilot*
**34** l'astina del pilota
– *pilot wire*
**35** l'astina di aggancio per la bretellina
– *tape wire*
**36** la bretellina
– *tape*
**37** il ceppo dello smorzatore
– *damper (damper block)*
**38** lo smorzatore
– *damper lifter*
**39** la barra di arresto degli smorzatori
– *damper rest rail*

**40** il pianoforte a coda (il pianoforte
a gran coda per sala da concerto;
*più piccolo:* il pianoforte a coda, i
pianoforte da appartamento; il
mezza coda)
– *grand piano (horizontal piano,
grand, concert grand, for the concert hall; smaller: baby grand
piano, boudoir piano; other form:
square piano, table piano)*
**41** i pedali del pianoforte a coda; il
pedale di destra per il sollevamento degli smorzatori, il pedale
di sinistra per lo spostamento
della tastiera verso destra: solo
una corda viene percossa e la
sonorità è minore
– *grand piano pedals; right pedal for
raising the dampers; left pedal for
softening the tone (shifting the
keyboard so that only one string is
struck 'una corda')*
**42** le bacchette dei pedali, la cetra, i
sostegni della cetra
– *pedal bracket*
**43** l'armonium (l'armonio)
– *harmonium (reed organ, melodi-
um)*
**44** il bottone del registro
– *draw stop (stop, stop knob)*
**45** il ginocchiere (lo schweller)
– *knee lever (knee swell, swell)*
**46** i pedali per azionare i mantici
– *pedal (bellows pedal)*
**47** la cassa dell'armonium
– *harmonium case*
**48** il manuale dell'armonium
– *harmonium keyboard (manual)*

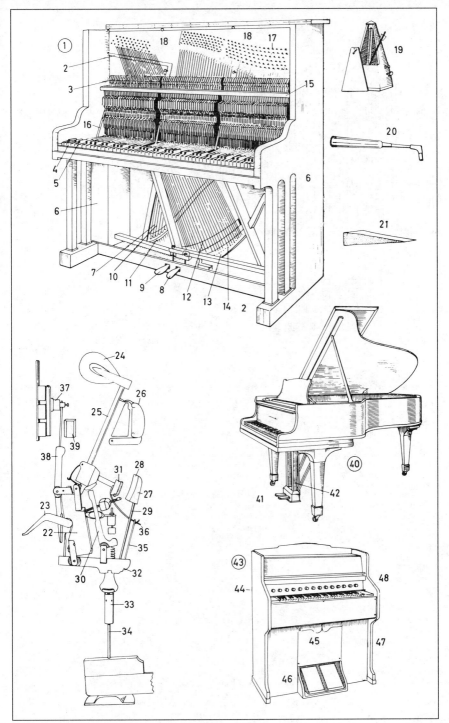

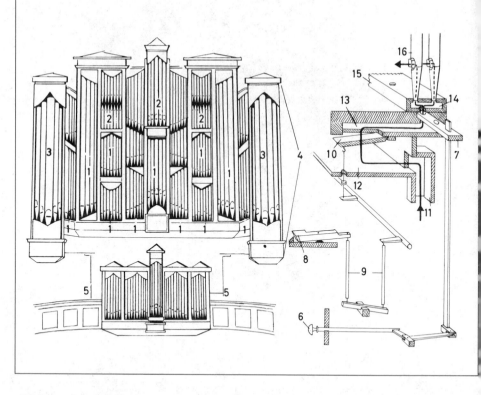

**1-52 l'organo** (organo da chiesa)
- *organ (church organ)*
**1-3** le canne di facciata
- *front view of organ (organ case)
[built according to classical princi-
ples]*
**1-5** la facciata (la cassa) dell'organo
- *display pipes (face pipes)*
**1** il grande organo
- *Hauptwerk* (approx. English equiva-
lent: *great organ*)
**2** l'organo recitativo
- *Oberwerk* (approx. English equiva-
lent: *swell organ*)
**3** le canne azionate dai pedali
- *pedal pipes*
**4** la torre del pedale
- *pedal tower*
**5** l'organo positivo
- *Rückpositiv* (approx. English equiv-
alent: *choir organ*)
**6-16** la trasmissione meccanica; *altri
sistemi:* trasmissione pneumatica,
trasmissione elettrica
- *tracker action (mechanical action);*
other systems: *pneumatic action,
electric action*
**6** il registro
- *draw stop (stop, stop knob)*
**7** la stecca (la coulisse)
- *slider (slide)*

**8** il tasto
- *key (key lever)*
**9** i pironi (le asticelle)
- *sticker*
**10** il ventilatore (il ventilabro)
- *pallet*
**11** il canale per l'aria
- *wind trunk*
**12-14** il somiere, un somiere a tiro con
catenacciatura; *altri tipi:* somiere a
vento, somiere a tiro, somiere a pis-
toni, somiere a membrane *f pl*
- *wind chest, a slider wind chest;* other
types: *sliderless wind chest (unit
wind chest), spring chest, kegellade
chest (cone chest), diaphragm chest*
**12** il cassone dell'aria
- *wind chest (wind chest box)*
**13** la scanalatura inferiore
- *groove*
**14** la scanalatura superiore
- *upper board groove*
**15** il piede della canna
- *upper board*
**16** la canna di un registro
- *pipe of a particular stop*
**17-35** le canne dell'organo
- *organ pipes (pipes)*
**17-22** la canna a ancia di metallo, un
trombone (una tromba, un corno)
- *metal reed pipe (set of pipes: reed
stop), a posaune stop*

**17** il piede
- *boot*
**18** la canaletta (la gola)
- *shallot*
**19** la linguetta
- *tongue*
**20** la noce (il ceppo di piombo)
- *block*
**21** il filo metallico per l'intonazione *f*
(la gruccia)
- *tuning wire (tuning crook)*
**22** il tubo di risonanza (il padiglione)
- *tube*
**23-30** la canna labiale aperta di metallo,
un salizionale
- *open metal flue pipe, a salicional*
**23** il piede
- *foot*
**24** la fessura
- *flue pipe windway (flue pipe duct)*
**25** la bocca
- *mouth (cutup)*
**26** il labbro inferiore
- *lower lip*
**27** il labbro superiore
- *upper lip*
**28** l'anima
- *languid*
**29** il corpo della canna
- *body of the pipe (pipe)*

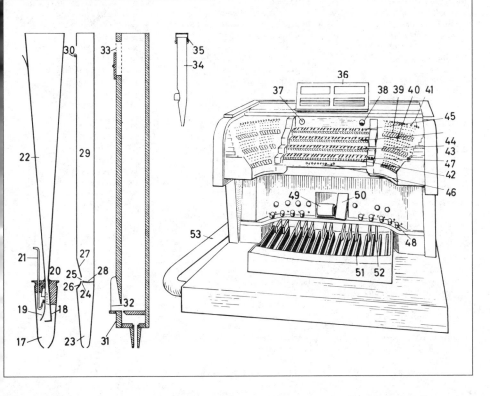

**30** la linguetta che regola l'accordatura della canna, un dispositivo per l'accordatura
– *tuning flap (tuning tongue), a tuning device*
**31-33** la canna labiale aperta di legno, un principale
– *open wooden flue pipe (open wood), principal (diapason)*
**31** il cappello
– *cap*
**32** l'orecchia
– *ear*
**33** il foro per l'accordatura con scivolo
– *tuning hole (tuning slot), with slide*
**34** la canna labiale chiusa
– *stopped flue pipe*
**35** la chiusura a scatola
– *stopper*
**36-52** la consolle dell'organo a comandi elettrici
– *organ console (console) of an electric action organ*
**36** il leggio
– *music rest (music stand)*
**37** l'indicatore *m* della posizione dei cilindri (indicatore *m* del crescendo)
– *crescendo roller indicator*
**38** il voltmetro
– *voltmeter*
**39** il tasto dei registri
– *stop tab (rocker)*

**40** il comando delle combinazioni libere
– *free combination stud (free combination knob)*
**41** gli annullatori delle lingue, dell'accoppiamento ecc.
– *cancel buttons for reeds, couplers etc.*
**42** il primo manuale agente sull'organo positivo
– *manual I, for the Rückpositiv (choir organ)*
**43** il secondo manuale agente sul grande organo
– *manual II, for the Hauptwerk (great organ)*
**44** il terzo manuale agente sull'organo recitativo
– *manual III, for the Oberwerk (swell organ)*
**45** il quarto manuale agente sulle canne a ancia
– *manual IV, for the Schwellwerk (solo organ)*
**46** i pistoncini per la registrazione manuale, le libere combinazioni, le combinazioni fisse e quelle predisposte dall'organaro
– *thumb pistons controlling the manual stops (free or fixed combinations) and buttons for setting the combinations*

**47** i pulsanti per azionare il meccanismo elettrico dei mantici
– *switches for current to blower and action*
**48** il pistone a piede *m* per l'accoppiamento
– *toe piston, for the coupler*
**49** il pedale dello schweller che inserisce gradualmente i registri
– *crescendo roller (general crescendo roller)*
**50** il pedale del crescendo
– *balanced swell pedal*
**51** il tasto a pedale *m* inferiore (suoni naturali)
– *pedal key [natural]*
**52** il tasto a pedale *m* superiore (suoni alterati)
– *pedal key [sharp or flat]*
**53** il cavo
– *cable (transmission cable)*

**1-61 figure** *f pl* **fantastiche** (animali *m pl* favolosi), animali *m pl* e figure *f pl* mitologiche
– *fabulous creatures (fabulous animals), mythical creatures*
**1** il drago
– *dragon*
**2** il corpo da serpente *m*
– *serpent's body*
**3** l'artiglio
– *claws (claw)*
**4** l'ala da pipistrello
– *bat's wing*
**5** la bocca con la lingua biforcuta
– *fork-tongued mouth*
**6** la lingua biforcuta
– *forked tongue*
**7** l'unicorno (simbolo della verginità)
– *unicorn [symbol of virginity]*
**8** il corno a spirale *f*
– *spirally twisted horn*
**9** la fenice
– *Phoenix*
**10** le fiamme e le ceneri della resurrezione
– *flames or ashes of resurrection*
**11** il grifone
– *griffin (griffon, gryphon)*
**12** la testa di aquila
– *eagle's head*
**13** l'artiglio del grifone
– *griffin's claws*
**14** il corpo di leone *m*
– *lion's body*
**15** l'ala
– *wing*
**16** la chimera, un mostro
– *chimera (chimaera), a monster*
**17** la testa di leone *m*
– *lion's head*
**18** la testa di capra
– *goat's head*
**19** il corpo di drago
– *dragon's body*
**20** la sfinge, una figura simbolica
– *sphinx, a symbolic figure*
**21** la testa umana
– *human head*
**22** il corpo leonino
– *lion's body*
**23** la sirena (la ninfa del mare, la ninfa delle acque, l'oceanina, la naiade, la ninfa delle fonti) *sim.:* la nereide, l'ondina (divinità marina); *masch.:* il tritone
– *mermaid (nix, nixie, water nixie, sea maid, sea maiden, naiad, water nymph, water elf, ocean nymph, sea nymph, river nymph); sim.: Nereids, Oceanids (sea divinities, sea deities, sea goddesses); male: nix (merman, seaman)*
**24** il corpo femminile
– *woman's trunk*

**25** la coda di pesce *m*
– *fish's tail (dolphin's tail)*
**26** il pegaso (il cavallo alato); *sim.:* l'ippogrifo
– *Pegasus (favourite, Am. favorite, steed of the Muses, winged horse); sim.: hippogryph*
**27** il corpo di cavallo
– *horse's body*
**28** le ali
– *wings*
**29** il cerbero
– *Cerberus (hellhound)*
**30** il corpo di cane *m* a tre teste *f pl*
– *three-headed dog's body*
**31** la coda di serpente *m*
– *serpent's tail*
**32** l'idra di Lerna
– *Lernaean (Lernean) Hydra*
**33** il corpo di serpente *m* a nove teste *f pl*
– *nine-headed serpent's body*
**34** il basilisco
– *basilisk (cockatrice) [in English legend usually with two legs]*
**35** la testa di gallo
– *cock's head*
**36** il corpo di drago
– *dragon's body*
**37** il titano, un gigante
– *giant (titan)*
**38** il macigno
– *rock*
**39** il piede di serpente *m*
– *serpent's foot*
**40** il tritone, una creatura marina
– *triton, a merman (demigod of the sea)*
**41** la conchiglia
– *conch shell trumpet*
**42** il piede di cavallo (il piede equino)
– *horse's hoof*
**43** la coda di pesce *m*
– *fish's tail*
**44** l'ippocampo (il cavallo marino)
– *hippocampus*
**45** il corpo di cavallo (il corpo equino)
– *horse's trunk*
**46** la coda di pesce *m*
– *fish's tail*
**47** il toro marino, un mostro marino
– *sea ox, a sea monster*
**48** il corpo di toro (il corpo taurino)
– *monster's body*
**49** la coda di pesce *m*
– *fish's tail*
**50** il drago a sette teste *f pl* dell'Apocalisse *f*
– *seven-headed dragon of St. John's Revelation (Revelations, Apocalypse)*
**51** l'ala
– *wing*

**52** il centauro, un mostro mezzo uomo e mezzo cavallo
– *centaur (hippocentaur), half man and half beast*
**53** il corpo di uomo con freccia e arco
– *man's body with bow and arrow*
**54** il corpo di cavallo
– *horse's body*
**55** l'arpia, un mostro alato
– *harpy, a winged monster*
**56** la testa di donna
– *woman's head*
**57** il corpo di uccello
– *bird's body*
**58** la sirena, un demone
– *siren, a daemon*
**59** il corpo femminile
– *woman's body*
**60** l'ala
– *wing*
**61** l'artiglio di uccello
– *bird's claw*

**1-40** reperti *m pl* preistorici
– *prehistoric finds*
**1-9 il paleolitico** e **il mesolitico**
– *Old Stone Age (Palaeolithic, Paleolithic, period) and Mesolithic period*
**1** il cuneo di selce *f* (il bifacciale acheuleano)
– *hand axe* (Am. *ax*) *(fist hatchet), a stone tool*
**2** la punta di lancia in osso
– *head of throwing spear, made of bone*
**3** l'arpione *m* in osso
– *bone harpoon*
**4** la punta
– *head*
**5** il giavellotto in corno di renna
– *harpoon thrower, made of reindeer antler*
**6** la selce dipinta
– *painted pebble*
**7** la testa del cavallo selvaggio, una scultura lignea
– *head of a wild horse, a carving*
**8** l'idolo dell'età della pietra, una statuetta in avorio
– *Stone Age idol, an ivory statuette*
**9** il bisonte, una pittura rupestre
– *bison, a cave painting (rock painting) [cave art, cave painting]*
**10-20 il neolitico**
– *New Stone Age (Neolithic period)*
**10** l'anfora [ceramica a cordicella]
– *amphora [corded ware]*
**11** il vaso in ceramica incisa [il gruppo della ceramica incisa]
– *bowl [menhir group]*
**12** il vaso con collo a imbuto [cultura del bicchiere imbutiforme]
– *collared flask [Funnel-Beaker culture]*
**13** il vaso con decorazioni *f pl* a spirale *f* [ceramica decorata a incisioni *f pl*]
– *vessel with spiral pattern [spiral design pottery]*
**14** il vaso in ceramica campaniforme [la cultura del vaso campaniforme]
– *bell beaker [bell beaker culture]*
**15** la palafitta, una costruzione su palafitte *f pl*
– *pile dwelling (lake dwelling, lacustrine dwelling)*
**16** il dolmen, una tomba megalitica; *altri tipi:* tomba a galleria; *coperto di terra, ghiaia, pietra:* il tumulo
– *dolmen (cromlech), a megalithic tomb ( coll.: giant's tomb); other kinds: passage grave, gallery grave (long cist); when covered with earth: tumulus (barrow, mound)*

**17** la tomba a cassa di pietra, una tomba con scheletro rannicchiato
– *stone cist, a contracted burial*
**18** il menhir, un monolito
– *menhir (standing stone), a monolith*
**19** l'ascia ricurva, un'ascia di guerra in pietra
– *boat axe* (Am. *ax), a stone battle axe*
**20** la figura umana in terracotta (un idolo)
– *clay figurine, an idol*
**21-40 l'età del bronzo** e **l'età del ferro;** *epoche:* l'epoca di Hallstatt, l'epoca di La-Tené
– *Bronze Age and Iron Age;* epochs: *Hallstatt period, La Tène period*
**21** la punta di lancia in bronzo
– *bronze spear head*
**22** il pugnale in bronzo con impugnatura
– *hafted bronze dagger*
**23** la scure a becco, un'ascia di bronzo con asta a occhiello
– *socketed axe* (Am. *ax), a bronze axe with haft fastened to rings*
**24** il disco ornamentale per cintura
– *girdle clasp*
**25** la lunula
– *necklace (lunula)*
**26** la collana dorata
– *gold neck ring*
**27** la fibula a arco di violino, una fibula
– *violin-bow fibula (safety pin)*
**28** la fibula a serpente *m; altri tipi:* la fibula a barca, la fibula a balestra
– *serpentine fibula;* other kinds: *boat fibula, arc fibula*
**29** la spilla con testa a sfera, una spilla di bronzo
– *bulb-head pin, a bronze pin*
**30** la fibula in due parti *f pl*, a doppia spirale *f; sim.:* la fibula a lastrine *f pl*
– *two-piece spiral fibula;* sim.: *disc (disk) fibula*
**31** il coltello di bronzo con impugnatura
– *hafted bronze knife*
**32** la chiave di ferro
– *iron key*
**33** il vomere
– *ploughshare* (Am. *plowshare)*
**34** la «situla» in lamierino di bronzo, un arredo funerario
– *sheet-bronze situla, a funerary vessel*
**35** una brocca a ansa [ceramica con intagli *m pl* a tacche *f pl*]
– *pitcher [chip-carved pottery]*

**36** un carro votivo in miniatura (carretto adibito al culto)
– *miniature ritual cart (miniature ritual chariot)*
**37** la moneta di argento celtica
– *Celtic silver coin*
**38** il canopo, un'urna cineraria; *altri tipi:* urna a forma di casa, urna a rilievo
– *face urn, a cinerary urn;* other kinds: *domestic urn, embossed urn*
**39** la tomba con urna in un tumulo di pietre *f pl*
– *urn grave in stone chamber*
**40** l'urna a collo cilindrico
– *urn with cylindrical neck*

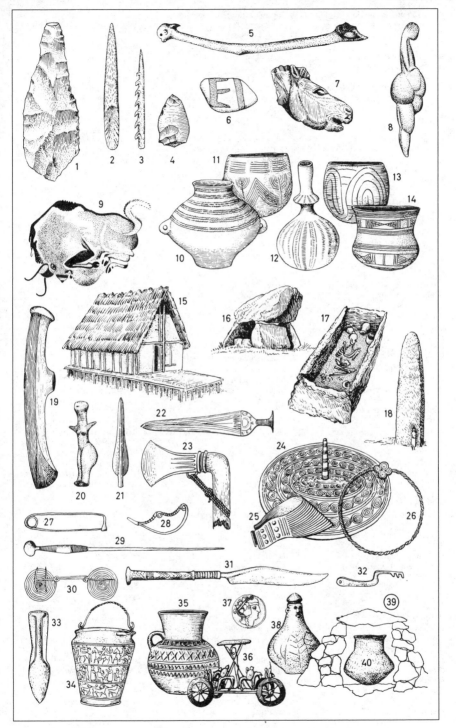

**1 il castello medievale** (la fortezza, il maniero)
- **knight's castle** *(castle)*
**2** la corte interna
- *inner ward (inner bailey)*
**3** il pozzo a carrucola
- *draw well*
**4** il masto (la torre principale, la torre di vedetta, la torre di guardia)
- *keep (donjon)*
**5** il carcere sotterraneo (le segrete del castello)
- *dungeon*
**6** la merlatura
- *battlements (crenellation)*
**7** il merlo
- *merlon*
**8** la piattaforma della torre
- *tower platform*
**9** la vedetta (la sentinella)
- *watchman*
**10** la caminata (la stanza fornita di camino, la camera delle dame)
- *ladies' apartments (bowers)*
**11** l'abbaino
- *dormer window (dormer)*
**12** il balcone (la terrazza)
- *balcony*
**13** il deposito delle provviste (il granaio)
- *storehouse (magazine)*
**14** il torrione di angolo
- *angle tower*
**15** il muro di cinta (la prima cinta di mura *f pl*)
- *curtain wall (curtains, enclosure wall)*
**16** il bastione (il baluardo)
- *bastion*
**17** la guardiola
- *angle tower*
**18** la feritoia
- *crenel (embrasure)*
**19** il muro di cortina *f*
- *inner wall*
**20** la bertesca
- *battlemented parapet*
**21** il parapetto
- *parapet (breastwork)*
**22** il corpo di guardia
- *gatehouse*
**23** la caditoia (la piombatoia)
- *machicolation (machicoulis)*
**24** la saracinesca
- *portcullis*
**25** il ponte levatoio
- *drawbridge*
**26** il contrafforte
- *buttress*
**27** i fabbricati rurali
- *offices and service rooms*
**28** la torretta
- *turret*
**29** la cappella
- *chapel*
**30** il palazzo
- *great hall*
**31** il cortile esterno (la corte esterna)
- *outer ward (outer bailey)*

**32** la porta esterna del castello
- *castle gate*
**33** il fossato esterno
- *moat (ditch)*
**34** la strada di accesso
- *approach*
**35** la torre di guardia (la torre di vedetta)
- *watchtower (turret)*
**36** la palizzata
- *palisade (pallisade, palisading)*
**37** il fossato interno
- *moat (ditch, fosse)*
**38-65 l'armatura del cavaliere**
- **knight's armour** *(Am. armor)*
**38** la corazza
- *suit of armour (Am. armor)*
**39-42** l'elmo
- *helmet*
**39** la cresta
- *skull*
**40** la visiera
- *visor (vizor)*
**41** la baviera
- *beaver*
**42** la goletta
- *throat piece*
**43** il camaglio
- *gorget*
**44** la gorgiera
- *épaulière*
**45** lo spallaccio
- *pallette (pauldron, besageur)*
**46** il petto della corazza
- *breastplate (cuirass)*
**47** il bracciale (la protezione per il braccio e l'avambraccio)
- *brassard (rear brace and vambrace)*
**48** la cubitiera
- *cubitière (coudière, couter)*
**49** la panziera
- *tasse (tasset)*
**50** la manopola
- *gauntlet*
**51** il fiancale
- *habergeon (haubergeon)*
**52** il cosciale
- *cuisse (cuish, cuissard, cuissart)*
**53** il ginocchietto
- *knee cap (knee piece, genouillère, poleyn)*
**54** la gambiera
- *jambeau (greave)*
**55** la scarpa
- *solleret (sabaton, sabbaton)*
**56** lo scudo oblungo
- *pavis (pavise, pavais)*
**57** lo scudo tondo
- *buckler (round shield)*
**58** la borchia dello scudo
- *boss (umbo)*
**59** il bacinetto
- *iron hat*
**60** il morione
- *morion*
**61** la barbuta veneziana
- *light casque*

**62** maglie *f pl*
- *types of mail and armour (Am. armor)*
**63** la maglia a catena
- *mail (chain mail, chain armour, Am. armor)*
**64** la maglia a scaglie *f pl*
- *scale armour (Am. armor)*
**65** la maglia piatta
- *plate armour (Am. armor)*
**66 la cerimonia di investitura** (l'accollata)
- **accolade** *(dubbing, knighting)*
**67** il signore del castello, un cavaliere
- *liege lord, a knight*
**68** lo scudiero
- *esquire*
**69** il coppiere
- *cup bearer*
**70** il trovatore (il menestrello)
- *minstrel (minnesinger, troubadour)*
**71 il torneo**
- **tournament** *(tourney, joust, just, tilt)*
**72** il crociato (il cavaliere dell'ordine *m* della Croce)
- *crusader*
**73** il templare (il cavaliere dell'ordine *m* del Tempio)
- *Knight Templar*
**74** la gualdrappa
- *caparison (trappings)*
**75** il buriasso
- *herald (marshal at tournament)*
**76** l'armatura da torneo incisa (la corazza incisa)
- *tilting armour (Am. armor)*
**77** l'elmo da torneo inciso
- *tilting helmet (jousting helmet)*
**78** il pennacchio
- *panache (plume of feathers)*
**79** lo scudo da torneo
- *tilting target (tilting shield)*
**80** la resta (un ferro applicato alla corazza per attaccarvi la lancia)
- *lance rest*
**81** la lancia
- *tilting lance (lance)*
**82** l'impugnatura
- *vamplate*
**83-88** l'armatura del cavallo (la barda)
- *horse armour (Am. armor)*
**83** il collo
- *neck guard (neck piece)*
**84** la testiera
- *chamfron (chaffron, chafron, chamfrain, chanfron)*
**85** la pettiera
- *poitrel*
**86** il fiancale
- *flanchard (flancard)*
**87** la sella da torneo
- *tournament saddle*
**88** la groppa
- *rump piece (quarter piece)*

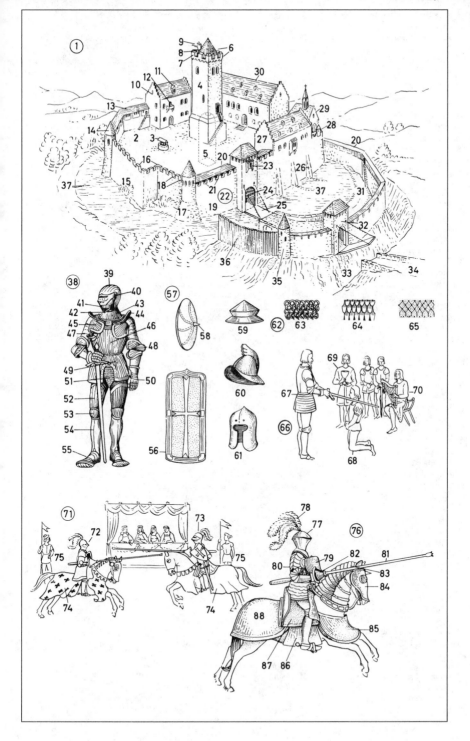

**1-30  la chiesa protestante (evangelica, luterana)**
- *Protestant church*
**1**  il presbiterio
- *chancel*
**2**  il leggio
- *lectern*
**3**  il tappeto davanti all'altare *m*
- *altar carpet*
**4**  l'altare *m*
- *altar (communion table, Lord's table, holy table)*
**5**  i gradini dell'altare *m*
- *altar steps*
**6**  la tovaglia dell'altare *m*
- *altar cloth*
**7**  la candela di altare *m*
- *altar candle*
**8**  la pisside
- *pyx (pix)*
**9**  la patena
- *paten (patin, patine)*
**10**  il calice
- *chalice (communion cup)*
**11**  la Bibbia (la Sacra Scrittura)
- *Bible (Holy Bible, Scriptures, Holy Scripture)*
**12**  il crocifisso
- *altar crucifix*
**13**  la pala di altare *m*
- *altarpiece*
**14**  la vetrata della chiesa
- *church window*
**15**  la pittura su vetro
- *stained glass*
**16**  la lampada murale
- *wall candelabrum*
**17**  la porta della sagrestia (della sacrestia, della sacristia)
- *vestry door (sacristy door)*
**18**  la scala per salire sul pulpito
- *pulpit steps*
**19**  il pulpito
- *pulpit*
**20**  il drappo
- *antependium*
**21**  il baldacchino
- *canopy, a soundboard (sounding board)*
**22**  il predicatore (il pastore, l'ecclesiastico, il ministro di culto) con i paramenti
- *preacher (pastor, vicar, clergyman, rector) in his robes (vestments, canonicals)*
**23**  la balaustra del pulpito
- *pulpit balustrade*
**24**  l'indicatore *m* con i numeri dei canti
- *hymn board showing hymn numbers*
**25**  il matroneo (la tribuna, la galleria)
- *gallery*

**26**  il sagrestano (il sacrestano)
- *verger (sexton, sacristan)*
**27**  la corsia centrale
- *aisle*
**28**  il banco, *insieme:* i banchi
- *pew; collectively: pews (seating)*
**29**  il fedele, *insieme:* la comunità dei fedeli
- *churchgoer (worshipper); collectively: congregation*
**30**  il libro dei canti
- *hymn book*
**31-62  la chiesa cattolica**
- *Roman Catholic church*
**31**  i gradini dell'altare *m*
- *altar steps*
**32**  il presbiterio
- *presbytery (choir, chancel, sacrarium, sanctuary)*
**33**  l'altare *m*
- *altar*
**34**  le candele dell'altare *m*
- *altar candles*
**35**  il crocifisso
- *altar cross*
**36**  la tovaglia di altare *m*
- *altar cloth*
**37**  l'ambone *m* (il leggio)
- *lectern*
**38**  il messale
- *missal (mass book)*
**39**  il prete (il sacerdote)
- *priest*
**40**  il chierico (il chierichetto)
- *server*
**41**  la sede (*ant.:* gli scranni)
- *sedilia*
**42**  il tabernacolo
- *tabernacle*
**43**  la stele
- *stele (stela)*
**44**  il cero pasquale
- *paschal candle (Easter candle)*
**45**  il candelabro del cero pasquale
- *paschal candlestick (Easter candlestick)*
**46**  la campanella della sagrestia
- *sanctus bell*
**47**  la croce processionale
- *processional cross*
**48**  gli ornamenti dell'altare *m* (piante *f pl* verdi, fiori *m pl*)
- *altar decoration (foliage, flower arrangement)*
**49**  la lampada perpetua
- *sanctuary lamp*
**50**  la pala di altare *m*, un'immagine *f* di Cristo
- *altarpiece, a picture of Christ*
**51**  la statua della Madonna
- *Madonna (statue of the Virgin Mary)*
**52**  il tavolo con i ceri votivi
- *pricket*

**53**  i ceri votivi
- *votive candles*
**54**  la stazione della Via Crucis
- *station of the Cross*
**55**  la cassetta per le offerte (per le elemosine)
- *offertory box*
**56**  l'espositore *m* per le pubblicazioni
- *literature stand*
**57**  le pubblicazioni religiose
- *literature (pamphlets, tracts)*
**58**  il sagrestano
- *verger (sexton, sacristan)*
**59**  la borsa per la questua
- *offertory bag*
**60**  l'elemosina (l'offerta)
- *offering*
**61**  il fedele (l'orante *m*)
- *Christian (man praying)*
**62**  il libro delle preghiere
- *prayer book*

1 **la chiesa**
– *church*
2 il campanile
– *steeple*
3 il gallo del campanile
– *weathercock*
4 la banderuola segnavento
– *weather vane (wind vane)*
5 la sfera sulla punta del campanile
– *spire ball*
6 la cuspide del campanile
– *church spire (spire)*
7 l'orologio del campanile
– *church clock (tower clock)*
8 la cella campanaria
– *belfry window*
9 la campana a funzionamento elettrico
– *electrically operated bell*
10 la croce sulla sommità del tetto
– *ridge cross*
11 il tetto della chiesa
– *church roof*
12 la cappella commemorativa
– *memorial chapel*
13 la sagrestia (la sacrestia), un annesso
– *vestry (sacristy), an annexe (annex)*
14 la lapide commemorativa (l'epitaffio)
– *memorial tablet (memorial plate, wall memorial, wall stone)*
15 l'ingresso laterale
– *side entrance*
16 il portale della chiesa
– *church door (main door, portal)*
17 il fedele
– *churchgoer*
18 il muro di cinta del cimitero (del camposanto)
– *graveyard wall (churchyard wall)*
19 l'ingresso del cimitero (del camposanto)
– *graveyard gate (churchyard gate, lichgate, lychgate)*
20 la casa del pastore (religione *f* evangelica); la canonica (religione *f* cattolica)
– *vicarage (parsonage, rectory)*
21-41 **il cimitero** (il camposanto)
– *graveyard (churchyard, God's acre,* Am. *burying ground)*
21 la camera mortuaria (l'obitorio)
– *mortuary*
22 il becchino
– *grave digger*
23 la tomba (la fossa)
– *grave (tomb)*
24 il tumulo
– *grave mound*
25 la croce sulla tomba
– *cross*
26 la lapide
– *gravestone (headstone, tombstone)*
27 la tomba di famiglia
– *family grave (family tomb)*
28 la cappella del cimitero
– *graveyard chapel*
29 la tomba di un bambino
– *child's grave*
30 la tomba con urne *f pl*
– *urn grave*
31 l'urna
– *urn*
32 il monumento tombale ai caduti
– *soldier's grave*
33-41 il funerale (la sepoltura, le esequie, l'inumazione *f* )
– *funeral (burial)*
33 i familiari e gli amici del defunto (i partecipanti al funerale)
– *mourners*
34 la fossa
– *grave*
35 la bara (il feretro)
– *coffin* (Am. *casket*)
36 la pala
– *spade*
37 il sacerdote
– *clergyman*
38 i familiari del defunto
– *the bereaved*
39 il velo della vedova, un velo da lutto
– *widow's veil, a mourning veil*
40 i necrofori (i becchini)
– *pallbearers*
41 il carrello per la bara
– *bier*
42-50 **la processione**
– *procession (religious procession)*
42 la croce processionale
– *processional crucifix*
43 il crucigero (*fam.:* il crocifero)
– *cross bearer (crucifer)*
44 lo stendardo, un gonfalone ecclesiastico
– *processional banner, a church banner*
45 il chierico
– *acolyte*
46 il portatore del baldacchino
– *canopy bearer*
47 il sacerdote (il prete)
– *priest*
48 l'ostensorio con il Santissimo
– *monstrance with the Blessed Sacrament (consecrated Host)*
49 il baldacchino
– *canopy (baldachin, baldaquin)*
50 le suore
– *nuns*
51 i partecipanti alla processione
– *participants in the procession*
52-58 **il convento** (il monastero, l'abazia, l'abbazia)
– *monastery*
52 il chiostro
– *cloister*
53 il giardino del convento
– *monastery garden*
54 il monaco (il frate), un benedettino
– *monk, a Benedictine monk*
55 il saio
– *habit (monk's habit)*
56 il cappuccio
– *cowl (hood)*
57 la tonsura
– *tonsure*
58 il breviario
– *breviary*
59 **la catacomba,** un complesso cimiteriale sotterraneo dei primi cristiani
– *catacomb, an early Christian underground burial place*
60 la nicchia (l'arcosolio)
– *niche (tomb recess, arcosolium)*
61 la lapide
– *stone slab*

**1** il battesimo cristiano
  – *Christian baptism (christening)*
**2** il fonte battesimale (il battistero)
  – *baptistery (baptistry)*
**3** il pastore protestante (evangelico)
  – *Protestant clergyman*
**4** i paramenti sacerdotali (la veste talare)
  – *robes (vestments, canonicals)*
**5** le bandelle
  – *bands*
**6** il colletto
  – *collar*
**7** il battezzando
  – *child to be baptized (christened)*
**8** l'abito da battesimo
  – *christening robe (christening dress)*
**9** il velo battesimale
  – *christening shawl*
**10** il fonte battesimale
  – *font*
**11** la vasca battesimale
  – *font basin*
**12** l'acqua lustrale
  – *baptismal water*
**13** il padrino/la madrina
  – *godparents*
**14** il matrimonio religioso
  – *church wedding (wedding ceremony, marriage ceremony)*
**15** u. **16** la coppia di sposi *m pl*
  – *bridal couple*
**15** la sposa
  – *bride*
**16** lo sposo
  – *bridegroom (groom)*
**17** l'anello (l'anello nuziale, l'anello matrimoniale, la fede, la vera)
  – *ring (wedding ring)*
**18** il bouquet della sposa
  – *bride's bouquet (bridal bouquet)*
**19** la coroncina nuziale (la coroncina di fiori *m pl* d'arancio)
  – *bridal wreath*
**20** il velo nuziale
  – *veil (bridal veil)*
**21** il fiore all'occhiello
  – *[myrtle] buttonhole*
**22** il sacerdote; *qui:* il celebrante
  – *clergyman*
**23** i testimoni
  – *witnesses [to the marriage]*
**24** la damigella
  – *bridesmaid*
**25** l'inginocchiatoio
  – *kneeler*
**26** la comunione (l'Eucarestia)
  – *Holy Communion*
**27** i comunicandi
  – *communicants*
**28** l'Ostia (l'Ostia consacrata)
  – *Host (wafer)*

**29** il calice
  – *communion cup*
**30** il rosario
  – *rosary*
**31** il grano del pater noster (il grano del padre nostro)
  – *paternoster*
**32** il grano dell'Ave Maria; ogni 10: una decina
  – *Ave Maria;* set of 10: *decade*
**33** il crocifisso
  – *crucifix*
**34-54** arredi *m pl* sacri (arredi *m pl* ecclesiastici)
  – *liturgical vessels (ecclesiastical vessels)*
**34** l'ostensorio
  – *monstrance*
**35** l'Ostia (l'Ostia consacrata, il Santissimo)
  – *Host (consecrated Host, Blessed Sacrament)*
**36** la lunetta
  – *lunula (lunule)*
**37** la raggiera
  – *rays*
**38** il turibolo (l'incensiere *m*), un recipiente liturgico per bruciare l'incenso
  – *censer (thurible), for offering incense (for incensing)*
**39** la catenella del turibolo
  – *thurible chain*
**40** il coperchio del turibolo
  – *thurible cover*
**41** il braciere del turibolo
  – *thurible bowl*
**42** la navicella per l'incenso
  – *incense boat*
**43** il cucchiaino per l'incenso
  – *incense spoon*
**44** le ampolline
  – *cruet set*
**45** l'ampollina per l'acqua
  – *water cruet*
**46** l'ampollina per il vino
  – *wine cruet*
**47** il secchiello per l'acqua santa
  – *holy water basin*
**48** il ciborio con le ostie
  – *ciborium containing the sacred wafers*
**49** il calice
  – *chalice*
**50** la coppetta offertoriale
  – *dish for communion wafers*
**51** la patena
  – *paten (patin, patine)*
**52** il campanello (il tintinnabolo)
  – *altar bells*
**53** la pisside
  – *pyx (pix)*
**54** l'aspersorio
  – *aspergillum*

**55-72** forme *f pl* di croci *f pl*
  – *forms of Christian crosses*
**55** la croce latina
  – *Latin cross (cross of the Passion)*
**56** la croce greca
  – *Greek cross*
**57** la croce russa
  – *Russian cross*
**58** la croce di San Pietro
  – *St. Peter's cross*
**59** la croce di Sant'Antonio (la croce a T)
  – *St. Anthony's cross (tau cross)*
**60** la croce di Sant'Andrea
  – *St. Andrew's cross (saltire cross)*
**61** la croce a forcella
  – *Y-cross*
**62** la croce di Lorena (lorenese)
  – *cross of Lorraine*
**63** la croce a ansa
  – *ansate cross*
**64** la croce doppia (la croce arcivescovile)
  – *patriarchal cross*
**65** la croce cardinalizia
  – *cardinal's cross*
**66** la croce pontificia
  – *papal cross*
**67** la croce di Costantino (un monogramma cristiano)
  – *Constantinian cross, a monogram of Christ (CHR)*
**68** la croce ripetuta
  – *crosslet*
**69** la croce a ancora
  – *cross moline*
**70** la croce a grucce *f pl*
  – *cross of Jerusalem*
**71** la croce tagliata (la croce pettorale)
  – *cross botonnée (cross treflée)*
**72** la croce di Gerusalemme
  – *fivefold cross (quintuple cross)*
**73** la croce celtica
  – *Celtic cross*

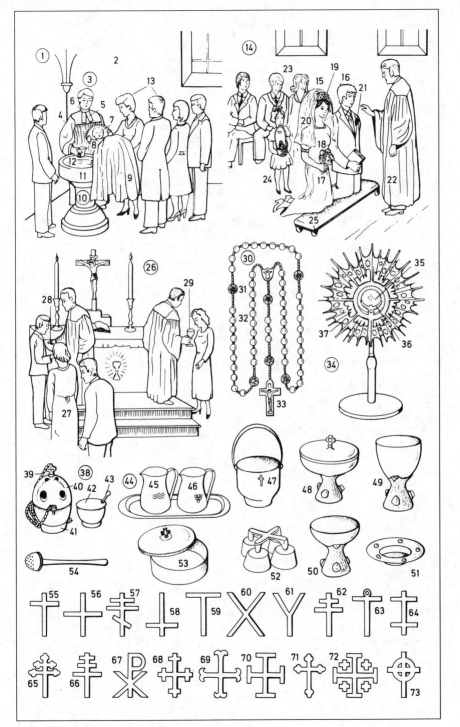

**1-18 arte** *f* **egizia**
- *Egyptian art*
1 la piramide, un monumento sepolcrale riservato ai faraoni
- *pyramid, a royal tomb*
2 la camera del re
- *king's chamber*
3 la camera della regina
- *queen's chamber*
4 il canale di areazione *f*
- *air passage*
5 la stanza del sarcofago
- *coffin chamber*
6 il complesso funerario
- *pyramid site*
7 il tempio funerario
- *funerary temple*
8 il tempio della valle dei re
- *valley temple*
9 il pilone
- *pylon, a monumental gateway*
10 gli obelischi
- *obelisks*
11 la sfinge
- *Egyptian sphinx*
12 il disco solare alato
- *winged sun disc (sun disk)*
13 la colonna a papiro chiuso
- *lotus column*
14 il capitello a germogli *m pl* di loto
- *knob-leaf capital (bud-shaped capital)*
15 la colonna papiriforme
- *papyrus column*
16 il capitello a forma di calice *m*
- *bell-shaped capital*
17 la colonna palmiforme
- *palm column*
18 la colonna decorata (la stele pilastro)
- *ornamented column*
**19 u. 20 arte** *f* **babilonese**
- *Babylonian art*
19 il fregio babilonese
- *Babylonian frieze*
20 il bassorilievo in piastrelle *f pl* smaltate
- *glazed relief tile*
**21-28 arte** *f* **persiana**
- *art of the Persians*
21 la tomba a torre *f*
- *tower tomb*
22 la piramide a gradini *m pl*
- *stepped pyramid*
23 la colonna sormontata da capitello a doppia testa di toro
- *double bull column*
24 la corolla
- *projecting leaves*
25 il capitello a palmette *f pl*
- *palm capital*

26 la voluta
- *volute (scroll)*
27 il fusto scanalato
- *shaft*
28 il capitello composito a doppia protome *f* animale; *qui:* tori *m pl* addossati
- *double bull capital*
**29-36 arte** *f* **assira**
- *art of the Assyrians*
29 la fortezza di Sargon, una cittadella
- *Sargon's Palace, palace buildings*
30 le mura della città
- *city wall*
31 la cinta interna delle mura
- *castle wall*
32 la ziggurat, una torre a gradini *m pl*
- *temple tower (ziggurat), a stepped (terraced) tower*
33 la scalinata esterna (la scala esterna)
- *outside staircase*
34 il portale principale
- *main portal*
35 il rivestimento della porta
- *portal relief*
36 la figura della porta
- *portal figure*
**37 arte** *f* **dell'Asia Minore**
- *art of Asia Minor*
38 la tomba rupestre
- *rock tomb*

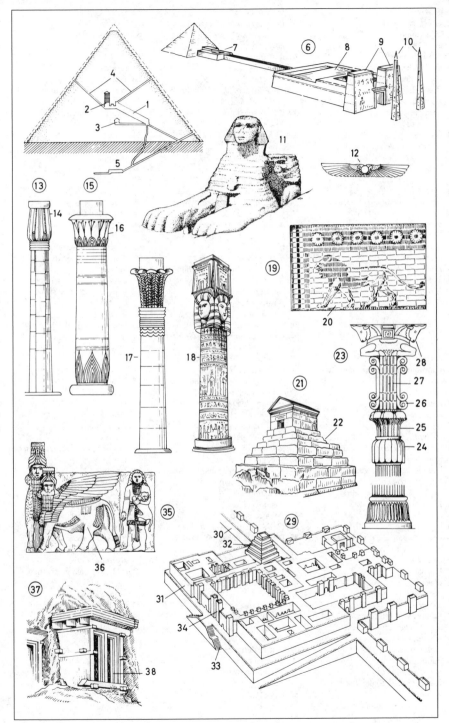

**1-48  arte *f* greca**
– *Greek art*
**1-7** l'acropoli *f*
– *the Acropolis*
**1** il Partenone
– *the Parthenon, a Doric temple*
**2** il peristilio (il porticato che cir-
conda il tempio)
– *peristyle*
**3** il timpano
– *pediment*
**4** la crepinide
– *crepidoma (stereobate)*
**5** la statua
– *statue*
**6** le mura del tempio
– *temple wall*
**7** i propilei (l'edificio d'ingresso del
tempio)
– *propylaea*
**8** la colonna dorica
– *Doric column*
**9** la colonna ionica
– *Ionic column*
**10** la colonna corinzia
– *Corinthian column*
**11-14** il cornicione
– *cornice*
**11** la sima con doccione *m*
– *cyma*
**12** il geison
– *corona*
**13** il mutulo (il gocciolatoio sotto il
cornicione)
– *mutule*
**14** il dentello
– *dentils*
**15** il triglifo
– *triglyph*
**16** la metopa, una scultura architet-
tonica
– *metope, a frieze decoration*
**17** la regula con gocce *f pl*
– *regula*
**18** l'architrave *m* (l'epistilio)
– *epistyle (architrave)*
**19** le gocce
– *cyma (cymatium, kymation)*
**20-25** il capitello
– *capital*
**20** l'abaco
– *abacus*
**21** l'echino
– *echinus*
**22** l'ipotrachelio (il collarino)
– *hypotrachelium (gorgerin)*
**23** la voluta
– *volute (scroll)*
**24** l'imbottitura
– *volute cushion*
**25** la ghirlanda di foglie d'acanto
– *acanthus*
**26** il fusto della colonna
– *column shaft*

**27** la scanalatura
– *flutes (grooves, channels)*
**28-31** la base della colonna
– *base*
**28** il toro
– *[upper] torus*
**29** il trochilo
– *trochilus (concave moulding, Am. molding)*
**30** il toro inferiore
– *[lower] torus*
**31** il plinto
– *plinth*
**32** lo stilobate
– *stylobate*
**33** la stele
– *stele (stela)*
**34** l'acroterio; *sul timpano:* figura scultorea
– *acroterion (acroterium, acroter)*
**35** l'erma (un busto applicato su un pilastro)
– *herm (herma, hermes)*
**36** la cariatide; *masch.:* il telamone (l'Atlante *m*)
– *caryatid; male: Atlas*
**37** il vaso greco
– *Greek vase*
**38-43** ornamenti *m pl* greci
– *Greek ornamentation (Greek decoration, Greek decorative designs)*
**38** le perle, un fregio ornamentale
– *bead-and-dart moulding (Am. molding), an ornamental band*
**39** il nastro con onde *f pl*
– *running dog (Vitruvian scroll)*
**40** il fregio a foglie *f pl*
– *leaf ornament*
**41** il fregio a palmette *f pl*
– *palmette*
**42** il fregio a ovoli *m pl*
– *egg and dart (egg and tongue, egg and anchor) cyma*
**43** il meandro
– *meander*
**44** il teatro greco
– *Greek theatre (Am. theater)*
**45** la scena (il palcoscenico)
– *scene*
**46** il proscenio (il loggiato)
– *proscenium*
**47** l'orchestra (lo spazio per la danza)
– *orchestra*
**48** il timele (l'ara sacrificale di Dioniso)
– *thymele (altar)*
**49-52  arte *f* etrusca**
– *Etruscan art*
**49** il tempio etrusco
– *Etruscan temple*
**50** il porticato
– *portico*
**51** la cella
– *cella*

**52** la trabeazione
– *entablature*
**53-60  arte *f* romana**
– *Roman art*
**53** l'acquedotto
– *aqueduct*
**54** il canale per l'acqua
– *conduit (water channel)*
**55** l'edificio a pianta centrale
– *centrally-planned building (centralized building)*
**56** il portico
– *portico*
**57** il timpano triangolare
– *reglet*
**58** la cupola
– *cupola*
**59** l'arco di trionfo
– *triumphal arch*
**60** l'attico superiore
– *attic*
**61-71  arte *f* paleocristiana**
– *Early Christian art*
**61** la basilica
– *basilica*
**62** la navata centrale (la navata principale)
– *nave*
**63** la navata laterale (la navata minore)
– *aisle*
**64** l'abside *f*
– *apse*
**65** il campanile
– *campanile*
**66** l'atrio
– *atrium*
**67** il colonnato
– *colonnade*
**68** la vasca per le abluzioni (il cantaro)
– *fountain*
**69** l'altare *m*
– *altar*
**70** il triforio
– *clerestory (clearstory)*
**71** l'arco trionfale
– *triumphal arch*
**72-75  arte *f* bizantina**
– *Byzantine art*
**72** *u.* **73** il sistema costruttivo a cupole *f pl*
– *dome system*
**72** la cupola centrale
– *main dome*
**73** la semicupola
– *semidome*
**74** il pennacchio sferico
– *pendentive*
**75** l'occhio, un'apertura per fare entrare la luce
– *eye, a lighting aperture*

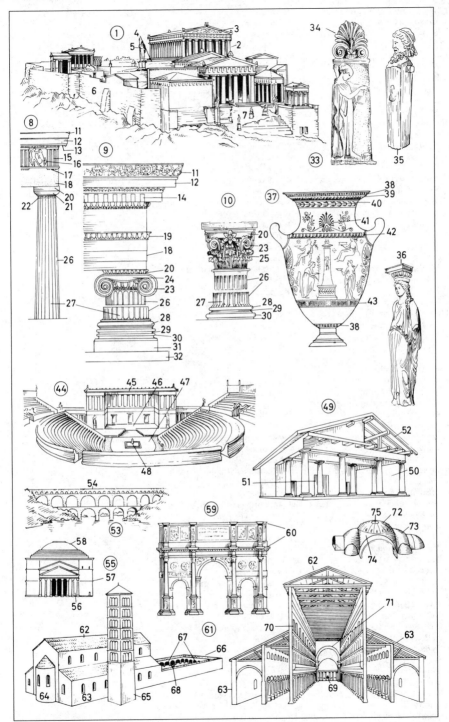

**1-21 arte** *f* **romanica** (il romanico)
– *Romanesque art*
**1-13** la chiesa romanica, un duomo
– *Romanesque church, a cathedral*
**1** la navata centrale
– *nave*
**2** la navata laterale
– *aisle*
**3** la cappella laterale
– *transept*
**4** il coro
– *choir (chancel)*
**5** l'abside *f*
– *apse*
**6** la torre sul quadrato
– *central tower* (Am. *center tower*)
**7** il tetto della torre
– *pyramidal tower roof*
**8** la loggia a arcatelle *f pl*
– *arcading*
**9** il fregio a archi *m pl* tondi
– *frieze of round arcading*
**10** l'arcata cieca
– *blind arcade (blind arcading)*
**11** la lesena, una fascia di muro verticale
– *lesene, a pilaster strip*
**12** la finestra circolare
– *circular window*
**13** il portale laterale (l'ingresso laterale)
– *side entrance*
**14-16** fregi *m pl* romanici
– *Romanesque ornamentation (Romanesque decoration, Romanesque decorative designs)*
**14** il fregio a scacchiera
– *chequered* (Am. *checkered) pattern (chequered design)*
**15** il fregio a squame *f pl*
– *imbrication (imbricated design)*
**16** il fregio con denti *m pl* a sega
– *chevron design*
**17** il sistema romanico delle volte
– *Romanesque system of vaulting*
**18** l'arco trasversale
– *transverse arch*
**19** l'arco perimetrale
– *barrel vault (tunnel vault)*
**20** il pilastro
– *pillar*
**21** il capitello a dado
– *cushion capital*
**22-41 arte** *f* **gotica** (il gotico)
– *Gothic art*
**22** la chiesa gotica (facciata occidentale), una cattedrale
– *Gothic church [westwork, west end, west façade], a cathedral*
**23** il rosone
– *rose window*
**24** il portale della chiesa, un portale a strombo
– *church door (main door, portal), a recessed portal*

**25** l'archivolto
– *archivolt*
**26** il timpano
– *tympanum*
**27** *u.* **28** i contrafforti
– *buttresses*
**27-35** il sistema costruttivo gotico
– *Gothic structural system*
**27** il pilastro rampante
– *buttress*
**28** l'arco rampante
– *flying buttress*
**29** il pinnacolo, una torretta ornamentale
– *pinnacle*
**30** il doccione
– *gargoyle*
**31** *u.* **32** la volta a crociera
– *cross vault (groin vault)*
**31** i costoloni della volta
– *ribs (cross ribs)*
**32** la chiave di volta
– *boss (pendant)*
**33** il triforio (il corridoio incassato)
– *triforium*
**34** il pilastro polistilo
– *clustered pier (compound pier)*
**35** la semicolonna
– *respond (engaged pillar)*
**36** il frontone ornamentale
– *pediment*
**37** il fiorone
– *finial*
**38** il fiore rampante (la foglia rampante)
– *crocket*
**39** *u.* **40** il traforo
– *tracery*
**39** *u.* **41** la finestra a traforo, una finestra sagomata
– *tracery window, a lancet window*
**39** il traforo quadrilobo (il quadrifoglio)
– *quatrefoil*
**40** il traforo pentalobo (il traforo a cinque foglie *f pl*)
– *cinquefoil*
**41** la colonnina
– *mullions*
**42-54 arte** *f* **del Rinascimento**
– *Renaissance art*
**42** la chiesa rinascimentale
– *Renaissance church*
**43** la crepidine, una parte emergente dell'edificio
– *projection, a projecting part of the building*
**44** il tamburo
– *drum*
**45** la lanterna
– *lantern*
**46** il pilastro (una parasta)
– *pilaster (engaged pillar)*
**47** il palazzo rinascimentale
– *Renaissance palace*

**48** il cornicione
– *cornice*
**49** la finestra con frontone *m* triangolare
– *pedimental window*
**50** la finestra con frontone *m* centinato
– *pedimental window [with round gable]*
**51** il bugnato
– *rustication (rustic work)*
**52** la cornice marcapiano
– *string course*
**53** il sarcofago (la tomba a sarcofago)
– *sarcophagus*
**54** il festone (la ghirlanda)
– *festoon (garland)*

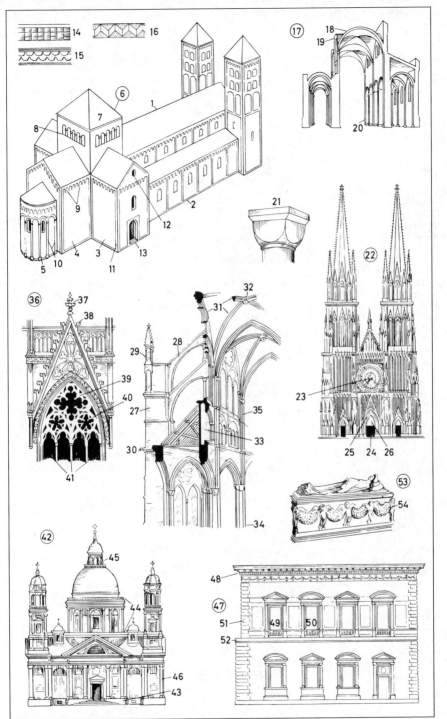

**1-8 arte** *f* **del barocco** (arte barocca)
– *Baroque art*
**1** la chiesa barocca
– *Baroque church*
**2** l'occhio di bue *m* (la lunetta)
– *bull's eye*
**3** la lanterna
– *bulbous cupola*
**4** la finestra circolare della cupola
– *dormer window (dormer)*
**5** il timpano semicircolare
– *curved gable*
**6** la colonna binata
– *twin columns*
**7** il cartoccio
– *cartouche*
**8** la decorazione a cartoccio
– *scrollwork*
**9-13 l'arte** *f* **rococò**
– *Rococo art*
**9** la parete rococò
– *Rococo wall*
**10** la modanatura, una cornice
ottenuta con membrature *f pl*
sporgenti
– *coving, a hollow moulding (Am.
molding)*
**11** la decorazione a cornice *f*
– *framing*
**12** la soprapporta
– *ornamental moulding (Am. molding)*
**13** la rocaille, un ornamento rococò
– *rocaille, a Rococo ornament*
**14** il tavolo stile *m* Luigi XVI
– *table in Louis Seize style (Louis
Seize table)*
**15** l'edificio stile *m* neoclassico, il
propileo
– *neoclassical building (building in
neoclassical style), a gateway*
**16** il tavolo stile *m* impero
– *Empire table (table in the Empire
style)*
**17** il divano stile *m* Biedermeier
– *Biedermeier sofa (sofa in the
Biedermeier style)*
**18** la poltroncina stile *m* art nouveau
– *Art Nouveau easy chair (easy
chair in the Art Nouveau style)*
**19-37 forme** *f pl* **di archi** *m pl*
– *types of arch*
**19** l'arco
– *arch*
**20** la spalla laterale
– *abutment*
**21** l'imposta
– *impost*
**22** il cuneo
– *springer, a voussoir (wedge stone)*
**23** la chiave di volta
– *keystone*

**24** il lato anteriore della spalla (la
testa)
– *face*
**25** l'intradosso (l'imbotte *f* )
– *intrados*
**26** l'estradosso
– *extrados*
**27** l'arco a tutto sesto
– *round arch*
**28** l'arco a monta depressa (l'arco
scemo)
– *segmental arch (basket handle)*
**29** l'arco parabolico
– *parabolic arch*
**30** l'arco a ferro di cavallo
– *horseshoe arch*
**31** l'arco acuto
– *lancet arch*
**32** l'arco trilobo
– *trefoil arch*
**33** l'arco con spalle *f pl* laterali
– *shouldered arch*
**34** l'arco convesso
– *convex arch*
**35** l'arco a dentelli *m pl*
– *tented arch*
**36** l'arco inflesso (*sim.* l'arco a dosso
di asino)
– *ogee arch (keel arch)*
**37** l'arco a quattro centri *m pl* (l'arco
Tudor)
– *Tudor arch*
**38-50 forme** *f pl* **delle volte**
– *types of vault*
**38** la volta a botte *f*
– *barrel vault (tunnel vault)*
**39** la chiave di volta
– *crown*
**40** il fianco della volta
– *side*
**41** la volta a padiglione *m*
– *cloister vault (cloistered vault)*
**42** la volta a crociera
– *groin vault (groined vault)*
**43** la volta a vela
– *rib vault (ribbed vault)*
**44** la volta stellare
– *stellar vault*
**45** la volta a nido di ape *f*
– *net vault*
**46** la volta a ventaglio
– *fan vault*
**47** la volta a padiglione *m*
– *trough vault*
**48** il padiglione
– *trough*
**49** la volta a chiglia
– *cavetto vault*
**50** la chiglia
– *cavetto*

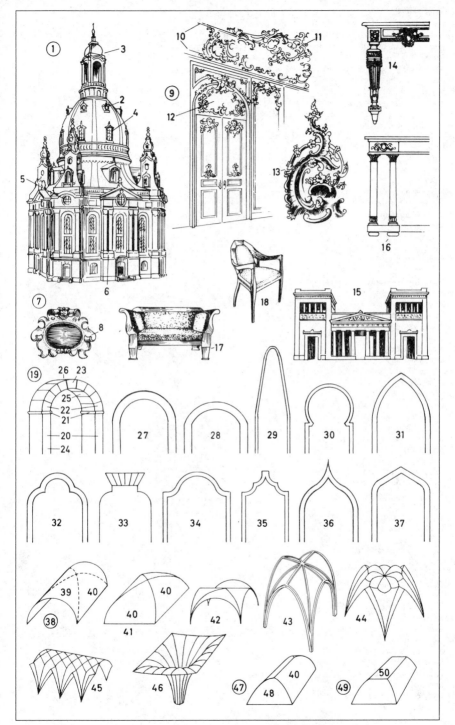

**1-6 arte *f* cinese**
- *Chinese art*
1 la pagoda (pagoda con tetto a più piani *m pl*), un tempio a forma di torre *f*
- *pagoda (multi-storey, multistory, pagoda), a temple tower*
2 il tetto a gradini *m pl*
- *storey (story) roof (roof of storey)*
3 il pailou, un portone di onore *m*
- *pailou (pailoo), a memorial archway*
4 l'ingresso
- *archway*
5 il vaso di porcellana
- *porcelain vase*
6 l'oggetto in lacca intagliata
- *incised lacquered work*

**7-11 arte *f* giapponese**
- *Japanese art*
7 il tempio
- *temple*
8 il campanile
- *bell tower*
9 la struttura portante (il sistema di trabeazione *f*)
- *supporting structure*
10 il Bodhisattva, un santo buddista
- *bodhisattva (boddhisattva), a Buddhist saint*
11 il torii, una porta
- *torii, a gateway*

**12-18 arte *f* islamica**
- *Islamic art*
12 la moschea
- *mosque*
13 il minareto, una torre di preghiera
- *minaret, a prayer tower*
14 il mihrab (la nicchia per la preghiera)
- *mihrab*
15 il mimbar (il pulpito)
- *minbar (mimbar, pulpit)*
16 il mausoleo, un monumento sepolcrale
- *mausoleum, a tomb*
17 il catino a stalattiti *f pl* (mugarnas)
- *stalactite vault (stalactitic vault)*
18 il capitello arabo
- *Arabian capital*

**19-28 arte *f* indiana**
- *Indian art*
19 Siva *m* danzante, un dio indiano
- *dancing Siva (Shiva), an Indian god*
20 la statua di Budda
- *statue of Buddha*
21 lo stupa (la pagoda indiana), una costruzione a cupola, una costruzione sacra buddista
- *stupa (Indian pagoda), a mound (dome), a Buddhist shrine*

22 il chatra (l'ombrello)
- *umbrella*
23 il recinto in pietra
- *stone wall (Am. stone fence)*
24 la porta d'ingresso
- *gate*
25 il complesso dei templi
- *temple buildings*
26 lo sikhara (la guglia del tempio)
- *shikara (sikar, sikhara, temple tower)*
27 l'interno del caityagrha, una grotta
- *chaitya hall*
28 il caityagrha, un piccolo stupa
- *chaitya, a small stupa*

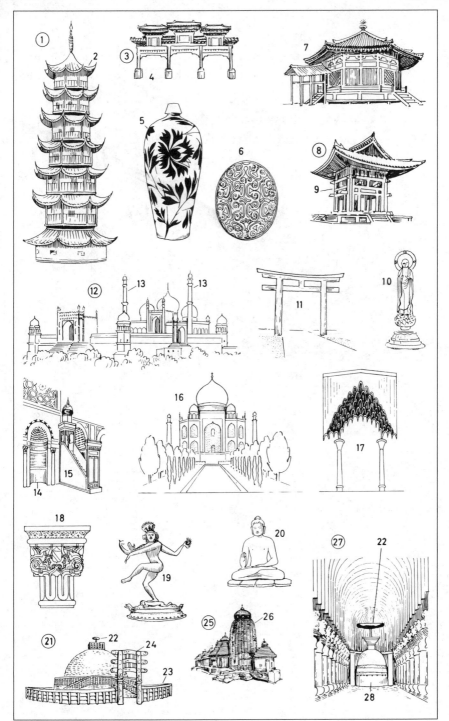

**1-43 l'atelier** *m* (lo studio)
– *studio*
**1** la finestra dell'atelier (il lucernario)
– *studio skylight*
**2** il pittore, un artista
– *painter, an artist*
**3** il cavalletto da studio
– *studio easel*
**4** lo schizzo a gessetto, con l'abbozzo del quadro
– *chalk sketch, with the composition (rough draft)*
**5** il gessetto
– *crayon (piece of chalk)*
**6-19** utensili *m pl* da pittore (attrezzi *m pl* per dipingere)
– *painting materials*
**6** il pennello piatto
– *flat brush*
**7** il pennello di setola
– *camel hair brush*
**8** il pennello rotondo
– *round brush*
**9** la pennellessa
– *priming brush*
**10** la scatola dei colori
– *box of paints (paintbox)*
**11** il tubetto con colore *m* a olio
– *tube of oil paint*
**12** la vernice
– *varnish*
**13** il solvente
– *thinner*

**14** il mestichino
– *palette knife*
**15** la spatola
– *spatula*
**16** il carboncino
– *charcoal pencil (charcoal, piece of charcoal)*
**17** il colore a tempera
– *tempera (gouache)*
**18** il colore a acquerello
– *watercolour (Am. watercolor)*
**19** il pastello
– *pastel crayon*
**20** il telaio
– *wedged stretcher (canvas stretcher)*
**21** la tela
– *canvas*
**22** il cartoncino con il fondo (la mestica)
– *piece of hardboard, with painting surface*
**23** la tavola di legno
– *wooden board*
**24** la tavola di legno compensato (la tavola di compensato)
– *fibreboard (Am. fiberboard)*
**25** il tavolo del pittore (il trespolo)
– *painting table*
**26** il cavalletto da campagna
– *folding easel*
**27** la natura morta, un tema (un soggetto)
– *still life group, a motif*
**28** la tavolozza
– *palette*

**29** lo scodellino della tavolozza
– *palette dipper*
**30** il piedestallo (il basamento)
– *platform*
**31** il manichino
– *lay figure (mannequin, manikin)*
**32** la modella per il nudo (la modella, il nudo)
– *nude model (model, nude)*
**33** il drappeggio
– *drapery*
**34** il cavalletto
– *drawing easel*
**35** il blocco da disegno (il blocco per gli schizzi)
– *sketch pad*
**36** lo studio a olio
– *study in oils*
**37** il mosaico
– *mosaic (tessellation)*
**38** la figura a mosaico
– *mosaic figure*
**39** i tasselli (le tessere) del mosaico
– *tesserae*
**40** l'affresco
– *fresco (mural)*
**41** il graffito
– *sgraffito*
**42** l'intonaco
– *plaster*
**43** lo schizzo (l'abbozzo, il cartone)
– *cartoon*

**1-38 l'atelier** *m* (lo studio)
– *studio*
1  lo scultore
– *sculptor*
2  il compasso per le proporzioni
– *proportional dividers*
3  il compasso per gli spessori
– *calliper (caliper)*
4  il modello di gesso, un calco in gesso
– *plaster model, a plaster cast*
5  il blocco di pietra (la pietra grezza)
– *block of stone (stone block)*
6  il modellatore (il modellatore in creta)
– *modeller (Am. modeler)*
7  la figura in creta, un torso
– *clay figure, a torso*
8  il rotolo di creta, una pasta per modellare
– *roll of clay, a modelling (Am. modeling) substance*
9  il treppiede per modellare
– *modelling (Am. modeling) stand*
10  la stecca da modellatore *m*
– *wooden modelling (Am. modeling) tool*
11  la miretta (una lama per modellare)
– *wire modelling (Am. modeling) tool*
12  la spatola di bosso
– *beating wood*
13  la gradina
– *claw chisel (toothed chisel, tooth chisel)*
14  lo scalpello per smussare
– *flat chisel*
15  la subbia
– *point (punch)*

16  il martello di ferro
– *iron-headed hammer*
17  la sgorbia
– *gouge (hollow chisel)*
18  il calcagnolo
– *spoon chisel*
19  lo scalpello piatto, uno scalpello da
legno
– *wood chisel, a bevelled-edge chisel*
20  il bedano (un attrezzo per scolpire il
legno)
– *V-shaped gouge*
21  il mazzuolo di legno
– *mallet*
22  l'armatura
– *framework*
23  la base dell'armatura
– *baseboard*
24  il sostegno dell'armatura
– *armature support (metal rod)*
25  i fili dell'armatura
– *armature*
26  la scultura in cera
– *wax model*
27  il blocco di legno
– *block of wood*
28  lo scultore in legno (l'intagliatore *m*)
– *wood carver (wood sculptor)*
29  il sacco con la scagliola (il gesso)
– *sack of gypsum powder (gypsum)*
30  la vasca per la creta
– *clay box*
31  la creta per modellare (la creta)
– *modelling (Am. modeling) clay*

32  la statua, una scultura
– *statue, a sculpture*
33  il bassorilievo
– *low relief (bas-relief)*
34  la lastra da modellare
– *modelling (Am. modeling) board*
35  l'armatura metallica, una rete metallica
– *wire frame, wire netting*
36  il medaglione (il tondo)
– *circular medallion (tondo)*
37  la maschera
– *mask*
38  la lastra (la lastrina)
– *plaque*

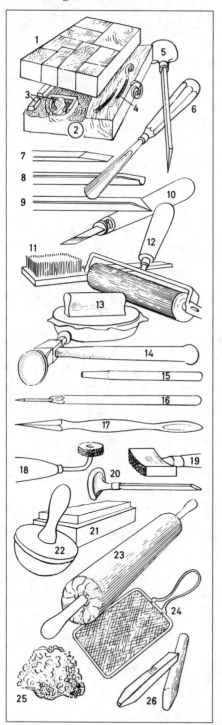

**1-13 l'incisione** *f* **su legno** (la silografia, la xilografia), un sistema di stampa rilievo-grafica
- *wood engraving (xylography), a relief printing method (a letterpress printing method)*
1 la lastra di legno tagliata trasversalmente per silografia, una base di legno
- *end-grain block for wood engravings, a wooden block*
2 la lastra di legno tagliata longitudinalmente, per silografica, un cliché di legno
- *wooden plank for woodcutting, a relief image carrier*
3 l'incisione *f* positiva
- *positive cut*
4 l'intaglio della lastra di legno tagliata longitudinalmente
- *plank cut*
5 il bulino
- *burin (graver)*
6 la sgorbia
- *U-shaped gouge*
7 lo scalpello a lama piatta
- *scorper (scauper, scalper)*
8 lo scalpello a lama concava
- *scoop*
9 lo scalpello a lama triangolare
- *V-shaped gouge*
10 il coltello per rifilare
- *contour knife*
11 la spazzola
- *brush*
12 il rullo per distribuire la gelatina
- *roller (brayer)*
13 l'inchiostratore *m* a mano
- *pad (wiper)*
**14-24 l'incisione** *f* **su rame** *m* (la calcografia), un procedimento di stampa in incavo; *tipi m pl:* l'acquaforte *f*, la mezzatinta (il mezzotinto), l'acquatinta
- *copperplate engraving (chalcography), an intaglio process;* kinds: *etching, mezzotint, aquatint, crayon engraving*
14 il martello per incavare
- *hammer*
15 il punzone
- *burin*
16 l'ago per incidere
- *etching needle (engraver)*
17 il brunitoio con scalpello
- *scraper and burnisher*
18 la ruota in osso (la ruota per brunire, la ruota per lucidare), un brunitoio
- *roulette*
19 la mezzaluna (il rocker)
- *rocking tool (rocker)*
20 il bulino rotondo, un arnese *m* per incidere
- *round-headed graver, a graver (burin)*
21 la pietra per affilare
- *oilstone*
22 il tampone
- *dabber (inking ball, ink ball)*
23 il rullo di cuoio
- *leather roller*
24 il setaccio
- *sieve*
**25** *u.* **26 la litografia** (la stampa su pietra), un procedimento di stampa piana
- *lithography (stone lithography), a planographic printing method*

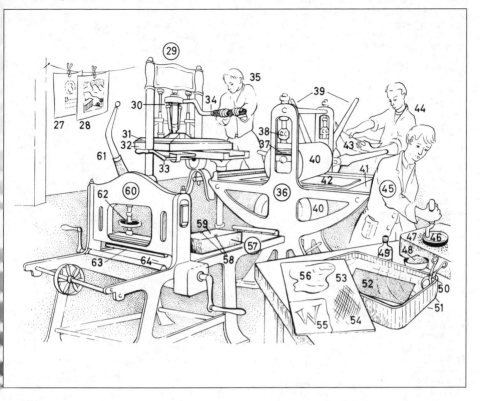

25 la spugna (la spugna naturale) per inu-
midire la pietra litografica
– *sponge for moistening the lithographic
stone*
26 il gesso litografico, un gesso
– *lithographic crayons (greasy chalk)*
27-64 **l'officina grafica,** una stamperia
– **graphic art studio,** *a printing office
(Am. printery)*
27 la stampa in bianco e nero
– *broadside (broadsheet, single sheet)*
28 la stampa a colori *m pl* (la cromoli-
tografia)
– *full-colour (Am. full-color) print
(colour print, chromolithograph)*
29 la platina, una pressa a mano
– *platen press, a hand press*
30 il giunto a ginocchiera
– *toggle*
31 il torchio, un piano di pressione *f*
– *platen*
32 la forma di stampa
– *type forme (Am. form)*
33 la manopola per lo scorrimento della
forma
– *feed mechanism*
34 la leva
– *bar (devil's tail)*
35 il tipografo (lo stampatore)
– *pressman*
36 il torchio calcografico
– *copperplate press*
37 gli spessori di cartone *m*
– *tympan*

38 il regolatore di pressione *f*
– *pressure regulator*
39 la ruota a stella
– *star wheel*
40 il cilindro
– *cylinder*
41 il piano di stampa
– *bed*
42 il feltro
– *felt cloth*
43 la bozza (la prova)
– *proof (pull)*
44 il calcografo (l'incisore *m* su rame *m*)
– *copperplate engraver*
45 il litografo mentre leviga la pietra
– *lithographer (litho artist), grinding the
stone*
46 la mola (il disco a smeriglio)
– *grinding disc (disk)*
47 la granulazione
– *grain (granular texture)*
48 lo smeriglio
– *pulverized glass*
49 la colla liquida
– *rubber solution*
50 la pinza
– *tongs*
51 il bagno di acido nitrico, per incidere la
lastra
– *etching bath for etching*
52 la lastra di zinco
– *zinc plate*
53 la lastra di rame *m* brunita
– *polished copperplate*

54 la retinatura
– *cross hatch*
55 la zona da incidere
– *etching ground*
56 il bitume di copertura
– *non-printing area*
57 la pietra litografica
– *lithographic stone*
58 le croci di registro
– *register marks*
59 la superficie di stampa
– *printing surface (printing image carrier)*
60 la stampa litografica
– *lithographic press*
61 la leva di pressione *f*
– *lever*
62 la vite di regolazione *f*
– *scraper adjustment*
63 l'inchiostratore *m* a mano
– *scraper*
64 il piano di appoggio per la pietra
– *bed*

**1-20 scritture** *f pl* **di vari popoli** *m pl*
- *scripts of various peoples*
**1** geroglifici *m pl* egiziani, una scrittura a disegni *m pl* stilizzati
- *ancient Egyptian hieroglyphics, a pictorial system of writing*
**2** arabo
- *Arabic*
**3** armeno
- *Armenian*
**4** georgiano
- *Georgian*
**5** cinese
- *Chinese*
**6** giappponese
- *Japanese*
**7** ebraico
- *Hebrew (Hebraic)*
**8** scrittura cuneiforme
- *cuneiform script*
**9** sanscrito
- *Devanagari, script employed in Sanskrit*
**10** siamese
- *Siamese*
**11** tamil *m*
- *Tamil*
**12** tibetano
- *Tibetan*
**13** scrittura del Sinai
- *Sinaitic script*
**14** fenicio
- *Phoenician*
**15** greco
- *Greek*
**16** romana capitale (scrittura capitale latina)
- *Roman capitals*
**17** onciale
- *uncial (uncials, uncial script)*
**18** minuscola carolina
- *Carolingian (Carlovingian, Caroline) minuscule*
**19** rune *f pl*
- *runes*
**20** cirillico
- *Cyrillic*
**21-26** antichi **strumenti** *m pl* **di scrittura**
- *ancient* **writing implements**
**21** stilo di acciaio indiano, uno strumento per incidere le foglie di palma
- *Indian steel stylus for writing on palm leaves*
**22** stilo di giunco appuntito dell'antico Egitto
- *ancient Egyptian reed pen*
**23** penna cava
- *writing cane*
**24** pennello per scrittura
- *brush*

**25** stilo romano
- *Roman metal pen (stylus)*
**26** penna di oca
- *quill (quill pen)*

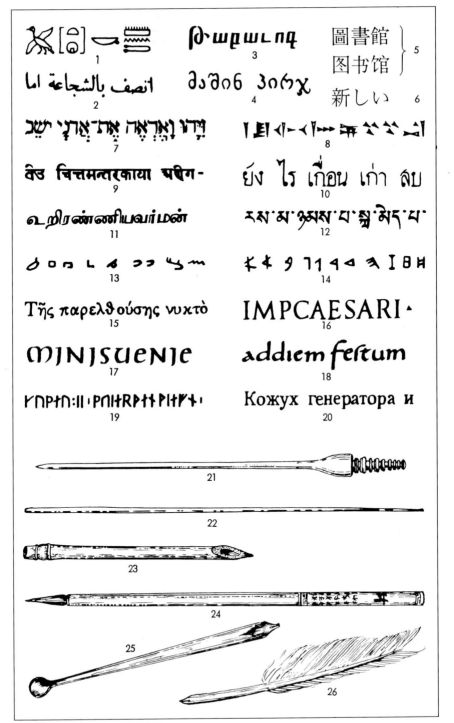

**1-15 caratteri** *m pl*
- *types (type faces)*
**1** il carattere gotico
- *Gothic type (German black-letter type)*
**2** il carattere schwabach
- *Schwabacher type (German black-letter type)*
**3** il gotico
- *Fraktur (German black-letter type)*
**4** il carattere romano rinascimentale
- *Humanist (Mediaeval)*
**5** il carattere preclassico (barocco)
- *Transitional*
**6** il carattere classico
- *Didone*
**7** il carattere grottesco
- *Sanserif (Sanserif type, Grotesque)*
**8** il carattere egiziano
- *Egyptian*
**9** il carattere dattilografico
- *typescript (typewriting)*
**10** il carattere inglese
- *English hand (English handwriting, English writing)*
**11** il carattere tedesco
- *German hand (German handwriting, German writing)*
**12** il carattere latino
- *Latin script*
**13** la stenografia
- *shorthand (shorthand writing, stenography)*
**14** la trascrizione fonetica
- *phonetics (phonetic transcription)*
**15** la scrittura Braille (il Braille)
- *Braille*
**16-29 segni** *m pl* **di interpunzione** *f*
- *punctuation marks (stops)*
**16** il punto
- *full stop (period, full point)*
**17** i due punti
- *colon*
**18** la virgola
- *comma*
**19** il punto e virgola
- *semicolon*
**20** il punto interrogativo (il punto di domanda)
- *question mark (interrogation point, interrogation mark)*
**21** il punto esclamativo
- *exclamation mark (Am. exclamation point)*
**22** l'apostrofo
- *apostrophe*
**23** le lineette
- *dash (em rule)*
**24** le parentesi tonde
- *parentheses (round brackets)*

**25** le parentesi quadre
- *square brackets*
**26** le virgolette
- *quotation mark (double quotation marks, paired quotation marks, inverted commas)*
**27** le virgolette francesi
- *guillemet (French quotation mark)*
**28** il trattino
- *hyphen*
**29** i puntini di sospensione *f*
- *marks of omission (ellipsis)*
**30-35 accenti** *m pl* **e segni** *m pl* **grafici per indicare una pronuncia alterata**
- *accents and diacritical marks (diacritics)*
**30** l'accento acuto
- *acute accent (acute)*
**31** l'accento grave
- *grave accent (grave)*
**32** l'accento circonflesso
- *circumflex accent (circumflex)*
**33** la cediglia (sotto la c)
- *cedilla [under c]*
**34** la dieresi (sopra la e)
- *diaeresis (Am. dieresis) [over e]*
**35** la tilde (sopra la n)
- *tilde [over n]*
**36** l'indicazione *f* di paragrafo
- *section mark*
**37-70 il giornale,** un quotidiano nazionale
- *newspaper,* a national daily newspaper
**37** la pagina del giornale
- *newspaper page*
**38** la prima pagina
- *front page*
**39** la testata del giornale
- *newspaper heading*
**40** l'occhiello
- *head rules and imprint*
**41** il sottotitolo
- *subheading*
**42** la data
- *date of publication*
**43** il numero postale del giornale
- *Post Office registration number*
**44** il titolo a caratteri *m pl* cubitali (a caratteri *m pl* di scatola)
- *headline*
**45** la colonna (l'articolo di spalla)
- *column*
**46** il titolo dell'articolo di spalla
- *column heading*
**47** il filetto tra due colonne
- *column rule*
**48** l'articolo di fondo
- *leading article (leader, editorial)*
**49** la continuazione dell'articolo
- *reference to related article*
**50** la notizia in breve
- *brief news item*

**51** la pagina politica
- *political section*
**52** il titolo della pagina
- *page heading*
**53** la caricatura (la vignetta)
- *cartoon*
**54** il servizio del corrispondente
- *report by newspaper's own correspondent*
**55** la sigla dell'agenzia di stampa
- *news agency's sign*
**56** l'inserzione *f* pubblicitaria (la pubblicità)
- *advertisement (coll. ad)*
**57** la pagina sportiva (la pagina dello sport)
- *sports section*
**58** l'illustrazione *f* (la fotografia)
- *press photo*
**59** la didascalia
- *caption*
**60** l'articolo sportivo
- *sports report*
**61** la notizia sportiva
- *sports news item*
**62** la pagina nazionale
- *home and overseas news section*
**63** la miscellanea
- *news in brief (miscellaneous news)*
**64** i programmi televisivi
- *television programmes (Am. programs)*
**65** le previsioni del tempo
- *weather report*
**66** la carta del tempo
- *weather chart (weather map)*
**67** il feuilleton (l'inserto)
- *arts section (feuilleton)*
**68** gli annunci mortuari
- *death notice*
**69** la parte riservata alle inserzioni
- *advertisements (classified advertising)*
**70** l'inserzione f, un'offerta di lavoro
- *job advertisement, a vacancy (a situation offered)*

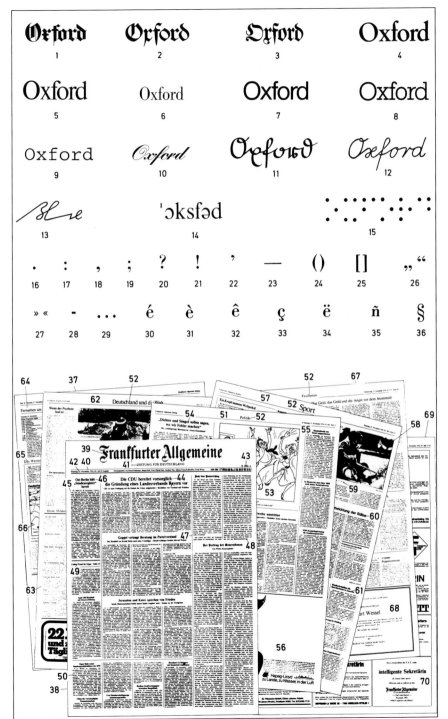

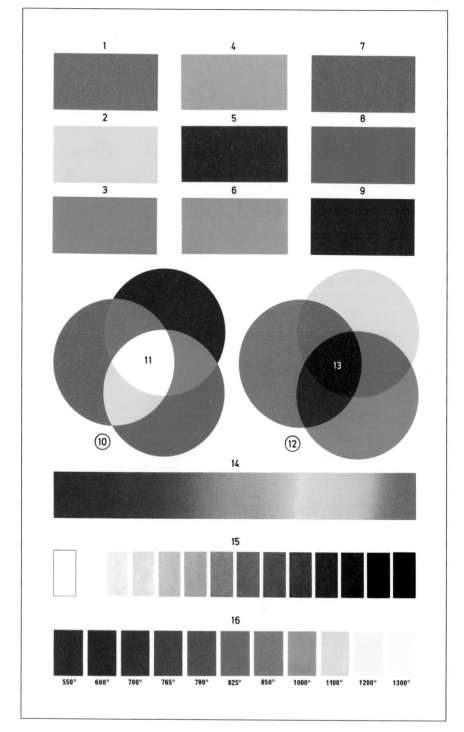

**1** rosso
– *red*
**2** giallo
– *yellow*
**3** blu
– *blue*
**4** rosa
– *pink*
**5** marrone
– *brown*
**6** celeste (azzurro)
– *azure (sky blue)*
**7** arancione
– *orange*
**8** verde
– *green*
**9** viola
– *violet*
**10** mescolanza additiva dei colori *m*
   *pl* (luce *f* colorata)
– *additive mixture of colours* (Am.
   *colors)*
**11** bianco
– *white*
**12** mescolanza sottrattiva dei colori
   *m pl* (i pigmenti)
– *subtractive mixture of colours*
   *(Am. colors)*
**13** nero
– *black*
**14** lo spettro solare (i colori
   dell'arcobaleno, i colori dell'iride *f* )
– *solar spectrum (colours,* Am. *col-*
   *ors, of the rainbow)*
**15** la scala del grigio
– *grey (Am. gray) scale*
**16** i colori dell'incandescenza
– *heat colours (Am. colors)*

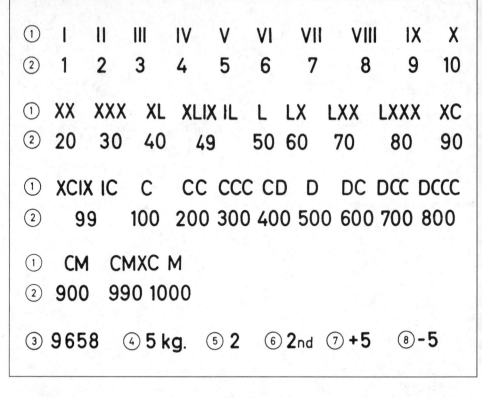

**1-26 aritmetica**
- *arithmetic*
**1-22 il numero**
- *numbers*
1 i numeri romani
- *Roman numerals*
2 i numeri arabi
- *Arabic numerals*
3 il numero naturale, un numero a quattro cifre *f pl* [*otto:* l'unità, *cinque:* la decina; *sei:* il centinaio; *nove:* il migliaio]
- *abstract number, a four-figure number [8: units; 5: tens; 6: hundreds; 9: thousands]*
4 il numero definito (grandezza fisica consistente del valore numerico e dell'unità e/o del segno di unità)
- *concrete number (physical quantity consisting of the numerical value and the unit or unit symbol)*
5 il numero cardinale
- *cardinal number (cardinal)*
6 il numero ordinale
- *ordinal number (ordinal)*
7 il numero relativo [con segno positivo]
- *positive number [with plus sign]*

8 il numero relativo [con segno negativo]
- *negative number [with minus sign]*
9 numeri *m pl* generali
- *algebraic symbols*
10 il numero misto [3: il numero interno, la parte intera; $^1/_3$ la frazione, la parte frazionaria]
- *mixed number [3: whole number (integer); $^1/_3$: fraction]*
11 numeri *m pl* pari
- *even numbers*
12 numeri *m pl* dispari
- *odd numbers*
13 numeri *m pl* primi
- *prime numbers*
14 il numero complesso [3: il numero razionale; $2\sqrt{-1}$: il numero irrazionale]
- *complex number [3: real part; $2\sqrt{-1}$: imaginary part]*
15 *u.* 16 frazioni *f pl* semplici
- *vulgar fractions*
15 la frazione propria [2: il numeratore, la linea di frazione *f*, 3: il denominatore]
- *proper fraction [2: numerator, horizontal line; 3: denominator]*

16 la frazione impropria, al tempo stesso: il reciproco (la frazione inversa) del 15
- *improper fraction, also the reciprocal of item 15*
17 la frazione a termini *m pl* frazionari
- *compound fraction (complex fraction)*
18 la frazione apparente [«semplificando» si ottiene un numero intero]
- *improper fraction [when cancelled down produces a whole number]*
19 frazioni *f pl* con denominatori *m pl* diversi [35 = il minimo comune denominatore]
- *fractions of different denominations [35: common denominator]*
20 la frazione decimale limitata con virgola e parte *f* decimale [3: il decimo; 5: il centesimo; 7: il millesimo]
- *proper decimal fraction with decimal point and decimal places [3: tenths; 5: hundredths; 7: thousandths]*

⑨ a, b, c ...     ⑩ $3\frac{1}{3}$    ⑪ 2, 4, 6, 8    ⑫ 1, 3, 5, 7

⑬ 3, 5, 7, 11    ⑭ $3 + 2\sqrt{-1}$    ⑮ $\frac{2}{3}$    ⑯ $\frac{3}{2}$

⑰ $\dfrac{\frac{5}{6}}{\frac{3}{4}}$    ⑱ $\frac{12}{4}$    ⑲ $\frac{4}{5} + \frac{2}{7} = \frac{38}{35}$    ⑳ $0\cdot357$

㉑ $0\cdot6666.... = 0\cdot\overline{6}$ ㉒    ㉓ $3 + 2 = 5$

㉔ $3 - 2 = 1$    ㉕ $3 \cdot 2 = 6$    ㉖ $6 \div 2 = 3$
                                $3 \times 2 = 6$

---

**21** la frazione decimale illimitata periodica
– *recurring decimal*
**22** il periodo
– *recurring decimal*
**23-26 il calcolo** (le quattro operazioni aritmetiche)
– *fundamental arithmetical operations*
**23** l'addizione *f* [3 e 2: gli addendi, + il segno di addizione *f*, = il segno di uguale, 5: la somma (il risultato)]
– *addition (adding) [3 and 2: the terms of the sum; +: plus sign; =: equals sign; 5: the sum]*
**24** la sottrazione [3: il minuendo, – il segno di sottrazione *f*, 2: il sottraendo, 1: il resto (la differenza)]
– *subtraction (subtracting); [3: the minuend; -: minus sign; 2: the subtrahend; 1: the remainder (difference)]*

**25** la moltiplicazione [3: il moltiplicando, x: il segno di moltiplicazione *f*, 2: il moltiplicatore, 2-3: fattori *m pl*, 6: il prodotto]
– *multiplication (multiplying); [3: the multiplicand; x : multiplication sign; 2: the multiplier; 2 and 3: factors; 6: the product]*
**26** la divisione [6: il dividendo, : = il segno di divisione *f*, 2: il divisore, 3: il quoziente]
– *division (dividing); [6: the dividend; ÷ : division sign; 2: the divisor; 3: the quotient]*

$$\text{①} \quad 3^2 = 9 \qquad \text{②} \quad \sqrt[3]{8} = 2 \qquad \text{③} \quad \sqrt{4} = 2$$

$$\text{④} \quad 3x + 2 = 12$$

$$\text{⑤} \quad 4a + 6ab - 2ac = 2a(2 + 3b - c) \qquad \text{⑥} \quad \log_{10} 3 = 0{\cdot}4771$$

$$\text{⑦} \quad \frac{P[\pounds 1000] \times R[5\%] \times T[2\,\text{years}]}{100} = I[\pounds 100]$$

**1-24 aritmetica**
- *arithmetic*
**1-10 operazioni** *f pl* **aritmetiche superiori**
- *advanced arithmetical operations*
**1** l'elevazione *f* a potenza [3 elevato alla seconda (tre al quadrato): la potenza, 3: la base, 2: l'esponente *m*, 9: il valore della potenza]
- *raising to a power [three squared ($3^2$): the power; 3: the base; 2: the exponent (index); 9: alue of the power]*
**2** l'estrazione *f* di radice *f* [radice *f* cubica di 8, 8: il radicando, 3: l'esponente *m* della radice, √: il segno di radice *f*, 2: il valore della radice]
- *e olution (extracting a root); [cube root of 8: cube root; 8: the radical; 3: the index (degree) of the root; √: radical sign; 2: alue of the root]*
**3** la radice quadrata
- *square root*
**4** *u.* **5** l'algebra (il calcolo letterale)
- *algebra*

**4** l'equazione *f* di primo grado [3, 2: i coefficienti, x: l'incognita]
- *simple equation [3, 2: the coefficients; x: the unknown quantity]*
**5** l'identità [a, b, c, i simboli algebrici]
- *identical equation; [a, b, c: algebraic symbols]*
**6** il calcolo logaritmico [*log.*: il simbolo di logaritmo, *lg.*: il simbolo del logaritmo a base *f* dieci, 3: il numero, 10: la base, 0: la caratteristica, 4771: la mantissa, 0,4771: il logaritmo]
- *logarithmic calculation (taking the logarithm, log); [log: logarithm sign; 3: number whose logarithm is required; 10: the base; 0: the characteristic; 4771: the mantissa; 0.4771: the logarithm]*

**7** il calcolo degli interessi (la formula dell'interesse *m* semplice) [K: il capitale (la somma investita), p: il tasso di interesse *m*, t: il tempo, z: gli interessi (le percentuali *f pl*, l'interesse *m*, il guadagno), %: il segno di percentuale *f*]
- *simple interest formula; [P: the principal; R: rate of inierest; T: time; I: interest (profit); %: percentage sign]*
**8-10** la regola del tre [≙ : comsponde a]
- *rule of three (rule-of-three sum, simple proportion)*
**8** l'impostazione *f* con l'incognita x
- *statement with the unknown quantity x*
**9** la proporzione
- *equation (conditional equation)*
**10** la soluzione
- *solution*
**11-14 matematica superiore**
- *higher mathematics*

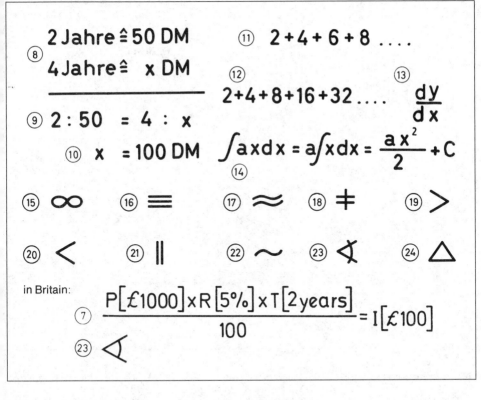

$$2\,\text{Jahre} \cong 50\,\text{DM}$$
$$4\,\text{Jahre} \cong \text{x}\,\text{DM}$$

⑧

⑨ $2 : 50 = 4 : x$

⑩ $x = 100\,\text{DM}$

⑪ $2 + 4 + 6 + 8 \ldots$

⑫ $2 + 4 + 8 + 16 + 32 \ldots$

⑬ $\dfrac{dy}{dx}$

⑭ $\int ax\,dx = a\!\int x\,dx = \dfrac{a x^2}{2} + C$

⑮ $\infty$    ⑯ $\equiv$    ⑰ $\approx$    ⑱ $\neq$    ⑲ $>$

⑳ $<$    ㉑ $\parallel$    ㉒ $\sim$    ㉓ $\sphericalangle$    ㉔ $\triangle$

in Britain:

⑦ $$\dfrac{P\,[£1000] \times R\,[5\%] \times T\,[2\,\text{years}]}{100} = I\,[£100]$$

㉓ $\sphericalangle$

---

**11** la serie aritmetica con gli elementi 2, 4, 6, 8
– *arithmetical series with the elements 2, 4, 6, 8*
**12** la serie geometrica
– *geometrical series*
**13** *u.* **14 il calcolo infinitesimale**
– *infinitesimal calculus*
**13** la derivata [dx, dy: i differenziali, d: il segno di differenziale *m*]
– *derivative [dx, dy: the differentials; d: differential sign]*
**14** l'integrale *m* [x: la variabile, c: la costante, ∫: il segno di integrale *m*, dx: il segno di differenziale *m*]
– *integral (integration); [x: the variable; C: constant of integration; ∫: the integral sign; dx: the differential]*
**15-24 simboli** *m pl* **matematici**
– *mathematical symbols*
**15** infinito
– *infinity*
**16** identico (il segno di identità)
– *identically equal to (the sign of identity)*
**17** approssimativamente uguale (il segno di uguaglianza con approssimazione *f* )
– *approximately equal to*

**18** diverso (il segno di disuguaglianza)
– *unequal to*
**19** maggiore di
– *greater than*
**20** minore di
– *less than*
**21-24 simboli** *m pl* geometrici
– *geometrical symbols*
**21** parallelo (il segno di parallelismo)
– *parallel (sign of parallelism)*
**22** simile (il segno di similitudine *f* )
– *similar to (sign of similarity)*
**23** il simbolo di angolo (in Italia ^)
– *angle symbol*
**24** il simbolo di triangolo
– *triangle symbol*

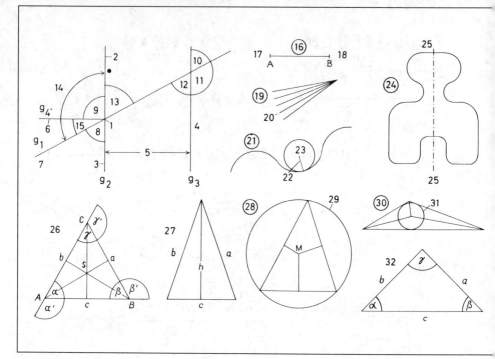

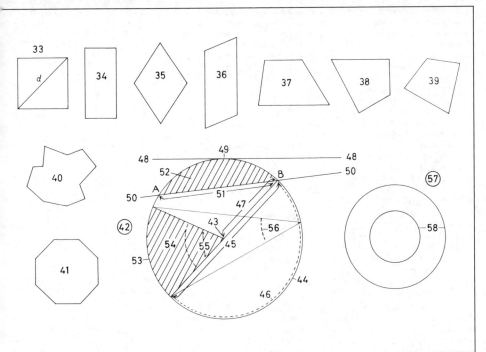

**29** la circonferenza circoscritta
– *circumcircle (circumscribed circle)*
**30** il triangolo ottusangolo con le bisettrici degli angoli
– *obtuse-angled triangle with bisectors of the angles*
**31** la circonferenza inscritta
– *inscribed circle*
**32** il triangolo rettangolo e le funzioni trigonometriche [a, b i cateti; c l'ipotenusa; γ l'angolo retto; a: c = sen α (seno); b: c = cos α (coseno); a: b = tg α (tangente *f* ); b: a = ctg. α (cotangente *f* )]
– *right-angled triangle and the trigonometrical functions of angles; [a, b: the catheti; c: the hypotenuse; γ: the right angle; a/c = sin α (sine); b/c = cos α (cosine); a/b = tan α (tangent); b/a = cot α (cotangent)]*
**33-39 quadrilateri** *m pl*
– *quadrilaterals*
**33-36 parallelogrammi** *m pl*
– *parallelograms*
**33** il quadrato (d una diagonale)
– *square [d: a diagonal]*
**34** il rettangolo
– *rectangle*

**35** il rombo
– *rhombus (rhomb, lozenge)*
**36** il romboide
– *rhomboid*
**37** il trapezio
– *trapezium*
**38** il deltoide
– *deltoid (kite)*
**39** il quadrilatero irregolare
– *irregular quadrilateral*
**40** il poligono
– *polygon*
**41** il poligono regolare
– *regular polygon*
**42 il cerchio**
– *circle*
**43** il centro
– *centre* (Am. *center*)
**44** la circonferenza
– *circumference (periphery)*
**45** il diametro
– *diameter*
**46** il semicerchio (la semicirconferenza)
– *semicircle*
**47** il raggio
– *radius (r)*
**48** la tangente
– *tangent*
**49** il punto di contatto (P)
– *point of contact (P)*

**50** la secante
– *secant*
**51** la corda AB
– *the chord AB*
**52** il segmento (il segmento circolare)
– *segment*
**53** l'arco di cerchio
– *arc*
**54** il settore (il settore circolare)
– *sector*
**55** l'angolo al centro
– *angle subtended by the arc at the centre* (Am. *center*) (*centre*, Am. *center, angle*)
**56** l'angolo alla circonferenza
– *circumferential angle*
**57** la corona circolare
– *ring (annulus)*
**58** i cerchi concentrici
– *concentric circles*

1 il sistema delle coordinate cartesiane (ortogonali *f pl* )
- *system of right-angled coordi-*
*nates*
2 *u.* 3 gli assi cartesiani
- *axes of coordinates (coordinate*
*axes)*
2 l'asse *m* delle ascisse (asse x)
- *axis of abscissae (x-axis)*
3 l'asse *m* delle ordinate (asse y)
- *axis of ordinates (y-axis)*
4 l'origine *f* degli assi cartesiani
- *origin of ordinates*
5 il quadrante [I–IV dal primo al
quarto quadrante]
- *quadrant [I-IV: 1st to 4th quad-*
*rant]*
6 il semiasse positivo
- *positive direction*
7 il semiasse negativo
- *negative direction*
8 i punti [P$_1$ e P$_2$] nel sistema delle
coordinate cartesiane; x$_1$ e y$_1$ [o x$_1$
e y$_1$] le loro coordinate
- *points [P$_1$ and P$_2$] in the system of*
*coordinates; x$_1$ and y$_1$ [and x$_2$ and*
*y$_2$ respectively] their coordinates*
9 il valore delle ascisse [x$_1$ o x$_2$] (le
ascisse)
- *values of the abscissae [x$_1$ and x$_2$]*
*(the abscissae)*
10 il valore delle ordinate [y$_1$ o y$_2$] (le
ordinate)
- *values of the ordinates [y$_1$ and y$_2$]*
*(the ordinates)*
11-29 le sezioni coniche
- *conic sections*
11 le curve nel sistema delle coordinate cartesiane
- *curves in the system of coordinates*
12 curve *f pl* algebriche piane (le
rette) [a l'intersezione *f* della
retta, b l'intersezione *f* della retta
con l'asse *m* delle ordinate, c
l'origine *f* della curva, l'intersezione *f* delle rette con l'asse *m*
delle ascisse]
- *plane curves [a: the gradient*
*(slope) of the curve; b: the ordi-*
*nates' intersection of the curve; c:*
*the root of the curve]*
13 curve *f pl*
- *inflected curves*
14 **la parabola,** una curva di secondo
grado
- ***parabola,*** *a curve of the second*
*degree*
15 i bracci della parabola
- *branches of the parabola*
16 il vertice della parabola
- *vertex of the parabola*
17 l'asse *m* della parabola
- *axis of the parabola*

18 una curva di terzo grado
- *a curve of the third degree*
19 il massimo della curva
- *maximum of the curve*
20 il minimo della curva
- *minimum of the curve*
21 il punto di flesso
- *point of inflexion (of inflection)*
22 **l'ellisse** *f*
- *ellipse*
23 l'asse *m* traverso (l'asse *m* maggiore)
- *transverse axis (major axis)*
24 l'asse *m* coniugato (l'asse *m*
minore)
- *conjugate axis (minor axis)*
25 i fuochi dell'ellisse *f* [F$_1$ e F$_2$]
- *foci of the ellipse [F$_1$ and F$_2$]*
26 **l'iperbole** *f*
- *hyperbola*
27 i fuochi [F$_1$ e F$_2$]
- *foci [F$_1$ and F$_2$]*
28 i vertici [S$_1$ e S$_2$]
- *vertices [S$_1$ and S$_2$]*
29 gli asintoti [a e b]
- *asymptotes [a and b]*
30-46 **solidi** *m pl* **geometrici**
- *solids*
30 il cubo
- *cube*
31 il quadrato, una faccia del cubo
- *square, a plane (plane surface)*
32 lo spigolo
- *edge*
33 il vertice
- *corner*
34 il prisma rettangolare
- *quadratic prism*
35 la base (la superficie di base *f* )
- *base*
36 il parallelepipedo
- *parallelepiped*
37 il prisma a base *f* triangolare
- *triangular prism*
38 il cilindro, un cilindro retto
- *cylinder, a right cylinder*
39 la base del cilindro, una circonferenza
- *base, a circular plane*
40 la superficie laterale
- *curved surface*
41 la sfera
- *sphere*
42 l'elissoide *m* di rotazione *f*
- *ellipsoid of revolution*
43 il cono
- *cone*
44 l'altezza del cono
- *height of the cone (cone height)*
45 il tronco di cono
- *truncated cone (frustum of a cone)*
46 la piramide a base *f* quadrangolare
- *quadrilateral pyramid*

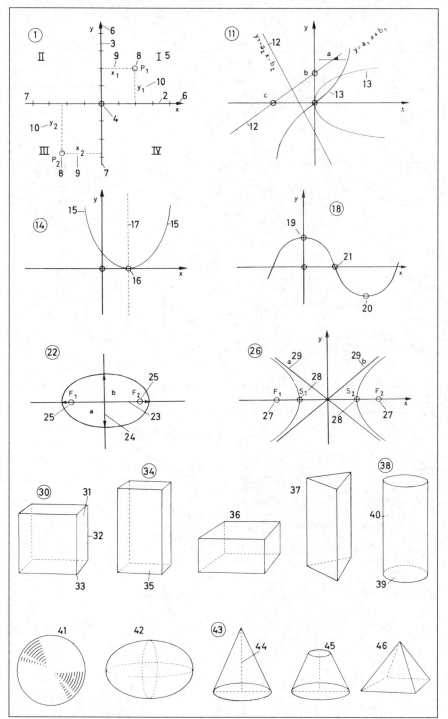

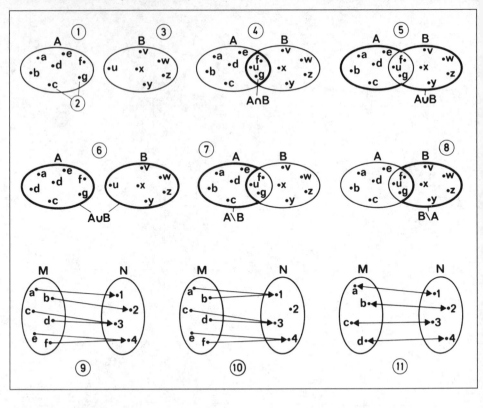

1 l'insieme *m* A, l'insieme *m* {a, b, c, d, e, f, g}
– *the set A, the set {a, b, c, d, e, f, g}*
2 gli elementi dell'insieme *m* A
– *elements (members) of the set A*
3 l'insieme *m* B, l'insieme *m* {u, v, w, x, y, z}
– *the set B, the set {u, v, w, x, y, z}*
4 l'intersezione *f* tra due insiemi *m* pl A ∩ B = {f, g, u}
– *intersection of the sets A and B, A ∩ B = {f, g, u}*
5 *u.* 6 l'unione *f* tra due insiemi *m* pl A ∪ B = {a, b, c, d, e, f, g, u, v, w, x, y, z}
– *union of the sets A and B, A ∪ B = {a, b, c, d, e, f, g, u, v, w, x, y, z}*
7 la differenza tra insiemi *m* pl A/B = {a, b, c, d, e}
– *complement of the set B, B' = {a, b, c, d, e}*
8 la differenza tra insiemi *m* pl B/A = {v, w, x, y, z}
– *complement of the set A, A' = {v, w, x, y, z}*
**9-11** relazioni *f* pl
– *mappings*

9 la relazione dell'insieme *m* M sull'insieme *m* N
– *mapping of the set M on to the set N*
10 la relazione dell'insieme *m* M nell'insieme *m* N
– *mapping of the set M into the set N*
11 la relazione biunivoca (equipotente) dell'insieme *m* M sull'insieme *m* N
– *one-to-one mapping of the set M on to the set N*

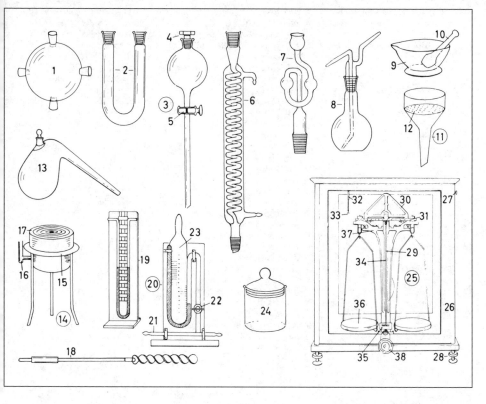

**1-38 gli apparecchi di laboratorio**
- *laboratory apparatus (laboratory equipment)*
1 il pallone di Scheidt
- *Scheidt globe*
2 il tubo a U
- *U-tube*
3 l'imbuto separatore
- *separating funnel*
4 il tappo smerigliato a testa ottagonale
- *octagonal ground-glass stopper*
5 il rubinetto
- *tap (Am. faucet)*
6 il condensatore a serpentina
- *coiled condenser*
7 il tubo di sicurezza
- *air lock*
8 la spruzzetta
- *wash-bottle*
9 il mortaio
- *mortar*
10 il pestello
- *pestle*
11 il filtro di Büchner
- *filter funnel (Büchner funnel)*
12 il setto bucherellato
- *filter (filter plate)*

13 la storta
- *retort*
14 il bagno di acqua (il bagnomaria)
- *water bath*
15 il treppiede
- *tripod*
16 l'indicatore *m* del livello dell'acqua
- *water gauge (Am. gage)*
17 gli anelli di sostegno
- *insertion rings*
18 l'agitatore *m*
- *stirrer*
19 il manometro
- *manometer for measuring positive and negative pressures*
20 il vacuometro, un manometro per pressioni *f pl* inferiori a quella atmosferica
- *mirror manometer for measuring small pressures*
21 il tubo di aspirazione *f*
- *inlet*
22 il rubinetto
- *tap (Am. faucet)*
23 la scala mobile
- *sliding scale*
24 il pesafiltri
- *weighing bottle*

25 la bilancia analitica
- *analytical balance*
26 l'armadietto
- *case*
27 il pannello anteriore sollevabile
- *sliding front panel*
28 il supporto a tre piedi *m pl*
- *three-point support*
29 la colonna
- *column (balance column)*
30 il giogo
- *balance beam (beam)*
31 la guida del cavaliere
- *rider bar*
32 il sostegno del cavaliere
- *rider holder*
33 il cavaliere
- *rider*
34 l'indice *m*
- *pointer*
35 la scala
- *scale*
36 il piatto della bilancia
- *scale pan*
37 l'arresto
- *stop*
38 la manopola di arresto
- *stop knob*

**1-63 gli apparecchi di laboratorio**
- *laboratory apparatus (laboratory equipment)*
1 il becco di Bunsen
- *Bunsen burner*
2 il tubo d'ingresso del gas
- *gas inlet (gas inlet pipe)*
3 il regolatore dell'aria
- *air regulator*
4 il becco di Teclu
- *Teclu burner*
5 il raccordo di collegamento
- *pipe union*
6 il regolatore del gas
- *gas regulator*
7 il tubo
- *stem*
8 il regolatore dell'aria
- *air regulator*
9 la lampada da soffiatore *m*
- *bench torch*
10 il rivestimento esterno
- *casing*
11 il tubo di entrata dell'ossigeno
- *oxygen inlet*
12 il tubo di entrata dell'idrogeno
- *hydrogen inlet*
13 l'ugello dell'ossigeno
- *oxygen jet*
14 il treppiede
- *tripod*
15 l'anello
- *ring (retort ring)*
16 l'imbuto
- *funnel*
17 il triangolo di argilla refrattaria
- *pipe clay triangle*
18 la reticella metallica
- *wire gauze*
19 la reticella in amianto
- *wire gauze with asbestos centre (Am. center)*
20 il becher (un recipiente resistente al fuoco)
- *beaker*
21 la buretta per misurare il volume dei liquidi
- *burette (for measuring the volume of liquids)*
22 il sostegno della buretta
- *burette stand*
23 il morsetto per la buretta
- *burette clamp*
24 la pipetta graduata
- *graduated pipette*
25 la pipetta
- *pipette*
26 il cilindro graduato
- *measuring cylinder (measuring glass)*
27 il cilindro graduato in cui mescolare i liquidi
- *measuring flask*

28 il matraccio, il pallone per misurare i liquidi
- *volumetric flask*
29 la capsula di porcellana per l'evaporazione *f*
- *evaporating dish (evaporating basin), made of porcelain*
30 il morsetto per tubo di gomma
- *tube clamp (tube clip, pinchcock)*
31 il crogiolo in argilla refrattaria con coperchio
- *clay crucible with lid*
32 la pinza da crogiolo
- *crucible tongs*
33 il morsetto
- *clamp*
34 la provetta
- *test tube*
35 il sostegno per provette *f pl*
- *test tube rack*
36 il pallone con fondo piano
- *flat-bottomed flask*
37 il collo smerigliato
- *ground glass neck*
38 il pallone con collo lungo
- *long-necked round-bottomed flask*
39 la beuta di Erlenmeyer
- *Erlenmeyer flask (conical flask)*
40 la beuta da vuoto per filtraggio
- *filter flask*
41 il filtro a pieghe *f pl*
- *fluted filter*
42 il rubinetto a una via
- *one-way tap*
43 il tubo contenente cloruro di calcio
- *calcium chloride tube*
44 il tappo a rubinetto
- *stopper with tap*
45 il cilindro
- *cylinder*
46 l'apparecchio per la distillazione *f*
- *distillation apparatus (distilling apparatus)*
47 il pallone da distillazione *f*
- *distillation flask (distilling flask)*
48 il condensatore
- *condenser*
49 il rubinetto di ritorno, un rubinetto a due vie *f pl*
- *return tap, a two-way tap*
50 il pallone di Claisen
- *distillation flask (distilling flask, Claisen flask)*
51 l'essicatore *m*
- *desiccator*
52 il coperchio del tubo
- *lid with fitted tube*
53 il rubinetto
- *tap*
54 il setto di porcellana per l'essicatore *m*
- *desiccator insert made of porcelain*

55 il pallone a tre colli *m pl*
- *three-necked flask*
56 il tubo a ipsilon
- *connecting piece (Y-tube)*
57 la bottiglia a tre colli *m pl*
- *three-necked bottle*
58 la bottiglia di lavaggio dei gas
- *gas-washing bottle*
59 l'apparecchio di sviluppo dei gas (l'apparecchio di Kipp)
- *gas generator (Kipp's apparatus, Am. Kipp generator)*
60 il pallone del troppo pieno
- *overflow container*
61 il recipiente per la sostanza
- *container for the solid*
62 il recipiente per l'acido
- *acid container*
63 l'uscita del gas
- *gas outlet*

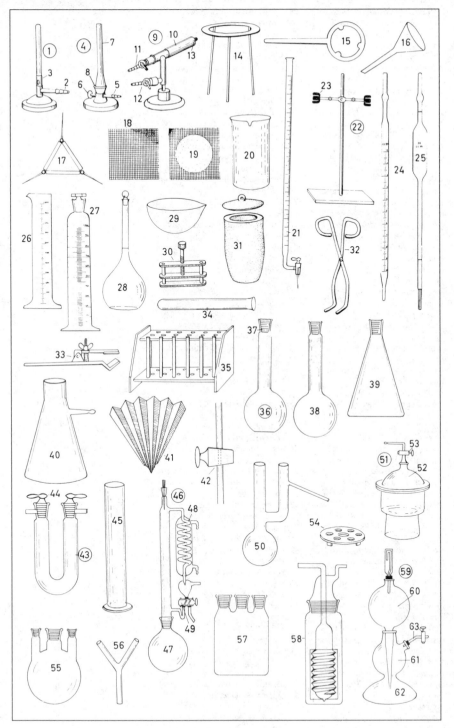

**1-26 forme** *f pl* **cristallografiche e combinazioni** *f pl* **dei cristalli** (struttura e formazione *f* dei cristalli)
– *basic crystal forms and crystal combinations [structure of crystals]*
**1-17 il sistema regolare** (cubico, monometrico)
– *regular (cubic, tesseral, isometric) crystal system*
**1** il tetraedro (il poliedro a quattro facce *f pl*) [tetraedrite *f*]
– *tetrahedron, (four-faced polyhedron) [tetrahedrite, fahlerz, fahl ore]*
**2** l'esaedro (il cubo, poliedro a sei facce *f pl*), un oloedro [salgemma]
– *hexahedron (cube, six-faced polyhedron), a holohedron [rock salt]*
**3** il centro di simmetria (il punto centrale del cristallo)
– *centre* (Am. *center*) *of symmetry (crystal centre)*
**4** un asse di simmetria
– *axis of symmetry (rotation axis)*
**5** un piano di simmetria
– *plane of symmetry*
**6** l'ottaedro (il poliedro a otto facce *f pl*) [oro]
– *octahedron (eight-faced polyhedron) [gold]*
**7** il rombododecaedro (granatoedro) [il granato]
– *rhombic dodecahedron [garnet]*
**8** il pentagonododecaedro [pirite *f*]
– *pentagonal dodecahedron [pyrite, iron pyrites]*
**9** un pentagono
– *pentagon (five-sided polygon)*
**10** il piramideottaedro [diamante *m*]
– *triakis-octahedron [diamond]*
**11** l'icosaedro (il poliedro a venti facce *f pl*), un poliedro regolare
– *icosahedron (twenty-faced polyhedron), a regular polyhedron*
**12** l'icositetraedro (il poliedro a ventiquattro facce *f pl*) [leucite *f*]
– *icositetrahedron (twenty-four-faced polyhedron) [leucite]*
**13** l'esacisottaedro (il poliedro a quarantotto facce *f pl*) [diamante *m*]
– *hexakis-octahedron (hexoctahedron, forty-eight-faced polyhedron) [diamond]*
**14** l'ottaedro con cubo [galena]
– *octahedron with cube [galena]*
**15** un esagono
– *hexagon (six-sided polygon)*
**16** il cubo con ottaedro [fluorite *f*]
– *cube with octahedron [fluorite, fluorspar]*
**17** un ottagono
– *octagon (eight-sided polygon)*

**18** *u.* **19 il sistema tetragonale**
– *tetragonal crystal system*
**18** la bipiramide tetragonale
– *tetragonal dipyramid (tetragonal bipyramid)*
**19** il protoprisma con protopiramide *f* [zircone *m*]
– *protoprism with protopyramid [zircon]*
**20-22 il sistema esagonale**
– *hexagonal crystal system*
**20** il protoprisma con proto e deuteropiramide *f* e base *f* [apatite *f*]
– *protoprism with protopyramid, deutero-pyramid and basal pinacoid [apatite]*
**21** il prisma esagonale
– *hexagonal prism*
**22** il prisma esagonale con romboedro [calcite *f*]
– *hexagonal (ditrigonal) biprism with rhombohedron [calcite]*
**23** la bipiramide rombica [zolfo]
– *orthorhombic pyramid (rhombic crystal system) [sulphur,* Am. *sulfur]*
**24** *u.* **25 sistema monoclino**
– *monoclinic crystal system*
**24** il prisma monoclino con clinopinacoide *m* e emipiramide *f* [gesso]
– *monoclinic prism with clinoprinacoid and hemipyramid (hemihedron) [gypsum]*
**25** l'ortopinacoide *m* (il cristallo geminato) [gesso]
– *orthopinacoid (swallowtail twin crystal) [gypsum]*
**26** pinacoidi triclini *m pl* (il sistema triclino) [solfato di rame *m*]
– *triclinic pinacoids (triclinic crystal system) [copper sulphate,* Am. *copper sulfate]*
**27-33 apparecchi** *m pl* **per la misurazione dei cristalli** (cristallometria)
– *apparatus for measuring crystals (for crystallometry)*
**27** il goniometro a contatto
– *contact goniometer*
**28** il goniometro a riflessione *f*
– *reflecting goniometer*
**29** il cristallo
– *crystal*
**30** il collimatore
– *collimator*
**31** il canocchiale di osservazione *f*
– *observation telescope*
**32** il cerchio graduato
– *divided circle (graduated circle)*
**33** la lente per la lettura dell'angolo di rotazione *f*
– *lens for reading the angle of rotation*

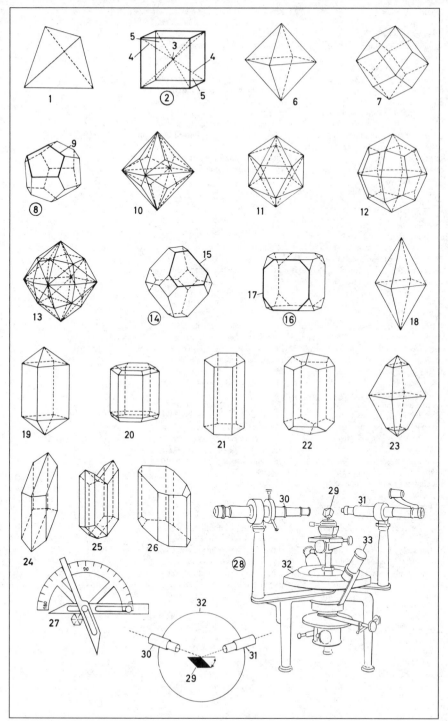

1 il palo totemico
– *totem pole*
2 il totem, una raffigurazione intagliata e dipinta, figurativa o simbolica
– *totem, a carved and painted pictorial or symbolic representation*
3 l'indiano della prateria
– *plains Indian*
4 il mustang, un cavallo della steppa
– *mustang, a prairie horse*
5 il lasso (il lazo), una lunga corda di cuoio con cappio (con nodo scorsoio)
– *lasso, a long throwing-rope with running noose*
6 il calumet (la pipa) della pace
– *pipe of peace*
7 la tenda indiana
– *wigwam (tepee, teepee)*
8 il palo della tenda
– *tent pole*
9 l'apertura per l'uscita del fumo
– *smoke flap*
10 la squaw, una donna indiana
– *squaw, an Indian woman*
11 il capo indiano
– *Indian chief*
12 l'ornamento del capo, una cuffia di piume *f pl*
– *headdress, an ornamental feather headdress*
13 la pittura di guerra
– *war paint*
14 la collana di zanne *f pl* d'orso
– *necklace of bear claws*
15 lo scalpo (il cuoio capelluto del cranio del nemico), un trofeo
– *scalp (cut from enemy's head), a trophy*
16 il tomahawk, un'ascia di guerra
– *tomahawk, a battle axe (Am. ax)*
17 i leggings, i gambali di pelle *f*
– *leggings*
18 il mocassino, una calzatura indiana (di pelle *f* e rafia)
– *moccasin, a shoe of leather and bast*
19 la canoa degli indiani della foresta
– *canoe of the forest Indians*
20 il tempio maya, una piramide a gradini *m pl*
– *Maya temple, a stepped pyramid*
21 la mummia
– *mummy*
22 il quipu (il registro a nodi *m pl*, scrittura con corde *f pl* degli Incas)
– *quipa (knotted threads, knotted code of the Incas)*

23 l'indio (indiano dell'America centrale e meridionale); *qui.* indiano dell'altopiano
– *Indio (Indian of Central and South America);* here: *highland Indian*
24 il poncho, un panno con apertura centrale per il passaggio della testa, usato come mantello senza maniche *f pl*
– *poncho, a blanket with a head opening used as an armless cloak-like wrap*
25 l'indiano della foresta tropicale
– *Indian of the tropical forest*
26 la cerbottana
– *blowpipe*
27 la faretra
– *quiver*
28 la freccia
– *dart*
29 la punta della freccia
– *dart point*
30 il tsanta (la testa rimpicciolita), un trofeo
– *shrunken head, a trophy*
31 le bolas, un'arma da getto e da cattura
– *bola (bolas), a throwing and entangling device*
32 la sfera di metallo o di pietra ricoperta di cuoio
– *leather-covered stone or metal ball*
33 la capanna sulle palafitte
– *pile dwelling*
34 il danzatore duk-duk, un membro di una società segreta maschile
– *duk-duk dancer, a member of a duk-duk (men's secret society)*
35 la piroga a bilanciere *m*
– *outrigger canoe (canoe with outrigger)*
36 il bilanciere
– *outrigger*
37 l'aborigeno australiano
– *Australian aborigine*
38 il perizoma di capelli *m pl* umani
– *loincloth of human hair*
39 il boomerang, un'arma da getto
– *boomerang, a wooden missile*
40 il propulsore (il woomer) con giavellotti *m pl*
– *throwing stick (spear thrower) with spears*

1 l'eschimese *m* (l'esquimese *m*)
 – *Eskimo*
2 il cane da slitta, un cane artico
 – *sledge dog (sled dog), a husky*
3 la slitta trainata dai cani *m pl*
 – *dog sledge (dog sled)*
4 l'igloo *m*, una capanna di neve *f* a
 cupola
 – *igloo, a dome-shaped snow hut*
5 il blocco di neve *f*
 – *block of snow*
6 il tunnel d'ingresso
 – *entrance tunnel*
7 la lampada a grasso
 – *blubber-oil lamp*
8 la tavoletta da lancio (uno strumento per lanciare gli arpioni)
 – *wooden missile*
9 l'arpione *m* da caccia
 – *lance*
10 l'arpione *m* a punta singola
 – *harpoon*
11 il galleggiante di pelle *f*
 – *skin float*
12 il kayak, un'imbarcazione monoposto leggera
 – *kayak, a light one-man canoe*
13 il telaio di legno o di osso ricoperto di pelle *f* di foca
 – *skin-covered wooden or bone*
 *frame*
14 la pagaia
 – *paddle*
15 i finimenti per la renna
 – *reindeer harness*
16 la renna
 – *reindeer*
17 l'ostiaco
 – *Ostyak (Ostiak)*
18 la slitta
 – *passenger sledge*
19 la yurta, una tenda da abitazione *f*
 delle tribù nomadi dell'Asia occidentale e centrale
 – *yurt (yurta), a dwelling tent of the*
 *western and central Asiatic*
 *nomads*
20 la copertura di feltro
 – *felt covering*
21 l'uscita per il fumo
 – *smoke outlet*
22 il kirghiso
 – *Kirghiz*
23 il berretto in pelle *f* di montone *m*
 – *sheepskin cap*
24 lo sciamano
 – *shaman*
25 le frange di ornamento
 – *decorative fringe*
26 il timpano
 – *frame drum*
27 il tibetano
 – *Tibetan*

28 il fucile con fiocina
 – *flintlock with bayonets*
29 la teca ruotante
 – *prayer wheel*
30 gli stivali di feltro
 – *felt boot*
31 il sampan (il sampang) (la casa
 battello)
 – *houseboat (sampan)*
32 la giunca
 – *junk*
33 la vela di stuoia
 – *mat sail*
34 il risciò
 – *rickshaw (ricksha)*
35 il coolie (il conducente del risciò)
 – *rickshaw coolie (cooly)*
36 la lanterna cinese
 – *Chinese lantern*
37 il samurai
 – *samurai*
38 la corazza imbottita
 – *padded armour (Am. armor)*
39 la geisha
 – *geisha*
40 il chimono
 – *kimono*
41 l'obi *m*
 – *obi*
42 il ventaglio
 – *fan*
43 il coolie
 – *coolie (cooly)*
44 il kris, un pugnale malese
 – *kris (creese, crease), a Malayan*
 *dagger*
45 l'incantatore *m* di serpenti *m pl*
 – *snake charmer*
46 il turbante
 – *turban*
47 il flauto
 – *flute*
48 il serpente danzante
 – *dancing snake*

1 la carovana dei cammelli
– *camel caravan*
2 l'animale *m* da sella (la cavalcatura)
– *riding animal*
3 l'animale *m* (la bestia) da soma
– *pack animal*
4 l'oasi *f*
– *oasis*
5 il palmeto
– *grove of palm trees*
6 il beduino
– *bedouin (beduin)*
7 il burnus
– *burnous*
8 il guerriero Masai
– *Masai warrior*
9 l'acconciatura
– *headdress (hairdress)*
10 lo scudo
– *shield*
11 il cuoio dipinto
– *painted ox hide*
12 la lancia con lama lunga
– *long-bladed spear*
13 il negro
– *negro*
14 il tamburo per accompagnare la danza
– *dance drum*
15 il coltello da lancio
– *throwing knife*
16 la maschera lignea
– *wooden mask*
17 la figura di antenato
– *figure of an ancestor*
18 il Tam-Tam, il tamburo per trasmettere messaggi *m pl* a distanza
– *slit gong*
19 la mazza da tamburo
– *drumstick*
20 la piroga, un'imbarcazione ricavata da un tronco di albero
– *dugout; a boat hollowed out of a tree trunk*
21 la capanna
– *negro hut*
22 la negra
– *negress*
23 il disco labiale
– *lip plug (labret)*
24 la macina
– *grinding stone*
25 la donna Herero
– *Herero woman*
26 il copricapo di cuoio
– *leather cap*
27 la zucca a fiaschetta
– *calabash (gourd)*
28 la capanna a forma di alveare *m*
– *beehive-shaped hut*
29 il boscimano
– *bushman*
30 l'orecchino a perno
– *earplug*
31 il perizoma
– *loincloth*
32 l'arco
– *bow*
33 la clava con testa rotonda e nodosa
– *knobkerry (knobkerrie), a club with round, knobbed end*
34 la donna boscimana che accende il fuoco per sfregamento
– *bushman woman making a fire by twirling a stick*
35 il paravento
– *windbreak*
36 lo zulù con gli ornamenti per la danza
– *Zulu in dance costume*
37 il bastone per la danza
– *dancing stick*
38 l'anello al polpaccio
– *bangle*
39 il corno da caccia in avorio
– *ivory war horn*
40 la collana di amuleti *m pl* e ossa *f pl*
– *string of amulets and bones*
41 il pigmeo
– *pigmy*
42 la pipa magica per esorcizzare gli spiriti
– *magic pipe for exorcising evil spirits*
43 il feticcio
– *fetish*

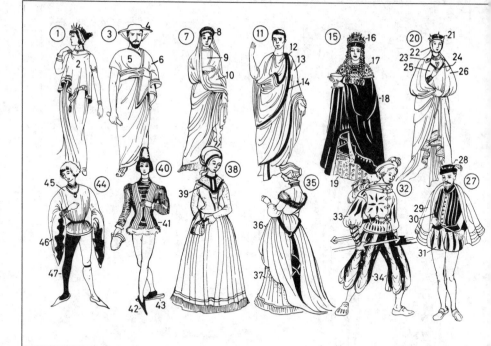

**1** donna greca, una greca
– *Greek woman*
**2** il peplo
– *peplos*
**3** uomo greco, un greco
– *Greek man*
**4** il petaso (cappello della Tessaglia)
– *petasus (Thessalonian hat)*
**5** il chitone, una tunica di lino indossata sotto l'abito
– *chiton, a linen gown worn as a basic garment*
**6** l'imazio, un mantello di lana
– *himation, woollen (Am. woolen)*
**7** donna romana, una romana
– *Roman woman*
**8** il posticcio (il toupet) frontale
– *toupee wig (partial wig)*
**9** la stola
– *stola*
**10** la palla, un mantello colorato
– *palla, a coloured (Am. colored) wrap*
**11** uomo romano, un romano
– *Roman man*
**12** la tunica
– *tunica (tunic)*
**13** la toga
– *toga*
**14** il bordo purpureo
– *purple border (purple band)*
**15** imperatrice bizantina
– *Byzantine empress*

**16** il diadema di perle *f pl*
– *pearl diadem*
**17** i pendenti preziosi
– *jewels*
**18** il manto di porpora
– *purple cloak*
**19** l'abito
– *long tunic*
**20** principessa tedesca [XIII secolo]
– *German princess [13th cent.]*
**21** il diadema
– *crown (diadem)*
**22** il sottogola (il soggolo)
– *chinband*
**23** la fibbia (il fermaglio)
– *tassel*
**24** l'allacciatura del manto
– *cloak cord*
**25** il vestito con la cintura
– *girt-up gown (girt-up surcoat, girt-up tunic)*
**26** il manto
– *cloak*
**27** tedesco in costume spagnolo [1575 circa]
– *German dressed in the Spanish style [ca. 1575]*
**28** il berretto
– *wide-brimmed cap*
**29** il mantello corto (la cappa)
– *short cloak (Spanish cloak, short cape)*
**30** il corsetto (il farsetto) imbottito
– *padded doublet (stuffed doublet, peasecod)*

**31** la braghetta imbottita
– *stuffed trunk-hose*
**32** il lanzichenecco [1530 circa]
– *lansquenet (German mercenary soldier) [ca. 1530]*
**33** il corsetto intagliato
– *slashed doublet (paned doublet)*
**34** i calzoni a sbuffo
– *Pluderhose (loose breeches, paned trunk-hose, slops)*
**35** donna di Basilea [1525 circa]
– *woman of Basle [ca. 1525]*
**36** la sopravveste
– *overgown (gown)*
**37** il sottabito
– *undergown (petticoat)*
**38** donna di Norimberga [1500 circa]
– *woman of Nuremberg [ca. 1500]*
**39** il fisciù (fazzoletto triangolare, incrociato sul petto)
– *shoulder cape*
**40** Borgognone (*stor.*: burgundo) [XV secolo]
– *Burgundian [15th cent.]*
**41** la giacca corta
– *short doublet*
**42** le scarpe a becco di anatra
– *piked shoes (peaked shoes, copped shoes, crackowes, poulaines)*
**43** la sottoscarpa di legno (la zeppa)
– *pattens (clogs)*
**44** giovane gentiluomo [1400 circa]
– *young nobleman [ca. 1400]*

45 la houppelande corta
– *short, padded doublet (short, quilted doublet, jerkin)*
46 le maniche a orli *m pl* festonati
– *dagged sleeves (petal-scalloped sleeves)*
47 la calzamaglia
– *hose*
48 nobildonna di Augsburg [1575 circa]
– *Augsburg patrician lady [ca. 1575]*
49 lo sbuffo delle maniche
– *puffed sleeve*
50 la sopravveste
– *overgown (gown, open gown, sleeveless gown)*
51 dama francese [1600 circa]
– *French lady [ca. 1600]*
52 la gorgiera (collare *m* increspato)
– *millstone ruff (cartwheel ruff, ruff)*
53 il vitino di vespa
– *corseted waist (wasp waist)*
54 gentiluomo [1650 circa]
– *gentleman [ca. 1650]*
55 il cappello svedese (il cappello piumato, il cappello da moschettiere *m*)
– *wide-brimmed felt hat (cavalier hat)*
56 il colletto di lino
– *falling collar (wide-falling collar) of linen*
57 la fodera bianca della manica
– *white lining*

58 gli stivali a imbuto con risvolto (gli stivali alla cavallerizza)
– *jack boots (bucket-top boots)*
59 gentildonna [1650 circa]
– *lady [ca. 1650]*
60 le maniche a sbuffo
– *full puffed sleeves (puffed sleeves)*
61 gentiluomo [1700 circa]
– *gentleman [ca. 1700]*
62 il tricorno
– *three-cornered hat*
63 lo spadino di gala
– *dress sword*
64 dama [1700 circa]
– *lady [ca. 1700]*
65 la cuffia di pizzo
– *lace fontange (high headdress of lace)*
66 la mantellina con guarnizioni *f pl* di pizzo
– *lace-trimmed loose-hanging gown (loose-fitting housecoat, robe de chambre, negligée, contouche)*
67 il bordo ricamato
– *band of embroidery*
68 dama [1880 circa]
– *lady [ca. 1880]*
69 la tournure (il cuscinetto, il cul de Paris)
– *bustle*
70 dama [1858 circa]
– *lady [ca. 1858]*
71 la cuffia (il cappello a sporta)
– *poke bonnet*

72 la crinolina
– *crinoline*
73 gentiluomo dell'epoca Biedermeier
– *gentleman of the Biedermeier period*
74 il colletto inamidato (il solino)
– *high collar (choker collar)*
75 il panciotto ricamato
– *embroidered waistcoat (vest)*
76 la giacca a falde *f pl*
– *frock coat*
77 la parrucca a codino
– *pigtail wig*
78 il nastro della parrucca
– *ribbon (bow)*
79 dame *f pl* in abito di corte *f* [1780 circa]
– *ladies in court dress [ca. 1780]*
80 lo strascico
– *train*
81 l'acconciatura rococò
– *upswept Rococo coiffure*
82 gli ornamenti dei capelli
– *hair decoration*
83 la sottogonna «a falbalà»
– *panniered overskirt*

**1**  il recinto
–  *outdoor enclosure*
**2**  la roccia naturale
–  *rocks*
**3**  il fossato di protezione *f*, un fossato
pieno di acqua
–  *moat*
**4**  il muro di protezione *f*
–  *enclosing wall*
**5**  gli animali dello zoo; *qui*: un gruppo
di leoni *m pl*
–  *animals on show; here: a pride of
lions*
**6**  il visitatore dello zoo
–  *visitor to the zoo*
**7**  il cartello indicatore
–  *notice*
**8**  la voliera (l'uccelliera)
–  *aviary*
**9**  il recinto degli elefanti
–  *elephant enclosure*
**10**  la gabbia (*per es.*: la gabbia degli animali feroci, delle giraffe, degli elefanti, delle scimmie)
–  *animal house (e.g. carnivore house,
giraffe house, elephant house, monkey house)*
**11**  la gabbia all'aperto
–  *outside cage (summer quarters)*
**12**  il recinto dei rettili *m pl*
–  *reptile enclosure*
**13**  il coccodrillo del Nilo
–  *Nile crocodile*

**14**  il terrario e l'acquario
–  *terrarium and aquarium*
**15**  la gabbia di vetro
–  *glass case*
**16**  la presa di aria
–  *fresh-air inlet*
**17**  l'uscita di aria
–  *ventilator*
**18**  il riscaldamento a pannelli *m pl*
–  *underfloor heating*
**19**  l'acquario
–  *aquarium*
**20**  la tavola sinottica
–  *information plate*
**21**  un paesaggio adeguato al clima, *qui*:
paessaggio tropicale
–  *flora in artificially maintained climate*

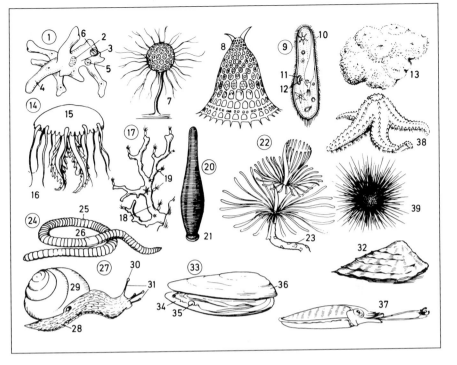

**1-12 organismi** *m pl* **unicellulari** (protozoi *m pl*)
- *unicellular (one-celled, single-celled) animals (protozoans)*
**1** l'ameba, una rhizopoda
- *amoeba, a rhizopod*
**2** il nucleo cellulare a disco
- *cell nucleus*
**3** il protoplasma
- *protoplasm*
**4** lo pseudopodio
- *pseudopod*
**5** il vacuolo escretore (il vacuolo pulsante, l'organello)
- *excretory vacuole (contractile vacuole, an organelle)*
**6** il vacuolo alimentare
- *food vacuole*
**7** l'actinophrys sol, un eliozoo
- *Actinophrys, a heliozoan*
**8** il radiolario; *qui:* lo scheletro siliceo
- *radiolarian; here: siliceous skeleton*
**9** il paramecio, un infusorio ciliato
- *slipper animalcule, a Paramecium (ciliate infusorian)*
**10** il ciglio
- *cilium*
**11** il macronucleo
- *macronucleus (meganucleus)*
**12** il micronucleo
- *micronucleus*
**13-39 organismi** *m pl* **pluricellulari** (metazoi *m pl*)
- *multicellular animals (metazoans)*

**13** la spugna, un porifero
- *bath sponge, a porifer (sponge)*
**14** la medusa, una discomedusa, un celenterato
- *medusa, a discomedusa, a coelenterate*
**15** l'ombrella
- *umbrella*
**16** il tentacolo
- *tentacle*
**17** il corallo, un autozoo
- *red coral (precious coral), a coral animal (anthozoan, reef-building animal)*
**18** il ramo di corallo
- *coral colony*
**19** il polipo coralligeno
- *coral polyp*
**20-26 vermi** *m pl*
- *worms (Vermes)*
**20** la sanguisuga, un anellide
- *leech, an annelid*
**21** la ventosa
- *sucker*
**22** lo spirografide, un anellide polichete
- *Spirographis, a bristle worm*
**23** il tubo
- *tube*
**24** il lombrico
- *earthworm*
**25** il segmento
- *segment*
**26** il clitello (la regione dell'accoppiamento)
- *clitellum [accessory reproductive organ]*

**27-36** molluschi *m pl*
- *molluscs (Am. mollusks)*
**27** la chiocciola dei giardini, un gasteropode terrestre
- *edible snail, a snail*
**28** il piede
- *creeping foot*
**29** la conchiglia globoide (il nicchio)
- *shell (snail shell)*
**30** l'occhio peduncolato
- *stalked eye*
**31** i tentacoli (le antenne, la coppia dei tentacoli)
- *tentacles (feelers)*
**32** l'ostrica
- *oyster*
**33** l'ostrica perlifera
- *freshwater pearl mussel*
**34** la madreperla
- *mother-of-pearl (nacre)*
**35** la perla
- *pearl*
**36** la conchiglia
- *mussel shell*
**37** la seppia comune, un cefalopode
- *cuttlefish, a cephalopod*
**38** u. **39** echinodermi *m pl*
- *echinoderms*
**38** la stella marina (la stella di mare *m*)
- *starfish (sea star)*
**39** il riccio di mare *m*
- *sea urchin (sea hedgehog)*

1 *u.* 2 **crostacei** *m pl* (granchi *m pl*)
– *crustaceans*
1 il granchio di mare *m*, un granchio
– *mitten crab, a crab*
2 l'asellus *m*
– *water slater*
3-39, 48-56 **insetti** *m pl*
– *insects*
3 la libellula, un odonato
– *water nymph (dragonfly), a homopteran (homopterous insect), a dragonfly*
4 lo scorpione acquatico; *sim.*: la nepa, un nepide, un idrocoride
– *water scorpion (water bug), a rhynchophore*
5 la coda a spada
– *raptorial leg*
6 la mosca effimera (l'effimera, l'efemera)
– *mayfly (dayfly, ephemerid)*
7 l'occhio composto
– *compound eye*
8 la cavalletta verde (la cavalletta, la locusta), un ortottero
– *green grasshopper, (green locust, meadow grasshopper), an orthopteron (orthopterous insect)*
9 la larva
– *larva (grub)*
10 l'insetto adulto
– *adult insect, an imago*
11 la zampa saltatoria
– *leaping hind leg*
12 la friganea, un tricottero
– *caddis fly (spring fly, water moth), a neuropteran*
13 l'afide *m*, un pidocchio delle piante
– *aphid (greenfly), a plant louse*
14 l'afide *m* adulto attero (aptero)
– *wingless aphid*
15 l'afide *m* alato
– *winged aphid*
16-20 **ditteri** *m pl*
– *dipterous insects (dipterans)*
16 la zanzara
– *gnat (mosquito, midge), a culicid*
17 la proboscide succhiante
– *proboscis (sucking organ)*
18 la mosca della carne, una mosca
– *bluebottle (blowfly), a fly*
19 la larva
– *maggot (larva)*
20 la pupa
– *chrysalis (pupa)*
21 *u.* 22 la formica
– *ant*
21-23 **imenotteri** *m pl*
– *Hymenoptera*
21 la femmina alata
– *winged female*

22 la formica operaia (l'operaia)
– *worker*
23 il bombo
– *bumblebee (humblebee)*
24-39 **coleotteri** *m pl*
– *beetles (Coleoptera)*
24 il cervo volante
– *stag beetle, a lamellicorn beetle*
25 le mandibole ramificate
– *mandibles*
26 i palpi labiali
– *trophi*
27 l'antenna
– *antenna (feeler)*
28 il capo
– *head*
29 *u.* 30 il torace
– *thorax*
29 il prototorace
– *thoracic shield (prothorax)*
30 lo scutello
– *scutellum*
31 l'addome *m*
– *tergites*
32 lo stimma (lo stigma)
– *stigma*
33 l'ala (l'ala posteriore)
– *wing (hind wing)*
34 la nervatura alare
– *nervure*
35 il punto di ripiegamento
– *point at which the wing folds*
36 l'elitra (l'ala anteriore)
– *elytron (forewing)*
37 la coccinella
– *ladybird (Am. ladybug), a coccinellid*
38 il cerambice, un coleottero
– *Ergates faber, a longicorn beetle (longicorn)*
39 lo scarabeo stercorario, un geotrupe
– *dung beetle, a lamellicorn beetle*
40-47 **aracnidi** *m pl*
– *arachnids*
40 lo scorpione
– *Euscorpius flavicandus, a scorpion*
41 il chelicero
– *cheliped with chelicer*
42 i pedipalpi
– *maxillary antenna (maxillary feeler)*
43 il pungiglione caudale
– *tail sting*
44-46 **araneidi** *m pl*
– *spiders*
44 la zecca dei cani, un acaro, una zecca
– *wood tick (dog tick)*
45 il ragno crociato, un aracnide
– *cross spider (garden spider), an orb spinner*
46 le filiere (le ghiandole sericigene)
– *spinneret*

47 la ragnatela
– *spider's web (web)*
48-56 **farfalle** *f pl* (lepidotteri *m pl*)
– *Lepidoptera (butterflies and moths)*
48 il baco da seta (il bombice del gelso), un lepidottero
– *mulberry-feeding moth (silk moth), a bombycid moth*
49 le uova
– *eggs*
50 la larva
– *silkworm*
51 il bozzolo
– *cocoon*
52 il macaone, una farfalla diurna
– *swallowtail, a butterfly*
53 l'antenna
– *antenna (feeler)*
54 l'ocello
– *eyespot*
55 la sfinge ligustrina, una sfingide
– *privet hawkmoth, a hawkmoth (sphinx)*
56 la proboscide
– *proboscis*

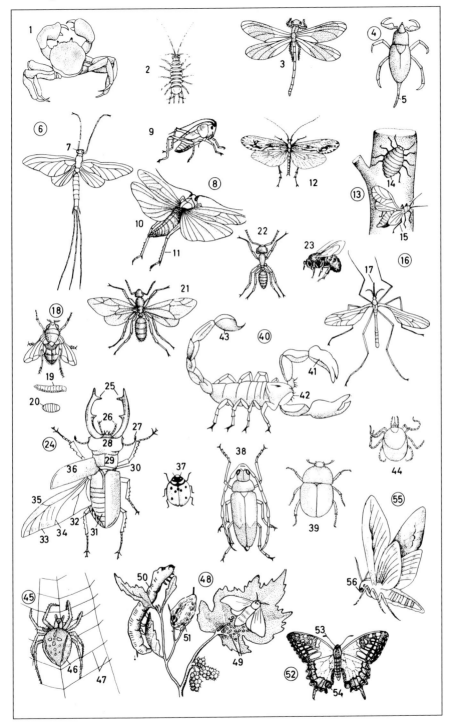

**1-3 struzioniformi** *m pl* (uccelli *m pl* inetti al volo)
- *flightless birds*
**1** il casuario, un casuariforme; *sim.:* l'emu
- *cassowary; sim.: emu*
**2** lo struzzo
- *ostrich*
**3** la covata dello struzzo [da 12 a 14 uova *f pl*]
- *clutch of ostrich eggs [12 - 14 eggs]*
**4** il pinguino imperatore, un pinguino (un uccello inetto al volo)
- *king penguin, a penguin, a flightless bird*
**5-10 palmipedi** *m pl*
- *web-footed birds*
**5** il pellicano, un pelecaniforme
- *white pelican (wood stork, ibis, wood ibis, spoonbill, brent goose, Am. brant goose, brant), a pelican*
**6** il piede palmato
- *webfoot (webbed foot)*
**7** la membrana interdigitale
- *web (palmations) of webbed foot (palmate foot)*
**8** il becco munito inferiormente di un sacco dilatabile (sacco membranoso)
- *lower mandible with gular pouch*
**9** la sula, un pelecaniforme
- *northern gannet (gannet, solan goose), a gannet*
**10** il marangone, un cormorano con ali *f pl* spiegate
- *green cormorant (shag), a cormorant displaying with spread wings*
**11-14 laridi** *m pl* (uccelli *m pl* acquatici, uccelli *m pl* tuffatori)
- *long-winged birds (seabirds)*
**11** il pesce rondine (la sterna), una rondine di mare *m* che si tuffa per prendere il cibo
- *common sea swallow, a sea swallow (tern), diving for food*
**12** la procellaria glaciale
- *fulmar*
**13** l'uria comune, un'uria, un'alcide *f*
- *guillemot, an auk*
**14** il gabbiano comune (il gabbiano tridattilo), un gabbiano
- *black-headed gull (mire crow), a gull*
**15-17 anserine** *f pl*
- *Anseres*
**15** l'anatra di mare *m*, uno smergo
- *goosander (common merganser), a sawbill*
**16** il cigno reale, un cigno
- *mute swan, a swan*

**17** il tubercolo alla base del becco
- *knob on the bill*
**18** l'airone *m* cinerino, un airone, una cicogna
- *common heron, a heron*
**19-21 caradriformi** *m pl*
- *plovers*
**19** il cavaliere d'Italia
- *stilt (stilt bird, stilt plover)*
**20** la folaga, un rallide
- *coot, a rail*
**21** la pavoncella
- *lapwing (green plover, peewit, pewit)*
**22** la quaglia, un galliforme
- *quail, a gallinaceous bird*
**23** la tortora, un colombiforme
- *turtle dove, a pigeon*
**24** il rondone, un apodiforme
- *swift*
**25** l'upupa, un coraciforme
- *hoopoe, a roller*
**26** il ciuffo erettile
- *erectile crest*
**27** il picchio (picchio nero, picchio verde, picchio grigio, picchio muratore), un piciforme
- *spotted woodpecker, a woodpecker; related: wryneck*
**28** il foro di entrata al nido
- *entrance to the nest*
**29** la camera di cova
- *nesting cavity*
**30** il cuculo (il cucù)
- *cuckoo*

**1, 3, 4, 5, 7, 9, 10**  uccelli *m pl* canori
– *songbirds*
**1**  il cardellino (il capirosso) un
passeriforme
– *goldfinch, a finch*
**2**  il gruccione (il grottaione)
– *bee eater*
**3**  il codirosso, un tordo
– *redstart (star finch), a thrush*
**4**  la cinciallegra, una cincia, un
uccello stanziale
– *bluetit, a tit (titmouse), a resident
bird (non-migratory bird)*
**5**  il ciuffolotto
– *bullfinch*
**6**  la ghiandaia marina
– *common roller (roller)*
**7**  il rigogolo, un uccello migratore
(l'oriolo)
– *golden oriole, a migratory bird*
**8**  il martin pescatore
– *kingfisher*
**9**  la ballerina bianca (il batticoda),
una cutrettola
– *white wagtail, a wagtail*
**10**  il fringuello
– *chaffinch*

**1-20 uccelli canori**
– *songbirds*
**1-3 corvidi** (corvi)
– *Corvidae (corvine birds, crows)*
**1** la ghiandaia
– *jay (nutcracker)*
**2** la cornacchia
– *rook, a crow*
**3** la gazza
– *magpie*
**4** la storno
– *starling (pastor, shepherd bird)*
**5** il passero
– *house sparrow*
**6-8 fringillidi** *m pl*
– *finches*
**6** *u.* **7** zigoli
– *buntings*
**6** lo zigolo giallo
– *yellowhammer (yellow bunting)*
**7** l'ortolano
– *ortolan (ortolan bunting)*
**8** il lucarino
– *siskin (aberdevine)*
**9** la cinciallegra, una cincia
– *great titmouse (great tit, ox eye), a titmouse (tit)*

**10** il regolo; *sim:* fiorrancino
– *golden-crested wren (goldcrest); sim.: firecrest, one of the Regulidae*
**11** il piccio muratore
– *nuthatch*
**12** lo scricciolo
– *wren*
**13-17 tordi** *m pl*
– *thrushes*
**13** il merlo
– *blackbird*
**14** l'usignolo
– *nightingale (poet.: philomel, philomela)*
**15** il pettirosso
– *robin (redbreast, robin redbreast)*
**16** il tordo bottaccio
– *song thrush (throstle, mavis)*
**17** l'usignolo maggiore
– *thrush nightingale*
**18** *u.* **19 alaudidi** *m pl*
– *larks*
**18** l'allodola
– *woodlark*
**19** la cappellaccia
– *crested lark (tufted lark)*

**20** la rondine
– *common swallow (barn swallow, chimney swallow), a swallow*

1-13 **uccelli** *m pl* **rapaci** (rapaci *m pl*
  diurni)
– *diurnal birds of prey*
1-4 falchi *m pl*
– *falcons*
1 lo smeriglio
– *merlin*
2 il falco pellegrino
– *peregrine falcon*
3 le zampe calzate
– *feathered legs*
4 il tarso
– *tarsus*
5-9 aquile *f pl*
– *eagles*
5 l'aquila di mare *m*
– *white-tailed sea eagle (white-tailed
  eagle, grey sea eagle, erne)*
6 il becco ricurvo (il rostro)
– *hooked beak*
7 l'artiglio
– *claw (talon)*
8 la coda
– *tail*
9 la poiana
– *common buzzard*
10-13 accipitridi *m pl*
– *accipiters*
10 l'astore *m*
– *goshawk*

11 il nibbio reale
– *common European kite (glede,
  kite)*
12 lo sparviero (lo sparviere)
– *sparrow hawk (spar-hawk)*
13 il falco di palude *f*
– *marsh harrier (moor buzzard,
  moor harrier, moor hawk)*
14-19 **uccelli** *m pl* rapaci notturni
– *owls*
14 il gufo comune
– *long-eared owl (horned owl)*
15 il gufo reale
– *eagle-owl (great horned owl)*
16 il ciuffo auricolare
– *plumicorn (feathered ear, ear tuft,
  ear, horn)*
17 il barbagianni
– *barn owl (white owl, silver owl,
  yellow owl, church owl, screech
  owl)*
18 il disco facciale cuoriforme
– *facial disc (disk)*
19 la civetta
– *little owl (sparrow owl)*

1  il cacatua dal ciuffo giallo (un
   pappagallo)
–  *sulphur-crested cockatoo, a parrot*
2  l'ara
–  *blue-and-yellow macaw*
3  l'uccello del paradiso (la paradisea)
–  *blue bird of paradise*
4  il colibrì (l'uccello mosca)
–  *sappho*
5  il cardinale (il richmondena cardi-
   nalis)
–  *cardinal (cardinal bird)*
6  il tucano, un ranfastide
–  *toucan (red-billed toucan), one of
   the Piciformes*

**1-18 pesci** *m pl*
- *fishes*
1 la verdesca (il verdone, lo squalo azzurro, la canosa) uno squalo (un pescecane)
- *man-eater (blue shark, requin), a shark*
2 il muso (il naso)
- *nose (snout)*
3 l'apertura branchiale
- *gill slit (gill cleft)*
4 la carpa a specchi *m pl*, una carpa
- *carp, a mirror carp (carp)*
5 l'apertura branchiale
- *gill cover (operculum)*
6 la pinna dorsale
- *dorsal fin*
7 la pinna pettorale
- *pectoral fin*
8 la pinna pelvica
- *pelvic fin (abdominal fin, ventral fin)*
9 la pinna anale
- *anal fin*
10 la pinna caudale
- *caudal fin (tail fin)*
11 la scaglia
- *scale*
12 il siluro di Europa
- *catfish (sheatfish, sheathfish, wels)*
13 il bargiglio
- *barbel*
14 l'aringa
- *herring*
15 la trota comune (la trota di ruscello), una trota
- *brown trout (German brown trout), a trout*
16 il luccio
- *pike (northern pike)*
17 l'anguilla
- *freshwater eel (eel)*
18 il cavalluccio marino (l'ippocampo)
- *sea horse (Hippocampus, horse-fish)*
19 le lofobranchie
- *tufted gills*
**20-26 anfibi** *m pl*
- *Amphibia (amphibians)*
**20-22 urodeli** *m pl* (salamandre *f pl*)
- *salamanders*
20 il tritone (il tritone crestato), una salamandra acquaiola
- *greater water newt (crested newt), a water newt*
21 la cresta dorsale
- *dorsal crest*
22 la salamandra maculata (la salamandra giallo-nero), una salamandra
- *fire salamander, a salamander*
**23-26 anuri** *m pl* (anfibi *m pl* privi di coda)
- *salientians (anurans, batrachians)*

23 il rospo comune (la botta), un rospo
- *European toad, a toad*
24 la raganella (l'ila)
- *tree frog (tree toad)*
25 il sacco vocale
- *vocal sac (vocal pouch, croaking sac)*
26 la ventosa
- *adhesive disc (disk)*
**27-41 rettili** *m pl*
- *reptiles*
**27 u. 30-37 lucertole** *f pl* (sauri *m pl*)
- *lizards*
27 la lucertola
- *sand lizard*
28 la tartaruga (la testuggine)
- *hawksbill turtle (hawksbill)*
29 lo scudo dorsale (la corazza, il carapace)
- *carapace (shell)*
30 il basilisco
- *basilisk*
31 il varano del deserto, un varano
- *desert monitor, a monitor lizard (monitor)*
32 l'iguana
- *common iguana, an iguana*
33 il camaleonte, un sauro con la lingua protrattile
- *chameleon, one of the Chamaeleontidae (Rhiptoglossa)*
34 la zampa prensile
- *prehensile foot*
35 la coda prensile
- *prehensile tail*
36 il geco muraiolo (la tarantola, lo stellione), un geco
- *wall gecko, a gecko*
37 l'orbettino, un rettile
- *slowworm (blindworm), one of the Anguidae*
**38-41 serpenti** *m pl* (serpi *f pl*, bisce *f pl*)
- *snakes*
38 la biscia dal collare (la natrice), una biscia d'acqua
- *ringed snake (ring snake, water snake, grass snake), a colubrid*
39 il collare
- *collar*
**40 u. 41 vipere** *f pl*
- *vipers (adders)*
40 la vipera comune, un serpente velenoso
- *common viper, a poisonous (venomous) snake*
41 l'aspide *m*
- *asp (asp viper)*

**1-6  farfalle** *f pl* **diurne**
- *butterflies*
**1**  la vanessa atalanta (il vulcano)
- *red admiral*
**2**  la vanessa io
- *peacock butterfly*
**3**  l'euchloe *f* cardamines
- *orange tip (orange tip butterfly)*
**4**  la cedronella (la gonepterix rhamni)
- *brimstone (brimstone butterfly)*
**5**  la nymphalis antiopa
- *Camberwell beauty (mourning
  cloak, mourning cloak butterfly)*
**6**  la lycaena arion
- *blue (lycaenid butterfly, lycaenid)*
**7-11  farfalle** *f pl* **notturne**
- *moths (Heterocera)*
**7**  l'arctia caja
- *garden tiger*
**8**  la catocala nupta
- *red underwing*
**9**  l'acherontia atropos (la sfinge
  testa di morto)
- *death's-head moth (death's-head
  hawkmoth), a hawkmoth (sphinx)*
**10**  la larva
- *caterpillar*
**11**  la pupa
- *chrysalis (pupa)*

**1** l'ornitorinco, un monotremo, oviparo
– *platypus (duck-bill, duck-mole), a monotreme (oviparous mammal)*
**2** u. **3 marsupiali** *m pl*
– *marsupial mammals (marsupials)*
**2** l'opossum *m* nordamericano, un opossum virginiano
– *New World opossum, a didelphid*
**3** il canguro gigante rosso, un canguro
– *red kangaroo (red flyer), a kangaroo*
**4-7 insettivori** *m pl* (entomofagi)
– *insectivores (insect-eating mammals)*
**4** la talpa
– *mole*
**5** il porcospino
– *hedgehog*
**6** l'aculeo
– *spine*
**7** il toporagno
– *shrew (shrew mouse), one of the Soricidae*
**8** l'armadillo
– *nine-banded armadillo (peba)*
**9** l'orecchione *m*, un vespertilionide, un pipistrello
– *long-eared bat (flitter-mouse), a flying mammal (chiropter, chiropteran)*
**10** il pangolino folidoto, uno squamato
– *pangolin (scaly ant-eater), a scaly mammal*
**11** il bradipo tridattilo
– *two-toed sloth (unau)*
**12-19 roditori** *m pl*
– *rodents*
**12** il porcellino d'India (la cavia)
– *guinea pig (cavy)*
**13** l'istrice *m*
– *porcupine*
**14** il castoro
– *beaver*
**15** il topo delle piramidi
– *jerboa*
**16** il criceto
– *hamster*
**17** il microto
– *water vole*
**18** la marmotta
– *marmot*
**19** lo scoiattolo
– *squirrel*
**20** l'elefante *m* africano, un proboscidato
– *African elephant, a proboscidean (proboscidian)*
**21** la proboscide
– *trunk (proboscis)*
**22** la zanna
– *tusk*

**23** un lamantino, una sirena (*sim.:* manato)
– *manatee (manati, lamantin), a sirenian*
**24** l'iracoideo sudafricano, un plantigrado
– *South African dassie (das, coney, hyrax), a procaviid*
**25-31 ungulati** *m pl*
– *ungulates*
**25-27 perissodattili** *m pl*
– *odd-toed ungulates*
**25** il rinoceronte nero, un rinoceronte
– *African black rhino, a rhinoceros (nasicorn)*
**26** il tapiro di pianura, un tapiro
– *Brazilian tapir, a tapir*
**27** la zebra
– *zebra*
**28-31 artiodattili** *m pl*
– *even-toed ungulates*
**28-30 ruminanti** *m pl*
– *ruminants*
**28** il lama
– *llama*
**29** il cammello (il cammello a due gobbe *f pl*)
– *Bactrian camel (two-humped camel)*
**30** il guanaco
– *guanaco*
**31** l'ippopotamo
– *hippopotamus*

**1-10 ungulati** *m pl*, ruminanti *m pl*
– *ungulates, ruminants*
**1** l'alce *m*
– *elk (moose)*
**2** il wapiti
– *wapiti (*Am. *elk)*
**3** il camoscio
– *chamois*
**4** la giraffa
– *giraffe*
**5** l'antilocapra, un'antilope *f*
– *black buck, an antelope*
**6** il muflone
– *mouflon (moufflon)*
**7** lo stambecco
– *ibex (rock goat, bouquetin, stein-bock)*
**8** il bufalo
– *water buffalo (Indian buffalo, water ox)*
**9** il bisonte
– *bison*
**10** il bue muschiato
– *musk ox*
**11-22 carnivori** *m pl*
– *carnivores (beasts of prey)*
**11-13 canidi** *m pl*
– *Canidae*
**11** lo sciacallo
– *black-backed jackal (jackal)*
**12** la volpe rossa
– *red fox*
**13** il lupo
– *wolf*
**14-17 mustelidi** *m pl*
– *martens*
**14** la martora
– *stone marten (beach marten)*
**15** lo zibellino
– *sable*
**16** la donnola
– *weasel*
**17** la lontra marina, una lontra
– *sea otter, an otter*
**18-22 foche** *f pl* (pinnipedi *m pl*)
– *seals (pinnipeds)*
**18** l'otaria dell'Alaska
– *fur seal (sea bear, ursine seal)*
**19** la foca
– *common seal (sea calf, sea dog)*
**20** il tricheco
– *walrus (morse)*
**21** le setole sul labbro (i baffi)
– *whiskers*
**22** la zanna
– *tusk*
**23-29 cetacei** *m pl*
– *whales*
**23** la focena
– *bottle-nosed dolphin (bottle-nose dolphin)*
**24** il delfino
– *common dolphin*

**25** il capidoglio (il capodoglio)
– *sperm whale (cachalot)*
**26** lo sfiatatoio
– *blowhole (spout hole)*
**27** la pinna dorsale
– *dorsal fin*
**28** la pinna pettorale
– *flipper*
**29** la pinna caudale
– *tail flukes (tail)*

**1-11 carnivori** *m pl*
- **carnivores** *(beasts of prey)*
**1** la iena striata, una iena
- *striped hyena, a hyena*
**2-8 felini** *m pl*
- **felines** *(cats)*
**2** il leone
- *lion*
**3** la criniera (la criniera del leone)
- *mane (lion's mane)*
**4** la zampa
- *paw*
**5** la tigre
- *tiger*
**6** il leopardo
- *leopard*
**7** il ghepardo
- *cheetah (hunting leopard)*
**8** la lince
- *lynx*
**9-11 orsi** *m pl*
- **bears**
**9** il procione (l'orso lavatore, l'orsetto lavatore)
- *raccoon (racoon, Am. coon)*
**10** l'orso bruno
- *brown bear*
**11** l'orso bianco
- *polar bear (white bear)*
**12-16 primati** *m pl*
- **primates**
**12** *u.* **13** scimmie *f pl*
- *monkeys*
**12** il reso (il macaus rhesus)
- *rhesus monkey (rhesus, rhesus macaque)*
**13** il babbuino
- *baboon*
**14-16 scimmie** *f pl* **antropomorfe**
- **anthropoids** *(anthropoid apes, great apes)*
**14** lo scimpanzé
- *chimpanzee*
**15** l'orangutan (l'orango)
- *orang-utan (orang-outan)*
**16** il gorilla
- *gorilla*

1 gigantocypris agassizi (ostracode *m* gigante), un cirripide
- *Gigantocypris agassizi*
2 macropharynx longicaudatus (l'anguilla pellicano), un anguilliforme
- *Eupharynx pelecanoides (pelican eel, pelican fish)*
3 metacrinus (il crinoide), un giglio di mare *m*, un echinoderma
- *Metacrinus (feather star), a sea lily, an echinoderm*
4 lycoteuthis diadema (la lampada magica), una seppia [luminosa]
- *Lycoteuthis diadema (jewelled squid), a cuttlefish [luminescent]*
5 atolla, una medusa degli abissi, un celenterato
- *Atolla, a deep-sea medusa, a coelenterate*
6 melanocetes, un pediculato [luminoso]
- *Melanocetes, a pediculate [luminescent]*
7 lophocalix philippensis, una spugna silicea
- *Lophocalyx philippensis, a glass sponge*
8 mopsea, una gorgonia (colonia)
- *Mopsea, a sea fan [colony]*
9 hydrallmania, un polipo idroide, un polipo, un celenterato [colonia]
- *Hydrallmania, a hydroid polyp, a coelenterate [colony]*
10 malacosteus indicus, uno stomatide [luminoso]
- *Malacosteus indicus, a stomiatid [luminescent]*
11 brisinga endecacnemos, una stella serpentina, un ofiuoride, un echinoderma [luminoso solo se eccitato]
- *Brisinga endecacnemos, a sand star (brittle star), an echinoderm [luminescent only when stimulated]*
12 pasiphaea, un gamberetto, un gambero
- *Pasiphaea, a shrimp, a crustacean*
13 echiostoma, uno stomiatide, un pesce [luminoso]
- *Echiostoma, a stomiatid, a fish [luminescent]*
14 umbellula encrinus, una pennatula (una penna di mare *m*), un celenterato [colonia luminosa]
- *Umbellula encrinus, a sea pen (sea feather), a coelenterate [colony, luminescent]*
15 polycheles, un gambero
- *Polycheles, a crustacean*
16 lithodes, un gambero, un granchio
- *Lithodes, a crustacean, a crab*

17 archaster, una stella marina, un echinoderma
- *Archaster, a starfish (sea star), an echinoderm*
18 oneirophanta, una oloturia (un cetriolo di mare *m*), un echinoderma
- *Oneirophanta, a sea cucumber, an echinoderm*
19 palaeopneustes niasicus, un riccio di mare, *m*, un echinoderma
- *Palaeopneustes niasicus, a sea urchin (sea hedgehog), an echinoderm*
20 chitonactis, un anemone di mare *m* (un'attinia), un celenterato
- *Chitonactis, a sea anemone (actinia), a coelenterate*

1 l'albero
– *tree*
2 il tronco
– *bole (tree trunk, trunk, stem)*
3 la chioma
– *crown of tree (crown)*
4 la cima
– *top of tree (treetop)*
5 il ramo
– *bough (limb, branch)*
6 il ramoscello
– *twig (branch)*
7 il fusto [sezione *f* trasversale]
– *bole (tree trunk) [cross section]*
8 la corteccia
– *bark (rind)*
9 il libro
– *phloem (bast sieve tissue, inner fibrous bark)*
10 il cambio (l'anello cambiale)
– *cambium (cambium ring)*
11 i raggi midollari
– *medullary rays (vascular rays, pith rays)*
12 l'alburno
– *sapwood (sap, alburnum)*
13 il durame
– *heartwood (duramen)*
14 il midollo
– *pith*
15 **la pianta**
– ***plant***
16-18 la radice
– *root*
16 la radice principale
– *primary root*
17 la radice laterale
– *secondary root*
18 il pelo radicale
– *root hair*
19-25 il germoglio (il getto)
– *shoot (sprout)*
19 la foglia
– *leaf*
20 il fusto
– *stalk*
21 la gemma laterale
– *side shoot (offshoot)*
22 la gemma apicale
– *terminal bud*
23 il fiore
– *flower*
24 la gemma fiorale
– *flower bud*
25 la foglia ascellare con la gemma ascellare
– *leaf axil with axillary bud*
26 **la foglia**
– ***leaf***
27 il picciolo
– *leaf stalk (petiole)*
28 il lembo fogliare
– *leaf blade (blade, lamina)*
29 la nervatura laterale
– *venation (veins, nervures, ribs)*
30 la nervatura principale
– *midrib (nerve)*
31-38 forme *f pl* delle foglie
– *leaf shapes*
31 lineare
– *linear*
32 lanceolata
– *lanceolate*
33 rotonda
– *orbicular (orbiculate)*
34 aghiforme
– *acerose (acerous, acerate, acicular, needle-shaped)*

35 cuoriforme
– *cordate*
36 ovata
– *ovate*
37 saettiforme
– *sagittate*
38 reniforme
– *reniform*
39-42 foglie *f pl* composte
– *compound leaves*
39 palmata
– *digitate (digitated, palmate, quinquefoliolate)*
40 pennato-saetta
– *pinnatifid*
41 pari-pennata
– *abruptly pinnate*
42 impari-pennata
– *odd-pinnate*
43-50 forme *f pl* dei margini fogliari
– *leaf margin shapes*
43 intera
– *entire*
44 seghettata
– *serrate (serrulate, saw-toothed)*
45 biseghettata
– *doubly toothed*
46 crenata
– *crenate*
47 dentata
– *dentate*
48 sinuata
– *sinuate*
49 cigliata
– *ciliate (ciliated)*
50 il ciglio
– *cilium*
51 **il fiore**
– ***flower***
52 il peduncolo
– *flower stalk (flower stem, scape)*
53 l'ovario
– *receptacle (floral axis, thalamus, torus)*
54 il ricettacolo
– *ovary*
55 lo stilo
– *style*
56 lo stigma
– *stigma*
57 lo stame
– *stamen*
58 il sepalo (il calice)
– *sepal*
59 il petalo (la corolla)
– *petal*
60 ovario e stame *m* (sezione *f* )
– *ovary and stamen [section]*
61 le pareti dell'ovario
– *ovary wall*
62 la cavità dell'ovario
– *ovary cavity*
63 l'ovulo
– *ovule*
64 il sacco embrionale
– *embryo sac*
65 il polline
– *pollen*
66 il tubo pollinico
– *pollen tube*
67-77 infiorescenze *f pl* (inflorescenze *f pl*)
– *inflorescences*
67 la spiga semplice
– *spike (racemose spike)*
68 la spiga composta
– *raceme (simple raceme)*
69 la pannocchia
– *panicle*

70 la cima ombrelliforme
– *cyme*
71 lo spadice
– *spadix (fleshy spike)*
72 l'ombrella semplice
– *umbel (simple umbel)*
73 il capolino
– *capitulum*
74 la calatide
– *composite head (discoid flower head)*
75 il capolino globoso
– *hollow flower head*
76 la cima elicoide
– *bostryx (helicoid cyme)*
77 la cima scorpioide
– *cincinnus (scorpioid cyme, curled cyme)*
78-82 radici *f pl*
– *roots*
78 le radici avventizie
– *adventitious roots*
79 la radice a fittone *m*
– *tuber (tuberous root, swollen taproot)*
80 le radici avventizie aeree
– *adventitious roots (aerial roots)*
81 le spine delle radici
– *root thorns*
82 gli pneumatofori
– *pneumatophores*
83-85 il filo di erba
– *blade of grass*
83 la guaina fogliare
– *leaf sheath*
84 la ligula fogliare
– *ligule (ligula)*
85 la lamina fogliare
– *leaf blade (lamina)*
86 l'embrione *m*
– *embryo (seed, germ)*
87 il cotiledone
– *cotyledon (seed leaf, seed lobe)*
88 la radichetta
– *radicle*
89 l'ipocotile *m*
– *hypocotyl*
90 la gemma apicale
– *plumule (leaf bud)*
91-102 frutti *m pl*
– *fruits*
91-96 frutti deiscenti
– *dehiscent fruits*
91 il follicolo
– *follicle*
92 il baccello (il legume)
– *legume (pod)*
93 la siliqua
– *siliqua (pod)*
94 la cassula (la capsula)
– *schizocarp*
95 la pisside
– *pyxidium (circumscissile seed vessel)*
96 il treto
– *poricidal capsule (porose capsule)*
97-102 frutti *m pl* indeiscenti
– *indehiscent fruits*
97 la bacca
– *berry*
98 la noce
– *nut*
99 la drupa (ciliegia)
– *drupe (stone fruit) (cherry)*
100 il sincarpio (cinorrodo)
– *aggregate fruit (compound fruit) (rose hip)*
101 la pluridrupa (lampone)
– *aggregate fruit (compound fruit) (raspberry)*
102 il frutto follicolare (mela *f* )
– *pome (apple)*

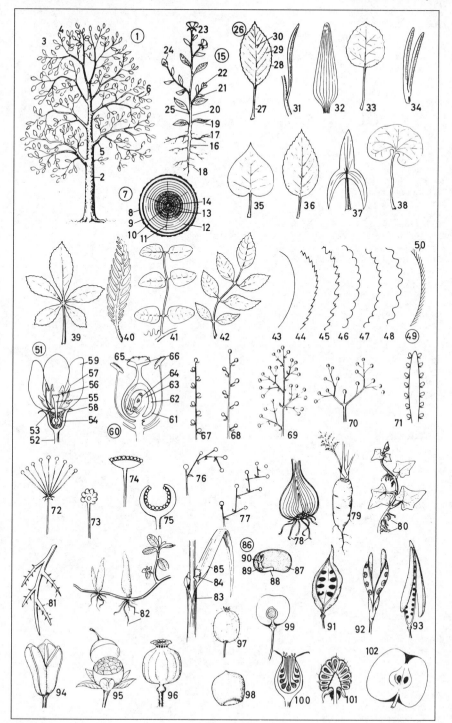

**1-73**  latifoglie *f pl*
– *deciduous trees*
**1**  la quercia
– *oak (oak tree)*
**2**  il ramo fiorito
– *flowering branch*
**3**  il ramo con frutto
– *fruiting branch*
**4**  il frutto (la ghianda)
– *fruit (acorn)*
**5**  la cupola
– *cupule (cup)*
**6**  il fiore femminile
– *female flower*
**7**  la brattea
– *bract*
**8**  l'inflorescenza *f* maschile
– *male inflorescence*
**9**  la betulla
– *birch (birch tree)*
**10**  il ramo con amenti *m pl* (gattini *m pl*), un ramo fiorito
– *branch with catkins, a flowering branch*
**11**  il ramo con frutto
– *fruiting branch*
**12**  la squama
– *scale (catkin scale)*
**13**  il fiore femminile
– *female flower*
**14**  il fiore maschile
– *male flower*
**15**  il pioppo
– *poplar*
**16**  il ramo fiorito
– *flowering branch*
**17**  il fiore
– *flower*
**18**  il ramo con frutto
– *fruiting branch*
**19**  il frutto
– *fruit*
**20**  il seme
– *seed*
**21**  la foglia del pioppo tremulo
– *leaf of the aspen (trembling poplar)*
**22**  l'infruttescenza
– *infructescence*
**23**  la foglia del pioppo bianco
– *leaf of the white poplar (silver poplar, silverleaf )*
**24**  il salice
– *sallow (goat willow)*
**25**  il ramo con gemme *f pl*
– *branch with flower buds*
**26**  l'amento con fiore *m*
– *catkin with single flower*
**27**  il ramo con foglie *f pl*
– *branch with leaves*
**28**  il frutto
– *fruit*
**29**  il ramo del vimine con foglie *f pl*
– *osier branch with leaves*

**30**  l'ontano
– *alder*
**31**  il ramo con frutto
– *fruiting branch*
**32**  il ramo fiorito con amento femminile vecchio
– *branch with previous year's cone*
**33**  il faggio
– *beech (beech tree)*
**34**  il ramo in fiore *m*
– *flowering branch*
**35**  il fiore
– *flower*
**36**  il ramo con frutto
– *fruiting branch*
**37**  la faggiola (l'achenio) (il frutto del faggio)
– *beech nut*
**38**  il frassino
– *ash (ash tree)*
**39**  il ramo fiorito
– *flowering branch*
**40**  il fiore
– *flower*
**41**  il ramo con frutto
– *fruiting branch*
**42**  il sorbo
– *mountain ash (rowan, quickbeam)*
**43**  l'inflorescenza
– *inflorescence*
**44**  l'infruttescenza
– *infructescence*
**45**  il frutto (sezione *f* longitudinale)
– *fruit [longitudinal section]*
**46**  il tiglio
– *lime (lime tree, linden, linden tree)*
**47**  il ramo con fiore *m*
– *fruiting branch*
**48**  l'inflorescenza
– *inflorescence*
**49**  l'olmo
– *elm (elm tree)*
**50**  il ramo con frutto
– *fruiting branch*
**51**  il ramo in fiore *m*
– *flowering branch*
**52**  il fiore
– *flower*
**53**  l'acero riccio
– *maple (maple tree)*
**54**  il ramo in fiore *m*
– *flowering branch*
**55**  il fiore
– *flower*
**56**  l'infruttescenza
– *fruiting branch*
**57**  la samara (il frutto maturo) a ali *f pl* opposte
– *maple seed with wings (winged maple seed)*
**58**  l'ippocastano (il castagno d'India)
– *horse chestnut (horse chestnut tree, chestnut, chestnut tree, buck-eye)*

**59**  il ramo con fiori *m pl* giovani
– *branch with young fruits*
**60**  la castagna amara (il seme)
– *chestnut (horse chestnut)*
**61**  il frutto maturo
– *mature (ripe) fruit*
**62**  il fiore (sezione *f* longitudinale)
– *flower [longitudinal section]*
**63**  il carpino bianco
– *hornbeam (yoke elm)*
**64**  il ramo con frutto
– *fruiting branch*
**65**  il seme
– *seed*
**66**  l'inflorescenza
– *flowering branch*
**67**  il platano comune
– *plane (plane tree)*
**68**  la foglia
– *leaf*
**69**  l'infruttescenza e il frutto
– *infructescence and fruit*
**70**  la robinia
– *false acacia (locust tree)*
**71**  il ramo fiorito
– *flowering branch*
**72**  parte *f* dell'infruttescenza
– *part of the infructescence*
**73**  il peduncolo delle foglie con spine *f pl* appaiate
– *base of the leaf stalk with stipules*

**1-71** conifere *f pl*
- *coniferous trees (conifers)*
**1** l'abete bianco
- *silver fir (European silver fir, common silver fir)*
**2** la pigna (il cono), uno strobilo
- *fir cone, a fruit cone*
**3** l'asse *f* del cono (l'asse della pigna)
- *cone axis*
**4** il cono femminile maturo
- *female flower cone*
**5** la squama del cono (la brattea protettiva)
- *bract scale (bract)*
**6** il cono maschile
- *male flower shoot*
**7** lo stame
- *stamen*
**8** la squama del cono (la squama fruttifera)
- *cone scale*
**9** il seme alato
- *seed with wing (winged seed)*
**10** il seme [sezione *f* longitudinale]
- *seed [longitudinal section]*
**11** l'ago dell'abete *m* bianco (l'ago)
- *fir needle (needle)*
**12** l'abete *m* rosso
- *spruce (spruce fir)*
**13** la pigna (il cono dell'abete *m* rosso)
- *spruce cone*
**14** la squama del cono (la squama fruttifera)
- *cone scale*
**15** il seme
- *seed*
**16** il cono femminile maturo
- *female flower cone*
**17** il cono maschile con polline *m*
- *male inflorescence*
**18** lo stame
- *stamen*
**19** l'ago dell'abete *m* rosso
- *spruce needle*
**20** il pino silvestre
- *pine (Scots pine)*
**21** il pino mugo
- *dwarf pine*
**22** il cono femminile maturo
- *female flower cone*
**23** il ciuffo di aghi *m pl* appaiati
- *short shoot with bundle of two leaves*
**24** i coni maschili
- *male inflorescences*
**25** il germoglio annuale
- *annual growth*
**26** il cono (la pigna) del pino silvestre
- *pine cone*
**27** la squama del cono (la squama della pigna)
- *cone scale*

**28** il seme
- *seed*
**29** il cono femminile maturo del pino cembro
- *fruit cone of the arolla pine (Swiss stone pine)*
**30** il cono femminile maturo del pino strobo (del pino di Weymouth)
- *fruit cone of the Weymouth pine (white pine)*
**31** il getto corto [sezione *f* trasversale]
- *short shoot [cross section]*
**32** il larice
- *larch*
**33** il ramo fiorito
- *flowering branch*
**34** la squama del cono femminile maturo
- *scale of the female flower cone*
**35** l'antera
- *anther*
**36** il ramo con i coni fruttiferi (con le pigne fruttifere) del larice
- *branch with larch cones (fruit cones)*
**37** il seme
- *seed*
**38** la squama del cono (della pigna)
- *cone scale*
**39** la thuya occidentale
- *arbor vitae (tree of life, thuja)*
**40** il ramo fruttifero
- *fruiting branch*
**41** il cono fruttifero (la pigna fruttifera)
- *fruit cone*
**42** la squama
- *scale*
**43** il rametto con fiori *m pl* maschili e femminili
- *branch with male and female flowers*
**44** l'inflorescenza maschile
- *male shoot*
**45** la squama con antere *f pl*
- *scale with pollen sacs*
**46** l'inflorescenza femminile
- *female shoot*
**47** il ginepro comune
- *juniper (juniper tree)*
**48** l'inflorescenza femminile [sezione *f* longitudinale]
- *female shoot [longitudinal section]*
**49** l'inflorescenza maschile
- *male shoot*
**50** la squama con antere *f pl*
- *scale with pollen sacs*
**51** il rametto col frutto
- *fruiting branch*
**52** le bacche di ginepro (i coni femminili maturi)
- *juniper berry*
**53** il frutto [sezione *f* trasversale]
- *fruit [cross section]*

**54** il seme
- *seed*
**55** il pino a ombrello (il pino domestico)
- *stone pine*
**56** l'inflorescenza maschile
- *male shoot*
**57** il cono fruttifero [la pigna fruttifera] con seme *m*
- *fruit cone with seeds [longitudinal section]*
**58** il cipresso
- *cypress*
**59** il ramo fruttifero
- *fruiting branch*
**60** il seme
- *seed*
**61** il tasso
- *yew (yew tree)*
**62** l'inflorescenza maschile e il cono (la pigna, la bacca) femminile maturo
- *male flower shoot and female flower cone*
**63** il ramo con frutti *m pl*
- *fruiting branch*
**64** il frutto
- *fruit*
**65** il cedro
- *cedar (cedar tree)*
**66** il ramo fruttifero
- *fruiting branch*
**67** la squama fruttifera
- *fruit scale*
**68** l'inflorescenza maschile e il cono (la pigna) femminile maturo
- *male flower shoot and female flower cone*
**69** la sequoia
- *mammoth tree (Wellingtonia, sequoia)*
**70** il ramo fruttifero
- *fruiting branch*
**71** il seme
- *seed*

1 la forsythia
– *forsythia*
2 l'ovario e lo stame
– *ovary and stamen*
3 la foglia
– *leaf*
4 il gelsomino con fiori *m pl* gialli
– *yellow-flowered jasmine (jasmin, jessamine)*
5 il fiore [sezione *f* longitudinale] con stilo, ovario e stami *m pl*
– *flower [longitudinal section] with styles, ovaries, and stamens*
6 il ligustro
– *privet (common privet)*
7 il fiore
– *flower*
8 l'inflorescenza
– *infructescence*
9 il fior di angelo (il fiorangiolo)
– *mock orange (sweet syringa)*
10 il pallone di Maggio (il viburno)
– *snowball (snowball bush, guelder rose)*
11 il fiore
– *flower*
12 i frutti *m pl*
– *fruits*
13 l'oleandro
– *oleander (rosebay, rose laurel)*
14 il fiore [sezione *f* longitudinale]
– *flower [longitudinal section]*
15 la magnolia rossa
– *red magnolia*
16 la foglia
– *leaf*
17 il cotogno del Giappone
– *japonica (japanese quince)*
18 il frutto
– *fruit*
19 il bosso
– *common box (box, box tree)*
20 il fiore femminile
– *female flower*
21 il fiore maschile
– *male flower*
22 il frutto [sezione *f* longitudinale]
– *fruit [longitudinal section]*
23 la weigela
– *weigela (weigelia)*
24 la yucca (la iucca) [parte *f* dell'inflorescenza]
– *yucca [part of the inflorescence]*
25 la foglia
– *leaf*
26 la rosa canina
– *dog rose (briar rose, wild briar)*
27 il frutto
– *fruit*
28 la spirea ulmaria (la filipendula ulmaria)
– *kerria*
29 il frutto
– *fruit*

30 il corniolo
– *cornelian cherry*
31 il fiore
– *flower*
32 il frutto (la corniola)
– *fruit (cornelian cherry)*
33 la mortella di Brabante (il mirto di Brabante)
– *sweet gale (gale)*

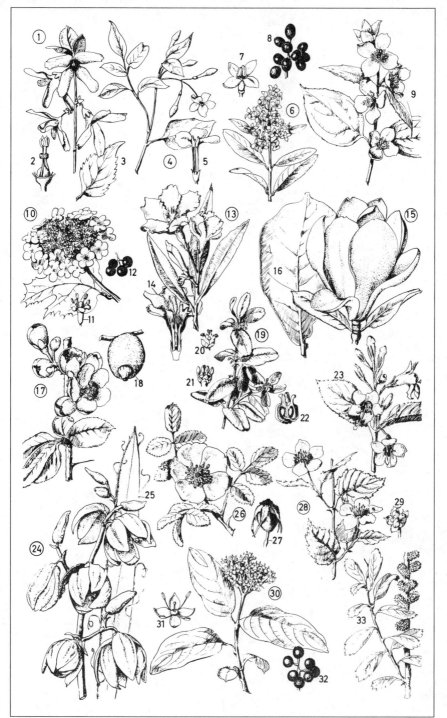

**1** la tulpifera (il liriodendro)
– *tulip tree (tulip poplar, saddle tree, whitewood)*
**2** i carpelli
– *carpels*
**3** lo stame
– *stamen*
**4** il frutto
– *fruit*
**5** l'issopo
– *hyssop*
**6** il fiore [visto anteriormente]
– *flower [front view]*
**7** il fiore
– *flower*
**8** il calice con frutto
– *calyx with fruit*
**9** l'agrifoglio
– *holly*
**10** il fiore ermafrodito (il fiore androgino)
– *androgynous (hermaphroditic, hermaphrodite) flower*
**11** il fiore maschile
– *male flower*
**12** il frutto con semi *m pl*
– *fruit with stones exposed*
**13** il caprifoglio (l'abbracciabosco, la madreselva, il vincibosco)
– *honeysuckle (woodbine, woodbind)*
**14** il bocciolo
– *flower buds*
**15** il fiore [sezione *f*]
– *flower [cut open]*
**16** la vite vergine (la vite del Canada)
– *Virginia creeper (American ivy, woodbine)*
**17** il fiore aperto
– *open flower*
**18** l'infruttescenza
– *infructescence*
**19** il frutto [sezione *f* longitudinale]
– *fruit [longitudinal section]*
**20** la ginestra dei carbonai
– *broom*
**21** il fiore dopo la rimozione *f* dei petali
– *flower with the petals removed*
**22** il baccello acerbo
– *immature (unripe) legume (pod)*
**23** la spirea
– *spiraea*
**24** il fiore [sezione *f* longitudinale]
– *flower [longitudinal section]*
**25** il frutto
– *fruit*
**26** il carpello
– *carpel*
**27** il prugnolo
– *blackthorn (sloe)*
**28** le foglie
– *leaves*
**29** i frutti
– *fruits*
**30** il biancospino dei boschi (il biancospino selvaggio)
– *single-pistilled hawthorn (thorn, may)*
**31** il frutto
– *fruit*
**32** il citiso (il maggiociondolo)
– *laburnum (golden chain, golden rain)*
**33** il grappolo di fiori *m pl*
– *raceme*
**34** i frutti
– *fruits*
**35** il sambuco
– *black elder (elder)*
**36** i fiori di sambuco, cime piane *f pl*
– *elder flowers*
**37** le bacche del sambuco
– *elderberries*

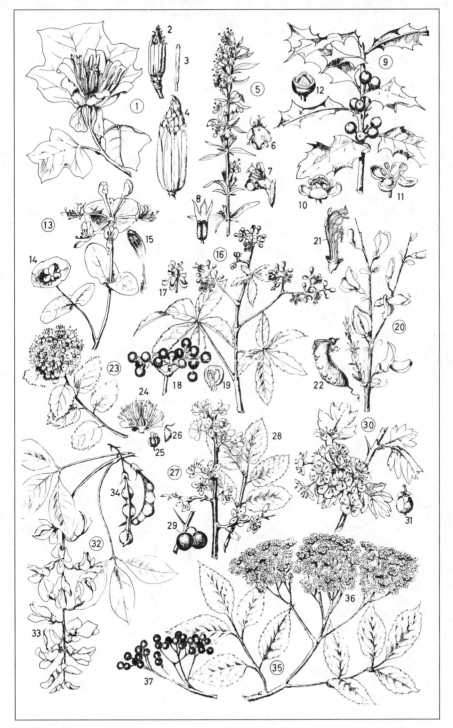

# 375 Fiori dei prati e dei campi I

1 la sassifraga granulata
– *rotundifoliate (rotundifolious) saxifrage (rotundifoliate break-stone)*
2 la foglia
– *leaf*
3 il fiore
– *flower*
4 il frutto
– *fruit*
5 l'anemone *m*
– *anemone (windflower)*
6 il fiore [sezione *f* longitudinale]
– *flower [longitudinal section]*
7 il frutto
– *fruit*
8 il ranuncolo (il botton d'oro)
– *buttercup (meadow buttercup, but-terflower, goldcup, king cup, crowfoot)*
9 la foglia basale
– *basal leaf*
10 il frutto
– *fruit*
11 il billeri dei prati
– *lady's smock (ladysmock, cuckoo flower)*
12 la foglia caulina
– *basal leaf*
13 il frutto (la siliqua)
– *fruit*
14 la campanula aperta
– *harebell (hairbell, bluebell)*
15 la foglia basale
– *basal leaf*
16 il fiore (sezione *f* longitudinale)
– *flower [longitudinal section]*
17 il frutto
– *fruit*
18 l'edera terrestre (glechoma hed-eracea)
– *ground ivy (ale hoof )*
19 il fiore (sezione *f* longitudinale)
– *flower [longitudinal section]*
20 il fiore (visto frontalmente)
– *flower [front view]*
21 la borracina
– *stonecrop*
22 la veronica maggiore
– *speedwell*
23 il fiore
– *flower*
24 il frutto
– *fruit*
25 il seme
– *seed*
26 la lisimachia (la nummalaria, la mazza d'oro)
– *moneywort*
27 la capsula (la cassula) deiscente
– *dehisced fruit*
28 il seme
– *seed*
29 la scabiosa (la scabbiosa)
– *small scabious*
30 la foglia basale
– *basal leaf*
31 il fiore periferico
– *ray floret (flower of outer series)*
32 il fiore interno
– *disc (disk) floret (flower of inner series)*
33 il calice con ariste *f pl*
– *involucral calyx with pappus bris-tles*
34 l'ovario aderente (l'ovario con calice *m*)
– *ovary with pappus*
35 il frutto
– *fruit*
36 il favagello
– *lesser celandine*
37 il frutto
– *fruit*
38 l'ascella della foglia con gemme *f pl* riproduttive
– *leaf axil with bulbil*
39 la gramigna dei prati
– *annual meadow grass*
40 il fiore
– *flower*
41 la spiga (la pannocchia) (vista lat-eralmente)
– *spikelet [side view]*
42 la spiga (la pannocchia) (vista frontalmente)
– *spikelet [front view]*
43 la cariosside
– *caryopsis, an indehiscent fruit*
44 il ciuffo di erba
– *tuft of grass (clump of grass)*
45 la consolida maggiore
– *comfrey*
46 il fiore (sezione *f* longitudinale)
– *flower [longitudinal section]*
47 il frutto
– *fruit*

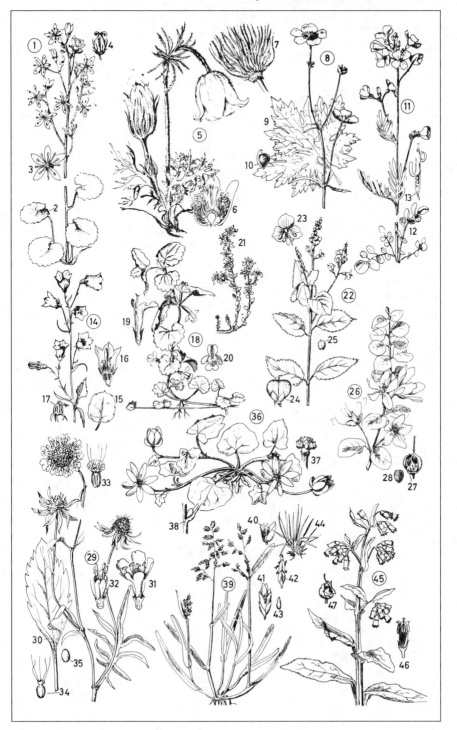

1 la margheritina (la pratolina)
– *daisy (*Am. *English daisy)*
2 il fiore
– *flower*
3 il frutto (l'achenio)
– *fruit*
4 la margherita
– *oxeye daisy (white oxeye daisy, marguerite)*
5 il fiore
– *flower*
6 il frutto (l'achenio)
– *fruit*
7 l'astranzia maggiore
– *masterwort*
8 la primavera odorosa (la primula)
– *cowslip*
9 il barabasco (il verbascum phlomoides)
– *great mullein (Aaron's rod, shepherd's club)*
10 la bistorta
– *bistort (snakeweed)*
11 il fiore
– *flower*
12 la centaurea minore (la biondella)
– *knapweed*
13 la malva a foglie *f pl* rotonde
– *common mallow*
14 il frutto (l'achenio)
– *fruit*
15 il millefoglie (l'achillea millefolium)
– *yarrow*
16 la brunella comune
– *self-heal*
17 la ginestrina comune (la trifoglina)
– *bird's foot trefoil (bird's foot clover)*
18 l'equiseto dei campi (un germoglio)
– *horsetail (equisetum) [a shoot]*
19 il fiore
– *flower (strobile)*
20 il licnide bianco
– *campion (catchfly)*
21 il fior del cuculo
– *ragged robin (cuckoo flower)*
22 l'aristolochia (*pop.:* gli strallogi)
– *birthwort*
23 il fiore
– *flower*
24 il geranio sanguigno
– *crane's bill*
25 la cicoria
– *wild chicory (witloof, succory, wild endive)*
26 la stellaria maggiore
– *common toadflax (butter-and-eggs)*
27 la pianella della Madonna
– *lady's slipper (Venus's slipper,* Am. *moccasin flower)*
28 l'orchidea latifoglia (un'orchidea)
– *orchis (wild orchid), an orchid*

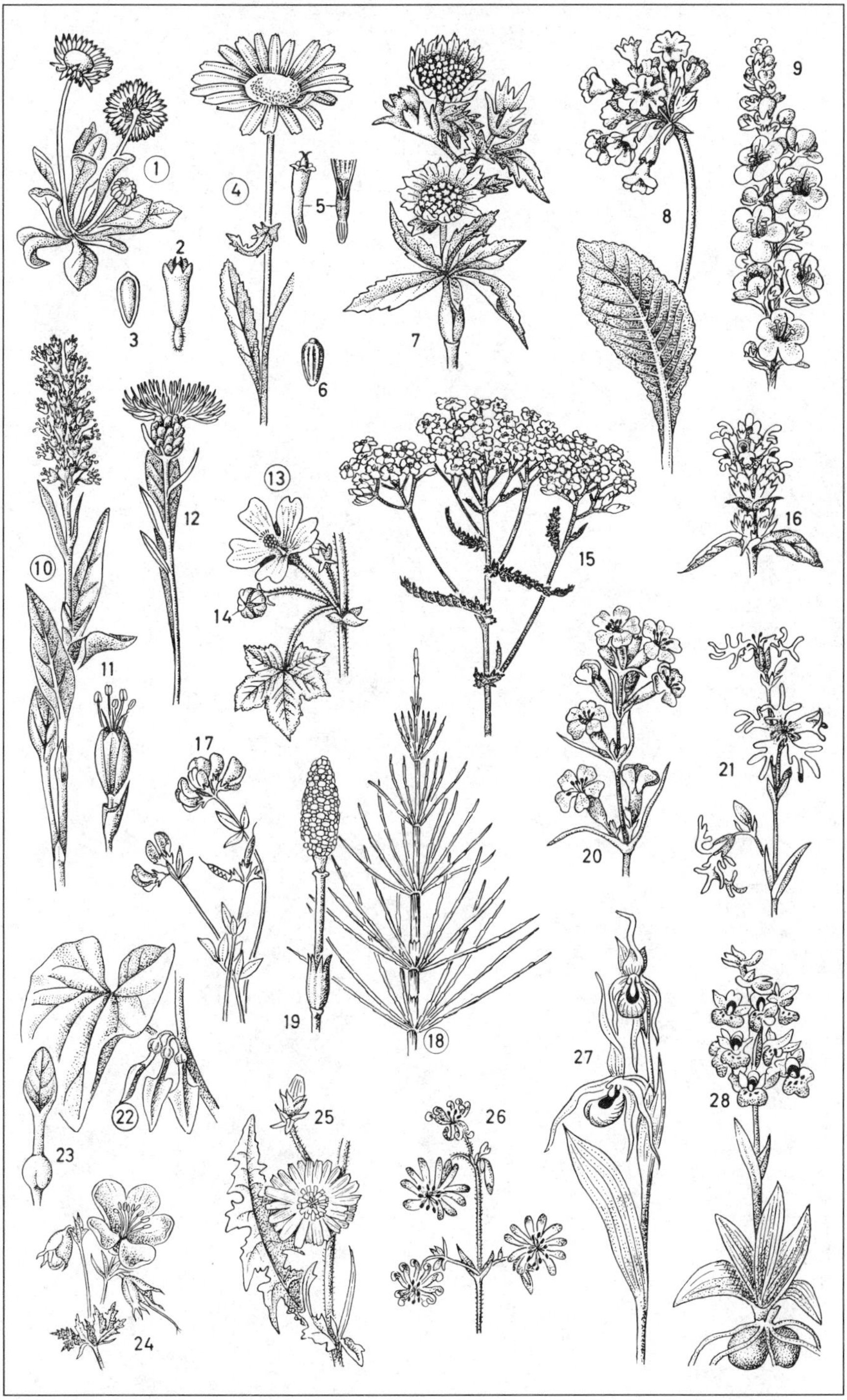
1
2
3
4
5
6
7
8
9
10
11
12
13
14
15
16
17
18
19
20
21
22
23
24
25
26
27
28

# 377 Piante di bosco, di palude e di brughiera

1 l'anemone *m* dei boschi
(l'anemone *m*)
– *wood anemone (anemone, wind-flower)*
2 il mughetto
– *lily of the valley*
3 l'antennaria dioica (la bambagia selvatica)
– *cat's foot (milkwort); sim.: sand-flower (everlasting)*
4 il giglio martagone (il riccio di dama)
– *turk's cap (turk's cap lily)*
5 la barba di capra
– *goatsbeard (goat's beard)*
6 l'aglio orsino
– *ramson*
7 la polmonaria
– *lungwort*
8 la consolida reale
– *corydalis*
9 l'erba di san Giovanni
– *orpine (livelong)*
10 il mezereo
– *daphne*
11 il noli me tangere
– *touch-me-not*
12 il licopodio
– *staghorn (stag horn moss, stag's horn, stag's horn moss, coral ever-green)*
13 la pinguicola comune, una pianta carnivora; *sim.:* il pigliamosche
– *butterwort, an insectivorous plant*
14 la rosolida (la drosera)
– *sundew; sim.: Venus's flytrap*
15 l'uva orsina
– *bearberry*
16 la felce dolce, una felce; *sim.:* felce *f* maschio, felce *f* aquilina, felce *f* imperiale
– *polypody (polypod), a fern; sim.: male fern, brake (bracken, eagle fern), royal fern (royal osmund, king's fern, ditch fern)*
17 il politrico volgare, un muschio
– *haircap moss (hair moss, golden maidenhair), a moss*
18 l'erioforo (il pennacchio)
– *cotton grass (cotton rush)*
19 l'erica; *sim.:* il brugo (il brentolo, la crecchia)
– *heather (heath, ling); sim.: bell heather (cross-leaved heather)*
20 l'eliantemo
– *rock rose (sun rose)*
21 il rosmarino di palude *f*
– *marsh tea*
22 il calamo aromatico
– *sweet flag (sweet calamus, sweet sedge)*

23 il mirtillo nero; *sim.:* il mirtillo rosso
– *bilberry (whortleberry, huckleber-ry, blueberry); sim.: cowberry (red whortleberry), bog bilberry (bog whortleberry), crowberry (crake-berry)*

**1-13 piante** *f pl* **alpine**
– *alpine plants*
1 il rododendro (la rosa delle Alpi)
– *alpine rose (alpine rhododendron)*
2 il ramo fiorito
– *flowering shoot*
3 la soldanella (la soldanella alpina)
– *alpine soldanella (soldanella)*
4 la corolla aperta
– *corolla opened out*
5 la capsula seminale con il pistillo
– *seed vessel with the style*
6 l'artemisia (il genepì)
– *alpine wormwood*
7 l'inflorescenza (l'infiorescenza)
– *inflorescence*
8 l'auricola (la primula auricola)
– *auricula*
9 la stella alpina (l'edelweiss)
– *edelweiss*
10 i tipi di fiori *m pl*
– *flower shapes*
11 il frutto con il pappo (l'achenio)
– *fruit with pappus tuft*
12 la sezione di un capolino
– *part of flower head (of capitulum)*
13 la genziana maggiore
– *stemless alpine gentian*

**14-57 piante** *f pl* **acquatiche e palustri**
– *aquatic plants (water plants) and marsh plants*
14 la ninfea
– *white water lily*
15 la foglia
– *leaf*
16 il fiore
– *flower*
17 la victoria regia
– *Queen Victoria water lily (Victoria regia water lily, royal water lily, Amazon water lily)*
18 la foglia
– *leaf*
19 la pagina inferiore della foglia
– *underside of the leaf*
20 il fiore
– *flower*
21 la stiancia (il biodo)
– *reed mace bulrush (cattail, cat's tail, cattail flag, club rush)*
22 la parte maschile della spiga
– *male part of the spadix*
23 il fiore maschile
– *male flower*
24 la parte femminile
– *female part*
25 il fiore femminile
– *female flower*
26 il non ti scordar di me (il miosotide, il miosotis)
– *forget-me-not*
27 lo stelo fiorito
– *flowering shoot*
28 il fiore [sezione *f* ]
– *flower [section]*

29 l'hydrocharis *f* morsus ranae
– *frog's bit*
30 il nasturzio (il tropeolo)
– *watercress*
31 lo stelo con fiori *m pl* e frutti *m pl* immaturi
– *stalk with flowers and immature (unripe) fruits*
32 il fiore
– *flower*
33 la siliqua con semi *m pl*
– *siliqua (pod) with seeds*
34 due semi *m pl*
– *two seeds*
35 la lenticchia d'acqua (la lemna)
– *duckweed (duck's meat)*
36 la pianta in fiore *m*
– *plant in flower*
37 il fiore
– *flower*
38 il frutto
– *fruit*
39 il giunco fiorito (l'aglio acquatico)
– *flowering rush*
40 l'ombrella fiorita
– *flower umbel*
41 le foglie
– *leaves*
42 il frutto
– *fruit*
43 la lattuga di mare
– *green alga*
44 la piantaggine d'acqua
– *water plantain*
45 la foglia
– *leaf*
46 l'inflorescenza (la pannocchia fiorita)
– *panicle*
47 il fiore
– *flower*
48 la laminaria, un'alga bruna
– *honey wrack, a brown alga*
49 il tallo
– *thallus (plant body, frond)*
50 il rizoide
– *holdfast*
51 l'erba saetta
– *arrow head*
52 le forme delle foglie
– *leaf shapes*
53 l'inflorescenza con fiori *m pl* maschili [in alto] e fiori *m pl* femminili [in basso]
– *inflorescence with male flowers [above] and female flowers [below]*
54 la zostera marina
– *sea grass*
55 l'inflorescenza
– *inflorescence*
56 la peste d'acqua (l'elodea)
– *Canadian waterweed (Canadian pondweed)*
57 il fiore
– *flower*

**1** l'aconito (il napello)
– *aconite (monkshood, wolfsbane, helmet flower)*
**2** la digitale
– *foxglove (Digitalis)*
**3** il colchico (la freddolina, lo zafferano bastardo)
– *meadow saffron (naked lady, naked boys)*
**4** la cicuta
– *hemlock (Conium)*
**5** l'erba morella
– *black nightshade (common nightshade, petty morel)*
**6** il giusquiamo
– *henbane*
**7** la belladonna, una solanacea
– *deadly nightshade (belladonna, banewort, dwale), a solanaceous herb*
**8** lo stramonio
– *thorn apple (stramonium, stramony,* Am. *jimson weed, jimpson weed, Jamestown weed, stinkweed)*
**9** il gigaro (l'aro, il piè vitellino)
– *cuckoo pint (lords-and-ladies, wild arum, wake-robin)*
**10-13** funghi *m pl* velenosi
– *poisonous fungi (poisonous mushrooms, toadstools)*
**10** l'ovolo malefico (l'ovolaccio), un fungo a lamelle *f pl*
– *fly agaric (fly amanita, fly fungus), an agaric*
**11** la tignosa verdognola
– *amanita*
**12** il porcino malefico (il boleto malefico)
– *Satan's mushroom*
**13** l'agarico torminoso (lactarius *m* torminosus)
– *woolly milk cap*

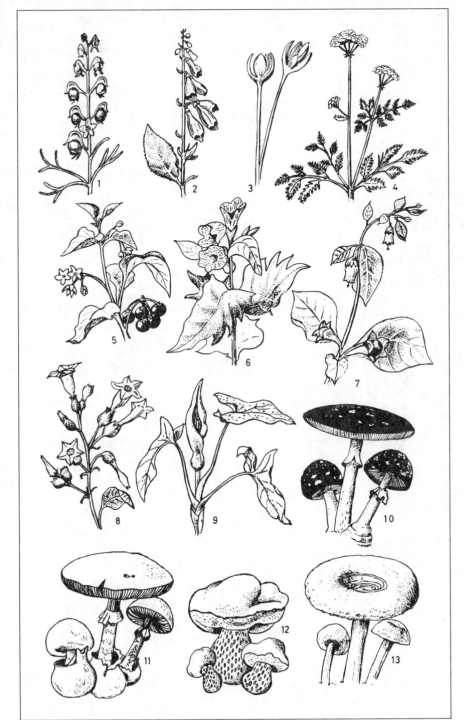

1 la camomilla
- *camomile (chamomile, wild camomile)*
2 l'arnica
- *arnica*
3 la menta piperita
- *peppermint*
4 l'assenzio
- *wormwood (absinth)*
5 la valeriana
- *valerian (allheal)*
6 il finocchio
- *fennel*
7 la lavanda
- *lavender*
8 il farfaro
- *coltsfoot*
9 il tanaceto
- *tansy*
10 la centaurea minore
- *centaury*
11 la piantaggine
- *ribwort (ribwort plantain, ribgrass)*
12 l'altea (la bismalva, il malvaccione)
- *marshmallow*
13 la frangola (l'alno nero)
- *alder buckthorn (alder dogwood)*
14 il ricino
- *castor-oil plant (Palma Christi)*
15 il papavero da oppio
- *opium poppy*
16 la sena (la cassia); *le foglie seccate:* foglie *f pl* di sena
- *senna (cassia); the dried leaflets: senna leaves*
17 la china
- *cinchona (chinchona)*
18 la canfora
- *camphor tree (camphor laurel)*
19 la pianta del betel
- *betel palm (areca, areca palm)*
20 la noce di betel
- *betel nut (areca nut)*

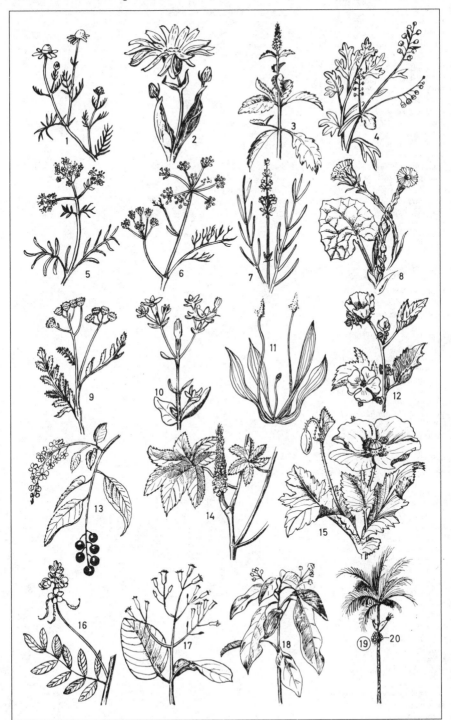

1 il fungo prataiolo
– *meadow mushroom (field mushroom)*
2 il micelio con corpi *m pl* fruttiferi (con funghi *m pl*)
– *mycelial threads (hyphae, mycelium) with fruiting bodies*
3 fungo [sezione *f sing.* longitudinale]
– *mushroom [longitudinal section]*
4 il cappello con lamelle *f pl*
– *cap (pileus) with gills*
5 il velo del fungo
– *veil (velum)*
6 la lamella [sezione *f sing.*]
– *gill [section]*
7 i basidi (*sing.* basidio) (del bordo delle lamelle con basidiospore *f pl*)
– *basidia [on the gill with basidiospores]*
8 le spore germinanti
– *germinating basidiospores (spores)*
9 il tartufo
– *truffle*
10 il tartufo (visto dall'esterno)
– *truffle [external view]*
11 il tartufo (sezione *f*)
– *truffle [section]*
12 interno con gli aschi contenenti le ascospore (sezione *f*)
– *interior showing asci [section]*
13 due aschi *m pl* con le ascospore
– *two asci with the ascospores (spores)*
14 il gallinaccio
– *chanterelle (chantarelle)*
15 il boleto dei castagni
– *Chestnut Boletus*
16 il porcino (il boleto edule; *regionale:* ceppatello)
– *cep (cepe, squirrel's bread, Boletus edulis)*
17 lo strato dei tubuli
– *layer of tubes (hymenium)*
18 il gambo
– *stem (stipe)*
19 la vescia
– *puffball (Bovista nigrescens)*
20 la vescia maggiore
– *devil's tobacco pouch (common puffball)*
21 il prataiolo (il pratolino)
– *Brown Ring Boletus (Boletus luteus)*
22 il porcinello
– *Birch Boletus (Boletus scaber)*
23 l'agarico delizioso
– *Russula vesca*
24 lo steccherino bruno
– *scaled prickle fungus*
25 la spugnola bastarda (il gallinaccio squamoso)
– *slender funnel fungus*

26 la spugnola rotonda (la morchella)
– *morel (Morchella esculenta)*
27 la spugnola conica
– *morel (Morchella conica)*
28 i chiodini (la famigliola buona)
– *honey fungus*
29 il verdone
– *saffron milk cap*
30 la mazza di tamburo (la bubbola maggiore)
– *parasol mushroom*
31 lo steccherino dorato
– *hedgehog fungus (yellow prickle fungus)*
32 la clavaria; *pop.:* la ditola, la manina
– *yellow coral fungus (goatsbeard, goat's beard, coral Clavaria)*
33 l'agarico cangiante (la famigliola gialla)
– *little cluster fungus*

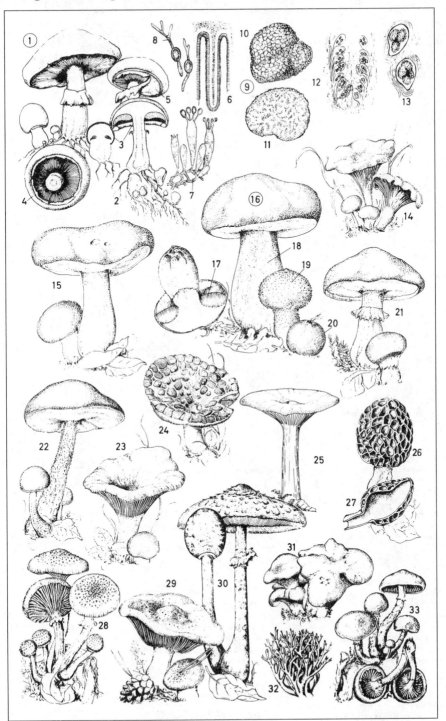

1 l'arbusto del caffé
- *coffee tree (coffee plant)*
2 il ramo con frutto
- *fruiting branch*
3 il ramo fiorito
- *flowering branch*
4 il fiore
- *flower*
5 il frutto con i due semi (chicchi *m pl*) [sezione *f* longitudinale]
- *fruit with two beans [longitudinal section]*
6 il chicco di caffé *m; dopo la lavorazione:* il caffé
- *coffee bean; when processed: coffee*
7 la pianta del té
- *tea plant (tea tree)*
8 il ramo fiorito
- *flowering branch*
9 la foglia del té; *dopo la lavorazione:* il té
- *tea leaf; when processed: tea*
10 il frutto
- *fruit*
11 l'albero del mate (*sim.:* il té del Paraguay)
- *maté shrub (maté, yerba maté, Paraguay tea)*
12 il ramo fiorito con i fiori ermafroditi
- *flowering branch with androgynous (hermaphroditic, hermaphrodite) flowers*
13 il fiore maschio
- *male flower*
14 il fiore ermafrodito
- *androgynous (hermaphroditic, hermaphrodite) flower*
15 il frutto
- *fruit*
16 l'albero del cacao
- *cacao tree (cacao)*
17 il ramo con fiori *m pl* e frutti *m pl*
- *branch with flowers and fruits*
18 il fiore [sezione *f* longitudinale]
- *flower [longitudinal section]*
19 i semi del cacao; *dopo la lavorazione:* il cacao, il cacao in polvere *f*
- *cacao beans (cocoa beans); when processed: cocoa, cocoa powder*
20 il seme [sezione *f* longitudinale]
- *seed [longitudinal section]*
21 l'embrione *m*
- *embryo*
22 la pianta di cannella
- *cinnamon tree (cinnamon)*
23 il ramo fiorito
- *flowering branch*
24 il frutto
- *fruit*
25 la scorza di cannella; *in polvere:* la cannella
- *cinnamon bark; when crushed: cinnamon*

26 la pianta del garofano
- *clove tree*
27 il ramo fiorito
- *flowering branch*
28 il boccio florale; *essiccato:* il chiodo di garofano
- *flower bud; when dried: clove*
29 il fiore
- *flower*
30 l'albero della noce moscata
- *nutmeg tree*
31 il ramo fiorito
- *flowering branch*
32 il fiore femminile [sezione *f* longitudinale]
- *female flower [longitudinal section]*
33 il frutto maturo
- *mature (ripe) fruit*
34 il seme della noce moscata, un seme con polpa avvolgente intagliata (macis)
- *nutmeg with mace, a seed with laciniate aril*
35 il seme [sezione *f* trasversale]; *essiccato:* la noce moscata
- *seed [cross section]; when dried: nutmeg*
36 l'arbusto del pepe
- *pepper plant*
37 il ramo fiorito
- *fruiting branch*
38 l'inflorescenza
- *inflorescence*
39 il frutto [sezione *f* longitudinale] con semi *m pl* (grani *m pl* di pepe *m*); *macinato:* il pepe
- *fruit [longitudinal section] with seed (peppercorn); when ground: pepper*
40 la pianta di tabacco della Virginia
- *Virginia tobacco plant*
41 il ramo fiorito
- *flowering shoot*
42 il fiore
- *flower*
43 la foglia di tabacco; *conciato:* il tabacco
- *tobacco leaf; when cured: tobacco*
44 il frutto maturo (la capsula matura)
- *mature (ripe) fruit capsule*
45 il seme
- *seed*
46 la pianta di vaniglia
- *vanilla plant*
47 il ramo fiorito
- *flowering shoot*
48 il baccello di vaniglia; *dopo la lavorazione:* la stecca di vaniglia
- *vanilla pod; when cured: stick of vanilla*
49 l'albero del pistacchio
- *pistachio tree*
50 il ramo fiorito coi fiori femminili
- *flowering branch with female flowers*

51 il pistacchio
- *drupe (pistachio, pistachio nut)*
52 la canna da zucchero
- *sugar cane*
53 la pianta durante la fioritura
- *plant (habit) in bloom*
54 l'inflorescenza a pannocchia
- *panicle*
55 il fiore
- *flower*

1 la colza
– *rape (cole, coleseed)*
2 la foglia caulinare
– *basal leaf*
3 il fiore [sezione *f* longitudinale]
– *flower [longitudinal section]*
4 la siliqua (il frutto maturo)
– *mature (ripe) siliqua (pod)*
5 il seme oleoso
– *oleiferous seed*
6 il lino
– *flax*
7 il ramo fiorito
– *peduncle (pedicel, flower stalk)*
8 la capsula
– *seed vessel (boll)*
9 la canapa
– *hemp*
10 la pianta femminile con frutto
– *fruiting female (pistillate) plant*
11 l'inflorescenza femminile
– *female inflorescence*
12 il fiore
– *flower*
13 l'inflorescenza maschile
– *male inflorescence*
14 il frutto
– *fruit*
15 il seme
– *seed*
16 il cotone (la pianta del cotone)
– *cotton*
17 il fiore
– *flower*
18 il frutto (la capsula aperta)
– *fruit*
19 la peluria (il cotone)
– *lint [cotton wool]*
20 il kapok (la pianta del kapok)
– *silk-cotton tree (kapok tree, capoc tree, ceiba tree)*
21 il frutto (la capsula)
– *fruit*
22 il ramo fiorito
– *flowering branch*
23 il seme
– *seed*
24 il seme [sezione *f* longitudinale]
– *seed [longitudinal section]*
25 la iuta
– *jute*
26 il ramo fiorito
– *flowering branch*
27 il fiore
– *flower*
28 il frutto
– *fruit*
29 l'olivo
– *olive tree (olive)*
30 il ramo fiorito
– *flowering branch*
31 il fiore
– *flower*
32 il frutto
– *fruit*

33 l'albero della gomma
– *rubber tree (rubber plant)*
34 il ramo con frutti *m pl*
– *fruiting branch*
35 il siconio (il fico)
– *fig*
36 il fiore
– *flower*
37 l'albero della guttaperca
– *gutta-percha tree*
38 il ramo fiorito
– *flowering branch*
39 il fiore
– *flower*
40 il frutto
– *fruit*
41 l'arachide *f*
– *peanut (ground nut, monkey nut)*
42 il ramo fiorito
– *flowering shoot*
43 la radice con frutti *m pl*
– *root with fruits*
44 il frutto [sezione *f* longitudinale]
– *nut (kernel) [longitudinal section]*
45 la pianta di sesamo (il sesamo)
– *sesame plant (simsim, benniseed)*
46 il ramo con fiori *m pl* e frutti *m pl*
– *flowers and fruiting branch*
47 il fiore [sezione *f* longitudinale]
– *flower [longitudinal section]*
48 la palma da cocco (il cocco)
– *coconut palm (coconut tree, coco palm, cocoa palm)*
49 l'inflorescenza
– *inflorescence*
50 il fiore femminile
– *female flower*
51 il fiore maschile [sezione *f* longi-tudinale]
– *male flower [longitudinal section]*
52 il frutto [sezione *f* longitudinale]
– *fruit [longitudinal section]*
53 la noce di cocco
– *coconut (cokernut)*
54 la palma da olio
– *oil palm*
55 lo spadice maschile con fiore *m*
– *male spadix*
56 l'infruttescenza con frutto
– *infructescence with fruit*
57 il seme con i fiori germinativi
– *seed with micropyles (foramina) (foraminate seed)*
58 la palma del sagù
– *sago palm*
59 il frutto
– *fruit*
60 la canna di bambù *m*
– *bamboo stem (bamboo culm)*
61 il ramo con le foglie
– *branch with leaves*
62 l'inflorescenza a pannocchia
– *spike*
63 la canna con nodi *m pl*
– *part of bamboo stem with joints*

64 il papiro
– *papyrus plant (paper reed, paper rush)*
65 l'inflorescenza in spiga
– *umbel*
66 l'inflorescenza a pannocchia
– *spike*

1 la palma da datteri *m pl*
– *date palm (date)*
2 la palma in frutto
– *fruiting palm*
3 il ramo di palma
– *palm frond*
4 l'inflorescenza a spadice *m* maschile
– *male spadix*
5 il fiore maschile
– *male flower*
6 l'inflorescenza a spadice *m* femminile
– *female spadix*
7 il fiore femminile
– *female flower*
8 l'infruttescenza
– *stand of fruit*
9 il dattero
– *date*
10 il seme del dattero
– *date kernel*
11 il fico
– *fig*
12 il ramo con siconi (*sing.* sicionio)
– *branch with pseudocarps*
13 il fico in fiore *m* [sezione *f* longitudinale]
– *fig with flowers [longitudinal section]*
14 il fiore femminile
– *female flower*
15 il fiore maschile
– *male flower*
16 il melograno
– *pomegranate*
17 il ramo in fiore *m*
– *flowering branch*
18 il fiore [sezione *f* longitudinale senza corolla]
– *flower [longitudinal section, corolla removed]*
19 il frutto
– *fruit*
20 il seme [sezione *f* longitudinale]
– *seed [longitudinal section]*
21 il seme [sezione *f* trasversale]
– *seed [cross section]*
22 l'embrione *m*
– *embryo*
23 il limone; *sim.:* mandarino, arancia, pompelmo
– *lemon; sim.: tangerine (mandarin), orange, grapefruit*
24 il ramo in fiore *m*
– *flowering branch*
25 il fiore di arancio [sezione *f* longitudinale]
– *orange flower [longitudinal section]*
26 il frutto
– *fruit*
27 l'arancia [sezione *f* trasversale]
– *orange [cross section]*

28 il banano
– *banana plant (banana tree)*
29 la corona del banano
– *crown*
30 il pseudotronco con foglie *f pl* inguainanti
– *herbaceous stalk with overlapping leaf sheaths*
31 l'inflorescenza con frutti giovani
– *inflorescence with young fruits*
32 il casco (l'infruttescenza)
– *infructescence (bunch of fruit)*
33 la banana
– *banana*
34 il fiore del banano
– *banana flower*
35 la foglia del banano [schema]
– *banana leaf [diagram]*
36 la mandorla
– *almond*
37 il ramo fiorito
– *flowering branch*
38 il ramo con frutti *m pl*
– *fruiting branch*
39 il frutto
– *fruit*
40 il nocciolo con il seme (la mandorla)
– *drupe containing seed [almond]*
41 il carrubo
– *carob*
42 il ramo con fiori *m pl* femminili
– *branch with female flowers*
43 il fiore femminile
– *female flower*
44 il fiore maschile
– *male flower*
45 il frutto
– *fruit*
46 il baccello [sezione *f* trasversale]
– *siliqua (pod) [cross section]*
47 il seme
– *seed*
48 il castagno
– *sweet chestnut (Spanish chestnut)*
49 il ramo fiorito
– *flowering branch*
50 l'inflorescenza femminile
– *female inflorescence*
51 l'inflorescenza maschile
– *male flower*
52 il riccio con i semi (le castagne, i marroni)
– *cupule, containing seeds*
53 la noce del Brasile
– *Brazil nut*
54 il ramo fiorito
– *flowering branch*
55 la foglia
– *leaf*
56 il fiore [visto dall'alto]
– *flower [from above]*
57 il fiore [sezione *f* longitudinale]
– *flower [longitudinal section]*

58 la cassula aperta con semi *m pl*
– *opened capsule, containing seeds*
59 la noce del Brasile [sezione *f* trasversale]
– *Brazil nut [cross section]*
60 la noce [sezione *f* longitudinale]
– *nut [longitudinal section]*
61 la pianta dell'ananas *m* (l'ananas, ant.: ananasso)
– *pineapple plant (pineapple)*
62 lo scapo con la rosetta di foglie *f pl*
– *pseudocarp with crown of leaves*
63 la spiga
– *syncarp*
64 il fiore dell'ananas
– *pineapple flower*
65 il fiore [sezione *f* longitudinale]
– *flower [longitudinal section]*

# Indice alfabetico

Per la consultazione del seguente indice si tenga presente che i numeri in neretto rimandano a quelli che contraddistinguono le tavole figurate, in testa alle pagine.

Il segno ~ indica ripetizione del nome che precede nell'ordine alfabetico. Quando necessario, è indicato il campo al quale un sostantivo appartiene. A tale scopo è usato il carattere corsivo con le abbreviazioni che elenchiamo.

capestro 322 5
capezzale 43 11
capezzolo 16 28; 75 19
capidoglio 367 25
capirosso 360 1
capitale 345 7
capitano 224 38
capitello Legatura 183 35;
 185 42
~ Arte 334 20-25
~ a dado 335 21
~ a forma di calice 333 16
~ a germogli di loto 333
 14
~ a palmette 333 25
~ arabo 337 18
~ composito 333 28
capo Anat. 16 1-18; 17
 42-55
~ Insetti 82 2
~ Artopodi 358 28
~ caccia 289 45
~ caricatore 206 29
~ ciurma 218 47
~ indiano 352 11
capocantiniere 79 17
capocchia di zolfo 107 23
capocollo 96 9
capocordata 300 25
capodoglio 367 25
capolino 61 14; 370 73
~ globoso 370 75
capomacchina 316 45
caporeparto 271 60
caposquadra 270 36
capostazione 205 41
capotasto superiore 323 20
capote Forze armate 257 4
~ Remare 283 57
~ richiusa 193 16
capoverso 175 16
capovoga 283 12
capovolta 308 43
~ al suolo 297 19
cappa Fabbro 137 7
~ Fabbr. della carta 173 27
~ Costumi 355 29
~ aspirante 39 17; 46 31
~ calda 74 3
~ filettata 127 35
~ rossa 319 27
~ termica 182 5
cappella Carta 15 61
~ Aeroporto 233 49
~ Cav. 329 29
~ commemorativa 331 12
~ del cimitero 331 28
~ laterale 335 3
cappellaccia 361 19
cappelleria 268 38
cappelli da uomo 35 22-40
~ e berretti per signora 35
 1-21
cappelliera 205 11
cappello Copricapi 35 7
~ Salvataggio 228 5
~ Strum. mus. 326 31
~ a cilindro 186 25
~ a larghe falde 35 38
~ a soffietto 35 36
~ a sporta 355 71

~ con lamelle 381 4
~ da cowboy 319 37
~ da donna 41 11
~ da moschettiere 355 55
~ da sole 29 16
~ da spiaggia 280 20
~ dei tubi lanciasiluri 259
 78
~ del matador 319 29
~ della Tessaglia 355 4
~ di banco 190 22
~ di carta 306 45
~ di feltro 35 15
~ di feltro di crine 35 24
~ di lana mohair 35 6
~ di loden 35 23
~ di paglia 35 16
~ di paglia di Firenze 35
 21
~ di tela cerata 35 30
~ di visone 35 18
~ estivo 35 37
~ maschile nastro canneté
 35 13
~ maschile nastro lavor-
 ato 35 14
~ piumato 355 55
~ pulitore 164 22
~ rotondo del picador 319
 20
~ svedese 355 55
capperi 98 42
cappio di appiglio 300 11
~ di appiglio per la discesa
 300 28
cappone 73 21
cappottatura del rullo 133
 32
cappotto 29 54; 271 41
~ di panno 30 61; 33 66
~ invernale 30 61
cappuccina 53 4
cappuccio Abb. 30 69
~ Ufficio 151 40
~ Alpinismo 300 19
~ Chiesa 331 56
~ del calcio 305 46
~ del falcone 86 44
~ della giacca a vento 300
 19
~ sbottonabile 31 21
capra 73 14
capriata 121 46, 52, 65
~ a padiglione 121 60
~ a parete piena 121 72
~ a traliccio 121 78
~ con (a) controcatena
 121 34
~ con arcarecci 121 42
~ del tetto 120 7
capriate in legno 121 27-83
Capricorno 3 36; 4 62
caprifoglio 374 13
caprinella 61 30
capriola 71 5
~ giovane senza corna 88
 34
~ vecchia non pregna 88
 34
caprioletta 88 39
caprioletto 88 39

capriolo 86 17; 88 28-39
~ femmina 88 34
~ giovane 88 39
~ maschio 88 28
caprolattame 170 28
capstan 117 34
capsula Erbe 61 5
~ Fabbr. della carta 173 7
~ Viaggi spaziali 234 65
~ Bot 370 94; 375 27; 383
 8, 21
~ aperta 383 18
~ «Apollo» 234 1, 2
~ dei campioni 161 2
~ del cotone 163 1
~ di metallo 166 31
~ di porcellana per l'evaporazione 350 29
~ fulminante 87 59
~ matura 382 44
~ per pistola giocattolo
 306 49
~ seminale con il pistillo
 378 5
~ spaziale 6 9
capsule 94 5
caradriformi 359 19-21
caraffa 79 15
~ del vino 266 32
~ thermos 40 5
carambola 277 7
caramella 98 75
~ al latte 98 77
caramelle 47 31
carapace 364 29
carattere 175 38; 249 29
~ classico 342 6
~ corsivo 175 7
~ dattilografico 342 9
~ egiziano 342 8
~ gotico 342 1
~ grottesco 342 7
~ inglese 342 10
~ latino 342 12
~ magro 175 8
~ maiuscolo 175 11
~ minuscolo 175 12
~ neretto 175 3
~ nerissimo 175 9
~ nero 175 2
~ nero stretto 175 10
~ preclassico 342 5
~ romano rinascimentale
 342 4
~ schwabach 342 2
~ tedesco 342 11
caratteri 174 7; 342 1-15
~ di scatola 342 44
~ mobili fusi 174 44
caratteristica 345 6
caravella 218 27-43
~ «Santa Maria» 220 37
carbon fossile 170 1
carbon cino 338 16
carbone attivo 270 58
~ di legna 278 48
~ negativo 312 41
~ positivo 312 40
carbonella 278 48
çarbonera 219 24

carbriolet a un cavallo 186
 29
carburante 188 10
~ Diesel 145 56; 196 1
carburatore 189 4; 192 1-15
~ esterno 190 79
~ invertito 192 1-15
carcere sotterraneo 329 5
carciofo 57 41
carda 163 34
~ a cappelli 163 34
cardamo del propulsore 6
 36
cardellino 360 1
cardias 20 41
cardigan 31 50
cardinale 363 5
cardo 61 32
~ asinino 61 32
~ selvatico 61 32
cardone 61 32
Carena 3 46
carena piatta 222 49
cariatide 334 36
carica di pallini 87 51
~ di polvere 87 57
caricaballe idraulico 63 37
caricamento 147 51; 176 17
~ automatico 110 24-35
~ dei dischetti 176 17
caricatore Ospedale 25 51
~ Caccia 87 17
~ Fotogr. 114 7, 15, 17;
 117 45
~ Ufficio 151 38
~ Fornace 159 7
~ Forze armate 255 7, 15
~ Film 313 9
~ a piccolo campo 112 35
~ circolare 114 77
~ del nastro adesivo 247
 27
~ della pistola 264 25
~ pellicola 115 53, 71
~ per la pellicola 116 6
caricatrice-pesatrice 163 33
caricatura 342 53
carico 73 5; 223 77; 226 9
~ container 221 22
~ del coke 156 15
~ di coperta 226 6
~ semovente 226 19
cariofillacea 69 12
cariosside 68 15, 25; 375 43
carne 99 53
~ affumicata 96 1
~ in scatola 98 20
~ macinata 96 16
~ tritata da salsiccia 96 41
carnera 308 27
carni 96 1-4
carnivori 367 11-22; 368
 1-11
Caronte 4 52
carota 57 17
~ di Liegi 57 18
carotide 18 1
carovana dei cammelli
 354 1
carpa 364 4
~ a specchi 364 4

cavaliere *Ufficio* 248 4
~ *Hotel* 267 42
~ *Cav.* 329 67
~ *Lab.* chimico 349 33
~ da rodeo 319 39
~ dell'ordine del Tempio 329 73
~ dell'ordine della Croce 329 72
~ d'Italia 359 19
cavalla 219 24
cavallerizzi acrobati 307 26
cavalletta 89 68; 358 8
~ verde 358 8
cavalletto *Mulini* 91 33
~ *Carp.* 120 18
~ *Idraulico* 126 11
~ *Cestaio* 136 10
~ *Bicicletta* 187 34; 188 51
~ *Ferrovia* 214 29
~ *Pittura* 338 34
~ centrale 189 21
~ da campagna 338 26
~ da studio 338 3
~ da tavolo 115 66
~ del tetto 122 66
~ di manovra a mano 202 17
~ di sostegno 67 2, 7
cavalli di posta 186 43
~ di ricambio 186 43
cavallina 296 17
cavallo *Anim. dom.* 73 2
~ *Carrozze* 186 28
~ *Giochi* 276 11
~ *Ginnastica* 296 1; 297 1
~ a dondolo 47 15
~ alato 327 26
~ ammaestrato 307 30
~ con maniglie 296 5
~ corazzato 319 18
~ da dressage 289 3
~ da salto 289 9
~ da trotto 289 28
~ del circo 307 30
~ della steppa 352 4
~ laterale 186 47
~ marino 327 44
~ pezzato 289 29
~ senza maniglie 296 1; 297 1
~ tra le stanghe 186 46
cavalluccio marino 364 18
cavarighe 174 14
cavatappi 40 18; 45 46
caverna 15 85
cavi della telecamera 239 2
~ di sollevamento 2 30
cavia 366 12
cavicchio 54 7; 56 1; 126 55
caviglia 126 55; 325 17
~ a becco 202 10
cavigliere 323 19; 324 10, 19
cavità ascellare 16 26
~ carsica 13 71
~ dell'ovario 370 62
~ faringea 19 24
~ nasale 17 53
~ orale 19 14-37

~ uterina 20 80
cavo *Ospedale* 25 43
~ *Cucina* 39 25; 50 66
~ *Fotogr.* 116 38; 117 72
~ *Energia nucleare* 153 41
~ *Fibre sin.* 169 28
~ *Fiume* 216 2; 217 23, 23
~ *Scherma* 294 31
~ *Strum. mus.* 326 53
~ a alta tensione 152 33; 153 42
~ allacciamento microfono 117 25
~ Bowde 189 12
~ da traino 216 24
~ del freno 189 12
~ del microfono 239 14; 310 32; 311 41
~ del poplite 16 51
~ del timone 283 52
~ della boa 90 3
~ della cornetta 237 3
~ della gru 222 13
~ della rete a strascico 90 12
~ dell'ancora 218 18
~ dell'elettrocardiogramma 25 43
~ dell'elettrodo 25 25
~ di adduzione elettrica 50 77
~ di alimentazione 142 25
~ di arresto 259 16
~ di collegamento *Ospedale* 25 56
~ di collegamento *Fotogr.* 117 8
~ di collegamento *Saldatore* 142 25
~ di controllo 271 53
~ di corrente 198 19
~ di diagnosi 195 3
~ di guida 288 69
~ di linea ad alta tensione 152 32
~ di perforazione 145 7
~ di sincronizzazione 313 29
~ di sollevamento 119 37
~ di traino 287 4
~ di uscita cinepresa 117 28
~ elettrico 56 32
~ elettrico di alimentazione 94 9
~ elettrico di collegamento 25 20
~ inferiore 90 9, 18
~ per la diagnosi 195 38
~ per la misurazione della temperatura dell'olio 195 16
~ per la temperatura dell'olio 195 40
~ per l'energia elettrica 198 14
~ per saldature 142 19
~ portante 215 40; 271 52
~ retrattile 128 45
~ sonda della rete 90 14
~ telefonico 198 15

~ traente 301 63
cavolaia maggiore 80 47
cavolfiore 57 31
cavolfiori 99 84
cavoli 57 28-34
cavolo 57 32
~ bianco 57 32
~ cappuccio 57 32
~ riccio 57 34
~ rosso 57 32
~ verzotto 57 33
cazzuola 118 52
~ del tappezziere 128 41
CD audio 243 38
~ player 242 28
~ video 243 39
cece 69 19
cecidomia 80 40
~ distruttrice 80 40
cediglia 342 33
~ della nota 320 5
cedola del dividendo 251 18
cedro 372 65
cedronella 365 4
cefalopode 357 37
celebrante 332 22
celenterato 357 14; 369 5, 9, 20
celesta 325 1
celeste 343 6
celetto 316 12
cella 77 27; 334 51
~ campanaria 331 8
~ della regina 77 37
~ frigorifera *Macello* 94 21-24
~ frigorifera *Navi* 223 56
celle dei fuchi 77 36
~ propellente 234 62
celletta dell'ape 77 26-30
~ di covata 77 31
~ opercolata con la pupa 77 32
cellette delle operaie 77 34
~ d'immagazzinamento 77 35
cellula germinativa 74 66
~ pulsante 110 38
~ solare 155 34
cellulosa alcalina 169 9
~ di faggio 169 1
cembalo 322 45
cemento 19 29
cenere di carbone 120 44
cengia 300 4
~ di ghiaccio 300 4
~ di massi 300 4
~ di neve 300 4
~ erbosa 300 4
~ rocciosa 300 4
cennamella 322 3
cenno torna al pontile 286 55
centaurea 61 1
~ minore 376 12; 380 10
Centauro 3 39
centauro 327 52
centesimi 252 15, 16, 19, 22, 23
centesimo 344 20
centina 230 46

~ ausiliaria 287 36
~ di ancoraggio 287 32
~ principale 287 35
centinaio 344 3
centinatura esterna 285 50
centrale 293 60
~ atomica 154 19
~ (dei) dati 248 43
~ di alimentazione elettrica 310 8
~ di comando 27 9
~ di distribuzione 217 45
~ di puntamento 255 56
~ elettrica 144 13; 152 1-28
~ elettronucleare 154 19
~ eolica 155 42
~ maremotrice 155 37
~ pressione idraulica 316 50
~ termoelettrica a vapore 152 1-28
centralina di comando *Seheria* 157 67
~ *Tess.* 168 32
centralino 267 5
~ privato 245 13
centratore 111 34
centrifuga 23 59
~ oscillante 168 14
~ per le lastre offset 179 1
centrifugazione 169 23
centro 346 26, 43
~ campo 291 2
~ del cerchio osculatore 346 23
~ della via d'acqua navigabile 224 98
~ di curvatura 346 23
~ di simmetria 351 3
~ residenziale agglomerato 37 54-57
centrocampista 291 14
cents 252 34
ceppatello 381 16
ceppo *Econ. forest.* 84 14
~ *Lattoniere* 125 21
~ *Viti* 143 100
~ *Tess.* 166 42
~ del freno *Fabbro* 138 12
~ del freno *Carrozze* 186 16
~ del freno *Autom.* 192 51
~ della pialla 132 24
~ dello smorzatore 325 37
~ di arresto 119 40
~ di fermo 166 44
~ di piombo 326 20
cera d'api 77 67
cerambice 358 38
ceramica a cordicella 328 10
~ con intagli a tacche 328 35
~ decorata ad incisioni 328 13
ceramista 161 9
cerbero 327 29
cerbiatta 88 1
cerbiatto 88 1
cerbottana 352 26

cercapoli 127 55
cerchi concentrici 346 58
~ in ferro 130 3
cerchiatura 130 24
cerchietto 280 32
~ del calcio di rigore 291 6
cerchio *Bicicletta* 187 28
~ *Equit.* 288 3
~ *Ginnastica* 297 46
~ *Sport* 305 31
~ *Circo* 307 58
~ *Mat.* 346 42
~ acrobatico 305 79
~ della botte 130 8
~ di rinforzo 130 16
~ graduato *Strum. ottici* 113 27
~ graduato *Cristalli* 351 32
~ grande del bersaglio 288 59
~ indicatore misurazione spot 115 33
~ delimitante le stelle circumpolari 3 5
~ medio del bersaglio 288 58
~ meridiano 113 26
~ piccolo del bersaglio 288 57
cerchione 189 25; 191 16; 192 77
~ di ferro 163 5
cerci dell'addome 81 12
cereali 68 1-37
cerimonia d'investitura 329 66
cerniera *Mecc.* 140 49
~ *Ufficio* 151 50
~ *Veicoli* 188 2
~ con molla 151 65
~ della susta 111 14
~ lampo 31 55
~ lampo interna 101 6
cernita a seconda delle categorie 74 44
cero pasquale 330 44
~ votivo 330 53
cerotto 21 7
~ adesivo 22 55
certificato azionario 251 11
~ elettorale 263 19
cerva 86 13; 88 1
~ non pregna 88 1
cervelletto 17 45
cervello 17 42; 18 22
cervice 16 21
cervo 88 1
~ giovane 88 1
~ in fregola 86 12; 88 4
~ volante 358 24
cesellatura 87 28
cesoia a ghigliottina 125 26
~ circolare 185 20
~ per il cartone 183 16
~ per lamiera 125 1
~ per lingotti 148 52
~ per mattoni 159 15
~ per profili 127 51
~ sagomata 125 2
cesoie 108 23

~ per cuoio 100 39
~ per siepi 56 17, 49
cespuglio 272 14
cesta 305 69
~ da viaggio 204 3
~ della frutta 266 57
~ delle patate 66 25
cestaio 136 33
cestella del polline 77 6
cestello 39 41; 40 42
~ dei pesci 89 25
~ per acquisti 271 15
cestino dei rifiuti *Stazione di servizio* 196 12
~ *Ferrovia* 205 55
~ *Città* 268 5
~ *Parco* 272 43; 273 25
~ del pane 45 20
~ di appoggio delle pratiche 245 30
~ in metallo 188 23
~ per la carta 46 25; 248 45
cesto *Superm.* 99 8
~ *Cestaio* 136 16
~ delle offerte speciali 96 18
~ di verdura 99 81
~ di vimini 309 10
~ fatto con strisce di corteccia 136 11
cetacei 367 23-29
cetra 322 15; 324 21
~ da tavolo 324 21
cetrioli 99 83
cetriolo 57 13
~ di mare 369 18
~ sotto aceto 98 29
chapiteau 307 1
char à bancs 186 33
chassis 191 2; 242 63
~ dell'impianto 241 3
chatra 337 22
chef de partie 275 3
cheimatobia 80 16
chelicero 358 41
chemisier 30 10
chenopodio 61 25
chermes dell'abete rosso 82 38
chiacchierino 102 19
chiamata del direttore di scena 315 52
~ d'emergenza 233 40
~ urgente 237 61
Chianti 98 61
chiatta 216 25; 225 8; 226 57
~ della draga 226 46
~ rinfusiera 226 35
chiatta-traghetto 216 15
chiavarda da muro 143 43
~ della serratura 246 23
chiave *Mecc.* 323 18, 32; 324 23
~ della camera 267 9
~ dell'arco 215 31
~ dell'idrante 270 27
~ di basso 320 9
~ di chiusura 87 25

~ di contralto 320 10
~ di do 320 10, 11
~ di fa 320 9
~ di ferro 328 32
~ di registrazione 323 59
~ di sicurezza 140 48
~ di sol 320 8
~ di tenore 320 11
~ di violino 320 8
~ di volta 335 32; 336 23, 39
~ dinamometrica 195 45
~ doppia 323 35
~ inglese 126 68
~ per dadi 195 44
~ per l'accordatura 325 20
~ prussiana 126 66
~ registrabile a doppio martello 126 67
~ registrabile a rullino 126 66
chiavetta a naso 143 74
~ piatta 143 73
chiavette incastrate 143 73-74
chiavi 320 8-11
chiavistello 140 39
Chicane-Allais 301 72
chicchi 382 5
chicco di caffè 382 6
~ di grano 68 13
chierichetto 330 40
chierico 330 40; 331 45
chiesa 15 53, 64; 331 1
~ barocca 336 1
~ cattolica 330 31-62
~ del paese 15 107
~ gotica 335 22
~ protestante 330 1-30
~ rinascimentale 335 42
~ romanica 335 1-13
chiglia *Navi* 222 22; 283 32, 50; 285 32, 47
~ *Arte* 336 50
~ a pinna 286 43
~ antirollio 222 47
~ di manovra 227 30
~ esterna 283 32
~ interna 283 50
~ mobile 285 41
chignon 34 29
chimera 327 16
chimono 353 40
china 380 17
chiocciola dei giardini 357 27
~ di alimentazione uscita grano 64 25
~ di mescolamento 64 21
chiodaia 137 17; 140 14
chiodatrice 138 27
chiodatura 143 56
chiodi 291 28
~ frontali 300 49
chiodini 381 28
chiodo 143 51
~ da pelliccia 131 22
~ da roccia 300 38
~ di garofano 382 28
~ di legno 121 92

~ grosso senza testa 121 93
~ per cartone catramato 122 96; 143 55
~ quadro 121 94
~ ribattuto 285 52
chioma 370 3
~ dell'albero 272 60
chiosco per bevande e generi alimentari 205 49
chiostro 15 63; 331 52
chip 237 41
chiromante 308 36
chitarra 318 8; 324 12
~ folk 324 73
chitarrista 318 9
chitarrone 324 1
chitonactis 369 20
chitone 355 5
chiusa 217 20, 77
~ a conche 15 58
~ d'argine 216 34
~ di tenuta 15 69
~ di ventilazione 144 38
chiusura a scatola 326 35
~ a turacciolo 147 31
~ del bacino 222 32
~ del coperchio 50 83
~ del corpo della cinepresa 313 33
~ della punta dello scambio 202 28
~ di sicurezza 50 25
~ frontale 50 30
~ vano inserimento scheda 115 21
chow-chow 70 21
ciac 310 35
ciacchista 310 34
ciambella 71 1
~ di pasta lievitata 97 42
ciano 61 1
cibi conservati 96 25
cibo surgelato 96 23
ciborio con le ostie 332 48
cicatricula 74 66
cicca 107 19
ciclamino 53 5
ciclismo 290 1-23
ciclista dietro motori 290 14
cicloesanolo 170 18
~ grezzo 170 16
ciclomotore 188 6, 24; 189 1
ciclone 9 5
ciclorama *Film* 310 12
~ *Teatro* 316 9
cicogna *Tetto* 122 32
~ *Uccelli* 359 18
cicoria 57 40; 376 25
cicuta 379 4
cieco 20 17
cielo a pecorelle 8 14
~ del doppio fondo 222 54
cifre scorrevoli 110 12
ciglia 19 41
cigliata 370 49
ciglio 63; 370 50
Cigno 3 23
cigno 272 54
~ reale 359 16

ciurma 218 48
civetta *Caccia* 86 48
~ *Denaro* 252 2
~ *Uccelli* 362 19
clacson 188 53
clarinettista 318 5
clarinetto 318 4; 323 34
~ basso 323 34
classe 284 57, 59
classi delle barche a vela
    284 49-65
~ sociali delle api 77 1--4-5
classificatore 172 50
clausola cambiaria 250 17
clava 354 33
clavaria 381 32
clavetta 297 38
clavicembalo 322 45
clavicola 17 6
clavicordo 322 36
~ legato o sciolto 322 36
cleono della barbabietola 80
    49
clessidra 110 23
cliché 178 38
~ di legno 340 2
cliente *Superm.* 98 43; 99 2,
    18
~ *Ottico* 111 2
~ *Ufficio* 248 18
~ *Ristorante* 266 25
~ *Gr. magazzini* 271 16,
    55
~ abituale 266 40
~ del bar 267 55
~ della banca 250 6
clienti del caffè 265 22-24
clima boreale 9 56
~ dei ghiacci perenni 9 58
~ della tundra 9 57
~ equatoriale 9 53
climi della terra 9 53-58
~ polari 9 57-58
clinch 299 31
clip 2 18
clitello 357 26
clitoride 20 88
clivia 53 8
cloche *Copricapi* 35 12
~ *Aeropl.* 230 24; 257 8;
    288 14
clog 101 44
cloro 170 7
clorobenzene 170 9, 11
clorobenzolo 170 9
clorurazione del benzolo
    170 8
cloruro di sodio 170 13
clown 307 24
~ musicista 307 23
club house 283 23
~ nautico 283 23
coach 292 57
coach-box 292 56
cocca *Navi* 218 18-26
~ *Sport* 305 63
~ anseatica 218 18-26
Cocchiere 3 27
cocchiere 186 40
~ con la mantellina 186 32
cocchiume 130 7

cocci 161 21
~ die porcellana 161 21
coccia 294 38, 43
coccige 17 5; 20 60
coccinella 358 37
cocciniglia di san José 80 35
~ perniciosa 80 35
cocco 383 48
coccodrillo del Nilo 356 13
cocheria 170 2
cockeria 170 2
cockpit *Veicoli* 188 40
~ *Aeropl.* 230 35; 231 19
~ *Remare* 283 8
~ *Sport del volo* 288 10
~ integrale 189 44
cocktail 317 33
coclea 17 63
~ di alimentazione 92 26
~ di riempimento serba-
    toio 64 24
~ grano 64 20
cocotte 306 37
cocuzzolo 16 1
coda *Cani* 70 12
~ *Selv.* 88 19, 47, 49, 62,
    75, 80
~ *Carni* 95 34
~ *Tetto* 122 89
~ *Uccelli* 362 8
~ a cavaturaccioli 73 12
~ a ciuffo 73 6
~ a lira 88 67
~ a nappa 73 6
~ a spada 358 5
~ a ventaglio 88 75
~ con piume falciformi 73
    25
~ del cavallo 72 38
~ della nota 320 5
~ dell'antenna 223 4
~ dell'aquilone 273 43
~ di cavallo 34 27
~ di pesce 327 25, 43, 49
~ di serpente 327 31
~ di volpe 60 21; 69 27
~ prensile 364 35
codice d'avviamento
    postale 236 43
codino *Accon.* 34 6
~ *Selv.* 88 58
~ *Corrida* 319 26
codirosso 360 3
codolo 45 52
~ dell'utensile 149 49
coefficienti 345 4
cofanetto dei prodotti igie-
    nici 28 18
~ delle fedi 36 6
cofano 191 8; 195 36; 304
    11
~ del bagagliaio 193 9
~ di protezione 138 9
~ motore posteriore 193
    35
coffa 219 54; 223 38
~ di maestra 219 52
~ di trinchetto 219 50
coincidenza 233 27
cokeria 144 7-11; 156 1-15
col buco 99 22

colata 147 54
~ continua 148 24-29
~ lavica 11 18
colatoio 300 3
colatore 148 8
colatrice di masselli 147
    34-44
colatura dell'impasto
    umido 161 15
colbacco 35 34
colchico 379 3
coleotteri 358 24-39
coleottero *Insetti* 82 1, 22,
    26, 42
~ *Artropodi* 358 38
~ del pane 81 23
~ del tabacco 81 25
~ parassita 80 10
colibrì 363 4
colino 96 45; 260 66
colla 48 4
~ a freddo 134 36
~ liquida 340 49
~ per grandi superfici 128
    28
~ per spalmatrici 128 26
~ per tappezzieri 128 23
~ speciale per tappezzieri
    128 24
collana 354 40
~ d'avorio 36 28
~ di corallo 36 34
~ di fiori 306 17
~ di perle 36 32
~ di perle coltivate 36 12
~ di zanne di orso 352 14
~ dorata 328 26
collant 32 12
collante per pellicole 312 22
collare *Cavallo* 71 15
~ *Selv.* 88 27
~ *Viti* 143 64
~ *Sport* 301 7
~ *Rettili* 364 39
~ del cane 70 13
~ di plastica 127 40
~ increspato 306 20; 355
    52
~ per cavo 127 40
collarino 334 22
collegamenti ai cavi 237 88
~ di presa 153 18
collegamento 25 43
~ a stella 153 20
~ a triangolo 153 21
~ al vuoto 145 51
~ comando a distanza 115
    13
~ dei trasformatori 153 19
~ della sede lampada 112
    60
~ dell'aria compressa 153
    53
~ per l'aria compressa 213
    20
~ per lo svuotamento 213
    21
collettame 226 11
colletto 332 6
~ alla coreana 30 43
~ con ruche 31 46

~ da Pierrot 306 20
~ della barbabietola 68 46
~ della vite 143 33
~ di carta 106 5
~ di lino 355 56
~ di maglia a coste 33 31
~ gallonato 186 22
~ inamidato 355 74
~ rovesciabile 31 69
~ rovesciato 30 5
collettore del vapore 210 21
~ della polvere 163 22
~ della valvola a farfalla
    190 15
~ dell'acque 198 27
~ dell'aria 75 32
~ di pioggia 10 46
~ di scarico 190 36
~ nero 155 29
colli 206 4
collier 31 28; 36 2, 16
collimatore 351 30
colline di sfondo 310 13
collo *Anat.* 16 19-21; 19
    1-13
~ *Abb.* 33 58
~ *Cavallo* 72 15
~ *Selv.* 88 3
~ *Carni* 95 6, 20, 47
~ *Stazione* 204 2; 329 83
~ a anello 30 3
~ a uomo 31 23
~ del calcio 87 7
~ del cinescopio 240 24
~ del remo 283 37
~ della nota 320 4
~ dell'amo 89 81
~ di pelliccia 30 63
~ smerigliato 350 37
collocazione delle superfici
    portanti 229 1-14
collottola 16 21
collutorio 49 36
colmata del doppiofondo
    120 44; 123 69
colmo 37 7
colofonia 323 11
colomba 73 33
colombiforme 359 23
Colombina 306 27
colon ascendente 20 19
~ discendente 20 21
~ traverso 20 20
colonia degli afidi 80 34
colonna *Ospedale* 26 5
~ *Tess.* 168 16
~ *Legatoria* 185 65
~ *Porto* 226 51
~ *Circo* 307 29, 45
~ *Scrittura* 342 45
~ *Lab. chimico* 349 29
~ a papiro chiuso 333 13
~ corinzia 334 10
~ decorata 333 18
~ del lavandino 49 27
~ delle affissioni 268 70
~ di carico 223 35
~ di comando 177 56
~ di distillazione 145 37,
    49
~ di mercurio 10 2

~ di sostegno **134** 54
~ dorica **334** 8
~ ionica **334** 9
~ mediana **114** 46
~ montante **269** 19
~ palmiforme **333** 17
~ papiriforme **333** 15
~ portante *Atomo* **2** 29
~ portante *Mulini* **91** 34
~ portante *Fotogr.* **116** 28
~ sonora **243** 24
~ sormontata da capitello **333** 23
~ vertebrale **17** 2-5
colonna-vetrinetta delle montature **111** 5
colonnato **334** 67
colonne a stantuffo **316** 60
~ binate **336** 6
colonnina *Stazione di servizio* **196** 1
~ *Arte* **335** 41
~ idrante **270** 26
colonnino della ringhiera **38** 29
~ di testa della ringhiera **123** 54
colorazione **23** 50
colore **129** 4
~ a tempera **338** 17
~ ad acquerello **338** 18
colori *Araldica* **254** 24-29
~ *Giochi* **276** 38-45
~ a stampo **260** 83
~ all'acquerello **48** 6
~ da distendere con le dita **260** 26
~ del fumaiolo **223** 2
~ dell'arcobaleno **343** 14
~ dell'incandescenza **343** 16
~ dell'iride **343** 14
colpa al centro **277** 2
colpi del biliardo **277** 2-6
colpo basso, un colpo proibito **299** 34
~ con effetto a destra **277** 6
~ con effetto a sinistra **277** 5
~ di testa *Biliardo* **277** 3
~ di testa *Calcio* **291** 46
~ dritto **294** 7
~ sotto **277** 4
colposcopio **23** 5
coltelli tagliatori **181** 42
coltellino da burro **45** 73
coltello *Tavola* **45** 7, 50
~ *Macelleria* **96** 31
~ a petto **120** 79
~ circolare **185** 22
~ da caccia a doppio taglio **87** 41
~ da caccia a taglio semplice **87** 42
~ da doratore *Verniciatore* **129** 51
~ da doratore *Legatura* **183** 7
~ da elettricista **127** 63
~ da formaggio **45** 72

~ da frutta **45** 71
~ da innesto **54** 31
~ da lancio **354** 15
~ da macellaio **96** 35
~ da macinato **96** 52
~ da pescatore **89** 39
~ da pesce **45** 64
~ da portata **45** 69
~ da sfilettare **89** 38
~ del legatore **183** 13
~ del rotore **85** 26
~ del sub **279** 8
~ di bronzo con impugnatura **328** 31
~ di taglio **173** 44
~ per caviale **45** 81
~ per disossare **94** 14
~ per lavorare il piombo **124** 12
~ per rifilare **94** 15; **340** 10
~ per rifilature **128** 38
~ per scuoiare **94** 13
~ per tappezziere **128** 37
~ scollettatore **64** 87
~ snodato **85** 20
~ superiore **183** 19
~ tagliaorli **100** 48
~ tagliasparagi **56** 10
~ universale **134** 28
coltivatore **65** 55
coltro **65** 11, 68
~ a dischi **64** 66
~ a disco **65** 69
~ dell'aratro **65** 10
coltura **84** 9
colza **383** 1
comando *Ferrovia* **210** 18; **211** 30
~ *Sport del volo* **288** 41
~ a distanza **157** 14
~ a leva ginocchiera **181** 16
~ a pedale **139** 27
~ areazione inferiore abitacolo **191** 81
~ del lampeggiatore **191** 68
~ del meccanismo di commutazione **211** 13
~ del reattore **154** 23
~ delle combinazioni libere **326** 40
~ dello scambio **202** 35
~ fanali **191** 64
~ indusi **211** 38
~ luci **191** 62
~ principale dell'asse orario **113** 15
~ riscaldamento lunotto posteriore **191** 82
~ timone di prua **224** 23
~ unifilare **288** 90
combinatore di marcia **197** 27
~ di marcia posteriore **197** 8
combinazione **127** 7
combinazioni dei cristalli **351** 1-26
combustibile nucleare **154** 4
comitato **263** 1-2

comizio elettorale **263** 1-15
commessa **97** 1; **98** 31; **99** 17; **271** 18
commesso **98** 13
commessura labiale **16** 14; **19** 19
commissario di Borsa **251** 7
~ di gara **299** 48
commutatore *Macch. utensili* **150** 28
~ *Radio* **238** 42
~ del nastro inchiostrato **249** 11
~ dell'autofocus **115** 22
~ di accensione **191** 75
~ per il misuratore **195** 4
~ selettivo **153** 13
comodino **43** 17
compact camera Super 8 **117** 51
~ disc **242** 61
compact-disc single **243** 37
comparsa cinematografica **310** 29
comparse **316** 39
compartimento **207** 13; **208** 22, 24
~ dell'espresso **207** 43
~ equipaggio **235** 16
~ riservato al personale di scorta al treno **205** 37
~ stagno **227** 26; **228** 27
compasso **151** 52
~ a verga **125** 11
~ da lavagna **260** 40
~ di spessore **135** 18
~ per esterni **135** 18
~ per fori **135** 23
~ per gli spessori **339** 3
~ per le proporzioni **339** 2
~ per vetro **124** 22
~ regolabile **151** 64
compattatore **199** 1
compendium **313** 3
compensatore a magazzeno **165** 51
~ di movimento **311** 27
complesso degli uffici **146** 14
~ dei templi **337** 25
~ dei tubi **26** 17
~ funerario **333** 6
completino **29** 12
completo abito e giacca **31** 6
~ da passeggio **29** 1
~ da spiaggia **33** 24
~ di lana **31** 49
~ di maglia **30** 33
~ due pezzi **31** 11
~ jeans **31** 58; **33** 20
~ pantalone **30** 57
~ per la culla **28** 31
~ per ragazza **29** 50
~ sportivo **33** 17
compluvio **122** 82
comportamento all'attrezzo **296** 22-39
compositoio **174** 13
compositore **174** 5; **176** 15
~ a mano **174** 5

compositrice monolineare **174** 19
composizione **174** 15; **175** 1-17; **181** 37
~ a due colonne **185** 64
~ a macchina **174** 27
~ a mano **174** 1
~ in piedi **174** 11
~ testi **176** 14
composta **55** 15
~ di frutta **45** 30
compresse sul viso **106** 25
compressione del nastro **163** 59
compressore *Verniciatore* **129** 33
~ *Fabbro* **138** 3
~ *Petrolio* **145** 45
~ *Fonti energetiche* **155** 4
~ *Ferrovia* **212** 34
~ *Strum. mus.* **325** 16
~ a alta pressione **232** 36
~ a bassa pressione **232** 35
~ a tiraggio indotto **152** 14
~ d'aria **211** 14
~ dei gas **156** 26
~ dell'aria **146** 23; **212** 58, 72
~ emostatico **26** 48
~ idraulico **108** 16
~ stradale **200** 36
compressori degli impianti frigoriferi **92** 22
comunicandi **332** 27
comunione **332** 26
comunità dei fedeli **330** 29
conca **13** 56; **217** 20
~ del bacino **222** 36
~ del «tritone» **146** 31
~ dell'acido **182** 16
~ di elevazione **217** 33
~ di ricezione della falda **163** 15
~ ribaltabile *Elettrodomestici* **50** 4
~ *Ferrovia* **213** 38
concatenazione a delta **153** 21
concentratore **172** 42, 48
~ dei liquidi di lavaggio **172** 44
concerto nel giardino delle terme **274** 21
conche **217** 17-25
conchiglia *Ferriera* **147** 32, 37
~ *Mercato delle pulci* **309** 46
~ *Fig. fant.* **327** 41
~ *Invertebrati* **357** 36
~ a colata **178** 22
~ globoide **357** 29
~ St. Jacques **309** 46
concime chimico **63** 14
concio **158** 30
Concorde **231** 15
concrezioni calcaree **13** 80-81
condensatore *Strum. ottici* **112** 8

~ non innestato 208 19
giuntura a becco di flauto 124 4
giunzione per la tubazione del freno 192 53
giuria 290 4
giusquiamo 379 6
glace di cioccolato 97 34
gladioli 51 28
gladiolo 60 11
glande 20 69
glechoma hederacea 375 18
globo oculare 19 45
~ terrestre 4 8
gloxinia 53 7
gluma 68 11
go-kart 273 33; 305 83
gocce 334 19
goccia 36 85, 86; 162 40
gocciolatoio 266 2
~ sotto il cornicione 334 13
gognometro 260 38
gola Geogr. 13 52
~ Anat. 16 19
~ Cavallo 72 16
~ Strum. mus. 326 18
gole 125 8
golena 216 41
goletta 254 2; 329 42
~ a gabbiola 220 11-13
~ a palo 220 18
~ a quattro alberi 220 28
golf 293 79-93
golfino 28 25; 29 9
golfo mistico 315 24
gomena 217 23; 218 18; 227 8
~ da traino 227 8
~ di salvataggio 228 12
~ galleggiante 90 4
gomito Anat. 16 45
~ Cavallo 72 20
~ Soffitto 123 49
~ Idraulico 126 52
~ con bocchettone 126 40
~ con bocchettone femmina 126 45
~ con giunti 67 6
~ del tubo della stufa 309 6
~ maschio femmina 126 51
~ ridotto 126 49
gomitolo di filo 183 11
gomma Ufficio 151 42
~ Bicicletta 187 30
~ a fibre di vetro 151 47
~ da cancellare 151 42
~ da corsa 290 19
~ di scorta 290 23
~ per macchina da scrivere 247 26
~ piuma 291 24
gommone Salvataggio 228 18
~ Campeggio 278 14
~ Surfing 279 27
~ Motoscafi 286 1
gondola 288 64
~ col motore 231 26

~ del carrello 256 15
~ del motore 256 25
~ motore di poppa 231 10
gonepterix rhamni 365 4
gonfalone 253 7-11, 12
~ ecclesiastico 331 44
gong 299 46
goniometro a contatto 351 27
~ a riflessione 351 28
gonna 29 46, 52; 31 24
~ a portafoglio 31 13
~ con pettorina e bretelle 29 41
~ con spacco laterale 30 51
~ da sera 30 56
~ del tailleur 31 3
~ di loden 30 67
~ pantaloni 31 48
~ plissettata 30 32
gonnellino hawaiano 306 18
gorgiera 329 44; 355 52
~ della maschera 294 14
gorgogliatore 156 22, 23, 24
gorgoglione 80 32
gorilla 368 16
gota 16 9
gotico Arte 335 22-41
~ Scrittura 342 3
gozzo 73 20
gradi 260 39
gradina 339 13
gradinate 307 15; 319 8
gradini 37 66
~ dell'altare 330 5, 31
~ di ferro 269 28
gradino Casa 38 27; 41 24; 50 38
~ Piscina 281 32
~ cuneiforme 123 31
~ di strato 13 49
~ d'imbarco 230 42
~ monoblocco 123 17
grado Dan 299 15
~ di pendenza 300 2
graduazione altimetrica 7 35
~ dell'alzo 87 68
~ in centimentiri e millimetri 247 36
~ in millibar 10 3
~ per la messa a punto del margine 249 12
~ termometrica 7 36
graffa a sella 126 53
~ a spazio doppio 126 57
graffito 338 41
grafico Navigazione 224 67
~ Ufficio 248 36
~ del volume d'affari 248 46
grafite 1 54
gramigna 61 30
~ dei prati 375 39
grammofono 309 31
gran fiocco 219 21
~ pavese 221 85
~ velaccio 218 53
~ volta dorsale 296 60
granaglie 68 1-37

granaio 329 13
granata Forze armate 255 23
~ Sport 302 43
granato 351 7
granatoedro 351 7
grancassa 323 55; 324 47
granchi 358 1-3
granchio Fal. 132 36
~ Fauna 369 16
~ di mare 358 1
grandangolo 115 45; 117 48
grande arco dell'aorta 18 10
~ campo autofocus 115 28
~ cane di peluche 47 41
Grande Carro 3 29
grande di Spagna 306 26
~ dorsale 18 59
~ fiocco 220 13
~ gluteo 18 60
~ nervo sciatico 18 30
~ obliquo addominale 18 43
~ onda 279 6
~ organo 326 1
~ palmare 18 40
~ pettorale 18 36
~ retto addominale 18 44
~ rotondo 18 55
grandezza fisica 344 4
grandi magazzini 268 41
grandine 9 36
grani 68 1-37
~ di pepe 382 39
grano 68 1
~ del padre nostro 332 31
~ del pater noster 332 31
~ dell'Ave Maria 332 32
~ di mais 68 37
~ di riso 68 30
granoturco 68 1, 31
~ duro 68 31
~ tenero 68 31
~ zuccherino 68 31
granulazione 340 47
grappa 121 97
~ per costruzioni edili 119 58
grappolo di fiori 58 15; 374 33
~ di ribes 58 11
~ d'uva 78 5
graspo 58 13
grassella 73 33
grassetto 175 3
grasso di cocco 98 23
~ vegetale 98 23
grata del cofano 304 12
graticcio 83 17
~ rotante 92 24
gratile 284 40
grattacielo 37 82
greco 341 15
green 293 82
grembiale 149 16
grembiule a volant 31 33
~ alla tirolese 31 31
~ da lavoro 33 56
~ da macellaio 96 39
~ di pelle 142 11
greppia 75 12

greyhound 70 24
grezzo 156 41
griffa 149 36
grifo 88 53
grifone 327 11
griglia Ortic. 55 13
~ Fil. del cotone 163 26
~ Divertimenti 308 33
~ a persiana 212 84
~ amovibile 199 34
~ da taglio 141 14
~ del preromptitore 163 54
~ del radiatore 191 11
~ del tamburo 163 55
~ di protezione Allev. del best. 75 43
~ di protezione Tess. 168 45
~ di protezione Stampa 181 24
~ di pulitura 64 76
~ di sterro 64 69
~ ingresso aria 191 47
~ paraneve 38 8
~ ribaltabile 210 5
grilletto 87 12; 255 5
grillo del focolare 81 7
gronda 37 8; 121 4
grondaia 37 6; 38 9; 122 28
~ di distribuzione 274 3
groom 186 27
groppa 329 88
~ del cavallo 72 31
groppiera 71 32
groschen 252 13
grotta 15 85; 272 1
~ carsica 13 79
grottaione 360 2
Gru 3 42
gru Bambini 47 39
~ Navi 222 34; 225 24
~ a carroponte 222 28
~ a cavalletto Segheria 157 27
~ a cavalletto Navi 222 25
~ a martello 222 7
~ a piattaforma girevole 222 23
~ a ponte 222 20
~ a portale Segheria 157 27
~ a portale Scalo merci 206 55
~ a rotazione concentrica 154 38
~ a tenaglia 148 47
~ a torre girevole 119 31
~ a tre gambe 222 6
~ ausiliaria 147 61
~ del forno a pozzo 148 47
~ della lancia 223 20
~ di ammarraggio 258 13
~ di bordo 259 10
~ di carico 85 28, 44
~ di coperta 221 5, 61
~ galleggiante 225 10
~ girevole 146 3
~ mobile 147 41

~ di alta tensione **127** 23
~ di arresto **268** 50
~ di battuta **293** 72
~ di colmo **121** 2
~ di combattimento **294** 9
~ di confine dello strato limite **256** 6
~ di contatto **197** 40
~ di corsa **292** 72
~ di demarcazione delle carreggiate **268** 72
~ di divisione dello strato limite **257** 13
~ di espansione **1** 61
~ di fallo **292** 48
~ di fede **224** 48
~ di fondo **291** 7; **292** 36; **293** 3-10
~ di frazione **344** 15
~ di galleggiamento **258** 27; **285** 31
~ di messa in guardia **294** 3
~ di metà campo **291** 3
~ di partenza **298** 3
~ di partenza e di arrivo **286** 30
~ di porta **292** 71
~ di posa delle lastre d'ardesia **122** 81
~ di posizione **224** 45
~ di servizio **293** 6-7
~ di tiro **292** 5
~ di tiro libero **292** 38
~ di trasporto del burro **76** 34
~ ferroviaria principale **15** 21
~ ferroviaria secondaria **15** 23
~ iperbolica di rilevamento 1 **224** 43
~ iperbolica di rilevamento 2 **224** 44
~ laterale **291** 9; **292** 17; **293** 55
~ laterale per il doppio **293** 2-3
~ laterale per il singolare **293** 4-5
~ meccanizzata smistamento oggetti **236** 33
~ mediana **293** 8-9, 54
~ miobara **9** 3
~ naso-commessura labiale **16** 11
~ pliobara **9** 2
~ scorrimento oggetti **236** 36
lineare **370** 31
linee della mano **19** 72-74
lineette **342** 23
linfonodo **19** 10
lingottiera **147** 32, 37
~ a mitraglia **147** 26
lingotto d'acciaio **147** 33; **148** 48
lingua *Anat.* **17** 52
~ *Selv.* **19** 25; **88** 2
~ biforcuta **327** 6
~ del ghiacciaio **12** 49

~ delle donne **308** 14
~ dello sci nautico **286** 49-55
~ di gatto di cioccolata **98** 84
~ di Menelik **308** 14
linguetta *Calzature* **100** 65; **101** 32
~ *Giochi* **291** 24
~ *Strum. mus.* **322** 52; **326** 19, 30
~ di accesso **6** 25
~ di accesso alla valvola **6** 21
~ prevenzione cancellazioni **242** 48
lino **383** 6
liquido **83** 8
~ detergente **111** 32
liquore **98** 58
Lira **3** 22
lira *Denaro* **252** 20, 21
~ *Strum. mus.* **322** 15
liriodendro **374** 1
liscia **128** 11
lisciatoio **128** 11
lisimachia **375** 26
lista delle vivande **266** 21
~ di carta da parati **128** 19
~ trasversale **136** 8
listelli **122** 17
listello **124** 3
~ di legatura **120** 53
~ intermedio **120** 51
~ reggigiornale **265** 26
listellone di sostegno **120** 45
listino dei cambi *Stazione* **204** 32
~ *Borsa* **251** 8
~ dei prezzi **98** 73
~ delle quotazioni **250** 8
~ delle valute estere **204** 32
~ di Borsa **251** 8
lithodes **369** 16
litografia **340** 25-26
litografo **340** 45
litosfera **11** 3
litweca **221** 115
liuto **324** 1
livella a bolla d'aria **126** 79; **134** 29
~ ad acqua **118** 63
~ trasversale **14** 61
livellatore di terreno **200** 19
livellatrice **201** 14
livellazione **14** 46
livello a cannocchiale **14** 48
~ del mare **146** 39
~ della falda freatica **269** 42
~ dell'acqua **269** 1
~ dell'acqua di sottosuolo **269** 63
~ dello strato di minerale **144** 29
~ di energia **1** 18
~ di trasformazione **23** 56
~ marino **11** 11
livrea **186** 21
lobbia **35** 22

lobo **73** 23
~ del fegato **20** 35
~ dell'orecchio **17** 57
~ superiore **20** 7
locale **266** 1-27
~ caldaia **38** 38-43
~ lavamani **207** 15
~ notturno **318** 1-33
~ per la preparazione degli insaccati **96** 31-59
~ per l'allevamento **74** 1
~ per macchinari **259** 56
~ radar **258** 60
locali con cuccette **259** 84
~ di abitazione **224** 108
locanda **266** 1-27
locomotiva a condensazione **210** 69
~ a scartamento ridotto **200** 24
~ ad accumulatore termico **210** 68
~ articolata **210** 64
~ di smistamento **206** 43
~ Diesel **200** 24
~ dieselidraulica **212** 1, 24; **213** 1
~ dieselidraulica a tre assi **212** 47
~ elettrica **205** 35; **208** 1; **211** 1; **214** 4
~ Garratt **210** 64
~ senza focolaio **210** 68
~ tender **210** 65
locomotive **212** 1-84
~ a vapore **210** 1-69
locusta **358** 8
loden **30** 64
lofobranchie **364** 19
logaritmo **345** 6
loggia ad arcatelle **335** 8
loggiato **334** 46
loggione **315** 16
loglio **61** 29; **69** 26
~ italico **69** 26
~ perenne **69** 26
logotipo **175** 6
lombata **95** 46; **96** 4
lombi *Anat.* **16** 24
~ *Cavallo* **72** 30
lombo **88** 18, 35
lombrico *Piscic.* **89** 67
~ *Invertebrati* **357** 24
long drink **317** 32
longarina **38** 26; **50** 36
~ esterna della scala **123** 44
longherone *Mulini* **91** 2
~ *Aeropl.* **230** 45; **287** 30
~ della fusoliera **235** 9
~ di rafforzamento **213** 12
~ laterale **235** 3
~ obliquo **287** 33
lontra marina **367** 17
looping **288** 1, 51
lophocalix philippensis **369** 7
l'orlo a giorno **102** 14
lotta **299** 6-12
~ greco-romana **299** 6-9
~ in piedi **299** 6

~ libera **299** 10-12
~ sul tappeto **299** 8
lottatore **299** 7
low speed aileron **229** 41
lozione dopobarba **49** 38; **106** 9
~ per capelli **106** 10
lubrificatore a pressione **195** 30
~ del bordino **211** 52
lubrificazione forzata **192** 16-27
lucarino **361** 8
lucchetto *Casa* **38** 21
~ *Posta* **237** 21
luccio **364** 16
luce **215** 13
~ azzurra **264** 11
~ bianca di poppa **286** 14
~ bianca di testa d'albero **286** 10
~ colorata **343** 10
~ del ponte **215** 26
~ della lampadina **127** 17
~ di arresto e posteriore **189** 9
~ di composizione **185** 59
~ di deflusso **217** 56
~ di posizione **230** 44, 50
~ inferiore **224** 101
~ intermittente **230** 64
~ rossa di sinistra **286** 12
~ superiore **224** 102
~ sussidiaria bianca **203** 15
~ verde della dritta **286** 11
~ verde-rossa di prua **286** 13
lucernaio **38** 2
lucernario *Allev. del best.* **75** 8
~ *Cant.* **118** 22
~ *Pittura* **338** 1
lucertola **364** 27
lucertole **364** 27-30-37
luci della ribalta **316** 26
~ di posizione **257** 36
~ d'ingombro **189** 56
~ direzionali **224** 101-102
~ psichedeliche **317** 13
lucidatura e verniciatura a spruzzo **129** 28
lucido da scarpe **50** 39
lucignolo **164** 29
luigi d'oro **252** 5
Luna **4** 1-9, 31, 45
luna calante **4** 7
~ crescente **4** 3
~ nuova **4** 2
~ park **308** 1-67
~ piena **4** 5
lunetta **332** 36; **336** 2
lungo estensore del radio **18** 56
~ fibulare **18** 64
~ peroneale **18** 64
lunotto **191** 32
lunula **19** 81; **328** 25
luogo di emissione **250** 13
~ di pagamento **250** 22
lupinella **69** 10

~ da croquet **292** 81
~ di stampaggio **139** 11
~ inferiore **139** 14
~ pneumatico **139** 24
~ superiore **139** 13
maglioncino **31** 51
maglione da sci **33** 52
magmatismo plutonico **11** 29-31
magnete *Atomo* **1** 63; **2** 51
~ *Orafo* **108** 32
~ *Ferrovia* **212** 38
~ di apertura del freno **143** 102
magnetofono per il programma registrato **261** 42
magnolia **373** 15
maiale *Agric.* **62** 10; **73** 9; **75** 39
~ *Carni* **95** 38-54
~ da macello **94** 11
maialino **75** 39, 42
mailcoach **186** 53
mais **68** 31
maiuscola **175** 11
maiuscoletti **175** 14
majorette **306** 67
malacosteus indicus **369** 10
malerba **61** 30
malleolo esterno **19** 59
~ interno **19** 60
mallo **59** 42
maltaggio **92** 1-41
maltazione **92** 1-41
malto verde **92** 23
malva a foglie rotonde **376** 13
malvaccione **380** 12
mamma con la carrozzina **272** 71
mammella **16** 28-29; **75** 18
manager **299** 45
mandarino *Carnevale* **306** 29
~ *Frutti* **384** 23
mandata **155** 10
mandibola **16** 17; **17** 35
mandibole ramificate **358** 25
mandolino **324** 16
mandorla **384** 36, 40
mandorle **45** 41
mandrino *Bricoleur* **134** 48
~ *Tornitore* **135** 6
~ *Macch. utensili* **149** 20; **150** 23
~ a due ganasce **135** 10
~ orizzontale **150** 32
~ portafresa **175** 60
~ verticale **150** 30
manganello **264** 19
mangiatoia **74** 13
~ all'aperto **62** 9
~ a tramoggia **74** 13
~ invernale per la selvaggina **86** 28
~ lineare **74** 4, 21
mangiatore di fuoco **308** 25
~ di spade **308** 26
manica a chimono **30** 36

~ a pagoda **30** 54
~ a pipistrello **31** 16
~ a sbuffo **31** 27
~ a vento **287** 11
~ a volant **29** 14
~ con il risvolto **30** 6
~ gallonata **186** 24
~ lunga **30** 15
~ rimboccata **31** 62
maniche a orli festonati **355** 46
~ a sbuffo **355** 60
manichino *Sarto* **103** 6
~ *Gr. magazzini* **271** 34
~ *Pittura* **338** 31
manici **28** 50
manico *Tavola* **45** 51, 59
~ *Econ. forest.* **85** 3
~ *Fal.* **132** 10
~ *Fabbro* **137** 30
~ *Scuola* **260** 8
~ *Strum. mus.* **324** 7, 18
~ del coltello **96** 34
~ del cucchiaio **45** 62
~ del rasoio **106** 39
~ del violino **323** 2
~ della falce **66** 16
~ della lima **108** 50
~ della scopa **38** 37; **50** 49
~ della zappa **66** 2
~ dell'annaffiatoio **55** 27
~ girevole **21** 16
~ per il trasporto **242** 39
manicotto *Ospedale* **25** 16
~ *Idraulico* **126** 43
~ *Città* **268** 31
~ del mozzo **187** 69
~ in pelle **191** 92
~ per l'aria viziata **142** 16
~ per l'insaccatura **83** 55
~ pneumatico **23** 34
~ scorrevole per la prima e seconda marcia **192** 35
~ scorrevole per la terza e la quarta marcia **192** 32
maniero **329** 1
manifesto **263** 12, 14
maniglia *Casa* **41** 28
~ *Idraulico* **126** 32
~ *Veicoli* **186** 12; **191** 5; **210** 63
~ *Ginnastica* **296** 6
~ del morsetto **260** 48
~ dell'aspirapolvere **50** 63
~ triangolare **298** 45
manina **381** 32
manipolatore a snodo sferico **2** 38
~ *Master-Slave* **2** 47
~ per fucinati **139** 32
mano **16** 47; **17** 15-17; **19** 64-83
~ di vernice protettiva **123** 5
manometro *Ospedale* **25** 22
~ *Irrigazione* **67** 10
~ *Lotta antiparass.* **83** 42
~ *Fabbro* **138** 15
~ *Galv.* **178** 8
~ *Stampa* **180** 74

~ *Autofficina* **195** 29; **196** 20
~ *Surfing* **279** 13
~ *Teatro* **316** 56
~ *Lab. chimico* **349** 19
~ a mercurio **25** 18
~ alta pressione **141** 4
~ bassa pressione **141** 6
~ carburante **230** 19
~ del cilindro freno **212** 7
~ del circuito di riscaldamento **210** 44
~ del freno **210** 50
~ del preriscaldatore **210** 43
~ della caldaia **210** 47
~ dell'aria **211** 24
~ dell'aria compressa **212** 8
~ olio **230** 20
~ per la condotta dell'aria **212** 6
~ pressione alimentazione **230** 7
~ pressione olio **157** 7
manopola *Fotogr.* **116** 33
~ *Ufficio* **151** 60
~ *Lav. a' maglia* **167** 41
~ *Bicicletta* **187** 3
~ *Cav.* **329** 50
~ *Arte* **340** 33
~ d'arresto **349** 38
~ d'avviamento **188** 31
~ dei programmi **50** 26
~ del gas **188** 30; **189** 29
~ del rullo **249** 22
~ di comando di ventilazione **26** 27
~ di serraggio **313** 8
~ micrometrica **14** 52
~ per avvolgere la pellicola **116** 7
~ per l'azzeramento **2** 7
~ per lo specchio riflettore **14** 58
~ per regolare i getti **83** 19
manopole **65** 2
manoscritto **174** 6
~ del film **310** 45
manovale **118** 19
manovella *Macch. agr.* **64** 43
~ *Pellicola* **117** 50
~ *Tess.* **168** 52
~ *Costr. stradale* **201** 9
~ *Posta* **237** 24
~ comando **149** 15
~ d'azionamento **201** 18; **309** 81
~ d'innalzamento della lama **132** 60
~ per la regolazione dell'altezza **64** 57
~ regolatrice della pressione **180** 81
manovratore **118** 32
~ capo **204** 45
manovre correnti **219** 67-71
~ dormienti **219** 10-19
manque **275** 22
mantella **30** 68

~ impermeabile **41** 4
mantellata in pietrame **216** 55
mantellina **30** 65; **105** 34; **355** 66
~ impermeabile **196** 26
mantello **88** 56; **254** 3
~ colorato **355** 10
~ corto **355** 29
~ del freno **187** 70
~ di argilla compressa **269** 39
mantice *Carrozze* **186** 42, 52
~ *Strum. mus.* **322** 58; **324** 37
~ di gomma di collegamento **207** 8; **208** 12
mantiglio **219** 47
~ della boma **219** 48
mantissa **345** 6
manto **355** 26
~ araldico **254** 14
~ coprente **198** 5
~ di porpora **355** 18
~ stradale **217** 1
manuale dell'armonium **325** 48
~ inferiore **322** 47
~ superiore **322** 46
manubrio **187** 2
~ da corsa **290** 18
~ dell'otturatore **87** 22
~ in due parti **188** 57
~ regolabile **188** 3
~ sollevato **188** 11
~ sportivo **188** 45
manzo **73** 1; **94** 2; **95** 14-37
maona **225** 60
mappa **140** 35
mappamondo *Geogr.* **14** 10-45
~ *Sala soggiorno* **42** 13
Mar Glaciale Antartico **14** 22
~ Glaciale Artico **14** 21
~ Mediterraneo **14** 25
maracas **324** 59
maragià **306** 28
marangone **359** 10
marazzo **94** 17
marca **187** 15
~ dell'auto **191** 12
~ di pescaggio **222** 73
~ d'immersione **222** 73
marcapianta **54** 4
marcato **321** 27
marcatore **273** 14
marcatura del foro **120** 23
~ del passaggio pedonale **268** 51
marchino **293** 90
marchio di controllo **94** 24
marciapiede *Casa* **37** 60
~ *Strada* **198** 9
~ *Ferrovia* **205** 1
~ *Navi* **219** 46
~ della stazione **214** 51
~ della stazione ferroviaria **205** 1
~ di servizio **205** 14
marco **252** 7

mare 13 26
Mare del Nord 14 25
maremoto 11 53
mareografo 225 37
margarina 98 21; 99 48
margherita 376 4
margherite 51 24
margheritina 376 1
marginale 222 51
marginatore 249 13, 14
marginatura 181 40
margine 185 55-57
~ del disco lunare 4 41
~ del recinto 289 2
~ di cucitura 185 55
~ di testa 185 56
~ esterno 185 57
~ inferiore 185 58
~ tracheale 72 16
margini 185 31
mari del mondo 14 19-26
marinaio 221 114
marionette 260 74
marmellata 98 52
marmitta 64 38
~ di scarico Autom. 191 29
~ di scarico Ferrovia 211 49; 212 69
marmotta 366 18
marna calcarea 160 1
~ iridata inferiore 154 57
marrone 343 5
marroni 384 52
marsina 33 13
marsupiali 366 2-3
marsupio 301 28
Marte 4 46
martelletto 322 34, 35; 325 3
~ di verifica ruote 205 40
martellina per le scorie 142 17
martello Anat. 17 61
~ Idraulico 126 78; 134 7
~ Mecc. 140 23
~ Atletica 298 42
~ Alpinismo 300 37
~ a doppio uso 300 37
~ da carpentiere 120 74
~ da cesello 108 41
~ da fucinatore 137 23
~ da ghiaccio 300 37
~ da muratore 118 53
~ da spianamento 137 33
~ da tegola 122 20
~ da vetraio 124 18
~ del calzolaio 100 37
~ del fabbro 134 40
~ di ferro 339 16
~ fenditore 85 5
~ per affilare la falce 66 9
~ per ardesia 122 73
~ per incavare 340 14
~ per lavorare il piombo 124 11
~ per le scorie Lattoniere 125 15
~ per le scorie Saldatore 141 25
~ per rilievi 125 14

~ per scanalare 137 34
~ per spianare 195 46
~ pneumatico perforatore 158 11
~ punteruolo 137 36
~ sagomato 108 40
martellone per serraggio 136 36
martin pescatore 360 8
martinetto idraulico Econ. forest. 84 25; 85 45
~ Fucina 139 41
martora 86 22; 367 14
marza 54 37
marzapane 98 82
marziano 126 35
mascella inferiore 16 17
~ superiore 19 27
maschera Ospedale 27 48
~ Radio 240 17
~ Surfing 279 10
~ Giochi 292 11
~ Scherma 294 13, 22
~ Carnevale 306 7
~ Film 312 4; 313 4
~ Teatro 315 10, 12
~ Scultore 339 37
~ antigas 270 40
~ da caratterista 306 33
~ da sub 279 10
~ di protezione Saldatore 142 3
~ di protezione Giochi 292 25
~ lignea 354 16
~ subacquea 280 38
mascheramento 199 11
~ delle cuciture 177 53
maschere di creta 260 75
mascherina 100 58; 101 16
~ per cancellare 151 35; 247 12
~ raffreddata ad aria 312 34
maschio Insetti 81 34
~ Mecc. 143 31; 150 34
~ del giunto 67 31
~ per filettare 140 60
massa isolante 153 38
~ oscillante 110 24
~ pendolare 11 43
masse d'aria 8 1-4
massello 147 40
massetere 19 7
massi 37 40; 51 6
massicciata 200 59
~ di ghiaia 200 60
massiccio montuoso 12 39
massimo della curva 347 19
mastello del copritetto 122 22
mastino 70 1
masto 329 4
mastra di boccaporto 222 64
matador 319 25, 31
matafione 90 5
matassa di giunco cinese 136 28
matematica superiore 345 11-14

materassino gonfiabile 278 31
~ paracadute 296 13
~ pneumatico 278 31; 280 17
materasso 43 10; 47 3
~ paracadute 296 18; 297 7
materia prima 169 1; 170 1
materiale 226 47
~ da laminare 148 51
~ da lavoro 260 81
~ da ufficio 247 1-44
~ di alimentazione 200 52
~ di medicazione 26 34
~ di riempimento 217 7
~ di sutura 22 56; 26 21
~ didattico 261 27
~ d'imballaggio 98 46-49
~ per la prima mano 128 6
~ pettinato 163 72
~ scaricato 200 12
materiali inerti 118 36
materie prime 160 1
matita Bambini 47 26
~ Ufficio 245 21
~ Scuola 260 5
~ colorata 47 26
~ da carpentiere 120 77
~ da disegno 260 5
~ da muratore 118 51
~ per cancellare 151 41
matite colorate 48 11
matraccio 350 28
~ conico Erlenmeyer 173 2
matrice Comp. 174 31; 175 55
~ Ufficio 247 5
~ a telaio 176 38, 45
~ incisa 175 37
~ metallica 178 6
~ per «Linotype» 174 29
matrici 174 47
~ a mano 174 28
matrimonio religioso 332 14
matroneo 330 25
mattone 159 20
~ crudo 159 16
~ lavorato per camini 159 28
~ pieno 159 20
~ pieno per stalle 159 27
~ solare 155 32
mattonelle combustibili 309 9
maturazione della cellulosa 169 7
mausoleo 337 16
mazza Idraulico 126 77
~ Fabbro 137 22
~ Cava 158 6
~ Giochi 292 62, 75
~ Strum. mus. 323 56
~ battente Fabbro 137 10; 139 26
~ battente Porto 226 38
~ battente inferiore 139 7
~ battente superiore 139 6
mazzaranga 200 26

~ con motore a scoppio 200 26
mazzettone 61 6
mazzuola 118 54
mazzuolo Carp. 120 67
~ Cava 158 36
~ Campeggio 278 25
~ di legno Lattoniere 125 18
~ Scultore 339 21
~ quadrangolare 132 5
meandro Geogr. 13 11
~ Arte 334 43
~ morto 15 75
meato della clavicembalo 322 48
meccanica del clavicembalo 322 48
~ del clavicordo 322 37
~ del pianoforte 325 2-18
~ del tasto del pianoforte 325 22-39
meccanico 140 1
~ auto 195 53
~ montatore 140 1
~ per chiavi 140 1
meccanismo a espansione 6 31
~ della scala 270 11
~ di alzo 255 53
~ di declinazione 113 4
~ di gettata degli aghi 167 59
~ di regolazione 148 61-65
~ di ritenuta 140 38
~ di spinta 148 69
~ d'inchiostrazione 249 51-52
~ motore 110 35
meccano 48 22
medaglione 339 36
mediano Selv. 88 8
~ Autom. 291 14; 293 76
medica 169 1
medicinali 25 14
medico generico 22 1-74; 23 2
medio 19 66
Mediterraneo 14 25
medium 308 9
medusa 357 14
~ degli abissi 369 5
megafono 283 21
meitura riportata 31 5
mela 58 56; 370 102
~ cotogna 58 49, 50
melanocetes 369 6
melario 77 45
melatonta 82 1
mele 99 86
melo 58 51
~ selvatico 58 51
melodica 320 48
melograno 384 16
meluggine 58 51
membra 16 43-54
membrana Apic. 77 23
~ Strum. mus. 323 52; 324 31
~ attraverso la quale parlare 204 38
~ del timpano 323 58

~ dell'otturatore 255 12
~ di avanzamento 157 44
~ di tensione 110 26
nottua 80 42
~ dei seminati 80 42
~ del pino 82 46
~ delle messi 80 42
nottuide 82 46
nougat 98 81
nove punti 175 26
novillero 319 2
nube a strati 8 3, 4
~ cumuliforme 8 1, 2
~ di bel tempo 8 1
nubi 8 1-19
~ nottilucenti 7 22
nuca 16 21; 95 20
nucleo 1 43, 53 17
~ atomico 1 2, 16, 29, 35, 49, 51
~ cellulare a disco 357 2
~ centrale della terra 11 5
~ del reattore 259 68
~ dell'elio 1 30-31
nudista 281 16
numeratore 344 15
numerazione 85 33
numeri arabi 344 2
~ dispari 344 12
~ generali 344 9
~ pari 344 11
~ per le chiamate di emergenza 237 6
~ primi 344 13
~ romani 344 1
numero 344 1-22; 345 6
~ a quattro cifre 344 3
~ cardinale 344 5
~ comico 307 25
~ complesso 344 14
~ definito 344 4
~ dei game 293 38
~ dei set 293 37
~ del binario 205 4
~ del cavallo ammaestrato 307 30-31
~ del conto 250 26
~ del posto tenda 278 42
~ del telaio 187 51
~ della carta Posta 237 39
~ della carta Banca 250 27
~ della pagina 185 63
~ della partita 163 6
~ della riparazione 195 48
~ della ripresa 310 35
~ dell'apparecchio 237 7
~ dell'inquadratura 310 35
~ dello spettacolo 307 25
~ di equilibrismo 307 44
~ di lancio dell'acrobata 307 43
~ di partenza Veicoli 189 18
~ di partenza Sport 301 37; 305 84
~ di registrazione 251 14
~ di serie 251 13
~ interno 344 10
~ intero 344 18

~ irrazionale 344 14
~ misto 344 10
~ naturale 344 3
~ ordinale 344 6
~ postale del giornale 342 43
~ razionale 344 14
~ relativo 344 7, 8
nummalaria, la mazza d'oro 375 26
nuotatore che opera il salvataggio 21 36
nuoto a braccio 282 37
~ a delfino 282 35
~ a dorso 282 36
~ a farfalla 282 34
~ a rana 282 33
~ a secco 282 20
~ subacqueo 282 38
nuova riga 175 15
nutazione 4 24
nuvola a cirri formata da cristalli di ghiaccio 8 7
~ a cumulo 287 22
~ a fiocchi 8 14
~ a strati 8 8, 9
~ apportatrice di precipitazioni 8 10
~ cumuliforme 8 17
~ cumulonembo 287 26
~ lanuginosa 8 15
nuvole 8 5-12, 13-17
~ lenticolari 287 19
~ temporalesche 7 2
nuvolosità 9 20-24
nuvoloso 9 23
nymphalis antiopa 365 5

# O

oasi 354 4
obbligazioni comunali 251 11-19
~ industriali 251 11-19
obelischi 333 10
obi 353 41
obice 255 29
~ corazzato 255 42
obiettive del mirino 114 25
obiettivi 114 52
~ AF 115 43
~ autofocus 115 43
~ intercambiabili 112 62; 115 43
~ primario e secondario 5 11
obiettivo Fotogr. 114 26; 115 57; 116 32
~ Video 243 3
~ Film 312 35; 313 2, 19
~ a focale variabile 117 2
~ a specchio 115 50
~ estraibile 114 5
~ grandangolo 115 45
~ grandangolare 117 48
~ macro-zoom 117 53
~ normale 115 46; 117 49
~ occhio di pesce 115 44
~ zoom 112 41; 115 23; 240 34; 313 23

~ zoom autofocus 115 23
~ zoom variabile 117 2
obitorio 331 21
obliterazioni 236 56-60
oboe 323 38
~ baritono 323 38
~ da caccia 323 38
~ d'amore 323 38
~ tenore 323 38
oca 73 34; 272 52
ocarina 324 32
occhi 88 43
~ composti laterali 77 2
occhiali 111 9
~ da corsa 303 15
~ da ghiacciaio 300 18
~ da saldatore 141 24
~ da sci 301 11
~ da sole 111 6; 301 19
~ de neve 300 18
~ di protezione 140 21
~ per saldatura 141 24
occhiellatrice 100 53
occhiello Calzolaio 100 63
~ Vetraio 124 23
~ Elettricista 127 30
~ Legatoria 185 44
~ Scrittura 342 40
occhio Anat. 16 7; 19 38-51
~ Ortic. 54 23, 34
~ Cavallo 72 4
~ Selv. 88 15, 33, 60
~ Fabbro 137 29
~ Arte 334 75
~ composto Apic. 77 20-24
~ composto Artropodi 358 7
~ del carattere 175 41
~ della macina 91 19
~ di bue 305 17
~ di cubia 222 75; 227 11
~ di pavone 73 32
~ magico 309 18
~ peduncolato 357 30
occhione di traino 152 48
occipite Anat. 16 2
~ Cavallo 72 12
occlusione 9 25
occorrente per la fasciatura d'emergenza 21 5
~ per scrivere 6 27
oceanina 327 23
Oceano Atlantico 14 20
~ Indiano 14 23
~ Pacifico 14 19
ocello 358 54
ochetta 273 30
ochiello 89 82
oculare Strum. ottici 113 20
~ Pellicola 117 14
~ Video 243 4
~ Film 311 9; 313 34
~ del microscopio 14 53
~ del mirino 313 6
oculari 112 19
odalisca 306 41
odonato 358 3
odontoiatra 24 1
öhre 252 25, 26
offerta 330 60
~ di lavoro 342 70

~ speciale 96 20
officina Mecc. 140 1-22
~ Trivell. offshore 146 30
~ Navi 222 4, 9
~ allestimento 222 3-4
~ del carpentiere 120 4
~ del fabbro 137 1-8
~ del tornitore 135 1-26
~ grafica 340 27-64
~ macchine 222 8
~ specializzata 195 1-55
offshore 221 32
ofiuoride 369 11
oftalmometro 111 44
oftalmoscopio 22 62
oggetto in lacca intagliata 337 6
ogiva dell'elica 230 33
oidio 80 20
oleandro 373 13
oleodotto 145 65
oliatore Orologiaio 109 4
~ Bicicletta 187 65
~ Stazione di servizio 196 16
oliera 45 42
olio 98 24; 99 66
~ combustibile leggero 145 58
~ combustibile pesante 145 59
~ da tavola 98 24
~ del motore 196 15
~ di arachidi 98 24
~ di girasole 98 24
~ di oliva 98 24
~ di semi 98 24
~ lubrificante 145 62
~ per cilindri 145 63
~ per doratura 129 44
~ per mandrini 145 61
olivo 383 29
olmo 371 49
oloedro 351 2
ologramma 250 28
~ di volume 250 28
~ in luce bianca 250 28
oloturia 369 18
ombelico 16 34
ombra 4 35
ombrella 357 15
~ fiorita 378 40
~ semplice 370 72
ombrello Casa 41 15
~ Ferrovia 205 12
~ Arte 337 22
~ pieghevole 41 12
ombrellone Casa 37 48
~ Città 268 61
~ Parco 272 58
omero 17 12
omnibus 186 37
~ a cavalli 186 37
omogeneizzatore 76 12
omoplata 16 23
onciale 341 17
onda artificiale 281 1
~ corta 7 26
~ di prua 223 81
onde di riva 13 36

~ di corrente doppia anticontatto **127** 6
~ di corrente per la dia-
gnosi **195** 39
~ di forza **64** 49; **65** 31
~ di gamba **299** 11
~ di moto **63** 21
~ di moto del tachimetro
**192** 38
~ di (per la) testa **21** 38
~ elettrica per il battita-
peto **50** 78
~ jack della cuffia **241** 57
~ motore **177** 54
~ per la cuffia **242** 18
~ Rautek **21** 18
~ sotto le ascelle **21** 37
~ tripolare **127** 13
presbiterio **330** 1, 32
presce femmina **89** 13
presco **59** 26-32
prese d'aria **258** 43
~ di alta tensione **153** 13
~ per il microfono **242** 17
~ per il trasporto a nuoto
**21** 37-38
presegnale con indicazione
di direzione **203** 20
~ con indicazione di velocità **203** 18
~ con luce sussidiaria **203**
17
~ con tavola ausiliaria **203**
12
~ in posizione «attesa di
via libera» **203** 23
~ in posizione «via impe-
dita» **203** 22
~ luminoso **203** 14
~ luminoso «via impe-
dita» **203** 9
presegnali **203** 7-24
presella per spianare **137** 35
presidente del seggio **263** 27
~ dell'assemblea **263** 1
presina da cucina **39** 18
presoffiatore **162** 24
pressa *Fucina* **139** 18
~ *Fabbr. del vetro* **162** 33
~ *Lav. a maglia* **167** 32
~ *Legatoria* **185** 13
~ *Giochi* **293** 32
~ a ginocchiera **183** 26
~ a mano **340** 29
~ collante **173** 24
~ idraulica *Fucina* **139** 35
~ idraulica *Fabbr. della
carta* **173** 37
~ idraulica *Galv.* **178** 7
~ manuale **183** 26
~ offset **173** 21
~ per balle **169** 33
~ per doratura e stampa
in rilievo **183** 26
~ per estrusione **159** 11
~ per impiallacciatura **133**
49
~ per le balle di paglia **63**
35
~ per mattoni **159** 11
~ per suole **100** 14

~ per telai **133** 42
~ umida **173** 19
pressatore **173** 49
pressione atmosferica **9** 4
~ barometrica **9** 4
~ sanguigna **25** 1
pressostato **269** 47
pressurazione **6** 26
prestiti **251** 11-19
~ convertibili **251** 11-19
presto **321** 28
prete **330** 39; **331** 47
pretorcitura **170** 45
prevendita dei biglietti **271**
26
previsioni del tempo **342** 65
prezzemolo **57** 19
prigioniero **143** 22
prima **321** 6
~ ballerina **314** 27
~ base **292** 46
~ bobina per il suono **117**
100
~ cinta di mura **329** 15
~ classe **207** 17
~ fila di palchi **315** 18
~ impilatura **157** 25
~ mola **111** 36
~ pagina **342** 38
~ posizione **314** 1
~ posizione per il saluto
**294** 18
primati **368** 12-16
primavera odorosa **376** 8
primo arbitro **292** 55; **293**
67
~ ballerino **314** 28
~ corso **118** 67
~ croupier **275** 6
~ e il secondo filo di
ordito **171** 17
~ giro **285** 19
~ gradino **123** 18
~ manuale agente
sull'organo positivo **326**
42
~ piano **37** 3
~ premio della tombola
**306** 11
~ quarto **4** 4
~ stadio S-IC **234** 3
~ sviluppo **116** 10
primula **376** 8
~ auricola **378** 8
primulacea **53** 5
principessa tedesca **355** 20
principio di esclusione di
Pauli **1** 7
~ di funzionamento **163**
51, 63
prisma a base triangolare
**347** 37
~ deviazione raggi **240** 35
~ esagonale **351** 21
~ esagonale con romboe-
dro **351** 22
~ monoclino con clinopi-
nacoide ed emipiramide
**351** 24
~ rettangolare **347** 34
prismi di deflessione **112** 13

privi di coda **364** 23-26
proboscidato **366** 20
proboscide *Aeroporto* **233**
12
~ *Artropodi* **358** 56
~ *Mammiferi* **366** 21
~ succhiante **358** 17
procedimento di soffiatura
e di pressione **162** 30
~ di tiraggio del vetro **162**
48
~ galvanoplastico **178** 1-6
procellaria glaciale **359** 12
processionaria **82** 14
processione **331** 42-50
processo di fermentazione
**92** 42-53
~ float **162** 12
Procione **3** 15
procione **368** 9
proctoclisi a gocce **26** 9
proctoscopio **23** 19
procuratore **299** 45
prodotti agricoli **68** 1-47
~ chimici per lo sviluppo
**116** 52
~ dei campi **68** 1-47
~ del vetro per fibre **162**
56-58
~ dolciari **98** 75-86
~ e utensili per le scarpe
**50** 39-43
~ igienici **99** 27-35
~ in scatola **98** 15-20
~ petroliferi **145** 52-64
~ surgelati **99** 58-61
prodotto **344** 25
produzione **170** 1-62
~ della carta a mano **173**
46-51
~ di acido solforico **156** 34
~ di benzolo **156** 41
~ di energia **1** 55
~ di fibre di raion **169** 1-34
~ di solfato di ammonio
**156** 35
~ di uova **74** 34-53
professore associato **262** 3
~ universitario **262** 3
profilati metallici **143** 3-7
profilatore **129** 46
profilo base **229** 45
~ del cuore **25** 39
~ del pneumatico **189** 27
profondità dell'ipocentro
**11** 34
programma **315** 13
programmatrice **248** 15
programmi televisivi **342** 64
proiettile **87** 55
~ diabolo **305** 34
proiettore *Astr.* **5** 23
~ *Scuola* **261** 8
~ *Film* **311** 22
~ a passo ridotto **117** 78
~ cinematografico **262** 8
~ del film sonoro **117** 81
~ overhead **262** 7
~ per diapositive **114** 76;
**309** 42
~ per film sonori **312** 24

proiezione **299** 17
~ cilindrica **14** 9
~ cinematografica **312**
1-23
~ conica **14** 8
prolunga *Casa* **50** 70
~ *Elettricista* **127** 10
~ *Ufficio* **151** 57
prolungamento del crivello
**64** 18
prominenza dell'articola-
zione metatarso-falan-
gea **19** 58
propagazione delle onde
acustiche **7** 14
~ delle onde sismiche **11**
35
~ mediante margotta **54**
18
propaggine **54** 11, 12
~ par bulbilli **54** 27
~ per stolone **54** 14
propilei **334** 7
propileo **336** 15
proporzione **345** 9
proprietario **266** 71
propulsione **223** 68-74
~ bielica **286** 2
~ degli anelli di filiera **164**
42
~ dei fusi **164** 31
propulsore **6** 30
~ a turbine **257** 15
~ a turboventola poste-
riore **232** 42
~ della locomotiva **210**
2-37
~ di assetto **6** 5
~ pilota **6** 3
~ principale **6** 3
~ turboventola frontale
**232** 33
prora **258** 3
proscenio *Teatro* **315** 15;
**316** 25
~ *Arte* **334** 46
prosciutto **95** 51; **96** 1; **99** 52
~ con lo stinco e lo zam-
petto **95** 38
prospetto della locomotiva
a tre assi **212** 51-67
~ laterale **37** 15
prostata **20** 76
proteggibraccia **142** 6
proteggiguancia **255** 25
proteggispalle **142** 5
protesi dentaria **24** 25
protettivo **2** 1
protezione antipolvere **2** 48
~ antisviamento **214** 75
~ degli alberi **118** 80
~ di gomma **289** 32
~ di plastica **289** 25
~ per i contraccolpi **132**
47
~ per il braccio e l'avambraccio **329** 47
protone **1** 2, 16, 31
protoplasma **357** 3

rami flessibili di salice 136 14
ramo 59 48; 370 5
~ biforcuto 54 13
~ con amenti 371 10
~ con fiore 371 47
~ con fiori 382 17
~ con fiori e frutti 383 46
~ con fiori femminili 384 42
~ con fiori giovani 371 59
~ con foglie 371 27
~ con frutti 372 63; 383 34; 384 38
~ con frutto 371 3, 11, 18, 31, 36, 41, 50, 64; 382 2
~ con gemme 371 25
~ con i coni fruttiferi 372 36
~ con le foglie 383 61
~ con siconi 384 12
~ del vimine con foglie 371 29
~ di albicocco 59 33
~ di ciliegio 59 1
~ di corallo 357 18
~ di melo 58 52
~ di nocciolo 59 44
~ di noce 59 37
~ di palma 384 3
~ di pero 58 32
~ fiorifero 59 26
~ fiorito 371 2, 16, 39, 71; 372 33; 378 2; 382 3, 8, 12, 23, 27, 31, 37, 41, 47, 50; 383 7, 22, 26, 30, 38, 42; 384 37, 49, 54
~ fruttifero 59 19, 30; 372 40, 59, 66, 70
~ in fiore 371 34, 51, 54; 384 17, 24
ramolaccio 57 16; 61 21
ramoscello 370 6
rampa d'accesso 307 20
~ del coke 156 12
~ del deposito 206 9
~ della scala 123 30, 42-44
~ dell'argine 216 47
~ di carico 206 1
~ di lancio 255 54
~ di lancio per bombe di profondità 258 34
~ di poppa 258 91
~ di prua 258 90
~ d'ingresso 199 15
~ per missili 259 50
~ per missili a corto raggio 259 26
rampone 270 15
ramponi 300 48
~ a dieci chiodi 300 48
~ a dodici chiodi 300 48
~ leggeri 300 48
rana 282 33
randa 220 1, 25; 284 44; 285 2
~ a trapezio 284 12
~ di maestra 220 11
~ di poppa 219 30
~ di trinchetto 220 12
ranghinatore rotante 63 26

ranuncolacea 60 13
ranuncolo 375 8
rapa 57 26
rapaci diurni 362 1-13
~ notturni 362 14-19
rapidi 207 1-21
rapportatore 120 81
rappresentazione del vento 9 9-19
raschiamento 26 52
raschiatoio 129 12
raschietto Ortic. 56 14
~ Tabacchi 107 45
~ Fal. 132 27
~ Cestaio 136 38
~ Mecc. 140 63
~ Uffico 151 43
~ Sport 301 24
~ da tappezziere 128 15
~ di ferro 303 24
~ triangolare 140 63
raschino d'acciaio 108 51
rasoio 105 9; 106 38
~ elettrico 49 37
~ per il taglio sfilato 106 41
raspa Fal. 132 1
~ Scuola 260 55
~ da colzolaio 100 49
~ da legno 134 8
raspo 58 13
rastello 272 67
raster image processor 176 27
rastrelliera Fil. del cotone 164 58
~ Strum. mus. 322 51
~ delle stecche 277 19
~ di spole 164 41
~ doppia 75 12
~ per le pipe 42 11
~ portaspole 164 28
rastrellina per patate 66 20
rastrello Ortic. 51 4; 56 4
~ Agric. 64 44; 66 23
~ a ventaglio 56 3
~ da fogliame 51 3
~ da stufa 38 42
~ del croupier 275 5
~ di legno 66 23
ravanello 57 15
ravastrello selvatico 61 21
razza del volante 191 58
razzi ausiliari 235 62
~ controllo assetto 234 48
~ di accelerazione 234 22, 48
~ stabilizzatori 6 40
razzo Salvataggio 228 2
~ Carnevale 306 54
~ ausiliario 235 58
~ mobile 255 52
~ vettore Saturno V 234 1, 2
re Giochi 276 8
~ Sport 305 7, 13
~ bemolle maggiore 320 67
~ del carnevale 306 58
~ maggiore 320 57
reale 95 19

reattore 154 3, 41, 50
~ a turbina 231 26
~ autofertilizzante 154 1
~ nucleare 1 48, 54 19
reattori di comando 237 73
reazione a catena 1 41, 48
receiver 241 61; 242 40; 318 18
reception 278 1
receptionist 267 7
recezione 267 1-26
recinto Econ. forest. 84 7
~ Zoo 356 1
~ con la sabbia 273 64
~ degli agenti di borsa 251 3
~ degli elefanti 356 9
~ dei rettili 356 12
~ in pietra 337 23
~ per gli animali 272 49
recinzione 15 39; 37 53
~ del cantiere 118 44
~ elettrica del prato 62 46
recipiente a pressione 170 33
~ dei rifiuti 37 63
~ delle patate da piantare 66 21
~ di captazione 10 40
~ graduato 267 60
~ per i rifiuti 207 55
~ per il miele 77 62
~ per la cove 89 17
~ per la maturazione 169 11
~ per la sostanza 350 61
~ per la vendemmia 78 10
~ per l'acido 350 62
~ per olio denso 109 5
~ resistente al fuoco 350 20
reciproco 344 16
reclusi 218 48
recorder per cassette 261 42
recuperatore di calore 147 15
~ di rinculo 255 47
redial 237 13
redini Cavallo 71 25, 33
~ Carrozze 186 31
~ Equit. 289 27
refe 185 20
refiner 172 73
refrigeratore 145 44
~ a torre 144 15
~ del gas 156 19
~ dell'olio Autom. 192 19
~ Ferrovia 211 11
reggia 143 11
reggicalze elastico 32 5
reggicavo 195 15
reggifoglio 249 17
regginipplo 126 63
reggipellicola mobile 117 90
reggipetto 318 29
reggiposata 45 11
reggiseno Abb. 32 1
~ Spiaggia 280 28
~ Locale notturno 318 29
regina Apic. 77 38
~ Giochi 276 9

~ di carnevale 306 61
reginetta di bellezza 306 64
regione del poplite 16 51
~ dell'epicentro 11 38
~ glutea 16 40
~ inguinale 16 38
~ lombare 16 24
~ sacrale 16 25
~ soprapubica 16 37
regista Film 310 40
~ Teatro 316 40
~ cinematografico 310 40
registratore a cassetta 117 73
~ a cassette 117 76
~ a doppio nastro 241 7
~ a due cassette 242 21, 43
~ a nastro 309 37; 317 21; 318 17
~ a valigetta 309 37
~ al quarzo 310 24
~ di cassa 99 93; 271 2
~ digitale a cassetta 242 66
~ magnetico 310 58; 311 1, 20
~ ottico per il suono 311 6
registrazione del comando 203 63
~ del suono 117 70
registri 322 51
registro Scuola 260 23
~ Strum. mus. 326 6
~ a nodi 352 22
~ azionario 251 14
~ dei clienti 267 8
~ elettorale 263 18
~ grave 324 44
~ melodico 324 41
regola del tre semplice 345 8-10
regolamento del parco 272 29
~ del traffico 268 30
~ elettorale 263 25
regolatore Fotoripr. 177 12
~ Ferrovia 210 52
~ Posta 237 58
~ a cursore 311 18
~ circolare 14 62
~ degli alti 241 53
~ dei bassi 241 52
~ del filtro 116 46
~ del filtro ciano 116 45
~ del filtro giallo 116 44
~ del filtro Magenta 116 43
~ del gas 350 6
~ del riscaldamento 207 54
~ del volano 224 56
~ del volume 117 85
~ del volume della cassetta 261 44
~ del volume di voce 261 43
~ della fasatura di immissione 190 58
~ della fiamma 107 31
~ della forza aspirante 50 72

~ da stampa **168** 62
~ di carico **206** 22
sagome di carico **213** 40
sagrestano **330** 26, 58
sagrestia **331** 13
sagù **98** 39
saio **331** 55
sala a tracciare **222** 3
~ Borsa **251** 1
~ caldaie **152** 1-21
~ cataloghi **262** 18
~ cinematografica **312** 1
~ controllo **152** 28
~ da ballo **306** 1
~ da biliardo **277** 7-19
~ da gioco **275** 1
~ da pranzo **223** 44
~ da té **265** 1-26
~ d'aspetto **22** 1; **204** 14
~ d'attesa **233** 28
~ della pompe **217** 43
~ delle proiezioni cinematografiche **5** 26
~ di angiografia **27** 12
~ di comando **153** 1-8
~ di consultazione **262** 17
~ controllo **25** 1-9
~ di doppiaggio **311** 34
~ di lettura **262** 13
~ di osservazione con lo spettrografo **5** 33
~ di prestito dei libri **262** 18
~ di radiografia **27** 1-35
~ di riunione **267** 39
~ di sincronizzazione **311** 37
~ di sterilizzazione **26** 34-54
~ di tracciatura **222** 3
~ macchine *Miniera* **144** 2
~ macchine *Centrale elettrica* **152** 22
~ macchine *Costr. idrauliche* **217** 21, 64
~ macchine *Navi* **221** 10; **222** 33; **223** 68, 70, 72; **227** 22
~ montata **212** 3; **213** 3
~ multiuffici **248** 1-48
~ nautica **223** 14; **228** 22
~ operatoria **26** 1-33
~ pompe **222** 33
~ ristorante **266** 73
~ saracinesche **217** 42, 63
~ sportelli **250** 1-11
~ turbine **152** 22; **217** 43
salamandra **364** 22
~ acquaiola **364** 20
~ giallo-nero **364** 22
~ maculata **364** 22
salatino **97** 31
saldatini di stagno **309** 52
saldatoio **134** 19, 57
~ a gas propano **125** 5
~ a martello **125** 5
~ a stagno **126** 73
saldatore *Orafo* **108** 14
~ *Elettricista* **127** 45
~ *Bricoleur* **134** 19, 57
~ elettrico **142** 2

~ rapido **134** 58
saldatrice a punti a pedale **142** 29
~ elettrica a gas inerte **138** 29
saldatura a punti **142** 22
~ a stagno **125** 5-7
sale **98** 40
~ da cucina **170** 13
~ e pepe **266** 77
salgemma **351** 2
~ inferiore **154** 64
~ superiore **154** 63
sali da bagno **49** 5; **99** 34
salice **371** 24
~ piangente **272** 63
salina **15** 32
saling **284** 13
saliscendi **140** 37
salita **194** 39
salizionale **326** 23-30
salone *Parruc.* **106** 1-42
~ *Navi* **223** 26
~ *Hotel* **267** 39
~ *Carnevale* **306** 1
~ per signora **105** 1-39
salopette **29** 19, 40; **30** 21
salotto **42** 21-26
salpinge uterina **20** 81
salsa remoulade **96** 29
salsiccia **96** 10; **99** 55
~ arrostita **96** 11; **308** 34
salsicciotto **96** 8
salsiera **45** 17
saltarello **322** 50
saltatore **289** 9
~ in alto **298** 10
~ nella fase di slancio **298** 29
saltello **297** 42
~ incrociato **297** 44
salterio tedesco **322** 32
salto *Equit.* **289** 21
~ *Sport* **295** 35; **297** 40; **298** 9-41; **301** 35; **302** 7
~ a forbice **295** 39; **298** 15
~ a gambe divaricate **295** 37
~ a gambe flesse **296** 53
~ a ostacoli **289** 8-14
~ alla corda **273** 15
~ alla Fosbury **298** 9
~ all'indietro raccolto **297** 15
~ all'indietro teso **297** 17
~ capovolto **297** 22
~ carpiato **295** 38
~ con l'asta **298** 28-36
~ del cervo **295** 40
~ in alto **298** 9-27
~ in avanti raccolto **297** 18
~ in lungo **298** 37-41
~ raccolto **295** 36
~ ventrale **298** 16
saltometro ritto **298** 13
salumi **96** 6-11; **98** 4; **99** 54
salvadanzara **77** 41
salvagente *Navi* **221** 124
~ *Salvataggio* **228** 13

~ *Spiaggia* **280** 3; **281** 6; **282** 19
salvamotore **269** 46
salvapattino **302** 25
salvataggio in incidenti su ghiaccio **21** 28-33
salvietta per il trucco **315** 44
salviette **106** 25
samara ad ali opposte **371** 57
sambuco **374** 35
sampan **353** 31
sampang **353** 31
samurai **353** 37
sandalo **101** 51, 53
~ alla greca **101** 48
~ con cinturino a collo **101** 27
~ da mare **280** 23
~ da spiaggia **280** 23
sandpipe **145** 13
sangallo **31** 32
sanguinaccio **99** 56
sanguisuga **357** 20
sanità **225** 26
sanscrito **341** 9
Santissimo **332** 35
santo buddista **337** 10
sapone **49** 22
saracco *Carp.* **120** 60
~ *Idraulico* **126** 72
~ *Fal.* **132** 44
~ *Bricoleur* **134** 27
saracinesca *Mulini* **91** 42
~ *Costr. idrauliche* **217** 53-56, 55
~ *Cav.* **329** 24
sarchiatore a mano **55** 21
~ a tre denti **56** 13
sarchiatrice a motore **56** 18
sarcofago **335** 53
sardine sott'olio **98** 19
sartia **284** 18
sartie di parrocchetto **219** 17
~ maggiori **219** 16
sartina **306** 21
sartiole di velaccino **219** 18
sarto **271** 37
~ da donna **103** 1
~ da uomo **104** 22
sartoria **268** 17
~ da donna **103** 1-27
~ da uomo **104** 1-32
sartorio **18** 45
sassi **269** 37
sassifraga granulata **375** 1
sassifragacee **58** 1-15
sassofono **324** 69
satellite **4** 45, 52
~ delle telecomunicazioni **237** 63
~ meteorologico **10** 64
~ per telecomunicazioni **237** 68
~ radiofonico **237** 80
Saturno **4** 49
sauna **281** 18
sauro **364** 33
sbarra *Ferrovia* **202** 40
~ *Ginnastica* **296** 7

~ del passaggio a livello apribile a chiamata **202** 47
~ della gabbia **307** 50
~ dentata di scomposizione **174** 30
~ di guida a inversione di marcia **164** 17
~ fissa **273** 32; **307** 5
sbarramento **15** 66
~ a portoni **217** 19
~ con paratoie piane **217** 73-80
sbarretta di legno **324** 64
sbattitore elettrico **39** 22
sbavatore **148** 43
sbilanciamento **299** 13
sbozzino **132** 16
scabbiosa **375** 29
scabiosa **375** 29
scacchi bianchi **276** 4
~ neri **276** 5
scacchiera **47** 20; **276** 1
~ per il gioco del filetto **276** 23
~ per il tric trac **276** 22
~ per la dama **276** 17
~ per l'Halma **276** 26
scacciamosche **83** 32
scacco matto **276** 15
scaffale **262** 12; **271** 27
~ dei quotidiani **262** 16
~ del materiale **100** 36
~ delle riviste **262** 15
~ incorporato **46** 19
~ pensile *Sarto* **104** 8
~ pensile *Ufficio* **248** 40
~ per i bicchieri **266** 9; **267** 65
~ per i libri **42** 3; **46** 7
~ per la posta **267** 2
~ per le bottiglie **266** 10
~ per pratiche **248** 10
~ pluriuso **248** 28
scaffali **98** 14
scafo *Aeropl.* **232** 2, 9
~ *Forze armate* **255** 33; **259** 22, 42
~ a coperta rasa **258** 2
~ con redan **286** 38-41
~ esterno **258** 66
~ portante **286** 27
scaglia **364** 11
scaglie di poliammide secco **170** 39
scala *Carta* **14** 29
~ *Carp.* **123** 75
~ *Ferrovia* **211** 43
~ *Gr. magazzini* **271** 44
~ *Lab. chimico* **349** 35
~ a cavalletto per tappezziere **128** 52
~ a chiocciola **123** 76, 77
~ a ganci **270** 16
~ a libretto **126** 2
~ a pioli *Soccorso* **21** 32
~ a pioli *Casa* **38** 15
~ a pioli *Cant.* **118** 41
~ a pioli *Parco giochi* **273** 22
~ a pioli da giardino **52** 8

~ retrovisore **188** 35; **189** 30; **191** 39
specchio *Casa* **41** 6; **43** 29; **49** 33
~ *Selv.* **88** 20, 36
~ *Sarto* **104** 1; **105** 20, 23
~ *Parruc.* **106** 6, 7
~ *Ottico* **111** 4
~ *Ferrovia* **207** 49
~ *Navi* **218** 58
~ *Gr. magazzini* **271** 33
~ *Vele* **285** 49
~ *Giochi* **292** 30
~ alare **88** 74
~ angolare **177** 28
~ concavo **5** 32; **308** 56
~ convesso **308** 57
~ deflettore **113** 11
~ di coronamento **218** 55
~ di poppa **285** 43, 48; **286** 26
~ fisso **224** 7
~ grande **224** 6
~ inferiore **218** 58
~ mobile **224** 6
~ per il trucco **315** 43
~ piano **5** 3
~ piccolo **224** 7
~ primario **5** 1
~ principale **113** 10
~ ribaltabile **115** 17
~ riflettore **14** 59
~ solare **5** 29
~ vaginale **23** 13
spechietto esterno **191** 40
specillo **26** 40
speck **96** 2
~ di prosciutto **95** 53
spedizione **170** 52
~ merci **206** 26
spedizioniere **206** 36
spegnitoio **137** 3
spelta verde **68** 25
spergula **69** 12
sperone *Anim. dom.* **73** 26
~ *Selv.* **88** 23, 57, 82
~ *Navi* **218** 9
~ a vomere **255** 34
~ da stivale **71** 51
~ da tacco **71** 50
~ della falce **66** 15
speronella **60** 13
speroni **71** 50-51
spessimetro **140** 53; **173** 10
spessore **202** 6
spessori di cartone **340** 37
spettatore **315** 8
spettatori **308** 29; **312** 5
spettografo a grata **5** 5
spettro solare **343** 14
spezzettatrice dell'impasto **97** 56, 63
spia *Casa* **38** 62
~ *Autom.* **191** 71, 72, 73, 76, 78, 80
~ del sacchetto **50** 61, 73
~ della batteria **237** 28
~ della portata **237** 29
~ dell'hard disc **244** 5
~ di controllo **50** 10
~ luminosa *Navi* **221** 125

~ luminosa *Ufficio* **249** 71
~ luminosa *Teatro* **315** 52
spiaggia **281** 2
~ sollevata **11** 54
spiario **77** 51
Spica **3** 18
spicchio di luna **88** 71
spider **193** 14
spie luminose **157** 62
spiedo **40** 33
spiegazione dei simboli **14** 27-29
spiga **375** 41, 42; **384** 63
~ composta **370** 68
~ della segale **68** 2
~ semplice **370** 67
spighetta **68** 3, 10; **69** 23
spigolo *Sport* **302** 21
~ *Mat.* **347** 32
~ a vista **151** 23
~ del marciapiede **198** 6
~ non in vista **151** 24
~ superiore del piano stradale **215** 8
spilla **36** 7, 18, 19
~ con testa a sfera **328** 29
~ d'avorio **36** 30
~ di bronzo **328** 29
spillo **143** 76
~ da cravatta **36** 22
spillone per l'esca **89** 41
spin **1** 4
spina **317** 8
~ anticontatto **127** 9
~ cilindrica **143** 40
~ conica **143** 37
~ della prolunga **127** 11
~ di arresto **140** 47
~ di rosa **60** 18
~ dorsale **17** 2-5
~ graduata per anelli **108** 25
~ per corrente trifase **127** 14
spinaci **57** 29
spine delle radici **370** 81
spinetta **322** 45
spintore **221** 93
spioncino **41** 29
~ della cabina **312** 15
spirale **297** 50
spirali della lenza **89** 21
spirea **374** 23
~ ulmaria **373** 28
spirografide **357** 22
spirografo **27** 36
spirometria **27** 36-50
spirometro **23** 31
spitz **70** 20
spogliarellista **318** 27
spogliarello **318** 27-32
spogliatoio **282** 3
spogliatore **84** 32
spoiler *Aeropl.* **229** 39
~ *Ciclismo* **290** 35
~ anteriore **193** 36
~ interno **229** 42
~ posteriore **193** 34
spola **165** 15; **166** 7; **167** 4
spolatore **104** 16
spole di torcitura **164** 60

~ incrociate **164** 58
sponda *Fattoria* **62** 25
~ *Fal.* **132** 35
~ *Biliardo* **277** 16
~ a griglia **62** 26
~ del letto **43** 5
~ di arresto **200** 34, 44
~ di protezione **118** 29; **119** 43
~ elastica **277** 16
sponderuola **132** 25
spore germinanti **381** 8
sporgenza dell'incudine **137** 14
sport cabrio **193** 26
~ del bob **303** 19-21
~ dello sci **301** 1-72
sportello *Carrozze* **186** 11
~ *Stazione* **204** 35
~ a vetri **44** 18
~ accettazione pacchi **236** 1
~ avvolgibile **245** 5
~ del blimp **313** 18
~ del cambio **250** 10
~ della cenere **38** 39
~ della cinepresa **313** 25
~ della'stufa **309** 7
~ di alimentazione **38** 61
~ di carico **139** 4
~ di chiusura **309** 27
~ di controllo **238** 38
~ per distribuzione automatica valori bollati **236** 19
~ per i versamenti **236** 25
~ per la vendita dei valori bollati **236** 15
~ posteriore **194** 11
~ ribaltabile **213** 25
~ ribaltabile della carrozzeria **249** 36
~ telescopico del forno **39** 14
sporto di fondazione **123** 3
sposa **332** 15
sposo **332** 16
spostamento di precisione **112** 5
~ grossolano **112** 4
~ molecolare **170** 23
spostare **54** 5
spranga di guida **85** 16
~ trasversale **119** 49
spranghetta di bloccaggio **247** 43
spray da scarpe **50** 40
~ nebulizzatore **50** 13
spremiagrumi **40** 9
spremitura **169** 5
~ del luccio **89** 11
sprinter **298** 5
sprone **33** 19
spruzzaglia **83** 8
spruzzata **67** 7
spruzzatore *Lotta antiparass.* **83** 58
~ *Parruc.* **106** 21
~ *Fabbr. della carta* **172** 72
~ a mano **83** 24
~ a polvere **181** 10

~ del profumo **43** 26
spruzzetta **349** 8
spugna *Ufficio* **247** 31
~ *Scuola* **260** 42
~ *Arte grafica* **340** 25
~ *Invertebrati* **357** 13
~ da bagno **49** 6
~ silicea **369** 7
spugnola bastarda **381** 25
~ conica **381** 27
~ rotonda **381** 26
spumante **98** 63
spuntasigari **107** 9
spunterbo **100** 58
sputacchiera **24** 12
squadra *Sarto* **103** 13
~ *Ufficio* **151** 7
~ *Scuola* **260** 37
~ *Ginnastica* **296** 49
~ a cappello **120** 69
~ a 30° **151** 8
~ da disegno **151** 7
~ da falegname **132** 6; **134** 26
~ dei giocatori **305** 25
~ di colata **148** 13
~ di salvataggio **270** 17
~ d'intervento **270** 34
~ in acciaio **108** 28
~ metallica **120** 78
~ per vetro **124** 20
~ semplice **140** 57
~ zoppa **120** 82
squadro **183** 17
squalo **364** 1
~ azzurro **364** 1
squama **371** 12; **372** 42
~ con antere **372** 45, 50
~ del cono **372** 5, 8, 14, 27, 38
~ del cono femminile maturo **372** 34
~ della pigna **372** 27
~ fruttifera **372** 8, 14, 67
squamato **366** 10
squaw **352** 10
stabbiolo da parto e da allevamento dei lattonzoli **75** 40
~ dei maialini **75** 36
stabilimenti **310** 1
~ di montaggio **310** 3
~ di sviluppo **310** 2
stabilimento **15** 37
~ di gradazione **274** 1
~ termale **274** 8
stabilizzatore *Autom.* **192** 71
~ *Aeropl.* **229** 26
~ *Vigili del fuoco* **270** 50
~ *Sport del volo* **288** 23
~ *Sport* **305** 58
~ di ossigeno **27** 42
stabilizzatori aerodinamici **234** 7
staccata frontale **295** 15
~ sagittale **295** 14
staccato **321** 34
stacchetta **121** 95; **122** 74
staccionata *Ortic.* **52** 10
~ *Cant.* **118** 44

**It 84**

~ di scorrimento in materiale plastico 301 52
~ di stampa 340 59
~ disboscata 84 13
~ freatica 13 77
~ ghiacciata 304 19
~ intonacata 123 72
~ laterale 347 40
~ lunare 6 13
~ non lavorata 151 20
~ portante 230 43; 287 29; 288 27
~ rifinita 151 22
~ terrestre 11 6-12
~ tratteggiata 151 29
supermercato 99 1-95
supinatore 18 39
supporti 164 42
~ a rulli 157 26
~ rettificatori 163 41
~ semplici 126 56
supporto Carta 14 50
~ Strum. ottici 112 55
~ Autom. 192 73
~ Ferrovia 202 29
~ Navi 221 102; 226 40
~ Giochi 292 31
~ a tre piedi 349 28
~ albero 91 10
~ anteriore 150 33
~ capillare 23 42
~ dati 176 5
~ degli irrigatori a pioggia 62 28
~ dei tubi 27 47
~ del cilindro 148 60
~ del cliché 178 44
~ del cuscinetto 177 61
~ del motore 190 38
~ del pantografo 175 53
~ del rotore 232 23
~ del telaio 132 70
~ della catena 226 26
~ della cuffia 261 41
~ della lastra 178 35
~ della meccanica 325 15
~ della mola 150 3
~ dell'albero portaelica 223 59
~ dell'antenna 237 65
~ dell'aspiratore 133 40
~ dell'avantreno 192 84
~ delle lastre 178 27
~ delle pipette 23 52
~ dell'obiettivo 112 18
~ dell'utensile 150 13
~ di gomma 192 82
~ di guida 113 14
~ filtri 112 57
~ idraulico 5 10; 310 50
~ in plastica del ventilatore 190 8
~ laterale 165 12
~ mediano 177 65
~ motore 191 53
~ per guanti 271 20
~ per i tronchi 157 31
~ per il rotolo di carta non stampata 180 3

~ per la carrozzeria 192 72
~ per la macchina fotografica 112 20
~ per la testina di registrazione 311 25
~ regolabile 67 22
~ rotaie di scorrimento 201 15
~ stellare dei rotoli 180 3, 19
surfer 279 5
surfing 279 1-6
surfista 284 1
surriscaldatore 152 9
susina 59 20
susino 59 19-23
susta 111 13
sveglia 110 11
~ elettrica 43 16
svenuto 270 24
svettatoio 56 11
sviluppatrice 116 1, 48
~ a luce solare 116 5
~ a più piani 116 3
~ a tamburo 116 20
~ automatica a rulli 116 60
sviluppo cromogeno 116 10
~ dei velieri in 400 anni 220 35-37
swing verticale 293 84

**T**

T-shirt 29 27; 31 38
tabaccheria 204 47
tabacchiera 107 20
tabacco 382 43
~ da masticare 107 19
~ da naso 107 20
~ ritorto 107 18
tabella dei prezzi 96 19
~ del sedimento urinario 23 58
~ del totalizzatore 289 35
tabellone 292 30; 293 70
~ dei risultati 293 34
~ illustrato della cavità oculare 22 32
tabernacolo 330 42
tabliatubo di piombo 126 65
tacca 175 47
~ di mira 87 66; 255 19
~ di ritegno a molla 87 70
~ direzionale 84 28
taccata di bacino 222 39
tacchina 73 28
tacchino 73 28
tacco Calzolaio 100 67; 101 28
~ Navi 222 40
tachigrafo 210 54
tachimetro Veicoli 188 19, 34; 189 40; 197 31
~ Ferrovia 212 9
~ con contachilometri parziale 191 74
~ con contafogli 181 54
~ della bicicletta 187 33

tagete 60 20
tagli 252 30-39
~ fantasia 36 68-71
tagliacartone 183 16
tagliando della cassa malattia 22 9
~ per il rinnovo del foglio cedole 251 19
tagliaorli 100 48
tagliapatate 40 43
tagliapietre 158 34
tagliardesia 122 84
tagliategole 122 33
tagliatelle 98 34
tagliatrice Pellicciaio 131 23
~ Fornace 159 15
~ per pelli 131 5
tagliatubi 126 84
tagliavetri 124 25-26
~ d'acciaio 124 26
taglierina Pellicola 117 95
~ Ufficio 151 15
~ Fibre sin. 169 30
~ Legatoria 183 16; 185 20
~ a rulli 173 42
~ con depolverizzatore 172 1
~ per bracciali in metallo 109 19
taglio Econ. forest. 84 29; 85 2
~ Parruc. 106 3
~ Mecc. 143 38
~ a botte 36 56, 75
~ a brillante 36 44
~ a cabochon 36 47
~ a navetta 36 55
~ a pera 36 54
~ a rosetta 36 45
~ a scacchiera 36 66
~ a T 54 32
~ a tavola 36 46
~ a tavola ottagonale 36 74
~ a tavola ovale 36 72
~ a tavola rettangolare 36 73
~ a trapezio incrociato 36 58
~ a triangolo 36 67
~ antico a cabochon 36 76
~ del bosco 84 15-37
~ del nastro 170 60
~ del perno a vite 143 49
~ della lima 140 28
~ incrociato a esagono 36 65
~ incrociato a esagono ovoidale 36 63
~ normale 36 48
~ ottagonale incrociato 36 53
~ rettangolare a cabochon 36 77
~ rotondo 36 42-43
~ scalare a esagono 36 62, 64
~ scalare a rombo 36 59
~ scalare a trapezio 36 57

~ scalare a triangolo 36 60 e 61
~ scalare ottagonale 36 52
~ scalare quadrato 36 51
~ scalare rettangolare 36 50
tagliola 87 48
tagliolo 137 32
~ a freddo 137 38
tailleur 31 1
talea 54 20, 24
~ a gemma 54 22
~ in acqua 54 19
~ legnosa 54 25
tallero imperiale 252 6
tallo 378 49
talpa 366 4
Tam-Tam 354 18
tamburello 317 27; 324 45
tamburo Fil. del cotone 163 43
~ Fabbr. della carta 173 35
~ Carnevale 306 70
~ Strum. mus. 323 55
~ Arte 335 44
~ Etnologia 354 14
~ addensatore 172 62
~ del freno 138 11
~ del freno a mano 192 50
~ della betoniera 118 34
~ della lavatrice 50 24
~ dell'asciugatrice 50 29
~ di accumulo 180 34
~ di avvolgimento 148 72
~ di schiusa 74 29
~ di tostatura 98 71
~ di trasferimento 180 36, 42
~ di trasferimento con sistema di pinze 180 65
~ di trasferimento dei fogli stampati 180 55
~ graduato 149 64
~ militare 323 55
~ miscelatore dell'asfalto 200 50
~ per fibre 162 55
~ per lo scarto 172 59
~ per lo spegnimento della calce viva 172 51
~ rotolante 273 45
~ rullante 323 51; 324 48
~ testina VHS 243 11
~ testina video 243 8
~ voltafogli 180 5, 20
tamil 341 11
tampone 340 22
~ del ponte elevatore 195 27
~ di pressione 133 47
~ per timbri 22 30
tana 86 26
~ del coniglio 86 26
tanaceto 380 9
tanaglia 140 69
tangente Strum. mus. 322 43
~ Mat. 346 32, 48
tanica 34 56
~ col manico 129 7
~ con il solvente 129 16

# Index

## Ordering
In this index the entries are ordered as follows:
1. Entries consisting of single words, e.g.: 'hair'.
2. Entries consisting of noun + adjective. Within this category the adjectives are entered alphabetically, e.g. 'hair, bobbed' is followed by 'hair, closely-cropped'. Where adjective and noun are regarded as elements of a single lexical item, they are not inverted, e.g.: 'blue spruce', not 'spruce, blue'.
3. Entries consisting of other phrases, e.g. 'hair curler', 'ham on the bone', are alphabetized as headwords.
Where a whole phrase makes the meaning or use of a headword highly specific, the whole phrase is entered alphabetically. For example 'ham on the bone' follows 'hammock'.

## References
The numbers in bold type refer to the sections in which the word many be found, and those in normal type refer to the items named in the pictures. Homonyms, and in some cases uses of the same word in different fields, are distinguished by section headings (in italics), some of which are abbreviated, to help to identify at a glance the field required. In most cases the full form referred to by the abbreviations will be obvious. Those which are not explained in the following list:

| | | | |
|---|---|---|---|
| *Agr.* | Agriculture / Agricultural | *Hydr. Engl.* | Hydraulic Engineering |
| *Alp. Plants* | Alpine Plants | *Impl.* | Implements |
| *Art. Studio* | Artist's Studio | *Inf. Tech.* | Information Technology |
| *Bldg.* | Building | *Intern. Combust. Eng.* | Internal Combustion Engine |
| *Carp.* | Carpenter | *Moon L.* | Moon Landing |
| *Cement Wks.* | Cement Works | *Music Not.* | Musical Notation |
| *Cost.* | Costumes | *Overh. Irrign.* | Overhead Irrigation |
| *Cyc.* | Cycle | *Platem.* | Platemaking |
| *Decid.* | Deciduous | *Plant. Propagn.* | Propagation of Plants |
| *D.I.Y.* | Do-it-yourself | *Rm.* | Room |
| *Dom. Anim.* | Domestic Animals | *Serv. Stat.* | Service Station |
| *Equest.* | Equestrian Sport | *Sp.* | Sports |
| *Fabul. Creat.* | Fabulous Creatures | *Text.* | Textile[s] |
| *Gdn.* | Garden | *Veg.* | Vegetable[s] |

## A

Aaron's rod 376 9
abacus 309 77
abacus *Art* 334 20
abattoir 94
abbreviated dialling key 237 13
abdomen *Man* 16 35-37, 36
abdomen *Bees* 77 10-19
abdomen *Forest Pests* 82 9
abdomen, lower ~ 16 37
abdomen, upper ~ 16 35
abductor hallucis 18 49
abductor of the hallux 18 49
aberdevine 361 8
aborigine, Australian ~ 352 37
abrasion platform 13 31
abrasive wheel combination 111 28, 35
abscissa 347 9
abseiling 300 28-30
abseil piton 300 39
abseil sling 300 28
absinth 380 4
absorber attachment 27 44
absorption dynamometer 143 97-107
absorption muffler 190 16
absorption silencer 190 16
abutment *Bridges* 215 27, 29, 45
abutment *Art* 336 20
abutment pier 215 29
acanthus 334 25

acceleration lane 15 16
acceleration rocket 234 22, 4
accelerator 191 46
accelerator lock 85 17
accelerator pedal 191 46, 94
accelerometer 230 10
accent, acute ~ 342 30
accent, circumflex ~ 342 32
accent, grave ~ 342 31
accent, strong ~ 321 27
accents 342 30-35
acceptance 250 12, 23
access arm 244 47
access balcony 37 72-76
access flap 62 1, 25
accessories 115 54-74
accessory shoe 114 4; 115 4
accessory shop 196 24
access ramp 199 15
access slot 244 42
acciaccatura 321 15
accipiters 362 10-13
accolade 329 66
accommodation 146 33
accommodation bureau 204 28
accommodation ladder 221 98
accomodation module 146 33
accompaniment side 324 43
accompaniment string 324 24
accordion 324 36
account, private ~ 250 4
accounting machine 236 26
account number 250 26
accumulator 309 41
accumulator *Theatre* 316 55
accumulator railcar 211 55

accuracy jump 288 55
acerate 370 34
acerose 370 34
acerous 370 34
acetylene connection 141 31
acetylene control 141 32
acetylene cylinder 141 2, 22
achene 58 23
achievement 254 1-6
achievement, marital ~ 254 10-13
achievement of arms 254 1-6
Achilles' tendon 18 48
acicular 370 34
acid container 350 62
acolyte 331 45
aconite 379 1
acorn 371 4
acorns 276 42
acoustic coupler 237 48; 244 66
acrobat 307 47
Acropolis 334 1-7
acroter 334 34
acroterion 334 34
acroterium 334 34
acting area light 316 16
acting area spotlight 316 16
actinia 369 20
Actinophrys 357 7
action 326 6-16
action lever 325 32
activated blade attachment 84 33
actor 316 37

actress 316 38
actuating transistor 195 19
actuator 244 47
acuity projector 111 47
acute 342 30
ad 342 56
Adam's apple 19 13
adapter 112 55
adapter, four-socket ~ 127 8
adapter, four-way ~ 127 8
adapter ring 115 55
added-feature telephone 237 9, 19, 22
adders 364 40 u. 41
adding 344 23
adding and subtracting machine 309 74
addition 344 23
address 236 42
address bus 244 52
address display 236 41
addressing machine, transfer-type ~ 245 7
address label 236 4
address system, ship's ~ 224 30
A-deck 223 28-30
adhesion railcar 214 1
adhesive, hot ~ 249 61
adhesive binder *Bookbind.* 184 1
adhesive binder *Office* 249 61
adhesive tape dispenser 247 27
adhesive tape dispenser, roller-type ~ 247 28
adhesive tape holder 247 28
adjusting cone 187 58

axis, normal ~ **230** 70
axis, polar ~ **113** 15, 18
axis, synclinal ~ **12** 19
axis, transverse ~ **347** 23
axis, vertical ~ **230** 70
axis mount, English-type ~ **113** 22
axis mounting, English-type ~ **113** 22
axis of abscissae **347** 2
axis of ordinates **347** 3
axis of rotation, instantaneous ~ **4** 25
axis of rotation, mean ~ **4** 27
axis of symmetry *Maths.* **346** 25
axis of symmetry *Crystals* **351** 4
axle **187** 61, 76, 81
axle, coupled ~ **210** 36
axle, floating ~ *Agr. Mach.* **65** 33
axle, floating ~ *Motorcycle* **189** 34
axle, live ~ **192** 65-71
axle, rigid ~ **192** 65-71
axle bearing **210** 10
axle drive shaft **201** 13
azalea **53** 12
azimuth **87** 74
azure *Heraldry* **254** 28
azure *Colour* **343** 6

# B

baboon **368** 13
baby **28** 5
baby bath **28** 3
baby carriage **28** 34; **272** 71; **273** 31
baby clothes **29** 1-12
baby doll **48** 25
baby grand piano **325** 40
baby pants **28** 22
baby pants, rubber ~ **29** 10
baby powder **28** 14
baby scales **22** 42
back *Man* **16** 22-25
back *Tablew. etc.* **45** 56
back *Horse* **72** 29
back *Mills* **91** 2
back *Roof* **122** 861
back *Bookbind.* **185** 41
back *Car* **193** 20, 35
back *Swim.* **282** 49
back *Ball Games* **293** 77
back *Sports* **305** 11
backband **71** 19
backboard **292** 30
backboard support **292** 31
backbone *Man* **17** 2-5
backbone *Bookbind.* **185** 41
back check **325** 27
back check felt **325** 28
backcloth **315** 33; **316** 10
back comb **105** 6
back cushion **42** 25
back cut **84** 29
backdrop **315** 33; **316** 10
backdrop light **316** 15
back fat **95** 40
backfilling **217** 7
back flip **297** 24
backgammon **276** 18
backgammon board **276** 22
back gauge **183** 17; **185** 4, 7
background *Films* **310** 33
background *Theatre* **316** 10
backhand stroke **293** 39
backing **269** 29
backing disc, rubber ~ **134** 22

backing paper *Photog.* **114** 21
backing paper *Paperhanger* **128** 5
back left second pin **305** 9
back loop **288** 50
back of the hand **19** 83
backpack unit **6** 20
back-pedal brake **187** 63
back pin **305** 11
back plate **140** 36
back-pressure valve, hydraulic ~ **141** 8
backrest *Weaving* **166** 37
backrest *Railw.* **207** 66
backrest, reclining ~ **191** 35
back right second pin **305** 10
back scouring valve **216** 61
backside **16** 40
back sight leaf **87** 67
back sight slide **87** 69
back standard adjustment **114** 55
backstay **219** 19
backstitch seam **102** 1
back support **295** 22; **296** 29
back-up ball **305** 20
back vault **297** 32
backward grand circle **296** 60
backward somersault *Swim.* **282** 42
backward somersault *Gymn.* **297** 15
backward underswing **296** 59
backward walkover **297** 23
backwater **172** 26
bacon **96** 2
Bactrian camel **366** 29
badge, fool's ~ **306** 60
badger **88** 48
badging **191** 12
badminton **293** 43 *u.* 44
badminton game **273** 6
badminton racket **293** 43
badminton racquet **293** 43
baffle board *Warships* **259** 27
baffle board **309** 17
baffle board, hinged ~ **259** 15
baffle board, movable ~ **259** 15
bag *Doc.* **22** 33
bag *Hunt* **86** 38
bag *Music. Instr.* **322** 9
bag, girl's ~ **29** 56
bag, heat-sealed ~ **76** 29
bag, paper ~ **98** 48
bag, postman's ~ **236** 54
bag filter **83** 54
bag-full indicator **50** 61, 73
baggage compartment **257** 15
baggage loader **233** 22
baggage man **267** 17
'baggage reclaim' **233** 38
baggage terminal **233** 5, 16
bagging nozzle **83** 55
bag net **77** 54
bagpipe **322** 8
bagsealer **40** 47
baguette **97** 12
bag wig **34** 4
bail **292** 70
bailey, inner ~ **329** 2
bailey, outer ~ **329** 31
bait **86** 21
bait, poisoned ~ **83** 31
bait, weighted ~ **89** 36
bait needle **89** 41
baits **89** 65-76
bait tin **89** 24
bakehouse **97** 55-74
baker's shop **97** 1-54
bakery **97**; **97** 55-74
baking ingredient **99** 62
baking ingredients **98** 8-11

balalaika **324** 28
Balance *Astron.* **3** 19; **4** 59
balance *Paperm.* **173** 9
balance beam **349** 30
balance cable **214** 46
balance cable sleeve **214** 74
balance column **349** 29
balance control **241** 54
balancer **307** 48
balance rail **322** 39
balance wheel **110** 31
balancing act **307** 44
balancing knob **116** 39
balancing pole **307** 42
balcony *Dwellings* **37** 18, 69, 73
balcony *Theatre* **315** 16; **315** 18
balcony *Chivalry* **329** 12
balcony, projecting ~ **218** 57
baldachin **331** 49
baldaquin **331** 49
bald patch **34** 21
bale **55** 31; **63** 34; **75** 7; **83** 13; **169** 34; **170** 62; **206** 10, 11, 23
bale arm **89** 62
bale breaker **163** 7
bale loader, hydraulic ~ **63** 37
bale opener **163** 7
baler, high-pressure ~ **63** 35
baling press **169** 33
balk **63** 3
ball *Infant Care etc.* **28** 16
ball *Bicycle* **187** 31
ball *Aircraft* **230** 12
ball *Ball Games* **292** 27
ball *Circus* **307** 60
ball, ivory ~ **277** 1
ball, metal ~ **352** 32
ball, paper ~ **306** 55
ball, plastic ~ **277** 1
ball, steel ~ **143** 70
ball, stone ~ **352** 32
ball and socket head **114** 47
ballast *Station* **205** 61
ballast *Railw.* **212** 66
ballast *Sailing* **285** 33
ballast *Airsports* **288** 65
ballast keel **285** 32
ballast tank **223** 78
ball bearing **143** 69; **187** 56, 68
ball boy **293** 22
ballerina **314** 26
ballet **314**
ballet dancer **314** 26
ballet positions **314** 1-6
ballet shoe **314** 30
ballet skirt **314** 31
ballet slipper **314** 30
ball games **291**; **292**; **293**
ballistics **87** 73
ball mill **161** 1
ball of clay **161** 9
ball of the foot **19** 58
ball of the thumb **19** 75
balloon **308** 13
balloon, gas ~ **288** 63
balloon, hot-air ~ **288** 79
balloon, manned ~ **7** 16
balloon basket **288** 64
ballooning **288** 63-84
ballot box **263** 28
ballot envelope **263** 21
ballot paper **263** 20
ball race **187** 68
ballroom **306** 1
Balmer series **1** 21
baluster **38** 29; **123** 51
balustrade **38** 25; **123** 22, 50
bamboo cane **136** 31
bamboo culm **383** 60
bamboo stem **383** 60, 63

banana **99** 90; **384** 33
banana flower **384** 34
banana-handling terminal **226** 22
banana leaf **384** 35
banana plant **384** 28
banana saddle **188** 59
banana tree **384** 28
band *Ball Games* **291** 25
band *Nightclub* **318** 3
band *Church* **332** 5
band, fluorescent ~ **199** 8
band, iron ~ **130** 16
band, ornamental ~ **334** 38
band, steel ~ **163** 5
bandage *First Aid* **21** 9
bandage *Equest.* **289** 15
bandages, emergency ~ **21** 1-13
band brake **143** 104
banderilla **319** 22
banderillero **319** 4, 21
band of barrel **130** 8
bandoneon **324** 36
bandora **322** 21
bandsaw **134** 50; **157** 48
bandsaw, horizontal ~ **157** 48
bandsaw blade **157** 53
band selection button **241** 45
bandstand **274** 19; **307** 9
band wheel **104** 15
band wheel cover **133** 32
banewort **37** 97
banger **306** 51
bangle *Jewell.* **36** 17
bangle *Ethnol.* **354** 38
bangle, asymmetrical ~ **36** 26
bangs **34** 36
banjo **324** 29
bank *Phys. Geog.* **13** 4
bank *Bank* **250**
bank *Roulette* **275** 11
bank acceptance **250** 12
bank branch **204** 31
bank clerk **250** 5
bank employee **251** 7
banknotes **252** 30-39
bank of circulation **252** 31
bank of issue **252** 31
bank of oars **218** 12
bank protection **216** 51-55
bank slope **217** 28
bank stabilization **216** 51-55
bank statement **247** 44
banner *Flags* **253** 12
banner *Election* **263** 12
banner, processional ~ **331** 44
banqueting hall **267** 39
bantam **74** 56
baptism, Christian ~ **332** 1
baptistery **332** 2
bar *Horse* **71** 41
bar *Office* **246** 29
bar *Restaurant* **266** 1-11
bar *Hotel* **267** 54
bar *Park* **272** 34
bar *Playground* **273** 32
bar *Gymn.* **296** 3, 8; **297** 4, 41
bar *Athletics* **298** 14, 34
bar *Winter Sp.* **303** 5
bar *Circus* **307** 50
bar *Disco* **317** 1, 9
bar *Nightclub* **318** 13, 15
bar *Music. Not.* **320** 42
bar *Graphic Art* **340** 34
bar, flat ~ **143** 10
bar, metal ~ **324** 77
bar, round ~ **143** 8
bar, sliding ~ **75** 21
bar arm **299** 10
barb *Bees* **77** 10
barb *Fish Farm.* **89** 80

climate, equatorial ~ **9** 53
climates **9** 53-58
climates, polar ~ **9** 57-58
climatic map **9** 40-58
climatology **9**
climber *Flower Gdn.* **51** 5
climber *Fruit & Veg. Gdn.* **52** 5
climber *Indoor Plants* **53** 2
climber *Veg.* **57** 8
climber *Mountain* **300** 5
climbing **300** 2-13
climbing boot **300** 44
climbing breeches **300** 7
climbing equipment **300** 31-57
climbing frame **273** 47
climbing harness **300** 56
climbing net **273** 50
climbing plant **53** 2
climbing roof **273** 60
climbing rope **273** 48; **296** 19
climbing tower **273** 17
clinch **299** 31
clinker cooler **160** 9
clinker pit **152** 8
clinker planking **285** 50-52
clinker store **160** 10
clinoprinacoid **351** 24
clip *Atom* **218**
clip *Bicycle* **187** 62
clip *Railw.* **202** 9
clipper display **238** 44
clippers, electric ~ **105** 21; **106** 32
clipper ship, English ~ **220** 36
clitellum **357** 26
clitoris **20** 88
Clivia minata **53** 8
cloak **355** 18, 26
cloak, red ~ **319** 27
cloak, short ~ **355** 29
cloak, Spanish ~ **355** 29
cloak, woollen ~ **355** 6
cloak cord **355** 24
cloakroom **48** 34; **207** 70; **315** 5; **318** 1
cloakroom attendant **315** 6; **318** 2
cloakroom hall **315** 5-11
cloakroom ticket **315** 7
cloche **35** 12
clock **191** 38; **211** 37; **212** 16
clock, double ~ **276** 16
clock, electric ~ **191** 79
clock, main ~ **245** 18
clock case **110** 18; **309** 57
clockmaker **109** 1
clocks **110**
clockwork **110** 28
clockwork drive **10** 14
clockwork mechanism **110** 28
clod **63** 7
clog **101** 44; **355** 43
cloister **331** 52
cloister vault **336** 41
closed vertical gate **301** 66
close-range surface-to-air missile **258** 62
close-up bellows attachment **115** 58
close-up lens **117** 55
closing gear **90** 27
closing head **143** 59
closure rail **202** 26
cloth **166** 12; **271** 59
cloth, damask ~ **45** 2
cloth, felt ~ **340** 42
cloth, flannel ~ **128** 48
cloth, linen ~ **206** 11
cloth, sterile ~ **26** 38
cloth, unraised ~ **168** 33
clothes, children's ~ **29**
clothes, teenagers' ~ **29** 48-68
clothes brush **50** 44; **104** 31

clothes closet **43** 1
clothes closet door **46** 2
clothes compartment **212** 63; **267** 30
clothes line **38** 23; **50** 33
clothes louse **81** 41
clothes moth **81** 13
clothes rack **271** 31
clothes rack, movable ~ **103** 7
clothes shop **268** 9
clothing, protective ~ **84** 26; **270** 46
cloth roller **166** 20
cloth-shearing machine, rotary ~ **168** 42
cloth take-up motion **166** 19
cloth take-up roller **166** 47
cloth temple **166** 13
cloud, lenticular ~ **287** 19
cloud chamber photograph **2** 26
cloud chamber track **2** 27
cloud cover **9** 20-24
clouds **8** 1-19, 1-4, 5-12, 13-17
clouds, luminous ~ **7** 22
clouds, noctilucent ~ **7** 22
clout **121** 94
clout nail **121** 94; **122** 96
clove **382** 28
clove carnation **60** 7
clove pink **60** 7
clover, four-leaf ~ **6** 95
clover broadcaster **66** 26
clove tree **382** 26
clown **306** 69; **307** 24
clown, musical ~ **307** 23
clown act **307** 25
club **283** 23
club hammer **126** 77
clubhouse **283** 23
club membership **286** 8
club rush **378** 21
clubs **276** 38
clump of grass **375** 44
cluster of eggs **80** 2, 30
cluster of grapes **78** 5
cluster of stars **3** 26
clutch **191** 44
clutch, dry ~ **190** 78
clutch, fluid ~ **65** 37
clutch, main ~ **65** 39
clutch, multi-plate ~ **190** 78
clutch, single-plate ~ **190** 71
clutch coupling **227** 23
clutch flange **177** 55
clutch lever **188** 32
clutch pedal **191** 44, 96; **192** 28
C major **320** 55, 62
C major scale **320** 45
C minor **320** 65
coach *Lorries etc.* **194** 17
coach *Ball Games* **291** 55; **292** 57
coach, four-axled ~ **208** 3
coach body **186** 5; **207** 2; **208** 6
coach bolt **202** 7
coach box **186** 8
coach door **186** 11
coaches **186** 1-3, 26-39, 45, 51-54
coach horse **186** 28
coachman **186** 32
coach screw **202** 7
coach step **186** 13
coach wagons **186** 1-3, 26-39, 45, 51-54
coagulating bath **169** 15
coal **170** 1
coal bunker **152** 2; **225** 19
coal conveyor **152** 1
coal distillation, dry ~ **170** 2
coal feed conveyor **199** 37
coal mill **152** 4

coal mine **144** 1-51
coal scuttle **309** 9
coal seam **144** 50
coal shovel **38** 43
coal tar **170** 3
coal tar extraction **156** 18
coal wharf **225** 18
coaming **283** 59
coarse dirt hose **50** 84
coarse fishing **89** 20-31
coastal cruiser **284** 60
coastal lake **13** 44
coaster **221** 99
coaster brake **187** 63
coasting vessel **221** 99
coat **29** 54; **30** 60; **33** 2
coat, black ~ **289** 4
coat, braided ~ **186** 23
coat, cloth ~ **30** 61; **33** 66
coat, dark ~ **289** 4, 13
coat, fur ~ **30** 60
coat, gallooned ~ **186** 23
coat, loden ~ **30** 64
coat, loose-fitting ~ **271** 41
coat, mink ~ **131** 24
coat, ocelot ~ **131** 25
coat, oilskin ~ **228** 7
coat, poncho-style ~ **30** 68
coat, poplin ~ **33** 60
coat, red ~ **289** 13
coat, three-quarter length ~ **271** 21
coat belt **33** 59
coat button **33** 64
coat collar **33** 58
coater **173** 31, 34
coat hanger **41** 3
coat hook **41** 2; **207** 50; **266** 14
coating, bituminous ~ **200** 58
coating of fluorescent material **240** 19
coat-of-arms **254** 1-6
coat-of-arms, marshalled ~ **254** 10-13
coat-of-arms, provincial ~ **252** 12, 14
coat pocket **33** 61
coat rack **41** 1
coat stand **266** 12
coat-tail **33** 14
cob **59** 49
cobalt bomb **2** 28
cobnut **59** 49
coccinellid **358** 37
coccyx **17** 5; **20** 60
cochlea **17** 63
cock *Farm Bldgs.* **62** 37
cock *Dom. Anim.* **73** 21
cockade **264** 8
cockatrice **327** 34
cockchafer **82** 1
cockchafer grub **82** 12
cocker spaniel **70** 38
cocking handle **255** 12
cocking lever **255** 12
cocking piece **121** 30
cock pheasant **88** 77
cock pigeon **73** 33
cockpit *Aircraft* **230** 1-31, 35; **231** 19
cockpit *Army* **255** 93
cockpit *Police* **264** 2
cockpit *Rowing* **283** 8
cockpit *Sailing* **285** 38
cockpit *Airsports* **288** 10
cockpit canopy **230** 39; **257** 4
cockpit coaming **283** 59
cockpit hood **230** 39; **257** 4
cockroach **81** 17
cockscomb **73** 22
cock's foot **69** 25
cock's head **69** 10
cock's tread **74** 65

cocktail **317** 33
cocktail fork **45** 76
cocktail glass **267** 56
cocktail shaker **267** 61
cocoa *Grocer* **98** 66
cocoa *Trop. Plants* **382** 19
cocoa bean **382** 19
cocoa palm **383** 48
cocoa powder **382** 19
coconut **383** 53
coconut oil **98** 23
coconut palm **383** 48
coconut tree **383** 48
cocoon *Forest Pests* **82** 21
cocoon *Arthropods* **358** 51
coco palm **383** 48
cocotte **306** 37
cod **90** 22
code flag halyard **223** 10
code flag signal **223** 9
cod end **90** 22
code pendant **253** 29
code pennant **253** 29
coding station **236** 35
cod line **90** 23
codling moth **58** 62
codlin moth **58** 62
coefficient **34** 54
coelenterate **357** 14; **369** 5, 9, 14, 20
coffee **98** 65-66, 67; **99** 68-70, 68; **265** 19
coffee *Trop. Plants* **382** 6
coffee, instant ~ **99** 70
coffee, pure ~ **98** 65
coffee bean **38** 26
coffee cup **44** 29
coffee grinder, electric ~ **39** 24; **98** 69
coffee machine **265** 2
coffee maker **39** 38
coffee plant **382** 1
coffee pot **44** 28
coffee roaster **98** 70
coffee service **44** 27
coffee set **44** 27; **265** 18
coffee table **42** 28
coffee tree **382** 1
coffee urn **265** 2
cofferdam **259** 19
coffin **331** 35
coffin chamber **33** 35
cog *Mach. Parts etc.* **143** 83
cog *Ship* **218** 18-26
cog, wooden ~ **91** 9
cognac **98** 59
cog railroad **214** 4 *u.* 5
cog railway **214** 4 *u.* 5
cog wheels **143** 82-96
coiffure, upswept ~ **355** 81
coiffures **34** 27-38
coil **89** 21
coiled-coil filament **127** 58
coiler **148** 72
coiler top **163** 62
coil spring **191** 28; **192** 68
coin **252** 1-29
coin, Celtic ~ **328** 37
coin, gold ~ **36** 37
coin, silver ~ **328** 37
coinage **252** 1-29, 40-44
coin-box telephone **236** 9
coin bracelet **36** 36
coin disc **252** 43
coining dies **252** 40 *u.* 41
coining press **252** 44
coins **252** 1-29
coins, aluminium ~ **252** 1-29
coins, copper ~ **252** 1-29
coins, gold ~ **252** 1-29
coins, nickel ~ **252** 1-29
coins, silver ~ **252** 1-29
coin setting **36** 38

railcar, short-distance ~ **208** 13
railcar, six-axle ~ **197** 13
railcar, twelve-axle ~ **197** 1
rail clip **202** 9
rail foot **202** 4
rail guard **210** 34
rail head **202** 2
railing *Bldg. Site* **118** 89
railing *Park* **272** 34
rail joint **202** 11
railroad *see* railway
railroad map **204** 33
railroad policeman **205** 20
railroad station **15** 41
railroad track **202; 203**
rail service, interurban ~ **197** 1
rail service, urban ~ **197** 13
railway, funicular ~ **214** 12
railway, light ~ **200** 23
railway, main line ~ **15** 21
railway, narrow-gauge ~ *Map* **15** 90
railway, narrow-gauge ~ *Road Constr.* **200** 23
railway employee **204** 45
railway guide, official ~ **204** 46
railway information clerk **204** 45
railway line **202; 203**
railway map **204** 33
railway policeman **205** 20
railway siding **225** 62
railway station **15** 41
railway vehicles **207; 208; 209; 210; 211; 212; 213**
rail web **202** 3
rain **8** 18; **9** 32
rainbow **7** 4
rainbow, colours of the ~ **343** 14
rainbow dressing **221** 85
rain cape **41** 4; **196** 26
rain cloud **8** 10
raincoat **29** 31
raincover **10** 41
rain gauge **10** 38, 44
rainwater pipe **37** 13; **38** 10; **122** 29
rain zone, temperate ~ **9** 55
rain zone, tropical ~ **9** 53
raisin **98** 8
raising of livestock **75**
raising to a power **345** 1
rake *Roof & Boilerr.* **38** 42
rake *Gdn. Tools* **56** 4
rake *Blacksm.* **137** 4
rake *Roulette* **275** 5
rake *Winter Sp.* **303** 24
rake, wire-tooth ~ **51** 3; **56** 3
rake, wooden ~ **66** 23
raking back **118** 61
Ram *Astron.* **4** 53
ram *Dom. Anim.* **73** 13
ram *Blacksm.* **137** 10
ram *Forging* **139** 12
ram *Ship* **218** 9
ram *Theatre* **316** 60
ram, lower ~ **139** 7
ram, upper ~ **139** 6
rambler **52** 5
ram guide **139** 8
ram longwall face **144** 36
rammer **200** 26
rammer, pneumatic ~ **148** 31
ramp *Bldg. Site* **119** 41
ramp *Floor etc. Constr.* **123** 30
ramp *Station* **206** 1
ramp *Ship* **221** 55
ram piston **65** 24
ramson **377** 6

randing **136** 1, 4
randing, oblique ~ **136** 3
rangefinder **255** 82
rangefinder, optical ~ **258** 37
rangefinder window **114** 40
range light, higher ~ **224** 102
range light, lower ~ **224** 101
range lights **224** 101-102
range selector **114** 59
range switch **114** 59
rape **383** 1
rapelling **300** 28-30
rapid adjustment compass **151** 64
rapid feeding system **74** 23
rapid-filter plant **269** 9
rapid heat-up cathode **240** 25
rapid scale **98** 12
rapid-veneer press **133** 49
rapping iron **136** 36
raptorial leg **358** 5
Raschel fabric **167** 29
rasp **260** 55
rasp, shoemaker's ~ **100** 49
raspberry **58** 28; **370** 101
raspberry bush **58** 25
raspberry flower **58** 26
raster image processor **176** 27
ratan chair cane **136** 32
rate-of-climb indicator **230** 14
rate of interest **345** 7
rattan chair cane **136** 32
rattle *Infant Care etc.* **28** 44
rattle *Carnival* **306** 40, 47
rattle, baby's ~ **28** 44
rat trap binding **301** 15
Rautek grip **21** 18
ravine **13** 52
raw coal bunker **144** 41
raw material *Cement Wks.* **160** 1, 4
raw material *Synth. Fibres* **169** 1-12
raw material store **160** 3
raw meal silo **160** 5
raw milk pump **76** 3
raw milk storage tank **76** 5
raw mill **160** 4, 7
ray *Church* **332** 37
ray *Maths.* **346** 20
ray, medullary ~ **370** 11
ray, vascular ~ **370** 11
ray floret **375** 31
rays, sun's ~ **4** 9
razor, open ~ **106** 38
razor, straight ~ **106** 38
razor handle **106** 39
R-class **284** 59
reach, lower ~ **217** 29
reach, upper ~ **217** 37
reaching leg **285** 24
reactor **154** 3, 41, 50
reactor, nuclear ~ **1** 48; **154** 19
reactor building **154** 20
reactor core **259** 68
reactor pressure vessel **154** 22
reader **260** 16
reading adjustment **10** 10
reading lamp **43** 15
reading microscope **113** 28
reading room **262** 13
reading room staff **262** 14
readout, digital ~ **110** 2; **112** 47
readout, fast ~ **195** 12
read-write head **244** 42, 48
read-write head drive motor **244** 51
ready position **305** 72
reamer **109** 8; **140** 31
reamer, angled ~ **125** 9
rear brace **329** 47

rearing of livestock **75**
rear of the railcar **197** 4
rearsight **255** 19
rear vault **297** 32
rear-view mirror **188** 35; **189** 30
rear-view mirror, inside ~ **191** 39
rearward horizontal stand **295** 31
rearward swing **296** 57
rear window heating switch **191** 82
rebate plane **132** 25
receipt **98** 44; **271** 7
receipt stamp **236** 29
receiver *Meteorol. Instr.* **10** 63
receiver *Hunt.* **87** 16
receiver *Docks* **226** 33
receiver *Post* **237** 10
receiver *Audio* **241** 5, 37, 61; **242** 16
receiver *Office* **246** 16
receiver *Ball Games* **293** 50
receiver *Nightclub* **318** 18
receiver, tilting-type ~ **148** 5
receiver cord **237** 3
receiver surface, blackened ~ **155** 29
receiving antenna **237** 66
receiving grids **244** 29
receiving hopper **147** 5
receiving table **249** 54
receiving tray **249** 47
receiving truck **226** 15
receptacle **370** 53
reception *Doc.* **22** 5
reception *Camping* **278** 1
reception hall **267** 1-26
receptionist, chief ~ **267** 7
recess **217** 70
reciprocal **344** 16
recirculation pump **154** 43, 54
recoil booster **255** 27
record **46** 15; **309** 32; **317** 24
record button **242** 11
record chamber, automatic ~ **241** 18
record deck **241** 4, 18
recorder *Meteorol. Instr.* **10** 61
recorder *Hosp.* **25** 3
recorder *Video* **243** 1
recorder *Music. Instr.* **322** 7
recorder, eight-channel ~ **27** 28
recorder, potentiometric ~ **23** 55
recording, photographic ~ **27** 33
recording amplifier **311** 11
recording and playback deck, single ~ **238** 58
recording and playback equipment **311** 23
recording arm **10** 7, 12, 15, 21
recording channel, central ~ **238** 1-6
recording drum **10** 5, 16, 20
recording engineer **310** 23, 55; **311** 36
recording head *Cine Film* **117** 33
recording head *Films* **311** 25
recording indicator light **242** 26
recording instrument **10** 61
recording level control **117** 16; **242** 16
recording level indicator **311** 14
recording loudspeaker **238** 37
recording mechanism **10** 42
recording meter **138** 19

recording paper **25** 4; **272** 9, 34, 40
recording pen **10** 13
recording rain gauge **10** 38
recording room **238** 16; **310** 54
recording room mixing console **238** 25
recording sensitivity selector **117** 16
recording space **177** 49
recording speaker **238** 37
record keeper **299** 48
record of posting book **236** 18
record player **46** 10; **241** 4, 18; **317** 19
record-protected cassette **242** 49
record rack **241** 10; **309** 36
record size selector **241** 30
record turntable **238** 24
recovery parachute **235** 60
rectangle **346** 34
rectifier *Blacksm.* **138** 30
rectifier *Electrotyp. etc.* **178** 2
rectifier *Films* **312** 18
rector **330** 22
rectory **331** 20
rectoscope **23** 16, 17
rectoscopy **23** 18
rectum **20** 22, 61
rectus abdominis **18** 44
red **343** 1
red admiral **365** 1
red-billed toucan **363** 6
redbreast **361** 15
redcap **205** 31
red card **291** 63
red clover **69** 1
red deer **88** 1-27, 1
red flyer **366** 3
red fox **88** 42; **367** 12
redial button, last number ~ **237** 12
red kangaroo **366** 3
red magnolia **373** 15
redstart **360** 3
red swing filter **116** 46
reducing coupler **126** 39, 41
reducing elbow **126** 49
reducing socket **126** 39, 41
reducing valve **141** 5
reduction drive lever **149** 3
reduction gear *Paperm.* **172** 69
reduction gear *Aircraft* **232** 59
reduction gear *Warships* **259** 61
reduction gearing, multi-step ~ **64** 71
reduction key **249** 40
red underwing **365** 8
red whortleberry **377** 23
red wine glass **45** 83
reed *Basketm.* **136** 28
reed *Weaving* **166** 10
reed *Music. Instr.* **326** 41
reed, double ~ **323** 29
reed mace **136** 27
reed mace bulrush **378** 21
reed organ **325** 43
reed pen **341** 22
reed pipe, metal ~ **326** 17-22
reed stop **326** 17-22
reed-threading draft **171** 6
reef **219** 72
reefer **221** 127
reel, fixed-spool ~ **89** 32, 61
reel, multiplying ~ **89** 59
reel, spring-tine ~ **64** 4
reel, stationary-drum ~ **89** 61
reel arm, foldaway ~ **117** 92
reel drum **312** 16
reel drum, fireproof ~ **312** 25
reel gearing **64** 5

rule, glazier's ~ **124** 21
rule of three **345** 8-10
rule-of-three sum **345** 8-10
rule pocket **33** 49
ruler **151** 33; **247** 35
ruling pen **151** 49
ruling pen attachment **151** 58, 61
rum **98** 57
ruminant **73** 1
ruminants **366** 28-30; **367** 1-10
rummer **45** 87
rump *Horse* **72** 31
rump *Game* **88** 20, 36
rump *Meat* **95** 14, 35
rump piece **329** 88
runch **61** 18
rune **341** 19
rung **38** 17; **50** 38
runner *Plant Propagn.* **54** 14, 16
runner *Soft Fruit* **58** 20
runner *Mills* **91** 22
runner *Iron Foundry etc.* **148** 21
runner *Rowing* **283** 45
runner *Ball Games* **292** 45, 66
runner *Athletics* **298** 5
runner, movable ~ **303** 10
runner, outrigged ~ **302** 46
runner bean **52** 28; **57** 8
runner gate **148** 21
running *Sailing* **285** 1
running *Athletics* **298** 1-8
running axle **210** 35
running-boar target **305** 33
running dog **334** 39
running gear, front ~ **191** 52
running head **185** 66
running light, side ~ **258** 15
running light indicator panel **224** 29
running posture **295** 2
running side **277** 5
running step **295** 41
running step indicator **211** 36
running take-off twist dive **282** 43
running three **305** 3, 5
running title **185** 66
running track **298** 6
running wheel **64** 41, 56; **214** 7, 70
runout **147** 54
runway *Hunt.* **86** 16
runway *Airport* **233** 1
runway *Gliding* **287** 15
rush *Phys. Geog.* **13** 17
rush *Basketm.* **136** 27
rusk **97** 54
*Russula vesca* **381** 23
rustication **335** 51
rusticwork **335** 51
rutting mane **88** 27
rutting season **86** 9-12
rye **68** 1, 2
rye bread **97** 10, 49; **99** 14
rye-bread roll **97** 16
rye flour **97** 52
ryegrass, perennial ~ **69** 26

# S

sabaton **329** 55
saber *see* sabre
sable *Ladies' Wear* **30** 60
sable *Heraldry* **254** 26
sable *Mammals* **367** 15
sabot **101** 47
sabre, light ~ **294** 20, 34

sabre fencer **294** 19
sabre fencing **294** 19-24
sabre gauntlet **294** 21
sabre glove **294** 21
sabre mask **294** 22
sabreur **294** 19
Sachsenwald class mine transport **258** 94
sack **38** 34
sacker **92** 39
Sacrament **331** 48
sacrarium **330** 32
sacristan **330** 26, 58
sacristy **331** 13
sacristy door **330** 17
sacrum **17** 21; **20** 59
saddle *Phys. Geog.* **12** 16, 42
saddle *Mach. Tools* **149** 13
saddle, adjustable ~ **188** 4
saddle, English ~ **71** 45-49
saddle, reciprocating ~ **185** 24
saddle, unsprung ~ **290** 17
saddle, western ~ **71** 37-44
saddle apron **149** 16
saddleback roof **37** 5; **121** 1
saddle clip **126** 53
saddle-pad **71** 17, 31
saddle roof **37** 5; **121** 11
saddles **71** 37-49
saddle seat **71** 37
saddle spring **187** 23
saddle stitching **31** 45
saddle tree **374** 1
safe **246** 22
safelight **116** 21
safety bar **301** 58
safety belt **191** 97
safety binding **301** 2
safety bonnet **85** 36
safety brake **85** 15
safety catch *Atom* **2** 40
safety catch *Household* **50** 25
safety catch *Hunt.* **87** 8, 24
safety catch *Army* **255** 14
safety catch, sliding ~ **87** 25
safety chain **126** 3
safety current **127** 2
safety curtain **316** 24
safety device **290** 13
safety equipment **316** 18
safety glass **124** 5
safety glasses **140** 21
safety helmet **84** 23; **140** 22; **158** 10; **300** 53
safety helmet, shock-resisting ~ **127** 48
safety hood **85** 36
safety jet **301** 53
safety key **140** 48
safety latch **50** 25
safety lighting **312** 6
safety lock **140** 44
safety net *Warships* **259** 18
safety net *Circus* **307** 14
safety nut **187** 64
safety pin **328** 27
safety rail **119** 43
safety valve *Roof & Boilerr.* **38** 70
safety valve *Railw.* **210** 3
safety wall **122** 35
saffron milk cap **381** 29
saggar **161** 2
sagger **161** 2
Sagittarius **3** 37; **4** 61
sagittate **370** 37
sago **98** 39
sago palm **383** 58
sail **219** 1-72; **283** 62; **284** 2; **285** 8
sail, brailed-up ~ **218** 21
sail, fore-and-aft ~ **220** 15

sail, furled ~ **218** 21
sail, square ~ **218** 21, 33; **219** 55-66; **220** 16
sail axle **91** 5
sailboat *Playground* **273** 29
sailboat *Camping* **278** 12
sailboat *Sailing* **284** 10-48
sailboat, single-masted ~ **220** 6-8
sailboats, mizzen-masted ~ **220** 9-10
sailboats, two-masted ~ **220** 11-17
sailing **284; 285**
sailing barge, ketch-rigged ~ **220** 9
sailing boat *Playground* **273** 29
sailing boat *Camping* **278** 12
sailing boat *Sailing* **284** 10-48
sailing boat, single-masted ~ **220** 6-8
sailing boats, mizzen-masted ~ **220** 9 *u.* 10
sailing boats, two-masted ~ **220** 11-17
sailing close-hauled **285** 10
sailing downwind **285** 1
sailing ship **219; 220**
sailing ships, development of ~ **220** 35-37
sailing ships, four-masted ~ **220** 28-31
sailing vessels, three-masted ~ **220** 18-27
sailing with free wind **285** 12
sailing with wind abeam **285** 11
sailor suit **309** 62
sailplane **287** 3
sailplane, high-performance ~ **287** 9
sails, fore-and-aft ~ **219** 20-31
sail shapes **220** 1-5
sail top **91** 6
sainfoin **69** 10
saint, Buddhist ~ **337** 10
Saint Andrew's cross bond **118** 65
salad **266** 51
salad bowl **45** 23
salad chicory **57** 40
salad cream **96** 29
salad drawer **39** 4
salad fork **45** 68
salad oil **98** 24; **99** 66
salad plants **57** 36-40
salad servers **45** 24
salad spoon **45** 67
salamander **364** 22
salamanders **364** 20-22
sal-ammoniac block **125** 6
sales area **99** 4
sales check **98** 44; **271** 7
salesclerk **98** 13
sales counter **271** 42, 61
salesgirl **97** 1; **98** 31; **99** 17; **271** 18
saleslady **97** 1; **98** 31; **99** 17; **271** 18
salesman **309** 29
sales premises **111** 1-19
sales shelf **99** 23
sales statistics **248** 46
salicional **326** 23-30
salientians **364** 23-26
salina *Map* **15** 32
salina *Spa* **274** 1-7
sallow **371** 24
salon, men's ~ **106** 1-42
salon mirror **105** 20; **106** 6
saloon **193** 1, 4-10, 4, 8
saloon, fastback ~ **193** 8
saloon, four-door ~ **193** 4-10

saloon, lower ~ **194** 37
saloon, stubback ~ **193** 8
saloon, upper ~ **194** 38
salt **98** 40
salt, common ~ **1** 9
salta **276** 20
salta piece **276** 21
salt cake storage tank **172** 36
salt cellar **266** 77
salt mine **154** 57-68, 72
saltstick **97** 31
salt water outlet **145** 33
salt water pipe **145** 33
salt water tank **146** 17
salt works *Map* **15** 32
salt works *Spa* **274** 1-7
salt works attendant **274** 5
salvage **227**
salvage tug **227** 5, 16
salvaging **227** 1
Salvator beer **93** 26
salving **227** 1
sampan **353** 31
sample sagger **161** 2
sample scoop **98** 72
samson post **223** 35
samson post, ventilator-type ~ **221** 58
samurai **353** 37
sanctuary **330** 32
sanctuary lamp **330** 49
sanctus bell **330** 46
sand *Map* **15** 6
sand *Bldg. Site* **118** 36; **119** 26
sandal **101** 51
sandal, ladies' ~ **101** 49
sandal court shoe **101** 27
sandbag **216** 50; **288** 65
sandbank **227** 3
sand bed **123** 8
sand belt, endless ~ **133** 15
sand box *Railw.* **212** 59, 76
sandbox *Playground* **273** 64
sand delivery pipe **148** 38
sand deposit **216** 52
sand dome **210** 14
sander **129** 30
sander, orbital ~ **134** 53
sander, single-belt ~ **133** 30
sander control **211** 32
sander switch **211** 32
sandhill **273** 66
sand hills **15** 6
sanding **129** 28
sanding attachment, orbital ~ **134** 53
sanding belt, endless ~ **133** 15
sanding belt regulator **133** 14
sanding disc **134** 25
sanding dust extractor **133** 28
sanding machine, single-belt ~ **133** 30
sanding table **133** 35
sanding valve **210** 55
sanding wheel **133** 27
sand lizard **364** 27
sandpaper **128** 14; **129** 25; **135** 25
sandpaper block **128** 13; **129** 26
sandpipe **210** 15, 19
sandpit **273** 64
sand star **369** 11
sand table **173** 13
sand track racing **290** 24-28
sand trap *Paperm.* **173** 13
sand trap *Ball Games* **293** 81
sand tube **210** 15
sandwich **45** 39
sandwich, open ~ **45** 37
sandwich board **308** 50
sandwich man **308** 49
sanitary articles **99** 35